Philosophy of Law

BLACKWELL PHILOSOPHY ANTHOLOGIES

Each volume in this outstanding series provides an authoritative and comprehensive collection of the essential primary readings from philosophy's main fields of study. Designed to complement the *Blackwell Companions to Philosophy* series, each volume represents an unparalleled resource in its own right, and will provide the ideal platform for course use.

PHILOSOPHY OF LAW
CLASSIC AND CONTEMPORARY READINGS

Edited by

Larry May

and

Jeff Brown

A John Wiley & Sons, Ltd., Publication

Editorial materials and organization © 2010 by Blackwell Publishing Ltd.

Blackwell Publishing was acquired by John Wiley & Sons in February 2007. Blackwell's publishing program has been merged with Wiley's global Scientific, Technical, and Medical business to form Wiley-Blackwell.

Registered Office
John Wiley & Sons Ltd, The Atrium, Southern Gate, Chichester, West Sussex, PO19 8SQ, United Kingdom

Editorial Offices
350 Main Street, Malden, MA 02148-5020, USA
9600 Garsington Road, Oxford, OX4 2DQ, UK
The Atrium, Southern Gate, Chichester, West Sussex, PO19 8SQ, UK

For details of our global editorial offices, for customer services, and for information about how to apply for permission to reuse the copyright material in this book please see our website at www.wiley.com/wiley-blackwell.

The right of Larry May and Jeff Brown to be identified as the author of the editorial material in this work has been asserted in accordance with the Copyright, Designs and Patents Act 1988.

Library of Congress Cataloging-in-Publication Data
Philosophy of law : classic and contemporary readings / edited by Larry May and Jeff Brown.
        p. cm. – (Blackwell philosophy anthologies)
    Includes bibliographical references and index.
    ISBN 978-1-4051-8388-8 (hardcover : alk. paper) – ISBN 978-1-4051-8387-1 (pbk. : alk. paper)
1. Law–Philosophy.   I. May, Larry.   II. Brown, Jeff.
    K235.P49 2009
    340′.1–dc22

                                                                                    2008041562

A catalogue record for this book is available from the British Library.
Set in 9.5/11.5pt Minion by Graphicraft Limited, Hong Kong
Printed in Singapore by Fabulous Printers Pte Ltd
02   2011

Contents

Preface

The aim of this textbook is to provide students with many diverse theoretical justifications for our legal rules, systems, and practices. With this in mind, we seek to introduce students both to the classical questions of philosophy of law, and to new emerging areas of theoretical dispute for legal theorists, philosophers, and lawyers. We provide introductions to all major areas of Anglo-American law, and the major philosophical underpinnings of each of these areas. This textbook also examines questions concerning the theoretical foundation and application of international law.

One important emphasis in the book is the relationship between morality and its application to law. Philosophers and legal theorists are split between those who take a moral approach to the law and those who reject a moral application of the law. We explore the relationship between morality and law in general, and also in sections devoted to specific areas of law, such as torts, property law, contract law, and constitutional law. In examining this important philosophical question, we include seminal essays from the history of philosophy, including works from Thomas Hobbes, John Locke, John Austin, Jeremy Bentham, Immanuel Kant, and John Stuart Mill. We also include many contemporary theorists, such as H. L. A. Hart, Ronald Dworkin, Robert Nozick, Richard Posner, Richard Epstein, A. M. Honore, and Michael Moore.

We will introduce students to diverse voices such as those of feminists, critical theorists, postmodernists, and critical race theorists. We explore viewpoints from the rest of the world, where Anglo-American law is not the norm; for example, Chinese conceptions of property law; Japanese conceptions of intellectual property; French and Canadian approaches to "bad Samaritanism"; and Indian, Irish, and Chinese approaches to fundamental constitutional rights.

In addition to introducing students to critics of contemporary Anglo-American law, we also explore the philosophical underpinnings of international law. In an increasingly interconnected world, important legal questions no longer simply concern the application of law within a specific society or legal system. This textbook introduces students to philosophical questions concerning the application of international law in a world immersed in diverse interests, global conflict, and war.

The essays on international law pervade most of the sections of the text. We begin with a section on legal reasoning, and even here we have included an essay on the use of custom in the reasoning of judges in international law. In the section on jurisprudence, we start with a piece from H. L. A. Hart's *The Concept of Law* and then begin the third section on the theory of international law with the final chapter of the same book by Hart. We also examine, for example, whether the use of force by one nation to stop an atrocity in another nation can be justified, and whether international criminal trials, like those that had Eichmann or Milosevic in the dock, were merely show trials. In the section on constitutional law, we have included discussion of *jus cogens* norms and basic human rights.

In these discussions, students will be exposed to a wide range of theoretical perspectives. By bringing as many different voices as possible into dialog with each other, we try to represent the philosophical foundations of various areas of law. And by exposing students to a wide range of theoretical views, this book also aims to challenge them to think critically about law within the US and other nations, as well as between nations.

The Structure of the Book

This book begins by looking at the principles of legal reasoning, especially how a consideration of the facts of particular cases can evolve into a settled body of abstract rules. Throughout the book, we introduce students to legal cases, interspersed with theoretical essays by philosophers and lawyers. As discussed in law, real-life cases are quite different from abstract, hypothetical cases, which philosophers trained in the analytic tradition rely on heavily. Although hypothetical cases are important and have their place, we believe it is important to introduce students to real patterns of fact for two reasons. First, a consideration of legal cases forces philosophers to think about concrete situations in which a decision has to be made about what is to be done. Having an abstract conception of justice is not enough; one must also be able to see how such a conception can be applied to adjudicate disputes between two equally well-defended parties. The problem is that fanciful hypothetical examples are often disengaged from the real world and its complexities. Although such examples have their place, we believe that the interaction between philosophy and law should be engaged with the real world and its problems. And second, a consideration of real-life legal fact patterns makes us aware of how a change in just one fact may make a huge difference in deciding which rules apply and what types of remedy are appropriate.

Unlike most of the standard texts in philosophy of law, we have organized our selections according to the areas of law that reflect how philosophical study of the subject relates to the normal set of courses taken at US law schools. Sections of our text correspond to the standard first-year courses in torts, criminal law, property law, and constitutional law. We also provide sections on jurisprudence, family law, and international law. Before each of these selections, we introduce students to the main concepts in these areas of law, as well as setting the stage for the detailed treatment of the various philosophical approaches to the core ideas in the essays that follow.

Our textbook tries to strike a balance between important philosophical essays in the analytic tradition and important non-traditional material; the latter includes a collection of essays that approach traditional topics in legal philosophy from the perspective of minority members within mainstream US culture as well as some non-Western material. Because law intersects in everyone's lives in so many ways, philosophical thinking on the subject is not simply an analytic exercise. It is a topic debated by lawyers, policy analysts, politicians, political activists, and philosophers alike. We believe that balancing traditional and non-traditional material helps us focus the student's attention on the interplay of voices and outlooks that constitute today's diverse world; a diversity that is deep both within countries and between them. Throughout, we have tried to offer readings that bring philosophical ideas alive by confronting them with real-life predicaments of people struggling to interact with one another in a diverse and pluralistic world.

Finally, we have included more readings than might be expected from law journals, as well as essays by prominent legal theorists teaching in US law schools. This has two advantages over most textbooks in this area. First, it introduces undergraduates to the way in which philosophy of law, or jurisprudence, is approached by lawyers as well as by philosophers. Second, for law students, it connects the philosophical study of law with some of the main figures in the area whom the students will already have encountered in their other courses.

In our view, philosophy of law has produced the richest literature of all the subfields of ethics and political philosophy. Philosophy of law is a rigorous field of inquiry in its own right, as one can see especially clearly when work by lawyers is brought together with work by philosophers in a single volume and then juxtaposed with the best work by contemporary critics of mainstream approaches. We hope that this book will inspire generations of students to bridge the gap between theory and practice and to look beyond the system of law in their own country when considering the exciting and diverse writings in philosophy of law.

Larry May

Jeff Brown

Source Acknowledgments

The editor and publisher gratefully acknowledge the permission granted to reproduce the copyright material in this book:

1. Edward H. Levi, "An Introduction to Legal Reasoning," from *An Introduction to Legal Reasoning* (The University of Chicago Press, 1949), © 1949 by the University of Chicago Press. Reprinted with permission from the University of Chicago Press.
2. Karl Llewellyn, "Remarks on the Theory of Appellate Decision and the Rules or Canons about how Statutes are to be Construed," *Vand L. Rev.*, vol. 3, 395 (1950).
3. Frederick Schauer, "Formalism," *Yale Law Journal*, vol. 97, no. 4, March 1988, pp. 508–48. © 1988. Reprinted with permission from The Yale Law Journal Co.
4. Cass R. Sunstein, "Incompletely Theorized Agreements," from *Legal Reasoning and Political Conflict* (Oxford University Press, 1996). © 1996 by Oxford University Press, Inc. Reprinted with permission from Oxford University Press.
5. Larry May, "Custom, *Opinio Juris*, and Consent," from *Crimes Against Humanity: A Normative Account* (Cambridge University Press, 2005), pp. 40–62. © 2005 by Larry May. Reprinted with permission from Cambridge University Press.
6. *Lochner v. New York*, 198 U.S. 45 (1905).
7. H. L. A. Hart, "Chapter 5: Law as the Union of Primary and Secondary Rules" and "Chapter 6: The Foundations of a Legal System," from *The Concept of Law*, 2nd edn. (Oxford: Clarendon Press, 1997), pp. 80–110. © 1961, 1994 by Oxford University Press. Reprinted with permission from Oxford University Press.
8. Ronald M. Dworkin, "The Model of Rules I," from *Taking Rights Seriously* (Cambridge, Mass: The Belknap Press of Harvard University Press, 1977), pp. 22–9, 39–45. © 1977, 1978 by Ronald Dworkin. Reprinted with permission from Harvard University Press and Gerald Duckworth & Co. Ltd.
9. Michael S. Moore, "Law as Justice," *Social Philosophy & Policy*, vol. 18, 2001, pp. 115–45. © 2001, Social Philosophy & Policy Foundation. Reprinted with permission from the author and Cambridge University Press.
10. Richard A. Posner, "The Economic Approach to Law," from *The Problems of Jurisprudence* (Cambridge, Mass: Harvard University Press, 1990), pp. 353–62, 391–2. © 1990 by the Presidents and Fellows of Harvard College. Reprinted with permission from Harvard University Press.
11. Duncan Kennedy, "The Distinction between Adjudication and Legislation," from *A Critique of Adjudication (fin de siècle)* (Cambridge, Mass: Harvard University Press,

1997), pp. 23–38. © 1997 by the Presidents and Fellows of Harvard College. Reprinted with permission from Harvard University Press.

12. Kimberlé Crenshaw, Neil Gotanda, Gary Peller, and Kendall Thomas, "Introduction," from *Critical Race Theory: The Key Writings that Formed the Movement* (New York: The New Press, 1995), pp. xii–xxxii. © 1995 by The New Press.

13. Patricia Smith, "Feminist Legal Critics: The Reluctant Radicals," in Stephen M. Griffin and Robert C. L. Moffat, eds., *Radical Critiques of the Law* (Lawrence, KS: University Press of Kansas, 1997), pp. 143–61. © 1997 by the University Press of Kansas.

14. *Riggs v. Palmer*, 22 N.E. 188 (1889).

15. H. L. A. Hart, "International Law," from *The Concept of Law*, 2nd edn. (Oxford: Clarendon Press, 1997), pp. 208–23. © 1961, 1994 by Oxford University Press. Reprinted with permission from Oxford University Press.

16. Mark W. Janis, "The Nature of *Jus Cogens*," *Connecticut Journal of International Law*, vol. 3, 1988, pp. 359–63. © 1988 Connecticut Journal of International Law. Reprinted with permission from the author and journal.

17. Fernando R. Tesón, *A Philosophy of International Law* (Westview Press, 1998), pp. 52–66. © 1998 by Fernando Tesón. Reprinted with permission of Westview Books, a member of Perseus Books Group.

18. Jack L. Goldsmith and Eric A. Posner, "Introduction," from *The Limits of International Law* (Oxford University Press, 2005), pp. 3–17. © 2005 by Oxford University Press, Inc. Reprinted with permission of Oxford University Press.

19. Allen Buchanan, "The Internal Legitimacy of Humanitarian Intervention," *Journal of Political Philosophy*, vol. 7, no. 1, 1999, pp. 71–87. © 2005 by Oxford University Press, Inc. Reprinted with permission of Oxford University Press.

20. Larry May, "Humanitarian Intervention: Problems of Collective Responsibility" adapted from from *Aggression and Crimes Against Peace* (Cambridge University Press, 2008). © 2008 by Larry May. Reprinted

with permission from Cambridge University Press.

21. Burleigh Wilkins, "Humanitarian Intervention: Some Doubts," in Aleksandar Jokic, ed., *Humanitarian Intervention: Moral and Philosophical Issues* (Broadview Press, 2003), pp. 35–44. © 2003 by Aleksandar Jokic. Reprinted with permission from Broadview Press.

22. *Prosecutor v. Tadić*, International Criminal Tribunal for the Former Yugoslavia, 1995, *Criminal Law Forum*, vol. 7, no. 1, 1996, pp. 51–3, 68–71.

23. John Locke, "Of Property," from *Second Treatise of Government*, chapter 5.

24. Robert Nozick, "Locke's Theory of Acquisition," from *Anarchy, State and Utopia* (New York: Basic Books, 1974), pp. 174–82. © 1974 by Basic Books, Inc. Reprinted with permission from Basic Books, a member of Perseus Books Group.

25. A. M. Honoré, "Property, Title and Redistribution," from Carl Wellman, ed., *Equality and Freedom* (Archiv fur Rechts- und Sozial-philosophie, 1977), pp. 107–15. © 1977. Reprinted with permission from Franz Steiner Verlag GmbH.

26. Richard Epstein, "Philosophical Implications," from *Takings: Private Property and the Power of Eminent Domain* (Harvard University Press, 1985), pp. 331–50. © 1985 by the President and Fellows of Harvard College. Reprinted with permission from Harvard University Press.

27. Dan Rosen and Chikako Usui, "The Social Structure of Japanese Intellectual Property Law," *UCLA Pacific Basin Law Journal*, vol. 13, Fall 1994, pp. 32–8, 69. © 1994. Reprinted with permission from the authors.

28. A. John Simmons, "Historical Rights and Fair Shares," *Law and Philosophy*, vol. 14, 1995, pp. 149–84. © 1995. Reprinted with permission from the author and Springer Science and Business Media.

29. *International New Service v. Associated Press*, Supreme Court of the United States (1918). 248 U.S. 215.

30. H. L. A. Hart and A. M. Honoré, "Causation and Responsibility," from *Causation in the Law*, 2nd edn. (Oxford University Press, 1985), pp. 62–83. © 1985 H. L. A. Hart

and A. M. Honoré. Reprinted with permission from Oxford University Press.

31. Joel Feinberg, "Sua Culpa," from *Doing and Deserving* (Princeton University Press, 1970), pp. 187–221. © 1970 by Joel Feinberg. Reprinted by kind permission of Betty Feinberg.

32. George P. Fletcher, "Fairness and Utility in Tort Theory," *Harvard Law Review*, vol. 85, no. 3, January 1972. © 1972 by Harvard Law Review Association. Reproduced with permission from Harvard Law Review Association in the format Textbook via Copyright Clearance Center.

33. Jules L. Coleman, "Tort Liability and the Limits of Corrective Justice," in Jules L. Coleman, ed., *In Harm's Way: Essays in Honor of Joel Feinberg* (Cambridge University Press, 1994), pp. 139–58. © 1994 by Cambridge University Press. Reprinted with permission from the author and Cambridge University Press.

34. Richard A. Epstein, "A Theory of Strict Liability," *Journal of Legal Studes*, vol. 2, no. 1, January 1973, pp. 151–204. © 1973 by Journal of Legal Studies. Reprinted with permission from the author and the University of Chicago Press.

35. Mitchell McInnes, "The Question of a Duty to Rescue in Canadian Tort Law: An Answer from France," *Dalhousie Law Journal*, vol. 13, no. 1, May 1990, pp. 85–122. © 1990 by Mitchell McInnes. Reprinted by kind permission of the author.

36. *Tarasoff v. Regents of Univ. of California*, 17 Cal. 3d 425, 551 P.2d 334, 131 Cal Rptr. 14 (1976).

37. John Stuart Mill, excerpts from chapters I, II, and IV of *On Liberty*.

38. Patrick Devlin, excerpts from *The Enforcement of Morals* (Oxford University Press, 1965). © 1965 by Patrick Devlin. Reprinted with permission from Oxford University Press.

39. Egbeke Aja, "Crime and Punishment: An Indigenous African Experience," *The Journal of Value Inquiry*, vol. 31, 1997, pp. 353–68. © 1997. Reprinted with permission from Springer Science and Business Media.

40. Anthony Kenny, "The Mind and the Deed," from *Freewill and Responsibility* (Routledge & Kegan Paul, 1978), pp. 1–21. © 1978 by Anthony Kenny. Reproduced with permission from Taylor & Francis Books UK.

41. Martti Koskenniemi, "Between Impunity and Show Trials," *Max Planck Yearbook of United Nations Law*, vol. 6, 2002, pp. 1–35. © 2002. Reprinted with permission from Koninklijke BRILL NV.

42. Mark Drumbl, chapter 6 from *Atrocity, Punishment and International Law* (Cambridge University Press, 2007), pp. 169–80. © 2007 by Mark A. Drumbl. Reprinted with permission from the author and Cambridge University Press.

43. Larry May, "Defending International Criminal Trials," from *Aggression and Crimes Against Peace* (Cambridge University Press, 2008). © 2008 by Larry May. Reprinted with permission from Cambridge University Press.

44. Justice Robert H. Jackson, "Opening Statement before the International Military Tribunal," International Military Tribunal, Nuremberg, November 21, 1945. *Source*: www.roberthjackson.org/Man/theman2-7-8-1/.

45. Thomas Hobbes, "Of the First and Second Natural Laws, and of Contracts" from *Leviathan*, Chapter 14.

46. P. S. Atiyah, "The Practice of Promising," from *Promises, Morals, and the Law* (Oxford University Press, 1981), pp. 138–76. © 1981 by P. S. Atiyah. Reprinted with permission from Oxford University Press.

47. Charles Fried, "Contract as Promise," from *Contract as Promise* (Harvard University Press, 1981), pp. 7–27. © 1981 by the President and Fellows of Harvard College. Reprinted with permission of Harvard University Press.

48. Michael D. Bayles, "Legally Enforceable Commitments," *Law and Philosophy*, vol. 4, no. 3 (December 1985), pp. 311–42 (excerpts). © 1985. Reprinted with permission from Springer Science and Business Media.

49. Alan Wertheimer, "Unconscionability and Contracts," *Business Ethics Quarterly*, vol. 2,

no. 4, October 1922, pp. 479–96. © 1922. Reprinted with permission from Business Ethics Quarterly.

50. Lynn Berat, "South African Contract Law: The Need for a Concept of Unconscionability," *Loyola of Los Angeles International and Comparative Law Journal*, vol. 14, 1992, pp. 507–27. © 1992. Reprinted with permission from ILR-Loyola Law School.

51. *Williams v. Walker-Thomas Furniture Co.*, 350 F.2d 445 (1965).

52. Ronald Dworkin, "Constitutional Cases," from *Taking Rights Seriously* (Cambridge, Mass: The Belknap Press of Harvard University Press, 1977), pp. 131–49. © 1977, 1978 by Ronald Dworkin. Reprinted with permission from Harvard University Press.

53. Stephen R. Munzer and James W. Nickel, "Does the Constitution Mean What It Always Meant?" *Columbia Law Review*, vol. 77, no. 7, November 1977, pp. 1029–62. © 1977 by Columbia Law Review Association, Inc. Reproduced with permission of Columbia Law Review Association, Inc. in the format Textbook via Copyright Clearance Center.

54. R. P. Peerenboom, "What's Wrong with Chinese rights? Toward a Theory of Rights with Chinese Characteristics," *Harvard Human Rights Journal*, vol. 6, 1993, pp. 29–57. © 1993. Reprinted with permission from Harvard Human Rights Journal.

55. Jeremy Cooper, "Poverty and Constitutional Justice: The Indian Experience," *Mercer Law Review*, vol. 44, 1993, pp. 611–35. © 1993. Reprinted with permission from Mercer Law Review.

56. Rory O'Connell, "Natural Law: Alive and Kicking? A Look at the Constitutional Morality of Sexual Privacy in Ireland," *Ratio Juris*, vol. 9, no. 3, Summer 1996, pp. 258–82. © 1996 by Ratio Juris. Reprinted with permission from Blackwell Publishing.

57. Alexander Orakhelashvili, *Peremptory Norms in International Law* (Oxford University Press, 2006), pp. 7–11, 48–53. © 2006 by A. Orakhelashvili. Reprinted with permission from Oxford University Press.

58. Hilary Charlesworth and Christine Chinkin, "The Gender of *Jus Cogens*," *Human Rights Quarterly*, vol. 15 (1993), pp. 63–76. © 1993 by The Johns Hopkins University Press. Reprinted with permission from The Johns Hopkins University Press.

59. *Plessy v. Ferguson*, 163 U.S. 537; 41 L. Ed. 256; 16 S. Ct. 1138 (1896).

Introduction

The Relationship Between Law and Philosophy

"Where there is law, there is injustice"

This quotation from Tolstoy is interestingly ambiguous. On one level, we are told that law's primary goal or aim is to confront and remedy injustice. In most societies, one of law's major functions is to act as the major institution entrusted with providing individual or collective remedies for people who have been harmed by the intentional or unintentional acts of others. On another level of meaning, we are told that where there are laws, there will be injustice. To some, this second meaning might sound a bit strange. Law can create injustice because it works through the application of general rules, but general rules do not easily fit specific patterns of facts. The rules always overlap or underdetermine the facts. This means that the application of law to facts may cause injustice to be done to someone. Law is based on an attempt to remedy injustice, but, by its very nature, law can create injustice as well. In both respects, we can see that law and justice are intertwined. This is one reason that philosophers have been intrigued by the ideas of both. For several thousands of years, the philosophical study of law has centered on the relationship between the concept of justice and the law. This volume will be no different. We provide many articles by both philosophers and lawyers who argue about the law's relationship with questions of justice.

Philosophical questions also extend to foundational questions concerning areas of law. In most contemporary law courses, the first few days are spent on the philosophical foundations of that legal subject. For example, property courses begin with discussions of how property rights are created in the state of nature, where there are no such rights. Contracts courses discuss the nature of promises and what it is about promises that creates an obligation in the world where none existed before. Torts and criminal law begin with discussions of why harm is considered such a bad thing in a society, as well as appropriate responses to acts that cause harm. Courses in constitutional law often begin with discussions of what is most foundational to any system of rules that calls itself law. Classes in international law often start with the question of whether "international law" is a meaningful concept at all. As these classes continue, there are additional discussions concerning "policy" considerations – namely, moral, social, political, and economic theorizing about the proper role of law in regulating our lives and the actions of other sovereign nations.

The study of philosophy intersects with the study of law in many different ways. As with the relationship between law and justice, the very idea, or concept, of law has been studied by philosophers since at least the ancient Greeks. Each branch of law has at least one question that has been rigorously explored by philosophers. What differentiates a contract from a promise? Is the government ever justified in redistributing property? Should tort law hold people liable for failing to help one another? Should constitutions be interpreted narrowly or liberally? Is punishment justified for reasons of retribution or deterrence? Are states ever justified in violating another state's sovereignty by force?

The Law's Goal of Stability in Social Relationships Among People and Nations

The various domestic fields of law all aim at one goal: providing the mechanisms that allow individuals to order their lives and plan for the future. International law works in a similar way. It allows states to put their interactions in order and plan for future relations between states. For example, contracts provide a mechanism by which obligations and rights can be created by mutual agreement. When you and I agree that you will clean my garage this weekend and that I will pay you 50 dollars to do so, the world for both of us has changed by our own free acts. You have an obligation to clean my garage, and I have an obligation to pay you 50 dollars. This contract gives us rights. I have a right to have my garage cleaned by you, and you have a right to be paid 50 dollars by me. Importantly, none of these rights existed until we exchanged promises. These rights are enforceable at law simply because we made an agreement, unless the contract violates some legal principle of fair dealing.

Property likewise provides a mechanism for regulating our lives concerning the acquisition and transfer of land and durable goods. Property law has helped create a base on which societies achieve a certain kind of economic stability. If on my deathbed I transfer the deed for my acre of homestead to my favorite grandchild, the law will generally recognize and enforce the peaceful transfer of title to this piece of property. Such transfer creates rights and obligations for my grandchild that she did not have before. Importantly, fights over who should inherit the land are

extinguished, and individuals can plan for the future with relative security. Most societies have established complex sets of rules regarding contract and property transfers. These rules allow individuals to regulate their own lives with minimal interference from the state.

Criminal and tort law also aim to secure a stable society, but in a very different way from that of contract or property law. Rather than helping people figure out how best to get what they want, the law intervenes to penalize or punish those who have acted in harmful and socially disruptive ways. The opportunity for individuals to be harmed by strangers or neighbors and loved ones creates a different kind of insecurity. For example, if you are lying on a stretcher in an operating room, unconscious and at the mercy of the medical team, we want some assurance that a doctor will not neglect to take good care of you or, at least, that you are not intentionally harmed or taken advantage of. Both tort and criminal law function to provide a basis for securing these goals. Importantly, how much protection the law provides varies from state to state and country to country. As you will read in this volume, different legal systems differ about whether there is a "duty to rescue" a stranger in need.

In constitutional law, we see attempts to regulate and stabilize societies concerning the behavior of high-placed political leaders. In the United States, constitutional law determines the stability of presidential office. In recent years, constitutional law has played a large role in presidential power. It was used to determine whether one president, Bill Clinton, should be removed from office for lying under oath and whether another, George W. Bush, should rightfully be president in a disputed election. Here, the US Constitution serves to provide for peaceful transfer of power and it also provides checks on the possible abuses of power by societies' most powerful members.

When we switch from areas of domestic law to international law more generally, we also see the role of law in trying to provide stability between nations. Given that we live in a world that is immersed in diverse interests, global conflict, and war, stability in international affairs is an important topic for international lawyers and philosophers. These questions have been raised during both the invasions of Iraq by the US and its allies. During the 1991 invasion, the coalition forces (led by the United States) had United Nations approval, but not in the more recent and ongoing Iraqi conflict. Due to the global and regional instability that war creates, international law looks to provide a stable mechanism to curtail the use of force by one nation against another. But there is still an important philosophical and legal question concerning that status of international law. How does international law "bind" a nation? If international law binds a nation, is there any conflict between international law and national sovereignty? Does it make sense to say that international law is "law" at all?

This book will explore significant areas of legal philosophy. We introduce the reader to important questions concerning law and justice,

the foundations of law and legal systems, and the foundations of specific areas of law, such as contracts, torts, criminal law, etc. The topics in this book reflect the intimate link between philosophy and law, a link going back to the earliest philosophers, such as Plato and Aristotle, and in our text, we continue in the same tradition. We strive to display a wider overlap between law and philosophy, where each of the main areas of law is shown to raise significant philosophical issues. Just as Tolstoy is correct to say that where there is law there is also injustice, so we would say that where there is injustice there have been philosophers. Whenever there have been debates about justice or injustice, injury and responsibility, desert and punishment, there has also been a dialog been philosophers and lawyers. The continuation of that dialog is what this book is about.

Part I

Legal Reasoning

Introduction

Legal reasoning is at the heart of law. It is what lawyers do when they argue court cases. It is also what judges do when they decide cases. Most philosophical theories of legal reasoning – that is, philosophical explanations and justifications of legal reasoning, including those presented here – focus on what judges do or should be doing when they decide court cases.

How judges create and use precedents is the central focus of Edward H. Levi's essay, which is taken from his seminal book, *An Introduction to Legal Reasoning* (1949). For Levi, the basic pattern of legal reasoning is reasoning by example, or reasoning from case to case. It proceeds in three basic steps: similarity is seen between two cases, the rule of law inherent in the first case is articulated, and the rule is applied to the second case. Finding similarities or differences between cases, a function of judges, is central to this conception of legal reasoning. Law is a system of rules that are discovered in the process of finding similarity and difference. Rather than being unchanging, rules are dynamic, changing in meaning with each new application to a case. Reasoning by example explains how new ideas for the community enter the law, as well as how litigants participate in law-making – for new ideas enter the law through arguments made by individual litigants in particular cases. Not only is reasoning by example the basic pattern of legal reasoning in case law, but it also applies with

minor adjustments to the reasoning involved in statutory and constitutional interpretation.

In "Remarks on the Theory of Appellate Decision and the Rules or Canons about how Statutes are to be Construed," Karl N. Llewellyn examines how judges interpret statutes. It is generally assumed that there is a "correct" way to read and construe a statute. Judges often use canons of statutory interpretation, which are to help guide them in making a proper reading of the statute. Llewellyn argues that canons will not help a judge find a "correct" way to understand a statute. To illustrate his point, he made a chart in which he aligned canons by "Thrusts" and "Parries." As he shows, for each canon labeled as a "Thrust," there is an opposite canon that acted as a "Parry." Each canon, then, also had an opposite counterpart. From this, Llewellyn argues that "if a statute is to make sense, it must be read in light of some assumed purpose." To assume that a statute just merely declares a rule is "nonsense."

In "Formalism," Frederick Schauer defends the theory of legal formalism. Schauer's insight is that decision-making according to rules lies at the heart of formalism. Because there is much to be said in favor of decision-making according to rules, there is much, also, to commend in formalism. According to Schauer, the main objection to formalism is that it conceals the fact that, in deciding cases, judges make choices. This is problematic because the legal system becomes unpredictable. In response, Schauer asks the reader to consider a legal system in which several conditions obtain. First, the meanings of legal rules are clear and settled. Second, the rules clearly apply in particular cases. Third, no escape routes exist. Fourth, no ways of creating escape routes exist. This kind of system, Schauer thinks, suggests a benign formalism – that is, a formalism that does not conceal judicial choices. This kind of system would display decision-making according to rules. What can be said on its behalf?

For one thing, one could predict the decisions made in such a system. But decision-making according to rules is predictable, Schauer argues, because of limited decisional jurisdiction. Decisional jurisdiction is the idea that the choices of decision-makers can be more or less restricted in scope. When one restricts decision-makers' scope of choice, one increases the predictability of their decisions by limiting the range of factors that can influence such decisions. A system with limited decisional jurisdiction is inherently more stable and conservative than one in which decision-makers have greater latitude of choice. A drawback of such a system is that it could tend toward rigidity and result in some absurd decisions. But formalism, Schauer claims, is not fundamentally about rigidity and absurdity. It is about power and its allocation. That formalism sometimes results in rigid and possibly absurd decisions might be offset by the fact that it requires modesty on the part of decision-makers. Formalism is less than optimal when it prevents wise judges from making good decisions, but it is beneficial when it prevents corrupt or foolish judges from abusing power. Schauer concludes his essay by arguing for a form of presumptive formalism.

In "Incompletely Theorized Agreements," Cass R. Sunstein argues that particular legal conclusions are and should be reached on the basis of incompletely theorized agreements. To explain what this means, Sunstein argues that one can identify several levels of abstraction in legal reasoning. At the most concrete or specific levels are particular conclusions of law – that is, the individual decisions that judges make. At the next level are low-level principles, such as the clear-and-present-danger rule. Mid-level principles and generalizations, such as freedom of speech, are even more abstract. At the highest level of abstraction are general ethical theories, such as Kantianism and utilitarianism, or commitments to quite abstract values, such as equality or personal autonomy. Sunstein focuses on incompletely theorized agreements on particular outcomes that are accompanied by agreement on the low-level principles that account for them. His view is that even when judges and other participants in the legal and political system disagree on higher-level principles and theories, they can agree on particular conclusions and lower-level principles.

In the next essay, "Custom, *Opinio Juris*, and Consent," by Larry May, we look at legal reasoning and international law. Much legal reasoning begins with a reference to custom or to common law considerations. The references to custom are especially common and yet also problematic in international law. One specific part of custom, *opinio juris*, is of special theoretical interest. *Opinio juris* concerns a longstanding custom where the states act in conformity with the custom and explain their actions in terms of being legally or morally obligated. In this essay, Larry May offers a critique of the use of custom based on *opinio juris* in reasoning about international law. Standing alone, custom cannot supply the justification for the kind of universal norms that international legal reasoning needs. *Opinio juris*, though, can supply evidence that universal norms already exist. Custom can be grounded in the consent of states, but it cannot be the ground of universal norms without something other than consent, which can of course be withdrawn as easily as it can be granted. Along the way, May considers a wide range of examples of the use of *opinio juris* and custom in international law.

We conclude this section with *Lochner v. New York* (1905), which is an example of legal formalism in action. In this case, Lochner, the plaintiff, appealed a ruling by the New York Court of Appeals upholding his conviction by a lower court. The lower court convicted Lochner of a misdemeanor for violating New York's labor law by permitting and requiring an employee to work in his bakery for more than 60 hours in one week. Writing for a majority of the Supreme Court (five to four), Justice Rufus

Peckham overruled the Court of Appeals' decision and struck down the labor law in question as a violation of the US Constitution. Central to Justice Peckham's disposition of the case is the bare assertion that the right to make business contracts is part of the liberty of the individual, which is protected by the Fourteenth Amendment. This assertion is bolstered by the subsidiary contentions that the freedom to make labor contracts extended to both parties, the employer and the employee, and that, in this case, there is no legitimate reason, such as public health concerns, for the state to restrict the hours of employment on which the parties agreed. Based on this reasoning, Justice Peckham concludes that New York's labor law is an unnecessary and unjustified intrusion of the police power of the state into the liberty of the individual as guaranteed by the Fourteenth Amendment, and strikes it down as unconstitutional.

Justice Peckham took it to be true by definition that the meaning of the term "liberty" in the Fourteenth Amendment includes the right of employer and employee to make labor contracts without government intrusion. However, one might argue, following Justice Holmes's dissent, that Justice Peckham chose an interpretation of the term liberty that supports his own favorite economic theory, laissez-faire, and used it in this case to combat the emergence of the modern welfare state by attacking protective labor laws.

1

An Introduction to Legal Reasoning

Edward H. Levi

I

This is an attempt to describe generally the process of legal reasoning in the field of case law and in the interpretation of statutes and of the Constitution. It is important that the mechanism of legal reasoning should not be concealed by its pretense. The pretense is that the law is a system of known rules applied by a judge; the pretense has long been under attack.[1] In an important sense legal rules are never clear, and, if a rule had to be clear before it could be imposed, society would be impossible. The mechanism accepts the differences of view and ambiguities of words. It provides for the participation of the community in resolving the ambiguity by providing a forum for the discussion of policy in the gap of ambiguity. On serious controversial questions, it makes it possible to take the first step in the direction of what otherwise would be forbidden ends. The mechanism is indispensable to peace in a community.

The basic pattern of legal reasoning is reasoning by example. It is reasoning from case to case. It is a three-step process described by the doctrine of precedent in which a proposition descriptive of the first case is made into a rule of law and then applied to a next similar situation. The steps are these: similarity is seen between cases; next the rule of law inherent in the first case is announced; then the rule of law is made applicable to the second case. This is a method of reasoning necessary for the law, but it has characteristics which under other circumstances might be considered imperfections.

These characteristics become evident if the legal process is approached as though it were a method of applying general rules of law to diverse facts – in short, as though the doctrine of precedent meant that general rules, once properly determined, remained unchanged, and then were applied, albeit imperfectly, in later cases. If this were the doctrine, it would be disturbing to find that the rules change from case to case and are remade with each case. Yet this change in the rules is the indispensable dynamic quality of law. It occurs because the scope of a rule of law, and therefore its meaning, depends upon a determination of what facts will be considered similar to those present when the rule was first announced. The finding of similarity or difference is the key step in the legal process.

The determination of similarity or difference is the function of each judge. Where case law is considered, and there is no statute, he is not bound by the statement of the rule of law made by the prior judge even in the controlling case. The statement is mere dictum, and this means that the judge in the present case may find irrelevant the existence or absence of facts which prior judges thought important. It is not what the prior judge intended that is of any importance; rather it is what the present judge, attempting to see the law as a fairly consistent whole, thinks should be the determining classification. In arriving at his result he will ignore what the past thought important; he will emphasize facts which prior judges would have thought made no difference. It is not alone that he could not see the law through the eyes of another, for he could at least try to do so. It is rather that the doctrine of dictum forces him to make his own decision.

Thus it cannot be said that the legal process is the application of known rules to diverse facts. Yet it is a system of rules; the rules are discovered in the process of determining similarity or difference. But if attention is directed toward the finding of similarity or difference, other peculiarities appear. The problem for the law is: When will it be just to treat different cases as though they were the same? A working legal system must therefore be willing to pick out key similarities and to reason from them to the justice of applying a common classification. The existence of some facts in common brings into play the general rule. If this is really reasoning, then by common standards, thought of in terms of closed systems, it is imperfect unless some overall rule has announced that this common and ascertainable similarity is to be decisive. But no such fixed prior rule exists. It could be suggested that reasoning is not involved at all; that is, that no new insight is arrived at through a comparison of cases. But reasoning appears to be involved; the conclusion is arrived at through a process and was not immediately apparent. It seems better to say there is reasoning, but it is imperfect.

Therefore it appears that the kind of reasoning involved in the legal process is one in which the classification changes as the classification is made. The rules change as the rules are applied. More important, the rules arise out of a process which, while comparing fact situations, creates the rules and then applies them. But this kind of reasoning is open to the charge that it is

classifying things as equal when they are somewhat different, justifying the classification by rules made up as the reasoning or classification proceeds. In a sense all reasoning is of this type, but there is an additional requirement which compels the legal process to be this way. Not only do new situations arise, but in addition people's wants change. The categories used in the legal process must be left ambiguous in order to permit the infusion of new ideas. And this is true even where legislation or a constitution is involved. The words used by the legislature or the constitutional convention must come to have new meanings. Furthermore, agreement on any other basis would be impossible. In this manner the laws come to express the ideas of the community and even when written in general terms, in statute or constitution, are molded for the specific case.

But attention must be paid to the process. A controversy as to whether the law is certain, unchanging, and expressed in rules, or uncertain, changing, and only a technique for deciding specific cases misses the point. It is both. Nor is it helpful to dispose of the process as a wonderful mystery possibly reflecting a higher law, by which the law can remain the same and yet change. The law forum is the most explicit demonstration of the mechanism required for a moving classification system. The folklore of law may choose to ignore the imperfections in legal reasoning, but the law forum itself has taken care of them.

What does the law forum require? It requires the presentation of competing examples. The forum protects the parties and the community by making sure that the competing analogies are before the court. The rule which will be created arises out of a process in which if different things are to be treated as similar, at least the differences have been urged. In this sense the parties as well as the court participate in the law-making. In this sense, also, lawyers represent more than the litigants.

Reasoning by example in the law is a key to many things. It indicates in part the hold which the law process has over the litigants. They have participated in the law-making. They are bound by something they helped to make. Moreover, the examples or analogies urged by the parties bring into the law the common ideas of the society. The ideas have their day in court, and they will have their day again. This is what makes the hearing fair, rather than any idea that the judge is completely impartial, for of course he cannot be completely so. Moreover, the hearing in a sense compels at least vicarious participation by all the citizens, for the rule which is made, even though ambiguous, will be law as to them.

Reasoning by example shows the decisive role which the common ideas of the society and the distinctions made by experts can have in shaping the law. The movement of common or expert concepts into the law may be followed. The concept is suggested in arguing difference or similarity in a brief, but it wins no approval from the court. The idea achieves standing in the society. It is suggested again to a court. The court this time reinterprets the prior case and in doing so adopts the rejected idea. In subsequent cases, the idea is given further definition and is tied to other ideas which have been accepted by courts. It is now no longer the idea which was commonly held in the society. It becomes modified in subsequent cases. Ideas first rejected but which gradually have won acceptance now push what has become a legal category out of the system or convert it into something which may be its opposite. The process is one in which the ideas of the community and of the social sciences, whether correct or not, as they win acceptance in the community, control legal decisions. Erroneous ideas, of course, have played an enormous part in shaping the law. An idea, adopted by a court, is in a superior position to influence conduct and opinion in the community; judges, after all, are rulers. And the adoption of an idea by a court reflects the power structure in the community. But reasoning by example will operate to change the idea after it has been adopted.

Moreover, reasoning by example brings into focus important similarity and difference in the interpretation of case law, statutes, and the constitution of a nation. There is a striking similarity. It is only folklore which holds that a statute if clearly written can be completely unambiguous and applied as intended to a specific case. Fortunately or otherwise, ambiguity is inevitable in both statute and constitution as well as with case law. Hence reasoning by example operates with all three. But there are important differences. What a court says is dictum, but what a legislature says is a statute. The reference of the

reasoning changes. Interpretation of intention when dealing with a statute is the way of describing the attempt to compare cases on the basis of the standard thought to be common at the time the legislation was passed. While this is the attempt, it may not initially accomplish any different result than if the standard of the judge had been explicitly used. Nevertheless, the remarks of the judge are directed toward describing a category set up by the legislature. These remarks are different from ordinary dicta. They set the course of the statute, and later reasoning in subsequent cases is tied to them. As a consequence, courts are less free in applying a statute than in dealing with case law. The current rationale for this is the notion that the legislature has acquiesced by legislative silence in the prior, even though erroneous, interpretation of the court. But the change in reasoning where legislation is concerned seems an inevitable consequence of the division of function between court and legislature, and, paradoxically, a recognition also of the impossibility of determining legislative intent. The impairment of a court's freedom in interpreting legislation is reflected in frequent appeals to the constitution as a necessary justification for overruling cases even though these cases are thought to have interpreted the legislation erroneously.

Under the United States experience, contrary to what has sometimes been believed when a written constitution of a nation is involved, the court has greater freedom than it has with the application of a statute or case law. In case law, when a judge determines what the controlling similarity between the present and prior case is, the case is decided. The judge does not feel free to ignore the results of a great number of cases which he cannot explain under a remade rule. And in interpreting legislation, when the prior interpretation, even though erroneous, is determined after a comparison of facts to cover the case, the case is decided. But this is not true with a constitution. The constitution sets up the conflicting ideals of the community in certain ambiguous categories. These categories bring along with them satellite concepts covering the areas of ambiguity. It is with a set of these satellite concepts that reasoning by example must work. But no satellite concept, no matter how well developed, can prevent the court from shifting its course, not only by realigning cases which impose certain restrictions, but by going beyond realignment back to the overall ambiguous category written into the document. The constitution, in other words, permits the court to be inconsistent. The freedom is concealed either as a search for the intention of the framers or as a proper understanding of a living instrument, and sometimes as both. But this does not mean that reasoning by example has any less validity in this field.

II

It may be objected that this analysis of legal reasoning places too much emphasis on the comparison of cases and too little on the legal concepts which are created. It is true that similarity is seen in terms of a word, and inability to find a ready word to express similarity or difference may prevent change in the law. The words which have been found in the past are much spoken of, have acquired a dignity of their own, and to a considerable measure control results. As Judge Cardozo suggested in speaking of metaphors, the word starts out to free thought and ends by enslaving it. The movement of concepts into and out of the law makes the point. If the society has begun to see certain significant similarities or differences, the comparison emerges with a word. When the word is finally accepted, it becomes a legal concept. Its meaning continues to change. But the comparison is not only between the instances which have been included under it and the actual case at hand, but also in terms of hypothetical instances which the word by itself suggests. Thus the connotation of the word for a time has a limiting influence – so much so that the reasoning may even appear to be simply deductive.

But it is not simply deductive. In the long run a circular motion can be seen. The first stage is the creation of the legal concept which is built up as cases are compared. The period is one in which the court fumbles for a phrase. Several phrases may be tried out; the misuse or misunderstanding of words itself may have an effect. The concept sounds like another, and the jump to the second is made. The second stage is the period when the concept is more or less fixed, although reasoning by example continues to classify items inside and out of the concept. The third stage is the breakdown of the concept, as reasoning by example has moved so far ahead as to make it clear that the suggestive influence of the word is no longer desired.

The process is likely to make judges and lawyers uncomfortable. It runs contrary to the pretense of the system. It seems inevitable, therefore, that as matters of kind vanish into matters of degree and then entirely new meanings turn up, there will be the attempt to escape to some overall rule which can be said to have always operated and which will make the reasoning look deductive. The rule will be useless. It will have to operate on a level where it has no meaning. Even when lip service is paid to it, care will be taken to say that it may be too wide or too narrow but that nevertheless it is a good rule. The statement of the rule is roughly analogous to the appeal to the meaning of a statute or of a constitution, but it has less of a function to perform. It is window dressing. Yet it can be very misleading. Particularly when a concept has broken down and reasoning by example is about to build another, textbook writers, well aware of the unreal aspect of old rules, will announce new ones, equally ambiguous and meaningless, forgetting that the legal process does not work with the rule but on a much lower level.

The movement of legal concepts in case law has frequently been shown by pointing to the breakdown of the so-called "inherently dangerous" rule. It is easy to do this because the opinion in *MacPherson v. Buick Motor Co.*[2] is the work of a judge acutely conscious of the legal process and articulate about it. But *MacPherson v. Buick* was only a part of a cyclical movement in which differences and similarities first rejected are then adopted and later cast aside. The description of the movement can serve as an example of case law. Roughly the problem has become: the potential liability of a seller of an article which causes injury to a person who did not buy the article from the seller. In recent times the three phases in the movement of the concepts used in handling this problem can be traced.

The first of these begins in 1816 and carries us to 1851. It begins with a loaded gun and ends with an exploding lamp. The loaded gun brought liability to its owner in the case of *Dixon v. Bell*.[3]

He had sent his thirteen- or fourteen-year-old servant girl to get the gun; in playing with the gun she had shot it off into the face of the plaintiff's son, who lost his right eye and two teeth. In holding that the plaintiff might recover, Lord Ellenborough attempted no classification of dangerous articles. He was content to describe the gun "as by this want of care . . . left in a state capable of doing mischief."[4] Thus the pattern begins with commodities mischievous through want of care.

The pattern becomes complicated in 1837 in the case of *Langridge v. Levy*,[5] where a plaintiff complained that the defendant had sold his father a defective gun for the use of himself and his sons. The gun had blown up in the plaintiff's hand. The court allowed recovery, apparently on the theory that the seller had falsely declared that the gun was safe when he knew it was defective and had sold the gun to the father knowing it was to be used by the plaintiff. It was therefore both a case of fraud and, in some sense, one of direct dealing between the seller and the plaintiff. The example used by the court was the case of a direct sale to the plaintiff, or where the instrument had been "placed in the hands of a third person for the purpose of being delivered to and then used by the plaintiff."[6] The direct dealing point is also emphasized by the statement of one of the judges during the argument to the effect that it would have helped the plaintiff's case if he had alleged that his father "was an unconscious agent in the transaction" because "the act of an unconscious agent is the act of the part who sets him in motion."[7]

In the argument of *Langridge v. Levy*, counsel for the defendant had pointed to a distinction between things "immediately dangerous or mischievous by the act of the defendant" and "such as may become so by some further act to be done to it."[8] They had urged what might be considered the pattern suggested by *Dixon v. Bell*. But the court rejected the use of any such distinction, although it remarked in passing that the gun was not "of itself dangerous, but . . . requires an act to be done, that is to be loaded, in order to make it so." It rejected not only the distinction but any category of dangerous articles, because it "should pause before we made a precedent by our decision which would be an authority for an action against the vendors, even of such

instruments and articles as are dangerous in themselves, at the suit of *any person* whomsoever into whose hands they might happen to pass and who should be injured thereby."[9]

Nevertheless the category of dangerous articles and the distinction between things of a dangerous nature and those which become so if improperly constructed (which need not be the same as requiring a further act to be done to make it dangerous) were again urged before the court five years later in *Winterbottom v. Wright*.[10] The court refused to permit a coachman to recover against the defendant who had provided a defective coach under contract with the Postmaster General. The plaintiff had been driving the coach from Hartford to Holyhead when it broke down due to some latent defect; the plaintiff was thrown from his seat and lamed for life. He could not recover because to extend liability this far would lead to "absurd and outrageous consequences." The court refused to discuss whether the defective coach was a weapon of a dangerous nature, even though defendant's counsel seemed to be willing to acknowledge the existence of a special rule of liability for that category. And as for the application of *Langridge v. Levy*, in that case there was "distinct fraud" and the plaintiff "was really and substantially the party contracting." The court refused to find similarity under the fraud concept in the fact that the defendant had sold a coach as safe when he did not know it to be in good condition, or under the direct dealing concept in *Langridge v. Levy* in that "there was nothing to show that the defendant was aware even of the existence of the particular son who was injured" whereas here the coach "was necessarily to be driven by a coachman."[11] The further argument that the plaintiff had no opportunity of seeing that the coach was sound and secure was insufficient to bring liability.

But in 1851, in *Longmeid v. Holliday*,[12] the concept of things dangerous in themselves, twice urged before the court and rejected, finally won out. Longmeid had bought a lamp for the use of himself and his wife from Holliday, the defendant storekeeper, who called the lamp "Holliday's Patent Lamp" and had it put together by other persons from parts which he had purchased. When Eliza Longmeid, the wife and plaintiff, tried to light the lamp, it exploded; the naphtha ran over her and scorched and burned her. She was not permitted to collect from the store-keeper. It had not been shown that the defendant knew the lamp was unfit and warranted it to be sound. And the lamp was not in its nature dangerous. In discussing those cases where a third person, not a party to a contract, might recover damages, the court said:

> And it may be the same when any one delivers to another without notice an instrument in its nature dangerous, or under particular circum-stances, as a loaded gun which he himself loaded, and that other person to whom it is delivered is injured thereby, or if he places it in a situation easily accessible to a third person, who sustains damage from it. A very strong case to that effect is *Dixon v. Bell*. But it would be going much too far to say that so much care is required in the ordinary intercourse of life between one individual and another, that, if a machine not in its nature dangerous, – a carriage for instance, – but which might become so by a latent defect entirely unknown, although discoverable by the exercise of ordinary care, should be lent or given by one person, even by the person who manufactured it, to another, the former should be answerable to the latter for a subsequent damage accruing by the use of it.[13]

Thus the doctrine of the distinction between things in their nature dangerous and those which become so by an unknown latent defect is announced as a way of explaining the difference between a loaded gun (which under the rule, however, is explained as a particular circum-stance) and a defective lamp. As applied in the case, the doctrine describes the classification of the lamp as dangerous only through a latent defect and results in no liability. But a court could have found as much direct dealing in the purchase of a lamp for the use of the purchaser and his wife as in the case of the purchase of a gun for the use of the purchaser and his sons. Under the rule as stated a carriage is not in its nature dangerous.

The second phase of the development of the doctrine of dangerous articles is the period dur-ing which the rule as announced in the *Longmeid* case is applied. The phase begins with mislabeled poison and ends with a defective automobile. During this time also there is the inevitable attempt to soar above the cases and to find some great overall rule which can classify the cases as though the pattern were really not a changing one.

It was the purchase of belladonna, errone-ously marked as extract of dandelion, which, in *Thomas v. Winchester*[14] in 1852, produced the first application and restatement of the rule announced in the *Longmeid* case. The poison had been bought at the store of Dr. Foord, but it had been put into its jar and incorrectly labeled in the shop of the defendant Winchester – prob-ably through the negligence of his employee. Mrs. Thomas, who used what she thought was the extract of dandelion, reacted by having "cold-ness of the surface and extremities, feebleness of circulation, spasms of the muscles, giddiness of the head, dilatation of the pupils of the eye and derangement of mind." She was allowed to recover against Winchester. The defendant's negligence had "put human life in imminent danger." No such imminent danger had existed in the *Winterbottom* case, the court explained. This was more like the case of the loaded gun in *Dixon v. Bell*. The imminent danger category would not include a defective wagon but it did include the poison.

Looking back, one might say today that the category of things by their nature dangerous or imminently dangerous soon came to include a defective hair wash. At least in *George v. Skivington*[15] in 1869, a chemist who com-pounded a secret hair wash was liable to the wife of the purchaser for injuries caused by the wash. But the court went about its business without explicit regard for the imminently dan-gerous category. It thought that the imperfect hairwash was like the imperfect gun in the *Langridge* case. It chose to ignore the emphasis in the *Langridge* case on the purported fact that the seller there knew the gun was defective and lied. It said, "substitute the word 'negligence' for fraud and the analogy between *Langridge v. Levy* and this case is complete." And as for the case of the defective lamp where there was no liability, that was different because negligence had not been found. In constructing a pattern for the cases, it appears that loaded guns, defective guns, poison, and now hair wash were in the imminently dangerous category. Defective wagons and lamps were outside.

The next year it became known that a defect-ive balance wheel for a circular saw was not imminently dangerous. The New York court stated: "Poison is a dangerous subject. Gunpowder is the same. A torpedo is a dangerous instrument, as is a spring gun, a loaded rifle or the like. . . . Not so, however, an iron wheel, a few feet in diameter and a few inches in thickness although one part may be weaker than another. If the article is abused by too long use, or by applying too much weight or speed, an injury may occur, as it may from an ordinary carriage wheel, a wagon axle, or the common chair in which we sit."[16] While applying the imminently dangerous category to defeat liability, the New York court took occasion to give a somewhat new emphasis to *Thomas v. Winchester*. It found that "the decision in *Thomas v. Winchester* was based upon the idea that the negligent sale of poisons is both at common law and by statute an indictable offense." And certainly that could be argued. At any rate, three years later the New York court said its opinion in the balance-wheel case showed that *Thomas v. Winchester* would not result in liability in a case where a boiler blew up.[17] But the imminently dangerous category received a new member in 1882 when the builder of a ninety-foot scaffold to be used in painting the dome of the courthouse was held liable to the estate of an employee-painter who was killed when the ledger gave way.[18] Yet if a defective scaffold was in, the court followed tradition in announcing that a defective carriage would be out.

In England, a defective scaffold was also put in the category. The plaintiff in *Heaven v. Pender*[19] was a ship painter who was injured, while engaged in his work, due to the breaking of defective ropes which held his support outside the ship. He was allowed to recover against the dock owner who had supplied the support and ropes. But the majority of the judges decided the case on the rather narrow point that the necessary workmen were in effect invited by the dock owner to use the dock and appliances. That could have been the explanation also for the American scaffold case. The most noteworthy feature of *Heaven v. Pender*, however, was the flight of one of the judges, Lord Esher, at that time Brett, toward a rule above the legal categories which would classify the cases.

Brett thought recovery should be allowed because:

Whenever one person supplies goods or machinery, or the like for the purpose of their being used by another person under such circumstances that everyone of ordinary sense would, if he thought, recognize at once that unless he used ordinary care and skill with regard to the condition of the thing supplied or the mode of supplying it, there will be danger of injury to the person or property of him for whose use the thing is supplied, and who is to use it, a duty arises to use ordinary care and skill as to the condition or manner of supplying such thing.[20]

This statement was concocted by Brett from two types of cases: first, the case where two drivers or two ships are approaching each other and due care is required toward each other, and second, where a man is invited into a shop or warehouse and the owner must use reasonable care "to keep his house or warehouse that it may not endanger the person or property of the person invited." Since these two different situations resulted in the same legal rule, or stated differently, since two general principles when applied resulted in the same legal rule, Brett thought there must be "some larger proposition which involves and covers both set of circumstances." This was because "the logic of inductive reasoning requires that where two propositions lead to exactly similar premises there must be a more remote and larger premise which embraces both of the major propositions." Brett's rule of ordinary care ran into some difficulty in looking back at the *Langridge* case and its insistence on both fraud and direct dealing. But Brett said of the *Langridge* case, "It is not, it cannot be accurately reported," and in any event the fact that recovery was allowed on the basis of fraud "in no way negatives the proposition that the action might have been supported on the ground of negligence without fraud."

The majority opinion in *Heaven v. Pender*, while proceeding on the invitee point, and while refusing to follow Brett in his flight, agrees that liability for negligence follows when the instrument is dangerous "as a gun" or when the instrument is in such a condition as to cause danger "not necessarily incident to the use of such an instrument" and no due warning is given. Approving this statement, the New York court in 1908 held that the question of a manufacturer's negligence could be left to a jury where the plaintiff lost an eye due to the explosion of a bottle of aerated water.[21] The next year a defective coffee urn or boiler which blew up and killed a man was permitted to join the aerated bottle in the danger concept.[22] The coffee-urn case provided the occasion for explaining two of the names given the dangerous category. Given an "inherently dangerous" article, the court explained, a manufacturer becomes liable for negligent construction which, when added to its inherent characteristics, makes it "imminently dangerous."

The categories by now were fairly well occupied. The dangerous concept had in it a loaded gun, possibly a defective gun, mislabeled poison, defective hair wash, scaffolds, a defective coffee urn, and a defective aerated bottle. The not-dangerous category, once referred to as only latently dangerous, had in it a defective carriage, a bursting lamp, a defective balance wheel for a circular saw, and a defective boiler. Perhaps it is not too surprising to find a defective soldering lamp in *Blacker v. Lake*[23] joining the not-dangerous class. But the English court, in the opinions of its two judges, experienced some difficulty. For the first judge there appears to have been no difficulty in classifying the soldering lamp as not dangerous. Yet the *Skivington* case caused trouble because it appeared to suggest that negligence could be substituted for fraud and perhaps liability would follow even though the article was not dangerous. But in that event the *Skivington* case should not be followed because it was in conflict with *Winterbottom v. Wright*. Accordingly, the soldering lamp not being dangerous, it was error to leave the question of negligence to the jury. The second judge suggested a more surprising realignment of the cases which threatened the whole danger category. He suggested that no recovery should be permitted even though the lamp fell into the class of things dangerous in themselves. The duty of the vendor in such a case, he pointed out, would be a duty to warn, but that duty is discharged if the nature of the article is obvious or known, as was true in this case. Indeed, the *Skivington* and *Thomas v. Winchester* cases were explainable on the very ground that the articles appeared harmless and their contents were unknown. One might almost say that recovery was permitted in those cases because the danger was only latent.

The period of the application of the doctrine of dangerous articles as set forth in the *Longmeid* case and adopted in *Thomas v. Winchester* may be thought to come to an end in 1915 with its application by a federal court – the Circuit Court of Appeals for the Second Circuit. This was the way the law looked to the court. "One who manufactures articles inherently dangerous, e.g. poisons, dynamite, gunpowder, torpedoes, bottles of water under gas pressure, is liable in tort to third parties which they injure, unless he has exercised reasonable care with reference to the articles manufactured. . . . On the other hand, one who manufactures articles dangerous only if defectively made, or installed, e.g., tables, chairs, pictures or mirrors hung on the walls, carriages, automobiles, and so on is not liable to third parties for injuries caused by them, except in cases of willful injury or fraud."[24] Accordingly, the court denied recovery in a suit by the purchaser of a car from a dealer against the manufacturer when the front right wheel broke and the car turned over.

MacPherson v. Buick[25] begins the third phase of the life of the dangerous instrument concept. The New York Court of Appeals in 1916 had before it almost a repetition of the automobile case passed upon by the federal court the previous year. The plaintiff was driving his car, carrying a friend to the hospital, when the car suddenly collapsed due to a defective wheel. The plaintiff was seriously injured. The Buick Motor Company, the defendant, had sold the car to a retail dealer who in turn had sold it to the plaintiff. The defective wheel had been sold to the Buick Company by the Imperial Wheel Company.

As was to be expected, counsel for the plaintiff urged that an automobile was "dangerous to a high degree."[26] It was, in fact, similar to a locomotive. It was much more like a locomotive than like a wagon. "The machine is a fair rival for the Empire Express," he said. "This is evidenced further by the fact that the person running an automobile must have a license of competency, equally with the locomotive engineer and by the legal restrictions imposed by law in the use of the automobile." It was "almost childish to say that an automobile at rest is not dangerous. Neither is a locomotive with the fire drawn" nor a battery of coffee boilers nor a 42-centimeter gun.

The automobile, propelled by explosive gases, was "inherently dangerous." The trial judge had charged the jury that "an automobile is not an inherently dangerous vehicle" but had said that they might find it "imminently dangerous if defective."[27] As to the difference between the two phrases, counsel said there was no point "juggling over definitions. 'Inherently' means 'inseparably.' 'Imminently' means 'threateningly.'" He did not comment on the request of the defendant that the judge charge the jury that recovery depended on the car being "eminently dangerous."[28] Counsel did write, however, that he "was powerfully impressed with a remark of Lord Chief Justice Isaacs, on his recent visit to this country, to the effect that in England they were getting away from merely abstract forms and were seeking to administer justice in each individual case."[29]

The New York Court of Appeals allowed recovery. Judge Cardozo recognized that "the foundations of this branch of the law ... were laid in *Thomas v. Winchester*." He said that some of the illustrations used in *Thomas v. Winchester* might be rejected today (having in mind no doubt the example of the defective carriage), but the principle of the case was the important thing. "There never has in this state been doubt or disavowal of the principle itself." Even while remarking that "precedents drawn from the days of travel by stagecoach do not fit the conditions of travel today," he was quick to add the explanation: "The principle that the danger must be imminent does not change, but the things subject to the principle do change." And in addition there were underlying principles. They were stated, more or less, Cardozo said, by Brett in *Heaven v. Pender*.

To be sure, Cardozo was not certain that this statement of underlying principles was an accurate exposition of the law of England. He thought "it may need some qualification even in our own state. Like most attempts at comprehensive definition, it may involve errors of inclusion and exclusion." He thought, however, that "its tests and standards, at least in their underlying principles, with whatever qualifications may be called for as they are applied to varying conditions, are the tests and standards of our law." He did not comment on the statement of Brett concerning *Thomas v. Winchester*

that it "goes a very long way. I doubt whether it does not go too far."

As to the cases, Cardozo recognized that the early ones "suggest a narrow construction of the rule." He had reference to the boiler and balance-wheel cases. But the way to set them aside had already been shown. They could be distinguished because there the manufacturer had either pointed out the defect or had known that his test was not the final one. The distinction was based upon a point unsuccessfully advanced by losing counsel in *Winterbottom v. Wright*. Other cases showed that it was not necessary to be destructive in order to be dangerous. "A large coffee urn ... may have within itself, if negligently made, the potency of danger, yet no one thinks of it as an implement whose normal function is destruction." And "what is true of the coffee urn is equally true of bottles of aerated water." *Devlin v. Smith* was important too. "A scaffold," Cardozo pointed out, "is not inherently a dangerous instrument." He admitted that the scaffold and the coffee-urn cases may "have extended the rule of *Thomas v. Winchester*," but "If so, this court is committed to the extension. The defendant argues that things inherently dangerous to life are poisons, explosives, deadly weapons, things whose normal function is to injure or destroy. But whatever the rule in *Thomas v. Winchester* may once have been, it has no longer that restricted meaning."

He showed a certain impatience for what he called "verbal niceties." He complained that "subtle distinctions are drawn by the defendant between things inherently dangerous and things imminently dangerous." As to this it was sufficient to say, "If danger was to be expected as reasonably certain, there was a duty of vigilance, and this whether you call the danger inherent or imminent." The rule was: "If the nature of a thing is such that it is reasonably certain to place life and limb in peril, when negligently made, it is then a thing of danger." But "there must be a knowledge of a danger not merely possible but probable." Thus what was only latently dangerous in *Thomas v. Winchester* now became imminently dangerous or inherently dangerous, or, if verbal niceties are to be disregarded, just plain or probably dangerous.

Elsewhere in commenting on the case, Cardozo seems to make somewhat less of the matter of principles. He wrote: "What, however, was the posture of affairs before the *Buick* case had been determined? Was there any law on the subject? A mass of judgments, more or less relevant, had been rendered by the same and other courts. A body of particulars existed in which an hypothesis might be reared. None the less, their implications were equivocal. . . . The things classified as dangerous have been steadily extended with a corresponding extension of the application of the remedy. . . . They have widened till they include a scaffold or an automobile or even pies and cakes when nails and other foreign substances have supplied ingredients not mentioned in the recipes of cook books." Cardozo described the legal process in connection with these cases as one in which "logic and utility still struggle for the mastery."[30] One can forgive Judge Cardozo for this language. It is traditional to think of logic as fighting with something. Sometimes it is thought of as fighting with history and experience.

In a reversal of itself, not so striking because the membership of the court was different, the same federal court hearing another appeal in the same case in which it had been decided that a defective automobile was not inherently dangerous now stated with new wisdom: "We cannot believe that the liability of a manufacturer of an automobile has any analogy to the liability of a manufacturer of 'tables, chairs, pictures, or mirrors hung on walls.' The analogy is rather that of a manufacturer of unwholesome food or of a poisonous drug."[31]

MacPherson v. Buick renamed and enlarged the danger category. It is usually thought to have brought the law into line with "social considerations."[32] But it did not remove the necessity for deciding cases. Later the New York courts were able to put into the category of things of danger or probably dangerous a defective bottle[33] and another coffee urn,[34] although one less terrifying than the coffee boiler of 1909. But for some reason or other, admission was denied to a defective automobile when the defect was a door handle which gave way, causing one of the doors to open with the result that the plaintiff was thrown through the door and under the car. The defective handle did not make the car a "thing of danger."[35] And if one is comparing cases and examples, it has to be admitted that a door handle is less closely connected with those things which make a car like a locomotive than is the wheel on which it runs.

Nevertheless, a new freedom follows from *MacPherson v. Buick.* Under it, as the Massachusetts court has said, the exception in favor of liability for negligence where the instrument is probably dangerous has swallowed up the purported rule that "a manufacturer or supplier is never liable for negligence to a remote vendee."[36] The exception now seems to have the same certainty the rule once had. The exception is now a general principle of liability which can be stated nicely in the Restatement, and text writers can criticize courts for not applying what is now an obvious rule of liability.[37]

A somewhat similar development has occurred in England. In *Donoghue v. Stevenson*[38] in 1932, the manufacturer of a bottle of ginger beer was held liable to the plaintiff who had purchased the bottle through a friend at a café. The bottle contained the decomposed remains of a snail. The opinions of the majority judges stressed the close and almost direct relationship between the manufacturer and the remote vendee. The control of the manufacturer of this type of article was thought to be "effective until the article reaches the consumer. . . . A manufacturer puts up an article of food in containers which he knows will be opened by the actual consumer. There can be no inspection by any purchaser and no reasonable preliminary inspection by the consumer." Lord Atkin, while stating that Brett's rule in *Heaven v. Pender* was too broad, found that the moral rule requiring the love of one's neighbour in law was translated into the injunction "you must not injure your neighbour." The question then was: "Who is my neighbour?" The practical rule evolved was of persons "closely and directly affected" and as to acts "which you can reasonably foresee would be likely to injure your neighbour." The emphasis on control and proximity revives the notion of the unconscious agent in *Langridge v. Levy*, as well as the inability to inspect, unsuccessfully urged in *Winterbottom v. Wright* and apparently implicit in the *Skivington* case.

As for other prior cases it was now said that the distinction between things dangerous and those dangerous in themselves was "an unnatural one" and anyway the fact that there might be a special duty for one category no longer meant that a duty might not exist for others. *Winterbottom* and *Longmeid* were no longer controlling because negligence had not been alleged and proved in those cases. And as for the *Blacker* case, Lord Atkin had read and re-read it but had difficulty "in formulating the precise grounds upon which the judgment was given." Thus prior cases were realigned out of the way despite the protest of dissenting judges who adhered to the view of the exception only for dangerous articles in the more traditional sense.

While the emphasis was on continuing control in the *Donoghue* case, and counsel urged that the *Donoghue* case applied only to articles intended for internal consumption, its rule was applied in *Grant v. Australian Knitting Mills*[39] in 1936 to underpants defective due to the presence of an irritating chemical. Here the emphasis could be more on the point that the defect was hidden. While the *Blacker* case was in a sense disregarded, the point made by one of its judges was in fact accepted. Reasoning in a manner not unlike *Skivington*, which substituted negligence for fraud, the court put secrecy in the place of control. Donoghue's case was now seen not to "depend on the bottle being stopped and sealed; the essential point in this regard was that the article should reach the consumer or user subject to the same defect as it had when it left the manufacturer." The court realized that in applying its test of directness, control, proximity and hidden defect, "many difficult problems will arise.... Many qualifying conditions and many complications of fact may in the future come before the Courts for decision." But "in their Lordships' opinion it is enough for them to decide this case on its actual facts."

With the breakdown of the inherently dangerous rule, the cycle from *Dixon v. Bell* was complete. But it would be a mistake to believe that the breakdown makes possible a general rule, such as the rule of negligence, which now can be applied. A rule so stated would be equivalent to the flight of Brett. Negligence itself must be given meaning by the examples to be included under it. Unlimited liability is not intended. As the comparison of cases proceeds, new categories will be stressed. Perhaps, for example, there will be a category for trade-marked, patented, advertised, or monopolized articles. The basis

for such a category exists. The process of reasoning by example will decide. [...]

Notes

1 The controlling book is Frank, *Law and the Modern Mind* (Anchor Books, Doubleday & Co., 1936).
2 217 N.Y. 382, 111 N.E. 1050 (1916); see Parker, *Attorneys at Law*, Ch. 8 (1942).
3 5 Maule & Selwyn 198 (1816).
4 Ibid., at 199.
5 2 Meeson & Welsby 519 (1837).
6 Ibid., at 531.
7 Alderson, B., ibid., at 525.
8 Ibid., at 528; note also the hypothetical case set forth by counsel for the plaintiff in *Langridge v. Levy* reported in 6 L.J. (N.S.) Ex. 137, 138 (1837). "A case might be put of a wrong medicine sent from a chemist, which is received by a person, and placed by him in a cupboard, and afterwards taken by a third person, who, in consequence receives an injury; can it be said that he has no remedy against the chemist?"
9 Ibid., at 530.
10 10 Meeson & Welsby 109 (1842).
11 Ibid., at 112.
12 155 Eng. Rep. 752 (1851).
13 Ibid., at 755. The opinion was by Parke, B.
14 6 N.Y. 397 (1852).
15 5 L.R. Ex. 1 (1869).
16 Loop v. Litchfield, 42 N.Y. 351, 359 (1870).
17 Losee v. Clute, 51 N.Y. 494 (1873).
18 Devlin v. Smith, 89, N.Y. 470 (1882).
19 11 L.R. Q.B. 503 (1883).
20 Ibid., at 510; see also rule as stated at 509.
21 Torgesen v. Schultz, 192 N.Y. 156, 84 N.E. 956 (1908).
22 Statler v. Ray, 195 N.Y. 478, 88 N.E. 1063 (1909).
23 106 L.T. 533 (1912).
24 Cadillac v. Johnson, 221 Fed. 801, 803 (C.C.A. 2d, 1915).
25 217 N.Y. 382, 111 N.E. 1050 (1916); see Bohlen, Liability of Manufacturers to Persons Other than Their Immediate Vendors, 45 L.Q. Rev. 343 (1929).
26 Brief for the Plaintiff 16, 17, 18.
27 217 N.Y. 382, 396, 111 N.E. 1050, 1055 (1916).
28 Ibid., at 399, 1056.
29 Brief for the Plaintiff 23.
30 Cardozo, *The Growth of the Law*, 40–1, 76–8 (Yale University Press, 1924).
31 Johnson v. Cadillac, 261 Fed. 878, 886 (C.C.A. 2d, 1919).

32 See Torts: Liability of Manufacturer to Consumer for Article Dangerous Because of Defective Construction, 9 Corn. L.Q. 494 (1924).

33 Smith v. Peerless Glass Co., 259 N.Y. 292, 181 N.E. 576 (1932); cf. Bates v. Batey & Co., [1913] 3 K.B. 351.

34 Hoenig v. Central Stamping Co., 273 N.Y. 485, 6 N.E. 2d 415 (1936).

35 Cohen v. Brockway Motor Corp., 240 App. Div. 18, 268 N.Y. Supp. 545 (1934).

36 Carter v. Yardley & Co., 319 Mass. 92, 64 N.E. 2d 693 (1946).

37 See Harper, Law of Torts § 106 (133).

38 [1932] A.C. 562. Note the reference to trade names and patents at 583.

39 [1936] A.C. 85.

2

Remarks on the Theory of Appellate Decision and the Rules or Canons about how Statutes are to be Construed

Karl N. Llewellyn

I

One does not progress far into legal life without learning that there is no single right and accurate way of reading one case, or of reading a bunch of cases. For

(1) Impeccable and correct doctrine makes clear that a case "holds" with authority only so much of what the opinion says as is absolutely necessary to sustain the judgment. Anything else is unnecessary and "distinguishable" and noncontrolling for the future. Indeed, if the judgment rests on two, three or four rulings, any of them can be rightly and righteously knocked out, for the future, as being thus "unnecessary." Moreover, any distinction on the facts is rightly and righteously a reason for distinguishing and therefore disregarding the prior alleged holding. But

(2) Doctrine equally impeccable and correct makes clear that a case "holds" with authority the rule on which the court there chose to rest the judgment; more, that that rule covers, with full authority, cases which are plainly distinguishable on their facts and their issue, whenever the reason for the rule extends to cover them. Indeed, it is unnecessary for a rule or principle to have led to the decision in the prior case, or even to have been phrased therein, in order to be seen as controlling in the new case: (a) "We there said . . ." (b) "That case necessarily decided . . ."

These divergent and indeed conflicting correct ways of handling or reading a single prior case as one "determines" what it authoritatively holds, have their counterparts in regard to the authority of a series or body of cases. Thus

(1) It is correct to see that "That rule is too well settled in this jurisdiction to be disturbed"; and so to apply it to a wholly novel circumstance. But

(2) It is no less correct to see that "The rule has never been extended to a case like the present"; and so to refuse to apply it: "We here limit the rule." Again,

(3) It is no less correct to look over the prior "applications" of "the rule" and rework them into a wholly new formulation of "the true rule" or "true principle" which knocks out some of the prior cases as simply "misapplications" and then builds up the others.

Karl Llewellyn, "Remarks on the Theory of Appellate Decision and the Rules or Canons about how Statutes are to be Construed," *Vand L. Rev.*, vol. 3, 395 (1950).

In the work of a single opinion-day I have observed 26 different, describable ways in which one of our best state courts handled its own prior cases, repeatedly using three to six different ways within a single opinion.

What is important is that *all* 26 ways (plus a dozen others which happened not to be in use that day) are correct. They represent not "evasion," but sound use, application and development of precedent. They represent not "departure from," but sound continuation of, our system of precedent as it has come down to us. The major defect in that system is a mistaken idea which many lawyers have about it – to wit, the idea that the cases themselves and in themselves, plus the correct rules on how to handle cases, provide one single correct answer to a disputed issue of law. In fact the available correct answers are two, three, or ten. The question is: *Which* of the available correct answers will the court *select* – and *why?* For since there is always more than one available correct answer, the court always has to select.

True, the selection is frequently almost automatic. The type of distinction or expansion which is always *technically* available may be psychologically or sociologically unavailable. This may be because of (a) the current tradition of the court or because of (b) the current temper of the court or because of (c) the sense of the situation as the court sees that sense. (There are other possible reasons a-plenty, but these three are the most frequent and commonly the most weighty.)

The *current tradition* of the court is a matter of period-style in the craft of judging. In 1820–50 our courts felt in general a freedom and duty to move in the manner typified in our thought by Mansfield and Marshall. "Precedent" guided, but "principle" controlled; and nothing was good "Principle" which did not look like wisdom-in-result for the welfare of All-of-us. In 1880–1910, on the other hand, our courts felt in general a prime duty to order within the law and a duty to resist any "outside" influence. "Precedent" was to control, not merely to guide: "Principle" was to be tested by whether it made for order in the law, not by whether it made wisdom-in-result. "Legal" Principle could not be subjected to "political" tests; even legislation was resisted as disturbing. Since 1920 the earlier style (the "Grand Style") has been working its way back into general use by our courts, though the language of the opinions moves still dominantly (though waningly) in the style (the "Formal Style") of the late 19th Century. In any particular court what needs study is how far along the process has gotten. The best material for study is the latest volume of reports, read in sequence from page 1 through to the end: the current mine-run of the work.

The *current temper* of the court is reflected in the same material, and represents the court's tradition as modified by its personnel. For it is plain that the two earlier period-styles represent also two eternal types of human being. There is the man who loves creativeness who can without loss of sleep combine risk-taking with responsibility, who sees and feels institutions as things built and to be built to serve functions, and who sees the functions as vital and law as a tool to be eternally reoriented to justice and to general welfare. There is the other man who loves order, who finds risk uncomfortable and has seen so much irresponsible or unwise innovation that responsibility to him means caution, who sees and feels institutions as the tested, slow-built ways which for all their faults are man's sole safeguard against relapse into barbarism, and who regards reorientation of the law in our polity as essentially committed to the legislature. Commonly a man of such temper has also a craftsman's pride in clean craftsman's work, and commonly he does not view with too much sympathy any ill-done legislative job of attempted reorientation.[1] Judges, like other men, range up and down the scale between the extremes of either type of temper, and in this aspect (as in the aspect of intellectual power and acumen or of personal force or persuasiveness) the constellation of the personnel on a particular bench at a particular time plays its important part in urging the court toward a more literal or a more creative selection among the available accepted and correct "ways" of handling precedent.

More vital, if possible, than either of the above is *the sense of the situation as seen by the court.* Thus in the very heyday of the formal period our courts moved into tremendous creative expansion of precedent in regard to the labor injunction and the due process clause. What they saw as sense to be achieved, and desperately needed, there broke through all trammels of the current period-style. Whereas the most creative-minded court working in the most creative period-style will happily and literally apply a formula without discussion, and even with relief, if the formula makes sense and yields justice in the situation and the case.

So strongly does the felt sense of the situation and the case affect the court's choice of techniques for reading or interpreting and then applying the authorities that one may fairly lay down certain generalizations:

A. In some six appealed cases out of ten the court feels this sense so clearly that lining up the authorities comes close to being an automatic job. *In the very process of reading an authority* a distinction leaps to the eye, and that is "all" that that case holds; or the language of another authority (whether or not "really" in point) shines forth as "clearly stating the true rule." Trouble comes when the cases do not line up this clearly and semi-automatically, when they therefore call for intellectual labor, even at times for a conclusion that the law as given will not allow the sensible result to be reached. Or trouble comes when the sense of the situation is not clear.

B. Technical leeways correctly available when the sense of the situation and the case call for their use cease to be correctly available *unless used in furtherance of what the court sees as such sense.* There is here in our system of precedent an element of uprightness, or conscience, of judicial responsibility: and motive becomes a factor in determining what techniques are correct and right. Today, in contrast with 1890, it may be fairly stated that even the literal application of a thoroughly established rule is not correct in a case or situation in which that application does not make sense unless the court in honest conscience feels forced by its office to make the application.

C. Collateral to B, but deserving of separate statement, is the proposition that *the greater the felt need, because of felt sense, the wider is the leeway correctly and properly available in reshaping an authority or the authorities.* What is both proper and to be expected in an extreme case would become abuse and judicial usurpation if made daily practice in the mine-run of cases. All courts worthy of their office feel this in their bones, as being

inherent in our system of precedent. They show the feeling in their work. Where differences appear is where they should appear; in divergent sizings up of what is sense, and of how great the need may be in any situation.

One last thing remains to be said about "sense."

There is a sense of *the type of situation* to be contrasted with the sense of *a particular controversy between particular litigants.* Which of these aspects of sense a court responds to more strongly makes a tremendous difference. Response primarily to the sense of the particular controversy is, in the first place, dangerous because a particular controversy may not be typical, and because it is hard to disentangle general sense from personalities and from "fireside" equities. Such response is dangerous in the second place because it leads readily to finding an out *for this case only* – and that leads to a complicating multiplicity of refinement and distinction, as also to repeated resort to analogies unthought through and unfortunate of extension. This is what the proverb seeks to say: "Hard cases make bad law."

If on the other hand the type of situation is in the forefront of attention, a solving rule comes in for much more thoughtful testing and study. Rules are thrust toward reasonable simplicity, and made with broader vision. Moreover, the idiosyncrasies of the particular case and its possible emotional deflections are set for judgment against a broader picture which gives a fair chance that accidental sympathy is not mistaken for long-range justice for all. And one runs a better chance of skirting the incidence of the other proverb: "Bad law makes hard cases."

On the case-law side, I repeat, we ought all thus to be familiar with the fact that the right doctrine and going practice of our highest courts leave them a very real leeway within which (a) to narrow or avoid what seem today to have been unfortunate prior phrasings or even rulings; or (b), on the other hand, to pick up, develop, expand what seem today to have been fortunate prior rulings or even phrasings.

It is silly, I repeat, to think of use of this leeway as involving "twisting" of precedent. The very phrase presupposes the thing which is not and which has never been. The phrase presupposes that there was in the precedent under consideration some one and single meaning. The whole experience of our case-law shows that that assumption is false. It is, instead, the business of the courts to use the precedents constantly to make the law always a *little* better, to correct old mistakes, to recorrect mistaken or ill-advised attempts at correction – but always within limits severely set not only by the precedents, but equally by the traditions of right conduct in judicial office.

What we need to see now is that all of this is paralleled, in regard to statutes, because of (1) the power of the legislature both to choose policy and to select measures; and (2) the necessity that the legislature shall, in so doing, use language – language fixed in particular words; and (3) the continuing duty of the courts to make sense, under and within the law.

For just as prior courts can have been skillful or unskillful, clear or unclear, wise or unwise, so can legislatures. And just as prior courts have been looking at only a single piece of our whole law at a time, so have legislatures.

But a court must strive to make sense *as a whole* out of our law *as a whole*. It must, to use Frank's figure,[2] take the music of any statute as written by the legislature; it must take the text of the play as written by the legislature. But there are many ways to play that music, to play that play, and a court's duty is to play it well, and in harmony with the other music of the legal system.

Hence, in the field of statutory construction also, there are "correct," unchallengeable rules of "how to read" which lead in happily variant directions.

This must be so until courts recognize that here, as in case-law, the real guide is Sense-for-All-of-Us. It must be so, so long as we and the courts pretend that there has been only one single correct answer possible. Until we give up that foolish pretense there must be a set of mutually contradictory *correct* rules on How to Construe Statutes: either set available as duty and sense may require.

Until then, also, the problem will recur in statutory construction as in the handling of case-law: *Which* of the technically correct answers (a) *should* be given: (b) *will* be given – and Why?

And everything said above about the temper of the court, the temper of the court's tradition, the sense of the situation and the case, applies here as well.

Thus in the period of the Grand Style of case-law statutes were construed "freely" to implement their purpose, the court commonly accepting the legislature's choice of policy and setting to work to implement it. (Criminal statutes and, to some extent, statutes on procedure, were exceptions.) Whereas in the Formal Period statutes tended to be limited or even eviscerated by wooden and literal reading, in a sort of long-drawn battle between a balky, stiff-necked, wrong-headed court and a legislature which had only words with which to drive that court. Today the courts have regained, in the main, a cheerful acceptance of legislative choice of policy, but they are still hampered to some extent in carrying such policies forward by the Formal Period's insistence on precise language.

II

One last thing is to be noted:

If a statute is to make sense, it must be read in the light of some assumed purpose. A statute merely declaring a rule, with no purpose or objective, is nonsense.

If a statute is to be merged into a going system of law, moreover, the court must do the merging, and must in so doing take account of the policy of the statute – or else substitute its own version of such policy. Creative reshaping of the net result is thus inevitable.

But the policy of a statute is of two wholly different kinds – each kind somewhat limited in effect by the statute's choice of measures, and by the statute's choice of fixed language. On the one hand there are the ideas consciously before the draftsmen, the committee, the legislature: a known evil to be cured, a known goal to be attained, a deliberated choice of one line of approach rather than another. Here talk of "intent" is reasonably realistic; committee reports, legislative debate, historical knowledge of contemporary thinking or campaigning which points up the evil or the goal can have significance.

But on the other hand – and increasingly as a statute gains in age – its language is called upon to deal with circumstances utterly uncontemplated at the time of its passage. Here the quest is not properly for the sense originally intended by the statute, for the sense sought originally to be *put into it*, but rather for the sense which *can be quarried out of it* in the light of the new situation. Broad purposes can indeed reach far beyond details known or knowable at the time of drafting. A "dangerous weapon" statute of 1840 can include tommy guns, tear gas or atomic bombs. "Vehicle," in a statute of 1840, can properly be read, when sense so suggests, to include an automobile, or a hydroplane that lacks wheels. But for all that, the sound quest does not run primarily in terms of historical intent. It runs in terms of what the words can be made to bear, in making sense in the light of the unforeseen.

III

When it comes to presenting a proposed construction in court, there is an accepted conventional vocabulary. As in argument over points of case-law, the accepted convention still, unhappily requires discussion as if only one single correct meaning could exist. Hence there are two opposing canons on almost every point. An arranged selection is appended. Every lawyer must be familiar with them all: they are still needed tools of argument. At least as early as Fortescue the general picture was clear, on this, to any eye which would see.

Plainly, to make any canon take hold in a particular instance, the construction contended for must be sold, essentially, by means other than the use of the canon: The good sense of the situation and a *simple* construction of the available language to achieve that sense, *by tenable means, out of the statutory language.*

Canons of construction

Statutory interpretation still speaks a diplomatic tongue. Here is some of the technical framework for maneuver.

THRUST	BUT	PARRY
1. A statute cannot go beyond its text.[3]		1. To effect its purpose a statute may be implemented beyond its text.[4]
2. Statutes in derogation of the common law will not be extended by construction.[5]		2. Such acts will be liberally construed if their nature is remedial.[6]
3. Statutes are to be read in the light of the common law and a statute affirming a common law rule is to be construed in accordance with the common law.[7]		3. The common law gives way to a statute which is inconsistent with it and when a statute is designed as a revision of a whole body of law applicable to a given subject it supersedes the common law.[8]
4. Where a foreign statute which has received construction has been adopted, previous construction is adopted too.[9]		4. It may be rejected where there is conflict with the obvious meaning of the statute or where the foreign decisions are unsatisfactory in reasoning or where the foreign interpretation is not in harmony with the spirit or policy of the laws of the adopting state.[10]
5. Where various states have already adopted the statute, the parent state is followed.[11]		5. Where interpretations of other states are inharmonious, there is no such restraint.[12]
6. Statutes *in pari materia* must be construed together.[13]		6. A statute is not *in pari materia* if its scope and aim are distinct or where a legislative design to depart from the general purpose or policy of previous enactments may be apparent.[14]
7. A statute imposing a new penalty or forfeiture, or a new liability or disability, or		7. Remedial statutes are to be liberally construed and if a retroactive interpretation will promote

creating a new right of action will not be construed as having a retroactive effect.[15]

8. Where design has been distinctly stated no
place is left for construction.[17]

9. Definitions and rules of construction contained in an interpretation clause are part of
the law and binding.[19]

10. A statutory provision requiring liberal
construction does not mean disregard of
unequivocal requirements of the statute.[21]

11. Titles do not control meaning; preambles
do not expand scope; section headings do not
change language.[23]

12. If language is plain and unambiguous
it must be given effect.[25]

13. Words and phrases which have received
judicial construction before enactment are to
be understood according to that construction.[27]

14. After enactment, judicial decision upon
interpretation of particular terms and phrases
controls.[29]

15. Words are to be taken in their ordinary
meaning unless they are technical terms or
words of art.[31]

16. Every word and clause must be given
effect.[33]

17. The same language used repeatedly in
the same connection is presumed to bear the
same meaning throughout the statute.[35]

18. Words are to be interpreted according
to the proper grammatical effect of their
arrangement within the statute.[37]

19. Exceptions not made cannot be read.[39]

20. Expression of one thing excludes
another.[41]

the ends of justice, they should receive such
construction.[16]

8. Courts have the power to inquire into real
– as distinct from ostensible – purpose.[18]

9. Definitions and rules of construction in
a statute will not be extended beyond their
necessary import nor allowed to defeat intention otherwise manifested.[20]

10. Where a rule of construction is provided
within the statute itself the rule should be
applied.[22]

11. The title may be consulted as a guide
when there is doubt or obscurity in the body;
preambles may be consulted to determine
rationale, and thus the true construction of
terms; section headings may be looked upon
as part of the statute itself.[24]

12. Not when literal interpretation would
lead to absurd or mischievous consequences
or thwart manifest purpose.[26]

13. Not if the statute clearly requires them to
have a different meaning.[28]

14. Practical construction by executive officers
is strong evidence of true meaning.[30]

15. Popular words may bear a technical
meaning and technical words may have a
popular signification and they should be so
construed as to agree with evident intention
or to make the statute operative.[32]

16. If inadvertantly inserted or if repugnant
to the rest of the statute, they may be rejected
as surplusage.[34]

17. This presumption will be disregarded
where it is necessary to assign different meanings to make the statute consistent.[36]

18. Rules of grammar will be disregarded
where strict adherence would defeat purpose.[38]

19. The letter is only the "bark." Whatever is
within the reason of the law is within the law
itself.[40]

20. The language may fairly comprehend
many different cases where some only are
expressly mentioned by way of example.[42]

21. General terms are to receive a general construction.[43]

22. It is a general rule of construction that where general words follow an enumeration they are to be held as applying only to persons and things of the same general kind or class specifically mentioned (*ejusdem generis*).[45]

23. Qualifying or limiting words or clauses are to be referred to the next preceding antecedent.[47]

24. Punctuation will govern when a statute is open to two constructions.[49]

25. It must be assumed that language has been chosen with due regard to grammatical propriety and is not interchangeable on mere conjecture.[51]

26. There is a distinction between words of permission and mandatory words.[53]

27. A proviso qualifies the provision immediately preceding.[55]

28. When the enacting clause is general, a proviso is construed strictly.[57]

21. They may be limited by specific terms with which they are associated or by the scope and purpose of the statute.[44]

22. General words must operate on something. Further, *ejusdem generis* is only an aid in getting the meaning and does not warrant confining the operations of a statute within narrower limits than were intended.[46]

23. Not when evident sense and meaning require a different construction.[48]

24. Punctuation marks will not control the plain and evident meaning of language.[50]

25. "And" and "or" may be read interchangeably whenever the change is necessary to give the statute sense and effect.[52]

26. Words imparting permission may be read as mandatory and words imparting command may be read as permissive when such construction is made necessary by evident intention or by the rights of the public.[54]

27. It may clearly be intended to have a wider scope.[56]

28. Not when it is necessary to extend the proviso to persons or cases which come within its equity.[58]

Notes

1 Intellectually, this last attitude is at odds with the idea that reorientation is for the legislature. Emotionally, it is not. Apart from the rather general resistance to change which normally companions orderliness of mind, there is a legitimate feeling that within a team team-play is called for, that it is passing the buck to thrust onto a court the labor of making a legislative job make sense and become workable.

2 Frank, "Words and Music: Some Remarks on Statutory Interpretation." 47 *Col. L. Rev.*, 1259 (1947).

3 First National Bank v. DeBerriz, 87 W. Va. 477, 105 S.E. 900 (1921); Sutherland, *Statutory Construction* §388 (2d ed. 1904); 59 C.J., *Statutes* §575 (1932).

4 Dooley v. Penn. R.R., 250 Fed. 142 (D. Minn. 1918); 59 C.J., *Statutes* §575 (1932).

5 Devers v. City of Seranton, 308 Pa. 13, 161 Atl. 540 (1932); Black, *Construction and Interpretation of Laws* §113 (2d ed. 1911); Sutherland, *Statutory Construction* §573 (2d ed. 1904); 25 R.C.L., *Statutes* §281 (1919).

6 Becker v. Brown, 65 Neb. 264, 91 N.W. 178 (1902); Black, *Construction and Interpretation of Laws* §113 (2d ed. 1911); Sutherland, *Statutory Construction* §§573–5 (2d ed. 1904); 59 C.J., *Statutes* §657 (1932).

7 Bandfield v. Bandfield, 117 Mich. 80, 75 N.W. 287 (1898); 25 R.C.L., *Statutes* §280 (1919).

8 Hamilton v. Rathbone, 175 U.S. 414, 20 Sup. Ct. 155, 44 L. Ed. 219 (1899); State v. Lewis, 142 N.C. 626, 55 S.E. 600 (1906); 25 R.C.L., *Statutes* §§280, 289 (1919).

9 Freese v. Tripp, 70 Ill. 496 (1873); Black, *Construction and Interpretation of Laws* §176 (2d ed. 1911); 59 C.J., *Statutes*, §§614, 627 (1932); 25 R.C.L., *Statutes* §294 (1919).

10 Bowers v. Smith, 111 Mo. 45, 20 S.W. 101 (1892); Black, *Construction and Interpretation of Laws*

§176 (2d ed. 1911); Sutherland, *Statutory Construction* §404 (2d ed. 1904); 59 C.J., *Statutes* §628 (1932).

11 Burnside v. Wand, 170 Mo. 531, 71 S.W. 337 (1902).

12 State v. Campbell, 73 Kan. 688, 85 Pac. 784 (1906).

13 Milner v. Gibson, 249 Ky. 594, 61 S.W.2d 273 (1933); Black, *Construction and Interpretation of Laws* §104 (2d ed. 1911); Sutherland, *Statutory Construction* §§443–8 (2d ed. 1904); 25 R.C.L., *Statutes* §285 (1919).

14 Wheelock v. Myers, 64 Kan. 47, 67 Pac. 632 (1902); Black, *Construction and Interpretation of Laws* §104 (2d ed. 1911); Sutherland, *Statutory Construction* §449 (2d ed. 1904); 59 C.J., *Statutes* §620 (1932).

15 Keeley v. Great Northern Ry., 139 Wis. 448, 121 N.W. 167 (1909); Black, *Construction and Interpretation of Laws* §119 (2d ed. 1911).

16 Falls v. Key, 278 S.W. 893 (Tex. Civ. App. 1925); Black, *Construction and Interpretation of Laws* §120 (2d ed. 1911).

17 Federoff v. Birks Bros., 75 Cal. App. 345, 242 Pac. 885 (1925); Sutherland, *Statutory Construction* §358 (2d ed. 1904); 59 C.J., *Statutes* §570 (1932).

18 Coulter v. Pool, 187 Cal. 181, 201 Pac. 120 (1921); 59 C.J., *Statutes* §570 (1932).

19 Smith v. State, 28 Ind. 321 (1867); Black, *Construction and Interpretation of Laws* §89 (2d ed. 1911); 59 C.J., *Statutes* §567 (1932).

20 *In re* Bissell, 245 App. Div. 395, 282 N.Y. Supp. 983 (4th Dep't 1935); Black, *Construction and Interpretation of Laws* §89 (2d ed. 1911); 59 C.J., *Statutes* §566 (1932).

21 Los Angeles County v. Payne, 82 Cal. App. 210, 255 Pac. 281 (1927); Sutherland, *Statutory Construction* §360 (2d ed. 1904); 59 C.J., *Statutes* §567 (1932).

22 State *ex rel.* Triay v. Burr, 79 Fla. 290, 84 So. 61 (1920); Sutherland, *Statutory Construction* §360 (2d ed. 1904); 59 C.J., *Statutes* §567 (1932).

23 Westbrook v. McDonald, 184 Ark. 740, 44 S.W. 2d 331 (1931); Huntworth v. Tanner, 87 Wash. 670, 152 Pac. 523 (1915); Black, *Construction and Interpretation of Laws* §§83–5 (2d ed. 1911); Sutherland, *Statutory Construction* §§339–42 (2d ed. 1904); 59 C.J., *Statutes* §599 (1932); 25 R.C.L., *Statutes* §§266–7 (1919).

24 Brown v. Robinson, 275 Mass. 55, 175 N.E. 269 (1931); Gulley v. Jackson, 165 Miss. 103, 145 So. 905 (1933); Black, *Construction and Interpretation of Laws* §§83–5 (2d ed. 1911); Sutherland, *Statutory Construction* §§339–42 (2d ed. 1904); 59 C.J., *Statutes* §§598–9 (1932); 25 R.C.L., *Statutes* §§266, 267 (1919).

25 Newhall v. Sanger, 92 U.S. 761, 23 L. Ed. 769 (1875); Black, *Construction and Interpretation of Laws* §51 (2d ed. 1911); 59 C.J., *Statutes* §569 (1932); 25 R.C.L., *Statutes* §§213, 225 (1919).

26 Clark v. Murray, 141 Kan. 533, 41 P.2d 1042 (1935); Sutherland, *Statutory Construction* §363 (2d ed. 1904); 59 C.J., *Statutes* §573 (1932); 25 R.C.L., *Statutes* §§214, 257 (1919).

27 Scholze v. Sholze, 2 Tenn. App. 80 (M.S. 1925); Black, *Construction and Interpretation of Laws* §65 (2d ed. 1911); Sutherland, *Statutory Construction* §363 (2d ed. 1904).

28 Dixon v. Robbins, 246 N.Y. 169, 158 N.E. 63 (1927); Black, *Construction and Interpretation of Laws* §65 (2d ed. 1911); Sutherland, *Statutory Construction* §363 (2d ed. 1904).

29 Eau Claire National Bank v. Benson, 106 Wis. 624, 82 N.W. 604 (1900); Black, *Construction and Interpretation of Laws* §93 (2d ed. 1911).

30 State *ex rel.* Bashford v. Frear, 138 Wis. 536, 120 N.W. 216 (1909); Black, *Construction and Interpretation of Laws* §94 (2d ed. 1911); 25 R.C.L., *Statutes* §274 (1919).

31 Hawley Coal Co. v. Bruce, 252 Ky. 455, 67 S.W.2d 703 (1934); Black, *Construction and Interpretation of Laws* §63 (2d ed. 1911); Sutherland, *Statutory Construction*, §§390, 393 (2d ed. 1904); C.J., *Statutes* §§577, 578 (1932).

32 Robinson v. Varnell, 16 Tex. 382 (1856); Black, *Construction and Interpretation of Laws* §63 (2d ed. 1911); Sutherland, *Statutory Construction* §395 (2d ed. 1904); 59 C.J., *Statutes* §§577, 578 (1932).

33 *In re* Terry's Estate, 218 N.Y. 218, 112 N.E. 931 (1916); Black, *Construction and Interpretation of Laws* §60 (2d ed. 1911); Sutherland, *Statutory Construction* §380 (2d ed. 1904).

34 United States v. York, 131 Fed. 323 (C.C.S.D.N.Y. 1904); Black, *Construction and Interpretation of Laws* §60 (2d ed. 1911); Sutherland, *Statutory Construction* §384 (2d ed. 1904).

35 Spring Canyon Coal Co. v. Industrial Comm'n, 74 Utah 103, 277 Pac. 206 (1929); Black, *Construction and Interpretation of Laws* §53 (2d ed. 1911).

36 State v. Knowles, 90 Md. 646, 45 Atl. 877 (1900); Black, *Construction and Interpretation of Laws* §53 (2d ed. 1911).

37 Harris v. Commonwealth, 142 Va. 620, 128 S.E. 578 (1925); Black, *Construction and Interpretation of Laws* §55 (2d ed. 1911); Sutherland, *Statutory Construction* §408 (2d ed. 1904).

38 Fisher v. Connard, 100 Pa. 63 (1882); Black, *Construction and Interpretation of Laws* §55 (2d ed. 1911); Sutherland, *Statutory Construction* §409 (2d ed. 1904).

39 Lima v. Cemetery Ass'n, 42 Ohio St. 128 (1884); 25 R.C.L., *Statutes* §260 (1919).

40 Flynn v. Prudential Ins. Co., 207 N.Y. 315, 100 N.E. 794 (1913); 59 C.J., *Statutes* §573 (1932).

41 Detroit v. Redford Twp., 253 Mich. 453, 235 N.W. 217 (1931); Black, *Construction and Interpretation of Laws* §72 (2d ed. 1911); Sutherland, *Statutory Construction* §§491–4 (2d ed. 1904).

42 Springer v. Philippine Islands, 277 U.S. 189, 48 Sup. Ct. 480, 72 L. Ed. 845 (1928); Black, *Construction and Interpretation of Laws* §72 (2d ed. 1911); Sutherland, *Statutory Construction* §495 (2d ed. 1904).

43 De Witt v. San Francisco. 2 Cal. 289 (1852); Black, *Construction and Interpretation of Laws* §68 (2d ed. 1911); 59 C.J., *Statutes* §580 (1932).

44 People *ex rel.* Krause v. Harrison, 191 Ill., 257, 61 N.E. 99 (1901); Black, *Construction and Interpretation of Laws* §69 (1911); Sutherland, *Statutory Construction* §347 (2d ed. 1904).

45 Hull Hospital v. Wheeler, 216 Iowa 1394, 250 N.W. 637 (1933); Black, *Construction and Interpretation of Laws* §71 (2d ed. 1911); Sutherland, *Statutory Construction* §§422–34 (2d ed. 1904); 59 C.J., *Statutes* §581 (1932); 25 R.C.L., *Statutes* §240 (1919).

46 Texas v. United States, 292 U.S. 522, 54 Sup. Ct. 819, 78 L. Ed. 1402 (1934); Grosjean v. American Paint Works, 160 So. 449 (La. App. 1935); Black, *Construction and Interpretation of Laws* §71 (2d ed. 1911); Sutherland, *Statutory Construction* §§437–41 (2d ed. 1904); 59 C.J., *Statutes* §581 (1932); 25 R.C.L., *Statutes* §240 (1919).

47 Dunn v. Bryan. 77 Utah 604, 299 Pac. 253 (1931); Black, *Construction and Interpretation of Laws* §73 (2d ed. 1911); Sutherland, *Statutory Construction* §§420, 421 (2d ed. 1904); 59 C.J., *Statutes* §583 (1932).

48 Myer v. Ada County, 50 Idaho 39, 293 Pac. 322 (1930); Black, *Construction and Interpretation of Laws* §73 (2d ed. 1911); Sutherland, *Statutory Construction* §§420, 421 (2d ed. 1904); 59 C.J., *Statutes* §583 (1932).

49 United States v. Marshall Field & Co., 18 C.C.P.A. 228 (1930); Black, *Construction and Interpretation of Laws* §88 (2d ed. 1911); Sutherland, *Statutory Construction* §361 (2d ed. 1904); 59 C.J., *Statutes* §590 (1932).

50 State v. Baird, 36 Ariz. 531, 288 Pac. 1 (1930); Black, *Construction and Interpretation of Laws* §87 (2d ed. 1911); Sutherland, *Statutory Construction* §361 (2d ed. 1904); 59 C.J., *Statutes* §590 (1932).

51 Hines v. Mills, 187 Ark. 465, 60 S.W.2d 181 (1933); Black, *Construction and Interpretation of Laws* §75 (2d ed. 1911).

52 Fulghum v. Bleakley, 177 S.C. 286, 181 S.E. 30 (1935); Sutherland, *Statutory Construction* §397 (2d ed. 1904); 25 R.C.L., *Statutes* §226 (1919).

53 Koch & Dryfus v. Bridges, 45 Miss. 247 (1871); Black, *Construction and Interpretation of Laws* §150 (2d ed. 1911).

54 Jennings v. Suggs, 180 Ga. 141, 178 S.E. 282 (1935); Ewing v. Union Central Bank, 254 Ky. 623, 72 S.W.2d 4 (1934); Black, *Construction and Interpretation of Laws* §151 (2d ed. 1911); 59 C.J., *Statutes* §631 (1932).

55 State *ex rel.* Higgs v. Summers, 118 Neb. 189, 223 N.W. 957 (1929); Black, *Construction and Interpretation of Laws* §130 (2d ed. 1911); Sutherland, *Statutory Construction* §352 (2d ed. 1904); 59 C.J., *Statutes* §640 (1932).

56 Reuter v. San Mateo County, 220 Cal. 314, 30 P.2d 417 (1934); Black, *Construction and Interpretation of Laws* §130 (2d ed. 1911).

57 Montgomery v. Martin, 294 Pa. 25. 143 Atl. 505 (1928); Black, *Construction and Interpretation of Laws* §131 (2d ed. 1911); Sutherland, *Statutory Construction* §322 (2d ed. 1904).

58 Forscht v. Green, 53 Pa. 138 (1866); Black, *Construction and Interpretation of Laws* §131 (2d ed. 1911).

3

Formalism

Frederick Schauer

With accelerating frequency, legal decisions and theories are condemned as "formalist" or "formalistic." But what *is* formalism, and what is so bad about it? Even a cursory look at the literature reveals scant agreement on what it is for decisions in law, or perspectives on law, to be formalistic, except that whatever formalism is, it is not good. Few judges or scholars would describe themselves as formalists, for a congratulatory use of the word "formal" seems almost a linguistic error. Indeed, the pejorative connotations of the word "formalism," in concert with the lack of agreement on the word's descriptive content, make it tempting to conclude that "formalist" is the adjective used to describe any judicial decision, style of legal thinking, or legal theory with which the user of the term disagrees.

Yet this temptation should be resisted. There *does* seem to be descriptive content in the notion of formalism, even if there are widely divergent uses of the term. At the heart of the word "formalism," in many of its numerous uses, lies the concept of decisionmaking according to *rule*. Formalism is the way in which rules achieve their "ruleness" precisely by doing what is supposed to be the failing of formalism: screening off from a decisionmaker factors that a sensitive decisionmaker would otherwise take into account. Moreover, it appears that this screening off takes place largely through the force of the language in which rules are written. Thus the tasks performed by rules are tasks for which the primary tool is the specific linguistic formulation of a rule. As a result, insofar as formalism is frequently condemned as excessive reliance on the language of a rule, it is the very idea of decisionmaking by rule that is being condemned, either as a description of how decisionmaking can take place or as a prescription for how decisionmaking should take place.

Once we disentangle and examine the various strands of formalism and recognize the way in which formalism, rules, and language are conceptually intertwined, it turns out that there is something, indeed much, to be said for decision according to rule – and therefore for formalism. I do not argue that formalism is always good or that legal systems ought often or even ever be formalistic. Nevertheless, I do want to urge a rethinking of the contemporary aversion to formalism. For even if what can be said for formalism is not in the end persuasive, the issues should be before us for inspection, rather than blocked by a discourse of epithets.

Frederick Schauer, "Formalism," *Yale Law Journal*, vol. 97, no. 4, March 1988, pp. 508–48. © 1988. Reprinted with permission from The Yale Law Journal Co.

Formalism as the Denial of Choice

A. *Choice within norms*

Few decisions are charged with formalism as often as *Lochner v. New York*. But what makes Justice Peckham's majority opinion in *Lochner* formalistic? Surely it is not just that the Court protected an unrestricted privilege of labor contracting against the first stirrings of the welfare state. For the Court to make such a political decision under the rubric of broad constitutional clauses like "liberty" is a far cry from what seems to be meant when decisions are criticized as being formal. To the extent that the charge of formalism suggests narrowness, *Lochner* is hardly a candidate. We criticize *Lochner* not for being narrow, but for being excessively broad.

Although *Lochner* is criticized for the length of its reach, a closer look reveals that it is not the result that is condemned as formalistic but rather the justification for that result. The formalism in *Lochner* inheres in its *denial* of the political, moral, social, and economic choices involved in the decision, and indeed in its denial that there was any choice at all. Justice Peckham simply announced that "[t]he general right to make a contract in relation to his business is part of the liberty of the individual protected by the Fourteenth Amendment"[1] and that "[t]he right to purchase or to sell labor is part of the liberty protected by this amendment."[2] To these pronouncements he added the confident statement that "[o]f course the liberty of contract relating to labor includes both parties to it."[3]

Justice Peckham's language suggests that he is explaining a precise statutory scheme rather than expounding on one word in the Constitution. It is precisely for this reason that his opinion draws criticism. We condemn *Lochner* as formalistic not because it involves a choice, but because it attempts to describe this choice as compulsion. What strikes us clearly as a political or social or moral or economic choice is described in *Lochner* as definitionally incorporated within the *meaning* of a broad term. Thus, choice is masked by the language of linguistic inexorability.

When I say that pelicans are birds, the truth of the statement follows inexorably from the meaning of the term "bird." If someone disagrees, or points at a living, breathing, flying pelican and says "That is not a bird," she simply does not know what the word "bird" means. We criticize *Lochner* as formalistic because it treats the word "liberty" (or the words "life, liberty, or property, without due process of law") as being like the word "bird" and the privilege of contracting as being like a pelican, i.e., subsumed in the broader category. According to the reasoning in *Lochner*, if you don't know that contracting for labor without governmental control is an example of liberty, then you just don't know what the word "liberty" means.

Lochner is condemned as formalistic precisely because the analogy between pelicans (as birds) and unrestricted contracting (as liberty) fails. One can understand much about the concept of liberty and about the word "liberty" and yet still deny that they include the privilege of unconstrained labor contracting. Thus, a decisionmaker who knows or should know that such a choice is open, but treats the choice as no more available than the choice to treat a pelican as other than a bird, is charged with formalism for treating as definitionally inexorable that which involves nondefinitional, substantive choices.

Lochner is merely one example in which a false assertion of inexorability is decried as formalistic. Much contemporary criticism of Blackstone, Langdell, and others of their persuasion attacks their jurisprudence on similar grounds. They stand accused of presenting contestable applications of general terms as definitionally incorporated within the meaning of the general term. It is important, however, to understand the relationship between the linguistic and the ontological questions for those of Blackstone's vision. Blackstone's view that certain abstract terms definitionally incorporate a wide range of specific results is tied intimately to his perception of a hard and suprahuman reality behind these general terms. If the word "property," for example, actually describes some underlying and noncontingent reality, then it follows easily that certain specific embodiments are necessarily part of that reality, just as pelicans are part of the underlying reality that is the universe of birds. These instantiations might still follow even if the general term is not a natural kind whose existence and demarcation is beyond the control of human actors. There is nothing natural or noncontingent about the term "basketball," but it is nevertheless an error in this culture at this time to apply that word to a group of people hitting small hard balls with one of a collection of fourteen different sticks. Still, linguistic clarity and rigidity are both facilitated insofar as the words track the natural kinds of the world. To the extent that Blackstone and others believed that categories like liberty, property, and contract were natural kinds rather than human artifacts, they were less likely to perceive the choices we would now not think to deny. When one believes that a general term reflects a deep reality beyond the power of human actors, the view that certain particulars are *necessarily* part of that reality follows with special ease.

Thus, one view of the vice of formalism takes that vice to be one of deception, either of oneself or of others. To disguise a choice in the language of definitional inexorability obscures that choice and thus obstructs questions of how it was made and whether it could have been made differently. Use of the word "formalism" in this sense hinges on the existence of a term (or phrase, sentence, or paragraph) whose contested application generates the choice. Some terms, like "liberty" and "equality," are *pervasively indeterminate*. It is not that such terms have no content whatsoever; it is that *every* application, every concretization, every instantiation requires the addition of supplementary premises to apply the general term to specific cases. Therefore, any application of that term that denies the choice made among various eligible supplementary premises is formalistic in this sense.

More commonly, however, the indeterminacy to be filled by a decisionmaker's choice is not pervasive throughout the range of applications of a term. Instead, the indeterminacy is encountered only at the edges of a term's meaning. As H. L. A. Hart tells us, legal terms possess a core of settled meaning and a penumbra of debatable meaning. For Hart, formalism derives from the denial of choice in the penumbra of meaning, where applying the term in question is optional. Thus, Hart conceives of formalism as the unwillingness to acknowledge in cases of doubtful application, such as the question of whether a bicycle is a vehicle for purposes of the prohibition on vehicles in the park, that choices must be made that go far beyond merely ascertaining the meaning of a word.

Hart's conception of formalism is closely aligned with that undergirding those who criticize both Blackstone and *Lochner*. Hart's formalist takes the penumbra to be as clear as the core, while the *Lochner* formalist takes the general term to be as determinate as the specific. Both deny the extent of actual indeterminacy, and thus neither admits that the application of the norm involves a choice not determined by the words of the norm alone.

B.   Choice among norms

Implicit in Hart's conception of formalism is the view that in the core, unlike in the penumbra, legal answers are often tolerably determinate. Even if this is true, and I will examine this claim presently, the possibility remains that a decisionmaker has a choice of whether or not to follow a seemingly applicable norm even in its core of meaning. The question in this case is not whether a bus is a vehicle, or even whether the core of the rule excludes buses from the park, but whether the rule excluding vehicles must be applied in this case. At times a decisionmaker may have a choice whether to apply the clear and specifically applicable norm. In such cases we can imagine a decisionmaker having and making a choice but denying that a choice was in any way part of the process. Thus, a variant on the variety of formalism just discussed sees formalism as involving not denial of the existence of choices within norms, but denial that there are frequently choices about whether to apply even the clear norms.

As an example of this type of formalism, consider the unreported and widely unknown case of *Hunter v. Norman*.[4] Hunter, an incumbent state senator in Vermont seeking re-election, filed his nominating petition in the Windsor County Clerk's office on July 21, 1986 at 5:03 p.m. In doing so he missed by three minutes the petition deadline set by title 17, section 2356, of the Laws of Vermont.[5] The statute provides, in its entirety, that "Primary petitions shall be filed not later than 5:00 p.m. on the third Monday of July preceding the primary election prescribed by section 2351 of this title, and not later than 5:00 p.m. of the forty-second day prior to the day of a special primary election."[6] The Windsor County Clerk, Jane Norman, duly enforced the statute by refusing to accept Hunter's petition, observing that "I have no intention of breaking the law, not for Jesus Christ himself."[7] Hunter's name, consequently, was to be withheld from appearing on the September Democratic primary election ballot.

Hunter, not surprisingly, took his disappointment to the courthouse and filed an action in equity against Norman for extraordinary relief.[8] He asked that the court order her to accept his petition and to ensure that his name would appear on the primary ballot. At the hearing, Hunter alleged that he had called the clerk's office earlier on the date in question and been told that he was required to deliver the petition in person because of the necessity of signing forms consenting to his nomination. In fact, these consent forms were not due until a later date. Hunter claimed that had he not been led to appear in person by receiving this erroneous advice, the petition would have been filed earlier in the day. He argued that in light of the erroneous information given to Hunter by the Clerk's office, the clerk (and the state) were estopped from relying on the statutory deadline. In support of this proposition, Hunter offered *Ryshpan v. Cashman*,[9] in which the Vermont Supreme Court, on similar facts, held that because "reliance on erroneous actions on behalf of the State has put . . . its citizens in inescapable conflict with the literal terms of one of the time requirements instituted by that same sovereignty . . . [t]he statutory time schedule must . . . as a matter of equity . . . yield."[10]

Ultimately, Hunter prevailed, and it appears that *Ryshpan v. Cashman* saved the day – or at least saved Hunter's day. *Ryshpan* therefore seems to have operated as an escape route from the rigors of the statute. Suppose, however, that everything in Hunter's case had been the same, including the existence of *Ryshpan*, but that the judge had ruled against Hunter solely on the basis of the statutory language. Had this hardly unrealistic alternative occurred, it would seem but a small step from the brand of formalism discussed above to a formalist characterization of this hypothetical decision. As long as *Ryshpan* exists, the judge has a choice whether to follow the letter of the statute or instead to employ the escape route. To make this choice and merely cite the statute as indicating the absence of choice would

therefore deny the reality of the choice that was made. The crux of the matter is that this choice was present as long as *Ryshpan* existed, whether the judge followed that case or not. The charge of formalism in such a case would be but a variation of formalism as the concealment of choice: Instead of a choice within a norm, as with either pervasively indeterminate language or language containing penumbras of uncertainty surrounding a core of settled meaning, here the choice is between two different norms.

This variation on *Ryshpan* reveals the reasons we condemn the masking of choice. When the statute and *Ryshpan* coexist, neither determines which will prevail. Thus, the choice of the escape route represented by *Ryshpan* over the result indicated by the statute, or vice versa, necessarily would be made on the basis of factors external to both. These factors might include the moral, political, or physical attractiveness of the parties; the particular facts of the case; the judge's own views about deadlines; the judge's own views about statutes; the judge's own views about the Vermont Supreme Court; the judge's own views about clerks of courts; and so on. Yet were any of these factors to cause a particular judge to decide that the statute should prevail, mere citation of the statute as inexorably dictating the result would conceal from the litigants and from society the actual determinative factors. Insofar as we expect the reasons for a decision to be open for inspection (and that, after all, is usually the reason judges write opinions), failure to acknowledge that a choice was made can be criticized because knowing how the choice was made helps to make legitimate the products of the system.

C. Is there always a choice?

Ryshpan v. Cashman is a trifle obscure, but it is hardly unique. Consider the number of *Ryshpan* equivalents that allow decisionmakers to avoid the specific mandates of a particular rule. A decisionmaker may determine that the literal language of a rule does not serve that rule's original intent, as the Supreme Court has interpreted the Civil Rights Act of 1964, the contracts clause of the Constitution, and the Eleventh Amendment. Or a decisionmaker may apply the "mischief rule" or its variants to determine that a literal application of the rule would not serve the rule's *purpose*. Or a decisionmaker may apply a more general rule that denies relief to a claimant entitled to relief under the most locally applicable rule; for example, she might apply the equitable principle of unclean hands or laches, the legal principle of *in pari delicto*, or the civil law principle of abuse of right. Any reader of this article could easily add to this list.

Yet, what if none of these established routes were available in a particular case – would a judge then be forced to apply the specifically applicable rule? To answer this question, let us examine another variation on *Hunter v. Norman*. Suppose that *Ryshpan v. Cashman* did *not* exist, but that everything else about the facts and the applicable law in *Hunter* remained the same. What choices, if any, would be open to the judge? The judge could, of course, simply hold that the statute applied and rule against Hunter. But must he? Could the judge instead "create" *Ryshpan* by concluding that Hunter should win because he was misled by the clerk's office?

This option of creating *Ryshpan* does not seem inconsistent with the way the American legal system operates. Despite the lack of any specific statute or case authorizing such a result, allowing Hunter to win because he was misled would raise no eyebrows in American legal circles. No one would call for an investigation of the judge's competence, as someone might had the judge ruled for Hunter because Hunter was a Capricorn and Norman a Sagittarius. If the creation of such an escape route would be consistent with American judicial traditions, then the judge can be seen to have had a choice between deciding for Hunter and deciding for Norman even without *Ryshpan*. Thus a judge who ruled against Hunter on the basis of the statute would be denying the extent to which there was still a choice to create *Ryshpan* and thereby rule for Hunter.

Of course, a judge who decided to "create" *Ryshpan* would probably not simply assert that Hunter should win because he relied on erroneous information from a state official. Rather, the judge would justify this conclusion by reference to general principles that lurk in various corners of the legal system. For example,

the judge might say that, as a general principle, parties are estopped from relying on laws whose contents they have misstated to the disadvantage of another; a decision against the clerk would be merely a specific instance of the application of that general principle. Or, the judge might cite other particular principles, such as the principle of reliance in securities law, and analogize this case to those. Under either analysis the judge would attempt to ground the new principle in some already existing principle.

On the basis of these variations, we can distinguish three possible models of escape route availability. Under one model, the existing escape routes in the system represent an incomplete list of principles to ameliorate the rigidity of rules, and the judge may add to this list where amelioration is indicated but no applicable ameliorative principle exists. In such instances, the judge might discuss justice or fairness or some other general value and explain why this value supports the creation of a principle like that in *Ryshpan v. Cashman*. The implicit ideal of this system is the availability of an ameliorative principle whenever the circumstances demand it. Thus the judge who creates a new ameliorative principle on an appropriate occasion furthers the goals of this system.

Alternatively, we could develop a model of a system in which there is already a more or less complete stock of ameliorative principles. In such a system, a judge would *always* have some escape route available if all the circumstances indicated that the applicable norm was not the best result to be reached in that case. If *Ryshpan* itself did not exist, the judge would be able to pick other extant ameliorative principles that would get Hunter's name on the ballot.

Both the first model, which resembles Dworkin's account of the law, and the second, which borrows from Llewellyn's, acknowledge the persuasiveness of judicial choice in their recognition of the judge's opportunity (or perhaps even obligation) to avoid the arguably unjust consequences of mechanical application of the most directly applicable legal rule. If either of these models is an accurate rendition of some legal system, then a decisionmaker within such a system who simply applies the most directly applicable legal rule without further thought or explanation either denies herself a choice that the system permitted or required, or denies to others an explanation of why she chose not to use the escape routes permitted by the system. This failure to explain the choice to apply the most locally applicable rule is simply a variation on the more egregious forms of formalism as denial of choice.

These two models – one allowing the creation of rule-avoiding norms, and the other presenting a complete list of such norms for use – must be contrasted with a third model. Under this third model, the stock of extant rule-avoiding norms is not temporarily incomplete but completable, as in the first model, nor is it complete, as in the second. Instead, it is both incomplete and closed. A decisionmaker will therefore be confronted with situations in which the immediately applicable rule generates a result the decisionmaker wishes to avoid but for which the system neither contains an escape route nor permits one to be created. Under this model, a judge who followed the rule – rather than the course she otherwise would have taken on the basis of *all* relevant factors – would not have acted formalistically in the sense now under discussion. Where there was no choice, a decisionmaker following the mandates of the most directly applicable norm could not be accused of having a choice but denying its existence.

If we can imagine a model in which a rule-avoiding norm is both nonexistent and precluded in some instances, then we can also imagine a model in which no rule-avoiding norms exist at all. In such a system, a decisionmaker would be expected simply to decide according to the rule when there was a rule dealing specifically with the situation. Because there was no choice to be made, the decisionmaker could not be charged with masking a choice.

This third model presents the conceptual possibility of a different type of formalism than that which has been the focus of this section. In this third model, the charge of "formalism" would possess a different significance than in the other two models, for the decisionmaker accused of being formalistic might not be denying a choice made in the decisionmaking process, but might never have had a choice at all. To investigate the possibility of this type of formalism we must determine whether a system can truly foreclose choices from the decisionmaker . . .

Should Choice be Restricted?

Let me recapitulate. One conception takes the vice of formalism to consist of a decisionmaker's denial, couched in the language of obedience to clear rules, of having made any choice at all. Yet rules, if followed, may not leave a decisionmaker free choice. Rules *can* limit decisional choice, and decisionmakers *can* abide by those limitations. Those limitations come in most cases from the literal language of a rule's formulation, for to take a rule as anything other than the rule's formulation, or at least the meaning of the rule's formulation, is ultimately to deny the idea of a rule.

Thus, formalism merges into ruleness, and both are inextricably intertwined with literalism, i.e., the willingness to make decisions according to the literal meaning of words or phrases or sentences or paragraphs on a printed page, even if the consequences of that decision seem either to frustrate the purpose behind those words or to diverge significantly from what the decisionmaker thinks – the rule aside – should be done. But does demonstrating that formalism is ruleness rescue formalism? Restated, what is so good about decision according to rules?

The simple answer to this question, and perhaps also the correct one, is "nothing." Little about decision constrained by the rigidity of rules seems intrinsically valuable. Once we understand that rules get in the way, that they gain their ruleness by cutting off access to factors that might lead to the best resolution in a particular case, we see that rules function as impediments to optimally sensitive decisionmaking. Rules doom decisionmaking to mediocrity by mandating the inaccessibility of excellence.

Nor is there anything essentially *just* about a system of rules. We have scarce reason to believe that rule-based adjudication is more likely to be just than are systems in which rules do not block a decisionmaker, especially a just decisionmaker, from considering every reason that would assist her in reaching the best decision. Insofar as factors screened from consideration by a rule might in a particular case turn out to be those necessary to reach a just result, rules stand in the way of justice in those cases and thus impede optimal justice in the long term. We equate Solomon's wisdom with justice not because Solomon followed the rules in solving the dispute over the baby but because Solomon came up with exactly the right solution for that case. We frequently laud not history's rule followers, but those whose abilities at particularized decisionmaking transcend the inherent limitations of rules.

Still, that rules may be in one sense unjust, or even that they may be inappropriate in much of what we call a legal system, does not mean there is nothing to be said for rules. One of the things that can be said for rules is the value variously expressed as predictability or certainty. But if we pursue the predictability theme, we see that what most arguments for ruleness share is a focus on disabling certain classes of decisionmakers from making certain kinds of decisions. Predictability follows from the decision to treat all instances falling within some accessible category in the same way. It is a function of the way in which rules decide ahead of time how *all* cases within a class will be determined.

Predictability is fostered to the extent that four different requirements are satisfied. The first of the factors contributing to predictability is the capacity on the part of those relying on a rule to identify certain particulars as instances of a given category (for example, that pelicans are birds). When there is a more or less uniform and uncontroversial ability to say that some item is a member of some category, little in the way of potentially variable judgment clouds the prediction of whether the rule will apply to this particular item. This relates to the second factor: that the decisionmakers in the system will perceive those particulars as being members of the same category perceived by the addressees and will be seen as so perceiving by those affected. That is, people perceive pelicans as birds; decisionmakers perceive pelicans as birds; and people know that decisionmakers will perceive pelicans as birds. Third, the rule must speak in terms of an accessible category. Predictability requires that a rule cover a category whose denotation is substantially noncontroversial among the class of addressees of the rule and common to the addressees of the rule and those who apply it. Finally, the rule must treat all members of a category in the same way. Only if the consequences specified in the apodosis of the rule are as accessible and noncontroversial as the

coverage specified in the protasis can a rule produce significant predictability of application. Thus, predictability comes from the knowledge that if this is a bird a certain result will follow, and from the confidence that what I now perceive to be a bird will be considered a bird by the ultimate decisionmaker.

This predictability comes only at a price. Situations may arise in which putting this particular into that category seems just too crude – something about this particular makes us desire to treat it specially. *This* vehicle is merely a statue, emits no fumes, makes no noise, and endangers no lives; it ought to be treated differently from those vehicles whose characteristics mesh with the purpose behind the rule. Serving the goal of predictability, however, requires that we ignore this difference, because to acknowledge this difference is also to create the power – the *jurisdiction* – to determine whether this vehicle or that vehicle serves the purpose of the "no vehicles in the park" rule. It is the jurisdiction to determine that only some vehicles fit the purpose of the rule that undermines the confidence that *all* vehicles will be prohibited. No longer is it the case that anything that is a *vehicle*, a moderately accessible category, is excluded. Instead, the category is now that of *vehicles whose prohibition will serve the purpose of the "no vehicle in the park" rule*, a potentially far more controversial category.

Thus, the key to understanding the relationship of ruleness to predictability is the idea of decisional jurisdiction. The issue is not whether the statue serves the purpose of the "no vehicles in the park" rule. It is whether giving some decisionmaker jurisdiction to determine what the rule's purpose is (as well as jurisdiction to determine whether some item fits that purpose) injects a possibility of variance substantially greater than that involved in giving a decisionmaker jurisdiction solely to determine whether some particular is or is not a vehicle. Note also that the jurisdictional question has a double aspect. When we grant jurisdiction we are first concerned with the range of equally correct decisions that might be made in the exercise of that jurisdiction. If there is no authoritative statement of the purpose behind the "no vehicles in the park" rule, granting jurisdiction to determine that purpose would allow a decisionmaker to decide whether the purpose is to preserve quiet, to prevent air pollution, or to prevent accidents, and each of these determinations would be equally correct In addition to increasing the range of correct decisions, however, certain grants of jurisdiction increase the likelihood of erroneous determination. Compare "No vehicles in the park" with "The park is closed to vehicles whose greatest horizontal perimeter dimension, when added to their greatest vertical perimeter dimension, exceeds the lesser of (a) sixty-eight feet, six inches and (b) the greatest horizontal perimeter dimension, added to the greatest vertical perimeter dimension, of the average of the largest passenger automobile manufactured in the United States by the three largest automobile manufacturers in the preceding year." The second adds no inherent variability, but it certainly compounds the possibility of decisionmaker error. Creating the jurisdiction to determine whether the purposes of a rule are served undermines predictability by allowing the determination of any of several possible purposes; in addition, the creation of that jurisdiction engenders the possibility that those who exercise it might just get it wrong.

Grants of decisional jurisdiction not only increase permissible variance and the possibility of "computational" error, they also involve decisionmakers in determinations that a system may prefer to have made by someone else. We may believe that courts are less competent to make certain decisions than other bodies; for example, we may feel that certain kinds of fact-finding are better done by legislatures. There may also be moral or political reasons to restrict the judge's discretion, for decisionmaking implicates profound questions of just who in a given domain may legitimately make certain decisions. It is, for example, a plausible position that the public rather than the University of Michigan philosophy department should make the moral determinations involved in governing the United States, even if the University of Michigan philosophy department would make better choices.

Although decreasing the possibility of variance and error by the decisionmaker contributes to the ability of addressees of rules to predict the consequences of application of those rules, limited variance can serve other values as well. If decisionmakers are denied jurisdiction to determine

whether a particular instance actually justifies its inclusion in a larger generalization or are denied jurisdiction to determine the best result on the basis of all germane factors, the part of the system inhabited by those decisionmakers becomes more stable. Treating a large group of different particulars in the same way – the inevitable byproduct of the generalization of rules – dampens the range of variance in result by suppressing consideration of a wide range of potentially relevant differences. Thus, stability, not as a necessary condition for predictability but as a value in its own right, is fostered by truncating the decisionmaking authority.

Because rule-bound decisionmaking is inherently stabilizing, it is inherently conservative, in the nonpolitical sense of the word. By limiting the ability of decisionmakers to consider every factor relevant to an event, rules make it more difficult to adapt to a changing future. Rules force the future into the categories of the past. Note the important asymmetry here, the way in which rules operate not to enable but only to disable. A decisionmaker can never exceed the optimal result based on all relevant factors. Thus, a rule-bound decisionmaker, precluded from taking into account certain features of the present case, can never do better but can do worse than a decisionmaker seeking the optimal result for a case through a rule-free decision.

Yet this conservatism, suboptimization, and inflexibility in the face of a changing future need not be universally condemned. Rules stabilize by inflating the importance of the classifications of yesterday. We achieve stability, valuable in its place, by relinquishing some part of our ability to improve on yesterday. Again the issue is jurisdiction, for those who have jurisdiction to improve on yesterday also have jurisdiction to make things worse. To stabilize, to operate in an inherently conservative mode, is to give up some of the possibility of improvement in exchange for guarding against some of the possibility of disaster. Whether, when, and where the game is worth the candle, however, cannot be determined acontextually.

In sum, it is clearly true that rules get in the way, but this need not always be considered a bad thing. It may be a liability to get in the way of wise decisionmakers who sensitively consider all of the relevant factors as they accurately pursue the good. However, it may be an asset to restrict misguided, incompetent, wicked, power-hungry, or simply mistaken decisionmakers whose own sense of the good might diverge from that of the system they serve. The problem, of course, is the difficulty in determining which characterization will fit decisionmakers; we must therefore decide the extent to which we are willing to disable good decisionmakers in order simultaneously to disable bad ones.

With these considerations in mind, let us approach formalism in a new light. Consider some of the famous marchers in formalism's parade of horribles, examples such as *R. v. Ojibway*, Fuller's statue of the truck in the park, and the poor Bolognese surgeon who, having opened the vein of a patient in the course of performing an emergency operation outdoors, was prosecuted for violating the law prohibiting "drawing blood in the streets." Each of these examples reminds us that cases may arise in which application of the literal meaning of words produces an absurd result. But now we can recast the question, for we must consider not only whether the result was absurd in these cases but also whether a particular decisionmaker should be empowered to determine absurdity. Even in cases as extreme as these, formalism is only superficially about rigidity and absurdity. More fundamentally, it is about power and its allocation.

Formalism is about power, but is also about its converse – modesty. To be formalistic as a decisionmaker is to say that something is not my concern, no matter how compelling it may seem. When this attitude is applied to the budget crisis or to eviction of the starving, it seems objectionable. But when the same attitude of formalism requires judges to ignore the moral squalor of the Nazis or the Ku Klux Klan in First Amendment cases, or the guilt of the defendant in Fourth Amendment cases, or the wealth of the plaintiff who seeks to recover for medical expenses occasioned by the defendant's negligence, it is no longer clear that refusal to take all factors into account is condemnable.

Modesty, of course, has its darker side. To be modest is at times good, but avoiding authority is also avoiding responsibility. In some circumstances we want our decisionmakers to take charge and accept the consequences of their actions. But it is by no means clear that just because it is good for some people to take charge some of the time, that taking charge, even accompanied by acceptance of responsibility, is a universal good. "I'm in charge here" has a long but not always distinguished history. Part of what formalism is about is its inculcation of the view that sometimes it is appropriate for decisionmakers to recognize their lack of jurisdiction and to defer even when they are convinced that their own judgment is best. The opposite of modesty is arrogance, not just responsibility. True, modesty itself carries responsibility, because an actor behaving modestly is participating and thus assisting in the legitimacy of the grant of authority to someone else. But this is a responsibility of a different and limited kind. That one accepts partial responsibility for the decisions of others does not entail the obligation to substitute one's judgment for that of others.

The distinctive feature of rules, therefore, lies in their ability to be formal, to exclude from consideration in the particular case factors whose exclusion was determined without reference to the particular case at hand. This formalism of rules is not only conceptually sound and psychologically possible, but it also, as I have tried to show, is on occasion normatively desirable. Insofar as formalism disables some decisionmakers from considering some factors that may appear important to them, it allocates power to some decisionmakers and away from others. Formalism therefore achieves its value when it is thought desirable to narrow the decisional opportunities and the decisional range of a certain class of decisionmakers.

I stress that all of this is compatible with agnosticism about how rulebound decisionmaking applies to legal systems in general, to particular legal systems, or to particular parts of legal systems. It is far from a necessary truth that legal systems must be exclusively or even largely operated as rule-governed institutions. Judgments about when to employ formalism are contextual and not inexorable, political and not logical, psychological and economic rather than conceptual. It would blunt my point about the simultaneously plausible and contingent nature of decision according to rule to offer in this acontextual setting my recommendations about what if any parts of the American or any other legal system should operate in such a fashion. My goal is only to rescue formalism from conceptual banishment. But having been readmitted to the community of respectable ideas, formalism, or decisionmaking according to rule in any strong sense, still has the burden of showing that it is appropriately used in a particular decisional domain. [. . .]

An alternative hypothesis posits some ground between no review and unfettered intrusiveness. There might be cases in which the presumption in favor of the result below would cause the decision to stand. Under this hypothesis, we can have rebuttable presumptions – cases in which the presumption might be overcome in particularly exigent circumstances but nevertheless controls in many or even most cases. [. . .]

If such instructions sometimes create presumptions, and if those presumptions sometimes work, then what does this say about the possibility of what we might call a *presumptive formalism*? In order to construct such a model, we would want to equate the literal mandate of the most locally applicable written rule with the judgment of the court below. The court below can be taken to have determined, for example, that in one case operable and operating automobiles are excluded from the park, in another case golf carts are excluded from the park, and in a third case immobile statues of trucks are excluded from the park. We can then equate the reviewing court with a determination of the correct result from the perspective of the reasons behind the rule rather than the literal language of the rule itself. We might conclude that in the first case even a de novo application of the reasons would generate the same result as generated by the formalistic reading, and therefore the formal mandate would prevail uncontroversially. In the second, a de novo application of reasons would generate a different result than that generated by the rule, but the result generated by the rule remains "in the ballpark" and therefore is upheld despite its divergence from the result that would be reached by direct application of the reasons. In the third, however, a de novo application of the reasons indicates that the result generated by the rule is so far out of bounds, so absurd, so preposterous that it is analogous to an abuse of discretion and would therefore be reversed – the rule would not be applied in this case.

Under such a theory of presumptive formalism there would be a presumption in favor of the result generated by the literal and largely acontextual interpretation of the most locally applicable rule. Yet that result would be presumptive only, subject to defeasibility when less locally applicable norms, including the purpose behind the particular norm, and including norms both within and without the decisional domain at issue, offered especially exigent reasons for avoiding the result generated by the presumptively applicable norm.

Such a system would bring the advantages of predictability, stability, and constraint of decisionmakers commonly associated with decision according to rule, but would temper the occasional unpleasant consequences of such a system with an escape route that allowed some results to be avoided when their consequences would be especially outrageous. Such a system would not be without cost. First of all, the escape route would necessarily decrease the amount of predictability, stability, and decisionmaker restraint. In short, it would diminish the amount of ruleness by placing more final authority in the decisionmaker than in the rule. Second, the presumptive force attached to the formalist reading of the applicable norms would still result in some odd or suboptimal results. In this sense, such a system would fail to honor all of the goals either of unrestrained particularism or unrestrained formalism. Finally, such a system would risk collapse into one in which the presumptions were for all practical purposes either absolute or nonexistent.

Even on the assumption that such a system might be desirable in some decisional domains, this does not mean that all or part of what we commonly call the legal system might be one of those domains. It might be that formalism, even only presumptively, is a good idea, but that the goals of the legal system, in light of the decisions we ask it to make, are such that it ought not to be designed along such a model. More likely, formalism ought to be seen as a tool to be used in some parts of the legal system and not in others. Determining which parts, if any, would be susceptible to such treatment is not my agenda here, for what I have attempted to offer is only an argument that formal systems are not necessarily to be condemned. That is not to say they are universally or even largely to be applauded, nor that they are to be pervasive or even frequent within that segment of society we call the legal system. To answer this last question we must ask what the legal system, in whole or in part, is supposed to do, for only when we answer that question can we determine what kinds of tools it needs to accomplish that task. [. . .]

Notes

1   198 U.S. 45 (1905) at 53.
2   *Id.*
3   *Id.* at 56.
4   No. S197-86-WrC (Vt. July 28, 1986). The following account of the case is drawn from Judge Cheever's brief opinion, the pleadings, news accounts in *Rutland Herald* of July 22, 23, 24, and 26,1986, and a conversation with Marilyn Signe Skoglund, Assistant Attorney General in the Office of the Attorney General, State of Vermont.
5   *Vt. Stat. Ann.* tit. 17, §2356 (1982).
6   *Id.*
7   *Rutland Herald*, July 23, 1986, at 5, col. 4.
8   The petition is unclear as to whether Hunter was seeking the extraordinary legal remedy of mandamus or a mandatory injunction in equity.
9   132 Vt. 628, 326 A.2d 169 (1974).
10   *Id.* at 630–1, 326 A.2d at 171.

4

Incompletely Theorized Agreements

Cass R. Sunstein

Incompletely theorized agreements play a pervasive role in law and society. It is quite rare for a person or group completely to theorize any subject, that is, to accept both a general theory and a series of steps connecting that theory to concrete conclusions. Thus we often have in law an *incompletely theorized agreement on a general principle* – incompletely theorized in the sense that people who accept the principle need not agree on what it entails in particular cases.

This is the sense emphasized by Justice Oliver Wendell Holmes in his great aphorism, "General principles do not decide concrete cases."[1] Thus, for example, we know that murder is wrong, but disagree about whether abortion is wrong. We favor racial equality, but are divided on affirmative action. We believe in liberty, but disagree about increases in the minimum wage. Hence the pervasive legal and political phenomenon of an agreement on a general principle alongside disagreement about particular cases. The agreement is incompletely theorized in the sense that it is *incompletely specified*. Much of the key work must be done by others, often through casuistical judgments at the point of application.

Often constitution-making becomes possible through this form of incompletely theorized agreement. Many constitutions contain incompletely specified standards and avoid rules, at least when it comes to the description of basic rights. Consider the cases of Eastern Europe and South Africa, where constitutional provisions include many abstract provisions on whose concrete specification there has been sharp dispute. Abstract provisions protect "freedom of speech," "religious liberty," and "equality under the law," and citizens agree on those abstractions in the midst of sharp dispute about what these provisions really entail.

Much lawmaking becomes possible only because of this phenomenon. Consider the fact that the creation of large regulatory agencies has often been feasible only because of incompletely specified agreements. In dealing with air and water pollution, occupational safety and health, or regulation of broadcasting, legislators converge on general, incompletely specified requirements – that regulation be "reasonable," or that it provide "a margin of safety." If the legislature attempted to specify these requirements – to decide what counts as reasonable regulation – there would be a predictably high level of dispute and conflict, and perhaps the relevant laws could not be enacted at all.

Cass R. Sunstein, "Incompletely Theorized Agreements," from *Legal Reasoning and Political Conflict* (Oxford University Press, 1996). © 1996 by Oxford University Press, Inc. Reprinted with permission from Oxford University Press.

Incompletely specified agreements thus have important social uses. Many of their advantages are practical. They allow people to develop frameworks for decision and judgment despite large-scale disagreements. At the same time, they help produce a degree of social solidarity and shared commitment. People who are able to agree on political abstractions – freedom of speech, freedom from unreasonable searches and seizures – can also agree that they are embarking on shared projects. These forms of agreement help constitute a democratic culture. It is for this reason that they are so important to constitution-making. Incompletely specified agreements also have the advantage of allowing people to show one another a high degree of mutual respect. By refusing to settle concrete cases that raise fundamental issues of conscience, they permit citizens to announce to one another that society shall not take sides on such issues until it is required to do so.

So much for incompletely specified provisions. Let us turn to a second phenomenon. Sometimes people agree on a mid-level principle but disagree about both general theory and particular cases. These sorts of agreements are also incompletely theorized, but in a different way. Judges may believe, for example, that government cannot discriminate on the basis of race, without having a large-scale theory of equality, and also without agreeing whether government may enact affirmative action programs or segregate prisons when racial tensions are severe. Judges may think that government may not regulate speech unless it can show a clear and present danger – but disagree about whether this principle is founded in utilitarian or Kantian considerations, and disagree too about whether the principle allows government to regulate a particular speech by members of the Ku Klux Klan.

My particular interest here is in a third kind of phenomenon, of special interest for law: incompletely theorized agreements on particular outcomes, accompanied by agreements on the narrow or low-level principles that account for them. These terms contain some ambiguities. There is no algorithm by which to distinguish between a high-level theory and one that operates at an intermediate or lower level. We might consider, as conspicuous examples of high-level theories, Kantianism and utilitarianism, and see

legal illustrations in the many distinguished (academic) efforts to understand such areas as tort law, contract law, free speech, and the law of equality as undergirded by highly abstract theories of the right or the good.[2] By contrast, we might think of low-level principles as including most of the ordinary material of legal "doctrine" – the general class of principles and justifications that are not said to derive from any large theories of the right or the good, that have ambiguous relations to large theories, and that are compatible with more than one such theory.

By the term "particular outcome," I mean the judgment about who wins and who loses a case. By the term "low-level principles," I refer to something relative, not absolute; I mean to do the same thing by the terms "theories" and "abstractions" (which I use interchangeably). In this setting, the notions "low-level," "high," and "abstract" are best understood in comparative terms, like the terms "big," "old," and "unusual." The "clear and present danger" standard is a relative abstraction when compared with the claim that members of the Nazi Party may march in Skokie, Illinois. But the "clear and present danger" idea is relatively particular when compared with the claim that nations should adopt the constitutional abstraction "freedom of speech." The term "freedom of speech" is a relative abstraction when measured against the claim that campaign finance laws are acceptable, but the same term is less abstract than the grounds that justify free speech, as in, for example, the principle of personal autonomy.

What I am emphasizing here is that when people diverge on some (relatively) high-level proposition, they might be able to agree when they lower the level of abstraction. Incompletely theorized judgments on particular cases are the ordinary material of law. And in law, the point of agreement is often highly particularized – absolutely as well as relatively particularized – in the sense that it involves a specific outcome and a set of reasons that do not venture far from the case at hand. High-level theories are rarely reflected explicitly in law.

Perhaps the participants in law endorse no such theory, or perhaps they believe that they have none, or perhaps they cannot, on a multi-member court, reach agreement on a theory. Perhaps they find theoretical disputes confusing or annoying. What is critical is that they agree on how a case must come out. The argument very much applies to rules, which are, much of the time, incompletely theorized; indeed, this is one of the major advantages of rules. People may agree that a 60-mile-per-hour speed limit makes sense, and that it applies to defendant Jones, without having much of a theory about criminal punishment. They may agree that to receive social security benefits, people must show that they earn less than a certain sum of money, without having anything like a theory about who deserves what. Thus a key social function of rules is to allow people to agree on the meaning, authority, and even the soundness of a government provision in the face of disagreements about much else.

Much the same can be said about rule-free decisions made under standards, factors, and analogical reasoning. Indeed, all of the lawyer's conventional tools allow incompletely theorized agreements on particular outcomes. Consider analogical thinking. People might think that A is like B and covered by the same low-level principle, without agreeing on a general theory to explain why the low-level principle is sound. They agree on the matter of similarity, without agreeing on a large-scale account of what makes the two things similar. In the law of discrimination, for example, many people think that sex discrimination is "like" race discrimination and should be treated similarly, even if they lack or cannot agree on a general theory of when discrimination is unacceptable. In the law of free speech, many people agree that a ban on speech by a Communist is "like" a ban on speech by a member of the Ku Klux Klan and should be treated similarly – even if they lack or cannot agree on a general theory about the foundations of the free speech principle.

Incomplete Theorization and the Constructive Uses of Silence

What might be said on behalf of incompletely theorized agreements, or incompletely theorized judgments, about particular cases? Some people think of incomplete theorization as quite unfortunate – as embarrassing or reflective of some important problem or defect. Perhaps people

have not yet thought deeply enough. When people theorize, by raising the level of abstraction, they do so to reveal bias, confusion, or inconsistency. Surely participants in a legal system should not abandon this effort.

There is a good deal of truth in these usual thoughts. Sometimes more in the way of abstraction does reveal prejudice or confusion. But this is not the whole story. On the contrary, incompletely theorized judgments are an important and valuable part of both private and public life. They help make law possible; they even help make life possible. Most of their virtues involve *the constructive uses of silence*, an exceedingly important social and legal phenomenon. Silence – on something that may prove false, obtuse, or excessively contentious – can help minimize conflict, allow the present to learn from the future, and save a great deal of time and expense. In law, as elsewhere, what is said is no more important than what is left unsaid. Certainly this is true for ordinary courts, which have limited expertise and democratic accountability, and whose limits lead them to be cautious.

My principal concern is the question of how judges on a multimember body should justify their opinions in public; the argument therefore has a great deal to do with the problem of collective choice. But some of the relevant points bear on other issues as well. They have implications for the question of how an individual judge not faced with the problem of producing a majority opinion – a judge on a trial court, for example – might write; they bear on the question of how a single judge, whether or not a member of a collective body, might think in private; and they relate to appropriate methods of both thought and justification wholly outside of adjudication and even outside of law.

Multimember institutions

Begin with the special problem of public justification on a multimember body. The first and most obvious point is that incompletely theorized agreements are well-suited to a world – and especially a legal world – containing social dissensus on large-scale issues. By definition, such agreements have the large advantage of allowing a convergence on particular outcomes by people unable to reach an accord on general principles.

This advantage is associated not only with the simple need to decide cases, but also with social stability, which could not exist if fundamental disagreements broke out in every case of public or private dispute.

Second, incompletely theorized agreements can promote two goals of a liberal democracy and a liberal legal system: to enable people to live together and to permit them to show each other a measure of reciprocity and mutual respect.[3] The use of low-level principles or rules generally allows judges on multimember bodies and hence citizens to find commonality and thus a common way of life without producing unnecessary antagonism. Both rules and low-level principles make it unnecessary to reach areas in which disagreement is fundamental.

Perhaps even more important, incompletely theorized agreements allow people to show each other a high degree of mutual respect, civility, or reciprocity. Frequently ordinary people disagree in some deep way on an issue – the Middle East, pornography, homosexual marriages – and sometimes they agree not to discuss that issue much, as a way of deferring to each other's strong convictions and showing a measure of reciprocity and respect (even if they do not at all respect the particular conviction that is at stake). If reciprocity and mutual respect are desirable, it follows that judges, perhaps even more than ordinary people, should not challenge a litigant's or another person's deepest and most defining commitments, at least if those commitments are reasonable and if there is no need for them to do so. Thus, for example, it would be better if judges intending to reaffirm *Roe v. Wade* could do so without challenging the judgment that the fetus is a human being.[4]

To be sure, some fundamental commitments might appropriately be challenged in the legal system or within other multimember bodies. Some commitments are ruled off-limits by the authoritative legal materials. Many provisions involving basic rights have this purpose. Of course it is not always disrespectful to disagree with someone in a fundamental way; on the contrary, such disagreements may sometimes reflect profound respect. When defining commitments are based on demonstrable errors of fact or logic, it is appropriate to contest them. So too when those commitments are rooted in a rejection of the basic dignity of all human beings, or when it is necessary to undertake the challenge to resolve a genuine problem. But many cases can be resolved in an incompletely theorized way, and that is all I am suggesting here.

Institutional arguments in law – especially those involving judicial restraint – are typically designed to bracket fundamental questions and to say that however those questions might be resolved in principle, courts should stand to one side. The allocation of certain roles has an important function of allowing outcomes to be reached without forcing courts to make decisions on fundamental issues. Those issues are resolved by reference to institutional competence, not on their merits.

In particular, the principle of stare decisis, which instructs courts to respect precedent, helps produce incompletely theorized agreements, and it helps to avoid constant struggle over basic principle. It serves this function precisely because it prevents people from having to build the world again, and together, every time a dispute arises. People can agree to follow precedent when they disagree on almost everything else. As a prominent example, consider the United States Supreme Court's refusal to overrule *Roe v. Wade*, where the justices emphasized the difficulties that would be produced by revisiting so large-scale a social controversy.[5] Members of the Court can accept the rule of precedent from diverse foundations and despite their many disagreements. Thus the justifications of the rule of precedent are diverse – involving predictability, efficiency, fairness, constraints on official discretion – and people who disagree on those justifications can agree on the practice, at least as a general rule.

Multimember institutions and individual judges

Turn now to reasons that call for incompletely theorized agreements whether or not we are dealing with a multimember body. The first consideration here is that incompletely theorized agreements have the crucial function of reducing the political cost of enduring disagreements. If judges disavow large-scale theories, then losers in particular cases lose much less. They lose a decision, but not the world. They may win on another occasion. Their own theory has not been rejected or ruled inadmissible. When the authoritative rationale for the result is disconnected from abstract theories of the good or the right, the losers can submit to legal obligations, even if reluctantly, without being forced to renounce their largest ideals. I have said that some theories should be rejected or ruled inadmissible. But it is an advantage, from the standpoint of freedom and stability, for a legal system to be able to tell most losers – many of whom are operating from foundations that have something to offer or that cannot be ruled out a priori – that their own deepest convictions may play a role elsewhere in the law.

The second point is that incompletely theorized agreements are valuable when we seek moral evolution over time. Consider the area of constitutional equality, where considerable change has occurred in the past and will inevitably occur in the future. A completely theorized judgment would be unable to accommodate changes in facts or values. If the legal culture really did attain a theoretical end-state, it would become too rigid and calcified; we would know what we thought about everything. This would disserve posterity.

Incompletely theorized agreements are a key to debates over constitutional equality, with issues being raised about whether gender, sexual orientation, age, disability, and others are analogous to race; such agreements have the important advantage of allowing a large degree of openness to new facts and perspectives. At one point, we might think that homosexual relations are akin to incest; at another point, we might find the analogy bizarre. Of course a completely theorized judgment would have many virtues if it is correct. But at any particular moment in time, this is an unlikely prospect for human beings, not excluding judges.

A particular concern here is the effect of changing understandings of both facts and values. Consider ordinary life. At a certain time, you may well refuse to make decisions that seem foundational in character – for example, whether to get married within the next year, whether to have two, three, or four children, or whether to live in San Francisco or New York. Part of the reason for this refusal is knowledge that your understandings of both facts and values may well change. Indeed, your identity may itself change in important and relevant ways and for

this reason a set of commitments in advance – something like a fully theorized conception of your life course – would make no sense.

Legal systems and nations are not so very different. If the Supreme Court is asked to offer a fully theorized conception of equality – in areas involving, for example, the rights of disabled people, children, and homosexuals – it may well respond that its job is to decide cases rather than to offer fully theorized accounts, partly because society should learn over time and partly because society's understandings of facts and values, in a sense its very identity, may well shift in unpredictable ways. This point bears on many legal issues. It helps support the case for incompletely theorized agreements.

The third point is practical. Incompletely theorized agreements may be the best approach that is available for people of limited time and capacities. Full theorization may be far too much to ask. A single judge faces this problem as much as a member of a multimember panel. Here too the rule of precedent is crucial; attention to precedent is liberating, not merely confining, since it frees busy people to deal with a restricted range of problems. Incompletely theorized agreements have the related advantage, for ordinary lawyers and judges, of humility and modesty. To engage in analogical reasoning, for example, one ordinarily need not take a stand on large, contested issues of social life, some of which can be resolved only on what will seem to many a sectarian basis. [. . .]

Fourth, incompletely theorized agreements are well adapted to a system that should or must take precedents as fixed points. This is a large advantage over more ambitious methods, since ambitious thinkers, in order to reach horizontal and vertical coherence, will probably be forced to disregard many decided cases. In light of the sheer number of decided cases and adjudicative officials, law cannot speak with one voice; full coherence in principle is unlikely in the extreme.

It is notable in this connection that for some judges and lawyers (lower court judges, for example), precedents truly are fixed (short of civil disobedience), whereas for others, including Supreme Court Justices, they are revisable, but only in extraordinary circumstances. If a judge or a lawyer were to attempt to reach full theorization, precedents would have at most the status of considered judgments about particular cases, and these might be revised when they run into conflict with something else that he believes and that is general or particular. This would cause many problems. Participants in a legal system aspiring to stability should not be so immodest as to reject judgments reached by others whenever those judgments could not be made part of reflective equilibrium for those particular participants. Thus the area of contract law is unlikely fully to cohere with the field of tort law or property; contract law is itself likely to contain multiple and sometimes inconsistent strands.

We can find many analogies in ordinary life. A parent's practices with his children may not fully cohere. Precedents with respect to bedtime, eating, homework, and much else are unlikely to be susceptible to systematization under a single principle. Of course, parents do not seek to be inconsistent. A child may feel justly aggrieved if a sibling is permitted to watch more hours of television for no apparent reason; but full coherence would be a lot to ask. The problem of reaching full consistency is all the more severe in law, where so many people have decided so many things, and where disagreements on large principles lurk in the background.

There is a more abstract point here. Human morality recognizes irreducibly diverse goods, which cannot be subsumed under a single "master" value.[6] The same is true for the moral values reflected in the law. Any simple, general, and monistic or single-valued theory of a large area of the law – free speech, contracts, property – is likely to be too crude to fit with our best understandings of the multiple values that are at stake in that area. It would be absurd to try to organize legal judgments through a single conception of value.

What can be said about law as a whole can be said about many particular areas of law. Monistic theories of free speech or property rights, for example, will fail to accommodate the range of values that speech and property implicate. Free speech promotes not simply democracy, but personal autonomy, economic progress, self-development, and other goals as well. Property rights are important not only for economic prosperity, but for democracy and autonomy too. We are unlikely to be able to appreciate the diverse values at stake, and to describe them with the specificity they deserve, unless we investigate the details of particular disputes.

This is not a decisive objection to general theories; a "top down" approach might reject monism and point to plural values.[7] Perhaps participants in democracy or law can describe a range of diverse values, each of them at a high level of abstraction; acknowledge that these values do not fall under a single master value; and use these values for assessing law. But even if correct, any such approach would run into difficulty because of an important practical fact: social disagreements about how best to describe or specify the relevant values. Moreover, any such approach is likely to owe its genesis and its proof – its point or points – to a range of particular cases on which it can build. Of course full theorization of an area of law would be acceptable, or even an occasion for great celebration, if it accounted for the plural values at issue. But this would be a most complex task, one that requires identification of a wide range of actual and likely cases. At least we can say that incompletely theorized judgments are well-suited to a moral universe that is diverse and pluralistic, not only in the sense that people disagree, but also in the sense that each of us is attuned to pluralism when we are thinking well about any area of law.

None of these points suggests that incompletely theorized agreements always deserve celebration. The virtues of such agreements are partial. Some incompletely theorized agreements are unjust. If an agreement is more fully theorized, it will provide greater notice to affected parties. Moreover, fuller theorization – in the form of wider and deeper inquiry into the grounds for judgment – may be valuable or even necessary to prevent inconsistency, bias, or self-interest. If judges on a panel have actually agreed on a general theory, and if they are really committed to it, they should say so. Judges and the general community will learn much more if they are able to discuss the true motivating grounds for outcomes. All these are valid considerations, and nothing I am saying here denies their importance.

Judges, Theory, and the Rule of Law

There is a close association between the effort to attain incompletely theorized agreements and the rule of law ideal. Insofar as a legal system involves rule by law rather than rule by individual human beings, it tries to constrain judgments in advance. Some people think that the rule of law, properly understood, is a law of rules. . . . For the moment we can understand the rule of law more modestly. It is opposed to rule by individual human beings, who should not be permitted to govern as they wish through making law entirely of their choice in the context of actual disputes. Insofar as the rule of law prevents this from happening, it tries to prevent people in particular cases from invoking their own theories of the right or the good so as to make decisions according to their own most fundamental judgments.

Indeed, a prime purpose of the rule of law is to rule off-limits certain deep ideas of the right or the good, on the view that those ideas ought not to be invoked, most of the time, by judges and officials occupying particular social roles. Among the forbidden or presumptively forbidden ideas are, often, high-level views that are taken as too hubristic or sectarian precisely because they are so high-level. The presumption against high-level theories is an aspect of the ideal of the rule of law to the extent that it is an effort to limit the exercise of discretion at the point of application.

In this way we might make distinctions between the role of high theory within the courtroom and the role of high theory in the political branches of government. To be sure, incompletely theorized agreements play a role in democratic arenas; consider laws protecting endangered species or granting unions a right to organize. But in democratic arenas, there is no taboo, presumptive or otherwise, on invoking high-level theories of the good or the right.[8] On the contrary, such theories have played a key role in many social movements with defining effects on American constitutionalism, including the Civil War, the New Deal, the women's movement, and the environmental movement. Abstract, high-level ideas are an important part of democratic discussion, and sometimes they are ratified publicly and placed in a constitution.

By contrast, development of large-scale theories by ordinary courts is problematic and usually understood as such within the judiciary. The skepticism about large-scale theories is partly a result of the fact that such theories may require large-scale social reforms, and courts

have enormous difficulties in implementing such reforms.[9] When courts invoke a large-scale theory as a reason for social change, they may well fail simply because they lack the tools to bring about change on their own. An important reason for judicial incapacity is that courts must decide on the legitimacy of rules that are aspects of complex systems. In invalidating or changing a single rule, courts may not do what they seek to do. They may produce unfortunate systemic effects, with unanticipated bad consequences that are not visible to them at the time of decision, and that may be impossible for them to correct thereafter.[10] Legislatures are in a much better position on this score. Consider, for example, an effort to reform landlord–tenant law. Judges may require landlords to provide decent housing for poor tenants, but the result may be to require landlords to raise rents, with detrimental effects on the poor. To say this is not to say that judge-initiated changes are always bad. But it is to say that the piecemeal quality of such changes is a reason for caution.

The claim that courts are ineffective in producing large-scale reform is a generalization, and it has the limits of all generalizations. The point does not count decisively against more ambitious judicial rulings when those rulings have a powerful legal and moral foundation. An ambitious ruling might announce an uncontestable high-level principle, and the announcement of the principle might be right even if courts lack implementing tools. What seems clear is that the difficulties of judge-led social reform provide a basis for judicial modesty. [. . .]

More fundamentally, it is in the absence of a democratic pedigree that the system of precedent, analogy, and incompletely theorized agreement has such an important place. The need to discipline judicial judgment arises from the courts' complex and modest place in any well-functioning constitutional system. To be sure, judges have, in some societies, a duty to interpret the Constitution, and sometimes that duty authorizes them to invoke relatively large-scale principles, seen as part and parcel of the Constitution as democratically ratified. Many people think that judicial activity is best characterized by reference to use of such principles.[11] Certainly there are occasions on which this practice is legitimate and even glorious.

To identify those occasions it would be necessary to develop a full theory of legal interpretation. For present purposes we can say something more modest. Most of judicial activity does not involve constitutional interpretation, and the ordinary work of common law decision and statutory interpretation calls for low-level principles on which agreements are possible. Indeed, constitutional argument itself is based largely on low-level principles, not on high theory, except on those rare occasions when more ambitious thinking becomes necessary to resolve a case or when the case for the ambitious theory is so insistent that a range of judges converge on it. And there are good reasons for the presumption in favor of low-level principles – having to do with the limited capacities of judges, the need to develop principles over time, the failure of monistic theories of the law, and the other considerations traced above. [. . .]

Hercules and Theory

An ambitious alternative

Enthusiasm for incompletely theorized agreements meets with many adversaries. Let us take Ronald Dworkin as an especially prominent example. In his illuminating work on legal reasoning, Dworkin urges, at least as an ideal, a high degree of theoretical self-consciousness in adjudication. Dworkin argues that when lawyers disagree about what the law is with respect to some hard question – Can the government ban hate speech? Cross-burning? – they are disagreeing about "the best constructive interpretation of the community's legal practice."[12] Thus Dworkin claims that interpretation in law consists of different efforts to make a governing text "the best it can be." This is Dworkin's conception of law as integrity. Under that conception, judges try to fit their rulings to preexisting legal materials, but they also invoke principle, in the sense that they try to cast those materials in their best light. The goal of the judge is to analyze the case at hand under the two dimensions of "fit" and "justification."

Hercules, Dworkin's infinitely patient and resourceful judge, approaches the law in this way. It is important for our purposes that on Dworkin's view, judges are obliged to account for the existing legal materials, whether judge-made or statutory, by weaving them together into a coherent framework. Hence judges are not supposed to impose large-scale theories of their own making. Here we might appear to have the makings of an appreciation for incompletely theorized agreements, for reliance on precedent is a large part of those agreements.

But Dworkin does not defend incompletely theorized agreements. On the contrary, his account appears to require judges to develop high-level theories and does not (to say the least) favor theoretical modesty. In Dworkin's hands, the relevant theories are large and abstract; they sound just like political philosophy or moral theory. On his view, the law of tort reflects a theory of equality, and the law of free speech a theory of autonomy. These theories are derived from and brought to bear on particular problems. But this is not how real lawyers proceed. They try to avoid broad and abstract questions. Such questions are too hard, large, and open-ended for legal actors to handle. They prevent people who disagree on large principles from reaching consensus on particular outcomes. In this way, Hercules could not really participate in ordinary judicial deliberations; he would be seen as a usurper, even an oddball.

In thinking about equal protection issues, for example, lawyers (and ordinary people) do not generate large-scale theories about the meaning of equality in a democracy. Instead they ask what particular sorts of practices seem clearly to violate the Fourteenth Amendment or the principle of equality, and then whether a measure discriminating against (for example) the handicapped is relevantly similar or relevantly different. Of course the description of relevant similarities and differences will have evaluative dimensions, and of course these should be made explicit. As we will see, an analogy depends for its plausibility on a principle of some sort. But lawyers and judges try not to engage in abstract political theorizing. They avoid such theorizing because it takes too much time and may be unnecessary; because it may go wrong insofar as it operates without close reference to actual cases; because it often prevents people from getting along at all; and because general theorizing can seem or be disrespectful insofar as it forces people to contend, unnecessarily, over their deepest and most defining moral commitments. Consider in this connection the idea that courts should not resolve constitutional issues unless they must in order to decide a case – an idea that imposes a presumptive taboo on judicial judgments about society's most basic or defining commitments.[13]

Dworkin anticipates an objection of this kind. He notes that it might be paralyzing for judges to seek a general theory for each area of law, and he acknowledges that Hercules is more methodical than any real-world judge can be. But Hercules, in Dworkin's view, "shows us the hidden structure of" ordinary "judgments and so lays these open to study and criticism."[14] Of course Hercules aims at a "comprehensive theory" of each area of law, whereas ordinary judges, unable to consider all lines of inquiry, must aim at a theory that is "partial." But Hercules's "judgments of fit and political morality are made on the same material and have the same character as theirs."

It is these points that I am denying here. The decisions of ordinary judges are based on different material and have a different character. They are less deeply theorized, not only because of limits of time and capacity, but also because of the distinctive morality of judging in a pluralistic society. I will qualify this claim below. But for the moment, the point suggests that the ordinary judge is no Hercules with less time on his hands, but a different sort of figure altogether.

Conceptual Ascent?

Borrowing from Henry Sidgwick's writings on ethical method,[15] an enthusiast for ambitious thinking might respond in the following way. There is often good reason for judges to raise the level of abstraction and ultimately to resort to large-scale theory. As a practical matter, concrete judgments about particular cases will prove inadequate for morality or law. Sometimes people do not have clear intuitions about how cases should come out; their intuitions are uncertain or shifting. Sometimes seemingly similar cases provoke different reactions, and it is necessary to raise the level of theoretical ambition to explain whether those different reactions are justified or

to show that the seemingly similar cases are different after all. Sometimes people simply disagree. By looking at broader principles, we may be able to mediate the disagreement. In any case there is a problem of explaining our considered judgments about particular cases, in order to see whether they are not just a product of accident,[16] and at some point the law will want to offer that explanation.

For these reasons, a judge who does not theorize might end up being Herculean too. At least he had better have that aspiration in mind. When our modest judge joins an opinion that is incompletely theorized, he has to rely on a reason or a principle, justifying one outcome rather than another. The opinion must itself refer to a reason or principle; it cannot just announce a victor. Perhaps the low-level principle is wrong because it fails to fit with other cases or because it is not defensible as a matter of (legally relevant) political morality.

In short, the incompletely theorized agreement may be nothing to celebrate. It may be wrong or unreliable. The fact that people converge may be a kind of coincidence or an accident, and when they start thinking more deeply, they may be able to tell whether the judgment is really right. Thus if a judge is reasoning well, he should have before him a range of other cases, c through z, in which the principle is tested against others and refined. At least if he is a distinguished judge, he will experience a kind of "conceptual ascent," in which the more or less isolated and small low-level principle is finally made part of a more general theory. Perhaps this would be a paralyzing task, and perhaps our judge need not often attempt it. But it is an appropriate model for understanding law and an appropriate aspiration for judges.

The conceptual ascent seems especially desirable in light of the fact that incompletely theorized agreements will allow large pockets of inconsistency. Some areas of the law may appear coherent and make internal sense, but they may run into each other if they are compared. We may have a coherent category of law involving sex equality (though this would be fortunate indeed), and a coherent category involving racial equality (same qualification), but these categories may have a very strange and unsatisfactory relation to the categories involving sexual orientation and the handicapped. Various subcategories of tort law may make sense, but they may not fit together at all. More ambitious forms of reasoning seem necessary in order to test the low-level principles. In this way we might conclude that judges should think of incompletely theorized agreements as an early step toward something both wider and deeper. Many academic understandings of law, including economic analysis, undertake the task of showing that wider and deeper conception.[17]

There is some truth in this response. Moral reasoners should try to achieve vertical and horizontal consistency, not just the local pockets of coherence offered by incompletely theorized agreements. In democratic processes it is appropriate and sometimes indispensable to challenge existing practice in abstract terms. But the response ignores some of the distinctive characteristics of the arena in which real-world judges must do their work. Some of these limits involve bounded rationality and thus what should happen in a world in which judges face various constraints; some of them involve limits of role and appropriate judicial morality in a world in which judges are mere actors in a complex system, and in which people legitimately disagree on first principles. In light of these limits, incompletely theorized agreements have the many virtues described above, including the facilitation of convergence, the reduction of costs of disagreement, and the demonstration of humility and mutual respect.

As I have noted, incompletely theorized agreements are especially well-adapted to a system that must take precedents as fixed points; lawyers could not try to reach full integrity without severely compromising the system of precedent. Usually local coherence is the most to which lawyers may aspire. Just as legislation cannot be understood as if it came from a single mind, so too precedents, compiled by many people responding to different problems in many different periods, will not reflect a single authorial voice.

There are many lurking questions. How do we know whether moral or political judgments are right? What is the relation between provisional or considered judgments about particulars and corresponding judgments about abstractions? Sometimes people write as if abstract theoretical judgments, or abstract theories, have a kind of

reality and hardness that particular judgments lack, or as if abstract theories provide the answers to examination questions that particular judgments, frail as they are, may pass or fail. On this view, theories are searchlights that illuminate particular judgments and show them for what they really are. But we might think instead that there is no special magic in theories or abstractions, and that theories are simply the (humanly constructed) means by which people make sense of the judgments that constitute their ethical and political worlds. The abstract deserves no priority over the particular; neither should be treated as foundational. A (poor or crude) abstract theory may be a confused way of trying to make sense of our considered judgments about particular cases, which may be much better than the theory. In fact it is possible that moral judgments are best described not as an emanation of a broad theory, but instead as part of a process of reflection about prototypical cases or "precedents" from which moral thinkers – ordinary citizens and experts – work.[18]

Legitimacy

There is a final issue. Dworkin's conception of law as integrity contains a theory of what it means for law to be legitimate. Hercules, Dworkin's idealized judge, can produce vertical and horizontal consistency among judgments of principle in law. The same cannot be said of those who urge incompletely theorized agreements. A legal system pervaded by such agreements need not yield anything like full coherence. Perhaps this is a decisive defect. Perhaps it suffers from the standpoint of those who seek legitimacy in law.

Of course principled consistency should not be disparaged, and of course a regime of principled judgments has many advantages over imaginable alternatives. Of course problems of legitimacy may arise precisely because of the absence of such consistency. If you are treated differently from someone else – if you are treated worse or better – there should be a reason for the difference in treatment. In fact, however, the idea of integrity – insofar as it is focused on the judiciary – does not provide a convincing theory of legitimacy. Integrity, if a product of good judicial judgment, is neither necessary nor sufficient for legitimacy.

Legitimacy stems not simply from principled consistency on the part of adjudicators, but from a justifiable exercise of authority, which requires a theory of just institutions. That theory should in turn be founded in democratic considerations, suitably constrained by an account of what interests should be immunized from democratic intrusion. Legitimacy is an outcome of well-functioning democratic processes, not of a system of distinction-making undertaken by judges. Even if done exceptionally well, distinction-making by principled judges is too court-centered as a source of legitimacy.

Those who stress incompletely theorized agreements insist that adjudication is part of a complex set of institutional arrangements, most prominently including democratic arenas. They attempt to design their theory of judicial judgment as an aspect of a far broader set of understandings about appropriate institutional arrangements and about forums in which the (suitably constrained) public can deliberate about its judgments. For reasons of both policy and principle, the development of large-scale theories of the right and the good is a democratic task, not a judicial one. These remarks should suggest the ingredients of an account of legitimacy of which incompletely theorized agreements would be a part. [. . .]

Notes

1 Lochner v. New York, 198 US 48, 69 (1908) (Holmes, J., dissenting).

2 See, e.g., Charles Fried, Contract as Promise: A Theory of Contractual Obligation (Cambridge: Harvard University Press, 1981); Ronald M. Dworkin, Law's Empire (Cambridge: Harvard University Press, 1986).

3 See John Rawls, Political Liberalism (New York: Columbia University Press, 1993), pp. 16–17, 50.

4 This is the goal of the equal protection argument. See Cass R. Sunstein, The Partial Constitution (Cambridge: Harvard University Press, 1993), ch. 9.

5 See Planned Parenthood v. Casey, 112 S. Ct. 2791 (1992). . . .

6 I borrow here from Joseph Raz, "The Relevance of Coherence," in Ethics in the Public Domain:

Essays in the Morality of Law and Politics (Oxford: Oxford University Press, 1994), p. 261.

7 See Amartya K. Sen, Commodities and Capabilities (Amsterdam: North-Holland, 1985).

8 I am putting to one side the questions raised by "comprehensive views," see Rawls, supra note [3].

9 See Gerald N. Rosenberg, The Hollow Hope: Can Courts Bring about Social Change? (Chicago: University of Chicago Press, 1991).

10 Examples are offered in R. Shep Melnick, Regulation and the Courts: The Case of the Clean Air Act (Washington, DC: Brookings Institution, 1983), and Donald Horowitz, The Courts and Social Policy (Washington, DC: Brookings Institution, 1977). The point is described from the theoretical point of view in Lon Fuller, The Forms and Limits of Adjudication, 92 Harv. L. Rev. 353 (1978), and Joseph Raz, "The Inner Logic of the Law," in Ethics in the Public Domain, supra note [6], at 224.

11 This is the vision of judicial review in Bruce A. Ackerman, We the People, vol. 1: Foundations (Cambridge: Harvard University Press, 1991). Note that it differs dramatically from the understanding in Ronald Dworkin, Law's Empire, in the sense that Ackerman insists that large-scale principles have sources in actual judgments of "we the people." There is, however, a commonality between Ackerman and Dworkin in the sense that both see the use of such principles as a large part of the Court's work. It is along that dimension that I am doubting both of their accounts. . . .

12 Dworkin, supra note 2, at 224.

13 See Alexander M. Bickel, The Least Dangerous Branch: The Supreme Court at the Bar of Politics (New Haven: Yale University Press, 1986).

14 Dworkin, supra note 2, at 265.

15 See Henry Sidgwick, The Methods of Ethics, 7th ed. (New York: Dover, 1966), pp. 96–104.

16 "[T]he resulting code seems an accidental aggregate of precepts, which stands in need of some rational synthesis." Sidgwick, supra note [15], at 102.

17 See Richard A. Posner, Economic Analysis of Law, 4th ed. (Boston: Little Brown, 1992); see also the discussion of the law of tort in Dworkin, supra note 2.

18 "One's ability to recognize instances of cruelty, patience, meanness, and courage, for example, far outstrips one's capacity for verbal definition of those notions." Paul M. Churchland, The Engine of Reason, the Seat of the Soul (Cambridge: MIT Press, 1995), p. 145; see also id. at 144, 293.

5

Custom, *Opinio Juris*, and Consent

Larry May

It is often said that many universal norms at the international level derive their authority from custom. One of the leading textbooks on international criminal law asserts:

> Unlike international agreement as such, customary international law is of a universally obligatory nature. Thus, what was at one time an international agreement binding merely signatories and their nationals can later become customary law for the entire international community.[1]

Jus cogens norms are here said to be nonconsensual, and yet sometimes to be also customary. But customary international norms are said to begin life as simply a matter of agreement – that is, arising from the acceptance of States over time.

Initially, it might seem that consensual norms of international law are a nice fit with my moral minimalism. Custom does not seem to be based in the questionable metaphysics of the natural law tradition, and custom seems to provide an easy way to limit the extent of binding norms – that is, to only those norms that reach a near-universal acceptance over time. Custom does indeed seem to limit the reach of international norms in a somewhat plausible way, thereby appealing to one aspect of my moral minimalism – namely, the substantive worry that we not overreach in proscribing every rights violation as a violation of international criminal law. But custom, as a source of *jus cogens* norms in international criminal law, is not consistent with another aspect of my moral minimalism – namely, that we not rely on controversial assumptions. As this chapter will show, customary international criminal norms are indeed suspect, even though not appealing to natural law principles, since they are initially grounded in consent, and yet are said to give rise to non-consensual norms.[2]

How can consensual norms give rise to non-consensual obligations? In this chapter, I take up this conceptual puzzle, ultimately arguing that if *jus cogens* norms are to be understood as truly universal norms, then they cannot be grounded in consensually based customs alone. More than acceptance, even over a long period of time, is necessary for having some norms in the international legal system that are to be treated as allowing no derogation, even by States that have not recognized these norms as legally binding. [. . .]

In international law, it is well established that for a customary norm to rise to the level of *a jus cogens* norm,[3] all or most States must recognize

Larry May, "Custom, *Opinio Juris*, and Consent," from *Crimes Against Humanity: A Normative Account* (Cambridge University Press, 2005), pp. 40–62. © 2005 by Larry May. Reprinted with permission from Cambridge University Press.

that norm as universally binding, they must behave as if they are bound by this norm, and they must meet the *opinio juris* test – namely, such felt bindingness must be based on a sense of legal or moral obligation.[4] The question posed in this chapter is whether such additional elements in an account of consensually based custom can ground *jus cogens* norms. I argue that consensually based custom and *opinio juris* cannot ground universal norms. The main reason is that such international custom, even when it meets the *opinio juris* test, remains a consensual basis for legally valid norms, yet what is needed for the justification of universally binding norms is a non-consensual basis. I also argue that while consensually based custom, standing alone, cannot supply the justification for such universally binding norms, consensually based custom, including the concept of *opinio juris*, can at least supply evidence of the existence of such norms. As [I have argued] an international harm principle could provide the support lacking in consensually based custom for universal norms in the international realm. But it is simply a mistake to think of universal *jus cogens* norms as merely arising from consensual customary international law. At the end of this chapter, I will consider what a non-consensually based custom might look like, and what it might be grounded in.

In the first section, I begin with some cautionary remarks drawn from the work of David Hume, who considered the attempt by his contemporaries to ground obligations in consent. Hume argued that such attempts were hopeless unless they were conjoined with non-consensual considerations. In the second section, a non-criminal model of understanding international customary norms is analyzed. I consider two cases concerning international contracts and property rights: the Texaco/Libya Arbitration[5] and the Kuwait/Aminoil Arbitration.[6] These cases were adjudicated by reference to international customary norms. In the third section, I will examine the case of Iraq, which had invaded Kuwait in 1990 to gain its oil resources, and was repelled by an international military force headed by the United States. In this third section, I will critically examine the supposed customary basis for the UN-imposed sanctions against Iraq after the Gulf War that were aimed at deterring Iraq from future aggression and punishing Iraq for its harmfully exploitative behavior toward Kuwait. In the fourth section, I will examine the conflicting opinions presented by two international judges on the role of custom and *opinio juris* in adjudicating international disputes concerning the use or threat of nuclear weapons.

In the fifth section, I directly confront the attempt to portray consensually based customary international law as providing universal norms that all states should obey. I argue that such custom, standing alone, cannot supply the justification for such norms, but that custom, including the concept of *opinio juris*, can at least supply evidence of the existence of legally valid norms. In the sixth section, the relationship between *jus cogens* norms and international customary law is further explored. I briefly examine six ways to save the consensual customary basis of universal norms, rejecting each in turn. By the end of this chapter, we can see the need for a non-consensual basis for universal norms [. . .].

I. Some Lessons from Hume

In David Hume's famous essay, "Of the Original Contract,"[7] several mistakes are identified among political philosophers of the eighteenth century. It seems to me that these mistakes have been repeated by contemporary theorists of international criminal law. I begin with a short discussion of Hume's arguments against the attempt to ground obligation in consent. Like Hobbes, Hume grants that one of the salient features of a state of nature is that all people are roughly equal. Since they are roughly equal to one another, "we must necessarily allow, that nothing but their own consent could, at first, associate them together, and subject them to any authority."[8] Consent is, on Hume's account, the obvious source of authority for binding obligations in the state of nature. But over time, as new people who had never consented come on the scene, problems arise for a consensual account of obligation.

We can also think of contemporary disputes in international criminal law as similar to the state-of-nature scenario that Hume envisions. [. . .] [T]here is a rough equality among States, giving rise to the problem of how one State can bind another State. Initially, the most obvious way to do this is through the mutual consent of States. This is why most of the major sources of international law in the twentieth century, such as the Charter of the United Nations or the Statute of the International Criminal Court, were initially established by multilateral treaties – that is, by States binding themselves, and thereby creating a basis by which one State could claim that another State is bound even given the rough equality of States. Hume and Hobbes are in agreement at this stage.

For Hume, the problem of consent arises from those philosophers who "assert not only that government in its earliest infancy arose from consent or rather the voluntary acquiescence of the people, but also even at present, when it has attained its full maturity, it rests on no other foundation."[9] In a telling analogy, Hume says that these same philosophers would be repelled by the idea that the "consent of the fathers" in one generation could "bind the children, even to the most remote generations."[10] Consent cannot provide a basis for binding universal norms, argues Hume, because with "every man every hour going out of the world, and another coming into it," original consent will not clearly bind all.[11] There must be some other ground of continuing obligation of non-consenting persons other than mere original consent.

Here, there is a similar problem to that of retroactive legislation.[12] In retroactive legislation, [...] a person is held accountable for actions taken in the past that are held to have violated a law only passed in the present. To say that one has violated a law that did not exist when one acted is to engage, at best, in a sleight of hand. There is now a law that exists, and on which prosecution proceeds. But if one could not have known about the law when one acted, it is patently unfair to use that law as a basis for judging past behavior. Similarly, to bind a State on the basis of an agreement or treaty that that State had not agreed to is similarly problematical. If a State did not sign on to the treaty, it is patently unfair to use the terms of the treaty to judge the behavior of a non-signatory State.

Hume argues that moral duties and obligations arise from sentiment "restrained by subsequent judgment or observation."[13] The "general interests or necessities" are sufficient to create the bindingness of such duties and obligations. For

our purposes, this recalls the Hobbesian point of the previous chapter that all people have a general interest in self-preservation and self-defense, and that such an interest can ground binding universal norms. Hume seems to be operating in a similar mode when he argues that moral duty arises out of general interests or necessities. The main point here is that the consent of others cannot replace these interests. The consent of some people cannot bind other people, and hence universally binding norms cannot be generated out of consensual norms.

Now, recall the quotation from a leading textbook on international criminal law with which I began this chapter. There the authors claim that customary international law is of "a universally binding nature." They claim that the support for such customary international law comes from binding international agreements. This is not itself problematical. States obviously think, with justification, that their treaties create binding obligations on one another. But Paust et al. go on to say that these treaty agreements later become binding for the "entire international community" – that is, even for those States that were not a party to these treaties. Yet from what they say, it is at best mysterious as to how such a transformation occurs. Again recall Hume's remark that such arguments seem to be like the argument that the consent of fathers binds successive generations of children. Why think that the consent of some States can come to bind other States, even those that explicitly decided not to sign on to the original agreement? This is the topic I will be exploring in the remainder of this chapter.

Of course it might be, as Hume seems to have held, that there are non-consensual customs that are binding on all, and that derive their bindingness from interest and necessity. Perhaps the test of *opinio juris* is supposed to allow us to pick out just such customs. This would all be fine if theorists of international criminal law had a clear idea of what it was that *opinio juris* added to original agreement to transform consensually based customs into non-consensual ones. But as we will see, *opinio juris* merely adds that some States not only consent but then act as if they are morally or legally bound. Then, once enough States so behave, binding universal norms arise. It often seems as if the sheer length of time by which a consensually based custom has lasted is sufficient to transform such a custom into a non-consensual, universally binding custom. Such a view obviously falls prey to the set of Humean objections I have just recited.

How does this Humean position square with the moral minimalist position with its Hobbesian leanings [. . .]? It is interesting to note that in a quotation from H. L. A. Hart mentioned earlier, Hobbes and Hume are linked as those who have understood the empirical good sense of a minimalist understanding of the natural law doctrine. And even from such a brief discussion of Hume so far, one can hopefully see why Hart linked Hume and Hobbes together. Hume diverged somewhat from Hobbes in thinking that it was the strong interest that individuals had in self-defense that ultimately was the rationale for the sovereign's authority, not merely what people actually consented to.

I wish to highlight a general lesson to be learned from our discussion of Hume. Consensually based custom does not mysteriously transform itself into non-consensual custom, even as it stands the test of time. Indeed, custom does not seem to be a very good basis at all for a stable understanding of what people are obligated to do, and much less for a universally binding set of norms. In what follows, I will build a parallel argument against deriving *jus cogens* norms from consensually based custom by reference to several major disputes in international law generally, and international criminal law in particular. Much confusion will be uncovered, as well as significant conceptual difficulties, when theorists of international law discuss the customary basis of *jus cogens* norms. I will illustrate the strains of that confusion, and then argue that other attempts to save the idea that custom can produce binding universal norms are also likely to fail.

II. A Non-Criminal Model: The Oil Nationalization Cases

The first problem with seeing consensually based custom as a source of universal legal norms is that it is too weak to justify these norms. Certain forms of custom are meant to pick out those norms that are universal, and yet the test for

custom seems to rely only on the consent of the parties involved, at least those that are most directly affected by the claimed rights and duties. Let us consider how an international arbitrator used the notion of custom to analyze Libya's right to nationalize a private corporation's assets to prevent exploitation of Libya's natural resources. The non-criminal *jus cogens* norm in question concerned the prohibition of the destruction of a State's natural resources. When custom originates from, and is justified by reference to, the empirical fact of consent, it cannot provide a ground for *universal* norms. At the end of this section, we consider the normative argument that is needed, and was supplied, in the second Libya case. By analyzing how this case succeeded and failed, we will find a rough model for how to proceed from consensual custom to universal legal norms.

In 1974, Texaco and Libya sought arbitration to resolve disputes stemming from Libya's contract deeding oil fields to Texaco in 1955. The deeds contained the following clause: "[C]ontractual rights expressly created by this concession shall not be altered except by mutual consent of the parties."[14] Yet, in 1974, Libya "nationalized the totality of the properties, rights, assets and interests of California Asiatic Oil Company and Texaco Overseas Petroleum Company arising out of the 14 Deeds of Concession held by those companies."[15] The ensuing dispute centered directly on the right of Libya to nullify a contract that had expressly guaranteed that no changes in the contract were allowed unless both parties consented. Libya argued that as a sovereign entity, it had the right to dispose of its natural resources as it saw fit. But Libya did allow for an international arbitrator to resolve its dispute with Texaco.

In the Texaco/Libya Arbitration case, the arbitrator cited approvingly UN General Assembly Resolutions that confirmed "that every State maintains a complete right to exercise full sovereignty over its natural resources and recognizes Nationalization as being a legitimate and internationally recognized method to ensure the sovereignty of the State upon such resources."[16] Although the arbitrator recognized that General Assembly resolutions are not legally binding, he declared that when the States most likely to be affected by the resolution have voted for the resolution, then these resolutions become a customary legal basis for obligations.[17]

Here we have a clear basis for determining international legal obligations – namely, look to the General Assembly resolutions, and also to the votes taken in that body. The General Assembly is treated like a legislative body duly authorized to make binding law. But since there is no international State, it is not clear who has authorized the General Assembly to make binding law. Indeed, as the arbitrator admitted, the General Assembly itself does not recognize its resolutions as anything other than advisory. This is why the arbitrator says that the case actually concerns whether there is a basis in customary international law for nationalization of resources. The arbitrator seemingly held that the General Assembly can establish a customary basis for binding law when a State both (1) is likely to be affected by the resolution, and (2) has voted for the resolution. If both these conditions are met, then a State is bound by the resolution.[18]

This opinion is conceptually unsettling in several respects. The most obvious conceptual difficulty concerns the favorable reference to General Assembly Resolutions about inherent or universal rights, and the failure to regard these Resolutions as creating binding legal obligations unless the States consent to them. There are two difficulties. First, either the General Assembly votes create binding custom – that is, new law – or the General Assembly votes merely acknowledge an already existing custom. In the former case, it is the consent of the parties that creates custom, and it is not clear why we need to talk of custom as playing a role at all. In the latter case, the General Assembly is largely irrelevant since the non-consensual custom would exist whether positive votes were taken by the General Assembly or not. Second, either the rights are universal or inherent, in which case they do not require the vote of the General Assembly or the consent of State parties most likely to be affected in order to be binding, or the Resolutions require the consent of State parties that are likely to be affected, in which case the rights declared in the Resolutions are consensual and not inherent or universal.

The arbitrator's opinion does in one sense conform to Hume's cautionary warnings, for the parties bound by the General Assembly votes are those States that voted positively and that understood they would likely be affected by the ensuing Resolution. But it is surely not the case that "universal" rights were created by these acts of "original" consent. It displays a serious conceptual confusion to think that the limited scope of what one consents to be bound to can create universally binding norms. We turn next to a much more successful attempt to ground a universal obligation not to exploit another State's natural resources, also at least begun in considerations of consent.

In another case, Liamco v. Libya,[19] Libya had first nationalized 51 percent of Liamco's concessions. Then, when Liamco failed to reach agreement with the new Libyan government concerning the use of natural resources in Libya, the remaining 49 percent of Liamco's concessions was nationalized.[20] Libya again claimed that its actions were justified in order to protect its natural resources from exploitation. Liamco claimed that the actions of the Libyan government were "politically motivated, discriminatory and confiscatory."[21] Both sides agreed to submit to international arbitration.

In the Liamco/Libya Arbitration, the international arbitrator specifically addressed one of the hardest questions: If a State owns natural resources and transfers ownership to another party, why does that other party not have the right to exploit those natural resources as part of its property right? According to the arbitrator, a property right has been defined since Roman times, as the right to use or abuse a given thing. The ancient notion of property rights granted to the property holder a right that could not be taken away without the property holder's consent. "In the light of that classical definition, the State could not expropriate any private property."[22] But the arbitrator does not follow this logic to its obvious conclusion.

In both Western conceptions of property and those that arise out of the Koran, "public necessity" is a ground for violation of property rights.[23] The Liamco arbitrator relies on an old Muslim legal maxim: "Private damage has to be suffered in order to fend off public damage." On the basis of such an understanding of property rights, the arbitrator says that a modern "social" view of property has emerged that sees a natural resource as property that is "subservient to the public interest of the Community represented by the State."[24] Nationalization of private property in order to advance the community interest can thereby be defended.[25]

The Liamco arbitrator concludes that "most publicists today uphold the sovereign right of a State to nationalize foreign property," even in contravention of "international treaties."[26] The writings of publicists are one of the chief sources of determining customary norms. As in the Texaco case, the principle that a State can abrogate private property rights for the community good is justified by reference to customary international law. In both the Texaco and Liamco Arbitrations, customary international law is considered the source of the legitimacy of nationalization. Nationalization becomes a legitimate response to exploitation of a State's natural resources by a foreign company. In both cases, customary international law is said to protect a State's right that its economic resources not be exploited. Since the advent of the Vienna Convention on Treaties that gave voice to the idea that there were non-consensual, *jus cogens* norms, such norms have been held to override those consensual rights and duties established by contracts and treaties.

The Liamco arbitrator seemed to acknowledge this point. An additional element was added to the analysis of State practices in order to determine the existence of a universal right of a State to protect its natural resources from exploitation. The arbitrator sought justification of universal rights by reference to normative arguments concerning property rights. Such arguments were then conjoined with the evidence of State practices, thereby putting the arbitrator on considerably firmer ground for claiming that economic exploitation was proscribed by universal (*jus cogens*) principles, not merely by reference to consensual customary practices. Thus the Liamco decision avoids the conceptual problems of the Texaco decision. The arbitrator appealed to non-consensual principles in order to justify the claim that universal prescriptions existed. Consensually based custom, standing alone, was not thought to be sufficient to ground universal rights and duties. So we have here a rough model of how to solve the main problem of this chapter. Something other than consensually based custom, perhaps a normative argument, seemed to be needed in order to make of certain

consensually based customs a source of non-consensually binding international law.

III.   Iraq's Invasion of Kuwait

The second problem with seeing consensually based custom as a source of international rights and duties is that it does not provide a clear basis to obligate those States that have not consented. A classic example of this problem comes in the various recent problems in Iraq. One of the most interesting aspects of the UN enforcement actions in Iraq is the attempt to justify the idea that non-member States, and hence States that have not explicitly consented to the United Nations Charter, can be obligated to act when Security Council resolutions call for universal adherence. How can the actions taken by the United Nations bind States that are not members of the United Nations? The answer cannot be drawn in the simple terms of consensually based custom.

In 1990, Iraq invaded Kuwait, laying claim to Kuwait's rich oil fields. The United Nations, through the Security Council, was quick to condemn Iraq's actions, and to call upon member States to defend the rights of Kuwait. A military response from a United States-led military force followed closely the Security Council resolutions.[27] Ten days after Iraq invaded Kuwait, the United States announced an interdiction policy – actually, a naval blockade – against Iraq. Eventually, a US-led military force confronted the Iraqi armies, and repelled them. The United States claimed to be justified in its military action by reference to Article 51 of the United Nations Charter. This action spurred the Security Council to pass another resolution, 665, authorizing such a use of force against Iraq.[28] It has been argued that Article 51 merely provides a codification of customary international law, and hence does not require explicit UN endorsement of a State's defensive acts. Indeed, Article 51 specifically says that the right of collective self-defense is an "inherent right" of member States.[29]

The recognition of a customary international norm condemning the use of economic exploitation and armed aggression by one State against another is an important development in international law. The Nicaragua case had clearly articulated the principle that armed aggression was a violation of *jus cogens* norms.[30] In the Iraq resolutions, the Security Council makes it even clearer that all States are obligated to aid the UN in preventing such aggression. While this statement does not apply to all human rights abuses, preventing armed aggression is here placed on the same footing with the *jus cogens* norms condemning slavery, genocide, and apartheid.

Security Council Resolution 661 decides that "all states" shall participate in the sanctions against Iraq. In Resolution 670, pursuant to Chapter VII of the UN Charter, the Security Council called "upon all states to carry out their obligations to ensure strict and complete compliance with resolution 661." In effect, the Security Council declared that cooperating with the UN in stopping unjustified State aggression is an obligation *erga omnes*, an obligation on all States based on universal *jus cogens* norms.[31]

Here we see some of the same problems as in the oil nationalization cases. The Security Council, like the General Assembly, acts by means of votes taken by its member States. The Security Council is not in a privileged position to identify universal norms, nor to create them. In addition, we have the problem of understanding how consensually based custom, standing alone, can bind those States that are not members of the United Nations, and hence could bind States that were not part of the Security Council's deliberative process. Iraq was one such nonmember State. And to make matters worse, Iraq claimed that its rights were also violated by the various Security Council actions.

After Iraq removed its troops from Kuwait, the Security Council passed additional resolutions creating continuing economic sanctions against Iraq. Yet Iraq complained vigorously about the denigration of its sovereignty by Resolution 687, which extended sanctions after the US-led forces left Iraq. Specifically, Iraq complained that it had been deprived "of its lawful right to acquire weapons and military materiel for defense . . . thus endangering the country's internal and external security."[32] Such a claim, as well as the claims that Iraq had acted unjustly, seem to me to be best defended not by reference to what Iraq had consented to do, for Iraq had consented to do very little. The issue seems to be better drawn in non-consensual terms: what Iraq owed to the other members of the international community, and what those members owed to Iraq as a matter of minimal morality.

One possible basis for Iraq's complaints, as well as the complaints made against Iraq, can be found in the universal right of a State to defend itself from external attack, and the universal obligation of a State to care for the bodily and spiritual welfare of its citizens. If this right and duty defended by Verdross, and also clearly recognized in the United Nations Charter, is indeed a *jus cogens* norm, it is very hard to see how it could be grounded in what Iraq or any other States consented to. What underlies Resolution 687 is that Iraq has violated the moral minimum of acceptable behavior of States. Such a basis for the claims against Iraq would not turn on whether Iraq was at the time a member of the United Nations and hence subject to the resolutions of the Security Council.

In the first two sections of this chapter, we have seen that the main problem of consensually based custom as a source of universal legally binding norms is that such a consensual source of putative law is not binding on States that have not consented. In addition, it is unclear how conflicts of custom can be adjudicated. Appeals to custom alone will not allow for the resolution of such problems. At most, customary practices of some States will tell us what those States think they are legally bound to do, not what other States that have rejected these customs are legally bound to do. In this sense, it is right to think that Security Council resolutions get their bindingness from the fact that they do, sometimes, reflect non-consensual norms of international law. Such resolutions also make binding norms, but only for those States that remain members and only for as long as the votes of the Security Council continue to declare such norms to be binding on its members. Non-consensual norms that could bind non-member States have to gain their justification from a source other than consensually based custom.

IV. The Threat to Use Nuclear Weapons

The third problem with seeing consensually based custom as a source of universal norms is that custom is not only normatively too weak to be much of a justification at all, but it is also so hard to meet the test for custom that custom will rarely be able to resolve disputes. The test for custom requires that all or most States engage in practices consistent with recognizing the norm as binding, and the *opinio juris* provision adds the notion that all or almost all States must indicate that they are motivated to follow the norm out of a sense of legal or moral obligation. Yet rarely, if ever, can such a high standard be achieved. Consensually based custom will then not be very useful in articulating duties and obligations in international law. And once again we see that consensually based custom will not provide a basis for non-derogable duties of the sort required for universal *jus cogens* norms.

In the ICJ's opinion on whether the threatened use of nuclear weapons can be justified to defend the rights of an aggrieved State, we see this problem in stark relief as two prominent international jurists disagreed about what is customary international law, and how if at all custom could resolve a dispute. In lodging dissents in the nuclear weapons case, Judge Schwebel and Judge Weeramantry debated the issue. Both of these jurists are highly respected as international law scholars. But, as will emerge, both failed to understand the difficulties with the concept of *opinio juris*, the concept that is supposed to provide a test for whether a norm rises to the level of customary international law with universally binding force.

According to the ICJ's majority opinion in the Advisory Opinion on Nuclear Weapons Use, the threat or use of nuclear weapons is generally contrary to international law. But the court left open the possibility that the threat or use of nuclear weapons might be justified "in an extreme circumstance of self-defense, in which the very survival of the state would be at stake."[33] The ICJ took up the issue of tactical nuclear weapons in paragraph 95 of its advisory opinion, and said, "the Court does not consider that it has sufficient basis for a determination on the validity" of the threat or use of tactical nuclear weapons. Thus the ICJ did not declare this use of nuclear weapons to be illegal. What is more important, though, is that the dissents spawned by this opinion give a rather clear idea of the conceptual problems that continue to plague the idea of customary international law.

Judge Schwebel, a United States judge sitting on the ICJ, argued in dissent that State practices and *opinio juris* demonstrate the support in customary international law for the legality of the threat or use of nuclear weapons. To support this claim, Schwebel points to the US-led war against Iraq in 1990. Citing statements by Iraqi Foreign Minister Tariq Aziz, Schwebel contends that the US threat of nuclear strikes deterred Iraq from using its chemical and biological weapons during the war with Iraq.[34] Schwebel argues that the threat of nuclear weapons allowed the United States to win the war, and thereby allowed the United Nations effectively to sanction Iraq for invading Kuwait. This shows that the threat of nuclear weapons can be rational, and acceptable to all. If Iraq had not been deterred by the threat, the United States would have been justified in using nuclear weapons in order to prevent the use by Iraq of prohibited weapons of mass destruction. According to Schwebel, it would be imprudent to prohibit the use of nuclear weapons as long as there are rogue States and terrorists who will only be deterred by nuclear threats.[35]

Judge Schwebel's use of the example of the invasion of Iraq does not support his claim that State practices and *opinio juris* favor the legality of nuclear weapons. First, there is no consensus that the United States would have been justified in using nuclear weapons to counter Iraq's use of chemical or biological weapons. Schwebel can cite no one outside of the United States who agrees with him about this point. Hence he is unable to show the nearly unanimous State practices he needs in support of his point, let alone the additional dimension of *opinio juris*. If the United States believed that it was justified in threatening the use of nuclear weapons, why was there then, as well as now, very little public discussion of this strategy? The United States may have been willing to use nuclear weapons, but it is unclear from what Schwebel shows that the United States felt it was clearly legally or morally justified in doing so.

Second, arguments about what would be prudent are not adequate for establishing *opinio juris*, which requires that a State act out of a sense of moral or legal obligation. Schwebel's argument misses the mark by failing to establish anything like the *opinio juris* dimension of customary international law. The chief conceptual problem with customary international law illustrated by Schwebel's opinion is that States often do things for unclear motives, and yet *opinio juris* requires a showing that a State's practice is based on a felt sense of legal or moral obligation. It is very hard to isolate the intentions and motives of a State, but it surely cannot be assumed that if a State clearly acts on prudential motives, it is thereby acting on the basis of a felt legal or moral obligation.

Prudence might provide a normative basis for a *jus cogens* norm, but only if prudence were linked to a moral minimum. Schwebel tries to make prudence a basis of custom, and then posits custom as a basis of a *jus cogens* norm. Such a strategy is simply confused. Prudence could motivate a state to support a custom, but the fact of consent is ultimately an empirical matter of whether many, or perhaps all, States support the custom. Even if all States support a custom on the basis of prudence, it is the prudence, as a normative matter, not the custom, as an empirical matter, that might ground a *jus cogens* norm.

Judge Weeramantry, also arguing in dissent, tries to counter Judge Schwebel's argument, by appealing to custom and *opinio juris* as well. Weeramantry bases much of his opinion on the Martens Clause of The Hague Convention in arguing that the threat or use of nuclear weapons "represents the very negation of . . . the structure of humanitarian law."[36] Such ultimate human values risk being wiped out, or at least massively and quite horribly destroyed, by "the advent of nuclear war."[37] Weeramantry says that the cornerstone of that branch of international customary law called humanitarian law is the Martens Clause's requirement that the dictates of public conscience must not be violated.[38] Here we see Weeramantry adding moral considerations to the arguments about State practice.

The part of the Martens Clause that seems most important to Weeramantry is the role that the "dictates of public conscience" play in filling the gaps left because we don't have a complete code of the laws of war. The "test" of what satisfies public conscience is "that the rule should be 'so widely and generally accepted that it can hardly be supposed that any civilized state would not support it,'"[39] and hence is contrary to common decency. And Weeramantry says that the public

conscience has spoken many times, in the most unmistakable terms, that the threat or use of nuclear weapons is unacceptable.[40] Weeramantry here seems to be influenced by natural law arguments, not by simple appeals to custom. The Martens Clause is presented as affirming a normative principle, not merely as one part of a previous multilateral treaty. [Elsewhere] I will explore the "public conscience" basis of *jus cogens* norms. But it should be here noted that this basis is not itself consensually customary, but rather morally normative, since what counts as a matter of public conscience is not simply a matter of what most States happen to believe.

While I share many of Weeramantry's sentiments, his argument leaves something to be desired. If we give a literal interpretation of his test for ascertaining when custom becomes a universal norm, there will then be no rule favoring or disfavoring the threat or use of nuclear weapons if there is just one civilized country that does not support it. But we know that several, if not many, "civilized" States do not support this rule. Indeed, the majority opinion in this case[41] also cites the Martens Clause. And the same is true of Judge Schwebel's opinion that mentions the Martens Clause approvingly on its very first page. Hence it seems that Weeramantry has set too stringent a test for what is necessary to ground universal international norms. He is right that whatever threatens the advent of nuclear war is indeed one of the worst of human disasters to be avoided at nearly any cost. But he is confused in thinking that the consensual practices of States plus *opinio juris* is unequivocal in supporting this idea, or is likely ever to be. The upshot is that the addition of *opinio juris* to consensually based custom does not help to arrive at *jus cogens* norms of international law.

V. What is the Relationship Between Custom and Universal Norms?

Customary international law is said to have two elements. First, there must be reasonably consistent and nearly universal practices of States to act in a certain way, such as not torturing people. Second, there must be *opinio juris* – that is, a general sense of legal or moral obligation on the part of the States that motivates them not to engage in a certain practice. As the ICJ held in the North Sea Continental Shelf Cases: "[t]he States concerned must therefore feel that they are conforming to what amounts to a legal obligation. The frequency, or even habitual character of the acts is not in itself enough."[42] Mark Janis calls *opinio juris* a "magic potion" that is added to the frequency of State practice. Janis says that the best sources of *opinio juris* are the statements made by jurists and judges because it is hard to tell what the motivation is for State action or practice.[43] As we saw earlier, even with the statements of jurists, there is often no consensus.

When a large number of States not only consent to be bound by a given custom, but also behave in ways that indicate that they have a sense of moral or legal obligation to obey that norm,[44] the customary norms are supposed to bind not only those States but also other non-consenting States. How is it possible for one State to bind another State by means of consent? Think of the prohibition of torture. What started out as a matter of mere consent by some States is said to have evolved into a norm that is binding on all States, and that cannot now be overturned by the express agreement of States. And this is supposed to be due to the fact that these States not only consent to the norm, but behave as if they are bound by it from a sense of obligation. But how can it happen that a norm that is based on the consent of various States can itself be transformed into a norm that is universally binding?

At least part of the answer is that in addition to the original consent, it must now be that all, or almost all, States regard a given norm as a universal norm. This appears to be a way to determine universal norms by asking all States what they think are universal norms, and this is indeed partially what is going on. But in addition, all, or nearly all, States must demonstrate by their behavior that they regard the norm as binding. And the bindingness needs to be one that is recognized as universal or somehow necessary in a sense that makes the norm a priori, as the ICJ recognized in the North Sea Continental Shelf Case.[45] In that case, the question was whether the equidistance principle was a "natural law of the continental shelf" evidenced in the customs of nations. The court asks: "[W]as the notion

of equidistance . . . an inherent necessity of continental shelf doctrine?"[46] It answers that this cannot be, since States have recognized two competing principles for determining the extent of a State's continental shelf.

The court then considers whether nonetheless "this emerging customary law became crystallized" as a result of being recognized in various treaties.[47] The treaties, though, would normally only provide a consensual basis for a given norm – after all, treaties are just elaborate contracts. But if the treaties recognized an existing norm thought to be universal, then this would be evidence for the existence of such a norm. Again, it would not be sufficient for the norm to be merely "accepted," but the States would also have to behave as if the norm were indeed a universal norm. So we are still left wondering how consensually based customary norms could become universal norms, and what might be the "magic potion" that could transform the former into the latter in international law.

At this stage, we need to draw an important distinction that will help us understand the relationship between customary and universal norms. We need to distinguish between *evidence* for the existence of a universal norm, and *justification* of that norm. Consensually based custom could provide evidence, although certainly not conclusive evidence, of the existence of a universal (*jus cogens*) norm, but consensually based custom cannot justify a *jus cogens* norm. The main reason for this is quite simple. Even if all States once consented to be bound by a given custom, and behaved as if this custom were universally binding, that would not make the norm universally binding since the States could change their views toward this custom. Paust et al. recognize this point when in their recent textbook of international law they assert that "customary law can be dynamic . . . What once was custom can change to non-custom . . . and what was not customary law can grow into customary law . . ."[48]

Let us say that a State is confronted with a supposedly universal norm based on a near-unanimous consensus among States. And a State is able to deny the universal bindingness of the norm merely by declaring that it does not now agree that the norm is binding. If even a small number of States change positions and now declare that they no longer acknowledge the norm as universal, then by these very declarations the norm would seem to lose its universal status.[49] Yet surely this cannot be. If the norm is to be universally binding now, it cannot also be true that now States can make that norm not universally binding. Either the norm is universally binding or it is not. States cannot make a norm currently more or less universally binding by their votes or by their practices, even if based on a sense of obligation.

This simple argument is not meant to deny that *opinio juris* may be the best evidence we have of the existence of a universal (*jus cogens*) norm of international law. If all or most States do acknowledge a norm as universally binding, and their behavior also displays such an acknowledgment, then this is indeed evidence of the existence of such a norm. Such evidence becomes even stronger if the reason that States do acknowledge such a norm is because of a sense of legal or moral obligation. And if States stop acknowledging a norm as universal, then this is very good evidence that such a norm may never have been universally binding. But in neither case is this evidence conclusive for establishing that a norm is or is not a universal legally binding norm.

So what might count as conclusive evidence of a universal legally binding norm? It might be conclusive if there is a morally normative argument based, for instance, on what reasonable States would accept. The very best evidence we have of a universal norm of international law is when there is both *opinio juris* and normative justification for such a norm. Normative justification may be enough, at least in the abstract, but in a highly diverse world, where the very premises of such a conceptual argument are highly contested, it is prudent to look to *opinio juris* in addition to normative justification in order to determine what the *jus cogens* norms of international law are. It is prudent because even if fully justified, the norm may not be respected by States unless it already also has fairly widespread support seen in the customary practices of these States. But such appeals to consensual custom, standing alone, cannot ground these norms. A norm cannot be said to be universally binding if, at the moment of a State's falling under the obligation, a State can evade this bindingness merely by declaring itself not bound.

VI. Defending Custom

The kind of custom we have been examining – namely, that which starts off as based in a multilateral treaty – is seemingly either justified by long-standing norms that reach back in time for their justification – that is, to the acceptance of certain norms at those historically distant times[50] – or is justified by the current acquiescence of States. In both cases, the customary norm is justified by the acceptance, and hence the consent, of States. Such norms cannot mysteriously change themselves into non-consensual norms unless something else is added. Perhaps the custom is based on hypothetical rather than actual consent. But in such cases, it is the morally normative argument underpinning the hypothetical consent that does the work, not the practices of States. In this section, I will explore various ways that one could still try to argue that consensually based custom might ground universal or inherent norms.

First, let us consider the "historical" argument. Customs are often defended on the grounds of having stood "the test of time" – namely, that the justification of the norm is acknowledged over different historical eras. Most customs start out as consensual in the sense that people regard the custom as binding because they accept it, or acquiesce in it. As a custom displays a staying power – that is, as generation after generation accepts or acquiesces in it, that custom demonstrates that it is acceptable to a broad constituency. In other words, customs gain in stature, and perhaps also in legal bindingness, the longer they last and as they gain more and more adherents. The more diverse the States that effectively "sign on" to a custom, and the longer those States remain "signatories," the stronger is the custom's bindingness. Having stood "the test of time," the custom demonstrates its "universal" acceptability. At some point, perhaps at that mystical point identified by Mark Janis, the custom itself ceases to be consensual and becomes non-consensual.

One significant problem with the historical argument concerns what have been called "persistent objectors."[51] Certain States may have dissented from the custom from the very beginning of the custom's history, and their dissent continues into the present day. By so objecting, these "persistent objectors" establish something like a counter-custom of their own. By the same reasoning as that provided by the consenters, the dissenters can claim that their dissent also gets stronger the longer it lasts, and perhaps also crystallizes into a countervailing non-consensual custom that is as strong as the original custom itself, since it is based on the same "test of time." Once it is acknowledged that the "persistent objector" is not bound by the customary norm to which it dissents, then the universal bindingness of the original customary norm is rendered suspect. This objection shows that a single State can, counter-intuitively, disrupt the move from historical consensual custom to universal norm.

Second, let us consider the "fairness" argument. Such an argument has its strongest support in reaction to the problem of the "persistent objectors." Take, for example, the custom that people not take advantage of those who are in vulnerable positions. If such a custom is not treated as universally binding, then some will choose not to follow the custom, and yet may well benefit from the custom, for instance, if they themselves are ever in a vulnerable position and hence in need of the restraint that the custom calls for. Those who do not follow the custom – the dissenters – will feel free to take advantage of the vulnerable to their own benefit, and yet will also count on the restraint of others if these dissenters are ever rendered vulnerable. In the parlance of social choice theory, this will allow the dissenters to become "free riders" in a society where most of the people restrain themselves. And because the dissenters benefit from their exploitation of this custom, it is unfair. The dissenters benefit from the adherence of others to a custom to which they themselves do not adhere. Fairness calls for the dissenters to be subject to the custom to avoid the free rider problem.

The fairness argument gives us a reason to treat some consensually based customs as universally binding norms, but it does not establish the principle that these customs, as opposed to any others, really are universally binding. Instead, we are given fairness-based reasons to apply certain norms to all, but no reason to think that the norms so applied have a special character by virtue of having been backed by custom. Indeed,

we have merely pushed the skeptical question back one level. Instead of asking why "persistent objectors" should be held to a custom that they dissented from, we now ask why the custom itself is thought to be so important that dissent from it is not to be allowed, even on the very good grounds provided by the "persistent objectors?" And the answer to this question cannot rely merely on the fact that a norm is supported by custom, but must appeal to fairness, or some other ground for thinking that the norm must be considered binding for all. Yet, such an argument is no longer basically a customary or historical argument but rather one of normative principle.

Third, a related strategy is to argue that customs should be seen as universally binding in order to solve certain coordination problems. Here it is not fairness but efficiency that makes the custom universally binding. On this strategy, perhaps custom is itself grounded in just one consensual principle – namely, a single rule of recognition that says that any norm that has satisfied the *opinio juris* criteria for being a custom is a proper basis of legal obligation. If all States accept such a rule, then any norm that meets the criteria becomes a binding norm on all States. If enough States accept a custom, then the other States are bound because all States have accepted the rule of recognition "tipping principle": as soon as n-number of States accept a norm, then, so as to solve a serious coordination problem, all other States accept that norm as binding on them, even those States that have not previously accepted it. And the basis for such a rule of recognition is that the world is simply a better place if there is a stable pattern of conduct than if there is not. Here is a way to link prudential considerations with morally normative ones that one would expect a moral minimalist like me to endorse.

Yet I still find myself skeptical. We would seem to need universal agreement to the rule of recognition, and yet this is not the case in international law. There has not been anything like the acceptance of an international rule of recognition, as Hart and others have pointed out.[52] Think of those States that never accepted the UN Charter or who never ratified the Rome Treaty. We have not solved the problems identified earlier since there are still persistent objectors to the rule of recognition, and yet these persistent objectors would find themselves nonetheless bound by the norms endorsed by that rule of recognition. As Hart also said, a rule of recognition is merely a fact. If some States do not accept a given rule of recognition, then it is not a rule of recognition for them.

Fourth, rather than being based on consent, perhaps custom derives its authority from a set of interdependent habits in a given population. These interlocking habits create a web of normative behavior in a society that is meant to ground *jus cogens* norms. Interdependent habits are not the same as consent. Indeed, it would be as odd to say that custom has been established by consent as it is to say that tradition has been established by a deliberate act. Rather, customs are established over time as more and more States find themselves acting in ways that are consistent with the custom. According to this defense of custom, it is not consent but a certain kind of implicit acceptance over time that is key, and the acceptance is seen in a State's behavior, not in some "mythical" consent. As long as States behave in interdependent and habitual ways, these habits are themselves a basis of custom that has normative force.

Whether acceptance is inferred from behavior or based on explicit consent, there is still the problem of how some States that behave in ways supportive of a custom can bind other States that do not behave in this way. I suppose it can be said that these other States simply already do behave this way (although perhaps unself-consciously) or that they will come to behave in this way down the road. Such a view denies the possibility of true "persistent objectors" to a given custom, and yet history is full of such examples. Persistent objectors consistently behave in ways that are opposed to a given custom. States that reject the custom against torture behave in ways, although probably not very often, that mark their objection to the custom. Of course, part of this is an empirical matter concerning how States actually do behave. But shifting to how States behave, and away from what States explicitly consent to, does not help account for the bind-ingness of certain norms, especially the binding-ness for the persistent objectors.

Fifth, custom could be considered to provide us with "as if" universal norms in the same way that scientists act as if they had "discovered" a new physical element – call it krypton. The act of those who accept the custom, and the act of the scientist, are similar in that they merely give us the best evidence of the existence of a univer-sal norm. This position is attractive in that it actually plays off my earlier discussion of the difference between evidence for, and justifica-tion of, a norm. Just as science doesn't need any more support, so also is this true for international norms. Here it is claimed that custom is the best evidence we can seek, and is not in need of supplementation by additional bases. Custom is then like a scientist's discovery of krypton in that custom is a kind of recognition by a society that a norm is binding. The society's recognition is not what makes the norm binding, just as the scientist's discovery of krypton is not what creates krypton. Both the norm and the krypton were already there. The society recognizes the existence of the norm by agreeing to, or acqui-escing in, a custom, just as the scientist recognizes the existence of krypton by "discovering" or naming it.

Yet I would want to insist that, even as evidence, consensual custom still does not provide a basis for a universal norm in the sense of providing a justification. Indeed, by the way this third position is articulated, it is clear that the custom does not provide a justification of the norm for those who would doubt that the norm does in fact exist, just as the skeptic is not answered by the scientist's reference to the "discovering" or naming of krypton. The skeptic will want to hear the reasons, and not just trust the scientist's word, just as the skeptic will not trust the "word" of the custom. Once again, our skeptical question is merely pushed back another level. Certainly no one denies that there are such putative customs and discoveries. The question is rather whether any putative custom or discovery really does pick out the universal norm or the krypton. To answer a skeptic at this level, one needs a different kind of argument than one that merely makes reference to some evidence. One needs an independent reason for the skeptic to trust that the society or the scientist is a reliable finder of actual, as opposed to illusory, norms or krypton.

Sixth, one could merely suggest that the defenders of *jus cogens* norms have simply overreached. *Jus cogens* norms are no different from norms in most societies proscribing murder or rape. That just these acts are proscribed is based on custom. That the proscription extends to all members in a society is based on utility, or some other value. In the international "society," *jus cogens* norms on this understanding would be simply those norms that are considered most fundamental, in terms of the benefits, or other values, that adherence to those norms is thought to provide for the world community. Once again, there are various ways to help pick out which of the international norms should have this designation. But the justification for them as universal or fundamental norms is simply that adherence to them does indeed benefit, or provide some other value to, that community. It is the value of these norms that gives them their universal bindingness and that goes beyond the mere criteria of identification of the norms.

Here we finally come to a position that is likely to produce a justification for universal norms in international law. But in the end it is a justification that is independent of the existence of the consensually based custom itself. For the justification is really based entirely on the utility, or other moral value, of a given norm, regardless of what its form happens to be, or regardless of its history. Hence this last attempt to save the customary basis of *jus cogens* norms either fails outright, or points us toward the type of justification that is based on moral principles, such as the principle of utility. [. . .] But this sixth attempt fails if it is thought to provide a justification based solely on the evidence of the existence of a norm rather than on the underlying justification for having the norm.

Consensually based customs thus do not justify the norms that they express. This said, it is also true that customs play a role in giving recognition to norms, perhaps even to universal norms. The custom of condemning murder can be said to give voice to the universal norm against the premeditated taking of innocent life. Therefore, to say that *jus cogens* norms are part of customary international law is not quite as odd as it first seemed. *Jus cogens* norms can be part of customary international law and still be non-consensual as long as the non-consensual nature of these norms is not thought to derive from their being originally consensual, as we

learned from David Hume. That universal *jus cogens* norms are customary is merely due to the way that they are sometimes recognized rather than anything having to do with their nature or justification.

The *opinio juris* test adds an important dimension to custom as a basis for international rights and duties. It is not enough that States behave as if there are universal rights and duties at stake. *Opinio juris* requires that the States behave in this way out of a sense of moral or legal obligation. Meeting this test will indeed greatly help in the identification of those customary norms of international law that are universally binding. But rather than looking at the behavior of States, and at the motivation of those States, why not look at the obligation itself, and ask whether there are good arguments based on normative principles to support such an obligation. Such a grounding will give us a direct basis for the identification and justification of non-consensual norms that does not depend on magically creating them out of consensually based customary norms.[53]

The non-consensual basis of *jus cogens* norms is especially important for practices that involve exploitation. Many States find themselves contractually bound to acquiesce in violating their own subjects' right not to be exploited. Because of the treaties and accords that those States have consented to, as was true in the two Libya cases discussed earlier, States are seemingly forced to exploit their subjects. If *jus cogens* norms are consensual, then they cannot easily be used to override other consensual norms, such as those imposed by treaty or contract.[54] Yet, as in the case of unconscionable domestic contracts, it is well recognized in international law that States do have a basis for rejecting exploitative treaties and contracts.[55] If this is to be a part of international law as well, the norms necessary for such an overriding will have to be non-consensual.

The conclusion to the argument of this chapter is that there is a serious conceptual confusion about custom and *opinio juris*, the supposed basis for universal *jus cogens* norms, in international law. Consensually based custom, standing alone, is not a clear basis for justifying the universal international norms, the violation of which will warrant international prosecutions. As in most justificatory matters, there is no substitute for moral support. I have hinted at what that normative support might look like, but the main point of this chapter has been a negative one: Consensually based custom and *opinio juris* are not sufficient bases for the condemnation of rights abuses and the ensuing crossing of borders to redress those rights violations. The most significant finding of this chapter is that there remains serious conceptual confusion about *opinio juris* as a cornerstone of universal *jus cogens* norms in international law.

Notes

1 Jordan J. Paust, M. Cherif Bassiouni, Michael Scharf, Jimmy Gurule, Leila Sadat, Bruce Zagaris, and Sharon A. Williams, *International Criminal Law: Cases and Materials*, 2nd edn., Durham, NC: Carolina Academic Press, 2000, p. 4.
2 I am very grateful to Andrew Altman and William Edmundson for helpful discussion of these points.
3 See Jerzy Sztucki, *Jus Cogens and the Vienna Convention on the Law of Treaties*, Vienna: Springer Verlag, 1974, for an excellent discussion of the historical development of the concept of *jus cogens* in international law.
4 North Sea Continental Shelf Cases, 1969 I.C.J. Reports 3, para. 37.
5 Texaco v. Libya, 17 International Legal Materials 1, 1978.
6 Kuwait v. Aminoil, 21 International Legal Materials 976, 1982.
7 David Hume, "Of the Original Contract," in *Hume's Ethical Writings*, Alasdair MacIntyre, ed., Notre Dame, IN: University of Notre Dame Press, 1979.
8 Ibid., p. 256.
9 Ibid., p. 257.
10 Ibid., p. 259.
11 Ibid., p. 264.
12 I am grateful to Kit Wellman for discussion of this point.
13 Hume, op. cit., p. 267.
14 Texaco/Libya Arbitration, Award of 19 January 1977, 17 International Legal Materials 1, 1978, para. 2.
15 Ibid., para. 7.
16 Ibid., para. 80.
17 Ibid., para. 83–4.
18 The international legal rights and duties of the United Nations come from the consent of its members. In the Reparations case, the ICJ held that the UN has both political and legal personality. Specifically, the court held that the UN "could not carry out the intentions of its founders if it was devoid of international personality." See *Reparations for Injuries Suffered in the Service of the United Nations*, Advisory Opinion, 11 April 1949, ICJ Reports, para. 174. The UN's legal capacity to act is based on the power vested in it by its members. To distinguish the UN from the unsuccessful League of Nations, the founding members of the UN gave to the Security Council, but not to the General Assembly, the power to initiate actions to promote international peace, including authorizing armed attacks. Until the 1990s, the Security Council was embroiled in ideological disputes between Communist and non-Communist countries that prevented it from acting according to its mandate. The end of the Cold War changed things – at least for the moment.
19 Liamco v. Libya, 20 International Legal Materials, 1, 1981.
20 It is interesting to note that the second Liamco nationalization occurred on the same day that Texaco's concessions were also nationalized.
21 Liamco v. Libya, para. 113.
22 Ibid., para. 47.
23 Ibid.
24 Ibid., para. 48.
25 Ibid., para. 48–9.
26 Ibid., para. 50.
27 The UN's swift and successful response to Iraq's invasion of Kuwait seems to be just what the UN was founded to do. The first sentence of Article 1(1) of the UN Charter says that the main goal of the UN is "[t]o maintain international peace and security." The Charter specifically calls for "the prevention and removal of threats to the peace, and for the suppression of acts of aggression." The swift action of the UN in enlisting member States to confront Iraq and force it to stop exploiting Kuwait is arguably the kind of "removal of threats to the peace" and "suppression of acts of aggression" that are the hallmark goals of the UN. See Charter of the United Nations, 1945, Article 1(1).
28 Frederic J. Kirgis, *International Organizations*, 2nd edn., St Paul, MN: West Publishing, 1993, p. 651.
29 Eugene Rostow, "Until What? Enforcement Action or Collective Self-Defense," *American Journal of International Law*, vol. 85, 1991, p. 506, contends that in any such Article 51 action, the key is to act on the basis of the provision of Article 51 that allows for "the inherent right of individual or collective self-defense . . . until the Security Council has taken measures necessary to maintain international peace and security."

30 Case Concerning Military and Paramilitary Activities in and against Nicaragua (Nicaragua v. United States), 1986, ICJ, 14, para. 190.

31 The Security Council claimed to be authorized to take these actions, and those actions proved to be important. Article 2(6) of the Charter says that the UN "shall ensure that states which are not members of the United Nations act in accordance with these principles so far as may be necessary for the maintenance of international peace and security." So, if the UN determines that an action requires conformity from non-members for its success in maintaining international peace and security, non-members can be required to act. This proposition can also be supported by reference to Article 35 of the Vienna Convention on the Law of Treaties, although Article 35 says that the third-party State must "expressly accept the obligation in writing."

32 Quoted in Kirgis, p. 678.

33 Advisory Opinion on the Legality of the Threat or Use of Nuclear Weapons, 1997 I.L.M. 814, ICJ, July 8, 1996, para. 105 E.

34 Ibid., Schwebel dissent, para. 10–12.

35 Ibid., Schwebel dissent, para. 12–13.

36 Ibid., Weeramantry dissent, para. 1.

37 Ibid., Weeramantry dissent, para. 11.

38 Ibid., Weeramantry dissent, para. 37.

39 Ibid., Weeramantry dissent, para. 40.

40 Ibid., Weeramantry dissent, para. 42.

41 Ibid., Majority Opinion, para. 87.

42 North Sea Continental Shelf Cases, 1969, ICJ Reports, 3, 44, quoted in Mark Janis, *An Introduction to International Law*, 1993, p. 46.

43 Ibid., pp. 47–8.

44 The most obvious way to show this is by the words uttered by the leaders of the State at the time the State acts. Another way, but much more controversial, is to look at how publicists and jurists interpret what the State's motivations are.

45 North Sea Continental Shelf Cases, 1969, ICJ Reports 3, para. 37. What the court seems to have meant by "a priori" is that states feel they cannot disregard the norm for reasons of self-interest.

46 Ibid., para. 55.

47 Ibid., para. 61.

48 Paust, Bassiouni et al., *International Criminal Law*, p. 5.

49 Even if we regard custom as a kind of tacit treaty, it will be the kind of treaty that States can "unsign," as happened when the United States decided to unsign the Rome Treaty establishing the ICC.

50 See John Ladd's entry, "Custom," in *The Encyclopedia of Philosophy*, New York: Macmillan, vol. 2, 1967.

51 See the discussion of this idea in Maurizio Ragazzi, *The Concept of International Obligations Erga Omnes*, Oxford: Oxford University Press, 1997, pp. 60–7. As Ragazzi notes, international law today only allows for the persistent objector to evade the bindingness of a custom if no "fundamental principles" are at stake. Of course, the topic of whether *jus cogens* norms are customary is deeply embedded in the discussion of whether a persistent objector can evade the bindingness of a custom.

52 See the final chapter of H. L. A. Hart's *The Concept of Law*, 2nd edn., Oxford: Oxford University Press, 1991.

53 This is not to say that such a moral grounding will be easy to achieve, or that this moral grounding will be universally acknowledged by everyone. We might need to settle for less than this, but we need to be clear that what is short of moral grounding will not truly justify.

54 Mark Janis argues in a similar vein that *jus cogens* norms should not be seen as grounded in customary international law. See Mark Janis, "The Nature of Jus Cogens," *Connecticut Law Review*, vol. 3, 1988, p. 360. Janis thinks that the only way to justify nonconsensual *jus cogens* norms is through natural law theory. As should be obvious by now, I have reservations about that view.

55 See Allen Wertheimer, "Unconscionability and Contracts," *Business Ethics Quarterly*, vol. 2, no. 4, October 1992, pp. 479–96, for a very good conceptual analysis of the basis, and limitations, of unconscionability in contracts in US law.

6

Lochner v. New York (1905)

Error to the County Court of Oneida County, State of New York

No. 292. Argued February 23, 24, 1905 – Decided April 17, 1905.

The general right to make a contract in relation to his business is part of the liberty protected by the Fourteenth Amendment, and this includes the right to purchase and sell labor, except as controlled by the State in the legitimate exercise of its police power.

Liberty of contract relating to labor includes both parties to it; the one has as much right to purchase as the other to sell labor.

There is no reasonable ground, on the score of health, for interfering with the liberty of the person or the right of free contract, by determining the hours of labor, in the occupation of a baker. Nor can a law limiting such hours be justified as a health law to safeguard the public health, or the health of the individuals following that occupation.

Section 110 of the labor law of the State of New York, providing that no employees shall be required or permitted to work in bakeries more than sixty hours in a week, or ten hours a day, is not a legitimate exercise of the police power of the State, but an unreasonable, unnecessary and arbitrary interference with the right and liberty of the individual to contract, in relation to labor, and as such it is in conflict with, and void under, the Federal Constitution.

This is a writ of error to the County Court of Oneida County, in the State of New York (to which court the record had been remitted), to review the judgment of the Court of Appeals of that State, affirming the judgment of the Supreme Court, which itself affirmed the judgment of the County Court, convicting the defendant of a misdemeanor on an indictment under a statute of that State. [. . .]

The indictment averred that the defendant "wrongfully and unlawfully required and permitted an employé working for him in his biscuit, bread and cake bakery and confectionery establishment, at the city of Utica, in this county, to work more than sixty hours in one week," after having been theretofore convicted of a violation of the same act; and therefore, as averred, he committed the crime or misdemeanor, second offense. The plaintiff in error demurred to the indictment on several grounds, one of which was that the facts stated did not constitute a crime. The demurrer was overruled, and the plaintiff in error having refused to plead further, a plea of not guilty was entered by order of the court and the trial commenced, and he was convicted of misdemeanor, second offense, as indicted, and sentenced to pay a fine of $50 and to stand committed until paid, not to exceed fifty days in the Oneida County jail. A certificate of reasonable doubt was granted by the county judge of Oneida County, whereon an appeal was taken to the Appellate Division of the Supreme Court, Fourth Department, where the judgment of conviction was affirmed. 73 App. Div. N.Y. 120. A further appeal was then taken to the Court of Appeals, where the judgment of conviction was again affirmed. 177 N.Y. 145. [. . .]

MR JUSTICE PECKHAM, after making the foregoing statement of the facts, delivered the opinion of the court.

The indictment, it will be seen, charges that the plaintiff in error violated the one hundred and tenth section of article 8, chapter 415, of the Laws of 1897, known as the labor law of the State of New York, in that he wrongfully and unlawfully required and permitted an employé working for him to work more than sixty hours in one week. There is nothing in any of the opinions delivered in this case, either in the Supreme Court or the Court of Appeals of the State, which construes the section, in using the word "required," as referring to any physical force being used to obtain the labor of an employé. It is assumed that the word means nothing more than the requirement arising from voluntary contract for such labor in excess of the number of hours specified in the statute. There is no pretense in any of the opinions that the statute was intended to meet a case of involuntary labor in any form. All the opinions assume that there is no real distinction, so far as this question is concerned, between the words "required" and "permitted." The mandate of the statute that "no employé shall be required or permitted to work," is the substantial equivalent of an enactment that "no employé shall contract or agree to work," more than ten hours per day, and as there is no provision for special emergencies the statute is mandatory in all cases. It is not an act merely fixing the number of hours which shall constitute a legal day's work, but an absolute prohibition upon the employer, permitting, under any circumstances, more than ten hours work

to be done in his establishment. The employé may desire to earn the extra money, which would arise from his working more than the prescribed time, but this statute forbids the employer from permitting the employé to earn it.

The statute necessarily interferes with the right of contract between the employer and employés, concerning the number of hours in which the latter may labor in the bakery of the employer. The general right to make a contract in relation to his business is part of the liberty of the individual protected by the Fourteenth Amendment of the Federal Constitution. *Allgeyer v. Louisiana*, 165 U.S. 578. Under that provision no State can deprive any person of life, liberty or property without due process of law. The right to purchase or to sell labor is part of the liberty protected by this amendment, unless there are circumstances which exclude the right. There are, however, certain powers, existing in the sovereignty of each State in the Union, somewhat vaguely termed police powers, the exact description and limitation of which have not been attempted by the courts. Those powers, broadly stated and without, at present, any attempt at a more specific limitation, relate to the safety, health, morals and general welfare of the public. Both property and liberty are held on such reasonable conditions as may be imposed by the governing power of the State in the exercise of those powers, and with such conditions the Fourteenth Amendment was not designed to interfere. *Mugler v. Kansas*, 123 U.S. 623; *In re Kemmler*, 136 U.S. 436; *Crowley v. Christensen*, 137 U.S. 86; *In re Converse*, 137 U.S. 624.

The State, therefore, has power to prevent the individual from making certain kinds of contracts, and in regard to them the Federal Constitution offers no protection. If the contract be one which the State, in the legitimate exercise of its police power, has the right to prohibit, it is not prevented from prohibiting it by the Fourteenth Amendment. Contracts in violation of a statute, either of the Federal or state government, or a contract to let one's property for immoral purposes, or to do any other unlawful act, could obtain no protection from the Federal Constitution, as coming under the liberty of person or of free contract. Therefore, when the State, by its legislature, in the assumed exercise of its police powers, has passed an act which seriously limits the right to labor or the right of contract in regard to their means of livelihood between persons who are *sui juris* (both employer and employé), it becomes of great importance to determine which shall prevail – the right of the individual to labor for such time as he may choose, or the right of the State to prevent the individual from laboring or from entering into any contract to labor, beyond a certain time prescribed by the State.

This court has recognized the existence and upheld the exercise of the police powers of the States in many cases which might fairly be considered as border ones, and it has, in the course of its determination of questions regarding the asserted invalidity of such statutes, on the ground of their violation of the rights secured by the Federal Constitution, been guided by rules of a very liberal nature, the application of which has resulted, in numerous instances, in upholding the validity of state statutes thus assailed. Among the later cases where the state law has been upheld by this court is that of *Holden v. Hardy*, 169 U.S. 366. A provision in the act of the legislature of Utah was there under consideration, the act limiting the employment of workmen in all underground mines or workings, to eight hours per day, "except in cases of emergency, where life or property is in imminent danger." It also limited the hours of labor in smelting and other institutions for the reduction or refining of ores or metals to eight hours per day, except in like cases of emergency. The act was held to be a valid exercise of the police powers of the State. A review of many of the cases on the subject, decided by this and other courts, is given in the opinion. It was held that the kind of employment, mining, smelting, etc., and the character of the employés in such kinds of labor, were such as to make it reasonable and proper for the State to interfere to prevent the employés from being constrained by the rules laid down by the proprietors in regard to labor. The following citation from the observations of the Supreme Court of Utah in that case was made by the judge writing the opinion of this court, and approved: "The law in question is confined to the protection of that class of people engaged in labor in underground mines, and in smelters and other works wherein ores are reduced and refined. This law applies only to the classes

subjected by their employment to the peculiar conditions and effects attending underground mining and work in smelters, and other works for the reduction and refining of ores. Therefore it is not necessary to discuss or decide whether the legislature can fix the hours of labor in other employments."

It will be observed that, even with regard to that class of labor, the Utah statute provided for cases of emergency wherein the provisions of the statute would not apply. The statute now before this court has no emergency clause in it, and, if the statute is valid, there are no circumstances and no emergencies under which the slightest violation of the provisions of the act would be innocent. There is nothing in *Holden v. Hardy* which covers the case now before us. Nor does *Atkin v. Kansas*, 191 U.S. 207, touch the case at bar. The *Atkin* case was decided upon the right of the State to control its municipal corporations and to prescribe the conditions upon which it will permit work of a public character to be done for a municipality. *Knoxville Iron Co. v. Harbison*, 183 U.S. 13, is equally far from an authority for this legislation. The employés in that case were held to be at a disadvantage with the employer in matters of wages, they being miners and coal workers, and the act simply provided for the cashing of coal orders when presented by the miner to the employer.

The latest case decided by this court, involving the police power, is that of *Jacobson v. Massachusetts*, decided at this term and reported in 197 U.S. 11. It related to compulsory vaccination, and the law was held valid as a proper exercise of the police powers with reference to the public health. It was stated in the opinion that it was a case "of an adult who, for aught that appears, was himself in perfect health and a fit subject for vaccination, and yet, while remaining in the community, refused to obey the statute and the regulation adopted in execution of its provisions for the protection of the public health and the public safety, confessedly endangered by the presence of a dangerous disease." That case is also far from covering the one now before the court.

Petit v. Minnesota, 177 U.S. 164, was upheld as a proper exercise of the police power relating to the observance of Sunday, and the case held that the legislature had the right to declare that, as matter of law, keeping barber shops open on Sunday was not a work of necessity or charity.

It must, of course, be conceded that there is a limit to the valid exercise of the police power by the State. There is no dispute concerning this general proposition. Otherwise the Fourteenth Amendment would have no efficacy and the legislatures of the States would have unbounded power, and it would be enough to say that any piece of legislation was enacted to conserve the morals, the health or the safety of the people; such legislation would be valid, no matter how absolutely without foundation the claim might be. The claim of the police power would be a mere pretext – become another and delusive name for the supreme sovereignty of the State to be exercised free from constitutional restraint. This is not contended for. In every case that comes before this court, therefore, where legislation of this character is concerned and where the protection of the Federal Constitution is sought, the question necessarily arises: Is this a fair, reasonable and appropriate exercise of the police power of the State, or is it an unreasonable, unnecessary and arbitrary interference with the right of the individual to his personal liberty or to enter into those contracts in relation to labor which may seem to him appropriate or necessary for the support of himself and his family? Of course the liberty of contract relating to labor includes both parties to it. The one has as much right to purchase as the other to sell labor.

This is not a question of substituting the judgment of the court for that of the legislature. If the act be within the power of the State it is valid, although the judgment of the court might be totally opposed to the enactment of such a law. But the question would still remain: Is it within the police power of the State? and that question must be answered by the court.

The question whether this act is valid as a labor law, pure and simple, may be dismissed in a few words. There is no reasonable ground for interfering with the liberty of person or the right of free contract, by determining the hours of labor, in the occupation of a baker. There is no contention that bakers as a class are not equal in intelligence and capacity to men in other trades or manual occupations, or that they are not able to assert their rights and care for themselves without the protecting arm of the State, interfering with their independence of judgment and of action. They are in no sense wards of the State. Viewed in the light of a purely labor law, with no reference whatever to the question of health, we think that a law like the one before us involves neither the safety, the morals nor the welfare of the public, and that the interest of the public is not in the slightest degree affected by such an act. The law must be upheld, if at all, as a law pertaining to the health of the individual engaged in the occupation of a baker. It does not affect any other portion of the public than those who are engaged in that occupation. Clean and wholesome bread does not depend upon whether the baker works but ten hours per day or only sixty hours a week. The limitation of the hours of labor does not come within the police power on that ground.

It is a question of which of two powers or rights shall prevail – the power of the State to legislate or the right of the individual to liberty of person and freedom of contract. The mere assertion that the subject relates though but in a remote degree to the public health does not necessarily render the enactment valid. The act must have a more direct relation, as a means to an end, and the end itself must be appropriate and legitimate, before an act can be held to be valid which interferes with the general right of an individual to be free in his person and in his power to contract in relation to his own labor. [. . .]

It is impossible for us to shut our eyes to the fact that many of the laws of this character, while passed under what is claimed to be the police power for the purpose of protecting the public health or welfare, are, in reality, passed from other motives. We are justified in saying so when, from the character of the law and the subject upon which it legislates, it is apparent that the public health or welfare bears but the most remote relation to the law. The purpose of a statute must be determined from the natural and legal effect of the language employed; and whether it is or is not repugnant to the Constitution of the United States must be determined from the natural effect of such statutes when put into operation, and not from their proclaimed purpose. *Minnesota v. Barber*, 136 U.S. 313; *Brimmer v. Rebman*, 138 U.S. 78. The court looks beyond the mere letter of the law in such cases. *Yick Wo v. Hopkins*, 118 U.S. 356.

It is manifest to us that the limitation of the hours of labor as provided for in this section of the statute under which the indictment was found, and the plaintiff in error convicted, has no such direct relation to and no such substantial effect upon the health of the employé, as to justify us in regarding the section as really a health law. It seems to us that the real object and purpose were simply to regulate the hours of labor between the master and his employés (all being men, *sui juris*), in a private business, not dangerous in any degree to morals or in any real and substantial degree, to the health of the employés. Under such circumstances the freedom of master and employé to contract with each other in relation to their employment, and in defining the same, cannot be prohibited or interfered with, without violating the Federal Constitution.

The judgment of the Court of Appeals of New York as well as that of the Supreme Court and of the County Court of Oneida County must be reversed and the case remanded to the County Court for further proceedings not inconsistent with this opinion.

Reversed.

Mr Justice Harlan, with whom Mr Justice White and Mr Justice Day concurred, dissenting.

While this court has not attempted to mark the precise boundaries of what is called the police power of the State, the existence of the power has been uniformly recognized, both by the Federal and state courts.

All the cases agree that this power extends at least to the protection of the lives, the health and the safety of the public against the injurious exercise by any citizen of his own rights. [. . .]

Granting then that there is a liberty of contract which cannot be violated even under the sanction of direct legislative enactment, but assuming, as according to settled law we may assume, that such liberty of contract is subject to such regulations as the State may reasonably prescribe for the common good and the well-being of society, what are the conditions under which the judiciary may declare such regulations to be in excess of legislative authority and void? Upon this point there is no room for dispute; for, the rule is universal that a legislative enactment, Federal or state, is never to be disregarded or held invalid unless it be, beyond question, plainly and palpably in excess of legislative power. In *Jacobson v. Massachusetts, supra,* we said that the power of the courts to review legislative action in respect of a matter affecting the general welfare exists *only* "when that which the legislature has done comes within the rule that if a statute purporting to have been enacted to protect the public health, the public morals or the public safety, has no real or substantial relation to those objects, or is, beyond all question, a plain, palpable invasion of rights secured by the fundamental law" – citing *Mugler v. Kansas,* 123 U.S. 623, 661; *Minnesota v. Barber,* 136 U.S. 313, 320; *Atkin v. Kansas,* 191 U.S. 207, 223. If there be doubt as to the validity of the statute, that doubt must therefore be resolved in favor of its validity, and the courts must keep their hands off, leaving the legislature to meet the responsibility for unwise legislation. If the end which the legislature seeks to accomplish be one to which its power extends, and if the means employed to that end, although not the wisest or best, are yet not plainly and palpably unauthorized by law, then the court cannot interfere. In other words, when the validity of a statute is questioned, the burden of proof, so to speak, is upon those who assert it to be unconstitutional. *McCulloch v. Maryland,* 4 Wheat. 316, 421.

Let these principles be applied to the present case. By the statute in question it is provided that, "No employé shall be required or permitted to work in a biscuit, bread or cake bakery or confectionery establishment more than sixty hours in any one week, or more than ten hours in any one day, unless for the purpose of making a shorter work day on the last day of the week; nor more hours in any one week than will make an average of ten hours per day for the number of days during such week in which such employé shall work."

It is plain that this statute was enacted in order to protect the physical well-being of those who work in bakery and confectionery establishments. It may be that the statute had its origin, in part, in the belief that employers and employés in such establishments were not upon an equal footing, and that the necessities of the latter often compelled them to submit to such exactions as unduly taxed their strength. Be this as it may, the statute must be taken as expressing the belief of the people of New York that, as a general rule, and in the case of the average man, labor in excess of sixty hours during a week in such establishments may endanger the health of those who thus labor. Whether or not this be wise legislation it is not the province of the court to inquire. Under our systems of government the courts are not concerned with the wisdom or policy of legislation. So that in determining the question of power to interfere with liberty of contract, the court may inquire whether the means devised by the State are germane to an end which may be lawfully accomplished and have a real or substantial relation to the protection of health, as involved in the daily work of the persons, male and female, engaged in bakery and confectionery establishments. But when this inquiry is entered upon I find it impossible, in view of common experience, to say that there is here no real or substantial relation between the means employed by the State and the end sought to be accomplished by its legislation, *Mugler v. Kansas, supra*. Nor can I say that the statute has no appropriate or direct connection with that protection to health which each State owes to her citizens, *Patterson v. Kentucky, supra*; or that it is not promotive of the health of the employés in question, *Holden v. Hardy, Lawton v. Steele, supra*; or that the regulation prescribed by the State is utterly unreasonable and extravagant or wholly arbitrary, *Gundling v. Chicago, supra*. Still less can I say that the statute is, beyond question, a plain, palpable invasion of rights secured by the fundamental law. *Jacobson v. Massachusetts, supra*. Therefore I submit that this court will transcend its functions if it assumes to annul the statute of New York. [...]

MR JUSTICE HOLMES dissenting.

I regret sincerely that I am unable to agree with the judgment in this case, and that I think it my duty to express my dissent.

This case is decided upon an economic theory which a large part of the country does not entertain. If it were a question whether I agreed with that theory, I should desire to study it further and long before making up my mind. But I do not conceive that to be my duty, because I strongly believe that my agreement or disagreement has nothing to do with the right of a majority to embody their opinions in law. It is settled by various decisions of this court that state constitutions and state laws may regulate life in many ways which we as legislators might think as injudicious or if you like as tyrannical as this, and which equally with this interfere with the liberty to contract. Sunday laws and usury laws are ancient examples. A more modern one is the prohibition of lotteries. The liberty of the citizen to do as he likes so long as he does not interfere with the liberty of others to do the same, which has been a shibboleth for some well-known writers, is interfered with by school laws, by the Post Office, by every state or municipal institution which takes his money for purposes thought desirable, whether he likes it or not. The Fourteenth Amendment does not enact Mr. Herbert Spencer's Social Statics. The other day we sustained the Massachusetts vaccination law. *Jacobson v. Massachusetts*, 197 U.S. 11. United States and state statutes and decisions cutting down the liberty to contract by way of combination are familiar to this court. *Northern Securities Co. v. United States*, 193 U.S. 197. Two years ago we upheld the prohibition of sales of stock on margins or for future delivery in the constitution of California. *Otis v. Parker*, 187 U.S. 606. The decision sustaining an eight hour law for miners is still recent. *Holden v. Hardy*, 169 U.S. 366. Some of these laws embody convictions or prejudices which judges are likely to share. Some may not. But a constitution is not intended to embody a particular economic theory, whether of paternalism and the organic relation of the citizen to the State or of *laissez-faire*. It is made for people of fundamentally differing views, and the accident of our finding certain opinions natural and familiar or novel and even shocking ought not to conclude our judgment upon the question whether statutes embodying them conflict with the Constitution of the United States.

General propositions do not decide concrete cases. The decision will depend on a judgment or intuition more subtle than any articulate major premise. But I think that the proposition just stated, if it is accepted, will carry us far toward the end. Every opinion tends to become a law. I think that the word liberty in the Fourteenth Amendment is perverted when it is held to prevent the natural outcome of a dominant opinion, unless it can be said that a rational and fair man necessarily would admit that the statute proposed would infringe fundamental principles as they have been understood by the traditions of our people and our law. It does not need research to show that no such sweeping condemnation can be passed upon the statute before us. A reasonable man might think it a proper measure on the score of health. Men whom I certainly could not pronounce unreasonable would uphold it as a first installment of a general regulation of the hours of work. Whether in the latter aspect it would be open to the charge of inequality I think it unnecessary to discuss.

Questions

1   According to Levi, legal reasoning is reasoning by example. Explain how reasoning by example works. Do you think that reasoning by example could lead to any problems for judges?

2   What is legal formalism? Critics of formalism claim that legal formalism leads to some "rigid" and absurd decisions. How does Schauer defend formalism against this charge?

3   What is legal realism? Assuming that the claims of legal realism are true, what does this mean for judicial decision-making?

4   How would Levi and Schauer respond to a legal realist?

5   What role should custom play in legal reasoning? Is May correct to think that custom is especially problematic in international legal reasoning?

Part II
Jurisprudence

Introduction

The fundamental question of jurisprudence is "What is the nature of law?" This question has fascinated thinkers since at least the time of the Greeks. In fact, Sophocles' famous play, *Antigone*, presents two opposing answers that become prominent in subsequent jurisprudence.[1] In the play, Antigone's brother, Polyneices, has been killed in battle against Thebes. Creon, the King of Thebes, has forbidden the burial of Polyneices' body. Creon claims the right to make this law because he is king. Antigone, however, refuses to obey; she attempts to bury Polyneices. As her authority, she cites a law higher than the one set by Creon – a law whose force derives from a divinely ordained natural order. This opposition represents two distinct answers to the nature-of-law question. Creon's view exemplifies what has come to be known as the tradition of legal positivism. This is the view that law is set by "position." The basic idea is that laws are made by the rulers of a political community and derive all their authority from that origin. According to this view, there is no essential connection between law and morality. The alternative, expressed by Antigone, has become known as the natural law tradition. Natural law theorists believe that the authority of positive law rests in part on its conformity to moral standards. An extreme version of this belief is expressed in Augustine's claim that "an unjust law is no law at all." According to this view, positive laws must conform to a higher moral law if they are to retain legitimacy.

Legal positivism is often defined as a command theory of law. A law is a command that obligates people either to act or to refrain from acting under the threat of punishment. The command theory of law is discussed by H. L. A. Hart in our first essay of this section. In "The Concept of Law," Hart compares the command theory to a gunman's threat. Just as a sovereign can issue a threat to obey, a gunman can express a desire that another act or refrain from acting, and this desire can be backed with the threat of sanction in the case of noncompliance. But no one thinks that the gunman's threat creates an obligation for the victim to comply. In Hart's terms, the victim is obliged, but not obligated, to obey the gunman's threat. So, too, is the case with the sovereign who commands: a subject might be obliged to obey the sovereign's command, but no obligation to obey has been created. At most, the command theory allows us to predict that certain forms of behavior will conform to the requirements of legal rules. It thereby provides us with an external perspective on legal rules – the perspective of an outside observer who, without participating in a social practice, can nonetheless detect regular patterns of behavior from which he or she can make predictions. To understand the nature of legal obligation and of social obligation more generally, we have to consider the internal perspective on rules. The *internal perspective* is that of a member of a social group who accepts and uses a rule or set of rules as a guide to conduct. Legal rules are a subset of obligations imposing social rules that members of a group accept as normative for certain kinds of conduct. Hart goes on to explain that in a legal system, legal rules are divided into two broad groups: primary rules that regulate action and secondary rules that are about primary rules.

Hart's theory of law as a union of primary and secondary rules is subject to rigorous criticism by Ronald Dworkin in "The Model of Rules I." Dworkin argues that law consists not only of rules, but also of standards. Standards are of two types: principles and policies. Principles articulate requirements of justice, fairness, or morality. They often express rights. Policies, in contrast, set out some desirable economic, social, or political goal to be achieved. In claiming that law consists of standards as well as rules, Dworkin rejects legal positivism because he argues that law has essential moral content.

Dworkin's view has implications for positivists' theory of judicial discretion, their analysis of legal obligation, and their theory of the rule of recognition. For example, if law is a system of primary and secondary rules, as Hart contends, then there is a point at which legal rules end. Positivist judges who must adjudicate cases at the margins of legal rules must therefore look beyond the rules to extralegal considerations to decide such a case. A Dworkinian judge, however, would be obligated to look to legal standards in addition to legal rules. In addition, positivists believe that legal obligations are created only by rules. But if standards are also a part of law, as Dworkin believes, then standards, too, can legally obligate.

In the next essay, we look at the natural law theory of Michael S. Moore. In "Law as Justice," Moore defends a natural law theory of legal adjudication. By "natural law" in legal theory, Moore means that (1) there are objective moral truths and (2) those moral truths are at least partly constitutive of the truth conditions for propositions of law. The first claim is a meta-ethical thesis of natural law, and the second claim is what Moore calls the "relational thesis" of natural law. He argues that the nature of law is such that, necessarily, if an institution is sufficiently unjust,

it is not a legal institution. What is legal must necessarily partake of morality. To defend his view of natural law in legal theory, Moore looks at the case of *Union Pacific Railway v. Cappier.*[2] He uses this case as an example to show how natural law principles have been used in the US common law when there is no controlling precedent and in overruling bad precedent.

In "The Economic Approach to Law," Richard A. Posner, a federal judge for the US Court of Appeals for the Seventh Circuit, argues that the nature of law is fundamentally economic. According to the economic analysis of law, all branches and activities of law can be explained in terms of a few basic economic assumptions and principles. The central assumption of economic analysis, according to Posner, is that all people, with a few exceptions,[3] are rational maximizers of their satisfactions. The putative fact grounds both the descriptive and normative claims of the law and economics movement, for economic analysts take as fundamental the notion that wealth maximization is and should be the overriding goal of the legal system. The "wealth" in "wealth maximization" does not refer to money only. Rather, it refers to the sum of all tangible and intangible goods and services, weighted by two kinds of prices: the offer price (the price someone is willing to pay for a good or service) and the asking price (the price someone wants to receive for a good or service). Posner argues that the activities of legislatures and judges and the operations of familiar common law rules can be understood as roughly conforming to the dictates of wealth maximization.

Positivism, natural law theory and economic approaches to the law have come under attack from the left. One such family of criticism, informed significantly by Marxist social theory is the Critical Legal Studies (CLS) movement. In "The Distinction between Adjudication and Legislation," Duncan Kennedy is concerned with ideological influences in judicial decision-making. According to the traditional distinction, judges follow the law and legislatures make the law. Judges do not make political decisions – that is what legislators do. This is a basic distinction between adjudication and legislation. Kennedy thinks that this is a false distinction. He is not concerned with whether judges should reach an outcome on the basis of their personal values.

Instead, Kennedy argues that judges' ideological commitments do in fact enter into rule-making and this is done over the denial of many of those involved in adjudication. Appellate adjudication, the discursive process by which rules of law are made, has ideological content.

The need for new legal and social realities is the leitmotif of Critical Race Theory (CRT), the historical, ideological, and methodological offspring of the CLS movement. Motivated by the persistent and pervasive presence of racism in law and society, critical race theorists have adopted the radical ideology and methods of the CLS movement in efforts to expose and transform the presently racist legal and social practice. The selection given here from *Critical Race Theory: The Key Writings that Formed the Movement* is part of an introduction to a volume of essays by critical race theorists. Foremost among them is disenchantment with the traditional civil rights discourse that emerged form the Civil Rights movement of the 1960s and early 1970s. Though it helped lead to the CRT movement, this discourse is firmly entrenched in mainstream political liberalism. One legacy of this discourse, according to CRT theorists, is that justice is conceptualized in a way that excluded the possibility of radical and transformative critique. In short, racism is narrowly defined from "the perpetrator's perspective," an intentional, but irrational, deviation by a conscious wrongdoer from an otherwise neutral, and therefore just, status quo. The legal conception of racism in terms of discrete, identifiable acts of prejudice is insulated from radical critiques that show racism to be pervasive and systematic and imbedded in the social institutions and everyday life.

In "Feminist Legal Critics: The Reluctant Radicals," Patricia Smith traces the philosophical history of the feminist movement in jurisprudential thought, which, like CRT theory, criticizes the prevailing liberal paradigm. Smith observes that in the early days of feminist legal analysis, feminist critics worked within the parameters of political liberalism. The liberal tradition in the United States began with the assumption that only white, Christian, property-owning men were entitled to rights. Persons who differed from the white-male standard, such as Negro slaves, Native Americans, Chinese immigrants, and women, were initially viewed as subhuman, inferior, and not entitled to the full panoply of rights and privileges enjoyed by white-male property-owners or equal treatment by the law. Early feminist battles, and significant gains for women, were won by extending to women the same legal rights and privileges accorded to white men under the dominant liberal paradigm. However, as Smith makes clear in her discussion of the evolution of sex discrimination in equal protection law, the central problem with liberalism is its reliance on allegedly neutral, impartial standards and principles. These standards are meant to apply with equal justice to men and women alike. Yet the standards themselves are not neutral; they incorporate a male bias. The inability of courts to recognize the basis of legal standard retards the courts' efforts to render unbiased justice in particular cases. Worse, it prevents courts from addressing systematic injustices that result from inherently patriarchal social institutions and norms. Thus, as with CLS and CRT scholars, feminist legal critics have challenged the liberal tradition's reliance on objectivism and formalism and have pushed toward increasingly radical critiques of the liberal paradigm in their pursuit of justice for women.

The final piece in this section is *Riggs v. Palmer*, decided in New York in 1889. In *Riggs*, the question before the court was whether a grandson who had murdered his grandfather could inherit under the terms of the will. The grandson was named as heir, and the statute of wills for New York State was silent on the question of whether a convicted murderer could inherit. The court admitted that the rules would allow the grandson to inherit, but it ruled against his claim on grounds of principle. In the court's opinion, the moral principle that no one should profit from his or her own wrongdoing controlled the statute of wills in this case, and thereby prevented the murderer from inheriting.

Notes

1 Sophocles, *Antigone*, ed. Brendan Kennelly (Newcaste upon Tyne: Bloodaxe Books, 1996).
2 *Union Pacific Railway v. Cappier*, 72 Pac. 281 (Kansas 1903).
3 Posner points to children, people with severe or mental impairments, and people suffering from temporary mental impairments.

7

The Concept of Law

H. L. A. Hart

CHAPTER 5: LAW AS THE UNION OF PRIMARY AND SECONDARY RULES

[. . .]

2. The Idea of Obligation

It will be recalled that the theory of law as coercive orders, notwithstanding its errors, started from the perfectly correct appreciation of the fact that where there is law, there human conduct is made in some sense non-optional or obligatory. In choosing this starting-point the theory was well inspired, and in building up a new account of law in terms of the interplay of primary and secondary rules we too shall start from the same idea. It is, however, here, at this crucial first step, that we have perhaps most to learn from the theory's errors.

Let us recall the gunman situation. A orders B to hand over his money and threatens to shoot him if he does not comply. According to the theory of coercive orders this situation illustrates the notion of obligation or duty in general. Legal obligation is to be found in this situation writ large; A must be the sovereign habitually obeyed and

the orders must be general, prescribing courses of conduct not single actions. The plausibility of the claim that the gunman situation displays the meaning of obligation lies in the fact that it is certainly one in which we would say that B, if he obeyed, was "obliged" to hand over his money. It is, however, equally certain that we should misdescribe the situation if we said, on these facts, that B "had an obligation" or a "duty" to hand over the money. So from the start it is clear that we need something else for an understanding of the idea of obligation. There is a difference, yet to be explained, between the assertion that someone *was obliged* to do something and the assertion that he *had an obligation* to do it. The first is often a statement about the beliefs and motives with which an action is done: B was obliged to hand over his money may simply mean, as it does in the gunman case, that he believed that some harm or other unpleasant consequences would befall him if he did not hand it over and he handed it over to avoid those consequences. In such cases the prospect of what would happen to the agent if he disobeyed has rendered something he would otherwise have preferred to have done (keep the money) less eligible.

H. L. A. Hart, "Chapter 5: Law as the Union of Primary and Secondary Rules" and "Chapter 6: The Foundations of a Legal System," from *The Concept of Law*, 2nd edn. (Oxford: Clarendon Press, 1997), pp. 80–110. © 1961, 1994 by Oxford University Press. Reprinted with permission from Oxford University Press.

Two further elements slightly complicate the elucidation of the notion of being obliged to do something. It seems clear that we should not think of B as obliged to hand over the money if the threatened harm was, according to common judgments, trivial in comparison with the disadvantage or serious consequences, either for B or for others, of complying with the orders, as it would be, for example, if A merely threatened to pinch B. Nor perhaps should we say that B was obliged, if there were no reasonable grounds for thinking that A could or would probably implement his threat of relatively serious harm. Yet, though such references to common judgments of comparative harm and reasonable estimates of likelihood, are implicit in this notion, the statement that a person was obliged to obey someone is, in the main, a psychological one referring to the beliefs and motives with which an action was done. But the statement that someone *had an obligation* to do something is of a very different type and there are many signs of this difference. Thus not only is it the case that the facts about B's action and his beliefs and motives in the gunman case, though sufficient to warrant the statement that B was obliged to hand over his purse, are *not sufficient* to warrant the statement that he had an obligation to do this; it is also the case that facts of this sort, i.e., facts about beliefs and motives, are *not necessary* for the truth of a statement that a person had an obligation to do something. Thus the statement that a person had an obligation, e.g., to tell the truth or report for military service, remains true even if he believed (reasonably or unreasonably) that he would never be found out and had nothing to fear from disobedience. Moreover, whereas the statement that he had this obligation is quite independent of the question whether or not he in fact reported for service, the statement that someone was obliged to do something, normally carries the implication that he actually did it.

Some theorists, Austin among them, seeing perhaps the general irrelevance of the person's beliefs, fears, and motives to the question whether he had an obligation to do something, have defined this notion not in terms of these subjective facts, but in terms of the *chance* or *likelihood* that the person having the obligation will suffer a punishment or "evil" at the hands of others in the event of disobedience. This, in effect, treats statements of obligation not as psychological statements but as predictions or assessments of chances of incurring punishment or "evil." To many later theorists this has appeared as a revelation, bringing down to earth an elusive notion and restating it in the same clear, hard, empirical terms as are used in science. It has, indeed, been accepted sometimes as the only alternative to metaphysical conceptions of obligation or duty as invisible objects mysteriously existing "above" or "behind" the world of ordinary, observable facts. But there are many reasons for rejecting this interpretation of statements of obligation as predictions, and it is not, in fact, the only alternative to obscure metaphysics.

The fundamental objection is that the predictive interpretation obscures the fact that, where rules exist, deviations from them are not merely grounds for a prediction that hostile reactions will follow or that a court will apply sanctions to those who break them, but are also a reason or justification for such reaction and for applying the sanctions. [. . .]

There is, however, a second, simpler, objection to the predictive interpretation of obligation. If it were true that the statement that a person had an obligation meant that he was likely to suffer in the event of disobedience, it would be a contradiction to say that he had an obligation, e.g., to report for military service but that, owing to the fact that he had escaped from the jurisdiction, or had successfully bribed the police or the court, there was not the slightest chance of his being caught or made to suffer. In fact, there is no contradiction in saying this, and such statements are often made and understood.

It is, of course, true that in a normal legal system, where sanctions are exacted for a high proportion of offences, an offender usually runs a risk of punishment; so, usually the statement that a person has an obligation and the statement that he is likely to suffer for disobedience will both be true together. Indeed, the connection between these two statements is somewhat stronger than this: at least in a municipal system it may well be true that, unless *in general* sanctions were likely to be exacted from offenders, there would be little or no point in making particular statements about a person's obligations. In this sense, such statements may be said to presuppose belief in the continued normal operation of the system of sanctions much as the statement "he is out" in cricket presupposes, though it does not assert, that players, umpire, and scorer will probably take the usual steps. None the less, it is crucial for the understanding of the idea of obligation to see that in individual cases the statement that a person has an obligation under some rule and the prediction that he is likely to suffer for disobedience may diverge.

It is clear that obligation is not to be found in the gunman situation, though the simpler notion of being obliged to do something may well be defined in the elements present there. To understand the general idea of obligation as a necessary preliminary to understanding it in its legal form, we must turn to a different social situation which, unlike the gunman situation, includes the existence of social rules; for this situation contributes to the meaning of the statement that a person has an obligation in two ways. First, the existence of such rules, making certain types of behavior a standard, is the normal, though unstated, background or proper context for such a statement; and, secondly, the distinctive function of such statement is to apply such a general rule to a particular person by calling attention to the fact that his case falls under it. [...] There is involved in the existence of any social rules a combination of regular conduct with a distinctive attitude to that conduct as a standard. We have also seen the main ways in which these differ from mere social habits, and how the varied normative vocabulary ("ought," "must," "should") is used to draw attention to the standard and to deviations from it, and to formulate the demands, criticisms, or acknowledgements which may be based on it. Of this class of normative words the words "obligation" and "duty" form an important sub-class, carrying with them certain implications not usually present in the others. Hence, though a grasp of the elements generally differentiating social rules from mere habits is certainly indispensable for understanding the notion of obligation or duty, it is not sufficient by itself.

The statement that someone has or is under an obligation does indeed imply the existence of a rule; yet it is not always the case that where rules exist the standard of behaviour required by them is conceived of in terms of obligation. "He ought to have" and "He had an obligation to" are not always interchangeable expressions, even though they are alike in carrying an implicit reference to existing standards of conduct or are used in drawing conclusions in particular cases from a general rule. Rules of etiquette or correct speech are certainly rules: they are more than convergent habits or regularities of behaviour; they are taught and efforts are made to maintain them; they are used in criticizing our own and other people's behaviour in the characteristic normative vocabulary. "You ought to take your hat off," "It is wrong to say 'you was.'" But to use in connection with rules of this kind the words "obligation" or "duty" would be misleading and not merely stylistically odd. It would misdescribe a social situation; for though the line separating rules of obligation from others is at points a vague one, yet the main rationale of the distinction is fairly clear.

Rules are conceived and spoken of as imposing obligations when the general demand for conformity is insistent and the social pressure brought to bear upon those who deviate or threaten to deviate is great. Such rules may be wholly customary in origin: there may be no centrally organized system of punishments for breach of the rules; the social pressure may take only the form of a general diffused hostile or critical reaction which may stop short of physical sanctions. It may be limited to verbal manifestations of disapproval or of appeals to the individuals' respect for the rule violated; it may depend heavily on the operation of feelings of shame, remorse, and guilt. When the pressure is of this last-mentioned kind we may be inclined to classify the rules as part of the morality of the social group and the obligation under the rules as moral obligation. Conversely, when physical sanctions are prominent or usual among the forms of pressure, even though these are neither closely defined nor administered by officials but are left to the community at large, we shall be inclined to classify the rules as a primitive or rudimentary form of law. We may, of course, find both these types of serious social pressure behind what is, in an obvious sense, the same rule of conduct; sometimes this may occur with no indication that one of them is peculiarly appropriate as primary and the other secondary, and then the question whether we are confronted with a rule of morality or rudimentary law may not be susceptible of an answer. But for the moment the possibility of drawing the line between law and morals need not detain us. What is important is that the insistence on importance or *seriousness* of social pressure behind the rules is the primary factor determining whether they are thought of as giving rise to obligations.

Two other characteristics of obligation go naturally together with this primary one. The rules supported by this serious pressure are thought important because they are believed to be necessary to the maintenance of social life or some highly prized feature of it. Characteristically, rules so obviously essential as those which restrict the free use of violence are thought of in terms of obligation. So too rules which require honesty or truth or require the keeping of promises, or specify what is to be done by one who performs a distinctive role or function in the social group are thought of in terms of either "obligation" or perhaps more often "duty." Secondly, it is generally recognized that the conduct required by these rules may, while benefiting others, conflict with what the person who owes the duty may wish to do. Hence obligations and duties are thought of as characteristically involving sacrifice or renunciation, and the standing possibility of conflict between obligation or duty and interest is, in all societies, among the truisms of both the lawyer and the moralist.

The figure of a *bond* binding the person obligated, which is buried in the word "obligation," and the similar notion of a debt latent in the word "duty" are explicable in terms of these three factors, which distinguish rules of obligation or duty from other rules. In this figure, which haunts much legal thought, the social pressure appears as a chain binding those who have obligations so that they are not free to do what they want. The other end of the chain is sometimes held by the group or their official representatives, who insist on performance or exact the penalty: sometimes it is entrusted by the group to a private individual who may choose whether or not to insist on performance or its equivalent in value to him. The first situation typifies the duties or obligations of criminal law and the second those of civil law where we think of private individuals having rights correlative to the obligations.

Natural and perhaps illuminating though these figures or metaphors are, we must not allow them to trap us into a misleading conception of obligation as essentially consisting in some feeling of pressure or compulsion experienced by those who have obligations. The fact that rules of obligation are generally supported by serious social pressure does not entail that to have an obligation under the rules is to experience feelings of compulsion or pressure. Hence there is no contradiction in saying of some hardened swindler, and it may often be true, that he had an obligation to pay the rent but felt no pressure to pay when he made off without doing so. To *feel* obliged and to have an obligation are different though frequently concomitant things. To identify them would be one way of misinterpreting, in terms of psychological feelings, the important internal aspect of rules. [...]

Indeed, the internal aspect of rules is something to which we must [...] refer before we can dispose finally of the claims of the predictive theory. For an advocate of that theory may well ask why, if social pressure is so important a feature of rules of obligation, we are yet so concerned to stress the inadequacies of the predictive theory; for it gives this very feature a central place by defining obligation in terms of the likelihood that threatened punishment or hostile reaction will follow deviation from certain lines of conduct. The difference may seem slight between the analysis of a statement of obligation as a prediction, or assessment of the chances, of hostile reaction to deviation, and our own contention that though this statement presupposes a background in which deviations from rules are generally met by hostile reactions, yet its characteristic use is not to predict this but to say that a person's case falls under such a rule. In fact, however, this difference is not a slight one. Indeed, until its importance is grasped, we cannot properly understand the whole distinctive style of human thought, speech, and action which is involved in the existence of rules and which constitutes the normative structure of society.

The following contrast again in terms of the "internal" and "external" aspect of rules may serve to mark what gives this distinction its great importance for the understanding not only of law but of the structure of any society. When a social group has certain rules of conduct, this fact affords an opportunity for many closely related yet different kinds of assertion; for it is possible to be concerned with the rules, either merely as an observer who does not himself accept them, or as a member of the group which accepts and uses them as guides to conduct. We may call these respectively the "external" and the "internal points of view." Statements made from the external point of view may themselves be of different kinds. For the observer may, without accepting the rules himself, assert that the group accepts the rules, and thus may from outside refer to the way in which *they* are concerned with them from the internal point of view. But whatever the rules are, whether they are those of games, like chess or cricket, or moral or legal rules, we can if we choose occupy the position of an observer who does not even refer in this way to the internal point of view of the group. Such an observer is content merely to record the regularities of observable behaviour in which conformity with the rules partly consists and those further regularities, in the form of the hostile reaction, reproofs, or punishments, with which deviations from the rules are met. After a time the external observer may, on the basis of the regularities observed, correlate deviation with hostile reaction, and be able to predict with a fair measure of success, and to assess the chances that a deviation from the group's normal behaviour will meet with hostile reaction or punishment. Such knowledge may not only reveal much about the group, but might enable him to live among them without unpleasant consequences which would attend one who attempted to do so without such knowledge.

If, however, the observer really keeps austerely to this extreme external point of view and does not give any account of the manner in which members of the group who accept the rules view their own regular behaviour, his description of their life cannot be in terms of rules at all, and so not in the terms of the rule-dependent notions of obligation or duty. Instead, it will be in terms of observable regularities of conduct, predictions, probabilities, and signs. For such an observer, deviations by a member of the group from normal conduct will be a sign that hostile reaction is likely to follow, and nothing more. His view will be like the view of one who, having observed the working of a traffic signal in a busy street for some time, limits himself to saying that when the light turns red there is a high probability that the traffic will stop. He treats the light merely as a natural *sign that* people will behave in certain ways, as clouds are a *sign that* rain will come. In so doing he will miss out a whole dimension of the social life of those whom he is watching, since for them the red light is not merely a sign that others will stop: they look upon it as a *signal for* them to stop, and so a reason for stopping in conformity to rules which make stopping when the light is red a standard of behaviour and an obligation. To mention this is to bring into the account the way in which the group regards its own behaviour. It is to refer to the internal aspect of rules seen from their internal point of view.

The external point of view may very nearly reproduce the way in which the rules function in the lives of certain members of the group, namely those who reject its rules and are only concerned with them when and because they judge that unpleasant consequences are likely to follow violation. Their point of view will need for its expression, "I was obliged to do it," "I am likely to suffer for it if . . . ," "You will probably suffer for it if . . . ," "They will do that to you if . . ." But they will not need forms of expression like "I had an obligation" or "You have an obligation" for these are required only by those who see their own and other persons' conduct from the internal point of view. What the external point of view, which limits itself to the observable regularities of behaviour, cannot reproduce is the way in which the rules function as rules in the lives of those who normally are the majority of society. These are the officials, lawyers, or private persons who use them, in one situation after another, as guides to the conduct of social life, as the basis for claims, demands, admissions, criticism, or punishment, viz., in all the familiar transactions of life according to rules. For them the violation of a rule is not merely a basis for the prediction that a hostile reaction will follow but a *reason* for hostility.

At any given moment the life of any society which lives by rules, legal or not, is likely to consist in a tension between those who, on the one hand, accept and voluntarily cooperate in maintaining the rules, and so see their own and other persons' behaviour in terms of the rules, and those who, on the other hand, reject the rules and attend to them only from the external point of view as a sign of possible punishment. One of the difficulties facing any legal theory anxious to do justice to the complexity of the facts is to remember the presence of both these points of view and not to define one of them out of existence. Perhaps all our criticisms of the predictive theory of obligation may be best summarized as the accusation that this is what it does to the internal aspect of obligatory rules.

3.   The Elements of Law

It is, of course, possible to imagine a society without a legislature, courts, or officials of any kind. Indeed, there are many studies of primitive communities which not only claim that this possibility is realized but depict in detail the life of a society where the only means of social control is that general attitude of the group towards its own standard modes of behaviour in terms of which we have characterized rules of obligation. A social structure of this kind is often referred to as one of "custom"; but we shall not use this term, because it often implies that the customary rules are very old and supported with less social pressure than other rules. To avoid these implications we shall refer to such a social structure as one of primary rules of obligation. If a society is to live by such primary rules alone, there are certain conditions which, granted a few of the most obvious truisms about human nature and the world we live in, must clearly be satisfied. The first of these conditions is that the rules must contain in some form restrictions on the free use of violence, theft, and deception to which human beings are tempted but which they must, in general, repress, if they are to coexist in close proximity to each other. Such rules are in fact always found in the primitive societies of which we have knowledge, together with a variety of others imposing on individuals various positive duties to perform services or make contributions to the common life. Secondly, though such a society may exhibit the tension, already described, between those who accept the rules and those who reject the rules except where fear of social pressure induces them to conform, it is plain that the latter cannot be more than a minority, if so

loosely organized a society of persons, approximately equal in physical strength, is to endure: for otherwise those who reject the rules would have too little social pressure to fear. This too is confirmed by what we know of primitive communities where, though there are dissidents and malefactors, the majority live by the rules seen from the internal point of view.

More important for our present purpose is the following consideration. It is plain that only a small community closely knit by ties of kinship, common sentiment, and belief, and placed in a stable environment, could live successfully by such a regime of unofficial rules. In any other conditions such a simple form of social control must prove defective and will require supplementation in different ways. In the first place, the rules by which the group lives will not form a system, but will simply be a set of separate standards, without any identifying or common mark, except of course that they are the rules which a particular group of human beings accepts. They will in this respect resemble our own rules of etiquette. Hence if doubts arise as to what the rules are or as to the precise scope of some given rule, there will be no procedure for settling this doubt, either by reference to an authoritative text or to an official whose declarations on this point are authoritative. For, plainly, such a procedure and the acknowledgement of either authoritative text or persons involve the existence of rules of a type different from the rules of obligation or duty which *ex hypothesi* are all that the group has. This defect in the simple social structure of primary rules we may call its *uncertainty*.

A second defect is the *static* character of the rules. The only mode of change in the rules known to such a society will be the slow process of growth, whereby courses of conduct once thought optional become first habitual or usual, and then obligatory, and the converse process of decay, when deviations, once severely dealt with, are first tolerated and then pass unnoticed. There will be no means, in such a society, of deliberately adapting the rules to changing circumstances, either by eliminating old rules or introducing new ones: for, again, the possibility of doing this presupposes the existence of rules of a different type from the primary rules of obligation by which alone the society lives. In an extreme case the rules may be static in a more drastic sense. This, though never perhaps fully realized in any actual community, is worth considering because the remedy for it is something very characteristic of law. In this extreme case, not only would there be no way of deliberately changing the general rules, but the obligations which arise under the rules in particular cases could not be varied or modified by the deliberate choice of any individual. Each individual would simply have fixed obligations or duties to do or abstain from doing certain things. It might indeed very often be the case that others would benefit from the performance of these obligations; yet if there are only primary rules of obligation they would have no power to release those bound from performance or to transfer to others the benefits which would accrue from performance. For such operations of release or transfer create changes in the initial positions of individuals under the primary rules of obligation, and for these operations to be possible there must be rules of a sort different from the primary rules.

The third defect of this simple form of social life is the *inefficiency* of the diffuse social pressure by which the rules are maintained. Disputes as to whether an admitted rule has or has not been violated will always occur and will, in any but the smallest societies, continue interminably, if there is no agency specially empowered to ascertain finally, and authoritatively, the fact of violation. Lack of such final and authoritative determinations is to be distinguished from another weakness associated with it. This is the fact that punishments for violations of the rules, and other forms of social pressure involving physical effort or the use of force, are not administered by a special agency but are left to the individuals affected or to the group at large. It is obvious that the waste of time involved in the group's unorganized efforts to catch and punish offenders, and the smouldering vendettas which may result from self-help in the absence of an official monopoly of "sanctions," may be serious. The history of law does, however, strongly suggest that the lack of official agencies to determine authoritatively the fact of violation of the rules is a much more serious defect; for many societies have remedies for this defect long before the other.

The remedy for each of these three main defects in this simplest form of social structure consists in supplementing the *primary* rules of obligation with *secondary* rules which are rules of a different kind. The introduction of the remedy for each defect might, in itself, be considered a step from the pre-legal into the legal world; since each remedy brings with it many elements that permeate law: certainly all three remedies together are enough to convert the regime of primary rules into what is indisputably a legal system. We shall consider in turn each of these remedies and show why law may most illuminatingly be characterized as a union of primary rules of obligation with such secondary rules. Before we do this, however, the following general points should be noted. Though the remedies consist in the introduction of rules which are certainly different from each other, as well as from the primary rules of obligation which they supplement, they have important features in common and are connected in various ways. Thus they may all be said to be on a different level from the primary rules, for they are all *about* such rules; in the sense that while primary rules are concerned with the actions that individuals must or must not do, these secondary rules are all concerned with the primary rules themselves. They specify the ways in which the primary rules may be conclusively ascertained, introduced, eliminated, varied, and the fact of their violation conclusively determined.

The simplest form of remedy for the *uncertainty* of the regime of primary rules is the introduction of what we shall call a "rule of recognition." This will specify some feature or features possession of which by a suggested rule is taken as a conclusive affirmative indication that it is a rule of the group to be supported by the social pressure it exerts. The existence of such a rule of recognition may take any of a huge variety of forms, simple or complex. It may, as in the early law of many societies, be no more than that an authoritative list or text of the rules is to be found in a written document or carved on some public monument. No doubt as a matter of history this step from the pre-legal to the legal may be accomplished in distinguishable stages, of which the first is the mere reduction to writing of hitherto unwritten rules. This is not itself the crucial step, though it is a very important one: what is crucial is the acknowledgement of reference to the writing or inscription as *authoritative*, i.e., as the *proper* way of disposing of doubts as to the existence of the rule. Where there is such an acknowledgement there is a very simple form of secondary rule: a rule for conclusive identification of the primary rules of obligation.

In a developed legal system the rules of recognition are of course more complex; instead of identifying rules exclusively by reference to a text or list they do so by reference to some general characteristic possessed by the primary rules. This may be the fact of their having been enacted by a specific body, or their long customary practice, or their relation to judicial decisions. Moreover, where more than one of such general characteristics are treated as identifying criteria, provision may be made for their possible conflict by their arrangement in an order of superiority, as by the common subordination of custom or precedent to statute, the latter being a "superior source" of law. Such complexity may make the rules of recognition in a modern legal system seem very different from the simple acceptance of an authoritative text: yet even in this simplest form, such a rule brings with it many elements distinctive of law. By providing an authoritative mark it introduces, although in embryonic form, the idea of a legal system: for the rules are now not just a discrete unconnected set but are, in a simple way, unified. Further, in the simple operation of identifying a given rule as possessing the required feature of being an item on an authoritative list of rules we have the germ of the idea of legal validity.

The remedy for the *static* quality of the regime of primary rules consists in the introduction of what we shall call "rules of change." The simplest form of such a rule is that which empowers an individual or body of persons to introduce new primary rules for the conduct of the life of the group, or of some class within it, and to eliminate old rules. [...] It is in terms of such a rule, and not in terms of orders backed by threats, that the ideas of legislative enactment and repeal are to be understood. Such rules of change may be very simple or very complex: the powers conferred may be unrestricted or limited in various ways: and the rules may, besides specifying the persons who are to legislate, define in more or less rigid terms the procedure to be followed in legislation. Plainly, there will be a very close connection between the rules of

change and the rules of recognition: for where the former exists the latter will necessarily incorporate a reference to legislation as an identifying feature of the rules, though it need not refer to all the details of procedure involved in legislation. Usually some official certificate or official copy will, under the rules of recognition, be taken as a sufficient proof of due enactment. Of course if there is a social structure so simple that the only "source of law" is legislation, the rule of recognition will simply specify enactment as the unique identifying mark or criterion of validity of the rules. [...]

We have already described in some detail the rules which confer on individuals power to vary their initial positions under the primary rules. Without such private power-conferring rules society would lack some of the chief amenities which law confers upon it. For the operations which these rules make possible are the making of wills, contracts, transfers of property, and many other voluntarily created structures of rights and duties which typify life under law, though of course an elementary form of power-conferring rule also underlies the moral institution of a promise. The kinship of these rules with the rules of change involved in the notion of legislation is clear, and as recent theory such as Kelsen's has shown, many of the features which puzzle us in the institutions of contract or property are clarified by thinking of the operations of making a contract or transferring property as the exercise of limited legislative powers by individuals.

The third supplement to the simple regime of primary rules, intended to remedy the *inefficiency* of its diffused social pressure, consists of secondary rules empowering individuals to make authoritative determinations of the question whether, on a particular occasion, a primary rule has been broken. The minimal form of adjudication consists in such determinations, and we shall call the secondary rules which confer the power to make them "rules of adjudication." Besides identifying the individuals who are to adjudicate, such rules will also define the procedure to be followed. Like the other secondary rules these are on a different level from the primary rules: though they may be reinforced by further rules imposing duties on judges to adjudicate, they do not impose duties but confer judicial powers and a special status on judicial declarations about the breach of obligations. Again these rules, like the other secondary rules, define a group of important legal concepts: in this case the concepts of judge or court, jurisdiction, and judgment. Besides these resemblances to the other secondary rules, rules of adjudication have intimate connections with them. Indeed, a system which has rules of adjudication is necessarily also committed to a rule of recognition of an elementary and imperfect sort. This is so because, if courts are empowered to make authoritative determinations of the fact that a rule has been broken, these cannot avoid being taken as authoritative determinations of what the rules are. So the rule which confers jurisdiction will also be a rule of recognition, identifying the primary rules through the judgments of the courts and these judgments will become a "source" of law. It is true that this form of rule of recognition, inseparable from the minimum form of jurisdiction, will be very imperfect. Unlike an authoritative text or a statute book, judgments may not be couched in general terms and their use as authoritative guides to the rules depends on a somewhat shaky inference from particular decisions, and the reliability of this must fluctuate both with the skill of the interpreter and the consistency of the judges.

It need hardly be said that in few legal systems are judicial powers confined to authoritative determinations of the fact of violation of the primary rules. Most systems have, after some delay, seen the advantages of further centralization of social pressure; and have partially prohibited the use of physical punishments or violent self-help by private individuals. Instead they have supplemented the primary rules of obligation by further secondary rules, specifying or at least limiting the penalties for violation, and have conferred upon judges, where they have ascertained the fact of violation, the exclusive power to direct the application of penalties by other officials. These secondary rules provide the centralized official "sanctions" of the system.

If we stand back and consider the structure which has resulted from the combination of primary rules of obligation with the secondary rules of recognition, change and adjudication, it is plain that we have here not only the heart of a legal system, but a most powerful tool for the analysis of much that has puzzled both the jurist and the political theorist.

Not only are the specifically legal concepts with which the lawyer is professionally concerned, such as those of obligation and rights, validity and source of law, legislation and jurisdiction, and sanction, best elucidated in terms of this combination of elements. The concepts (which bestride both law and political theory) of the state, of authority, and of an official require a similar analysis if the obscurity which still lingers about them is to be dissipated. The reason why an analysis in these terms of primary and secondary rules has this explanatory power is not far to seek. Most of the obscurities and distortions surrounding legal and political concepts arise from the fact that these essentially involve reference to what we have called the internal point of view: the view of those who do not merely record and predict behavior conforming to rules, but *use* the rules as standards for the appraisal of their own and others' behaviour. This requires more detailed attention in the analysis of legal and political concepts than it has usually received. Under the simple regime of primary rules the internal point of view is manifested in its simplest form, in the use of those rules as the basis of criticism, and as the justification of demands for conformity, social pressure, and punishment. Reference to this most elementary manifestation of the internal point of view is required for the analysis of the basic concepts of obligation and duty. With the addition to the system of secondary rules, the range of what is said and done from the internal point of view is much extended and diversified. With this extension comes a whole set of new concepts and they demand a reference to the internal point of view for their analysis. These include the notions of legislation, jurisdiction, validity, and, generally, of legal powers, private and public. There is a constant pull towards an analysis of these in the terms of ordinary or "scientific," fact-stating or predictive discourse. But this can only reproduce their external aspect: to do justice to their distinctive, internal aspect we need to see the different ways in which the law-making operations of the legislator, the adjudication of a court, the exercise of private or official powers, and other "acts-in-the-law" are related to secondary rules.

[handwritten top margin: identifying rule = referencing previous enactments]

[handwritten: rules provided: (sources).]

In the next chapter we shall show how the ideas of the validity of law and sources of law, and the truths latent among the errors of the doctrines of sovereignty may be rephrased and clarified in terms of rules of recognition. But we shall conclude this chapter with a warning: though the combination of primary and secondary rules merits, because it explains many aspects of law, the central place assigned to it, this cannot by itself illuminate every problem. The union of primary and secondary rules is at the centre of a legal system; but it is not the whole, and as we move away from the centre we shall have to accommodate, in ways indicated in later chapters, elements of a different character.

CHAPTER 6: THE FOUNDATIONS OF A LEGAL SYSTEM

[handwritten left margin: Hart 212]

1. Rule of Recognition and Legal Validity

[handwritten left margin: Legal system = society habitually obeys orders of sovereign who itself doesn't obey anyone.]

[...] The foundations of a legal system consist of the situation in which the majority of a social group habitually obey the orders backed by threats of the sovereign person or persons, who themselves habitually obey no one. This social situation is, for this theory, both a necessary and a sufficient condition of the existence of law. We have already exhibited in some detail the incapacity of this theory to account for some of the salient features of a modern municipal legal system: yet none the less, as its hold over the minds of many thinkers suggests, it does contain, though in a blurred and misleading form, certain truths about certain important aspects of law. These truths can, however, only be clearly presented, and their importance rightly assessed, in terms of the more complex social situation where a secondary rule of recognition is accepted and used for the identification of primary rules of obligation. It is this situation which deserves, if anything does, to be called the foundations of a legal system. In this chapter we shall discuss various elements of this situation which have received only partial or misleading expression in the theory of sovereignty and elsewhere.

[handwritten left margin: → misleading theory of sovereignty]

[handwritten left margin: secondary rules + primary rules = legal system]

Wherever such a rule of recognition is accepted, both private persons and officials are provided with authoritative criteria for identifying primary rules of obligation. The criteria so provided may, as we have seen, take any one or more of a variety of forms: these include reference to an authoritative text; to legislative enactment; to customary practice; to general declarations of specified persons, or to past judicial decisions in particular cases. In a very simple system like the world of Rex I [...] where only what he enacts is law and no legal limitations upon his legislative power are imposed by customary rule or constitutional document, the sole criterion for identifying the law will be a simple reference to the fact of enactment by Rex I. The existence of this simple form of rule of recognition will be manifest in the general practice, on the part of officials or private persons, of identifying the rules by this criterion. In a modern legal system where there are a variety of "sources" of law, the rule of recognition is correspondingly more complex: the criteria for identifying the law are multiple and commonly include a written constitution, enactment by a legislature, and judicial precedents. In most cases, provision is made for possible conflict by ranking these criteria in an order of relative subordination and primacy. It is in this way that in our system "common law" is subordinate to "statute."

It is important to distinguish this relative *subordination* of one criterion to another from *derivation*, since some spurious support for the view that all law is essentially or "really" (even if only "tacitly") the product of legislation, has been gained from confusion of these two ideas. In our own system, custom and precedent are subordinate to legislation since customary and common law rules may be deprived of their status as law by statute. Yet they owe their status of law, precarious as this may be, not to a "tacit" exercise of legislative power but to the acceptance of a rule of recognition which accords them this independent though subordinate place. Again, as in the simple case, the existence of such a complex rule of recognition with this hierarchical ordering of distinct criteria is manifested in the general practice of identifying the rules by such criteria.

In the day-to-day life of a legal system its rule of recognition is very seldom expressly formulated as a rule; though occasionally, courts in England may announce in general terms the relative place

[handwritten bottom margin: (precedent is sub. to legislation)   Common law is subordinate to statute   subordination vs. derivation   • Law ≠ tacit legislative power   • Law = accepting]

(margin note, top left): • RoR = existence shown in the ways in which particular rules are identified, either by courts or other officials [unstated]

of one criterion of law in relation to another, as when they assert the supremacy of Acts of Parliament over other sources or suggested sources of law. For the most part the rule of recognition is not stated, but its existence is shown in the way in which particular rules are identified, either by courts or other officials or private persons or their advisers. There is, of course, a difference in the use made by courts of the criteria provided by the rule and the use of them by others: for when courts reach a particular conclusion on the footing that a particular rule has been correctly identified as law, what they say has a special authoritative status conferred on it by other rules. In this respect, as in many others, the rule of recognition of a legal system is like the scoring rule of a game. In the course of the game the general rule defining the activities which constitute scoring (runs, goals, &c.) is seldom formulated; instead it is *used* by officials and players in identifying the particular phases which count towards winning. Here too, the declarations of officials (umpire or scorer) have a special authoritative status attributed to them by other rules. Further, in both cases there is the possibility of a conflict between these authoritative applications of the rule and the general understanding of what the rule plainly requires according to its terms. This [. . .] is a complication which must be catered for in any account of what it is for a system of rules of this sort to exist.

The use of unstated rules of recognition, by courts and others, in identifying particular rules of the system is characteristic of the internal point of view. Those who use them in this way thereby manifest their own acceptance of them as guiding rules and with this attitude there goes a characteristic vocabulary different from the natural expressions of the external point of view. Perhaps the simplest of these is the expression, "It is the law that . . . ," which we may find on the lips not only of judges, but of ordinary men living under a legal system, when they identify a given rule of the system. This, like the expression "Out" or "Goal," is the language of one assessing a situation by reference to rules which he in common with others acknowledges as appropriate for this purpose. This attitude of shared acceptance of rules is to be contrasted with that of an observer who records *ab extra* the fact that

(margin note, bottom left): • RoR = shared acceptance from internal point of view.

a social group accepts such rules but does not himself accept them. The natural expression of this external point of view is not "It is the law that . . ." but "In England they recognize as law . . . whatever the Queen in Parliament enacts. . . ." The first of these forms of expression we shall call an *internal statement* because it manifests the internal point of view and is naturally used by one who, accepting the rule of recognition and without staring the fact that it is accepted, applies the rule in recognizing some particular rule of the system as valid. The second form of expression we shall call an *external statement* because it is the natural language of an external observer of the system who, without himself accepting its rule of recognition, states the fact that others accept it.

(margin note): internally accepting RoR.

(margin note): external view of RoR (not accepting RoR, but acknowledging that others accept it).

If this use of an accepted rule of recognition in making internal statements is understood and carefully distinguished from an external statement of fact that the rule is accepted, many obscurities concerning the notion of legal "validity" disappear. For the word "valid" is most frequently, though not always, used, in just such internal statements, applying to a particular rule of a legal system, an unstated but accepted rule of recognition. To say that a given rule is valid is to recognize it as passing all the tests provided by the rule of recognition and so as a rule of the system. We can indeed simply say that the statement that a particular rule is valid means that it satisfies all the criteria provided by the rule of recognition. This is incorrect only to the extent that it might obscure the internal character of such statements; for, like the cricketers' "Out," these statements of validity normally apply to a particular case a rule of recognition accepted by the speaker and others, rather than expressly state that the rule is satisfied.

(margin note): valid rule = passing all criteria of RoR internally

Some of the puzzles connected with the idea of legal validity are said to concern the relation between the validity and the "efficacy" of law. If by "efficacy" is meant that the fact that a rule of law which requires certain behaviour is obeyed more often than not, it is plain that there is no necessary connection between the validity of any particular rule and *its* efficacy, unless the rule of recognition of the system includes among its criteria, as some do, the provision (sometimes referred to as a rule of obsolescence) that no rule is to count as a rule of the system if it has long ceased to be efficacious.

(margin note): RoR must be efficacious (obeyed more often than not)
↳ rule of obsolescence
(no rule is a rule unless it is efficacious).

From the inefficacy of a particular rule, which may or may not count against its validity, we must distinguish a general disregard of the rules of the system. This may be so complete in character and so protracted that we should say, in the case of a new system, that it had never established itself as the legal system of a given group, or, in the case of a once-established system, that it had ceased to be the legal system of the group. In either case, the normal context or background for making any internal statement in terms of the rules of the system is absent. In such cases it would be generally *pointless* either to assess the rights and duties of particular persons by reference to the primary rules of a system or to assess the validity of any of its rules by reference to its rules of recognition. To insist on applying a system of rules which had either never actually been effective or had been discarded would, except in special circumstances mentioned below, be as futile as to assess the progress of a game by reference to a scoring rule which had never been accepted or had been discarded.

[margin note: if ROR is not efficacious then it is pointless]

One who makes an internal statement concerning the validity of a particular rule of a system may be said to *presuppose* the truth of the external statement of fact that the system is generally efficacious. For the normal use of internal statements is in such a context of general efficacy. It would however be wrong to say that statements of validity "mean" that the system is generally efficacious. For though it is normally pointless or idle to talk of the validity of a rule of a system which has never established itself or has been discarded, none the less it is not meaningless nor is it always pointless. One vivid way of teaching Roman Law is to speak *as if* the system were efficacious still and to discuss the validity of particular rules and solve problems in their terms; and one way of nursing hopes for the restoration of an old social order destroyed by revolution, and rejecting the new, is to cling to the criteria of legal validity of the old regime. This is implicitly done by the White Russian who still claims property under some rule of descent which was a valid rule of Tsarist Russia.

A grasp of the normal contextual connection between the internal statement that a given rule of a system is valid and the external statement of fact that the system is generally efficacious, will help us see in its proper perspective the common

theory that to assert the validity of a rule is to predict that it will be enforced by courts or some other official action taken. In many ways this theory is similar to the predictive analysis of obligation which we considered and rejected in the last chapter. In both cases alike the motive for advancing this predictive theory is the conviction that only thus can metaphysical interpretations be avoided: that either a statement that a rule is valid must ascribe some mysterious property which cannot be detected by empirical means or it must be a prediction of future behaviour of officials. In both cases also the plausibility of the theory is due to the same important fact: that the truth of the external statement of fact, which an observer might record, that the system is generally efficacious and likely to continue so, is normally presupposed by anyone who accepts the rules and makes an internal statement of obligation or validity. The two are certainly very closely associated. Finally, in both cases alike the mistake of the theory is the same: it consists in neglecting the special character of the internal statement and treating it as an external statement about official action.

This mistake becomes immediately apparent when we consider how the judge's own statement that a particular rule is valid functions in judicial decision; for, though here too, in making such a statement, the judge presupposes but does not state the general efficacy of the system, he plainly is not concerned to predict his own or others' official action. His statement that a rule is valid is an internal statement recognizing that the rule satisfies the tests for identifying what is to count as law in his court, and constitutes not a prophecy of but part of the *reason* for his decision. There is indeed a more plausible case for saying that a statement that a rule is valid is a prediction when such a statement is made by a private person; for in the case of conflict between unofficial statements of validity or invalidity and that of a court in deciding a case, there is often good sense in saying that the former must then be withdrawn. Yet even here, [. . .] to investigate the significance of such conflicts between official declarations and the plain requirements of the rules, it may be dogmatic to assume that it is withdrawn as a statement now shown to be *wrong*, because it has falsely *predicted* what a court would say. For there are more reasons for withdrawing statements than the fact that they are wrong, and also more ways of being wrong than this allows.

The rule of recognition providing the criteria by which the validity of other rules of the system is assessed is in an important sense, which we shall try to clarify, an *ultimate* rule: and where, as is usual, there are several criteria ranked in order of relative subordination and primacy one of them is *supreme*. These ideas of the ultimacy of the rule of recognition and the supremacy of one of its criteria merit some attention. It is important to disentangle them from the theory, which we have rejected, that somewhere in every legal system, even though it lurks behind legal forms, there must be a sovereign legislative power which is legally unlimited.

Of these two ideas, supreme criterion and ultimate rule, the first is the easiest to define. *supreme* We may say that a criterion of legal validity or source of law is supreme if rules identified by reference to it are still recognized as rules of the system, even if they conflict with rules identified by reference to the other criteria, whereas rules identified by reference to the latter are not so recognized if they conflict with the rules identified by reference to the supreme criterion. A similar explanation in comparative terms can be given of the notions of "superior" and "subordinate" criteria which we have already used. It is plain that the notions of a superior and a supreme criterion merely refer to a (relative) place on a scale and do not import any notion of legally *unlimited* legislative power. Yet "supreme" and "unlimited" are easy to confuse – at least in legal theory. One reason for this is that in the simpler forms of legal system the ideas of ultimate rule of recognition, supreme criterion, and legally unlimited legislature seem to converge. For where there is a legislature subject to no constitutional limitations and competent by its enactment to deprive all other rules of law emanating from other sources of their status as law, it is part of the rule of recognition in such a system that enactment by that legislature is the supreme criterion of validity. This is, according to constitutional theory, the position in the United Kingdom. But even systems like that of the United States in which there is no such legally unlimited legislature may perfectly well contain an ultimate rule of recognition which provides

a set of criteria of validity, one of which is supreme. This will be so, where the legislative competence of the ordinary legislature is limited by a constitution which contains no amending power, or places some clauses outside the scope of that power. Here there is no legally unlimited legislature, even in the widest interpretation of "legislature"; but the system of course contains an ultimate rule of recognition and, in the clauses of its constitution, a supreme criterion of validity.

The sense in which the rule of recognition is the *ultimate* rule of a system is best understood if we pursue a very familiar chain of legal reasoning. If the question is raised whether some suggested rule is legally valid, we must, in order to answer the question, use a criterion of validity provided by some other rule. Is this purported by-law of the Oxfordshire County Council valid? Yes: because it was made in exercise of the powers conferred, and in accordance with the procedure specified, by a statutory order made by the Minister of Health. At this first stage the statutory order provides the criteria in terms of which the validity of the by-law is assessed. There may be no practical need to go farther; but there is a standing possibility of doing so. We may query the validity of the statutory order and assess its validity in terms of the statute empowering the minister to make such orders. Finally, when the validity of the statute has been queried and assessed by reference to the rule that what the Queen in Parliament enacts is law, we are brought to a stop in inquiries concerning validity: for we have reached a rule which, like the intermediate statutory order and statute, provides criteria for the assessment of the validity of other rules; but it is also unlike them in that there is no rule providing criteria for the assessment of its own legal validity.

There are, indeed, many questions which we can raise about this ultimate rule. We can ask whether it is the practice of courts, legislatures, officials, or private citizens in England actually to use this rule as an ultimate rule of recognition. Or has our process of legal reasoning been an idle game with the criteria of validity of a system now discarded? We can ask whether it is a satisfactory form of legal system which has such a rule at its root. Does it produce more good than

• rules being valid

to need to find a rule to provide criteria for the assessment of the validity of other rules.

(1) *supreme relative to other rules when there is a conflict. (not unlimited)*

evil? Are there prudential reasons for supporting it? Is there a moral obligation to do so? These are plainly very important questions; but, equally plainly, when we ask them about the rule of recognition, we are no longer attempting to answer the same kind of question about it as those which we answered about other rules with its aid. When we move from saying that a particular enactment is valid, because it satisfies the rule that what the Queen in Parliament enacts is law, to saying that in England this last rule is used by courts, officials, and private persons as the ultimate rule of recognition, we have moved from an internal statement of law asserting the validity of a rule of the system to an external statement of fact which an observer of the system might make even if he did not accept it. So too when we move from the statement that a particular enactment is valid, to the statement that the rule of recognition of the system is an excellent one and the system based on it is one worthy of support, we have moved from a statement of legal validity to a statement of value. [. . .]

In the simple system of primary rules of obligation sketched in the last chapter, the assertion that a given rule existed could only be an external statement of fact such as an observer who did not accept the rules might make and verify by ascertaining whether or not, as a matter of fact, a given mode of behaviour was generally accepted as a standard and was accompanied by those features which, as we have seen, distinguish a social rule from mere convergent habits. It is in this way also that we should now interpret and verify the assertion that in England

a rule – though not a legal one – exists that we must bare the head on entering a church. If such rules as these are found to exist in the actual practice of a social group, there is no separate question of their validity to be discussed, though of course their value or desirability is open to question. Once their existence has been established as a fact we should only confuse matters by affirming or denying that they were valid or by saying that "we assumed" but could not show their validity. Where, on the other hand, as in a mature legal system, we have a system of rules which includes a rule of recognition so that the status of a rule as a member of the system now depends on whether it satisfies certain criteria provided by the rule of recognition, this brings with it a new application of the word "exist." The statement that a rule exists may now no longer be what it was in the simple case of customary rules – an external statement of the *fact* that a certain mode of behaviour was generally accepted as a standard in practice. It may now be an internal statement applying an accepted but unstated rule of recognition and meaning (roughly) no more than "valid given the system's criteria of validity." In this respect, however, as in others a rule of recognition is unlike other rules of the system. The assertion that it exists can only be an external statement of fact. For whereas a subordinate rule of a system may be valid and in that sense "exist" even if it is generally disregarded, the rule of recognition exists only as a complex, but normally concordant, practice of the courts, officials, and private persons in identifying the law by reference to certain criteria. Its existence is a matter of fact. [. . .]

8

The Model of Rules I

Ronald Dworkin

[handwritten annotations:]

Dworkin: attacking Hart's positivism:
↳ in penumbral cases, lawyers don't use rules, but use principles (other standards than rules).
↳ positivism = rules; but misses the roles of principles.

• policy = goal to be reached; improving economic, political, or social features of society.
• principle = requirement of justice or fairness or some other dimension of morality.

Ex:

[...]

Rules, Principles, and Policies

I want to make a general <u>attack on positivism</u>, and I shall use H. L. A. H<u>art's version as a target</u>, when a particular target is needed. My strategy will be organized around the fact that <u>when lawyers</u> reason or dispute about legal rights and obligations, particularly in those hard cases when our problems with these concepts seem most acute, <u>they make use of standards that do not function as rules, but operate differently as principles, policies, and other sorts of standards. Positivism</u>, I shall argue, <u>is a model of and for a system of rules</u>, and its central notion of a single fundamental test for law forces us t<u>o miss the important roles of these standards that are not rules</u>.

I just spoke of "principles, policies, and other sorts of standards". Most often I shall use the term "<u>principle</u>" generically, to refer to the whole set of these standards other than rules; occasionally, however, I shall be more precise, and distinguish between principles and policies. Although nothing in the present argument will turn on the distinction, I should state how I draw it. I call a <u>"policy" that kind of standard that sets out a goal to be reached, generally an improvement in some</u> economic, political, or social feature of the community (though some goals are negative, in that they stipulate that some present feature is to be protected from adverse change). <u>I call a "principle" a standard that is to be observed, not because it will advance or secure an economic, political, or social situation deemed desirable, but because it is a requirement of justice or fairness or some other dimension of morality.</u> Thus the standard that automobile accidents are to be decreased is a (policy) and the <u>standard that no man may profit</u> by his own wrong a (principle). The distinction can be <u>collapsed by construing a principle as stating</u> a <u>social goal</u> (*i.e.,* the goal of a society in which no man profits by his own wrong), or by <u>construing</u> a <u>policy as stating a principle</u> (*i.e.,* the principle that the goal the policy embraces is a worthy one) or by adopting the utilitarian thesis that prin<u>ciples of justice are disguised statements</u> of goals (securing the greatest happiness of the greatest number). In some contexts the distinction has uses which are lost if it is thus collapsed.[1]

My immediate purpose, however, is to distinguish principles in the generic sense from rules,

[handwritten box:] rules vs. principles

Ronald M. Dworkin, "The Model of Rules I," from *Taking Rights Seriously* (Cambridge, Mass: The Belknap Press of Harvard University Press, 1977), pp. 22–9, 39–45. © 1977, 1978 by Ronald Dworkin. Reprinted with permission from Harvard University Press and Gerald Duckworth & Co. Ltd.

and I shall start by collecting some examples of the former. The examples I offer are chosen haphazardly; almost any case in a law school casebook would provide examples that would serve as well. In 1889 a New York court, in the famous case of *Riggs v. Palmer*,[2] had to decide whether an heir named in the will of his grandfather could inherit under that will, even though he had murdered his grandfather to do so. The court began its reasoning with this admission: "It is quite true that statutes regulating the making, proof and effect of wills, and the devolution of property, if literally construed, and if their force and effect can in no way and under no circumstances be controlled or modified, give this property to the murderer."[3] But the court continued to note that "all laws as well as all contracts may be controlled in their operation and effect by general, fundamental maxims of the common law. No one shall be permitted to profit by his own fraud, or to take advantage of his own wrong, or to found any claim upon his own iniquity, or to acquire property by his own crime."[4] The murderer did not receive his inheritance.

In 1960, a New Jersey court was faced, in *Henningsen v. Bloomfield Motors, Inc.*[5] with the important question of whether (or how much) an automobile manufacturer may limit his liability in case the automobile is defective. Henningsen had bought a car, and signed a contract which said that the manufacturer's liability for defects was limited to "making good" defective parts – "this warranty being expressly in lieu of all other warranties, obligations or liabilities." Henningsen argued that, at least in the circumstances of his case, the manufacturer ought not to be protected by this limitation, and ought to be liable for the medical and other expenses of persons injured in a crash. He was not able to point to any statute, or to any established rule of law, that prevented the manufacturer from standing on the contract. The court nevertheless agreed with Henningsen. At various points in the court's argument the following appeals to standards are made: (a) "[W]e must keep in mind the general principle that, in the absence of fraud, one who does not choose to read a contract before signing it cannot later relieve himself of its burdens."[6] (b) "In applying that principle, the basic tenet of freedom of competent parties to contract is a

factor of importance."[7] (c) "Freedom of contract is not such an immutable doctrine as to admit of no qualification in the area in which we are concerned."[8] (d) "In a society such as ours, where the automobile is a common and necessary adjunct of daily life, and where its use is so fraught with danger to the driver, passengers and the public, the manufacturer is under a special obligation in connection with the construction, promotion and sale of his cars. Consequently, the courts must examine purchase agreements closely to see if consumer and public interests are treated fairly."[9] (e) "'[I]s there any principle which is more familiar or more firmly embedded in the history of Anglo-American law than the basic doctrine that the courts will not permit themselves to be used as instruments of inequity and injustice?'"[10] (f) "'More specifically the courts generally refuse to lend themselves to the enforcement of a "bargain" in which one party has unjustly taken advantage of the economic necessities of other . . .'"[11]

The standards set out in these quotations are not the sort we think of as legal rules. They seem very different from propositions like "The maximum legal speed on the turnpike is sixty miles an hour" or "A will is invalid unless signed by three witnesses". They are different because they are legal principles rather than legal rules.

The difference between legal principles and legal rules is a logical distinction. Both sets of standards point to particular decisions about legal obligation in particular circumstances, but they differ in the character of the direction they give. Rules are applicable in an all-or-nothing fashion. If the facts a rule stipulates are given, then either the rule is valid, in which case the answer it supplies must be accepted, or it is not, in which case it contributes nothing to the decision.

This all-or-nothing is seen most plainly if we look at the way rules operate, not in law, but in some enterprise they dominate – a game, for example. In baseball a rule provides that if the batter has had three strikes, he is out. An official cannot consistently acknowledge that this is an accurate statement of a baseball rule, and decide that a batter who has had three strikes is not out. Of course, a rule may have exceptions (the batter who has taken three strikes is not out if the catcher drops the third strike). However, an accurate statement of the rule would take this exception into account, and any that did not would be incomplete. If the list of exceptions is very large, it would be too clumsy to repeat them each time the rule is cited; there is, however, no reason in theory why they could not all be added on, and the more that are, the more accurate is the statement of the rule.

If we take baseball rules as a model, we find that rules of law, like the rule that a will is invalid unless signed by three witnesses, fit the model well. If the requirement of three witnesses is a valid legal rule, then it cannot be that a will has been signed by only two witnesses and is valid. The rule might have exceptions, but if it does then it is inaccurate and incomplete to state the rule so simply, without enumerating the exceptions. In theory, at least, the exceptions could all be listed, and the more of them that are, the more complete is the statement of the rule.

But this is not the way the sample principles in the quotations operate. Even those which look most like rules do not set out legal consequences that follow automatically when the conditions provided are met. We say that our law respects the principle that no man may profit from his own wrong, but we do not mean that the law never permits a man to profit from wrongs he commits. In fact, people often profit, perfectly legally, from their legal wrongs. The most notorious case is adverse possession – if I trespass on your land long enough, some day I will gain a right to cross your land whenever I please. There are many less dramatic examples. If a man leaves one job, breaking a contract, to take a much higher paying job, he may have to pay damages to his first employer, but he is usually entitled to keep his new salary. If a man jumps bail and crosses state lines to make a brilliant investment in another state, he may be sent back to jail, but he will keep his profits.

We do not treat these – and countless other counter-instances that can easily be imagined – as showing that the principle about profiting from one's wrongs is not a principle of our legal system, or that it is incomplete and needs qualifying exceptions. We do not treat counter-instances as exceptions (at least not exceptions in the way in which a catcher's dropping the third strike is an exception) because we could not

hope to capture these counter-instances simply by a more extended statement of the principle. They are not, even in theory, subject to enumeration, because we would have to include not only these cases (like adverse possession) in which some institution has already provided that profit can be gained through a wrong, but also those numberless imaginary cases in which we know in advance that the principle would not hold. Listing some of these might sharpen our sense of the principle's weight (I shall mention that dimension in a moment), but it would not make for a more accurate or complete statement of the principle.

A principle like 'No man may profit from his own wrong' does not even purport to set out conditions that make its application necessary. Rather, it states a reason that argues in one direction, but does not necessitate a particular decision. If a man has or is about to receive something, as a direct result of something illegal he did to get it, then that is a reason which the law will take into account in deciding whether he should keep it. There may by other principles or policies arguing in the other direction – a policy of securing title, for example, or a principle limiting punishment to what the legislature has stipulated. If so, our principle may not prevail, but that does not mean that it is not a principle of our legal system, because in the next case, when these contravening considerations are absent or less weighty, the principle may be decisive. All that is meant, when we say that a particular principle is a principle of our law, is that the principle is one which officials must take into account, if it is relevant, as a consideration inclining in one direction or another.

The logical distinction between rules and principles appears more clearly when we consider principles that do not even look like rules. Consider the proposition, set out under '(d)' in the excerpts from the *Henningsen* opinion, that 'the manufacturer is under a special obligation in connection with the construction, promotion and sale of his cars'. This does not even purport to define the specific duties such a special obligation entails, or to tell us what rights automobile consumers acquire as a result. It merely states – and this is an essential link in the *Henningsen* argument – that automobile

• principles = no legal consequences
that follow automatically.
⟶ take into consideration illegal actions to make
a decision decisive.

[handwritten: Courts take into consideration fairness, not just statutes in penumbral cases.]

manufacturers must be held to higher standards than other manufacturers, and are less entitled to rely on the competing principle of freedom of contract. It does not mean that they may never rely on that principle, or that courts may rewrite automobile purchase contracts at will; it means only that if a particular clause seems unfair or burdensome, courts have less reason to enforce the clause than if it were for the purchase of neckties. The 'special obligation' counts in favor of, but does not in itself necessitate, a decision refusing to enforce the terms of an automobile purchase contract.

This first difference between rules and principles entails another. Principles have a dimension that rules do not – the dimension of weight or importance. When principles intersect (the policy of protecting automobile consumers intersecting with principles of freedom of contract, for example), one who must resolve the conflict has to take into account the relative weight of each. This cannot be, of course, an exact measurement, and the judgment that a particular principle or policy is more important than another will often be a controversial one. Nevertheless, it is an integral part of the concept of a principle that it has this dimension, that it makes sense to ask how important or how weighty it is.

Rules do not have this dimension. We can speak of rules as being *functionally* important or unimportant (the baseball rule that three strikes are out is more important than the rule that runners may advance on a balk, because the game would be much more changed with the first rule altered than the second). In this sense, one legal rule may be more important than another because it has a greater or more important role in regulating behavior. But we cannot say that one rule is more important than another within the system of rules, so that when two rules conflict one supersedes the other by virtue of its greater weight.

If two rules conflict, one of them cannot be a valid rule. The decision as to which is valid, and which must be abandoned or recast, must be made by appealing to considerations beyond the rules themselves. A legal system might regulate such conflicts by other rules, which prefer the rule enacted by the higher authority, or the rule enacted later, or the more specific rule, or some-

[handwritten left margin: principle = dimension of weight or importance ‼ when principles intersect, need to ask how important each principle is.]

[handwritten left margin: rules do not have this (↑) dimension. (no conflict) ↓ when rules conflict, one supersedes the other. (one of them cannot be valid).]

thing of that sort. A legal system may also prefer the rule supported by the more important principles. (Our own legal system uses both of these techniques.)

It is not always clear from the form of a standard whether it is a rule or a principle. 'A will is invalid unless signed by three witnesses' is not very different in form from 'A man may not profit from his own wrong', but one who knows something of American law knows that he must take the first as stating a rule and the second as stating a principle. In many cases the distinction is difficult to make – it may not have been settled how the standard should operate, and this issue may itself be a focus of controversy. The first amendment to the United States Constitution contains the provision that Congress shall not abridge freedom of speech. Is this a rule, so that if a particular law does abridge freedom of speech, it follows that it is unconstitutional? Those who claim that the first amendment is 'an absolute' say that it must be taken in this way, that is, as a rule. Or does it merely state a principle, so that when an abridgement of speech is discovered, it is unconstitutional unless the context presents some other policy or principle which in the circumstances is weighty enough to permit the abridgement? That is the position of those who argue for what is called the 'clear and present danger' test or some other form of 'balancing'.

Sometimes a rule and a principle can play much the same role, and the difference between them is almost a matter of form alone. The first section of the Sherman Act states that every contract in restraint of trade shall be void. The Supreme Court had to make the decision whether this provision should be treated as a rule in its own terms (striking down every contract 'which restrains trade', which almost any contract does) or as a principle, providing a reason for striking down a contract in the absence of effective contrary policies. The Court construed the provision as a rule, but treated that rule as containing the word "unreasonable", and as prohibiting only "unreasonable" restraints of trade.[12] This allowed the provision to function logically as a rule (whenever a court finds that the restraint is "unreasonable" it is bound to hold the contract invalid) and substantially as a principle (a court must take into account a variety of other *[handwritten margin note at top: these terms make application of rules depend on principles (room for interpretation).]*

principles and policies in determining whether a particular restraint in particular economic circumstances is "unreasonable").

Words like "reasonable", "negligent", "unjust" and "significant" often perform just this function. Each of these terms makes the application of the rule which contains it depend to some extent upon principles or policies lying beyond the rule, and in this way makes that rule itself more like a principle. But they do not quite turn the rule into a principle, because even the least confining of these terms restricts the *kind* of other principles and policies on which the rule depends. If we are bound by a rule that says that "unreasonable" contracts are void, or that grossly "unfair" contracts will not be enforced, much more judgment is required than if the quoted terms were omitted. But suppose a case in which some consideration of policy or principle suggests that a contract should be enforced even though its restraint is not reasonable, or even though it is grossly unfair. Enforcing these contracts would be forbidden by our rules, and thus permitted only if these rules were abandoned or modified. If we were dealing, however, not with a rule but with a policy against enforcing unreasonable contracts, or a principle that unfair contracts ought not to be enforced, the contracts could be enforced without alteration of the law.

Principles and the Concept of Law

[handwritten margin note: Legal principles ≠ Legal rules]

Once we identify legal principles as separate sorts of standards, different from legal rules, we are suddenly aware of them all around us. Law teachers teach them, lawbooks cite them, legal historians celebrate them. But they seem most energetically at work, carrying most weight, in difficult lawsuits like *Riggs* and *Henningsen*. In cases like these, principles play an essential part in arguments supporting judgments about particular legal rights and obligations. After the case is decided, we may say that the case stands for a particular rule (e.g., the rule that one who murders is not eligible to take under the will of his victim). But the rule does not exist before the case is decided; the court cites principles as its justification for adopting and applying a new rule. In *Riggs*, the court cited the principle that no man

[handwritten note at bottom: Riggs: principles used to justify the adoption of a new rule.]

may profit from his own wrong as a background standard against which to read the statute of wills and in this way justified a new interpretation of that statute. In *Henningsen*, the court cited a variety of intersecting principles and policies as authority for a new rule respecting manufacturers' liability for automobile defects.

An analysis of the concept of legal obligation must therefore account for the important role of principles in reaching particular decisions of law.

[. . .]

[handwritten margin note: • principles are important for reaching legal decisions.]

Would we also have to abandon or modify the first tenet, the proposition that law is distinguished by tests of the sort that can be set out in a master rule like Professor Hart's rule of recognition? If principles of the *Riggs* and *Henningsen* sort are to count as law, and we are nevertheless to preserve the notion of a master rule for law, then we must be able to deploy some test that all (and only) the principles that do count as law meet. Let us begin with the test Hart suggests for identifying valid *rules* of law, to see whether these can be made to work for principles as well.

Most rules of law, according to Hart, are valid because some competent institution enacted them. Some were created by a legislature, in the form of statutory enactments. Others were created by judges who formulated them to decide particular cases, and thus established them as precedents for the future. But this test of pedigree will not work for the *Riggs* and *Henningsen* principles. The origin of these as legal principles lies not in a particular decision of some legislature or court, but in a sense of appropriateness developed in the profession and the public over time. Their continued power depends upon this sense of appropriateness being sustained. If it no longer seemed unfair to allow people to profit by their wrongs, or fair to place special burdens upon oligopolies that manufacture potentially dangerous machines, these principles would no longer play much of a role in new cases, even if they had never been overruled or repealed. (Indeed, it hardly makes sense to speak of principles like these as being "overruled" or "repealed". When they decline they are eroded, not torpedoed.)

[handwritten margin note: Hart: rule is valid if institution enacted them. (legislature judges) ≠ principles]

[handwritten margin note: principle valid if they are developed in profession and in the public over time (applied in real life.]

[Handwritten margin notes top: "principle of law = institutional support." and "principles valid = having support of other principles."]

True, if we were challenged to back up our claim that some principle is a principle of law, we would mention any prior cases in which that principle was cited, or figured in the argument. We would also mention any statute that seemed to exemplify that principle (even better if the principle was cited in the preamble of the statute, or in the committee reports or other legislative documents that accompanied it). Unless we could find some such institutional support, we would probably fail to make out our case, and the more support we found, the more weight we could claim for the principle.

Yet we could not devise any formula for testing how much and what kind of institutional support is necessary to make a principle a legal principle, still less to fix its weight at a particular order of magnitude. We argue for a particular principle by grappling with a whole set of shifting, developing and interacting standards (themselves principles rather than rules) about institutional responsibility, statutory interpretation, the persuasive force of various sorts of precedent, the relation of all these to contemporary moral practices, and hosts of other such standards. We could not bolt all of these together into a single "rule", even a complex one, and if we could the result would bear little relation to Hart's picture of a rule of recognition, which is the picture of a fairly stable master rule specifying "some feature or features possession of which by a suggested rule is taken as a conclusive affirmative indication that it is a rule . . ."[13]

Moreover, the techniques we apply in arguing for another principle do not stand (as Hart's rule of recognition is designed to) on an entirely different level from the principles they support. Hart's sharp distinction between acceptance and validity does not hold. If we are arguing for the principle that a man should not profit from his own wrong, we could cite the acts of courts and legislatures that exemplify it, but this speaks as much to the principle's acceptance as its validity. (It seems odd to speak of a principle as being valid at all, perhaps because validity is an all-or-nothing concept, appropriate for rules, but inconsistent with a principle's dimension of weight.) If we are asked (as we might well be) to defend the particular doctrine of precedent, or the particular technique of statutory interpretation, that we used in this argument, we should certainly

cite the practice of others in using that doctrine or technique. But we should also cite other general principles that we believe support that practice, and this introduces a note of validity into the chord of acceptance. We might argue, for example, that the use we make of earlier cases and statutes is supported by a particular analysis of the point of the practice of legislation or the doctrine of precedent, or by the principles of democratic theory, or by a particular position on the proper division of authority between national and local institutions, or something else of that sort. Nor is this path of support a one-way street leading to some ultimate principle resting on acceptance alone. Our principles of legislation, precedent, democracy, or federalism might be challenged too; and if they were we should argue for them, not only in terms of practice, but in terms of each other and in terms of the implications of trends of judicial and legislative decisions, even though this last would involve appealing to those same doctrines of interpretation we justified through the principles we are now trying to support. At this level of abstraction, in other words, principles rather hang together than link together.

So even though principles draw support from the official acts of legal institutions, they do not have a simple or direct enough connection with these acts to frame that connection in terms of criteria specified by some ultimate master rule of recognition. Is there any other route by which principles might be brought under such a rule? Hart does say that a master rule might designate as law not only rules enacted by particular legal institutions, but rules established by *custom* as well. He has in mind a problem that bothered other positivists, including Austin. Many of our most ancient legal rules were never explicitly created by a legislature or a court. When they made their first appearance in legal opinions and texts, they were treated as already being part of the law because they represented the customary practice of the community, or some specialized part of it, like the business community. (The examples ordinarily given are rules of mercantile practice, like the rules governing what rights arise under a standard form of commercial paper.)[14] Since Austin thought that all law was the command of a determinate sovereign, he held that these customary practices were not law until the _(acceptance)._

courts (as agents of the sovereign) recognized them, and that the courts were indulging in a fiction in pretending otherwise. But that seemed arbitrary. If everyone thought custom might in itself be law, the fact that Austin's theory said otherwise was not persuasive.

critique Austin

Hart reversed Austin on this point. The master rule, he says, might stipulate that some custom counts as law even before the courts recognize it. But he does not face the difficulty this raises for his general theory because he does not attempt to set out the criteria a master rule might use for this purpose. It cannot use, as its only criterion, the provision that the community regard the practice as *morally* binding, for this would not distinguish legal customary rules from moral customary rules, and of course not all of the community's long-standing customary moral obligations are enforced at law. If, on the other hand, the test is whether the community regards the customary practice as *legally* binding, the whole point of the master rule is undercut, at least for this class of legal rules. The master rule, says Hart, marks the transformation from a primitive society to one with law, because it provides a test for determining social rules of law other than by measuring their acceptance. But if the master rule says merely that whatever other rules the community accepts as legally binding are legally binding, then it provides no such test at all, beyond the test we should use were there no master rule. The master rule becomes (for these cases) a non-rule of recognition; we might as well say that every primitive society has a secondary rule of recognition, namely the rule that whatever is accepted as binding is binding. Hart himself, in discussing international law, ridicules the idea that such a rule could be a rule of recognition, by describing the proposed rule as "an empty repetition of the mere fact that the society concerned ... observes certain standards of conduct as obligatory rules."[15]

Hart's treatment of custom, amounts, indeed, to a confession that there are at least some rules of law that are not binding because they are valid under standards laid down by a master rule but are binding – like the master rule – because they are accepted as binding by the community. This chips at the neat pyramidal architecture we admired in Hart's theory: we can no longer say that only the master rule is binding because of its acceptance, all other rules being valid under its terms.

This is perhaps only a chip, because the customary rules Hart has in mind are no longer a very significant part of the law. But it does suggest that Hart would be reluctant to widen the damage by bringing under the head of "custom" all those crucial principles and policies we have been discussing. If he were to call these part of the law and yet admit that the only test of their force lies in the degree to which they are accepted as law by the community or some part thereof, he would very sharply reduce that area of the law over which his master rule held any dominion. It is not just that all the principles and policies would escape its sway, though that would be bad enough. Once these principles and policies are accepted as law, and thus as standards judges must follow in determining legal obligations, it would follow that *rules like* those announced for the first time in *Riggs* and *Henningsen* owe their force at least in part to the authority of principles and policies, and so not entirely to the master rule of recognition.

Dworkin

So we cannot adapt Hart's version of positivism by modifying his rule of recognition to embrace principles. No tests of pedigree, relating principles to acts of legislation, can be formulated, nor can his concept of customary law, itself an exception to the first tenet of positivism, be made to serve without abandoning that tenet altogether. One more possibility must be considered, however. If no rule of recognition can provide a test for identifying principles, why not say that principles are ultimate, and *form* the rule of recognition of our law? The answer to the general question "What is valid law in an American jurisdiction?" would then require us to state all the principles (as well as ultimate constitutional rules) in force in that jurisdiction at the time, together with appropriate assignments of weight. A positivist might then regard the complete set of these standards as the rule of recognition of the jurisdiction. This solution has the attraction of paradox, but of course it is an unconditional surrender. If we simply designate our rule of recognition by the phrase "the complete set of principles in force", we achieve only the tautology that law is law. If, instead, we tried actually to list all the principles in force we would fail. They are controversial, their

?

confusion with H's view of rule of recognition. Dworkin rejects ROR. legally binding vs. binding because community sees it as binding. customary laws (those that a community regularly practices).

weight is all important, they are numberless, and they shift and change so fast that the start of our list would be obsolete before we reached the middle. Even if we succeeded, we would not have a key for law because there would be nothing left for our key to unlock.

I conclude that if we treat principles as law we must reject the positivists' first tenet, that the law of a community is distinguished from other social standards by some test in the form of a master rule. We have already decided that we must then abandon the second tenet – the doctrine of judicial discretion – or clarify it into triviality. What of the third tenet, the positivists' theory of legal obligation?

This theory holds that a legal obligation exists when (and only when) an established rule of law imposes such an obligation. It follows from this that in a hard case – when no such established rule can be found – there is no legal obligation until the judge creates a new rule for the future. The judge may apply that new rule to the parties in the case, but this is *ex post facto* legislation, not the enforcement of an existing obligation.

The positivists' doctrine of discretion (in the strong sense) required this view of legal obligation, because if a judge has discretion there can be no legal right or obligation – no entitlement – that he must enforce. Once we abandon that doctrine, however, and treat principles as law, we raise the possibility that a legal obligation might be imposed by a constellation of principles as well as by an established rule. We might want to say that a legal obligation exists whenever the case supporting such an obligation, in terms of binding legal principles of different sorts, is stronger than the case against it.

Of course, many questions would have to be answered before we could accept that view of legal obligation. If there is no rule of recognition, no test for law in that sense, how do we decide which principles are to count, and how much, in making such a case? How do we decide whether one case is better than another? If legal obligation rests on an undemonstrable judgment of that sort, how can it provide a justification for a judicial decision that one party had a legal obligation? Does this view of obligation square with the way lawyers, judges and laymen speak, and is it consistent with our attitudes about moral obligation? Does this analysis help us to deal

with the classical jurisprudential puzzles about the nature of law?

These questions must be faced, but even the questions promise more than positivism provides. Positivism, on its own thesis, stops short of just those puzzling, hard cases that send us to look for theories of law. When we read these cases, the positivist remits us to a doctrine of discretion that leads nowhere and tells nothing. His picture of law as a system of rules has exercised a tenacious hold on our imagination, perhaps through its very simplicity. If we shake ourselves loose from this model of rules, we may be able to build a model truer to the complexity and sophistication of our own practices.

Notes

1   [. . .] See also Dworkin, "Wasserstrom: The Judicial Decision", 75 *Ethics* 47 (1964), reprinted as "Does Law Have a Function?", 74 *Yale Law Journal* 640 (1965).
2   115 N.Y. 506, 22 N.E. 188 (1889).
3   *Id.* at 509, 22 N.E. at 189.
4   *Id.* at 511, 22 N.E. at 190.
5   32 N.J. 358, 161 A.2d 69 (1960).
6   *Id.* at 386, 161 A.2d at 84.
7   *Id.*
8   *Id.* at 388, 161 A.2d at 86.
9   *Id.* at 387, 161 A.2d at 85.
10 *Id.* at 389, 161 A.2d at 86 (quoting Frankfurter, J., in *United States v. Bethlehem Steel*, 315 U.S. 289, 326 [1942]).
11 *Id.*
12 *Standard Oil v. United States*, 221 U.S. 1, 60 (1911); *United States v. American Tobacco Co.*, 221 U.S. 106, 180 (1911).
13 H. L. Hart, *The Concept of Law*, 92 (1961).
14 See Note, "Custom and Trade Usage: Its Application to Commercial Dealings and the Common Law", 55 *Columbia Law Review* 1192 (1955), and materials cited therein at 1193 n.l. As that note makes plain, the actual practices of courts in recognizing trade customs follow the pattern of applying a set of general principles and policies rather than a test that could be captured as part of a rule of recognition.
15 H. L. A. Hart, *The Concept of Law*, 230 (1961). A master rule might specify some particular feature of a custom that is independent of the community's attitude; it might provide, for example, that all customs of very great age, or all customs

having to do with negotiable instruments count as law. I can think of no such features that in fact distinguish the customs that have been recognized as law in England or America, however. Some customs that are not legally enforceable are older than some that are, some practices relating to commercial paper are enforced and others not, and so forth. In any event, even if a distinguishing feature were found that identified all rules of law established by custom, it would remain unlikely that such a feature could be found for principles which vary widely in their subject matter and pedigree and some of which are of very recent origin.

Hart: rules are binding to people because of the rule of recognition

⟶ Dworkin: rules also binding because they are customary to communities. ?
⟶ there are also principles that people conform to.
= accepted as law.

Dworkin's argument ☆ rules owe their force at least in part to the authority of principles and policies, and so not entirely to the master rule of recognition.

☆ in penumbral cases, when there is no legal obligation, a judge must create a new rule based on the relevant principles.
(ex post facto).
⟶ depends on facts of case (which side's argument is stronger).

⟶ th(a)rs that positivism stops short of difficult cases.

9

Law as Justice

Michael S. Moore

I. Natural Law's Relational Thesis

A perennial question of jurisprudence has been whether there is a relationship between law and morality. Those who believe that there is no such relationship are known as "legal positivists," while those who hold that some such relationship exists are usually tagged with the label "natural lawyers." Unfortunately, the latter phrase has been used in quite divergent senses. Sometimes it is used to designate any objectivist position about morality; as often, it labels the view that human nature determines what is objectively good or right; and perhaps as often, it labels the view that some natural facts other than facts about human nature determine what is objectively good or right; and sometimes the label presupposes some divine origins to both morality and human law.

In light of these differences in what is meant by "natural law," both in ancient as well as contemporary literature, I shall begin by stipulating the usage that I have found convenient for some time.[1] By "natural law" in legal theory, I understand one to mean the claims that: (1) there are objective moral truths; and (2) those moral truths are at least partly constitutive of the truth conditions for propositions of law. I have called the first claim the *metaethical thesis of natural law*

and the second claim the *relational thesis of natural law*. In this essay I am concerned solely with the relational thesis.[2]

The relational thesis asserts there to be some relation between human law and the laws of morality. In an earlier paper, I took some pains to clarify this thesis.[3] The bottom line of that analysis was the following construal of the natural lawyer's relational thesis: the nature of law is such that necessarily, if some institution is sufficiently unjust, it is not a *legal* institution. Legality, in other words, necessarily partakes of morality.

Legality is an attribute of four different sorts of institutions. Most generally, it can be an attribute of some kind of system within society. When we ask, "Does this island society have law?" we are inquiring as to whether the essential attributes of a *legal system* are in place.[4] By contrast, when we speak of law within some particular system that we acknowledge to be a legal system, we are often asking about *laws*. For example, we may wonder whether the custom that the public have access to ocean beaches is a law. In such cases, we are inquiring about the legality of some individual rule or other kind of discrete, individuated standard.[5] The third possible venue for legality judgments has to do with classes of rules. Here we ask whether rules of a certain sort are *legal* rules

Michael S. Moore, "Law as Justice," *Social Philosophy & Policy*, vol. 18, 2001, pp. 115–45. © 2001, Social Philosophy & Policy Foundation. Reprinted with permission from the author and Cambridge University Press.

or not. For example, one might urge, as did Bentham, that rules made by courts as they decided cases were not law, and that the idea of a common law of decided cases was wholly illusory.[6] The fourth item calling for some judgment of legality has to do with what lawyers call the "law of the case."[7] Such law consists of singular propositions of law, such as "This contract is valid." These propositions apply only to the particular facts of a given legal dispute, but on those facts they are dispositive; they declare the legal rights and legal duties of particular parties in particular situations.

There is even a fifth sort of judgment we make that is closely related to these four. This is the judgment we make about *areas* of law. That is, admitting that we are in a *legal* system and that some rule or other institution is *legal* in character, we may nevertheless be puzzled about whether this rule or institution is part of one area of law rather than another.[8] The sort of judgments I have in mind include whether punitive-damages rules are part of criminal law or of tort law and whether rules for construing leases are part of contract law or property law. In such cases, doubt is not felt about the legality of the rules, but rather about what *kind* of law the rules are.

The relational thesis of natural law may be asserted at any of these five levels. That is, a natural lawyer may assert: (a) that a social system is a legal system only if it exceeds some threshold of justice in its overall operation; (b) that a rule is a law only if in content or in its operation it is not too unjust; (c) that a class of rules is part of the law only if as a class the rules serve some overall good; (d) that some actual (or predicted) judicial order is the law of the case for which it is (or will be) made only if that order is not too unjust; or (e) that an individual law is part of some discrete area of law only if this individual law serves the value(s) distinctive of that area of law. The natural lawyer who interests me asserts all five of these varieties of the relational thesis. I shall not in this essay attempt to analyze the natural law position with respect to all five of these varieties. Rather, I shall focus on the second and fourth, that is, on laws and laws of cases. My hope is that the problems and solutions explored in these more particular areas can be broadened to the more general topics of law (as legal system), kinds of law, and areas of law.

Before turning to the relational thesis with respect to laws and laws of cases, I shall explore some preliminary matters in the immediately succeeding sections. In Section II, I lay out the traditional argument for the natural lawyer's relational thesis, an argument that focuses on the idea of legal obligation. In Section III, I explore the typical way that natural lawyers have argued for law's necessarily obligating force, a mode of argument based on a functional analysis of law, laws, laws of cases, etc. In Section IV, I deal with two rather general objections to the functionalist program outlined in Section III, objections that cut across all five of the varieties of the natural lawyer's relational thesis. After these general preliminaries, I then turn to the relational thesis for laws of cases (Section V) and for laws (Section VI).

II.   The Traditional Argument for the Relational Thesis

The dominant mode of arguing for the relational thesis (at all levels of generality) has centered on the idea of obligation, an idea thought to be crucial to legality. The idea is that law must be distinct from the order of a gunman writ large (to paraphrase Augustine[9]) and that what makes law distinct from mere force lies in the ability of law to obligate obedience rather than merely coerce it. Let us call this step one of the natural lawyer's argument for the relational thesis. As Aquinas summarized this step: law necessarily binds the conscience.[10]

The second step of the argument is to assert that only that which is morally just (or at least "good enough for government work") can bind the conscience. The first idea here is that there is only one kind of obligation, and that is moral obligation.[11] It is not that we cannot give sense to the idea of a legal obligation. A legal obligation, on this view, just is a moral obligation with respect to some legal institution. This makes legal obligation a kind of moral obligation, rather than something distinct from moral obligation. The second idea here, one that is more central, is that legal obligations – moral obligations created by man-made rules – can exist only if those rules are not too unjust in content. The plausible thought is that no one can be morally obligated by morally evil rules.

The two-step argument to the natural lawyer's conclusion is thus:

(1)   Something is legal only if it obligates.
(2)   Something obligates only if it is not unjust.
(3)   Therefore, something is legal only if it is not unjust.

There are other routes to establishing the natural lawyer's conclusion. One might urge a conventionalist semantic thesis by purporting to discover in the usages of "law," "*droit*," "*recht*," etc. a common criterion of correct usage that is moral in character.[12] Alternatively, one might view law as an "interpretive concept," and then urge that the best interpretation of that concept is one linking law to morality.[13] One might also do a cosmopolitan sociology, abstracting from social practices the world over those universally treated as *legal* practices in their respective cultures, and discover that practices are treated as legal only if such practices are also moral.[14]

The traditional argument of the natural lawyer as I have reconstructed it above is different than these semantic, interpretive, or sociological modes of argument. In contrast to all of these, the traditional argument is refreshingly *practical*. In its first step, it treats law as something of practical relevance – law changes what we have reason to do.[15] If the argument's first premise is correct, then theorizing about law's nature will not be an academic pursuit in any pejorative sense, for what such theorizing seeks is the nature of one of the things that obligate us as rational and moral people. There is no "academic chalk dust" involved in such an approach, as there easily can be when one uses the semantic, interpretive, and sociological approaches sketched above.

Our practical interest in the traditional argument will be maintained no matter *who* it is that is necessarily obligated by law. There are two possibilities worth distinguishing here:[16] we might think that law *qua* law obligates everyone in the system, citizens to whom the law is applied as well as the judges who do the application of law to citizens. Alternatively, we might think that law necessarily obligates only judges; citizens, on this weaker view, might be obligated by various laws, but such items could be laws even if they did not obligate citizens to obey them. In either

case, the nature of law would be of practical interest to us. If the stronger view is true, of course, the law is of practical interest because we have an interest in knowing what we are obligated to do. Even on the weaker view, we would all have prudential reasons for wanting to know what judges are obligated to do, for even though few of us are judges, it is judges who sanction our behavior.

III.   The Functionalist Argument for Law's Binding Force

It is the argument for the first premise in the traditional argument above that interests me here. Specifically, my focus is on what I shall call the *functionalist argument*. This is the argument used by natural lawyers to establish that something can be law only if it obligates someone, citizens or (at least) judges.

The general form of the functionalist argument is best displayed as having three premises:

(1)   Something X is law only if it serves the distinctive function(s) of law.
(2)   The distinctive function(s) of law is Y.
(3)   Y is served only if X obligates.
(4)   Therefore, something is law only if it obligates.

In more colloquial English, the first premise asserts that law is a *functional kind*, that is, a kind whose essence is to be found in the value(s) it serves more than by the unique structural features it may possess. This functionalist premise applies to the various aspects of law; consider, for example, legal systems. Just like a human heart may have quite diverse structural realizations and still be a heart because it performs the function distinctive of hearts (i.e., pumping blood), so legal systems may be realized through quite different institutions and still be legal systems because they perform the function(s) distinctive of such systems.

One can carry the functionalist premise down to laws, kinds of law, the laws of cases, and areas of law. The premise would hold, for example, that one decides if some rule is a law by examining the purpose such a rule serves (that is, its value or function) rather than the rule's structural features, such as its exact wording in some statute or precedent court's opinion. Analogously, rules used by courts to decide cases make up a distinctive kind of law ("common law") because they serve a common function or value. A law governing the rights and duties of particular parties in some particular case is what it is by virtue of the value(s) it serves, not in virtue of, say, the fact that it was stated by some judge at a certain point in proceedings involving the parties. Finally, an individual law is part of criminal law, for example, if the law serves the function distinctive of criminal law, irrespective of whether the law is called "criminal" and irrespective of things like the sanction attached to the law.

The second premise involves specification of the value that makes something into a legal system, a law, a certain kind of law, a law of a case, or an area of law. About legal systems, for example, one might claim that the function of law as such is, among other possibilities, the preservation of order;[17] the coordination of individual goods into the common good;[18] the furtherance of community made possible by an "integrated" treatment of all citizens;[19] or the enhancement of liberty made possible by clear, prospective rules.[20] About laws, the values served may be as diverse as the legitimate ends of legislation. The functionalist claim about a statute forbidding vehicles in a park, for example, might be that the application of such a rule is to be guided by the promotion of pedestrian safety more than by the literal meaning of the terms of such a statute – in which case, "what the law is" depends more on the values served by the statute in question than on its formal features.[21] About kinds of law, the values served are less various. With respect to common law, for example, the functionalist claim might be that such law serves the value of equality sloganized in the principle of formal justice that "like cases are to be treated alike."[22] We find more diversity of values when we consider areas of law. The functionalist claim here could be that criminal law, for example, serves a distinctive kind of justice, retributive justice,[23] whereas tort law serves another kind of justice, corrective justice, etc. When we finally consider the laws of a case, the values served may be even more various. Indeed, as I shall argue, any value whatsoever may be the value served by the law of a particular case.

The third premise asserts the truth of an instrumental calculation, a calculation about the means needed in order for law to serve its distinctive function. Specifically, the assertion is that the various goods of legal systems, laws, kinds of laws, areas of law, and laws of cases are served only if these items obligate obedience.

IV. Two General Problems with the Functionalist Argument for Natural Law

A. The alleged lack of any role for the obligatoriness of law in the functionalist argument for natural law

It may seem that a functionalist view of law is sufficient for the natural lawyer's conclusion, and that it therefore renders unnecessary the claim that something is legal only if it obligates. The idea here is that if law is a functional kind, then something must serve the values of law in order to be law, that is, only good law can be law at all.[24] This, it is urged, is the natural law conclusion, achieved without need of some intermediate premise of law's necessary obligatoriness.

There is this much truth to the charge: if law is a functional kind, then law must be of *some* value to be law at all. Yet that law is necessarily of some value is a very weak natural law thesis. Meticulous Nazis who dutifully observed the procedural niceties associated with the rule of law would create a system having *some* value, even though the content of their rules would be horribly unjust. If one identified the function of law as securing the procedural values of the rule of law, then one could say that such Nazis would have law. Yet any natural law worth talking about should resist being satisfied with this conclusion, and should deny that the system these Nazis would create is a legal system. An acceptable natural law theory should maintain that there is law only if the overall justice of a system reaches a level that obligates at least judges within the system, and this will require that the natural lawyer depend on a premise involving law's obligatoriness.

One might well think that there is some life to the objection, even conceding this reply. Suppose some function for law is discovered that does guarantee that if something is law, it is sufficiently just so as to obligate obedience. In such a case, the obligatoriness of law would do no work in the natural lawyer's argument. That is, the functionalist would have shown that law and morality are necessarily connected because anything, to be law, must be strongly moral. Because anything strongly moral is also plausibly thought to be obligatory, the functionalist would have therefore shown that law is obligatory. But the claim that something is legal only if it obligates would be logically epiphenomenal to the natural law conclusion, not a necessary step in the argument for that conclusion.

What this amended objection reveals is that the functionalist approach to natural law could proceed in a manner analogous to the semantic, interpretive, or sociological approaches mentioned earlier. Such a direct functionalist approach to jurisprudence would dispense with the traditional natural law argument and cut straight to its conclusion upon the discovery of a functionalist essence to law. This would occur in much the same way that the semantic, interpretive, and sociological approaches proceed directly to the natural lawyer's conclusion from, respectively, certain linguistic facts about usage of "law," the discoveries that law is an interpretive concept and that "law as integrity" is the best interpretation of it, or some social facts about law in all cultures.

Like these other approaches, a direct functionalist approach to the essence of law is certainly possible. However, like those other approaches, the direct functionalist approach does not include a role for legal obligation and therefore does not show that law has practical relevance. The virtue of the traditional argument's focus on someone's (judge or citizen) obligation is that this focus does give law such relevance. This relevance, in turn, gives us argumentative tools that we lack if we adopt the more abstract, direct approaches. The philosopher Joel Feinberg once confessed that he was at a loss in considering how to establish the natural lawyer's relational thesis if one left aside the obligations of some role, such as a judge.[25] While this may be too strong, Feinberg nicely captures the argumentative advantage provided by the traditional argument's focus on legal obligation, particularly the legal obligations of judges.

B.   The alleged incompatibility between law's necessary obligating character and its functionalist nature

In contrast to the previous objection, which construed the functionalist approach to be so *strong* that it begged the question of law's nature as value-laden, another objection regards the approach as necessarily too *weak*. According to this objection, no system can actually obligate obedience unless it is in the service of all the values there are. One can see this objection most clearly by adverting to the third premise in the functionalist argument. This premise not only says that obligation is a *necessary* condition of something serving law's distinctive value(s); it equivalently says that something serving law's distinctive value(s) is a *sufficient* condition for that thing to be obligatory. Yet how can this be? After all, it is highly implausible to think that there is some one value that is so good that it outweighs all other values when they conflict, and less plausible still to think that this dominant value is *the* value served by law. What anyone is actually obligated to do is plausibly a function of all the values there are, so if the values law necessarily serves are limited in the way functionalism asserts, how could law always be obligating?

The only way the functionalist argument can go through in the face of this objection is if the distinctive value(s) that makes an institution legal is connected to all the values there are in such a way that to serve law's value is to serve all values. Then legality could plausibly be sufficient for obligation in the way asserted by the functionalist's argument. The history of post-World War II natural law jurisprudence can be seen as the search for just such a value. Lon Fuller, for example, held that law has a procedural goal as its essential function.[26] For Fuller, the function of all law is the exercise of social control through general rules. If rules are prospective, clear, general, consistently applied, possible to comply with, stable, public, etc., then citizens know what is expected of them, the administration of justice is not ad hoc and arbitrary, and law is efficiently self-executing for properly motivated citizens.

Considering Fuller's account, Herbert Hart put forth a version of the objection we are considering here, claiming that the procedural goal of law could be attained by a regime whose laws were nevertheless ruthlessly evil in their content.[27] In such a "Hell where due process was meticulously observed,"[28] there would be no obligation of citizens to obey the edicts of the regime, nor would even judges have an obligation to enforce them.

Fuller's response to Hart's version of the objection reveals clearly what the natural lawyer needs here. Fuller's faith was that if people "do things the right way" (i.e., fulfill law's procedural goals), then they will "do the right things" (i.e., have laws that are substantively just).[29] Few have shared Fuller's faith in the power of good procedure to make for good substance, but his answer illustrates clearly the problem facing a functionalist natural lawyer. The problem is to derive obligation (of citizens or even judges) out of the limited values thought to be law's essential function; for when those limited values conflict with the many other values that exist, why are citizens or even judges obligated by only those values giving law its point?

One sees the same problem driving John Finnis in his resuscitation of Aquinas's view that the function of human law is to serve the common good.[30] The common good occupies a special place in Finnis's theory of value. It is not one of the seven basic goods that Finnis believes exist. Rather, the common good is that set of conditions that enables members of political communities to attain for themselves the seven basic goods, not just individually but through coordinated activities; these conditions also enable individuals to enjoy the good of cooperating with others generally, which is itself part of the common good.[31] Importantly, Finnis seeks to link this goal of law to the seven basic goods: "There is a 'common good' for human beings, inasmuch as life, knowledge, play, aesthetic experience, friendship, religion, and freedom in practical reasonableness are good for any and every person. And each of these human values is itself a 'common good'."[32] If this is right, then to serve the goal of law – the common good – is to serve something good for its own sake – human cooperation – which is also good because it serves all the values there are. This is both a plausible basis for obligation and a strong version of natural law.

As a last example, consider Ronald Dworkin's attempt to show that all law serves the function of "integrity."[33] Integrity is not one of the four

political goods that Dworkin posits (these goods, he says, are distributive justice, fairness, procedural fairness, and fraternity). Rather, integrity is the good of a political community speaking with one voice. It is a mode of promoting the four political goods, a mode that is distinctively that of law. Integrity is thus served only when all political goods are served, and for the law to serve integrity will be for it to serve such goods. If this is true, then again, law exists only when it strongly serves the good, and law can plausibly be supposed to obligate (necessarily) both citizen obedience and judicial enforcement.

It is not my purpose here to assess the adequacy of these three contemporary functionalist natural law accounts, nor even to consider whether any such general account of law can succeed. Rather, I shall pursue the functionalist strategy at a much lower level of generality. In the succeeding sections, I shall deal with the laws of cases and with laws, suggesting as I go how one might generalize what we learn there to legal systems, kinds of law, or areas of law.

V.   The Functionalist Account of the Laws of Cases

One may plausibly suppose that the law of a case before a formal decision in that case is rendered by a judge differs from the law of a case after such a decision. I shall therefore divide my discussion along this temporal dimension.

A.   The law of the case prior to decision

Here we are met at the outset with the claim that there is no law of the case until the judge in that case decides it. According to this claim, there may be "predicted law" or "probable law," but there is no "actual law" until a judicial order is entered.[34] This view of law is analogous to the view of a baseball umpire whose slogan is "They ain't nothing 'til I call 'em." Even Hart held this view at one time; this was when he was under the sway of J. L. Austin's developing views of "performative utterances."[35] Hart urged that singular propositions of law, such as "This contract is valid," have no truth value until the requisite performance by a judge makes them true by assertion.[36]

Yet this old legal realist view of the law of cases cannot be sustained. Judges do not (always and necessarily) create legal rights and legal duties at the time of adjudication; in some cases, at least, they discover the antecedently existing rights and duties of the parties, rights and duties that existed when the parties acted prior to adjudication. In these cases, then, the parties had legal obligations with respect to each other prior to any judicial pronouncement, and the judge's obligation is to describe accurately what those citizens' obligations were.

One could, of course, drive a wedge between citizen/judicial obligation, on the one hand, and law, on the other. That is, one could insist that there is no law for a particular case until a judge makes some, even while conceding that citizens are obligated as if there is law and judges are obligated to *make* law consistent with such citizen obligations. But what would be the point of such insistence? If citizens are obligated by some standards, and if judges in their role as judges are obligated to decide against those breaking these obligations, then why should we refuse to call such standards law? With such refusal, theorizing about law's nature would lose the practical significance discussed earlier, and such theorizing would become a pejoratively academic enterprise.

Let us assume, then, that there are laws of cases prior to judicial decisions. We next need to flesh out the functionalist account of such laws. Consider the law of a case arising under a statute. In such cases, whether the singular proposition of law that decides the case is law wholly depends on a valid interpretation of the statute. If valid interpretations of statutes always involve values, then so do the laws of cases arising under such statutes.

We need an example; consider one presented by Fuller.[37] Two citizens are arrested under a city ordinance forbidding anyone to "sleep in the train station." The first defendant is a ticketed passenger waiting for his train; he nodded off while he was seated. The second defendant is a homeless person ("bum," in Fuller's day) who had spread out his belongings on the floor of the station and lain down, but was arrested before he had actually fallen asleep.

The first defendant presents what Aquinas would call a tension between the "letter" and the "spirit" of the city ordinance.[38] The letter of the ordinance is its literal meaning; literally, defendant one was asleep, so the letter of the ordinance would require his conviction. The spirit of the ordinance is the function or value it serves; if that function is to prevent the use of the railroad station for overnight accommodations, defendant one's conviction would not serve the spirit of the ordinance. Aquinas persuasively argues that in cases where the letter and spirit of a statute conflict, the spirit should prevail. The correct law of the case here is thus, "Defendant one is not guilty of sleeping in the train station."

Much ink has been spilt defending and attacking Aquinas's theory of interpretation.[39] By my lights, its defenders have the better case and have carried the day with most judges in most legal systems. "Purposive interpretation" is now a staple of American jurisprudence. The result is that in our legal system, the truth value of the singular legal proposition, "Defendant one is not guilty of sleeping in the train station," depends as much on a matter of value (what this statute is good for) as on matters of value-neutral fact (such as the historical fact that such an ordinance was passed, or the semantic fact that "sleep" in ordinary English covers what defendant one did but not what defendant two did).

If Aquinas is both correct and generally followed by our judges, then some connection between law and morality has been made out. The singular propositions that decide concrete cases are propositions of *law* only insofar as they further the value behind certain general propositions of law (such as that supplied by the ordinance in the above example).

Legal positivists have three routes open to them to deny this connection between law and morality. One is to deny that the spirit of a statute should trump the letter of that statute. Although Fuller thought Hart advocated such a "plain meaning" approach,[40] clearer examples of this sort of positivism are to be found elsewhere. Particularly with the Reagan/Bush appointments to the federal bench in America, one increasingly encounters the view that the law of some case under a statute is a function exclusively of the historical facts surrounding a statute's passage and of the semantic facts giving the words of a statute their normal meaning. Under this view, when a statute's meaning is plain, judges should not hesitate to flout the purpose of the statute if it conflicts with this meaning; when the meaning is not plain, there is no law of cases brought up under that statute until judges make some law for those cases through their orders.[41]

Fortunately, this plain meaning route (also called "literalism" or "strict constructionism") is mouthed more than it is actually applied. Few judges can actually stomach applying a statute so as to fulfill its literal meaning while frustrating its purpose.[42] Justice Oliver Wendell Holmes lampooned this sort of statutory application, noting that judges who engaged in it would in effect be saying to the legislature, "I see what you are driving at but you have not said it so we shall go on as before."[43]

A second route for the legal positivist here is to deny that the function or purpose of a statute is a value. On this view, the purpose of a statute is just another value-neutral fact of history – it is what the legislature intended to achieve in passing the statute. If judges decide the laws of cases under statutes by referring to this factual criteria, then nothing in these decisions depends on a connection between law and morality.[44]

The problems with this "originalist" kind of positivism are legion and well known.[45] It is unclear what sense can be given to the idea of a legislature's intention. If fictionalized, it loses its status as merely a historical fact.[46] If reduced to the intentions held by a majority of individual legislators, it rarely exists and has little normative appeal because the legislature's job in passing a statute is not to have a "moment of shared intention," but to express, in some shared language, whatever mix of different intentions there might be.[47] In addition, even if one can make complete sense of a normatively attractive model of legislative intent, such intent would not prevent the laws of cases under statutes from having a connection to values. Suppose, for example, the town council's intent in passing the no-sleeping ordinance described above was to avoid the annoyance, overcrowding, and danger that would be created were the train station to become a de facto shelter for the homeless. This could give a judge the line of march in applying the ordinance, but it does not tell her how far to go in this direction. Achieving the ordinance's end has to be balanced against the costs (to other values) of such achievement. It is not obvious, for example, that a judge should prevent the station from

being used as a shelter in cases where people are dazed or injured in the aftermath of a train wreck or other disaster. As a second example, consider defendant two in Fuller's hypothetical. Although his conviction would serve the purpose of the ordinance, he was not literally asleep and the heightened importance we attach to notice in criminal cases might well prevent his conviction.

Hart charted a third route to denying the connection of laws of cases to morality. This was based on the observation that even putting the best possible moral face on a thoroughly iniquitous statute could result in very unjust applications of that statute.[48] For example, a judge could attribute the best possible purpose to the antebellum fugitive slave laws in America and still end up applying such laws in a way that involves little justice.[49]

Both Hart's objection and the previous objection reveal something touched on earlier: they both show how weakly connected law may be to morality under the functionalist approach to natural law. According to these objections, that the law of some case serves *some* good (i.e., the function of that law) does not generate much confidence that this law of a case serves *the* good in any comprehensive sense. The point here is a perfectly general one about functional kinds. It is plausible to suppose that mousetraps have a function (namely, catching mice), and that the service of this function is what makes something a mousetrap. Even so, the best mousetrap may not be the device that is best at catching mice, for other values may intrude when one is judging whether a mousetrap is good enough for service.[50] For example, a safety-catch that decreases something's efficiency of mouse-catching but increases the safety of humans who use it may make the thing in question a better mousetrap. The unsafe mousetrap *is* a mousetrap, because it serves the function distinctive of mousetraps; yet this does not guarantee that it is good enough to use.

At the level of legal systems, as we have seen, contemporary theorists have sought to connect the attainment of law's general function to the service of all the values there are. With regard to mousetraps, this move would be analogous to asserting that a mousetrap good at catching mice could not be unsafe for human use (because, e.g., even if it were somewhat less safe than other mousetraps, its greater effectiveness would lead to it being used less frequently, and hence to overall safer mouse-catching). For the laws of cases, however, such a move is implausible. The value served by the law of a particular case is too discrete to permit one to have much confidence that the law of a particular case respects all of the values there are.

Consider, in this regard, the case of *Kirby v. United States*.[51] In *Kirby*, the defendant had stopped a steamboat in order to detain a federal mail carrier. The defendant was accordingly arrested and convicted of the federal crime of "obstructing or retarding the passage of the US Mail." He was convicted despite the fact that he was a sheriff and despite the fact that he stopped the steamboat in order to arrest the mail carrier for murder under a valid state bench warrant.

By my lights, the defendant sheriff satisfied the literal meaning of the words used in the federal statute – literally, he did obstruct and retard the passage of the US mail. In addition, his conviction would serve the seeming purpose of the federal statute, which was to secure the passage of federal mail in a federal system made up of independent state authorities. Nonetheless, the law of the case that the judge was obligated to apply was that the defendant did not obstruct or retard the passage of the US mail. Another value intrudes here, namely, the value of getting murderers off the street (or, as it happened, the river). This value easily trumps the slightly increased speed in the passage of the mail that is attainable, if murderous mail carriers are considered immune to state arrest while carrying the mail. Moreover, this intruding value can in no sense be encapsulated within the purpose of the obstruction statute. Making certain that murderers get their just deserts is a real good, as is making sure they are not free to murder again. However, these are not the goods that are the function of the obstruction statute; they are extraneous to that statute's purpose and for that reason I call judgments using such extraneous values "safety-valve judgments."

The functionalist approach to the laws of cases is thus unable to generate a natural law view of such laws without some external support. The functionalist approach connects the laws

of cases to values, but only weakly so, and too weakly to make the laws of cases congruent with judicial obligation. Cases like *Kirby* make explicit that the obligation of a judge in a particular case is to balance (1) the political values that are served by adhering to the ordinary semantic meaning of words used in the relevant statute, (2) the function this statute should be seen to serve, and (3) all values impacted by a provisional interpretation of the statute that is based solely on that statute's semantics or function.[52] The outcome of this balance of values constitutes the law of the case: it is a judge's obligation to find this law, and a citizen's obligation to obey it. This is a natural law conclusion about the laws of cases, a conclusion that functionalism by itself cannot generate.

This conclusion seems to be established instead by some nonfunctionalist argument for the first step of the traditional argument for natural law, namely, the claim that something needs to obligate to be law. Aquinas himself attempts to establish the necessary obligatoriness of law with some dubious etymology of "*ligare*," the Latin word for law.[53] Even if his etymology were correct, however, such a semantic approach to the question could not establish the point.

The point is better supported by three different observations. First, at least when dealing with the laws of cases within some legal system, law should be a concept holding our practical interest. One possibility here is that our concept of the laws of cases should answer to a citizen's purely prudential interest in avoiding legal sanctions. Such a prudential interest easily generates Holmes's famous predictive theory of the laws of cases: the law is a prediction of judicial force.[54] As is well known, however, such a prudentially oriented notion of law is wholly inadequate for judges or other legal officials, for it is not plausible to suppose that they are engaged in the task of predicting either their own decisions or the decisions of those with power to discipline them.[55]

A concept of law of practical interest to both judges and citizens will therefore be tied to what judges *should* do in some cases, not to what they *will* do. For law to be practically interesting, then, it must generate reasons for action for at least some actors within a legal system. This poses a problem for legal positivists, for if law is not obligatory in nature, as they argue, then it is hard to see how law could provide reasons and therefore be practically interesting. Legal positivists who see this problem respond by claiming that they can remain unengaged (or "detached"[56]) in their jurisprudence. Such positivists argue that the law must "claim" to create reasons for action for certain people,[57] or that certain actors must believe or "accept" that law creates such reasons for action, without such positivists themselves asserting that law does actually create reasons for action.[58]

This detachment might be possible when one does jurisprudence externally, that is, outside any particular legal system.[59] When dealing with singular propositions of law from inside a legal system, however, we cannot remain so detached. If, for example, an American citizen or judge wishes to apply the positivists' concept of law in general to American law, he will have to drop the detachment. This is because these "unengaged" positivist concepts of law require us to believe that if some singular proposition is one of law, then we must believe that this proposition *describes* a reason for us to act. If we believe this, however, then we must believe that the proposition actually *gives* us a reason to act. That is, we are committed to the proposition in fact giving us a reason for action because it is a proposition *of law*. The upshot at this point is that if one wishes to have a notion of law that is of practical interest, but wants to avoid the Holmesian identification of the laws of cases with predicted judicial force, then one is committed to the view that if a singular proposition is part of the law of one's jurisdiction, then that proposition necessarily gives someone a reason for action.

The second point suggesting that laws of cases are obligatory has to do with the kind of reason for action that law generates. Law will hold some practical interest for us if it simply generates *a* reason for someone within our legal system to act in one way rather than another. Yet law will hold much more practical interest for us if it generates not only *a* reason for action, but a *conclusive* (or nearly conclusive) reason for such action, the kind of reason we commonly call an obligation. If law generates this kind of reason, then the question of whether some proposition is one of law grabs our attention in the way that the question of whether we promised to do

something grabs our attention: answers to each of these questions often tell us what we ought to do.

Perhaps one can derive this obligatoriness of the laws of cases from the function of law in general. Consider, again, the analogy of promises. One argument for why promises create an obligation to do the promised act, as opposed to merely creating a reason to do that act, stems from a functionalist view of promising. Suppose the practice of promise-making has as its function the good of social cooperation, both for its own sake and for the further good such cooperation makes possible. The functionalist argument would be that social cooperation is only possible if the parties to a promise believe that promises create obligations, a belief the parties can sustain only if promises do in fact create obligations. The good that gives promising its point justifies regarding promises as obligation-creating acts and not merely reason-creating acts. Analogously, one might think that law in general has the function of serving the common good or of making social cooperation possible, and that for this good to be served, the laws of cases must be regarded as obligatory, and therefore must actually be obligatory.

Putting aside this very general functionalist argument, which proceeds from some controversial views of law's general function, let us consider, as a kind of *reductio* argument, the alternative to identifying singular propositions of law with someone's obligation. Suppose in a case like *Kirby*, we identify the singular proposition of law for that case as the singular proposition that is logically derivable from that general proposition consisting of the plain meaning of the federal obstruction statute. On a literal reading of "obstruction," Sheriff Kirby literally obstructed the passage of the US mail when he arrested the murderous mail carrier; thus, the singular proposition of law in this case would be "Kirby is guilty of obstructing the passage of the US mail." Now suppose that we divorce the law from judicial obligation by saying that Kirby is guilty according to the law, but that Kirby's legal obligation was to do just what he did and that the trial judge's legal obligation according to the law is to hold Kirby not guilty of obstructing the passage of the US mail. This view is one held by some positivists, including, notably, legal philosopher Andrei Marmor.[60]

It is pretty clear that what motivates views such as Marmor's is the desire to keep singular propositions of law free from the contamination of value judgments, specifically, those value judgments needed to assess a statute's "spirit" and the "all-things-considered safety-valve judgments" mentioned earlier. Yet Marmor, like others, is unwilling to stomach the preposterous results reached if one truly follows a plain meaning interpretive theory. So he cleaves judicial obligation from the law, and the judge is therefore obligated – *qua* judge, *legally* obligated – to decide contrary to law!

Surely we do not want to do this to our concept of law. If one identifies the law of the case in *Kirby* as the exclusive dictate of the ordinary meaning of "obstruct" in the relevant statute, then the "law" created only *a* reason for Kirby to act in one way, and *a* reason for a judge to sanction him if he acted the other way. Stronger reasons *not* of the law's creation urged Kirby not to act as the law dictated, and those same non-law-created reasons urged the judge not to sanction Kirby for violating the law. What the law is, on this view of law, simply is not a very interesting question. The law, on this view of it, is simply a bit player in the balance of reasons justifying both citizen and judicial behavior. Indeed, one would be hard-pressed to make much sense of the ideal of the "rule of law" because in no sense would law (so conceived) rule anyone's behavior.

The third point in favor of the obligatoriness of laws of cases has to do with who it is that is necessarily obligated by law. The traditional jurisprudential answer, common to both natural lawyers and legal positivists, has been *judges*: the law necessarily obligates judges to decide in accordance with it. Even Hart, who was openly critical of American jurisprudence for its "obsession" with judges,[61] himself created a general theory of law in which the obligations (real or perceived) of judges are central.[62]

Whether the real or perceived obligations of judges are indeed central to there being a legal system is an interesting question, but it is not our question here. Whatever one thinks of judicial obligation as the touchstone of the legality of whole social systems, surely *judicial* obligation is intuitively most closely connected to the legality of singular propositions. If the law of the *Kirby* case was that Kirby was not guilty of obstructing

the passage of the US mail, then surely the judge's obligation was to find just that.[63]

In summary, then, I take the traditional argument for a natural law view of those singular legal propositions derived from statutes to be quite strong. This is because I find both steps of the natural lawyer's argument (which I reverse in order here in order to correspond with the argument of this section) to be intuitive at this level of legality. First, judges are obligated in cases like *Kirby* and Fuller's sleeping hypothetical to decide in accordance with "safety-valve" and "spirit" value judgments; second, the laws of such cases are to be identified with these value-laden decisions, not with some supposedly value-free ingredient in them (such as the relevant statutes' "plain meaning"). Functionalism, as we have seen, cannot sufficiently establish either step of the argument. The need to take into account the value or function served by some statute shows that a judge's obligation includes the obligation to make value judgments in his decisions, but cases like *Kirby* remind us that simply serving such a function is an insufficient basis on which to justify a judicial decision. Some general function of all law might support the obligation of a judge to decide in accordance with the law of some case, but this obligation seems supportable without reliance on some general function of all law. Functionalism, in short, supports but does not itself generate a natural law theory of the singular propositions of law arising under statutes.

B.   The law of a case after a final judicial decision

The status of the law of a particular case may seem to change radically after a judge renders a decision. If the time for appeal has expired, or if no appeal can be taken because the court making the decision is the highest court, then the judge's decision is final. This decision, whatever it is, seems to fix the rights and duties of the parties irrevocably; moreover, it seems to do so all by itself.

The irrevocability of such a decision is termed its "*res judicata* effect." Even if the decision is later "strictly confined to its facts," or even overruled in another case, the decision stands with respect to the parties in the original case. For example, even if a judge's conclusion that there is a valid contract between two parties is erroneous, once that decision is final, the parties have the rights and duties of contracting parties.

The seeming sufficiency of the decision to constitute the law of the case may be seen by supposing a completely erroneous decision. If the parties are stuck with such a decision as determinative of their rights and duties, that would show the sufficiency of the decision itself, whatever it is, to constitute the law of their case. Prior to such an erroneous decision, we may suppose that everything (plain meaning, spirit, safety-valve considerations) supported the claim that the truth value of the singular legal proposition "This contract is invalid" was "true"; after the erroneous decision, the truth value of that proposition, nonetheless, seems to be "false." The decision itself seems fully determinative of what the law of this case now is.

Legal positivists should like this account of the law of a case quite a bit. After all, on this account the truth of such singular propositions of law seems to turn on a pure matter of nonmoral fact, namely, the historical fact that the relevant judge decided as she did. The clarity and simplicity of this view, then, inclines the positivist toward the legal realist idea that until the judge makes a decision, there is no law of a particular case.

Unfortunately for the positivist, however, none of this is as it seems. To begin with, we have good reasons, as discussed above, for saying that there is a law for a case prior to some judge deciding it. Furthermore, although a judgment in a case is almost always given res judicata effect as the law of the case, that this is so is due to a balancing of values (not solely because of some historical fact), *and*, when that balance tips the other way, it is not so at all.

The doctrine that a legal judgment, once rendered, should conclude the dispute between the parties is justified by important considerations. These include the undesirability of favoring the tireless and the wealthy in disputes, the undesirability of allowing multiple attempts at establishing liability, and the desirability of promoting efficient adjudication by giving litigants incentives to present their best case on the first try. We might think of these considerations as the additional functions served by the law of a case once a decision has been reached ("additional" because the basic function essential to the law of a case,

irrespective of whether a judge has actually decided the matter, is the fixing of the legal rights and duties of the parties). Such considerations supporting res judicata may well be so strong that they almost always justify both a judge in refusing to "overrule" a prior ruling on the law of a case and a citizen subject to the ruling from disobeying it. The considerations are not so strong, however, as to make res judicata into the hard and fast rule many lawyers pretend it to be.

Consider a case in which (1) the mother is declared unfit in a child custody proceeding because the judge concludes, erroneously under the laws of his jurisdiction, that the mother's full-time employment disqualifies her from being a fit parent; (2) the father is erroneously declared fit because the judge does not know that the father has sexually abused the child; and (3) the judge, on the basis of the determinations mentioned in (1) and (2), enters a judgment awarding exclusive custody to the father. It is clear to me that the mother in this case is not obligated to obey the court's judgment. Indeed, her obligation is to do whatever she can to protect her child; this includes secreting the child away from the father at the first opportunity. It is almost as clear that a judge who knows what the mother knows – that is, he knows how erroneous the custody judgment is in both law and fact – is obligated not to enforce it against the mother.[64] This position, of course, raises a procedural worry in that it will encourage litigants to reopen matters of fact and law that are already concluded, but this must be balanced against the worry that severe injustice can be caused if judges are given authority to fix irrevocably the legal rights and obligations of litigants.

What cases like the custody example show us is that when the level of injustice about to be caused by some judgment in a case is quite high, even the strong considerations in favor of res judicata yield. Thus, the judgment does not by itself obligate either citizen or judicial obedience. Rather, the content of such obligations is determined by a balance between the considerations behind res judicata and the considerations disserved by the judgment. Even when that balance tips in favor of the res judicata considerations – as it usually will in a reasonably just legal system – obligation follows this balance of values, not some value-free historical fact.

Here we again face a familiar possibility, that of cleaving obligation from the law of the case. Certainly an idiomatic way of describing the mother's obligation in a case like that above is to say, "She was obligated not to follow the law." We might even say this of the judge – that is, we might say that he was obligated not to enforce the law of that case. It is preferable, however, to keep citizen and judicial obligation in line with the law. If both judge and citizen were obligated to keep the child away from the abusive father before any judgment was entered, and they are similarly obligated after the judgment, then the law of the case did not change when the judgment was entered.

This way of looking at the matter is reinforced by the fact that when we determine that an earlier judgment was erroneous, it is desirable to be able to say that our later determination correcting this judgment is retroactively applicable.[65] Suppose that in the custody case, a later court finds that the initial judgment discussed above was erroneous. Between the time that the initial judgment was entered and the time that it is declared erroneous, what was the law of the case? Was it the erroneous judgment, which therefore both changed the pre-judgment law of the case and was itself changed by the subsequent determination of error? If so, then contempt charges would still be appropriate against the disobedient mother, and disciplinary proceedings would still be appropriate against a judge who had refused to enforce the custody order before the determination of error. Because these consequences are undesirable, it is better to treat the judgment subsequently determined to be erroneous as if it had never been the law of the case. On this view, the law of the case never changed, and no one can be punished for doing what he was obligated to do according to that law. Such a view requires us *not* to divorce obligation from legality, and thus *not* to see a judgment as itself constituting the law for its case.

The law of a case after a judgment is entered should thus be a function of exactly the same mixture of value judgments and historical/semantic facts that it was a function of prior to judgment. The difference is that to determine the law of a case after a judgment is entered, the balance of considerations that determined the law of the case prior to judgment must then itself be balanced against the considerations favoring finality of judgments. This view of the law of a case as a complex balance of values is still a natural law view. It is a view partly supported by a functionalist approach to the law of a case; however, just as functionalism is unable to ground the natural law view of cases prior to judgment, it is also insufficient for grounding a natural law view of the law of adjudicated cases.

VI. The Functionalist Account of Laws

As with the laws of cases, when we speak of the legality of general standards, it is helpful to separate discussion of laws prior to enactment from discussion of laws after positive enactment by some legal institution (i.e., a court, legislature, constitutional convention, administrative agency, etc.). Having used statutes previously in my discussion of the laws of cases, in this section I shall focus on the laws that arise from court decisions – what Anglo-American lawyers call the common law.

A.   Common law without controlling precedent

In this subsection, I shall suppose what common law lawyers call a "case of first impression." These are cases where there is no precedent case "on all fours" with the case under consideration, nor is there some entrenched rule of the common law. Of thousands of possible examples in American law, I shall consider *Union Pacific Railway v. Cappier*.[66]

Decided in 1903, *Cappier* put before the Kansas Supreme Court the issue of Good Samaritan duties in tort where the defendant had innocently caused the victim to be in peril. The Union Pacific Railway had nonnegligently run down a trespassing youth named Cappier; the railroad engine severed one of the boy's arms and one of his legs. The railroad's employees stopped its train, ascertained Cappier's injuries, moved him to the side of the track, and went on. Cappier subsequently bled to death, and his mother brought suit.

By 1903, the Kansas courts had not yet spoken on the question of whether strangers who

nonculpably place another in peril have a positive duty to rescue the victim from that peril. Prior
to 1903, it had been established that in general,
strangers owe one another no positive duties
of aid in either criminal law or tort; with few
exceptions, Kansas tort law held there to be only
negative duties not to cause injury to others
through our actions. Yet the question of whether
those who nonculpably place a stranger in peril
might owe that stranger a positive duty of rescue
had not been faced by the Kansas courts.

In a situation like this, some legal positivists
are tempted by the view that there are no laws
governing such cases. They would argue for this
view here by noting that no statutory or constitutional rule dealt with this province of the
common law, and that no common law rule
had been established by prior cases in Kansas.
Yet this view runs afoul of Dworkin's well-
known arguments that parties to lawsuits such
as *Cappier* have legal rights and legal duties even
in the absence of any obvious legal rules governing their case.[67] Dworkin's long-held "rights
thesis" holds that there are legal rights even in
the hardest of cases, and that the generation of
such legal rights requires that there be more laws
than meet the eye.[68]

Dworkin's argument for the rights thesis
was partly derived from observations of Anglo-
American legal practice. Litigants like Mrs.
Cappier do not appear before judges as suppli-
cants of judicial favor, pleading for a favorable
exercise of the judge's discretion to *create* a legal
right for them. Rather, such litigants appear as
claimants of legal rights, legal rights whose existence must predate any declaration by the judge
that they exist. Supplementing this inference
from legal practice were Dworkin's arguments
from certain ideals about the rule of law. Judges,
he noted, do not make law (a job for the legislature); instead, they apply antecedently existing laws
to the facts of cases. Furthermore, judges do not
retroactively apply laws to transactions that took
place before such laws came into existence; they
apply laws that existed when the parties acted.

In other work, I have sought to supplement
Dworkin's arguments here in two ways.[69] First, no
one, to my knowledge, urges that judges should
resolve cases of first impression by flipping
coins, holding contests of strength between the
litigants, using medieval flotation tests, or in any

other way utilizing an admittedly arbitrary decision procedure. Hart and the contemporary legal
positivists who have followed Hart's lead universally concede that when judges run out of
obvious law in hard cases, they should repair
to various standards such as utility, efficiency,
liberty, and the like. However, positivism forces
these theorists to urge that such standards are not
legal standards, and that the rights such standards
generate are thus not *legal* rights until the judge
makes them so by his decision. Yet notice that
judges are obligated to use these standards; they
do not have any discretion in the matter. Since
this obligation arises for a judge in her role as
judge, we have every reason to think of the judge's
obligation to decide in favor of one party rather
than another as a *legal* obligation, to think of the
rights of the winning litigant as *legal* rights, and
to think of the standards that justify such legal
rights as *legal* standards, that is, laws.[70]

My second argument bolstering Dworkin's
rights thesis rests on the observation that the
standards judges do and ought to repair to in order
to decide hard cases in a nonarbitrary way satisfy
certain functional tests for laws. As part of law
generally, all laws serve at least the function of
making our obligations clearer to us than they
would be in the absence of laws. By serving such
a certainty-enhancing function, the general
standards used by judges in hard cases merit the
title "law."[71]

Assuming, then, that there are laws governing hard cases such as *Cappier*, we next need to
inquire into the status of these laws under the
natural law/legal positivism debate and the degree
to which the functionalist approach can support
the natural law view of the matter. Prima facie,
the natural law account of the laws governing
hard cases looks quite plausible. In *Cappier*, the
standards at issue included, among others, some
principle of liberty that makes it immoral for
the state to force us to do some positive action
that would prevent harm, even though the state
can properly force us to refrain from doing any
act that would cause that harm; some principle
according to which the causing of a peril that
ultimately becomes realized is enough causal
involvement in the victim's situation so as to
make the creator of the peril obliged to prevent
the harm whose risk he has created; and some
principle of corrective justice according to which

a duty to correct a harm (by paying compensation) arises whenever one is morally obliged to prevent that harm. If one holds that these are all *legal* principles because they are good moral principles, then this is pretty straightforwardly a natural law position about such standards.

There are two maneuvers that legal positivists might use to avoid the unwanted conclusion that the standards that decide hard cases are legal standards only insofar as they are moral standards. I will call these maneuvers the shallow positivist response and the deep positivist response.

A shallow positivist urges that the law contains default rules of the following form: if an act is not clearly prohibited by some law, then that act is permitted.[72] In *Cappier*, on this view, there is a standard that preexists the judge's decision and which decides the case, but it is not any of the moral principles listed earlier. Rather, the deciding standard is a default rule for torts: if an act is not one described by the existing causes of action for tort, then the law is that there is no tort cause of action. Since there was no common law rule granting Cappier a cause of action against a lapsed Good Samaritan who had caused the victim's condition of peril, the law of Kansas (i.e., the alleged default rule) provided that there was no cause of action against such lapsed Good Samaritans.

This shallow positivist response has both descriptive and normative problems. Descriptively, Anglo-American tort law does not contain such a default rule. As the late William Prosser noted in his famous hornbook on tort law, "There is no magic inherent in the name given to a tort, or in any arbitrary classification[.]" Rather, Prosser urged, Anglo-American tort law had proceeded on the basis that "it is the business of the law to remedy wrongs that deserve it[.]"[73] Normatively, any default rule that would bar novel (and therefore nameless) torts is a bad idea. As J. L. Austin once quipped, "fact is richer than diction."[74] The ways in which a culpable person can injure an innocent person have not all been tried; it being desirable that culpable people pay for the harms they cause innocent people, it is undesirable that the tort causes of action be frozen at the types of wrongdoing hitherto attempted.

The deep positivist response is very different from that of the shallow positivist. The deep positivist admits that there are nonobvious legal standards like the principle of liberty described above, but denies that these standards are part of the law because they are moral standards. Instead, the deep positivist says these standards are laws because they pass a value-free test of pedigree. If such principles are "incorporated by," "implied by," or "exemplified by" the more obvious common law rules, then by this test of logic and history alone, those principles are legal in character.[75]

The deep positivist tenders an extraordinary claim. About the common law, the claim is that in a well-established legal system such as ours, with its multitude of past decisions, even where there seemingly is no common law rule on point for a case of first impression, one unique principle adequate to decide that case can nonetheless be extracted from the existing rules by these value-free methods of incorporation, implication, and exemplification.

This claim runs head-on into undetermination worries. For any finite set of decided cases, there are an infinite number of general standards that would cover these cases as instances.[76] Moreover, with respect to any particular novel case to be decided, some of these standards will generate one result, while other standards will generate the opposite result. In other words, value-free extrapolation from past cases is indeterminate with respect to cases of first impression. The upshot of this is that there can be no purely factual pedigree for the legal standards used to decide hard cases. Such standards are in fact what they appear to be on their face: moral standards that are also legal standards because of their moral status.

This is a natural law conclusion about the laws that generate legal rights in hard cases, but the functional approach does little to establish it. True enough, one might conclude that some standard like the principle of liberty is a *legal* standard in part because of the increased certainty in hard cases that use of this principle makes possible. Yet surely judges should pick – and do pick – standards to resolve hard cases more by looking to the all-things-considered moral correctness of these standards than to the enhanced certainty that use of such principles makes possible. This certainty-enhancing function may be common to all legal principles that resolve hard cases, yet their service of this function cannot be the major reason for their selection.

B. Common law with precedent squarely on point

As with singular propositions of law, so here, once courts have issued a rule in prior cases that bears directly on some present case, things seem to be quite different. Except for those who identify law exclusively with either (1) singular propositions of law that decide cases (as did the legal realists), or (2) statutes (as did Bentham), everyone would admit there are laws here. Therefore, we again may put aside any worry that there is no law here to have a natural law theory about.

In the actual *Cappier* case, the Kansas Supreme Court held that the defendant railroad owed the deceased boy no positive duty of aid, despite the railroad's having nonculpably caused the boy's condition of peril. Suppose a similar case arises in Kansas in 1904, one year after the *Cappier* decision. In asking what the law is that governs my hypothesized 1904 case, we need to ask and answer two distinct questions. The first question is about the breadth of the rule laid down in *Cappier*: how similar must the 1904 case be to the facts of *Cappier* for the former to be governed by the common law rule that *Cappier* established? A narrow rule would require a great deal of similarity; a broader rule, less. The second question asks whether it is possible that the rule established in *Cappier* was not the law of Kansas – not in 1904, nor even in 1903. These two questions correspond to the two jurisprudential concerns about common law rules: (1) determining how one fixes the holding (or "*ratio decidendi*") of a precedent case like *Cappier*, and (2) ascertaining the force or "weight" of that holding for future cases. I consider each in turn.

1. *Extracting rules from precedent cases.* The two leading theories of holding are the classical theory and the legal realist theory.[77] According to the classical theory, the general proposition of law for which a precedent stands is the proposition stated as the holding in the precedent court's opinion. According to the legal realist theory of precedent, the holding of a precedent case is to be constructed by describing the facts of the precedent case and by noting what legal

action the precedent court took on those facts; the rule, on this view, is one enjoining future judges to take similar action when deciding cases with similar facts. There are variations and mixtures of these two views,[78] but this simple characterization will suffice for our purposes.

Which of these views one adopts depends on what one takes to be the function of giving precedential force to past decisions. To use Dickens's somber phraseology, why is it good that "dead men sit on our benches"? One response to this question is to say that this practice of *stare decisis* increases the predictability of judicial behavior, and that this is good because it makes adjudication more efficient, cuts down on the chilling of liberty that occurs when sanctions are uncertain, and reduces unfair surprise of citizens. Arguably at least, the classical theory serves these values best, because on this theory, to know the common law one need but open the case reports and read the stated rules.

Some, such as myself, have argued that the main value justifying *stare decisis* is equality.[79] The ideal of formal justice is that like cases should be treated alike, and this is achieved only if judges follow the judges who preceded them on some issue. It allows present judges to treat litigants equally (by coordinating around a salient past decision), and it treats present litigants the same way that earlier litigants were treated.

If formal equality is the function served by common law, then this argues against regarding the holding stated by the precedent court in its opinion to be the actual holding of the case. This is because of the fact that on this sort of formal-equality account, judging whether or not a subsequent case is like the precedent case (and thus deserving of like treatment) requires one to judge whether the cases are truly alike in morally relevant respects. Such equality judgments cannot simply adopt the categories stated in the precedent court opinion; instead, equality requires the subsequent court to penetrate the announced reach of the precedent court opinion and decide for itself what makes a relevant difference and what does not. Suppose, for example, that the Kansas Supreme Court had said in its *Cappier* opinion, "We hold that those who innocently cause a condition of peril for another owe that other no positive duty of rescue." By its terms, the stated holding does not apply to *culpable* causers of conditions of peril. Yet suppose a subsequent court deciding the 1904 case sees no relevant difference between innocent and culpable causers of some peril; in the court's view, neither sort of defendant involves himself so much in the victim's plight that he owes that victim a positive duty of rescue. Equality demands that the 1904 court ignore the limits on the holding of *Cappier* stated by the 1903 court, and substitute a broader rule for which *Cappier* stands: "causing a condition of peril, whether culpably or innocently, generates no positive duties of rescue." Only under this broader holding of *Cappier* can we treat the 1904 case like *Cappier* itself, because only under this broader holding can we use a nonarbitrary likeness between the facts of the two cases to judge whether the two cases are deserving of like treatment.

This formal-equality account is a natural law theory of the common law. This is because on this view the general rules that make up the common law are a blend of historical fact (what was decided in prior cases) and moral fact (how far the treatment accorded to litigants in the precedent cases should be projected to other, somewhat different cases, a matter of moral judgment). Such a natural law view, when generated exclusively by the functionalist argument, still presents the worry we have seen before: if precedent decisions are bad enough, there may be little one can do to construct a common law that is sufficiently moral to obligate the obedience of citizens and judges. It is via a doctrine of overruling that the common law surmounts this worry.

2. Overruling bad precedents. In addition to being able to broaden the apparent holding of precedent cases like *Cappier*, the common law has always had a variety of devices for *narrowing* the class of future cases to which precedent cases will apply. Precedent cases that have very expansive implications for future cases can nonetheless be narrowed by the time-honored expedient of distinguishing. Cases that are wrongly decided, root and branch, but which still deserve to be followed because of the values served by *stare decisis*, are often severely narrowed in their reach and may even be "confined to their facts," as lawyers often say. These narrowing techniques, along with the broadening techniques discussed above, are part of the common law's insistence on

continually rejudging what laws have been established by precedent cases.

Sometimes a precedent case is sufficiently in error such that neither the value it promotes nor the values promoted by *stare decisis* can obligate obedience to it. *Cappier* was such a case. The liberty not to be forced to aid another, which motivated the court's decision, is a real good. Other real goods, like treating others alike and furthering certainty, are served by following precedents generally, and thus would have been served had *Cappier* been followed. Yet the decision flouted values of even greater importance. It was not merely an ought of supererogation that the railroad ignored when it abandoned young Cappier; it was an ought of moral obligation. Moreover, it was not a weak moral obligation such as one owes to any stranger; it was a strong obligation arising out of the fact that it was the railroad's actions that placed Cappier in peril of death. By breaching this strong primary obligation, the railroad had a secondary obligation to correct the injustice it had done in leaving Cappier to die. This good of corrective justice outweighed any liberty interest of the railroad in not being coerced by law to do its duty.

For these reasons, American tort law has by and large overruled cases like *Cappier*. One way to view this is to say that Kansas tort law changed once *Cappier* was overruled. Suppose that this overruling took place via a Kansas Supreme Court opinion issued in 1905. The view that regards overrulings as changing the law would say that cases arising out of facts occurring in 1904 – after the 1903 *Cappier* decision, but before the 1905 overruling – would be governed by the "no positive duty" rule laid down in *Cappier*. Yet with occasional exceptions, mostly in criminal procedure, this is not how overruling works in common law systems. What we actually find is that once a precedent is overruled, no pending case, no matter when its facts arose, is treated as being controlled by the original rule. For our example, this implies that the law of Kansas in 1904 was not the no-duty rule of *Cappier*, but rather the 1905 rule that one does have a duty to those one places in peril. *Cappier*, in other words, was never the law of Kansas, not even in 1903. At most, the holding in *Cappier* was only the law of that case – and as we saw in Section V, even that might not be true.

What this shows is that a common law rule, such as that of *Cappier*, is not simply a matter of historical fact. Furthermore, such a rule is also more than just a blend of historical fact, the values that justify the rule, and the values that justify common law in general. Rather, the common law at any given time is a function of all three of these items, and of an all-things-considered value judgment on the rule in question. The rule in cases like *Cappier* is the law only if the values behind the announced rule, together with the values of having common law rules at all, are stronger than the values disserved by continuing such a rule.

This safety-valve function of overruling a precedent court's holding is quite parallel to the safety-valve function of overruling both the letter and spirit of a statute with a similar all-things-considered value judgment, as in cases like *Kirby v. United States* discussed above. In both situations, the function of the rule in question, together with the function of the relevant kind of rules (i.e., the function of statutes or the common law) has to be balanced against all possible competing values. Only rules that reflect such a balance are obligating of judges and citizens – that is, only they are *laws*.

VII. Closing Ruminations

From Aristotle through Aquinas to post-World War II theorists such as Fuller, we have inherited a tradition of natural law that is functionalist (that is, "teleological") in its orientation. So strong is this tradition that many assume that while "one need not be a teleologist about everything in order to be a natural law theorist . . . one must be a teleologist about law itself" in order to qualify.[80]

If this were true, natural law would be problematic. As we have seen with respect to both the laws of cases arising under statutes and the laws that consist of common law rules, the functionalist approach is too weak to generate the natural law conclusion by itself. Arguments that proceed from various functions of laws of cases, of particular statutes, of particular common law rules, of the common law in general, of statutes in general, or of law in general do not establish that either laws or laws of cases are necessarily

so good that they can obligate obedience. To establish such obligation, functionalism needs to be supplemented by other arguments about how law is best practiced.

These considerations do not settle the question of whether the more ambitious functionalist approach to law in general can sustain a natural law view. In my opinion, neither Fuller's rule-of-law virtues nor Dworkin's notion of "integrity" has much chance of making law good enough to obligate obedience necessarily; both are far too procedural to guarantee substantive justice in systems that conform to them. The common good of Aquinas and Finnis holds more promise here, but perhaps this is only because the common good threatens to collapse into the good of each citizen, and thus into the good *tout court*. Exploration of these matters, however, is beyond the ambitions of this essay.

Notes

1   Michael Moore, "Law as a Functional Kind," in Robert George, ed., *Natural Law Theories* (Oxford: Oxford University Press, 1992), reprinted as chap. 9 of Michael Moore, *Educating Oneself in Public: Critical Essays in Jurisprudence* (Oxford: Oxford University Press, 2000).

2   My views on the metaethical thesis are presented in Michael Moore, "Moral Reality," *Wisconsin Law Review* 1982, no. 6 (November/December 1982): 1061–156; Michael Moore, "Moral Reality Revisited," *Michigan Law Review* 90, no. 8 (August 1992): 2424–533; and Michael Moore, "Good without God," in Robert George, ed., *Natural Law, Liberalism, and Morality* (Oxford: Oxford University Press, 1995).

3   Moore, "Law as a Functional Kind."

4   These attributes are the concern of H. L. A. Hart, *The Concept of Law* (Oxford: Clarendon Press, 1961); and Joseph Raz, *The Concept of a Legal System* (Oxford: Clarendon Press, 1970).

5   Herbert Hart nicely distinguished this concern about laws from more general concerns about legal systems, in his "Positivism and the Separation of Law and Morality," *Harvard Law Review* 71, no. 4 (February 1958): 593–629.

6   On Bentham's distaste for the common law, see A. W. B. Simpson, "The Common Law and Legal Theory," in A. W. B. Simpson, ed., *Oxford Essays in Jurisprudence*, 2d ser. (Oxford: Oxford University Press, 1973); and Gerald Postema, *Bentham and*

the Common Law Tradition (Oxford: Clarendon Press, 1984).

7   When Michael Detmold urges the unity of *law* and morality, this is what he seems to have in mind. See M. J. Detmold, *The Unity of Law and Morality* (London: Routledge and Kegan Paul, 1987).

8   On areas of law, see Michael Moore, "A Theory of Criminal Law Theories," in Dan Friedmann, ed., *Tel Aviv University Studies in Law*, vol. 8 (Tel Aviv, Israel: Tel Aviv University Press, 1990), revised and reprinted as chap. 1 of Moore, *Placing Blame: A General Theory of the Criminal Law* (Oxford: Clarendon Press, 1997).

9   Augustine, *De Libero Arbitrio*, I.v.ll.

10   Thomas Aquinas, *Summa Theologiae*, I–II, q. 90, a. 4, in Anton C. Pegis, *Basic Writings of Saint Thomas Aquinas* (New York: Random House, 1945), 2:746–7.

11   We can contrast this position with the legal positivism of Austin and Bentham, for whom there were two kinds of obligations: moral obligations and legal obligations. For them, legal obligations were not a kind of moral obligation; legal obligations were simply liability to legal sanctions. This is a very Pickwickian sense of "obligation," because in no real sense is one obligated by threats of painful consequences. As Hart put it, one may be *obliged* to yield to such threats without being *obligated* to yield to them. See Hart, *The Concept of Law*.

12   John Austin argues against a natural law position by using this sort of semantic analysis to analyze the meaning of "law." John Austin, *The Province of Jurisprudence Determined*, ed. H. L. A. Hart (New York: Noonday Press, 1954).

13   See, for example, Ronald Dworkin, *Law's Empire* (Cambridge, MA: Harvard University Press, 1986).

14   This is Hart's method in *The Concept of Law*.

15   In contemporary jurisprudence, this approach is most closely associated with Joseph Raz. See particularly Raz, *Practical Reason and Norms* (Oxford: Oxford University Press, 1975).

16   These two roles are worth distinguishing for purposes of argument even if one accepts Heidi Hurd's thesis that the obligation of judge and of citizen correspond with one another. Heidi Hurd, *Moral Combat* (Cambridge: Cambridge University Press, 1999). There are expository advantages served if we separate the roles because in various instances the tugs of intuition are different for the two roles.

17   See, for example, Thomas Hobbes, *Leviathan* (Oxford: Clarendon Press, 1909).

18   See Aquinas, *Summa Theologiae*; and John Finnis, *Natural Law and Natural Rights* (Oxford: Clarendon Press, 1980).

19   See Dworkin, *Law's Empire*.

20   See Lon Fuller, *The Morality of Law*, 2d ed. (New Haven, CT: Yale University Press, 1969).

21   This is the example used in the Hart/Fuller debate. Hart, "Positivism and the Separation of Law and Morality"; Lon Fuller, "Positivism and Fidelity to Law – A Reply to Professor Hart," *Harvard Law Review* 71, no. 4 (February 1958): 630–72.

22   See Michael Moore, "Precedent, Induction, and Ethical Generalization," in Laurence Goldstein, ed., *Precedent in Law* (Oxford: Oxford University Press, 1988).

23   See Moore, "A Theory of Criminal Law Theories."

24   Ruth Gavison suggests this objection. Ruth Gavison, "Natural Law, Positivism, and the Limits of Jurisprudence: A Modern Round," *Yale Law Journal* 91, no. 6 (May 1982): 1266–7. See also Daniel Robinson, "Antigone's Defense: A Critical Study of *Natural Law Theory: Contemporary Essays*," *Review of Metaphysics* 45, no. 2 (December 1991): 382.

25   Joel Feinberg, "The Dilemmas of Judges Who Must Interpret 'Immoral Laws,'" in Joel Feinberg and Jules Coleman, eds., *Philosophy of Law*, 6th ed. (Belmont, CA: Wordsworth/Thomson Learning, 2000), 108–29.

26   Fuller, *The Morality of Law*.

27   H. L. A. Hart, "Book Review – *The Morality of Law*," *Harvard Law Review* 78, no. 6 (April 1965): 1281–96.

28   Grant Gilmore's nice paraphrase of Hart's point. Grant Gilmore, *The Ages of American Law* (New Haven, CT: Yale University Press, 1974), 111.

29   Lon Fuller, "What the Law Schools Can Contribute to the Making of Lawyers," *Journal of Legal Education* 1, no. 2 (Winter 1948): 204; Fuller, *The Morality of Law*, 152–86, 223–4; Fuller, "Fidelity to Law," 636, 643, 661; and Lon Fuller, "A Reply to Professors Cohen and Dworkin," *Villanova Law Review* 10, no. 4 (Summer 1965): 661–6.

30   Finnis, *Natural Law and Natural Rights*.

31   Ibid., 154–5.

32   Ibid.

33   Dworkin, *Law's Empire*.

34   This is the view of Jerome Frank, *Law and the Modern Mind* (New York: Brentano's, 1930).

35   J. L. Austin, "A Plea for Excuses," *Proceedings of the Aristotelian Society* 57 (1957): 1–30.

36   H. L. A. Hart, "The Ascription of Responsibility and Rights," *Proceedings of the Aristotelian Society* 49 (1949): 171–94.

37   Fuller, "Fidelity to Law."

38   Aquinas, *Summa Theologiae*, I–II, q. 96, a. 6.

39   On Aquinas's side, see Fuller, "Fidelity to Law"; and Max Radin, "Statutory Interpretation," *Harvard*

Law Review 43, no. 6 (April 1930): 863–90. On the other side, see, e.g., Frank Easterbrook, "Statute's Domains," *University of Chicago Law Review* 50, no. 2 (Spring 1983): 533–52.

40 Fuller, "Fidelity to Law."

41 See, e.g., Easterbrook, "Statute's Domains."

42 Compare Easterbrook's preaching in "Statute's Domains" with his practice in *In re Erickson*, 815 F.2d 1090 (7th Cir. 1987).

43 Oliver Wendell Holmes, Jr., quoted in Learned Hand, *The Bill of Rights* (Cambridge, MA: Harvard University Press, 1958), 18.

44 See, e.g., Joseph Raz, "Authority and Consent," *Virginia Law Review* 67, no. 1 (February 1981): 103–31.

45 For one of many critiques, see Michael Moore, "The Semantics of Judging," *Southern California Law Review* 54, no. 2 (January 1981): 256–70.

46 Dworkin stresses this point in his "The Forum of Principle," *New York University Law Review* 56, nos. 2–3 (May/June 1981): 469–518, reprinted in *A Matter of Principle* (Cambridge, MA: Harvard University Press, 1985). See also Moore, "The Semantics of Judging."

47 See Radin, "Statutory Interpretation"; Moore, "The Semantics of Judging"; and Antonin Scalia, *A Matter of Interpretation*, ed. Amy Gutmann (Princeton, NJ: Princeton University Press, 1997), 17.

48 Hart made this point against both Fuller and Dworkin. Hart, "Book Review – *The Morality of Law*"; Hart, "Comment," in Ruth Gavison, ed., *Issues in Contemporary Legal Philosophy* (Oxford: Oxford University Press, 1987).

49 This is one of Dworkin's favorite examples. Compare Dworkin, "Review of Cover's *Justice Accused*," *Times Literary Supplement*, December 5, 1975, with J. L. Mackie, "The Third Theory of Law," *Philosophy and Public Affairs* 7, no. 1 (Autumn 1977): 3–16; and with Joel Feinberg, "The Dilemmas of Judges Who Must Interpret 'Immoral Laws.'"

50 This example is Kenneth Stern's, from his "Either-or or Neither-nor," in Sidney Hook, ed., *Law and Philosophy* (New York: New York University Press, 1963), 249–50.

51 *Kirby v. United States*, 74 U.S. (7 Wall.) 482 (1869).

52 I defend this view of statutory interpretation at length in Michael Moore, "A Natural Law Theory of Interpretation," *Southern California Law Review* 58, no. 2 (January 1985): 277–398.

53 Aquinas, *Summa Theologiae*, I–II, q. 90, a. 1.

54 Oliver Wendell Holmes, "The Path of the Law," *Harvard Lam Review* 10, no. 8 (March 1897): 457–68.

55 See, e.g., Hart, *The Concept of Law*.

56 This is Raz's term. Joseph Raz, *The Authority of Law* (Oxford: Oxford University Press, 1979).

57 Ibid.

58 This is Hart's view in *The Concept of Law*.

59 I defend the possibility of this kind of external jurisprudence against Dworkin and others in Michael Moore, "Hart's Concluding Scientific Postscript," *Legal Theory* 4, no. 3 (September 1998): 301–27; and in Moore, *Educating Oneself in Public*, chaps. 1, 3.

60 Andrei Marmor, *Interpretation and Legal Theory* (Oxford: Oxford University Press, 1992).

61 H. L. A. Hart, "American Jurisprudence through English Eyes: The Nightmare and the Noble Dream," *Georgia Law Review* 11, no. 5 (September 1977): 969–89, reprinted in H. L. A. Hart, *Essays in Jurisprudence and Philosophy* (Oxford: Clarendon Press, 1983).

62 In Hart's *The Concept of Law*, judges must regard the rule of recognition as obligatory for a legal system to exist.

63 It is perhaps almost as intuitive that Kirby's legal rights and obligations were the same as those the judge was obligated to discover in his decision. Still, I leave for another day the question of whether the laws of cases necessarily obligate citizens as well as judges. (In this regard, however, see Hurd, *Moral Combat*.) If they do, this stronger first step of the traditional argument for natural law makes the second step easier, since in comparison to judicial obligations, which express just those values defining a discrete role, citizens' obligations are more easily seen as an expression of all the values there are.

64 In the Anglo-American legal system, we have for centuries tempered the desire for finality in legal judgments with a desire to reopen "final" judgments in order to correct serious substantive or procedural errors. At common law, this was accomplished procedurally by the ancient writs of *coram nobis* and *audita querela*, and in Equity, by bills in equity seeking injunctions against the enforcement of legal judgments. (See J. W. Moore, *Moore's Federal Practice*, 3rd ed. [New York: M. Bender, 1999], secs. 60 App. 105–8.) Even under current federal American law, the old view that courts have inherent power to reopen their own judgments survives; Federal Rule of Civil Procedure 60(b) enumerates five traditional grounds for reopening a judgment and then adds a safety-valve provision specifying that a judgment can also be reopened for "any other reason justifying relief from the operation of the judgment." Under this provision, "[t]he degree

of unfairness may properly be considered in determining whether a court is justified in disturbing the finality of a judgment." Moore, *Moore's Federal Practice*, sec. 60 App. 37. As courts recognize, this "catch-all" or safety-valve provision is a "grand reservoir of equitable power to do justice in a particular case." *Compton v. Alton Steamship* Co., 608 F.2d 96, 106 (5th Cir. 1979).

Currently, the above-referenced procedures for reopening a judgment are available only to the court that rendered the judgment. However, when the degree of injustice caused by an erroneous judgment is serious enough, a "collateral attack" on that judgment can be launched from a different court. See, e.g., *Fay v. Noia*, 372 U.S. 391 (1963), and *Townsend v. Sain*, 372 U.S. 293 (1963), where collateral review of state court factual findings was allowed by the US Supreme Court in order to protect constitutional values. In a civil context, see Feinberg, "The Dilemmas of Judges Who Must Interpret 'Immoral Laws,'" for a discussion of the various techniques used by state court judges in the antebellum North to avoid giving "full faith and credit" to Southern court findings pertaining to escaped slaves.

65 Anglo-American law, as formally stated, is different from what I am arguing for in this essay. See, e.g., *United States v. United Mine Workers*, 330 U.S. 258, 294 (1947), in which it is stated that "[a]n injunction . . . must be obeyed . . . however erroneous the action of the court may be[.]" If our law really means this, it is bad law. I doubt, however, that our law does mean this. To give the proper incentives to most people, it is doubtlessly useful to utter such categorical, exceptionless pronouncements; in actuality, however, courts merely slap on the wrists actors like Martin Luther King when those actors violate judicial orders (subsequently determined to be erroneous for very good reasons).

66 *Union Pacific Ry. v. Cappier*, 72 Pac. 281 (Kansas 1903)
67 Ronald Dworkin, "The Model of Rules," *University of Chicago Law Review* 35, no. 1 (Autumn 1967): 14–54.
68 Ronald Dworkin, "Hard Cases," *Harvard Law Review* 88, no. 6 (April 1975): 1057–109.
69 Michael Moore, "Legal Principles Revisited," *Iowa Law Review* 82, no. 3 (March 1997): 867–91, reprinted as chap. 7 of Moore, *Educating Oneself in Public*.
70 Ibid., 873 n. 40.
71 Ibid., 875–6.
72 This is Hans Kelsen's view. See Hans Kelsen, "The Pure Theory of Law," *Law Quarterly Review* 51, no. 203 (July 1935): 528. "There is no such thing, of course; as a genuine gap, in the sense that a legal dispute could not be decided according to the valid norms, owing to the omission of a provision directed to the concrete case. . . . The law says not only that a person is obligated to a certain behavior . . . but also that a person is free to do or not to do what he is not obligated to do."
73 W. Page Keeton, *Prosser and Keeton on Torts*, 5th ed. (St. Paul, MN: West Publishing Co., 1984), 56–7.
74 Austin, "A Plea for Excuses."
75 A good example of such deep positivism can be found in Rolph Sartorius, *Individual Conduct and Social Norms* (Encino, CA: Dickenson Publishing, 1975).
76 See Moore, *Placing Blame*, 14–18.
77 See generally Moore, "Precedent."
78 Ibid.
79 Ibid. See also Moore, "Legal Principles Revisited," discussing Dworkin's commitment to seeing equality (rather than integrity) as the function of the common law.
80 Susan Dimock, "The Natural Law Theory of St. Thomas Aquinas," in Feinberg and Coleman, eds., *Philosophy of Law*, 31.

10

The Economic Approach to Law

Richard A. Posner

The most ambitious and probably the most influential effort in recent years to elaborate an overarching concept of justice that will both explain judicial decision making and place it on an objective basis is that of scholars working in the interdisciplinary field of "law and economics," as economic analysis of law is usually called.[1] I am first going to describe the most ambitious version of this ambitious effort and then use philosophy to chip away at it and see what if anything is left standing.

The Approach

The basic assumption of economics that guides the version of economic analysis of law that I shall be presenting is that people are rational maximizers of their satisfactions – *all* people (with the exception of small children and the profoundly retarded) in *all* of their activities (except when under the influence of psychosis or similarly deranged through drug or alcohol abuse) that involve choice. Because this definition embraces the criminal deciding whether to commit another crime, the litigant deciding whether to settle or litigate a case, the legislator

deciding whether to vote for or against a bill, the judge deciding how to cast his vote in a case, the party to a contract deciding whether to break it, the driver deciding how fast to drive, and the pedestrian deciding how boldly to cross the street, as well as the usual economic actors, such as businessmen and consumers, it is apparent that most activities either regulated by or occurring within the legal system are grist for the economic analyst's mill. It should go without saying that nonmonetary as well as monetary satisfactions enter into the individual's calculus of maximizing (indeed, money for most people is a means rather than an end) and that decisions, to be rational, need not be well thought out at the conscious level – indeed, need not be conscious at all. Recall that "rational" denotes suiting means to ends, rather than mulling things over, and that much of our knowledge is tacit.

Since my interest is in legal doctrines and institutions, it will be best to begin at the legislative (including the constitutional) level. I assume that legislators are rational maximizers of their satisfactions just like everyone else. Thus nothing they do is motivated by the public interest as such. But they want to be elected and reelected, and they need money to wage an effective campaign.

Richard A. Posner, "The Economic Approach to Law," from *The Problems of Jurisprudence* (Cambridge, Mass: Harvard University Press, 1990), pp. 353–62, 391–2. © 1990 by the Presidents and Fellows of Harvard College. Reprinted with permission from Harvard University Press.

This money is more likely to be forthcoming from well-organized groups than from unorganized individuals. The rational individual knows that his contribution is unlikely to make a difference; for this reason and also because voters in most elections are voting for candidates rather than policies, which further weakens the link between casting one's vote and obtaining one's preferred policy, the rational individual will have little incentive to invest time and effort in deciding whom to vote for. Only an organized group of individuals (or firms or other organizations – but these are just conduits for individuals) will be able to overcome the informational and free-rider problems that plague collective action.[2] But such a group will not organize and act effectively unless its members have much to gain or much to lose from specific policies, as tobacco farmers, for example, have much to gain from federal subsidies for growing tobacco and much to lose from the withdrawal of those subsidies. The basic tactic of an interest group is to trade the votes of its members and its financial support to candidates in exchange for an implied promise of favorable legislation. Such legislation will normally take the form of a statute transferring wealth from unorganized taxpayers (for example, consumers) to the interest group. If the target were another interest group, the legislative transfer might be effectively opposed. The unorganized are unlikely to mount effective opposition, and it is their wealth, therefore, that typically is transferred to interest groups.

On this view, a statute is a deal [. . .]. But because of the costs of transactions within a multi-headed legislative body, and the costs of effective communication through time, legislation does not spring full-grown from the head of the legislature; it needs interpretation and application, and this is the role of the courts. They are agents of the legislature. But to impart credibility and durability to the deals the legislature strikes with interest groups, courts must be able to resist the wishes of current legislators who want to undo their predecessors' deals yet cannot do so through repeal because the costs of passing legislation (whether original or amended) are so high, and who might therefore look to the courts for a repealing "interpretation." The impediments to legislation actually facilitate rather than retard the striking of deals, by giving interest groups some assurance that a deal struck with the legislature will not promptly be undone by repeal. An independent judiciary is one of the impediments.

Judicial independence makes the judges imperfect agents of the legislature. This is tolerable not only for the reason just mentioned but also because an independent judiciary is necessary for the resolution of ordinary disputes in a way that will encourage trade, travel, freedom of action, and other highly valued activities or conditions and will minimize the expenditure of resources on influencing governmental action. Legislators might appear to have little to gain from these widely diffused rule-of-law virtues. But if the aggregate benefits from a particular social policy are very large and no interest group's ox is gored, legislators may find it in their own interest to support the policy. Voters understand in a rough way the benefits to them of national defense, crime control, dispute settlement, and the other elements of the night watchman state, and they will not vote for legislators who refuse to provide these basic public services. It is only when those services are in place, and when (usually later) effective means of taxation and redistribution develop, that the formation of narrow interest groups and the extraction by them of transfers from unorganized groups become feasible.

The judges thus have a dual role: to interpret the interest-group deals embodied in legislation and to provide the basic public service of authoritative dispute resolution. They perform the latter function not only by deciding cases in accordance with preexisting norms, but also – especially in the Anglo-American legal system – by elaborating those norms. They fashioned the common law out of customary practices, out of ideas borrowed from statutes and from other legal systems (for example, Roman law), and out of their own conceptions of public policy. The law they created exhibits, according to the economic theory that I am expounding, a remarkable (although not total – remember the extension of the rule of capture to oil and gas) substantive consistency. It is as if the judges *wanted* to adopt the rules, procedures, and case outcomes that would maximize society's wealth.

I must pause to define "wealth maximization," a term often misunderstood. The "wealth" in "wealth maximization" refers to the sum of all tangible and intangible goods and services, weighted by prices of two sorts: offer prices (what people are willing to pay for goods they do not already own); and asking prices (what people demand to sell what they do own). If A would be willing to pay up to $100 for B's stamp collection, it is worth $100 to A. If B would be willing to sell the stamp collection for any price above $90, it is worth $90 to B. So if B sells the stamp collection to A (say for $100, but the analysis is qualitatively unaffected at any price between $90 and $100 – and it is only in that range that a transaction will occur), the wealth of society will rise by $10. Before the transaction A had $100 in cash and B had a stamp collection worth $90 (a total of $190); after the transaction A has a stamp collection worth $100 and B has $100 in cash (a total of $200). The transaction will not raise measured wealth – gross national product, national income, or whatever – by $10; it will not raise it at all unless the transaction is recorded, and if it is recorded it is likely to raise measured wealth by the full $100 purchase price. But the real addition to social wealth consists of the $10 increment in *nonpecuniary* satisfaction that A derives from the purchase, compared with that of B. This shows that "wealth" in the economist's sense is not a simple monetary measure, and explains why it is a fallacy (the Earl of Lauderdale's fallacy) to think that wealth would be maximized by encouraging the charging of monopoly prices. The wealth of producers would increase but that of consumers would diminish – and actually by a greater amount, since monopoly pricing will induce some consumers to switch to goods that cost society more to produce but, being priced at a competitive rather than a monopoly price, appear to the consumer to be cheaper. The fallacy thus lies in equating business income to social wealth.[3]

Similarly, if I am given a choice between remaining in a job in which I work forty hours a week for $1,000 and switching to a job in which I would work thirty hours for $500, and I decide to make the switch, the extra ten hours of leisure must be worth at least $500 to me, yet GNP will fall when I reduce my hours of work. Suppose the extra hours of leisure are worth $600 to me, so that my full income rises from $1,000 to $1,100 when I reduce my hours. My former employer presumably is made worse off

by my leaving (else why did he employ me?), but not more than $100 worse off; for if he were, he would offer to pay me a shade over $1,100 a week to stay – and I would stay. (The example abstracts from income tax.)

Wealth is *related* to money, in that a desire not backed by ability to pay has no standing – such a desire is neither an offer price nor an asking price. I may desperately desire a BMW, but if I am unwilling or unable to pay its purchase price, society's wealth would not be increased by transferring the BMW from its present owner to me. Abandon this essential constraint (an important distinction, also, between wealth maximization and utilitarianism – for I might derive greater utility from the BMW than its present owner or anyone else to whom he might sell the car), and the way is open to tolerating the crimes committed by the passionate and the avaricious against the cold and the frugal.

The common law facilitates wealth-maximizing transactions in a variety of ways. It recognizes property rights, and these facilitate exchange. It also protects property rights, through tort and criminal law. (Although today criminal law is almost entirely statutory, the basic criminal protections – for example, those against murder, assault, rape, and theft – have, as one might expect, common law origins.) Through contract law it protects the process of exchange. And it establishes procedural rules for resolving disputes in these various fields as efficiently as possible.

The illustrations given thus far of wealth-maximizing transactions have been of transactions that are voluntary in the strict sense of making everyone affected by them better off, or at least no worse off. Every transaction has been assumed to affect just two parties, each of whom has been made better off by it. Such a transaction is said to be Pareto superior, but Pareto superiority is not a necessary condition for a transaction to be wealth maximizing. Consider an accident that inflicts a cost of $100 with a probability of .01 and that would have cost $3 to avoid. The accident is wealth-maximizing "transaction" (recall Aristotle's distinction between voluntary and involuntary transactions) because the expected accident cost ($1), is less than the cost of avoidance. (I am assuming risk neutrality. Risk aversion would complicate the analysis but

not change it fundamentally.) It is wealth maximizing even if the victim is not compensated.
The result is consistent with Learned Hand's
formula, which defines negligence as the failure
to take cost-justified precautions. If the only precaution that would have averted the accident
is not cost-justified, the failure to take it is
not negligent and the injurer will not have to
compensate the victim for the costs of the
accident.

If it seems artificial to speak of the accident
as the transaction, consider instead the potential
transaction that consists of purchasing the safety
measure that would have avoided the accident.
Since a potential victim would not pay $3 to
avoid an expected accident cost of $1, his offer
price will be less than the potential injurer's
asking price and the transaction will not be
wealth maximizing. But if these figures were
reversed – if an expected accident cost of $3
could be averted at a cost of $1 – the transaction
would be wealth maximizing, and a liability
rule administered in accordance with the Hand
formula would give potential injurers an incentive to take the measures that potential victims
would pay them to take if voluntary transactions
were feasible. The law would be overcoming
transaction-cost obstacles to wealth-maximizing
transactions – a frequent office of liability rules.

The wealth-maximizing properties of common
law rules have been elucidated at considerable
length in the literature of the economic analysis
of law.[4] Such doctrines as conspiracy, general
average (admiralty), contributory negligence,
equitable servitudes, employment at will, the
standard for granting preliminary injunctions,
entrapment, the contract defense of impossibility, the collateral-benefits rule, the expectation
measure of damages, assumption of risk, attempt,
invasion of privacy, wrongful interference with
contract rights, the availability of punitive
damages in some cases but not others, privilege
in the law of evidence, official immunity, and
the doctrine of moral consideration have been
found – at least by some contributors to this
literature – to conform to the dictates of wealth
maximization. [. . .] It has even been argued that
the system of precedent itself has an economic
equilibrium. Precedents are created as a by-
product of litigation. The greater the number of
recent precedents in an area, the lower the rate

of litigation will be. In particular, cases involving
disputes over legal as distinct from purely factual
issues will be settled. The existence of abundant,
highly informative (in part because recent)
precedents will enable the parties to legal disputes
to form more convergent estimates of the likely
outcome of a trial, and as noted in previous
chapters, if both parties agree on the outcome of
trial they will settle beforehand because a trial
is more costly than a settlement. But with less
litigation, fewer new precedents will be produced, and the existing precedents will obsolesce
as changing circumstances render them less apt
and informative. So the rate of litigation will
rise, producing more precedents and thereby
causing the rate of litigation again to fall.

This analysis does not explain what drives
judges to decide common law cases in accordance with the dictates of wealth maximization.
Prosperity, however, which wealth maximization
measures more sensitively than purely monetary
measures such as GNP, is a relatively uncontroversial policy, and most judges try to steer clear
of controversy: their age, method of compensation, and relative weakness vis-à-vis the other
branches of government make the avoidance of
controversy attractive. It probably is no accident,
therefore, that many common law doctrines
assumed their modern form in the nineteenth century, when laissez-faire ideology, which resembles
wealth maximization, had a strong hold on the
Anglo-American judicial imagination [. . .].

It may be objected that in assigning ideology
as a cause of judicial behavior, the economist
strays outside the boundaries of his discipline;
but he need not rest on ideology. The economic
analysis of legislation implies that fields of law left
to the judges to elaborate, such as the common
law fields, must be the ones in which interest-group
pressures are too weak to deflect the legislature
from pursuing goals that are in the general interest. Prosperity is one of these goals, and one that
judges are especially well equipped to promote.
The rules of the common law that they pro-
mulgate attach prices to socially undesirable
conduct, whether free riding or imposing social
costs without corresponding benefits.[5] By doing
this the rules create incentives to avoid such
conduct, and these incentives foster prosperity.
In contrast, judges can, despite appearances, do
little to redistribute wealth. A rule that makes it

easy for poor tenants to break leases with rich land-lords, for example, will induce landlords to raise rents in order to offset the costs that such a rule imposes, and tenants will bear the brunt of these higher costs. Indeed, the principal redistribu-tion accomplished by such a rule may be from the prudent, responsible tenant, who may derive little or no benefit from having additional legal rights to use against landlords – rights that en-able a tenant to avoid or postpone eviction for nonpayment of rental – to the feckless tenant. That is a capricious redistribution. Legislatures, how-ever, have by virtue of their taxing and spending powers powerful tools for redistributing wealth. So an efficient division of labor between the legislative and judicial branches has the legislative branch concentrate on catering to interest-group demands for wealth distribution and the judicial branch on meeting the broad-based social demand for efficient rules governing safety, property, and transactions. Although there are other possible goals of judicial action besides efficiency and redistribution, many of these (various conceptions of "fairness" and "justice") are labels for wealth maximization,[6] or for redistribution in favor of powerful interest groups; or else they are too controversial in a heterogeneous society, too ad hoc, or insufficiently developed to provide judges who desire a reputation for objectivity and disinterest with adequate grounds for their decisions.

Finally, even if judges have little commitment to efficiency, their inefficient decisions will, by definition, impose greater social costs than their efficient ones will. As a result, losers of cases decided mistakenly from an economic stand-point will have a greater incentive, on average, to press for correction through appeal, new litiga-tion, or legislative action than losers of cases decided soundly from an economic standpoint – so there will be a steady pressure for efficient results. Moreover, cases litigated under inefficient rules tend to involve larger stakes than cases litigated under efficient rules (for the inefficient rules, by definition, generate social waste), and the larger the stakes in a dispute the likelier it is to be litigated rather than settled; so judges will have a chance to reconsider the inefficient rule.

Thus we should not be surprised to see the com-mon law tending to become efficient, although since the incentives of judges to perform well along any dimension are weak (this is a by-product of judicial independence), we cannot expect the law ever to achieve perfect efficiency. Since wealth maximization is not only a guide in fact to common law judging but also a genuine social value and the only one judges are in a good posi-tion to promote, it provides not only the key to an accurate description of what the judges are up to but also the right benchmark for criticism and reform. If judges are failing to maximize wealth, the economic analyst of law will urge them to alter practice or doctrine accordingly. In addition, the analyst will urge – on any legislator sufficiently free of interest-group pressures to be able to leg-islate in the public interest – a program of enact-ing only legislation that conforms to the dictates of wealth maximization.

Besides generating both predictions and pre-scriptions, the economic approach enables the common law to be reconceived in simple, coher-ent terms and to be applied more objectively than traditional lawyers would think possible. From the premise that the common law does and should seek to maximize society's wealth, the economic analyst can deduce in logical – if you will, formalist – fashion (economic theory is formulated nowadays largely in mathematical terms) the set of legal doctrines that will express and perfect the inner nature of the common law, and can compare these doctrines with the actual doctrines of common law. After translat-ing from the economic vocabulary back into the legal one, the analyst will find that most of the actual doctrines are tolerable approximations to the implications of economic theory and so are formalistically valid. Where there are discrepan-cies, the path to reform is clear – yet the judge who takes the path cannot be accused of making rather than finding law, for he is merely con-tributing to the program of realizing the essen-tial nature of the common law.

The project of reducing the common law – with its many separate fields, its thousands of separate doctrines, its hundreds of thousands of reported decisions – to a handful of mathematical formu-las may seem quixotic, but the economic analyst can give reasons for doubting this assessment. Much of the doctrinal luxuriance of common law is seen to be superficial once the essentially economic nature of the common law is under-stood. A few principles, such as cost–benefit analysis, the prevention of free riding, decision under uncertainty, risk aversion, and the promotion of mutually beneficial exchanges, can explain most doctrines and decisions. Tort cases can be translated into contract cases by recharacterizing the tort issue as finding the implied pre-accident contract that the parties would have chosen had transaction costs not been prohibitive, and contract cases can be translated into tort cases by asking what remedy if any would maximize the expected benefits of the contractual undertaking considered ex ante. The criminal's decision whether to commit a crime is no different in principle from the prosecutor's decision whether to prosecute; a plea bargain is a contract; crimes are in effect torts by insolvent defendants because if all criminals could pay the full social costs of their crimes, the task of deterring antisocial behavior could be left to tort law. Such examples suggest not only that the logic of the common law really is economics but also that the teaching of law could be simplified by exposing students to the clean and simple economic structure beneath the particolored garb of legal doctrine.

If all this seems reminiscent of Langdell, it differs fundamentally in being empirically verifiable. The ultimate test of a rule derived from economic theory is not the elegance or logicality of the derivation but the rule's effect on social wealth. The extension of the rule of capture to oil and gas was subjected to such a test, flunked, and was replaced (albeit through legislative rather than judicial action) by efficient rules. The other rules of the common law can and should be tested likewise.
[. . .]

[. . .] Wealth maximization is an ethic of productivity and social cooperation – to have a claim on society's goods and services you must be able to offer something that other people value – while utilitarianism is a hedonistic, unsocial ethic [. . .]. And an ethic of productivity and cooperation is more congruent with the values of the dominant groups in our society than the pure utilitarian ethic would be. Unfortunately, wealth maximization is not a pure ethic of productivity and cooperation, not only because even lawful efforts at maximizing wealth often make some other people worse off, but more fundamentally because luck plays a big

role in the returns to market activities. What is worse, it is always possible to argue that the distribution of productivity among a population is itself the luck of the genetic draw, or of upbringing, or of where one happens to have been born, and that these forms of luck have no ethical charge. There are counterarguments, of course, but they are not decisive. So, once again, the foundations of an overarching principle for resolving legal disputes are rotten, and one is driven back to the pragmatic ramparts.

Notes

1   The literature is vast; for diverse viewpoints, see *The Economic Approach to Law* (Paul Burrows and Cento G. Veljanovski eds. 1981); Robert Cooter and Thomas Ulen, *Law and Economics* (1988); Mark Kelman, *A Guide to Critical Legal Studies*, chs. 4–5 (1987); A Mitchell Polinsky, *An Introduction to Law and Economics* (2d ed. 1989); Steven Shavell, *Economic Analysis of Accident Law* (1987); "Symposium: The Place of Economics in Legal Education," 33 *Journal of Legal Education* 183 (1983); and my book *Economic Analysis of Law* (3d ed. 1986).

2   A free rider is someone who derives a benefit without contributing to the cost of creating the benefit. For example, even if A and B both favor the enactment of a statute, X, each will prefer the other to invest what is necessary in getting X enacted, since the benefit of X to A or to B will be the same whether or not he contributes to the cost of obtaining it. [. . .]

3   On these and other technical details of wealth maximization, see my article "Wealth Maximization Revisited," 2 *Notre Dame Journal of Law, Ethics, and Public Policy* 85 (1985).

4   See *Economic Analysis of Law*, note 1 above, pt. 2 and ch. 21; William M. Landes and Richard A. Posner, *The Economic Structure of Tort Law* (1987).

5   Such imposition is well illustrated by acquisitive crimes: the time and money spent by the thief in trying to commit thefts and the property owner in trying to prevent them have no social product, for they are expended merely in order to bring about, or to prevent, a redistribution of wealth. Overall wealth decreases, as in the case of monopoly, discussed earlier.

6. For example, it is unclear whether Weinrib's Kantian theory of tort law has different substantive implications from the economic theory; the differences may be in vocabulary only.

11

The Distinction between Adjudication and Legislation

Duncan Kennedy

a. The process of marking

b.

This chapter takes up one of the "great dichotomies"[1] of political theory in general and legal theory in particular, that between adjudication and legislation. I have already suggested that the ideological element in adjudication is "denied" by many, and that judges operate in "bad faith." The denial is in part a response to the critique of judging, the "viral" element in American legal thought. Jurisprudence theorizes denial by explaining how adjudication can be nonideological, and it is now time to examine the variety of ways in which it does this.

It is important to distinguish at the outset between denying the ideological element in judging and denying that judges make decisions that are important to ideological intelligentsias. I don't think many people would deny that liberals and conservatives care about what rules the US Supreme Court adopts about abortion, and care in a way that is well described as ideologically motivated. I don't think many people would deny that ideological intelligentsias care ideologically about which rule courts adopt when they are working out the details of products liability.

But it is a different matter to claim that the discursive process by which the rules are made, here appellate adjudication, has ideological content and significance in its own right. It is different because many liberals and conservatives believe, some of the time, to some extent, usually in bad faith, that although there are ideological stakes in rule definition, the discursive process that disposes the stakes by choosing the rule (appellate decision) is not or ought not to be ideological. Judges, moreover, always claim that they themselves are proceeding according to a discursive procedure that positively excludes ideology, though of course it is commonplace for them to accuse other judges of failing to make this exclusion.

There are two quite different conventional ways to state the idea that appellate court discursive practices for choosing rules do or should exclude ideology. These will figure heavily in the future discussion. One is to say that the rule-making process is or ought to be "objective"; the other is to say, much more modestly, that it ought not to be "personal."

Within legal culture, since the late nineteenth century, there has been debate about the objectivity of the procedures that judges use in choosing rules of law. *For lawyers*, I assert, the main thing at stake in these discussions has been whether or not judges are, or have to be or ought to be,

Duncan Kennedy, "The Distinction between Adjudication and Legislation," from *A Critique of Adjudication (fin de siècle)* (Cambridge, Mass: Harvard University Press, 1997), pp. 23–38. © 1997 by the Presidents and Fellows of Harvard College. Reprinted with permission from Harvard University Press.

ideological actors. To say that judicial law making produces rule choices that are objectively correct is simply to say that it produces rule choices that cannot be attributed to the ideological sympathies of the judges. It is sometimes asserted that there are other stakes, like the nonpolitical value of certainty as a facilitator of legal transactions, but these turn out to be makeweights in the legal debate, though occasionally appealing to outsiders.

An amusing sideshow to this debate has been staged by philosophers (of many persuasions and ideologies) who have been interested in objectivity "in general" and who address the question in law as an analogue to the question as it arises elsewhere. Often, they haven't understood the lawyers' stakes, and so propose that law is objective according to an account of objectivity that doesn't respond to the issue of the preclusion of ideological determination, thinking they are thereby clarifying things for us philosophical illiterates.[2] Because they miss the point, these interventions don't usually get incorporated into the lawyers' debate.

Stanley Fish made the opposite mistake in his debate with Ronald Dworkin.[3] He seemed to think it should comfort us that, though law is certainly not objective, there is no way for judges to escape control by their context. But the mode of "always already constrained" that he proposed was patently a constraint that couldn't exclude ideology.

The parallel debate about whether legal decision making is not or ought not to be "personal" has the same stakes. Nonlawyers sometimes interpret the exclusion of the personal as aimed at corruption, or at the random preferences of judges, say, for litigants wearing blue shirts. But the only real issue is the personal understood as the ideological. The following passage is highly typical, not least in its equivocation as to whether judges "really do not" decide on the basis of personal values, or are only "deterred" from so doing, so that they can make "massive doctrinal shifts" only "rarely."

[T]he fact that judges are protected in significant ways from the popular will . . . make[s] it inappropriate for them to reach outcomes on the basis of their personal (and possibly idiosyncratic) values. Despite all the palaver that this is

what judges really do, *the truth is that they really do not*. The institutional constraints I have already mentioned – combined with the requirement of reasoned decision and a moral obligation of candor – are *checks that deter* the imposition of judges' personal values and that confine the courts to "molecular motions." *Massive doctrinal shifts are rare*. When they do occur, they are *usually* a long time building, and, if they touch sensitive moral nerves, are at least as long a time commanding the general acceptance needed to make them effective.[4]

I want to state forcefully that at the present time in American legal culture this version of adjudication (David Shapiro's) is not "mainstream" because there isn't a mainstream view of the issue. Lawyers vary from perfect cynicism to perfect late-nineteenth-century Langdellianism, with a surprisingly large and idiosyncratic range of variations in between. Legal academics are the same. Legal theorists, who are often professionally concerned with the issue, unanimously reject "nihilism" (whatever that means) but equally unanimously reject any kind of "formalism." Their range of intermediate variants is more organized into schools than the random variants of lawyers but no less baroque.

Shapiro's article does represent an orthodoxy, a view that was once merely common sense but that has become tradition, embattled but faithful to first principles amidst a sea of heretics, backsliders, and cranks.

I will not be arguing about whether judges do or should reach outcomes (make rules) on the basis of their personal or idiosyncratic values, if we take personal in the sense of "preference between chocolate and vanilla ice cream," or preference for litigants wearing blue shirts or carrying bribes. What I am interested in is the way in which judges' ideological commitments (including the commitment not to be ideological) enter into rule making, and the consequences of their presence, if they are present, under erasure or denial. It seems clear to me that *sometimes* judges choose rules on the basis of deduction from other rules, and that *sometimes* they are (I'm happy to say "improperly") influenced by truly idiosyncratic factors. But ideological orientation [. . .] is never something "merely personal."

Adjudication versus Legislation

The distinction between adjudication and legislation is closely related to a number of others, and it is impossible to explain it without reference to them. They include the distinctions between a court and a legislature, between applying and making law, between law and politics, between objective and subjective questions, between rights and powers, and between professionally and electorally accountable officials. In one way of looking at it, adjudication is what courts do and legislation is what legislatures do. In this version, the distinction is parasitic on the prior one between the two institutions of court and legislature and is merely descriptive. Whatever courts do is adjudication; whatever legislatures do is legislation.

It is much more common, however, to see the two as *methods of decision* that might or might not characterize any given activity of a court or a legislature. In the oldest and simplest version of this view, though not in the current understanding of lawyers, what legislatures do when they legislate is make law, and what courts do when they adjudicate is apply law to facts. But it is perfectly possible for a legislature to adjudicate and for a court to legislate. In this version of the distinction, adjudication and legislation are mutually exclusive concepts – an actor cannot be doing both at the same time, deciding a question in one way precludes deciding it in the other, applying existing law to existing facts is different from making new law to apply to future (or past) facts.

The distinction remains sharp even if we recognize that application will often require reformulation of the rule before it can be applied to the facts. We are unsure at first blush how to apply the rule to the facts; we resolve the question by appealing to the definitions of the words. As long as the process of reformulation is understood to be "semantic," or "deductive," in the sense of looking for the "meaning" of the words that compose the rule to be applied, it is not, in this understanding, rule making, even if the case is a hard one. "Questions of law," as conventionally distinguished from "questions of fact," fall within the judge's province, in this view, because they involve objective questions of meaning rather than the subjective judgments that are required

when we make the political choice to apply one rule or another to a given fact situation.

The distinction between adjudication and legislation has often been a building block in the larger normative theory of Liberalism (capitalized to distinguish it from "liberalism," the political ideology that is opposed to conservatism). By "Liberalism" I mean belief in individual rights, majority rule, and the rule of law. Liberal theories of the rule of law require the separation of powers as one means to protect individual rights in a regime of majority rule. The separation between legislative and judicial institutions corresponds exactly to the distinction between legislation and adjudication as methods of decision. Legislatures *should* legislate and only legislate; courts *should* adjudicate and only adjudicate, even though they may in fact violate these role constraints.

In this normative view, the law-making process requires value judgments, which are inescapably subjective, and therefore political. Because law making is political, it should be done by elected officials (possibly subject to constraints imposed by the people as a whole through constitutional law making), operating under a norm of accountability to their constituents.

Conversely, legislatures should not adjudicate. Adjudication (law application) determines the rights of the parties to disputes. Liberals of both the positivist and natural rights schools agree that the rule of law means that the parties have a right to determination of their rights, however established, by a process that is not tainted by the subjective political preferences of the majority. As I noted above, these writers are concerned not so much with the eccentric, the truly "personal," as with the ideological, what James Madison called "faction."

Adjudication, in the old view, need not be political, because it involves questions of meaning and questions of fact that are independent of value judgments (objective). Since the determination of questions of right can be done objectively, rather than ideologically, it seems obvious that it should be. Therefore it should be entrusted to trained professionals operating under a norm of "independent" fidelity to law. Courts constituted to perform this function should not legislate because they are not elected.

Within this normative vision, the phrase "judicial legislation" has an invariably negative normative meaning, as in this sentence from a sophisticated journalist commentator on a Supreme Court nominee: "Although Breyer's instincts are moderate rather than activist, his pragmatism raises questions about judicial legislation that might be useful to explore."[5] This theory takes the rule of law to mean that the exercise of force or violence against citizens must be justified in two ways: first, by appeal to a norm produced by the democratic decision-making process that is embodied in the legislature or the process of constitution making; second, by the application of the norm to the facts in a process that is independent of the very decision process that generated it. Judicial legislation is problematic because it violates the first requirement, just as the trial of cases in the legislature would violate the second.

This version of the distinction between legislation and adjudication and of its place in Liberal theory plays a substantial role in American popular political culture, but it has little credence among the intelligentsia and even less in the specifically legal intelligentsia. The reason is that it seems implausible to describe the actual activity of judges as nothing more than applying law, at least as the notion of law application is generally understood.

Of course, judges do apply law all the time, in the sense of taking a norm that everyone involved understands to be "valid" and asking whether its factual predicates have been proved. But it seems equally obvious that judges constantly have to do something better described as making than as applying law. At a minimum, judges often have the job of resolving gaps, conflicts, or ambiguities in the system of legal norms. In some cases, no amount of reformulation based on the underlying definitions of the words composing the arguably applicable rules produces a deductively valid resolution. When it is agreed that there is a gap, conflict, or ambiguity in this sense, then it is also agreed that the judge who resolves it "makes" a new rule and then applies it to the facts, rather than merely applying a preexisting rule.[6]

When identified with the contrast between law making and law application, the legislation/adjudication dichotomy seems to admit of no middle term. But as soon as we shift to this broader notion of legal interpretation, it follows that adjudication involves both making and applying. But it does not follow, and is controverted, that judicial law making must be or is in fact "judicial legislation" and therefore abhorrent to the part of the theory of the rule of law that requires a democratic (legislative) legitimation for the use of force against the citizen.

American judges vigorously deny that what they do even in "hard cases" has to be or is in fact judicial legislation, though they often concede that they make law. They argue for particular rule choices in a rhetoric of nonpolitical necessity. I think it fair to say, however, that their case-by-case claims that they are constrained by the legal materials to reach results to which their politics are irrelevant are not convincing.

First, it is a convention of judicial opinion writing, and a political requirement of popular culture, that judges represent themselves as neutral with respect to the content of the law they make. Second, any individual judge making any particular rule has an interest, an interest in his or her rule prevailing, in presenting the rule choice as not judicial legislation. Third, many particular claims of legal necessity in judicial opinions are unconvincing on their face, and therefore raise the question of what is "really" determining the outcome.

In stark contrast with the view that judges present in their opinions, the standard practice of sophisticated journalism treats judges, at least of the Supreme Court, as political actors whose views and alignments can be analyzed through the conventional vocabulary of politics. Indeed, as in the following quotation, the journalistic treatment of the Court uses the language of ideology with more confidence than would a parallel treatment of legislative disputes, given the prevailing sense that straightforward left-right divisions only partially describe legislative politics. Linda Greenhouse is describing the 1993 Supreme Court term for the Sunday *New York Times* "News of the Week in Review":

> [M]any of the decisions [the justices] produced revealed deep divisions and some bore the marks of raw ideological combat . . .
>
> . . . [T]he exchange . . . highlighted the Court's current dynamic: Justices Thomas and Scalia at

the extreme conservative end of the Court's spectrum, and Justices Blackmun, Stevens, Souter and Ginsburg occupying a place that, while certainly not classically liberal, can be defined as liberal relative to where the Court is today...

...Justice Kennedy occupied the gravitational center of the Court.[7]

It is worth noting that in the only substantive argumentative exchange she mentions, the "liberal" wing attacks the "conservatives" for making "a 'radical' attempt to argue policy rather than law." The judges, in other words, attack one another for judicial legislation even as the commentators tell the story in strict ideological terms. A week later, a *Boston Globe* journalist portrayed the "general ideological makeup" of the Court on a spectrum including the categories liberal, moderate liberal, moderate, moderate conservative, and conservative, and predicted that Stephen Breyer would be a moderate liberal.[8]

A large part of American legal academic work is concerned with whether there is a politically legitimate method of judicial law making through the interpretation of legal materials – in other words, a middle term between law application and judicial legislation. This literature is both descriptive and normative. A good deal of it might be described as simultaneously reassuring and celebratory. It presents famous judges, for example, as paragons exactly because they manage to contribute mightily to law (that is, make a lot of "good" law) without falling into the trap of ideology. Here is John Noonan, a judge who was first a law professor, reviewing, for the general intelligentsia readership of the *New York Times Book Review*, a law professor's celebratory biography of Judge Learned Hand:

The craftsman was committed to neither a conservative nor a liberal agenda, but to a creed of judicial restraint... reinforced by his own experience of democracy. Judicial restraint was the watchword of liberals when conservatives dominated the courts; it continued to be the watchword of judges like Hand and Felix Frankfurter even after liberals were in judicial ascendancy. The result is that Hand's opinions do not wholly please either left or right... Political correctness was not his concern. He sought to produce the right decision.[9]

A few months later, Vincent Blasi, also a law professor, reviewed a biography of Justice Lewis Powell in exactly the same vein:

In an age that generated fierce pressures to interpret the Constitution to serve one or another partisan agenda, Lewis Powell probably did as much as anyone to keep alive the ideal of judicial independence. Few Justices in history have succeeded so well at separating their political predilections from their judgments regarding what the Constitution means. Justice Powell's performance disappointed many conservatives... Because his view prevailed in a large number of closely contested decisions, Justice Powell's independence had a major impact on the development of the law.[10]

A letter writer was concerned that the review might mislead the "educated layman" into thinking that "independence" was rare rather than the rule on the Supreme Court, but agreed that Powell's "ability to place the law ahead of any ideological or political considerations is what made him a noteworthy jurist."[11]

The Jurisprudence of Adjudication

Though in neither the reassuring nor the celebratory mode, this chapter addresses the anxiety implicit in these reviewers' particular choice of praise. If what makes a judge great is his ability to resist not only other people's but also his own ideological predilections, then it seems to follow, as the letter writer sees, that lesser judges don't manage this. In building their normative theories, legal philosophers take positions about what it is possible for judges to do and appeal constantly to ideas about what they do in fact. In the process, they provide a typology of approaches to the ideological "underside" of adjudication.

We can distinguish no fewer than five general strategies for dealing with the problem. The first, associated with classical positivism through H. L. A. Hart,[12] is to deny or at least to ignore the possibility of a middle term, arguing that what is not law application is for all intents and purposes judicial legislation. A basic problem with this approach is that there is a large number of cases in which the judge at least reformulates the existing rule of law.

Is it plausible that whenever the judge's reformulation is other than a deduction from the "core meanings" of words in an earlier valid formulation, we should understand him as behaving as he would if he were a legislator? No one interested in the political analysis of the content of the legal system would adopt such a hypothesis. It seems too obvious to argue that the institutional contexts of adjudication and legislation are so different that identical ideological motives in judges and legislators will produce very different substantive rule-making outcomes. But the question is, different in what way?[13]

The second position, which I associate with Hans Kelsen,[14] Roberto Unger,[15] Mark Tushnet,[16] Gary Peller,[17] and James Boyle,[18] collapses the distinction between rule making and rule application by showing that rule application cannot be insulated from "subjective" influence, including ideological influence. It seems to follow a fortiori that the far less structured activity of resolving gaps, conflicts, and ambiguities is similarly porous. There are a number of arguments as to why rule application "cannot be objective," relying on linguistic philosophers as diverse as John Locke, Ludwig Wittgenstein, Richard Rorty, and Jacques Derrida, but one example will suffice here.

It is often asserted that "no rule can determine the scope of its own application," meaning that applying, say, "close the door at five" will require judgments about whether particulars in the order of events correspond or don't correspond to the concepts "close," "door," and "five." As a logical matter, the basis for these judgments can't be found in the concepts themselves. But there are no "objective" tests of correspondence outside the text of the rule, once one agrees that language is not the mirror of nature.

It is common to respond (as Owen Fiss[19] has) that when the rule applier acts, he does so according to something other than a deductive process, relying on "practical reason," the consensus of the "interpretive community," or whatever. The critics reply that whatever method one chooses as a solution to the "application problem," that is, however one grounds rule application, that method will not have the demonstrable or objective quality that would be necessary to guarantee that the decision maker's ideology played no role in the choice of an outcome.[20]

The collapse of even the hardest core of rule application into rule making, and its consequent opening to ideological influence, were important events in the general cultural contests about role constraint and about "being right." But the collapsing strategy is less important to the enterprise we are pursuing here – that of trying to assess the particular character of judicial as opposed to legislative law making.

It is already widely recognized in our legal culture that judges make law through legal interpretation. Moreover, it is obvious that in many or most cases the application process is experienced by all involved not just as unproblematic, but also as unproblematizable, no matter how clearly nondeductive. And we have a choice in formulating norms between using terms that will be "easy" ("you can vote at age 21") and those that will be "hard" ("when you achieve good character") to apply. The experience of core meanings survives the loss of its metaphysical grounding.[21] Although problematic cases of rule application remain common in spite of our best efforts, they pose less of a problem for the claim of ideological neutrality in adjudication than does the acknowledged openness of the interpretive process.

Judges' choices among new rules proposed to resolve gaps, conflicts, and ambiguities are contestable (and contested) within a distinct normative discourse of statutory and constitutional interpretation, precedent, and "policy." This discourse may sometimes falsely presuppose that whatever rules judges adopt can be applied "neutrally," and it is certainly true that how rules get applied is sometimes as important as what they "are." In a common law, but not in a code system, when judges reformulate rules in the process of applying them in particular cases, the reformulations become part of the body of "sources" of law in later cases. Common lawyers interested in judicial law making have always been interested in this process and in how we might compare it with the legislative process. Showing that law is made even in the most routine application of rule to facts is important, but it seems more important to try to figure out how the rules get made in the first place.

The third position is that while there is no middle term, in the sense of a method distinct from both application and legislation, judicial law making is nonetheless distinct from legislation because it is bounded in its substance. A classic statement would be Oliver Wendell Holmes's: "I recognize without hesitation that judges do and must legislate, but they can do so only interstitially; they are confined from 'molar to molecular motions.' "[22] Another would be Felix Frankfurter's list of the doctrines that confine constitutional adjudication and thereby restrain its political impact (standing, case or controversy, political question doctrine).[23] Yet another would be Joseph Raz's list of institutional constraints on adjudication.[24]

A solution of this kind accepts that what is not rule application is methodologically indistinguishable from judicial legislation, and perhaps acknowledges that the nondemocratic character of judging makes this problematic. A further concession would be that the second-level rules that confine judicial law making within a "sphere" are open to the same critique as the judge's first-order rule making. In other words, what guarantees a nonideological distinction between "interstitial" and "macro" law making, or between "political" and "judicial" questions? The minute the judge is doing something more than applying (searching for the meaning of) the rules that confine the scope of his legislative law making, he is engaged in judicial legislation about the scope of judicial legislation.[25]

The fourth solution addresses this problem by proposing a genuine middle term between law application and judicial legislation. This is the method of "coherence" or "fit," through which the judge can make new rules of law without consulting his own legislative preferences. I associate this solution with the work of Benjamin Cardozo,[26] Karl Llewellyn,[27] Lon Fuller,[28] Henry Hart and Albert Sacks,[29] Neil MacCormick,[30] J. M. Finnis,[31] and Ronald Dworkin.[32] Fit or coherence rule making is distinct from the method of developing the definitions of the words in legal rules as an aid to applying them, because it is focused on the choice among different rules proposed to resolve a gap, conflict, or ambiguity in the legal system seen as an ensemble of rules. It is clear that the judge is making law. He does so by treating the whole existing corpus of rules (rather than the words of a particular rule) as the product of an implicit rational plan, and asks which of the rules proposed best furthers that plan.

If he employs the method of coherence, he will make law that is not influenced by his personal convictions, simply because he will follow the rational plan even when he doesn't agree with it.

The method of coherence permits the judge to do ideological work when he furthers a particular legal regime by developing it in the face of a gap, conflict, or ambiguity. The regime may be incomprehensible except as the working out of an ideological conception, in the sense of a liberal or conservative conception. In the familiar case, the legislature has enacted a comprehensive statute, say the National Labor Relations Act, which self-consciously rejects a preexisting conservative regime of labor relations and equally self-consciously adopts a rival liberal regime. The judge who wants to resolve a case in a way that "fits" the statutory scheme has to pursue the liberal conception. But it is not his "personal" ideology but that of the legislative (or constitutional) boss that guides him. The coherence conception permits similar analysis of bodies of case law. The judge does the ideological bidding of the prior judges, relying on the legislature to change that ideology if it wants to.

A coherence theorist might believe, as does Dworkin, that the legal regime taken as a whole is intelligible only as the expression of a particular combination of political theoretical conceptions. If this is the case, coherence requires the categorical exclusion from the interpretative process of *other* political conceptions: "A judge who accepts this constraint, and whose own convictions are Marxist or anarchist or taken from some eccentric religious tradition, cannot impose these convictions on the community under the title of law, however noble or enlightened he believes them to be, because they cannot provide the coherent general interpretation he needs."[33] I find this statement odd (possibly because of my own combination of Marxist, anarchist, and eccentric religious convictions) but typical of the narrowing aspirations of coherence theorists (explored below).

The position that there is a middle methodology between law application and judicial legislation is consistent with the idea (the third solution above) that there are rules that constrain the scope of judicial law making and thereby serve to limit the impact of ideology on adjudication. Indeed, the method of coherence provides a response to the fear that such rules only push the problem of judicial legislation back from the interpretation of substantive norms to the interpretation of the supposedly constraining rules. The judge who interprets the political question doctrine or the vaguer notion of "interstitiality" through the requirement of coherence with prior cases and other rules of the system is enacting "the system's" ideology of judicial constraint or judicial activism, rather than his personal view.

One can distinguish two variants of the position that there is a methodological middle term. The English version remains true to its Benthamite positivist heritage by positing that there is a limit to the range of cases that correspond to the method of coherence. The judges are obliged to decide all cases that come before them, and some of these are beyond the middle range – in other words, the law "runs out" and the judge must legislate. Of course, he does so subject to the various constraints, such as the requirement of a case or controversy, described above.

In this version, there are two forms of judicial legislation, only one of which has a negative connotation. If, on the one hand, the judge fails to perform his function of judicial law making according to the method of coherence, and particularly if he makes a rule that corresponds to his legislative preference rather than to the preference implicit in the legal materials, then the rule of law is in jeopardy. On the other hand, where the law "runs out," he is simply the victim of a contradiction between the role constraints proposed by popular political culture. He is supposed to decide the case without judicial legislation, but this is impossible. Since not deciding is also impossible (walking away means that the defendant wins), the right thing for him to do is what he thinks is right, leaving it to the legislature or (in the United States) to the constitutional amendment process to correct him if he is wrong.

In the American version, the method of coherence will give a "right answer" to any dispute over which the judge has jurisdiction. There may be types of cases for which the adjudicative method is inappropriate (Fuller,[34] Hart and Sacks[35]), but legal doctrine itself defines these cases and forbids the judge deciding them, rather than requiring him

to do so. The defendant wins "as a matter of law," rather than by refusal of justice. The judge never has to legislate, and judicial legislation is *always* bad. The conventional judicial rhetoric of constraint by law can be honored, rather than treated in the positivist manner as a pious fraud. In this version, the judge can do his job.

With the passage from Cardozo to Fuller and Llewellyn through Hart and Sacks to Dworkin, there is a noticeable evolution of this position. It moves in the direction of blurring the difference between the middle term of coherence and judicial legislation, while at the same time vigorously affirming its importance. Dworkin and many other modern American legal theorists concede (even affirm) the political character of adjudication. They affirm the possibility of "rightness" in even the "hardest" cases, while progressively abandoning any claim that this rightness is "objective," or demonstrable in the sense that any rational practitioner of legal reasoning would have to accept it, let alone noncontroversial within the canons of good legal reasoning. They nonetheless retain a sharp distinction between judging and legislating:

> [L]egal practice is an exercise in interpretation not only when lawyers interpret particular documents or statutes but generally. Law so conceived is deeply and thoroughly political. Lawyers and judges cannot avoid politics in the broad sense of political theory. But law is not a matter of personal or partisan politics, and a critique of law that does not understand this difference will provide poor understanding and even poorer guidance.[36]

For Dworkin, a hard case may require judgments of "political theory" because there may be more than one solution that meets the requirement of coherence or fit. Moreover, the operation of investigating whether a proposed solution passes the initial test of fit will be influenced by the same political theories that the judge appeals to if at the end of the day he has to choose between outcomes that are equally coherent. There is no metacriterion for choosing between political theories, or between versions of coherence influenced by those theories, other than the judge's conviction that a given theory is the best.

As Gerald Postema points out,[37] this is an extreme "protestant" version of "rightness" in interpretation. In hard cases, the judge cannot rely on external authority or even on the idea of objectivity, and cannot hope to compel the agreement of others; but he is never to succumb to doubt as to whether the truth he seeks "really exists" outside himself. "[J]udges deciding difficult constitutional cases are [not] simply voting their personal political convictions as much as [sic] if they were legislators or delegates to a new constitutional convention."[38] If the judge is doing "ordinary politics in disguise," he is "incompetent or in bad faith."[39]

Contrast, finally, the civil law version of adjudication, a fifth strategy that combines all of these elements in yet another way. On the Continent, the official story is that the role of the judge is to apply the relevant Code to the facts of the case using a presumption of gaplessness. If the case cannot be resolved by semantic or deductive analysis of the meanings of the terms in a validly enacted rule, the judge deploys interpretive techniques based on the presumption that the Code is the coherent working out of a particular conceptual structure. He does the best he can but does not entertain the possibility that "there is no right answer." In the official version, the judge can always do his job, though some cases are harder than others. In this respect, Dworkin is a Continental.

But the official version[40] denies, first, that the judge will ever have to go beyond coherence, or fit, into Dworkin's realm of personally held general political theory, and, second, that these general theories legitimately influence the operation of determining coherence in the first place. The more radical Continental thinkers suggest that it may sometimes be necessary for the judge to appeal beyond the conceptual form of coherence to the notion of "progress" or "social evolution," but they underplay rather than emphasize the controversial character of these ideas. Even the Continentals of the free law school took the convention of judicial necessity far more seriously than does the current American academic mainstream.[41]

Typology of Theories of Adjudication

Deduction + judicial legislation	Hart
Judicial legislation	Unger
Deduction + limiting rules + judicial legislation	Raz
Deduction + coherence + judicial legislation	MacCormick
Deduction + coherence + personal political theory	Dworkin
Deduction + coherence	Civilians

It is pretty plain that the development of each of these theories of adjudication has been part of a broader political project. As soon as we shift from understanding adjudication as rule application to understanding it as interpretation, we threaten to destabilize the larger Liberal conceptual structure that distinguishes courts from legislatures, law from politics, technical from democratic decision making, and the rule of law from tyranny. The larger structure, whether understood as a prescription or as a description of reality, plays a central role in ideological controversies among various conservativisms, liberalisms, and radicalisms, including the Marxist variants. The question of the role of ideology in adjudication is an ideological question.

[. . .]

Notes

1 Norberto Bobbio, *Stato, governo, societa: Per una teoria generale della politica* (Turin: Einaudi, 1980).

2 See Jules L. Coleman and Brian Leiter, "Determinacy, Objectivity, and Authority," 142 *U. Pa. L. Rev.* 549 (1993); Heidi L. Feldman, "Objectivity in Legal Judgment," 92 *Mich. L. Rev.* 551 (1994).

3 Stanley Fish, "Working on the Chain Gang: Interpretation in Law and Literature," 60 *Texas L. Rev.* 551 (1982).

4 David L. Shapiro, "Courts, Legislatures, and Paternalism," 74 *Va. L. Rev.* 519, 556–7 (1988) (emphasis mine).

5 Jeffrey Rosen, "Breyer Restraint," *New Republic*, June 11, 1994, p. 20.

6 I don't mean to be taking sides in any extant debate here. Even Ronald Dworkin agrees that judges make law in the minimal sense indicated in the text. Ronald Dworkin, *Law's Empire* (Cambridge, Mass.: Harvard University Press, 1986), p. 6.

7 Linda Greenhouse, "Fierce Combat on Fewer Battlefields," *New York Times*, July 3, 1994, s. 4, p. 1.

8   Anthony Flint, "Breyer Set for Senate Hearings," *Boston Globe*, July 10, 1994, s. 1, pp. 1, 16.

9   John Noonan, "Master of Restraint," *New York Times Book Review*, May 1, 1994, p. 7.

10   Vincent Blasi, "Judge Him Unpredictable," *New York Times Book Review*, June 19, 1994, p. 3.

11   Adam Levine, letter to the editor, "Unpredictable Justice Powell," *New York Times Book Review*, July 10, 1994, p. 31.

12   H. L. A. Hart, *The Concept of Law*, 2d ed. (Oxford: Clarendon Press, 1994).

13   Hart's attitude toward this question is perhaps well represented by this statement: "At this point [where the law runs out] judges may again make a choice that is neither arbitrary nor mechanical; and here often display characteristic judicial virtues, the special appropriateness of which to legal decision explains why some feel reluctant to call such judicial activity 'legislative.' These virtues are: impartiality and neutrality in surveying the alternatives; consideration for the interest of all who will be affected; and a concern to display some acceptable general principle as a reasoned basis for decision." Ibid., p. 200.

14   Hans Kelsen, *Introduction to the Problems of Legal Theory*, trans. B. Litschewski Paulson and S. L. Paulson (Oxford: Clarendon Press, 1992), s. 36. For an interesting collection of essays on Kelsen's theory of interpretation, see *Cognition and Interpretation of Law*, ed. Letizia Gianformaggio and Stanley Paulson (Turin: G. Giapichelli, 1995).

15   Roberto M. Unger, *Knowledge and Politics* (New York: Free Press, 1975), p. 88.

16   Mark V. Tushnet, *Red, White, and Blue: A Critical Analysis of Constitutional Law* (Cambridge, Mass.: Harvard University Press, 1988), pp. 52–7.

17   Gary Peller, "The Metaphysics of American Law," 73 *Cal. L. Rev.* 1151, 1181 (1985).

18   James Boyle, "The Politics of Reason: Critical Legal Theory and Local Social Thought," 133 *U. Pa. L. Rev.* 685, 710–11 (1985).

19   Owen Fiss, "Objectivity and Interpretation," 34 *Stan. L. Rev.* 739 (1982).

20   Paul Brest, "Interpretation and Interest," 34 *Stan. L. Rev.* 765 (1982).

21   Duncan Kennedy, "Legal Formality," 2 *J. Legal Studies* 351, 364, nn. 21, 22 (1973); Duncan Kennedy, "Form and Substance in Private Law Adjudication," 89 *Harv. L. Rev.* 1685, 1687–8 (1976).

22   Southern Pacific v. Jensen, 244 U.S. 205, 221 (1917) (Holmes, J., dissenting). See Thomas C. Grey, "Molecular Motions: The Holmesian Judge in Theory and Practice," 37 *Wm. & Mary L. Rev.* 19 (1995).

23   Felix Frankfurter, "The Supreme Court of the United States," in *Law and Politics: Occasional Papers of Felix Frankfurter*, ed. Archibald Macleish and E. F. Pritchard, Jr. (New York: Harcourt, Brace, 1939), p. 21.

24   Joseph Raz, *The Authority of Law: Essays on Law and Morality* (Oxford: Clarendon Press, 1979), ch. 10.

25   See Lon Fuller, "Positivism and Fidelity to Law – A Reply to Professor Hart," 71 *Harv. L. Rev.* 630, 666 (1958).

26   Benjamin Cardozo, *The Nature of the Judicial Process* (New Haven: Yale University Press, 1957).

27   Karl Llewellyn, *The Common Law Tradition: Deciding Appeals* (Boston: Little, Brown, 1960).

28   Lon Fuller, "The Forms and Limits of Adjudication," 92 *Harv. L. Rev.* 353 (1978).

29   Henry M. Hart and Albert Sacks, *The Legal Process: Basic Problems in the Making and Application of Law*, ed. William Eskridge and Phillip Frickey (Westbury, NY: Foundation Press, 1994).

30   Neil MacCormick, *Legal Reasoning and Legal Theory* (Oxford: Clarendon Press, 1978), chs. 7 and 8.

31   J. M. Finnis, "On 'The Critical Legal Studies Movement,'" 30 *Am. J. Jurisprudence* 21, 38 (1985).

32   Dworkin, *Law's Empire*.

33   Ronald Dworkin, *A Matter of Principle* (Cambridge, Mass.: Harvard University Press, 1985), p. 2.

34   Fuller, "The Forms and Limits of Adjudication," pp. 393–405.

35   Hart and Sacks, *The Legal Process*, pp. 646–7.

36   Dworkin, *A Matter of Principle*, p. 147.

37   Gerald Postema, "'Protestant' Interpretation and Social Practices," 6 *Law & Phil.* 283, 289 (1987).

38   Dworkin, *A Matter of Principle*, p. 2.

39   Dworkin, *Law's Empire*, p. 411.

40   See Mitchel Lasser, "Judicial (Self-)Portraits: Judicial Discourse in the French Legal System," 104 *Yale L.J.* 1325, 1343 (1995).

41   André-Jean Arnaud, *Les juristes face à la société du XIXe siècle à nos jours* (Paris: Presses Universitaires de France, 1975).

12

Critical Race Theory:
The Key Writings that
Formed the Movement

Kimberlé Crenshaw, Neil Gotanda,
Gary Peller, and Kendall Thomas

Introduction

This volume offers a representative, though by no means exhaustive, compilation of the growing body of legal scholarship known as Critical Race Theory (CRT). As we conceive it, Critical Race Theory embraces a movement of left scholars, most of them scholars of color, situated in law schools, whose work challenges the ways in which race and racial power are constructed and represented in American legal culture and, more generally, in American society as a whole. In assembling and editing these essays, we have tried both to provide a sense of the intellectual genesis of this project and to map the main methodological directions that Critical Race Theory has taken since its inception. Toward these ends, the essays in the first few parts are arranged roughly in the chronological order of their publication. The remaining parts, however, are devoted to the most important methodological strands of Critical Race Theory today. We have chosen to present the substance of the original essays rather than small portions of a greater number of works, in the interest of providing the reader with texts that retain as much of their complexity, context, and nuance as possible.

As these writings demonstrate, there is no canonical set of doctrines or methodologies to which we all subscribe. Although Critical Race scholarship differs in object, argument, accent, and emphasis, it is nevertheless unified by two common interests. The first is to understand how a regime of white supremacy and its subordination of people of color have been created and maintained in America, and, in particular, to examine the relationship between that social structure and professed ideals such as "the rule of law" and "equal protection." The second is a desire not merely to understand the vexed bond between law and racial power but to *change* it. The essays gathered here thus share an ethical commitment to human liberation – even if we reject conventional notions of what such a conception means, and though we often disagree, even among ourselves, over its specific direction.

This ethical aspiration finds its most obvious concrete expression in the pursuit of engaged, even adversarial, scholarship. The writings in this collaboration may be read as contributions to what Edward Said has called "antithetical knowledge," the development of counteraccounts of social reality by subversive and subaltern elements of the reigning order. Critical Race Theory – like the

Critical Legal Studies movement with which we are often allied – rejects the prevailing orthodoxy that scholarships should be or could be "neutral" and "objective." We believe that legal scholarship about race in America can never be written from a distance of detachment or with an attitude of objectivity. To the extent that racial power is exercised legally and ideologically, legal scholarship about race is an important site for the construction of that power, and thus is always a factor, if "only" ideologically, in the economy of racial power itself. To use a phrase from the existentialist tradition, there is "no exit" – no scholarly perch outside the social dynamics of racial power from which merely to observe and analyze. Scholarship – the formal production, identification, and organization of what will be called "knowledge" – is inevitably political. Each of the texts in this volume seeks in its own way not simply to explicate but also to intervene in the ideological contestation of race in America, and to create new, oppositionist accounts of race.

The aspect of our work which most markedly distinguishes it from conventional liberal and conservative legal scholarship about race and inequality is a deep dissatisfaction with traditional civil rights discourse. As several of the authors in this collection demonstrate, the reigning contemporary American ideologies about race were built in the sixties and seventies around an implicit social compact. This compact held that racial power and racial justice would be understood in very particular ways. Racial justice was embraced in the American mainstream in terms that excluded radical or fundamental challenges to status quo institutional practices in American society by treating the exercise of racial power as rare and aberrational rather than as systemic and ingrained. The construction of "racism" from what Alan Freeman terms the "perpetrator perspective" restrictively conceived racism as an intentional, albeit irrational, deviation by a conscious wrongdoer from otherwise neutral, rational, and just ways of distributing jobs, power, prestige, and wealth. The adoption of this perspective allowed a broad cultural mainstream both explicitly to acknowledge the fact of racism and, simultaneously, to insist on its irregular occurrence and limited significance. As Freeman concludes, liberal race reforms thus served to legitimize the basic myths of American meritocracy.

In Gary Peller's depiction, this mainstream civil rights discourse on "race relations" was constructed in this way partly as a defense against the more radical ideologies of racial liberation presented by the Black Nationalist and Black Consciousness movements of the sixties and early seventies, and their less visible but intellectually subversive scholarly presentations by people such as James Turner, now a teacher in black studies at Cornell. In the construction of "racism" as the irrational and backward bias of believing that someone's race is important, the American cultural mainstream neatly linked the black left to the white racist right: according to this quickly coalesced consensus, because race-consciousness characterized both white supremacists and black nationalists, it followed that both were racists. The resulting "center" of cultural common sense thus rested on the exclusion of virtually the entire domain of progressive thinking about race within colored communities. With its explicit embrace of race-consciousness, Critical Race Theory aims to reexamine the terms by which race and racism have been negotiated in American consciousness, and to recover and revitalize the radical tradition of race-consciousness among African-Americans and other peoples of color – a tradition that was discarded when integration, assimilation and the ideal of color-blindness became the official norms of racial enlightenment.

The image of a "traditional civil rights discourse" refers to the constellation of ideas about racial power and social transformation that were constructed partly by, and partly as a defense against, the mass mobilization of social energy and popular imagination in the civil rights movement of the late fifties and sixties. To those who participated in the civil rights movements firsthand – say, as part of the street and body politics engaged in by Reverend Martin Luther King, Jr.'s cadres in town after town across the South – the fact that they were part of a deeply subversive movement of mass resistance and social transformation was obvious. Our opposition to traditional civil rights discourse is neither a criticism of the civil rights movement nor an attempt to diminish its significance. On the contrary, as Anthony Cook's radical reading of King's theology and social theory makes explicit, we draw much of our inspiration and sense of direction from that courageous, brilliantly conceived, spiritually inspired, and ultimately transformative mass action.

Of course, colored people made important social gains through civil rights reform, as did American society generally: in fact, but for the civil rights movement's victories against racial exclusion, this volume and the Critical Race Theory movement generally could not have been taught at mainstream law schools. The law's incorporation of what several authors here call "formal equality" (the prohibition against explicit racial exclusion, like "whites only" signs) marks a decidedly progressive moment in US political and social history. However, the fact that civil rights advocates met with some success in the nation's courts and legislatures ought not to obscure the central role the American legal order played in the deradicalization of racial liberation movements. Along with the suppression of explicit white racism (the widely celebrated aim of civil rights reform), the dominant legal conception of racism as a discrete and identifiable act of "prejudice based on skin color" placed virtually the entire range of everyday social practices in America – social practices developed and maintained throughout the period of formal American apartheid – beyond the scope of critical examination or legal remediation.

The affirmative action debate [. . .] provides a vivid example of what we mean. From its inception, mainstream legal thinking in the US has been characterized by a curiously constricted understanding of race and power. Within this cramped conception of racial domination, the evil of racism exists when – and only when – one can point to specific, discrete acts of racial discrimination, which is in turn narrowly defined as decision-making based on the irrational and irrelevant attribute of race. Given this essentially negative, indeed, dismissive view of racial identity and its social meanings, it was not surprising that mainstream legal thought came to embrace the ideal of "color-blindness" as the dominant moral compass of social enlightenment about race. Mainstream legal argument regarding "race relations" typically defended its position by appropriating Dr King's injunction that a person should be judged "by the content of his character rather than the color of his skin" and wedding it to the regnant ideologies of equal opportunity

and American meritocracy. Faced with this state of affairs, liberal proponents of affirmative action in legal and policy arenas – who had just successfully won the formal adoption of basic antidiscrimination norms – soon found themselves in a completely defensive ideological posture. Affirmative action requires the use of race as a socially significant category of perception and representation, but the deepest elements of mainstream civil rights ideology had come to identify such race-consciousness as racism itself. Indeed, the problem here was not simply political and strategic: the predominant legal representation of racism as the mere recognition of race matched the "personal" views of many liberals themselves, creating for them a contradiction in their hearts as well as their words.

Liberal antidiscrimination proponents proposed various ways to reconcile this contradiction: they characterized affirmative action as a merely "exceptional" remedy for past injustice, a temporary tool to be used only until equal opportunity is achieved or a default mechanism for reaching discrimination that could not be proved directly. Separate but related liberal defenses of affirmative action hold that its beneficiaries have suffered from "deprived" backgrounds that require limited special consideration in the otherwise fully rational and unbiased competition for social goods, or that affirmative action promotes social "diversity," a value which in the liberal vision is independent of, perhaps even at odds with, equality of opportunity or meritocracy.

The poverty of the liberal imagination is belied by the very fact that liberal theories of affirmative action are framed in such defensive terms, and so clearly shaped by the felt need to justify this perceived departure from purportedly objective findings of "merit" (or the lack thereof). These apologetic strategies testify to the deeper ways civil rights reformism has helped to legitimize the very social practices – in employment offices and admissions departments – that were originally targeted for reform. By constructing "discrimination" as a deviation from otherwise legitimate selection processes, liberal race rhetoric affirms the underlying ideology of just deserts, even as it reluctantly tolerates limited exceptions to meritocratic mythology. Despite their disagreements about affirmative action, liberals and conservatives who embrace dominant civil rights discourse treat the category of merit itself as neutral and impersonal, outside of social power and unconnected to systems of racial privilege. Rather than engaging in a broad-scale inquiry into why jobs, wealth, education, and power are distributed as they are, mainstream civil rights discourse suggests that once the irrational biases of race-consciousness are eradicated, everyone will be treated fairly, as equal competitors in a regime of equal opportunity.

What we find most amazing about this ideological structure in retrospect is how very little actual social change was imagined to be required by "the civil rights revolution." One might have expected a huge controversy over the dramatic social transformation necessary to eradicate the regime of American apartheid. By and large, however, the very same whites who administered explicit policies of segregation and racial domination kept their jobs as decision makers in employment offices of companies, admissions offices of schools, lending offices of banks, and so on. In institution after institution, progressive reformers found themselves struggling over the implementation of integrationist policy with the former administrators of segregation who soon regrouped as an old guard "concerned" over the deterioration of "standards."

The continuity of institutional authority between the segregationist and civil rights regimes is only part of the story. Even more dramatic, the same criteria for defining "qualifications" and "merit" used during the period of explicit racial exclusion continued to be used, so long as they were not directly "racial." Racism was identified only with the outright formal exclusion of people of color; it was simply assumed that the whole rest of the culture, and the de facto segregation of schools, work places, and neighborhoods, would remain the same. The sheer taken-for-grantedness of this way of thinking would pose a formidable and practically insurmountable obstacle. Having rejected race-consciousness in toto, there was no conceptual basis from which to identify the cultural and ethnic character of mainstream American institutions; they were thus deemed to be racially and culturally neutral. As a consequence, the deeply transformative potential of the civil rights movement's interrogation of racial power was

successfully aborted as a piece of mainstream American ideology.

Within the predominantly white law school culture where most of the authors represented in this volume spend professional time, the law's "embrace" of civil rights in the Warren Court era is proclaimed as the very hallmark of justice under the rule of law. In our view, the "legislation" of civil rights movement and its "integration" into the mainstream commonsense assumptions in the late sixties and early seventies were premised on a tragically narrow and conservative picture of the goals of racial justice and the domains of racial power. In the balance of this introduction, we describe as matters both of institutional politics and intellectual inquiry how we have come to these kinds of conclusions.

In his essay on the Angelo Herndon case, Kendall Thomas describes and pursues a central project of Critical Race scholarship: the use of critical historical method to show that the contemporary structure of civil rights rhetoric is not the natural or inevitable meaning of racial justice but, instead, a collection of strategies and discourses born of and deployed in particular political, cultural, and institutional conflicts and negotiations. Our goal here is similar. We hope to situate the strategies and discourses of Critical Race Theory within the broader intellectual and social currents from which we write, as well as within the specific work place and institutional positions where we are located and from which we struggle.

The emergence of Critical Race Theory in the eighties, we believe, marks an important point in the history of racial politics in the legal academy and, we hope, in the broader conversation about race and racism in the nation as a whole. As we experienced it, mostly as law students or beginning law professors, the boundaries of "acceptable" race discourse had become suddenly narrowed, in the years from the late sixties to the late seventies and early eighties, both in legal institutions and in American culture more generally. In the law schools we attended, there were definite liberal and conservative camps of scholars and students. While the debate in which these camps engaged was clearly important – for example, how the law should define and identify illegal racial

What is it to hold a belief and not act on it?.

I A B C .
II
III

power – the reigning discourse seemed, at least to us, ideologically impoverished and technocratic.

In constitutional law, for example, it was well settled that government-sanctioned racial discrimination was prohibited, and that legally enforced segregation constituted such discrimination. That victory was secured in *Brown v. Board of Education* and its progeny. In the language of the Fourteenth Amendment, race is a "suspect classification" which demands judicial strict scrutiny. "Race relations" thus represent an exception to the general deference that mainstream constitutional theory accords democratically elected institutions. Racial classifications violate the equal protection clause unless they both serve a compelling governmental interest and further, are no broader than necessary to achieve that goal. Within the conceptual boundaries of these legal doctrines, mainstream scholars debated whether discrimination should be defined only as intentional government action [. . .] or whether the tort-like "de facto" test should be used when government actions had predictable, racially skewed results [. . .] or whether the racial categories implicit in affirmative action policy should be legally equivalent to those used to burden people of color and therefore also be subject to strict scrutiny [. . .] and then whether remedying past social discrimination was a sufficiently compelling and determinate goal to survive strict scrutiny [. . .] and so on.

In all these debates we identified, of course, with the liberals against the intent requirement established in *Washington v. Davis*, the affirmative action limitations of *Bakke* (and later *Croson*), the curtailment of the "state action" doctrine resulting in the limitation of sites where constitutional antidiscrimination norms would apply, and so on. Yet the whole discourse seemed to assume away the fundamental problem of racial subordination whose examination was at the center of the work so many of us had spent our college years pursuing in Afro-American studies departments, community mobilizations, student activism, and the like.

The fact that affirmative action was seen as such a "dilemma" or a "necessary evil" was one symptom of the ultimately conservative character of even "liberal" mainstream race discourse. More generally, though, liberals and conservatives seemed to see the issues of race and law from within the same structure of analysis – namely, a policy that legal rationality could identify and eradicate the biases of race-consciousness in social decision-making. Liberals and conservatives as a general matter differed over the degree to which racial bias was a fact of American life: liberals argued that bias was widespread where conservatives insisted it was not; liberals supported a disparate effects test for identifying discrimination, where conservatives advocated a more restricted intent requirement; liberals wanted an expanded state action requirement, whereas conservatives wanted a narrow one. The respective visions of the two factions differed only in scope: they defined and constructed "racism" the same way, as the opposite of color-blindness.

In any event, however compelling the liberal vision of achieving racial justice through legal reform overseen by a sympathetic judiciary may have been in the sixties and early seventies, the breakdown of the national consensus for the use of law as an instrument for racial redistribution rendered the vision far less capable of appearing even merely pragmatic. By the late seventies, traditional civil rights lawyers found themselves fighting, and losing, rearguard attacks on the limited victories they had only just achieved in the prior decade, particularly with respect to affirmative action and legal requirements for the kinds of evidence required to prove illicit discrimination. An increasingly conservative judiciary made it clear that the age of ever expanding progressive law reform was over.

At the same time that these events were unfolding, a predominantly white left emerged on the law school scene in the late seventies, a development which played a central role in the genesis of Critical Race Theory. Organized by a collection of neo-Marxist intellectuals, former New Left activists, ex-counter-culturalists, and other varieties of oppositionists in law schools, the Conference on Critical Legal Studies established itself as a network of openly leftist law teachers, students, and practitioners committed to exposing and challenging the ways American law served to legitimize an oppressive social order. Like the later experience of Critical Race writers vis-à-vis race scholarship, "crits" found themselves frustrated with the presuppositions of the conventional scholarly legal discourse: they opposed not only conservative legal work but also the dominant liberal varieties. Crits contended that liberal and conservative legal scholarship operated in the narrow ideological channel within which law was understood as qualitatively different from politics. The faith of liberal lawyers in the gradual reform of American law though the victory of the superior rationality of progressive ideas depended on a belief in the central ideological myth of the law/politics distinction, namely, that legal institutions employ a rational, apolitical, and neutral discourse with which to mediate the exercise of social power. This, in essence, is the role of law as understood by liberal political theory. Yet politics was embedded in the very doctrinal categories with which law organized and represented social reality. Thus the deeply political character of law was obscured in one way by the obsession of mainstream legal scholarship with technical discussions about standing, jurisdiction and procedure; and the political character of judicial decision-making was – or could be – determined by preexisting legal rules, standards, and policies, all of which were applied according to professional craft standards encapsulated in the idea of "reasoned elaboration." Law was, in the conventional wisdom, distinguished from politics because politics was open-ended, subjective, discretionary, and ideological, whereas law was determinate, objective, bounded, and neutral.

This conception of law as rational, apolitical, and technical operated as an institutional regulative principle, defining what was legitimate and illegitimate to pursue in legal scholarship, and symbolically defining the professional, businesslike culture of day-to-day life in mainstream law schools. This generally characterized the entire post-war period in legal education, with virtually no organized dissent. Its intellectual and ideological premises had not been seriously challenged since the Legal Realist movement of the twenties and thirties – a body of scholarship that mainstream scholars ritually honored for the critique of the "formalism" of turn-of-the-century legal discourse but marginalized as having "gone too far" in its critique of the very possibility of a rule of law. Writing during the so-called liberty of contract period (characterized by the Supreme Court's invalidation of labor reform legislation on the grounds that it violated the "liberty" of workers and owners to contract

with each other over terms of employment) the legal realists set out to show that the purportedly neutral and objective legal interpretation of the period was really based on politics, on what Oliver Wendell Holmes called the "hidden and often inarticulate judgments of social policy."

The crits unearthed much of the Legal Realist work that mainstream legal scholars had ignored for decades, and they found the intellectual and theoretical basis for launching a full-scale critique of the role of law in helping to rationalize an unjust social order. While the Realist critique of American law's pretensions to neutrality and rationality was geared toward the right-wing libertarianism of an "Old Order" of jurists, crits redirected it at the depoliticized and technocratic assumptions of legal education and scholarship in the seventies. Moreover, in the sixties tradition from which many of them had come, they extended the intellectual and ideological conflict they engendered to the law school culture to which it was linked.

By the late seventies, Critical Legal Studies existed in a swirl of formative energy, cultural insurgency, and organizing momentum: It had established itself as a politically, philosophically, and methodologically eclectic but intellectually sophisticated and ideologically left movement in legal academia, and its conferences had begun to attract hundreds of progressive law teachers, students, and lawyers; even mainstream law reviews were featuring critical work that reinterpreted whole doctrinal areas of law from an explicitly ideological motivation. Moreover, in viewing law schools as work-places, and thus as organizing sites for political resistance, "CLSers" actively recruited students and left-leaning law teachers from around the country to engage in the construction of left legal scholarship and law school transformation. CLS quickly became the organizing hub for a huge burst of left legal scholarly production and for various oppositional political challenges in law school institutional life. Several left scholars of color identified with the movement, and most important for the eventual genesis of Critical Race Theory a few years later, CLS succeeded in at least one aspect of its frontal assault on the depoliticized character of legal education. By the late seventies, explicitly right-wing legal scholarship had developed its own critique of the conventional assumptions, just as the national mood turned to the right with the election of Ronald Reagan. The law school as an institution was, by then, an obvious site for ideological contestation as the apolitical pretensions of the "nonideological" center began to disintegrate.

Critical Race Theory emerged in the interstices of this political and institutional dynamic. Critical Race Theory thus represents an attempt to inhabit and expand the space between two very different intellectual and ideological formations. Critical Race Theory sought to stage a simultaneous encounter with the exhausted vision of reformist civil rights scholarship, on the one hand, and the emergent critique of left legal scholarship on the other. Critical Race Theory's engagement with the discourse of civil rights reform stemmed directly from our lived experience as students and teachers in the nation's law schools. We both saw and suffered the concrete consequences that followed from liberal legal thinkers' failure to address the constrictive role that racial ideology plays in the composition and culture of American institutions, including the American law school. Our engagement with progressive left legal academics stemmed from our sense that their focus on legal ideology, legal scholarship and politics of the American law school provided a language and a practice for viewing the institutions in which we studied and worked both as sites and targets for our developing critique of law, racism, and social power.

In identifying the liberal civil rights tradition and the Critical Legal Studies movement as key factors in the emergence of Critical Race Theory, we do not mean to offer an oversimplified genealogy in which Critical Race Theory appears as a simple hybrid of the two. We view liberal civil rights scholarship and the work of the critical legal theorists not so much as rudimentary components of Critical Race Theory, but as elements in the conditions of its possibility. In short, we intend to evoke a particular atmosphere in which progressive scholars of color struggled to piece together an intellectual identity and a political practice that would take the form both of a left intervention into race discourse and a race intervention into left discourse. [. . .]

13

Feminist Legal Critics:
The Reluctant Radicals

Patricia Smith

Feminist legal criticism began not as a radical critique, but as a liberal argument for the universal application of traditional legal categories.[1] The early campaigns for universal suffrage are the first obvious examples. The arguments for women's suffrage were radical only in the limited sense that they tended to restrict traditional patriarchal power and to equalize the political power of women in a very limited way. Women's suffrage was in that sense socially radical, but this fact was hardly recognized at the time. That is, giving women the vote was not widely expected to change the social, legal, or political situation of women in any radical way at all.

And conceptually, the arguments for women's suffrage were not radical in any sense; they were liberal. It was not necessary for them to be radical. This was because of an interesting contradiction between universal liberal rhetoric and patriarchal social structures that depended for its resolution on ultimately unsustainable factual assumptions about the differences between the basic nature of men and women. These assumptions were explicitly built into law in the form of overt prohibitions against the participation of women in various aspects of public life.

In the case of voting, for examples, the prohibition against women voting was most generally based on the view that women were incapable of understanding political issues. Incompetence (along with danger, including moral danger) has been the most common argument throughout all of history against women doing almost everything. The incompetence argument has struck contemporary feminists as ironic in the face of apparently powerful counterexamples, such as Cleopatra and Queen Elizabeth, to name only two powerful female leaders who seemed to understand not only political issues but political strategy quite as well as any man. But human beings have never allowed powerful but inconvenient counterexamples to stand in the way of powerful and convenient theories, and we still do not. We call them exceptions, and early political thinkers called them exceptions too. Queens didn't count. But eventually, as women gradually became more generally educated, the exceptions overpowered the rule of incompetence as to voting, and the prohibition was overcome. This development was based on a liberal rather than a radical view. The liberal view is that all human beings are presumptively entitled to

Patricia Smith, "Feminist Legal Critics: The Reluctant Radicals," in Stephen M. Griffin and Robert C. L. Moffat, eds., *Radical Critiques of the Law* (Lawrence, KS: University Press of Kansas, 1997), pp. 143–61. © 1997 by the University Press of Kansas.

equal treatment, or equality before the law. Eighteenth-century political rhetoric speaks this way about human rights, often referred to as the "rights of man." Now, the fact is that a significant portion of the human population was excluded from these "human" rights. Apparently you had to prove you were human. Native Americans, Chinese immigrants, and African-American slaves had no more rights than women; and the justification was that these groups of individuals were different. (What they were different from was left unspecified, but the assumption was that they were different from the norm, which was taken as given, and which in this country had the characteristics of white, male, heterosexual Christians of European heritage.) The presumption of equality was overridden when it came to the rights of others or did not apply to them because of "intrinsic" differences of race and sex.

Thus, the great liberal debate of the nineteenth and twentieth centuries has been over who gets included in the ranks of personhood, citizenship, and humanity. Over time the circle was expanded to include more and more groups that had previously been considered unfit for rights: non-property owners, working men, different nationalities, different races, and finally even women. In all of these cases the decision to include these groups was based on the conclusion that differences that were previously thought significant were not significant after all. For purposes of law it was decided that differences between the excluded groups and the included group were largely irrelevant. What never changed was the norm – the standard of evaluation or the standard of comparison. That standard was based on the status quo founded in the assumptions of those in power. The standard was never questioned because it was assumed to be necessary, neutral and universal – simply a description of the world. Thus, the great liberal debate was over which classes of people are factually or materially (as opposed to morally) equal (that is, psychologically, dispositionally, and intellectually equal to the norm), then and only then were you entitled to formal equality or equality before the law.

That was the forum entered by liberal feminists, and it is in fact the forum of greatest advance in the cause of women's rights. One thing that shows is that much of the liberal ideal is correct – most differences between groups of people should be considered irrelevant to law. But in recent decades women have discovered that the liberal program has certain serious limitations, and that discovery has led many feminists to a more radical evaluation of law and to the greatest intellectual contribution that feminists have made to legal analysis, namely the critique of traditional discriminatory norms. Nowadays, feminists are asking why, as a matter of justice, those in power are entitled to formulate standards that favor themselves by which to measure all others. As a matter of power this is easily understood. As a matter of justice it is quite puzzling. The answer to the puzzle is that the norms formulated by those in power are not characterized as favoring themselves, but as neutral descriptions of necessary features of the world. So the current challenge for feminist scholars is to show how norms traditionally considered neutral are actually biased. The feminist critique of equal protection law provides the clearest illustration of both the liberal approach and its limits, while some recent work of feminist legal critics in this area and others demonstrates the new and radicalized challenge feminism now presents to previously unexamined discriminatory legal norms. In the next two sections I consider each of these to illustrate the development of feminist legal analysis as a certain form of radical legal critique.

The Evolution of Sex Discrimination in Equal Protection Law

The 1950s and 1960s marked the first serious consideration among the American people of the possibility that a legal system overall might be biased against an entire class of people, and in particular an entire race of people. (Of course, the Marxists had been making the class argument for years, but it had very little impact in the United States.) With the struggle for civil rights for American blacks came the realization that law itself was at least sometimes used systematically to disadvantage an entire group with no apparent justification, because by the 1960s it had become embarrassing to argue that blacks are not human beings, or not human "in the relevant sense."

It is interesting that it took more than a decade for any serious analogies to be drawn between the legal treatment of blacks and the legal treatment of women, but at least by the 1970s effective arguments were being made that sexism was in some sense analogous to racism. In 1971 the Supreme Court struck down for the first time a sex-based classification as a violation of the equal protection clause of the Fourteenth Amendment.[2] The arguments made in this case and others of the time were analogous to the liberal arguments being made against race discrimination. For example, in 1973 ACLU counsel Ruth Bader Ginsberg argued in *Frontiero v. Richardson* that sex-based classifications, like racially based classifications, should be recognized as constitutionally suspect on three grounds. First, historically women have been subjugated and restricted as a class. Second, women ought to be judged on their individual merits rather than on the basis of stereotypes that are often inaccurate, and even if accurate in general may be inaccurate as applied to a particular individual. (In other words, if an individual woman meets the standard norm she ought not to be eliminated by a blanket prohibition against women as a class.) Third, sex is an immutable characteristic that often bears no relation to the ability to perform or contribute.[3]

Thus, the typical argument for the advancement of women's rights in the early 1970s was the liberal argument that challenged the dominant power to make good on its universal claims for impartiality and justice by opposing historical oppression, recognizing the value of individuality, and avoiding the individual unfairness of frequently inaccurate stereotypes. This argument worked well initially, at least in blatant cases of overt discrimination, and well it should since it employs the dominant ideology of the classical liberal tradition, which is central to western legal thought. However, it did not take long for problems to crop up.

Since the basis of sex discrimination claims was the traditional idea of similarly situated persons being differentially treated on irrelevant grounds, the Court saw no basis for deciding cases in which persons were not similarly situated. Thus, when *Roe v. Wade* was decided shortly after *Frontiero*, the woman's right to choose abortion

was based on the right to privacy, with no mention of a foundation in equal protection law based on sex.[4] Similarly, when mandatory unpaid maternity leaves for schoolteachers were challenged in *Cleveland Board of Education v. LaFleur*, the Court avoided the sex discrimination claim by striking down the policy on other grounds.[5] Having thus hemmed itself into an analysis of sex discrimination based only on the differential treatment of similarly situated persons, when the Court was faced squarely and unavoidably with the sex discrimination claims of pregnant women in *Geduldig v. Aiello* in 1974, it reached the stunning conclusion that discrimination based on pregnancy does not involve a sex-based classification.[6] *Geduldig* does not represent one of the Court's shining hours. It generated an enormous wave of critical commentary. The extension of the reasoning in *Geduldig* to a Title VII case prompted a swift amendment (the Pregnancy Disability Act) by Congress, repudiating the Court's reasoning. And the Court itself in more recent decisions has backed away from this holding, though it has not changed its general rationale for sex discrimination under the equal protection clause.[7]

The problems caused by the general rationale that bases a discrimination claim solely on the differential treatment of similarly situated persons show that it cannot deal with questions of fair treatment where differences are real. There is something so obviously wrong with the idea that where differences are real equal protection of the law cannot apply, that a raft of critical commentary has been generated which has led to a more radical feminist critique of law. What feminists have realized is that equal protection law itself, while claiming to be neutral, in fact assumes a male standard of what is normal. For example, the average working woman will be pregnant twice during her working career. Pregnancy is abnormal only for a working man. Thus, the standard of normality that discounts pregnancy for working persons is male. The question, of course, is why should that be the standard?

Christine Littleton has summarized the feminist critique of current equality analysis in the following three points that demonstrate its male bias. First, it defines as beyond its scope precisely those issues that women find crucial to their concrete experience as women (such as pregnancy). Second, it construes difference (which is created by the relationship of women to particular, contingent social structures, such as home and work responsibilities) as natural (that is, unchangeable and inherent) and as located solely in the woman herself (women are naturally domestic). Third, it assumes (without evidence) the gender neutrality of social institutions, as well as the notion that practices must distinguish themselves from "business as usual" in order to be seen as unequal.[8]

More briefly put, equality analysis is biased against women in three respects: (1) it is inapplicable once it encounters a "real" difference from men; (2) it locates the difference in women, rather than in relationships; and (3) it fails to question the assumption that social institutions are gender neutral, and that women and men are therefore similarly related to those institutions.

This analysis made many feminists acutely aware of the arbitrariness of norms and of the fact that the inability of the courts to deal with sex discrimination in many cases is directly related to the inability to evaluate biased norms. And some feminists reasoned that if the liberal presumption of neutral legal processes retards the ability to evaluate norms as biased, then the liberal approach is sharply limited in its ability to correct systematic injustice, such as that which grows out of systematic patriarchal norms.

The Development of Feminist Legal Critique as Radical Reform

Feminists have recognized that a significant part of law is the legitimation of the dominant ideology and that a significant part of the dominant ideology of most societies is patriarchal. This is the focus of some recent feminist legal critique. It is the embodiment of the observation that norms are often systematically biased in ways that reinforce the subordination of women to men by assuming a male standard of what is normal, or a male perspective of what is real, and then entrenching these assumptions by characterizing them as neutral. A number of feminists have developed this position in a variety of ways.

Perhaps the best known are the views of Catherine MacKinnon. In a recent book,

MacKinnon sets out a radical feminist thesis of law and jurisprudence.[9] She is concerned with the transformation of belief into reality. Law, she points out, is a crucial factor in that transformation. Virtually all societies, she notes, are organized in social hierarchies that subordinate women to men on the basis of sex, as well as subordinating certain people to others on the basis of race and class. These facts of social organization which institutionalize social power are embodied in the organization of states as law. That is, through law, social domination is made both legitimate and invisible. It becomes reality – just the way things are. Liberal legalism or positivist jurisprudence buries the embodiment of patriarchal dominance even further by insisting that the proper domain of jurisprudence is descriptive, not evaluative or normative. As she puts it:

> Liberal legalism [i.e., legal positivism] is thus a medium for making male dominance both invisible and legitimate by adopting the male point of view in law at the same time as it enforces that view on society. . . . Through legal mediation, male dominance is made to seem a feature of life, not a one-sided construct imposed by force for the advantage of a dominant group. To the degree it succeeds ontologically, male dominance does not look epistemological: control over being produces control over consciousness. . . . Dominance reified becomes difference. Coercion legitimated becomes consent. . . . In the liberal state, the rule of law – neutral, abstract, elevated, pervasive – both institutionalizes the power of men over women and institutionalizes power in its male form.[10]

There are many variations on this theme. Quite a number of feminists have suggested that legal standards often uncritically reinforce social disadvantages imposed on women. For example, Deborah Rhode[11] and Christine Littleton[12] have both suggested moderate versions of the radical thesis that recognize the need to address structural problems of patriarchy that entrench inequality, but argue for addressing them in terms of disadvantage rather than domination. Both are examples of feminist theories that call for accepting diversity in all its forms, using law to ensure that diversity is not penalized. Both require the equal acceptance of cultural differences and concentrate on eliminating the unequal consequences of sex differences, whatever their origin or nature. One of the attractive features of this approach is that it makes no particular assumptions about the intrinsic psychological nature of men or women. It does not presume that we can know what the intrinsic differences or similarities might be, or what the sexes would be like if social conditioning were different. It holds only that no cultural position should be penalized – it should not be a disadvantage to be one sex or race or nationality rather than another. The idea, as Littleton puts it, is to embrace diversity and make difference costless.

In another interesting proposal from a rather different direction, Nadine Taub and Wendy Williams[13] have suggested one way in which the courts could formulate in legal doctrine the ideal that difference should not be penalized. Taub and Williams advocate the expansion of what the Court has called the *Griggs* doctrine of discriminatory impact.[14] Very generally speaking, the *Griggs* doctrine says that if a norm or practice has a disproportionate impact on a suspect class (such as a race or sex) then that norm or practice is subject to reevaluation. Unfortunately, the Court has chosen to restrict rather than expand the *Griggs* doctrine, but suggestions like that of Taub and Williams show that equal protection could be made an effective device for the protection of disadvantaged classes if the dominant class saw fit to develop it in that direction.

Whether these critiques are formulated in terms of disproportionate impact, the domination of women or their disadvantage, all represent a shift from liberal claims for inclusion in traditional norms to a radical critique of those norms as fundamentally biased. Martha Minow[15] has generalized this position to a critique of the inability of courts (and particularly the Supreme Court's inability) to deal with the problem of differences in a pluralistic society. Unexamined assumptions create what Minow calls dilemmas of difference for the courts. Minow points out that the Supreme Court is often faced with the apparent dilemma of reinforcing disadvantage no matter which choice it makes. If it recognizes a disadvantage so as to correct it, it may reinforce stereotypes that perpetuate it. On the other hand, if the Court ignores the difference so as to counter the stereotypes associated with it, then there is no way to address the disadvantage

attached to the difference.[16] This is a serious problem for all classes that are systematically disadvantaged, since the "neutral" (that is, disinterested and detached) application of biased standards simply reproduces systematic disadvantage, thus calling into question the very meaning of neutrality. Minow suggests that courts could defuse these dilemmas by recognizing the unexamined assumptions that generate them.

First, she points out, we commonly assume that differences are intrinsic rather than relational or comparative. Women are considered intrinsically different rather than different as compared to men. Jews are intrinsically different rather than different as compared to Christians, and so forth. As Minow points out, men are as different from women as women are from men; Christians are as different from Jews as Jews are from Christians. The question is why the norm should be male and Christian? Second, we typically adopt an unstated norm as a point of reference in evaluating others. This norm is not neutral or inevitable, but it seems so when left unstated and unexamined. It is taken as given rather than recognized as chosen. It is assumed universal rather than recognized as particular. Third, we treat the perspective of the person doing the judging as objective, even though in fact no one can see fully from someone else's point of view or without a point of view. Fourth, we assume that the perspective of those being judged is either irrelevant or already covered by the supposedly objective and universal perspective of the judge. Fifth, it is assumed that the status quo – the existing social and economic arrangement – is natural, neutral, inevitable, uncoerced, and good. So departures from the status quo risk non-neutrality and interference with individual freedom. Minow believes that making these assumptions explicit will require judges to examine the foundations of their own perspectives, which are often not recognized as perspectives at all. Once recognized as perspectives, the views must be defended as compared to other perspectives rather than being erroneously assumed as universal.[17]

The above examples illustrate that many feminists today recognize that a significant part of law is the legitimation of the status quo (which is to say, the dominant power or ideology) and that a significant part of the dominant ideology of our society (and most others) is patriarchal. Thus, standard traditional norms must be examined and defended in terms of the interests of all people rather than assumed as inevitable and neutral.

However, a fact that many feminists do not mention but most presume is that patriarchy is not the only or the entire dominant ideology of this society. Our society is also individualist, committed to justice and freedom, committed to the ideals of impartiality, the rule of law and equality before the law. These are not patriarchal ideals as such.[18] They are universal, humanistic ideals. In fact, they are not particularly compatible with patriarchy; and this contradiction between what is often called liberal ideology (but what might be called humanist ideology) and patriarchy can still be exploited in the cause of justice for women. That is, the contradiction between patriarchy and humanistic liberal ideals that are both embodied in Anglo-American law enables even radical feminists to advocate reform rather than revolution. Thus, even radical feminists are radical only in the sense of advocating far-reaching reforms. They need not advocate the overthrow of government, or even the amendment of the Constitution. On the other hand, a commitment to the elimination of patriarchy is a commitment to revolutionize fundamental social and legal institutions.

The view of Taub and Williams illustrates this clearly. On the one hand, the proposal they make is very moderate – a simple and reasonable extension of a doctrine already formulated by the Court and regularly used in one form in Title VII cases. In another respect the proposal is a radical one because the effect of it would be to counteract the disadvantages imposed on certain classes of people by social organization itself. Yet, the rationale is perfectly compatible with humanistic liberal ideals verbally expressed in the Anglo-American legal tradition for two hundred years.

Similarly, Minow's suggestions would have a radical impact on the process of judging itself, yet on the other hand, all she is really arguing is that those in power should be accountable to the point of examining their own assumptions. This is so reasonable a requirement that one wonders how anyone committed to rational thinking could argue against it. Certainly, liberals would not.

Even MacKinnon, one of the most radical of feminists, utilizes the distinction between humanistic liberal rhetoric and patriarchal practices. In her recent analysis of equality, MacKinnon argues that the law of equality provides a peculiar opportunity for challenging the inequality of law on behalf of women, since law does not usually guarantee rights to something that does not exist. Equality in law is understood formally, and so it is presumed that by and large women already have it. Many, if not most, formal legal barriers for women have been dismantled. Women can now own property, execute contracts, attend universities, and engage in businesses and professions without formal prohibition. But, as many feminists have observed, this formal equality does not eliminate informal discrimination, nor does it provide equal opportunity in fact. MacKinnon argues that it is up to feminists to make equality law meaningful for women by defining it in terms of the concrete experience of women's lives, and challenging the male forms of power that are affirmatively embodied as rights in law. MacKinnon recognizes that equality is not about character traits or even human nature. It is not about "sameness and difference," as it is so often construed, but about domination and subordination. Equality and inequality are about the distribution of power. To confront that distribution of power directly, recognizing it for what it is, and to remove the mask of legitimacy raised by its legalization is the critical task of feminist jurisprudence, according to MacKinnon.[19]

These positions recognize implicitly or explicitly that there are serious contradictions between the universal values that we profess and the patriarchal institutions that structure our lives. This is a consistent factor in feminist legal analysis that connects recent work with early liberal feminist views. But early liberal feminist criticism was effective only while it was directed at explicitly patriarchal legal doctrines. These patriarchal legal doctrines made the contradiction explicit and clear.[20]

However, feminists today recognize that the form of the contradiction has changed. It is no longer an explicit contradiction between two clearly articulated legal rules. At least much of the time the contradiction is now between two (or more) rather vaguely understood legal norms that are the embodiment of traditional social standards. Thus, traditional standards cannot simply be taken as given. Rebutting false claims of factual difference between men and women is not enough. The contradictions between universal values and patriarchal practices cannot be effectively utilized for freedom and justice for women until the bias of certain norms is recognized.

These problems are far from over, and a major aggravating factor in their solution is the common claim that they have already been solved.[21] I believe that the remaining problems can be usefully characterized in the form of two remaining hurdles.

The first hurdle is simply a development of the original liberal battle: how to keep the discrimination that used to come in overtly through the front door from sneaking covertly through the back door. Old stereotypes die hard, and despite our best efforts to combat unfounded and untestable assumptions about differences between men and women, these assumptions seem able to reinstitute themselves like chameleons in new forms.

The second hurdle is how to get those who occupy positions of power to see that the norms they use are, after all, just the norms they choose, and that many traditional norms in fact benefit men at the expense of women and/or reinforce traditional social arrangements that restrict the freedom of women. Negotiating this hurdle requires a more radical approach to challenging basic norms. Such an approach is not incompatible with classical liberal ideals of justice and equality, but does set up serious tensions with traditional presumptions of neutral legal processes.

The case of *EEOC v. Sears*[22] provides a good example of the issues involved in the first hurdle. This case involved a Title VII class action lawsuit charging Sears Roebuck and Co. with employment discrimination against women in hiring and promotion. The charge was based on statistical evidence that women were greatly underrepresented in higher-paying commission sales positions although the pool of applicants was more or less equal, and lower-paying jobs were predominantly filled by women. This approach relied on a typical focus of Title VII class action suits which utilizes statistics that indicate a disproportionate impact from facially neutral practices as presumptive evidence of discrimination. In other words, if a disproportionate impact is shown, Title VII presumes that discrimination is the reason for it. This, then, shifts the burden of proof to the defendant to provide nondiscriminatory reasons for the differences shown by the statistics.

To meet this burden of proof, Sears argued successfully that women were not underrepresented in the high-paying commission sales jobs because of discrimination, but because women as a class really are not interested in such jobs.[23] Ironically, Sears used the language of certain feminist scholars to support its claim that women dislike competition and value good relationships more than money. According to this view, women tend to sacrifice monetary advancement for less stressful working conditions and more limited hours that enable them to meet their responsibilities at home. So disparities in high-paying jobs are not due to discrimination but to women's own choices. This argument was accepted by the court, even in the face of contradicting testimony from women who had actually applied to Sears for commission sales positions.[24]

Joan Williams[25] has done a good job of pointing out that this reasoning simply re-enshrines old stereotypes of women as passive, domestic, and self-sacrificing. These old stereotypes are powerful and entrenched. It is always easier to fall back into them than it is to get rid of them. What is particularly distressing about the *Sears* case is that it inserts sexist stereotypes into precisely the legislation that was enacted to counteract them. Even if the stereotypes are true as generalizations, Title VII was designed to protect those women who do not fit that generalization, specifically those women who applied for the commission sales positions at Sears. Sears simply discounted these women and so did the court. That is, Sears assumed that those women who applied for commission sales and supervisory positions did not really want those jobs. They were padding their applications to increase their chances of getting hired, it was claimed.[26] Since most women applied for low-level clerking positions, Sears reasoned, that must be what all women prefer. That outrageously invalid argument is the argument that the court accepted as the basis of its interpretation of Title VII. This will disadvantage all future claimants. Furthermore, if actual testimony cannot rebut the Sears argument that women are not interested in competitive work, how could any plaintiff overcome that argument on the part of any employer? One wonders how any woman can ever win a Title VII claim based on disproportionate impact again. Cases like *Sears* show how easy it is to go backward, even with regard to the old liberal argument that we are all human and are entitled to equal treatment based on our individual merits. We have far to go before men and women will be presumed equal, and discriminatory assumptions about the "intrinsic" differences in male and female disposition and intellect are overcome.

There are no easy examples of the issues connected with the second hurdle, because in the evaluation of traditional norms what seems normal is what everyone is used to, and that is the status quo. The challenge always carries the burden of persuasion, always seems at least initially less plausible than the norm, and that is true whether or not the norm is just.[27] Feminists have found that norms are most difficult to challenge where the differences (physical or social) between men and women are real, and where the interests of men and women are perceived to be at odds. In such cases it is the status quo itself that disadvantages women, and it cannot be corrected unless the norm is changed. This involves new evaluations at very fundamental levels.

Consider, for example, the formulation of harm or injury. What constitutes an injury is central to legal action. It has long been a truism that justice and law require interpersonal respect, at least to the extent that we may not intentionally harm, defraud, or interfere with the freedom of other individuals. We are not entitled to cause injury. Virtually all moral and legal theories agree that this is the core of interpersonal responsibility. One person's freedom ends with the freedom and bodily integrity of another. Any individual's rights are limited by the basic rights of all other persons. Thus, coercion, intimidation, fraudulent deception, and bodily injury are prohibited by justice and law without question. That is the settled core of our

moral tradition, but it does not specify what counts as harm or injury, or what qualifies as coercion, intimidation, or deception at a level that can be prohibited.

Somehow injury does not apply the same way to women, at least with respect to men who are related to them or even who know them. If assault is prohibited, why are husbands so often not prosecuted for beating their wives? If exploitation is wrong, why are employers so often not prosecuted for pressuring their employees into sexual relations? If rape is illegal, why are men so often not prosecuted if they are acquainted with the women they coerce into sex? If bodily integrity is a fundamental right, how could decisions regarding pregnancy rest ultimately with anyone other than the women whose body is involved? All of these are areas that involve real differences between men and women, and they are areas in which the interests of men and women can now be interpreted as possibly conflicting.

As Minow has pointed out, contrary to assumptions of universality, all law is formulated from a perspective. So we can hardly be surprised if it turns out to be the perspective of those who formulated it, which is to say, the perspective of powerful men – the traditional patriarchs. It is difficult to assume the perspective of someone else. It takes a level of self-awareness that is truly rare. Nor is it more common for people in power to recognize the limits of their own views and the value of understanding and accommodating the views of others.

Until almost the twentieth century, women were not considered to have interests or views of their own. Women were not independent or free. In fact, they were not separate individuals legally. A woman could not have an interest that conflicted with the interests of her husband or father. Thus, she could not be harmed or injured by her husband or father (unless he killed her). The man to whom she was related was responsible for her and in charge of her.

So it is hardly surprising that wife beating was construed as discipline, which is not a harm. It is not surprising that rape, unlike any other crime, was defined from the perspective of the perpetrator rather than the victim. Nor is it surprising that until recently sexual harassment simply did not exist, and procreation (both in terms of contraception and abortion) was controlled by government rather than by women. Women did not have separate interests; their interests were defined by men, from the perspective of men, in terms of the interests of men, because that is who formulated the law. This was not a commitment of liberalism. It is not even compatible with liberalism. It was an assumption of patriarchy that was left unexamined because it was the norm (a) that women had no interests separate from their husbands or fathers, and (b) that the law should not intrude into family matters. The challenge for feminists is then how to change such norms and others like them, which have been taken as given – as normal – for hundreds or even thousands of years.

The very fact that such issues are now being addressed, that such topics are being publicly discussed, is the first sign of social progress. Yet we have far to go before women are recognized as entitled to bodily integrity that cannot be coercively usurped by men who know them and by legislators who presume to define their interests. The great divide between the protection of women from strangers and the nonprotection of women from men who know them reflects old and deeply embedded notions of male supremacy, domination, and the ownership of women. Until recently these views were supported by overt acceptance of male authority and supremacy. Today, many people say that these old presumptions of patriarchy no longer hold. Today we say that women are entitled to determine their own physical integrity by their own voluntary choices.

Yet these abstract ideals have serious concrete limits. Powerful forces have mobilized to oppose reproductive freedom for women on the assumption that women are not entitled to make such choices. The physical integrity of women does not include the right to control their reproductive capacities. Pregnancy is not a harm; it is a blessing. Thus, the norm is still that women are essentially mothers, first and foremost. The choice not to be a mother (i.e., to be in actual control of one's reproductive capacities), while formally acknowledged in law, is still highly controversial and is flatly rejected by many. The long-standing commitment to individual autonomy is a fundamental norm of our society

that has never been and still is not applied equally to men and women. That is because (a) men and women are different, so deciding what an equal commitment to autonomy means is not a simple matter; (b) autonomy was never considered important for women in the past; and (c) those who decided legal, moral, and religious policy about motherhood and procreation were not the same people who were subject to the disadvantages of such policies. So the fight over who should be in control of women's bodies is still far from settled.

And old patterns of social interaction based on norms that subordinate women are perpetuated, largely by denial and by blaming the victim. If a woman is raped or beaten not by a stranger but in the course of normal life, then she must have brought it on herself. If she is harassed by her employer she must have led him on. And anyway, date rape has to be rare. Wife battering is surely uncommon. Sexual harassment must be largely imaginary. We do not want to hear about these problems.

Statistical surveys clearly indicate that women are harmed much more often by men who know them than by any other cause. For example, 4 million women are battered in their homes in the United States each year. Women are harassed, beaten, raped, and killed by men who know them far more often than by strangers. Yet these offenses, with the exception of killing, are still largely unprosecuted. Why? Because we the people excuse the abuse of women as a form of control or an outlet for frustration ("If you can't beat your wife who can you beat?"). This behavior is a hangover from an earlier and more overtly sexist day, and we don't want to know about it. So we pretend that it is a rarity committed by a few outlaws like ordinary crimes. But it is not.[28]

The pervasiveness of these abusive practices attests to the worst features of the continuing sexism of our society. Old norms die hard. Physical coercion and violence remain an option for male domination in personal relations as a last resort. The more women struggle for freedom and equality, the more some men will respond with violence. The more women compete, the more they will be harassed by those who feel threatened or offended by the changing status quo.

And the failure to prosecute attests to the continuing sexism of our law.[29] This will not change significantly until traditional norms are changed that condone it. Until police and prosecutors, judges and juries recognize such injuries as serious harms and stop making excuses for them, women will not be protected. But police and prosecutors, judges and juries by and large reflect the attitudes of the general public.

So long as overpowering your date is not the same as raping a stranger, and beating your wife is not as serious as assaulting someone on the street, and pressuring your secretary into sex is just the way life is, and pregnancy is characterized by Supreme Court justices as an inconvenience, the physical integrity of women will not be determined by their own voluntary choices. Thus, many women today are still dominated by physical force and restrictive legislation, denied the most basic protections of justice by a society and a legal system that pretends that some physical coercion is not real harm, and in any case that women can avoid it by "proper behavior," by understanding their limits. Such a view is not compatible with the liberal commitment to freedom and equal treatment, as liberal feminists have argued for many years. It can only be made compatible by assuming the normative commitments of patriarchy as a fact of life. And that is not actually hard to do (in fact it is actually harder not to do) since patriarchal assumptions have set the standard of normal social relations, religious ideals, moral expectations, and legal standards for thousands of years. Patriarchy is the norm – or more accurately, it is an enormously complex network of norms. It is challenging those norms and that network that constitutes the radical agenda of modern feminists. It is an agenda that does not conflict with liberal values; it does not require overthrow of the government, or even amending the Constitution, but it does require the eventual transformation of our most fundamental institutions, including extensive legal reform.

Notes

1 "Radical" and "liberal" are terms of multiple definition and use. I consider a radical critique to be one that calls for revolutionary or funda-

mental change of some sort, but not necessarily military overthrow, or political upheaval, or even immediate social change. That is, on my view, a radical critique can call for incremental or evolutionary change, so long as the ultimate goal is monumental or profound. "Liberal" is harder to define because it standardly encompasses a broad swath of views ranging from communitarian to libertarian. But usually liberals are thought to fall somewhere between those two poles. I believe that all liberals are committed to freedom, justice, and the significance of individuals, although they may interpret these values in very different ways. Thus, on my view, it is possible for a radical critique to rest on liberal values. The two positions are not categorically antagonistic. However, whether a particular radical critique is compatible with a particular liberal view depends on the particulars of both. I will use the term "liberal" to stand for a commitment to freedom, justice in the form of equal treatment, and the significance of individuals.

2 *Reed v. Reed*, 404 U.S. 71 (1971).

3 411 U.S. 677 (1973).

4 410 U.S. 113 (1973).

5 414 U.S. 632 (1974).

6 417 U.S. 484 (1974).

7 See *Newport News Ship, and Dry Dock v. E.E.O.C.*, 103 S. Ct. 2622 (1983). The general rationale is that individuals cannot be treated differently on the basis of sex unless there is some clearly specifiable difference that justifies different treatment. Thus, so long as the sexes are similar they must be treated the same.

8 C. Littleton, "Reconstructing Equality," *Calif. L. Rev.* 75 (1987): 1279.

9 C. MacKinnon, *Toward a Feminist Theory of the State* (Cambridge: Harvard University Press, 1989).

10 Ibid., 237–8.

11 D. Rhode, *Justice and Gender* (Cambridge: Harvard University Press, 1989).

12 Littleton, "Reconstructing Equality."

13 N. Taub and W. Williams, "Will Equality Require More...?" *Rutgers L. Rev./Civ. Rts. Dev.* 37 (1985): 825.

14 See *Griggs v. Duke Power*, 401 U.S. 424 (1971).

15 M. Minow, "Foreword: Justice Engendered," *Harvard L. Rev* 101 (1987): 10.

16 The common formulation of the early debate over women's rights illustrates the problem. It was asked whether women, being different, should argue for equal rights or for special rights. Equal rights (i.e., identical rights) seemed to disadvantage women sometimes (e.g., as to pregnancy benefits), and so some argued that

special rights were needed to accommodate women's special needs and circumstances. Others argued that only equal (i.e., identical) rights should be claimed because any special needs or differences acknowledged by women are always used to limit women in the long run, and special rights will be viewed as special favors that accommodate women's deficiencies. The problem is that if that is the way the issue is formulated, then women lose either way because the (unstated) norm is male. After all, who is it that women are different from? Whose rights (if equality is the standard) should women's rights be equal to? And if women's rights should sometimes be different from men's, why is it women's rights that are characterized as special? Why not formulate rights in terms of women's needs and characterize men's rights as special? One way makes as much sense as the other. The question is, who is the norm?

17 Minow, "Justice Engendered."

18 Some feminists consider all these principles to be patriarchal, but most feminists either do not specify their position on this point or hold a more contextually based view rather like that expressed here.

19 MacKinnon, *Toward a Feminist Theory*.

20 In *Reed v. Reed*, for example, it was held that a woman could not be barred from being the executrix of an estate on the basis of her sex, since there was no demonstrable difference between men and women in regard to administering an estate. The (patriarchal) state law that excluded all women as a class from that activity was clearly contradicted by our supposedly universal commitment to freedom and equal treatment and by our constitutional commitment to equal protection of the law.

21 See, e.g., D. Rhode, "The 'No Problem' Problem: Feminist Challenges and Cultural Change," *Yale L. J.* 100 (1991): 1731.

22 628 F. Supp. 1264 (N.D. Ill. 1986).

23 It is worth noting that in *Castro v. Beecher*, 334 F. Supp. 930, 936 (D. Mass. 1976), an almost identical argument, that the underrepresentation of blacks in law enforcement was simply due to their lack of interest, was rejected by the court as racist. And in *Glover v. Johnson*, 478 F. Supp. 1075, 1086–8 (E.D. Mich. 1979), the argument that women did not need vocational training since women preferred unskilled jobs anyway was also rejected as prejudice. Thus, in the past courts have rejected justifications of disparities based on supposed lack of interest.

24 The court also ignored expert testimony from a historian who argued that history shows that women accept more competitive jobs whenever

they become available. See J. Williams, "Deconstructing Gender," *Mich. L. Rev.* 87 (1989): 797.

25 Ibid.

26 The Sears managers, the statistical analyst, and the guidebook for hiring all systematically discounted applications of women for traditionally male positions (such as commission sales). The statistical analyst explained on the witness stand exactly how she went about discounting all applications of women for "male" jobs. Yet the court accepted this approach as appropriately reflecting the (supposed) interests of women, despite conflicting testimony by women that they had in fact wanted commission sales positions. This demonstrates the power of stereotypes, once accepted. See ibid., 813–20.

27 For example, in *Plessy v. Ferguson*, 163 U.S. 537, the case that established the legitimacy of racial segregation under the equal protection clause, the Court said (among other things): "The object of the amendment was undoubtedly to enforce the absolute equality of the two races before the law, but, in the nature of things, it could not have been intended to abolish distinctions based upon color, or to enforce social, as distinguished from political, equality, or a commingling of the two races upon terms unsatisfactory to either." Segregation was the norm. A mere constitutional amendment requiring racial equality could not rebut the presumption of the legitimacy of the status quo, hence the Court's interpretation of "equal protection" allowed the norm to stand. It appears clearly unjust to us today, but at the time it seemed perfectly reasonable, which attests to the strength of the status quo. How many reasonable and defensible sexist judgments of the 1980s and 1990s will seem similarly outrageous fifty years from now? We haven't the distance to tell.

28 During the Vietnam War 59,000 soldiers were killed, causing a storm of public outrage. During the same period 54,000 women were killed by their male partners, without so much as a whisper of public protest. We can say we didn't know. (That's what the Germans said about the Jews.) But why didn't we know? It was public record. We didn't want to know. And we still don't. Women's voices are louder now, but we still mostly ignored the recent Senate report (Senate Report no. 197, 102nd Cong., 1st Sess. (1991)) noting that both rape and domestic violence have sharply increased in the past decade. Four million women are severely battered every year, the leading cause of injury for US women (much greater than assault by strangers). From 2,000 to 4,000 women are now murdered by their male partners yearly. In 1990 more

women were beaten by their male partners than were married. Nor can the increase of rape and battery be fully explained by better reporting, because the government systematically under-estimates the numbers of such victims. See Senate Report no. 197.

29 Again using domestic violence as my example, women cannot escape this harm without legal intervention. Three-fourths of all reported domestic violence assaults occur after a woman has left her partner, and the majority of murdered battered women are killed after they leave.

Between 1983 and 1987 battered women shelters reported over a 100 percent increase in women seeking refuge, and 1 million per year were turned away for lack of space. Yet funding in the past five years has been decreased. Half of all homeless women in the United States in the past decade were refugees of domestic violence. But legal response has been slow. Only fifteen states have laws that prosecute batterers and protect victims. See gen. K. Culliton, "Domestic Violence Legislation in Chile and the US" (unpublished manuscript).

14

Riggs v. Palmer (1889)

[handwritten note, top right:] grandson (Elmer) poisoned his grandfather (Francis) so that he could possess the property in the will faster.

Opinion by: Earl

OPINION: Earl, J.   On the 13th day of August 1880, Francis B. Palmer made his last will and testament, in which he gave small legacies to his two daughters, Mrs Riggs and Mrs Preston, the plaintiffs in this action, and the remainder of his estate to his grandson, the defendant, Elmer E. Palmer, subject to the support of Susan Palmer, his mother, with a gift over to the two daughters, subject to the support of Mrs Palmer, in case Elmer should survive him and die under age, unmarried and without any issue. The testator at the date of his will owned a farm and considerable personal property. He was a widower, and thereafter, in March 1882, he was married to Mrs Bresee, with whom before his marriage he entered into an ante-nuptial contract in which it was agreed that, in lieu of dower and all other claims upon his estate in case she survived him, she should have her support upon his farm during her life, and such support was expressly charged upon the farm. At the date of the will, and, subsequently, to the death of the testator, Elmer lived with him as a member of his family, and at his death was sixteen years old. He knew of the provisions made in his favor in the will and, that he might prevent his grandfather from revoking such provisions, which he had manifested some intention

to do, and to obtain the speedy enjoyment and immediate possession of his property, he willfully murdered him by poisoning him. He now claims the property, and the sole question for our determination is, can he have it? The defendants say that the testator is dead; that his will was made in due form and has been admitted to probate and that, therefore, it must have effect according to the letter of the law.

It is quite true that statutes regulating the making, proof and effect of wills, and the devolution of property, if literally construed, and if their force and effect can in no way and under no circumstances be controlled or modified, give this property to the murderer.

The purpose of those statutes was to enable testators to dispose of their estates to the objects of their bounty at death, and to carry into effect their final wishes legally expressed; and in considering and giving effect to them this purpose must be kept in view. It was the intention of the law-makers that the donees in a will should have the property given to them. But it never could have been their intention that a donee who murdered the testator to make the will operative should have any benefit under it. If such a case had been present to their minds, and it had been supposed necessary to make some provision of law to meet it, it cannot be doubted that they would have

[handwritten note, bottom:] – According to law, [literal] Elmer is entitled to the property.

[handwritten note, bottom:] – should murderer benefit from his crime and recive the property?

Riggs v. Palmer, 22 N.E. 188 (1889).

[handwritten: lawmakers could not make laws for every specific case → need interpretation of law]

provided for it. It is a familiar canon of construction that a thing which is within the intention of the makers of a statute is as much within the statute as if it were within the letter; and a thing which is within the letter of the statute is not within the statute, unless it be within the intention of the makers. The writers of laws do not always express their intention perfectly, but either exceed it or fall short of it, so that judges are to collect it from probable or rational conjectures only, and this is called rational interpretation; and Rutherforth, in his Institutes (p. 407) says: "When we make use of rational interpretation, sometimes we restrain the meaning of the writer so as to take in less, and sometimes we extend or enlarge his meaning so as to take in more than his words express."

Such a construction ought to be put upon a statute as will best answer the intention which the makers had in view, for *qui haeret in litera, haeret in cortice.* In Bacon's Abridgment (Statutes I, 5); Pufendorf (book 5, chapter 12), Rutherforth (pp. 422, 427), and in Smith's Commentaries (814), many cases are mentioned where it was held that matters embraced in the general words of statutes, nevertheless, were not within the statutes, because it could not have been the intention of the law-makers that they should be included. They were taken out of the statutes by an equitable construction, and it is said in Bacon: "By an equitable construction, a case not within the letter of the statute is sometimes holden to be within the meaning, because it is within the mischief for which a remedy is provided. The reason for such construction is that the law-makers could not set down every case in express terms. In order to form a right judgment whether a case be within the equity of a statute, it is a good way to suppose the law-maker present, and that you have asked him this question, did you intend to comprehend this case? Then you must give yourself such answer as you imagine he, being an upright and reasonable man, would have given. If this be that he did mean to comprehend it, you may safely hold the case to be within the equity of the statute; for while you do no more than he would have done, you do not act contrary to the statute, but in conformity thereto." In some cases the letter of a legislative act is restrained by an equitable construction; in others it is enlarged; in others the

construction is contrary to the letter. The equitable construction which restrains the letter of a statute is defined by Aristotle, as frequently quoted, in this manner: *Aequitas est correctio legis generaliter latoe qua parti deficit.* If the law-makers could, as to this case, be consulted, would they say that they intended by their general language that the property of a testator or of an ancestor should pass to one who had taken his life for the express purpose of getting his property? In 1 Blackstone's Commentaries (91) the learned author, speaking of the construction of statutes, says: "If there arise out of them any absurd consequences manifestly contradictory to common reason, they are, with regard to those collateral consequences, void. When some collateral matter arises out of the general words, and happens to be unreasonable, then the judges are in decency to conclude that the consequence was not foreseen by the parliament, and, therefore, they are at liberty to expound the statute by equity and only *quoad hoc* disregard it"; and he gives as an illustration, if an act of parliament gives a man power to try all causes that arise within his manor of Dale, yet, if a cause should arise in which he himself is party, the act is construed not to extend to that because it is unreasonable that any man should determine his own quarrel.

[handwritten: X ? should be what reasonable or rational man would do]

There was a statute in Bologna that whoever drew blood in the streets should be severely punished, and yet it was held not to apply to the case of a barber who opened a vein in the street. It is commanded in the Decalogue that no work shall be done upon the Sabbath, and yet, giving the command a rational interpretation founded upon its design, the Infallible Judge held that it did not prohibit works of necessity, charity or benevolence on that day.

What could be more unreasonable than to suppose that it was the legislative intention in the general laws passed for the orderly, peaceable and just devolution of property, that they should have operation in favor of one who murdered his ancestor that he might speedily come into the possession of his estate? Such an intention is inconceivable. We need not, therefore, be much troubled by the general language contained in the laws.

[handwritten: J answers question]

Besides, all laws as well as all contracts may be controlled in their operation and effect by

[handwritten: → maxim of common law.]

[handwritten margin note, top: — Crazy to think that one who murdered and prematurely caused the death, to be entitled to inheritance.]

general, fundamental maxims of the common law. No one shall be permitted to profit by his own fraud, or to take advantage of his own wrong, or to found any claim upon his own iniquity, or to acquire property by his own crime. These maxims are dictated by public policy, have their foundation in universal law administered in all civilized countries, and have nowhere been superseded by statutes. They were applied in the decision of the case of the *New York Mutual Life Insurance Company* v. *Armstrong* (117 U.S. 591). There it was held that the person who procured a policy upon the life of another, payable at his death, and then murdered the assured to make the policy payable, could not recover thereon. Mr Justice Field, writing the opinion, said: "Independently of any proof of the motives of Hunter in obtaining the policy, and even assuming that they were just and proper, he forfeited all rights under it when, to secure its immediate payment, he murdered the assured. It would be a reproach to the jurisprudence of the country if one could recover insurance money payable on the death of a party whose life he had feloniously taken. As well might he recover insurance money upon a building that he had willfully fired."

[handwritten margin note: common law maxims → help people obey moral laws. (common laws)]

These maxims, without any statute giving them force or operation, frequently control the effect and nullify the language of wills. A will procured by fraud and deception, like any other instrument, may be decreed void and set aside, and so a particular portion of a will may be excluded from probate or held inoperative if induced by the fraud or undue influence of the person in whose favor it is. (*Allen* v. *M'Pherson*, 1 H.L. Cas. 191; *Harrison's Appeal*, 48 Conn. 202.) So a will may contain provisions which are immoral, irreligious or against public policy, and they will be held void.

Here there was no certainty that this murderer would survive the testator, or that the testator would not change his will, and there was no certainty that he would get this property if nature was allowed to take its course. He, therefore, murdered the testator expressly to vest himself with an estate. Under such circumstances, what law, human or divine, will allow him to take the estate and enjoy the fruits of his crime? The will spoke and became operative at the death of the testator. He caused that death, and thus by his crime made it speak and have operation. Shall it speak and operate in his favor? If he had met the testator and taken his property by force, he would have had no title to it. Shall he acquire title by murdering him? If he had gone to the testator's house and by force compelled him, or by fraud or undue influence had induced him to will him his property, the law would not allow him to hold it. But can he give effect and operation to a will by murder, and yet take the property? To answer these questions in the affirmative, it seems to me, would be a reproach to the jurisprudence of our state, and an offense against public policy.

Under the civil law evolved from the general principles of natural law and justice by many generations of jurisconsults, philosophers and statesmen, one cannot take property by inheritance or will from an ancestor or benefactor whom he has murdered. [...] In the Civil Code of Lower Canada the provisions on the subject in the Code Napoleon have been substantially copied. But, so far as I can find, in no country where the common law prevails has it been deemed important to enact a law to provide for such a case. Our revisers and law-makers were familiar with the civil law, and they did not deem it important to incorporate into our statutes its provisions upon this subject. This is not a *casus omissus*. It was evidently supposed that the maxims of the common law were sufficient to regulate such a case and that a specific enactment for that purpose was not needed.

For the same reasons the defendant Palmer cannot take any of this property as heir. Just before the murder he was not an heir, and it was not certain that he ever would be. He might have died before his grandfather, or might have been disinherited by him. He made himself an heir by the murder, and he seeks to take property as the fruit of his crime. What has before been said as to him as legatee applies to him with equal force as an heir. He cannot vest himself with title by crime.

My view of this case does not inflict upon Elmer any greater or other punishment for his crime than the law specifies. It takes from him no property, but simply holds that he shall not acquire property by his crime, and thus be rewarded for its commission.

[handwritten margin note, bottom: — giving him property would reward him for murder → he might not have been the heir if he didn't kill him.]

[handwritten top-left: under any law: common? civil, natural]

Our attention is called to *Owens v. Owens* (100 N.C. 240), as a case quite like this. There a wife had been convicted of being an accessory before the fact to the murder of her husband, and it was held that she was, nevertheless, entitled to dower. I am unwilling to assent to the doctrine of that case. The statutes provide dower for a wife who has the misfortune to survive her husband and thus lose his support and protection. It is clear beyond their purpose to make provision for a wife who by her own crime makes herself a widow and willfully and intentionally deprives herself of the support and protection of her husband. As she might have died before him, and thus never have been his widow, she cannot by her crime vest herself with an estate. The principle which lies at the bottom of the maxim, *volenti non fit injuria*, should be applied to such a case, and a widow should not, for the purpose of acquiring, as such, property rights, be permitted to allege a widowhood which she has wickedly and intentionally created.

The facts found entitled the plaintiffs to the relief they seek. The error of the referee was in his conclusion of law. Instead of granting a new trial, therefore, I think the proper judgment upon the facts found should be ordered here. The facts have been passed upon twice with the same result, first upon the trial of Palmer for murder, and then by the referee in this action. We are, therefore, of opinion that the ends of justice do not require that they should again come in question.

The judgment of the General Term and that entered upon the report of the referee should, therefore, be reversed and judgment should be entered as follows: That Elmer E. Palmer and the administrator be enjoined from using any of the personalty or real estate left by the testator for Elmer's benefit; that the devise and bequest in the will to Elmer be declared ineffective to pass the title to him; that by reason of the crime of murder committed upon the grandfather he is deprived of any interest in the estate left by him; that the plaintiffs are the true owners of the real and personal estate left by the testator, subject to the charge in favor of Elmer's mother and the widow of the testator, under the ante-nuptial agreement, and that the plaintiffs have costs in all the courts against Elmer.

Dissent by: Gray

[handwritten: (appealling)]

DISSENT: Gray, J. (dissenting)   This appeal presents an extraordinary state of facts, and the case, in respect of them, I believe, is without precedent in this state.

The respondent, a lad of sixteen years of age, being aware of the provisions in his grandfather's will, which constituted him the residuary legatee of the testator's estate, caused his death by poison in 1882. For this crime he was tried and was convicted of murder in the second degree, and at the time of the commencement of this action he was serving out his sentence in the state reformatory. This action was brought by two of the children of the testator for the purpose of having those provisions of the will in the respondent's favor canceled and annulled.

The appellants' argument for a reversal of the judgment, which dismissed their complaint, is that the respondent unlawfully prevented a revocation of the existing will, or a new will from being made, by his crime, and that he terminated the enjoyment by the testator of his property and effected his own succession to it by the same crime. They say that to permit the respondent to take the property willed to him would be to permit him to take advantage of his own wrong.

To sustain their position the appellants' counsel has submitted an able and elaborate brief, and, if I believed that the decision of the question could be affected by considerations of an equitable nature, I should not hesitate to assent to views which commend themselves to the conscience. But the matter does not lie within the domain of conscience. We are bound by the rigid rules of law, which have been established by the legislature and within the limits of which the determination of this question is confined. The question we are dealing with is, whether a testamentary disposition can be altered, or a will revoked, after the testator's death, through an appeal to the courts, when the legislature has, by its enactments, prescribed exactly when and how wills may be made, altered and revoked, and apparently, as it seems to me, when they have been fully complied with, has left no room for the exercise of an equitable jurisdiction by courts over such matters. Modern jurisprudence, in recognizing the right of the individual, under more or less restrictions, to dispose of his

[handwritten bottom: Defendant argues that the matter does not lie within conscience or morality; they are bound by rules of law which do not state that will can be revoked.]

[handwritten margin note top: —there are exceptions to revoke wills; but murdering the old man is not one of them.]

property after his death, subjects it to legislative control, both as to extent and as to mode of exercise. Complete freedom of testamentary disposition of one's property has not been and is not the universal rule; as we see from the provisions of the Napoleonic Code, from those systems of jurisprudence in other countries which are modeled upon the Roman law, and from the statutes of many of our states. To the statutory restraints, which are imposed upon the disposition of one's property by will, are added strict and systematic statutory rules for the execution, alteration and revocation of the will; which must be, at least, substantially, if not exactly, followed to insure validity and performance. The reason for the establishment of such rules, we may naturally assume, consists in the purpose to create those safeguards about these grave and important acts, which experience has demonstrated to be the wisest and surest. That freedom, which is permitted to be exercised in the testamentary disposition of one's estate by the laws of the state, is subject to its being exercised in conformity with the regulations of the statutes. The capacity and the power of the individual to dispose of his property after death, and the mode by which that power can be exercised, are matters of which the legislature has assumed the entire control, and has undertaken to regulate with comprehensive particularity.

[handwritten margin note: Defendant; "one shall not benefit from his own wrongs" does not apply to the legal system]

The appellants' argument is not helped by reference to those rules of the civil law, or to those laws of other governments, by which the heir or legatee is excluded from benefit under the testament, if he has been convicted of killing, or attempting to kill, the testator. In the absence of such legislation here, the courts are not empowered to institute such a system of remedial justice. The deprivation of the heir of his testamentary succession by the Roman law, when guilty of such a crime, plainly, was intended to be in the nature of a punishment imposed upon him. The succession, in such a case of guilt, escheated to the exchequer. [. . .]

[handwritten margin note: courts are not empowered to institute such rules.]

I concede that rules of law, which annul testamentary provision made for the benefit of those who have become unworthy of them, may be based on principles of equity and of natural justice. It is quite reasonable to suppose that a testator would revoke or alter his will, where his mind has been so angered and changed as to make him

unwilling to have his will executed as it stood. But these principles only suggest sufficient reasons for the enactment of laws to meet such cases.

The statutes of this state have prescribed various ways in which a will may be altered or revoked; but the very provision, defining the modes of alteration and revocation, implies a prohibition of alteration or revocation in any other way. The words of the section of the statute are: "No will in writing, except in the cases hereinafter mentioned, nor any part thereof, shall be revoked or altered otherwise," etc. Where, therefore, none of the cases mentioned are met by the facts, and the revocation is not in the way described in the section, the will of the testator is unalterable. I think that a valid will must continue as a will always, unless revoked in the manner provided by the statutes. Mere intention to revoke a will does not have the effect of revocation. The intention to revoke is necessary to constitute the effective revocation of a will; but it must be demonstrated by one of the acts contemplated by the statute. As Woodworth, J., said in *Dan* v. *Brown* (4 Cow. 490): "Revocation is an act of the mind, which must be demonstrated by some outward and visible sign of revocation." The same learned judge said in that case: "The rule is that if the testator lets the will stand until he dies, it is his will; if he does not suffer it to do so, it is not his will." (*Goodright* v. *Glasier*, 4 Burr. 2512, 2514; *Pemberton* v. *Pemberton*, 13 Ves. 290.)

The finding of fact of the referee, that, presumably, the testator would have altered his will, had he known of his grandson's murderous intent, cannot affect the question. We may concede it to the fullest extent; but still the cardinal objection is undisposed of, that the making and the revocation of a will are purely matters of statutory regulation, by which the court is bound in the determination of questions relating to these acts. Two cases in this state and in Kentucky, at an early day, seem to me to be much in point. *Gains* v. *Gains* (2 Marshall, 190), was decided by the Kentucky Court of Appeals in 1820. It was there urged that the testator intended to have destroyed his will, and that he was forcibly prevented from doing so by the defendant in error or devisee, and it was insisted that the will, though not expressly, was thereby virtually revoked. The court held, as the act concerning wills prescribed the manner in which a will might be revoked, that as none of the acts evidencing revocation were done, the intention could not be substituted for the act. In that case the will was snatched away and forcibly retained. In 1854, Surrogate Bradford, whose opinions are entitled to the highest consideration, decided the case of *Leaycraft* v. *Simmons* (3 Bradf. 35). In that case the testator, a man of eighty-nine years of age, desired to make a codicil to his will, in order to enlarge the provisions for his daughter. His son having the custody of the instrument, and the one to be prejudiced by the change, refused to produce the will, at testator's request, for the purpose of alteration. The learned surrogate refers to the provisions of the civil law for such and other cases of unworthy conduct in the heir or legatee, and says, "our statute has undertaken to prescribe the mode in which wills can be revoked (citing the statutory provision). This is the law by which I am governed in passing upon questions touching the revocation of wills. The whole of this subject is now regulated by statute, and a mere intention to revoke, however well authenticated, or however defeated, is not sufficient." And he held that the will must be admitted to probate. I may refer also to a case in the Pennsylvania courts. In that state the statute prescribed the mode for repealing or altering a will, and in *Clingan* v. *Mitcheltree* (31 Pa. State Rep. 25) the Supreme Court of the state held, where a will was kept from destruction by the fraud and misrepresentation of the devisee, that to declare it canceled as against the fraudulent party would be to enlarge the statute.

I cannot find any support for the argument that the respondent's succession to the property should be avoided because of his criminal act, when the laws are silent. Public policy does not demand it, for the demands of public policy are satisfied by the proper execution of the laws and the punishment of the crime. There has been no convention between the testator and his legatee, nor is there any such contractual element in such a disposition of property by a testator, as to impose or imply conditions in the legatee. The appellants' argument practically amounts to this: That as the legatee has been guilty of a crime, by the commission of which he is placed in a position to sooner receive the benefits of the testamentary provision, his rights to the property should be forfeited and he should be divested of his estate. To allow their argument to prevail would involve the diversion by the court of the testator's estate into the hands of persons, whom, possibly enough, for all we know, the testator might not have chosen or desired as its recipients. Practically the court is asked to make another will for the testator. The laws do not warrant this judicial action, and mere presumption would not be strong enough to sustain it.

But more than this, to concede appellants' views would involve the imposition of an additional punishment or penalty upon the respondent. What power or warrant have the courts to add to the respondent's penalties by depriving him of property? The law has punished him for his crime, and we may not say that it was an insufficient punishment. In the trial and punishment of the respondent the law has vindicated itself for the outrage which he committed, and further judicial utterance upon the subject of punishment or deprivation of rights is barred. We may not, in the language of the court in *People* v. *Thornton* (25 Hun. 456), "enhance the pains, penalties and forfeitures provided by law for the punishment of crime."

The judgment should be affirmed, with costs.

Questions

1 How does Hart's positivism differ from the command theory of law?

2 What are legal principles and how are they a challenge to positivist theories of law?

3 Explain why Posner thinks that wealth maximization is the basis of legal decision-making? Do you think that wealth maximization also accounts for Dworkin's idea of legal principles?

4 What does Moore mean when he argues that legality must take part in morality? How would Kennedy disagree with Moore?

5 How do you think Hart would decide in the *Riggs* case?

Part III

International Law

Introduction

Jeremy Bentham coined the term "international law" to stand for the law governing the relations of states. Since Bentham's time, international law has been a perennial topic in jurisprudence, at least in part because it remains unclear whether and to what extent international law is really law. There are significant normative issues as well, including whether international law is binding, and upon whom, as well as whether various practices such as humanitarian intervention are consistent with principles of international law. We agree with H. L. A. Hart that international law is a hard case for any concept of law. Indeed, we begin this section with a chapter from Hart's *The Concept of Law*.

Hart closes his book with a chapter on international law. In excerpts from this book that are in an earlier reading (see chapter 7), we saw that Hart holds the view that law is best seen as a union of primary and secondary rules. The problem is that international law lacks secondary rules. Hart now asks whether a somewhat wider use of the term "law" might not be justifiable and whether international law could then fit under that category, just as is true in common usage. In addition, Hart asks whether international law is binding. He argues that international law is indeed properly called law and that it is binding in a certain sense as well. Hart also argues that states can be sovereign and still allow for the existence of binding international law. He ends

this excerpt by indicating that international law is not merely international morality.

Mark W. Janis asks what the relationship is between international law and morality by investigating one of the most difficult of all international law concepts, the idea of *jus cogens* norms. While Hart works within the tradition of legal positivism, Janis works within the natural law tradition. He contends that international law has focused too much on what states declare to be binding, rather than what are overriding principles. And he points out that international law already recognizes a category of norms that cannot be overridden by treaties and other acts of states. To make sense of such norms, Janis thinks that we must make reference to natural law concepts. Janis suggests that natural law principles might provide a kind of constitutional order for the international legal realm. This topic is taken up later in our book in the constitutional law section.

Fernando R. Tesón defends a third alternative, a Kantian approach that is an alternative to positivism and natural law theory. Tesón contrasts his view with the tradition of realism in international relations theory, the dominant school of thought opposed to moral theories like natural law theory and Kantianism. Realism asserts that international relations are governed by the self-interests of states, not by universal moral norms. Tesón offers criticisms of this view, and then defends an alternative. His Kantian thesis stipulates that "an international act is in principle immoral when it violates human rights." In his view, international intervention into a sovereign state can occur when that state or its government is illegitimate, for instance when it is no longer accountable to its people, when it has become corrupt, or when the state violates the principles of its constitution.

Jack L. Goldsmith and Eric A. Posner defend the view that self-interest not morality is the key consideration in international law. They approach international law from the perspective of the law and economics movement that we explored in earlier readings. Goldsmith and Posner rightly say that the state is an abstraction, since what it does is completely dependent on what individuals do. States act on the self-interests of their members, and international law emerges as an avenue for states to pursue their self-interests. In general, they deny that talk of moral obligations of states can make sense in this realm of self-interest maximization. According to Goldsmith and Posner, states respect each other's borders or decide to cross those borders based on elaborate calculations of self-interest, not on the basis of moral considerations of the sort that Janis and Tesón discussed.

We then turn to a specific debate in international law, concerning the justification of humanitarian intervention. Humanitarian intervention is the use of force by one state against another state for the sake of preventing human rights violations. Allen Buchanan begins this debate by asking whether a state can ever have good moral reasons to justify to its own citizens attacking another state so as to promote a humanitarian objective. Buchanan considers and rejects the view that states exist merely to serve the bidding of their members. Instead, he defends the view that states have legitimacy insofar as they serve the goal of justice, but, given that view, humanitarian intervention can be justified to a state's own citizens because there is no significant difference between promoting justice for its own people and promoting it for some other people.

Larry May is much more skeptical about humanitarian intervention than Buchanan. At least in part, this is because May is worried about the adverse consequences of the use of force by one state against another, namely that civilians will be put in serious jeopardy. Humanitarian intervention should only occur when these risks are outweighed by the benefits of the intervention, and this will only be true in a limited number of cases. In the majority of cases, humanitarian intervention is actually unjustified aggression. Nonetheless, May argues that leaders of states that engage in this form of aggression should generally not be prosecuted since normally their motives are good ones.

Burleigh Wilkins provides us with a very good summary of the various reasons that states could give for engaging in humanitarian intervention. Wilkins finds fault with all the rationales. He is especially concerned that humanitarian intervention appears to be a very serious violation of international law, since it fails to respect the sovereignty of states. Nonetheless, even Wilkins allows that there may be some rare cases where humanitarian intervention is justified, but only where the international community explicitly endorses it. Unilateral humanitarian intervention is not justified because it represents such a serious violation of the rules of the international community.

We end with a brief excerpt from the first case to be decided by the International Criminal Tribunal for the former Yugoslavia. In this case, the defendant challenged the legitimacy of the international tribunal in ways that parallel some of the challenges to international law in general that we have seen in other essays. This excerpt provides a very good example of how the powers originally conveyed to the United Nations Security Council by multilateral treaty have been expanded to incorporate new tribunals and courts that were not even contemplated at the time of the founding of the United Nations. The opinion stresses the role that the United Nations is supposed to play in providing peace and security in the world. The specific way that this is accomplished, by means of a criminal tribunal that will rule on individual culpability for atrocities committed in Yugoslavia in the early 1990s, well illustrates both the positions of those who support, but also those who oppose, the moral underpinnings of international law.

15

International Law

H. L. A. Hart

1. Sources of Doubt

The idea of a union of primary and secondary rules to which so important a place has been assigned in this book may be regarded as a mean between juristic extremes. For legal theory has sought the key to the understanding of law sometimes in the simple idea of an order backed by threats and sometimes in the complex idea of morality. With both of these law has certainly many affinities and connexions; yet, as we have seen, there is a perennial danger of exaggerating these and of obscuring the special features which distinguish law from other means of social control. It is a virtue of the idea which we have taken as central that it permits us to see the multiple relationships between law, coercion, and morality for what they are, and to consider afresh in what, if any, sense these are necessary.

Though the idea of the union of primary and secondary rules has these virtues, and though it would accord with usage to treat the existence of this characteristic union of rules as a sufficient condition for the application of the expression "legal system", we have not claimed that the word "law" must be defined in its terms. It is because we make no such claim to identify or regulate

in this way the use of words like "law" or "legal", that this book is offered as an elucidation of the *concept* of law, rather than a definition of "law" which might naturally be expected to provide a rule or rules for the use of these expressions. Consistently with this aim, we investigated [elsewhere] the claim made in the German cases, that the title of valid law should be withheld from certain rules on account of their moral iniquity, even though they belonged to an existing system of primary and secondary rules. In the end we rejected this claim; but we did so, not because it conflicted with the view that rules belonging to such a system must be called "law", nor because it conflicted with the weight of usage. Instead we criticized the attempt to narrow the class of valid laws by the extrusion of what was morally iniquitous, on the ground that to do this did not advance or clarify either theoretical inquiries or moral deliberation. For these purposes, the broader concept which is consistent with so much usage and which would permit us to regard rules however morally iniquitous as law, proved on examination to be adequate.

International law presents us with the converse case. For, though it is consistent with the

H. L. A. Hart, "International Law," from *The Concept of Law*, 2nd edn. (Oxford: Clarendon Press, 1997), pp. 208–23. © 1961, 1994 by Oxford University Press. Reprinted with permission from Oxford University Press.

usage of the last 150 years to use the expression "law" here, the absence of an international legislature, courts with compulsory jurisdiction, and centrally organized sanctions have inspired misgivings, at any rate in the breasts of legal theorists. The absence of these institutions means that the rules for states resemble that simple form of social structure, consisting only of primary rules of obligation, which, when we find it among societies of individuals, we are accustomed to contrast with a developed legal system. It is indeed arguable, as we shall show, that international law not only lacks the secondary rules of change and adjudication which provide for legislature and courts, but also a unifying rule of recognition specifying "sources" of law and providing general criteria for the identification of its rules. These differences are indeed striking and the question "Is international law really law?" can hardly be put aside. But in this case also, we shall neither dismiss the doubts, which many feel, with a simple reminder of the existing usage; nor shall we simply confirm them on the footing that the existence of a union of primary and secondary rules is a necessary as well as a sufficient condition for the proper use of the expression "legal system". Instead we shall inquire into the detailed character of the doubts which have been felt, and, as in the German case, we shall ask whether the common wider usage that speaks of "international law" is likely to obstruct any practical or theoretical aim.

Though we shall devote to it only a single chapter some writers have proposed an even shorter treatment for this question concerning the character of international law. To them it has seemed that the question "Is international law really law?" has only arisen or survived, because a trivial question about the meaning of words has been mistaken for a serious question about the nature of things: since the facts which differentiate international law from municipal law are clear and well known, the only question to be settled is whether we should observe the existing convention or depart from it; and this is a matter for each person to settle for himself. But this short way with the question is surely too short. It is true that among the reasons which have led theorists to hesitate over the extension of the word "law" to international law, a too simple, and indeed absurd view, of what justifies the

application of the same word to many different things has played some part. The variety of types of principle which commonly guide the extension of general classifying terms has too often been ignored in jurisprudence. Nonetheless, the sources of doubt about international law are deeper, and more interesting than these mistaken views about the use of words. Moreover, the two alternatives offered by this short way with the question ("Shall we observe the existing convention or shall we depart from it?") are not exhaustive; for, besides them, there is the alternative of making explicit and examining the principles that have in fact guided the existing usage.

The short way suggested would indeed be appropriate if we were dealing with a proper name. If someone were to ask whether the place called "London" is *really* London, all we could do would be to remind him of the convention and leave him to abide by it or choose another name to suit his taste. It would be absurd, in such a case, to ask on what principle London was so called and whether this principle was acceptable. This would be absurd because, whereas the allotment of proper names rests *only* on an *ad hoc* convention, the extension of the general terms of any serious discipline is never without its principle or rationale, though it may not be obvious what that is. When as, in the present case, the extension is queried by those who in effect say, "We know that it is called law, but is it really law?", what is demanded – no doubt obscurely – is that the principle be made explicit and its credentials inspected.

We shall consider two principal sources of doubt concerning the legal character of international law and, with them, the steps which theorists have taken to meet these doubts. Both forms of doubt arise from an adverse comparison of international law with municipal law, which is taken as the clear, standard example of what law is. The first has its roots deep in the conception of law as fundamentally a matter of orders backed by threats and contrasts the character of the *rules* of international law with those of municipal law. The second form of doubt springs from the obscure belief that states are fundamentally incapable of being the subjects of legal obligation, and contrasts the character of the *subjects* of international law with those of municipal law.

2. Obligations and Sanctions

The doubts which we shall consider are often expressed in the opening chapters of books on international law in the form of the question "How can international law be binding?" Yet there is something very confusing in this favourite form of question; and before we can deal with it we must face a prior question to which the answer is by no means clear. This prior question is: what is meant by saying of a whole system of law that it is "binding"? The statement that a particular rule of a system is binding on a particular person is one familiar to lawyers and tolerably clear in meaning. We may paraphrase it by the assertion that the rule in question is a valid rule, and under it the person in question has some obligation or duty. Besides this, there are some situations in which more general statements of this form are made. We may be doubtful in certain circumstances whether one legal system or another applies to a particular person. Such doubts may arise in the conflict of laws or in public international law. We may ask, in the former case, whether French or English Law is binding on a particular person as regards a particular transaction, and in the latter case we may ask whether the inhabitants of, for example, enemy-occupied Belgium, were bound by what the exiled government claimed was Belgian law or by the ordinances of the occupying power. But in both these cases, the questions are questions of law which arise *within* some system of law (municipal or international) and are settled by reference to the rules or principles of that system. They do not call in question the general character of the rules, but only their scope or applicability in given circumstances to particular persons or transactions. Plainly the question, "Is international law binding?" and its congeners "How can international law be binding?" or "What makes international law binding?" are questions of a different order. They express a doubt not about the applicability, but about the general legal status of international law: this doubt would be more candidly expressed in the form "Can such rules as these be meaningfully and truthfully said ever to give rise to obligations?" As the discussions in the books show, one source of doubt on this point is simply the absence from the system of centrally organized sanctions.

This is one point of adverse comparison with municipal law, the rules of which are taken to be unquestionably "binding" and to be paradigms of legal obligation. From this stage the further argument is simple: if for this reason the rules of international law are not "binding", it is surely indefensible to take seriously their classification as law; for however tolerant the modes of common speech may be, this is too great a difference to be overlooked. All speculation about the nature of law begins from the assumption that its existence at least makes certain conduct obligatory.

In considering this argument we shall give it the benefit of every doubt concerning the facts of the international system. We shall take it that neither Article 16 of the Covenant of the League of Nations nor Chapter VII of the United Nations Charter introduced into international law anything which can be equated with the sanctions of municipal law. In spite of the Korean war and of whatever moral may be drawn from the Suez incident, we shall suppose that, whenever their use is of importance, the law enforcement provisions of the Charter are likely to be paralysed by the veto and must be said to exist only on paper.

To argue that international law is not binding because of its lack of organized sanctions is tacitly to accept the analysis of obligation contained in the theory that law is essentially a matter of orders backed by threats. This theory, as we have seen, identifies "having an obligation" or "being bound" with "likely to suffer the sanction or punishment threatened for disobedience". Yet, as we have argued, this identification distorts the role played in all legal thought and discourse of the ideas of obligation and duty. Even in municipal law, where there are effective organized sanctions, we must distinguish, for the variety of reasons given in Chapter III [of *The Concept of Law*], the meaning of the external predictive statement "I (you) are likely to suffer for disobedience", from the internal normative statement "I (you) have an obligation to act thus" which assesses a particular person's situation from the point of view of rules accepted as guiding standards of behaviour. It is true that not all rules give rise to obligations or duties; and it is also true that the rules which do so generally call for some sacrifice of private interests, and are generally supported by serious demands for conformity and insistent criticism of deviations. Yet once we free ourselves from the predictive analysis and its parent conception of law as essentially an order backed by threats, there seems no good reason for limiting the normative idea of obligation to rules supported by organized sanctions.

We must, however, consider another form of the argument, more plausible because it is not committed to definition of obligation in terms of the likelihood of threatened sanctions. The sceptic may point out that there are in a municipal system, as we have ourselves stressed, certain provisions which are justifiably called necessary; among these are primary rules of obligation, prohibiting the free use of violence, and rules providing for the official use of force as a sanction for these and other rules. If such rules and organized sanctions supporting them are in this sense necessary for municipal law, are they not equally so for international law? That they are may be maintained without insisting that this follows from the very meaning of words like "binding" or "obligation".

The answer to the argument in this form is to be found in those elementary truths about human beings and their environment which constitute the enduring psychological and physical setting of municipal law. In societies of individuals, approximately equal in physical strength and vulnerability, physical sanctions are both necessary and possible. They are required in order that those who would voluntarily submit to the restraints of law shall not be mere victims of malefactors who would, in the absence of such sanctions, reap the advantages of respect for law on the part of others, without respecting it themselves. Among individuals living in close proximity to each other, opportunities for injuring others, by guile, if not by open attack, are so great, and the chances of escape so considerable, that no mere natural deterrents could in any but the simplest forms of society be adequate to restrain those too wicked, too stupid, or too weak to obey the law. Yet, because of the same fact of approximate equality and the patent advantages of submission to a system of restraints, no combination of malefactors is likely to exceed in strength those who would voluntarily co-operate in its maintenance. In these circumstances, which constitute the background of municipal law,

sanctions may successfully be used against malefactors with relatively small risks, and the threat of them will add much to whatever natural deterrents there may be. But, just because the simple truisms which hold good for individuals do not hold good for states, and the factual background to international law is so different from that of municipal law, there is neither a similar necessity for sanctions (desirable though it may be that international law should be supported by them) nor a similar prospect of their safe and efficacious use.

This is so because aggression between states is very unlike that between individuals. The use of violence between states must be public, and though there is no international police force, there can be very little certainty that it will remain a matter between aggressor and victim, as a murder or theft, in the absence of a police force, might. To initiate a war is, even for the strongest power, to risk much for an outcome which is rarely predictable with reasonable confidence. On the other hand, because of the inequality of states, there can be no standing assurance that the combined strength of those on the side of international order is likely to preponderate over the powers tempted to aggression. Hence the organization and use of sanctions may involve fearful risks and the threat of them add little to the natural deterrents. Against this very different background of fact, international law has developed in a form different from that of municipal law. In a population of a modern state, if there were no organized repression and punishment of crime, violence and theft would be hourly expected; but for states, long years of peace have intervened between disastrous wars. These years of peace are only rationally to be expected, given the risks and stakes of war and the mutual needs of states; but they are worth regulating by rules which differ from those of municipal law in (among other things) not providing for their enforcement by any central organ. Yet what these rules require is thought and spoken of as obligatory; there is general pressure for conformity to the rules; claims and admissions are based on them and their breach is held to justify not only insistent demands for compensation, but reprisals and countermeasures. When the rules are disregarded, it is not on the footing that they are not binding; instead efforts are made to conceal the facts. It may of course be said that such rules are efficacious only so far as they concern issues over which states are unwilling to fight. This may be so, and may reflect adversely on the importance of the system and its value to humanity. Yet that even so much may be secured shows that no simple deduction can be made from the necessity of organized sanctions to municipal law, in its setting of physical and psychological facts, to the conclusion that without them international law, in its very different setting, imposes no obligations, is not "binding", and so not worth the title of "law".

3. Obligation and the Sovereignty of States

Great Britain, Belgium, Greece, Soviet Russia have rights and obligations under international law and so are among its subjects. They are random examples of states which the layman would think of as independent and the lawyer would recognize as "sovereign". One of the most persistent sources of perplexity about the obligatory character of international law has been the difficulty felt in accepting or explaining the fact that a state which is sovereign may also be "bound" by, or have an obligation under, international law. This form of scepticism is, in a sense, more extreme than the objection that international law is not binding because it lacks sanctions. For whereas that would be met if one day international law were reinforced by a system of sanctions, the present objection is based on a radical inconsistency, said or felt to exist, in the conception of a state which is at once sovereign and subject to law.

Examination of this objection involves a scrutiny of the notion of sovereignty, applied not to a legislature or to some other element or person *within* a state, but to a state itself. Whenever the word "sovereign" appears in jurisprudence, there is a tendency to associate with it the idea of a person above the law whose word is law for his inferiors or subjects. We have seen ·in the early chapters of this book how bad a guide this seductive notion is to the structure of a municipal legal system; but it has been an even more potent source of confusion in the theory of international law. It is, of course, *possible* to think of a state along such lines, as if it were a species of Superman – a Being inherently lawless but the source of law for its subjects. From the sixteenth century onwards, the symbolical identification of state and monarch ("L'état c'est moi") may have encouraged this idea which has been the dubious inspiration of much political as well as legal theory. But it is important for the understanding of international law to shake off these associations. The expression "a state" is not the name of some person or thing inherently or "by nature" outside the law; it is a way of referring to two facts: first, that a population inhabiting a territory lives under that form of ordered government provided by a legal system with its characteristic structure of legislature, courts, and primary rules; and, secondly, that the government enjoys a vaguely defined degree of independence.

The word "state" has certainly its own large area of vagueness but what has been said will suffice to display its central meaning. States such as Great Britain or Brazil, the United States or Italy, again to take random examples, possess a very large measure of independence from both legal and factual control by any authorities or persons outside their borders, and would rank as "sovereign states" in international law. On the other hand, individual states which are members of a federal union, such as the United States, are subject in many different ways to the authority and control of the federal government and constitution. Yet the independence which even these federated states retain is large if we compare it with the position, say, of an English county, of which the word "state" would not be used at all. A county may have a local council discharging, for its area, some of the functions of a legislature, but its meagre powers are subordinate to those of Parliament and, except in certain minor respects, the area of the county is subject to the same laws and government as the rest of the country.

Between these extremes there are many different types and degrees of dependence (and so of independence) between territorial units which possess an ordered government. Colonies, protectorates, suzerainties, trust territories, confederations, present fascinating problems of classification from this point of view. In most cases the dependence of one unit on another is expressed in legal forms, so that what is law in the territory of the dependent unit will, at least on certain issues, ultimately depend on law-making operations in the other.

In some cases, however, the legal system of the dependent territory may not reflect its dependence. This may be so either because it is merely formally independent and the territory is in fact governed, through puppets, from outside; or it may be so because the dependent territory has a real autonomy over its internal but not its external affairs, and its dependence on another country in external affairs does not require expression as part of its domestic law. Dependence of one territorial unit on another in these various ways is not, however, the only form in which its independence may be limited. The limiting factor may be not the power or authority of another such unit, but an international authority affecting units which are alike independent of each other. It is possible to imagine many different forms of international authority and correspondingly many different limitations on the independence of states. The possibilities include, among many others, a world legislature on the model of the British Parliament, possessing legally unlimited powers to regulate the internal and external affairs of all; a federal legislature on the model of Congress, with legal competence only over specified matters or one limited by guarantees of specific rights of the constituent units; a régime in which the only form of legal control consists of rules generally accepted as applicable to all; and finally a régime in which the only form of obligation recognized is contractual or self-imposed, so that a state's independence is legally limited only by its own act.

It is salutary to consider this range of possibilities because merely to realize that there are many possible forms and degrees of dependence and independence, is a step towards answering the claim that because states are sovereign they "*cannot*" be subject to or bound by international law or "*can*" only be bound by some specific form of international law. For the word "sovereign" means here no more than "independent"; and, like the latter, is negative in force: a sovereign state is one *not* subject to certain types of control, and its sovereignty is that area of conduct in which it is autonomous. Some measure of autonomy is imported, as we have seen, by the very meaning of the word "state" but the contention that this "*must*" be unlimited or "*can*" only be limited by certain types of obligation is at best the assertion of a claim that states ought to be free of all other restraints, and at worst is an unreasoned dogma. For if in fact we find that there exists among states a given form of international authority, the sovereignty of states is to that extent limited, and it has just that extent which the rules allow. Hence we can only know which states are sovereign, and what the extent of their sovereignty is, when we know what the rules are; just as we can only know whether an Englishman or an American is free and the extent of his freedom when we know what English or American law is. The rules of international law are indeed vague and conflicting on many points, so that doubt about the area of independence left to states is far greater than that concerning the extent of a citizen's freedom under municipal law. Nonetheless, these difficulties do not validate the *a priori* argument which attempts to deduce the general character of international law from an absolute sovereignty, which is assumed, without reference to international law, to belong to states.

It is worth observing that an uncritical use of the idea of sovereignty has spread similar confusion in the theory both of municipal and international law, and demands in both a similar corrective. Under its influence, we are led to believe that there *must* in every municipal legal system be a sovereign legislator subject to no legal limitations; just as we are led to believe that international law *must* be of a certain character because states are sovereign and incapable of legal limitation save by themselves. In both cases, belief in the necessary existence of the legally unlimited sovereign prejudges a question which we can only answer when we examine the actual rules. The question for municipal law is: what is the extent of the supreme legislative authority recognized in this system? For international law it is: what is the maximum area of autonomy which the rules allow to states?

Thus the simplest answer to the present objection is that it inverts the order in which questions must be considered. There is no way of knowing what sovereignty states have, till we know what the forms of international law are and whether or not they are mere empty forms. Much juristic debate has been confused because this principle has been ignored, and it is profitable to consider in its light those theories of international law which are known as "voluntarist" or theories of "auto-limitation". These attempted to reconcile the (absolute) sovereignty of states with the existence of binding rules of international law, by treating all international obligations as self-imposed like the obligation which arises from a promise. Such theories are in fact the counterpart in international law of the social contract theories of political science. The latter sought to explain the facts that individuals, "naturally" free and independent, were yet bound by municipal law, by treating the obligation to obey the law as one arising from a contract which those bound had made with each other, and in some cases with their rulers. We shall not consider here the well-known objections to this theory when taken literally, nor its value when taken merely as an illuminating analogy. Instead we shall draw from its history a threefold argument against the voluntarist theories of international law.

First, these theories fail completely to explain how it is known that states "*can*" only be bound by self-imposed obligations, or why this view of their sovereignty should be accepted, in advance of any examination of the actual character of international law. Is there anything more to support it besides the fact that it has often been repeated? Secondly, there is something incoherent in the argument designed to show that states, because of their sovereignty, *can* only be subject to or bound by rules which they have imposed upon themselves. In some very extreme forms of "auto-limitation" theory, a state's agreement or treaty engagements are treated as mere declarations of its proposed future conduct, and failure to perform is not considered to be a breach of any obligation. This, though very much at variance with the facts, has at least the merit of consistency: it is the simple theory that the absolute sovereignty of states is inconsistent with obligation of any kind, so that, like Parliament, a state cannot bind itself. The less extreme view that a state may impose obligations on itself by promise, agreement, or treaty is not, however, consistent with the theory that states are subject only to rules which they have thus imposed on themselves. For, in order that words, spoken or written, should in certain circumstances function as a

promise, agreement, or treaty, and so give rise to obligations and confer rights which others may claim, *rules* must already exist providing that a state is bound to do whatever it undertakes by appropriate words to do. Such rules presupposed in the very notion of a self-imposed obligation obviously cannot derive *their* obligatory status from a self-imposed obligation to obey them.

It is true that every specific *action* which a given state was bound to do might in theory derive its obligatory character from a promise; none the less this could only be the case if the *rule* that promises, &c., create obligations is applicable to the state independently of any promise. In any society, whether composed of individuals or states, what is necessary and sufficient, in order that the words of a promise, agreement, or treaty should give rise to obligations, is that rules providing for this and specifying a procedure for these self-binding operations should be generally, though they need not be universally, acknowledged. Where they are acknowledged the individual or state who wittingly uses these procedures is bound thereby, whether he or it chooses to be bound or not. Hence, even this most voluntary form of social obligation involves some rules which are binding independently of the choice of the party bound by them, and this, in the case of states, is inconsistent with the supposition that their sovereignty demands freedom from all such rules.

Thirdly there are the facts. We must distinguish the *a priori* claim just criticized, that states *can* only be bound by self-imposed obligations, from the claim that though they could be bound in other ways under a different system, in fact no other form of obligation for states exists under the present rules of international law. It is, of course, possible that the system might be one of this wholly consensual form, and both assertions and repudiations of this view of its character are to be found in the writings of jurists, in the opinions of judges, even of international courts, and in the declarations of states. Only a dispassionate survey of the actual practice of states can show whether this view is correct or not. It is true that modern international law is very largely treaty law, and elaborate attempts have been made to show that rules which appear to be binding on states without their prior consent do in fact rest on consent, though this may have been given only "tacitly" or has to be "inferred". Though not all are fictions, some at least of these attempts to reduce to one the forms of international obligation excite the same suspicion as the notion of a "tacit command" which, as we have seen, was designed to perform a similar, though more obviously spurious, simplification of municipal law.

A detailed scrutiny of the claim that all international obligation arises from the consent of the party bound, cannot be undertaken here, but two clear and important exceptions to this doctrine must be noticed. The first is the case of a new state. It has never been doubted that when a new, independent state emerges into existence, as did Iraq in 1932, and Israel in 1948, it is bound by the general obligations of international law including, among others, the rules that give binding force to treaties. Here the attempt to rest the new state's international obligations on a "tacit" or "inferred" consent seems wholly threadbare. The second case is that of a state acquiring territory or undergoing some other change, which brings with it, for the first time, the incidence of obligations under rules which previously it had no opportunity either to observe or break, and to which it had no occasion to give or withhold consent. If a state, previously without access to the sea, acquires maritime territory, it is clear that this is enough to make it subject to all the rules of international law relating to the territorial waters and the high seas. Besides these, there are more debatable cases, mainly relating to the effect on non-parties of general or multilateral treaties; but these two important exceptions are enough to justify the suspicion that the general theory that all international obligation is self-imposed has been inspired by too much abstract dogma and too little respect for the facts.

4.   International Law and Morality

In Chapter V [of *The Concept of Law*] we considered the simple form of social structure which consists of primary rules of obligation alone, and we saw that, for all but the smallest most tightly knit and isolated societies, it suffered from grave defects. Such a régime must be static,

its rules altering only by the slow processes of growth and decay; the identification of the rules must be uncertain; and the ascertainment of the fact of their violation in particular cases, and the application of social pressure to offenders must be haphazard, time-wasting, and weak. We found it illuminating to conceive the secondary rules of recognition, change, and adjudication characteristic of municipal law as different though related remedies for these different defects.

In form, international law resembles such a régime of primary rules, even though the content of its often elaborate rules are very unlike those of a primitive society, and many of its concepts, methods, and techniques are the same as those of modern municipal law. Very often jurists have thought that these formal differences between international and municipal law can best be expressed by classifying the former as "morality". Yet it seems clear that to mark the difference in this way is to invite confusion.

Sometimes insistence that the rules governing the relations between states are only moral rules, is inspired by the old dogmatism, that any form of social structure that is not reducible to orders backed by threats can only be a form of "morality". It is, of course, possible to use the word "morality" in this very comprehensive way; so used, it provides a conceptual wastepaper basket into which will go the rules of games, clubs, etiquette, the fundamental provisions of constitutional law and international law, together with rules and principles which we ordinarily think of as moral ones, such as the common prohibitions of cruelty, dishonesty, or lying. The objection to this procedure is that between what is thus classed together as "morality" there are such important differences of both form and social function, that no conceivable purpose, practical or theoretical, could be served by so crude a classification. Within the category of morality thus artificially widened, we should have to mark out afresh the old distinctions which it blurs.

In the particular case of international law there are a number of different reasons for resisting the classification of its rules as "morality". The first is that states often reproach each other for immoral conduct or praise themselves or others for living up to the standard of international morality. No doubt *one* of the virtues which states may show or fail to show is that of abiding by international law, but that does not mean that that law is morality. In fact the appraisal of states' conduct in terms of morality is recognizably different from the formulation of claims, demands, and the acknowledgements of rights and obligations under the rules of international law. In Chapter V [of *The Concept of Law*] we listed certain features which might be taken as defining characteristics of social morality: among them was the distinctive form of moral pressure by which moral rules are primarily supported. This consists not of appeals to fear or threats of retaliation or demands for compensation, but of appeals to conscience, made in the expectation that once the person addressed is reminded of the moral principle at stake, he may be led by guilt or shame to respect it and make amends.

Claims under international law are not couched in such terms though of course, as in municipal law, they may be joined with a moral appeal. What predominate in the arguments, often technical, which states address to each other over disputed matters of international law, are references to precedents, treaties and juristic writings; often no mention is made of moral right or wrong, good or bad. Hence the claim that the Peking Government has or has not a right under international law to expel the Nationalist forces from Formosa is very different from the question whether this is fair, just, or a morally good or bad thing to do, and is backed by characteristically different arguments. No doubt in the relations between states there are halfway houses between what is clearly law and what is clearly morality, analogous to the standards of politeness and courtesy recognized in private life. Such is the sphere of international "comity" exemplified in the privilege extended to diplomatic envoys of receiving goods intended for personal use free of duty.

A more important ground of distinction is the following. The rules of international law, like those of municipal law, are often morally quite indifferent. A rule may exist because it is convenient or necessary to have some clear fixed rule about the subjects with which it is concerned, but not because any moral importance is attached to the particular rule. It may well be but one of a large number of possible rules, any one of which would have done equally well. Hence legal rules, municipal and international, commonly contain much specific detail, and draw arbitrary distinctions, which would be unintelligible as elements in moral rules or principles. It is true that we must not be dogmatic about the possible content of social morality: as we saw in Chapter V [of *The Concept of Law*] the morality of a social group may contain much by way of injunction which may appear absurd or superstitious when viewed in the light of modern knowledge. So it is possible, though difficult, to imagine that men with general beliefs very different from ours, might come to attach *moral* importance to driving on the left instead of the right [. . .].

16

The Nature of *Jus Cogens*

Mark W. Janis

Jus cogens, compelling law, is the modern concept of international law that posits norms so fundamental to the public order of the international community that they are potent enough to invalidate contrary rules which might otherwise be consensually established by states. The most notable appearance of *jus cogens* is, of course, in article 53 of the Vienna Convention on the Law of Treaties,[1] where the term is rendered in English as "peremptory norm":

> A treaty is void if, at the time of its conclusion, it conflicts with a peremptory norm of general international law. For the purposes of the present Convention, a peremptory norm of general international law is a norm accepted and recognized by the international community of States as a whole as a norm from which no derogation is permitted and which can be modified only by a subsequent norm of general international law having the same character.[2]

The Vienna Convention further provides that: "If a new peremptory norm of general international law emerges, any existing treaty which is in conflict with that norm becomes void and terminates."[3]

Looking at the Vienna Convention, it is sometimes (but I think wrongly) presumed that *jus cogens* must be a form of customary international law, the law developed by state practice in international relations and by implicit state consent. For example, the Restatement of the Foreign Relations Law of the United States (Revised) opines that *jus cogens* "is now widely accepted . . . as a principle of customary law (albeit of higher status)."[4] To base this conclusion on the definition of "peremptory norm" in the Vienna Convention, one must make a number of assumptions: 1) that despite the limitation "[f]or the purposes of the present Convention," the provision can be generally applied to international law; 2) that there is an equivalence between the term "peremptory norm" and the term "*jus cogens*"; and 3) that there is a further equivalence between the term "general international law" and the term "customary international law." Putting aside the first two assumptions (I have no problem at all with the second) it strikes me that the third is insupportable.

The central problem with equating "general international law" and "customary international law" is, I think, that customary international law is by its very nature not an apt instrument

Mark W. Janis, "The Nature of *Jus Cogens*," *Connecticut Journal of International Law*, vol. 3, 1988, pp. 359–63 © 1988 Connecticut Journal of International Law. Reprinted with permission from the author and journal.

for the development of non-derogable rules, norms with a potency superior even to treaty rules. As usually conceived customary international law is the weak sister of conventional international law. Both are based on state practice, but treaties show the practice explicitly in the form of written rules, while the rules of custom must be drawn awkwardly from the various evidences of state diplomacy or pronouncements. Both treaty and custom are grounded on the idea of agreement. Here again, treaties are stronger, since consent is shown by a ratification process, while the consensual foundations of custom must be demonstrated more uncertainly by expressions of the law-like character of the rules, the vague notion of *opinio juris*. That any form of customary international law can be said to be so firmly rooted that it can be employed to prospectively repudiate subsequent treaty rules is, I think, a proposition that makes nonsense of the usual theory of customary and conventional international law.[5]

It is more reasonable, I think, to understand the Vienna Convention's term "general international law" to signify not customary international law, but rather, and more precisely, those non-derogable rules described in the text of the Vienna Convention itself. We are thus saved the improbable task of elaborating two sorts of customary international law: the one making ordinary consensual rules, the other creating rules with a permanence which even treaties cannot supersede. The term "customary international law" could have been employed in article 53, but was not. The special definition of *jus cogens* as a peremptory norm in the Vienna Convention takes the concept out from the bounds of customary international law and gives it its own character and essence.

The distinctive character essence of *jus cogens* is such, I submit, as to blend the concept into traditional notions of natural law. Such a blending makes sense both historically and functionally. Historically, it is significant that the proponents of the idea of peremptory norms invalidating treaty rules were, in no small measure, reacting to the abuses of Nazism during the Second World War.[6] They rejected the positivist proposition that state acts, even the making of treaties, should be always thought capable of making binding law. Verdross, one of *jus cogens'*

earliest advocates,[7] explained that the concept of *jus cogens* was quite alien to legal positivists, but "[t]he situation was quite different in the natural law school of international law."[8] Natural lawyers were ready to accept "the idea of a necessary law which all states are obliged to observe . . . , [that is, an] ethics of the world."[9]

When the first drafts of what were to become the Vienna Convention's peremptory norm provisions were introduced in the International Law Commission by Lauterpacht in 1953, he made a clear distinction between the new notion, as yet untermed, and customary international law: "the test was not inconsistency with customary international law pure and simple but inconsistency with such overriding principles of international law which may be regarded as constituting principles of international public policy."[10] And as Schwelb noted, though the term *jus cogens* may be new, "the concept of an international *ordre public* has been advocated for a very long time."[11] *Jus cogens* is a legal emanation which grew out of the naturalist school, from those who were uncomfortable with the positivists' elevation of the state as the sole source of international law.

Functionally, a rule of *jus cogens* is, by its nature and utility, a rule so fundamental to the international community of states as a whole that the rule constitutes a basis for the community's legal system. Perforce and per article 53, a rule of *jus cogens* is ordinarily non-derogable and invalidates subsequent norms generated by treaty or by custom, that is, by the ordinary consensual forms of international legislation. Thus it is a sort of international law that, once ensconced, cannot be displaced by states, either in their treaties or in their practice. *Jus cogens* therefore functions like a natural law that is so fundamental that states, at least for the time being, cannot avoid its force.

Partly because of its perceived potency, a peremptory norm is even more difficult to prove and establish than a usually controversial rule of customary international law. In the *North Sea Continental Shelf* cases, the International Court of Justice explicitly put itself on record as not "attempting to enter into, still less pronounce upon any question of *jus cogens*."[12] There seems to be no example in modern international practice of a treaty being voided by a peremptory norm.[13]

Nonetheless, there have been frequent assertions by states and others that certain principles of law are so fundamental as to be considered *jus cogens*. For example, there are the principles of articles 1 and 2 of the Charter of the United Nations, which guarantee the sovereignty of states. Some human rights, too, are claimed to be protected by rules of *jus cogens*.[14]

Probably no rule better fits the definition of a norm of *jus cogens* than *pacta sunt servanda*, for it is essential to the theory of both conventional and customary international law that contracts between states be legally binding. However, it is difficult to understand how the obligatory force of agreements can be attributed to either treaty or custom without making a circular argument. If either a treaty or a customary rule be said to impose the rule *pacta sunt servanda*, why should that treaty or customary rule be valid unless it relied upon that very rule of legal obligation that is itself at issue?

It makes much better sense to argue that the *pacta sunt servanda* rule is neither a rule of conventional nor customary international law, but rather a norm fundamental to the legal system from which both treaty and customary rules derive. Indeed, it might do to conceive of the *pacta sunt servanda* norm as just the kind of non-derogable rule described as a peremptory norm in the Vienna Convention. In effect, this compelling law, *jus cogens*, is not a form of customary international law, but a form of international constitutional law, a norm which sets the very foundations of the international legal system.

In a sense, *pacta sunt servanda* rules may be seen to be a form of natural law if we take an organic view of the term "natural." A rule such as *pacta sunt servanda* is natural to the international community of states because there would be no such community without such a rule. The norm is intrinsic to the very existence of the given community. This does not mean that the rule is one prescribed by nature to every community or every legal system or to any given community's legal system at any given time. Rather, the word "natural" has to do with the organic or constitutional aspect of the rule: that it concerns the fundamental order of the community and its legal system.

Notes

1   May 23, 1969, UN Doc. A/Conf. 39/27, UN Sales No. E.70.V.6 (1970), *reprinted in* 63 Am. J. Int'l L. 875 (1969).
2   Id. art. 53.
3   Id. art. 64.
4   Restatement of the Foreign Relations Law of the United States (Revised) §102 reporter's note 6 (Tent. Draft No. 6, 1985).
5   I more fully explore the nature of customary international law in M. W. Janis, International Law 35–46 (1988).
6   See E. Jiménez de Arechaga, El Derecho Internacional Contemporaneo 79 (1980).
7   See Verdross, *Forbidden Treaties in International Law*, 31 Am. J. Int'l L. 571 (1937).
8   Verdross, *Jus Dispositivum and Jus Cogens in International Law*, 60 Am. J. Int'l L. 55, 56 (1966).
9   Id.
10 Schwelb, *Some Aspects of International* Jus Cogens *As Formulated by the International Law Commission*, 61 Am. J. Int'l L. 946, 949 (1967).
11 Id.
12 North Sea Continental Shelf Cases (W. Ger. v. Den.; W. Ger. v. Neth.), 1969 I.C.J. 4, 42 (Judgment of Feb. 20).
13 See Gaja, Jus Cogens *Beyond the Vienna Convention*, 172 Hague Recueil 271, 286–9 (1981).
14 See Robledo, *Le* jus cogens *international: sa génese, sa nature, ses fonctions*, 172 Hague Recueil 9, 167–87 (1981).

17

A Philosophy of International Law

Fernando R. Tesón

A Critique of Realism

Much of the literature on nonforcible inter-vention (or low-intensity conflict) focuses on what strategies would best serve the national interest and is thus wedded to the normative Realist model just discussed. But is normative Realism a morally sound principle? I submit that it is not; advancing the national interest is neither a sufficient nor a necessary condition to justify international acts.

I will start with utilitarian Realism. This version of Realism, as suggested above, has considerable appeal because it is based on democratic prin-ciples. What could be more attractive than the suggestion that a government that we institute to defend our interests should do just that? Yet utilitarianism as a general moral theory has well-known fatal flaws. In the philosophical literature, the most important critique of utilitarianism comes from a deontological perspective.[1] Inter-national acts may serve the national interest in a utilitarian sense yet may be immoral. Just as an individual is expected to refrain from immoral acts even when they advance his self-interest, so in international relations governments must refrain from immoral acts even when they serve the national interest. The deontological critique thus disagrees with the often unstated premise of Realism that there is no international morality.

This flaw of utilitarian Realism can be clearly seen in a well-known problem of utilitarianism generally: its failure to take into account human rights. Surely someone committed to liberal principles would not accept the proposition that a government may blatantly violate the rights of persons in other countries, provided only that in doing so it advances the interests of its own citizens. For example, a government cannot justify killing or oppressing people in other countries simply in order to improve the economic con-dition of its citizens. The premise of utilitarian Realism is thus fatally incomplete: the role of government is not simply to maximize the inter-ests of the citizens who appointed it but rather to maximize these interests *consistently with respect for human rights*. A morally justified democracy is a rights-constrained democracy, not a pure democracy where the majority does as it pleases.[2] It is correct to say government may have a *primary* duty to uphold *our* rights and *our* just institutions. But because human rights are inter-national and universal[3] our government also has a duty to respect the rights of *all* people, foreigners included. Just as the majority may not oppress minorities within a state, so the majority may not

Fernando R. Tesón, *A Philosophy of International Law* (Westview Press, 1998), pp. 52–66. © 1998 by Fernando Tesón. Reprinted with permission of Westview Books, a member of Perseus Books Group.

legitimately direct its own government to ignore the rights of individuals in other states. Therefore a government's duty to maximize the preferences of its citizens cannot be a paramount international duty that excludes consideration of how people in foreign countries are treated. To be sure, utilitarian Realism has a role to play in the justification of foreign policy. When a government performs an international act (such as an act of intervention) that seriously *harms* the national interest even if the behavior serves worthy purposes, the citizens of the government's state have a claim against it for not doing its job properly.[4]

Communitarian Realism, unlike utilitarian Realism, shares with the Kantian thesis the view that valid principles trump actual interests and preferences. Yet despite its antiutilitarian, foundationalist approach, communitarian Realism is also untenable because it upholds a collective value and is, for that reason, also indifferent to human rights. Under communitarian Realism, an international act is justified when it is consonant with the tradition and the communal values of the state performing the act. Communitarian Realism does not take into account the resulting harms, including human rights violations, suffered by citizens and noncitizens alike. Because communitarian Realism favors the realization of a national interest that looms over and above the actual preferences of citizens, it is far more dangerous than utilitarian Realism, in spite of its current vogue. Indeed, communitarian Realism is too closely akin to the spurious and destructive themes of nationalism. Perhaps for that reason, communitarianism is also hopelessly relativistic. There is no internal principle to prevent the doctrine from being used to justify appalling regimes of oppression and frightful foreign policies, so long as those practices spring from the tradition of the society in question. In addition, communitarians lack the moral tools to come to the defense of *dissenters* from the tradition. For example, communitarians are bereft of arguments to defend the victims of the Tiananmen Square massacre, since arguably despotism has traditionally been part of the "intimation" of Chinese tradition. They also lack the moral tools to oppose the claim by the religious community[5] of Islamic fundamentalists to forcibly convert infidel nations, if that is part

of the Islamic tradition. Communitarianism is incompatible with international human rights because the very premise of the theory rejects the notion of international justice or morality.

Unlike utilitarianism, communitarianism does not depend on principles of democratic representation. Communitarians have no reason to prefer a democratically elected government who fails to uphold that tradition to an undemocratic government who does. In the earlier example regarding the critique of the CIA's involvement in overthrowing Chilean president Salvador Allende, an appeal to community seemed acceptable because *the tradition it was based on was morally worthy on grounds other than the simple fact that it was a tradition* – it was a *liberal* tradition. In such a case, the communitarian Realist arrives at a morally desirable outcome but for the wrong reasons. One can of course argue that the CIA's help in ousting Allende was immoral because it was inconsistent with the American tradition of respect for human rights and the popular will. But what about the people most directly affected? It seems that the operation must be condemned for the effects it had on *Chileans*, not for the self-regarding reason that it was inconsistent with the tradition of the United States.[6]

A just tradition must be defended because it is just, not because it is a tradition; conversely, unjust traditions deserve no respect. A communitarian may reply that the relevant community should be defined as the *international* community. Because that community has agreed to an international law of human rights, international human rights are now part of the "intimations of the tradition" that determine the community interest.[7] This position, however, amounts to unconditional surrender, since it makes communitarian Realism true but trivial. If human rights are universal, then communitarianism is tantamount to liberalism. The communitarian can no longer identify a relevant community as legitimately denying human rights, since that community would also be part of the international community and therefore governed by the imperative to honor human rights.

Normative Realism, then, fails to supply a *sufficient* justification for international acts. Moreover, the pursuit of national interest, in either the utilitarian or communitarian versions, does not seem to be a *necessary* condition to justify international acts either. If we conclude that there is a duty to assist people in distress, or that there is a duty to transfer wealth to the needy under appropriate principles of distributive justice, international morality may mandate international aid by governments even when those acts do not advance the national interest. In conclusion, normative Realism is unappealing in any of its versions because of its indifference to universal principles of justice, human rights in particular. Utilitarian Realists are correct in seeking a liberal democratic foundation of national interest, but they lack deontological constraints on governmental behavior. Communitarian Realists, in contrast, are right to take a foundational approach, thereby rejecting the utilitarian determination of the national interest; however, they choose a faulty foundational principle – appeal to tradition. Both communitarian and utilitarian principles are insensitive to human rights.

The Kantian Justification of International Acts

The task then is to provide a theoretical basis for international morality and especially for legitimate intervention, one that avoids the pitfalls of Realism. Under the Kantian thesis, *an international act is in principle immoral when it violates human rights.* If we accept this suggestion we can see why the national interest alone cannot possibly justify acts of intervention that violate the rights of individuals in the target state. The reason is simply that *universal* human rights trump the pursuit of interest. A justified foreign policy, therefore, may be described as follows: *a government is entrusted by the citizens of the state with the conduct of foreign affairs so that the interests of the citizens will be served, provided that global human rights are respected.* The Kantian thesis is thus compatible with the pursuit of the national interest in the utilitarian sense, with human rights operating as a side-constraint to that pursuit.

The foremost interest of citizens in a democracy is to uphold and defend their just institutions; the government, therefore, has a duty to defend the state's just institutions. In a sense, this interest may seem to correspond to that offered by communitarian Realists, because the morality of defending just institutions does not depend on citizens actually wanting to defend them at any particular time. We praise a government that has the foresight to defend just institutions against the popular will.[8] As suggested above, the Kantian thesis differs from communitarian Realism, even though they may at times prescribe the same course of action. In those cases where an appeal to tradition is desirable, such as when the American tradition of defense of freedom and democracy is invoked, the communitarian interest is simply coincidentally in accord with the defense of just institutions. Liberals, however, will *already* have decided on independent grounds that freedom is worth defending. The government of a just state has a duty to defend its just institutions because they are *just* institutions, not because they are *its* institutions.

The second duty of a democratic government is to uphold and promote human rights and democracy *globally*. This tenet is supported by the two reasons discussed in Chapter 1.[9] The first reason is simply that human rights are universal, as indicated above. Human rights accrue to every human being, regardless of history, culture, or geographical circumstance. Every person has an equal claim to be treated with dignity and respect: this is the ethical foundation of international human rights. The second reason why governments must uphold human rights and democracy globally is that, as we saw, this is the only way to secure peace. By encouraging the creation and preservation of democratic societies abroad, the democratic government is building the liberal alliance, which alone can serve as the basis for a stable international community. Liberal democracies are far less prone to make war than illiberal regimes. The coexistence of democratic and undemocratic regimes is the main cause of conflict, because those two radically different political systems do not easily coexist.

We can now summarize the normative basis of foreign policy. A democratic government has a three-fold international duty: (1) to defend its own just institutions; (2) to respect the rights of all persons at home and abroad; and (3) to promote the preservation and expansion of human rights and democracy globally. These three ways of upholding human rights differ, however. The first duty of a government is to defend *its* just institutions; this duty is perhaps the only *absolute* duty that governments have. The second duty of a democratic government is to respect human rights, including protection of the rights of foreign persons when it conducts otherwise permissible acts of intervention. This duty is very strong although perhaps not always absolute.[10] The third duty of a democratic government, which is related to the second, is to defend and promote respect for human rights *by foreign governments.* This duty is strong yet constrained by moral and prudential considerations that relate to the rights of innocent people in the target state, as well as to the capabilities of the acting state, its resources, and the safety of its citizens.[11]

The corollary of the foregoing considerations is that *an act of intervention will be justified if, and only if, it is consistent with respect for international human rights.* A government may pursue the national interest, either in the utilitarian sense (defined as the satisfaction of the aggregate preferences or interests of the citizens of the state), or in the (putative) communitarian sense of defending just institutions, provided that in doing so it respects the rights of everybody. *This* version of moderate Realism is acceptable because the protection of human rights and the defense of just institutions operate as moral constraints on the pursuit of national interest.

The human rights approach helps us analyze many kinds of international acts. Take the case of insurgency and counterinsurgency. The Kantian thesis includes a theory of just war; it is the war waged in defense of human rights.[12] In most wars, international or civil, there is a side that is morally right. That side may be waging a war to defend itself from an aggressor, or to overthrow a tyrannical government (at home or abroad), or justly to secede from a parent state.[13] Insurgency operations by a democratic state designed to assist just revolutionaries are justified, provided that the help is welcome by the insurgents themselves. For example, a response to a request for assistance by Iraqi revolutionaries aimed at overthrowing Saddam Hussein would be morally justified. Similarly, counterinsurgency operations to assist legitimate, rights-respecting governments against illiberal uprisings are morally justified, provided that the government welcomes the assistance.[14]

Assistance to illegitimate governments, or illiberal groups in civil wars, on the grounds that they are friends of the legitimate government carrying out the operation, is forbidden in principle. A very important corollary of the human rights theory of international law and relations is that, normally, only legitimate governments may be supported.[15] The *liberal alliance* envisioned by Kant, and hopefully taking shape in the post-Cold War international society, is the only plausible foundation of international law, and illegitimate governments are excluded from its benefits. This point sharply brings out the contrast between Kantianism and Realism. Many Realists have maintained that, in foreign policy, we should support our "friends," even if they are despicable dictators.[16] Leaving aside for the moment the very plausible claim that in Realism's own terms such a policy is disastrous in the long run, the Kantian thesis condemns this view as profoundly immoral.[17]

The human rights-based justification of international acts is still very general, and at first blush many will find it unsatisfactory. One possible objection draws on principles of state sovereignty. An act of intervention may be conducted in such a surgical way that no one's rights are violated, yet the sovereignty of the target state would still have been punctured. That violation of sovereignty, it is argued, suffices to condemn all or most acts of intervention. In order to assess this objection, one must examine the ethical foundations of state sovereignty. So far I discussed the morality of foreign policy, that is, the moral considerations relative to the potential intervenor. I must now examine the morality of state sovereignty, that is, the moral considerations relative to the target state.

The Justification of State Sovereignty

I will now outline the principles I think underlie the concepts of state sovereignty and intervention. The twin principles of state sovereignty and nonintervention are among the best established principles of international law. A liberal conception of politics is one for which the justified civil society protects and recognizes basic human rights, of the type named in modern constitutions and pertinent international instruments.[18] A liberal conception of state sovereignty has to be congruent with the justification it offers for the legitimacy of the state generally. I suggest that a state is *sovereign* when it is *internally legitimate*.[19]

The best way to approach the question of the legitimacy of the state is to draw on the distinction between the horizontal social contract and the vertical social contract.[20] Citizens of the state are bound to one another by the principles of justice that underlie a just constitution – this is the *horizontal* social contract. Meaningful social cooperation requires the creation of government, that is, of institutions and offices to which political power is attached. These offices are occupied by persons who are democratically chosen by the citizens of the state. These persons enter, therefore, into an *agency* relationship with the people who have elected them. This agency relationship is the *vertical* social contract. In a democracy, the government is accountable to the people and has to remain faithful to the terms of the vertical contract.

It follows that illegitimacy may take place in two ways. First, the vertical contract may be breached, in which case the *government* is illegitimate. This occurs when the government is unrepresentative or, even if it was originally representative, it engages in serious and disrespectful human rights violations. The government has lost its standing since it no longer represents the citizens. Second, the horizontal social contract may break down, so that the *state* is illegitimate. This situation could result in anarchy, as in Somalia in the early 1990s, or in a fragmentation of the parent state into several independent states, as happened to the Soviet Union and Yugoslavia.

Sovereignty is the outward face of legitimacy. A government is legitimate when it genuinely represents the people and generally respects human rights. Such a government must be respected by foreigners, in particular foreign governments. A state is legitimate, and must be respected, when it is the result of a genuine horizontal social contract. In turn, a legitimate social contract, for instance a legitimate constitution, is one that, at the very least, protects the basic human rights of its citizens. Such a state must likewise be respected by foreigners, in particular foreign governments. A group of people residing in a territory, bound by a legitimate

horizontal contract, may rescind the vertical contract as a result of a breach by their government. This may occur violently, as by revolution, or peacefully. The government in power becomes illegitimate; in other words, the vertical contract has collapsed. In these cases, citizens have not lost their rights. They have not forfeited their human rights or their civil society, which is the result of the social contract that protects such rights. The horizontal social contract, I emphasize, is derivative from individual rights. They have given up neither their individual rights nor their life in common, their commitment to social cooperation. The illegitimate *government*, however, is not morally protected. Foreigners, therefore, have a duty to respect human rights and a life in common in the state but do not owe a similar duty to the illegitimate government, because that government does not legitimately represent the state and its people anymore. In addition, an illegitimate government is not entitled to respect[21] because by hypothesis, if international law offered protection to this government, it could remain in power and oppress its people without fear of political pressure from the international community.[22]

It is possible, however, that the horizontal contract itself may collapse, causing civil society to disintegrate. There may be an illegitimate, spurious social contract – one that does not provide for respect for basic human rights. In these cases, the *state* is illegitimate. Of course, a fortiori the government will be illegitimate, since the vertical contract exists at the sufferance of the horizontal contract. In this case also, as in the case of collapse of the vertical contract, the former citizens – now stateless people, persons in the state of nature – maintain their individual rights.[23] Foreigners, and in particular foreign governments, must respect the human rights of the individuals that reside in that putative state, notwithstanding the collapse of the horizontal social contract. If the horizontal contract collapses, citizens do not have a claim to life in common anymore. Foreigners, therefore, are not under as stringent a duty to respect that "society" as in the case of collapse of the vertical contract. They must respect individual human rights, but there is no longer a social contract to respect. A group of individuals, not a state or a society, is all that is left.

In summary, a state is entitled to the complete protection of state sovereignty afforded by international law when it is founded upon a legitimate horizontal contract *and* a legitimate vertical contract. A state is entitled to less protection of its sovereignty when the *vertical* contract has collapsed. While human rights and the right to a life in common ought to be respected, the illegitimate government and its instrumentalities are not entitled to protection. Finally, when both the horizontal and vertical contract have collapsed, there is no sovereignty whatsoever, but the individuals that reside within the boundaries of the defunct state retain their rights, which foreigners should still respect.

We turn now to the application of the principles that support state sovereignty and how they can trump the behavior of foreign governments. I shall start with the somewhat easier question of the moral standing to intervene.

Who Can Intervene

Two conditions apply to the potential intervenor: its cause has to be just and its government has to be legitimate. We saw that the only legitimate aim of the intervenor is the protection of human rights. In some cases, as discussed above, there are moral reasons to make war, and, a fortiori, to perform less intrusive international acts. The overriding aim of a just war is the protection of human rights. A government's war to defend the rights of its citizens, when they are being violated by a foreign aggressor, is called self-defense. A government's war to defend the citizens of the target state from human rights violations by their own government is called humanitarian intervention. The second condition is that only a legitimate government has moral standing to carry out a legitimate operation (military or otherwise) *as a government*. Dictators may not validly perform acts of intervention. The reason is straightforward. The vertical contract is invalid and the agency relationship is spurious; consequently, the government cannot validly act on behalf of the citizens of the state. Its international acts, and in particular its coercive acts, such as war and acts of intervention, are invalid qua acts of the state.

At first blush, this conclusion seems counterintuitive. Why can't the illegitimate government

of state A send a group of people to train and advise the combatants led by the legitimate government of state B in *its* fight against illiberal insurgents? Surely B will use all the help it can get. This, however, will not do – the government of A cannot validly order *citizens of* A to fight and perhaps risk their lives in another state, even for a just cause! Because A's is an illegitimate government, it lacks the moral standing to command. The citizens of A are not legitimately subordinate to the government and have no duty to obey. Of course, any individual has a right to join in a just war fought in another state when invited by the just warriors.[24] If people in A decide voluntarily, and are not deployed by A, to join the just counterinsurgency in B, they could do so in their private capacity. The illegitimate government may not engage the people and the collective resources of the state in any war or other coercive action.

The position defended here is in sharp contrast with Realism. Realists, especially communitarians, claim that every state has a national interest that is as legitimate and important as any other state's national interest against which it competes in the international arena. Realists do not seriously consider the possibility that a government carrying out an operation may simply be unrepresentative. There are many ways in which the Realist bypasses this inconvenient fact. For example, a Realist might argue that there are political or sociological reasons why the tyrant remains in power, or that tyranny is a natural phenomenon.[25] They might, more plausibly, distinguish between the dictator's domestic illegitimacy and his international standing to pursue the national interest. This justification ignores the fact that the international act performed by the dictator purports to engage the collective responsibility of the citizenry. Typically, the act may put the population at grave risk. Other governments may then legitimately challenge the authority of the dictator so to act, and this can be done only by resorting to some notion of domestic legitimacy.

When Intervention Is Justified

The question whether or not an act of intervention violates the target state's sovereignty is answered by applying the principles suggested in the foregoing discussion. First, I will make a terminological clarification. I use the word "intervention" in this chapter to denote any act that punctures the sovereignty of the target state. It includes military operations, but it is not restricted to them. The term includes non-forcible acts (whether or not they involve *some* degree of coercion on persons) performed in another state without the latter's consent. My aim is to explore to what extent such acts are morally precluded by the principle of state sovereignty. War is but an extreme case of coercion. Because war is subject to independent legal and moral constraints, it raises special problems. Yet I believe that intervention is governed by the same principles throughout the spectrum of coercion.

There are three possible cases relative to the target state. First, the target state is fully legitimate, meaning that both the state and the government are legitimate. Second, the target state rests on a valid horizontal contract, but the vertical contract is invalid, with the consequence that the government is illegitimate. Finally, the target "state" does not have a valid horizontal social contract – both the state and the government are illegitimate.

Intervention against a fully legitimate state

Assuming the justice of the cause and conformity to the other moral constraints (i.e., proportionality and modus operandi), an act of intervention will violate the sovereignty of the target state when both the horizontal and the vertical contracts are legitimate.

The single exception, more apparent than real, to this principle arises when the legitimate government of the target state *authorizes* the operation, as is often the case with justified counterinsurgency. For example, whether US efforts to help the government of El Salvador in the 1980s were barred by sovereignty considerations, other things being equal, depends on whether that government was legitimate. If the government was illegitimate, aid to that government was morally prohibited, come what may, because even express authorization by an illegitimate government is invalid. If the government was legitimate, the morality of the operation does not depend on sovereignty considerations, because of the authorization. Recall, however,

that for the operation to be legitimate, the intervenor must fulfill other requirements, particularly the requirement of a just cause. A legitimate government may not always espouse a just cause, so the operation may be illegitimate on those grounds. In addition, the envisaged operation may be banned for being disproportionate, or intrinsically odious, or otherwise violative of human rights.

The Eichmann case may illustrate this point.[26] In 1960, Israeli agents located the infamous Nazi war criminal, Adolf Eichmann, living under a false name in Argentina. They abducted him in Argentina and took him to Israel, where he was tried, convicted, sentenced to death, and hanged. At the time, both the Israeli and the Argentine governments were legitimate.[27] Was the operation morally justified? This is a particularly instructive case, because punishing a war criminal is a worthy aim, especially for those, such as myself, who sympathize with retributivism. I believe, nevertheless, that the Israeli government was *not* justified in kidnapping Eichmann, as was recognized by the United Nations Security Council and the Israelis themselves, who apologized to Argentina.

First, it is necessary to examine the underlying aim of the operation. I have indicated that the main justification of international acts, and international coercion in particular, is the defense of human rights. The punishment of a war criminal, even one as evil as Eichmann, is a less compelling aim than a *direct* defense of human rights. The Israelis had two possible justifications for punishing Eichmann: retributive justice and deterrence. Retributive justice is an abstract idea of just desert that cannot easily be linked to the defense of human rights, even if one otherwise accepts the retributivist justification of punishment.[28] Deterrence is only *indirectly* linked to the defense of human rights. A deterrence argument would justify punishment of Eichmann in order to show potential war criminals and mass murderers that they will suffer should they violate human rights. Since the fear of punishment will prevent some war crimes, so the argument goes, the probability of rights violations will decrease.

Under either deterrence or retributivism, the goals pursued by the Israeli government, while morally worthy, are insufficient to outweigh a legitimate state's sovereignty. The Israelis should have requested authorization from the Argentine government before they abducted Eichmann. Even if the Argentines had refused to help the Israeli cause, and there is no evidence that they would have, I believe that the moral foundations that support the sovereignty of a fully legitimate state defeat legitimate retributive interests. Of course, given the horrific nature of Eichmann's crimes, the Argentine government would have acted immorally had it refused to surrender or, in the alternative, prosecute Eichmann. Even then, Israel could not justifiably seek a remedy that violated a legitimate state's sovereignty. Members of the liberal alliance have a duty to resort to rational methods of solving disputes. Abductions have no place *within* the alliance, no matter how noble the cause or how vile the target of the operation.[29]

What about the Alvarez-Machain case, mentioned above? Assuming the most favorable facts for the US government, that is, that Alvarez-Machain was in fact guilty of complicity in acts of torture, the Alvarez-Machain case is indistinguishable from the Eichmann case. Mexico is a legitimate state, and the Mexican government a legitimate government. Mexico is a member of the liberal alliance; therefore, its sovereignty must be respected. The United States has no right to intervene in Mexico; moreover, it had a solemn duty to resort to the agreed-upon methods of dealing with criminal fugitives, such as the extradition treaty in force between the two nations.[30] Had Mexico refused to extradite Alvarez-Machain, the United States would not have been justified in using coercion. Only diplomatic and judicial remedies, such as a case in the World Court, are available among liberal republics. It is unfortunate that the US Supreme Court refused to give even the slightest consideration to this central question of international morality.

Intervention against an illegitimate government

The second situation, in which the targeted state is legitimate but its government is not, is more complex. In such cases, assuming all other necessary conditions are met, acts of intervention are *legitimate only if they are directed against the government itself and its instrumentalities*. This means that the operations may not violate the human rights of the citizens or disrupt their life in common. The example of Iraq may serve to illustrate this point. I already indicated that a legitimate government's assistance to an insurgency of Iraqi citizens aimed at ousting the Iraqi dictator would be morally justified.[31] Suppose that the United States contemplates an operation to destroy the arsenal of Iraq, in particular all those facilities and materiel that may increase its nuclear capabilities. State sovereignty does not preclude this operation, because it is directed against the government and its instrumentalities and not against the citizens of Iraq.[32] In such cases, the citizens have not waived their human rights or their right to have a state or a life in common. Therefore, the operation must respect these rights and the local institutions that represent their freely chosen life in common. The intervention must be tailored as narrowly as possible as an action against the government, not the people. Some cases are relatively clear, as when a democratic government aids revolutionaries against a tyrannical ruler, or protects imminent victims of genocide, or rescues nationals in danger.

Even in these clear cases the citizens of the target state have not given up their state. The operation must respect the local institutions reflective of their life in common. One hypothetical example may help clarify this principle. Suppose the US government has detected in Cuba a notorious drug lord suspected of very serious crimes in the United States. Is the United States morally justified in abducting this person from Cuba? The Cuban government, we shall assume, is illegitimate, but the Cuban *state* is not. In other words, Cubans have a right against foreigners that their life in common be respected. This may include institutions such as the judicial system. The answer to our question will depend on whether the courts in Cuba are independent or subservient to the Castro regime. If the former, the US may not act and must instead utilize diplomatic channels, such as a request for extradition. If the latter, the courts are not an institution to administer justice to the Cuban people but rather a mere instrumentality of the illegitimate regime. In this case, I suggest that the United States may act, provided the operation satisfies the other requirements. Action is justifiable because the United States would be doing no more than capturing a suspected criminal from his hideout among a gang of outlaws of the international community. After all, illegitimate governments are no more than gangs of outlaws, usurpers.

Because the citizens in the target state retain their individual rights, acts of intervention are complicated by the very difficult and virtually unavoidable problem that some innocent people may be injured or killed during an otherwise justified operation. The most prominent doctrine to justify incidental killing of innocent people in a just military action is the doctrine of double effect, which is in part recognized by modern international law. According to this doctrine, incidental loss of lives in war is not prohibited if the *intent* of the just warrior is to obtain a military advantage, not to victimize innocents, even if he can *foresee* the deaths of innocent people.[33]

The doctrine of double effect, however, has been recently challenged by Judith J. Thomson. Her critique is skeptical of the moral relevance of the doctrine's crucial distinction between specific intent to kill bystanders and mere foresight that bystanders will die. In her view, if there is any justification for the incidental loss of lives of bystanders in a war, it must depend on the justice of the cause – on the larger purpose of the operation.[34] Thomson, however, bypasses this question as too complicated, *et pour cause*: justifying the loss of innocent lives is perhaps the major challenge faced by any nonutilitarian theory of just war.[35] Providing a satisfactory defense of the doctrine of double effect is beyond the scope of this discussion. I will, however, make three observations. First, unless we find *some* justification for the incidental killing of innocent people, no war or revolution could ever be justified. I am aware, of course, that this begs the larger question of the justification of war: maybe pacifists are right, and no violence is ever justified; or maybe utilitarians are right, and the only plausible thing to do is to weigh costs and benefits of war. But *if* one rejects utilitarianism, and *if* one accepts as a point of departure that sometimes fighting a war or a revolution is the morally right thing to do, then we must come up with some rights-based justification for the incidental killing of bystanders. Second, the justification for the incidental loss of innocent lives in a nonforcible act of intervention does

not differ from the justification given for such loss in conventional war. Whether one chooses the doctrine of double effect or the larger cause doctrine to justify incidental loss of innocent lives in a just war, the same rationale is available for justified acts of nonforcible intervention. Recall that the other constraints, such as proportionality and modus operandi, always apply. Finally, there is an important difference in blameworthiness between the warrior fighting for a just cause who diligently tries to protect innocents and the just warrior who chooses to terrorize and victimize them in his pursuit of the just end. An operation against an illegitimate government, then, must not be *aimed* at innocent people, even if that is conducive to the demise of the tyrant. Moreover, the agents conducting the operation must design it with the protection of bystanders in mind.

Intervention against an illegitimate state

When a state is illegitimate the social contract has collapsed and sovereignty considerations no longer apply. In some instances when the horizontal contract has disintegrated, anarchy reigns and different groups may control different parts of the territory.[36] The intervention still has to have a just cause and, as always, the individual rights of the residents ought to be respected. All the considerations regarding innocent bystanders discussed in the previous section apply here as well. In these cases the people must be allowed to rebuild a legitimate state if they wish to do so. Humanitarian intervention must be accompanied by measures facilitating the political reorganization of local forces on the basis of free elections and respect for human rights. People who traditionally have lived in a region must be permitted freely to enter into a social contract.[37] These are not easy questions to answer, and the solutions will vary considerably depending on the facts.

Necessity, Proportionality, and Decency

The main purpose of this chapter has been to suggest principles with which to evaluate acts of intervention in light of state sovereignty. Two other conditions, however, further restrict the legitimacy of these acts. The first is the customary requirement of *necessity* and *proportionality*. Acts of intervention satisfy the requirement of necessity only if no less intrusive means are available to accomplish the same goal. Proportionality involves calculations of the costs and benefits of the operation in a way that is not solely dependent upon the national interest, however measured. The general rule is that the coercion used in the operation and the consequent harm done by it have to be proportionate to the importance of the interest that is being served, both in terms of the intrinsic moral weight of the goal and in terms of the extent to which that goal is served.

The second of these final conditions for a morally defensible act of intervention is that the modus operandi must not be so odious as to be corruptive of the virtues that people must exhibit in a liberal democracy. The operation should not be morally self-defeating.[38] This requirement rests upon an important moral insight: there are things we cannot do to others because of what *they* are (i.e., they hold rights), and there are things we cannot do to others because of what *we* are.[39] What are we? As individuals having inherent dignity and value, and as members of a just civil society – a liberal democracy – we must act in such a way as to cultivate our civic virtues and best character traits. This applies, a fortiori, to actions by the government, which is supposed to act for the *polis*. In part, the insistence on governmental virtue in the conduct of foreign policy derives from self-interest; we cannot expect our government to behave honorably with *us* if it goes around the world sending hit squads to assassinate and torture people, even for just causes.[40]

An example may help illustrate this proposition. Is it morally permissible to assassinate Saddam Hussein? I would think not. The proper course of action is to help the Iraqis overthrow him, capture him, and bring him to trial before Iraqi courts or an international court in accordance with internationally accepted norms of fair trial. Assassination is banned, not because the punishment is necessarily inappropriate in light of Hussein's crimes but rather because agents of a liberal democracy must conduct themselves in a way that honors the civic virtues for

which they stand. Criminal punishment can only be imposed through the mechanisms allowed by liberal society. The same reasoning applies to other intrinsically contemptible modes of action, such as torture and terrorism, regardless of sovereignty considerations, just cause, or national interest.[41]

A Note on Neoliberalism and International Relations

In recent years an energetic school of thought has reacted against the predominant Realist model. This movement, which calls itself "neoliberalism," has challenged the Realist assumption that states ought to be considered as closed and self-contained units in international relations. In the words of a representative of this trend: "All governments represent some segment of domestic society, whose interests are reflected in state policy.... The behavior of states... reflects the nature and configuration of state preferences [i.e., as shaped by their domestic origin and configuration]."[42] Not all governments, therefore, are the same. Above all, the national interest is determined not by the anarchical nature of international relations, but by the domestic features of the state. This view is an important improvement over Realism. It removes the theoretical obstacle that obsessed Realists, namely the apparent united front presented by states in the international arena. Neoliberals correctly observe instead that the people who rule states are political actors and that therefore what they do and say internationally is intimately related to their domestic origin and role. Neoliberals thus attempt to puncture, in a descriptive sense, the barrier of sovereignty. For that they deserve ample credit.

Yet in spite of its name, this view is still far from the liberal view espoused in this book. Neoliberalism is quite close to Realism because it accepts the premise that states act out of interest alone. The only amendment to Realism, albeit an important one, is that domestic politics adetermine the national interest and consequently the foreign policy of the state interest. This seems to me correct yet insufficient on two grounds. First, the dynamics of the relationship between domestic politics and the national interest that projects itself outwards is quite complex, and it is not captured by the surprisingly neo-Marxist assertion that the ruling elite transposes its domestic interests into the international arena. Second, and most important, this view fails to address the crucial dimension of *legitimacy*. While liberalism is compatible with several possible views of human nature, it is not a theory about the dynamics of politics, domestic or international. It is a theory about the *justification* of political power of any kind. It is a normative thesis about rights, obligations, and principles. So even though this new school of thought is an improvement over Realism because, in a descriptive sense, it pierces the veil of state sovereignty, it says nothing about legitimacy in the international system (or the domestic, for that matter). For that reason, the theory seems to be a misnomer: the link between neoliberalism and liberalism in the tradition, say, of Kant, Locke, and Rawls, seems quite weak.

Defenders of the thesis, in response, make two points: first, the label "liberalism" emphasizes the importance of international institutions (or regimes) in facilitating cooperation among states.[43] Second, liberal states get along better with one another (the Kantian empirical argument described in Chapter 1). As to the first point, international institutions may or may not serve liberal values (as exemplified by the highly illiberal United Nations during the 1970s). As to the second point, one can ask what is the basis for preferring the liberal alliance over other arrangements. After all, liberal governments are also carriers of class or other interests. In order to privilege liberal states and governments, one has to say that they are morally legitimate while illiberal states and governments are not. The neoliberals reply, with Kant, that the liberal alliance should be privileged over their illiberal colleagues because liberal states do not go to war. But, as I discussed in Chapter 1, this reason for preferring the liberal alliance is precarious. If someone could show that an evil world empire is even *more* likely than a liberal alliance to maintain a *pax romana*, then these writers should prefer that arrangement. In short: there is no escape from normative theory, from the question of legitimacy. The liberal alliance that seems to be emerging from the Cold War is not to be praised only, or primarily, because it is

more apt to maintain peace: it is to be preferred because it reflects morally just political arrangements.

Notes

1 The seminal works in this regard are John Rawls, *A Theory of Justice* (1971) and Ronald Dworkin, *Taking Rights Seriously* (1978).

2 See Immanuel Kant, "To Perpetual Peace: A Philosophical Sketch" [1795], in *Perpetual Peace and Other Essays*, 107, 114 (Ted Humphrey trans., 1983).

3 The concept of the universality of human rights has been persistently challenged over the years (especially by governments who wish to violate them), but I believe that such universality holds both as a matter of morality and as a matter of positive international law. More recently, the otherwise quite deficient Vienna Declaration has reaffirmed the principle of universality. See Vienna Declaration and Programme of Action, 25 June 1993 (copy furnished to the author by the US Department of State), part II, paragraph 1 ("The universal nature of [human] rights is beyond question").

4 When an agent, such as a lawyer, fails to serve the interests of his client, the client has a claim against the lawyer, even though the lawyer be motivated by the noblest of concerns.

5 While community may often be seen as defined by national borders, community may or may not coincide with nations – witness religious communities, or the moral community of Europe defined by the European Convention on Human Rights.

6 The coup opened the door to years of oppressive military government.

7 I take this to be the thrust of the New Haven school, with its emphasis on clarification of global community policies. See Myres S. McDougal et al., "The World Constitutive Process of Authoritative Decision," in *International Law Essays*, 191 (Myres S. McDougal & W. Michael Reisman eds., 1981). For my critique, see Fernando R. Tesón, *Humanitarian Intervention: An Inquiry Into Law and Morality*, 17–21 (2nd ed. 1997).

8 An example of this is the refusal of the French government in exile to accept the surrender of the French people to the Nazi occupiers during World War II.

9 See Fernando R. Tesón, *A Philosophy of International Law*, ch. 1 (1998).

10 There are a number of reasons to support the view that states legitimately have lesser duties

vis-à-vis foreigners. These are analogous to the reasons that individuals have a greater duty toward their family members than to others. Yet even these subordinate duties are absolute within their proper compass: the fact that we normally do more things for the people that are close to us does not mean that we can violate the rights of others.

11 Notice that I am talking here about duties, not rights. I take for granted, at this stage of development of international law, that democratic governments have a *right* to demand human rights compliance from other governments and, in some extreme cases, even to intervene by force to help victims of serious oppression. See generally Tesón, *Humanitarian Intervention*.

12 See id. at 121–2; see also David Luban, "Just War and Human Rights," 9 *Philosophy and Public Affairs* 60 (1980).

13 See generally Allen Buchanan, *Secession: The Morality of Political Divorce From Fort Sumter to Lithuania and Quebec* (1991) (advocating various arguments as moral grounds for the right to secede).

14 This proviso derives from considerations of autonomy, which apply to acts in defense of others. See Judith J. Thomson, "Self-Defense," 20 *Philosophy and Public Affairs*, 283, 305–6 (1991). But self-defense of the state is always, in effect, defense of others. In repelling an aggressor, the government assists citizens who are being victimized by aggression, and individuals fight in defense of fellow citizens. It follows that, as I have tried to show elsewhere, the rationale for self-defense does not differ in substance from the rationale for humanitarian intervention. See Tesón, *Humanitarian Intervention*, 119–20; see also Fernando R. Tesón, "International Obligation and the Theory of Hypothetical Consent," 15 *Yale Journal of International Law* 84, 117 (1990).

15 I say "in principle" and "normally" because one can imagine a situation where the only way to avoid a moral catastrophe is to temporarily support an illegitimate government. An interesting case arises when two tyrants are fighting each other. Here the liberal democracy must refrain from helping either, except in very extreme situations, such as when one tyrant, if victorious, will drop a nuclear bomb or cause a similar catastrophe. But it is never morally right to support a tyrant against a democracy, or a tyrant against democratic forces resisting him, or illiberal rebels against a democratic government.

16 Even in the midst of the current global democratic revolution, we can see the endurance of this ruthless approach: Western governments befriend the Syrian dictator Hafez al-Assad and the current Chinese leadership, on account of spurious *national interest*.

17 We do not even need a very deep theory of morality to condemn the Realist's advocacy of help to *friendly* dictators. Whether one relies on the universality of human rights (as I do), or on an American or Western communitarian tradition, or on pure compassion, the result is the same.

18 See, e.g., Universal Declaration of Human Rights, General Assembly Resolution 217A (III), 3 United Nations General Assembly (Resolutions, part 1) at 71, *United Nations Document* A/810 (1948).

19 I made this point in Tesón, *Humanitarian Intervention*, 77–9, 81–99, 117–21. See also Charles R. Beitz, *Political Theory and International Relations* (1979).

20 The distinction between the two kinds of social contracts was suggested by Hannah Arendt, "Civil Disobedience," in *Crises of the Republic*, 49, 85–87 (1969). I elaborate the idea here in more detail.

21 I realize that this is not the thrust of international law, which tends to protect any government that has succeeded in subduing the population. See Tesón, *Humanitarian Intervention*, ch. 4.

22 This is not to say that foreigners may do *anything* with regard to an illegitimate government. In particular, they may not overthrow it without the consent of the citizens of the state. Id. at 126–9.

23 Imagine that in an unexplored area of the globe we discover individuals who do not have any political or social organization, who just wander in the region. Human rights, I believe, would pertain to them, although I will not attempt to prove this point.

24 I believe that people have a *duty* to assist, to the extent possible, their fellow citizens (i.e. citizens of the same state) against an unjust aggression; this is the only possible justification of conscription enforced by legitimate governments. I will not, however, attempt to demonstrate this difficult point here.

25 Cf. Michael Walzer, "The Moral Standing of States: A Response to Four Critics," in *International Ethics*, 217, 229 (Charles R. Beitz et al., eds., 1985).

26 Attorney-General of the Government of Israel v. Eichmann, 36 *International Legal Reports* 5 (District Court of Jerusalem 1961), reprinted in D. J. Harris, *Cases and Materials on International Law*, 266–74 (4th ed. 1990).

27 This was one of the brief periods of civilian government in Argentina.

28 See Jeffrie G. Murphy, "Retributivism, Moral Education, and the Liberal State," *Criminal Justice Ethics*, Winter–Spring 1985, at 3. Kant's reason for rejecting deterrence and adopting retribution is unsatisfactory. See Immanuel Kant, *Metaphysical Elements of Justice*, 99–106 (John Ladd trans., 1965) (criminals must be punished because if we don't, we share in their blood guilt).

29 Of course, the situation changes radically when we change the dateline. Suppose Eichmann is residing in Buenos Aires in 1978, sheltered by the fascist military régime. The considerations against abducting him do not apply here and Israel would have had a strong moral case for conducting the operation. The requirement that the operation be as surgical as possible still applies.

30 See Extradition Treaty, May 4, 1978, United States–Mexico, 31 *United States Treaties* 5059.

31 See supra text accompanying note 19.

32 Recall that the other conditions must obtain. In this case, the aim – prevention of aggression by a tyrannical government – is justified.

33 An updated version of the doctrine is offered in Warren S. Quinn, "Actions, Intentions, and Consequences: The Doctrine of Double Effect," 18 *Philosophy and Public Affairs* 334, 334–6 (1989).

34 See Thomson, "Self-Defense," 292–6.

35 In *Humanitarian Intervention*, I adopted Daniel Montaldi's suggestion that incidental loss of lives in an otherwise justified war can sometimes be justified by reference to the nature of the evil that the just warriors are attempting to suppress. I suggested that the suppression of serious and disrespectful human rights violations was an interest compelling enough to outweigh, sometimes, the bystanders' right to life. Tesón, *Humanitarian Intervention*, 103–8. Although I think I was on the right track, this view (which is consistent with

Thomson's "larger cause" suggestion) needs to be elaborated further.

36 Lebanon in the 1970s and Somalia and Yugoslavia in the early 1990s may be examples of this situation.

37 By "freely," I refer to *individual freedom*.

38 Virtue theory is usually traced back to Aristotle. See generally Nancy Sherman, *The Fabric of Character: Aristotle's Theory of Virtue* (1989). For a contemporary account, see Alasdair C. MacIntyre, *After Virtue: A Study in Moral Theory* (2nd ed. 1984). The effect of adding virtue considerations to rights considerations is that the scope of morality is enlarged. In that sense, virtue theory provides important insights and supplements to liberal rights theory. However, contrary to virtue theorists, I regard civic virtues as parasitic on the values that underlie a liberal democracy, not the other way round.

39 See Robert A. Nozick, *Philosophical Explanations*, 400–2 (1981).

40 See generally Thomas Nagel, "Ruthlessness in Public Life," in *Public and Private Morality*, 75, 78–9 (Stuart Hampshire ed., 1978) (discussing whether public morality can be derived from public morality).

41 Of course, Saddam Hussein may die at the hands of agents sent to arrest him if he chooses to resist, and the action will not thereby become illegitimate.

42 Anne-Marie Slaughter Burley, "International Law and International Relations Theory: A Dual Agenda," 87 *American Journal of International Law* 205, 228 (1993) (citing Andrew Moravcsik, "Liberalism and International Relations Theory" (working paper, Center for International Affairs, Harvard University, 1992)). This article contains further references on neoliberalism and its debate with Realism.

43 A representative author is Robert O. Keohane, *After Hegemony* (1989).

18

The Limits of International Law

Jack L. Goldsmith and Eric A. Posner

International law has long been burdened with the charge that it is not really law. This misleading claim is premised on some undeniable but misunderstood facts about international law: that it lacks a centralized or effective legislature, executive, or judiciary; that it favors powerful over weak states; that it often simply mirrors extant international behavior; and that it is sometimes violated with impunity. International law scholarship, dominated for decades by an improbable combination of doctrinalism and idealism, has done little to account for these characteristics of international law. And it has made little progress in explaining how international law works in practice: how it originates and changes; how it affects behavior among very differently endowed states; when and why states act consistently with it; and why it plays such an important role in the rhetoric of international relations.

This book seeks to answer these and many other related questions. It seeks to explain how international law works by integrating the study of international law with the realities of international politics. Our theory gives pride of place to two elements of international politics usually neglected or discounted by international law scholars: state power and state interest. And it uses a methodological tool infrequently used in

international law scholarship, rational choice theory, to analyze these factors. Put briefly, our theory is that international law emerges from states acting rationally to maximize their interests, given their perceptions of the interests of other states and the distribution of state power. We are not the first to invoke the idea of state interest to explain the rules of international law (Oppenheim 1912). But too often this idea is invoked in a vague and conclusory fashion. Our aim is to integrate the notion of state interest with simple rational choice models in order to offer a comprehensive theory of international law. We also draw normative lessons from our analysis.

This introduction discusses the assumptions of our analysis, sketches our theory in very general terms, and locates our position among the various schools of international law and international relations scholarship.

Assumptions

The assumption that states act rationally to further their interests is not self-evident. All components of this assumption – that the state is the relevant agent, that a state has an identifiable interest, and that states act rationally to

Jack L. Goldsmith and Eric A. Posner, "Introduction," from *The Limits of International Law* (Oxford University Press, 2005), pp. 3–17. © 2005 by Oxford University Press, Inc. Reprinted with permission of Oxford University Press.

further these interests – are open to question. Nonetheless, we believe state-centered rational choice theory, used properly, is a valuable method for understanding international law. What follows is a brief discussion of our use of the concepts of state, state interest, and rationality. Further detail is provided in subsequent chapters.

State

The existence of a state depends on the psychology of its citizens. If all US citizens stopped believing that the United States was a state, and instead began to believe that they were citizens of Indiana or Texas or some other subunit, then the United States would cease to exist and numerous new states would come into existence. (This is in effect what happened when the Soviet Union and Yugoslavia disintegrated in the 1990s.) Moreover, "the state" is an abstraction. Although the identity of the state is intuitively clear, the distinction between the state and the influences on it sometimes blurs. Relatedly, the state itself does not act except in a metaphorical sense. Individual leaders negotiate treaties and decide whether to comply with or breach them. Because the existence of a state and state action ultimately depend on individuals' beliefs and actions, one could reject the assumption that states have agency and insist that any theory about the behavior of states must have microfoundations in a theory of individual choice.

Despite these considerations, we give the state the starring role in our drama. The main reason for doing so is that international law addresses itself to states and, for the most part, not to individuals or other entities such as governments. NAFTA did not confer international legal obligations on President Clinton or the Clinton administration, but rather on the United States. The United States remains bound by these obligations until a future government withdraws the United States from the treaty. Moreover, although states are collectivities, they arrange themselves to act like agents, just as corporations do. Corporations are generally easier to understand than states. Corporate interests – to make money for the shareholders, subject to agency costs resulting from the delegation of authority to individuals who run the firm – are (usually) easier to identify. And it is easier to assume that

corporate obligations remain in force despite the turnover of managers, directors, and shareholders because the obligations are enforced by domestic courts regardless of who happens to be in control of the corporation. Still, state interests can be identified (as we explain later), and through various domestic institutions states can and do maintain their corporate identity. Both ordinary language and history suggest that states have agency and thus can be said to make decisions and act on the basis of identifiable goals.

The placement of the state at the center of analysis necessarily limits the scope of analysis. We do not discuss, except in passing, difficult and important topics at the margins of international law about how states form and disintegrate. Many scholars view European Union integration as a possible model for a more ambitious public international law. Although the EU project is in some respects constituted by international law, we think it is more usefully viewed as an example of multistate unification akin to pre-twentieth-century unification efforts in the United States (which, during its Articles of Confederation period, was viewed by some as a federation governed by international law), Germany, and Italy. In any event, we offer no theory of state unification or integration. Nor [...] do we have much to say about the opposite claim that the state is losing power downward to smaller state units (for example, the disintegration of the Soviet Union and the former Yugoslavia), to substate units (for example, the devolution movements throughout Europe), and to multinational corporations and transnational NGOs.

State interest

By state interest, we mean the state's preferences about outcomes. State interests are not always easy to determine, because the state subsumes many institutions and individuals that obviously do not share identical preferences about outcomes. Nonetheless, a state – especially one with well-ordered political institutions – can make coherent decisions based upon identifiable preferences, or interests, and it is natural and common to explain state action on the international plane in terms of the primary goal or goals the state seeks to achieve.

We generally identify state interests in connection with particular legal regimes by looking, based on many types of evidence, to the preferences of the state's political leadership. This assumption is a simplification and is far from perfect. But it is parsimonious, and it is appropriate because a state's political leadership, influenced by numerous inputs, determines state actions related to international law. In some contexts in the book – for example, in explaining the significance of the ratification process for treaties, or in analyzing the domestic interest groups that affect a state's international trade policy – we will depart from this simplifying assumption and consider how various domestic groups and institutions influence the political leadership's decisions related to international law.

We avoid strong assumptions about the content of state interests and assume that they can vary by context. This distinguishes our work from the work of some realists, who assume that a state's interests are limited to security and (perhaps) wealth. Our relative agnosticism about the content of state interests has led some critics of our previous work to argue that we can adjust state interests as necessary to fit the conclusions we want to reach. It is true that the power of our explanations depends on the accuracy of our identification of state interests, and that state interests are in some contexts difficult to identify or controversial. We have tried to identify as objectively as possible state leaders' preferences in connection with particular legal regimes; we leave it to our critics to determine whether we have succeeded.

The concept of state interest used in this book must not be confused with the policy that promotes state welfare. In every state, certain individuals or groups – elites, corporations, the military, relatives of dictators – have disproportionate influence on leaders' conduct of state policy. Even in democratic states, the institutions that translate individual preferences into particular policies are always imperfect, potentially derailed by corruption, incompetence, or purposeful hurdles (like separation of powers), and sometimes captured by interest groups. The inevitable presence of these distorting mechanisms means that the "state interest" as we use the term is not necessarily, or even usually, the policy that would maximize the public good

within the state. Any descriptive theory of international law must account for the agency slack of domestic politics, and we do so primarily by focusing on what leaders maximize (see Krasner 1999). One consequence of this approach is that our use of the term "state interest" is merely descriptive of leaders' perceived preferences and is morally neutral. To take an extreme example, when we analyze a leader's interest in committing human rights abuses, we refer only to what the leader perceives as the best policy to maintain his or her authority; we do not suggest that human rights abuses are ever morally justifiable.

Rational choice

It is uncontroversial that state action on the international plane has a large instrumental component. Rational choice theory provides useful models for understanding instrumental behavior. Political scientists' use of rational choice tools has brought considerable insight to many aspects of international relations and has opened many fruitful research agendas. We believe rational choice can shed similar light on international law.

Our theory of international law assumes that states act rationally to maximize their interests. This assumption incorporates standard premises of rational choice theory: the preferences about outcomes embedded in the state interest are consistent, complete, and transitive. But we do not claim that the axioms of rational choice accurately represent the decision-making process of a "state" in all its complexity, or that rational choice theory can provide the basis for fine-grained predictions about international behavior. Rather, we use rational choice theory pragmatically as a tool to organize our ideas and intuitions and to clarify assumptions. No theory predicts all phenomena with perfect accuracy. And we do not deny that states sometimes act irrationally because their leaders make mistakes, because of institutional failures, and so forth. Our claim is only that our assumptions lead to better and more nuanced explanations of state behavior related to international law than other theories do.

There is a massive literature critical of rational choice theory, three components of which we address here. First, a word on collective rationality. As understood by economics, rationality is primarily an attribute of individuals, and even then only as an approximation. The term's application to collectivities such as corporations, governments, and states must be performed with care. For some of the reasons mentioned earlier, social choice theory casts doubt on the claim that collectivities can have coherent preferences. But if this critique were taken seriously, any explanation of international law, or, for that matter, even domestic law, would be suspect. Cycling is probably most prevalent not in states but in pre- or nonstates, that is, in aggregations of people who cannot develop stable institutions. As explained earlier, when states exist, people have adopted institutions that ensure that governments choose generally consistent policies over time – policies that at a broad level can be said to reflect the state's interest as we understand the term.

Another challenge to rational choice theory comes from cognitive psychologists, who have shown that individuals make cognitive errors, sometimes systematically. We do not deny the empirical claims of this literature. History is full of examples of state leaders committing errors while acting on the international stage, and it is conceivable that these errors can be traced to the standard list of cognitive biases (McDermott 1998). The problem is that the cognitive psychology literature has not yet produced a comprehensive theory of human (or state) behavior that can guide research in international law and relations (Levy 1997). Such a theory might well result in a more refined understanding of international law and relations. But it might not; individual cognitive errors might have few if any macro effects on international relations. Economic theory has produced valuable insights based on its simplifying assumptions of rationality. Our theory should be judged not on the ontological accuracy of its methodological assumptions, but on the extent to which it sheds light on problems of international law.

Finally, there is the constructivist challenge from international relations scholarship (Wendt 1999). To the extent that constructivism shares similarities with traditional international law scholarship – for example, its commitment to noninstrumental explanations of state behavior – we address its claims throughout the book. Here we address its critique of state preferences. As is usual (but not necessary) in rational choice theory, we take state interests at any particular time

to be an unexplained given. Constructivists challenge this assumption. They seek to show that the preferences of individuals, and therefore state interests, can be influenced by international law and institutions. To the extent this is true, it would call into question our theory's ability to explain international law in terms of state interests. We doubt it is true to any important degree, but we cannot prove the point. On the other hand, constructivists have not shown that international law transforms individual and state interests. The relevant question is whether the endogenization of the state's interest, assuming it could be done in a coherent fashion, would lead to a more powerful understanding of how states behave with respect to international law. We provide our theory in the pages that follow, and we leave it to critics to decide whether constructivism provides a better theory of international law.

There is a related point. We consistently exclude one preference from the state's interest calculation: a preference for complying with international law. Some citizens, perhaps many, want their states to comply with international law, and leaders, especially in liberal democracies that tend to reflect citizen preferences, might act on this basis. A rational choice theory could incorporate this preference into the state's utility function. Nonetheless, for two reasons we reject a preference for complying with international law as a basis for state interests and state action on the international plane.

First, even on the assumption that citizens and leaders have a preference for international law compliance, preferences for this good must be compared to preferences for other goods. State preferences for compliance with international law will thus depend on what citizens and leaders are willing to pay in terms of the other things that they care about, such as security or economic growth. We think that citizens and leaders care about these latter goods more intensely than they do about international law compliance; that preferences for international law compliance tend to depend on whether such compliance will bring security, economic growth, and related goods; and that citizens and leaders are willing to forgo international law compliance when such compliance comes at the cost of these other goods. If we are correct about this – and the limited polling data are consistent with our view (Chicago Council on Foreign Relations 2002, 19) – compliance with international law will vary predictably with the price of other goods, the wealth of the state, and other relevant parameters.

Ultimately, the extent to which citizens and leaders have a preference for compliance with international law is an empirical question that we do not purport to resolve in this book. But there is a second, methodological reason why we exclude a preference for complying with international law from the state's interest calculation. It is unenlightening to explain international law compliance in terms of a preference for complying with international law. Such an assumption says nothing interesting about when and why states act consistently with international law and provides no basis for understanding variation in, and violation of, international law. A successful theory of international law must show why states comply with international law rather than assuming that they have a preference for doing so.

A related methodological point is that a theory's explanatory power depends, at least in part, on its falsifiability. Some critics of our earlier work have claimed that our theory is not falsifiable. We disagree. While we do not make fine-grained predictions, throughout the book we make claims – for example, that international law does not shift power or wealth from powerful to weak states, and that states cannot solve large-scale collective action problems through customary international law – that empirical evidence could contradict. These predictive claims are not as precise as, say, those made by sophisticated economic analyses. But that level of methodological sophistication is not our aim here. Our aim is, rather, to give a simple but plausible descriptive account for the various features of international law (including many that have been ignored) in terms of something other than a state's propensity to comply with international law.

Theory

With these preliminaries in mind, we now provide a skeleton of our theory of international law. We put flesh on these bones in subsequent chapters.

Consider two states, A and B. At time 1, the two states have certain capacities and interests. The capacities include military forces, economic institutions, natural resources, and human capital. The interests are determined by leaders who take account in some way of the preferences of citizens and groups. At time 1, the states divide available resources in some stable fashion. They divide territory along a border, and they divide collective goods such as airwaves, fisheries, and mineral deposits in ways that might or might not prevent overexploitation.

At time 2, as a result of a shock, the time 1 status quo becomes unstable. In the simplest case, A's power increases (for any number of reasons) relative to B's, and state A demands a greater share of resources from state B. In the past, this demand might have been for territory or tribute. In the modern world, A will often demand something less tangible, such as access to markets, greater protection for intellectual property, military assistance, base rights, foreign aid, or diplomatic assistance. State A might also threaten to close its own markets, violate B's intellectual property rights, reduce the military assistance or foreign aid it had been rendering B, cut back on diplomatic assistance to B, and so forth. Any of these might happen because A had provided these benefits to B in return for benefits that it no longer wants or needs.

If A and B had perfect information about each other (if, that is, each knew the other's interests and capacities completely), and if transaction costs were zero, their relations would adjust smoothly and quickly to the shock, and at time 3 there would be a new division of resources: a new border, new diplomatic activities, a new level of military assistance in one direction or the other, a new level of foreign aid, or new trade patterns. In the real world of transaction costs and imperfect information, their adjustments will be slow and suboptimal. There might be significant conflict, including war, as the states learn about one another and bluff and bargain over the new order, exaggerating their strengths and concealing their weaknesses. Eventually, the situation between the two states will stabilize.

The relations between the two states at any time can be described as a set of rules. But here care must be used, for several very different things might be going on. Consider a border between A and B. The border is a rule that delineates the territory of each state, where it is understood that neither state can send individuals or objects across the border without the permission of the other state. Territorial borders are generally thought to be constituted and governed by international law. Assume that states A and B respect the border. Our theory of international law posits that one of four things might explain this behavioral regularity.

First, it is possible that neither of the two states has an interest in projecting power across the border. State A does not seek resources in state B's territory and would not seek them even if B were unable to resist encroachment. A is barely able to control its own territory and wants to have nothing to do with B's. State B has the same attitude to state A. When a pattern of behavior – here, not violating the border – results from each state acting in its self-interest without any regard to the action of the other state, we call it a *coincidence of interest.*

There is a second possible explanation for the border. State A might be indifferent between one border and another border deeper in what is now state B's territory. The additional territory might benefit state A, but it would also bring with it costs. The main concern for the states is to clarify the point at which state A's control ends and state B's begins, so that the two states can plan accordingly and avoid conflict. State B has the same set of interests and capacities. Once the two states settle on a border, neither violates the border because if either did, conflict would result. This state of affairs is called *coordination.* In cases of coordination, states receive higher payoffs if they engage in identical or symmetrical actions than if they do not. A classic coordination game from domestic life is driving: all parties do better if they coordinate on driving on the right, or driving on the left, than if they choose different actions.

A third possible explanation for the border is *cooperation.* States A and B would each benefit by having some of the other's territory, all things being equal. But each knows that if it tried to obtain more territory, the other state would resist, and a costly breakdown in relations, and possibly war, would result, making both states worse off. Thus, the states agree (implicitly or explicitly) on a border that reflects their interests and capacities, and the border is maintained by mutual threats to retaliate if the other state violates the border. In such cases of cooperation, states reciprocally refrain from activities (here, invasion or incursion) that would otherwise be in their immediate self-interest in order to reap larger medium- or long-term benefits.

The final possibility is *coercion.* State A is satisfied with the existing border, but state B seeks to expand its territory at A's expense. If B is sufficiently powerful, it can dictate the new border. Because state A is weaker and state B benefits from the extra territory whether or not state A resists, state A yields (either before or after military conflict) and a new border is created. Other states might or might not object: they also might benefit from the new border or be powerless to resist it. Coercion results when a powerful state (or coalition of states with convergent interests) forces weaker states to engage in acts that are contrary to their interests (defined independently of the coercion).

This book[1] argues that some combination of these four models explains the state behaviors associated with international law. These models do not exhaust the possibilities of international interaction. But they provide a simple and useful framework for evaluating a range of international legal regimes. As we explain throughout the book, each model has different characteristics that make it more or less stable and effective, depending on the circumstances. Taken together, however, the four models offer a different explanation for the state behaviors associated with international law than the explanation usually offered in international law scholarship. The usual view is that international law is a check on state interests, causing a state to behave in a way contrary to its interests. In our view, the causal relationship between international law and state interests runs in the opposite direction. International law emerges from states' pursuit of self-interested policies on the international stage. International law is, in this sense, *endogenous* to state interests. It is not a check on state self-interest; it is a product of state self-interest. This does not mean, as critics of our earlier work have suggested, that we think that international law is irrelevant or unimportant or in some sense unreal. As we will explain, international law, especially treaties, can play an important role in helping states achieve mutually beneficial outcomes by clarifying what counts as cooperation or coordination in interstate interactions. But under our theory, international law does not pull states toward compliance contrary to their interests, and the possibilities for what international law can achieve are limited by the configurations of state interests and the distribution of state power.

The bulk of the book is devoted to applying this framework to various regimes of international law. The argument unfolds in three parts. Part 1 analyzes customary international law. We are skeptical of the traditional claim that customary international law reflects universal behavioral regularities. And, we argue, the actual patterns of state behavior associated with customary international law reflect either coincidence of interest or *bilateral* cooperation, coercion, or coordination. We bolster these arguments with case studies of four areas of customary international law.

Part 2 analyzes treaties, the second form of international law. The main puzzle here is: Why do states use treaties instead of customary international law? We offer two general answers. First, treaties – which result from self-conscious negotiation and bargaining, and which are almost always embodied in written form that reduces ambiguity – are more effective than customary international law at specifying what counts as cooperation or coordination. Second, the institutions associated with treaties, including domestic ratification processes and the default rules of treaty interpretation, can provide valuable information that improves cooperation and coordination between states. In addition, part 2 explains how nonlegal agreements relate to legalized agreements; what multilateral treaties accomplish and why their efficacy tends to depend on the logic of bilateral monitoring and enforcement; and the relative roles of retaliation and reputation in treaty compliance. We support our arguments with case studies of international human rights treaties and trade treaties.

Part 3 addresses several external challenges to our theory of international law. Some scholars claim that the pervasive use of international legal rhetoric demonstrates the efficacy of international law that cannot be explained in instrumental terms. We argue that this claim is wrong and show why it would be rational for states to talk to each other in the language of international law even if they were not motivated by a desire to comply with it. Another challenge to our thesis comes from those who claim that, even if states comply with international law only when it is in their interest to do so, they nonetheless have a moral obligation to comply with it against their interest. We argue, to the contrary, that states have no such moral obligation. We also address a related challenge from cosmopolitan theory, which argues that states have a duty in crafting international law to act on the basis of global rather than state welfare. Such duties cannot, we think, be reconciled with cosmopolitans' commitment to liberal democracy, a form of government that is designed to ensure that foreign policy, including engagement with international law, serves the interests of citizens, and that almost always produces a self-interested foreign policy.

International Law Scholarship

Most scholarship on international law has been written by law professors. Although these scholars have proposed many different theories, most of them share an assumption that we reject: that states comply with international law for noninstrumental reasons. Doctrinally, this assumption is reflected in the international law rules of *opinio juris* (the "sense of legal obligation" that makes customary international law binding) and *pacta sunt servanda* (the rule that treaties must be obeyed). Theoretically, the assumption is expressed in various ways, but they all reduce to the idea that a state is drawn toward compliance with international law because compliance is the morally right or legitimate thing to do. Mainstream international law scholarship does not deny that states have interests and try to pursue them. But it claims that international law puts a significant brake on the pursuit of these interests.

Many international law scholars do not question the assumption that states follow international law for noninstrumental reasons. For them, the premise is enough to justify their research agenda, which is that of doctrinalism: identifying the "black letter law" of international law in any given domain, independent of actual behaviors. Other scholars seek to explain the conditions under which international law "exerts a pull toward compliance," that is, exercises normative influence on state behavior (Franck 1990, 24–5).

Brierly (1963) says states obey international law because they have consented to it. Franck (1990, 24) says they do so because international law rules came into existence through a legitimate (transparent, fair, inclusive) process. Koh (1997, 2603) says that international law becomes part of a state's "internal value set." This theorizing often fuels, and is overtaken by, normative speculation about improving international law.

In our view, this research agenda is unfruitful. The assumption of a tendency toward compliance has little if any explanatory value. The narrower view – that states are pulled to comply with international law because it reflects morally valid procedures, or consent, or internal value sets – is not supported by the evidence, as we show in subsequent chapters. Noninstrumental accounts of international law also mask many different reasons why states act consistently with international law, and result in an impoverished theory of compliance. Finally, the theories do not provide good explanations for the many important features of international law unrelated to compliance, including variation and change in international law.

There is a more sophisticated international law literature in the international relations subfield of political science. The methodological commitments of international relations theorists in political science are different from those of most international lawyers. Positive analysis is the hallmark of international relations literature; international relations scholars seek primarily to explain, rather than prescribe, international behaviors. For this reason, among others, international relations scholars take theoretical, methodological, and empirical issues more seriously than international lawyers do, and they draw more generously on economics, sociology, and history.

Until recently, international relations theorists did not study international law as a category apart from the institutions embodied by international law. The dominant American theory of international relations – realism – treated international law as inconsequential or as outside its research agenda (Mearsheimer 2001; Waltz 1979). (A major exception is Hans Morgenthau 1948.) Other political science theories, such as the English School's theory of international society (Bull 1977), were more optimistic about

international cooperation but did not focus on international law as a distinctive institution.

A different strand of international relations theory – institutionalism – uses the tools of rational choice theory to understand international relations. This tradition dates back at least as far as Schelling's (1963) work. Institutionalism's major contribution was to show how states could productively cooperate in the absence of a centralized lawmaker or law enforcer (Keohane 1984; Snidal 1985; Oye 1986). The object of institutionalist analysis was the "regime," a term denned in the literature as "sets of implicit or explicit principles, norms, rules, and decision-making procedures around which actors' expectations converge in a given area of international relations" (Krasner 1983, 2). The original institutionalism movement did not focus on international law as a category distinct from international politics.

In recent years, political scientists have begun to study international law in its own right (Goldstein et al. 2000). A related development is a growing interest among some international law scholars in the tools of international relations theory (Slaughter, Tulumello, and Wood 1998; Burley 1993; Setear 1996; Abbott 1989). There is also a small but growing rational choice literature in international law being developed by economists and lawyers influenced by economics (Dunhoff and Trachtman 1999; Setear 1996; Sykes 1991; Guzman 2002; Stephan 1996; Posner 2003; Sykes 2004 is a survey).

Our approach falls closer to the political science international relations tradition, and in particular to institutionalism, than to the mainstream international law scholarship tradition. But, as will become clear, our views differ from international relations institutionalism, from the newer international relations "legalization" movement, and from other rational choice approaches to international law in several respects. Ours is a comprehensive analysis of international law. The greatest overlap between extant international relations and rational choice international law scholarship and our book comes in part 2, on treaties. But international relations scholarship has ignored customary international law (the topic of part 1) altogether, and it has said relatively little about the normative issues discussed in part 3. In addition, we are more skeptical about the role of international law in advancing international cooperation than most (but not all) international relations institutionalists and most rational choice-minded lawyers. And our methodological assumptions are more consistently instrumental than those found in this literature, which frequently mixes instrumental and non-instrumental explanations (Abbott et al. 2000). Finally, unlike the political scientists, whose focus remains the realm of international politics, we are interested primarily in the nuts and bolts of international law.

Editor's Note

[1]   Goldsmith and Posner's *The Limits of International Law*, from which this reading is taken.

References

Abbott, Kenneth W. 1989. Modern International Relation Theory: A Prospectus for International Lawyers. *Yale Journal of International Law* 14: 335.

Abbott, Kenneth W., Robert O. Keohane, Andrew Moraucsik, Anne-Marie Slaughter, and Duncan Snidal. 2000. The Concept of Legalization. *International Organization* 54: 401.

Brierly, James Leslie. 1963. *The Law of Nations: An Introduction to the International Law of Peace.* Oxford: Clarendon Press.

Bull, Hedley. 1977. *The Anarchical Society: A Study of Order in World Politics.* New York: Columbia University Press.

Burley, Anne-Marie Slaughter. 1993. International Law and International Relations Theory: A Dual Agenda. *American Journal of International Law* 86: 205.

Chicago Council on Foreign Relations. 2002. *Worldview 2002: American Public Opinion and Foreign Policy.* Chicago: Chicago Council on Foreign Relations.

Dunhoff, Jeffrey L. and Joel Trachtman 1999. Economic Analysis of International Law: Microanalysis of Macro-Institutions. *Yale Journal of International Law* 24: 1.

Franck, Thomas M. 1990. *The Power of Legitimacy Among Nations.* New York: Oxford University Press.

Goldstein, Judith, Miles Kahler, Robert O. Keohane, and Anne-Marie Slaughter. 2000. Legalization & World Politics. *International Organization* 54: 3.

Guzman, Andrew. 2002. A Compliance-Based Theory of International Law. *California Law Review* 90: 1823.

Keohane, Robert O. 1984. *After Hegemony.* Princeton, NJ: Princeton University Press.

Koh, Harold Hongju. 1997. Why Do Nations Obey International Law? *Yale Law Journal.* 106: 2599.

Krasner, Stephen. 1983. *International Regimes.* Ithaca, NY: Cornell University Press.

Krasner, Stephen. 1999. *Sovereignty: Organized Hypocrisy.* Princeton, NJ: Princeton University Press.

Levy, Jack S. 1997. Prospect Theory, Rational Choice, and International Relations. *International Studies Quarterly* 41: 87.

McDermott, Rose. 1998. *Risk-Taking in International Politics: Prospect Theory in American Foreign Policy.* Ann Arbor: University of Michigan Press.

Mearsheimer, John. 2001. *The Tragedy of Great Power Politics.* New York: Norton.

Morgenthau, Hans. 1948. *Politics Among Nations: The Struggle for Power and Peace.* New York: Knopf.

Oppenheim, L. 1912. *International Law, Volume I.* London: Longmans, Green.

Oye, Kenneth A. ed. 1986. *Cooperation under Anarchy.* Princeton, NJ: Princeton University Press.

Posner, Eric A. 2003. A Theory of the Law War. *University of Chicago Law Review* 70: 297.

Schelling, Thomas. 1963. *The Strategy of Conflict.* New York: Oxford University Press.

Setear, John K. 1996. An Iterative Perspective on Treaties: A Synthesis of International Relations Theory and International Law. *Harvard International Law Journal* 37: 139.

Slaughter, Anne-Marie, Andrews S. Tulumello, and Stephan Wood. 1998. International Law and International Relations Theory: A New Generation of Interdisciplinary Scholarship. *American Journal of International Law* 92: 367.

Snidal, Ducan. 1985. Coordination vs. Prisoners' Dilemma: Implications for International Cooperation and Regimes. *American Political Science Review* 79: 923.

Stephan, Paul B. 1996. Accountability and International Law Making: Rules, Rents and Legitimacy. *Northwestern Journal of International Laws and Business* 17: 681.

Sykes, Alan O. 1991. Protectionism as a "Safe Guard": A Positive Analysis of GATT "Escape Clause" with Normative Speculations. *University of Chicago Law Review* 58: 255.

Sykes, Alan O. 2004. "International Law," in *The Handbook of Law and Economics*, ed. A Mitchell Polinksy and Steven Shavell. Amsterdam: Elsevier.

Waltz, Kenneth Neal. 1979. *Theory of International Politics.* Reading, Mass.: Addison-Wesley.

Wendt, Alexander. 1999. *Social Theory of International Politics.* New York: Cambridge University Press.

19

The Internal Legitimacy of Humanitarian Intervention

Allen Buchanan

I. The Problem of Internal Legitimacy

Humanitarian intervention is often defined as infringement of a state's sovereignty by an external agent or agents for the sake of preventing human rights violations.[1] The term "infringement" in this definition is carefully chosen: the implied contrast is between infringements and violations; not all infringements are unjust, so the definition remains neutral as to whether, or under what conditions, intervention is justified.

On a stricter definition, humanitarian intervention is limited to the use of force, as distinguished from economic sanctions. Some writers add the stipulation that humanitarian intervention must be purely humanitarian in intent, that the sole or at least the primary goal of the intervention must be to protect the welfare and freedom of those in another state, rather than some advantage to the intervening state or its citizens.[2]

The ethics of humanitarian intervention is a complex and passionately disputed topic. Familiar issues include the following. (1) Given the centrality of state sovereignty in international law, when, if ever, is humanitarian intervention legal, and under what conditions is it morally permis-sible to engage in illegal humanitarian interven-tion? (2) When, if ever, is unilateral, as opposed to collective, humanitarian intervention morally justified? (3) Does any persistent violation of human rights justify intervention, or only extreme violations, such as genocide? (4) Even if persistent human rights violations (or violations of certain basic human rights) constitute a *prima facie* justification for intervention, what other conditions must be satisfied? (Proposals include a requirement of proportionality, such that the human rights violations that result from the inter-vention should be considerably less than those it is designed to prevent, and requirements of pro-cedural justice for impartially identifying targets of intervention and for selecting disinterested agents of intervention.)

There is another fundamental issue of the ethics of humanitarian intervention that seems largely to have gone unnoticed in the contemporary scholarly debate: the problem of the internal legitimacy of humanitarian intervention.[3] This problem remains after all the familiar questions are answered satisfactorily; yet it precedes them all because, unless it can be answered affirmat-ively, the other questions do not arise. It is this problem that is the focus of this paper.

Allen Buchanan, "The Internal Legitimacy of Humanitarian Intervention," *Journal of Political Philosophy*, vol. 7, no. 1, 1999, pp. 71–87. © 2005 by Oxford University Press, Inc. Reprinted with permission of Oxford University Press.

The problem is this: How can the government of a state morally justify humanitarian intervention to its own citizens? Like the questions listed above, this is a question about moral justification, but unlike them it directs the question of justification inward. The other, more familiar questions concerning humanitarian intervention are questions about external legitimacy: they assume that there is no problem of internal legitimacy or, if there is, that it has been solved; they concentrate on whether intervention by one state or by a collection of states can be justified to the state that is the object of intervention, or to the community of states as a whole.

The failure to address the problem of the internal legitimacy of humanitarian intervention is a major deficiency, not only in the moral theory of intervention, but in the doctrine of human rights as well. Evolving human rights law specifies the conditions under which it is legally permissible for states to intervene to protect human rights when they choose to do so. In addition, under the basic principle that agreements are to be kept (*pacta sunt servanda*), international law recognizes that states that have signed human rights treaties have obligations under those treaties. Yet such treaties (including the International Covenant on Civil and Political Rights) only impose on signatories duties to protect the human rights of their own citizens and merely encourage states to "promote" human rights in other states.[4]

In other words, existing international human rights law does not establish clear obligations of humanitarian intervention on the part of states.[5] Human rights activists and some international legal scholars have advocated that international law should be modified so that it imposes clear obligations to engage in humanitarian intervention on states. However, it can be argued that unless humanitarian intervention is internally legitimate, the imposition of a duty of humanitarian intervention would itself be a moral wrong. Like the ethical literature on humanitarian intervention, international legal doctrine for the most part slides over the problem of internal legitimacy.

At this juncture a cautionary word is in order. The problem of the internal legitimacy of humanitarian intervention, as I have defined it,

is a problem about the morality, not the legality, of humanitarian intervention. International legal writers have rightly noted that at least for some states the legality of participation in some aspects of international human rights enforcement efforts is questionable. In some cases, as with Japan and Germany, the constitution of a state prohibits the use of military force abroad, even for humanitarian intervention. It has also been argued that participation in some international efforts to implement human rights norms, including war crimes trials, may be incompatible with the stringent demands of the equal protection and due process provisions of the US Constitution.[6] The question I shall focus on here, however, is not whether humanitarian intervention is internally legal (that is, lawful according to the legal system of the state that intervenes) but whether the government can provide an adequate moral justification to its own citizens when it intervenes on humanitarian grounds.

An immediate response may well be: There is no problem here; if the intervening state is legitimate, then its legitimacy justifies its interventions to its people, at least if those interventions are justifiable externally (that is, to the target of intervention and the world community). However, this response begs the question. It assumes, without argument, that among the legitimate activities of a state are undertakings whose primary aim is to protect the rights of persons who are not its citizens. But, as I shall argue, this assumption is unjustifiable from the perspective of what is arguably the dominant understanding of the nature of the state and the role of government in liberal political thought: the idea that the state is an association for the mutual advantage of its members and that the government is simply an agent whose fiduciary duty is to serve the interests, or to realize the will of those citizens.

Exploring the problem of the internal legitimacy of humanitarian intervention leads us back, then, to what is perhaps the most basic question of political philosophy: what are states for? I shall argue that the dominant understanding of the nature of the state and the role of government, what I shall refer to as the "discretionary association" view, makes internally legitimate humanitarian intervention impossible (except, perhaps, in the special case where it is explicitly authorized by democratic processes). And I will indicate that the dominant way of thinking about justice – the view that justice is a matter of relations among members of a cooperative scheme – reinforces the discretionary association view's inability to account for the internal legitimacy of humanitarian intervention. I will also articulate the features of the "discretionary association" view that explain its perennial attraction.

However, I will then argue that humanitarian intervention can be internally legitimate. First, I will raise several serious objections to the "discretionary association view" that makes the internal legitimacy of humanitarian intervention problematic. Second, I will show that the attractions of the discretionary association view can be preserved in an alternative understanding of "the state as an instrument for justice" in such a way as to provide a solution to the problem of the internal legitimacy of humanitarian intervention.

II. The Discretionary Association View of the State

The internal legitimacy of humanitarian intervention is an intelligible problem regardless of what view of the state one takes, but within the dominant view of the state in liberal political thought it is an especially daunting problem. According to the dominant view, the state is a discretionary association for the mutual advantage of its members. The government is simply the agent of the associated individuals, an instrument to further *their* interests. Or, on a more complex, democratic variant of that dominant view, the state is a framework not simply for serving the interests of the citizens but also for articulating their will, through democratic processes, and the role of the government is not only to serve the citizens' interests but to realize their will (or rather the will of the majority of the citizens).

Perhaps the clearest proponent of the discretionary association view is Locke. For him the state is a discretionary association in this sense: Although there is no moral obligation to enter into political society, it is permissible and even advisable for individuals who interact together in a state of nature to avoid its "inconveniences"

– especially those attendant on private enforcement of the moral rules – by forming a political society and authorizing a group of individuals to be the government, to serve as the agent of the people.[7] For Locke political association is discretionary, not only in the sense that there is no moral obligation to form a state, but also in that individuals may choose with whom they wish to associate politically. There is no suggestion of what I have referred to elsewhere as an "obligation of inclusion" – a moral duty to help ensure that all persons have access to institutions that will protect their basic rights.[8]

The very idea of a social contract so central to liberal theorizing about justice suggests the discretionary association view. The state is understood as the creation of a hypothetical contract among those who are to be its citizens, and the terms of the contract they agree on are justified by showing how observance of those terms serves *their* interests. No one else's interests are represented, so legitimate political authority is naturally defined as authority exercised for the good of the parties to the contract, the citizens of this state. Even in variants of the contract doctrine that view the parties as representatives of future generations, such as Rawls's, it is only insofar as future generations are presumed to be citizens of *this* state that their interests are considered in the making of the contract. The state is understood to be the enforcer of principles of justice, and principles of justice are thought of as specifying the terms of cooperation among those who are bound together in one political society, rather than as specifying how persons generally must be treated.

The discretionary association view usually includes a distinction between the state and the government. The justifying function of the state – what justifies the interference with liberty that it entails – is the wellbeing and freedom of its members. There is no suggestion that the state must do anything to serve the cause of justice in the world at large. What makes a government legitimate is that it acts as the faithful agent of its own citizens. And to that extent, government acts legitimately only when it occupies itself exclusively with the interests of the citizens of the state of which it is the government.

The enduring popularity of the discretionary association view is no accident. It has several signal attractions, at least from the standpoint of a liberal political philosophy. First, the discretionary association view puts government in its place. It makes it clear who is master, namely, the people. Thus the discretionary association view is a powerful expression of the idea of popular sovereignty: the government, being the instrument of the people, serves at their pleasure. The government has no independent moral status, no rights on its own account. Second, the discretionary association view implies the equal freedom of the citizens. Individuals freely decide whether to enter into association with one another. Third, the state itself – the structure of institutions that create and sustain political society – is justified because it serves the interests of the people and for no other reason. Especially at a time when states (and even subjects) were seen as the property of dynastic families whose interests they were to serve, and when rulers used their power to uphold a hierarchy of rank among subjects, these features of the discretionary association view represented a profound moral revolution in political thought.

According to the simpler version of the discretionary association view, a government that engages in what I referred to earlier as pure humanitarian intervention violates its fiduciary obligation: it fails to act in the best interest of its citizens. This failure is momentous, because it is a violation of the fiduciary duty of the government, which in turn is founded on the justifying function of the state – the fact that the state serves the interests of its citizens.

On the more complex, democratic version of the discretionary association view, the mere fact that a government engages in pure humanitarian intervention by definition shows that it acts contrary to the best interests of its citizens, but it is apparently a further question as to whether the government acts illegitimately. For the citizens might democratically authorize pure humanitarian intervention even though they are aware that it is not in their best interest. Such would be the case if the majority gave higher priority to justice than to their own interests.

One should not be too quick to assume, however, that pure humanitarian intervention is within the sphere of legitimate democratic authorization allowed by the discretionary association view. For according to this view the state is not

an instrument for moral progress. It has a much more limited purpose: the advancement of the interests of its citizens. Hence a proponent of the discretionary association view might hold that the function justifying the state places an antecedent constraint on what may be authorized by democratic processes, just as a list of individual rights places an antecedent constraint on what may be decided by majority rule. On this interpretation of the democratic variant of the discretionary association view, the majority is sovereign only over choices concerning which interests of the citizens are to be given priority and how they are to be pursued. At least so long as there is one citizen who votes against it, pure humanitarian intervention is illegitimate, because the purpose of the state (the goal which unites all citizens in one political association) is limited to the advantage of those citizens, and the effective pursuit of this goal limits the sphere of legitimate democratic decision making.

It will do no good to say that democratic processes define the citizens' interests – that if the majority votes for humanitarian intervention then *ipso facto* humanitarian intervention is in the citizens' interest, and that therefore humanitarian intervention democratically approved lies within the proper sphere of state action according to the discretionary association view. Such a claim is nothing more than verbal sleight of hand. At most, democratic endorsement of humanitarian intervention establishes that the majority of citizens, not even all citizens, prefer such intervention. It does not establish that it is in the interest of all citizens or even that the majority of the citizens believe it is in their interest. Furthermore, our question is whether pure humanitarian intervention – intervention that is not in the interests of the citizens (or even in the interests of a majority of them) – can be internally justified. At the very least, the assumption that democratic authorization legitimizes pure humanitarian intervention requires a departure from a strict interpretation of the discretionary association view's central tenet, which is that the state is an arrangement for the mutual advantage of its citizens. Instead the discretionary association view would have to be reformulated as follows: the state is first and foremost an arrangement for the mutual advantage of its members; however, once the basic interests of all the citizens are secured, it is permissible, through democratic processes, to authorize actions that do not serve the best interests of the citizens.

Suppose that this modification is acceptable. Suppose, that is, that the discretionary association view can be reasonably interpreted to include an understanding of democratic authorization according to which legitimate democratic decisions are not limited to those that serve the best interests of the citizens. This only means that there are conditions under which pure humanitarian intervention is permissible. There is still nothing in the democratic variant of the discretionary association view that requires citizens ever to forgo their own interests for the sake of preventing human rights violations abroad. This is part of what is meant by calling it the discretionary association view.

If the citizens' will, duly expressed through democratic processes, is that their government should refrain from pure humanitarian intervention, then this is permissible, according to the dominant view. However, once democratic processes have expressed the people's desire not to engage in pure humanitarian intervention, pure humanitarian intervention by the government is illegitimate. From the standpoint of the discretionary association view of the state, pure humanitarian intervention is not only non-obligatory. It is in fact morally impermissible, unless there is a clear democratic mandate.

A consistent policy of avoiding pure humanitarian intervention would, of course, require that the state in question refrain from signing any human rights conventions or other agreements that create obligations of pure humanitarian intervention. Call this mode of state practice "the Swiss model."[9] From the standpoint of the discretionary association view, even on its democratic variant, there would be nothing morally defective about a world in which *every* state adopted the "Swiss model."

I noted earlier that an awareness of the problem of the internal legitimacy of humanitarian intervention is conspicuously absent in much of the contemporary scholarly literature on the ethics of intervention. However, so-called political realists, of which Hans J. Morgenthau and George F. Kennan are perhaps the most influential modern examples, have typically opposed pure humanitarian intervention.[10]

The realists have not fared well at the hands of recent moral theorists of international relations. They present easy targets, in great part because they often fail to give rigorous arguments in favor of their views and sometimes even appear muddled in their thinking.[11] My aim here is not to untangle the various threads of realist thinking in a systematic way, but only to indicate that there is one strand that is securely anchored in the discretionary association view of the nature of the state and the role of government. If this is so, then at least some realist arguments against pure humanitarian intervention cannot be convincingly refuted without rejecting a dominant paradigm of liberal political thought.

There are two quite different ways to understand the realist's antipathy to pure humanitarian intervention. According to the first, what might be called the moral nihilist view, all moral action in international relations is irrational, because the conditions for moral behavior being rational do not obtain in the international sphere.

According to the second realist view, which might be called the "fiduciary obligation" position, there is at least one moral concept that is applicable to international relations: the concept of an overriding fiduciary obligation on the part of the leaders of states to serve the interests of their peoples, even when doing so violates other putative moral principles. On this second realist view, the ruthless leader is not a stranger to morality. He is the dedicated servant of a higher morality.

Unlike the international moral nihilist or Hobbesian, the fiduciary realist does not make the mistake of assuming that there is no room for moral concepts or for rational moral behavior at all in international relations. However, the fiduciary realist view constricts the morality of international relations almost to the vanishing point. Government officials not only may but ought to transgress any moral principle for the sake of fulfilling their fiduciary obligations.

Critics of this variety of realism have been quick to point out that it is vulnerable to two serious objections. First, fiduciary obligations are not absolute. By undertaking fiduciary duties government officials do not thereby wipe the slate clean of all pre-existing obligations they may have as individuals, including obligations not to violate human rights. So the fact that government officials have fiduciary obligations to their own citizens does not show that it is permissible for them to violate other moral principles, much less that they act wrongly if they act on other moral principles. Second, at least for some states some of the time, survival is not at stake in international relations. At least the more powerful states can engage in pure humanitarian intervention without risking their survival.

These objections are telling against the fiduciary realist position as it is usually presented. But they leave one important element of the fiduciary realist position untouched – its opposition to pure humanitarian intervention. The fiduciary realist can argue as follows: It is true that fiduciary obligations are not absolute; they can be overridden by weightier obligations. From this it follows that government leaders do not have moral *carte blanche* to do whatever is necessary to further the interests of their citizens. But that is not to say that they may use the resources of the state to further the interests of individuals who are not citizens of the state, and the discretionary association view provides no explanation of why they should be allowed to do so. (Similarly, if I hire you to be my agent, it is true that you do not thereby escape other obligations you may have, but the mere fact that you have other obligations does not entitle you to use my resources to fulfill them.) Yes, the realist continues, it is quite correct to point out that not all pure humanitarian interventions put the state's survival interests at risk. But this is irrelevant to the question of pure humanitarian intervention. The fact remains that government officials ought only to serve the interests of their own states.

Fiduciary realism, stripped of the implausible assumptions to which critics have rightly objected, has the merit of taking seriously the idea that the government is the agent of the people – the people of its state – and that the fact that it is their agent makes a difference to what it may do. It is crucial to understand that this strand of realist thought is not a muddled aberration, a *sui generis* confusion or free-floating anomaly in Western political thought. It is nurtured by the dominant discretionary association paradigm, which includes the idea that the government is only an agent, bound by a fiduciary obligation. Unless we are willing to reject or modify the discretionary association view, there will be no convincing reply to the fiduciary normative realist's objection to pure humanitarian intervention.

III.   The Moral Costs of the Discretionary Association View

Despite its several attractions, noted above, the discretionary association view is subject to four serious problems. Two have already been mentioned. It not only leaves us without a convincing reply to the fiduciary normative realist, but also implies that there would be nothing morally wrong with a world in which every state adopted "the Swiss model." In such a world, the enforcement of human rights standards abroad would be regarded as purely optional. The language of moral obligation would be out of place in debates about humanitarian intervention.

A third problem is that the discretionary association view is afflicted by a deep incoherence, if not an outright inconsistency. It justifies the state as a coercive apparatus by appeal to the need to protect *universal* interests, while at the same time limiting the right of the state to use its coercive power to the protection of a particular group of persons, identified by the purely contingent characteristic of happening to be members of the same political society.

According to the most plausible version of this view, the most important interests that states are to serve are basic human interests, not special interests that citizens of this or that particular state have but that the citizens of other states might not have. Thus for Locke, for example, government best serves the interests of its citizens by protecting life, liberty and property. If the interests whose protection justifies the state are human interests, common to all persons, then surely a way of thinking about the nature of states and the role of government that provides no basis for obligations to help ensure that the interests of all persons are protected is fundamentally flawed.

This point can be put even more forcefully if it is framed in terms of individuals' rights. According to the more influential examples of the discretionary association view such as Locke's and Rawls's, the state is to ensure that the cooperative framework it supplies works to the mutual advantage of all citizens by protecting every citizen's basic human rights. And it is the fact that the state protects all citizens' basic human rights that is supposed to justify its use of coercion: because these rights are so important for all persons as persons, the interferences with liberty that this coercion involves are justified. So on the one hand the discretionary association view bases its conception of the nature of the state and the role of government on a universalist conception of which kinds of interests are worth protecting by the coercive power of the state, while on the other hand it provides no basis for imputing any obligation to use the resources of the state to implement this universalist conception beyond the boundaries of the state. The discretionary association view rules out obligations of pure humanitarian intervention in principle at the same time that it implicitly embraces a universalist conception of the worth of the individual that recognizes no boundaries.

A fourth problem with the discretionary association view takes the form of a dilemma. Either that view must deny that states have any obligations toward citizens of other states, including negative duties not to kill or injure them wantonly, in which case it is in stark conflict both with some of our most basic and widely held moral intuitions and with one of the most basic principles of international law; or else that view must acknowledge that states have such negative duties, making it then vulnerable to the charge that it provides no reasonable basis for not recognizing some positive duties as well. Let us consider each alternative in turn.

Taken literally, the discretionary association view holds that the state may not do anything except serve the best interests of its citizens. This would mean that if it were the case that an unprovoked attack on another state would promote its citizens' interests, then the state may undertake such an attack. Such an implication is squarely at odds with what is perhaps one of our most confident and widely shared moral intuitions, namely, that it is wrong to harm the innocent. It is also in conflict with one of the most basic principles of international law, namely, that wars of aggression are prohibited. Not surprisingly, most proponents of the discretionary association view would acknowledge that a state's efforts to serve the interests of its citizens must be con-

strained by certain basic negative duties toward others. Let us call this the softened discretionary association view.

The difficulty is that once the discretionary association view makes this concession, it is hard to see how it can avoid going further, toward the recognition of at least some positive duties toward noncitizens. The most plausible reasons for holding that states have negative duties toward noncitizens appeal to the moral importance of human beings as such, and to the role which the fulfillment of the negative duties in question plays in protecting certain fundamental interests in liberty and wellbeing that human beings as such have. But, as has been convincingly argued in many other contexts, the protection of those fundamental interests also requires the fulfillment of positive duties as well, including duties to ensure that all have access to resources for subsistence and to basic educational opportunities. Libertarian attempts to limit duties to those that are negative either fail to appreciate that the same considerations that ground negative rights also ground positive ones or assume that the only morally significant sort of liberty is freedom from coercion. In brief, the same arguments that show that the state has positive as well as negative duties to its own citizens show that it is arbitrary to soften the harsh implications of the discretionary association view by admitting negative duties to noncitizens while denying any positive duties to noncitizens.

Suppose that the proponent of the discretionary association view could somehow avoid the objection that acknowledging negative duties to noncitizens while denying positive ones is arbitrary. The softened discretionary association view would still conflict with some rather basic moral intuitions. For example, it cannot explain what is wrong with a rich and powerful state refusing to exert even the most minimal efforts, at virtually no risk to itself, to prevent genocide in a neighboring state. In a world in which the discretionary association view were taken seriously no one could appeal to an obligation to engage in humanitarian intervention even as a *prima facie* obligation that might be overridden by practical considerations.

Whether or not the international legal system should impose legal obligations to cooperate in pure humanitarian interventions upon states that democratically decide not to engage in pure humanitarian interventions is another matter. There might be sound reasons for refraining from efforts to impose such international legal obligations. My point is that the discretionary association view makes it impossible to argue that even the most powerful and rich state has any moral obligation, no matter how limited, to cooperate in pure humanitarian intervention efforts, even when doing so is necessary to stop the most egregious violations of human rights and even when the costs of doing so are minimal.

Indeed, the discretionary association view cannot make sense of the fact that we experience the question of pure humanitarian intervention as a moral conflict. We experience a moral conflict because we feel the pull not only of moral reasons against pure humanitarian intervention, but in favor of it as well. On the discretionary association view, there are not two sides to the matter and hence there can be no conflict, because there can be no moral obligation to engage in pure humanitarian intervention.

One can, of course, construct practical arguments for why states should only attend to the interests of their own citizens and the fulfillment of negative duties toward noncitizens. One could argue that, even though there is a *prima facie* obligation to engage in pure humanitarian intervention, such intervention is never justifiable all things considered because any serious effort at pure humanitarian intervention would be excessively costly to the citizens of the intervening state, or because it is doomed to failure for lack of the resources and knowledge required for success, or because it is likely to be a disguised imperialist adventure, and not a pure humanitarian intervention at all. But we are not concerned here with whether pure humanitarian intervention meets standards of practicality. We are asking whether it can even in principle be internally justified, given the dominant liberal model of what states are for and what the role of government is. Even if all the foregoing practical problems disappeared, our question would remain.

In addition, the same features of the discretionary association view that preclude it from recognizing that the people of one state sometimes have at least a *prima facie* obligation to intervene on humanitarian grounds in another state also make it unable to account for what I take to be

a relatively uncontroversial moral intuition about the ethics of immigration. According to the discretionary association view, it is simply a confusion to argue that the people of a very rich and secure state have even a *prima facie* moral obligation to accept even a small number of refugees from genocide occurring just across the border, even when their acceptance carries no risks to the people of the state. It is one thing to say that the obligation to accept political refugees is limited – for example, that a people need not accept refugees if doing so will embroil them in a war or will create ethnic conflict within their state or will undermine the dominant culture of the state. But it is quite another to say that there is no obligation at all. Yet, on the discretionary association view, there is no such obligation.

IV.   The State as an Instrument for Justice

For all of these reasons it is worth asking whether the attractions of the discretionary association view can be preserved while avoiding these costs. The chief moral cost of the discretionary association view is not that it implies that *governments* should not undertake pure humanitarian intervention except (perhaps) when explicitly authorized to do so by democratic processes. The more basic problem is that it provides no basis for believing that the *people* of any particular state have any obligation to use the resources of their state to undertake pure humanitarian intervention or to accept refugees even under the least painful circumstances. On the contrary, the discretionary association model portrays pure humanitarian intervention and the acceptance of refugees as aberrations, as inexplicable departures from what political action ought to be. Even on the democratic variant of the discretionary association view there is still a problem, as we have seen: how can a majority voting in favor of pure humanitarian intervention justify their decision to a dissenting minority, given that the justifying function of the state is to serve the interests of its citizens, not to protect the rights of others?

There is a radically different conception of the nature of the state and the role of government that avoids the moral and theoretical costs of the discretionary association view while at the same time preserving its attractions. We may call it the "state-as-the-instrument-for-justice" view. It rests upon the premise that there is a natural duty of justice that requires us to help ensure that all persons have access to institutions for the protection of their basic moral rights.[12]

In *A Theory of Justice* Rawls articulates a natural duty of justice as having two parts: "first, we are to comply with and do our fair share in just institutions when they exist and apply to us; and second, we are to assist in the establishment of just arrangements when they do not exist, at least when this can be done with little cost to ourselves."[13] The duty is said to be natural in the sense that individuals have it independently of any special undertakings and independently of the institutional roles they may occupy.

The scope of the second clause is perhaps not altogether clear. It could mean that we are to help establish just institutions that will apply to us, where no just institutions now apply to us. Or it could mean that we are to help establish justice institutions for all persons.

In fact, three different understandings of the second clause can be distinguished. In each case the qualifier "if one can do so without excessive costs" is to be understood as being included (for brevity I will not repeat it each time).

NDJ1:   Each person has a duty to contribute to the creation of just arrangements to include himself and his fellow citizens.

NDJ2:   Each person has a duty to contribute to the creation of just arrangements to include himself and all those with whom he will interact (which may include some who are not his fellow citizens).

NDJ3:   Each person has a duty to contribute to the inclusion of all persons in just arrangements.

It is the third, most demanding understanding of the "natural duty of justice" upon which I will focus. It alone provides a secure foundation for an obligation of pure humanitarian intervention, and only it provides a convincing solution to the problem of the internal legitimacy of pure humanitarian intervention.

The natural duty of justice (hereafter understood as NDJ3) is such a fundamental principle that it may seem impossible to provide an argument for it that does not assume at least one premise that is more controversial than the principle itself. However, even if no convincing argument can be presented for it, it has considerable intuitive appeal, at least if, as I have suggested, it is understood as imposing a limited obligation, not an obligation to help ensure that all have access to just institutions regardless of cost. Given its intuitive appeal, showing that the natural duty of justice provides the basis for a view of the nature of the state and the role of government that avoids the costs of the discretionary association view while preserving its attractions would be a valuable exercise, even if no argument for it could be supplied. Nevertheless, although I cannot attempt to provide a conclusive case for the natural duty NDJ3 here, I will indicate one plausible line of argument in support of it.

Before doing so, however, I would like to emphasize that proponents of the discretionary association view typically do not provide explicit arguments to support it. Instead, support for the discretionary association view is indirect. Its plausibility appears to depend solely upon what it implies: namely, that citizens are free and equal; that the state is to serve their interests, rather than the interests of the ruler or the citizens of some other state; and that the government is merely their agent, with no rights or moral standing of its own. Yet these attractive implications, I shall argue, also follow from what I have referred to as the instrument for justice view.

Perhaps the best way to argue for the natural duty of justice is to tease out the incoherence of denying that this duty exists while at the same time affirming that persons as such have rights. I take it that the assertion that persons as such have rights means that we all have a duty to treat persons in certain ways, and that this duty is owed to persons because it is grounded in the nature of persons. Different moral theories may provide somewhat different accounts of what it is about persons that is the source of their rights and hence of our duties toward them (Kantian theories, for instance, hold that it is the capacity for moral agency). But what is important is that the duties that correlate with the rights of persons as such are *owed to* persons. They are not merely duties *regarding* persons (such as we would have if, for example, the sole basis for moral constraints on the way we may treat people were the commands of God or the relationships we happen to have toward persons).

To say that persons as such have certain rights, then, means that because of certain characteristics that all persons have they are entitled to certain treatment. But if this is so, then surely one ought not only to respect persons' rights by not violating them. One ought also to contribute to creating arrangements that will ensure that persons' rights are not violated. To put the same point somewhat differently, respect for persons requires doing something to ensure that they are treated respectfully.

Consider the alternative. Suppose that the ground of our duties regarding persons were external to them – that we are required to treat them in certain ways only because God commands us to do so, for example. We would have duties regarding persons but not owed to them. In this case there would be no incoherence or oddness at all about acknowledging that we are obligated to treat persons in certain ways while at the same time denying that we have any obligation whatsoever, no matter how limited, to help ensure that others treat them similarly. For although God *might* command us to see that our fellows treat persons as he commands us to treat them, he also might not.

Alternatively, suppose that the ground of one's duty not to violate persons' rights lay only in some relationship one happens to bear to them, such as being a fellow citizen or being co-participants in some international economic arrangement for our mutual advantage. If some such relationship were the sole basis of the duty, then one would not have a duty to persons as such to respect their rights, and there would be no presumption that there is a duty to help ensure that all persons' rights are respected.

In contrast, if the basic moral rights of persons are grounded in the morally important characteristics that all persons possess, then it is difficult to maintain a separation between respecting persons' rights and making some effort to see that their rights are respected. At the very least, the same appreciation for the nature of persons that is supposed to ground their most basic rights and hence our duty to respect those rights

carries a presumptive duty to help ensure that all persons can live in conditions in which their basic rights are respected, at least if we can do so without excessive costs to ourselves.

I would not presume to assert that these considerations provide an unassailable foundation for the natural duty of justice. But let us suppose, for the sake of drawing out the implications of this duty for how we conceive of the nature of the state and the role of government, that each of us has an obligation to help ensure that all persons have access to rights-protecting institutions. The extent of what we are actually required to do to fulfill that obligation will vary with the costs of fulfilling it. If this is the case, then those individuals who are politically organized, who can collectively command the resources of a state, will have greater capacity to help ensure that others have access to a justice-protecting regime, without excessive costs.

With this greater capacity comes greater responsibility for alleviating the condition of other persons whose rights are imperilled. As individuals commanding only our own private resources, there may be little that any of us can do to help ensure that all persons can live in a rights-protecting regime. But when we are organized in a state our collective capacity for promoting just institutions abroad is greatly enhanced. And if we live in a powerful and rich state, there will surely be cases in which our collective resources can be used to further the cause of justice in the world, without excessive costs to us.

Because it is a natural duty, NDJ3 places a constraint on how we may use our institutional resources, upon what we may do with the state, and hence what our government, our agent, may do. Given the fact that having a state of our own enables us to act on the natural duty, we are not morally free to use our state merely as a framework for *our* mutual advantage. Thus if we were to adopt the "Swiss model," we would fail to acknowledge the natural duty of justice and ignore the fact that in our world at present states are the chief instrumentalities by which individuals can help ensure that all persons have access to institutions that protect their rights.

This is not to say that the sole legitimate purpose, or even the primary legitimate purpose of particular political associations is to promote justice for all of humanity. Because the natural duty includes an excessive cost proviso, it can accommodate the idea that citizens may rightly show partiality to their own interests. (Moreover, there are sound practical reasons for first seeking to establish justice locally, within the boundaries of existing states, working from within them.[14]) But what the natural duty does imply is that the state cannot be viewed simply as an arrangement for the mutual benefit of its members alone. And this suffices to rebut the fiduciary realist's claim that humanitarian intervention is in principle illegitimate.

The assumption that there is a natural duty of justice allows us to develop a view of the state that preserves the attractive implications of the discretionary association view, while avoiding its moral and theoretical costs. If we suppose that there is a natural duty of justice (NDJ3), then we must acknowledge that those who collectively control effective political institutions have responsibilities to others and that consequently the state is not merely an association for the mutual advantage of its members, but a resource for ensuring that all persons' rights are protected. Given this view of the state, we can explain the moral conflict we feel when we consider the pros and cons of pure humanitarian intervention.

A view of the state as an instrument for justice is clearly compatible with what is probably the single most attractive feature of the discretionary association view: a proper understanding of the status of government – that government is simply an agent, not a moral being with rights of its own. It also captures the idea that citizens are free and equal by affirming that all persons' rights matter. For even though the state-as-the-instrument-for-justice view places some constraints on the use of state resources for enhancing the condition of the citizens, it does not do so in the name of any assumption of unequal worth. On the contrary, the constraints it imposes follow from the assumption that all persons are of equal moral worth and that consequently all are entitled to protection of their rights. Finally, the state-as-the-instrument-for-justice view, like the discretionary association view, rules out any arrangements that sacrifice the interests of the citizens for the sake of benefitting anyone else, whether it be the rulers or the citizens of some other state. For according to the instrument for justice view, the proper business of the state is to benefit its members, within the constraints imposed by the natural duty of justice, and these constraints recognize that there are limits on the costs that the citizens of one state must bear to protect the rights of other persons.

Acknowledging that there is a robust natural duty of justice that requires citizens to use their state's resources to help ensure that all have access to a rights-protecting regime is an important theoretical advance in the doctrine of human rights. But from this alone it does not follow that it would be legitimate for the international legal system to *enforce* a duty on the part of states to contribute to the establishment of justice for all persons. For the natural duty of justice might be viewed as an imperfect duty rather than an enforceable one – merely an indeterminate and hence unenforceable duty to do something to help provide just institutions for all persons. Although I can only sketch the argument here, I will conclude by suggesting that a conscientious effort to act on the natural duty of justice will require states to work together to create international legal institutions that will articulate determinate duties and assign them to states in such a way as to distribute fairly the costs of ensuring that all persons have access to rights-protecting institutions. If this were accomplished, the enforcement of duties of humanitarian intervention would be morally justifiable.

Notes

1 See, for example, Jack Donnelly, "Human rights, humanitarian intervention and American foreign policy: law, morality, and politics," *Journal of International Affairs*, 37 (1984), 311.

2 See, for example, Fernando Teson, *Humanitarian Intervention*, 2nd edn (Irvington-on-Hudson, NY: Transnational Publishers, 1992), pp. 1–6.

3 I borrow the term "internal legitimacy" from Ronald Sanders. In an unpublished paper Sanders distinguishes between internal and external legitimacy. On his view, a state is internally legitimate if its citizens (or the majority of them) accept it as having rightful political authority. My use of the term does not follow his, however. I only use it to focus on which party the justification for humanitarian intervention is directed toward.

4 Article 2, Part II, International Covenant on Civil and Political Rights (1966), in James Nickel, *Making Sense of Human Rights* (Berkeley: University of California Press, 1987), p. 212.

5 As opposed to those that might be generated by other more specific treaties into which states have entered.

6 Alfred Rubin, *Ethics and Authority in International Law* (Cambridge: Cambridge University Press, 1997), p. 93.

7 John Locke, *Second Treatise of Civil Government*, ed. C. B. Macpherson (Indianapolis, Ind.: Hackett, 1980), pp. 1–2.

8 Allen Buchanan, "The morality of inclusion," *Social Philosophy & Policy*, 10 (1993), 242–7.

9 This label is not intended to suggest that Switzerland actually pursues a purely self-interested foreign policy (all the time). The point rather is that this country, whether rightly or wrongly, has the reputation of sufficiently approximating such a policy to make the label a handy one.

10 George F. Kennan, *Realities of American Foreign Policy* (Princeton, NJ: Princeton University Press, 1954). Hans J. Morgenthau, *In Defense of the National Interest* (New York: Knopf, 1952), and *Politics Among Nations*, 5th edn (New York: Knopf, 1973).

11 For excellent critiques of realist thinking, see: Marshall Cohen, "Moral skepticism and international relations," *Philosophy & Public Affairs*, 13 (1984), 299–346; and Charles Beitz, *Political Theory & International Relations* (Princeton, NJ: Princeton University Press, 1979), pp. 15–50.

12 The remainder of this section of the paper draws on my paper "Political legitimacy and the natural duty of justice" (unpublished).

13 John Rawls, *A Theory of Justice* (Cambridge, Mass.: Harvard University Press, 1971), p. 334.

14 For an illuminating and systematic elaboration of this important point, see Jeremy Waldron, "Special ties and natural duties," *Philosophy & Public Affairs*, 22 (1993), 22–30.

20

Humanitarian Intervention: Problems of Collective Responsibility

Larry May

Humanitarian intervention has replaced self-defensive war and become the new favored example of those who think there are clear cases of morally justified wars. Surely if there are morally justified wars, then wars fought to stop a genocide or to curtail crimes against humanity are more likely to be the ones, rather than say wars fought to gain territory or convert the heathens. Wars fought in self-defense look less justifiable than wars fought to save innocent parties from being slaughtered – even Augustine, the founder of the Just War tradition, thought that wars fought for defense of others were more justifiable, because more selfless, than wars fought in self-defense. But there is an unfortunate part of most wars fought for humanitarian reasons: innocent people will be killed. This is the inevitable result of all wars, and even more likely to occur in humanitarian wars since there is often no clear military target that needs to be destroyed, such as a supply depot. In order to win most humanitarian wars, one must try to break the will of a part of a population that is oppressing another part of a population, rather than merely to defeat the enemy army in certain military campaigns. Yet, if it is true that a large part of a population is complicit in causing, or

allowing, a genocidal campaign, perhaps a war that must target that civilian population is not so difficult to justify after all.[1] Humanitarian intervention also raises other issues involving collective responsibility, including how to understand the responsibility of states for rescuing distant peoples, and whether individual human persons should be held liable for what their states do.

Humanitarian interventions raise four distinct collective responsibility issues. First, is the question of whether states can have collective responsibilities to go to the aid of fellow states. Second, there is the question of whether a people can be collectively liable for atrocities committed in their states that would then weaken the normal immunity from attack that people have. Third, is the question of whether a state is responsible for the civilian casualties that are caused by its bombing campaigns in a just war. Fourth, is the question of which individuals share in responsibility and should be prosecuted when the state is responsible for engaging in humanitarian war.

I wish to consider criticisms of so-called humanitarian wars, such as NATO's war to stop Serbs from engaging in ethnic cleansing against Kosovar Albanians. In the first section, I will set the stage for our discussion by briefly assessing the current state of international law regarding humanitarian intervention today. I will then examine two arguments often used to justify humanitarian wars. In the second section, I will look at the argument based on collective liability of those otherwise innocent people who will die in a humanitarian war. [. . .] In the fourth section, I will discuss in what sense states are responsible for humanitarian wars. In the fifth section, I will provide a brief defense of humanitarian wars. In the final section, I will address the problem of who, if anyone, should be prosecuted for humanitarian wars. In general, I argue that theorists today are too quick to replace self-defensive wars with humanitarian wars as paradigmatically justified wars, and that attention to collective responsibility issues makes this clear.

I. Humanitarian Intervention in International Law

Consider the state of international law today regarding the case of humanitarian interventions. In the 1986 Nicaragua case,[2] the International Court of Justice points to a problem with humanitarian intervention. The case concerned the mining of Nicaragua's harbors by the CIA, and by "contras," who were merely paid operatives of the US. The US tried to topple the Nicaraguan government in the early 1980s, as a means to prevent what it predicted would be massive human rights violations by the communist government of Nicaragua in the region. Here is part of the Court's judgment:

> In any event, while the United States might form its own appraisal of the situation as to respect for human rights, the use of force could not be the appropriate method to monitor or ensure such respect. With regard to the steps actually taken, the protection of human rights, a strictly humanitarian objective, cannot be compatible with mining of ports . . . which is based on the right of collective self-defense.

This ICJ opinion seems to see humanitarian intervention to prevent human rights abuses as just one form of aggression. Yet, there has been

a controversy about how to interpret this ICJ opinion, some reading it narrowly as applying only to the unusual factual circumstances of this case, and others seeing in it a broad condemnation of humanitarian intervention.

Ian Brownlie, writing in 1963, says this of the doctrine of humanitarian intervention:

> The state practice justifies the conclusion that no genuine case of humanitarian intervention has occurred with the . . . embarrassing exception provided by Germany [by its claim to be going to the aid of Czechoslovakia], the institution has disappeared from modern state practice. As a matter of legal international policy this is a beneficial development. The institution did not conspicuously enhance state relations and was applied only against weak states. It belongs to an era of unequal relations. Many modern authorities either ignore humanitarian intervention or expressly deny that such a right to intervene exists.[3]

Brownlie points to the fact that even when discussions "in the Sixth Committee of the General Assembly" in the 1960s considered "whether action taken by a state to prevent genocide against a racially related minority in a neighboring state" would be aggression, many of the delegates said that it would.[4] And if stopping genocide was not then considered to be sufficient to justify the initiation war, it is hard to imagine any other humanitarian goal that could have done so.

From 1960 to the present day, sentiments have changed but it is probably fair to say that the vast majority of international law scholars still find wars waged for humanitarian reasons to be illegal. Indeed, most of the authorities today continue to think of humanitarian intervention as a form of aggression. Wars waged for humanitarian reasons, such as NATO's attempt to stop ethnic cleansing in Kosovo by its brief war against Serbia, are sometimes described as paradigmatically justified wars. Yet, this is a very recent movement, although one that is often strongly represented in the media and in moral and political theory.

The reason why humanitarian intervention has been so controversial is that it is hard to characterize the acts by the state that has caused the humanitarian crisis as having threatened either the state that intervenes or the world community. And for this reason it is hard to see that the offending state has engaged in a first strike or otherwise provoked the attack by the intervening state. And without any provocation, at least based on the traditional elements of what constitutes state aggression, where unprovoked first strikes are paradigmatically cases of state aggression, it looks like the state that has engaged in humanitarian intervention has itself engaged in an act of aggression.

Of course, since the state has gone to war for defense of the rights of others, it is not clearly an example of state aggression. Yet, what is in question is whether this kind of defense of others, where the other in question is not itself a state that is being attacked, can justify intervention. It is odd indeed to call the humanitarian actions of a state by the name aggression since that implies that there is some hostility behind the intervention. If the intervention is truly motivated by humanitarian concerns, then calling it aggression and therefore also hostile seems out of place.

It is also hard to see that humanitarian interventions constitute wrongs at all, let alone the most important of wrongs in the international arena, and hence we have reason to think that crossing state borders is not always wrong. Humanitarian intervention may indeed often be ill advised since anything that contributes to the horrors of war is to be avoided at nearly all costs. But if the motivation for the humanitarian intervention is to stop genocide, then the war may not be ill advised even though there is a serious risk of the kind of major loss of civilian life that occurs in most wars. Here we might do some rudimentary utilitarian calculation in order to see that stopping genocide by means of a war could be justified.

I would be hard pressed though to see humanitarian intervention that risks the horrors of war as a paradigmatically good thing to do or as an example of a paradigmatically justified war. Anything that increases the likelihood of major loss of civilian lives must at best be a necessary evil, surely not a paradigmatically justified war. The morally ambiguous character of humanitarian intervention is made even more clear when one realizes, as we will see, that humanitarian wars are more likely than other wars to involve massive civilian casualties. Such considerations contribute to the continuing debate today about how to regard humanitarian intervention.

Some legal scholars have recently supported the idea that some humanitarian wars can be legally fought. Art. 2/4 of the UN Charter declares that "All members shall refrain in their international relations from the threat or use of force against the territorial integrity or political independence of any state, or in any other manner inconsistent with the purposes of the United Nations." Michael Reisman argues that humanitarian wars are not straightforward violations of Article 2/4 of the UN Charter:

> Since a humanitarian intervention seeks neither a territorial change nor a challenge to the political independence of the State involved and is not only not inconsistent with the purposes of the United Nations but is rather in conformity with the most fundamental peremptory norms of the charter, it is a distortion to argue that it is precluded by Article 2(4).[5]

If the intent is to save a people from annihilation, it is possible that there was no additional intent to change the territorial boundaries or political independence of a state.

Critics of this legal argument respond that any humanitarian war will cross borders and this is surely a violation of the territorial integrity of the state. Here is one common response, provided by Oscar Schachter: "The idea that wars waged in a good cause such as democracy and human rights would not involve a violation of territorial integrity or political independence demands an Orwellian construction of those terms."[6] And this view seems reasonable if we just look at the wording of the UN Charter.

While a growing number of scholars in moral and political theory argue that some humanitarian wars are justified,[7] the majority of legal scholars continue to follow Schachter here, and the Nicaragua case continues to be cited as the main precedent in international law, despite the failure of the international community to condemn NATO's humanitarian war against Serbia to stop its persecution of the Kosovar Albanians. In general, while international law may be in flux about humanitarian intervention, legal scholars have not followed their colleagues in political and moral philosophy in urging whole-scale changes in what appear to be straightforward applications of *jus ad bellum* concepts.

II. Immunity, Complicity, and Collective Liability

Humanitarian intervention seems to be morally problematic, especially since large loss of civilian life is a nearly inevitable result of such wars. One strategy for dealing with the inevitable loss of innocent lives in a humanitarian war is to argue that the members of a society engaged in oppression of its own citizens have lost their immunity and hence ceased to be innocent. Perhaps the otherwise innocent members of a political society that engages in such abhorrent practices as ethnic cleansing have lost their immunity from attack, even though these people may not straightforwardly deserve to be attacked. Some, like Erin Kelly, as well as Seumas Miller and David Rodin, have recently argued that the people who will inevitably lose their lives in humanitarian wars may not suffer injustice since they are collectively liable for such things as ethnic cleansing that have precipitated the need for the humanitarian wars in the first place. Since I have also defended the idea of collective responsibility in the past, and since I find the application of these arguments to the justifiability of humanitarian war to be unsettling, I will take this subtle issue up in some detail.

Kelly contends that "the liability of the perpetrators allows us to focus primarily on the needs of the victims, even at serious costs to the perpetrators."[8] And she has an expansive view of who is liable for an injustice. As she says, "it is not necessary that members of a liable group should each have acted with the intention of causing the result that they together in fact caused. Nor is it necessary that they knew the result would ensue. But it is important that they could have foreseen that unjust harms would occur."[9] While I have written in a similar vein concerning collective moral responsibility, I am not willing to follow Kelly in thinking that such considerations translate into liability of the sort that could result in a person losing his or her immunity to be attacked. Shared or collective

moral responsibility does not translate well into such legal or quasi-legal notions of liability.

Employing a concept of distributive collective liability, Kelly argues that individuals are liable for injustices as long as they are part of a collective agent in which:

(1)   The group or some of its members are causally responsible for an injustice via the political and social arrangements they impose or perpetuate.

(2)   Passive members of the group, that is, members who do not actively promote the offending result, benefit from the injustice and could together have played a role in preventing it.

(3)   Members of the group could have foreseen the possibility that some injustice or other could result.

(4)   Members of the group have had an opportunity, weakly construed, to exit the group, to take political action to combat the injustice, or to refuse the benefits that accrue to them as a result of the injustice.[10]

I have no trouble accepting these conditions for assigning shared or distributive collective *moral* responsibility. Indeed, Kelly claims to be indebted to me for just such an argument. But I worry when such conditions are employed to justify, quoting Kelly again, "loosening moral prohibitions on the use of violence in response to injustice."[11]

Shared or distributive collective moral responsibility is a strong tool – indeed one that many people find counterintuitive. I have employed it in the past as a way to get people to take more responsibility for their actions as well as their omissions. I have also suggested that such considerations may warrant the instilling of shame, but I have been very reluctant to think that legal guilt or liability follows from the ascription of shared or distributive collective moral responsibility. For me, this would create an undue burden. Things come to a head when ascriptions of collective agency are said to lead to collective liability and then to a weakening of the immunity from attack and death that we all normally have.

In US domestic criminal law, merely having foreseen the possibility that an injustice could occur, in conjunction with being able when acting with many others to have prevented the injustice, would not count to make one liable for punishment. One could argue that suffering injury or death in a just war is not equivalent to punishment. In the next section I examine in more detail the relationship between punishment and humanitarian intervention. Suffice it here to say that with the possible exception of conspiracy laws, punishment is not justified on such weak grounds of liability as those proposed by Kelly to justify loss of life during war. And even when thinking about conspiracies in domestic criminal law, there has to be some wrongful act on the part of the defendant for him or her to be subject to punishment.

Yet, Kelly argues that there is no such act component required on the part of previously innocent people in order for them to lose their immunity from attack in societies where serious injustice is occurring. On her view, it is sufficient that a passive member of a group benefit from the injustice that other members of the group are actively perpetrating, in order to make the passive members liable in a way that loses their immunity from attack. Such benefiting seemingly makes the individual complicit in the injustices and thereby makes her liable in a way that would affect her status as "innocent" as well as her corresponding immunity from attack.

Yet, the idea that people are immune from attack unless they have actively done something wrong is a cornerstone of liberal moral and political theory, as far back at least as Grotius in the early seventeenth century. We do not hold someone liable for merely having thoughts of a certain kind and we do not typically hold a person liable merely because he or she benefited from a wrongful act. Liability to be punished or attacked is such a serious matter that we look for much more than merely having had immoral thoughts or having benefited. Having immoral thoughts might warrant moral criticism of various sorts, but it does not warrant criminal punishment or other forms of sanctioned violence. And while having benefited from a wrong is often quite a serious matter, typically it triggers some kind of monetary or civil liability rather than liability to punishment or attack, if it triggers a legal response at all – think of unjust enrichment cases. Of course, this statement of how things are is only mentioned to give a beginning intuitive

basis for an argument, not a replacement for that argument.

The argument against Kelly's view begins with the idea that there is a division of labor in the moral domain. We reserve the most strongly condemnatory responses for the worst of wrongs committed by individuals. If one individual intentionally, and inexcusably, harms another, criminal sanction is the appropriate response. If one conspires with others intentionally, and inexcusably, to cause harm, I am willing to agree with Kelly that punishment or some forms of force, or in rare cases, violence, might be justified as a response here as well. But the conspiring must involve some explicit act on the part of the agent in question. From all I can tell, Kelly would disagree with this point since she seems to require only that one not have exited from a group that one could have predicted would cause harm. This is, as she recognizes, to make passive participation a basis for the most serious of responses, and this seemingly denies that there is a division of labor in the moral domain concerning proper responses.

One of the main reasons to preserve a division of labor in the moral domain is to deter the worst of wrongs, the intentional decision directly to cause harm to another. While it is surely true that great harm in the world is indeed caused by those who passively participate, the passive actors would not cause nearly as much harm if it were not for the active participators. Most people simply go along, and while it would be good to get people to be more active in the prevention of harm, surely the more important thing is to get the active participators to stop. Holding passive members of groups to the same standards as those who are active sends the wrong message, and seems unfair in that in many instances the passive participants could have chosen to be more active in the perpetration of the harm, but did not so choose. So while their choice, not to try to prevent the harm, or not to distance themselves from the group causing harm, may be morally wrong, treating them as if they did the same as those active members of the group fails to take morally relevant factors into account and hence is unfair.

Another problem with the argument by Kelly and others we have been considering is that humanitarian wars do not only kill adult civilians who might be complicit in genocide or ethnic cleansing. Humanitarian wars also kill children. Young children, say those who are under the age of seven, cannot possibly be said to be complicit in the genocide of ethnic cleansing campaigns, and so they will be innocent deaths regardless of the arguments we have been considering. Hugh LaFollette and I have made a similar point about those who try to argue that the poor and starving of the world are not owed help because they should have helped themselves. The case of children makes this, and the arguments about humanitarian war, not seem very plausible after all.[12]

Kelly and others who employ collective liability strategies to justify the killing of the innocent in humanitarian wars also fail to distinguish between criminal sanctions and the sanctions of war. One could agree that being a passive member of a group that causes harm makes one subject to criminal sanctions, perhaps on the basis of a conspiracy theory. But criminal sanctions and war sanctions should not be treated the same. Criminal sanctions are only meted out after extensive consideration of the facts, with attention paid to mitigating circumstances and various excuses that the agent has. There is in the end a determination of guilt by an independent fact-finder, that is, the judge or jury.

In war, there is no such determination of the guilt or liability of a particular person. At best there is a non-independent determination of such guilt, but more often there is no serious attempt to make this determination at all. Rather, bombing campaigns are launched with little regard for the particular liability of an otherwise innocent person who is likely to be killed. Because of this, even if one agreed that collective liability schemes could be used to eliminate the immunity from criminal punishment we all normally have, more would be needed before similar arguments could justify the loss of immunity from attack in war.

[. . .]

IV. Collective Responsibility and States

Humanitarian intervention is a difficult case because it involves a state initiating war against a state that has not attacked or even threatened it. There is no invasion that is imminent, and no population group of the attacking state has been jeopardized. To be sure, there are people who are being attacked or threatened, but they reside normally within the confines of a sovereign state that has not by and large acted hostilely toward its neighbors. And yet, if the only way to prevent large-scale harm to a population is for one state to wage war against the state that so threatens this population, it seems that this is indeed a just cause for war. But, there will be, as we will see, problems of proportionality as well as other serious problems that make this case a very difficult one indeed.

Central to the questions raised in this paper is how we are to understand the collective responsibility of states. We could proceed as I have suggested in some of my earlier writings, to treat the collective responsibility of a state in a non-distributive way. This strategy is attractive especially when considering questions of responsibility for waging aggressive war, since war is something that no individual can mount on his or her own, and is clearly best understood as something that states do. I would contend that war is one of the best examples of something that collectivities do, rather than what individuals, or at least rather than what individuals, acting in isolation from one another, do. And humanitarian wars raise the issue of what states are responsible for in particularly graphic ways.

There is of course a serious debate about whether states or other collectivities can have non-distributive responsibilities. In my earlier writings I said that this issue turns on whether states can act in a non-distributive way, or at least can have actions attributed to them in this way.[13] Waging war is the kind of action that makes sense to attribute, if anything does, to a collectivity, and specifically to a state. For war to be waged there must be highly coordinated actions of many individual human persons, and these actions must be occurring in the midst of certain circumstances. War is not best seen as a duel writ large, unless by the phrase "writ large," we mean that it is best seen as a duel among states.

If it makes sense to attribute actions to states, such as the action of waging aggressive or humanitarian war, then it also makes sense to blame or praise these states, and in general to talk of these states being responsible for waging war. The only other person or entity that it might make sense to blame for waging aggressive war is the individual human person who is often most associated with the state, the head of state. I will address this point in the final section of this paper. Aside from this person, there is really no one else who is responsible for the highly coordinated action that constitutes war. And this perhaps explains why for so many centuries discussion of war has almost always focused on the actions and responsibilities of states rather than on the members of states. Indeed, it is very hard even to talk about war as a function of what individual human persons do without elliptical language. The idea that states have responsibilities for waging war is not a difficult one conceptually, if we are receptive to the idea of collectivities acting at all.

Let us return to the issue of collective liability that we discussed in section two. If a state could but did not go to the aid of a state or sub-group of that state to stop oppression or aggression, there is a sense in which that state as well as other similarly placed states, and even the international community, could be collectively liable for failing to supply such aid. When the aid in question is providing military force to stop aggressive troops from carrying out oppression, it still seems as if it would be wrong not to do so, and the collective failure to aid people in such places as Darfur is a collective liability of the state, or other institution, that could help. We must not allow another Holocaust to occur because states and other institutions do not understand their collective responsibilities.

So, as you can see, the idea of collective responsibility has been used on both sides of the debate concerning humanitarian intervention. For there are at least two collectivities in play: the State, as we have just seen, and the international community. If there is anything like an international community, the members of this community have both collective responsibilities for what they do toward one another and collective responsibilities if they fail to do what they should do. And for our purposes this raises two questions: first, are states the proper members of the international community; and second, are the members of the international community implicated in the moral responsibilities of the international community? International law is

premised on international enforcement of rules at the international level. Those who support humanitarian intervention see it as one source of enforcement of international law. Those who oppose humanitarian intervention see that states have a collective responsibility not to violate the UN Charter and jeopardize the sovereignty of fellow states.

In addition to the issues of non-distributive collective responsibility raised by humanitarian intervention, there are also distributive collective responsibility issues as well. I will here address moral issues, and leave legal issues until the final section of this paper. Morally, we need to ascertain whether the responsibility of a state for waging aggressive or humanitarian war gives rise to moral responsibility for the members of states, that is, individual human persons. And here we face one of the greatest challenges, namely to explain why every member of a state does not share responsibility, and to the same extent, for what the state is responsible for. My view, defended elsewhere, is that the better approach is to talk of differential moral responsibility based on the different roles that the members of a state played, where the greater the participation normally means the greater the moral responsibility.

Individual human persons will share moral responsibility for what their states do not merely because of group membership but also because of participation in what the state does. This thesis is easy to accept when we talk of shared individual moral responsibility for war. In some wars, all of the members of a state participate, in other wars only a small number of people participate. But participation is the key component that links the individual human person to the state in moral terms, and perhaps also in legal terms as we will explore later. Since state action is only the coordinated action of the state's members, and since the action of its members is best understood as participation, when we move from non-distributive to distributive responsibility, the best strategy is to do so by reference to individual participation.[14]

V. Defending Humanitarian Wars

I wish to mount a limited defense of humanitarian wars based on some of the ideas of the eighteenth-century theorist, Emer de Vattel, and in light of what we learned in other earlier sections as well. Perhaps humanitarian wars can be justified by reference to Vattel's principle of humanity, namely, when it is in a state's power to help other states without risking greater harm to itself, it is permissible (perhaps even obligatory) to do so.[15] Vattel worried about how the application of this principle could disrupt sovereignty. And we have also wondered about the risk of civilian casualties from humanitarian war. One way to modify the Vattelian principle to respond to such worries is to stipulate that one has a responsibility to act only if one does not risk greater harm to self *or others*. We should also stipulate that the states have very good grounds for thinking that the state or people to be rescued are truly in need of, and desire, rescue.

Vattel worried that humanitarian wars would often jeopardize whatever good there is from having stable sovereign states. I would agree with his analysis. But Vattel also said that the most obvious case where such worries were not clearly overriding concerned situations where there was a civil war or at least where it was not clear where sovereignty resided. We could expand on his idea, extrapolating to emergency situations generally, and say that humanitarian wars should only be allowed where what is to be gained is not overridden by the negative effects on sovereignty that occur due to such intervention. Such considerations would naturally fall under the category of potential harm to others by waging humanitarian wars. Only when the risks incumbent on intrusion on sovereignty are less than the gains in such intrusion, can humanitarian wars be justified on this reconstruction of Vattel's position. Proportionality consideration would be key here.

When discussing Kelly's arguments about collective liability, we encountered a worry about the loss of life to civilians in humanitarian wars. I tried to show that Kelly's argument did not work to justify such civilian losses. But these losses may nonetheless be justified, yet only in very few cases, if the sheer extent of the humanitarian crisis is so large as to outweigh considerations of the lives of the innocent that are risked by the attempt to stop the crisis through military means. If innocent lives are on both sides of the balance sheet, there is no reason to think that greater saving of lives cannot justify lesser loss of lives, assuming that there is no other way to save the greater number of lives than by war.

When discussing the doctrine of double effect we also saw how some, although again very few, humanitarian wars might be justified by reference to this doctrine. When the war is aimed at civilian targets, the doctrine of double effect will not help much. But we might be able to justify even the targeting of civilians if it could be shown that this was necessary to save many more lives than those that were risked by the targeting. It is sometimes said that the intentional targeting of civilians can never be justified. But I follow Vattel in thinking that there can be emergency situations where such a large number of innocent people is threatened by the actions of a state, or where there is so much potential harm to the world community, say by a genocidal campaign, that what is normally banned may sometimes be allowed. Of course, emergency situations do not have much precedent. But that is just to reaffirm what has been thought at least since Augustine, namely, that all war, even humanitarian war, can only be justified, if at all, in the most extreme cases of harm that can be prevented in no other way.

What we have come to see is that it is next to impossible to justify all humanitarian wars, but that at least some humanitarian wars may be justified, even strongly so. Many humanitarian wars will violate the proportionality principle in that more harm to the civilian population or to the security of the region will occur from these wars than the good that is risked by waging them. But some humanitarian wars will not run afoul of the proportionality principle since they will confront genocides and other mass crimes with less loss of life through the conduct of the war itself. In addition, many humanitarian wars do not meet the last resort principle since war has rarely been able to stop, at least not for very long, mass crimes like genocide from occurring in ways that diplomacy often can. But there surely are some humanitarian wars that seem to satisfy the last resort principle and are likely to have some efficacy. And the justification of such wars will indeed be best grounded in collective responsibility principles.

Think of a war waged to stop the genocide in the Darfur region of the Sudan. The Sudanese government, if we can even refer to the near anarchy in the Sudan as having a government, has shown itself unwilling or unable to stop the slaughter. Diplomatic efforts have been tried and have all failed miserably. The United Nations' attempts to put peace-keeping troops in place have met with strong resistance and the death of many peace-keepers. Threats of economic boycotts and incentives of economic aid have similarly failed to achieve a stop to the carnage in the refugee camps. This is the kind of case where it looks like war might be the last resort to ending the genocide and doing what the international community has a collective responsibility to do.

Indeed, it seems that the failure to go to war to end genocides of the sort that are occurring in Darfur would indicate a failure of the international community to enforce its most widely praised multi-lateral treaty, namely the Genocide Convention, and hence a serious failure of international law itself. If law is not enforced then it ceases to have any claim to be called law. In international law, an area of law already thought of as contro- versially labeled "law" at best, there is an especially pressing reason to demonstrate that there is enforcement of the most widely accepted provi- sions of international law. Failure to intervene in places like Darfur, in order to stop the flagrant violation of the Genocide Convention is also a major failure of international law.

Humanitarian wars can at least be prima facie defended in such circumstances as the genocide in Darfur. Such wars might be technically aggres- sive in that they involve invasion by one State against another state that is resisting rather than consenting to the invasion. Yet, since there is no "hostility" that motivates the invading state, and if the international community in effect consents to allow the invasion to occur, it seems as if the designation of aggression is the kind of technical characterization that doesn't bear much norm- ative weight. Aggression is not itself a trigger of normative disapproval, since some aggression, such as that form that stops worse aggression can be a very good thing indeed, as theorists from the Just War tradition and contemporary international law have claimed. And this is even clearer when it is realized that there are often such strong normative reasons in favor of humanitarian wars as well, such as when a humanitarian war is waged to stop genocide.

The major problem with humanitarian inter- vention wars is that despite their lofty aims they are still wars. And because they are wars there will be innocent civilians who will be killed, perhaps in very large numbers. And the horrors of war do not stop just with the killing of the innocent, no matter how unintended, but extend to massive injuries and infrastructure damage that may take a generation to overcome. Because of the general horrors involved, wars of humanitarian intervention remain morally and legally prob- lematical. Yet, when it really does seem like the last hope for saving many lives and preventing widescale injury, and saving property from mass destruction, then sometimes such wars seem worth it. And those who initiate and wage such wars have not clearly done wrong when they pursue humanitarian intervention as a strategy for promoting international law.

VI.   Should Anyone Be Prosecuted for Initiating a Humanitarian War?

Despite the difficulty of condemning or justify- ing all humanitarian wars, I wish to argue that it is not difficult to say whether or not anyone should be prosecuted for waging such wars. In my view, it is very rare that an individual, even a political or military leader of a state, should be prosecuted for initiating and waging human- itarian wars regardless of the fact that at least some of these wars could be characterized as aggressive. We should think of the principle of just cause, and the corresponding idea of state aggression, as a bifurcated principle. We should only prosecute individuals for clear-cut cases of aggressive war, and from what we have seen in this paper, humanitarian war is anything but clear-cut. While we might want to condemn and even sanction states for waging humanitarian wars, it is rarely justified to prosecute even the state's top leaders for the crime of aggression.

In contemporary international law, the ele- ments of the crime of aggression are not well settled. But there seems to be agreement that there are at least three elements of this crime. First, the prosecution must show that there is state aggression. This is often highly contentious, and especially so when considering wars waged for humanitarian reasons. State aggression is an element of the crime of aggression where that means that in order to convict an individual for the crime of participating in an aggressive war one must first prove that the war in question was indeed a war that a state was waging aggressively. Second, there is the matter of *actus reus*, and normally this means that one had a fairly high level of participation in the waging of the war of aggression. Third, one must also prove that the individual in question had *mens rea*, that is that he or she intended to participate in a war of aggression. And while any individual human person could be prosecuted for such a crime, the ICC has made it clear that only state leaders will be so prosecuted, if anyone is.

One of the main reasons to think that we should rarely if ever prosecute state leaders for waging humanitarian war comes from considerations of *mens rea*. For most wars this is the stumbling block for individual prosecutions in any event. State leaders are often doing what they think is in the best interest of their country, or are doing their patriotic duty, or merely following orders by those who are even higher up the chain of command. These intentions and motives make it hard to show that state leaders had a guilty mind when they participated in initiating or waging aggressive war. And this is especially true since it is often hard for state leaders to figure out whether a given war is indeed a war of aggression, and whether these leaders meant to be participating in an aggressive war.

When humanitarian war is being initiated or waged, it is even harder than it normally is to prove *mens rea* of state leaders. For at very least there will be mixed intentions or motives, as the state leader seeks to aid another state, or a sub-population within a state. Coming to the aid of others is certainly not a straightforwardly guilt-making act. Indeed, given the rich tradition about the good Samaritan, many would find humanitarian intervention to be the opposite of something for which an individual should be judged guilty. And when we add to this the extreme difficulty of telling whether a given war of humanitarian intervention is also a war of aggression, proving *mens rea* of state leaders will be very difficult indeed.

The *actus reus* component also now looks very difficult to prove as well in humanitarian wars.

Participation in such wars will be no harder to prove than normal, I suppose. But that only means that the act part is no more difficult than normal. Establishing that the act was guilty depends even more on the circumstances in humanitarian intervention than in other types of war. For it is very unclear what exactly are the illegal circumstances within which individual acts of participation are to be located. Specifically, it will matter quite a bit whether or not the individual human person in question saw his or her participation as part of an aggressive war, and this will indeed turn on the state of mind of this individual human person.

The circumstances of humanitarian intervention concern such things as an ongoing genocide or ethnic cleansing campaign, as well as the normal circumstances of planning for war. So we could see the acts of state leaders either as participating in stopping genocide or ethnic cleansing, or as participating in the preparation for war. The first set of circumstances may not imply anything guilty about the acts; while the second set of circumstances may do so. But if the war is clearly waged purely for humanitarian reasons, then it is hard not to see the second colored by the first. Because of these mixed considerations, it is especially hard to convict state leaders in such cases, even though the consensus in international law remains in favor of the illegality of humanitarian intervention.

The state aggression element is of course also very hard to prove in cases of humanitarian intervention. Indeed, it is even a bit controversial whether humanitarian intervention should count as war at all, as I said at the beginning of this paper. Not all invasions by the police into a person's home violate the rights of that person. If the person has committed a crime and is seen fleeing the scene by hiding in his or her own home, there is no trespass if the police enter the home to confront the suspect. Similarly, not all use of force by one state against another is a war, especially if they are not aimed at overthrowing the political order of a state. And peace-keeping missions that cross borders are by definition not wars as long as there is no attempt to violate the territorial integrity of a state. Armies can be on peace-keeping or law-enforcement missions and not necessarily engage in war by crossing into a sovereign state's territory.

Because humanitarian intervention does not look like normal cases of state aggression, it will be harder for the prosecution to prove the state aggression element in such cases, just as it is also harder than normal to prove *mens rea* and *actus reus*. One might argue that prosecutions of individuals for participating in humanitarian wars should take place even if it is unlikely that convictions can be secured so as to make a statement about the wrongness of such wars. It is surely not a good normative reason to fail to prosecute just because conviction is unlikely. On pragmatic grounds, most prosecutors do take likelihood of conviction into account, but that is normally because the prosecutors have too many other possible cases to prosecute waiting in the wings. But at the international level, this may not be as big a practical problem as in the domestic sphere, since at least for the foreseeable future few cases will be referred to the ICC. Nonetheless, it is normatively odd to urge that prosecutions not take place because they will be hard to bring to convictions. Shouldn't prosecutions for crimes of aggression be undertaken so as to deter individual leaders from waging war?

My view is that the answer to this question would normally be yes, but that there is a countervailing consideration in the case of humanitarian wars. Yes, it is true that we want to discourage states from waging wars, but it is also true that we want to encourage states to go to the aid of other states or sub-groups within states that are experiencing serious and sustained oppression. Morally, it would be a mistake to discourage individuals from going to the aid of other individuals who are in serious trouble and are unlikely to extricate themselves on their own. Indeed, encouraging state leaders to be good Samaritans seems like just the kind of thing that international law should aim at, just as it also should aim at minimizing use of force. And legally there are also similar reasons to worry about such countervailing considerations, especially considerations tied to deterrence.

In this paper, I have tried to explain how difficult a case humanitarian intervention is when we are considering the crime of aggression. For all three elements, humanitarian intervention is problematic. But, I argued that it makes sense to think that some wars of humanitarian intervention can be justified. I also argued that

on similar grounds it rarely makes sense to prosecute state leaders for participating in such wars, if wars they are. Humanitarian intervention will remain very controversial at the level of asking about whether states should be condemned and sanctioned for engaging in them. But it is much less controversial concerning prosecutions, since there are many reasons to think that state leaders and other individual human persons should not be convicted in humanitarian intervention cases than in other cases of aggressive war. The participation is less likely to be guilty in that it is so hard to tell whether the war is aggressive that one participates in, and the motives and intentions are more likely to be admirable, than in other types of war. For these reasons, it will be rare indeed that prosecutions for humanitarian interventions should go forward.[16]

Notes

1   See Deen K. Chatterjee and Don E. Scheid, *Ethics and Foreign Intervention*, New York: Cambridge University Press, 2003.
2   See Case Concerning Military and Paramilitary Activities in and Against Nicaragua (*Nicaragua v. United States*), 1986, International Court of Justice Advisory Opinion, paragraph 268.
3   Ian Brownlie, *International Law and the Use of Force by States*, Oxford: Oxford University Press, 1963, pp. 340–1.
4   Ibid.
5   W. Michael Reisman with the collaboration of Myres McDougal, "Humanitarian Intervention to Protect the Ibos," in Richard Lillich, ed., *Humanitarian Intervention and the United Nations*, Charlottesville, VA: University Press of Virginia, p. 177.
6   Oscar Schachter, "The Legality of Pro-democratic Invasion," *American Journal of International Law*, vol. 78, 1984, p. 649. This quotation and the previous one are taken from the excellent article on this topic by J. L. Holzgrefe, "The Humanitarian Intervention Debate," in J. L. Holzgrefe and Robert O. Keohane, ed., *Humanitarian Intervention*, New York: Cambridge University Press, 2003, pp. 15–52.
7   The most prominent scholar to argue in this vein is Allen Buchanan.
8   Erin Kelly, "The Burdens of Collective Liability," in Chatterjee and Scheid, *Ethics and Foreign Intervention*, p. 132.
9   Ibid., p. 127.

10 Ibid., pp. 131–2.

11 Ibid., p. 133.

12 "Suffer the Little Children," co-authored with Hugh LaFollette, *World Hunger and Morality*, ed. William Aiken and Hugh LaFollette, Englewood Cliffs, NJ: Prentice-Hall, 1996, pp. 70–84.

13 See Larry May, *The Morality of Groups*, Notre Dame, IN: University of Notre Dame Press, 1987; Larry May, *Sharing Responsibility*, Chicago, IL: University of Chicago Press, 1992; Larry May, *The Socially Responsive Self*, Chicago, IL: University of Chicago Press, 1996.

14 For a similar strategy, see Christopher Kutz, *Complicity*, New York: Cambridge University Press, 2000. Also see *Individual and Collective Responsibility*, ed. Peter French, New York: Schenkman Publishing, 1972.

15 Emer de Vattel, *Le Droit des gens, ou Principes de la loi naturelle* (The Laws of Nations or the Principles of Natural Law) (1758), trans. Charles Fenwick, Washington, DC: Carnegie Institute, 1916, p. 130.

16 This paper is cut from my book, *Aggression and Crimes Against Peace*. Versions of this paper were read at the APA Pacific meetings in Portland, as keynote addresses at conferences in Helsinki and Louisville, and at philosophy department colloquia at the University of Northern Illinois, the University of South Florida, and Texas A&M University, in 2006.

21

Humanitarian Intervention: Some Doubts

Burleigh Wilkins

If Locke was correct, and I think he was, revolution is justified when there is systematic violation of the rights to life, liberty, and property with no peaceful redress in sight. I believe that secession and even terrorism are also justified when these conditions obtain. But what about humanitarian intervention? Is it also justified in such a situation? Many of us hesitate when confronted by this question, but why? Is it because humanitarian intervention involves military action by some state or states against another state? Is it because it may raise questions about the legitimacy of a state's sovereignty, questions which even the most secure liberal democracy may feel uncomfortable in addressing? Are even more egregious violations of human rights required in the case of humanitarian intervention than in the cases of revolution, secession, and terrorism? Of course, attempted justifications of humanitarian intervention may focus upon issues other than human rights violations, such as the need to establish or reestablish a democracy or to put an end to a vicious civil war, but these issues, although separate from the issue of human rights violations, may nevertheless be related to it. For purposes of this chapter, I shall be concerned only with

human rights violations as a possible ground for humanitarian intervention.

Although it involves the violation of a state's independence and territorial integrity, humanitarian intervention is usually distinguished from war on the ground that the loss of independence and territorial integrity is limited in time and scope. Also it is regarded as a means and not an end, with the end being not conquest or the acquisition of land but the restoration or establishment of protection for basic human rights. But how long before a temporary incursion becomes an occupation? And does not the protection of human rights necessitate at times a change of government, as part of what is sometimes called "a comprehensive settlement"? And what, if anything, can the intervening power(s) do about the culture or way of life which may underlie a government's violation of human rights?

International law seems committed to respect for the sovereignty of states, to the protection of human rights, and to the maintenance of peaceful relations among states. In an ideal world where, say, all states are liberal democracies, all three of these commitments would presumably be honored. There is Michael Doyle's "law" that

Burleigh Wilkins, "Humanitarian Intervention: Some Doubts," in Aleksandar Jokic, ed., *Humanitarian Intervention: Moral and Philosophical Issues* (Broadview Press, 2003), pp. 35–44. © 2003 by Aleksandar Jokic. Reprinted with permission from Broadview Press.

no democracies ever fight one another, but is this a law or just a trend? In any event, in the real world it may be impossible to provide equal protection for sovereignty, human rights, and peaceful co-existence among states. Here we can note the temptation to treat human rights violations in one state as a threat to the peace and security of all states, or at least of neighboring states, and to use this as a justification for the violation of a nation's sovereignty, although this may in some cases seem farfetched and even disingenuous.

Perhaps humanitarian intervention isn't war, but is it enough like war that the doctrine of just war – with its requirements that a war be fought for a just cause and in a just manner, with an expectation of success, and with a respect for proportionality between the means being employed and the end being sought – can be applied? Would a little fine-tuning help? Justice can be cashed in terms of human rights, with the stipulation that the intervention will not become an all-out war and that it will not last too long. *Jus ad interventionem*. It has a fine ring to it! And the numbers are simply appalling: four times as many deaths in the twentieth century at the hands of the victims' own government or as a result of civil strife than from all the wars between states.[1]

Is the model of Good Samaritan intervention by an individual person(s) to assist an individual under attack by another at all helpful here? But these interventions, in those jurisdictions where they are legally mandated, are called for only in cases where the convenience and not the lives of third-party interveners is at risk. Here the law seems to follow common morality: if an individual chooses to risk his or her life to come to the aid of another, this is not considered a duty but a supererogatory act. Does this help explain the cautious manner in which political philosophers speak only of a right of intervention and the silence of philosophers such as Walzer and Rawls on whether humanitarian intervention may be a duty?[2] Make no mistake: humanitarian intervention involves a high probability that the intervening party will take casualties. Sometimes the mere presence of troops may lead to casualties, as "mission creep" is a fact of geopolitical life. This is what happened in Somalia where American troops who were initially dispatched to protect humanitarian aid supplies for a starving populace got caught in a struggle between rival warlords.

However, consider the case where an intervening party takes no casualties, as for example the US–NATO intervention in Kosovo which relied entirely upon high altitude bombings to achieve its objectives. This kind of attack, which critics have likened to shooting fish in a barrel, raises fundamental questions of fairness in how an intervention is conducted.

Might not humanitarian intervention sometimes yield just the opposite effect where the protection of human rights is concerned? There are two real possibilities. An oppressive government may be prompted to become even more oppressive in response to an intervention, with confidence that its supporters and even some of its previous critics will "rally round the flag." Or, once intervention occurs, the leadership of an opposition group may become more militant and disrespectful of the rights of others, or the leadership may pass into the hands of a more militant faction with even less respect for human rights than the oppressive regime with which we started out.

Almost everyone agrees that humanitarian intervention might be justified in some cases, but real world examples may prove troublesome. Take the example of the persecution of Jews in Nazi Germany. When would humanitarian intervention have been justified? Before or after *Kristallnacht*? Or only after the Holocaust had begun? By then the West was already at war with Germany for other reasons. What this example shows is the difficulty in pointing to the time when intervention would have become justified, and the certainty that early intervention would have inevitably escalated into an all-out war that the West was not prepared, militarily or psychologically, to fight. The same is true today when we raise the question of what to do about Tibet or Chechnya. The answer is that we can do very little with powers that have nuclear weapons at their disposal. And, of course, we would not pressure allies such as Turkey over its mistreatment of the Kurds as much as we would pressure non-allies over less severe mistreatment of some of their citizens.

Michael J. Smith in a defense of humanitarian intervention candidly admits that there "simply won't be consistency" in our reactions to human rights violations, but he asks, "Is it more ethical to say that, since I cannot do everything everywhere consistently, I should do nothing?"[3] Smith proposes that we adopt a scale of evil where human rights abuses are concerned; on this scale Virginia's frequent use of the death penalty would rank far below the massacres in Rwanda and Cambodia since "few disinterested observers would urge or welcome the forcible landing of an international military force to prevent Virginia's next execution." Smith seems to believe that there is nothing problematic about how rankings on a scale of evil would be determined. This might be true if the executions in Virginia and the massacres in Rwanda and Cambodia were placed at opposite ends of the scale, but other cases might prove more difficult to rank.

There are, as Smith points out, a few success stories for humanitarian intervention, such as India's intervention in East Pakistan and Tanzania's intervention in Uganda. But India's role in the liberation of Bangladesh, according to some observers, only made matters worse, and, given the history of India–Pakistan relations, it may be that India's intervention was not driven mainly by humanitarian concerns. This leaves us with Tanzania's overthrow of the monstrous Idi Amin in Uganda. Such a small success can hardly lend much support to the principle of humanitarian intervention, and large successes are not to be expected. Undoubtedly, as Smith reminds us, there are moral evils far greater than inconsistency, and to do nothing in the face of evil may well be one of them. It is not, however, the problem of consistency per se that concerns me but the problem of how targets for humanitarian intervention get selected.

Scholars agree that there are no instances of purely humanitarian intervention, and, given what we know about the complexity of human motivation and of the relations among states, this is scarcely surprising. Of course, some cases of allegedly humanitarian intervention are clearly bogus, e.g., Hitler's invasion of Czechoslovakia on the ground of protecting the human rights of the German minority. We all know that for Hitler human rights stopped with German rights, but other cases are more subtle. Sometimes humanitarian intervention may be used in part to

settle old grudges, as was alleged against Boutros Boutros-Ghali where Somalia was concerned, or humanitarian intervention may be used against states which have previously fallen upon disfavor in our eyes. Serbia needs to be taught a lesson, as the American Secretary of State put it during the US–NATO intervention in Kosovo. Intervention may also be used in restoring a state's moral standing in the eyes of others. For example, American intervention in Bosnia was undoubtedly influenced by the desire to overcome anti-American sentiments in the Muslim world arising from the Gulf War and to restore the American "reputation" for fairness and even-handedness. One thing we can be sure of is that humanitarian intervention will not occur if there is a risk of a major conflict in which the intervening power(s) can be expected to take significant casualties. It may be possible to devise a scale of evil, as Smith believes, but there already is a scale of power, and no one seriously believes that evils of great magnitude will trump considerations of relative power.

Because of my doubts about humanitarian intervention I shall not explore in any detail the crucial question of who might best decide whether humanitarian intervention is warranted and who should carry out the intervention. Unilateral intervention by a single state has the advantage of swiftness but runs the risk of partiality and of appearing to be a species of "gunboat diplomacy." Regional organizations should be better at filtering out biases, but they may be dominated by a single great power. The UN may take too long in its decision-making, but it is less likely to be biased and has enjoyed, at least until recently, great moral stature. The UN seems to be the best organization for making a decision about intervention, but the problem of consensus is troubling. Kofi Annan in his report on the tragedy of Srebrenica took responsibility for the UN and the part it played. But politicians and bureaucrats are adroit at taking responsibility in such a way as to shift responsibility. In the "lessons" to be learned from the tragedy, Annan ranked the lack of a common "political will" high on his list of causes which will need to be addressed to avoid future Srebrenicas.[4] However, the lack of a common political will has not been present in all of the activities of the UN as, for example, in the Gulf War which turned on the conquest of one state by another. In cases where there is no common political will, is doing nothing not preferable to the kind of bungling which contributes to disasters like Srebrenica?

The lack of a common political will is, of course, not necessarily confined to the international arena. Domestic support in a state for humanitarian intervention may ebb and flow, depending on the strength of opposed political parties and upon their commitment to a particular humanitarian intervention. One concern I have is the following: once it has been decided that humanitarian intervention is warranted in a particular situation, crucial steps that a more patient diplomacy might pursue may be slapped. An example of this is the haste with which the US and NATO decided to attack Serbia before negotiations were given a real chance – negotiations which were, in fact, a form of ultimatum. There is also the danger of self-righteousness which may lead the UN or other state to make demands which no self-respecting state could possibly accept, such as permitting foreign troops to travel at will throughout its territory or the holding of a plebiscite concerning independence for a contested region.

The current international situation can be characterized as follows. Friends and foes alike are nervous over the US–NATO intervention in Kosovo. How long will troops continue to be deployed there? What will count as a successful termination of the mission? Does it set a precedent for future interventions elsewhere in the name of human rights? Whatever happened to the duty of non-intervention, and what kind of duty is it anyway?

One possible reading of the duty of non-intervention is that it is an absolute duty, and various UN agreements including the Charter appear to support this interpretation. However, many moral philosophers would deny that a duty – or a right – can be absolute, that is, obtaining under all circumstances. Perhaps we should try to move in one of two other directions. We could say that the duty of non-intervention is *prima facie*, that is, that there is a strong presumption against intervention but one that can be overridden when there are compelling reasons to do so. Or we could try to write out a list of exceptions and make this list an explicit part of the formulation of the duty of non-intervention. What are some of these exceptions? Cases where we are invited to intervene by the legitimate government of a state? Cases where we can prevent or suppress systematic violations of human rights? Cases where we can assist in struggles for "national liberation"? But, except for the case where the intervention is invited, all other cases will be controversial and will call for further elaboration or refinement. The question still remains of whether these elaborations and refinements would be stated as explicit parts of the duty of non-intervention. For various reasons the project of a definitive list of exceptions to any duty – including that of non-intervention – seems doomed to failure. Seeing the duty of non-intervention as *prima facie* becomes a more attractive alternative if only by default. However, it might still be argued that the duty of non-intervention is absolute and that we only need add "except in the case of an emergency." All deontological rules, it is sometimes argued, are properly construed in this way, and the emergency exception would be difficult to satisfy. This may be part of the problem: although some non-emergency but justifiable reasons for intervention may be compelling, one person's emergency may be another person's difficulty which can be resolved short of intervention.

A final possibility is an openly purposive or teleological reading of the duty of non-intervention: it is to be respected except when intervention serves an end or purpose deemed morally justifiable, in accordance with, for example, utilitarianism or Marxism. However, where international law is concerned this purposive or teleological reading of the duty of non-intervention would strain the associative model of the UN and other forms of cooperation among states, as described by Terry Nardin.[5] What is to prevent the protection and especially the promotion of human rights from becoming as divisive as any other teleological reading of the duty of non-intervention? The protection and promotion of human rights might be divisive not only between states that champion human rights and those that do not, but also among states that support human rights but fail to agree on the appropriateness of particular interventions. Consider, for example, the controversies surrounding the Reagan administration's policies in Nicaragua and especially that administration's refusal to acknowledge that the American bombing of Nicaragua's harbors fell under the jurisdiction of the International Court of Justice.

I admit to having grown weary, or at least wary, of disjunctions between doing something and doing nothing. In the present case there are many things which can be done to advance the cause of human rights which fall short of humanitarian intervention. One way to ameliorate conflicts between liberal and decent societies on the one hand and outlaw states on the other is, simply put, trade. There is Thomas Friedman's "law" that no two countries with McDonald's have ever gone to war with one another. Where human rights issues are concerned the strategy, which sounds simple in the abstract, is to link trading privileges with the acceptance of human rights covenants, as, for example, was the case with the European Council when it granted trading privileges to Russia. In the eighteenth century, the Chinese Emperor wrote to the emissary of King George III that he did not wish to trade with the British since the Chinese had no interest in Britain's clever gadgets. Fortunately for us, and the prospects of a stable world order, all the world seems mad to have the US's clever gadgets. The question of how to take this market for American goods and use it to promote the cause of human rights is, however, a question of statecraft to which, as a philosopher, I have nothing to contribute beyond counsels of prudence. However, in the remainder of this paper I shall explore some conceptual matters which may help clarify the connections between morality and international law.

One possible way to approach this problem is to underscore the moral content of international law and to see it as being in itself an ethical tradition. Of course, this interpretation of international law runs counter to the "realist" school of thought, which reduces all relations among states to questions of national interest. Treaties are made to be broken, according to the realist, whenever one side sees an advantage in doing so, and states are expected to spy not only upon their enemies but upon their friends as well. Trust no one, and promote national self-interest by whatever means are judged to be necessary. Against this bleak picture of the relations among states, which, of course, is not entirely mistaken,

it is possible to think of international law as an ethical tradition in its own right similar to natural law theory, Kantianism, utilitarianism, Marxism, etc. This is Terry Nardin's position: ethical traditions evolve over time, and they involve judgments about the application of principles to particular situations.[6] Certainly Nardin is right, since one would be hard pressed to articulate a sharp distinction between legal and moral principles and the ways in which they are applied to particular cases. In what follows, however, I shall be concerned with international law not as an ethical tradition but with the moral obligations to which it gives rise where the conduct of states is concerned.

I begin this final portion of my paper with a confession about international law. I find it to be a perplexing mixture of treaties among states, customary practices among states, the charters and instruments of the United Nations and several regional organizations, the decisions of various international tribunals, and even the writings of international lawyers. International law is so complex and in such a state of change that it cannot, according to some scholars, readily be codified. Then, of course, there is the problem of sanctions or enforcement, a problem so important some commentators have concluded that, strictly speaking, international law is not law at all. Thus, there is something very tentative in what I say when I speak of international law as a legal system.

A municipal legal system differs from mere orders and commands in that it imposes moral duties and obligations upon all members of a society, and there is a general recognition, not limited to legal philosophers, that there is a moral obligation to obey all the laws of a municipal legal system. You cannot pick and choose which laws you will obey. Transposing this picture to international law results in the following: all states are morally bound to respect the provisions of international law, just as individuals are morally bound to respect the provisions of municipal law. But are states the kinds of things that can have moral duties and obligations? Why not, provided we see them as organized groups of individuals bound together by common rules? At the very least it is coherent to say that organized groups of individuals can undertake or enter into agreements with other organized groups of individuals. In fact, this seems to be what actually happens on a daily basis where, for example, the transactions of business corporations are concerned. Where international law is concerned, the agreements between organized groups can be understood in terms of treaties and even customary practices among states.

It is noteworthy that the principles governing the relations among peoples which we find in John Rawls's *The Law of Peoples* are themselves taken from international law. According to Rawls, these principles are: peoples are to observe a duty of non-intervention, peoples are to honor human rights, peoples are to observe treaties and undertakings, and peoples are equal and are parties to the agreements that bind them. Rawls writes that "These familiar and largely traditional principles I take from the history and usage of international law and practice. The parties are not given a menu of alternative principles and ideals from which to select, as they are in *Political Liberalism* or in *A Theory of Justice*. Rather, the representatives of well-ordered peoples simply reflect on the advantages of these principles of equality among peoples and see no reason to depart from them or to propose alternatives."[7] In Rawls's second Original Position, the representatives of liberal and decent hierarchical peoples select principles that are binding upon all peoples, including outlaw states. (Could there ever be an outlaw people for Rawls? Perhaps not, given, for example, the careful way in which he tries to distinguish the Nazi state from the German people. Here he disagrees with David Goldhagen's position in *Hitler's Willing Executioners*. The possibility that a coercive demonic political leadership could in time produce a demonic people merits careful consideration.)[8] If I am correct, both Rawls's account of the principles governing the relations of peoples and international law as *it already is* presuppose the idea of international law conceived of as a legal system.

The duty of non-intervention is on my interpretation a moral duty binding upon all states, and it is one of many such duties. Here we should note once more the importance of our conceiving of international law as a legal system. It would be nonsensical to speak of a moral obligation to obey a single principle or to abide by a single agreement standing in isolation from a system of principles or agreements. (There is an analog

here, I think, with science where scientific laws are seen as part of a system.) All states are morally bound not to intervene in the domestic affairs of other states. Of course all states are also bound to respect human rights; this would be especially true of the member states of the UN and even more so of those states which have signed the two UN Human Rights Covenants. However there are no provisions in the UN Charter or in these covenants for humanitarian intervention in the domestic affairs of states that do not respect human rights. In the past any such intervention clearly would have been illegal, but now things seem less certain. Perhaps in some circumstances humanitarian intervention may trump the obligation of states not to interfere in the domestic affairs of other states. In this connection it is regrettable, though understandable, that the International Court of Justice refused to rule on the legality of US–NATO intervention in Kosovo. At the risk of sounding like a democratic populist in international law when I am emphatically not a democratic populist where American domestic law is concerned, I think humanitarian intervention gives rise to such complex issues that it should be referred to the legislature. Let the member states of the UN address directly the question of whether humanitarian intervention is permissible, and if need be let us amend the Charter. Let us vote humanitarian intervention up or down, but let us not leave it to be decided on a case-by-case basis. Law, ideally, should satisfy the requirements of justice, but at the very least states no less than individuals need to know what the legal consequences of certain courses of conduct may be.[9]

I want to conclude on a cautiously optimistic note, which I think is consistent with the interpretation of international law as a legal system. According to *Political Liberalism*,[10] John Rawls's history of how the West evolved in a liberal and tolerant direction, two variables were highlighted as important. First was luck, and second was a growing appreciation on the part of individuals with different belief systems of the mutual advantages arising from limited *modus vivendi* agreements. From this it was a short step, historically speaking, to the moral quest for fair rules of social cooperation. Where relations among states are concerned, the world today has an additional advantage in international law, conceived of as a legal system that gives rise to moral obligations among states. However the question of humanitarian intervention is resolved, whether or not it is seen as a right or even as a duty, all states – not just liberal or decent states – are under an obligation to abide by international law.

Notes

1 See Sean O. Murphy, *Humanitarian Intervention* (Philadelphia: University of Pennsylvania Press, 1996).

2 Michael Walzer, *Just and Unjust Wars* (New York: Basic Books, 1997). John Rawls, *The Law of Peoples* (Cambridge, MA: Harvard University Press, 1999), 81, 93–4n. Stanley Hoffmann in *The Ethics and Politics of Intervention* (Notre Dame, IN: University of Notre Dame Press, 1996), 12–39, claims that he is more Kantian than Rawls because he believes there is a duty of intervention, but both are more Kantian than Kant who did not believe in intervention.

3 Michael J. Smith, "Humanitarian Intervention: An Overview of the Ethical Issues," *Ethics and International Affairs* 12 (1998): 78.

4 Report of the Secretary General Pursuant to General Assembly Resolution 53/35 (1998).

5 Terry Nardin, *Law, Morality, and the Relations of States* (Princeton, NJ: Princeton University Press, 1983).

6 Terry Nardin, "Ethical Traditions in International Affairs," *Traditions of International Ethics*, ed. Terry Nardin and David R. Mapels (Cambridge: Cambridge University Press, 1992), 1–23.

7 Rawls, *The Law of Peoples*, 41.

8 Ibid., 100–1n.

9 Anthony Ellis thinks the small states in the UN would probably defeat any amendment permitting humanitarian intervention. I am not sure this is so, but, if it is, this would reflect a failure by the UN to respect the moral equality of all member states, a failure which could perhaps be alleviated by other changes in the way the UN operates, for example, by changes in the veto powers of the permanent members of the Security Council.

10 John Rawls, *Political Liberalism* (New York: Columbia University Press, 1993).

22

Prosecutor v. Tadić (1995)

Decision on the Defence Motion for Interlocutory Appeal on Jurisdiction

International Tribunal for the Prosecution of Persons Responsible for Serious Violations of International Humanitarian Law Committed in the Territory of the Former Yugoslavia since 1991

PROSECUTOR V. DUŠKO TADIĆ A/K/A "DULE" CASE NO. IT-94-1-AR72 (2 OCTOBER 1995)

In the appeals chamber, before Judge Cassese, Presiding; Judge Abi-Saab; Judge Deschênes; Judge Li; Judge Sidhwa.

I. Introduction

A. The Judgment under Appeal

1. The Appeals Chamber of the International Tribunal for the Prosecution of Persons Responsible for Serious Violations of International Humanitarian Law Committed in the Territory of Former Yugoslavia since 1991 (hereinafter "International Tribunal") is seized of an appeal lodged by the Defence against a judgment rendered by Trial Chamber II on 10 August 1995. By that judgment, Appellant's motion challenging the jurisdiction of the International Tribunal was denied.

2. Before the Trial Chamber, Appellant had launched a three-pronged attack;

(a) illegal foundation of the International Tribunal;
(b) wrongful primacy of the International Tribunal over national courts;
(c) lack of jurisdiction *ratione materiae*.

The judgment under appeal denied the relief sought by Appellant; in its essential provisions, it reads as follows:

> "THE TRIAL CHAMBER [...] HEREBY DISMISSES the motion insofar as it relates to primacy jurisdiction and subject-matter jurisdiction under Articles 2, 3 and 5 and otherwise decides it to be incompetent insofar as it challenges the establishment of the International Tribunal.

Prosecutor v. Tadić, International Criminal Tribunal for the Former Yugoslavia, 1995, *Criminal Law Forum*, vol. 7, no. 1, 1996, pp. 51–3, 68–71.

HEREBY DENIES the relief sought by the Defence in its Motion on the Jurisdiction of the Tribunal." (Decision on the Defence Motion on Jurisdiction in the Trial Chamber of the International Tribunal, 10 Aug. 1995 (Case No. IT-94-1-T), at 33 (hereinafter "Decision at Trial"))

Appellant now alleges error of law on the part of the Trial Chamber.

3.   As can readily be seen from the operative part of the judgment, the Trial Chamber took a different approach to the first ground of contestation, on which it refused to rule, from the route it followed with respect to the last two grounds, which it dismissed. This distinction ought to be observed and will be referred to below.

From the development of the proceedings, however, it now appears that the question of jurisdiction has acquired, before this Chamber, a two-tier dimension:

(a)   the jurisdiction of the Appeals Chamber to hear this appeal;
(b)   the jurisdiction of the International Tribunal to hear this case on the merits.

Before anything more is said on the merits, consideration must be given to the preliminary question: whether the Appeals Chamber is endowed with the jurisdiction to hear this appeal at all.

[. . .]

The second reason, which is more particular to the case at hand, is that Appellant has amended his position from that contained in the Brief submitted to the Trial Chamber. Appellant no longer contests the Security Council's power to determine whether the situation in the former Yugoslavia constituted a threat to the peace, nor the determination itself. He further acknowledges that the Security Council "has the power to address to [*sic*] such threats [. . .] by appropriate measures." ([Defence] Brief to Support the Notice of (Interlocutory) Appeal, 25 Aug. 1995 (Case No. IT-94-1-AR72), ¶ 5.1 (hereinafter "Defence Appeal Brief")) But he continues to contest the legality and appropriateness of the measures chosen by the Security Council to that end.

2.   The Range of Measures Envisaged under Chapter VII

31.   Once the Security Council determines that a particular situation poses a threat to the peace or that there exists a breach of the peace or an act of aggression, it enjoys a wide margin of discretion in choosing the course of action: as noted above (¶ 29) it can either continue, in spite of its determination, to act via recommendations, *i.e.*, as if it were still within Chapter VI ("Pacific Settlement of Disputes") or it can exercise its exceptional powers under Chapter VII. In the words of Article 39, it would then "decide what measures shall be taken in accordance with Articles 41 and 42, to maintain or restore international peace and security." (United Nations Charter art. 39)

A question arises in this respect as to whether the choice of the Security Council is limited to the measures provided for in Articles 41 and 42 of the Charter (as the language of Article 39 suggests), or whether it has even larger discretion in the form of general powers to maintain and restore international peace and security under Chapter VII at large. In the latter case, one of course does not have to locate every measure decided by the Security Council under Chapter VII within the confines of Articles 41 and 42, or possibly Article 40. In any case, under both interpretations, the Security Council has a broad discretion in deciding on the course of action and evaluating the appropriateness of the measures to be taken. The language of Article 39 is quite clear as to the channelling of the very broad and exceptional powers of the Security Council under Chapter VII through Articles 41 and 42. These two Articles leave to the Security Council such a wide choice as not to warrant searching, on functional or other grounds, for even wider and more general powers than those already expressly provided for in the Charter.

These powers are *coercive vis-à-vis* the culprit State or entity. But they are also *mandatory vis-à-vis* the other Member States, who are under an obligation to cooperate with the Organization (*id.*, art. 2, ¶ 5; arts. 25, 48) and with one another (*id.* art. 49), in the implementation of the action or measures decided by the Security Council.

3. The Establishment of the International Tribunal as a Measure under Chapter VII

32.   As with the determination of the existence of a threat to the peace, a breach of the peace or an act of aggression, the Security Council has a very wide margin of discretion under Article 39 to choose the appropriate course of action and to evaluate the suitability of the measures chosen, as well as their potential contribution to the restoration or maintenance of peace. But here again, this discretion is not unfettered; moreover, it is limited to the measures provided for in Articles 41 and 42. Indeed, in the case at hand, this last point serves as a basis for Appellant's contention of invalidity of the establishment of the International Tribunal.

   In its resolution 827, the Security Council considers that "in the particular circumstances of the former Yugoslavia," the establishment of the International Tribunal "would contribute to the restoration and maintenance of peace" and indicates that, in establishing it, the Security Council was acting under Chapter VII. (S.C. Res. 827 (25 May 1993)) However, it did not specify a particular Article as a basis for this action.

   Appellant has attacked the legality of this decision at different stages before the Trial Chamber as well as before this Chamber on at least three grounds:

(a)   that the establishment of such a tribunal was never contemplated by the framers of the Charter as one of the measures to be taken under Chapter VII; as witnessed by the fact that it figures nowhere in the provisions of that Chapter, and more particularly in Articles 41 and 42, which detail these measures;

(b)   that the Security Council is constitutionally or inherently incapable of creating a judicial organ, as it is conceived in the Charter as an executive organ, hence not possessed of judicial powers which can be exercised through a subsidiary organ;

(c)   that the establishment of the International Tribunal has neither promoted, nor was capable of promoting, international peace as demonstrated by the current situation in the former Yugoslavia.

[. . .]

In sum, the establishment of the International Tribunal falls squarely within the powers of the Security Council under Article 41.

(b)   Can the Security Council Establish a Subsidiary Organ with Judicial Powers?

37.   The argument that the Security Council, not being endowed with judicial powers, cannot establish a subsidiary organ possessed of such powers is untenable: it results from a fundamental misunderstanding of the constitutional set-up of the Charter.

   Plainly, the Security Council is not a judicial organ and is not provided with judicial powers (though it may incidentally perform certain quasi-judicial activities such as effecting determinations or findings). The principal function of the Security Council is the maintenance of international peace and security, in the discharge of which the Security Council exercises both decision-making and executive powers.

38.   The establishment of the International Tribunal by the Security Council does not signify, however, that the Security Council has delegated to it some of its own functions or the exercise of some of its own powers. Nor does it mean, in reverse, that the Security Council was usurping for itself part of a judicial function which does not belong to it but to other organs of the United Nations according to the Charter. The Security Council has resorted to the establishment of a judicial organ in the form of an international criminal tribunal as an Instrument for the exercise of its own principal function of maintenance of peace and security, *i.e.,* as a measure contributing to the restoration and maintenance of peace in the former Yugoslavia.

   The General Assembly did not need to have military and police functions and powers in order to be able to establish the United Nations Emergency Force in the Middle East ("UNEF") in 1956. Nor did the General Assembly have to be a judicial organ possessed of judicial functions and powers in order to be able to establish UNAT. In its advisory opinion in the *Effect of Awards*, the International Court of Justice, in addressing practically the same objection, declared:

> "[T]he Charter does not confer judicial functions on the Genera Assembly [. . .] By establishing the Administrative Tribunal, the General Assembly was not delegating the performance of its own functions: it was exercising a power which it had under the Charter to regulate staff relations." (*Effect of Awards* at 61)

(c) Was the Establishment of the International Tribunal an Appropriate Measure?

39. The third argument is directed against the discretionary power of the Security Council in evaluating the appropriateness of the chosen measure and its effectiveness in achieving its objective, the restoration of peace.

Article 39 leaves the choice of means and their evaluation to the Security Council, which enjoys wide discretionary powers in this regard; and it could not have been otherwise, as such a choice involves political evaluation of highly complex and dynamic situations.

It would be a total misconception of what are the criteria of legality and validity in law to test the legality of such measures *ex post facto* by their success or failure to achieve their ends (in the present case, the restoration of peace in the former Yugoslavia, in quest of which the establishment of the International Tribunal is but one of many measures adopted by the Security Council).

40. For the aforementioned reasons, the Appeals Chamber considers that the International Tribunal has been lawfully established as a measure under Chapter VII of the Charter.

Questions

1 Why does Hart regard international law as a hard case for understanding the concept of law? In what ways is international law to be thought of as law proper and in what ways is it not to be thought of as law?

2 Is humanitarian intervention justifiable on liberal principles? If so, which liberal principles are especially important here?

3 Can collective responsibility ever be justified? Can war be understood strictly as a matter of individual responsibility?

4 When violations of *jus cogens* norms occur, can such violations be understood from a strict legal positivist perspective, or must moral considerations also be appealed to?

5 From the standpoint of law and economics, how is custom understood? How might one argue against such a position?

Part IV
Property

Introduction

Issues of property have long intrigued philosophers. Not only have they questioned how we form property, but they have also explored the implications of property for humanity. Some philosophers have argued that property instigated the move away from a more peaceful state of nature; others have argued for a less pessimistic view of property and a less idyllic view of the state of nature. Philosophers have also explored the role that the state should play in enforcing property rights. One key question is whether or not the state should ever play a role in the redistribution of property even if society would benefit from such redistribution.

To begin to explore these questions, we start with John Locke's work "Of Property," which is a section from his *Second Treatise of Government*. Here, Locke presents his theory on the origin of property. Originally, Locke argues that God gave the earth and the creatures on it to all humankind. While these items were owned in common, each individual owned his or her own person and labor. Thus, when an individual takes an item from the state of nature and mixes her labor with it, she creates private property. Locke also argues that each individual is entitled to take as much as she wants from the commons, if she uses the items before they spoil.

Locke argues that we may also apply this theory to the ownership of land. Each individual may enclose a plot of land for personal cultivation and then the land becomes his private property. The only limit to the enclosure of land for personal use is that no one should take more land than he or she can use; to take more is robbery. Locke claims that the appropriation of land actually improves life for all of humankind because cultivated land produces crop yields that far outstrip those of uncultivated land. Moreover, it is the privatization of land that leads to the use of money. Finally, Locke argues that money is what allows for the unequal possession of land that exists in a modern society. With the use of money, an individual can possess more land and produce more crops than he alone can use, because he can trade those crops for non-perishable money. Without money, having too much surplus would lead to the general harm of spoilage.

Robert Nozick offers an analysis of Locke's theory of property in a section from his *Anarchy, State, and Utopia*. In exploring a variety of questions that he believes Locke's theory leaves unanswered, Nozick focuses on what he finds to be the crucial question: does appropriation of property worsen the plight of others? This question hinges on Locke's assertion that, in any appropriation of property, there should be "enough and as good left in common for others." Nozick focuses on two possible ways one's appropriation might worsen others' circumstance. First, the lack of opportunity for appropriation might prevent an individual from improving her situation through appropriating property. Second, the appropriation might worsen an individual because he can no longer use property freely as he once did. Nozick argues that a stringent proviso will exclude both possibilities, while a weaker proviso will exclude only the second possibility.

While Nozick explores the position that Locke's proviso is a stringent one, he claims that its characterization as a weak proviso is more accurate because of the variety of benefits that flow from the appropriation of property. For example, appropriation provides alternative sources of employment and increases the total amount of social product because those who can best use them possess the means of production. Nozick also claims that all adequate theories of justice in appropriation need a proviso similar to this weaker model. Nevertheless, while Nozick claims the need for a proviso modeled after the weak version, he argues that there are legitimate ways of circumventing such a proviso. For example, a person who wishes to appropriate some item might compensate others whom such an appropriation would harm so that she does not worsen their situation. Additionally, Nozick argues that if we include such a proviso to regulate justice in acquisition, there must be a similar proviso to regulate justice in transfer. Nevertheless, Nozick claims this concern does not illustrate that whenever someone owns all of something, others are left worse off. He argues that if someone appropriates a small amount of chemicals and invents a drug, he makes no one worse off, because there are still chemicals available for appropriation. For Nozick, the Lockean proviso will allow for the free operation of a market system.

In "Property, Title, and Redistribution," A. M. Honoré focuses on Robert Nozick's argument that the state has no duty to redistribute benefits equally throughout society, as confined to property. Honoré claims that this view rests on the idea that a person is allowed to keep "exclusively and indefinitely" for her own use whatever she makes or produces. This, Honoré argues, can be true of a person in isolation, but no argument illustrates that this is true for a social being. In Honoré's opinion, Nozick's attempt to reproduce Western property law assumes and omits too much. For example, Nozick's theory rests on the assumption that we can determine just title to property in abstraction from the historical or social context. This means that a just acquisition 200 years ago remains the just root for a title held today. As such, we are forced to say, for example, either that the acquisition of slaves was always unjust or that the descendants of slaveholders are entitled to own the descendants of slaves today. If we argue the former, Honoré questions how we are to know that there are no similarly unjustified forms of acquisition and ownership today. In fact, Honoré claims that outside Utopia, Nozick's theory has little application. Finally, he argues that Nozick is too quick to reject other systems of property law.

Richard A. Epstein, in a section from *Takings: Private Property and the Power of Eminent Domain*, defends the use of eminent domain as a government tool. In Epstein's opinion, eminent domain is key to the development of a state, because the need for such a power motivates the move from a voluntary protective association to a true state. Epstein defines the power of eminent domain as the state's right to force exchanges of property rights, but these exchanges must leave the individuals with rights that are more valuable than the ones that the government has taken. Additionally, there are two limitations to this right: the forced exchanges are only for public use, and the exchanges require compensation.

Epstein also defends his view of eminent domain by comparing it that of Robert Nozick. Under Nozick's version of libertarianism, the government cannot be allowed to exercise forced exchanges, but Epstein finds this view lacking. Without forced exchanges, Epstein argues, society cannot achieve true social order because there will be too many holdouts and free-riders. Finally, Epstein critiques the view that eminent domain ignores the role of civic virtue. Epstein argues that civic virtue is a by-product of sound institutional arrangements. As such, eminent domain works toward civic virtue by attempting to achieve such sound institutional arrangements. According to Epstein, eminent domain is a necessary part of just government because it connects private property and public law.

In "The Social Structure of Japanese Intellectual Property Law," Dan Rosen and Chikako Usui explore the basis for Japanese attitudes toward intellectual property laws. Rosen and Usui suggest that, given widespread use of Western intellectual property laws by Japanese businesses, many might think that the Japanese would argue for intellectual property law. Yet, when the authors examine Japanese intellectual property law, they find them to be weak and Japanese attitudes toward them ambivalent. Rosen and Usui argue that the reason for this lack of support within Japan is due to the larger social system; moreover, looking at the law as a small part of the large culture is the best way to understand law overall.

Rosen and Usui suggest that, within the United States, copyright law functions as a sort of bribe, in that the government gives inventors exclusive access to the economic benefits of their work in the hope that this economic incentive will motivate them to produce more. Further, free-riders in the United States must show "strong reasons" why the holder of the copyright ought not to benefit. In Japan, the law does not assume exclusive access by the inventor; instead, the law gives wide consideration to fair exploitation by others. This wide consideration allows both widespread personal and privileged uses that benefit society overall, such as allowing fixed fees from textbook manufacturers for copyrighted material. This difference in attitude, according to Rosen and Usui, arises from Chinese Confucianism. Following Confucianism, Japanese society recognizes the interdependence that exists among all its members. This attitude allows for intellectual property laws that are much less protective of individual rights than are similar laws within the United States.

The next essay looks at the issues of property claims and redistribution in the case of American Indians. In "Historical Rights and Fair Shares," A. John Simmons offers two approaches to dealing with property claims of American Indians based on past property right violations. First, the state can treat American Indians like any other group, with the fact of their original occupation excluded as irrelevant. Second, the state can take seriously American Indians' historical claims to land and see these claims as the basis of the persistent right to rectification. Simmons argues that the second method is the more acceptable of the two because it both preserves the particularity of the American Indian claims and can be sensitive to the changing circumstances because

the content of these historical rights can be particularized fair shares. For example, American Indian historical rights are to fair portions of the actual land that they used; yet, if the state or any of its citizens have destroyed or irreversibly altered those lands, then the native tribes are due the closest approximations.

Finally, *International News Service v. Associated Press* is provided as an example of theoretical disputes over property law. Here, both parties are competitors in gathering and selling the news to individual newspapers. The main value of this news is in its promptness or freshness. The International News Services admitted that it was pirating the Associated Press's news, by copying it from news billboards and early editions of subscribing newspapers, but claimed that this was lawful because the news is not property. The Associated Press responded by arguing that International News Service violated its property rights. Additionally, such practices constituted unfair competition in business, because the International News Service was benefiting at the expense of the Associated Press's time and money.

The Supreme Court ruled for the Associated Press. It addressed three main questions: (1) is there property in the news? (2) if there is, does it survive publication? and (3) is this practice unfair competition in trade? As for the first question, the Court ruled that the news is not property in the way in which a literary novel is property. The news is not a creation, but a recording of events. However, because both parties pay to collect and distribute it and receive money for it like any other type of merchandise, the Court ruled that the news takes a form of "quasi-property." Given this characterization, the Court focused on the final question, expanding it as follows. Does someone who gathers news for sale at considerable pain and expense have an interest in publication without interference? The Court ruled that the defendant was essentially a free-rider engaged in unfair business practice. Because the Associated Press fairly paid the necessary price for the news, it should have the benefit of the news just as any property-owner who justly paid for her property should have the benefit of it.

23

Of Property

John Locke

25.   Whether we consider natural reason, which tells us that men, being once born, have a right to their preservation, and consequently to meat and drink and such other things as nature affords for their subsistence; or revelation, which gives us an account of those grants God made of the world to Adam, and to Noah and his sons; it is very clear that God, as King David says (Psalm cxv. 16), "has given the earth to the children of men," given it to mankind in common. But this being supposed, it seems to some a very great difficulty how any one should ever come to have a property in anything. I will not content myself to answer that if it be difficult to make out property upon a supposition that God gave the world to Adam and his posterity in common, it is impossible that any man but one universal monarch should have any property upon a supposition that God gave the world to Adam and his heirs in succession, exclusive of all the rest of his posterity. But I shall endeavor to show how men might come to have a property in several parts of that which God gave to mankind in common, and that without any express compact of all the commoners.

26.   God, who has given the world to men in common, has also given them reason to make use of it to the best advantage of life and convenience. The earth and all that is therein is given to men for the support and comfort of their being. And though all the fruits it naturally produces and beasts it feeds belong to mankind in common, as they are produced by the spontaneous hand of nature; and nobody has originally a private dominion exclusive of the rest of mankind in any of them, as they are thus in their natural state; yet, being given for the use of men, there must of necessity be a means to appropriate them some way or other before they can be of any use or at all beneficial to any particular man. The fruit or venison which nourishes the wild Indian, who knows no enclosure and is still a tenant in common, must be his, and so his, i.e., a part of him, that another can no longer have any right to it before it can do him any good for the support of his life.

27.   Though the earth and all inferior creatures be common to all men, yet every man has a property in his own person; this nobody has any right to but himself. The labor of his body and the work of his hands, we may say, are properly his. Whatsoever then he removes out of the state that nature has provided and left it in, he has mixed his labor with, and joined to it something that is his own, and thereby makes it his property. It being by him removed from the common state nature has placed it in, it has by this labor something annexed to it that excludes

John Locke, "Of Property," from *Second Treatise of Government*, chapter 5.

the common right of other men. For this labor being the unquestionable property of the laborer, no man but he can have a right to what that is once joined to, at least where there is enough and as good left in common for others.

28. He that is nourished by the acorns he picked up under an oak, or the apples he gathered from the trees in the wood, has certainly appropriated them to himself. Nobody can deny but the nourishment is his. I ask, then, When did they begin to be his? When he digested or when he ate or when he boiled or when he brought them home? Or when he picked them up? And it is plain, if the first gathering made them not his, nothing else could. That labor put a distinction between them and common; that added something to them more than nature, the common mother of all, had done; and so they became his private right. And will anyone say he had no right to those acorns or apples he thus appropriated because he had not the consent of all mankind to make them his? Was it a robbery thus to assume to himself what belonged to all in common? If such a consent as that was necessary, man had starved, notwithstanding the plenty God had given him. We see in commons, which remain so by compact, that it is the taking any part of what is common and removing it out of the state nature leaves it in which begins the property, without which the common is of no use. And the taking of this or that part does not depend on the express consent of all the commoners. Thus the grass my horse has bit, the turfs my servant has cut, and the ore I have digged in any place where I have a right to them in common with others, become my property without the assignation or consent of anybody. The labor that was mine, removing them out of that common state they were in, has fixed my property in them.

29. By making an explicit consent of every commoner necessary to any one's appropriating to himself any part of what is given in common, children or servants could not cut the meat which their father or master had provided for them in common without assigning to every one his peculiar part. Though the water running in the fountain be every one's, yet who can doubt but that in the pitcher is his only who drew it out? His labor has taken it out of the hands of nature where it was common and belonged equally to all her children, and has thereby appropriated it to himself.

30. Thus this law of reason makes the deer that Indian's who has killed it; it is allowed to be his goods who has bestowed his labor upon it, though before it was the common right of every one. And amongst those who are counted the civilized part of mankind, who have made and multiplied positive laws to determine property, this original law of nature, for the beginning of property in what was before common, still takes place; and by virtue thereof what fish any one catches in the ocean, that great and still remaining common of mankind, or what ambergris any one takes up here, is, by the labor that removes it out of that common state nature left it in, made his property who takes that pains about it. And even amongst us, the hare that anyone is hunting is thought his who pursues her during the chase; for, being a beast that is still looked upon as common and no man's private possession, whoever has employed so much labor about any of that kind as to find and pursue her has thereby removed her from the state of nature wherein she was common, and has begun a property.

31. It will perhaps be objected to this that "if gathering the acorns, or other fruits of the earth, etc., makes a right to them, then any one man may engross as much as he will." To which I answer: not so. The same law of nature that does by this means give us property does also bound that property, too. "God has given us all things richly" (1 Tim. vi. 17), is the voice of reason confirmed by inspiration. But how far has he given it us? To enjoy. As much as any one can make use of to any advantage of life before it spoils, so much he may by his labor fix a property in; whatever is beyond this is more than his share and belongs to others. Nothing was made by God for man to spoil or destroy. And thus considering the plenty of natural provisions there was a long time in the world, and the few spenders, and to how small a part of that provision the industry of one man could extend itself and engross it to the prejudice of others, especially keeping within the bounds set by reason of what might serve for his use, there could be then little room for quarrels or contentions about property so established.

32. But the chief matter of property being now not the fruits of the earth and the beasts that subsist on it, but the earth itself, as that which takes in and carries with it all the rest, I think it is plain

that property in that, too, is acquired as the former. As much land as a man tills, plants, improves, cultivates, and can use the products of, so much is his property. He by his labor does, as it were, enclose it from the common. Nor will it invalidate his right to say everybody else has an equal title to it, and therefore he cannot appropriate, he cannot enclose, without the consent of all his fellow commoners – all mankind. God, when he gave the world in common to all mankind, commanded man also to labor, and the penury of his condition required it of him. God and his reason commanded him to subdue the earth, i.e., improve it for the benefit of life, and therein lay out something upon it that was his own, his labor. He that in obedience to this command of God subdued, tilled, and sowed any part of it, thereby annexed to it something that was his property, which another had no title to, nor could without injury take from him.

33.   Nor was this appropriation of any parcel of land by improving it any prejudice to any other man, since there was still enough and as good left, and more than the yet unprovided could use. So that, in effect, there was never the less left for others because of his enclosure for himself; for he that leaves as much as another can make use of does as good as take nothing at all. Nobody could think himself injured by the drinking of another man, though he took a good draught, who had a whole river of the same water left him to quench his thirst; and the case of land and water, where there is enough for both, is perfectly the same.

34.   God gave the world to men in common; but since he gave it them for their benefit and the greatest conveniences of life they were capable to draw from it, it cannot be supposed he meant it should always remain common and uncultivated. He gave it to the use of the industrious and rational – and labor was to be his title to it – not to the fancy or covetousness of the quarrelsome and contentious. He that had as good left for his improvement as was already taken up needed not complain, ought not to meddle with what was already improved by another's labor; if he did, it is plain he desired the benefit of another's pains which he had no right to, and not the ground which God had given him in common with others to labor on, and whereof there was as good left as that already possessed, and more than he knew what to do with, or his industry could reach to.

35.   It is true, in land that is common in England or any other country where there are plenty of people under government who have money and commerce, no one can enclose or appropriate any part without the consent of all his fellow commoners; because this is left common by compact, i.e., by the law of the land, which is not to be violated. And though it be common in respect of some men, it is not so to all mankind, but is the joint property of this country or this parish. Besides, the remainder after such enclosure would not be as good to the rest of the commoners as the whole was when they could all make use of the whole; whereas in the beginning and first peopling of the great common of the world it was quite otherwise. The law man was under was rather for appropriating. God commanded, and his wants forced, him to labor. That was his property which could not be taken from him wherever he had fixed it. And hence subduing or cultivating the earth and having dominion, we see, are joined together. The one gave title to the other. So that God, by commanding to subdue, gave authority so far to appropriate; and the condition of human life which requires labor and material to work on necessarily introduces private possessions.

36.   The measure of property nature has well set by the extent of men's labor and the conveniences of life. No man's labor could subdue or appropriate all, nor could his enjoyment consume more than a small part, so that it was impossible for any man, this way, to entrench upon the right of another, or acquire to himself a property to the prejudice of his neighbor, who would still have room for as good and as large a possession – after the other had taken out his – as before it was appropriated. This measure did confine every man's possession to a very moderate proportion, and such as he might appropriate to himself without injury to anybody, in the first ages of the world, when men were more in danger to be lost by wandering from their company in the then vast wilderness of the earth than to be straitened for want of room to plant in. And the same measure may be allowed still without prejudice to anybody, as full as the world seems; for supposing a man or family in the state they were at first peopling of the world by the children of Adam or Noah, let him plant in some inland, vacant places of America; we shall find that the possessions he could make

himself, upon the measures we have given, would not be very large, nor, even to this day, prejudice the rest of mankind, or give them reason to complain or think themselves injured by this man's encroachment, though the race of men have now spread themselves to all the corners of the world and do infinitely exceed the small number which was at the beginning. Nay, the extent of ground is of so little value without labor that I have heard it affirmed that in Spain itself a man may be permitted to plough, sow, and reap, without being disturbed, upon land he has no other title to but only his making use of it. But, on the contrary, the inhabitants think themselves beholden to him who by his industry on neglected and consequently waste land has increased the stock of corn which they wanted. But be this as it will, which I lay no stress on, this I dare boldly affirm – that the same rule of property, viz., that every man should have as much as he could make use of, would hold still in the world without straitening anybody, since there is land enough in the world to suffice double the inhabitants, had not the invention of money and the tacit agreement of men to put a value on it introduced – by consent – larger possessions and a right to them; which, how it has done, I shall by-and-by show more at large.

37. This is certain, that in the beginning, before the desire of having more than man needed had altered the intrinsic value of things which depends only on their usefulness to the life of man, or had agreed that a little piece of yellow metal which would keep without wasting or decay should be worth a great piece of flesh or a whole heap of corn, though men had a right to appropriate, by their labor, each one to himself as much of the things of nature as he could use, yet this could not be much, nor to the prejudice of others, where the same plenty was still left to those who would use the same industry. To which let me add that he who appropriates land to himself by his labor does not lessen but increase the common stock of mankind; for the provisions serving to the support of human life produced by one acre of enclosed and cultivated land are – to speak much within compass – ten times more than those which are yielded by an acre of land of an equal richness lying waste in common. And therefore he that encloses land, and has a greater plenty of the conveniences of life from ten acres than he could have from a hundred left to nature, may truly be said to give ninety acres to mankind; for his labor now supplies him with provisions out of ten acres which were by the product of a hundred lying in common. I have here rated the improved land very low in making its product but as ten to one, when it is much nearer a hundred to one; for I ask whether in the wild woods and uncultivated waste of America, left to nature, without any improvement, tillage, or husbandry, a thousand acres yield the needy and wretched inhabitants as many conveniences of life as ten acres of equally fertile land do in Devonshire, where they are well cultivated.

Before the appropriation of land, he who gathered as much of the wild fruit, killed, caught, or tamed as many of the beasts as he could; he that so employed his pains about any of the spontaneous products of nature as any way to alter them from the state which nature put them in, by placing any of his labor on them, did thereby acquire a propriety in them; but, if they perished in his possession without their due use, if the fruits rotted or the venison putrified before he could spend it, he offended against the common law of nature and was liable to be punished; he invaded his neighbor's share, for he had no right further than his use called for any of them and they might serve to afford him conveniences of life.

38. The same measures governed the possession of land, too: whatsoever he tilled and reaped, laid up and made use of before it spoiled, that was his peculiar right; whatsoever he enclosed and could feed and make use of, the cattle and product was also his. But if either the grass of his enclosure rotted on the ground, or the fruit of his planting perished without gathering and laying up, this part of the earth, notwithstanding his enclosure, was still to be looked on as waste and might be the possession of any other. Thus, at the beginning, Cain might take as much ground as he could till and make it his own land, and yet leave enough to Abel's sheep to feed on; a few acres would serve for both their possessions. But as families increased and industry enlarged their stocks, their possessions enlarged with the need of them; but yet it was commonly without any fixed property in the ground they made use of till they incorporated, settled themselves together, and built cities; and then, by consent, they came

in time to set out the bounds of their distinct territories, and agree on limits between them and their neighbors, and by laws within themselves settled the properties of those of the same society; for we see that in that part of the world which was first inhabited, and therefore like to be best peopled, even as low down as Abraham's time they wandered with their flocks and their herds, which was their substance, freely up and down; and this Abraham did in a country where he was a stranger. Whence it is plain that at least a great part of the land lay in common, that the inhabitants valued it not, nor claimed property in any more than they made use of. But when there was not room enough in the same place for their herds to feed together, they, by consent, as Abraham and Lot did (Gen. xiii. 5), separated and enlarged their pasture where it best liked them. And for the same reason Esau went from his father and his brother and planted in Mount Seir (Gen. xxxvi. 6).

39. And thus, without supposing any private dominion and property in Adam over all the world exclusive of all other men, which can in no way be proven, nor any one's property be made out from it; but supposing the world given, as it was, to the children of men in common, we see how labor could make men distinct titles to several parcels of it for their private uses, wherein there could be no doubt of right, no room for quarrel.

40. Nor is it so strange, as perhaps before consideration it may appear, that the property of labor should be able to overbalance the community of land; for it is labor indeed that put the difference of value on everything; and let anyone consider what the difference is between an acre of land planted with tobacco or sugar, sown with wheat or barley, and an acre of the same land lying in common without any husbandry upon it, and he will find that the improvement of labor makes the far greater part of the value. I think it will be but a very modest computation to say that, of the products of the earth useful to the life of man, nine-tenths are the effects of labor; nay, if we will rightly estimate things as they come to our use and cast up the several expenses about them, what in them is purely owing to nature, and what to labor, we shall find that in most of them ninety-nine hundredths are wholly to be put on the account of labor.

41. There cannot be a clearer demonstration of anything than several nations of the Americans are of this, who are rich in land and poor in all the comforts of life; whom nature having furnished as liberally as any other people with the materials of plenty, i.e., a fruitful soil, apt to produce in abundance what might serve for food, raiment, and delight, yet for want of improving it by labor have not one-hundredth part of the conveniences we enjoy. And a king of a large and fruitful territory there feeds, lodges, and is clad worse than a day-laborer in England.

42. To make this a little clear, let us but trace some of the ordinary provisions of life through their several progresses before they come to our use and see how much of their value they receive from human industry. Bread, wine, and cloth are things of daily use and great plenty; yet, notwithstanding, acorns, water, and leaves, or skins must be our bread, drink, and clothing, did not labor furnish us with these more useful commodities; for whatever bread is more worth than acorns, wine than water, and cloth or silk than leaves, skins, or moss, that is wholly owing to labor and industry: the one of these being the food and raiment which unassisted nature furnishes us with; the other, provisions which our industry and pains prepare for us, which how much they exceed the other in value when anyone has computed, he will then see how much labor makes the far greatest part of the value of things we enjoy in this world. And the ground which produces the materials is scarce to be reckoned in as any, or at most but a very small, part of it; so little that even amongst us land that is left wholly to nature, that has no improvement or pasturage, tillage, or planting, is called, as indeed it is, "waste"; and we shall find the benefit of it amount to little more than nothing.

This shows how much numbers of men are to be preferred to largeness of dominions; and that the increase of lands and the right employing of them is the great art of government; and that prince who shall be so wise and godlike as by established laws of liberty to secure protection and encouragement to the honest industry of mankind, against the oppression of power and narrowness of party, will quickly be too hard for his neighbors; but this by the bye.

To return to the argument in hand.

43. An acre of land that bears here twenty bushels of wheat, and another in America which with the same husbandry would do the like, are, without doubt, of the same natural intrinsic value; but yet the benefit mankind receives from the one in a year is worth £5, and from the other possibly not worth a penny if all the profit an Indian received from it were to be valued and sold here; at least, I may truly say, not one-thousandth. It is labor, then, which puts the greatest part of the value upon land, without which it would scarcely be worth anything; it is to that we owe the greatest part of all its useful products; for all that the straw, bran, bread of that acre of wheat is more worth than the product of an acre of as good land which lies waste is all the effect of labor. For it is not barely the ploughman's pains, the reaper's and thresher's toil, and the baker's sweat [that] is to be counted into the bread we eat; the labor of those who broke the oxen, who digged and wrought the iron and stones, who felled and framed the timber employed about the plough, mill, oven, or any other utensils, which are a vast number requisite to this corn, from its being seed to be sown to its being made bread, must all be charged on the account of labor, and received as an effect of that; nature and the earth furnished only the almost worthless materials as in themselves. It would be a strange "catalogue of things that industry provided and made use of, about every loaf of bread" before it came to our use, if we could trace them: iron, wood, leather, bark, timber, stone, bricks, coals, lime, cloth, dyeing drugs, pitch, tar, masts, ropes, and all the materials made use of in the ship that brought any of the commodities used by any of the workmen to any part of the work; all which it would be almost impossible, at least too long, to reckon up.

44. From all which it is evident that, though the things of nature are given in common, yet man, by being master of himself and proprietor of his own person and the actions or labor of it, had still in himself the great foundation of property; and that which made up the greater part of what he applied to the support or comfort of his being, when invention and arts had improved the conveniences of life, was perfectly his own and did not belong in common to others.

45. Thus labor, in the beginning, gave a right of property wherever anyone was pleased to employ it upon what was common, which remained a long while the far greater part and is yet more than mankind makes use of. Men, at first, for the most part contented themselves with what unassisted nature offered to their necessities; and though afterwards, in some parts of the world – where the increase of people and stock, with the use of money, had made land scarce and so of some value – the several communities settled the bounds of their distinct territories and, by laws within themselves, regulated the properties of the private men of their society, and so, by compact and agreement, settled the property which labor and industry began. And the leagues that have been made between several states and kingdoms either expressly or tacitly disowning all claim and right to the land in the others' possession have, by common consent, given up their pretenses to their natural common right which originally they had to those countries, and so have, by positive agreement, settled a property amongst themselves in distinct parts and parcels of the earth; yet there are still great tracts of ground to be found which – the inhabitants thereof not having joined with the rest of mankind in the consent of the use of their common money – lie waste, and are more than the people who dwell on it do or can make use of, and so still lie in common; though this can scarce happen amongst that part of mankind that have consented to the use of money.

46. The greatest part of things really useful to the life of man, and such as the necessity of subsisting made the first commoners of the world look after, as it does the Americans now, are generally things of short duration, such as, if they are not consumed by use, will decay and perish of themselves; gold, silver, and diamonds are things that fancy or agreement has put the value on, more than real use and the necessary support of life. Now of those good things which nature has provided in common, every one had a right, as has been said, to as much as he could use, and property in all that he could effect with his labor; all that his industry could extend to, to alter from the state nature had put it in, was his. He that gathered a hundred bushels of acorns or apples had thereby a property in them; they were his goods as soon as gathered. He was only to look that he used them before they spoiled, else he took more than his share and robbed others. And indeed it was

a foolish thing, as well as dishonest, to hoard up more than he could make use of. If he gave away a part to anybody else so that it perished not uselessly in his possession, these he also made use of. And if he also bartered away plums that would have rotted in a week for nuts that would last good for his eating a whole year, he did no injury; he wasted not the common stock, destroyed no part of the portion of the goods that belonged to others, so long as nothing perished uselessly in his hands. Again, if he would give his nuts for a piece of metal, pleased with its color, or exchange his sheep for shells, or wool for a sparkling pebble or a diamond, and keep those by him all his life, he invaded not the right of others; he might heap as much of these durable things as he pleased; the exceeding of the bounds of his just property not lying in the largeness of his possession, but the perishing of anything uselessly in it.

47.   And thus came in the use of money – some lasting thing that men might keep without spoiling, and that by mutual consent men would take in exchange for the truly useful but perishable supports of life.

48.   And as different degrees of industry were apt to give men possessions in different proportions, so this invention of money gave them the opportunity to continue and enlarge them; for supposing an island, separate from all possible commerce with the rest of the world, wherein there were but a hundred families, but there were sheep, horses, and cows, with other useful animals, wholesome fruits, and land enough for corn for a hundred thousand times as many, but nothing in the island, either because of its commonness or perishableness, fit to supply the place of money; what reason could anyone have there to enlarge his possessions beyond the use of his family and a plentiful supply to its consumption, either in what their own industry produced or they could barter for like perishable, useful commodities with others? Where there is not something both lasting and scarce, and so valuable to be hoarded up, there men will not be apt to enlarge their possessions of land were it ever so rich, ever so free for them to take. For, I ask, what would a man value ten thousand or a hundred thousand acres of excellent land, ready cultivated and well stocked, too, with cattle, in the middle of the inland parts of America where

he had no hopes of commerce with other parts of the world to draw money to him by the sale of the product? It would not be worth the enclosing, and we should see him give up again to the wild common of nature whatever was more than would supply the conveniences of life to be had there for him and his family.

49.   Thus in the beginning all the world was America, and more so than that is now; for no such thing as money was anywhere known. Find out something that has the use and value of money amongst his neighbors, you shall see the same man will begin presently to enlarge his possessions.

50.   But since gold and silver, being little useful to the life of man in proportion to food, raiment, and carriage, has its value only from the consent of men, whereof labor yet makes, in great part, the measure, it is plain that men have agreed to a disproportionate and unequal possession of the earth, they having, by a tacit and voluntary consent, found out a way how a man may fairly possess more land than he himself can use the product of, by receiving in exchange for the overplus gold and silver which may be hoarded up without injury to any one, these metals not spoiling or decaying in the hands of the possessor. This partage of things in an inequality of private possessions men have made practicable out of the bounds of society and without compact, only by putting a value on gold and silver, and tacitly agreeing in the use of money; for, in governments, the laws regulate the right of property, and the possession of land is determined by positive constitutions.

51.   And thus, I think, it is very easy to conceive how labor could at first begin a title of property in the common things of nature, and how the spending it upon our uses bounded it. So that there could then be no reason of quarreling about title, nor any doubt about the largeness of possession it gave. Right and convenience went together; for as a man had a right to all he could employ his labor upon, so he had no temptation to labor for more than he could make use of. This left no room for controversy about the title, nor for encroachment on the right of others; what portion a man carved to himself was easily seen, and it was useless, as well as dishonest, to carve himself too much or take more than he needed.

24

Locke's Theory of Acquisition

Robert Nozick

Before we turn to consider other theories of justice in detail, we must introduce an additional bit of complexity into the structure of the entitlement theory. This is best approached by considering Locke's attempt to specify a principle of justice in acquisition. Locke views property rights in an unowned object as originating through someone's mixing his labor with it. This gives rise to many questions. What are the boundaries of what labor is mixed with? If a private astronaut clears a place on Mars, has he mixed his labor with (so that he comes to own) the whole planet, the whole uninhabited universe, or just a particular plot? Which plot does an act bring under ownership? The minimal (possibly disconnected) area such that an act decreases entropy in that area, and not elsewhere? Can virgin land (for the purposes of ecological investigation by high-flying airplane) come under ownership by a Lockean process? Building a fence around a territory presumably would make one the owner of only the fence (and the land immediately underneath it).

Why does mixing one's labor with something make one the owner of it? Perhaps because one owns one's labor, and so one comes to own a previously unowned thing that becomes permeated with what one owns. Ownership seeps over into the rest. But why isn't mixing what I own with what I don't own a way of losing what I own rather than a way of gaining what I don't? If I own a can of tomato juice and spill it in the sea so that its molecules (made radioactive, so I can check this) mingle evenly throughout the sea, do I thereby come to own the sea, or have I foolishly dissipated my tomato juice? Perhaps the idea, instead, is that laboring on something improves it and makes it more valuable; and anyone is entitled to own a thing whose value he has created. (Reinforcing this, perhaps, is the view that laboring is unpleasant. If some people made things effortlessly, as the cartoon characters in *The Yellow Submarine* trail flowers in their wake, would they have lesser claim to their own products whose making didn't *cost* them anything?) Ignore the fact that laboring on something may make it less valuable (spraying pink enamel paint on a piece of driftwood that you have found). Why should one's entitlement extend to the whole object rather than just to the *added value* one's labor has produced? (Such reference to value might also serve to delimit the extent of ownership; for example, substitute "increases the value of" for "decreases entropy in" in the above entropy criterion.)

Robert Nozick, "Locke's Theory of Acquisition," from *Anarchy, State and Utopia* (New York: Basic Books, 1974), pp. 174–82. © 1974 by Basic Books, Inc. Reprinted with permission from Basic Books, a member of Perseus Books Group.

No workable or coherent value-added property scheme has yet been devised, and any such scheme presumably would fall to objections (similar to those) that fell the theory of Henry George.

It will be implausible to view improving an object as giving full ownership to it, if the stock of unowned objects that might be improved is limited. For an object's coming under one person's ownership changes the situation of all others. Whereas previously they were at liberty (in Hohfeld's sense) to use the object, they now no longer are. This change in the situation of others (by removing their liberty to act on a previously unowned object) need not worsen their situation. If I appropriate a grain of sand from Coney Island, no one else may now do as they will with *that* grain of sand. But there are plenty of other grains of sand left for them to do the same with. Or if not grains of sand, then other things. Alternatively, the things I do with the grain of sand I appropriate might improve the position of others, counterbalancing their loss of the liberty to use that grain. The crucial point is whether appropriation of an unowned object worsens the situation of others.

Locke's proviso that there be "enough and as good left in common for others" (sect. 27) is meant to ensure that the situation of others is not worsened. (If this proviso is met is there any motivation for his further condition of non-waste?) It is often said that this proviso once held but now no longer does. But there appears to be an argument for the conclusion that if the proviso no longer holds, then it cannot ever have held so as to yield permanent and inheritable property rights. Consider the first person Z for whom there is not enough and as good left to appropriate. The last person Y to appropriate left Z without his previous liberty to act on an object, and so worsened Z's situation. So Y's appropriation is not allowed under Locke's proviso. Therefore the next to last person X to appropriate left Y in a worse position, for X's act ended permissible appropriation. Therefore X's appropriation wasn't permissible. But then the appropriator two from last, W, ended permissible appropriation and so, since it worsened X's position, W's appropriation wasn't permissible. And so on back to the first person A to appropriate a permanent property right.

This argument, however, proceeds too quickly. Someone may be made worse off by another's appropriation in two ways: first, by losing the opportunity to improve his situation by a particular appropriation or any one; and second, by no longer being able to use freely (without appropriation) what he previously could. A *stringent* requirement that another not be made worse off by an appropriation would exclude the first way if nothing else counterbalances the diminution in opportunity, as well as the second. A *weaker* requirement would exclude the second way, though not the first. With the weaker requirement, we cannot zip back so quickly from Z to A, as in the above argument; for though person Z can no longer *appropriate*, there may remain some for him to *use* as before. In this case Y's appropriation would not violate the weaker Lockean condition. (With less remaining that people are at liberty to use, users might face more inconvenience, crowding, and so on; in that way the situation of others might be worsened, unless appropriation stopped far short of such a point.) It is arguable that no one legitimately can complain if the weaker provision is satisfied. However, since this is less clear than in the case of the more stringent proviso, Locke may have intended this stringent proviso by "enough and as good" remaining, and perhaps he meant the non-waste condition to delay the end point from which the argument zips back.

Is the situation of persons who are unable to appropriate (there being no more accessible and useful unowned objects) worsened by a system allowing appropriation and permanent property? Here enter the various familiar social considerations favoring private property: it increases the social product by putting means of production in the hands of those who can use them most efficiently (profitably); experimentation is encouraged, because with separate persons controlling resources, there is no one person or small group whom someone with a new idea must convince to try it out; private property enables people to decide on the pattern and types of risks they wish to bear, leading to specialized types of risk bearing; private property protects future persons by leading some to hold back resources from current consumption for future markets; it provides alternate sources of employment for unpopular persons who don't have to convince any one person or small group to hire them, and so on. These considerations enter a Lockean theory to support the claim that appropriation of private property satisfies the intent behind the "enough and as good left over" proviso, *not* as a utilitarian justification of property. They enter to rebut the claim that because the proviso is violated no natural right to private property can arise by a Lockean process. The difficulty in working such an argument to show that the proviso is satisfied is in fixing the appropriate base line for comparison. Lockean appropriation makes people no worse off than they would be *how?* This question of fixing the baseline needs more detailed investigation than we are able to give it here. It would be desirable to have an estimate of the general economic importance of original appropriation in order to see how much leeway there is for differing theories of appropriation and of the location of the baseline. Perhaps this importance can be measured by the percentage of all income that is based upon untransformed raw materials and given resources (rather than upon human actions), mainly rental income representing the unimproved value of land, and the price of raw material *in situ*, and by the percentage of current wealth which represents such income in the past.[1]

We should note that it is not only persons favoring *private* property who need a theory of how property rights legitimately originate. Those believing in collective property, for example those believing that a group of persons living in an area jointly own the territory, or its mineral resources, also must provide a theory of how such property rights arise; they must show why the persons living there have rights to determine what is done with the land and resources there that persons living elsewhere don't have (with regard to the same land and resources).

The Proviso

Whether or not Locke's particular theory of appropriation can be spelled out so as to handle various difficulties, I assume that any adequate theory of justice in acquisition will contain a proviso similar to the weaker of the ones we have attributed to Locke. A process normally giving rise to a permanent bequeathable property right in a previously unowned thing will not do so if the position of others no longer at liberty to use the thing is thereby worsened. It is important to specify *this* particular mode of worsening the situation of others, for the proviso does not encompass other modes. It does not include the worsening due to more limited opportunities to appropriate (the first way above, corresponding to the more stringent condition), and it does not include how I "worsen" a seller's position if I appropriate materials to make some of what he is selling, and then enter into competition with him. Someone whose appropriation otherwise would violate the proviso still may appropriate provided he compensates the others so that their situation is not thereby worsened; unless he does compensate these others, his appropriation will violate the proviso of the principle of justice in acquisition and will be an illegitimate one.[2] A theory of appropriation incorporating this Lockean proviso will handle correctly the cases (objections to the theory lacking the proviso) where someone appropriates the total supply of something necessary for life.[3]

A theory which includes this proviso in its principle of justice in acquisition must also contain a more complex principle of justice in transfer. Some reflection of the proviso about appropriation constrains later actions. If my appropriating all of a certain substance violates the Lockean proviso, then so does my appropriating some and purchasing all the rest from others who obtained it without otherwise violating the Lockean proviso. If the proviso excludes someone's appropriating all the drinkable water in the world, it also excludes his purchasing it all. (More weakly, and messily, it may exclude his charging certain prices for some of his supply.) This proviso (almost?) never will come into effect; the more someone acquires of a scarce substance which others want, the higher the price of the rest will go, and the more difficult it will become for him to acquire it all. But still, we can imagine, at least, that something like this occurs: someone makes simultaneous secret bids to the separate owners of a substance, each of whom sells assuming he can easily purchase more from the other owners; or some natural catastrophe destroys all of the supply of something except that in one person's possession. The total supply could not be permissibly appropriated by one person at the beginning. His later acquisition of it all does not show that the original appropriation violated the proviso (even by a reverse argument similar to the one above that tried to zip back from Z to A). Rather, it is the combination of the original appropriation *plus* all the later transfers and actions that violates the Lockean proviso.

Each owner's title to his holding includes the historical shadow of the Lockean proviso on appropriation. This excludes his transferring it into an agglomeration that does violate the Lockean proviso and excludes his using it in a way, in coordination with others or independently of them, so as to violate the proviso by making the situation of others worse than their baseline situation. Once it is known that someone's ownership runs afoul of the Lockean proviso, there are stringent limits on what he may do with (what it is difficult any longer unreservedly to call) "his property." Thus a person may not appropriate the only water hole in a desert and charge what he will. Nor may he charge what he will if he possesses one, and unfortunately it happens that all the water holes in the desert dry up, except for his. This unfortunate circumstance, admittedly no fault of his, brings into operation the Lockean proviso and limits his property rights.[4] Similarly, an owner's property right in the only island in an area does not allow him to order a castaway from a shipwreck off his island as a trespasser, for this would violate the Lockean proviso.

Notice that the theory does not say that owners do have these rights, but that the rights are overridden to avoid some catastrophe. (Overridden rights do not disappear; they leave a trace of a sort absent in the cases under discussion.) There is no such external (and *ad hoc*?) overriding. Considerations internal to the theory of property itself, to its theory of acquisition and appropriation, provide the means for handling such cases. The results, however, may he coextensive with some condition about catastrophe, since the baseline for comparison is so low as compared to the productiveness of a society with private appropriation that the question of the Lockean proviso being violated arises only in the case of catastrophe (or a desert-island situation).

The fact that someone owns the total supply of something necessary for others to stay alive does *not* entail that his (or anyone's) appropriation of anything left some people (immediately or later) in a situation worse than the baseline one. A medical researcher who synthesizes a new substance that effectively treats a certain disease and who refuses to sell except on his terms does not worsen the situation of others by depriving them of whatever he has appropriated. The others easily can possess the same materials he appropriated; the researcher's appropriation or purchase of chemicals didn't make those chemicals scarce in a way so as to violate the Lockean proviso. Nor would someone else's purchasing the total supply of the synthesized substance from the medical researcher. The fact that the medical researcher uses easily available chemicals to synthesize the drug no more violates the Lockean proviso than does the fact that the only surgeon able to perform a particular operation eats easily obtainable food in order to stay alive and to have the energy to work. This shows that the Lockean proviso is not an "end-state principle"; it focuses on a particular way that appropriative actions affect others, and not on the structure of the situation that results.

Intermediate between someone who takes all of the public supply and someone who makes the total supply out of easily obtainable substances is someone who appropriates the total supply of something in a way that does not deprive the others of it. For example, someone finds a new substance in an out-of-the-way place. He discovers that it effectively treats a certain disease and appropriates the total supply. He does not worsen the situation of others; if he did not stumble upon the substance no one else would have, and the others would remain without it. However, as time passes, the likelihood increases that others would have come across the substance; upon this fact might be based a limit to his property right in the substance so that others are not below their baseline position; for example, its bequest might be limited. The theme of someone worsening another's situation by depriving him of something he otherwise would possess may also illuminate the example of patents. An inventor's patent does not deprive others of an object which would not exist if not for the inventor. Yet patents would have this effect on others who independently invent the object. Therefore, these independent inventors, upon whom the burden of proving independent discovery may rest, should not be excluded from utilizing their own invention as they wish (including selling it to others). Furthermore, a known inventor drastically lessens the chances of actual independent invention. For persons who know of an invention usually will not try to reinvent it, and the notion of independent discovery here would be murky at best. Yet we may assume that in the absence of the original invention, sometime later someone else would have come up with it. This suggests placing a time limit on patents, as a rough rule of thumb to approximate how long it would have taken, in the absence of knowledge of the invention, for independent discovery.

I believe that the free operation of a market system will not actually run afoul of the Lockean proviso. (Recall that crucial to our story in Part I of how a protective agency becomes dominant and a *de facto* monopoly is the fact that it wields force in situations of conflict, and is not merely in competition, with other agencies. A similar tale cannot be told about other businesses.) If this is correct, the proviso will not play a very important role in the activities of protective agencies and will not provide a significant opportunity for future state action. Indeed, were it not for the effects of previous *illegitimate* state action, people would not think the possibility of the proviso's being violated as of more interest than any other logical possibility. (Here I make an empirical historical claim; as does someone who disagrees with this.) This completes our indication of the complication in the entitlement theory introduced by the Lockean proviso.

Notes

1 I have not seen a precise estimate. David Friedman, *The Machinery of Freedom* (New York: Harper & Row, 1973), pp. xiv, xv, discusses this issue and suggests 5 percent of US national income as an upper limit for the first two factors mentioned. However he does not attempt to estimate the percentage of current wealth which is based upon such income in the past. (The vague notion of "based upon" merely indicates a topic needing investigation.)

2 Fourier held that since the process of civilization had deprived the members of society of certain liberties (to gather, pasture, engage in the chase), a socially guaranteed minimum provision for the persons was justified as compensation for the loss (Alexander Gray, *The Socialist Tradition* (New York: Harper & Row, 1968), p. 188). But this puts the point too strongly. This compensation would be due those persons, if any, for whom the process of civilization was a *net loss*, for whom the benefits of civilization did not counterbalance being deprived of these particular liberties.

3 For example, Rashdall's case of someone who comes upon the only water in the desert several miles ahead of others who also will come to it and appropriates it all. Hastings Rashdall, "The Philosophical Theory of Property," in *Property: Its Duties and Rights* (London: Macmillan, 1915).

We should note Ayn Rand's theory of property rights ("Man's Rights," in *The Virtue of Selfishness* (New York: New American Library, 1964), p. 94), wherein these follow from the right to life, since people need physical things to live. But a right to life is not a right to whatever one needs to live; other people may have rights over these other things. [. . .] At most, a right to life would be a right to have or strive for whatever one needs to live, provided that having it does not violate anyone else's rights. With regard to material things, the question is whether having it does violate any right of others. (Would appropriation of all unowned things do so? Would appropriating the water hole in Rashdall's example?) Since special considerations (such as the Lockean proviso) may enter with regard to material property, one *first* needs a theory of property rights before one can apply any supposed right to life (as amended above). Therefore the right to life cannot provide the foundation for a theory of property rights.

4 The situation would be different if his waterhole didn't dry up, due to special precautions he took to prevent this. Compare our discussion of the case in the text with Hayek, *The Constitution of Liberty*, p. 136; and also with Ronald Hamowy, "Hayek's Concept of Freedom; A Critique," *New Individualist Review*, April 1961, pp. 28–31.

25

Property, Title, and Redistribution

A. M. Honoré

This discussion paper is concerned with the relationship between the institution of private property and the notion of economic equality. Is it inconsistent, or morally obtuse to recognize the value of the institution and at the same time to argue that each member of a society is entitled to an equal or approximately equal standard of living? I shall be particularly concerned with the argument of R. Nozick, in *Anarchy, State, and Utopia*[1] to the effect that under a system of "just entitlements" such as he specifies there is no room to admit that the state has the right or duty to redistribute benefits so as to secure an equal or more equal spread, because "the particular rights over things fill the space of rights, leaving no room for general rights to be in a certain material condition."[2] Though Nozick's "just entitlements"[3] are not confined to titles to property I shall so confine myself. Rights of a more personal character could in theory be the subjects of redistribution and indeed Nozick discusses the case for transplanting organs from A to B in order to correct physical maldistribution of parts of the body.[4] Fascinating as such speculations may be, the physical and technical difficulties involved in such a programme would be stupendous and the moral objections to the invasion of

people's bodies for whatever purpose are much stronger than they are when what is proposed is to tax or, in some cases, to expropriate. Nor can one concede the argument that the redistribution of part of what A has earned to B goes beyond the invasion of property rights and amounts to a system of forced labour[5] by which A is compelled to work part of his day for B, so that redistribution of property is really an invasion of the status and freedom of the person taxed or expropriated. This is no more compelling than the Marxist argument that a wage-earner whose surplus product is appropriated by the employer is a sort of wage slave. The objection to this is not that the income-earner freely works under a system in which he knows that part of what he produces will be appropriated by his employer or transferred to other people by means of taxes. He may have no choice, if he is to earn a living, but to accept a system which he dislikes. The argument is open to attack rather because it rests on the morally questionable view that a person is entitled to keep exclusively and indefinitely for himself whatever he makes or produces. This would be true of a man working in complete isolation; no serious argument has been advanced to show that it is true of a social being.

A. M. Honoré, "Property, Title and Redistribution," from Carl Wellman, ed., *Equality and Freedom* (Archiv fur Rechts- und Sozial-philosophie, 1977), pp. 107–15. © 1977. Reprinted with permission from Franz Steiner Verlag GmbH.

Nozick's argument depends on accepting this questionable view. Against those who favour a principle of social justice by which things are to be distributed according to need, desert, the principle of equal claims or the like, he argues that the just allocation is the historically justifiable one. This can be ascertained, in relation to any given item of property, by asking whether the holder acquired it by a just title or derived his title justly from another who so held it, either originally or by derivation from such a just acquirer. Consequently just distribution depends on just acquisition and transfer, and redistribution is confined to those instances in which the original acquisition or the subsequent transmission of the property was unjust.

All therefore turns on what count as just principles of acquisition and transfer of title. According to Nozick:

1   A person who acquires a holding in accordance with the principle of justice in acquisition is entitled to that holding.
2   A person who acquires a holding in accordance with the principle of justice in transfer from some one else entitled to the holding is entitled to the holding.
3   No one is entitled to a holding except by (repeated) applications of 1 and 2.

The complete principle of distributive justice would say simply that a distribution is just if everyone is entitled to the holdings they possess under the distribution.

What is presupposed by this set of rules for tracing title is apparently only that the principles of acquisition and transfer should be morally respectable. For acquisition something like Locke's theory of property is understood.[6] Transfers in a free society will be consensual. But that is only the appearance. What Nozick additionally pre-supposes, without seeking to justify, is that the interest acquired and transmitted is the owner-ship of property as conceived in western society on the model of Roman law.[7] He is assuming, first, that the acquirer obtains an exclusive right to the thing acquired, that he is entitled, having cleared the land, made the tool etc. to deny access and use to everyone else. Secondly he is supposing that the right acquired is of indefinite duration. The man who has made the clearing can remain

there for his lifetime. He is not obliged to move on after so many years, and leave the fruits of his labour to another, nor does he lose his right by leaving. Thirdly the right is supposed to be transmissible inter vivos and on death, so that it can be sold, given, inherited, mortgaged and the like again without limit of time. Under such a system of property law, of course, the initial acquisition is decisive. Once A has cleared the land his neighbours, friends, associates and, if it comes to that, his family are obliged to look on while he enjoys and transmits his "entitlement" to whomsoever he chooses, irrespective of the fact that in a wider context they, along with him, form part of a single group[8] which is dedicated, among other objects, to the preservation of all. This system of property law, whatever its economic merits, is not self-evidently just. If the interest acquired (western-type ownership) is greater than can be morally justified, then however just the methods by which A acquires the thing in ques-tion and transfers it to X, the distribution of property under which the thing is allocated to X is not thereby saved from criticism. Indeed, quite the contrary. If the interest awarded to owners under the system is greater than can reasonably be justified on moral, as opposed to economic, grounds, any distribution of property will be inherently unjust. Hence the intervention of the state will be needed if justice is to be done.

There is no doubt that the Nozick rules about just acquisition, transfer and distribution repro-duce in outline western systems of property law based on the liberal conception of ownership. According to these notions, ownership is a per-manent, exclusive and transmissible interest in property. But this type of property system is neither the only conceivable system, nor the easiest to justify from a moral point of view, nor does it predominate in those societies which are closest to a "state of nature."

In so far as the Nozick principles are meant to reproduce western property law they are incom-plete in that they omit provision for lapse of title and for compulsory acquisition. Lapse of title is not perhaps of great moral importance, but it is worth noting that legal rules about limitation of actions and prescription embody the idea that an owner who neglects his property may be deprived of it. The acquirer (squatter or the like) obtains it by a sort of private expropriation.

More important is expropriation by the state or public authority. It is not at all clear why the parts of western property law favourable to the private owner should be reproduced in the system of entitlements to the exclusion of those which favour the claims of the community. The latter, after all, balance the former. The individualistic bias of property law is corrected by the admission of state claims to tax and expropriate.

Aside from the omission of rules about lapse and compulsory acquisition one may note that Nozick's principles rest on the assumption that whether a justification exists for acquiring or transferring property can be decided in abstraction from the historical and social context. A just acquisition in 1066 or 1620 remains a just root of title in 1975. If this were really so one would have to say either that the acquisition of slaves is seen in retrospect always to have been unjust and that the state would have been justified in intervening in a slave-owning society to correct the injustice, or that the descendants of slave-owners are entitled to own the descendants of freed slaves. So with colonies, *mutatis mutandis*. Are we to say that as a result of the post-war movement to free colonies we now see that the acquisition of colonies, apparently valid at the time in international law and morality, was always wrong and that the international society would have been justified, had it been so minded, in intervening even in the nineteenth century to free the existing colonies and prevent further acquisitions? If so, how can we be sure that there are not equally unjustified forms of property ownership in present-day society which in fact justify state intervention in a redistributive sense? And how can we be sure in any future society that these objectionable forms of acquisition are not present? In which case, outside Utopia, the thesis advanced by Nozick has no application. But if the acquisition of slaves and colonies was initially just, surely some provision should be made in his system for the redistribution of entitlements when the moral basis on which they originally rested has become eviscerated. These instances would count morally as cases of lapse of title owing to changing views of right and wrong. Legally they would furnish examples of just expropriation. There would have to be a further exception in Nozick's system to cater for changing conditions of fact. Suppose, apart from any

question of the justification for colonies, that in the nineteenth century Metropolitania occupied a deserted tract which it proceeded to colonize, building roads and irrigating the land. As a result a numerous indigenous population crowded in from the neighbouring areas. These people now claim to be free and to decide their own destinies. Whether or not colonization is in general thought a permissible form of "entitlement" the changed situation must surely change one's moral evaluation of Metropolitania's title to the formerly deserted tract. So with the Mayflowerite who bagged a large stretch of unoccupied land in 1620. If the situation is now that irrespective of title the tracts in question are occupied by people who have nowhere else to live surely the moral basis of the title of the Mayflowerite's successors must at least be open to debate. Once there was more than enough to go round, now there is not. And is the case very different if the thousands without property instead of occupying the colonies or tracts in question crowd the periphery and make claims on the unused resources inside: All this is intended to make the simple point that it is obtuse to suppose that the justification for acquiring or transmitting property could be settled once and for all at the date of acquisition or transfer. Legally it may be so, subject to the rules of lapse and expropriation. This is because of the need to frame rules of law in such a way as to ensure certainty of title. They are meant however to be applied in a context in which social and moral criticism may be directed against their operation and in which their defects may be corrected by legislation or similar means. Apart from positive law, can it seriously be maintained that the rules about what constitutes a just acquisition or transfer both express unchanging verities and, in their application to the facts of a given acquisition or transfer, are exempt from reassessment in the light of changed circumstances?

Systems of property law which diverge from the orthodox western type based on liberal conceptions of ownership are conceivable, morally defensible and have actually obtained in certain societies. To begin with the conceivable, let us take an imaginary case. Suppose that, in a "state of nature" a group of people live near a river and subsist on fish, which they catch by hand, and berries. There is great difficulty in catching fish by hand. Berries are however fairly plentiful. There are bits of metal lying around and I discover how to make one of them into a fishhook. With this invention I quadruple my catch of fish. My neighbours cannot discover the knack and I decline to tell them. They press me to lend them the fishhook or to give them the lessons in acquiring the technique. I have however acquired western notions of property law and Lockean ideas about entitlement, I point out that I have a just title to the fishhook, since according to Nozick's version of Locke they are no worse off as a result of my invention. I am therefore entitled to the exclusive, permanent and transmissible use of the fishhook. My neighbours may try their hands at finding out how to make one, of course, but if they fail they may look forward to eating berries and from time to time a bit of fish while I and those persons whom I choose to invite to a meal propose to enjoy ourselves with daily delicacies. If they object that this is unfair I shall point out (though the relevance is not obvious) that they are not actually starving. Nor am I monopolizing materials. There are other pieces of metal lying around. They are no worse off than they were before or than they would have been without my find (in fact they *are* worse off, relatively to me). As to the parrot cry that they protect me and my family from marauders, wild animals and the like, so that I ought to share my good fortune with them, I reply that they have not grasped what is implied by a system of just entitlements. Are they saying that I am not entitled to the fishhook?

One of my brighter neighbours might well answer me as follows. "I do not deny that you have a right to the fishhook. As you say you made it and you invented the system of using it to catch fish. But it does not follow that, as you assert, your right to it is exclusive, permanent and transmissible. Your views seem to be coloured by reading books about sophisticated societies. In those societies men are dedicated to increasing production, come what may, and in order to achieve that they accept institutions which to us seem very unfair. We are simple people used to sharing our fortunes and misfortunes. We recognize that you have a right to the fishhook but not that the right has the unlimited content which you assign to it. You ought to allow each of us to use it in turn. Naturally as the maker and inventor you are

entitled to a greater share in the use than the rest of us individually, and if you like to call that share 'ownership' we shall not object. But please stop looking up the definition of 'ownership' in foreign books. These notions will only disrupt our way of life."

The point my neighbour is making is that a system of private property can be inherently distributive. In the system envisaged there is an "owner" in the sense of a person whose right to the use of the thing is greater than that of others, who has a residual claim if others do not want to use the thing, and in whom powers of management will be vested. He will be responsible for lending the fishhook out, it will be returned to him each evening, he will keep it in repair. But these powers of use, management and reversion fall short of western conception of ownership. In such a system the redistributive power of the state will be unnecessary unless the members of the group fail to keep the rules. For the rules themselves ensure an even distribution of property, subject to the recognition of desert and choice – a recognition which is not allowed to subvert the principle of sharing.

Is the projected system of property law obviously unjust? How does it compare with western notions of ownership? From the point of view of justice, though perhaps not of economic efficiency, it seems to compare rather favourably. It is designed to give effect to the interdependence of the members of the group and to recognize overtly that they cannot survive in isolation. It rejects the notion that I do no harm to a member of my group if as a result of my effort I am better off, and he is no worse off than he would otherwise be. That notion, which is common to the outlook of Nozick and Rawls, however much they otherwise differ, rests on the assumption that a person who is *comparatively* worse off is not worse off. But he is, and the precise wrong he suffers is that of being treated as an unequal by the more fortunate member or members of the group.

The fruits of an invention which raises production have therefore, in the projected system, to be shared, either by a system of compulsory loan or, in a weaker version, by a system of surplus sharing, under which what an owner "has in excess of his needs or is not using must be made available to other members of his group."[9]

The sort of system envisaged is unlikely to survive the division of labour, viz. specialisation. The members of the group other than the inventor are likely to feel that he can fish better than they and that they would do well to get him to fish for them. But then they must pay him. At first perhaps the payment is a fraction of the catch. Later the inventor is bemused by the idea that he is entitled to the whole product of his invention. So he argues that his neighbours owe him the whole of his catch and, if they want any of it, must pay in some other way, as by repairing his hut. As he has possession on his side his views may prevail. We slide insensibly, therefore, from a participatory to an exclusive system of property law, and it is difficult to keep alive, in a society of economic specialisation, the notion that each participates in a common enterprise. The remedy for this is not, or is only to a minor extent, a return to rotatory labour. It is rather that the community as a whole, the state, must act as the surrogate of the participatory principles. The inventor of the fishhook will have to be taxed. In that way the economic advantages of specialisation can be combined with a just, or juster distribution of the benefits derived from it. The tax will be used to give the other members of the group benefits corresponding to their former rights to use the fishhook.

There is no point in attempting to work out in detail what a participatory system of property law would be like. The idea is easy to grasp. If such a system is morally sound, then it follows that in a western-type system the intervention of the state, so far from being, as Nozick thinks, ruled out except in peripheral instances, (initially unjust acquisitions, subsequently unjust transfers) is essential in order to achieve justice in distribution.[10] Whether one says that this is because in a western-type system all the holdings are unjust (because they are holdings of an unjust sort of property interest) or that they were initially just but that their permanent retention cannot be justified, is debatable: the former seems more appealing. In any event either Nozick's conclusion is empty because the premises are never fulfilled, or if the premises are fulfilled, they do not lead to the conclusion to which they seem to lead.

If it is accepted that the sort of property system described is conceivable and morally defensible, that is sufficient to rebut the argument which denies a redistributive function to the state. It is not irrelevant, however, to draw attention to the fact that among the variety of property arrangements found in simple societies there are some which approximate to the distributive arrangement outlined. Among other things this will serve to rebut any argument that I am relying on a gimmicky obligatory principle of transfer.[11] A convenient outline of the variety of such property systems is to be found in M. J. Herskowitz's work.[12] They are of course multifold: apart from arrangements which resemble the western institution of ownership there are to be found types of group (e.g. family or clan) ownership, public ownership, rotating individual use (e.g. of fishing grounds) and also the sort of arrangement here envisaged, namely what may be called private ownership subject to compulsory loan or sharing. Thus among the Bushmen[13] "all kinds of food are private property" and "one who takes without the permission of the owner is liable to punishment for theft" but "one who shoots a buck or discovers a terrain where vegetable food is to be gathered is nevertheless expected to share with those who have nothing," so that "all available food, though from the point of view of customary law privately owned, is actually distributed among the members of a given group." The dividing is done by the owner and the skin, sinews etc. belong to him to deal with as he pleases. Among the Indians of the Pacific North-West[14] a man is said to have "owned" an economically important tract and this "ownership" was expressed by his "giving permission," to his fellows to exploit the locality each season but "no instance was ever heard of an 'owner' refusing to give the necessary permission. Such a thing is inconceivable." The individual "ownership" is a sort of stewardship or ownership in trust carrying with it management and the right to use but not excluding the right of others to a similar use. Among certain tribes of Hottentots[15] a person who dug a waterhole or opened a spring made this his property and all who wished to use it had to have his permission, but he was under an obligation to see that no stranger or stranger's stock was denied access to it. Among then Tswana[16] where the chief allocates (and in that sense "owns") the land he will allot cattle-posts to individuals, but not exclusively. The allocee, whose position is closest to that of the private owner, "must share with a number of other people the pastures of the place where his cattle-post is situated, although no one else may bring his cattle there without permission." Yet occupation does give a certain prior right. "If a man builds a hut and so indicates that it is not merely for temporary use, he established a form of lien over the place, and can return to it at any time."

There are also examples of what I have termed surplus sharing, which give effect to the principle that what a person has in excess of his needs, or is not using must be made available to other members of the group. Among the Eskimos the principle that "personal possession is conditioned by actual use of the property" comes into play. A fox-trap lying idle may be taken by anyone who will use it. In Greenland a man already owning a tent or large boat does not inherit another, since it is assumed that one person can never use more than one possession of this type. "Though what a person uses is generally acknowledged to be his alone any excess must be at the disposal of those who need it and can make good use of it."[17]

These examples show that there is nothing unnatural about distributive property arrangements in a simple society. The mechanism, or one of the possible mechanisms by which such arrangements are secured, is that of what it seems preferable to call private ownership subject to a trust or a duty to permit sharing. The "ownership" is not of course ownership of the classical western type, but neither is it "primitive communism." Its essential feature is that the titles to acquisition are much the same as in modern societies – finding, invention, occupation, making and the like – and the types of transfer – sale, gift, inheritance – are not necessarily dissimilar, but the type of interest acquired and transmitted is different. The principle of sharing is written into the delineation of interests of property.

There is no special reason to think that our moral consciousness is superior to that of simple societies. So if compulsory sharing commends itself to some of them it should not be dismissed out of hand for societies in which the division of

labour has made those simple arrangements out of date: but in these, given the weakened social cohesion which the division of labour introduces, the central authority (the state) is needed to see that sharing takes place.

Notes

1   Oxford, 1974.
2   Ibid., p. 238.
3   Ibid., pp. 150–82.
4   Ibid., p. 206.
5   Ibid., pp. 169f, arguing that redistributive arrangements give B a sort of Property right in A. This mistake stems from the Lockean argument that we own ourselves and *hence* what we make etc. If human beings are free they cannot own themselves; their relationship to themselves and their bodies is more like one of "sovereignty" which cannot be alienated or foregone, though it can be restricted by (lawful) contract or treaty.
6   Ibid., pp. 174ff.
7   For an analysis, see Honoré, "Ownership," in: Guest, *Oxford Essays in Jurisprudence* (London, 1961).
8   For an analysis see Honoré, *ARSP* 61 (1975), p. 161.
9   M. J. Herskowitz, *Economic Anthropology* (New York, 1952), p. 372
10 Nozick, *Anarchy, State, and Utopia*, pp. 174ff. However one interprets Locke's requirement that the acquirer must leave enough and as good in common for others (Second Treatise, sec. 27) the intention behind is not satisfied unless entitlements are adjusted from time to time according to what *then* remains for others.
11 Ibid., p. 157.
12 M. J. Herskowitz, *Economic Anthropology* (New York, 1952), part IV: Property.
13 Ibid., pp. 321–2, citing L. Schapera, *The Khosian Peoples of South Africa, Bushmen and Hottentots* (London, 1930), p. 148.
14 Ibid., pp. 332–3, citing P. Drucker "Rank, Wealth and Kinship in Northwest Coast Society," *Amer. Anth.* 41 (1939), p. 59.
15 Ibid., pp. 343–4, citing Schapera, *The Khosian Peoples*, pp. 286–91.
16 Ibid., p. 344, citing *The Khosian Peoples*, Schapera, and A. J. H. Goodwin, "Work and Wealth," in *The Bantu-Speaking Tribes of South Africa* (ed. L. Schapera), pp. 156–7.
17 Ibid., pp. 373–4, citing K. Birket-Smith, *The Eskimos* (London, 1936), pp. 148–51.

26

Philosophical Implications

Richard A. Epstein

A Summing Up

The explication of the eminent domain clause in the previous nineteen chapters has covered cases that range from outright acquisition of land to the manifold modes of regulation and taxation so characteristic of the modern state. My central concern in this concluding chapter is not with the legal status of the takings clause, but with the larger questions of normative political theory: what are the intrinsic merits of the eminent domain provision when it is stripped of its present constitutional authority? If we were now in a position to organize a government from scratch, would its constitution include an eminent domain clause as interpreted here? My thesis is that the eminent domain approach, as applied both to personal liberty and private property, offers a principled account of both the functions of the state and the limitations upon its powers.

Representative government begins with the premise that the state's rights against its citizens are no greater than the sum of the rights of the individuals whom it benefits in any given transaction. The state qua state has no independent set of entitlements, any more than a corporation has rights qua corporation against any of its

shareholders.[1] All questions of public right are complex amalgams of questions of individual entitlements, so the principles of property, contract, and tort law can be used to explain the proper extent of government power. These rules determine the proper relationships among private individuals, which are preserved when the state intervenes as an agent on one side of the transaction. These entitlement principles obey very simple rules of summation and hence apply with undiminished vigor to large-number situations involving modifications of liability rules, regulation, and taxation. A system of private rights provides an exhaustive and internally consistent normative baseline of entitlements against which all the complex schemes of governance can be tested. As there are no gaps in rights when ownership is first established, no gaps emerge when private ownership is transformed by state intervention, whatever its form.

The state, however, cannot simply arise (even conceptually) out of a series of voluntary transactions from an original distribution of rights. Free riders, holdouts, and radical uncertainty thwart any omnibus agreement before its inception. The question then arises, what minimum of additional power that must be added for the state

Richard Epstein, "Philosophical Implications," from *Takings: Private Property and the Power of Eminent Domain* (Harvard University Press, 1985), pp. 331–50. © 1985 by the President and Fellows of Harvard College. Reprinted with permission from Harvard University Press.

to become more than a voluntary protective association and to acquire the exclusive use of force within its territory? The eminent domain analysis provides the answer: the only additional power needed is the state's right to force exchanges of property rights that leave individuals with rights more valuable than those they have been deprived of. The specter of the unlimited Hobbesian sovereign is averted by two critical limitations upon the nature of the exchanges that the state can force. First, the eminent domain logic allows forced exchanges only for the public use, which excludes naked transfers from one person to another. Second, it requires compensation, so everyone receives something of greater value in exchange for the *rights* surrendered.

In the final analysis the two conditions blend into one, because the power to coerce is limited to cases in which positive-sum games may go forward with a pro rata division of the surplus they generate. It is always easy to construct examples whereby some individuals with distinctive personal tastes will be worse off in fact, because they will lose the power to rape, kill, pillage, and plunder. Yet the baseline for forced exchanges is individual entitlements to personal autonomy, not individual preferences regardless of their content. Aggrieved parties cannot complain if they lose under the state something they were not entitled to against other individuals as a matter of right. No requirement of unanimous consent prevents the move to a system of governance.[2] The single pervert cannot block the state. Once organized, the state has the power to govern because within its own territory it has the monopoly of force sufficient to protect all persons against aggression in all its forms. Finally, by a system of unbiased judges (long recognized as part of the tradition of natural justice) the state insures that all disputes can be resolved. The gains of final adjudication are the substantial gains of social order, while the errors tend to be randomly distributed, so all persons share pro rata in the surplus created.[3]

This eminent domain framework does not depend upon a hidden assumption that before the formation of a government all individuals, real or hypothetical, reside in a "state of nature." Quite the contrary, political theory is quite unintelligible if it assumes that prior to the establishment of a government, individuals have no common language, no conception of right and wrong, no common culture or tradition, and no means of socialization outside the state. The question of the state is narrower than is sometimes supposed. The state is not the source of individual rights or of social community. It presupposes that these exist and are worth protecting, and that individuals reciprocally benefit from their interactions with one another. A unique sovereign emerges solely in response to the demands to preserve order. The state becomes a moral imperative precisely because there is something of value that is worth protecting from the unbridled use of force by those who foresake tradition, family, and friends. A set of forced exchanges from existing rights does not create the original rights so exchanged; like the constitutional vision of private property, forced exchanges presuppose them. A forced exchange does not create culture and sense of community, it protects them by removing the need for compelling or allowing everyone to act as a policeman in his own cause. The state arises because the rates of error and abuse in pure self-help regimes become intolerable. The strength of a natural law theory is in its insistence that individual rights (and their correlative obligations) exist independent of agreement and prior to the formation of the state.

Rival Theories

To get some sense of the power of the eminent domain approach, it is instructive to compare this view with two rival theories that have been very influential in recent times, theories with which it has both important similarities and important differences. These theories are the one associated with the work of Robert Nozick in *Anarchy, State, and Utopia* and that of John Rawls in *A Theory of Justice*. After reviewing them, I shall consider whether the theory of eminent domain is consistent with a vision of civic virtue in public life or is nullified by past acts that violate the theory itself.

Nozick

Nozick's theory incorporates the first part of the eminent domain approach in its respect for the principles of individual rights. Nozick relies heavily upon "historical" principles of justice to account for the institution of private property and the inequalities in wealth it engenders. At one time those principles were widely accepted in both common and constitutional discourse.[4] Nozick's rules of acquisition have close affinity to the first-possession rules of property. His principles of rectification cover the terrain of the law of tort, and those of transfer cover the law of contract.[5] One great attraction of his normative theory is its powerful congruence with basic social institutions and human practices which provides a convenient data base on which to examine its implications. Another strong point is that by striking a responsive chord, the theory requires no great cost to be legitimated, because people do not need to be persuaded to abandon their customary moral views, as they would to embrace a highly abstract theory (like Rawls's) that cuts against the grain and commits them to outcomes they cannot understand by procedures they sorely distrust.

But there are difficulties with Nozick's theory. The first concerns its origin and the status of individual rights. Nozick follows closely in the Lockean and common law tradition, for his historical theory of justice begins with the proposition that ownership is acquired by taking possession of an unowned thing. Nonetheless, the proposition that possession is the root of title is not a necessary truth.[6] The linkage between possession and title can be denied without self-contradiction. Arguably, all things in an initial position are subject to some form of collective ownership. Some nondeductive procedure must be available to let us choose between competing visions of the correct original position. Nozick's view depends upon an intuitive appreciation of the need for autonomy and self-determination. In one sense his position looks like a bare assertion: private property and personal liberty are important because they are important or because they are inherent in human nature. Such efforts at self-justification are always uneasy, but they are not for that reason wrong. One way to look at Nozick's simple theory is to ask what the world would look like if the popular conception of autonomy was abandoned. On what grounds could one categorically condemn murder, rape, mayhem, theft, and pillage? Our instincts of revulsion are so powerful that one is loathe to adopt a theory of individual rights that rests solely upon the shifting sands of utilitarian calculation. Slavery by conquest is regarded as a categorical evil.[7] Do we want even to consider the argument that slavery is justified if the agency costs of control and supervision are small in comparison with the resource gains from subjecting an incompetent slave to the will of a competent master? Or is the incompetence of one person only an argument for guardianship by another? Is it really an open question whether the parent–child relationship is one of guardianship or ownership? Simple faith may not serve as the ideal foundation of an ethical theory, but it may be much better than the next best alternative.

Nozick writes in an antiutilitarian vein that places his historical theory in sharp opposition to a consequentialist one. Yet in one sense the intuitive base for much libertarian doctrine might be strengthened by a direct appeal to considerations of utility. Utilitarianism does not purport to rest upon mere assertion or past practice but seeks to show how these rules can be harmonized in the service of an end that is itself justified. If everyone is better off in World One than they are in World Two, who would want to interpose an argument about rights that, if respected, consigned everyone to the inferior world? A utilitarian argument is always filled with gigantic pitfalls because it makes all small decisions turn upon some vast social construct. Still, we shall not be too quick to attack a theory for mistakes in its application, especially if these can be corrected without abandoning the major premise.

Indeed, a sensible utilitarian theory does provide powerful support for Nozick's substantive commitment to individual liberty and private property. The simplicity of Nozick's system is surely commendable, for it cuts down the number of negative-sum games by setting boundary lines that other persons cannot cross without the owner's consent. The theory also tends to foster many separate sources of power, whether in personal talents or external things. It thereby tends to create competitive structures and to prevent the concentration of wealth and power in a few hands. Thus the first-possession rule itself makes it highly unlikely that any one person will reduce all things to ownership, especially when others enjoy the same privilege of original acquisition. Unifying the possession, use, and disposition of a determinate thing in the hands of individuals makes it far easier to organize subsequent transactions to correct original errors of allocation. Similarly, leaving things with their initial possessor creates a system of ownership that does not begin with state entanglements and that removes the dead-weight costs of shifting property from its present possessor to it rightful owner under the new system.[8] A utilitarian theory, especially of the indirect sort, thus looks quite consistent with the simple rules of thumb to which common practice conforms and to which libertarians gave great respect.[9]

Utilitarian theory is often criticized because it is said to ignore differences between persons and to make rights turn on consequences, not origins. But quite the opposite is true. A good utilitarian should be driven to respect differences among persons, if only to avoid the common pool problems that the principle of autonomy is able in large measure to overcome. Similarly, future happiness depends upon a system of stable and well-defined rights. These can be had only if entitlements are made to turn upon individual past actions which, once their consequences are understood, can offer the signposts for intelligent planning. The contrast between ontological and consequentialist theories in ethics is much overdrawn.

The defense of liberty and property can be made in either libertarian or utilitarian terms, yet it does not follow that distributional issues are ignored. Even before the advent of the welfare state, many social institutions developed to share and pool risk. Certainly the family has this function, and the same role can be ascribed to the large clans of primitive society. Friendly societies and fraternal organizations have had a similar role, and voluntary support for charitable activities has worked to preserve the social fabric against all sorts of external shocks. There is a certain amount of luck as to who is born smart and who is not, who has a congenital defect and who has great talent. No libertarian could consistently oppose voluntary aid to the poor and needy, or the complex private arrangements used to secure it. This obligation can be recognized as an "imperfect" one that is not simply a matter of ordinary consumption, even if the dangers of state coercion in principle make transfer payments an improper function of the state.

The original position taken first by Locke and adopted by Nozick has enormous appeal. Everyone does own himself, and no one owns any external things, and there are natural status obligations of support within the family. Nonetheless, Nozick's libertarian theory fails in its central mission because it cannot justify the existence of the state. Its chief weakness is that it views all entitlements as absolute, so all forced exchanges are ruled out of bounds, regardless of their terms. Yet without forced exchanges, social order cannot be achieved, given the holdout and free-rider problems. Nozick presents a wonderful discussion of the invisible-hand mechanisms that lead to the creation of multiple collective protection associations.[10] But no invisible-hand mechanism explains the emergence of an exclusive sovereign within any given territory. The need for forced exchanges makes this last leap from many associations to a single state, and the eminent domain argument supplies this step. Individual entitlements are respected always as claims for compensation and frequently, but not uniformly, as absolutes.

There are still limits on what the eminent domain theory can do. It cannot explain *which* protective association should become the exclusive one; for example, the place of honor might be awarded to the association with the most members. (Even here the specification of the territory can be decisive in choosing between rival claims.) The critical point is that any association which assumes power is hemmed in by a nondiscrimination provision: it owes the same obligations toward outsiders that it owes to its own members. Exploitation is made more difficult, if not precluded, when those who are bound without their consent must on average be left better off in their entitlement than before. The libertarian theory augmented by a willingness to tolerate some forced exchanges is vastly richer than a libertarian theory that wholly shuns them.

Rawls

The theory of governance implicit in the eminent domain clause also has strong elements of similarity to, and distinction from, the contractarian theory of justice most prominently associated with John Rawls. Rawls has two central principles: liberty and the difference principle.[11] According to the first, the proper purpose of social organization is to expand the liberties of all individuals to act, without interfering with others' liberties. By the second principle, any adjustment in the position of the original liberties must work to the advantage of the most disadvantaged in society. These substantive principles are justified by an appeal to the idea of reflective equilibrium, which itself depends upon a set of procedures to determine the proper substantive rules. Rawls's recurrent question is, what practices would all members in society adopt if they made their fundamental choices about the social structure behind a veil of ignorance? So located, their only knowledge is of human nature in general and of the laws of physical and social interaction, such as that most individuals are risk averse and are motivated by an uneasy mix of self-interest, family affections, and a sense of obligation. They are systematically denied knowledge of their own personal preferences and social niche.

Rawls's contractarian theory permits a richness of discussion that cannot be generated by simple libertarian premises, but it is open to powerful and familiar criticisms of a different sort, which I need not recount at length. First, it is quite impossible to understand Rawls's use of contract as it relates to abstractions.[12] Contract within the private law is an effort to vindicate the unique tastes of discrete persons who are far more concerned with their particular places and preferences than with the general social good. The Hobbesian cry, "The value of all things contracted for, is measured by the Appetite of the Contractors; and therefore the just value, is that which they be contented to give,"[13] is as succinct a statement and justification of freedom of contract as one can hope to give. Voluntary exchanges presuppose that in general every person has reliable information as to what he values and how much he values it or, at least, that he has better information about those things than those who would limit his choices. Trades are a positive-sum game because each person attaches greater value to what he receives than to what he surrenders. To argue for contracts by disinterested, indeed disembodied, persons is simply to strain a metaphor beyond its breaking point. By removing all traces of psychological struggle and individual self-interest, the theory departs radically from any plausible view of the

private agreements based upon personal knowledge that lie at its analogical root. The metaphor of contract is best dropped altogether from Rawls's conception, because a single composite individual could do everything that is required of a contracting group. Indeed it is only the residual allure of the contract idea of consensus that drives Rawls to consider the preferences of hypothetical groups. By the terms of his theory, the choice of the single mean (or median?) person should suffice as well.

A second line of criticism is that Rawls's method of inquiry suffers from radical, indeed fatal, uncertainty. What results does the procedure generate, and how do these tie in with any common intuitions of individual rights and duties that are supposed to be generated? Rawls admitted that he could not be certain whether his view of the system tolerated the private ownership of productive property,[14] a startling indeterminacy in itself and a troublesome admission for anyone committed either to human freedom or to the power of normative discourse. Will the most ordinary of transactions – getting married to the spouse of one's own choice, having children, buying a home – be permissible under his theory? Nozick rightly points out that the theory offers no clear and powerful linkages between the micro level and the macro level.[15]

By degrees, the difference principle becomes the spider's web that traps the individual. Every individual's action will influence the utility others derive from their own holdings, whatever they may be. The irony should become apparent. The original objection to utilitarian thought was that it failed to respect the differences between persons. Yet that same objection can be leveled against Rawls's position, as the philosophical doctrine of internal relations is thus pressed into service to make the independence of human action, and with it individual liberty, a logical impossibility. If those left worse off are viewed as being harmed, then every human action contains a built-in justification for government intervention, even under the restrictive Millian principle that governments may intervene only to prevent harm to others. The libertarian position on rights does not suffer from this embarrassment. It contains a strong threshold condition – against the taking of private property, against the use of force or fraud – which must be crossed before one can regard the loss in welfare sustained by others as an actionable wrong. The proposition that all decisions must be collective because every action creates external harm can be rejected on principled grounds.[16]

The eminent domain approach to the question of political obligation meets these two central objections to Rawls's theory. The eminent domain theory does not have to deal with the entitlements of lifeless abstractions. Instead of relying upon a set of complex procedures to generate the needed substantive rights, it starts with a substantive account of individual rights, beginning with first possession and covering every aspect of the use and disposition of property. The radical uncertainty of Rawlsian procedures is thereby averted.

The eminent domain approach also eliminates the need to resort to hypothetical persons with incomplete personal knowledge. All persons are treated as their own masters, who are entitled to the full benefits of their natural talents and abilities. When a person takes possession of that which was previously unowned, he does not do so both as an agent for himself *and* as trustee for all other persons with claims upon him. He does so only for himself. In contrast, the Rawlsian approach regards the distribution of original talents (and hence the gains derived from their application) as morally arbitrary, the product of luck, and thus worthy of no protection. The opposition to Locke's view that each person owns his own labor cannot be more vivid.

Rawls's position has none of the operational simplicity of Locke's, but instead gives each person a lien upon the product of every other person, so that the personal destinies of all persons, present and future, are forever intertwined. His position forces upon every individual obligations that run contrary to biological instincts of egoism, whereby some special genetic linkage, such as parent to child, helps explain why one person takes into account another's gain or loss. The strong opposition between obligations within the family and within society at large is largely suppressed in Rawls's picture of human obligation. It is as if every person enjoyed the fruits of his own labor by leave of some central authority, so taxation becomes no longer a charge on individual wealth for supplying public goods but an efficient means for the state to reclaim the

product of human talents that it already owns as trustee for the public at large. This conception strikes at the very heart of personal self-definition and individual self-expression. It presupposes the kind of detachment from, and impartiality toward, self that no human being emerging from his evolutionary past of remorseless self-interest can hope to achieve.[17] Each person becomes so enmeshed in the affairs of others that even heroic efforts will never get them out. The theory is advanced in the cause of freedom, but the totalitarian abuse that it risks should be evident, for what happens if the wrong people gain control of the central machinery of social control?

The problems are also economic. The Rawlsian view is that personal talents are arbitrarily distributed in nature. That observation is used to justify social efforts to correct for the original imbalance, thereby expanding the occasions for social intervention. At common law the class of individual wrongs only reaches harms inflicted by one person against another. Acts of God and of the injured person himself are outside the domain of legal rectification, either by courts or by legislatures. But once the distribution of native talents becomes a matter of social concern, then coercion is necessary to neutralize natural differences attributable to the luck of the draw. In principle, social intervention will now be routinely justified to correct for acts of God, that is, for all harms caused by natural events, running the gamut from birth defects to injury by lightning, and even some forms of self-inflicted harm, at least if not deliberately caused. On either view, the scope of legitimate government actions is expanded enormously, without any clear indication of their form or content. It is quite impossible to say that rectification of acts of God requires the return to some status quo ante, because there is no benchmark to return to. Before the levels of overall compensation are set, there must be some assurance that the resources are there to allow the transfers to take place, for it is no longer enough to say that where the defendant wrongdoer is insolvent the matter comes to an end. There need not be any wrongdoer in the sense that the private law uses that term; all assets are held in social solution, even if in possession of those who claim to be their natural owners.

This collectivization of risk in turn leads to the very types of managerial problems that well-functioning markets seek to avoid. If an individual does not own himself, then there is a classic agency-cost question, because he must bear all the costs of his own labor while retaining only some portion of the gain. When everyone perceives the conflict between production and yield, the problems become additive. If individual misfortune is socialized, then some common pool must be formed to determine what fraction of each risk each person must bear. This pooling is designed to remove arbitrary individual differences that are distasteful to risk-averse parties. But the diversification of this risk comes at a very high cost. Transactional freedom is reduced because no one has clear title to anything that he wishes to purchase or sell, so property rights remain ill defined over time. The system downplays the natural, if imperfect, form of risk pooling provided by family and religious units.

The system also tends to cut against the formation of voluntary insurance markets. In the effort to control the problems of adverse selection (that is, only a small number of self-selected people being part of the insurance pool) the system increases the risks of moral hazard – the tendency of individuals to take steps to reduce their share of the total burden while keeping their full share of the benefits. The lesson derived from the development of natural resources is that pooling should be undertaken only when that solution is dictated by the nature of the resource. Where individual property rights can be well defined, pooling should be avoided – hence the difference between land and oil. The Rawlsian instinct runs the opposite way. Every thing is thrown into a common pool, even though the natural limits of the human body make it an ideal candidate for individual ownership, which the classical liberal theories provide.

The dangers of totalitarian excess become greater because of the built-in justifications for extensive social control. The creation of collective enterprises where none existed before does not eliminate self-interest; it only finds new and destructive avenues of expression. Individuals blessed with natural talents will seek to conceal them to escape the taxation or external controls that are the concrete expressions of the social lien.

Their conduct offers an ironclad justification for other persons to monitor their "personal" affairs, which can never be wholly personal because they always involve the use and deployment of collective goods, to wit, unearned individual talents. The Rawlsian system is designed to yield fairer distributions, but if it takes people as they are, then the price is paid in the enormous shrinkage of the pie, which goes along with the implicit truncation of any sense of individual responsibility and self-worth, the indispensable glue of any social order. Why opt for a system of cross-ownership of persons? The Lockean creed of individual ownership of individual labor is a far simpler and more profound starting point. When meshed with a system of forced exchanges, it gives a far more consistent and well-ordered vision of both government and society.

All of this is not to say that the eminent domain approach does not incorporate elements of Rawlsian theory. Determining implicit in-kind compensation often turns on whether parties lie behind a veil of ignorance. With Rawls the veil is a construct, but under the eminent domain clause it is a simple fact of life, and the doubts about hypothetical constructs disappear. Concrete individuals are free to seek their own self-interest with whatever vigor they possess. But there are certain general rules (as with tort liability), which in the future are as apt to help as to hurt them, in the same proportions that they help or hurt others in society. Acting out of self-interest, the individual will maximize the wealth of the whole because that is the best way to maximize his own slice of the pie.

Second, the difference principle bears a close kinship to the disproportionate impact test, sometimes called the equal protection dimension of the eminent domain clause. Within Rawls's system the difference principle is a way of judging the soundness of institutional arrangements by improving the position of the worst off in society. Yet the difference principle works far better when it is moored to a system of Lockean entitlements, where it sorts out permissible from impermissible forced exchanges. The object of the rule is to move everyone to a more valuable set of fixed rights. Where the increase in wealth is accompanied by a radical shift in shares, compensation is required to ensure that all participate evenly in the social gains, so that wealth orderings are left unaffected by collective action. In contrast, Rawls's difference principle tends to compress the distribution of wealth and other benefits, compromising the position of the well-off for the benefit of the less fortunate. The redistributive element in the difference principle is plain. Yet one can invoke (as Rawls indeed does) ideas of insurance and risk aversion to suggest that, ex ante, all will accept that arrangement because when everyone is behind the veil of ignorance the gains of extreme success are smaller than the losses of great privation. But the benefits of the bedrock foundation of personal autonomy and private property remain secure, as it is far easier to work transformations with an existing baseline than without one. Risk aversion still remains relevant because it requires a downward evaluation of compensation packages that contain contingent benefits and a more favorable attitude to government actions that substitute fixed payouts for uncertain ones. Nonetheless, risk aversion is still only one element in the package, not the package itself.

Civic virtue

A final critique of the eminent domain theory comes from a very different quarter. It is often said that a theory that stresses the importance of private property and the fragility of government institutions ignores the role of civic virtue – devotion to public service, protection of the weak, advancement of the arts, participation in public life – which is central to understanding the highest aspirations of political life.[18] To be sure, there is something wrong with a view of the world that treats the renunciation of force and fraud as the noblest of human endeavors. Music, art, literature, science, and humanitarian endeavors speak eloquently against such a view. But civic virtue in public affairs is akin to happiness in private affairs. To make it the direct end of human conduct is to guarantee that it will not be obtained. Discreet indirection becomes the order of the day. As personal happiness is the by-product of a rich and productive life, so civic virtue is the by-product of sound institutional arrangements. The eminent domain approach works toward civic virtue, not by trumpeting its evident goodness, but by creating a sound institutional environment where it can flourish.

Consider the point that virtue and poverty do not go well together. Persons who are pressed to the edge of subsistence cannot render aid to others. Hunger breeds fear; fear breeds aggression; aggression, conflict; and conflict, civil disorder and decay. Civic virtue, then, depends upon sufficient personal liberty, security, and wealth to keep most people far from the thin edge. What set of institutions will tend to guarantee these political conditions? The first is the facilitation of voluntary transactions, which are generally positive-sum games, because people deal only with their own property. The second is control of legislatures, which have a propensity for negative-sum games because they allow people to deal in the property of others. To speak of the protection of markets is not to speak of unlicensed liberty to act as one pleases. At the very least, the ordinary law of contract rules out all forms of force, duress, misrepresentation, and sharp practice. Contract law forbids many things, and its commands are not easy to comply with, judging from the frequency of their violation. Nor is it necessary to license every voluntary transaction: the antitrust laws find their most powerful voice in preventing voluntary transactions with negative social yields, such as monopoly. Similarly, to speak of the dangers of legislation is not to condemn all legislative practices, for there are public goods that private markets cannot provide, such as police, highways, and regulation of common pool resources.

Civic virtue will be under constant siege if factions have free rein in the public arena. Those who possess civic virtue must constantly fend off initiatives, such as endless farm subsidies or import protection, that should be ruled out of bounds at the start. When the virtuous people fail, they are bound to feel cynical: why shouldn't I get mine too? Degenerative noncooperative games emerge in which everyone is a net loser. It is a subdued version of the war of all against all, transformed into a more genteel, but still destructive, game in a different arena. In such a world everyone can plausibly claim that he should get his because everyone else has, or will, get his too. How can civic virtue survive persistent temptation? The bad will drive out the good in a Gresham's law of political life.

The only way to foster virtue is to reduce the opportunities for illicit gains from legislative intrigue. Civic virtue can emerge in private charitable behavior. It can emerge in responsible participation in the provision of public goods – deciding how much should be spent on defense, highways, and courts or when war should be declared or peace negotiated – matters which cannot, by any stretch of the imagination, be regulated by the eminent domain clause. Civic virtue does not prosper in a world in which courts refuse to protect either personal autonomy or property rights. The eminent domain clause thus improves the soil from which civic virtue can grow. It controls abuse by demanding that losers in the legislative process retain rights that leave them as well off as they were before.

Past injustices

Thus far the theory has talked about the principle of eminent domain against rival conceptions of political order. But it may be said that the theory is incomplete because it does not account for prior injustices in the distribution of rights. These prior errors undermine all present entitlements, even if sound normative theory protects private property while allowing forced exchanges. Much of the current stores of wealth were acquired by improper means, and these imperfections necessarily infect the system as it now stands. To insist that the game now be played straight (which assumes, rightly, that we know how to play it straight) is to entrench for all time the present imperfections. Since the preconditions of the normative theory are not met, the theory must be rejected no matter what strength it has on the blank slate, the state of nature.

This argument stands in opposition to the parallel problem [. . .] on welfare rights, where the question was whether the power of embedded expectations was so great that one could not undo, especially by constitutional means, the social legislation of the New Deal and beyond, no matter how infirm its constitutional foundations. Nonetheless, there is a curious reversal, as the present argument places the claims of original justice above those of subsequent reliance on the current order. Yet the question has no conclusive answer.

One way to approach the argument, is to consider its principled analogy within the framework of the private law: the problem of *ius tertii*.[19] In the simplest case A owns property, which is then taken by B. C then takes the property from B. The question is whether the infirmity in B's title is sufficient to defeat his action to recover possession of the thing from C. The common law answer is no. Note what happens if the rule is otherwise. If B cannot recover from C, there is no way to prevent C taking the thing from B in the first place. Yet C secures no title hence he cannot prevent D from taking the thing from him. Denying B's action has the unhappy consequence that once the possession of property deviates from the proper chain of title, it must forever remain beyond the pale of private ownership. The common pool problem that the law tries to avoid is now created with a vengeance. The consequences for economic development and social peace are easy to envision, given that it is impossible to make productive use of an ever-increasing fraction of resources.

The doctrine of *relative title*, then, is the common law response to the problem. B by his wrong has title superior to all the world save A and those persons who claim through A. Let C, a stranger, take B's property, and B may recover it or its proceeds. Yet both of these actions may be trumped by A, either by a suit against B or a direct action against the party in possession. Nor does the story end here. B may die and leave his cause of action to D. C may die and leave his property to E. To the extent of assets descended, D has a cause of action against E, as the relative title extends across persons and across generations.

Still, A or his successors cannot always have the right of action. With property titles as with contract claims, some statute of limitations is needed to wipe ancient titles off the books. As the classical article on adverse possession notes,[20] barring old valid claims is the price worth paying to protect valid titles against ceaseless attack. The social gains from forcing quick resolution of disputes are so enormous that everyone is better off with the limitation than without it. The abrogation of property rights by these statutes is fully and easily justified by the theories of implicit in-kind compensation already discussed. The private law can specify the consequences of wrongful conduct, chiefly by drawing a radical distinction between the claims of the original owner and those of the rest of the world: flawed possession counts for naught against the owner but is dispositive against the world. Once the flawed title is cleared by a statute of limitations, the normal process of mutually beneficial transactions can improve everyone's lot, notwithstanding the initial deviation from the ideal position.

As befits the subject, this theory can be carried into the public domain. Statutes of limitation may cut off (by our principle of summation) all claims for compensation demanded by one group for the property that was taken from another group. The fact that property was taken from the Indians, for example, affords no principled reason why the property should be redistributed from the present owners to the non-Indian poor. But the question is usually not so simple, for it must be asked whether each individual claimant is in the position of A, the original owner, or of C, the stranger to the title. The factual question may often prove intractable, as some of the claimants will be descendants of original owners, and others will be strangers, and still others a bit of both. Sorting out the claims introduces both administrative and error costs that come quickly to dominate the analysis. The doctrines of adverse possession and *ius tertii* depend upon being able to trace benefits and burdens across generations. There have been, in fact, so many false steps between the original error and the current position that it is quite impossible to go back and do things right, just as it is impossible to undo a system of Social Security after it has been in effect for fifty years. Any such efforts could well generate more errors than they eliminate. Can everyone claim to be the victim and not the perpetrator of improper government action? Efforts to sort out individual claims are wholly unpersuasive. Categorical efforts, those to assist blacks because of slavery and Indians because of dispossession, are likewise met with very powerful obstacles. Should other claimants be admitted to the list, given the vast amount of unjust regulation that falls short of total confiscation? Is it worth reducing total wealth, including that held by innocent parties, in an effort to run a compensation scheme that is sure to go awry if it is ever implemented?

Consider the practical obstacles to trying the large claims on their merits. It is not easy to figure out where the injured parties would have been if they had not been harmed in the first place. Is life in America for the descendants of slaves worse than life in Africa? Would migration have taken place on other and better terms? Would the Indian tribes subdued by the United States have been slaughtered by rivals, as happened in many tribal wars? If a cause of action can be established, what is the remedy? Is it possible to restore the property taken when it cannot be identified and when it has been improved by good-faith purchasers who reasonably believed that their claims were incontestable? Do we limit recoveries to damages? From whom and in what amount? Should some setoff be given for payments under government welfare programs, which were perhaps designed to offset these past injustices? How much have blacks, disadvantaged by slavery, received by block grants or welfare payments or private charitable actions? What about the efforts of the federal government on behalf of, or against, Indians? No one could ever get the information to answer these questions if they were litigated under the set of applicable private law rules, aggregated over all individuals.

Not only is the baseline of rights insecure, but the source of the compensation is likewise problematic. One can say that the burdens of compensation all fall on the state, but this only conceals the persistent problem that the state must tax (and hence take) from individuals who have no direct responsibility for past wrongs. Many Americans reached this country after the abolition of slavery, in the great migrations from Eastern Europe between 1880 and 1920, for example. Many who were here earlier fought and gave their lives to abolish slavery. The costs of undoing the past are greater than the cost of trying to reshape the future. It may be possible to take limited steps at feasible cost to rectify the greatest abuse. Doing this would be more easily justified in a country that has been plagued with recent caste discrimination or apartheid than in our own. My own judgment is that any effort to use massive social transfers to right past wrongs will create far more tensions than it is worth, so treating all errors as a giant wash is the best of a bad lot. In contrast to my stand on welfare rights, I would give zero weight to the reliance claims of those who want to maintain a system of caste or segregation. But it is best to recognize the limits of any principle of rectification and to set about building from the base we have instead of trying to reconstruct its foundations anew.

We have thus come a complete circle. It is possible, both as a matter of constitutional law and political theory, to articulate common conceptions of right and wrong to resolve disputes that individuals have with each other and with the state. These principles do not rest upon any single value but seek to merge the three dominant strands of thought – libertarian, utilitarian, and even redistributive – into a coherent theory of individual rights and political obligations. The difficulties that remain are factual, given the complexity of our history and the legal institutions we have organized. As constructed, this argument about the eminent domain clause provides a decisive linkage between private property and public law. The received judicial wisdom about the linkage recognizes all the important parts of the picture but combines them in ways that are indefensible to anyone who is seriously concerned with either private property or limited government. The extensive discussion of the decided cases is designed to show how to reconstruct the link between individual rights and political institutions in order to demonstrate the intellectual and cultural unity of private and public law.

Notes

1   It is precisely on this view that limited liability has been often attacked as an anomaly. Within the framework of a liberty-based analysis, there is no particular difficulty with the position of contract claimants, for the agreement to reach only corporate assets in satisfaction of a claim is no more problematic than a nonrecourse mortgage which limits the mortgagee's rights of collection only to the subject property. Tort claims are a very different matter. Here the legitimation of the corporate form is best understood as a set of complex forced exchanges. As a quid pro quo for limited liability, a corporation can be properly compelled to have liability insurance to meet its anticipated risks. And more generally, without limited liability no one could venture into any pooled investment, given the general rules of agency that hold all investors responsible for the actions of their employees. Limited liability thus channels

suits for and against responsible parties, reducing transaction costs. Given its general nature and the positive welfare effects, it is very easy to conclude that limited liability meets the standards for implicit in-kind compensation.

2   The insistence upon subjective preferences is developed in Frank I. Michelman, "Ethics, Economics and the Law of Property," in *Ethics, Economics, and the Law* 3 (J. Roland Pennock and John W. Chapman eds.) (NOMOS Monograph No. 24, 1982), but is forcefully criticized by Harold Demsetz, "Professor Michelman's Unnecessary and Futile Search for the Philosopher's Touchstone," id. at 41.

3   In principle one could argue that judges do not need absolute immunity, but that they should be liable when they act beyond their jurisdiction or with malice. Yet the dangers of that are great, because any disappointed litigant could seize on some exception. For this reason absolute immunity has remained inviolate even under statutes, such as Section 1983 of the Civil Rights Act, which on their face seem to subject judges to suit for decisions that wrongly award the property of A to B. See *Pierson v. Ray*, 386 US 547 (1967). For my views on the relationship between official immunity to private suit and other forms of control of judicial abuse, see Richard A. Epstein, "Private-Law Models for Official Immunity," 1978 *Law and Contemp. Probs.* 53.

4   See *Coppage v. Kansas*, 236 US 1 (1915).

5   See Robert Nozick, *Anarchy, State, and Utopia*, ch. 7 (1974).

6   For a deeper exploration of the theme, see Richard A. Epstein, "Possession as the Root of Title," 13 *Ga. L. Rev.* 1221 (1979).

7   The question of slavery by contract is far more difficult, but two points do stand out. First, the illustrations of it in practice are so infrequent that one can doubt whether it ever comes about except by force or fraud. Even indentured servant contracts were of limited duration and imposed special duties upon the master. Second, and less often noticed, slaves also bargain away the rights of their offspring and thus are in breach of their natural obligations. Third, slavery has a corrosive effect on individual participation in public governance. None of these points is decisive, and each has counterexamples, but their combined weight supports the view that everyone is better off, ex ante, if slavery is banned altogether, as the theory of forced exchanges and implicit in-kind compensation allows.

8   Donald Wittman, "Liability for Harm or Restitution for Benefit?" 13 *J. Legal Stud.* 57 (1984).

9   See John Gray, "Indirect Utility and Fundamental Rights," 1 *Soc. Phil. and Pol.* 73 (1984).

10 Nozick, supra note 5, at 12–25.

11 John Rawls, *A Theory of Justice* (1971).

12 See Ronald Dworkin, "The Original Position," 40 *U. Chi. L. Rev* 500 (1973).

13 Thomas Hobbes, *Leviathan*, ch. 15 (1651).

14 Rawls, supra note 11, at 270–4.

15 Nozick, supra note 5, at 204–13.

16 For development, see Richard A. Epstein, "Intentional Harms," 4 *J. Legal Stud.* 391, 421–2 (1975), which deals with the question of *damnum absque iniuria* – harm without legal injury – which was the common law technique of restricting compensable harms so that all purposive human conduct does not become actionable.

17 See, generally, Jack Hirschleifer, "Economics from a Biological Viewpoint," 20 *J. Law & Econ.* 1 (1977). For my views, see Richard A. Epstein, "A Taste for Privacy? Evolution and the Emergence of a Naturalistic Ethic," 9 *J. Legal Stud.* 665 (1980). "One central contribution of sociobiology to economics lies in demonstrating that tastes themselves are governed by discernible principles, and that self-interest, far from being merely an economic premise, is in the guise of inclusive fitness a biological conclusion." Id. at 679.

18 See, e.g., Frank I. Michelman, "Politics and Values or What's Really Wrong with Rationality Review?" 13 *Creighton L. Rev.* 487 (1979). Frank I. Michelman, "Property as a Constitutional Right," 38 *Washington & Lee Law Rev.* 1097 (1981); Carol Rose, "*Mahon* Reconstructed: Or Why the Takings Issue Is Still a Muddle" 57 *So. Cal. L. Rev.* 561 (1984).

19 See, e.g., F. Pollock and R. Wright, *Possession in the Common Law* 91–3 (1888); The Winkfield [1902], p. 42.

20 Henry Ballantine, "Title by Adverse Possession," 32 *Harv. L. Rev.* 135 (1918). "The statute [of limitations in adverse possession cases] has not for its object to reward the diligent trespasser for his wrong nor yet to penalize the negligent and dormant owner for sleeping upon his rights; the great purpose is automatically to quiet all titles which are openly and consistently asserted, to provide proof of meritorious titles, and correct errors in conveyancing." In other words, good titles can be protected against false claims of prior ownership only if bad claims are so protected as well.

27

The Social Structure of Japanese Intellectual Property Law

Dan Rosen and Chikako Usui

I. Introduction

In a documentary entitled "The Japanese Version,"[1] the film-makers introduce us to a bar in Tokyo. The bar is dedicated to American cowboy culture. Western memorabilia hang on the walls; country and western music plays on the loudspeakers; and classic films play on video monitors. One customer in the bar, a dentist, regularly dresses like a character out of a Hoot Gibson movie. When asked why American Westerns are so popular in Japan, he answers without hesitation. The cowboy represents traditional Japanese society, the dentist says. Whenever there's trouble, the cowboys all gather together into a group and take care of each other's interests, just like people in Japan.

Of course, in America, the cowboy is the quintessential individualist, roaming the prairies alone and living by his own rules. Like the Lone Ranger, he rides into town, confronts evil, and then rides off into the sunset.

If both Japanese and Americans see an image as well-defined as the American cowboy so differently, it should come as no surprise that they also see intellectual property very differently.[2]

To say that Japan is a group-oriented culture and America is an individualistic one is a cliché, but there is enough truth in the stereotypes to retain them despite the exceptions that can be found. With intellectual property, as with American Westerns, what you see depends on who you are.

In general, the intellectual property world is divided along two axes: (1) importing versus exporting nations, and (2) private enterprise versus non-market economies. On both of these scales, one would expect Japan to be a strong proponent of patent, trademark, and copyright laws. In the US, six of the top ten companies receiving patents are Japanese.[3] In Germany, as well, Japanese companies constitute the most prominent foreign applicants for patents, having applied for 2,910 in 1992, compared with 1,139 applications from American companies.[4] Japanese companies benefit greatly from trademark laws that prevent others from calling their cars "Honda Accord" or tape players "Sony Walkman." And although Japanese artistic works do not command worldwide audiences (because of the lack of knowledge of the Japanese language, not because of quality), Japanese corporations now

Dan Rosen and Chikako Usui, "The Social Structure of Japanese Intellectual Property Law," *UCLA Pacific Basin Law Journal*, vol. 13, Fall 1994, pp. 32–8, 69. © 1994. Reprinted with permission from the authors.

export music and movies through their acquisition of American companies such as Columbia (Sony) and MCA (Matsushita), as well as the European EMI (Toshiba).

So, by all conventional measures, Japan should be a bastion of protection for intellectual property. And yet, compared with many Western countries and particularly the United States, the Japanese version of intellectual property law is porous and the attitude is often ambivalent. The roots of this lie in social attitudes towards the role of individuals within a society, interlocking relationships, the speed of progress, and interaction with outside entities. The argument put forward here is not that culture causes legal form, but rather that the law can best be understood as part of a much larger social system. This article will follow the threads of Japanese sociological thought and how they wind their way through patent, trade secret, trademark, and copyright.

II. Traditional Japanese Thought and the Role of Intellectual Property

In the United States, the copyright clause to the Constitution reveals the purpose of intellectual property law: "To promote the Progress of Science and the useful Arts, by securing for limited Times to Authors and Inventors the exclusive Right to their respective Writings and Discoveries."[5] Copyright is a social bribe, or at least a payoff. We promise to give the artists or inventors the sole ability to make money from their work[6] to encourage them to continue producing.[7] In a system predicated on private gain, such an incentive seems not only appropriate, but also necessary. Without it, the fear is that talented people would select other ways to use their skills – ways in which they could maximize their own economic rewards.

In contrast, Japan's copyright law reveals a balancing of interests between individual inventors and society. Rather than securing exclusive rights, the law's purpose "is to prescribe the rights of authors."[8] Unlike American patent and copyright law, which assumes exclusive rights from the outset, Japanese copyright law speaks of "promot[ing] the protection of the rights of authors, etc., giving consideration to

a fair exploitation of these cultural products, and thereby . . . contributing to the development of culture."[9]

In America, the most scarred battlefield of copyright law is the fair use doctrine. Section 107 of the Copyright Act attempts to consider the interests of the public within the context of the author's exclusive rights, but it does so in a hesitant and, at best, Delphic manner. A variety of factors are to be considered, none of which is talismanic.[10] Wars over photocopying,[11] home videorecording,[12] and getting a scoop on the memoirs of an ex-President have been waged over the interpretation of these factors.[13] The law assumes that the private right of the copyright holder prevails unless the would-be copier can show a strong reason to be allowed a "free ride." In most fair use disputes, neither the plaintiff nor the defendant can be sanguine about the outcome.[14]

Japan takes a very different approach: simple and direct – one that prescribes the rights of authors and defines a fair exploitation. A copyrighted work "may be reproduced by a user for the purpose of his personal use, family use, or other use similar thereto within a limited area. . . ."[15] Japan does not make the interest of the public an exception to copyright; it includes the public interest in the allocation of rights. Article 33 further clarifies this "public welfare" idea. Article 33 provides publishers of government-approved school textbooks an absolute right to copy copyrighted material "for the use of children or pupils in their education in primary schools, junior and senior high schools or other similar schools."[16] The Commissioner of the Agency for Cultural Affairs then fixes an appropriate amount of payment for the use. In American copyright parlance, this is known as a compulsory license.[17] What is crucial here is that the ability to use the material is never in doubt because the public purpose is compelling.[18]

This illustrates a more general point that Japanese copyright law, like Japanese society, considers the interaction of individuals and the society simultaneously and values the correlative responsibilities at least as highly as the individual rights. American copyright law, like American society, begins with the premise that the whole prospers by giving as much protection to the individual as possible.[19]

The origins of this theme may be found in Chinese Confucianism which even today exerts a strong (if perhaps silent) influence on Japanese society. Confucianism posits a good society by mutual consideration of the needs of others. I take care of your needs; you take care of mine.[20] American thought is dominated by looking out for oneself. "Look out for number one." "Every man for himself." "It's a dog eat dog world." These are not idle proverbs.

Several writers, most notably Robert Whiting, have noted how this cultural difference affects the playing of America's national pastime in Japan. American players are accustomed to doing their best, and, by doing so, helping the entire team. The Japanese train their players to work incrementally for the progress of the team, each person sacrificing his personal goals (such as more home runs) to the immediate team objectives (bunt).[21] . . .

Takeo Doi's book, *The Anatomy of Dependence*,[22] is so often cited for this proposition that perhaps no more elaboration is necessary. Unfortunately, the translation of the title of his work obscures Doi's point that the Japanese are trained from birth to rely on others rather than to operate independently. The Japanese word in question is *amaeru*. It is not simply dependence, but rather interdependence – an elaborate interlocking system in which people look to one another (often as a kind of surrogate family) to have their needs fulfilled while they, in turn, fulfill the needs of others.

What bedevils many Western nations is that Japan's economy operates this way as well. It is an oversimplification to say that American antitrust law discourages the conglomeration of corporate power while Japanese law encourages it,[23] but not much of one.[24] Banks all offer the same services at the same cost, despite ongoing deregulation.[25] A taxi company in Kyoto recently incurred the wrath of all of its competitors by lowering prices by ten percent at a time when the others wanted a rate increase. The government gave permission to offer the discount as an experiment. The government also regulates the prices of airline flights in Japan. Prices are higher than in the US, and business has been bad in recent years, but the quality of service is high.[26]

Shigenori Matsui has described succinctly the difference between the American and the Japanese views of uniformity and unbridled competition. "Whereas in the United States the governmental regulation tends to be deemed justified only where the market failure or malfunction exists, it tends to be deemed justified in Japan even when no market failure or malfunction exists. . . . The role of the Government as a promoter and protector of the economy has long been accepted in Japan."[27]

Until quite recently, most Japanese corporations followed the lead of the Ministry of International Trade and Industry ("MITI"), in setting their goals. MITI set these goals by instigating interaction between corporate players, rather than by passing down Stalinistic decrees.[28] John Haley has called this process of Japanese administration "consensual administrative management."[29] The government would decide generally the most beneficial direction for industry, and then "Japan Inc.," as it was called sometimes, would head in that direction together; not like the legs of the same animal, but rather like the parade of different animals all headed toward Noah's ark. Everyone would be able to get on board, but each in its own way. Those who wanted more space, or who wished to steer the boat a different way, however, would be cast overboard quickly.

Frank Upham's retelling of the tale of Sato Taiji illustrates the point. Sato, a born iconoclast, decided it would be a good idea to import gas and sell it cheaply. Good for business and good for consumers. MITI, however, saw his plan differently. In its eyes, Sato's success would undermine the carefully maintained balance of oil company profitability, employment, and stability of supply. And so, MITI, through "administrative guidance" (*gyō-sei shidō*)[30] and its network of influence throughout the economy made sure that he would be stopped.[31]

In recent years, increased trading with countries that do not share this worldview has caused some breakdown in this system. [. . .]

Notes

1 *The Japanese Version* (The Center for New American Media 1990).
2 See generally Samson Helfgott, "Cultural Differences *Between* the US and Japanese Patent Systems," 72 *J. Pat.* [& Trademark] *Off. Soc'y* 231–8 (1990).

3 "IBM Won Most US Patents in '93," *UPL*, Jan. 10, 1994. [. . .]

4 In Germany, however, domestic companies are at the top of the list. The most active applicants, in order, in 1992 were Siemens AG, Boscho (Robert) Gmbh, Bayer AG, BASF AG, IBM (US), Hoechest AG, and Canon (Japan). "Japan Tops German Patent List," *Japan Times*, Apr. 21, 1993, at 10.

5 US Const. art. I, §8, cl.8.

6 See Alfred C. Yen, "Restoring the National Law: Copyright as Labor and Possession," 51 *Ohio St. LJ* 517 (1990).

7 The other competing viewpoint, especially associated with France, provides intellectual property rights not as an incentive but rather as a recognition of the creator's dignity. See Dan Rosen, "Artists' Moral Rights: A European Evolution," 2 *Cardozo Arts & Ent. LJ* 155 (1983). Despite the theoretical aversion to the moral rights concept, it has made its way into American law, adjacent to copyright. See, e.g., Russ VerSteeg, "Moral Rights for the Visual Artist: Contract Theory and Analysis," 67 *Wash. L. Rev.* 827 (1992); Edward J. Damich, "The Visual Artists Rights Act of 1990: Toward a Federal System of Moral Rights Protection for the Visual Arts," 39 *Cath. UL Rev.* 945 (1990). See generally Carl H. Settlemeyer III, "Between Thought and Possession: 'Artists' 'Moral Rights' and Public Access to Creative Works," 81 *Geo. LJ* 2291 (1993).

8 Chosaku-ken Hō [Copyright Law], Law No. 48 of 1970, art. 1 (Japan).

9 Id.

10 *Notwithstanding the provision of sections 106 and 106A, the fair use of a copyrighted work . . . for purposes such as criticism, comment, news reporting, teaching (including multiple copies for classroom use), scholarship, or research is not an infringement of copyright. In determining whether the use made of a work in any particular case is a fair use the factors to be considered shall include –*

   1. *the purpose and character of the use, including whether such use is of a commercial nature or is for nonprofit educational purposes;*
   2. *the nature of the copyrighted work;*
   3. *the amount and substantiality of the portion used in relation to the copyrighted work as a whole; and*
   4. *the effect of the use upon the potential market for or value of the copyrighted work.*

   17 USC. §107 (1988 & Supp. IV 1992).

11 *Williams & Wilkins Co. v. United States*, 487 F.2d 1345 (Ct.Cl. 1973), aff'd by an equally divided court, 420 U.S. 376 (1975).

12 *Sony Corp. of Am. v. Universal City Studios, Inc.*, 464 U.S. 417 (1984).

13 *Harper & Row, Publishers, Inc. v. Nation Enters.*, 471 U.S. 539 (1985).

14 See, e.g., L. Ray Patterson, "Understanding Fair Use," 55 *Law & Contemp. Probs.* 249 (1992); Jay Dratler, Jr., "Distilling the Witches' Brew of Fair Use in Copyright Law," 43 *Miami L. Rev.* 233 (1988).

15 Chosaku-ken Hō, *supra* note 9, art. 30.

16 Id. art. 33.

17 Examples of compulsory license in American copyright law have included cable television retransmission of broadcast signals (17 USC §111) (1988 & Supp. IV 1992), retransmission of satellite signals to home receiving dishes (17 USC §119) (1988 & Supp. IV 1992), jukeboxes (17 USC §§116, 116A) (1988 & Supp. IV 1992) and the use of copyrighted nondramatic works by public broadcasting (17 USC §118) (1988 & Supp. IV 1992).

18 American practice, in contrast, is the product of a compromise agreement reached among publishers', authors', educators', and trade organizations. It sets numerical limits on the amount of material that can be copied for classroom use, e.g., "an excerpt from any prose work of not more than 1,000 words or 10% of the work, whichever is less, but in any event a minimum of 500 words." "Agreement on Guidelines for Classroom Copying in Not-for-Profit Educational Institutions II (ii) (b)," in *Copyright for the Nineties*, 645, 646 (Alan Latman et al. eds., 1989).

19 Recent cases to the contrary seem to result from an inability to control the technology, rather than from any redefinition of the rights of copyright holders. See generally Dan Rosen, "A Common Law for the Ages of Intellectual Property," 38 *U. Miami L. Rev.* 769 (1984).

20 Confucianism, however, frequently has been misused to justify rigid stratification and inflexible government. Some would argue that the Tokugawa shogunate in Japan adopted this approach implicitly. In seventeenth century China, it was used explicitly to strengthen the government's control. See Jonathan D. Spence, *The Search for Modern China*, 58–60 (1990).

21 Robert Whiting, *You Gotta Have Wa* (1989); Robert Whiting, *The Chrysanthemum and the Bat* (1977).

22 Takeo Doi, *The Anatomy of Dependence* (John Bester trans., 1971).

23 See generally Mitsuo Matsushita, *Introduction to Japanese Antimonopoly Law* (1990); Alex Y. Seita & Jiro Tamura, *The Historical Background of Japan's Antimonopoly Law*, 1994 *U. Ill. L. Rev.* 115 (1994).

24 See generally J. D. Richards, Comment, "Japan Fair Trade Commission Guidelines Concerning Distribution Systems and Business Practices: An Illustration of Why Antitrust Law is a Weak Solution to US Trade Problems With Japan," 2 *Wis. L. Rev.* 921 (1993).

25 For example, the Japanese subsidiary of Citibank, from the United States, is the only bank in Japan that has 24-hour automatic teller machines (ATMs).

26 Maintaining quality and guarding against the ill effects of unrestrained price competition are the main reasons given for government control of "excessive competition." See generally Daniel Okimoto, *Between MITI and the Market: Japanese Industrial Policy for High Technology* (1989). It should be noted that the airline business in the deregulated US market has been bad too, with many carriers going out of business and others struggling. See generally *Airline Deregulation: The Early Experience* (John R. Meyer & Clinton V. Oster, Jr. eds., 1981); Anthony E. Brown, *The Politics of Airline Deregulation* (1987); Steven Morrison & Clifford Winston, *The Economic Effects of Airline Deregulation* (1986).

27 Shigenori Matsui, "*Lochner v. New York* in Japan: Protecting Economic Liberties in a Country Governed by Bureaucrats," in *Law and Technology in the Pacific Community*, 199, 299 (Philip S. C. Lewis ed. 1994). Professor Matsui, however, believes that "it is more likely that the term 'excessive competition' is used as a pretext for protectionist regulation for the industry." See also J. Mark Ramseyer, "The Cost of the Consensual Myth: Antitrust Enforcement and Institutional Barriers to Litigation in Japan," 94 *Yale LJ* 604 (1985).

28 Western writers, especially, have many different interpretations of MITI's role. See, e.g., Chalmers Johnson, *MITI and the Japanese Miracle* (1982); David Friedman, *The Misunderstood Miracle: Industrial Development and Political Change in Japan* (1988).

29 John O. Haley, *Authority Without Power: Law and the Japanese Paradox*, 144 (1991).

30 See id. at 160–6 (1991).

31 MITI's network of influence throughout the economy may extend as far as China – one of Sato's shipments never made it on the ship. Frank K. Upham, "The Man Who Would Import: A Cautionary Tale About Bucking the System in Japan," 17 *J. Japanese Stud.* 323 (1991) (reviewing Sato Taiji, *Ore Wa Tsūsansho ni Barasareta! [I Was Butchered by MITI!]* (1986)).

In May of 1994, Nagoya-based Kanare Beikoku – a rice retailer – opened a discount gas station in Akomaki, Aichi prefecture, without a government license. It was said to be the first gas station in Japan to sell gas for less than ¥100 per liter. MITI refused the company's registration papers twice because it was unsatisfied with the documentation of the source of the gasoline. Eventually, in late June, MITI relented and the station received authorized status. See "Cheap Gas Fuels Debate Over Regulations," *Daily Yomiuri*, June 14, 1994, at 9; "Gas Station Gets License," *Japan Times*, July 1, 1994, at 14.

28

Historical Rights and Fair Shares

A. John Simmons

[...] There are, I think, two broadly liberal approaches to dealing with the claims and problems of groups like the Native American peoples, only one of which is historical in the sense discussed here. Some theorists treat Native Americans simply as one of a number of disadvantaged groups in our society, all of whom need to be made better off until they enjoy the social and economic rights and goods that justice demands be provided to all. Native Americans may require some special rights, based on the special vulnerability of their cultural context; but their tribes' historical standings as the original occupants of the Americas are irrelevant to their current moral claims.[1] The alternative liberal approach to this end-state view is to take seriously the historical claims of Native Americans to land and resources as the basis of persistent rights to rectification, beyond anything to which they are entitled simply as equal citizens (or persons).[2] The virtue of the historical approach, as I see it, is that it preserves the particularity of Native American claims. Their rights are not, I think, just rights to some fair share of American resources; they are rights to a particular (or a particularized) fair share. Treating Native American rights as exclusively end-state rights means denying that the actual arguments made by Native American

tribes for historical rights to particular lands and resources have any moral force at all, or any appeal beyond ungrounded emotionalism. But I do not think most of us regard Native American demands for control over portions of their historical homelands simply as unmotivated, sentimental nonsense.

It is tempting to embrace the nonhistorical, end-state view if we think that passing time and changing circumstances simply wipe out such historical rights. But I have suggested some ways in which historical rights can be sensitive to changing circumstances without simply dissolving in the face of change. I've argued that we can have genuinely historical rights whose content is nonetheless imprecise. This imprecision of content, however, does not reduce such rights to general, nonhistorical (i.e., end-state) rights to any fair share. Rather, such rights can be to particularized, though not particular, fair shares of land or resources.

These arguments enable us to defend a conception of Native American rights to rectification that preserves at least some of the particularity of the claims actually advanced in lawsuits and published arguments by (or on behalf of) Native American tribes. There is, I think, a range of acceptable rectificatory outcomes in these cases. Native

A. John Simmons, "Historical Rights and Fair Shares," *Law and Philosophy*, vol. 14, 1995, pp. 149–84. © 1995. Reprinted with permission from the author and Springer Science and Business Media.

American historical rights are to particularized shares; but the relevant entitlements were seldom made precise by any freely chosen (or otherwise responsibly accomplished) just downsizing of holdings. This means the historical rights of Native Americans are in certain ways imprecise (in addition to being exceptionally difficult to trace). But their rights are to (currently) fair portions of the actual lands they lived, hunted, and worked on, not to generic fair shares of American land. And these particularized rights are to portions of what were once their central holdings – for instance, to portions of lands they held sacred, lands on which they resided, or lands in which they invested labor through agriculture or other improvements (like ecological management). Where lands or resources within the acceptable range of particularized shares have been destroyed or irreversibly altered (by commercial development, say), the best rectification will be accomplished by returning land or goods that most closely approximate those to which Native Americans have particularized rights, or lands or goods that best facilitate duplicating the condition they would have enjoyed in the absence of the original injustice. Our counterfactual judgments in these cases should be conservative, assuming an absence of rashness and of extraordinary developments. And additional compensation for losses incurred during the changing of circumstances that required downsizing must also be considered.

It will certainly turn out that some past property injustices are simply unrectifiable. And it will certainly turn out as well that our judgments about just rectification will be fuzzy at best, complicated as they are both by evidentiary problems and by the imprecision of historical rights to shares (and of the concept of a fair share generally). The calculations required to determine even a reasonably specific range of acceptable rectificatory outcomes will be, to say the least, extraordinarily complex. But the principles noted here can at least provide some very broad guidelines for the proper way to particularize the reparations made to Native American peoples. We will always face, of course, the problems of conflicting claims by current generations of (largely) innocent third parties, those "newcomers" to the Americas whose expectations are firmly based on an assumed continuation of current distributions of land and resources. Those of us in this group are not, of course, quite like the completely innocent person who unwittingly builds his life around holdings that just turn out to have been stolen by an earlier possessor. For we all know the history of theft, broken agreements, and brutal subjugation on which our holdings in land and natural resources historically rest. But the claims of current generations of Americans must still be taken seriously. They can only be taken seriously in the right measure, however, if we first understand at least some of the force of the historical rights of Native Americans with which these claims are alleged to conflict.

Now it may seem that in these suggestions I have blithely ignored the two largest obstacles to understanding or accepting historical rights: the changes in cast that accompany long passages of time, and the dramatically different conceptions of property in fact favored by most Native American tribes. I will close this discussion with a few brief remarks on these two problems. Taking changes of cast first, there are obviously two central, relevant possibilities of this sort: those involving the death of the victim of wrongdoing and those involving the death of the wrongdoer. Both sorts of cases are complicated. When the wrongdoer dies, he may leave behind nothing that could adequately compensate his victim for the wrong, in which case rectification will simply be impossible. Where land is at issue, of course, this will generally not be the case (though we will still need to deal with the conflicting claims on the land of the children or dependents of the wrongdoer or of innocent third party holders of stolen land). But set all of this aside for now; the impossibility of full rectification in certain kinds of cases is not, I think, any more of a problem here than is the impossibility of retributive justice in cases where offenders die before they can be punished. The more troubling questions, I believe, clearly concern those cases in which the victim of wrongdoing dies. If the victim's rights die with him, of course, then Native American rights cannot possibly have persisted through the centuries in the ways my previous remarks suggested.

And why should we suppose that rights of rectification have simply been passed down family lines, from the original victims of injustice all the way to their current descendants? After all, those original victims might, in the absence of the injustice, have later sold their holdings or lost them in a poker game or given them to a needy friend, so that the relevant rights never would have passed to their children anyway. Why should inheritance of rights to rectification simply be assumed in this way,[3] particularly when we know that inherited property is the source of many apparent social injustices?[4] To this I think there are three appropriate responses. First, our counterfactual judgments about how things would have gone on in the absence of the wrong should be conservative. [. . .] Second, I think children have rights against their parents to the receipt of property (including in this "property" parental rights to the return of stolen property) that is needed by those children for a decent life; and in the case of the children of hunter-gatherers, this will invariably mean rights to use of the land and natural resources. Even if the parents did freely give away or sell the land their children needed for a decent life, then, the children would still have claims against the recipients of that land to the portions they needed.[5] Their parents were not entitled to dispose of the land without regard for the needs of their offspring. Finally, and perhaps most obviously relevant, we have the fact that the land and resources at issue were taken by Native Americans to be tribal property, not individual property.[6] If the property was thus held jointly, so were the relevant rights to rectification of injustice; and then, of course, the death of individual Native Americans was irrelevant to the question of persisting historical rights, as was the question of inheritance of rights (since the tribe as a whole never died, in at least many actual historical cases).

Now this last response may seem to solve the problem of the changing cast of characters only at the price of introducing new difficulties into our attempts to make sense of historical rights. First, there is no doubt that most Native American tribes understood the nature of their property in land and resources quite differently than, say, Locke and Nozick understand property rights. Tribes regarded themselves as inseparably connected to certain territories, so that their identities depended on continued and in some cases exclusive use of the land. Tribal ownership (or, better, stewardship) of the land was typically viewed as essential and inalienable, with ownership not so much derived from productive use as demanding productive uses that harmonized with the land.[7] And this amounts, of course, to a view of property in land which is more national than simply joint or collective. On such a conception of property in land, mandatory downsizing to make room for newcomers makes no clear sense. Newcomers may be permitted to use (nonsacred) tribal lands, but they cannot come to have any kind of property in the land that excludes tribal use.

From a Lockean historical perspective, this Native American conception of property rights will probably be viewed as in certain ways simply mistaken. Persons have rights of fair access to land and natural resources, and even a nation is not entitled to insist on control over a territory of inflexible size.[8] We must make room for everyone.[9] Native American beliefs that they need not yield to newcomers exclusive control over portions of their territories would then be viewed as a kind of nonculpable moral ignorance, an ignorance that perhaps excuses their acts of resistance to settlement of their territories, but that in no way limits the rights of fair access (and self-defense) of newcomers. The alternative (i.e., non-Lockean) historical perspectives are either conventionalist, relativizing property claims within a territory to those acknowledged by the dominant conventions in that territory,[10] or use-oriented, denying that exclusive private property in land or natural resources is possible.

But it may seem that the problems for a Lockean historical theory run still deeper. We might think, for example, that Lockeans simply can't handle joint or collective property claims at all, that all Lockean property is individual. This view, I think, is clearly confused. Joint property is certainly possible on a Lockean view.[11] Any individual property that individuals freely join together is then the (private) joint property of that collective. And further, if property acquisition turns on labor or on the incorporation of objects into purposive activities, joint property will be produced wherever objects are incorporated into collective projects. Thus, Native American tribes can certainly be supposed even on a Lockean view to have joint property in bodies of land or in natural resources. They can thus have historical rights to land or resources that can persist through time; they can have rights to the rectification of property injustices (i.e., injustices consisting in violations of those historical rights); and they can have rights that may be affected (in the ways we have discussed) by changing circumstances.

This conclusion needs two final points of clarification. First, even joint or collective property is subject to the individualistic limit set by the idea of a fair share. Collectives may hold no more property than the sum of the fair shares of their individual members.[12] And mandatory downsizing will be determined in terms of the proportionate downsizing of individual shares. Second, our Lockean conclusions about Native American tribal property cannot be derived by strict adherence to the letter of Locke's own arguments. Locke himself took Native Americans to have property only in their artifacts and in the products of their hunting and gathering. They had no property in land, for they did not use the land itself in any efficient way, as did the European settlers who enclosed and cultivated portions of the earth. Thus, for Locke there was no question of required reparations for encroachments on tribal lands, for those lands constituted vacant waste still awaiting original appropriation.[13]

If, though, we take seriously the idea that property can be acquired by incorporation into our purposive activities, then the collective tribal activities of hunting, fishing, migratory residence, nonsedentary agriculture, and the like, could certainly have grounded tribal property rights in land and resources. But while Locke may have been wrong on that point, he was certainly right about the inefficiency of aboriginal land use, at least in this one sense – there is not enough land in the world to support us all at the population density levels characteristic of original Native American tribal life. Even if hunting and gathering remain legitimate sources of property in land, the fair shares of land available for exclusive use by hunter-gatherers must be far smaller than those originally occupied by aboriginal Americans. Thus, mandatory downsizing enters our theory even if we reject Locke's assumptions about which activities constituted productive (hence, appropriative) uses of the land.

We are left, then, with a characteristically liberal idea, one that we can now see is embraced by both purely historical and purely end-state theories of property rights and social justice (and so, we can surmise, one that will be embraced by any hybrid theory as well). Justice cares about insuring to all persons (access to) their fair share of goods and resources; it cares far less about the manner in which persons use these goods to advance their life plans and particular projects, or in the perceived virtues of those plans or projects themselves.

Notes

1 This is roughly the approach taken by Will Kymlicka in *Liberalism, Community, and Culture* (Oxford: Oxford University Press, 1989). See especially the long footnote on pp. 158–61 in which Kymlicka expresses scepticism about the moral importance of "the fact of original occupancy." Lyons also concludes that "it is highly doubtful that [Native Americans] have any special claims based upon their distant ancestors' original occupation of the land" ("The New Indian Claims . . .": 268). Waldron seems sympathetic to this approach as well ("Superseding Historic Injustice": 26–8).
2 A good recent example of this approach can be found in James Tully, "Rediscovering America: the *Two Treatises* and Aboriginal Rights," in *An Approach to Political Philosophy: Locke in Contexts* (Cambridge: Cambridge University Press, 1993).
3 Waldron, "Superseding Historic Injustice": 15.
4 Lyons, "The New Indian Claims . . .": 258.
5 I discuss this view in *The Lockean Theory of Rights*, pp. 204–12.
6 Waldron, "Superseding Historic Injustice": 15; Lyons, "The New Indian Claims . . .": 257.
7 Tully, "Rediscovering America," pp. 138, 153–4. This view of property thus had more in common with pre-Lockean (than with Lockean) European conceptions of property, according to which land was sometimes taken to define the family that possessed it and consequently to be inalienable for that family.
8 Locke himself regarded national territories as set by understandings or contracts (treaties) between nations, in which members of each society give up rights of fair access to land within the agreed-upon boundaries of other societies (*Second Treatise*, §45). But it is unclear why such agreements should be taken to bind or protect (a) new

residents of these societies (prior to their consenting to membership); (b) individuals in the state of nature (such as Locke imagined Native Americans to be); or (c) nations that lack this understanding or were not otherwise party to any tacit or express agreements concerning national territory. Locke could, of course, have tried recognizing the Native American nations as genuine political societies, and then placed them with the nations in group (c), thus justifying appropriation of their territories by European settlers. But this would have entailed that those same Native Americans were free to appropriate European territory. It was thus safer from Locke's perspective (which included his desire to defend European settlement of the Americans) to place Native Americans in class (b), as Locke in fact did.

9   This implication for national property is one of the least discussed features of historical rights theories. A Lockean alternative is to view the right of fair access as a right of access not to land and natural resources, but to the means for living a decent life. This right of fair access might, then, in developed societies entail, not rights to land for newcomers, but rights to wealth or to nonalienating opportunities for paid employment. See *The Lockean Theory of Rights*, pp. 293–4.

10 The Lockean view "naturalizes" property rights, I think, precisely to avoid such conventionalism. For if property rests simply on social convention, our property cannot be secure, given the possibility of simple alterations in social convention. The Lockean has to argue that while agreements between persons or within groups may change property relations between those involved, such agreements cannot change the rights of those not party to the agreements – such as white settlers, who could insist, on natural moral grounds, on their rights of fair access to land and resources.

11 Indeed, national territory is for Locke in one sense all joint, for though it is composed of private land holdings, this private land is "united" to the commonwealth (*Second Treatise*, §120). And the commons within each nation's boundaries is the pure joint property of all the nation's members (ibid., §35). On the acquisition of collective property in Pufendorf and Locke, see my "Original Acquisition Theories," section III.

12 The truth of this claim rests on (at least) three assumptions. First, of course, I assume that collectives are the kinds of things that can possess rights. Second, I assume no insuperable difficulties are introduced by the changing composition of the collectives. Third, I assume that members of a collective may hold in trust the rights to fair shares of other members who have been wrongfully killed or who have died after being unjustly deprived of their shares. Thus, we cannot reduce the fair share of a tribe by killing off its members or by stealing their land and waiting for them to die off. Tribes are entitled to hold shares in trust for future members under such circumstances (for some reasonable time period, at least), just as family members are entitled to do in cases of joint familial property. Morris has objected to the second of these assumptions by suggesting that since the collective will have "radically different" histories in the possible worlds containing and not containing the injustice, the actual and the possible collectives cannot be identical ("Existential Limits": 181). But here, unlike the case of individuals conceived after the injustice, the identity of the group across possible worlds can be supported by continuity with the previous (i.e., pre-injustice) history of the group in all similar worlds. Even more obviously, the "counterpart relation" (that can be used instead of identity in such cases) can be supported by that same previous history.

13 Tully, "Rediscovering America," pp. 148, 162.

29

International News Service v. Associated Press (1918)

Mr Justice Pitney delivered the opinion of the court.

The parties are competitors in the gathering and distribution of news and its publication for profit in newspapers throughout the United States. The Associated Press, which was complainant in the District Court, is a cooperative organization, incorporated under the Membership Corporations Law of the State of New York, its members being individuals who are either proprietors or representatives of about 950 daily newspapers published in all parts of the United States. . . .

Complainant gathers in all parts of the world, by means of various instrumentalities of its own, by exchange with its members, and by other appropriate means, news and intelligence of current and recent events of interest to newspaper readers and distributes it daily to its members for publication in their newspapers. The cost of the service, amounting approximately to $3,500,000 per annum, is assessed upon the members and becomes a part of their costs of operation, to be recouped, presumably with profit, through the publication of their several newspapers. Under complainant's by-laws each member agrees upon assuming membership that news received through complainant's service is received exclusively for publication in a particular newspaper, language, and place specified in the certificate of membership, that no other use of it shall be permitted, and that no member shall furnish or permit anyone in his employ or connected with his newspaper to furnish any of complainant's news in advance of publication to any person not a member. And each member is required to gather the local news of his district and supply it to the Associated Press and to no one else.

Defendant is a corporation organized under the laws of the State of New Jersey, whose business is the gathering and selling of news to its customers and clients, consisting of newspapers published throughout the United States, under contracts by which they pay certain amounts at stated times for defendant's service. It has wide-spread news-gathering agencies; the cost of its operations amounts, it is said, to more than $2,000,000 per annum; and it serves about 400 newspapers located in the various cities of the United States and abroad, a few of which are represented, also, in the membership of the Associated Press.

The parties are in the keenest competition between themselves in the distribution of news throughout the United States; and so, as a rule, are the newspapers that they serve, in their several districts.

International New Service v. Associated Press, Supreme Court of the United States (1918), 248 U.S. 215.

Complainant in its bill, defendant in its answer, have set forth in almost identical terms the rather obvious circumstances and conditions under which their business is conducted. The value of the service and of the news furnished, depends upon the promptness of transmission, as well as upon the accuracy and impartiality of the news; it being essential that the news be transmitted to members or subscribers as early [as] or earlier than similar information can be furnished to competing newspapers by other news services, and that the news furnished by each agency shall not be furnished to newspapers which do not contribute to the expense of gathering it. And further, to quote from the answer: "Prompt knowledge and publication of worldwide news is essential to the conduct of a modern newspaper, and by reason of the enormous expense incident to the gathering and distribution of such news, the only practical way in which a proprietor of a newspaper can obtain the same is, either through cooperation with a considerable number of other newspaper proprietors in the work of collecting and distributing such news, and the equitable division with them of the expenses thereof, or by the purchase of such news from some existing agency engaged in that business."

The bill was filed to restrain the pirating of complainant's news by defendant in three ways:

[...] and Third, by copying news from bulletin boards and from early editions of complainant's newspapers and selling this, either bodily or after rewriting it, to defendant's customers.

* * *

The only matter that has been argued before us is whether defendant may lawfully be restrained from appropriating news taken from bulletins issued by complainant or any of its members, or from newspapers published by them, for the purpose of selling it to defendant's clients. Complainant asserts that defendant's admitted course of conduct in this regard both violates complainant's property right in the news and constitutes unfair competition in business. And notwithstanding the case has proceeded only to the stage of a preliminary injunction, we have deemed it proper to consider the underlying questions, since they go to the very merits of the action and are presented upon facts that are

not in dispute. As presented in argument these questions are: 1. Whether there is any property in news; 2. Whether, if there be property in news collected for the purpose of being published, it survives the instant of its publication in the first newspaper to which it is communicated by the news-gatherer; and 3. Whether defendant's admitted course of conduct in appropriating for commercial use matter taken from bulletins or early editions of Associated Press publications constitutes unfair competition in trade.

The federal jurisdiction was invoked because of diversity of citizenship, not upon the ground that the suit arose under the copyright or other laws of the United States. Complainant's news matter is not copyrighted. It is said that it could not, in practice, be copyrighted, because of the large number of dispatches that are sent daily; and, according to complainant's contention, news is not within the operation of the copyright act. Defendant, while apparently conceding this, nevertheless invokes the analogies of the law of literary property and copyright, insisting as its principal contention that, assuming complainant has a right of property in its news, it can be maintained (unless the copyright act be complied with) only by being kept secret and confidential, and that upon the publication with complainant's consent of uncopyrighted news by any of complainant's members in a newspaper or upon a bulletin board, the right of property is lost, and the subsequent use of the news by the public or by defendant for any purpose whatever becomes lawful.

* * *

In considering the general question of property in news matter, it is necessary to recognize its dual character, distinguishing between the substance of the information and the particular form or collocation of words in which the writer has communicated it.

No doubt news articles often possess a literary quality, and are the subject of literary property at the common law; nor do we question that such an article, as a literary production, is the subject of copyright by the terms of the act as it now stands. [...]

But the news element – the information respecting current events contained in the literary production – is not the creation of the writer, but is a report of matters that ordinarily are *publici juris*; it is the history of the day. It is not to be supposed that the framers of the Constitution, when they empowered Congress "to promote the progress of science and useful arts, by securing for limited times to authors and inventors the exclusive right to their respective writings and discoveries" (Const., Art. I, §8, par. 8), intended to confer upon one who might happen to be the first to report a historic event the exclusive right for any period to spread the knowledge of it.

We need spend no time, however, upon the general question of property in news matter at common law, or the application of the copyright act, since it seems to us the case must turn upon the question of unfair competition in business. And, in our opinion, this does not depend upon any general right of property analogous to the common-law right of the proprietor of an unpublished work to prevent its publication without his consent; nor is it foreclosed by showing that the benefits of the copyright act have been waived. We are dealing here not with restrictions upon publication but with the very facilities and processes of publication. The peculiar value of news is in the spreading of it while it is fresh; and it is evident that a valuable property interest in the news, as news, cannot be maintained by keeping it secret. Besides, except for matters improperly disclosed, or published in breach of trust or confidence, or in violation of law, none of which is involved in this branch of the case, the news of current events may be regarded as common property. What we are concerned with is the business of making it known to the world, in which both parties to the present suit are engaged. That business consists in maintaining a prompt, sure, steady, and reliable service designed to place the daily events of the world at the breakfast table of the millions at a price that, while of trifling moment to each reader, is sufficient in the aggregate to afford compensation for the cost of gathering and distributing it, with the added profit so necessary as an incentive to effective action in the commercial world. The service thus performed for newspaper readers is not only innocent but extremely useful in itself, and indubitably constitutes a legitimate business. The parties are

competitors in this field; and, on fundamental principles, applicable here as elsewhere, when the rights or privileges of the one are liable to conflict with those of the other, each party is under a duty so to conduct its own business as not unnecessarily or unfairly to injure that of the other. [. . .]

Obviously, the question of what is unfair competition in business must be determined with particular reference to the character and circumstances of the business. The question here is not so much the rights of either party as against the public but their rights as between themselves. [. . .] And although we may and do assume that neither party has any remaining property interest as against the public in uncopyrighted news matter after the moment of its first publication, it by no means follows (that there is no remaining property interest in it as between themselves). For, to both of them alike, news matter, however little susceptible of ownership or dominion in the absolute sense, is stock in trade, to be gathered at the cost of enterprise, organization, skill, labor, and money, and to be distributed and sold to those who will pay money for it, as for any other merchandise. (Regarding the news, therefore, as but the material out of which both parties are seeking to make profits at the same time and in the same field, we hardly can fail to recognize that for this purpose, and as between them, it must be regarded as *quasi* property, irrespective of the rights of either as against the public.)

In order to sustain the jurisdiction of equity over the controversy, we need not affirm any general and absolute property in the news as such. The rule that a court of equity concerns itself only in the protection of property rights treats any civil right of a pecuniary nature as a property right [. . .] and the right to acquire property by honest labor or the conduct of a lawful business is as much entitled to protection as the right to guard property already acquired. [. . .] It is this right that furnishes the basis of the jurisdiction in the ordinary case of unfair competition.

The question, whether one who has gathered general information or news at pains and expense for the purpose of subsequent publication through the press has such an interest in its publication as may be protected from interference, has been raised many times, although never, perhaps, in the precise form in which it is now presented.

Board of Trade v. Christie Grain & Stock Co., 198 U.S. 236, 250, related to the distribution of quotations of prices on dealings upon a board of trade, which were collected by plaintiff and communicated on confidential terms to numerous persons under a contract not to make them public. This court held that, apart from certain special objections that were overruled, plaintiff's collection of quotations was entitled to the protection of the law; that, like a trade secret, plaintiff might keep to itself the work done at its expense, and did not lose its right by communicating the result to persons, even if many, in confidential relations to itself, under a contract not to make it public; and that strangers should be restrained from getting at the knowledge by inducing a breach of trust.

In National Tel. News Co. v. Western Union Tel. Co., 119 Fed.Rep. 294, the Circuit Court of Appeals for the Seventh Circuit dealt with news matter gathered and transmitted by a telegraph company, and consisting merely of a notation of current events having but a transient value due to quick transmission and distribution; and, while declaring that this was not copyrightable although printed on a tape by tickers in the offices of the recipients, and that it was a commercial not a literary product, nevertheless held that the business of gathering and communicating the news – the service of purveying it – was a legitimate business, meeting a distinctive commercial want and adding to the facilities of the business world, and partaking of the nature of property in a sense that entitled it to the protection of a court of equity against piracy.

*   *   *

Not only do the acquisition and transmission of news require elaborate organization and a large expenditure of money, skill, and effort; not only has it an exchange value to the gatherer, dependent chiefly upon its novelty and freshness, the regularity of the service, its reputed reliability and thoroughness, and its adaptability to the public needs; but also, as is evident, the news has an exchange value to one who can misappropriate it.

The peculiar features of the case arise from the fact that, while novelty and freshness form so important an element in the success of the business, the very processes of distribution and publication necessarily occupy a good deal of time. Complainant's service, as well as defendant's, is a daily service to daily newspapers; most of the foreign news reaches this country at the Atlantic seaboard, principally at the City of New York, and because of this, and of time differentials due to the earth's rotation, the distribution of news matter throughout the country is principally from east to west; and, since in speed the telegraph and telephone easily outstrip the rotation of the earth, it is a simple matter for defendant to take complainant's news from bulletins or early editions of complainant's members in the eastern cities and at the mere cost of telegraphic transmission cause it to be published in western papers issued at least as early as those served by complainant. Besides this, and irrespective of time differentials, irregularities in telegraphic transmission on different lines, and the normal consumption of time in printing and distributing the newspaper, result in permitting pirated news to be placed in the hands of defendant's readers sometimes simultaneously with the service of competing Associated Press papers, occasionally even earlier.

Defendant insists that when, with the sanction and approval of complainant, and as the result of the use of its news for the very purpose for which it is distributed, a portion of complainant's members communicate it to the general public by posting it upon bulletin boards so that all may read, or by issuing it to newspapers and distributing it indiscriminately, complainant no longer has the right to control the use to be made of it; that when it thus reaches the light of day it becomes the common possession of all to whom it is accessible; and that any purchaser of a newspaper has the right to communicate the intelligence which it contains to anybody and for any purpose, even for the purpose of selling it for profit to newspapers published for profit in competition with complainant's members.

The fault in the reasoning lies in applying as a test the right of the complainant as against the public, instead of considering the rights of complainant and defendant, competitors in business, as between themselves. The right of the purchaser of a single newspaper to spread knowledge of its contents gratuitously, for any legitimate purpose not unreasonably interfering with complainant's right to make merchandise of it, may be admitted; but to transmit that news for commercial use, in competition with complainant – which is what defendant has done and seeks to justify – is a very different matter. In doing this defendant, by its very act, admits that it is taking material that has been acquired by complainant as the result of organization and the expenditure of labor, skill, and money, and which is salable by complainant for money, and that defendant in appropriating it and selling it as its own is endeavoring to reap where it has not sown, and by disposing of it to newspapers that are competitors of complainant's members is appropriating to itself the harvest of those who have sown. Stripped of all disguises, the process amounts to an unauthorized interference with the normal operation of complainant's legitimate business precisely at the point where the profit is to be reaped, in order to divert a material portion of the profit from those who have earned it to those who have not; with special advantage to defendant in the competition because of the fact that it is not burdened with any part of the expense of gathering the news. The transaction speaks for itself, and a court of equity ought not to hesitate long in characterizing it as unfair competition in business.

The underlying principle is much the same as that which lies at the base of the equitable theory of consideration in the law of trusts – that he who has fairly paid the price should have the beneficial use of the property. [. . .] It is no answer to say that complainant spends its money for that which is too fugitive or evanescent to be the subject of property. That might, and for the purposes of the discussion we are assuming that it would, furnish an answer in a common-law controversy. But in a court of equity, where the question is one of unfair competition, if that which complainant has acquired fairly at substantial cost may be sold fairly at substantial profit, a competitor who is misappropriating it for the purpose of disposing of it to his own profit and to the advantage of complainant cannot be heard to say that it is too fugitive or evanescent to be regarded as property. It has all the attributes of property necessary for

determining that a misappropriation of it by a competitor is unfair competition because contrary to good conscience.

The contention that the news is abandoned to the public for all purposes when published in the first newspaper is untenable. Abandonment is a question of intent, and the entire organization of the Associated Press negatives such a purpose. The cost of the service would be prohibitive if the reward were to be so limited. No single newspaper, no small group of newspapers, could sustain the expenditure. Indeed, it is one of the most obvious results of defendant's theory that, by permitting indiscriminate publication by anybody and everybody for purposes of profit in competition with the news-gatherer, it would render publication profitless, or so little profitable as in effect to cut off the service by rendering the cost prohibitive in comparison with the return. The practical needs and requirements of the business are reflected in complainant's by-laws which have been referred to. Their effect is that publication by each member must be deemed not by any means an abandonment of the news to the world for any and all purposes, but a publication for limited purposes; for the benefit of the readers of the bulletin or the newspaper as such; not for the purpose of making merchandise of it as news, with the result of depriving complainant's other members of their reasonable opportunity to obtain just returns for their expenditures.

Mr Justice Holmes:

When an uncopyrighted combination of words is published there is no general right to forbid other people repeating them – in other words there is no property in the combination or in the thoughts or facts that the words express. Property, a creation of law, does not arise from value, although exchangeable – a matter of fact. Many exchangeable values may be destroyed intentionally without compensation. Property depends upon exclusion by law from interference, and a person is not excluded from using any combination of words merely because someone has used it before, even if it took labor and genius to make it. If a given person is to be prohibited from making the use of words that his neighbors are free to make some other ground must be found. One such ground is vaguely expressed in the phrase unfair trade. This means that the words are repeated by a competitor in business in such a way as to convey a misrepresentation that materially injures the person who first used them, by appropriating credit of some kind which the first user has earned. The ordinary case is a representation by device, appearance, or other in direction that the defendant's goods come from the plaintiff. But the only reason why it is actionable to make such a representation is that it tends to give the defendant an advantage in his competition with the plaintiff and that it is thought undesirable that an advantage should be gained in that way. Apart from that the defendant may use such unpatented devices and uncopyrighted combinations of words as he likes. The ordinary case, I say, is palming off the defendant's product as the plaintiff's, but the same evil may follow from the opposite falsehood – from saying, whether in words or by implication, that the plaintiff's product is the defendant's, and that, it seems to me, is what has happened here.

Fresh news is got only by enterprise and expense. To produce such news as it is produced by the defendant represents by implication that it has been acquired by the defendant's enterprise and at its expense. When it comes from one of the great news-collecting agencies like the Associated Press, the source generally is indicated, plainly importing that credit; and that such a representation is implied may be inferred with some confidence from the unwillingness of the defendant to give the credit and tell the truth. If the plaintiff produces the news at the same time that the defendant does, the defendant's presentation impliedly denies to the plaintiff the credit of collecting the facts and assumes that credit to the defendant. If the plaintiff is later in western cities it naturally will be supposed to have obtained its information from the defendant. The falsehood is a little more subtle, the injury a little more indirect, than in ordinary cases of unfair trade, but I think that the principle that condemns the one condemns the other. It is a question of how strong an infusion of fraud is necessary to turn a flavor into a poison. The dose seems to me strong enough here to need a remedy from the law. But as, in my view, the only

ground of complaint that can be recognized without legislation is the implied misstatement, it can be corrected by stating the truth; and a suitable acknowledgment of the source is all that the plaintiff can require. I think that within the limits recognized by the decision of the Court the defendant should be enjoined from publishing news obtained from the Associated Press for hours after publication by the plaintiff unless it gives express credit to the Associated Press; the number of hours and the form of acknowledgment to be settled by the District Court.

Mr. Justice McKenna concurs in this opinion.

Mr. Justice Brandeis dissenting.

News is a report of recent occurrences. The business of the news agency is to gather systematically knowledge of such occurrences of interest and to distribute reports thereof. The Associated Press contended that knowledge so acquired is property, because it costs money and labor to produce and because it has value for which those who have it not are ready to pay; that it remains property and is entitled to protection as long as it has commercial value as news; and that to protect it effectively the defendant must be enjoined from making, or causing to be made, any gainful use of it while it retains such value. An essential element of individual property is the legal right to exclude others from enjoying it. If the property is private, the right of exclusion may be absolute; if the property is affected with a public interest, the right of exclusion is qualified. But the fact that a product of the mind has cost its producer money and labor, and has a value for which others are willing to pay, is not sufficient to ensure to it this legal attribute of property. The general rule of law is, that the noblest of human productions – knowledge, truths ascertained, conceptions, and ideas – become, after voluntary communication to others, free as the air to common use. Upon these incorporeal productions the attribute of property is continued after such communication only in certain classes of cases where public policy has seemed to demand it. These exceptions are confined to productions which, in some degree, involve creation, invention, or discovery. But by no means all such are endowed with this attribute of property. The creations which are recognized as property by the common law are literary, dramatic, musical, and other artistic creations; and these have also protection under the copyright statutes. The inventions and discoveries upon which this attribute of property is conferred only by statute, are the few comprised within the patent law. There are also many other cases in which courts interfere to prevent curtailment of plaintiff's enjoyment of incorporeal productions; and in which the right to relief is often called a property right, but is such only in a special sense. In those cases, the plaintiff has no absolute right to the protection of his production; he has merely the qualified right to be protected as against the defendant's acts, because of the special relation in which the latter stands or the wrongful method or means employed in acquiring the knowledge or the manner in which it is used. Protection of this character is afforded where the suit is based upon breach of contract or of trust or upon unfair competition.

The knowledge for which protection is sought in the case at bar is not of a kind upon which the law has heretofore conferred the attributes of property; nor is the manner of its acquisition or use nor the purpose to which it is applied such as has heretofore been recognized as entitling a plaintiff to relief.

* * *

The great development of agencies now furnishing country-wide distribution of news, the vastness of our territory, and improvements in the means of transmitting intelligence, have made it possible for a news agency or newspapers to obtain, without paying compensation, the fruit of another's efforts and to use news so obtained gainfully in competition with the original collector. The injustice of such action is obvious. But to give relief against it would involve more than the application of existing rules of law to new facts. It would require the making of a new rule in analogy to existing ones. The unwritten law possesses capacity for growth; and has often satisfied new demands for justice by invoking analogies or by expanding a rule or principle. This process has been in the main wisely applied and should not be discontinued. Where the problem is relatively simple, as it is apt to be when private interests only are involved, it generally proves adequate. But with the increasing complexity of society, the public interest tends to become omnipresent; and the problems presented by new demands for justice cease to be simple. Then the creation or recognition by courts of a new private right may work serious injury to the general public, unless the boundaries of the right are definitely established and wisely guarded. In order to reconcile the new private right with the public interest, it may be necessary to prescribe limitations and rules for its enjoyment; and also to provide administrative machinery for enforcing the rules. It is largely for this reason that, in the effort to meet the many new demands for justice incident to a rapidly changing civilization, resort to legislation has latterly been had with increasing frequency.

The rule for which the plaintiff contends would effect an important extension of property rights and a corresponding curtailment of the free use of knowledge and of ideas; and the facts of this case admonish us of the danger involved in recognizing such a property right in news, without imposing upon news-gatherers corresponding obligations. [...]

A legislature, urged to enact a law by which one news agency or newspaper may prevent appropriation of the fruits of its labors by another, would consider such facts and possibilities and others which appropriate enquiry might disclose. Legislators might conclude that it was impossible to put an end to the obvious injustice involved in such appropriation of news, without opening the door to other evils, greater than that sought to be remedied.

* * *

Or legislators dealing with the subject might conclude, that the right to news values should be protected to the extent of permitting recovery of damages for any unauthorized use, but that protection by injunction should be denied, just as courts of equity ordinarily refuse (perhaps in the interest of free speech) to restrain actionable libels, and for other reasons decline to protect by injunction mere political rights; and as Congress has prohibited courts from enjoining the illegal assessment or collection of federal taxes. If a legislature concluded to recognize property in published news to the extent of permitting recovery at law, it might, with a view to making the remedy more certain and adequate, provide a fixed measure of damages, as in the case of copyright infringement.

Or again, a legislature might conclude that it was unwise to recognize even so limited a property right in published news as that above indicated; but that a news agency should, on some conditions, be given full protection of its business; and to that end a remedy by injunction as well as one for damages should be granted, where news collected by it is gainfully used without permission. If a legislature concluded, [. . .] that under certain circumstances news-gathering is a business affected with a public interest, it might declare that, in such cases, news should be protected against appropriation, only if the gatherer assumed the obligation of supplying it, at reasonable rates and without discrimination, to all papers which applied therefor. If legislators reached that conclusion, they would probably go further, and prescribe the conditions under which and the extent to which the protection should be afforded; and they might also provide the administrative machinery necessary for ensuring to the public, the press, and the news agencies, full enjoyment of the rights so conferred.

Courts are ill-equipped to make the investigations which should precede a determination of the limitations which should be set upon any property right in news or of the circumstances under which news gathered by a private agency should be deemed affected with a public interest. Courts would be powerless to prescribe the detailed regulations essential to full enjoyment of the rights conferred or to introduce the machinery required for enforcement of such regulations. Considerations such as these should lead us to decline to establish a new rule of law in the effort to redress a newly-disclosed wrong, although the propriety of some remedy appears to be clear.

Questions

1   How does Nozick expand on Locke's theory of property? Does Nozick argue for a strong or a weak proviso? What are his reasons?

2   According to Rosen and Usui, why does US copyright law function as a sort of bribe? How is the Japanese system different? Give reasons in support of both systems? What do you prefer and why?

3   How would Locke respond to Simmons's argument in "Historical Rights and Fair Shares"? What would Simmons say to Locke about past property right violations?

4   How does Honoré evaluate Nozick's theory of property rights? Explain why Honoré thinks that the historical and social context is important to determine a just title to property.

5   What is eminent domain? Why does Epstein think that the power of eminent domain is a necessary part of a just government?

Part V
Torts

Introduction

[handwritten annotations in margins: "Tort wrongdoing harm", "Common Tort Law → reasonable man standard", "Sense", "Moral judgment of the consequences tracing part of law."]

Although difficult to define, broadly speaking a tort is a "civil wrong."[1] In part, some of the difficulties in defining torts concern the fact that tort law is connected to many, if not all, other areas of law. Many attempts have been made to define the domain of tort law. Some, such as Sir John Salmond, have argued that there is no law of tort, only unconnected torts that, when combined, form tort law as we know it. Others have argued that there are general principles at work even though formulating those general principles is difficult or seems impossible. Still others claim that a single principle, rather than many principles, operates in tort law: "Any harm done to another is wrong, and calls for redress unless 'justification' for it can be shown."[2]

The function of tort law is easier to define. Tort law is designed to help compensate individuals for the losses they have incurred as the result of the activities of another. This definition is quite broad, but it is aided by what people commonly hold as the guiding principle of tort law, namely, that "liability must be based on conduct which is socially unreasonable."[3] The notion of unreasonableness is specified in this manner to avoid being too individualized, because, without general standards, *all* activity might be considered unreasonable. The "reasonable person" standard often implements this principle in tort law.

Perhaps because of its vagueness, tort law has been an especially rich area for philosophers, as evidenced by the variety of philosophical views presented in this volume. Issues, such as causation, responsibility, retribution, and reasonableness – to name only a few – are brought up multiple times throughout these essays. For example, in "Causation and Responsibility," H. L. A. Hart and A. M. Honoré focus on the role of causation in determining legal as compared to moral responsibility. They focus on three cases that illustrate the potential difficulties in tracing the consequences from what seems initially to be simple causes. In case one, the investigation of a forest fire reveals that person A flung a lighted cigarette into the bracken at the forest's edge, the bracken caught fire, and a breeze sprang up, fanning the flames toward the forest. Though saying that A caused the forest fire seems easy, Hart and Honoré point out that to do so means that we have not taken the breeze to be a cause in the same way that we have taken A's fling of the lighted cigarette to be a cause. In case two, A flings the lighted cigarette into the bracken. Just as the flames are about to die out, person B deliberately pours gasoline onto the dying embers. The fire then spreads and burns down the forest. Here, Hart and Honoré state that, unlike case one, A is not the cause of the forest fire – B is. Because B has exploited the circumstances, B is the cause of the fire no matter what we think of either A's or B's actions. In case three, A hits B and B falls to the ground, stunned. At the very moment B falls, a tree also falls to the ground and kills B. According to Hart and Honoré, while A is the cause of any bruises B might have sustained in hitting the ground, A is not the cause of B's death. While the fall of the three resembles the breeze in case one, in that it is independent and subsequent to A's actions, the falling tree holds a very different place in the causal chain from that of the breeze. In a sense, the falling tree causes B's death.

In the section, "Sua Culpa," Joel Feinberg explores the more specific notion of "his fault" and defends the procedure of levying liability on the basis of fault. When harm has occurred, blame often needs to be fixed through a careful examination of the actions of those who are potentially at fault. This allows determination of who is in possession of the fault or, in other words, which fault is "his fault." Feinberg fixes blame in this fashion by using the "triconditional analysis." This allows us to conclude that the harm is "his fault" if (1) the person was at fault in action, (2) the faulty act caused the harm, and (3) the aspect that made the act faulty was also one of the aspects that caused the harm. According to Feinberg, this manner of fixing blame is necessary so that the innocent do not have to bear the costs of injustice; instead, the faulty injurer must bear these costs so as to protect the innocence of the injured party. Feinberg claims that liability should be fixed in this way, which he calls the "weak retributive principle," rather than under a more conventional retributive account designed to punish any person at fault. He argues that the latter, which he calls a "strong retributive principle," does not take into account the fact that we are all faulty at one time or another.

In "Fairness and Utility in Tort Theory," George P. Fletcher argues that there are two opposed paradigms for resolving tort disputes: reciprocity and reasonableness. The paradigm of reciprocity compares the risk-creating activity of both parties and the possibility of an excuse. If there is not an equal creation of risk and a basis for excuse, then the risk-creator is liable. A simple cost–benefit analysis determines the notion of reasonableness. Fletcher finds that though the paradigm of reasonableness has a certain allure, given its appeal in the modern US legal system, the paradigm of reciprocity is overall a better tort theory. According to Fletcher, the latter paradigm offers a greater overall level of protection for individuals than that provided by the former.

Jules L. Coleman, in "Tort Liability and the Limits of Corrective Justice," disagrees with Feinberg's weak retributive principle for imposing fault. Finding this principle too limited, Coleman proposes allocating costs on the basis of fault according to a method that rests on the principle of corrective justice. Under this principle, liability is not imposed to protect the innocence of the victims; rather, justice lies in the duties that the injurer owes to the victim. This means that an individual may owe a duty to a victim because the victim has suffered a loss, even if she is not at fault for creating that loss. For example, Coleman holds that someone may be an optimal risk-reducer and thus may be found to owe a duty to the victim although she is not directly responsible for creating the victim's loss. Yet, the duty owed to the victim is not the same in every case. Coleman states that the duties owed to a particular victim depend on the surrounding social and legal practices. For example, with a no-fault plan used to compensate victims from a pool that all pay into, no additional duty is owed to the victim, except perhaps an apology.

Richard A. Epstein begins the next selection, "A Theory of Strict Liability," by pointing out an oppositional relationship between common law notions of common sense and fairness within tort law and the more recent economic theory of torts. While some prefer an economic theory of torts because it reduces the need for an examination of the fairness question, there are some questions of fairness that cannot be answered in economic terms. Epstein points out that this argument contains a presupposition regarding the theory of fairness itself – namely, that one can explain it in such a way that leaves room for economic theory. Given this supposition, Epstein attempts to raise these fairness questions within traditional legal theory so as to determine whether the argument for economic theory holds. To accomplish this task, he focuses on the conflict between negligence and strict liability theories.

In "The Question of a Duty to Rescue in Canadian Tort Law: An Answer from France," Mitchell McInnes argues that Canadian tort law can be expanded to include a general duty to rescue. This is due in part to the possibility of expanding the many currently existing exceptions to the general lack of a duty to rescue in Canadian tort law. For example, the Canadian courts have found that a duty to rescue can arise in a relationship of economic benefits, relationships of control or benefit, creations of danger, gratuitous undertakings, and statutory duties. Through some theories attempt to explain these exceptions, McInnes, believes that these exception are simply a product of policy decisions. Further, though some policy arguments reject the duty to rescue, McInnes finds overall stronger policy arguments in favor of the duty to rescue. Thus, he claims the lack of a duty to rescue in Canadian law is an "anachronism" that ought to be changed.

Finally, we provide the *Tarasoff v. Regents of University of California* case as an example of theoretical controversy about tort law. Here, Prosenjit Poddar, while under the care of the psychologist Dr Lawrence Moore, killed Tatiana

Tarasoff. Poddar had informed Dr Moore of his intention to kill Tarasoff. Dr Moore had Poddar detained by campus police, but Poddar was released when he seemed rational. Moreover, Dr Moore never informed Tarasoff of Poddar's intention. In this appeal, Dr Moore's employer is found liable for Dr Moore's failure to warn Tarasoff of the immediate danger posed by his patient. The court's justification for this ruling is based on a notion of a professional's duty to exercise reasonable care. Because he failed in this duty, Dr Moore is found by the court to be negligent. This has been regarded as a highly controversial decision.

Notes

1 W. Paige Keeton, ed., *Prosser and Keeton on Torts*, 5th edn. (St Paul, MN: West, 1984), 2.
2 Ibid., 4.
3 Ibid., 6.

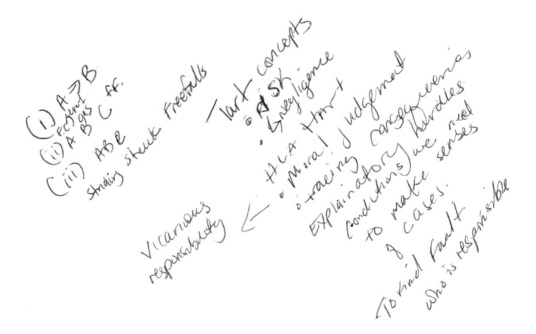

30

Causation and Responsibility

H. L. A. Hart and A. M. Honoré

I Responsibility in Law and Morals

[. . .] In the moral judgments of ordinary life, we have occasion to blame people because they have caused harm to others, and also, if less frequently, to insist that morally they are bound to compensate those to whom they have caused harm. These are the moral analogues of more precise legal conceptions; for, in all legal systems, liability to be punished or to make compensation frequently depends on whether actions (or omissions) have caused harm. Moral blame is not of course confined to such cases of causing harm. We blame a man who cheats or lies or breaks promises, even if no one has suffered in the particular case: this has its legal counterpart in the punishment of abortive attempts to commit crimes, and of offences constituted by the unlawful possession of certain kinds of weapons, drugs, or materials, for example, for counterfeiting currency. When the occurrence of harm is an essential part of the ground for blame the connection of the person blamed with the harm may take any of the forms of causal connection we have examined. His action may have initiated a series of physical events dependent on each other and culminating in injury to persons or property, as in wounding and killing. These simple forms are paradigms for the lawyer's talk of harm "directly" caused. But we blame people also for harm which arises from or is the consequence of their neglect of common precautions; we do this even if harm would not have come about without the intervention of another human being deliberately exploiting the opportunities provided by neglect. The main legal analogue here is liability for "negligence." The wish of many lawyers to talk in this branch of the law of harm being "within the risk of" rather than "caused by" the negligent conduct manifests appreciation of the fact that a different form of relationship is involved in saying that harm is the consequence, on the one hand, of an explosion and, on the other, of a failure to lock the door by which a thief has entered. Again, we blame people for the harm which we say is the consequence of their influence over others, either exerted by non-rational means or in one of the ways we have designated "interpersonal transactions." To such grounds for responsibility there correspond many important legal conceptions: the instigation of crimes ("commanding" or "procuring") constitutes an important ground of criminal responsibility and the concepts of

H. L. A. Hart and A. M. Honoré, "Causation and Responsibility," from *Causation in the Law*, 2nd edn. (Oxford University Press, 1985), pp. 62–83. © 1985 H. L. A. Hart and A. M. Honoré. Reprinted with permission from Oxford University Press.

enticement and of inducement (by threats or misrepresentation) are an element in many civil wrongs as well as in criminal offences.

The law, however, especially in matters of compensation, goes far beyond these casual grounds for responsibility in such doctrines as the vicarious responsibility of a master for his servant's civil wrongs and that of the responsibility of an occupier of property for injuries suffered by passers-by from defects of which the occupier had no knowledge and which he had no opportunity to repair. There is a recognition, perhaps diminishing, of this non-causal ground of responsibility outside the law; responsibility is sometimes admitted by one person or group of persons, even if no precaution has been neglected by them, for harm done by persons related to them in a special way, either by family ties or as members of the same social or political association. Responsibility may be simply "placed" by moral opinion on one person for what others do. The simplest case of such vicarious moral responsibility is that of a parent for damage done by a child; its more complex (and more debatable) form is the moral responsibility of one generation of a nation to make compensation for their predecessors' wrong, such as the Germans admitted in payment of compensation to Israel.

At this point it is necessary to issue a caveat about the meaning of the expression "responsible" if only to avoid prejudicing a question about the character of *legal* determinations of causal connection. [. . .] Usually in discussion of the law and occasionally in morals, to say that someone is responsible for some harm means that in accordance with legal rules of moral principles it is at least permissible, if not mandatory, to blame or punish or exact compensation from him. In this use[1] the expression "responsible for" does not refer to a factual connection between the person held responsible and the harm but simply to his liability under the rules to be blamed, punished, or made to pay. The expressions "answerable for" or "liable for" are practically synonymous with "responsible for" in *this* use, in which there is no implication that the person held responsible actually *did* or *caused* the harm. In this sense a master is (in English law) responsible for the damage done by his servants acting within the scope of their authority and a parent (in French and German

law) for that done by his children; it is in this sense that a guarantor or surety is responsible for the debts or the good behaviour of other persons and an insurer for losses sustained by the insured. Very often, however, especially in discussion of morals, to say that someone is responsible for some harm is to assert (*inter alia*) that he *did* the harm or *caused* it, though such a statement is perhaps rarely confined to this for it usually also carries with it the implication that it is at least permissible to blame or punish him. This double use of the expression no doubt arises from the important fact that doing or causing harm constitutes not only the most usual but the primary type of ground for holding persons responsible in the first sense. We still speak of inanimate or natural causes such as storms, floods, germs, or the failure of electricity supply as "responsible for" disasters; this mode of expression, now taken only to mean that they caused the disasters, no doubt originated in the belief that all that happens is the work of spirits when it is not that of men. Its survival in the modern world is perhaps some testimony to the primacy of causal connection as an element in responsibility and to the intimate connection between the two notions.

We shall consider later an apparent paradox which interprets in a different way the relationship between cause and responsibility. Much modern thought on causation in the law rests on the contention that the statement that someone has caused harm either means no more than that the harm would not have happened without ("but for") his action or where (as in normal legal usage and in all ordinary speech), it apparently means more than this, it is a disguised way of asserting the "normative" judgment that he is responsible in the first sense, i.e. that it is proper or just to blame or punish him or make him pay. On this view to say that a person caused harm is not really, though ostensibly it is, to give a *ground* or *reason* for holding him responsible in the first sense; for we are only in a position to say that he has caused harm when we have decided that he is responsible. Pending consideration of the theories of legal causation which exploit this point of view we shall use the expression "responsible for" only in the first of the two ways explained, i.e. without any implication as to the type of factual connection between the person held responsible and the harm; and we shall provisionally, though without prejudicing the issue, treat statements that a person caused harm as one sort of non-tautologous ground or reason for saying that he is responsible in this sense.

[. . .] Yet, in order to understand the extent to which the causal notions of ordinary thought are used in the law, we must bear in mind the many factors which must differentiate moral from legal responsibility in spite of their partial correspondence. The law is not only bound to follow the moral patterns of attribution of responsibility but, even when it does, it must take into account, in a way which the private moral judgments need not and does not, the general social consequences which are attached to its judgments of responsibility; for they are of a gravity quite different from those attached to moral censure. [. . .] Always to follow the private moral judgment here would be far too expensive for the law: not only in the crude sense that it would entail a vast machinery of courts and officials, but in the more important sense that it would inhibit or discourage too many other valuable activities of society. To limit the *types* of harm which the law will recognize is not enough; even if the types of harm are limited it would still be too much for any society to punish or exact compensation from individuals whenever their connection with harm of such types would justify moral censure. Conversely, social needs may require that compensation should be paid and even (though less obviously) that punishment be inflicted where no such connection between the person held responsible and the harm exists. [. . .]

II Tracing Consequences

"To consequences no limit can be set": "Every event which would not have happened if an earlier event had not happened is the consequence of that earlier event." These two propositions are not equivalent in meaning and are not equally or in the same way at variance with ordinary thought. They have, however, both been urged sometimes in the same breath by the legal theorist[2] and the philosopher: they are indeed sometimes said by lawyers to be "the philosophical doctrine" of causation. It is perhaps not difficult even for the layman to accept the first

proposition as a truth about certain physical events; an explosion may cause a flash of light which will be propagated as far as the outer nebulae; its effects or consequences continue indefinitely. It is, however, a different matter to accept the view that whenever a man is murdered with a gun his death was the consequence of (still less an "effect" of or "caused by") the manufacture of the bullet. The first tells a perhaps unfamiliar tale about unfamiliar events; the second introduces an unfamiliar, though, of course, a possible way of speaking about familiar events. It is not that this unrestricted use of "consequence" is unintelligible or never found; it is indeed used to refer to bizarre or fortuitous connections or coincidences: but the point is that the various causal notions employed for the purposes of explanation, attribution of responsibility, or the assessment of contributions to the course of history carry with them implicit limits which are similar in these different employments.

It is, then, the second proposition, defining consequence in terms of "necessary condition," with which theorists are really concerned. This proposition is the corollary of the view that, if we look into the past of any given event, there is an infinite number of events, each of which is a necessary condition of the given event and so, as much as any other, is its cause. This is the "cone"[3] of causation, so called because, since any event has a number of simultaneous conditions, the series fans out as we go back in time. [. . .]

Legal theorists have developed this account of cause and consequence to show what is "factual," "objective," or "scientific" in these notions: this they call "cause in fact" and it is usually stressed as a preliminary to the doctrine that any more restricted application of these terms in the law represents nothing in the facts or in the meaning of causation, but expresses fluctuating legal policy or sentiments of what is just or convenient. Moral philosophers have insisted in somewhat similar terms that the consequences of human action are "infinite." [. . .] The point is that though we could, we do not think in this way in tracing connections between human actions and events. Instead, whenever we are concerned with such connections, whether for the purpose of explaining a puzzling occurrence, assessing responsibility, or giving an intelligible historical narrative, we employ a set of concepts restricting in various ways what counts as a consequence. These restrictions colour *all* our thinking in causal terms; when we find them in the law we are not finding something invented by or peculiar to the law, though of course it is for the law to say when and how far it will use them and, where they are vague, to supplement them. [...]

[...] [W]e shall consider the detail of three simple cases.

(i)   A forest fire breaks out, and later investigation shows that shortly before the outbreak A had flung away a lighted cigarette into the bracken at the edge of the forest, the bracken caught fire, a light breeze got up, and fanned the flames in the direction of the forest. If, on discovering these facts, we hesitate before saying that A's action caused the forest fire this would be to consider the alternative hypothesis that in spite of appearances the fire only succeeded A's action in point of time, that the bracken flickered out harmlessly and the forest fire was caused by something else. To dispose of this it may be necessary to examine in further detail the process of events between the ignition of the bracken and the outbreak of fire in the forest and to show that these exemplified certain types of continuous change. If this is shown, there is no longer any room for doubt: A's action *was* the cause of the fire, whether he intended it or not. This seems and is the simplest of cases. Yet it is important to notice that even in applying our general knowledge to a case as simple as this, indeed in regarding it as simple, we make an implicit use of a distinction between types of factor which constitute a limit in tracing consequences and those which we regard as mere circumstances "through" which we trace them. For the breeze which sprang up after A dropped the cigarette, and without which the fire would not have spread to the forest, was not only subsequent to his action but entirely independent of it: it was, however, a common recurrent feature of the environment, and, as such, it is thought of not as an "intervening" force but as merely part of the circumstances in which the cause "operates." The decision so to regard it is implicitly taken when we combine our knowledge of the successive stages of the process and assert the connection.

It is easy here to be misled by the natural metaphor of a causal "chain," which may lead us to think that the causal process consists of a series of single events each of which is dependent upon (would not have occurred without) its predecessor in the "chain" and so is dependent upon the initiating action or event. In truth in any causal process we have at each phase not single events but complex sets of conditions, and among these conditions are some which are not only subsequent to, but independent of the initiating action or event. Some of these independent conditions, such as the evening breeze in the example chosen, we classify as mere conditions in or on which the cause operates; others we speak of as "interventions" or "causes." To decide how such independent elements shall be classified is also to decide how we shall combine our knowledge of the different general connections which the successive stages exemplify, and it is important to see that nothing *in* this knowledge itself can resolve this point. We may have to go to science for the relevant general knowledge before we can assert with proper confidence that A's action did cause the fire, but science, though it tells us that an air current was required, is silent on the difference between a current in the form of an evening breeze and one produced by someone who deliberately fanned the flames as they were flickering out in the bracken. Yet an air current in this deliberately induced form is not a "condition" or "mere circumstance" through which we can trace the consequence; its presence would force us to revise the assertion that A caused the fire. Conversely if science helped us to identify as a necessary factor in producing the fire some condition or element of which we had previously been totally ignorant, e.g. the persistence of oxygen, this would leave our original judgment undisturbed if this factor were a common or pervasive feature of the environment or of the thing in question. There is thus indeed an important sense in which it is true that the distinction between cause and conditions is not a "scientific" one. It is not determined by laws or generalizations concerning connections between events.

When we have assembled all our knowledge of the factors involved in the fire, the residual question which we then confront (the attributive question) may be typified as follows: Here is A's action, here is the fire; can the fire be attributed to A's action as its consequence given that there is also this third factor (the breeze or B's intervention) without which the fire would not have happened? It is plain that, both in raising questions of this kind and in answering them, ordinary thought is powerfully influenced by the analogy between the straightforward cases of causal attribution (where the elements required for the production of harm in addition to the initiating action are all "normal" conditions) and even simpler cases of responsibility which we do not ordinarily describe in causal language at all but by the simple transitive verbs of action. These are the cases of the direct manipulation of objects involving changes in them or their position: cases where we say "He pushed it," "He broke it," "He bent it." The cases which we do confidently describe in causal language ("The fire was caused by his carelessness," "He caused a fire") are cases where no other human action or abnormal occurrence is required for the production of the effect, but only normal conditions. Such cases appear as mere long-range or less direct versions or extensions of the most obvious and fundamental case of all for the attribution of responsibility: the case where we can simply say "He did it." Conversely in attaching importance to thus causing harm as a distinct ground of responsibility and in taking certain kinds of factor (whether human interventions or abnormal occurrences), without which the initiating action would not have led to harm, to preclude the description of the case in simple causal terms, common sense is affected by the fact that here, because of the manner in which the harm eventuates, the outcome cannot be represented as a mere extension of the initiating action; the analogy with the fundamental case for responsibility ("He did it") has broken down. [. . .]

(ii) A throws a lighted cigarette into the bracken which catches fire. Just as the flames are about to flicker out, B, who is not acting in concert with A, deliberately pours petrol on them. The fire spreads and burns down the forest. A's action, whether or not he intended the forest fire, was not the cause of the fire: B's was.

The voluntary intervention of a second human agent, as in this case, is a paradigm among those factors which preclude the assimilation in causal judgments of the first agent's connection with the eventual harm to the case of simple direct manipulation. Such an intervention displaces the prior action's title to be called the cause and, in the persistent metaphors found in the law, it "reduces" the earlier action and its immediate effects to the level of "mere circumstances" or "part of the history." B in this case was not an "instrument" through which A worked or a victim of the circumstances A has created. He has, on the contrary, freely exploited the circumstances and brought about the fire without the co-operation of any further agent or any chance coincidence. Compared with this the claim of A's action to be ranked the cause of the fire fails. That this and not the moral appraisal of the two actions is the point of comparison seems clear. If A and B both intended to set the forest on fire, and this destruction is accepted as something wrong or wicked, their moral wickedness, judged by the criterion of intention, is the same. Yet the causal judgment differentiates between them. If their moral guilt is judged by the outcome, this judgment though it would differentiate between them cannot be the source of the causal judgment; for it presupposes it. The difference just is that B has caused the harm and A has not. Again, if we appraise these actions as good or bad from different points of view, this leaves the causal judgments unchanged. A may be a soldier of one side anxious to burn down the enemy's hide-out: B may be an enemy soldier who has decided that his side is too iniquitous to defend. Whatever is the moral judgment passed on these actions by different speakers it would remain true that A had not caused the fire and B had.

There are, as we have said, situations in which a voluntary action would not be thought of as an intervention precluding causal connection in this way. These are the cases discussed further below where an opportunity commonly exploited for harmful actions is negligently provided, or one person intentionally provides another with the means, the opportunity, or a certain type of reason for wrongdoing. Except in such cases a voluntary intervention is a limit past which consequences are not traced. By contrast, actions which in any of a variety of different ways are less than fully voluntary are assimilated to the means by which or the circumstances in which the earlier action brings about the consequences.

Such actions are not the outcome of an informed choice made without pressure from others, and the different ways in which human action may fall short in this respect range from defective muscular control, through lack of consciousness or knowledge, to the vaguer notions of duress and predicaments, created by the first agent for the second, in which there is no "fair" choice.

In considering examples of such actions and their bearing on causal judgments there are three dangers to avoid. It would be folly to think that in tracing connections through such actions instead of regarding them, like voluntary interventions, as a limit, ordinary thought has clearly separated out their non-voluntary aspect from others by which they are often accompanied. Thus even in the crude case where A lets off a gun (intentionally or not) and startles B, so that he makes an involuntary movement of his arm which breaks a glass, the commonness of such a reaction as much as its compulsive character may influence judgment that A's action was the cause of the damage.

Secondly we must not impute to ordinary thought all the fine discriminations that could be made and in fact are to be found in a legal system, or an equal willingness to supply answers to complex questions in causal terms. Where there is no precise system of punishment, compensation or reward to administer, ordinary men will not often have faced such questions as whether the injuries suffered by a motorist who collides with another in swerving to avoid a child are consequences attributable to the neglect of the child's parents in allowing it to wander on to the road. Such questions courts have to answer and in such cases common judgments provide only a general, though still an important indication of what are the relevant factors.

Thirdly, though very frequently non-voluntary actions are assimilated to mere conditions or means by which the first agent brings about the consequences, the assimilation is never quite complete. This is manifested by the general avoidance of many causal locutions which are appropriate when the consequences are traced (as in the first case) through purely physical events. Thus even in the case in which the second agent's role is hardly an "action" at all, e.g. where A hits B, who staggers against a glass window and breaks it, we should say that A's blow made B stagger and break the glass, rather than that A's blow caused the glass to break, though in any explanatory or attributive context the case would be *summarized* by saying that A's action was the cause of the *damage*.

In the last two cases where B's movements are involuntary in the sense that they are not part of any action which he chose or intended to do, their connection with A's action would be described by saying that A's blow *made* B stagger or *caused* him to stagger or that the noise of A's shot *made* him jump or *caused* him to jump. This would be true, whether A intended or expected B to react in this way or not, and the naturalness of treating A's action as the cause of the ultimate damage is due to the causal character of this part of the process involving B's action. The same is, however, true where B's actions are not involuntary movements but A is considered to have made or caused B to do them by less crude means. This is the case if, for example, A uses threats or exploits his authority over B to make B do something, e.g. knock down a door. At least where A's threats are of serious harm, or B's act was unquestionably within A's authority to order, he too has made or forced or (in formal quasi-legal parlance) "caused" B to act.

Outside the area of such cases, where B's will would be said either not to be involved at all, or to be overborne by A, are cases where A's act creates a predicament for B *narrowing* the area of choice so that he has either to inflict some harm on himself or others, or sacrifice some important interest or duty. Such cases resemble coercion in that A narrows the area of B's choice but differ from it in that this predicament need not be intentionally created. A sets a house on fire (intentionally or unintentionally): B to save himself has to jump from a height involving certain injury, or to save a child rushes in and is seriously burned. Here, of course, B's movements are not involuntary; the "necessity" of his action is here of a different order. His action is the outcome of a choice between two evils forced on him by A's action. In such cases, when B's injuries are thought of as the consequence of the fire, the implicit judgment is made that his action was the lesser of two evils and in this sense a "reasonable" one which he was obliged to make to avoid the greater evil. This is often paradoxically, though understandably, described by saying that here the agent "had no choice" but to do what he did. Such judgments involve a comparison of the importance of the respective interests sacrificed and preserved, and the final assertion that A's action was the cause of the injuries rests on evaluations about which men may differ.

Finally, the ground for treating some harm which would not have occurred without B's action as the consequence of A's action may be that B acted in ignorance of or under a mistake as to some feature of the situation created by A. Poisoning offers perhaps the simplest example of the bearing on causal judgments of actions which are less than voluntary in this Aristotelian sense. If A intending B's death deliberately poisons B's food and B, knowing this, deliberately takes the poison and dies, A has not, unless he coerced B into eating the poisoned food, caused B's death: if, however, B does not know the food to be poisoned, eats it, and dies, A has caused his death, even if he put the poison in unwittingly. Of course only the roughest judgments are passed in causal terms in such cases outside law courts, where fine degrees of "appreciation" or "reckless shutting of the eyes" may have to be discriminated from "full knowledge." Yet, rough as these are, they indicate clearly enough the controlling principles.

Though in the foregoing cases A's initiating action might often be described as "the cause" of the ultimate harm, this linguistic fact is of subordinate importance to the fact that, for whatever purpose, explanatory, descriptive, or evaluative, consequences of an action are traced, discriminations are made (except in the cases discussed later) between free voluntary interventions and less than voluntary reactions to the first action or the circumstances created by it.

(iii) The analogy with single simple actions which guides the tracing of consequences may be broken by certain kinds of conjunctions of physical events. A hits B who falls to the ground stunned and bruised by the blow; at that moment a tree crashes to the ground and kills B. A has certainly caused B's bruises but not his death: for though the fall of the tree was, like the evening breeze in our earlier example, independent of and subsequent to the initiating action, it would be differentiated from the breeze in any description in causal terms of the connection

of B's death with A's action. It is to be noticed that this is not a matter which turns on the intention with which A struck B. Even if A hit B inadvertently or accidentally his blow would still be the cause of B's bruises: he would have caused them, though unintentionally. Conversely even if A had intended his blow to kill, this would have been an attempt to kill but still not the cause of B's death, unless A knew that the tree was about to fall just at that moment. On this legal and ordinary judgments would be found to agree; and most legal systems would distinguish for the purposes of punishment an attempt with a fatal upshot, issuing by such chance or anomalous events, from "causing death" – the terms in which the offences of murder and manslaughter are usually defined.

Similarly the causal description of the case does not turn on the moral appraisal of A's action or the wish to punish it. A may be a robber and a murderer and B a saint guarding the place A hoped to plunder. Or B may be a murderer and A a hero who has forced his way into B's retreat. In both cases the causal judgment is the same. A had caused the minor injuries but not B's death, though he tried to kill him. A may indeed be praised or blamed but not for causing B's death. However intimate the connection between responsibility and causation, it does not determine causal judgments in this simple way. Nor does the causal judgment turn on a refusal to attribute grave consequences to actions which normally have less serious results. Had A's blow killed B outright and the tree, falling on his body, merely smashed his watch we should still treat the coincidental character of the fall of the tree as determining the form of causal statement. We should then recognize A's blow as the cause of B's death but not the breaking of the watch.

The connection between A's action and B's death in the first case would naturally be described in the language of *coincidence*. "It was a coincidence: it just happened that, at the very moment when A knocked B down, a tree crashed at the very place where he fell and killed him." The common legal metaphor would describe the fall of the tree as an "extraneous" cause. This, however, is dangerously misleading, as an analysis of the notion of coincidence will show. It suggests merely an event which is subsequent to and independent of some other contingency, and of course the fall of the tree has both these features in relation to A's blow. Yet in these respects the fall of the tree does not differ from the evening breeze in the earlier case where we found no difficulty in tracing causal connection.[4] The full elucidation of the notion of a coincidence is a complex matter for, though it is very important as a limit in tracing consequences, causal questions are not the only ones to which the notion is relevant. The following are its most general characteristics. We speak of a coincidence whenever the conjunction of two or more events in certain spatial or temporal relations (1) is very unlikely by ordinary standards and (2) is for some reason significant or important, provided (3) that they occur without human contrivance and (4) are independent of each other. It is therefore a coincidence if two persons known to each other in London meet without design in Paris on their way to separate independently chosen destinations; or if two persons living in different places independently decide to write a book on the same subject. The first is a coincidence of time and place ("It just happened that we were at the same place at the same time"), and the second a coincidence of time only ("It just happened that they both decided to write on the subject at the same time"). [...]

One further criterion in addition to these four must be satisfied if a conjunction of events is to rank as a coincidence and as a limit when the consequences of the action are traced. This further criterion again shows the strength of the influence which the analogy with the case of the simple manipulation of things exerts over thought in causal terms. An abnormal *condition* existing at the time of a human intervention is distinguished both by ordinary thought and, with a striking consistency, by most legal systems from an abnormal event or conjunction of events subsequent to that intervention; the former, unlike the latter, are not ranked as coincidences or "extraneous" causes when the consequences of the intervention come to be traced. Thus A innocently gives B a tap over the head of a normally quite harmless character, but because B is then suffering from some rare disease the tap has, as we say, "fatal results." In this case A has caused B's death though unintentionally. The scope of the principle which thus distinguishes contemporaneous abnormal conditions from subsequent events is unclear; but at least where a human being initiates some physical change in a thing, animal, or person, abnormal physical states of the object affected, existing at the time, are ranked as part of the circumstances in which the cause "operates." In the familiar controlling imagery these are part of "the stage already set" before the "intervention." [...]

Notes

1 Cf. *OED sub tit.* Responsible: Answerable, accountable (*to* another *for* something); liable to be called to account: "being responsible to the King for what might happen to us," 1662; Hart, "Varieties of Responsibility" (1967) 83 *LQR* 346, reprinted with additions as "Responsibility and Retribution" in Hart, *Punishment and Responsibility* (Oxford, 1968), chap. IX.

2 F. H. Lawson, *Negligence in the Civil Law* (Oxford, 1950), p. 53.

3 Glanville Williams, *Joint Torts and Contributory Negligence* (London, 1951), p. 239.

4 Above, p. 308.

31

Sua Culpa

Joel Feinberg

I

[...] It may seem that most of those who quibble and quarrel about "his fault" are either children or lawyers; and even lawyers, therefore, can seem childish when they are preoccupied with the question. But investigators, editorialists, and executives must assign blame for failures and thereby judge the faults of their fellows. (Indeed, their inquiries and debates are most childish when they do *not* carefully consider fault and instead go scapegoat-hunting.) My assumption in what follows is that the faults that concern nonlawyers, both children and adults, are faults in the same sense of the word as those that concern the lawyer, that the concept of "his fault" is imported into the law from the world of everyday affairs. On the other hand, "proximate cause" (to pick just one of a thousand examples) is a technical term of law invented by lawyers to do a special legal job and subject to continual refashioning in the interests of greater efficiency in the performance of its assigned legal task. To explain this term to a layman is precisely to explain what *lawyers* do with it; if it should ever happen that a child, or a sportswriter, or an historian should use the expression, that fact would be of no relevance to its proper analysis. But to explain the concept of "his fault," we must give an account that explains what both lawyers and laymen do with it and how it is possible for each to understand and to communicate with the other by means of it.

An equivalent way of saying that some result is a man's fault is to say that he is to *blame* for it. Precisely the same thing can also be said in the language of *responsibility*. Of course, to be responsible for something (after the fact) may also mean that one did it, or caused it, or now stands answerable, or accountable, or liable to unfavorable responses from others for it. One can be responsible for a result in all those senses without being to blame for it. One can be held liable for a result either because it is one's fault or for some quite different kind of reason; and one can be to blame for an occurrence and yet escape all liability for it. Still, when one is to blame for a harm, one can properly be said to be "responsible for it *really*"; that is, there is a sense of "responsible for" that simply means "chargeable to one as one's fault." One of the commonest uses of the expression "*morally* responsible for" is for being responsible for something in this sense. (Another is for chargeability to a fault of a distinctively moral kind. Still another is for being *liable* to responses of a distinctively moral kind.)

Joel Feinberg, "Sua Culpa," from *Doing and Deserving* (Princeton University Press, 1970), pp. 187–221. © 1970 by Joel Feinberg. Reprinted by kind permission of Betty Feinberg.

II

The word "fault" occurs in three distinct idioms. We can say of a man that *he has a fault*, or that he is (or was) *at fault*, or that he is "to blame" for a given harm, which is to say that the harm is (or was) *his fault*. In this essay I shall be directly concerned only with the last of these idioms. [. . .]

III

We come now to the main business at hand: the analysis of the concept of "his fault." It should be clear at the outset that, in order for a given harm to be someone's fault, he must have been somehow "at fault" in what he did or omitted to do, and also that there must have been some sort of causal connection between his action or omission and the harm. It is equally obvious that neither of these conditions by itself can be sufficient. Thus a motorist may be at fault in driving with an expired license or in exceeding the speed limit by five miles per hour, but unless his faulty act is a cause of the collision that ensues, the accident can hardly be his fault. Fault without causally determining action, then, is not sufficient. Similarly, causation without fault is not sufficient for the caused harm to be the causer's fault. It is no logical contradiction to say that a person's action caused the harm yet the harm was not his fault.

The triconditional analysis

It is natural at this point to conclude that a harm is "his fault" if and only if (1) he was at fault in acting (or omitting) and (2) his faulty act (or omission) caused the harm. This analysis, however, is incomplete, being still vulnerable to counterexamples of faulty actions causing harm that is nevertheless not the actor's fault. Suppose that *A* is unlicensed to drive an automobile but drives anyway, thereby "being at fault." The appearance of him driving in an (otherwise) faultless manner causes an edgy horse to panic and throw his rider. His faultily undertaken act caused a harm that cannot be imputed to him because the respect in which his act was faulty was causally irrelevant to the production of the harm. (When we come to give a causal explanation of the

harm, we will not mention the fact that the driver had no license in his pocket. *That* is not what scared the horse.) This example suggests that a further condition is required to complete the analysis: (3) the aspect of the act that was faulty was also one of the aspects in virtue of which the act was a cause of the harm. [. . .]

We can refer to this account as "the triconditional analysis" and to its three conditions as (in order) "the fault condition," "the causal condition" (that the act was a cause of the harm), and "the causal relevance condition" (that the faulty aspect of the act was its causal link to the harm). I shall conclude that the triconditional analysis goes a long way toward providing a correct account of the commonsense notion of "his fault" and that its three conditions are indeed necessary to such an account even if, in the end, they must be formulated much more carefully and even supplemented by other conditions in an inevitably more complicated analysis. The remainder of this section discusses difficulties for the analysis as it stands which, I think, it can survive (at least after some tinkering, modifying, and disclaiming). One of these difficulties stems from a heterogeneous group of examples of persons who, on our analysis, would be blamed for harms that are clearly not their fault. I try to sidestep these counterexamples by affixing a restriction to the fault condition and making corresponding adjustments in the formulation of the relevance condition. The other difficulties directly concern the causal condition and the relevance condition. Both of these can involve us quickly in some fundamental philosophical problems.

Restrictions on the fault condition

There are some exceptional cases (but readily accessible to the philosophical imagination) in which a person who is clearly not to blame for a given harm nevertheless is the sole person who satisfies the conditions of the tripartite analysis. These cases, therefore, constitute counterexamples to that analysis if it is taken to state not only necessary but sufficient conditions for blame. Nicholas Sturgeon has suggested an especially ingenious case:

> *A* has made a large bet that no infractions of the law will occur at a certain place in a certain

period of time; but *B*, at that place and time, opens a pack of cigarettes and fails to destroy the federal tax seal thereby breaking the law. *A*, seeing *B*'s omission, is so frustrated that he suffers a fatal heart attack on the spot. (To simplify matters, we may suppose that no one has any reason to suppose *A* is endangering his health by gambling in this way.)[1]

Clearly, *A*'s death is not *B*'s fault. Yet (1) *B* was at fault in acting contrary to law; (2) his faulty act frustrated *A*, causing the heart attack; and (3) the aspects of *B*'s act (omission) that were faulty (the illegality of his omission to destroy the tax stamps) were also among the aspects of it in virtue of which there was a causal connection between it and the harm. [. . .]

[. . .] We can attempt to avoid counter-examples of the sort Sturgeon [. . .] suggested by tampering with the first condition (the fault condition). We can say now (of course, only tentatively and not without misgiving) that, for the purpose of this analysis, the way of being at fault required by the fault condition is to be understood as the harm-threatening way, not the nonbenefiting, offense-threatening, harmless faith-breaking, or law-violating ways. The fault condition then can be reformulated as follows (in words suggested by Sturgeon): a given harm is *A*'s fault only if (1) *A* was at fault in acting or omitting to act and "the faultiness of his act or omission consisted, at least in part, in the creation of either a certainty or an unreasonable risk of harm. [. . .]"[2] Now the faulty smoker in Sturgeon's example [. . .] [is] no longer "at fault" in the requisite way, and the revised analysis no longer pins the blame for coincidental harms on [him]. To open a cigarette package in an overly fastidious fashion is not to endanger unduly the health of others. [. . .]

[. . .] We can now say that the (harm-threatening) "faulty aspect" of an act is a cause of subsequent harm when the risk or certainty of harm in virtue of which the act was at fault was a risk or certainty of "just the sort of harm that was in fact caused,"[3] and not harm of some other sort. The resultant harm, in other words, must be within the scope of the risk (or certainty) in virtue of which the act is properly characterized as faulty. This is more than a mere explication of the original way of putting the third condition.

It is a definite modification designed to rule out cases of *coincidence* where the faulty aspect of an act, even when it is of the harm-threatening sort, may be causally linked to a subsequent harm via such adventitious conditions as standing wagers. [. . .] Under the revised formulation, the very same considerations involved in the explanation of *why* the act is faulty are also involved, essentially and sufficiently, in the explanation of *how* the harm was caused. [. . .]

Fault and cause: dependent and independent determinations

Can we tell whether an act caused a given harm independently of knowing whether the actor was at fault in acting? The answer seems to be that we can determine the causal question independently of the fault question in some cases but not in others. Part of our problem is to explain this variation. Consider first some examples. [. . .] [T]he motorist in our earlier example, by driving (whether with or without fault is immaterial to this point) along a rarely traveled stretch of country road, caused a nervous horse to bolt. That is, it was his activity as he conducted it then and there, with its attendant noise and dust, that caused the horse to bolt; and we can know this independently of any determination of fault.

Examples provided by J. L. Mackie [. . .] however, seem to cut the other way. Mackie[4] describes an episode in which a motorcyclist exceeded a speed limit and was chased by a policeman, also on a motorcycle, at speeds up to seventy miles per hour. An absentminded pedestrian stepped off a bus into the policeman's path and was killed instantly. The newspapers for the next few days were full of debates over the question of whose conduct was the "real cause" of the death, debates that seemed to center on the question of whose conduct was the least *reasonable* intrusion into the normal course of events. To express an opinion at all on the causal question seemed to be to take a stand, plain and simple, about the *propriety* of pursuits by police in heavily populated areas. [. . .]

To clarify the relations between cause and fault, it will be necessary to digress briefly and remind ourselves of certain features of causal judgments as they are made in ordinary life. That one condition is causally necessary or, in a given context, sufficient for the occurrence of a given event is normally a question simply for empirical investigation and the application of a scientific theory. Normally, however, there will be a plurality of distinguishable causal conditions (often called "causal factors") for any given event, and the aim of a causal inquiry will be to single out one[5] of these to be denominated "the cause" of the event in question.[6] A judgment that cites one of the numerous eligible causal conditions for an event as "the cause" I call a *causal citation*. The eligibility of an event or state as a causal factor is determined empirically via the application of inductive criteria.[7] On the other hand, the citation of one of the eligible candidates as "the cause" is normally made, as we shall see, via the application of what Dray calls "pragmatic criteria." In Dray's convenient phrase, the inductive inquiry establishes the "importance of a condition to the event," whereas the causal citation indicates its "importance to the inquirer."

The point of a causal citation is to single out one of the certified causal candidates that is especially *interesting* to us, given our various practical purposes and cognitive concerns. These purposes and concerns provide a convenient way of classifying the "contexts of inquiry" in which causal citations are made. The primary division is between explanatory and nonexplanatory contexts. The occasion for an explanatory citation is one in which there is intellectual puzzlement of a quite specific kind. A surprising or unusual event has occurred which is a deviation from what is understood to be the normal course of things. [. . .]

Very often one of the causal conditions for a given upshot is a faulty human action. [. . .]

[. . .] [C]ausal citations can be divided into those made from explanatory and those made from nonexplanatory standpoints, and the latter group into those made from the "engineering" and those made from the "blaming" standpoints. Explanatory citations single out abnormal interferences with the normal course of events or hitherto unknown missing links in a person's understanding. They are designed simply to remove puzzlement by citing the causal factor that can shed the most light. Hence we can refer to the criterion of selection in explanatory contexts (for short) as *the lantern criterion*. Causal citations made from the "engineering standpoint" are

made with a view to facilitating control over future events by citing the most efficiently and economically manipulable causal factor. The criterion for selection in engineering contexts can thus be called (for short) *the handle criterion*. The point of causal citations in purely blaming contexts is simply to pin the label of blame on the appropriate causal factor for further notice and practical use. These judgments cite a causal factor that is a human act or omission "stained" (as an ancient figure of speech would have it) with fault. The criterion in blaming contexts can be called (for short) *the stain criterion*. When we look for "the cause," then, we may be looking for the causal factor that has either a lantern, a handle, or a stain on it.

Purely blaming citations can be interpreted in two different ways. On the first model, to say that a person's act was the cause of the harm is precisely equivalent to saying that he is to blame for the harm, that is, that the harm is his fault. The causal inquiry undertaken from the purely blaming perspective, according to this view, is one and the same as the inquiry into the question of who was to blame or of whose fault it was. On this model, then, causal citation is not a condition for the fixing of blame; it is, rather, precisely the same thing. [. . .]

On the second model of interpretation, which is also sometimes *a propos*, the truth of the causal citation "His act was the cause of the harm" is only one of the *conditions* for the judgment that "The harm was his fault." Here we separate cause and fault before bringing them together again in a "his fault" judgment, insisting that the harm was his fault *only if* his action caused it. The causal inquiry, so conceived, is undertaken for the sake of the blame inquiry, but its results are established independently. [. . .]

The causal relevance condition: is it always necessary?

Does the analysis of commonsense "his fault" judgments really require a causal relevance condition? Many people, I suspect, are prepared to make "his fault" judgments in particular cases even when they know that a causal relevance condition has not been satisfied; and many puzzling cases are such as to make even most of us hesitate about the matter. [. . .]

[. . .] [O]thers might prefer to reject the causal relevance condition out of hand as too restrictive and urge instead that the blame always be placed on the person *most at fault*, whether the fault is causally relevant or not, providing his faulty action was a genuine causal factor. [. . .] It does not commend itself to the intuitive understanding in a quiet reflective hour, however, and seems to me to have no other merit than that of letting the indignation and vindictiveness occasioned by harm have a respectable outlet in our moral judgments. [. . .] Rather, if we are vindictively inclined, we can say that to impose liability on a person to enforced compensation or other harsh treatment for some harm does not always require that the harm be his fault. This would be the moral equivalent of a departure from what is called "the fault principle" in the law of torts. It is an attempt to do justice to our spontaneous feelings, without confusing our concepts, and has the merits at least of openness and honesty.

Disinterested parties might reject causal relevance as a condition for being to blame in a skeptical way, offering as an alternative to it a radical contextual relativism. [. . .] This skeptical theory, however, strikes me as a combined insight and *non sequitur*. The insight is that we are not *forced* to pinpoint blame unless some practical question like liability hinges on it and that it is often the better part of wisdom to decline to do so when one can. But it does not follow from the fact that "his fault" judgments can sometimes be avoided that it is logically open to us to make them in any way we wish when we do make them. I hold, therefore, to the conclusion that, in fixing the blame for harm, we are restricted by our very concepts to the person(s) whose faulty act was a causal factor in the production of the harm in virtue of its causally relevant faulty aspect.

There often is room for discretion in the making of "his fault" judgments, but it comes at a different place and is subject to strict limitations. The person whose fault the harm is said to be *must* satisfy the conditions of the triconditional analysis (and perhaps others as well); but when more than one person is so qualified, the judgment-maker may sometimes choose between them on "pragmatic grounds," letting some of them off the hook. When this discretion is proper, the three conditions of our analysis must be honored as necessary, but they are no longer taken to be sufficient. [. . .] [I]f it is given that we must, for some practical purpose, single out a wrongdoer more narrowly, then we have discretion to choose among those (but only those) who satisfy the necessary conditions of the tripartite analysis.[8]

Fault and tort liability

Suppose we accept the revised triconditional analysis of "his fault" but jettison the causal relevance condition as a requisite for tort *liability*. [. . .] The prime consequence of dropping the causal relevance condition is to downgrade the role of causation as a ground for liability and to increase the importance of simply being at fault. If causal relevance is not required, it would seem that being at fault is the one centrally important necessary condition for liability, and indeed so important as to render the causal condition itself a mere dispensable formality. To upgrade the fault condition to that extent is most likely to seem reasonable when the fault is disproportionately greater than the harm it occasions. [. . .]

It is another matter, however, when the harm is disproportionately greater than the fault, when a mere slap causes an unsuspected hemophiliac to bleed to death, or a clumsy slip on the sidewalk leads one to bump an "old soldier with an egg shell skull," causing his death. Hart and Honoré suggest that even here commonsense considerations can help justify abandonment, in some cases at least, of the causal relevance condition by mitigating its apparent harshness:

> The apparent unfairness of holding a defendant liable for a loss much greater than he could foresee to some extent disappears when we consider that a defendant is often negligent without suffering punishment or having to pay compensation. I may drive at an excessive speed a hundred times before the one occasion on which my speeding causes harm. The justice of holding me liable, should the harm on that occasion turn out to be extraordinarily grave, must be judged in the light of the hundred other occasions on which, without deserving such luck, I have incurred no liability.[9]

[. . .] If justice truly requires (as the Hart–Honoré argument suggests) that blame and liability be properly apportioned to *all* a person's faults as accumulated in the long run, causal linkage to harm aside, why not go all the way in this direction and drop the "causal factor" condition altogether in the interest of Aristotelian "due proportion" and fairness? To say that we are all negligent is to say that on other occasions, at least, we have all created unreasonable risk of harms, sometimes great harms, of one kind or another, to other persons. Even in circumstances where excessive harm actually results, we may have created other risks of a different kind to other individuals, risks which luckily failed to eventuate in harm. [. . .]

The system just described could be called a system of "liability without *contributory* fault," since it bypasses a causation requirement. It is a system of liability based on fault simply, whether or not the fault contributes to harm. It thus differs sharply from the traditional system of liability based in part upon what is called *the fault principle*, which requires that accidental losses be borne by the party whose fault the accident was. This is liability based on "his fault" ascriptions, rather than "at fault" imputations. In contrast, the principle underlying a system of liability based on fault without causation might well be called the *retributive theory of torts*. [. . .]

One way to understand the retributive theory of torts is to relate it to, or derive it from, a general moral theory that bears the name of retributivism. In treating of this more general theory, it is very important to distinguish a strong from a weak version, for failure to do so has muddled discussions of retribution in criminal law and would very likely do the same in discussions of principles of tort liability. According to the strong version of the general retributive principle, *all* evil or, more generally still, all *fault* deserves its comeuppance; it is an end in itself, quite apart from other consequences, that all wrongdoers (or faulty doers) be made to suffer some penalty, handicap, or forfeiture as a requital for their wrongdoing. Similarly, it is an end in itself, morally fitting and proper irrespective of other consequences, that the meritorious be rewarded with the means to happiness. [. . .]

The weaker version of general retributivism, on the other hand, is essentially a comparative principle, applying to situations in which it is given that someone or other must do without, make a sacrifice, or forfeit his interest. The principle simply asserts the moral priority, *ceteris paribus*, of the innocent party. Put most pithily, it is the principle that *fault forfeits first*, if forfeit there must be. If someone must suffer, it is better, *ceteris paribus*, that it be the faulty than the meritorious. This weaker version of retributivism, which permeates the law, especially the criminal law, has strong support in common sense. It commonly governs the distribution of that special kind of benefit called "the benefit of the doubt," so that, where there is doubt, for example, about the deterrent efficacy of a particular mode of punishment for a certain class of crimes, the benefit of that doubt is given to potential victims instead of convicted criminals.

I find the weaker version of retributivism much more plausible intuitively than the stronger, though even it is limited – for example, by the values of intimacy and friendship. [. . .]

Now let us return to our tort principles, What is called the "fault principle" (or, better, the "his fault" principle) does not derive from, and indeed is not even compatible with, the strong version of general retributivism. As we have seen, the causal component of "his fault" ascriptions introduces a fortuitous element, repugnant to pure retributivism. People who are very much at fault may luckily avoid causing proportionate harm, and unlucky persons may cause harm in excess of their minor faults. In the former case, little or no harm may be a person's fault even though he is greatly at fault; hence his liability, based on "his fault," will not be the burden he deserves, and the moral universe will be out of joint. In the latter case, unhappily coexistent circumstances may step up the normal magnitude of harm resulting from a minor fault, and again the defendant's liability will not do proper justice to his actual fault.

The tort principle that is called for by strong retributivism is that which I have called "the retributive theory of torts." Being at fault gets its proper comeuppance from this principle, whether or not it leads directly to harm; and the element of luck – except for luck in escaping detection – is largely eliminated. Hence fault suffers its due penalty, and if that is an end in itself, as strong retributivism maintains, then the retributive theory of torts is well recommended indeed. But the lack of intuitive persuasiveness of the general theory, I think, diminishes the plausibility of its offshoot in torts. Weak retributivism, which is generally more plausible, in my opinion, than its strong counterpart, does not uniquely favor either the retributive theory of torts or the "his fault" principle. Except in straightforwardly comparative contexts where the necessity of forfeiture is given, it takes no stand whatever about principles of tort liability. [. . .]

One final point remains to be made. If we hold that we are all more or less equally sinners in respect to a certain area of conduct or a certain type of fault – if, for example we are all as likely, more or less, to be erring defendants as wronged plaintiffs in driving accident suits – then the principle of strong retributivism itself would call for the jettisoning of the "his fault" principle in that area of activity. If fault is distributed equally, the "his fault" principle, in distributing liability *unequally* among a group, will cause a lack of correspondence between fault and penalty. On the assumption of equal distribution of fault, the use of the "his fault" principle would lead to *less* correspondence, less exact proportioning of penalty to fault, even than various principles of social insurance that have the effect of spreading the losses as widely as possible among a whole community of persons presumed to be equally faulty. But then these schemes of nonfault liability are supported by strong reasons of their own, principles both of justice and economy,[10] and hardly need this bit of surprising added support from the principle of strong retributivism.

Notes

1 The example is from a very helpful letter sent to me by Professor Sturgeon after I read an earlier version of this paper at Cornell in May 1969.

2 Ibid.

3 Ibid.

4 "Responsibility and Language," *Australasian Journal of Philosophy*, 33 (1955), 145.

5 In unusual cases, two or three.

6 The distinction in common sense between a "causal factor" and "the cause" corresponds roughly – very roughly – to the technical legal distinction between "cause in fact" and "proximate cause."

7 A causal factor is an earlier necessary condition in at least the weaker sense of "necessary condition," viz., a member of a set of jointly sufficient conditions whose presence was necessary to the sufficiency of the set; but it need not be necessary in the stronger sense, viz., a necessary element in every set of conditions that would be jointly sufficient, as oxygen is necessary to every instance of combustion. Not all prior necessary conditions, of course, are genuine causal factors. Analytic connections ("But for his having been born, the accident would not have happened") are ruled out, and so are "incidental connections" (earlier speeding bringing one to a given point just at the moment a tree falls on the road). Unlike necessary conditions connected in a merely incidental way to results, causal factors are "necessary elements in a set of conditions generally connected through intermediate stages with it." See H. L. A. Hart and A. M. Honoré, *Causation in the Law* (Oxford: Clarendon Press, 1959), 114. See also Robert Keeton, *Legal Cause in the Law of Torts* (Columbus: Ohio State University Press, 1963), 62.

8 If it is given that a particular "his fault" judgment on a particular occasion must single out one or a small number to be assigned the blame, then the concept of "his fault" can perhaps be understood to limit discretion by providing two additional necessary conditions to the triconditional analysis: (4) there is no other person to whom conditions (1)–(3) apply who was substantially more at fault than the present assignee(s); and (5) there is no other person to whom conditions (1)–(3) apply whose act was a more striking deviation from routine, or of a kind patently more manipulable, or otherwise a more "direct" or "substantial" cause. [. . .]

9 Hart and Honoré, op. cit., 243.

10 E.g., the *benefit principle* (of commutative justice) that accidental losses should be borne according to the degree to which people benefit from an enterprise or form of activity; the *deep pocket principle* (of distributive justice) that the burden of accidental losses should be borne by those most able to pay in direct proportion to that ability; the *spread-it-out principle* that the cost of accidental losses should be spread as widely as possible "both interpersonally and intertemporally"; the *safety* or *loss-diminution principle* that the method of distributing losses that leads to the smallest net amount of loss to be distributed is the best one.

32

Fairness and Utility in Tort Theory

George P. Fletcher

I Two Paradigms of Liability

[. . .] [T]ort theorists tend to regard the existing doctrinal framework of fault and strict liability as sufficiently rich to express competing views about fairly shifting losses. This conceptual framework accounts for a number of traditional beliefs about tort law history. One of these beliefs is that the ascendancy of fault in the late nineteenth century reflected the infusion of moral sensibility into the law of torts. That new moral sensibility is expressed sometimes as the principle that wrongdoers ought to pay for their wrongs. Another traditional view is that strict tort liability is the analogue of strict criminal liability, and that if the latter is suspect, so is the former. The underlying assumption of both these tenets is that negligence and strict liability are antithetical rationales of liability. This assumed antithesis is readily invoked to explain the ebbs and flows of tort liability. Strict liability is said to have prevailed in early tort history, fault supposedly held sway in the late nineteenth century, with strict liability now gaining ground.

These beliefs about tort history are ubiquitously held, but to varying degrees they are all false or at best superficial. There has no doubt been a deep ideological struggle in the tort law of the last century and a half. But, as I shall argue, it is not the struggle between negligence and fault on the one hand, and strict liability on the other. Rather, the confrontation is between two radically different paradigms for analyzing tort liability – paradigms which represent a complex of views about (1) the appropriate standard of liability, (2) the appropriate style of legal reasoning, and (3) the relationship between the resolution of individual disputes and the community's welfare.

These paradigms of liability cut across traditional doctrinal lines, creating a deep ideological cleavage between two ways of resolving tort disputes. [. . .]

Of the two paradigms, I shall call the first the paradigm of reciprocity. According to this view, the two central issues of tort law – whether the victim is entitled to recover and whether the defendant ought to pay – are distinct issues, each resolvable without looking beyond the case at hand. Whether the victim is so entitled depends exclusively on the nature of the victim's activity when he was injured and on the risk created by the defendant. The social costs and utility of the risk are irrelevant, as is the impact of the judgment on socially desirable forms of behavior.

George P. Fletcher, "Fairness and Utility in Tort Theory," *Harvard Law Review*, vol. 85, no. 3, January 1972. © 1972 by Harvard Law Review Association. Reproduced with permission from Harvard Law Review Association in the format Textbook via Copyright Clearance Center.

Further, according to this paradigm, if the victim is entitled to recover by virtue of the risk to which he was exposed, there is an additional question of fairness in holding the risk creator liable for the loss. This distinct issue of fairness is expressed by asking whether the defendant's creating the relevant risk was excused on the ground, say, that the defendant could not have known of the risk latent in his conduct. To find that an act is excused is in effect to say that there is no rational, fair basis for distinguishing between the party causing harm and other people. Whether we can rationally single out the defendant as the loss-bearer depends on our expectations of when people ought to be able to avoid risks. As will become clear in the course of this discussion, these expectations should not always depend upon the social utility of taking risks; rather they should often depend on non-instrumentalist criteria for judging when men ought to be able to avoid excessive risks of harm. For example, the standard of uncommon "ultra-hazardous activities," introduced by the first *Restatement* is apparently a non-instrumentalist standard: one looks only to the risk and not to its social utility to determine whether it is ultra-hazardous. Yet it is never made clear by the *Restatement* why extra-hazardous risks warrant "strict liability" while ordinarily hazardous risks do not.

As part of the explication of the first paradigm of liability, I shall propose a specific standard of risk that makes sense of the *Restatement*'s emphasis on uncommon, extra-hazardous risks, but which shows that the *Restatement*'s theory is part of a larger rationale of liability that cuts across negligence, intentional torts, and numerous pockets of strict liability. The general principle expressed in all of these situations governed by diverse doctrinal standards is that a victim has a right to recover for injuries caused by a risk greater in degree and different in order from those created by the victim and imposed on the defendant – in short, for injuries resulting from nonreciprocal risks. Cases of liability are those in which the defendant generates a disproportionate, excessive risk of harm, relative to the victim's risk-creating activity. For example, a pilot or an airplane owner subjects those beneath the path of flight to non-reciprocal risks of harm. Conversely, cases of nonliability are those of reciprocal risks, namely those in which the victim and the defendant subject each other to roughly the same degree of risk. For example, two airplanes flying in the same vicinity subject each other to reciprocal risks of a mid-air collision. Of course, there are significant problems in determining when risks are nonreciprocal, and we shall turn to these difficulties later. For now, it is sufficient to note that the paradigm of reciprocity represents (1) a bifurcation of the questions of who is entitled to compensation and who ought to pay, (2) a commitment to resolving both of those issues by looking only to the activity of the victim and the risk-creator, and (3) a specific criterion for determining who is entitled to recover for loss, namely all those injured by nonreciprocal risks.

The conflicting paradigm of liability – which I shall call the paradigm of reasonableness – represents a rejection of noninstrumentalist values and a commitment to the community's welfare as the criterion for determining both who is entitled to receive and who ought to pay compensation. Questions that are distinct under the paradigm of reciprocity – namely, is the risk nonreciprocal and was it unexcused – are collapsed in this paradigm into a single test: was the risk unreasonable? The reasonableness of the risk thus determines both whether the victim is entitled to compensation and whether the defendant ought to be held liable. Reasonableness is determined by a straightforward balancing of costs and benefits. If the risk yields a net social utility (benefit), the victim is not entitled to recover from the risk-creator; if the risk yields a net social disutility (cost), the victim is entitled to recover.[1] The premises of this paradigm are that reasonableness provides a test of activities that ought to be encouraged and that tort judgments are an appropriate medium for encouraging them. [. . .]

II The Paradigm of Reciprocity

A The victim's right to recover

Our first task is to demonstrate the pervasive reliance of the common law on the paradigm of reciprocity. The area that most consistently reveals this paradigm is the one that now most lacks doctrinal unity – namely, the disparate pockets of strict liability. [. . .]

I shall attempt to show that the paradigm of reciprocity accounts for the typical cases of strict liability – crashing airplanes,[2] damage done by wild animals,[3] and the more common cases of blasting, fumigating and crop dusting.[4] To do this, I shall consider in detail two leading, but seemingly diverse instances of liability for reasonable risk-taking – *Rylands v. Fletcher*[5] and *Vincent v. Lake Erie Transportation Co.*[6] The point of focusing on these two cases is to generate a foundation for inducing the claim that unexcused nonreciprocity of risk is the unifying feature of a broad spectrum of cases imposing liability under rubrics of both negligence and strict liability.

In *Rylands v. Fletcher* the plaintiff, a coal mine operator, had suffered the flooding of his mine by water that the defendant had pumped into a newly-erected reservoir on his own land. The water broke through to an abandoned mine shaft under the defendant's land and thus found its way to the plaintiff's adjoining mine. The engineers and contractors were negligent in not providing stronger supports for the reservoir; yet because they were independent contractors, the defendant was not liable for their negligence. Though the defendant's erecting and maintaining the reservoir was legally permissible, the Exchequer Chamber found for the plaintiff,[7] and the House of Lords affirmed.[8] Blackburn's opinion in the Exchequer Chamber focused on the defendant's bringing on to his land, for his own purposes, "something which, though harmless whilst it remain there, will naturally do mischief if it escape."[9] Lord Cairns, writing in the House of Lords, reasoned that the defendant's activity rendered his use of the land "non-natural"; accordingly, "that which the Defendants were doing they were doing at their own peril."[10]

Neither Blackburn's nor Cairns' account provides an adequate rationale for liability. It may be that a body of water will "naturally do mischief if it escapes," but so may many other things, like water in a pipe, oil in a furnace tank, and fire in a fireplace. It is unlikely that Blackburn would favor liability for the harmful consequences of these risky practices. Cairns' rationale of non-natural use, for all its metaphysical pretensions, may be closer to the policy issue at stake in the dispute.

The fact was that the defendant sought to use his land for a purpose at odds with the use of land then prevailing in the community. He thereby subjected the neighboring miners to a risk to which they were not accustomed and which they would not regard as a tolerable risk entailed by their way of life. Creating a risk different from the prevailing risks in the community might be what Lord Cairns had in mind in speaking of a non-natural use of the land. A better term might have been "abnormal" or "inappropriate" use. Indeed these are the adjectives used in the proposed revision of the *Restatement* to provide a more faithful rendition of the case law tradition of strict liability.[11]

A seemingly unrelated example of the same case law tradition is *Vincent v. Lake Erie Transportation Co.*, a 1910 decision of the Minnesota Supreme Court.[12] The dispute arose from a ship captain's keeping his vessel lashed to the plaintiff's dock during a two-day storm when it would have been unreasonable, indeed foolhardy, for him to set out to sea. The storm battered the ship against the dock, causing damages assessed at five hundred dollars. The court affirmed a judgment for the plaintiff even though a prior case had recognized a ship captain's right to take shelter from a storm by mooring his vessel to another's dock, even without consent.[13] The court's opinion conceded that keeping the ship at dockside was justified and reasonable, yet it characterized the defendant's damaging the dock as "prudently and advisedly [availing]" himself of the plaintiff's property. Because the incident impressed the court as an implicit transfer of wealth, the defendant was bound to rectify the transfer by compensating the dock owner for his loss.[14]

The rationales of *Rylands* and *Vincent* are obviously not interchangeable. Building a reservoir is not availing oneself of a neighbor's property. And mooring a ship to a wharf is not an abnormal or "non-natural" use of either the ship or the wharf. Yet by stripping the two cases of their rhetoric and by focusing on the risks each defendant took, one can bring the two cases within the same general principle. The critical feature of both cases is that the defendant created a risk of harm to the plaintiff that was of an order different from the risks that the plaintiff imposed on the defendant. [. . .]

Expressing the standard of strict liability as unexcused, nonreciprocal risk-taking provides an account not only of the *Rylands* and *Vincent* decisions, but of strict liability in general. It is apparent, for example, that the uncommon, ultra-hazardous activities pinpointed by the *Restatement* are readily subsumed under the rationale of nonreciprocal risk-taking. If uncommon activities are those with few participants, they are likely to be activities generating nonreciprocal risks. Similarly, dangerous activities like blasting, fumigating, and crop dusting stand out as distinct, nonreciprocal risks in the community. They represent threats of harm that exceed the level of risk to which all members of the community contribute in roughly equal shares.

The rationale of nonreciprocal risk-taking accounts as well for pockets of strict liability outside the coverage of the *Restatement*'s sections on extra-hazardous activities. For example, an individual is strictly liable for damage done by a wild animal in his charge, but not for damage committed by his domesticated pet.[15] Most people have pets, children, or friends whose presence creates some risk to neighbors and their property. These are risks that offset each other; they are, as a class, reciprocal risks. Yet bringing an unruly horse into the city goes beyond the accepted and shared level of risks in having pets, children, and friends in one's household. If the defendant creates a risk that exceeds those to which he is reciprocally subject, it seems fair to hold him liable for the results of his aberrant indulgence. [...]

Negligently and intentionally caused harms also lend themselves to analysis as nonreciprocal risks. As a general matter, principles of negligence liability apply in the context of activities, like motoring and sporting ventures, in which the participants all normally create and expose themselves to the same order of risk. These are all pockets of reciprocal risk-taking. [...] To establish liability for harm resulting from these activities, one must show that the harm derives from a specific risk negligently engendered in the course of the activity. Yet a negligent risk, an "unreasonable" risk, is but one that unduly exceeds the bounds of reciprocity. [...]

To complete our account of the paradigm of reciprocity, we should turn to one of its primary expressions: intentional torts, particularly the torts of battery and assault. [...] An intentional assault or battery represents a rapid acceleration of risk, directed at a specific victim. These features readily distinguish the intentional blow from the background of risk. Perceiving intentional blows as a form of nonreciprocal risk helps us understand why the defendant's malice or animosity toward the victim eventually became unnecessary to ground intentional torts.[16] The nonreciprocity of risk, and the deprivation of security it represents, render irrelevant the attitudes of the risk-creator.

All of these manifestations of the paradigm of reciprocity – strict liability, negligence and intentional battery – express the same principle of fairness: all individuals in society have the right to roughly the same degree of security from risk. By analogy to John Rawls' first principle of justice,[17] the principle might read: we all have the right to the maximum amount of security compatible with a like security for everyone else. This means that we are subject to harm, without compensation, from background risks, but that no one may suffer harm from additional risks without recourse for damages against the risk-creator. [...]

B   Excusing nonreciprocal risks

If the victim's injury results from a nonreciprocal risk of harm, the paradigm of reciprocity tells us that the victim is entitled to compensation. Should not the defendant then be under a duty to pay? Not always. For the paradigm also holds that nonreciprocal risk-creation may sometimes be excused, and we must inquire further, into the fairness of requiring the defendant to render compensation. We must determine whether there may be factors in a particular situation which would excuse this defendant from paying compensation.

Though the King's Bench favored liability in its 1616 decision of *Weaver v. Ward*,[18] it digressed to list some hypothetical examples where directly causing harm would be excused and therefore exempt from liability. [...]

The hypotheticals of *Weaver v. Ward* correspond to the Aristotelian excusing categories of compulsion and unavoidable ignorance.[19] Each of these has spawned a line of cases denying liability in cases of inordinate risk-creation. The excuse of compulsion has found expression in the emergency doctrine, which excuses excessive risks created in cases in which the defendant is caught in an unexpected, personally dangerous situation. In *Cordas v. Peerless Transportation Co.*, for example, it was thought excusable for a cab driver to jump from his moving cab in order to escape from a threatening gunman on the running board. In view of the crowd of pedestrians nearby, the driver clearly took a risk that generated a net danger to human life. It was thus an unreasonable, excessive, and unjustified risk. Yet the overwhelmingly coercive circumstances meant that he, personally, was excused from fleeing the moving cab. An example of unavoidable ignorance excusing risk-creation is *Smith v. Lampe*, in which the defendant honked his horn in an effort to warn a tug that seemed to be heading toward shore in a dense fog. As it happened, the honking coincided with a signal that the tug captain expected would assist him in making port. Accordingly the captain steered his tug toward the honking rather than away from it. That the defendant did not know of the pre-arranged signal excused his contributing to the tug's going aground. Under the facts of the case, the honking surely created an unreasonable risk of harm. If instantaneous injunctions were possible, one would no doubt wish to enjoin the honking as an excessive, illegal risk. Yet the defendant's ignorance of that risk was also excusable. Under the circumstances he could not fairly have been expected to inform himself of all possible interpretations of honking in a dense fog. [...]

[...] [W]e can formulate two significant claims about the role of excuses in cases decided under the paradigm of reciprocity. First, excusing the risk-creator does not, in principle, undercut the victim's right to recover. In most cases it is operationally irrelevant to posit a right to recovery when the victim cannot in fact recover from the excused risk-creator. [...]

Secondly, an even more significant claim is that these excuses – compulsion and unavoidable ignorance – are available in all cases in which the right to recovery springs from being subjected to a nonreciprocal risk of harm. We have already pointed out the applicability of these excuses in negligence cases like *Cordas* and *Smith v. Lampe*. What is surprising is to find them applicable in

cases of strict liability as well; strict liability is usually thought of as an area where courts are insensitive to questions of fairness to defendants. [...] In *Madsen v. East Jordan Irrigation Co.*,[20] for example, the defendant's blasting operations frightened the mother mink on the plaintiff's farm, causing them to kill 230 of their offspring. The Utah Supreme Court affirmed a demurrer to the complaint. In the court's judgment, the reaction of the mother mink "was not within the realm of matters to be anticipated."[21] This is precisely the factual judgment that would warrant saying that the company's ignorance of this possible result was excused, yet the rubric of proximate cause provided a doctrinally acceptable heading for dismissing the complaint.

It is hard to find a case of strict liability raising the issue of compulsion as an excuse. Yet if a pilot could flee a dangerous situation only by taking off in his plane, as the cab driver in *Cordas* escaped danger by leaping from his moving cab, would there be rational grounds for distinguishing damage caused by the airplane crash from damage caused by *Cordas*' cab? One would think not. Both are cases of nonreciprocal risk-taking and both are cases in which unusual circumstances render it unfair to expect the defendant to avoid the risk he creates. [...]

III   The Paradigm of Reasonableness

[...] In the course of the nineteenth century, [...] the concepts underlying the paradigm of reciprocity gradually assumed new contours. A new paradigm emerged, which challenged all traditional ideas of tort theory. [...]

The core of this revolutionary change was a shift in the meaning of the word "fault." At its origins in the common law of torts, the concept of fault served to unify the medley of excuses available to defendants who would otherwise be liable in trespass for directly causing harm. As the new paradigm emerged, fault came to be an inquiry about the context and the reasonableness of the defendant's risk-creating conduct. [...]

The difference between justifying and excusing conditions is most readily seen in the case of intentional conduct, particularly intentional crimes. Typical cases of justified intentional conduct are self-defense and the use of force to effect an arrest. These justificatory claims assess the reasonableness of using force under the circumstances. The questions asked in seeking to justify an intentional battery as self-defense relate to the social costs and the social benefits of using force and to the wrongfulness of the initial aggressor's conduct in attacking the defendant. The resolution of this cost–benefit analysis speaks to the legal permissibility and sometimes to the commendability of the *act* of using force under the circumstances. Excuses, in contrast, focus not on the costs and benefits of the *act*, but on the degree of the *actor's* choice in engaging in it. Insanity and duress are raised as excuses even to concededly wrongful acts. To resolve a claim of insanity, we are led to inquire about the *actor's* personality, his capacities under stress and the pressures under which he was acting. Finding that the *actor* is excused by reason of insanity is not to say that the *act* was right or even permissible, but merely that the actor's freedom of choice was so impaired that he cannot be held accountable for his wrongful deed. [...]

That the fault requirement shifted its orientation from excusing to justifying risks had the following consequences: (1) fault became a judgement about the risk, rather than about the responsibility of the individual who created the risk; (2) fault was no longer a question of fairness to the individual, but an inquiry about the relative costs and benefits of particular risks; (3) fault became a condition for recognizing the right of the victim to recover. These three postures of the fault requirement diverged radically from the paradigm of reciprocity. Together, they provided the foundation for the paradigm of reasonableness, a way of thinking that was to become a powerful ideological force in tort thinking of the late nineteenth and twentieth centuries.

The reasonable man became a central, almost indispensable figure in the paradigm of reasonableness. By asking what a reasonable man would do under the circumstances, judges could assay the issues both of justifying and excusing risks. Reasonable men, presumably, seek to maximize utility; therefore to ask what a reasonable man would do is to inquire into the justifiability of the risk. [...]

No single appellate decision ushered in the paradigm of reasonableness. It derived from a variety of sources. If there was a pivotal case, however, it was *Brown v. Kendall*, decided by the Massachusetts Supreme Judicial Court in 1850. [...]

[...] Chief Justice Shaw's opinion created possibilities for an entirely new and powerful use of the fault standard, and the judges and writers of the late nineteenth and early twentieth centuries responded sympathetically.

Shaw's revision of tort doctrine made its impact in cases in which the issue was not one of excusing inadvertent risk-creation, but one of justifying risks of harm that were voluntarily and knowingly generated. Consider the following case of risk-creation: [...] the defendant police officer shoots at a fleeing felon, knowing that he thereby risks hitting a bystander. [...] All of these victims could receive compensation for their injuries under the paradigm of reciprocity, as incorporated in the doctrine of trespassory liability; the defendant or his employees directly and without excuse caused the harm in each case. Yet as *Brown v. Kendall* was received into the tort law, the threshold of liability became whether, under all the circumstances, the defendant acted with ordinary, prudent care. But more importantly, the test of ordinary care transcended its origins as a standard for determining the acceptability of ignorance as an excuse, and became a rationale for determining when individuals could knowingly and voluntarily create risks without responsibility for the harm they might cause. The test for justifying risks became a straightforward utilitarian comparison of the benefits and costs of the defendant's risk-creating activity. The assumption emerged that reasonable men do what is justified by a utilitarian calculus, that justified activity is lawful, and that lawful activities should be exempt from tort liability.

In the case mentioned above, the arguments are readily at hand for maximizing utility by optimizing accidents: [...] capturing fleeing felons is sufficiently important to warrant a few risks to onlookers. [...] More generally, if promoting the general welfare is the criterion of rights and duties of compensation, then a few individuals must suffer. One might fairly wonder, however, why [...] law enforcement [...] should prosper at the expense of innocent victims.

IV Utility and the Interests of the Individual

The accepted reading of tort history is that the rise of the fault standard in the nineteenth century manifested a newly found sensitivity to the morality of legal rules. James Barr Ames captured orthodox sentiments with his conclusion that "[t]he ethical standard of reasonable conduct has replaced the unmoral standard of acting at one's peril."[22] [. . .]

But the issue in the nineteenth century was not the choice between strict liability on the one hand and liability based on fault on the other. Nor was it a simplistic choice between an "unmoral" standard and an ethical one. Rather, the question of the time was the shape that the fault standard would take. Should the absence of fault function as an excuse within a paradigm of reciprocity? Or should it function as a standard for exempting from liability risks that maximize utility? That was the moral and policy question that underlay the nineteenth century revolution in tort thinking. The question posed by the conflict of paradigms was whether traditional notions of individual autonomy would survive increasing concern for the public welfare. If the courts of the time had clearly perceived and stated the issue, they would have been shaken by its proportions. [. . .]

V The Interplay of Substance and Style

The conflict between the paradigm of reasonableness and the paradigm of reciprocity is, in the end, a struggle between two strategies for justifying the distribution of burdens in a legal system. [. . .]

On the whole, however, the paradigm of reasonableness still holds sway over the thinking of American courts. The reasonable man is too popular a figure to be abandoned. The use of litigation to pursue social goals is well entrenched. Yet the appeal to the paradigm might well be more one of style than substance. [. . .]

The paradigm of reciprocity, on the other hand, for all its substantive and moral appeal, puts questions that are hardly likely to engage the contemporary legal mind: When is a risk so excessive that it counts as a nonreciprocal risk? When are two risks of the same category and thus reciprocally offsetting? [. . .]

[. . .] Yet why should the rhetoric of reasonableness and foreseeability appeal to lawyers as a more scientific or precise way of thinking? The answer might lie in the scientific image associated with passing through several stages of argument before reaching a conclusion. The paradigm of reasonableness requires several stages of analysis: defining the risk, assessing its consequences, balancing costs and benefits. The paradigm of reciprocity requires a single conclusion, based on perceptions of similarities, of excessiveness, and of directness. If an argument requires several steps, it basks in the respectability of precision and rationality. Yet associating rationality with multistaged argumentation may be but a spectacular lawyerly fallacy. [. . .]

Notes

1 This is a simpler statement of the balancing test known as the "Learned Hand formula," defined in United States v. Carroll Towing Co., 159 F.2d 169 (2d Cir. 1947). [. . .]

2 See [. . .] *Prosser and Keeton on Torts* (West, 1984), 514–16.

3 E.g., Collins v. Otto, 149 Colo. 489, 369 P.2d 564 (1962) (coyote bite); Filburn v. People's Palace & Aquarium Co., 25 Q.B.D. 258 (1890) (escaped circus elephant). See generally *Prosser and Keeton*, 496–503.

4 E.g., Exner v. Sherman Power Constr. Co., 54 F.2d 510 (2d Cir. 1931) (storing explosives); Western Geophysical Co. of America v. Mason, 240 Ark. 767, 402 S.W.2d 657 (1966) (blasting); Luthringer v. Moore, 31 Cal. 2d 489, 190 P.2d 1 (1948) (fumigating); Young v. Darter, 363 P.2d 829 (Okla. 1961) (crop dusting).

5 159 Eng. Rep. 737 (Ex. 1865), *rev'd*, L.R.1 Ex. 265 (1866), *aff'd*, L.R. 3 H.L. 330 (1868).

6 109 Minn. 456, 124 N.W. 221 (1910).

7 L.R. 1 Ex. 265 (1866).

8 L.R. 3 H.L. 330 (1868).

9 L.R. 1 Ex. at 279.

10 L.R. 3 H.L. at 339.

11 Restatement (Second) of Torts §520 (Tent. Draft No 10, 1964).

12 109 Minn. 456, 124 N.W. 221 (1910).

13 See Ploof v. Putnam, 81 Vt. 471, 71 A. 188 (1908) (defendant dock owner, whose servant unmoored the plaintiff's ship during a storm, held liable for the ensuing damage to the ship and passengers).

14 109 Minn. at 460, 124 N.W. at 222.

15 See, e.g., Fowler v. Helck, 278 Ky. 361, 128 S.W. 2d 564 (1939); Warrick v. Farley, 95 Neb. 565, 145 N.W. 1020 (1914).

16 See Vosburg v. Putney, 80 Wis. 523, 50 N.W. 403 (1891). Animosity would obviously be relevant to the issue of punitive damages, see *Prosser and Keeton*, 9–10, the formal rationales for which are retribution and deterrence, not compensation.

17 Rawls, "Justice as Fairness," 67 *Philosophical Rev.*, 164, 165 (1958) ("[E]each person participating in a practice, or affected by it, has an equal right to the most extensive liberty compatible with a like liberty for all."). [. . .]

18 80 Eng. Rep 284 (K.B. 1616).

19 *The Nicomachean Ethics of Aristotle* (Ross transl. World Classics ed. 1954), Book III, ch. 1, at 48 ("Those things, then, are thought involuntary, which take place under compulsion or owing to ignorance").

20 101 Utah 552, 125 P.2d 794 (1942).

21 *Id.* at 555, 125 P.2d at 795.

22 J. B. Ames, "Law and Morals," 22 *Harv. L. Rev.* 97, 99 (1908).

33

Tort Liability and the Limits of Corrective Justice

Jules L. Coleman

This essay tries to make sense of and defend both of the following claims: [. . .] (1) Many of the important rights and duties sustained in tort law are justifiable departures from tort law's corrective justice core; and (2) the extent to which corrective justice (as a moral principle) creates reasons for acting in a community depends on the nature and scope of nonmoral, including legal, practices. So it is a mistake to think of law only in terms of the extent to which it implements or is otherwise influenced by morality. The scope of morality can itself be determined in part by legal practice; or so I will argue.

Four Kinds of Cases

With regard to the claim that many of the duties sustained in tort law do not implement corrective justice, it will be helpful to distinguish among four different kinds of cases.

1   The victim has suffered a loss owing to the fault of the injurer or as a result of a right of his being invaded. The victim's loss is imposed on the injurer whose fault or conduct is responsible for it.

2   The victim has suffered a loss owing to the fault of the injurer or as a result of a right of his being invaded. The victim's loss is imposed on someone other than his injurer, someone who is not responsible for the occurrence.

3   The victim has suffered a loss that is no one's fault and which does not involve a right of his being invaded. (For example, he loses out to another in a competitive business context.) The victim's loss is imposed on the party whose conduct is causally responsible for the loss, but who is otherwise faultless.

4   The victim has suffered a loss that is no one's fault and which does not involve a right of his being invaded. But instead of the loss being imposed on the party whose conduct is causally responsible for the loss (as in case 3), it is imposed on someone else altogether.

Whereas tort law provides us with examples of all four kinds of cases, only cases of the first sort implicate corrective justice. If I am right that corrective justice represents the core of tort law, then these other cases must be departures from corrective justice. The question is whether, and under what conditions, these departures are justifiable or defensible.

Jules L. Coleman, "Tort Liability and the Limits of Corrective Justice," in Jules L. Coleman, ed., *In Harm's Way: Essays in Honor of Joel Feinberg* (Cambridge University Press, 1994), pp. 139–58. © 1994 by Cambridge University Press. Reprinted with permission from the author and Cambridge University Press.

Suppose a manufacturer provides an ineffective (or inefficient) warning. It is inefficient because it fails fully or adequately to warn and, therefore, to deter. Someone uses the product and injures himself as a result. In order for his loss to be wrongful under corrective justice, the warning would have had to be ineffective; the victim would have had to have read it; had the warning been adequate it would have deterred him from using the product; he would have had to use the product believing that it was safe for him and so on. An optimal warning would have deterred him from using the product had he read it. The warning on the product would not have. In fact, the victim never read the warning. The warning is not optimal, but it does not in fact contribute to the victim's loss. Though there is no denying that the manufacturer is at fault, the victim's loss is not the manufacturer's fault. The victim has suffered a loss, but not one for which he has a claim in corrective justice to repair. One might even say that the loss is his own fault.

Nevertheless, a court might well impose liability on the product manufacturer for the purpose of encouraging more efficient warnings. Though he has no right to it, compensation provides the victim with an incentive to litigate. By litigating, he acts as a private regulator. The manufacturer has a defective warning that needs to be improved. If part of the goal of the law is to encourage product manufacturers to provide optimal warnings, why should a court wait until a victim comes along who has a valid claim to repair in justice? The goal of encouraging efficient warnings does not discriminate between those victims who have suffered wrongful losses and those who have not.

Presumably few would object if the state fined the manufacturer an amount equal to the damage that results from a defective warning. Suppose the money from that fine were to go toward funding the relevant public regulatory scheme. In private litigation, the victim is acting as a private prosecutor. The liability judgment works like a fine. Instead of funding the public regulatory scheme, it funds a private regulatory scheme. On what grounds could one object to holding the manufacturer liable to the "victim"? He is being paid to "prosecute."

The plausibility or desirability of the private prosecutor approach does not depend on the legitimacy of the underlying claim. Whether or not the victim has a right in corrective justice to repair, imposing his loss on the manufacturer can be defended on the grounds that it creates an attractive system of incentives to litigate and to invest in safety.

Here, then, is a case in which the plaintiff recovers against a defendant, though they are not brought together by considerations of corrective justice. The defendant has acted wrongfully, but his wrongdoing is not responsible for the plaintiff's loss. The plaintiff has no right to repair in justice; the defendant has no duty either.

This sort of case differs, therefore, from others in which the plaintiff has a right to repair in justice, but liability for his loss is imposed on someone other than the wrongdoer or injurer. Let's now consider such cases.

Liability and the Cheapest Cost-Avoider

In the case I am imagining, the victim has a claim in justice to repair, but the defendant does not have a duty in justice to him. The interesting feature of this case is that someone other than the defendant owes a duty of repair to the victim. Thus, there are the victim who has the sort of claim that would be valid under the principle of corrective justice, as well as an agent who has the duty to the victim because he is responsible for having created the loss, and some third party who the court is prepared to hold liable to the victim because he is the cheapest cost-avoider, though he is in no way responsible for the harm. (For example, suppose you wrongfully injure me causing me substantial damage, but instead of me suing you, I sue your Dean who is not responsible for my loss or your conduct, but who, I believe, might be a good person to sue for a variety of reasons. Perhaps he has "deeper" pockets, or he is the cheapest cost-avoider, that is, he can optimally reduce (in the future) the probability of harm at the lowest cost.)

Were the court to impose liability on the cheapest cost-avoider, it would be enforcing a claim valid in corrective justice, but it would not otherwise be implementing corrective justice (it would not be imposing the loss on someone who has the duty to repair it). The question here is whether in imposing the victim's loss on the third party tort law violates corrective justice.

One reason for thinking that imposing the victim's loss on someone other than the individual who has the moral duty to repair it is wrong in that the third party does not volunteer to have the loss imposed upon him; another is that the third party is innocent of wrongdoing. Suppose Donald Trump volunteers to pay all my debts of repair. If he pays them off, all claims against me are extinguished thereby; no injustice is done. The example suggests that someone other than the injurer can shoulder the victim's loss without violating corrective justice. In that example, however, Trump volunteers to bear my costs, and it is for that reason, one might say, that no violation of corrective justice occurs. Had my costs been imposed on him without his consent, our moral assessment of the situation would have been very different. This suggests that corrective justice is violated when the costs of accidents are imposed on someone who does not agree so to bind herself.

Involuntariness is not an adequate criterion of wrongfulness, however. [...]

Neither the cheapest cost-avoider nor the wrongdoer agrees to bear the victim's costs. Though neither agrees to shoulder the relevant costs, there is an obvious difference between them; the cheapest cost-avoider is, ex hypothesi, innocent of mischief, the wrongdoer is not. This suggests that the reason that it is permissible to impose the victim's loss upon the wrongdoer, but not on the cheapest cost-avoider (if he is not the wrongdoer), is that the latter is innocent of wrongdoing, whereas the former is not. The reason that imposing the victim's loss on the cheapest cost-avoider violates corrective justice, then, is that corrective justice prohibits imposing losses on innocent persons. Thus, imposing the loss on the wrongdoer is compatible with corrective justice (even required by it perhaps), but imposing the same loss on the cheapest cost-avoider violates justice.

In fact, imposing liability on someone innocent of wrongdoing need not constitute a corrective injustice. Innocent individuals can sometimes have a duty in corrective justice to repair. Far from being an offense to justice, imposing liability on them may be required by it. An individual who justifiably infringes the right of another may have a duty in justice to repair, a duty grounded in the fact that his conduct constitutes a wrong to the person injured. [...]

By showing that it is not always permissible to impose a loss on an innocent and unwilling party, we have not shown that the state would always be justified in doing so. [...] For all we have shown, the state may have authority to impose liability on someone only if they have a duty in corrective justice to repair. It's just that innocence and voluntariness are not essential to determining whether a person has such a duty.

On the other hand, we could view these examples as illustrating a different point, namely that the state must have a good reason for imposing liability. If it does not, then it acts beyond the scope of its authority, and in doing so, it may impose its own corrective injustices. [...]

The manufacturing example shows that creating a system of effective incentives to reduce the incidence of accidents could count as a good reason for imposing liability. In that case imposing the victim's loss on the cheapest cost-avoider would not violate corrective justice.

If the state is free to impose liability on the wrongdoer (under the auspices of corrective justice) or on the cheapest cost-avoider (under the auspices of efficiency consistent with corrective justice), then, provided the costs of searching out the best risk reducer are low enough, why would the state ever choose to implement corrective justice?[1] If the state chooses to implement corrective justice, then it will miss an opportunity to create a scheme of accident-cost-minimizing incentives, and for no good reason. As long as the victim who has a claim in corrective justice is compensated, why should the state foolishly impose the loss on the person with the moral duty in corrective justice to make repair if imposing it on the cheapest cost-avoider promises to accomplish some good and does not itself violate corrective justice? And, remember, imposing the loss on the cheapest cost-avoider does not violate corrective justice because the state has a good reason for imposing the loss on him, and therefore does him (the cheapest cost-avoider) no wrong.

If this is a sound argument, then it is problematic that a state would ever concern itself with making sure that the victim's loss is imposed on the party who has the duty in corrective justice to repair it. As long as the victim is compensated and some good is accomplished by imposing the loss on someone who can do something about such losses, why bother? But the argument may not be sound. Imposing the loss on an innocent cheapest cost-avoider may in fact violate corrective justice. What might the argument that it does look like?

[...] Perhaps the real problem with imposing the victim's loss on the cheapest cost-avoider is that it is unjust to do so *when there is someone else who has the duty in corrective justice to make repair*. It may be permissible to impose a loss on the cheapest cost-avoider, even if that person is free of mischief and unwilling to bear the costs voluntarily – provided there is no individual who has a duty in justice to bear those costs. If there is such a person, as there is in our example, then imposing the loss on the cheapest cost-avoider is wrongful for exactly that reason. [...]

[...] This, conclusion follows only if corrective justice demands an absolute priority with respect to all other goals the state may legitimately pursue within a tort system. This conclusion cannot be sustained, however.

We might distinguish between two different ways in which imposing liability on someone unconnected or otherwise not responsible for an accident's occurrence might be viewed as imposing a wrongful loss. In one case there are no good reasons whatsoever for imposing the loss on her. She did not cause the harm; she was not negligent or otherwise at fault in any way; nor is she in a good position to reduce or spread risk. In this sense, the loss is imposed on her for no good reason connected to any plausible account of the point or purpose of accident law; it is imposed entirely without justification, and is wrongful in that sense. [...]

Suppose, instead, that there exist good reasons of the sort recognized as legitimate within the relevant political morality for imposing the loss on her. Perhaps, she is the optimal risk-reducer. In the sense of wrongful just characterized, imposing liability would not be wrongful. However, we can imagine another sense of the term or criterion for its application that makes it wrongful to impose liability (even if there are good reasons of the sort the state is authorized to implement for doing so), that is, whenever liability

could have been imposed on someone else who has the duty in corrective justice to make repair. Because there are good reasons for imposing the loss in some way other than that dictated by corrective justice, the only ground for holding that doing so is wrongful is that any such liability judgment forgoes the opportunity to do corrective justice. And that in turn can be wrongful only if doing corrective justice has some kind of absolute priority over other legitimate goals the state may pursue through its tort system.

I accept the first and reject the second way in which imposing losses on third parties can constitute a corrective injustice. The state must allocate costs for a reason that is within its authority to implement, and it must do so in a way that falls within the constraints of the relevant principles of justice and political morality. If it has no good reason of the relevant sort for imposing liability, it violates corrective justice, and, very likely, other principles of justice as well. On the other hand, if it acts on the basis of good reasons within the scope of its authority, it does not violate corrective justice, even though it does not implement it. Imposing the loss on an innocent third party may not be a good idea on other grounds, but it is not wrongful just because in doing so the state misses a chance to impose the loss on that person who has the duty in corrective justice. On the other hand, imposing the loss on a third party who is not a good risk-reducer or -spreader may create a wrongful loss, whether or not there is someone who has the duty in corrective justice to make repair, simply because there exists no justification for imposing the loss on him. The fact that someone has a duty to make repair in corrective justice has little, if anything, to do with the wrongfulness of imposing liability without a good reason for doing so.

In this account, corrective justice does not invariably or absolutely cancel or override reasons for acting that the state may be otherwise authorized to implement. It has no absolute priority with respect to the state's other legitimate goals. [...]

Limiting Corrective Justice

[...] Implementing corrective justice requires a set of substantive liability rules, for example, a rule of liability for negligence. In addition to substantive liability rules, implementing corrective justice requires administrative rules establishing burdens of proof and evidence. [...]

Two cases famous in torts case books help to illustrate the relationship between administrative rules and the principles they are designed to implement. Consider first *Ybarra v. Spangard*.[2] In *Ybarra*, the plaintiff undergoes surgery, and, while under general anesthetic, is apparently mistreated. The plaintiff can establish neither negligence or responsibility. He can prove that he suffered an injury. The court holds that the most plausible explanation of his injury suggests negligence on someone's part. The court applies the doctrine of res ipsa loquitur in order to shift the burden of proof to the defendants to show that no negligence transpired. In effect, the court holds that under the circumstances, each of the named parties within the operating room should have the burden of showing that he or she was not the responsible party. A defendant who cannot show that he or she was not responsible will remain subject to liability. And this will be true even if that defendant is not someone who has the duty in corrective justice to repair; even if, moreover, that person is not in a good position to reduce or spread the relevant risk.

Nevertheless, it is easy to see how such a rule for shifting the burden of proof could be thought of as constituting a plausible way of implementing corrective justice. In *Ybarra*, the best way for a defendant to free herself of the burden of liability is to identify the party who is responsible for the plaintiff's misfortune. Presumably, at least some of the defendants know who that person is. Being excused from liability provides each defendant with the incentive to reveal that information. If the information is revealed, then that person who is in fact responsible for the loss will be solely liable for it, and corrective justice will have been served.[3]

Summers v. Tice[4] can be given a similar rationale. In that case, two hunters negligently fire in the direction of a third. The plaintiff is hit by one bullet, but there is no way he can determine whose bullet is responsible for his injury. If, in order to recover, he had to identify the responsible party, he would be out of luck. Instead, the court allows the burden to be shifted to the defendants, both of whom acted negligently.

Either could free himself of liability by showing that his bullet was not the effective one. In that case the other party whose bullet is responsible for the damage would be solely liable and corrective justice done. As it happens, the defendants are in no better position to identify the responsible bullet than is the plaintiff. Neither can free himself of liability. Both are liable to the plaintiff, when in fact only one has the duty in corrective justice to repair. Still, it is a mistake to infer that *Summers* marks a departure from corrective justice simply because someone other than the person who has the relevant duty must bear some of the costs. Rather, the outcome in *Summers* is a predictable consequence of applying evidentiary rules designed to implement corrective justice under conditions of uncertainty.

It is tempting to extend the rationale of *Summers* to modern tort cases like *Sindell*[5] and *Hymowitz*.[6] If *Summers* can be understood as an effort to extend the ambit of corrective justice, then *Sindell* and *Hymowitz* might be subject to a similar analysis. In each case plaintiffs had been injured as the result of diethylstilbestrol (DES) administered to their mothers during pregnancy as a miscarriage preventive, and the defendants were the manufacturers and marketers of the drug. During the period the defendants marketed DES, they knew or should have known that it causes cancerous or precancerous vaginal and cervical growths in the daughters of the mothers who took it, but they failed to test for efficacy and safety or to warn of its potential danger. Because of the passage of time between ingestion of the drug by the mother and harm to the daughter, and the large number of manufacturers using the same drug formula, the plaintiffs in DES cases usually are not able to identify which defendant manufactured the drug ingested by their respective mothers.

Although the court in *Sindell* found inapplicable theories of "alternate liability," "concert of action" liability, and industry-wide ("enterprise") liability, it adopted a "market share" theory in order to find for the plaintiffs. Under the court's market share formula, the plaintiff joins as defendant the manufacturers of a substantial share of the particular market of DES from which her mother might have taken. Damages are apportioned to each defendant's share of that particular market, and each defendant may cross-claim against other manufacturers or demonstrate that it, in fact, could not have produced the particular drug ingested by the plaintiff's mother. [. . .]

Following the line of reasoning in *Ybarra* and *Summers*, one could argue that the burden can be shifted legitimately to each of the many defendants to show that he is not responsible for anyone's wrongdoing. Indeed, that is part of the holding in *Sindell*. In other words, if a particular defendant can show that none of the drugs he manufactures is responsible for any of the harms suffered by members of the plaintiff class, he can free himself of liability. Because there is no practical way of determining which harms are the responsibility of those manufacturers who are not able to free themselves of liability, the court adopts the principle that each should be liable for that percentage of the total damages that corresponds to its share of the market. This is the principle of market share liability. If market share is a reasonable proxy for causal responsibility, then one can view *Sindell* as an extension of *Summers* and *Ybarra*, which in turn can be understood as efforts to pursue the overarching goal of corrective justice when facing substantial epistemic obstacles.

The problem with this, the standard interpretation of *Sindell*, is revealed by the ruling in *Hymowitz*. In *Hymowitz*, one of the defendants in fact establishes that his product is not causally responsible for any of the harms suffered by members of the plaintiff class. Under the *Sindell* formula, any defendant who can establish his freedom from causal responsibility is able to free himself of liability. The *Hymowitz* court, however, rejects this option, and allows the defendant liability reflecting his share of the national market.

One response to *Hymowitz* is to treat it as a mistake that does not conform to the administration of corrective justice story we have been weaving. Another alternative is to contend that *Hymowitz* in fact fits within the corrective justice account of tort law. This is Richard Wright's view.[7] According to Wright, *Hymowitz* establishes that the relevant *harm* for which people can be justly held liable in torts (in cases of this sort) is the *wrongful imposition of risk*. The defendant in *Hymowitz* cannot show that he did not impose

unjustifiable risks. Indeed, he did. All he can show is that the risks he imposed did not mature into full blown harms of the relevant sort. [. . .]

The problem with Wright's argument is that it is unmotivated and ad hoc. It is not helpful to say that *Hymowitz* introduces another category of harms particularly appropriate to cases of a certain sort (market share cases). Either the imposition of unjustifiable risk is the relevant harm in all cases, both those in which the risk matures and those in which it does not, or it is not. One cannot claim that in the uncomplicated torts case, the relevant harm is the injury the victim suffers whereas in other cases in which this conception of the harm is problematic – those like *Hymowitz* – the relevant harm is the risk imposed. This is simply an ad hoc solution to a difficult problem. [. . .]

The standard interpretation rejects *Hymowitz* as a mistake, an unjustifiable departure from tort law's preoccupation with implementing corrective justice under the conditions of uncertainty bound to obtain. To his credit, Wright rejects this interpretation. His mistake is in thinking that *Hymowitz* can be defended as a form of corrective justice in which the relevant harm is the wrongful imposition of risk. The best interpretation of *Hymowitz*, however, does not view it as a mistake or as an attempt to implement corrective justice for a distinct category of harms. To understand *Hymowitz* and *Sindell*, we have to consider the principle of corrective justice once again.

Suppose that we all lived in New Zealand or that our community, wherever it was, decided to implement a no-fault plan like New Zealand's. Let's now set aside all questions about whether doing so would be a smart or otherwise desirable thing to do. The question we need to address is in what way does this no-fault plan affect or otherwise relate to the principle of corrective justice? [. . .]

[. . .] The New Zealand plan neither affronts corrective justice, nor is its existence irrelevant to corrective justice [. . .] [because] whether or not corrective justice in fact imposes moral duties on particular individuals is *conditional* upon the existence of other institutions for making good victims' claims to repair. The capacity within a particular community of corrective justice to impose the relevant *moral* duties depends on the existence of certain *legal* or *political* institutions or social practices. [...]

The view I am suggesting is that whether or not corrective justice itself imposes moral duties on individuals in a community will depend on other practices that are in effect. The reason is this. Corrective justice links agents with losses. It provides individuals with agent-relative reasons for acting. These reasons for acting can be superseded by other practices that create reasons for acting, both agent-neutral and agent-relative. Such practices can sometimes sever the relationship between agents and losses. The victim's wrongful loss may give her a right to recover. That right is part of the normative basis for imposing a duty to repair. The nature and scope of the duty depend on the practices in place. The content of the duty and the reasons for acting to which it gives rise do not follow logically from the nature of the right to repair, but from the normative practices in place within the community, practices that, in conjunction with the victim's right, give rise to specific obligations.

My view is not that other social and legal practices sever all of the relationships between wrongdoer and victim. After all, the wrongdoer may be responsible for the victim's loss. The question is to which duties does this relationship give rise. And my argument is that the nature and scope of the duties depend on the prevailing practices. Moreover, even if no-fault practices exist for handling accident costs, the injurer, and no one else, may have the duty to apologize, or the like.

The question before the state is not whether to forgo corrective justice; instead, it is, what ought to be done about losses including those that result from wrongful conduct. If there is a comprehensive plan put into effect for dealing with those losses by imposing them on everyone or on all those individuals who are at fault, whether or not their fault results in harm to others, then corrective justice itself imposes no duties within that community.[8] Thus, although corrective justice is private justice – justice between the parties – whether or not it imposes obligations between the parties depends on other social, political and legal practices. This, I take it, is a controversial, but I think inescapable truth about corrective justice. It may be true of other moral principles as well.

If corrective justice is conditional in this sense, then the state may choose to allocate accident costs in any number of ways. [...]

With this discussion in mind, let's return to the troubling cases of *Sindell* and *Hymowitz*. [...]

The problem comes from trying to reconcile *Sindell* with *Hymowitz*. According to *Sindell*, although at fault, a defendant who could establish that his fault was not responsible for anyone's damage would free himself of liability. In *Hymowitz*, the absence of responsibility is inadequate to free the defendant of liability. *Hymowitz* is, in fact, the correct interpretation of the basic principles set forth in *Sindell*. *Sindell* is not an extension of corrective justice. Instead, it involves a localized at-fault plan. [...]

[...] One can have either a corrective justice scheme or an at-fault pool but not both at the same time. For that reason, *Sindell* does not fully comprehend the underlying principles of liability that it creates. It is caught between two paradigms: corrective justice and at-fault liability. Perhaps, the *Sindell* court fails to see that the two cannot be reconciled; perhaps the court believes that imposing liability on the basis of fault or market share is at the heart of corrective justice, and that because it is, any defendant who can in fact show that he did not cause any harm should be able to free himself of liability. Whatever the reason, *Sindell* is torn between two conflicting approaches to allocating the relevant costs: one that imposes the duty in corrective justice; the other that imposes losses according to a localized at-fault scheme. Therefore, rather than being an unjustifiable departure from the logic of *Sindell*, *Hymowitz* represents the correct understanding of *Sindell*'s underlying logic.

Notes

1   For the sake of this argument we are assuming that the wrongdoer is not the cheapest cost-avoider, although there is no reason to think that the two will always be different individuals. We are concerned with that case in which they are different, however, because we want to know whether imposing the loss on the cheapest cost-avoider violates corrective justice, and it could only if the two were different individuals.

2   Ybarra v. Spangard, 25 Cal. 2d 486, 154 P.2d 687 (1944).

3   It is a further question whether such a burden shifting rule will actually prove effective. The point here is simply to illustrate how various rules can still be interpreted as part of a general plan to implement an ideal, say, of corrective justice, even if the results the rules generate in particular cases do not fully correspond to the results corrective justice would require.

4   Summers v. Tice, 33 Cal. 2d. 80, 199 P.2d 1 (1948).

5   Sindell v. Abbott Laboratories, 26 Cal. 3d 588, 607 P.2d 924, 163 Cal. Rptr. 132 (1980).

6   Hymowitz v. Eli Lilly and Co., 73 N.Y. 2d 487, 539 N.E. 2d 941 (1989), cert, denied sub nom. Rexall Drug Co. v. Tigue, 110 S. Ct. 350 (1989).

7   Richard W. Wright, "Responsibility, risk, probability, naked statistics, and proof: Pruning the bramble bush by clarifying the concepts," 73 *Iowa L. Rev.* 1001 (1988).

8   There are some conditions that must be satisfied before this is valid. First, the victims must be fully compensated under the alternative plan, or they must be as fully compensated under the alternative as they would be under a scheme that implements corrective justice. Second, the alternative must accomplish some additional goals not secured by a corrective justice plan. Third, the alternative must conform to the relevant demands of justice and morality.

In my earlier work, I claimed that the duties in corrective justice could be discharged by parties other than those who are responsible for creating wrongful losses. Thus, my claim was that no-fault plans were ways of discharging duties in corrective justice (provided other conditions like those mentioned above were met). I still accept the claim that it is possible for someone other than the wrongdoer to discharge the wrongdoer's obligations, otherwise insurance would be unthinkable, but I reject the idea that no-fault plans are ways of meeting the demands of corrective justice. Instead, certain practices simply mean that no duties in corrective justice arise in a particular community. Thus, it is not as if New Zealand has an unusual approach to meeting the demands of corrective justice with respect to accident-related losses. Rather, in New Zealand, there is no practice of corrective justice with respect to such losses. After all, in corrective justice, the faulty injurer has a duty to repair, and under the plans we are talking about, there simply is no agent-relative duty of any sort. The victim's right grounds a duty, but the duty it grounds depends on the practice. The practice of corrective justice imposes that duty on the faulty injurer. Other practices or social conventions might well impose different duties.

Whereas I used to say that other practices can *discharge* the wrongdoer's duty, I now say that such practices either *extinguish* duties in corrective justice that would otherwise arise or that duties in corrective justice simply do not arise. The difference between the latter two approaches is important. In one view, corrective justice is like a default rule. If no other practices of the appropriate sort exist, then corrective justice does, and it imposes duties of a certain agent-relative kind. In the other, if there is no practice of corrective justice, there are no duties of corrective justice, whatever other practices may exist. I have settled on a view about which of these alternatives is correct, but everything I have said so far is compatible with both interpretations.

34

A Theory of Strict Liability

Richard A. Epstein

[handwritten marginalia: "Possibly Duty to rescue (no) Canadian law"]

[handwritten marginalia: "moral factor for liability?"]

[handwritten marginalia: "If consent Negligence principles are prob red principles of"]

Introduction

Torts is at once one of the simplest and one of the most complex areas of the law. It is simple because it concerns itself with fact patterns that can be understood and appreciated without the benefit of formal legal instruction. [. . .]

But the simplicity of torts based upon its use of ordinary language is deceptive. [. . .] While an intuitive appreciation of the persistent features of ordinary language may help decide easy cases, more is required for the solution of those difficult cases where the use of ordinary language pulls in different directions at the same time. There is need for a systematic inquiry which refines, but which does not abandon, the shared impressions of everyday life. The task is to develop a normative theory of torts that takes into account common sense notions of individual responsibility. [. . .]

This common sense approach to torts as a branch of common law stands in sharp opposition to much of the recent scholarship on the subject because it does not regard economic theory as the primary means to establish the rules of legal responsibility. A knowledge of the economic consequences of alternative legal arrangements can be of great importance, but even

among those who analyze tort in economic terms there is acknowledgment of certain questions of "justice" or "fairness" rooted in common sense beliefs that cannot be explicated in terms of economic theory.[1] [. . .] But once it is admitted that there are questions of fairness as between the parties that are not answerable in economic terms, the exact role of economic argument in the solution of legal questions becomes impossible to determine. It may well be that an acceptable theory of fairness can be reconciled with the dictates of economic theory in a manner that leaves ample room for the use of economic thought. But that judgment presupposes that some theory of fairness has been spelled out, which, once completed, may leave no room for economic considerations of any sort.

In order to raise these fairness questions in the context of traditional legal doctrine, I shall focus on the conflict that has persisted in the common law between theories of negligence and theories of strict liability. [. . .]

I.   A Critique of Negligence

The development of the common law of tort has been marked by the opposition between two

Richard A. Epstein, "A Theory of Strict Liability," *Journal of Legal Studies*, vol. 2, no. 1, January 1973, pp. 151–204.

major theories. The first holds that a plaintiff should be entitled, prima facie, to recover from a defendant who has caused him harm only if the defendant intended to harm the plaintiff or failed to take reasonable steps to avoid inflicting the harm. The alternative theory, that of strict liability, holds the defendant prima facie liable for the harm caused whether or not either of the two further conditions relating to negligence and intent is satisfied. [. . .]

But the law of negligence never did conform in full to the requisites of the "moral" system of personal responsibility invoked in its behalf. In particular, the standard of the reasonable man, developed in order to insure injured plaintiffs a fair measure of protection against their fellow citizens, could require a given person to make recompense even where no amount of effort could have enabled *him* to act in accordance with the standard of conduct imposed by the law. [. . .]

Even if these exceptions to the general rule of negligence affect only a few of the cases to be decided, they do indicate a theoretical weakness that helps to explain efforts to find alternative justifications for the law of negligence couched in economic rather than moral terms. Thus, it was suggested that a defendant should be regarded as negligent if he did not take the precautions an economically prudent man would take in his own affairs, and, conversely, that where the defendant *did* conduct himself in an economically prudent manner, he could successfully defend himself in an action brought by another person whom he injured.

Although positions of this sort had been suggested from the beginning of this century, they received their most famous exposition in the opinion of Learned Hand in *United States v. Carroll Towing Co.*[2] The narrow point for decision in *Carroll Towing* was whether the owner of a barge owed to others a duty to keep a barge or attendant on board while his barge was moored inside a harbor. [. . .] Hand expresses his conclusion in mathematical terms in order to demonstrate its applicability to the entire law of tort:

> if the probability be called P; the injury, L; and the burden, B; liability depends upon whether B is less than L multiplied by P: i.e., whether B [is less than] PL.[3]

[. . .] Hand proceeds to examine the conduct, not of the owner, but of the bargee and in the traditional manner so often used to decide the "reasonableness" of the defendant's conduct in negligence cases. The evidence showed that the bargee had been off the ship for a period in excess of twenty-one hours before the accident took place. Moreover, all he had to offer to explain his absence was some "fabricated" tale.[4] There was "no excuse for his absence," and it followed:

> In such circumstances we hold – and it is all that we do hold – that it was a fair requirement that the Conners Company should have a bargee aboard (unless he had some excuse for his absence), during the working hours of daylight.[5]

The use of the concept of "excuse" in Hand's formulation of the particular grounds for decision suggests that some of the elements material to determining "blameworthiness" in the moral sense are applicable with full force even after the statement of the general economic formula. But it is unclear what counts for Hand as an appropriate excuse within the framework of the law of tort. [. . .]

But even if the notion of "excuse" is put to one side, Hand's formula is still not free from difficulty. It is difficult to decide how to apply the formula when there is a need for but a single precaution which one party is no better suited to take than the other. If, for example, there were two boats in a harbor, and need for but a single bargee, what result is appropriate if the two boats collide when both are unmanned? Is there negligence, or contributory negligence, or both? The formula is silent on the question of which ship should be manned. Yet that is the very question which must be answered, since in economic terms no bargee provides too little accident protection while two bargees provide too much. [. . .]

[. . .] In any system of common law liability, a court must allocate, explicitly or implicitly, a loss that has already occurred between the parties – usually two – before it. It could turn out that neither of the parties acted in a manner that was unreasonable or improper from either an economic or a moral point of view, but a decision that the conduct of both parties was "proper" under the circumstances does not necessarily decide the legal case; there could well be other reasons why one party should be preferred to another.

The point is illustrated by the famous case of *Vincent v. Lake Erie Transport Co.*[6] During a violent storm, defendant ordered his men to continue to make the ship fast to the dock during the course of the storm in order to protect it from the elements. The wind and waves repeatedly drove it into the dock, damaging it to the extent of $500. Although there had been a prior contract between the plaintiff and defendant, the case was treated by the court as though the parties to the suit were strangers, since the terms of the contract did not cover the incident in question. Moreover, it was accepted without question that the conduct of the defendant was reasonable in that there was no possible course of action open to the captain of the ship that would have enabled him to reduce the aggregate damage suffered by the ship and the dock. On these facts the court concluded that the defendant had to pay the plaintiff for the $500 damage.

The result in *Vincent* seems inconsistent with either of the customary explanations, moral or economic, of negligence in the law of tort. There is no argument that the conduct of the defendant was "blameworthy" in any sense. [. . .] Similarly, if the economic conception of negligence is adopted, the same result must be reached once it is admitted that the conduct of the defendant served to minimize the total amount of damage suffered; the expected benefits of further precautions were outweighed by their costs.

Had the Lake Erie Transportation Company owned both the dock and the ship, there could have been no lawsuit as a result of the incident. [. . .] The action in tort in effect enables the injured party to require the defendant to treat the loss he has inflicted on another as though it were his own. If the Transportation Company must bear all the costs in those cases in which it damages its own property, then it should bear those costs when it damages the property of another. The necessity may justify the decision to cause the damage, but it cannot justify a refusal to make compensation for the damage so caused. [. . .]

II. An Analysis of Causation

Implicit in the development of the prior arguments is the assumption that the term causation has a content which permits its use in a principled manner to help solve particular cases. In order to make good on these arguments that concept must be explicated and shown to be a suitable basis for the assignment of responsibility. Those two ends can be achieved only if much of the standard rhetoric on causation in negligence cases is first put to one side.

Under the orthodox view of negligence, the question of causation is resolved by a two-step process. The first part of the inquiry concerns the "cause in fact" of the plaintiff's injury. The usual test to determine whether or not the plaintiff's injury was in fact caused by the negligence of the defendant is to ask whether, "but for the negligence of the defendant, the plaintiff would not have been injured." But this complex proposition is not in any sense the semantic equivalent of the assertion that the defendant caused the injury to the plaintiff. The former expression is in counterfactual form and requires an examination of what *would have* been the case if things had been otherwise. The second expression simply asks in direct indicative form what in fact *did* happen. The change in mood suggests the difference between the two concepts.

The "but for" test does not provide a satisfactory account of the concept of causation if the words "in fact" are taken seriously. *A* carelessly sets his alarm one hour early. When he wakes up the next morning he has ample time before work and decides to take an early morning drive in the country. While on the road he is spotted by *B*, an old college roommate, who becomes so excited that he runs off the road and hurts *C*. But for the negligence of *A*, *C* would never have been injured, because *B* doubtless would have continued along his uneventful way. Nonetheless, it is common ground that *A*, even if negligent, is in no way responsible for the injury to *C*, caused by *B*.

Its affinity for absurd hypotheticals should suggest that the "but for" test should be abandoned as even a tentative account of the concept of causation. But there has been no such abandonment. [. . .] [T]here is no merit, philosophic or otherwise, to an account of any concept

A caused B *IF I stopped A cause*

which cannot handle the simplest of cases, and only a mistaken view of philosophic inquiry demands an acceptance of an account of causation that conflicts so utterly with ordinary usage.

Once the "philosophical" account of causation was accepted, it could not be applied in legal contexts without modification because of the unacceptable results that it required. The concept of "cause in law" or "proximate" cause became necessary to confine the concept within acceptable limits. [...] [T]he question of proximate cause has been said to reduce itself to the question whether the conduct of the defendant is a "substantial factor" contributing to the loss of the plaintiff, or whether the harm suffered was "reasonably foreseeable." But these formulations of the test of proximate cause do not give much guidance for the solution of particular cases. One might think that this would be treated as a defect in an account of a concept like causation, but in large measure it has been thought to be its strength. Once it is decided that there is no hard content to the term causation, the courts are free to decide particular lawsuits in accordance with the principles of "social policy" under the guise of the proximate-cause doctrine.

[...] But the term [proximate cause] cannot be banished from the lexicon on the ground that it is "metaphysical." The concept is dominant in the law because it is dominant in the language that people, including lawyers, use to describe conduct and to determine responsibility.[7] [...]

[...] [T]he concept of causation, as it applies to cases of physical injury, can be analyzed in a matter that both renders it internally coherent and relevant to the ultimate question who shall bear the loss.

There will be no attempt to give a single semantic equivalent to the concept of causation. Instead, the paper will consider in succession each of four distinct paradigm cases covered by the proposition "*A caused B* harm." [...] Briefly put, they are based upon notions of force, fright, compulsion and dangerous conditions.

Force

We begin with the simplest instance of causation: the application of force to a person or thing. In a physical sense, the consequences of the application of force may be quite varied. In some cases the object acted upon will move; in others it will be transformed; in still others it will be damaged. It is this last case that will be of exclusive concern here, because it is accepted without question that the minimum condition of tort liability is damage to the person or property of the plaintiff.

The identification of causation with force does not of itself complete the first instance of the proposition "*A caused harm to B.*" It is still necessary to show that the force in question was applied by human and not natural agencies, and thus to tie the concept of force to that of human volition. The term "volition" is a primitive in the language whose function is to mark off the class of human acts from the class of events; to distinguish between "I raised my arm," and "my arm went up." But even if the term cannot be defined, its function can be made clear by some simple examples. In the old case of *Smith v. Stone*,[8] the defendant was carried on to the plaintiff's land by a band of armed men. The court held that the plaintiff could not recover in trespass, because it was "the trespasse of the party that carried the defendant upon the land, and not the trespasse of the defendant." True, the physical requirement of entrance was satisfied in the case, but the defendant's movement was in no sense an "action" because, if anything, it was contrary to his will. [...]

The combination of force and volition is expressed in the simple transitive sentence, *A hit B*. It is true that this proposition as stated is consistent with the assertion that *A* did not harm *B*. But in many contexts the implication of harm follows fairly from the assertion, as anyone hit by a car will admit. Where the issue is in doubt, the verb can be changed, even as the form of the proposition remains constant, to bring the element of harm more sharply into relief. Thus instead of "*A hit B*," another proposition of the requisite form could be "*A pummeled B*," or "*A beat B*." But since the specifics of the harm go only to the measure of damages and not to the issue of liability, the proposition "*A hit B*" will serve as the model of the class of propositions to be considered.

The grammatical structure of the proposition "*A hit B*" is crucial to analysis of the problem of causation because it describes a situation both where the parties are *linked* to each other and where their respective roles are still *differentiated*. [...] But it may well be necessary as a matter of fact to assess the role of those forces that are *instruments* of the defendant. Take a simple case where *A* drives his car into *B*. It could be argued that *A*'s act extended no further than the depression of the gas pedal or, perhaps, *A*'s movement of his leg muscles. But the constant and inveterate use of the English language militates against the restriction of an act to the physical movements of *A*'s body. "*A* drove his car into *B*" is a true description of the event; we might explain its significance away, but we can never deny it in good faith. Reference to those subsequent mechanical complications does not falsify that description. [...]

Finally, the proposition of the form "*A* hit *B*" does not depend upon the two-part theory of causation developed by the law of negligence. No question of "but for" is ever raised, much less answered. [...]

Once this simple causal paradigm is accepted, its relationship to the question of responsibility for the harm so caused must be clarified. Briefly put, the argument is that proof of the proposition *A* hit *B* should be sufficient to establish a prima facie case of liability.[9] [...] The doctrine of strict liability holds that proof that the defendant caused harm creates that presumption because proof of the nonreciprocal source of the harm is sufficient to upset the balance where one person must win and the other must lose. There is no room to consider, as part of the prima facie case, allegations that the defendant intended to harm the plaintiff, or could have avoided the harm he caused by the use of reasonable care. The choice is plaintiff or defendant, and the analysis of causation is the tool which, prima facie, fastens responsibility upon the defendant. [...]

Fright and shock

The structure of the prima facie case for assault – the historical companion to trespass to the person – parallels the paradigm for the prima facie case of the tort of trespass, and illustrates the means by which the concept of causation can be extended in a principled manner. The case in assault is *A* frightened *B*. That paradigm indicates, as in trespass, that *A* and *B* do not have

symmetrical roles. There is the same close connection between the conduct of the defendant and the harm of the plaintiff. There is, however, a difference between the cases of assault and those of trespass. In trespass actions the plaintiff's conduct is not in issue in the prima facie case. But the *reactions* of the plaintiff must be taken into account before the prima facie case of assault can be completed. Still, the roles of the parties are not identical. The reactions of the plaintiff do not rise to the level of acts because they are in no sense volitional.

Nonetheless, the paradigm does raise some troublesome issues. Suppose, for example, the defendant frightened the plaintiff when he raised his hand to mop the sweat off his face at a time when the plaintiff was standing about fifty yards away. Do facts such as these disclose a prima facie case of assault? Our first response to the allegation does not address the issue of substantive law at all. Rather, it says that the harm suffered by the plaintiff is so trivial that it is inappropriate to use, at public expense, the legal machinery to resolve the case. [...]

But the case can be made more difficult by assuming that the plaintiff has suffered serious injuries as a result of his fright. If anyone could be frightened by that kind of conduct, however, most likely he could not have survived long enough in life's hustle and bustle to be injured by the defendant. [...]

But even after these odd cases are put to one side, the paradigm of assault does raise problems of proof that are not present in trespass cases since the allegation "*A* frightened *B*," unlike the allegation "*A* hit *B*," can be proved in the given case only after the responses of *B* are taken into account. [...]

[...] The crucial question is that of causation and if a defendant frightens or shocks a plaintiff, the recovery should, prima facie, be allowed. [...]

A compelled B to hit C.

Compulsion

The concept of causation is not limited to cases of the form "*A* hit *B*" or "*A* frightened *B*." There are other relationships that exhibit more complex grammatical forms to which it also applies. Indeed, the proposition "*A* hit *B*" represents only a special case of a more complex

[handwritten: Criteria you need to meet]

[handwritten: explanatory nurdles explain and get passed. not vague ? up or genett]

relationship, capable of indefinite extension, which for three persons takes the form "A compelled B to hit C." [. . .]

[. . .] In the analysis of this more complex proposition and its relationship to the question of responsibility, there is the same interaction between nonreciprocity and causation as in the simple cases already analyzed. In order to unpack these relationships, consider the case from the standpoint of the injured party, C. If the proposition "A compelled B to hit C" is true, then it follows that "B hit C." The last proposition can be analyzed in accordance with the notions of causation based upon force and volition that have already been developed. Given that paradigm, it follows that C has a prima facie case against B. B cannot escape liability by showing that he did not hit C, for a demonstration that he acted under compulsion is not the same as a demonstration that he did not act at all. [. . .] Nor, if the observations about the defense of "necessity" made earlier are sound, can B plead as a defense that he was compelled by A to hit C. Even if this conduct were reasonable, it does not follow that B need not pay. [. . .] B will have an action over against A after he has paid C, on the theory that A compelled him (to his loss) to hit C.

The analysis is not yet complete, because C is not limited to an action against B. He can bring in the alternative an action against A. That action, however, could not rely on trespassory theories of causation. A did not hit C; B did. But the roles of A and C are still both linked, and differentiated, because A compelled B to hit C; C did not compel B to hit A. [. . .]

The changes in causal theory have their effect on questions of proof. Proof of compulsion upon B is crucial if C's action against A is to succeed. [. . .]

In particular, two points must be observed. First, the question whether B was negligent under the circumstances is, at best, evidence on the question of compulsion. [. . .] Second, it is not strictly material whether B intended to harm C, because he could have been compelled to act as he did whether or not that harm was intended. [. . .]

One further problem remains. Suppose C is able to bring actions against both A and B. He will not be entitled to a double recovery for the single harm, so it will be necessary to decide whether A or B will be saddled with the ultimate loss. Here again the causal paradigm permits us to link and differentiate the roles of the parties to the suit. A compelled B to hit C; B did not compel A to hit C. Hence it follows that, prima facie, B should prevail over A. [. . .]

Causation and dangerous conditions

The forms of causation thus far developed are the easiest to comprehend and accept. But an analysis of causation is seriously incomplete if made only in terms of force, fright, and compulsion. Both ordinary thought and legal theory also use a causal paradigm which covers cases involving the creation of dangerous conditions that result in harm to either person or property. [. . .]

[. . .] [T]here are significant differences between this paradigm and those that have come before. First, it makes use of the expression, "result in." While it could be objected that this term defines causation in terms of itself, that is not the case. The term "result in" is intended to cover only those cases of causation – force, fright, and compulsion – already developed in previous sections of this paper. [. . .]

Second, this paradigm applies only to dangerous conditions. It is possible to divide the most common instances of dangerous conditions into three classes.[10] The first includes things that are "inherently" dangerous, of which stored explosives are the most common example. They are inherently dangerous because they retain their *potential* energy in full, even if they are stored or handled with the highest possible care. [. . .]

The second kind of dangerous condition is created when a person places a thing – not dangerous in itself – in a dangerous position. Instances of this form of dangerous condition are of two sorts. The first class presupposes the recognition of rights of way: highways, footpaths, and the like. [. . .]

Other situations in this class involve any unstable position where the application of a small force will permit the release of some greater force. [. . .]

The third kind of dangerous situation concerns products or other things dangerous because defective. [. . .]

[handwritten: what you have to answer for to make your case / prima facie case / cashin (on first face)]

It can [...] be shown that this account of causation is consistent with the rules of strict liability. It is true that the term "dangerous" often carries with it suggestions of both the degree of risk and the probability of harm, but in the restricted sense the term is used here – with the emphasis upon the "potential" to cause harm in the narrow sense of that term – more than a verbal mutation is at stake. The law of negligence, as expressed in the formula of Learned Hand, requires balancing the risk and probable extent of harm against the burden of the costs needed either to eliminate or reduce it. No cost–benefit analysis is required, however, when the theories of dangerous conditions are used to establish the causal connection between the defendant's conduct and the plaintiff's harm. It could well be that the defendant acts in a reasonable manner when he creates a dangerous condition that results in harm to the plaintiff. It may not be worthwhile for him to see that all of his manufactured products are free from defects; but nonetheless he will be held liable if any of them should prove defective and cause harm. [...]

III. The Problem of the Good Samaritan

[...] The theories of strict liability explain and justify, as the rules of reasonableness cannot, the common law's refusal to extend liability in tort to cases where the defendant has not harmed the plaintiff by his affirmative action.[11] The problem arises in its starkest form in the case of the good Samaritan. A finds himself in a perilous situation which was not created by B, as when A is overwhelmed by cramps while swimming alone in a surging sea. B, moreover, is in a position where he could, without any danger of injury to himself, come to A's assistance with some simple and well-nigh costless steps, such as throwing a rope to the plaintiff. The traditional common law position has been that there is no cause of action against B solely because B, in effect, permitted A to drown.

It is important to note the manner in which such cases should be decided under a negligence system. [...]

[If] one considers the low costs of prevention to B of rescuing A, and the serious, if not deadly,

harm that A will suffer if B chooses not to rescue him, there is no reason why the *Carroll Towing* formula or the general rules of negligence should not require, under pain of liability, the defendant to come to the aid of the plaintiff. Nonetheless, the good Samaritan problem receives special treatment even under the modern law of torts. [...] No matter how the facts are manipulated, it is not possible to argue that B caused A harm in any of the senses of causation which were developed in the earlier portions of this article when he failed to render assistance to A in his time of need. In typical negligence cases, all the talk of avoidance and reasonable care may shift attention from the causation requirement, which the general "but for" test distorts beyond recognition. But its importance is revealed by its absence in the good Samaritan cases where the presence of all those elements immaterial to tortious liability cannot, even in combination, persuade judges who accept the negligence theory to apply it in the decisive case.

The principles of strict liability do more than explain the reasons behind the general common law refusal to require men to be good Samaritans. They also explain why it is that in some cases there are strong arguments to support apparent exceptions to the common law position. [...]

[...] *Montgomery v. National C. & T.*, is described by Gregory as follows:

> Consider this situation: Two of defendant's trucks, due to no fault of the drivers, became stalled on a narrow road, completely blocking the highway. Also, without fault, the men were unable to get the trucks started again. This was at the foot of a short hill, which obscured the view of approaching drivers. Moreover, the hill was somewhat icy. Plaintiff came driving along at a normal speed. By the time he saw the stalled trucks, he was unable to stop and crashed into them. Had one of defendant's truck drivers climbed the hill and posted a warning, this accident would not have happened.[12]

[...] [T]he South Carolina court found that the defendant could be held liable on account of the actionable negligence of its employees in the course of their employment, because on the facts of the case the employees had both the opportunity and the means to place warnings in some form at the top of the hill which would have enabled the plaintiff to avoid the crash in question. The court insisted that this duty rested upon the defendant's employees even though two propositions are settled: first, that no passerby would have been charged with that duty, even if he had the time and means to have taken those steps; and second, that the defendant's employees would have been under no duty to place those warnings if the road had been blocked, say, by a falling tree.[13] In effect, the position of the court is that simply because the defendant's employees blocked the road, they were under a duty to take those precautions reasonably calculated to prevent possible injury to other users of the highway. [. . .]

[. . .] The defendant is liable because harm resulted when the plaintiff's car ran into its truck after his employees blocked the road. It is immaterial that the defendant's employees had an opportunity to place warnings at the top of the hill, because the theory of dangerous conditions, too, is a theory of strict liability. Once it is shown that the plaintiff's conduct (he hit the defendant's truck) only serves to complete the prima facie case, the liability follows, because the facts do not even suggest the basis for an affirmative defense.[14]

Theories of strict liability, therefore, support the result [. . .] in a simple and direct fashion. But it is not clear that these results are correct under a system of negligence which accepts as one of its premises that a man is under no duty to confer aid upon a stranger. [. . .]

[. . .] Defendant's drivers would have been under no duty to warn oncoming vehicles of the possible danger if the road had been blocked by a falling tree. Once it is accepted that an allegation that the defendant blocked the highway does not create a prima facie case, then [. . .] it seems improper to take refuge in a halfway house which says that the conduct of the defendant is nonetheless sufficient to obligate him to take reasonable steps for the benefit of the plaintiff. [. . .] [T]he act of the defendant must be treated like an Act of God. [. . .]

These variations on the good Samaritan rule illustrate the evasive responses that courts are prepared to make in order to restrict a rule that they accept but do not like. [. . .]

There is a further class of exceptions to the good Samaritan rule, motivated by the same judicial distaste for the doctrine, which also cannot be rationalized by an appeal to the theories of strict liability. Consider the case where the defendant gratuitously takes steps to aid the plaintiff only to discontinue his efforts before the plaintiff is moved to a position of comparative safety. For example, A sees B lying unconscious on the public street. Immediately, he runs to the phone, dials an emergency room, and then hangs up the receiver. Or, in the alternative, he picks B up and places him in his automobile, only to return him to his original position on the sidewalk when he thinks, for whatever reason, better of the involvement.

It has often been argued that the good Samaritan doctrine in these situations is of no application on the ground that once the defendant undertakes to assist the plaintiff in distress, he can no longer claim that his conduct amounted to a "simple nonfeasance," no longer maintain that the two were still strangers in the eyes of the law. [. . .]

This position must be rejected. The act requirement in the law of tort is but a combination of the volition and the causation requirements already discussed. The law of tort cannot be invoked simply because the defendant has done something; it must be shown that the act in question has caused harm to the plaintiff. Where the defendant has dialed the phone only to put the receiver back on the hook, he has acted, but those acts have not caused harm. The theories of force, fright, compulsion, and dangerous condition are inapplicable, either alone or in combination, to the facts as described. [. . .]

Properly conceived, these situations should be discussed together with other forms of gratuitous undertakings and the obligations they generate. The common law has never found a home for such obligations. They should not be part of the law of tort because they do not satisfy the causation requirement; and the unfortunate doctrine of consideration prevents their easy inclusion in the law of contracts. [. . .]

The same issue involved in the good Samaritan problem frequently arises when it is the *defendant* who claims in effect that the plaintiff was under an affirmative duty to take steps for his, the defendant's, benefit. The point is most clearly raised in connection with the maxim that a tortfeasor takes his victim as he finds him. The maxim applies where the defendant has tortiously harmed the plaintiff, and the issue is whether the latter is entitled to recover for those injuries which would not have occurred had the plaintiff had, in all material respects, a "normal" constitution.

The situation is illustrated by the facts of *Vosburg v. Putney*.[15] The plaintiff was suffering from the after effects of a prior injury to his leg. The defendant kicked the leg at its sore point and caused a serious inflammation. Little or no harm would have been done to an individual with a sound leg. Once it is accepted that the plaintiff has a prima facie case against the defendant, whether on a theory of strict liability, negligence, or "wrongful" intent, the question arises whether the plaintiff should be able to recover for that portion of the damages that would not have been suffered by a plaintiff with a healthy constitution. If he takes no precaution to protect his knee, it should be possible for the defendant to argue that the plaintiff's negligence bars his recovery if the *Carroll Towing* formula is used to determine the reasonableness of the plaintiff's conduct. [. . .]

If this line of reasoning is accepted, the defendant in cases like *Vosburg v. Putney* could argue that the plaintiff was in breach of his duties to the defendant when he failed, say, to wear a shinguard which at low cost would protect him from accidental harm. [. . .] But the law does not take this position. It holds instead that the plaintiff is under no duty to package and bandage himself (though the costs are low) in order to reduce the damages to be paid by those who might harm him. Where the plaintiff is in a weakened condition, he has not caused the harm in any of the senses developed in part II, even if he had the opportunity to prevent them from occurring. As in the case of the good Samaritan, one man is not under a common law duty to take steps to aid a stranger. [. . .]

[. . .] Strong arguments can be advanced to show that the common law position on the good Samaritan problem is in the end consistent with both moral and economic principles.

The history of Western ethics has been marked by the development of two lines of belief. One line

of moral thought emphasizes the importance of freedom of the will. It is the intention (or motive) that determines the worth of the act; and no act can be moral unless it is performed free from external compulsion.[16] Hence the expansion of the scope of positive law could only reduce the moral worth of human action. [. . .]

On the other hand there are those theories that concern themselves not with the freedom of the will, but with the external effects of individual behavior. There is no room for error, because each act which does not further the stated goals (usually, of the maximization of welfare) is in terms of these theories a bad act. Thus a system of laws must either require the individual to act, regardless of motive, in the socially desired manner, or create incentives for him to so behave. [. . .]

[. . .] [M]ost systems of conventional morality try to distinguish between those circumstances in which a person should be compelled to act for the benefit of his fellow man, and those cases where he should be allowed to do so only if prompted by the appropriate motives. To put the point in other terms, the distinction is taken between that conduct which is required and that which, so to speak, is beyond the call of duty. If that distinction is accepted as part of a common morality, then the argument in favor of the good Samaritan rule is that it, better than any possible alternatives, serves to mark off the first class of activities from the second. [. . .]

The defense of the good Samaritan rule in economic terms takes the same qualified form. [. . .]

[. . .] [T]he incentive effects created by the absence of a good Samaritan rule must be examined in the context of other rules of substantive law. Thus it is critical to ask about the incentives which are created by rules which permit a rescuer to bring an action against the person he saved on quasi-contractual theories. It is also important to ask what modifications of behavior could be expected if the scope of this kind of action were expanded, and important, too, to know about the possible effects of systems of public honors and awards for good Samaritans. None of these arguments is designed to show that the common law approach can be justified on economic grounds, but they do show how perilous it is to attempt to justify legal rules by the incentives that they create. [. . .]

But it is a mistake to dwell too long upon questions of cost, for they should not be decisive in the analysis of the individual cases. Instead it is better to see the law of torts in terms of what might be called its political function. The arguments made here suggest that the first task of the law of torts is to define the boundaries of individual liberty. To this question and the rules of strict liability based upon the twin notions of causation and volition provide a better answer than the alternative theories based upon the notion of negligence, whether explicated in moral or economic terms. In effect, the principles of strict liability say that the liberty of one person ends when he causes harm to another. Until that point he is free to act as he chooses, and need not take into account the welfare of others.

But the law of tort does not end with the recognition of individual liberty. Once a man causes harm to another, he has brought himself within the boundaries of the law of tort. It does not follow, however, that he will be held liable in each and every case in which it can be showed that he caused harm, for it may still be possible for him to escape liability, not by an insistence upon his freedom of action, but upon a specific showing that his conduct was either excused or justified. Thus far in this paper we have only made occasional and unsystematic references to the problems raised by both pleas of excuses and justification. Their systematic explication remains crucial to the further development of the law of tort. That, task, however, is large enough to deserve special attention of its own.

Notes

1 See Guido Calabresi & A. Douglas Melamed, "Property Rules, Liability Rules, and Inalienability: One View of the Cathedral," 85 *Harv. L. Rev.* 1089, 1102–5 (1972). But see Richard A. Posner, "A Theory of Negligence," 1 *J. Leg. Studies* 29 (1972).
2 159 F. 2d 169 (2d Cir. 1947)
3 *Id.* at 173.
4 *Id.* at 173–4
5 *Id.* at 174.
6 109 Minn. 456, 124 N.W. 221 (1910).
7 H. L. A. Hart & A. M. Honoré, *Causation in the Law* (1959), at 59–62.
8 Style 65, 82 Eng. Rep. 533 (1647).
9 The argument depends upon "a deep sense of common law morality that one who hurts another should compensate him." Leon Green, "Foreseeability in Negligence Law," 61 *Colum. L. Rev.* 1412 (1961).
10 The classification that follows was developed in John Charlesworth, *Liability for Dangerous Things* (1992).
11 I put aside here all those cases in which there are special relationships between the plaintiff and the defendants: parent and child, invitor and invitee, and the like.
12 Charles O. Gregory, "The Good Samaritan and the Bad," in *The Good Samaritan and the Law*, 22, 27 (James Ratcliff, ed., 1966).
13 *Id.* at 27.
14 If the owner of the truck brought an action against the driver, claiming as its prima facie case, "you struck my truck," that action would fail because the defendant could plead as its affirmative defense, "you (plaintiff) blocked my right of way." Observe that there is no appeal here to a notion of contributory negligence, even though the defense puts plaintiff's conduct into issue.
15 80 Wis. 523, 50 N.W. 403 (1891). [. . .]
16 See, *e.g.*, James Street Fulton, "The Free Person and Legal Authority," in *Responsibility in Law and in Morals*, 1–11 (Arthur L. Harding, ed., 1960).

35

The Question of a Duty to Rescue in Canadian Tort Law: An Answer from France

Mitchell McInnes

I Introduction

A man witnesses a canoeist drowning a short distance from the shore.[1] For over forty minutes the tenants of an apartment complex listen to the tortured screams of a woman being murdered in the streets below.[2] A handful of railway employees watch a boy bleed to death for want of medical attention after he was struck by a passing car.[3] The owner of a pleasure craft learns that one of his passengers has fallen overboard into an icy lake.[4] An innocent party to a motor vehicle accident finds that the driver at fault was injured as a result of the mishap.[5] In each of these examples the first mentioned party (or parties) could have safely rendered assistance to the helpless victim. The aim of the present discussion is to show that there ought to be a *legal* obligation to do so in Canadian tort law. [. . .]

II History of Duty to Act at Common Law and in French Law

[. . .]
Before 1941 the law in France was much the same as it was in the common law world – generally speaking, legal sanctions would not follow upon a refusal to rescue someone. [. . .]

While an increasing number of European countries had come to impose a positive obligation to render aid,[6] remarkable and unfortunate circumstances provided French legislators with a unique impetus.

In 1941 a German officer serving in France was murdered while witnesses stood idly by, refusing to intervene. By way of reprisal, the Nazis executed 50 hostages. The Vichy government, coerced by the Germans, hoped to obviate the future need for such drastic measures by providing a means of redress through the more humane channels of the French courts.[7] The result was the enactment of a statute which required intervention for the prevention of crimes and for the assistance of persons in peril.[8] [. . .] A free French government, declaring the law void, sought not to repudiate the existence of the duty, but rather to retain it in an expanded form. The year 1945 saw the implementation of articles 61–63 of the Penal Code,[9] of which article 63 §2 is, for the present purposes, the most pertinent. It provides that:

> Whoever abstains voluntarily from giving such aid to a person that he would have been able to give him without risk to himself or third persons by his personal action or by calling help . . .

shall be liable.

Mitchell McInnes, "The Question of a Duty to Rescue in Canadian Tort Law: An Answer from France," *Dalhousie Law Journal*, vol. 13, no. 1, May 1990, pp. 85–122. © 1990 by Mitchell McInnes. Reprinted by kind permission of the author.

The statute is primarily penal in nature, the criminal punishment for a breach being a term of imprisonment of between three months and five years, or a fine of between 36,000 and 1,500,000 francs, or both. Of more relevance for the present purposes, of course, is the fact that a breach can also give rise to civil liability. [. . .]

III Article 63 §2 of the French Penal Code and a Proposed Duty

Professor Tunc has distilled from the statute and related case law four conditions which must be met before liability can be incurred.[10] First, the person must be in danger. [. . .] Second, the statute is breached only where something *could* have been done, though that "something" is not exhausted by possibilities of personal intervention. [. . .] Third, one is required to act only in the absence of risk to himself or third parties. [. . .] Finally, the refusal to rescue must be voluntary. It will not be so where one is unaware of the need for assistance. [. . .]

The French statute provides a sensible, comprehensive model for the duty which should be imposed in Canada. First of all, the policy underlying a duty to rescue would not be well served if an obligation existed only where the victim's *life* was in danger. [. . .] Further, while there will be instances where the gravity of the situation will be readily apparent, it would seem to invite problems to restrict the imposition of a duty to such cases. [. . .] The French statute should also be followed insofar as it does not require the rescue of property which is at risk. Whereas the imposition of a duty is justified where a person is facing danger, it may not be where a *thing* is facing danger. [. . .]

On whom should a duty be imposed? Again, the French legislation gives an appropriate response, congruent with the policy of a duty. Some have suggested that only those actually witness to the peril should be obliged to act. It is not at all clear, however, why a duty should be so dependant on chance. [. . .] Of course, the line must be drawn at some point – but it is a point which French courts have been able to locate. Thus, a duty should be imposed on one who is either present at the scene or who is "reliably informed." The "reasonable man" standard should be used in deciding whether a person so informed assessed the circumstances and the need for help properly. [. . .]

Depending on the nature of the situational demands, the requirement under French law is to personally intervene, or obtain help, or both. This is sensible. The spirit of the duty would not be observed if one could walk away simply because personal involvement was impossible if others, who could help, were summonable. Whatever action is called for, however, the rescuer should not be expected to satisfy too high a standard of care. [. . .]

IV Current Law: General Absence of Duty and Exceptions

Common law courts have long felt uncomfortable with the law's general denial of a duty to assist one in peril. [. . .] Inevitably, time began to see the crystallization of conscience into law as the number of "exceptional" situations in which a duty would be imposed grew even larger. Today liability for a failure to act will lie in widely disparate circumstances, many of which would not have been actionable under the traditional common law position. [. . .]

1 Exceptions to the general rule

(i) Relationships of economic benefit
The Supreme Court of Canada has on a number of occasions recognized that a duty *may* arise where a relationship of economic benefit exists. In *Jordan House Ltd.* v. *Menow*,[11] Mr. Justice Laskin (as he then was) agreed with the lower court's decision to impose liability upon a hotel which had served beer to a patron who was past the point of visible intoxication and later ejected him out into the night. The action was brought by the patron after he was struck by a vehicle as he weaved his way down a much-traveled highway on foot. It was held that while motorists might be expected to succumb to Good Samaritan impulses and take steps to ensure that the plaintiff safely reached his destination, they were under no legal duty to do so. The hotel, on the other hand, was under such a duty. The basis for the difference seems primarily

to have been that the hotel stood in an invitor–invitee relationship with its patron, although, significantly, it was stressed that "a great deal turned on the knowledge of the [hotel] of the patron and his conditions...."[12] Not every tavern-owner would be obliged to "act as a watch dog for all patrons who enter his place of business and drink to excess."[13] The litigants in the *Jordan House* case were particularly well acquainted, and the plaintiff's propensity to over-consumption and subsequent reckless behaviour was well known to the defendant. Indeed, the defendant had earlier ordered its employees not to serve the plaintiff unless he was accompanied by a responsible person.[14] [...]

(ii)   Relationships of control or supervision
Individuals often stand in a relationship of control or supervision in which one is dominant over the other. In some instances the price consequent on that power is the obligation to protect the subordinate party from harm. [...] [I]n an employer–employee relationship where the former may dictate working conditions, a duty exists.[15] An obligation has also been recognized as between school and pupil,[16] innkeeper and guest,[17] ship master and passenger,[18] jail and prisoner,[19] and hospital and patient.[20]
     Frequently a relationship of control or supervision may give rise to a duty which is owed not to the party under control, but rather to a third party. Thus, a parent owes a duty to ensure that a child does not cause injuries to third parties,[21] and prisons and psychiatric institutions are obliged to protect the public from escaped prisoners[22] and patients.[23] [...] Finally, an affirmative obligation may also be imposed on one who has control over a dangerous object.[24]

(iii)   Creation of danger
Related to the idea that a duty will be imposed on one who has control over an instrument of danger is the idea that a duty will be imposed on one who non-negligently creates a danger. In *Oke* v. *Weide Transport and Carra*[25] the defendant non-negligently collided with a sign post, leaving it bent and protruding from the pavement at right angles. The deceased was later "speared" by the post when it penetrated the floor boards of his car and deflected up into his chest. The majority of the Manitoba Court

of Appeal dismissed the plaintiff's action on the grounds of foreseeability, reserving judgment on the question of whether or not the defendant was under a duty to the deceased to do anything about the post. In a celebrated dissent Freedman, J.A. argued that the defendant should be held liable. [...] The essence of Mr Justice Freedman's opinion is supported elsewhere, affirmative obligations being imposed in various circumstances where a defendant's actions created a situation of peril.[26]

(iv)   Gratuitous undertakings
[...]
     Generally, a mere promise, unsupported by consideration, will not ground an action in either tort or contract. There is, however, an underdeveloped body of law which suggests that where the undertaking is coupled with reliance, a tortious duty may be imposed. In effect, a party, through past conduct, may create a self-imposed obligation to act. Such was the case in *Mercer* v. *South Eastern and Chatham Railway Co.*[27] The defendant there had voluntarily commenced a routine of locking a gate which opened onto its railway tracks whenever a train passed by. The object of the practice was to prevent that which in fact occurred. The plaintiff, aware of and relying on the defendant's custom, was run down by a locomotive after passing through the unlocked gate. Regrettably, through carelessness the defendant had deviated from its usual procedure. Liability followed. [...]
     The second issue to be addressed in regards to gratuitous undertakings concerns the standard of care which will be imposed on one who commences to effect a rescue in the absence of a duty to do so. On the one hand, the famous American case of *Zelenko* v. *Gimbel Bros.*[28] stands for the proposition that one who gratuitously undertakes a rescue must not fail to do what "an ordinary man would do in performing the task." A different approach was adopted in *East Suffolk Catchment Board* v. *Kent*[29] where it was held that a public body would not be liable for failing to expediently continue on with a rescue operation unless by doing so it inflicted injury on the plaintiff. The Ontario Court of Appeal subsequently expanded that principle to cover private individuals who gratuitously intervene. [...]

(v)   Statutory duties

[. . .] While much of the legislation imposing positive obligations is only peripherally related to the issue of a duty to rescue [. . .], "hit-and-run" statutes bear directly on the matter. Illustrative is the Alberta Motor Vehicle Administration Act:[30]

> 76(1) When an accident occurs on a highway, the driver or other person in charge of the vehicle that was directly or indirectly involved in the accident . . .
> (b) shall render all reasonable assistance. . . .

Failure to do so may result in a fine of $500 or imprisonment for a term not exceeding six months.[31] Significantly, the statute is also said to ground a civil action if breached.[32] The provision is interesting for its scope of applicability. [. . .] More to the point, one must render aid regardless of fault,[33] and even though one's involvement in the accident may only be "indirect". [. . .]

The policy of section 76(1) of the Alberta Motor Vehicle Administration Act, and of similar legislation, is clear. Parliament and provincial legislatures have indicated a new direction for the law by getting involved in the business of encouraging, nay, requiring Good Samaritanism. [. . .]

2   Summary of the exceptions

A number of commentators have sought to distil from the various exceptions a common basis upon which affirmative obligations are imposed and can be rationalized. Most popular is the "benefit theory" which holds that a duty will be placed upon one who has "voluntarily brought himself into a certain relationship with others from which he obtains or expects a benefit."[34] [. . .] It is suggested, however, that unless stretched to an untenable extent, the existence of a benefit (actual or potential) moving to obligor provides at best only a partial explanation. [. . .]

[. . .] However, the mere fact that one derives an economic benefit does not inevitably lead to the conclusion that a duty will be incurred, nor does the incurrence of a duty necessarily depend on the presence of a benefit. Mr Justice Laskin (as he then was), while holding that a duty did exist on the facts before the court in *Jordan House Ltd. v. Menow*, went on to say that not every tavern owner would be under a similar duty to all his customers. "A great deal turns on the knowledge of the operator (or his employees) of the patron and his condition. [. . .]"[35]

The benefit analysis is most unacceptable in regards to parent–child relationships. There is something very distasteful about a legal system which would purportedly downplay altruistic behaviour within the family unit, and seek rather to explain the duty owed by a mother or father as the price to be paid for some benefit actually or potentially moving to the parent. [. . .]

Gratuitous undertakings by definition cannot be explained by the benefit principle, a fact which even the most forceful advocates of the theory concede.[36] [. . .]

Other theories as to why or when tort law will impose a duty to act are similarly unsatisfying. Professor Weinrib, starting from the proposition that "[the] common law position on non-feasance generally relies on contract law, and hence on the market, to regulate the provision of aid to others for independently existing dangers,"[37] goes on to argue that an affirmative obligation will be imposed in tort where there is an absence of any social value in the liberty to contract. The evidence offered in defence of this thesis, while somewhat supportive, is sparse and ultimately unpersuasive. Weinrib begins by offering an explanation for the decision of the Supreme Court of Canada in *O'Rourke v. Schacht*[38] in which a police officer was held to be under a duty to warn drivers of dangerous conditions on a highway. [. . .] Similarly, duties owed by family members to one another are explained on the basis that "family relations [are] never appropriate for market regulation."[39] Finally it is noted that contracts which have been made between rescuers and rescuees have been declared unenforceable as unconscionable or made under duress.[40]

The theory is fatally flawed. First of all, it is rather limited in scope. Weinrib does not, for example, even attempt to explain the basis of the duty found in cases like *Jordan House Ltd. v. Menow*. [. . .]

On a more fundamental level it appears that whether or not a duty will be imposed is a policy decision. Neither the benefit theory nor Weinrib's theory are capable of adequately explaining all of the affirmative obligations which exist in tort law, though both may represent factors which, along with others, are at play in the policy field. [...]

V   Policy Basis of Tort Development

A duty to rescue could be either judicially or statutorily created. Although both approaches have features which recommend them, it is the former which is preferred here. [...]

A general duty to rescue, if it is to be recognized judicially, rather than statutorily, will find its home in the tort of negligence. That it could fit within the test set forth by Lord Atkin's famous dictum in *Donoghue* v. *Stevenson* seems clear.[41]

> The rule that you are to love your neighbour becomes in law that you are not to injure your neighbour, and the lawyer's question is, Who is my neighbour? receives a restricted reply. You must take reasonable care to avoid acts or *omissions* which you can reasonably foresee would be likely to injure your neighbour. Who, then, in law is my neighbour? The answer seems to be – persons who are so closely and directly affected by my act that I ought reasonably to have them in contemplation as being so affected when I am directing my mind to the acts or *omissions* which are called in question. (Emphasis added) [...]

VI   Policy Considerations

1   Policy arguments against a duty to rescue

Reflecting the values and attitudes of the times, the development of the early common law was premised upon a philosophy of "rugged individualism."[42] [...] Quite naturally it was considered inappropriate for the government or the courts to intervene in regards to omissions – their function was more narrowly aimed at preventing *positive* harm from being done.[43] [...]

[...] Such harsh judgements are today unlikely. Condemnation is unlikely to follow upon a cry for help if the situation was truly one of imminent danger. Indeed, silence in such

circumstances might be regarded as obstinate and irresponsible. From all that has been said, it seems clear that modern Canadian society is not based on a philosophy of rugged individualism.[44] The view that a duty to rescue is unnecessary and undesirable, so typical of the earlier era, should similarly seem anachronistic. [...]

Implicit throughout the discussion so far has been the assumption that a general duty to rescue would be consistent with commonly held notions of morality. [...]

The best indicator that a duty to rescue would be consistent with morality or conscience, however, is seen in the possible responses to a call for help. Basically, two are possible. First of all, the bystander may become involved and personally provide relief or summon one who is better equipped to do the job. Morality would surely underlie the altruistic response. Alternatively, the bystander may pass by. [...] If, as in most cases, the bystander later tried to justify his inaction, the role of morality is again evident. "I'm not a doctor – I couldn't have helped." "Someone else will stop for the poor guy." "It's none of my business." Such responses are unfortunately familiar to all but the most saintly among us. What is clear is that if not for the pangs of guilt, if not for the need to placate one's bothersome conscience, if not for the knowledge that the morally correct choice was not made, such rationalizations would be pointless and would not occur.

Epstein has argued that in a society in which the government can force one to gratuitously confer a benefit upon another, "it becomes impossible to tell where liberty ends and obligation begins."[45] [...] True, if Canadian society is to retain its basic nature, liberty must at some point prevail over the call for personal sacrifice. However, practically speaking, the duty advocated would seldomly be invoked, and when it was, it would only require action which would not expose the rescuer to danger. The extent to which freedom would be threatened would not be great. [...]

In defence of the traditional common law view it has been said that the law should not require one to jeopardize his pocket-book or safety in an attempt to save a person in peril.[46] This argument is no longer supportable because recent developments have seen tort law soften its attitude towards rescuers, and also because it assumes the imposition of a duty in *all* cases. First, while the early common law did invoke the concepts of *volenti*[47] and causation[48] to deny the claims of rescuers who are injured as a result of their efforts, jurists of the 20th century have increasingly come to praise and encourage Good Samaritans.[49] Consequently, compensation is available to the reasonable[50] rescuer from one who negligently created the perilous situation [. . .] or from a third party responsible for supervening negligence. [. . .]

Secondly, while it is inevitable that mishaps would occur under the proposed duty, a bystander need not court disaster in order to fulfil his obligations. To reiterate, the model advocated, based on the French experience, would only require that which could be done safely. [. . .]

2   Policy arguments in favour of a duty to rescue

Most of what has been said up to this point has simply rebutted arguments made against the imposition of a duty to rescue. That, of course, only takes the issue half of the way home. It is necessary to show not only that bad things would not come from a duty, but also that good things would.

From a practical viewpoint, the best possible result which could come from the imposition of a duty would be an increase in the number of rescues which are undertaken. [. . .]

Assuming that people would be aware of a duty to rescue if it existed, the question then becomes whether they would more often aid those in peril. Posner's suggestion that the existence of an obligation would paradoxically lead to fewer rescuers is, in the absence of empirical support, difficult to accept.[51] First, his prediction that (for example) a strong swimmer would avoid the beach because there might be a call for help is dubious to say the least. Given that the sacrifice required would be minimal and non-life threatening, it seems unlikely that such a person would shun the water and the pleasure that it brings her, as well as the possibility of glory and personal pride which would follow upon a rescue. Secondly, Posner's prediction that

altruists, who would otherwise become involved, would refuse on the grounds that a legal duty would be coercive and would deprive them of the power of choice, is untenable. It is certainly a cynical view, but beyond that it seems to fly in the face of common sense. How likely is it that a person, otherwise predisposed to benevolent behaviour, would be so offended by legal recognition of his own values that he would consciously commit a tort and incur liability and public condemnation? [. . .] [I]t does seem far more probable that, if anything, a duty would lead to more, not fewer, rescues. [. . .]

The imposition of a duty to rescue would also be a positive development in that it would serve the various goals of tort law. It would likely lessen the incidence of socially undesirable behaviour as it would provide an incentive (the avoidance of liability) to those who are capable of action and who are aware of the moral call for help, but who are simply callous or recalcitrant. That is, it would act as a deterring factor. [. . .]

VII   Conclusions

[. . .] From all that has been said, however, it appears abundantly clear that the view embodied in the law's general denial of a duty to undertake a rescue is an anachronism. Accordingly, the law should be altered so as to reflect the settled convictions of Canadians today.

Admittedly, effecting such a change would not be easy. Developments might continue to be slow and uncertain as judges and legislators cautiously invoke various devices as means of justifying their progressive steps. . . .

The policy considerations which must be accounted for in answering this question are many. On the basis of the experience in France over the past four decades it has been shown that the administrative and philosophical fears of those who oppose a duty are largely unfounded. So, too, it has been shown that the existence of an obligation to assist those in peril would have many positive effects. Prosser has said that "changing social conditions lead constantly to the recognition of new duties."[52] One can hope.

Notes

1 *Osterlind* v. *Hill* (1928), 263 Mass. 73, 160 N.E. 301.

2 These were the facts surrounding the murder of Kitty Genovese in New York City, March 26, 1964. [. . .]

3 *Union Pacific R.R.* v. *Cappier* (1903), 66 Kan. 649, 72 P. 281.

4 *Horsley* v. *McLaren* (1972), S.C.R. 441, 22 D.L.R. (3d) 545; *affg.* [1970] 2 O.R. 487, 11 D.L.R. (3d) 277; *revg.* (1969), 2 O.R. 137, 4 D.L.R. (3d) 557.

5 See e.g. Alberta Motor Vehicle Administration Act, R.S.A. 1980, c. M-22, s.76 (1).

6 Portugal (1867), Switzerland (1808), Netherlands (1881), Italy (1889), Norway (1902), Russia (1903), Turkey (1926), Denmark (1930), Poland (1932), Germany (1871, 1935). Rudzinski's seminal survey, "The Duty to Rescue: A Comparative Analysis," in *The Good Samaritan and the Law* (J. Ratcliffe ed., 1966), should be consulted for a detailed discussion.

7 Magnol (1946) Semaine Juridique I. 531.

8 Tunc, Commentaire (1946) Dalloz Legislation 33, 38.

9 (1947) Dalloz Legislation 130. The most significant difference between the two versions is that the later one does not require proof that serious bodily harm or death actually resulted from the failure to give succour.

10 Tunc, "The Volunteer and the Good Samaritan," in Ratcliffe, ed., *The Good Samaritan and the Law supra*, 47.

11 [1974] S.C.R. 239, 38 D.L.R. (3d) 105; *affg.* (1971), 1 O.R. 129, 14 D.L.R. (3d) 345; *affg.* (1970), 1 O.R. 54, 7 D.L.R. (3d) 494.

12 *Id.* at 113. Mr. Justice Ritchie, concurring on the result based his decision on narrower grounds. For him the duty imposed was simply to not serve the plaintiff alcohol when he was drunk.

13 *Id.* at 113.

14 *Id.* at 107.

15 Fleming, *Law of Torts* (1983), 142; *Remedies in Tort* (1987), 16.1–102.

16 *Williams* v. *Eady* (1893), 10 T.L.R. 41; *Moddejonge* v. *Huron Couty Bd. of Educ.*, [1972] 2 O.R. 437 (HC.J.); *Portelance* v. *Bd. of Trustees R.C. Sep. Sch. of Grantham*, [1962] 2 O.R. 365, 32 D.L.R. (2d) 337 (C.A.).

17 Fleming, *Law of Torts*, 142; *Remedies in Tort*, 16.1–102.

18 *Horsley* v. *McLaren*.

19 *Timm* v. *R.* (1965) 1 Ex. C.R. 174; *Ellis* v. *Home Office* (1953), 2 All E.R. 149; *Howley* v. *R.* (1973), F.C. 184.

20 *Lawson* v. *Wellesley* (1975), 9 O.R. (2d) 677; *affd. on other grounds* (1978), 1 S.C.R. 893.

21 *Hatfield* v. *Pearson* (1956), 6 D.L.R. (2d) 593; *Starr* v. *Crone* (1950), 4 D.L.R. 433.

22 *Home Office* v. *Dorset Yacht Co.* (1970), A.C. 1004 (1970), 2 W.L.R. 1140 (1970), 2 All E.R. 294; *affg.* (1969), 2 Q.B. 412 (1969), 2 All E.R. 564.

23 *Holgate* v. *Lancashire Mental Hosp. Bd.* (1937), 4 All E.R. 19. In the United States the duty is even broader. *See Tarasoff* v. *Regents of Univ. of Calif.* (1976), 131 Cal. Rptr. 14. [. . .]

24 See e.g. *Stermer* v. *Lawson* (1977), 79 D.L.R. (3d) 366; *affd.* (1979), 11 C.C.L.T. (B.C.C.A.) lending a motorcycle to a young, unlicensed driver; Rudolph, "The Duty to Act: A Proposed Rule" (1965), 503; *Ayers* v. *Hicks* (1942), 40 N.E. 2d. 334.

25 (1963), 41 D.L.R. (2d) 53.

26 *Jordan House* v. *Menow*; *Depeu* v. *Flatau* (1907), 100 Minn. 299, 11 N.W. 1 [. . .] *Ontario Hospital Services Commission* v. *Borsoski* (1973), 54 D.L.R. (3d) 339, 7 O.R. (2d) 83 [. . .] *Haynes* v. *Harwood* (1935), 1 K.B. 146 (1934), All E.R. Rep. 103. [. . .]

27 (1922), K.B. 549.

28 (1935), 287 N.Y.S. 134; *affd. without reasons* (1935), 287 N.Y.S. 136.

29 (1941), A.C. 74, (1940), 4 All E.R. 527. The case has been much criticized, and subsequent decisions have put its status into doubt. *City of Kamloops* v. *Nielsen* (1984), 2 S.C.R. 2, 29 C.C.L.T. 97 (1984) 2 W.W.R.1 (*per* Wilson J.), *Anns* v. *Merton London Borough Council* (1978), A.C. 728, (1977), 2 W.L.R. 1024, (1977), 2 All E.R. 492.

30 *Supra* n. 5. See also Canadian Criminal Code R.S.C. 1985, c. C-46, s.252(1); Highway Traffic Act R.S.O. 1980, c. 198, s.174(1)(6); Motor Vehicle Act R.S.B.C. 1979, c. 288, s. 62(1).

31 R.S.A. 1980, c. M-22, s. 101(1).

32 Linden, *Canadian Tort Law* (4th ed. 1988), 283.

33 There exists, independently of the statute, a duty to render aid where the driver was tortiously responsible for the injury of the other. *Racine* v. *CNR* (1923), 2 D.L.R. 572 (1923), 1 W.W.R. 1439, 19 Alta. L.R. 529 (C.A.).

34 McNeice & Thornton, "Affirmative Duties in Tort" (1949), 58 *Yale L.J.* 1282–3; Bohlen, "The Moral Duty to Aid Others As a Basis of Tort Liability" (1908), 56 *U.Pa.L.Rev.* 217 and 316, 220.

35 [. . .] 38 D.L.R. (3d) 113.

36 McNeice & Thornton, "Affirmative Duties in Tort," 1286–7.

37 Weinrib, "The Case for a Duty to Rescue" (1980), 90 *Yale L.J.* 247, 269.

38 (1976), 1 S.C.R. 53 D.L.R. (3d) 96; *affg.* (1973), 1 O.R. 221, 30 D.L.R. (3d) 641.

39 *Supra* n. 37, at 271.

40 *Id.* [. . .]

41 [1932] A.C. 562, 580. Similar statements appeared in earlier decisions, but it is Lord Atkin's which has withstood the test of time, *Heaven* v. *Pender* (1883), 11 Q.B.D. 503 as limited by *LaLievre* v. *Gould* (1893), 1 Q.B. 491; *Buckley* v. *Mott* (1920), 50 D.L.R. 508 (N.S.).

42 Hope, "Officiousness" (1929), 15 *Cornell L.Q.* 25, 29.

43 Hale, "Prima Facie Torts, Combination and Non-feasance" (1946), 46 *Col. L. Rev.* 196, 214.

44 *Crocker* v. *Sundance Northwest Resorts Ltd.* (1988), 1 S.C.R. 1186, 51 D.L.R. (4th); 321, 44 C.C.L.L. 225, *revg.* (1985), 20 D.L.R. (4th) 552, 33 C.C.L.T. 73, *which revd.* (1983), 150 D.L.R. (3d) 178, 25 C.C.L.T. 201.

45 Epstein, "A Theory of Strict Liability" (1973), 2 *J. Legal Stud.* 151, at 199.

46 McNeice & Thornton, "Affirmative Duties in Tort" (1949), 58 *Yale L.J.* 1288; Linden, "Tort Liability for Criminal Nonfeasance" (1966), 44 *Can. Bar Rev.* 25, 30.

47 See e.g. *Kimball* v. *Butler Bros.* (1910), 15 O.W.R. 221 (C.A.).

48 See e.g. *Anderson* v. *Northern Ry. Co.* (1875), 25 U.C.C.P. 301 (C.A.).

49 See e.g. *Attorney General for Ontario* v. *Crompton* (1976), 1 C.C.L.T. 81. A detailed analysis of the position in civil law countries can be found in Dawson, "Rewards for the Rescue of Human Life?" in Ratcliffe, ed., *The Good Samaritan and the Law*, 62.

50 The "foolhardy" and the "rash" will not be compensated. *Baker* v. *Hopkins* (1958), 3 All E.R. 147 (Q.B.D.); *affd.* (1959), 1 W.L.R. 966 (1959), 3 All E.R. 225 (C.A.); *Haigh* v. *Grand Trunk Pacific Ry. Co.* (1914), 7 W.W.R. (N.S.) 806. Recent developments suggest that the courts may also be willing to employ the doctrine of contributory negligence to deny compensation in part. See e.g. *Sayers* v. *Harlow Urban District Council* (1958), 2 All E.R. 342 (C.A.); *Holomis* v. *Dubuc* (1974), 56 D.L.R. (3d) 351.

51 Posner, *Economic Theory of Law* (1986), §6.9.

52 *Handbook on the Law of Torts* (1964), 334.

36

Tarasoff v. Regents of University of California (1976)

TOBRINER, J. On October 27, 1969, Prosenjit Poddar killed Tatiana Tarasoff. Plaintiffs, Tatiana's parents, allege that two months earlier Poddar confided his intention to kill Tatiana to Dr Lawrence Moore, a psychologist employed by the Cowell Memorial Hospital at the University of California at Berkeley. They allege that on Moore's request, the campus police briefly detained Poddar, but released him when he appeared rational. They further claim that Dr Harvey Powelson, Moore's superior, then directed that no further action be taken to detain Poddar. No one warned plaintiffs of Tatiana's peril.

Concluding that these facts set forth causes of action against neither therapists and policemen involved, nor against the Regents of the University of California as their employer, the superior court sustained defendants' demurrers to plaintiffs' second amended complaints without leave to amend. This appeal ensued.

[Plaintiffs' second amended complaints set forth four causes of action: (1) a claim that defendants negligently failed to detain a dangerous patient; (2) a claim that defendants negligently failed to warn Tatiana's parents; (3) a claim for punitive damages on the ground that defendants acted "maliciously and oppressively"; and (4) a claim that defendants breached their duty to their patient and the public. The court concludes that plaintiffs' first and fourth causes of action are barred by governmental immunity, and that plaintiffs' third cause of action is barred by a rule precluding exemplary damages in a wrongful death action. Therefore, the court addresses the question of whether plaintiffs' second cause of action can be amended to state a basis for recovery.]

The second cause of action can be amended to allege that Tatiana's death proximately resulted from defendants' negligent failure to warn Tatiana or others likely to apprise her of her danger. Plaintiffs contend that as amended, such allegations of negligence and proximate causation, with resulting damages, establish a cause of action. Defendants, however, contend that in the circumstances of the present case they owed no duty of care to Tatiana or her parents and that, in the absence of such duty, they were free to act in careless disregard of Tatiana's life and safety.

In analyzing this issue, we bear in mind that legal duties are not discoverable facts of nature, but merely conclusory expressions that, in cases of a particular type, liability should be imposed for damage done. As stated in Dillon v. Legg (1968) 68 Cal. 2d 728, 734, 69 Cal. Rptr. 72, 76, 441 P.2d 912, 916: "The assertion that liability must

Tarasoff v. Regents of Univ. of California, 17 Cal. 3d 425; 551 P.2d 334; 131 Cal. Rptr. 14 (1976).

... be denied because defendant bears no 'duty' to plaintiff 'begs the essential question – whether the plaintiff's interests are entitled to legal protection against the defendant's conduct. . . . [Duty] is not sacrosanct in itself, but only an expression of the sum total of those considerations of policy which lead the law to say that the particular plaintiff is entitled to protection.' (Prosser, Law of Torts [3d ed. 1964] at pp. 332–3.)"

In the landmark case of Rowland v. Christian (1968) 69 Cal. 2d 108, 70 Cal. Rptr. 97, 443 P.2d 561, Justice Peters recognized that liability should be imposed "for an injury occasioned to another by his want of ordinary care or skill" as expressed in section 1714 of the Civil Code. Thus, Justice Peters, quoting from Heaven v. Pender (1883) 11 Q.B.D. 503, 509 stated: "'whenever one person is by circumstances placed in such a position with regard to another . . . that if he did not use ordinary care and skill in his own conduct . . . he would cause danger of injury to the person or property of the other, a duty arises to use ordinary care and skill to avoid such danger.'"

We depart from "this fundamental principle" only upon the "balancing of a number of considerations"; major ones "are the foreseeability of harm to the plaintiff, the degree of certainty that the plaintiff suffered injury, the closeness of the connection between the defendant's conduct and the injury suffered, the moral blame attached to the defendant's conduct, the policy of preventing future harm, the extent of the burden to the defendant and consequences to the community of imposing a duty to exercise care with resulting liability for breach, and the availability, cost and prevalence of insurance for the risk involved."

The most important of these considerations in establishing duly is foreseeability. As a general principle, a "defendant owes a duty of care to all persons who are foreseeably endangered by his conduct, with respect to all risks which make the conduct unreasonably dangerous." As we shall explain, however, when the avoidance of foreseeable harm requires a defendant to control the conduct of another person, or to warn of such conduct, the common law has traditionally imposed liability only if the defendant bears some special relationship to the dangerous person or to the potential victim. Since the relationship between

a therapist and his patient satisfies this requirement, we need not here decide whether foreseeability alone is sufficient to create a duty to exercise reasonable care to protect a potential victim of another's conduct.

Although, as we have stated above, under the common law, as a general rule, one person owed no duty to control the conduct of another, nor to warn those endangered by such conduct, the courts have carved out an exception to this rule in cases in which the defendant stands in some special relationship to either the person whose conduct needs to be controlled or in a relationship to the foreseeable victim of that conduct. Applying this exception to the present case, we note that a relationship of defendant therapists to either Tatiana or Poddar will suffice to establish a duty of care; as explained in section 315 of the Restatement Second of Torts, a duty of care may arise from either "(a) a special relation . . . between the actor and the third person which imposes a duty upon the actor to control the third person's conduct, or (b) a special relation . . . between the actor and the other which gives to the other a right of protection."

Although plaintiffs' pleadings assert no special relation between Tatiana and defendant therapists, they establish as between Poddar and defendant therapists the special relation that arises between a patient and his doctor or psychotherapist. Such a relationship may support affirmative duties for the benefit of third persons. Thus, for example, a hospital must exercise reasonable care to control the behavior of a patient which may endanger other persons. A doctor must also warn a patient if the patient's condition or medication renders certain conduct, such as driving a car, dangerous to others.

Although the California decisions that recognize this duty have involved cases in which the defendant stood in a special relationship *both* to the victim and to the person whose conduct created the danger, we do not think that the duty should logically be constricted such situations. Decisions of other jurisdictions hold that the single relationship of a doctor to his patient is sufficient to support the duty to exercise reasonable care to protect others against dangers emanating from the patient's illness. The courts hold, that a doctor is liable to persons infected by his patient if he negligently fails to diagnose a contagious disease or, having diagnosed the illness, fails to warn members of the patient's family. [. . .]

Defendants contend, however, that imposition of a duty to exercise reasonable care to protect third persons is unworkable because therapists cannot accurately predict whether or not a patient will resort to violence. In support of this argument amicus representing the American Psychiatric Association and other professional societies cites numerous articles which indicate that therapists, in the present state of the art, are unable reliably to predict violent acts; their forecasts, amicus claims, tend consistently to overpredict violence, and indeed are more often wrong than right. Since predictions of violence are often erroneous, amicus concludes, the courts should not render rulings that predicate the liability of therapists upon the validity of such predictions.

The role of the psychiatrist, who is indeed a practitioner of medicine, and that of the psychologist who performs an allied function, are like that of the physician who must conform to the standards of the profession and who must often make diagnoses and predictions based upon such evaluations. Thus the judgment of the therapist in diagnosing emotional disorders and in predicting whether a patient presents a serious danger of violence is comparable to the judgment which doctors and professionals must regularly render under accepted rules of responsibility.

We recognize the difficulty that a therapist encounters in attempting to forecast whether a patient presents a serious danger of violence. Obviously we do not require that the therapist, in making that determination, render a perfect performance; the therapist need only exercise "that reasonable degree of skill, knowledge, and care ordinarily possessed and exercised by members of [that professional specialty] under similar circumstances." Within the broad range of reasonable practice and treatment in which professional opinion and judgment may differ, the therapist is free to exercise his or her own best judgment without liability; proof, aided by hindsight, that he or she judged wrongly is insufficient to establish negligence.

In the instant case, however, the pleadings do not raise any question as to failure of defendant therapists to predict that Poddar presented a serious danger of violence. On the contrary, the present complaints allege that defendant therapists did in fact predict that Poddar would kill, but were negligent in failing to warn.

Amicus contends, however, that even when a therapist does in fact predict that a patient poses a serious danger of violence to others, the therapist should be absolved of any responsibility for failing to act to protect the potential victim. In our view, however, once a therapist does in fact determine, or under applicable professional standards reasonably should have determined, that a patient poses a serious danger of violence to others, he bears a duty to exercise reasonable care to protect the foreseeable victim of that danger. While the discharge of this duty of due care will necessarily vary with the facts of each case, in each instance the adequacy of the therapist's conduct must be measured against the traditional negligence standard of the rendition of reasonable care under the circumstances. [. . .]

Contrary to the assertion of amicus, this conclusion is not inconsistent with our recent decision in People v. Burnick, supra, 14 Cal. 3d 306, 121 Cal. Rptr. 488, 535 P.2d 352. Taking note of the uncertain character of therapeutic prediction, we held in *Burnick* that a person cannot be committed as a mentally disordered sex offender unless found to be such by proof beyond a reasonable doubt. The issue in the present context, however, is not whether the patient should be incarcerated, but whether the therapist should take any steps at all to protect the threatened victim; some of the alternatives open to the therapist, such as warning the victim, will not result in the drastic consequences of depriving the patient of his liberty. Weighing the uncertain and conjectural character of the alleged damage done the patient by such a warning against the peril to the victim's life, we conclude that professional inaccuracy in predicting violence cannot negate the therapist's duty to protect the threatened victim.

The risk that unnecessary warnings may be given is a reasonable price to pay for the lives of possible victims that may be saved. We would hesitate to hold that the therapist who is aware that his patient expects to attempt to assassinate the President of the United States would not be obligated to warn the authorities because the therapist cannot predict with accuracy that his patient will commit the crime.

Defendants further argue that free and open communication is essential to psychotherapy; that "Unless a patient . . . is assured that . . . information [revealed by him] can and will be held in utmost confidence, he will be reluctant to make the full disclosure upon which diagnosis and treatment . . . depends." (Sen. Com. on Judiciary, comment on Evid. Code, §1014.) The giving of a warning, defendants contend, constitutes a breach of trust which entails the revelation of confidential communications. [. . .]

We realize that the open and confidential character of psychotherapeutic dialogue encourages patients to express threats of violence, few of which are ever executed. Certainly a therapist should not be encouraged routinely to reveal such threats; such disclosures could seriously disrupt the patient's relationship with his therapist and with the persons threatened. To the contrary, the therapist's obligations to his patient require that he not disclose a confidence unless such disclosure is necessary to avert danger to others, and even then that he do so discreetly, and in a fashion that would preserve the privacy of his patient to the fullest extent compatible with the prevention of the threatened danger.

The revelation of a communication under the above circumstances is not a breach of trust or a violation of professional ethics; as stated in the Principles of Medical Ethics of the American Medical Association (1957), section 9: "A physician may not reveal the confidence entrusted to him in the course of medical attendance . . . *unless he is required to do so by law or unless it becomes necessary in order to protect the welfare of the individual or of the community.*" (Emphasis added.) We conclude that the public policy favoring protection of the confidential character of patient–psychotherapist communications must yield to the extent to which disclosure is essential to avert danger to others. The protective privilege ends where the public peril begins.

Our current crowded and computerized society compels the interdependence of its members. In this risk-infested society we can hardly tolerate the further exposure to danger that would result from a concealed knowledge of the therapist that his patient was lethal. If the exercise of reasonable care to protect the threatened victim requires the therapist to warn the endangered party or those who can reasonably be expected to notify him, we see no sufficient societal interest that would protect and justify concealment. The containment of such risks lies in the public interest. For the foregoing reasons, we find that plaintiffs' complaints can be amended to state a cause of action against defendants Moore, Powelson, Gold, and Yandell and against the Regents as their employer, for breach of a duty to exercise reasonable care to protect Tatiana.

[The majority concludes that the police defendants did not have a special relationship to either Tatiana or Poddar to impose upon them a duty to warn. The court also concludes that the defendant therapists are not protected by governmental immunity in connection with their failure to warn Tatiana's parents because their decisions were not "basic policy decisions" within the meaning of earlier precedent.]

For the reasons stated, we conclude that plaintiffs can amend their complaints to state a cause of action against defendant therapists by asserting that the therapists in fact determined that Poddar presented a serious danger of violence to Tatiana, or pursuant to the standards of their profession should have so determined, but nevertheless failed to exercise reasonable care to protect her from that danger. To the extent, however, that plaintiffs base their claim that defendant therapists breached that duty because they failed to procure Poddar's confinement, the therapists find immunity in Government Code section 856. Further, as to the police defendants we conclude that plaintiffs have failed to show that the trial court erred in sustaining their demurrer without leave to amend.

The judgment of the superior court in favor of defendants Atkinson, Beall, Brownrigg, Hallernan, and Teel is affirmed. The judgment of the superior court in favor of defendants Gold, Moore, Powelson, Yandell, and the Regents of the University of California is reversed, and the cause remanded for further proceedings consistent with the views expressed herein.

WRIGHT, C. J., and SULLIVAN and RICHARDSON, JJ., concur.

MOSK, J. (concurring and dissenting).

I concur in the result in this instance only because the complaints allege that defendant therapists did in fact predict that Poddar would kill and were therefore negligent in failing to warn of that danger. Thus the issue here is very narrow: we are not concerned with whether the therapists, pursuant to the standards of their profession, "should have" predicted potential violence; they allegedly did so in actuality. Under these limited circumstances I agree that a cause of action can be stated.

Whether plaintiffs can ultimately prevail is problematical at best. As the complaints admit, the therapist *did* notify the police that Poddar was planning to kill a girl identifiable as Tatiana. While I doubt that more should be required, this issue may be raised in defense and its determination is a question of fact.

I cannot concur, however, in the majority's rule that a therapist may be held liable for failing to predict his patient's tendency to violence if other practitioners, pursuant to the "standards of the profession," would have done so. The question is, what standards? Defendants and a responsible amicus curiae, supported by an impressive body of literature demonstrate that psychiatric predictions of violence are inherently unreliable. [. . .]

I would restructure the rule designed by the majority to eliminate all reference to conformity to standards of the profession in predicting violence. If a psychiatrist does in fact predict violence, then a duty to warn arises. The majority's expansion of that rule will take us from the world of reality into the wonderland of clairvoyance.

CLARK, J. (dissenting).

Until today's majority opinion, both legal and medical authorities have agreed that confidentiality is essential to effectively treat the mentally ill, and that imposing a duty on doctors to disclose patient threats to potential victims would greatly impair treatment. [. . .] Moreover, [. . .] imposing the majority's new duty is certain to result in a net increase in violence.

Overwhelming policy considerations weigh against imposing a duty on psychotherapists to warn a potential victim against harm. While offering virtually no benefit to society, such a duty will frustrate psychiatric treatment, invade fundamental patient rights and increase violence.

The importance of psychiatric treatment and its need for confidentiality have been recognized by this court. [. . .]

Assurance of confidentiality is important for three reasons.

Deterrence from Treatment

First, without substantial assurance of confidentiality, those requiring treatment will be deterred from seeking assistance. It remains an unfortunate fact in our society that people seeking psychiatric guidance tend to become stigmatized. Apprehension of such stigma – apparently increased by the propensity of people considering treatment to see themselves in the worst possible light – creates a well-recognized reluctance to seek aid. This reluctance is alleviated by the psychiatrist's assurance of confidentiality.

Full Disclosure

Second, the guarantee of confidentiality is essential in eliciting the full disclosure necessary for effective treatment. The psychiatric patient approaches treatment with conscious and unconscious inhibitions against revealing his innermost thoughts. "Every person, however well-motivated, has to overcome resistances to therapeutic exploration. These resistances seek support from every possible source and the possibility of disclosure would easily be employed in the service of resistance." (Goldstein & Katz, supra, 36 Conn. Bar J. 175, 179; see also, 118 Am. J. Psych. 734, 735.) Until a patient can trust his psychiatrist not to violate their confidential relationship, "the unconscious psychological control mechanism of repression will prevent the recall of past experiences." (Butler, Psychotherapy and Griswold: Is Confidentiality a Privilege or a Right? (1971) 3 Conn. L. Rev. 599, 604.)

Successful Treatment

Third, even if the patient fully discloses his thoughts, assurance that the confidential relationship will not be breached is necessary to maintain his trust in his psychiatrist – the very means by which treatment is effected. "[T]he essence of much psychotherapy is the contribution of trust in the external world and ultimately in the self, modeled upon the trusting relationship established during therapy." (Dawidoff, The Malpractice of Psychiatrists, 1966 Duke L.J.

696, 704). Patients will be helped only if they can form a trusting relationship with the psychiatrist. All authorities appear to agree that if the trust relationship cannot be developed because of collusive communication between the psychiatrist and others, treatment will be frustrated.

Given the importance of confidentiality to the practice of psychiatry, it becomes clear the duty to warn imposed by the majority will cripple the use and effectiveness of psychiatry. Many people, potentially violent – yet susceptible to treatment – will be deterred from seeking it; those seeking it will be inhibited from making revelations necessary to effective treatment; and, forcing the psychiatrist to violate the patient's trust will destroy the interpersonal relationship by which treatment is effected.

Violence and Civil Commitment

By imposing a duty to warn, the majority contributes to the danger to society of violence by the mentally ill and greatly increases the risk of civil commitment – the total deprivation of liberty – and those who should not be confined. The impairment of treatment and risk of improper commitment resulting from the new duty to warn will not be limited to a few patients but will extend to a large number of the mentally ill. Although under existing psychiatric procedures only a relatively few receiving treatment will ever present a risk of violence, the number making threats is huge, and it is the latter group – not just the former – whose treatment will be impaired and whose risk of commitment will be increased. [...]

Neither alternative open to the psychiatrist seeking to protect himself is in the public interest. The warning itself is an impairment of the psychiatrist's ability to treat, depriving many patients of adequate treatment. It is to be expected that after disclosing their threats, a significant number of patients, who would not become violent if treated according to existing practices, will engage in violent conduct as a result of unsuccessful treatment. In short, the majority's duty to warn will not only impair treatment of many who would never become violent but worse, will result in a net increase in violence.

The second alternative open to the psychiatrist is to commit his patient rather than to warn. Even in the absence of threat of civil liability, the doubts of psychiatrists as to the seriousness of patient threats have led psychiatrists to over-commit to mental institutions. This overcommitment has been authoritatively documented in both legal and psychiatric studies. [...]

Given the incentive to commit created by the majority's duty, this already serious situation will be worsened, contrary to Chief Justice Wright's admonition "that liberty is no less precious because forfeited in a civil proceeding than when taken as a consequence of a criminal conviction." (In re W. (1971) 5 Cal. 3d 296, 307, 96 Cal Rptr. 1, 9, 486 P.2d 1201, 1209.) [...]

[T]he majority impedes medical treatment, resulting in increased violence from – and deprivation of liberty to – the mentally ill.

We should accept [...] medical judgment, relying upon effective treatment rather than on indiscriminate warning.

The judgment should be affirmed.

McComb, J., concurs.

Questions

1 Why does Epstein think that the rules of strict liability provide a better model of tort liability than does negligence theory? Do you agree?

2 Explain why a negligence theory of torts can support good Samaritan laws, but a strict liability theory of torts does not.

3 Explain what Hart and Honoré mean by "tracing consequences" in tort law.

4 What does Feinberg mean by "his fault" in tort liability? Why does he think that fixing blame is necessary for tort law?

5 What does Coleman mean by "corrective justice?" How does his theory differ from Feinberg's?

Part VI
Criminal Law

Introduction

Criminal law is rich in philosophical interest. Any serious study of criminal law should begin with some basics. First, what is a crime? Broadly speaking, a crime is an act or omission that violates criminal law. Though this definition has the virtue of relativizing what counts as a crime to specific criminal codes, aside from that, it is not very illuminating or helpful. However, some traditional distinctions and typologies shed more light on what constitutes a crime. For example, English jurist William Blackstone distinguished between crimes that are *mala in se* – that is, evil in themselves or crimes against nature, such as murder – and those that are *mala prohibita* – that is, acts or omissions that are not intrinsically evil but count as crimes only because they have been prohibited by criminal law, such as certain regulatory offenses.[1] Another useful typology is suggested by Lawrence M. Friedman, who identifies property crimes, crimes against persons, moral offenses such as gambling and certain forms of sexual activity (often called "victimless crimes" because they usually involve the consent of participants), offense against public order, and regulatory crimes.[2] Another familiar distinction is between felonies that are relatively more serious crimes, such as aggravated assault, and misdemeanors, which are deemed less serious crimes, such as simple assault.

Many, though not all, crimes can be analyzed into two components: an *actus reus*, or guilty act, and a *mens rea*, or guilty mind. The *actus reus* is the act or omission that has been prohibited by law, and the *mens rea* is the culpable mental state, identified by law, that the offender was in at the time of acting. For a person to be charged with a crime, a guilty act must have been committed, but the specific crime with which an alleged offender is charged often depends on both the accused's mental state at the time of acting and the circumstances in which the act was committed. Consider homicide. In general, "a person is guilty of criminal homicide if he or she purposely, knowingly, recklessly or negligently caused the death of another human being."[3] The words *purposely, knowingly, recklessly*, and *negligently* refer to the accused's mental state at the time of acting and influences the degree of seriousness of the crime as well as the specific crime – such as murder or voluntary or involuntary manslaughter – with which the accused is charged. The circumstances in which the guilty act is committed can also affect both the seriousness of the crime with which an accused is charged and the severity of the sentence if the accused is convicted. Aggravating circumstances increase the severity of a crime and/or penalty, whereas mitigating circumstances can have the opposite effect. For example, the crime of simple rape becomes aggravated rape, a more serious crime, when a weapon is present. In some states, a convicted murderer becomes eligible for the death penalty if the victim was a police officer killed in the line of duty. Sometimes the circumstances of the act provide a legal excuse or justification for the act; that is, they furnish a reason for acting that shows that the act is not one that the law prohibits. Killing in self-defense, intentional killing from necessity in the line of duty, and sometimes accidental killing are all cases in point.

Armed with these introductory remarks about crime and criminal law, we can now turn to a more detailed discussion of the essays presented in this section. Among the most fundamental philosophical questions we can ask is: "What is the function or purpose of criminal law?"

The essays by John Stuart Mill and Patrick Devlin, with which Part VI begins, offer contrasting answers to these questions. Their answers have important implications both for what constitutes a crime, and the proper reach that the law should have into private lives of individuals. Mill's piece, an excerpt from his famous work, *On Liberty*, sets forth the "harm principle," according to which the government may intervene in the private affairs of individuals only for the sake of preventing harms to non-consenting third parties. The state may not intervene for the good of the individual, nor may it intrude in the private activities of consenting rational adults. Mill makes clear that the harm principle applies only to mature adults of undiminished rational capacities, and, to Mill's discredit, primitive people living in quasi-barbaric states are not protected by the harm principle. Because of their lack of rational capacity, those people need, and, in Mill's view, are rightly subject to, regulation by others, including the state.

Motivating these limits on the power of government to intervene in the affairs of rational adults is a commitment to the autonomy of the individual. Mill firmly believes in the right of people to make their own choices, set their own goals, and frame their own life plans. He advocates a list of liberties that comprises some of the most basic freedoms of the liberal political tradition: the right to freedom of thought and conscience, or speech and opinion, of expression and publication; the right to cultivate one's preferences and tastes and to frame one's life plan as one chooses; and the freedom to unite. All these liberties are constrained by the proviso that engaging in them should not cause harm to others. Mill offers an optimistic vision of the value of personal autonomy, of the possibilities of human flourishing, and of the limited role of government.

Patrick Devlin takes a different perspective on the function of the criminal law as well as on the limits of the law's right to intervene in the private affairs of consenting adults. In this excerpt from *The Enforcement of Morals*, he argues that the function of the criminal law is to enforce society's morals. This view has been called *legal moralism*. As his primary defense of this position, he offers an argument from analogy. Just as political structures (such as forms of government), are essential to the continuation of society, so too are ongoing moral institutions, practices, and beliefs. Moral institutions, such as monogamous marriage, and moral beliefs, such as the Christian belief in the sanctity of family (father and mother, united in holy wedlock and their children), are the bonds that hold society together. Just as treason threatens the government and may be prohibited by criminal law for the sake of preserving society, so, too, whatever threatens the moral institutions and beliefs that hold society together may also be criminally prohibited. Following this argument, Devlin claims that homosexuality ought to be criminalized. Far from being a victimless "moral crime," the "victim" of homosexual behavior is the institution of heterosexual marriage, which is weakened by homosexual practices. By threatening marriage, homosexuality threatens society's morals and should be criminally prohibited. Devlin goes on to explain that there are no theoretical limits to the law's right to enforce morality, only practical limits. We must look to legislatures to determine the practical limits of the law's reach into private affairs; legislatures, in turn, must look to the opinions of the average reasonable person to ascertain the limits of society's tolerance for a particular practice. If a practice would elicit from the average reasonable "man on the street" genuine feelings of disgust, coupled with a deliberate judgment that it is injurious to society, then, Devlin thinks, the practice lies beyond the limits of what society can tolerate, and legislation should criminalize it.

In "Crime and Punishment: An Indigenous African Experience," Egbeke Aja provides an interesting non-Western perspective on legal moralism, and this piece provides a perspective on crime in punishment that challenges the traditional Western ways of thinking. Aja offers an example of the traditional, pre-colonial morality of the Igbo, an ethnic group in Nigeria with a population of about 10 million.

Traditional Igbo morality stresses the primacy of the world order over the individual. Personal morality does not exist in traditional Igbo thinking. Moral action consists in acts intended to maintain harmony among the various forces of nature: animal, vegetable, and mineral. There is, moreover, an ontological dimension to Igbo morality: to do wrong is not merely to be an individual in disharmony with natural forces, but to disrupt the natural order itself. An individual's actions matter only insofar as they affect the larger socio-natural scheme.

In the Igbo society, any deliberate or unconscious harm to the fabric of society constituted a crime. Aja gives examples of three main types of crime – capital, minor crimes, and abomination – and their respective punishments. Because they bear on the conception of responsibility central to the Igbo notion of crime, two features of these crimes are noteworthy. First, guilt for a crime was not limited to an individual perpetrator. The guilt or pollution associated with a crime affected a person's entire household, contaminating anything that was related to him or her – people, animals, or property. Second, the Igbo idea of the guilty mind, or *mens rea*, as an element of criminal offense evidently differed from the idea of Western criminal law. This is seen in the Igbo idea that newborn infants, even fetuses, were held responsible for certain crimes. For example, a breach baby was to be thrown into the evil forest after birth. The baby was judged to have the intention to take the life of the mother. This essay provides a perspective on crime and punishment that challenges the traditional Western ways of thinking.

Anthony Kenny's piece, "The Mind and the Deed," defends the traditional Western common law conception of criminal responsibility. Recall that, according to the traditional view, two elements compose a criminal offense: an *actus reus*, or guilty act, and *mens rea*, or guilty mind. Kenny defends the traditional conception against several objections that he believes are conceptually confused. First, he argues against the use of

strict liability in criminal law. He argues that the use of strict liability would lead to a host of absurd consequences.

Another objection to the traditional conception of criminal law is epistemological. How can we know for sure that someone has a particular mental state at the time of committing a criminal act? Here Kenny invokes the view of philosopher Ludwig Wittgenstein to argue that (1) observing certain forms of physical behavior can allow us to infer a person's mental state and (2) assuming that someone is in a certain mental state can enable us to make sense of his or her physical actions. For example, if I see tears running down your face and I hear you sobbing, I can infer that you are grief-stricken. If I am puzzled by the fact that you suddenly drop to the floor and begin feeling the carpet with your hands, I can make sense of this behavior by hypothesizing that you have lost a contact lens and want to find it.

In an interesting twist on the usual problem, Kenny discusses a 1967 case from the High Court of Malawi, *Nyuzi and Kudemera v. Republic*. Alarmed at the high infant mortality rate, a village in Malawi suspected that witchcraft had caused the deaths. The villagers employed Nyuzi and his assistant to determine whether a group of suspects were witches. Several people died after ingesting a non-poisonous substance administered by Nyuzi. In Malawi (at the time), witchcraft was a strict liability offense. Consequently, Nyuzi and one of his assistance were convicted. Kenny raises the question of whether the two were also guilty of killing the deceased – that is, whether an *actus reus* had occurred. Questions of *mens rea* at least appear to be more tractable. Among the cluster of questions that *Nyuzi* raises is the reasonableness of the defendants' belief that they were intervening to prevent deaths. This query underscores the difficulty of using the "average reasonable man" standard in multicultural contexts. According to whose standard of reasonableness should the defendants' beliefs be judged – the average Westerner or the average Malawian?

The remaining essays in this section concern international criminal law. We begin with a piece by the distinguished Finnish legal theorist, Martti Koskenniemi, "Between Impunity and Show Trials." Koskenniemi provides a thorough critique of the idea of punishing individuals for violations of international criminal law. He argues that trials rarely provide for the truth and that it is especially hard to justify punishing international criminals. Indeed, he contends that international criminal trials are quite likely to end up being more like show trials than regular criminal trials. This is because the political leaders in the dock are likely to play to nationalist sentiments back home and are unlikely to see the international court or tribunal as anything other than an affront to national sovereignty. Even in well-publicized cases like that of Adolph Eichmann, Koskenniemi argues that it is unlikely that anything resembling justice was served by his trial.

In "Atrocity, Punishment, and International Law," Mark Drumbl is also critical of international criminal trials, largely because they fail to satisfy the normal rationales for criminal punishment, especially deterrence and expressivism. Concerning deterrence, Drumbl points out that many international criminals act out of ideological reasons, not out of self-interest or greed. As a result, it is hard to figure out how to deter them using criminal punishment. And as far as expressing the strong negative sentiments of a community for what the perpetrator has done, Drumbl thinks there is more cause for hope of success, even as he sees several major problems here as well. International trials can only convey part of the truth of atrocities since they must only deal with who is in the dock. In addition, the narrative to be told is often interrupted because of illness or explicit strategies of the defendant. And the expression of community condemnation is often rendered difficult by the need for plea bargaining to reduce the cost of very expensive international trials.

In "Defending International Criminal Trials," Larry May tries to rebut the arguments of Koskenniemi and Drumbl, arguing that international criminal trials face no more serious difficulties than domestic criminal trials, at least high-profile ones. In part of his essay, May argues that Koskenniemi and other critics of international trials head off on the wrong track

by asking for a single norm, such as deterrence, to provide a rationale for criminal punishment, when it might be that a combination of norms can provide such a rationale. May also argues that Drumbl has failed to note that military leaders, who often stand in the dock in international trials, are not often driven by ideological considerations, and may be more subject to deterrence than are political leaders. May ends by suggesting some changes that might make international trials and punishment of those who are in the dock more palatable, including making sure that the trials are scrupulously fair.

We end this section with Justice Robert H. Jackson's "Opening Statement before the International Military Tribunal." Justice Jackson was one of the chief prosecutors at Nuremberg, where the main Nazi leaders and architects of the Holocaust were tried by the Allies who had defeated Germany in the Second World War. He provided one of the most significant defenses of international tribunals as he gave the United States' opening statement at the Nuremberg trial. The most quoted line from this speech is that the purpose of international trials is to "stay the hand of vengeance" that had too often characterized victor's justice in the past. Jackson called the Nuremberg trials "one of the most significant tributes that Power has ever paid to Reason." Jackson was aware that many would be critical of the Nuremberg trial, especially since it was the first of its kind. And in a stirring speech he defends not only the Nuremberg tribunal but also the very idea of international criminal trials, in a way that has continued to resonate over many years since the trial at Nuremberg took place in 1945.

Notes

1 See Blackstone, *Commentaries on the Laws of England*, vol. 4 (University of Chicago Press, 1979), 7–8.

2 See Friedman, *Crimes and Punishment in American History* (Basic Books, 1993), 7.

3 Henry Campbell Black, *Black's Law Dictionary*, 5th edn. (West, 1979), 661.

37

On Liberty

John Stuart Mill

Chapter I: Introductory

[. . .] The object of this Essay is to assert one very simple principle, as entitled to govern absolutely the dealings of society with the individual in the way of compulsion and control, whether the means used be physical force in the form of legal penalties, or the moral coercion of public opinion. That principle is, that the sole end for which mankind are warranted, individually or collectively, in interfering with the liberty of action of any of their number, is self-protection. That the only purpose for which power can be rightfully exercised over any member of a civilized community, against his will, is to prevent harm to others. His own good, either physical or moral, is not a sufficient warrant. He cannot rightfully be compelled to do or forbear because it will be better for him to do so, because it will make him happier, because, in the opinions of others, to do so would be wise, or even right. These are good reasons for remonstrating with him, or reasoning with him, or persuading him, or entreating him, but not for compelling him, or visiting him with any evil in case he do otherwise. To justify that, the conduct from which it is desired to deter him must be calculated to produce evil to some one else. The only part of the conduct of any one, for which he is amenable to society, is that which concerns others. In the part which merely concerns himself, his independence is, of right, absolute. Over himself, over his own body and mind, the individual is sovereign.

It is, perhaps, hardly necessary to say that this doctrine is meant to apply only to human beings in the maturity of their faculties. We are not speaking of children, or of young persons below the age which the law may fix as that of manhood or womanhood. Those who are still in a state to require being taken care of by others, must be protected against their own actions as well as against external injury. For the same reason, we may leave out of consideration those backward states of society in which the race itself may be considered as in its nonage. The early difficulties in the way of spontaneous progress are so great, that there is seldom any choice of means for overcoming them; and a ruler full of the spirit of improvement is warranted in the use of any expedients that will attain an end, perhaps otherwise unattainable. Despotism is a legitimate mode of government in dealing with barbarians, provided the end be their improvement, and the means justified by actually effecting that end. Liberty, as a principle, has no application to any

John Stuart Mill, excerpts from chapters I, II, and IV of *On Liberty*.

state of things anterior to the time when mankind have become capable of being improved by free and equal discussion. Until then, there is nothing for them but implicit obedience to an Akbar or a Charlemagne, if they are so fortunate as to find one. But as soon as mankind have attained the capacity of being guided to their own improvement by conviction or persuasion (a period long since reached in all nations with whom we need here concern ourselves), compulsion either in the direct form or in that of pains and penalties for non-compliance, is no longer admissible as a means to their own good, and justifiable only for the security of others.

It is proper to state that I forego any advantage which could be derived to my argument from the idea of abstract right, as a thing independent of utility. I regard utility as the ultimate appeal on all ethical questions; but it must be utility in the largest sense, grounded on the permanent interests of a man as a progressive being. Those interests, I contend, authorize the subjection of individual spontaneity to external control, only in respect to those actions of each, which concern the interest of other people. If any one does an act hurtful to others, there is a *prima facie* case for punishing him, by law, or, where legal penalties are not safely applicable, by general disapprobation. There are also many positive acts for the benefit of others, which he may rightfully be compelled to perform; such as to give evidence in a court of justice; to bear his fair share in the common defense, or in any other joint work necessary to the interest of the society of which he enjoys the protection; and to perform certain acts of individual beneficence, such as saving a fellow-creature's life, or interposing to protect the defenseless against ill-usage, things which whenever it is obviously a man's duty to do, he may rightfully be made responsible to society for not doing. A person may cause evil to others not only by his actions but by his inaction, and in either case he is justly accountable to them for the injury. The latter case, it is true, requires a much more cautious exercise of compulsion than the former. To make any one answerable for doing evil to others is the rule; to make him answerable for not preventing evil is, comparatively speaking, the exception. Yet there are many cases clear enough and grave enough to justify that exception. In all things

which regard the external relations of the individual, he is *de jure* amenable to those whose interests are concerned, and, if need be, to society as their protector. There are often good reasons for not holding him to the responsibility; but these reasons must arise from the special expediencies of the case: either because it is a kind of case in which he is on the whole likely to act better, when left to his own discretion, than when controlled in any way in which society have it in their power to control him; or because the attempt to exercise control would produce other evils, greater than those which it would prevent. When such reasons as these preclude the enforcement of responsibility, the conscience of the agent himself should step into the vacant judgment seat, and protect those interests of others which have no external protection; judging himself all the more rigidly, because the case does not admit of his being made accountable to the judgment of his fellow-creatures.

But there is a sphere of action in which society, as distinguished from the individual, has, if any, only an indirect interest; comprehending all that portion of a person's life and conduct which affects only himself, or if it also affects others, only with their free, voluntary, and undeceived consent and participation. When I say only himself, I mean directly, and in the first instance; for whatever affects himself, may affect others through himself; and the objection which may be grounded on this contingency, will receive consideration in the sequel. This, then, is the appropriate region of human liberty. It comprises, first, the inward domain of consciousness; demanding liberty of conscience in the most comprehensive sense; liberty of thought and feeling; absolute freedom of opinion and sentiment on all subjects, practical or speculative, scientific, moral, or theological. The liberty of expressing and publishing opinions may seem to fall under a different principle, since it belongs to that part of the conduct of an individual which concerns other people; but, being almost of as much importance as the liberty of thought itself, and resting in great part on the same reasons, is practically inseparable from it. Secondly, the principle requires liberty of tastes and pursuits; of framing the plan of our life to suit our character; of doing as we like, subject to such consequences as may follow: without impediment from fellow-creatures, so long as what we do does not harm them, even though they should think our conduct foolish, perverse, or wrong. Thirdly, from this liberty of each individual, follows the liberty, within the same limits, of combination among individuals; freedom to unite, for any purpose not involving harm to others: the persons combining being supposed to be of full age, and not forced or deceived.

No society in which these liberties are not, on the whole, respected, is free, whatever may be its form of government; and none is completely free in which they do not exist absolute and unqualified. The only freedom which deserves the name, is that of pursuing our own good in our own way, so long as we do not attempt to deprive others of theirs, or impede their efforts to obtain it. Each is the proper guardian of his own health, whether bodily, or mental and spiritual. Mankind are greater gainers by suffering each other to live as seems good to themselves, than by compelling each to live as seems good to the rest. [. . .]

Chapter II: Of the Liberty and Thought and Discussion

[. . .] We have now recognised the necessity to the mental well-being of mankind (on which all their other well-being depends) of freedom of opinion, and freedom of the expression *of* opinion, on four distinct grounds; which we will now briefly recapitulate.

First, if any opinion is compelled to silence, that opinion may, for aught we can certainly know, be true. To deny this is to assume our own infallibility.

Secondly, though the silenced opinion be an error, it may, and very commonly does, contain a portion of truth; and since the general or prevailing opinion on any subject is rarely or never the whole truth, it is only by the collision of adverse opinions that the remainder of the truth has any chance of being supplied.

Thirdly, even if the received opinion be not only true, but the whole truth; unless it is suffered to be, and actually is, vigorously and earnestly contested, it will, by most of those who receive it, be held in the manner of a prejudice, with little comprehension or feeling of its rational

grounds. And not only this, but, fourthly, the meaning of the doctrine itself will be in danger of being lost, or enfeebled, and deprived of its vital effect on the character and conduct: the dogma becoming a mere formal profession, inefficacious for good, but cumbering the ground, and preventing the growth of any real and heartfelt conviction, from reason or personal experience. [. . .]

Chapter IV: Of the Limits to the Authority of Society Over the Individual

[. . .] What, then, is the rightful limit to the sovereignty of the individual over himself? Where does the authority of society begin? How much of human life should be assigned to individuality, and how much to society?

Each will receive its proper share, if each has that which more particularly concerns it. To individuality should belong the part of life in which it is chiefly the individual that is interested; to society, the part which chiefly interests society.

Though society is not founded on a contract, and though no good purpose is answered by inventing a contract in order to deduce social obligations from it, every one who receives the protection of society owes a return for the benefit, and the fact of living in society renders it indispensable that each should be bound to observe a certain line of conduct towards the rest. This conduct consists, first, in not injuring the interests of one another; or rather certain interests, which, either by express legal provision or by tacit understanding, ought to be considered as rights; and secondly, in each person's bearing his share (to be fixed on some equitable principle) of the labours and sacrifices incurred for defending the society or its members from injury and molestation. These conditions society is justified in enforcing, at all costs to those who endeavour to withhold fulfillment. Nor is this all that society may do. The acts of an individual may be hurtful to others, or wanting in due consideration for their welfare, without going to the length of violating any of their constituted rights. The offender may then be justly punished by opinion, though not by law. As soon as any part of a person's conduct affects prejudicially the interests of others, society has jurisdiction over it, and the question whether the general welfare will or will not be promoted by interfering with it, becomes open to discussion. But there is no room for entertaining any such question when a person's conduct affects the interests of no persons besides himself, or needs not affect them unless they like (all the persons concerned being of full age, and the ordinary amount of understanding). In all such cases, there should be perfect freedom, legal and social, to do the action and stand the consequences.

It would be a great misunderstanding of this doctrine to suppose that it is one of selfish indifference, which pretends that human beings have no business with each other's conduct in life, and that they should not concern themselves about the well-doing or well-being of one another, unless their own interest is involved. Instead of any diminution, there is need of a great increase of disinterested exertion to promote the good of others. But disinterested benevolence can find other instruments to persuade people to their good than whips and scourges, either of the literal or the metaphorical sort. I am the last person to undervalue the self-regarding virtues; they are only second in importance, if even second, to the social. It is equally the business of education to cultivate both. But even education works by conviction and persuasion as well as by compulsion, and it is by the former only that, when the period of education is passed, the self-regarding virtues should be inculcated. Human beings owe to each other help to distinguish the better from the worse, and encouragement to choose the former and avoid the latter. They should be forever stimulating each other to increased exercise of their higher faculties, and increased direction of their feelings and aims towards wise instead of foolish, elevating instead of degrading, objects and contemplations. But neither one person, nor any number of persons, is warranted in saying to another human creature of ripe years, that he shall not do with his life for his own benefit what he chooses to do with it. He is the person most interested in his own well-being: the interest which any other person, except in cases of strong personal attachment, can have in it, is trifling, compared with that which he himself has; the interest which society

has in him individually (except as to his conduct to others) is fractional, and altogether indirect; while with respect to his own feelings and circumstances, the most ordinary man or woman has means of knowledge immeasurably surpassing those that can be possessed by any one else. The interference of society to overrule his judgment and purposes in what only regards himself must be grounded on general presumptions; which may be altogether wrong, and even if right, are as likely as not to be misapplied to individual cases, by persons no better acquainted with the circumstances of such cases than those are who look at them merely from without. In this department, therefore, of human affairs, Individuality has its proper field of action. In the conduct of human beings towards one another it is necessary that general rules should for the most part be observed, in order that people may know what they have to expect: but in each person's own concerns his individual spontaneity is entitled to free exercise. Considerations to aid his judgment, exhortations to strengthen his will, may be offered to him, even obtruded on him, by others: but he himself is the final judge. All errors which he is likely to commit against advice and warning are far outweighed by the evil of allowing others to constrain him to what they deem his good.

I do not mean that the feelings with which a person is regarded by others ought not to be in any way affected by his self-regarding qualities or deficiencies. This is neither possible nor desirable. If he is eminent in any of the qualities which conduce to his own good, he is, so far, a proper object of admiration. He is so much the nearer to the ideal perfection of human nature. If he is grossly deficient in those qualities, a sentiment the opposite of admiration will follow. There is a degree of folly, and a degree of what may be called (though the phrase is not unobjectionable) lowness or depravation of taste, which, though it cannot justify doing harm to the person who manifests it, renders him necessarily and properly a subject of distaste, or, in extreme cases, even of contempt: a person could not have the opposite qualities in due strength without entertaining these feelings. Though doing no wrong to any one, a person may so act as to compel us to judge him, and feel to him, as a fool, or as a being of an inferior order: and since this judgment and feeling are a fact which he would prefer to avoid, it is doing him a service to warn him of it beforehand, as of any other disagreeable consequence to which he exposes himself. It would be well, indeed, if this good office were much more freely rendered than the common notions of politeness at present permit, and if one person could honestly point out to another that he thinks him in fault, without being considered unmannerly or presuming. We have a right, also, in various ways, to act upon our unfavorable opinion of any one, not to the oppression of his individuality, but in the exercise of ours. We are not bound, for example, to seek his society; we have a right to avoid it (though not to parade the avoidance), for we have a right to choose the society most acceptable to us. We have a right, and it may be our duty, to caution others against him, if we think his example or conversation likely to have a pernicious effect on those with whom he associates. We may give others a preference over him in optional good offices, except those which tend to his improvement. In these various modes a person may suffer very severe penalties at the hands of others for faults which directly concern only himself; but he suffers these penalties only in so far as they are the natural and, as it were, the spontaneous consequences of the faults themselves, not because they are purposely inflicted on him for the sake of punishment. A person who shows rashness, obstinacy, self-conceit – who cannot live within moderate means – who cannot restrain himself from hurtful indulgences – who pursues animal pleasures at the expense of those of feeling and intellect – must expect to be lowered in the opinion of others, and to have a less share of their favourable sentiments; but of this he has no right to complain, unless he has merited their favour by special excellence in his social relations, and has thus established a title to their good offices, which is not affected by his demerits towards himself.

What I contend for is, that the inconveniences which are strictly inseparable from the unfavourable judgment of others, are the only ones to which a person should ever be subjected for that portion of his conduct and character which concerns his own good, but which does not affect the interest of others in their relations with him. Acts injurious to others require a totally different treatment. Encroachment on their rights; infliction on them of any loss or damage not justified by his own rights; falsehood or duplicity in dealing with them; unfair or ungenerous use of advantages over them; even selfish abstinence from defending them against injury – these are fit objects of moral reprobation, and, in grave cases, of moral retribution and punishment. And not only these acts, but the dispositions which lead to them, are properly immoral, and fit subjects of disapprobation which may rise to abhorrence. Cruelty of disposition; malice and ill-nature; that most anti-social and odious of all passions, envy; dissimulation and insincerity, irascibility on insufficient cause, and resentment disproportioned to the provocation; the love of domineering over others; the desire to engross more than one's share of advantages (the πλεονεξια of the Greeks); the pride which derives gratification from the abasement of others; the egotism which thinks self and its concerns more important than everything else, and decides all doubtful questions in its own favour; – these are moral vices, and constitute a bad and odious moral character: unlike the self-regarding faults previously mentioned, which are not properly immoralities, and to whatever pitch they may be carried, do not constitute wickedness. They may be proofs of any amount of folly, or want of personal dignity and self-respect; but they are only a subject of moral reprobation when they involve a breach of duty to others, for whose sake the individual is bound to have care for himself. What are called duties to ourselves are not socially obligatory, unless circumstances render them at the same time duties to others. The term duty to oneself, when it means anything more than prudence, means self-respect or self-development, and for none of these is any one accountable to his fellow-creatures, because for none of them is it for the good of mankind that he be held accountable to them.

The distinction between the loss of consideration which a person may rightly incur by defect of prudence or of personal dignity, and the reprobation which is due to him for an offence against the rights of others, is not a merely nominal distinction. It makes a vast difference both in our feelings and in our conduct towards him whether he displeases us in things in which we think we have a right to control him, or in things in which we know that we have not. If he displeases us, we may express our distaste, and we may stand aloof from a person as well as from a thing that displeases us; but we shall not therefore feel called on to make his life uncomfortable. We shall reflect that he already bears, or will bear, the whole penalty of his error; if he spoils his life by mismanagement, we shall not, for that reason, desire to spoil it still further: instead of wishing to punish him, we shall rather endeavour to alleviate his punishment, by showing him how he may avoid or cure the evils his conduct tends to bring upon him. He may be to us an object of pity, perhaps of dislike, but not of anger or resentment; we shall not treat him like an enemy of society: the worst we shall think ourselves justified in doing is leaving him to himself, if we do not interfere benevolently by showing interest or concern for him. It is far otherwise if he has infringed the rules necessary for the protection of his fellow-creatures, individually or collectively. The evil consequences of his acts do not then fall on himself, but on others; and society, as the protector of all its members, must retaliate on him; must inflict pain on him for the express purpose of punishment, and must take care that it be sufficiently severe. In the one case, he is an offender at our bar, and we are called on not only to sit in judgment on him, but, in one shape or another, to execute our own sentence: in the other case, it is not our part to inflict any suffering on him, except what may incidentally follow from our using the same liberty in the regulation of our own affairs, which we allow to him in his.

The distinction here pointed out between the part of a person's life which concerns only himself, and that which concerns others, many persons will refuse to admit. How (it may be asked) can any part of the conduct of a member of society be a matter of indifference to the other members? No person is an entirely isolated being; it is impossible for a person to do anything seriously or permanently hurtful to himself, without mischief reaching at least to his near connections, and often far beyond them. If he injures his property, he does harm to those who directly or indirectly derived support from it, and usually diminishes, by a greater or less amount, the general resources of the community. If he deteriorates his bodily or mental faculties, he not only brings evil upon all who depended on him for any portion of their happiness, but disqualifies himself for rendering the services which he owes to his fellow-creatures generally; perhaps becomes a burden on their affection or benevolence; and if such conduct were very frequent, hardly any offence that is committed would detract more from the general sum of good. Finally, if by his vices or follies a person does no direct harm to others, he is nevertheless (it may be said) injurious by his example; and ought to be compelled to control himself, for the sake of those whom the sight or knowledge of his conduct might corrupt or mislead.

And even (it will be added) if the consequences of misconduct could be confined to the vicious or thoughtless individual, ought society to abandon to their own guidance those who are manifestly unfit for it? If protection against themselves is confessedly due to children and persons under age, is not society equally bound to afford it to persons of mature years who are equally incapable of self-government? If gambling, or drunkenness, or incontinence, or idleness, or uncleanliness, are as injurious to happiness, and as great a hindrance to improvement, as many or most of the acts prohibited by law, why (it may be asked) should not law, so far as is consistent with practicability and social convenience, endeavour to repress these also? And as a supplement to the unavoidable imperfections of law, ought not opinion at least to organise a powerful police against these vices, and visit rigidly with social penalties those who are known to practise them? There is no question here (it may be said) about restricting individuality, or impeding the trial of new and original experiments in living. The only things it is sought to prevent are things which have been tried and condemned from the beginning of the world until now; things which experience has shown not to be useful or suitable to any person's individuality. There must be some length of time and amount of experience after which a moral or prudential truth may be regarded as established: and it is merely desired to prevent generation after generation from falling over the same precipice which has been fatal to their predecessors.

I fully admit that the mischief which a person does to himself may seriously affect, both through their sympathies and their interests, those nearly connected with him and, in a minor degree, society at large. When, by conduct of this sort, a person is led to violate a distinct and assignable obligation to any other person or persons, the case is taken out of the self-regarding class, and becomes amenable to moral disapprobation in the proper sense of the term. If, for example, a man, through intemperance or extravagance, becomes unable to pay his debts, or, having undertaken the moral responsibility of a family, becomes from the same cause incapable of supporting or educating them, he is deservedly reprobated, and might be justly punished; but it is for the breach of duty to his family or creditors, not for the extravagance. If the resources which ought to have been devoted to them had been diverted from them for the most prudent investment, the moral culpability would have been the same. George Barnwell murdered his uncle to get money for his mistress, but if he had done it to set himself up in business, he would equally have been hanged. Again, in the frequent case of a man who causes grief to his family by addiction to bad habits, he deserves reproach for his unkindness or ingratitude; but so he may for cultivating habits not in themselves vicious, if they are painful to those with whom he passes his life, or who from personal ties are dependent on him for their comfort. Whoever fails in the consideration generally due to the interests and feelings of others, not being compelled by some more imperative duty, or justified by allowable self-preference, is a subject of moral disapprobation for that failure, but not for the cause of it, nor for the errors, merely personal to himself, which may have remotely led to it. In like manner, when a person disables himself, by conduct purely self-regarding, from the performance of some definite duty incumbent on him to the public, he is guilty of a social offence. No person ought to be punished simply for being drunk; but a soldier or a policeman should be punished for being drunk on duty. Whenever, in short, there is a definite damage, or a definite risk of damage, either to an individual or to the public, the case is taken out of the province of liberty, and placed in that of morality or law.

But with regard to the merely contingent, or, as it may be called, constructive injury which a person causes to society, by conduct which neither violates any specific duty to the public, nor occasions perceptible hurt to any assignable individual except himself; the inconvenience is one which society can afford to bear, for the sake of the greater good of human freedom. If grown persons are to be punished for not taking proper care of themselves, I would rather it were for their own sake, than under pretence of preventing them from impairing their capacity of rendering to society benefits which society does not pretend it has a right to exact. But I cannot consent to argue the point as if society had no means of bringing its weaker members up to its ordinary standard of rational conduct, except waiting till they do something irrational, and then punishing them, legally or morally, for it. Society has had absolute power over them during all the early portion of their existence: it has had the whole period of childhood and nonage in which to try whether it could make them capable of rational conduct in life. The existing generation is master both of the training and the entire circumstances of the generation to come; it cannot indeed make them perfectly wise and good, because it is itself so lamentably deficient in goodness and wisdom; and its best efforts are not always, in individual cases, its most successful ones; but it is perfectly well able to make the rising generation, as a whole, as good as, and a little better than, itself. If society lets any considerable number of its members grow up mere children, incapable of being acted on by rational consideration of distant motives, society has itself to blame for the consequences. Armed not only with all the powers of education, but with the ascendancy which the authority of a received opinion always exercises over the minds who are least fitted to judge for themselves; and aided by the *natural* penalties which cannot be prevented from falling on those who incur the distaste or the contempt of those who know them; let not society pretend that it needs, besides all this, the power to issue commands and enforce obedience in the personal concerns of individuals, in which, on all principles of justice and policy, the decision ought to rest with those who are to abide the consequences. Nor is there anything which tends more to discredit and frustrate the better means of influencing conduct than a resort to the worse. If there be among those whom it is attempted to coerce into prudence or temperance any of the material of which vigorous and independent characters are made, they will infallibly rebel against the yoke. No such person will ever feel that others have a right to control him in his concerns, such as they have to prevent him from injuring them in theirs; and it easily comes to be considered a mark of spirit and courage to fly in the face of such usurped authority, and do with ostentation the exact opposite of what it enjoins; as in the fashion of grossness which succeeded, in the time of Charles II, to the fanatical moral intolerance of the Puritans. With respect to what is said of the necessity of protecting society from the bad example set to others by the vicious or the self-indulgent; it is true that bad example may have a pernicious effect, especially the example of doing wrong to others with impunity to the wrong-doer. But we are now speaking of conduct which, while it does no wrong to others, is supposed to do great harm to the agent himself: and I do not see how those who believe this can think otherwise than that the example, on the whole, must be more salutary than hurtful, since, if it displays the misconduct, it displays also the painful or degrading consequences which, if the conduct is justly censured, must be supposed to be in all or most cases attendant on it.

But the strongest of all the arguments against the interference of the public with purely personal conduct is that, when it does interfere, the odds are that it interferes wrongly, and in the wrong place. On questions of social morality, of duty to others, the opinion of the public, that is, of an overruling majority, though often wrong, is likely to be still oftener right; because on such questions they are only required to judge of their own interests; of the manner in which some mode of conduct, if allowed to be practised, would affect themselves. But the opinion of a similar majority, imposed as a law on the minority, on questions of self-regarding conduct, is quite as likely to be wrong as right; for in these cases public opinion means, at the best, some

people's opinion of what is good or bad for other people; while very often it does not even mean that; the public, with the most perfect indifference, passing over the pleasure or convenience of those whose conduct they censure, and considering only their own preference. There are many who consider as an injury to themselves any conduct which they have a distaste for, and resent it as an outrage to their feelings; as a religious bigot, when charged with disregarding the religious feelings of others, has been known to retort that they disregard his feelings, by persisting in their abominable worship or creed. But there is no parity between the feeling of a person for his own opinion, and the feeling of another who is offended at his holding it; no more than between the desire of a thief to take a purse, and the desire of the right owner to keep it. And a person's taste is as much his own peculiar concern as his opinion or his purse. It is easy for any one to imagine an ideal public which leaves the freedom and choice of individuals in all uncertain matters undisturbed, and only requires them to abstain from modes of conduct which universal experience has condemned. But where has there been seen a public which set any such limit to its censorship? Or when does the public trouble itself about universal experience? In its interferences with personal conduct it is seldom thinking of anything but the enormity of acting or feeling differently from itself; and this standard of judgment, thinly disguised, is held up to mankind as the dictate of religion and philosophy, by nine-tenths of all moralists and speculative writers. These teach that things are right because they are right; because we feel them to be so. They tell us to search in our own minds and hearts for laws of conduct binding on ourselves and on all others. What can the poor public do but apply these instructions, and make their own personal feelings of good and evil, if they are tolerably unanimous in them, obligatory on all the world? [. . .]

38

The Enforcement of Morals

Patrick Devlin

[. . .] I think it is clear that the criminal law as we know it is based upon moral principle. In a number of crimes its function is simply to enforce a moral principle and nothing else. The law, both criminal and civil, claims to be able to speak about morality and immorality generally. Where does it get its authority to do this and how does it settle the moral principles which it enforces? Undoubtedly, as a matter of history, it derived both from Christian teaching. But I think that the strict logician is right when he says that the law can no longer rely on doctrines in which citizens are entitled to disbelieve. It is necessary therefore to look for some other source.

In jurisprudence, as I have said, everything is thrown open to discussion and, in the belief that they cover the whole field, I have framed three interrogatories addressed to myself to answer:

1   Has society the right to pass judgment at all on matters of morals? Ought there, in other words, to be a public morality, or are morals always a matter for private judgment?
2   If society has the right to pass judgment, has it also the right to use the weapon of the law to enforce it?

3   If so, ought it to use that weapon in all cases or only in some; and if only in some, on what principles should it distinguish?

I shall begin with the first interrogatory and consider what is meant by the right of society to pass a moral judgment, that is, a judgment about what is good and what is evil. The fact that a majority of people may disapprove of a practice does not of itself make it a matter for society as a whole. Nine men out of ten may disapprove of what the tenth man is doing and still say that it is not their business. There is a case for a collective judgment (as distinct from a large number of individual opinions which sensible people may even refrain from pronouncing at all if it is upon somebody else's private affairs) only if society is affected. Without a collective judgment there can be no case at all for intervention. Let me take as an illustration the Englishman's attitude to religion as it is now and as it has been in the past. His attitude now is that a man's religion is his private affair; he may think of another man's religion that it is right or wrong, true or untrue, but not that it is good or bad. In earlier times that was not so; a man was denied the right to practise what was thought of as heresy, and heresy was thought of as destructive of society.

The language used in the passages I have quoted from the Wolfenden Report suggests the view that there ought not to be a collective judgment about immorality *per se*. Is this what is meant by "private morality" and "individual freedom of choice and action"? Some people sincerely believe that homosexuality is neither immoral nor unnatural. Is the "freedom of choice and action" that is offered to the individual, freedom to decide for himself what is moral or immoral, society remaining neutral; or is it freedom to be immoral if he wants to be? The language of the Report may be open to question, but the conclusions at which the Committee arrive answer this question unambiguously. If society is not prepared to say that homosexuality is morally wrong, there would be no basis for a law protecting youth from "corruption" or punishing a man for living on the "immoral" earnings of a homosexual prostitute, as the Report recommends.[1] This attitude the Committee make even clearer when they come to deal with prostitution. In truth, the Report takes it for granted that there is in existence a public morality which condemns homosexuality and prostitution. What the Report seems to mean by private morality might perhaps be better described as private behavior in matters of morals.

This view – that there is such a thing as public morality – can also be justified by *a priori* argument. What makes a society of any sort is community of ideas, not only political ideas but also ideas about the way its members should behave and govern their lives; these latter ideas are its morals. Every society has a moral structure as well as a political one: or rather, since that might suggest two independent systems, I should say that the structure of every society is made up both of politics and morals. Take, for example, the institution of marriage. Whether a man should be allowed to take more than one wife is something about which every society has to make up its mind one way or the other. In England we believe in the Christian idea of marriage and therefore adopt monogamy as a moral principle. Consequently the Christian institution of marriage has become the basis of family life and so part of the structure of our society. It is there not

because it is Christian. It has got there because it is Christian, but it remains there because it is built into the house in which we live and could not be removed without bringing it down. The great majority of those who live in this country accept it because it is the Christian idea of marriage and for them the only true one. But a non-Christian is bound by it, not because it is part of Christianity but because, rightly or wrongly, it has been adopted by the society in which he lives. It would be useless for him to stage a debate designed to prove that polygamy was theologically more correct and socially preferable; if he wants to live in the house, he must accept it as built in the way in which it is.

We see this more clearly if we think of ideas or institutions that are purely political. Society cannot tolerate rebellion; it will not allow argument about the rightness of the cause. Historians a century later may say that the rebels were right and the Government was wrong and a percipient and conscientious subject of the State may think so at the time. But it is not a matter which can be left to individual judgment.

The institution of marriage is a good example for my purpose because it bridges the division, if there is one, between politics and morals. Marriage is part of the structure of our society and it is also the basis of a moral code which condemns fornication and adultery. The institution of marriage would be gravely threatened if individual judgments were permitted about the morality of adultery; on these points there must be a public morality. But public morality is not to be confined to those moral principles which support institutions such as marriage. People do not think of monogamy as something which has to be supported because our society has chosen to organize itself upon it; they think of it as something that is good in itself and offering a good way of life and that it is for that reason that our society has adopted it. I return to the statement that I have already made, that society means a community of ideas; without shared ideas on politics, morals, and ethics no society can exist. Each one of us has ideas about what is good and what is evil; they cannot be kept private from the society in which we live. If men and women try to create a society in which there is no fundamental agreement about good and evil they will fail; if, having based it on common agreement, the agreement goes, the society will disintegrate. For society is not something that is kept together physically; it is held by the invisible bonds of common thought. If the bonds were too far relaxed the members would drift apart. A common morality is part of the bondage. The bondage is part of the price of society; and mankind, which needs society, must pay its price. [. . .]

[. . .] You may think that I have taken far too long in contending that there is such a thing as public morality, a proposition which most people would readily accept, and may have left myself too little time to discuss the next question which to many minds may cause greater difficulty: to what extent should society use the law to enforce its moral judgments? But I believe that the answer to the first question determines the way in which the second should be approached and may indeed very nearly dictate the answer to the second question. If society has no right to make judgments on morals, the law must find some special justification for entering the field of morality: if homosexuality and prostitution are not in themselves wrong, then the onus is very clearly on the lawgiver who wants to frame a law against certain aspects of them to justify the exceptional treatment. But if society has the right to make a judgment and has it on the basis that a recognized morality is as necessary to society as, say, a recognized government, then society may use the law to preserve morality in the same way as it uses it to safeguard anything else that is essential to its existence. If therefore the first proposition is securely established with all its implications, society has a prima facie right to legislate against immorality as such.

The Wolfenden Report, notwithstanding that it seems to admit the right of society to condemn homosexuality and prostitution as immoral, requires special circumstances to be shown to justify the intervention of the law. I think that this is wrong in principle and that any attempt to approach my second interrogatory on these lines is bound to break down. I think that the attempt by the Committee does break down and that this is shown by the fact that it has to define or describe its special circumstances so widely that they can be supported only if it is accepted that the law *is* concerned with immorality as such.

The widest of the special circumstances are described as the provision of "sufficient safeguards against exploitation and corruption of others, particularly those who are specially vulnerable because they are young, weak in body or mind, inexperienced, or in a state of special physical, official or economic dependence."[2] The corruption of youth is a well-recognized ground for intervention by the State and for the purpose of any legislation the young can easily be defined. But if similar protection were to be extended to every other citizen, there would be no limit to the reach of the law. The "corruption and exploitation of others" is so wide that it could be used to cover any sort of immorality which involves, as most do, the cooperation of another person. Even if the phrase is taken as limited to the categories that are particularized as "specially vulnerable," it is so elastic as to be practically no restriction. This is not merely a matter of words. For if the words used are stretched almost beyond breaking-point, they still are not wide enough to cover the recommendations which the Committee make about prostitution.

Prostitution is not in itself illegal and the Committee do not think that it ought to be made so.[3] If prostitution is private immorality and not the law's business, what concern has the law with the ponce or the brothelkeeper or the householder who permits habitual prostitution? The Report recommends that the laws which make these activities criminal offences should be maintained or strengthened and brings them (so far as it goes into principle; with regard to brothels it says simply that the law rightly frowns on them) under the head of exploitation.[4] There may be cases of exploitation in this trade, as there are or used to be in many others, but in general a ponce exploits a prostitute no more than an impresario exploits an actress. The Report finds that "the great majority of prostitutes are women whose psychological makeup is such that they choose this life because they find in it a style of living which is to them easier, freer and more profitable than would be provided by any other occupation. [. . .] In the main the association between prostitute and ponce is voluntary and operates to mutual advantage."[5] The Committee would agree that this could not be called exploitation in the ordinary sense. They say: "It is in our view an over-simplification to think that those who live on the earnings of prostitution are exploiting the prostitute as such. What they are really exploiting is the whole complex of the relationship between prostitute and customer; they are, in effect, exploiting the human weaknesses which cause the customer to seek the prostitute and the prostitute to meet the demand."[6]

All sexual immorality involves the exploitation of human weaknesses. The prostitute exploits the lust of her customers and the customer the moral weakness of the prostitute. If the exploitation of human weaknesses is considered to create a special circumstance, there is virtually no field of morality which can be defined in such a way as to exclude the law.

I think, therefore, that it is not possible to set theoretical limits to the power of the State to legislate against immorality. It is not possible to settle in advance exceptions to the general rule or to define inflexibly areas of morality into which the law is in no circumstances to be allowed to enter. Society is entitled by means of its laws to protect itself from dangers, whether from within or without. Here again I think that the political parallel is legitimate. The law of treason is directed against aiding the king's enemies and against sedition from within. The justification for this is that established government is necessary for the existence of society and therefore its safety against violent overthrow must be secured. But an established morality is as necessary as good government to the welfare of society. Societies disintegrate from within more frequently than they are broken up by external pressures. There is disintegration when no common morality is observed and history shows that the loosening of moral bonds is often the first stage of disintegration, so that society is justified in taking the same steps to preserve its moral code as it does to preserve its government and other essential institutions. The suppression of vice is as much the law's business as the suppression of subversive activities; it is no more possible to define a sphere of private morality than it is to define one of private subversive activity. It is wrong to talk of private morality or of the law not being concerned with immorality as such or to try to set rigid bounds

to the part which the law may play in the suppression of vice. There are no theoretical limits to the power of the State to legislate against treason and sedition, and likewise I think there can be no theoretical limits to legislation against immorality. You may argue that if a man's sins affect only himself it cannot be the concern of society. If he chooses to get drunk every night in the privacy of his own home, is anyone except himself the worse for it? But suppose a quarter or a half of the population got drunk every night, what sort of society would it be? You cannot set a theoretical limit to the number of people who can get drunk before society is entitled to legislate against drunkenness. The same may be said of gambling. The Royal Commission on Betting, Lotteries, and Gaming took as their test the character of the citizen as a member of society. They said: "Our concern with the ethical significance of gambling is confined to the effect which it may have on the character of the gambler as a member of society. If we were convinced that whatever the degree of gambling this effect must be harmful we should be inclined to think that it was the duty of the state to restrict gambling to the greatest extent practicable."[7]

In what circumstances the State should exercise its power is the third of the interrogatories I have framed. But before I get to it I must raise a point which might have been brought up in any one of the three. How are the moral judgments of society to be ascertained? By leaving it until now, I can ask it in the more limited form that is now sufficient for my purpose. How is the law-maker to ascertain the moral judgments of society? It is surely not enough that they should be reached by the opinion of the majority; it would be too much to require the individual assent of every citizen. English law has evolved and regularly uses a standard which does not depend on the counting of heads. It is that of the reasonable man. He is not to be confused with the rational man. He is not expected to reason about anything and his judgment may be largely a matter of feeling. It is the viewpoint of the man in the street – or to use an archaism familiar to all lawyers – the man in the Clapham omnibus. He might also be called the right-minded man. For my purpose I should like to call him the man in the jury box, for the moral judgment of society must be something about which any twelve men or women drawn at random might after discussion be expected to be unanimous. This was the standard the judges applied in the days before Parliament was as active as it is now and when they laid down rules of public policy. They did not think of themselves as making law but simply as stating principles which every right-minded person would accept as valid. It is what Pollock called "practical morality," which is based not on theological or philosophical foundations but "in the mass of continuous experience half-consciously or unconsciously accumulated and embodied in the morality of common sense." He called it also "a certain way of thinking on questions of morality which we expect to find in a reasonable civilized man or a reasonable Englishman, taken at random."

Immorality then, for the purpose of the law, is what every right-minded person is presumed to consider to be immoral. Any immorality is capable of affecting society injuriously and in effect to a greater or lesser extent it usually does; this is what gives the law its *locus standi*. It cannot be shut out. But – and this brings me to the third question – the individual has a *locus standi* too; he cannot be expected to surrender to the judgment of society the whole conduct of his life. It is the old and familiar question of striking a balance between the rights and interests of society and those of the individual. [. . .]

[. . .] [I]t is possible to make general statements of principle which it may be thought the legislature should bear in mind when it is considering the enactment of laws enforcing morals.

I believe that most people would agree upon the chief of these elastic principles. There must be toleration of the maximum individual freedom that is consistent with the integrity of society. It cannot be said that this is a principle that runs all through the criminal law. Much of the criminal law that is regulatory in character – the part of it that deals with *malum prohibitum* rather than *malum in se* – is based upon the opposite principle, that is, that the choice of the individual must give way to the convenience of the many. But in all matters of conscience the principle I have stated is generally held to prevail. It is not confined to thought and speech; it

extends to action, as is shown by the recognition of the right to conscientious objection in war-time; this example shows also that conscience will be respected even in times of national danger. The principle appears to me to be peculiarly appropriate to all questions of morals. Nothing should be punished by the law that does not lie beyond the limits of tolerance. It is not nearly enough to say that a majority dislike a practice; there must be a real feeling of reprobation. Those who are dissatisfied with the present law on homosexuality often say that the opponents of reform are swayed simply by disgust. If that were so it would be wrong, but I do not think one can ignore disgust if it is deeply felt and not manufactured. Its presence is a good indication that the bounds of toleration are being reached. Not everything is to be tolerated. No society can do without intolerance, indignation and disgust; they are the forces behind the moral law, and indeed it can be argued that if they or something like them are not present, the feelings of society cannot be weighty enough to deprive the individual of freedom of choice. I suppose that there is hardly anyone nowadays who would not be disgusted by the thought of deliberate cruelty to animals. No one proposes to relegate that or any other form of sadism to the realm of private morality or to allow it to be practised in public or private. It would be possible no doubt to point out that until a comparatively short while ago nobody thought very much of cruelty to animals and also that pity and kindliness and the unwillingness to inflict pain are virtues more generally esteemed now than they have ever been in the past. But matters of this sort are not determined by rational argument. Every moral judgment, unless it claims a divine source, is simply a feeling that no right-minded man could behave in any other way without admitting that he was doing wrong. It is the power of a common sense and not the power of reason that is behind the judgments of society. But before a society can put a practice beyond the limits of tolerance there must be a deliberate judgment that the practice is injurious to society. There is, for example, a general abhorrence of homosexuality. We should ask ourselves in the first instance whether, looking at it calmly and dispassionately, we regard it as a vice so abominable that its mere presence is an offence. If that is the genuine feeling of the society in which we live, I do not see how society can be denied the right to eradicate it. Our feeling may not be so intense as that. We may feel about it that, if confined, it is tolerable, but that if it spread it might be gravely injurious; it is in this way that most societies look upon fornication, seeing it as a natural weakness which must be kept within bounds but which cannot be rooted out. It becomes then a question of balance, the danger to society in one scale and the extent of the restriction in the other. On this sort of point the value of an investigation by such a body as the Wolfenden Committee and of its conclusions is manifest.

The limits of tolerance shift. This is supplementary to what I have been saying but of sufficient importance in itself to deserve statement as a separate principle which law-makers have to bear in mind. I suppose that moral standards do not shift; so far as they come from divine revelation they do not, and I am willing to assume that the moral judgments made by a society always remain good for that society. But the extent to which society will tolerate – I mean tolerate, not approve – departures from moral standards varies from generation to generation. It may be that overall tolerance is always increasing. The pressure of the human mind, always seeking greater freedom of thought, is outwards against the bonds of society forcing their gradual relaxation. It may be that history is a tale of contraction and expansion and that all developed societies are on their way to dissolution. I must not speak of things I do not know; and anyway as a practical matter no society is willing to make provision for its own decay. I return therefore to the simple and observable fact that in matters of morals the limits of tolerance shift. Laws, especially those which are based on morals, are less easily moved. It follows as another good working principle that in any new matter of morals the law should be slow to act. By the next generation the swell of indignation may have abated and the law be left without the strong backing which it needs. But it is then difficult to alter the law without giving the impression that moral judgment is being weakened. This is now one of the factors that is strongly militating against any alteration to the law on homosexuality.

A third elastic principle must be advanced more tentatively. It is that as far as possible privacy should be respected. This is not an idea that has ever been made explicit in the criminal law. Acts or words done or said in public or in private are all brought within its scope without distinction in principle. But there goes with this a strong reluctance on the part of judges and legislators to sanction invasions of privacy in the detection of crime. The police have no more right to trespass than the ordinary citizen has; there is no general right of search; to this extent an Englishman's home is still his castle. The Government is extremely careful in the exercise even of those powers which it claims to be undisputed. Telephone tapping and interference with the mails afford a good illustration of this. A Committee of three Privy Councillors who recently inquired into these activities found that the Home Secretary and his predecessors had already formulated strict rules governing the exercise of these powers and the Committee were able to recommend that they should be continued to be exercised substantially on the same terms. But they reported that the power was "regarded with general disfavour."

This indicates a general sentiment that the right to privacy is something to be put in the balance against the enforcement of the law. Ought the same sort of consideration to play any part in the formation of the law? Clearly only in a very limited number of cases. When the help of the law is invoked by an injured citizen, privacy must be irrelevant; the individual cannot ask that his right to privacy should be measured against injury criminally done to another. But when all who are involved in the deed are consenting parties and the injury is done to morals, the public interest in the moral order can be balanced against the claims of privacy. The restriction on police powers of investigation goes further than the affording of a parallel; it means that the detection of crime committed in private and when there is no complaint is bound to be rather haphazard and this is an additional reason for moderation. These considerations do not justify the exclusion of all private immorality from the scope of the law. I think that, as I have already suggested, the test of "private behaviour" should be substituted for "private morality" and the influence of the factor should be reduced from that of a definite limitation to that of a matter to be taken into account. Since the gravity of the crime is also a proper consideration, a distinction might well be made in the case of homosexuality between the lesser acts of indecency and the full offence, which on the principles of the Wolfenden Report it would be illogical to do. [. . .]

Notes

1 Para. 76.
2 Para. 13.
3 Paras. 224, 285, and 318.
4 Para. 223.
5 Paras. 302 and 320.
6 Para. 306.
7 (1951) Cmd. 8190, para. 159.

39

Crime and Punishment: An Indigenous African Experience

Egbeke Aja

1. Introduction

This essay is an attempt to peep through rather a small keyhole into the phenomena of crime and punishment in an indigenous African society – the Igbo society – an ethnic group in Nigeria with an estimated population of about ten million. My concern is not merely a theoretical one. Behind the analyses and issues raised are proffered answers to the nagging questions of:

1   How can the Igbo harmonize borrowed values with the indigenous ones; and
2   What are the effective ways of dealing with the alarming increase in crime with its bewildering sophistication, without running foul of inherited law?

2. Morality in the Indigenous Igbo Society

A people's happiness and even their survival depend on the degree of harmony between them and the other beings or forces that inhabit their world. Morality, for the Igbo consisted in all acts and usages intended to maintain harmony among the various forces: human, vegetable, and mineral. Humankind is at the vortex of these forces. Moral goodness, therefore, has an onto-logical dimension: To do wrong in the indigenous Igbo society means not merely to be individually in disharmony with the order in nature but to harm and disorganize this order itself. Igbo morality is objective morality, for "The objective ethics of the Africans is an ontological ethics, immanent and intrinsic. It is attached to the essence of things ontologically perceived."[1] There is an intrinsic order of things which is the essential condition for the integrity of being. Hence, in the indigenous Igbo society, and African society generally, there is no purely personal morality.

We might say that, what an individual does has no importance in itself, but only on account of the deleterious influence the action is likely to have on the group and on the forces of nature which ensure the group's survival: rain, health, fertility, etc. Herein lies the basis of Igbo moral-ity. The *summum bonum* for an indigenous Igbo is the performance of those acts which will enhance the ontological well-being of the Igbo community. All ethical concepts hinge on this. Consequently, the indigenous Igbo morality is

Egbeke Aja, "Crime and Punishment: An Indigenous African Experience," *The Journal of Value Inquiry*, vol. 31, 1997, pp. 353–68. © 1997. Reprinted with permission from Springer Science and Business Media.

a metaphysical ethics because (1) it emphasizes the innate harmony between human beings and the universe; (2) it respects the mechanism of the interaction among beings; and most importantly, (3) it has as its centerpiece, the community or the group. It can be described as "ethical communalism."[2]

Little wonder that in the indigenous Igbo society the perfect person was the person with a good heart, that is, a person who has learned the art of living and promoting the essential harmonies in life. Human beings, for the traditional Igbo, reach their full stature only in the solidarity of their community.

I have argued that the underlying factor of all African (Igbo) indigenous moral conduct was ontological. The greatest happiness and good of the group was the end and aim of each individual member of the indigenous Igbo society. The morality was utilitarian. However, it was not egoistic utility. It was communal and to a large extent, altruistic in outlook.[3] The Yorubas, another major ethnic group in Nigeria, share the same view of the interrelatedness of beings inhabiting the universe. For the Yorubas, "Gentle character it is which enables the rope of life to stay unbroken in one's hand."[4]

The indigenous Igbo morality, in essence, was a morality of conduct rather than that of being. It was a dynamic morality, for it defined what X did rather than what X was. A person was what she was because of what she did. Human beings, for the Igbo, were not by nature either good or bad except in terms of what they did or did not do. As a result, the traditional Igbo morality was characterized by the following features:

1 *Prohibitions* – which include general prescriptions such as: Do not take the life of another person; do not steal; do not commit incest; do not defraud strangers, etc. These, though moral in content, were religious in expression. They were all rooted in religious beliefs and observances connected with *Ala*, the earth divinity.

2 *Taboos* – these were either general or specific. General taboos were applicable to all persons and included such taboos observed at various moments demanded by tradition or divination irrespective of time and place. For example, during a designated period of the year a man was

not allowed to beat up his wife. Another example is that one kind of snake, the green snake, was not to be killed or eaten by a member of the Igbo community.

Specific taboos were for special people. For example, the traditional medical practitioner was not allowed to eat *ojukwu* – the yellow palm fruits which render her or his medicine powerless. Some priests were not to eat any food cooked by a mother of twins, nor were they expected to be under the same roof with such a mother.

3 *Customs* – the *Omenala* constituted the customs. Like the taboos, and prohibitions, they were couched in religious practices. The values of the indigenous Igbo society were summed up by the *Omenala*, that is, that which happens or is approved of in the community. Customs ranged from serious subjects like moral sanctions used to maintain social control to matters of etiquette and polite behavior. For example, anybody who picked up a fallen fruit which was not hers/his was accounted as having stolen. A child dared not beat up her parents or even elders. A woman or a man was not to have a child before marriage. All these values made up the Igbo tradition – a pattern of thought and action expressed in religious or social customs. The values made for cultural continuity in communal attitudes and institutions. They formed the index of what was accepted in the traditional Igbo culture. The essential requirement of *Omenala*, or tradition, on the part of the individual was the identification of self with the totality of beings. This identification was manifested in the individual's compliance with the specific beliefs and customs prevalent in the community.

3. What Constituted Crime in the Indigenous Igbo Society

In the pre-colonial Igbo society, influences – natural and artificial – were steady, uniform, harmonious, and consistent. The individual was a member, not only of her immediate family, but also of her extended family, of the village at large, and even of the Igbo race. This group-membership, though mythical, was accepted by the Igbo as real and as such had reality. Each member belonged to the group in a very practical sense. Hence, to be out adrift from one's kith and kin was a living death; thus, the sanctions of ostracism was like outlawry in feudal England.

However, the indigenous Igbo society had little or no contact with the outside world. Each community was self-supporting and self-contained. "This 'splendid' isolation was conducive to consistency in behavior patterns of the individual members of the group."[5] Within the group, few crimes were possible, and as a result less crimes were committed because "society prepares the crime, the criminal commits it." Though in modern societies crime may just be a revolt by the criminal against the ills and shortcomings of the society, in the indigenous Igbo society, it was a kink on the ontological well-being of the group, a negation or violation of what ought-to-be. In the traditional Igbo society, there were no white collar crimes, like forgery and fraud; no bank robberies, since the communities had no banks. Property was sparse, and stealing was rare and limited in scope. Morality was high, since the individual would not dare break the moral norms of the community. The Igbo were so closely knit by consanguinity that strife was scarcely present and violence was strenuously avoided. Yet, there were limited areas of individual and group offenses.

For the indigenous Igbo, moral goodness had an ontological dimension. It was utilitarian, for all acts and usages were geared toward the attainment of perfect harmony which ought to exist in and between the physical, social, and religious dimensions of life. This, in the main, constituted the ontological locus of the traditional Igbo conscience. In the traditional Igbo society, a plurality of co-ordinated forces occur. The order in which these forces occur and interact comes from God. It must be respected and religiously maintained.[6] But, just as one stone thrown into a pond breaks up the reflections you could previously see in the water, so any criminal act can disrupt the existential harmony in the traditional Igbo society. Such an act effectively breaks the ontological harmony of the community of forces.

Crime was, in the indigenous Igbo society, "a disruptive factor in the fabric of the universe, a kink in the normal web of relationships between beings or an obstruction in the lines of flow of the life-forces which keep the social order alive."[7] That is, any deliberate or unconscious harm to the fabric of the organized society itself constituted crime. The principles at stake were basic to the ordering of society, and a breach of those principles impinged on the well-being of the entire community. With this understanding, for the indigenous Igbo, the unborn child or the newly born child could be a criminal. A disturbance of the ontological order, whether by the individual or by the corporate group, was ultimately an offense by the corporate body – the Igbo society. Hence, for the traditional Igbo,

> The guilt of one person involves his entire household including his animals and property. The pollution of the individual is corporately the pollution of those related to him whether they are human beings, animals or material goods.[8]

Any breach in the unity of *Omenala* – customs and traditions – was recognized by the indigenous Igbo, and Africans generally, as a breach of peace likely to result in tragedy for the community. A breach, therefore, was treated as a community affair. For instance, if a person committed a crime, the Igbo of old did not wait for the police to come to start mulling over the matter under the pretense of conducting a high-powered investigation. Instead, the first person to catch a glimpse of the culprit instantaneously pounced on him or her and exerted the appropriate justice once and for all. This instantaneous action was based on the principle that delaying justice was breaking the tradition or *Omenala* whose fundamental *raison d'être* was ensuring peace and harmony in the community of beings.

4.   Kinds of Crimes

In the indigenous Igbo society crimes could be categorized into three main kinds:

1.   *Capital crimes.* These involve one taking the life of a member of one's community either by omission or commission. They also included other offenses that attracted capital punishment. For instance, if a baby presents a breach position during birth, such a baby after birth is thrown away

into the evil forest. The baby is deemed to have had the intention of taking the life of its mother. This, for the Igbo, was a heinous crime on the part of the baby. The traditional Igbo was and is still at pains to understand the modern English criminal procedure adopted in our courts where a person known to be a murderer is pronounced not guilty and set free for want of evidence and some other technicalities. Up till now, these are beyond the comprehension of the traditional Igbo who is still of a piece with the philosophy of the group. For the traditional Igbo, only one law exists for murder: death by hanging.

In Igbo thought, the word is a force. As a force, it influences and is being influenced by other forces in the Igbo universe. Thoughts or words wishing that someone be harmed in some way, are seen as an ill-wind that blows no good either on the individual who expressed the word, or the entire Igbo society. The word must be directed toward the maintenance of the group's ontological solidarity and harmony – the highest good. For, "the whole tone of the philosophy of most African people is distinctly life affirming."[9] Hearsay, therefore, was enough evidence in determining the guilt of a suspect.

The traditional Igbo distinguished four kinds of murder or *Ochu.*

(1) *Accidental killing.* In modern legal language, this is referred to as manslaughter. In traditional Igbo society, the slayer was notified of the death of the victim of the act. The slayer was given an opportunity to flee the community. The criminal remained in exile – uprooted from his roots – for a specific period. After the period, he may return if he so desired. If he returned, he then paid compensation to the relatives of the deceased. This is known as *Igwa ochu.* In keeping with the people's life-affirming philosophy, the compensation to the relatives of the deceased often ended in the family of the criminal giving a young girl in marriage to a member of the family of the deceased. The children of such a marriage are reckoned by the deceased family to have adequately redressed the social and ontological imbalance caused by the loss of their relative at the hand of the manslayer.

(2) *Killing in a fight.* In the indigenous Igbo society, dangerous weapons were not allowed in a fight between relatives or people of the same town or ethnic group. However, machetes, spears,

bows and arrows, and similar weapons, though dangerous weapons, were permitted in a fight between communities. But care was exercised in the use of these weapons. If it happened that a member of one community was killed in a fight by a member of another community, members of the offending community would flee their village to another. The Igbo refer to this as *Iso ochu.* While in flight, the property left behind will be confiscated by the relatives of the deceased. More often than not, the offending community was sacked, their huts burnt down, their walls pulled down, and their economic trees felled all in the bid to restore the loss of joy of life sustained by the bereaved. The community remained desolate for a specified period, say three years, after which the offending community would pay compensation, such as grant of land known as *Ala ochu,* or female members of the community would be given away into forced marriage into the deceased person's community or village.

(3) *Decapitation.* For the traditional Igbo, to kill a human being was an odious crime; to decapitate the deceased was an unpardonable crime. The traditional Igbo could not imagine the prospect of their relatives going to the spirit world headless. As a result, the cutting off of the head amounted to an ontological sacrilege and led to eternal enmity between the opposing communities.

To forestall this singular crime, in tribal wars, it was customary to conclude a treaty between the belligerents whereby it was agreed that in the event of a member being killed, the corpse must not be decapitated.

(4) *Willful murder.* It was an atrocity for you to willfully and deliberately kill a member of your community. The houses and property of your entire family were then destroyed. You, the slayer, would in addition be expected to hang yourself. Should you delay in taking the rope, your relatives would be prompted to hand to you a suitable rope showing you, symbolically, the way you were to go. But, if the murderer was a coward and ran away, he remained in exile until the bitter feelings toward him had died down. In some cases, the criminal was exiled for life; in others, it lasted only for seven years. However, should any of the deceased relatives see the murderer return to the community, they had a right to kill her or him at sight.

But after the stipulated period of exile, negotiations are opened. If these succeed, the fugitive
returned to the community, and before he was
integrated into the community, he performed
all the appropriate sacrifices and made all prescribed restitutions.

In some cases, the criminal could run into
the sanctuary of some local juju shrine where
no one can touch her or him in retaliation.
This phenomenon is one of the origins of the
Osu caste system in some parts of Igboland.
The fugitive, having surrendered to a shrine,
becomes sacred and immune to human attacks.
But the whole family's property was destroyed
or forbidden to be used by anyone in the community as a sign of reparation.

A person with the Western mind-set would
criticize these measures as drastic and unjust.
In contradistinction to the European conception of justice which measures liability in terms
of material damage, the traditional Igbo conception measures liability in terms of the loss
in the joy of life. That is what is evaluated. For
the Igbo, the taking of the life of a member of
one's community was an ontological sacrilege;
it was just like breaking off one of the cogs in a
wheel. The whole system will no longer work
smoothly, for a gap has been created in the
traditional cobweb relationship. Anything that
affects a member of the traditional society,
affects the whole group. Hence, no price was
deemed too grave for reinstating the group's
ontological equilibrium.

2. *Minor crimes.* These are called minor in that
they do not directly involve the taking of someone's life. Instead, they are acts that disturb the
ontological harmony of the individual and the
whole group. But some of them could attract
capital punishment. This category of crimes
concerns violations of other people's right over
property. They include stealing, witchcraft,
adultery, and breaking of taboos.

Stealing. Notorious thieves, wicked traditional
medical practitioners, those who engaged in
the nefarious practice of witchcraft, those who
betrayed and sold out community secrets, those
who were unruly and also refused to submit to
the protests of relatives or who acted in such
a manner that they placed the family or the
community in jeopardy, were treated as criminals.

The indigenous Igbo society got rid of this class
of criminals by putting them to death.

In respect of the thief, the article stolen was
of importance in determining the gravity of the
punishment. For instance, yam theft was and is
still regarded as a serious crime against not just
humanity but also *Ala*, the earth goddess. The Igbo
regard yam as the chief of all crops in Igboland.
As such, yam is not expected to be subjected to
a mean act such as stealing. So, a yam thief was
punished severely in traditional Igbo society.
But if the criminal is proved not a habitual
offender, in some Igbo communities, she or he
was made to dance around the village naked.
The criminal was taunted, beaten, stoned, and
jeered at as she or he went round the town-
squares. In the indigenous Igbo society, loss of
face was counted a grave punishment. But a
notorious yam thief was required to take her or
his life. Or, the relatives would be advised to
arrange with people of another community to rid
the family of the nuisance. Under one pretext
or another the criminal was induced to pass a
chosen pathway where hired executioners, lying
in ambush, would get rid of her or him. After they
finished with the criminal a tuber of yam would
be placed on the chest of the slain criminal.
People who indulged in habitual stealing of
other people's property suffered a similar fate
in traditional Igbo cultures.

Adultery was also judged an offense against
humanity and the gods. Adultery with the wife
of a Chief was adjudged more grievous than with
the wife of an ordinary member of the society.
For the Igbo, a Chief is the spiritual head of the
people. He is the link between the dead and
the living. Anything, therefore, that disturbs
his well-being affects the entire society, even
the spirit world. As a result, adultery with his
wife attracted the death penalty. Though the
adulterer was held responsible, the wife of the
Chief might be forgiven. But the same offense
committed with the wife of any other member
of the society demanded sacrifice and propitiation on the part of the man and the woman
adulterers.

Nowadays, though still practiced in many
Igbo communities, such killings would amount
to murder, but in the indigenous Igbo culture
they were justifiable homicide. It was a crude
justice but an effective deterrent to evil-doing. The

action was to forestall the Igbo adage that *Otu mkpisi aka ruta manu, ozue umuaka dum*. When one finger is oiled, it spreads to the others. In consonance with the Biblical injunction that if one part of one's body would make you sin, you should cut it off. The Igbo society got rid of any member of the society who habitually violated the rights of others over property. A person who tampered with the people's main source of sustenance, yam, or source of joy, deserved no other punishment than severance from the kith and kin.

3. *Abomination* consists of crimes which may or may not have been committed through the actions of the criminal. They include child infanticide and the breaking of taboos and customs of the people. They are acts or events which are contrary to what used to be – a deviation from the normal state of affairs.

In the indigenous Igbo society, any abnormality in child-bearing was regarded as an abomination and by deduction, a crime or *aru*. The practice was to kill such a baby immediately after birth. This practice, dictated by and deeply rooted in the people's customs, was a common phenomenon; examples of *aru* in Igbo culture included the following:

(1) *Twin delivery or ejima*. The unfortunate twins were usually placed in a water pot and deposited in a "bad bush" or otherwise destroyed.

(2) *Nwa oghom* (Accidental birth). A child born before an elder brother or sister has been weaned committed an abomination. The baby was deemed to have interfered with the progress and well-being of its predecessor. For the Igbo, the first to be born has a greater right to live than the later "intruder," an indication of the high premium the indigenous Igbo placed on seniority of birth, and the order in the ontological hierarchy of beings or forces.

(3) *A breach birth – Iji okpa puta*. This was considered an abomination, and, therefore, demanded the death of the baby who chose to come into the world by that way whether the mother survived or not.

(4) A baby born with teeth or a child cutting the upper teeth first. In either case the penalty was death for the child or baby. The baby born with teeth is referred to as *Nwa pu eze n'afo*;

while the child who cuts upper teeth first is known as *Nwa ezc clu*.

Other minor crimes or abominations that could be committed by a baby or a child included failure to cry vigorously at birth, being born with six toes or six fingers. In the first case, the baby forfeited its life; whereas, as a general rule, in the second case, the baby was abandoned to die on its own.

The above crimes indicate fundamental beliefs among the indigenous Igbo. For the Igbo, a human fetus becomes a human being directly it is conceived and must be accorded that status. The idea of an age of reason is alien to traditional Igbo jurisprudence, which holds that a superior force or being is always the guardian of an inferior force or being. Maintenance of the intrinsic harmony in nature is paramount in the mind of the indigenous Igbo. Any act of omission or commission that threatened the corporate existence of the society never went unpunished. Anything that would anger the gods was counted an abomination; so to be safe from the wrath of the gods, the indigenous society did everything to guard its members against the group's declared abominations.

By certain acts of speech, one could commit an abomination. It was a crime or abomination for any man to beat up his wife at a particular period of the year. For instance, in Chinua Achebe's *Things Fall Apart*, Okonkwo beat up Ekwefi, his wife, during the holy week.[10] By that singular act, Okonkwo offended both the community, *Umuofia*, and the gods. That amounted to a disruption of the desired peace, quiet, and harmony in both the human and spirit world, of *Umuofia*. When such an offense was committed, an appropriate propitiation was made to appease both the living and the dead. Okonkwo, of *Things Fall Apart*, atoned for the beating of his wife during the holy week.

By killing and eating a revered animal or totem, an indigenous Igbo was deemed to have committed a crime. Specific sacrifice was demanded. In Igbo thought, the animal world is part and parcel of the human world. Killing a python, a totem in some Igbo communities, called for a compensation and a befitting burial rite for the slain python. Such were some of the crimes and punishment in the simple, harmonious, indigenous Igbo culture.

5. Proof in the Indigenous Igbo Cultures

In Igbo jurisprudence, grave suspicion amounts to *prima facie* proof. Should a murderer not admit guilt, the onus to establish her or his innocence was on that person. Proof in such cases was usually by means of trial by ordeal or by the invocation and the intervention of the gods in juju-swearing. The gods were needed because for the Igbo, and the Africans in general, the departed and the gods are the guardians of morality. In ordeal or juju-swearing, the gods decided on the issue of the guilt or the innocence of the accused. One popular form of ordeal was to wash a corpse and collect the bath-water. A relative of the deceased took a sip of the water to assure witnesses that no poison had been mixed with it, then the accused person took a mouthful of the water. A period, usually twelve months, was agreed upon. If the suspected murderer died within the period, then her or his guilt would have been confirmed by the gods. If the suspect did not die, then she or he danced around the village, proclaiming her or his innocence. Relatives and friends of the suspect were advised to refrain from interacting with her or him till after the expiration of the agreed period. In some cases, the water used in washing the corpse was poured across the road along which the suspect lived.

By modern standards, these means of detecting and punishing criminals may seem crude. But in a society with deep and tender religious feelings, such as the indigenous Igbo, ordeals and juju-swearing are accepted methods of proof. Admittedly, a guilty criminal may die by sheer auto-suggestion or by qualms of conscience, but for the traditional Igbo, the juju or the gods would have done their job as guardians of indigenous Igbo morals.

6. Crime in Contemporary Igbo Culture

Colonialism had a tremendous influence on the Igbo in spite of their resilience to change. Western civilization, with its money economy and materialism, descended on the indigenous Igbo society which was hitherto homogeneous, simple, and with few incidences of crime. From colonialism resulted a cultural synthesis which has produced a curious cultural hybrid. This, in turn, has produced conflict of norms, divergent aims, and disparate rules of conduct.

The erstwhile simple society has gradually been undermined and progressively eroded and is threatened to be over-thrown. Consequently, the contemporary Igbo society is rife with sophisticated crimes. The group ideology that characterized the traditional Igbo culture has been replaced with a new one which is individualist in concept and materialist in content. The emphasis has shifted to individual enterprise and to the acquisition of material wealth. As a result, the average Igbo has started to disregard the old traditional system of social welfare which is fast giving way to the advancing avalanche of self-satisfaction. With the new materialism, wealth has soon been identified with worth. Hence, the saying in Igbo: *Onye nkirika akwa bu onye nkirika okwu*, meaning that the poor cannot possibly make any meaningful contribution to public debate.

Worse still, the traditional distinction between a rich and a virtuous person is fast disappearing in the contemporary Igbo society. Little wonder that the desire now is for more personal wealth which is both the key to and the symbol of success. The desire and trend obviously have led to more conflicts of interest and ultimately to more crime. A high crime rate is expected generally in a social system in which great emphasis is placed on the success goal and the attainment of wealth, whereas little or no emphasis is placed upon the proper means of achieving those goals.

The new neighborhood-township created by Western ideas and civilization has failed to function as an effective check on crime, since it is lacking in those pressures for conformity dictated by similar customs, religions, etc. reminiscent of the primordial indigenous Igbo neighborhood. The confusion has been compounded by the increase in commerce and travel as well as by the impact of newspapers, radio, and television. The danger of criminal contact and criminal contamination have become greater, when control over behavior has become weaker and more ineffective.

Expectedly, the Igbo of today is caught up in intense cultural conflict; he is called upon by existential conditions to dance to the rhythm of new religions, new values, new world views, and new political and legal systems. The Igbo value system has thus become distorted. Consequently, the crime rate is on the increase. The society appears unable to check the ugly trend; nor is it able to administer commensurate punishments to criminals. The Western legal system, with its emphasis on evidence, is responsible for the inability of the society to cope with crime in contemporary Igbo societies. [. . .]

Notes

1 Placide Temples, *Bantu Philosophy* (Paris: Presence Africaine, 1959), p. 81.

2 Egbeka Aja, "The Ontological Foundations of African Communalism." Unpublished MA Philosophy Dissertation (University of Nigeria, Nsukka, 1986), p. 98.

3 Edmund Ilogu, *Igbo Life and Thought* (Onitsha: University Publishing Company, 1985), p. 29.

4 John S. Mbiti, *African Religions and Philosophy* (London: Heinemann, 1969), p. 212.

5 C. A. Oputa, "Crime and the Nigerian Society," T. O. Elias et al., eds., *African Indigenous Laws* (Nsukka: Institute of African Studies, University of Nigeria, Nsukka, 1975), p. 8

6 Tempels, *Bantu Philosophy*, p. 80.

7 K. C. Anyanwu and E. A. Ruch, *African Philosophy* (Rome: Catholic Book Agency, 1980), p. 135.

8 Mbiti, *African Religions and Philosophy*, p. 206.

9 E. C. Parrinder, *West African Psychology* (London: Lutterworth Press, 1951), p. 223.

10 Chinua Achebe, *Things Fall Apart* (London: Heinemann, 1980), ch. 5.

40

The Mind and the Deed

Anthony Kenny

The topic of responsibility is an area in which the interests of the philosopher and of the lawyer overlap. One branch of philosophy is the philosophy of mind and action, and one of the concerns of the criminal lawyer is the mental element in crime. This area of overlap will be the subject of this book.

Philosophers of mind are concerned with the analysis of the relationship between mind and behavior. When we understand, respond to, and evaluate each other's actions we make constant use of mentalistic concepts. On the basis of what people do, and in order to explain what they do, we attribute to them certain desires and beliefs. We ascribe their actions to choices, and we invoke, to explain their conduct, various intentions, motives, and reasons. These mentalistic concepts, such as *desire*, *belief*, *intention*, *motive*, and *reason*, are the subject matter of the philosophy of mind. In human action we look for a mental element; in the philosophy of human action we study the relationship between the mental element and the overt behaviour.

Actions are sometimes the subject of moral and legal evaluation: some actions we regard as admirable and praiseworthy; others we condemn and punish as criminal. Those human actions which are crimes are of special interest and have long been a subject of special study. Crimes, like other actions, involve a mental element. For this mental element lawyers have a special name: *mens rea*, which is the Latin for "guilty mind." There was a maxim of the English common law: *actus non facit reum nisi mens sit rea*: an act does not make a man guilty unless his mind is guilty too. The "guilty mind" need not be any consciousness of wickedness nor any malevolent intent: in most cases it is simply a knowledge of what one is doing, where what one is doing is something illegal. But where *mens rea* is required, no act can be criminal unless accompanied by a certain mental state. The particular mental state indicated by *mens rea* differs, as we shall see, from crime to crime: the expression means, in general, the state of mind which must accompany an act which is on the face of it criminal if the agent is to be held responsible, and therefore liable for punishment, for the action.

This notion of responsibility will be the major topic of this book. The scope and method of the chapters will be philosophical in the narrow sense of the word current in Anglo-American academic circles: I shall be engaged in the analysis

Anthony Kenny, "The Mind and the Deed," from *Freewill and Responsibility* (Routledge & Kegan Paul, 1978), pp. 1–21.

and clarification of certain concepts which are central to our understanding of human nature and activity. I shall not be advancing empirical hypotheses about human behaviour, nor reporting scientific discoveries about human mental processes. Nor shall I be offering an elementary course in aspects of criminal law. But I shall constantly draw upon actual legal cases to illustrate the conceptual points that I wish to make. This is not because I believe that the notions of belief, intention, choice, and the like are only at home in the formal context of criminal proceedings: on the contrary, as I have said, I believe that the use of them is indispensable at every step when we endeavour to understand and communicate with each other. But the reports of the courts and the decisions of judges provide a fund of material for philosophical study which is more concrete, vivid, and credible, while at the same time often more extraordinary and thought-provoking, than any product of philosophers' imaginations. Moreover, the needs of the courts to reach a decision, and the experience of legal systems over long periods of practical operation, have in some areas brought a precision into legal concepts which can contrast favourably with the achievement of philosophers. Finally, by concentrating on legal cases in which matters of life and death are considered and in which the lifetime fate of the accused may be in the balance, we remind ourselves that the philosophy of action, while it may operate at a very abstract level, is a subject of great practical importance whose aim is to dispel confusions that can have far-reaching social consequences.

For several reasons the notion of responsibility and the cluster of concepts that combine to provide its habitat have been looked on with disfavour in recent years. To many people the apparatus of responsibility as administered in the criminal courts seems antiquated and inhumane: many social reformers look forward to a day when the courts of the criminal law have gone the way of rotten boroughs and ordeal by combat. They look forward to a time when law courts are replaced by something more scientific and clinical: when the determination of responsibility and the handing down of penalties by judicial bodies is replaced by the diagnosis of social illness and the prescription of appropriate medicinal procedures by teams of social scientists.

In these lectures I shall argue that many attacks on the common-law notion of responsibility are based on misunderstandings of an essentially philosophical nature. Conceptual confusions, I shall argue, often distort the benevolent and liberal intentions of social reformers and ensnare them into making proposals whose effects are abhorrent.

To illustrate the type of objection made by social reformers to the notions of *mens rea* and responsibility I shall quote from the evidence laid by the National Association for Mental Health before the Butler Committee which inquired into the treatment of mentally abnormal offenders and which reported in 1974. Under the heading "The Determination of Criminal Responsibility" the Association submitted as follows:[1]

Until very recently the concept of "*mens rea*" was the basis of all decisions regarding responsibility. This position was eroded by the introduction of the concept of diminished responsibility in the 1958 Homicide Act. We recognise and applaud the liberal intention behind the concept, but it is all the same a difficult one, particularly as in some cases of mental illness the diminution of responsibility may be periodic and not permanent. The position is further complicated by the fact that there are now a number of "absolute" offences, where a person may be found guilty although he had no knowledge that what he was doing was an offence and no intention of committing an offence. Examples of such offences range from parking offences to being in possession of dangerous drugs.

The Association has considerable reservations about the present confused situation. The difficulty arises over the imprecise nature of psychiatric definition of mental disorder. This means that we constantly see the unedifying clash of psychiatric experts for the defense and the prosecution in an effort to determine the state of man's mind, when this is very often not susceptible of scientific proof. Indeed such proof would only be obtainable in the highly unlikely event of a psychiatrist observing and assessing the offender at the precise time of his offence.

We accordingly suggest for the Committee's consideration that the accused's state of mind could more profitably be taken into account in the disposal of his case than in assessing his responsibility. The disposal of cases of this kind ought to follow a very careful statement of psychiatric opinion and a full review of me social history.

Given adequate provision for taking into account a convicted person's state of mind in the decision about disposal, we suggest that the concept of "*mens rea*" and criminal responsibility could be dispensed with in favour of the concept of strict accountability for one's actions in criminal charges. We recognise, however, the radical change in sentencing procedure that would be required in this case.

The Association, therefore, wished the requirement of *mens rea* as an ingredient in crime to be replaced by a system of strict accountability for action plus a professional investigation into the accused's state of mind at the time of sentencing. In attacking *mens rea*, the Association does not seem to have had a single target in mind. It devotes itself in the paper to the consideration of when it is proper to consider an accused person's "state of mind." But by this expression it clearly meant several different things. Most commonly the expression is used in the paper to refer to the accused's state of mental health: Is he or she sane or insane, mentally normal or abnormal? This is naturally what the Association is most interested in and what it wants professionally investigated at the time of disposal. But in other places, by "state of mind" the Association means such things as whether the accused knew that what he was doing was an offence and whether he had any intention of committing an offence. To investigate a state of mind in this sense is very different from inquiring into a person's state of mental health. To decide whether someone is mentally ill may well call for difficult expert inquiry by a psychiatrist – an inquiry whose difficulties would not necessarily be resolved by "observing and assessing the offender at the precise time of his offence." To discover whether someone knew a particular place to be a No Parking zone does not call for similar professional expertise.

The Association seems to have believed that "*mens rea*" meant knowledge that one is committing an offence, or the intention to commit an offence. This is not correct. Certainly for many crimes one needs to know that one is doing the action which is, as a matter of fact, an offence;

but one does not need to know *that* it is an offence. The common law, which imposed the requirement of *mens rea*, contained also the maxim that ignorance of law was no defence. The *mens rea* which is needed for most crimes is not knowledge that X, which one is doing, is a crime; but simply the knowledge that one is doing X.

The state of mind which constitutes *mens rea* in fact varies from crime to crime. Let us suppose that the law wishes to prohibit a certain action, and let us suppose further that it gives a description of the prohibited action in terms which contain no reference to the agent's state of mind: e.g., a description such as "being in charge of a motor vehicle" or "entering a prohibited place." There are many different provisos which the law can go on to make concerning what the mental state of the agent must be if his performance of the prohibited act is to constitute a crime.

1 Let us suppose the law makes no such proviso at all, so that the act will be punishable no matter whether the accused did know or could have known what he was doing. In that case no *mens rea* will be required for the crime and it will be an "absolute" offence, an offence of "strict liability."

2 If the law does not wish it to be punishable absolutely in this manner, let us next suppose that it wishes it to be punishable whether or not the agent actually knows that he is performing the action, provided only that he could and should have known that he was. In that case the crime will be a crime of negligence. Where there is negligence, there is voluntary unawareness of the nature of one's action. The question arises. Is negligence a form of *mens rea*? Some argue that unawareness is not a state of mind and so negligence is not *mens rea*; others argue that because negligence is voluntary and culpable unawareness, the requirement of *mens rea* is present in crimes of negligence. The terminological point is perhaps not of great importance: what is important is to distinguish crimes of negligence from crimes of strict liability.

3 If the law does not thus wish an act to be punishable when performed by an agent who is unaware that he is performing it, let us next suppose that it wishes it to be punishable

whether or not the agent intends to perform it (in the sense of wanting to perform it as an end in itself or as a means to some other end), provided only that he believes or thinks it likely that he is performing it. In that case the crime will be one of recklessness: recklessness will be the *mens rea* required for the action to be punishable.

4   If the law does not wish an action to be punishable whenever performed by an agent with this degree of awareness, it may wish it to be punishable only when performed intentionally by an agent as an end in itself or as a means to some other end. In this case the *mens rea* required will be the act's being intentional.

5   Finally, the law may not wish any and every intentional performance of an action to be punishable, but only in cases where the action is done with a particular intention which the law goes on to specify. In this case the *mens rea* will be the specific intent mentioned in the definition of the crime; crimes of this kind are called crimes of specific intent, and are contrasted with the crimes in the previous category which are sometimes called crimes of basic intent.

"Mens rea," then, may mean anything from mere negligence to a specific intention such as the intention to assist the enemy in wartime. Later, we shall have occasion to give detailed examples of types of crime in each of these five categories, and indeed on the borderlines between them. For the moment it is enough to note that as we go from the beginning to the end of this scale, the requirement of *mens rea* becomes more strict: as we go further in the scale the prosecution has to establish more and more about the accused's state of mind in order to secure conviction. The issue of soundness or unsoundness of mind is a quite separate issue, which may apply differently to different categories of crime, as we shall see later. But the general background assumption to these gradations of *mens rea* is that the accused is of sound mind: even in the cases of strict liability this is so.

The nature of strict liability is misleadingly represented in the National Association for Mental Health's submission quoted above. It is in no way a special feature of crimes of strict liability that the accused can be convicted though he has no knowledge that he is committing an offence: this is so in the great majority of crimes. Nor is it peculiar to crimes of strict liability that one can be convicted even though one did not know that one was doing the act which is, as a matter of fact, an offence: this is the case with all offences of negligence. One can, for instance, be guilty of driving without due care and attention even though at the time one did not know that one's driving was careless. The peculiar feature of absolute offences is that one can be found guilty even though one did not know, and could not reasonably have known, that one was performing the prohibited action. Selling adulterated milk and driving a motor car uninsured have been held in English law to be offences of this kind. A supplier of milk may be guilty of the former offence if milk reaches his customer in an adulterated form even though he delivered it in sound condition to a reputable carrier. If the requirement to provide third-party insurance is interpreted strictly, then I can be found guilty of driving a car uninsured if my insurers go bankrupt as I drive along the motorway.

It is not clear whether the National Association of Mental Health wishes *mens rea* to be replaced in all offences with liability that is absolute in this strict sense. If so, the proposal is surely totally unacceptable. If it were accepted, many innocent people could find themselves convicted and then – if the psychiatrists decided that it was in their or the public interest – detained against their will for indefinite periods. Suppose that I absentmindedly walk out of a bookstore with a book I have not paid for, and that as soon as I leave the store I realize what I have done and instantly go back to pay. According to the Association's proposal I would be guilty of theft, having appropriated the property of another, and evidence that I had no dishonest intent would be neither here nor there. When I had been found guilty, there would then follow "a very careful statement of psychiatric opinion and a full review of the social history." If the psychiatrists discovered that I had a history of odd, though not criminal, behaviour, then in accordance with a proposal of the Association not reproduced above, I would be liable to be committed to a special secure hospital.

It has been often remarked that the undesirable consequences of any proposal to abolish the requirement of *mens rea* come out particularly clearly in the case of the law of perjury. In any situation in which witnesses contradict each other on oath, one of them is making a statement which is objectively false. As things are, of course, no perjury is involved in this utterance of falsehood as long as the witness honestly believes that he is speaking the truth. But if the consideration of the accused's state of mind were to be abolished in the criminal law, then such things as his beliefs and his intentions would become irrelevant. In every clash between two witnesses one at least would be guilty of perjury and could be handed over to the psychiatrists at the Queen's pleasure forthwith.

Consider again the law of treason. English wartime defence regulations made it an offence to do an act likely to assist the enemy with intent to assist the enemy. On the reformers' proposal, of course, the mentalistic proviso, "with intent to assist the enemy," would have to be omitted. This would no doubt have the advantage of securing rapid promotion for junior officers, as their seniors were tried for treason and removed to strict security hospitals for mistaken orders in the field. Few, indeed, at any level would be secure. During the German invasion of Greece in 1941, Churchill ordered several British North African divisions to Greece. This act, as was foreseeable, materially assisted the German war effort: it failed to prevent the conquest of Greece, and it enabled the Axis to make substantial gains in Libya and Egypt. If the question of intent were to be ruled immaterial, this order, and countless others like it, could count as treasonable.

Objections to the notion of responsibility, I have claimed, are often based on conceptual confusion. But the objections, and the confusions on which I claim they are based, are of several different kinds. The principal ones can be grouped into three classes: the epistemological, the metaphysical, and the ethical. The epistemological objection to the notion of *mens rea* stems from the idea that it is impossible, or at least impracticably difficult, to ascertain the state of mind of a man in a way sufficient to determine *mens rea*. The metaphysical one starts from a presumption that science has shown, or made it extremely likely, that determinism is true. If every act of every human

being is determined in advance by inexorable laws of nature – so the objection runs – then it seems unfair to single out particular actions for judgment and reprobation. Moreover, it may well seem pointless to try to change or affect people's actions by punishments or the threat of punishments, if everything they will ever do is predictable in advance from laws and conditions that obtained before ever they were born. Finally, the ethical objection to the notion of responsibility envisages it as tied up with a theory of retributive punishment, a view of punishment as allotting to a criminal his strict deserts, rendering evil for evil, an eye for an eye and a tooth for a tooth, in a barbarously vindictive manner.

[. . .] In this chapter I will attack the epistemological root of the objection to responsibility, which is the philosophical error often called by professional philosophers "dualism."

Dualism is the idea that mental events and states belong to a private world which is inaccessible to public observation: the belief in two separate realms of mental and physical realities which interact, if at all, only in a highly mysterious manner that transcends the normal rules of causality and evidence. The most impressive modern presentation of dualism was the philosophy of Descartes in the seventeenth century. Most contemporary philosophers reject such Cartesian dualism but its influence is great even upon those who explicitly renounce it. In extreme reaction to Cartesian ideas there grew up in the present century a school of behaviourists, who denied the existence of the mental realm altogether, maintaining that when we attribute mental states or events to people we are really making roundabout statements about their actual or hypothetical bodily behaviour. Behaviourism was for long very influential among psychologists; and among the philosophers a subtle and not quite thoroughgoing form of behaviourism was espoused in our own times by Gilbert Ryle.

The most significant philosopher of mind in the twentieth century, however, was Ludwig Wittgenstein: and Wittgenstein thought that both dualists and behaviourists were victims of confusion. Wittgenstein's own position was a middle stance between dualism and behaviourism. Mental events and states, he believed, were neither reducible to their bodily expressions (as the behaviourists had argued) nor totally separable from them (as the dualists had concluded). According to Wittgenstein the connection between mental processes and their manifestations in behaviour is not a causal connection discoverable, like other causal connections, from the regular concomitance between the two types of events. To use Wittgenstein's technical term, the physical expression of a mental process is a *criterion* for that process: that is to say, it is part of the concept of a mental process of a particular kind (a sensation such as pain, for instance, or an emotion such as grief) that it should have a characteristic manifestation. To understand the very notion of a given mental state, one has to understand what kinds of behaviour count as evidence for its occurrence; and the relation between the behavioural evidence and the mental state is not an inductive one, not, that is to say, a connection established by the observation of the co-occurrence of two sets of independently identifiable events.

I do not intend here to expound or to defend Wittgenstein's philosophy of mind: I have tried to do so elsewhere.[2] I merely observe that in so far as the epistemological objection to the notion of responsibility rests upon philosophical presuppositions, those presuppositions have in recent times been the subject of decisive criticism within philosophy itself. If Wittgenstein is right, there is no epistemological reason to reject the mentalistic concepts which are used in the legal assessment of responsibility, and no reason to think that we are setting judges and juries an impossible task in requiring them to have regard to the state of mind of an accused at the time of the commission of a criminal act. When we infer from behaviour and testimony to mental states and activities, we are not making a shaky inductive inference to events in an inaccessible realm; the very concepts of mental states have as their function to enable us to interpret and understand the conduct of human beings. The mind itself can be defined as the capacity to acquire the abilities to behave in the complicated and symbolic ways which constitute the linguistic, social, moral, cultural, economic, scientific, and other characteristically human activities of men in society.[3]

The mentalistic concepts which are used in the law cannot be understood apart from their function in explaining and rendering intelligible the behaviour of human agents. But this must not be misunderstood. When we explain action in terms of desires and beliefs we are not putting forward any explanatory *theory* to account for action. It is true that desires and beliefs explain action; but the explanation is not of any causal hypothetical form. It is not as if the actions of human beings constitute a set of raw data – actions identifiable on their faces as the kinds of actions they are – for which we then seek an explanatory hypothesis. On the contrary, many human actions are not identifiable as actions of a particular kind unless they are already seen and interpreted as proceeding from a particular set of desires and beliefs. Brief reflection suffices to show this in the case of such human actions as buying and selling, promising and marrying, lying and story-telling. But it can be true also of the most basic, apparently purely physical, actions, such as killing and letting die. In legal contexts it may well be easier to identify the state of mind of the accused and of others involved than it is to decide what, in purely physical terms, they actually did.

I would like to illustrate this by a detailed consideration of an African trial: the case of *Nyuzi and Kudemera* v *Republic*, heard on appeal by the High Court of Malawi in February 1967.[4] The case demonstrates clearly that it may be easier to decide whether an accused's state of mind fulfills the requirements of *mens rea* than to decide whether his actions answer to the description of a particular *actus reus* [. . .]

I quote from the African Law Reports:

The appellants were charged jointly in the Resident Magistrate's Court, Mwanza, with (a) agreeing to hold a trial by ordeal contrary to s.3(2) of the Witchcraft Ordinance (*cap.* 31) and (b) directing, controlling and presiding at a trial by ordeal contrary to s.3(1) of the Ordinance.

The evidence revealed that the inhabitants of a certain village called on the first appellant, who professed to be a witchdoctor, to find out why the children born in the village were dying soon after birth. The first appellant agreed to hold a trial by ordeal to discover whether there were any witches in the village who might be responsible for the deaths. Sixteen people submitted themselves voluntarily for a test by *muabvi*, the belief being that the *muabvi* would kill any witches who drank it but would not affect the innocent. The first appellant prepared the *muabvi* which was handed to the 16 participants by the second appellant. Four of the 16 died and several others became ill as a result of the trial. The *muabvi* was submitted to a government analyst, who reported that it was not poisonous, and the pathologist who examined the deceased found no cause of death and no trace of poison in the bodies. The first appellant was convicted on both counts; the second appellant was acquitted on the first count but convicted on the second.

The first appellant appealed on the grounds that he was an experienced witchdoctor who, in holding the trial by ordeal, was performing a useful service at the villagers' own request, and that the deaths were caused by magic because the deceased were magicians. The second appellant appealed on the ground that he did not profess to be a witchdoctor and had merely acted as an assistant to the first appellant.

One of the issues before the Court was whether the second appellant – the acolyte – had been rightly convicted: his conviction was in fact varied on appeal, for reasons of no current interest. I will consider only questions which arise concerning the first appellant, Nyuzi; and I shall concentrate on three questions: Did he kill the deceased? If he did kill them, did he kill them intentionally? If he did kill them intentionally, did he murder them?

First, then, did the witchdoctor kill, or cause the deaths of the villagers who died? From several remarks in the course of his judgment it is clear that the High Court judge, Cram J., thought it correct to say that Nyuzi had killed his victims. But this must be something of a question, given what we are told in the course of the judgment:

A government analyst examined bark and powder found in the possession of the appellant but reported that they were not poisonous; experiments on animals showed that *muabvi* was not fatal, at least to guinea pigs. The pathologist found no cause of death in the deceased, but she believed that the cause of death might be poison. She conceded, however, that she found no poison.

The judge referred to an interesting, but unsubstantiated, theory that *muabvi* while not in itself fatal to human beings becomes toxic when associated with adrenalin: so that a person frightened by the ordeal, whose glands were activated, would internally manufacture a poison. The defence case was, in a manner, parallel to this: that the deaths were the result not of Nyuzi's action but of the internal activity of the witches' magic.

Among the members of seminars and classes to whom I have described this case in England and the USA I have found that opinion is fairly evenly divided on the question, Did Nyuzi kill the deceased? Some feel strongly in favour of an affirmative answer, some feel strongly in favour of a negative answer, and some are undecided. By contrast, it is usually easy to secure unanimous agreement about the description of Nyuzi's state of mind: he intended to submit the villagers to a test which, if they were witches, would lead to their death. Here is a case, then, in which it is much easier to reach a decision about a relatively complicated form of *mens rea* than about a relatively simple type of *actus reus*.

Those of us who feel, as the judge did, that it is natural on the facts of the case to say that Nyuzi killed his victims must admit, as the judge did, that no one knows how he did it. The reason that we say, if we do, that he killed the deceased is that we know that he believed the application of the ordeal could cause the death of witches, and that he intended to apply the ordeal. The action can only be identified as a killing because we have previously identified the state of mind as a type of conditional intent to kill. It might be objected that we do not need to identify the witchdoctor's state of mind in order to regard his action as a killing: we need merely believe that he possesses mysterious powers which he exercised in this case. But this suggestion does not, in fact, escape the route through a judgment about the witchdoctor's mind: for the only reason we say – if we do – that he possesses special powers is that this kind of thing happens when he *wants* it to happen.

It was not, in fact, necessary in the case of *Nyuzi* to decide whether the accused had caused the death of the deceased, since the trial was not for murder but for violation of the law against witchcraft. The Malawi witchcraft ordinance reads, in part: "trial by the ordeal of *muabvi* . . . or by any ordeal which is likely directly or indirectly to result in the death of or bodily injury to any person shall be and is hereby prohibited." Directing a trial by ordeal, if death results, is punishable by life imprisonment; if not, by seven years' hard labor.

No doubt it is in part at least because *muabvi* is non-toxic that witchfinders who administer it are not charged with murder: there must arguably be ground for reasonable doubt as to whether the administration of it actually causes death. In earlier times, witchdoctors offering *muabvi* have been charged and convicted of murder. One such, Palamba, had his appeal against conviction allowed by the Court of Appeal for Eastern Africa in 1947: not, however, because he did not cause death, but because he had no intent to kill.[5] *Muabvi*, the court argued, was not believed in the appellant's culture to be poison: an additional element was needed to cause death: the guilt of sorcery in the person who died after taking it. But witchcraft, the court went on to say, did not exist; therefore the deceased was innocent of witchcraft. "On the basis that the deceased was innocent of witchcraft, where was malice aforethought in the appellant who, *ex hypothesi*, believed that the administration of *muabvi* to a person innocent of witchcraft would not cause death?"

The argument of the court in *Palamba* seems to have been that the accused's intent can be expressed thus: I intend to kill X if X is a witch. This is a conditional intention, not an absolute intention. But it is a conditional the antecedent of which is necessarily false, since there are no such things as witches. Therefore it is a tantamount to no intent at all.

There is no doubt that, if a witchfinder has an intent to kill, it is only a conditional intent; and conditional intention is a difficult topic. [. . .] But there seems to be no doubt that a conditional intent can be a sufficient *mens rea* in murder as in other crimes; and whether the antecedent of the conditional is necessarily false seems to be less to the point than whether the accused believes it to be necessarily false. The argument of the court in *Palamba* was brushed aside by the judge in *Nyuzi* with the words: "This hardly takes account of the intent to kill a guilty witch."

"The real defence," the judge continued, "even with intent to kill, is self-defence or defence of the person of others." The trial, to repeat, was not a murder trial: but if self-defence can provide a defence to murder, clearly it can provide one against the lesser offence prohibited by the witch-craft ordinance. It is well established in English and Malawi law that defence of the person of others against a felonious attack is as legitimate a defence in law as self-defence: but the difficulty of admitting the defence in the present case is that the belief in the existence of the threat which is to be warded off depends upon the belief in witchcraft, and the question arises: Is this belief a reasonable one?

The deaths of the children complained of by the villagers were, no doubt, explicable in scientific terms, such as invasion of their bodies by a harmful organism, genetic defects, lack of care and attention or malnutrition. A person in ignorance of scientific knowledge, believing the deaths caused by sorcery, can regard the killing of the witch reputed responsible for the deaths as justified in defense of person. In this culture to destroy the witch may be considered non-culpable and even meritorious. In the light of knowledge of a modern scientific culture, he acts under a mistake of fact. Section 10 of the Penal Code (*cap.* 23) runs:

"A person who does . . . an act under an honest and reasonable, but mistaken, belief in the existence of any state of things is not criminally responsible for the act . . . to any greater extent than if the real state of things had been such as he believed to exist. . . ."

The kernel of the problem appears in the word "reasonable." To what or to whom can what is "reasonable" be related?

The issue of the reasonableness of belief in witchcraft has been raised in a number of African cases which were murder cases, in which the death of supposed witches had been brought about not by an ordeal but by perfectly normal means. In *Jackson* the accused believed that an elderly female relation had put a spell on him, and he killed her with a bow and arrow and a hoe in the belief that this was the only way of averting his own imminent death.[6] His defence of self-defence was allowed at the trial, on the grounds that there was "no difference in principle between a physical and a metaphysical attack." On appeal, however, by the Attorney-General, it was held that the proper verdict should have been one of murder: the Federal Supreme Court was of the opinion that under the English common law a belief in the efficacy of witchcraft was unreasonable because it would not be accepted by the man in the street in England. This decision was queried by a number of courts before it was finally overruled in 1967 by the Supreme Court of Appeal of Malawi. As the High Court judge put it in the case of *Lufazema* which led to the overruling of *Jackson*:[7]

> Granted that the use of force in defense of person or property is governed by the principles of the English common law, does that, however, necessitate going the further step of choosing the average man in an English street? ... Surely one does no violence to the principle (that the test of reasonableness is the reaction of the man in the street) by insisting that when it is applied in Malawi, it must mean a Malawi street.

On the other hand, a court argued in a parallel case (*Ifereonwe*),[8] the mere prevalence of a belief does not make it reasonable.

> It would be a dangerous precedent to recognise that because of a superstition, which may lead to a terrible result as is disclosed by the facts of this case, is generally prevalent among a community, it is therefore reasonable.

The case with which we have been principally concerned, *Nyuzi*, was heard before *Jackson* had been overruled; but the judge did not hesitate to dissent from it, remarking that what seems reasonable according to today's science in Manchester might not be the appropriate criterion by which to judge a person whose pre-scientific beliefs had been inculcated in the bush on the banks of the Zambesi river. In the view of the pre-scientific culture in which he was steeped, the appellant was intervening to prevent felonious deaths by the evil powers of witchcraft. "The common law requires *mens rea* as an element of a criminal offence. If a person, however, does not know the factual basis for the criminality of his act, how can he know his act is wrong?"

The judge eventually upheld the conviction, though clearly with grave misgivings about the ethical propriety of his decision. The legislature, he said, had enacted an absolute statutory liability for acts of witchcraft: "inherent in the statute

is the requirement that the actor realises what he is doing, but he need not have *mens rea*." He concluded:

> What is required is some solution which will keep this potentially dangerous person under some sort of control until he can be safely released on society, but which will also meet the ethical objection raised when a person without moral guilt is used as an example to others. It must be conceded that this kind of control simply does not exist. The only power the court has to segregate or to restrain is by imprisonment. The court must be guided as to the extent of loss of liberty by the certain risk to the community should the appellant be released in the present state of his beliefs. In all these circumstances, although a sentence of seven years' imprisonment with hard labour may offend ethical principles, it does give a practical solution to the risk to the community. Were the appellant to receive and accept some scientific explanations or to renounce his beliefs, consideration might be given in another place to a release upon licence, but not otherwise. For these reasons the appeal against conviction and sentence is dismissed.

The case was clearly a very difficult one, and the judge's manifest efforts to be fair to all concerned and his embarrassment at the apparent impossibility of doing so cannot but evoke sympathy and admiration. None the less, there is something rather puzzling both about his own account of the effect of his decision and the reasons which he gives for reaching it. The effect of the decision was to rule out self-defence as a defence to the charge of holding a trial by ordeal, and this decision was clearly necessary if the entire prohibition on ordeals was not to be nullified, since if the defence applied once it would apply always. But this does not make the offence into an absolute one: the intent to perform the prohibited action must be there, and that is the form that *mens rea* takes in the majority of crimes. Moreover, in order to rule out self-defence there is no need to make the test of a reasonable belief the reactions of an English man in the street. As was observed by the court in *Lufazema*: "belief in the efficacy of witchcraft might have been held unreasonable for the average man in Malawi also." If legislation is imposed with the express purpose of stamping out a system of beliefs with evil social consequences – whether it be the belief in witchcraft or the belief in the superiority of one race over another – then the belief that it is introduced to eliminate cannot be regarded as reasonable. The reference is not to English culture or to expediency in contrast with justice, but with reference to what the Malawi legislature wished to obtain in Malawi. Assuming that the Malawi legislature was right in imposing the witchcraft statute, then a court would surely be right in holding that a belief in witchcraft was not a reasonable belief.

If there is something wrong with punishing an accused such as Nyuzi, it is surely not that he believed what he was doing to be morally right, nor that the majority of the members of his community would share his belief. The question which really imposes an objection to the enforcement of witchcraft statutes in cases such as *Nyuzi* is rather: Is it right to punish someone for an action undertaken in the light of beliefs which in his situation he could not help but have? This is a particular form of the very general question of whether it is justifiable to blame or punish a person for something he has done when he could not have done otherwise.

Whether in truth the members of communities such as Nyuzi's are in such a condition of unshakeable conviction of the truth of witchcraft is a matter of fact on which it would be impudent for one unacquainted with them to express an opinion. But the question of general

principle is one of the most fundamental philosophical questions that arise concerning the criminal law [. . .] The metaphysical objection to responsibility, as I have said, arises from the supposition of determinism. If determinism is true, and if people should not be held responsible in cases where they could not do otherwise than they have done, then it seems that no one should ever be held responsible for anything. Supposing, then, that determinism is true – and surely many intelligent and well-informed people believe that it is – how can we any longer uphold the notion of responsibility in our courts of law?

Notes

1   The National Association for Mental Health, *Evidence for Submission to the Committee on Mentally Abnormal Offenders* unpublished paper, pp. 1–2.
2   In A. Kenny, *Wittgenstein*, Penguin, Harmondsworth, 1975.
3   This account of the mind is expounded in the first chapter of A. Kenny, *Will, Freedom and Power*, Blackwell, Oxford, 1975.
4   *Nyuzi and Kudemera* v *Republic*, (1966–8) *African Law Reports*, 249.
5   (1947), 14 E. A. C. A. 96.
6   (1923–60) A. L. R. Malawi 488.
7   High Court of Malawi, 1 May 1967.
8   West African Court of Appeal, unreported; considered in *Nyuzi and Kudemera, op. cit.*, p. 259.

41

Between Impunity and Show Trials

Martti Koskenniemi

When former President Milosevic began his defence at The Hague on Tuesday, 12 February 2002, there was no reason to be surprised by his chosen tactics. By turning the accusing finger towards the West, in particular the members of the North Atlantic Treaty Organization (NATO), for their alleged complicity in first destroying what Milosevic called "mini-Yugoslavia" (Bosnia–Herzegovina) and in 1999 conducting an aggression against his own country, he aimed to avoid conducting his defence under conditions laid down by his adversaries. At the same time, his manoeuvre highlights, once again, the difficulty of grappling with large political crises by means of individual criminal responsibility and gives reason to question the ability of criminal trial to express or conserve the "truth" of a complex series of events involving the often erratic action by major international players, Great Powers, the European Union, the United Nations, and so on. The Milosevic trial – like international criminal law generally – oscillates ambivalently between the wish to punish those individually responsible for large humanitarian disasters and the danger of becoming a show trial.

I. Why Punish?

Bringing Milosevic to The Hague has been celebrated as the most significant event in the international efforts to end the culture of impunity, under way since the establishment of the Yugoslavian and Rwandan war crimes tribunals in 1993 and 1994, the adoption of the Statute of the International Criminal Court in 1998 and the commencement of criminal procedures in several countries against former domestic or foreign political leaders. The record of these events is mixed. But there is no doubt that they manifest a renewed urge today to think about international politics in terms of domestic categories. The universalisation of the Rule of Law calls for the realisation of criminal responsibility in the international as in the domestic sphere. In the liberal view, there should be no outside-of-law: everyone, regardless of place of activity or formal position, should be accountable for their deeds.[1]

Yet, as Hannah Arendt pointed out during the Nuremberg trials, "[h]anging Göring is certainly necessary but totally inadequate. For this

Martti Koskenniemi, "Between Impunity and Show Trials," *Max Planck Yearbook of United Nations Law*, vol. 6, 2002, pp. 1–35. © 2002. Reprinted with permission from Koninklijke BRILL NV.

culpability . . . transcends and destroys all legal order."[2] What she meant, of course, was that sometimes a tragedy may be so great, a series of events of such political or even metaphysical significance, that punishing an individual does not come close to measuring up to it. In nearly all the criminal prosecutions concerned with crimes against humanity committed during or after World War II, some observers have doubted the ability of the criminal law to deal with the events precisely in view of their enormous moral, historical, or political significance.

The philosopher Karl Jaspers, for instance, wrote to Arendt in 1960, a few months before the opening of the Eichmann trial, pointing to the extent to which the events for which he was accused "stand outside the pale of what is comprehensible in human and moral terms" and that "[s]omething other than law [was] at stake here – and to address it in legal terms [was] a mistake."[3] The same argument was heard occasionally in connection with the more recent trials in France of Klaus Barbie, "the butcher of Lyon" in 1987, and of the two Frenchmen Paul Touvier and Maurice Papon, in 1994 and 1998 respectively. And today, it seems clear that whether or not Milosevic goes to prison is in no way an "adequate" response to the fact that over 200,000 people lost their lives – while millions more were affected – by the succession of wars in the former Yugoslavia. If the trial has significance, then that significance must lie elsewhere than in the punishment handed out to him.

Because this is so plainly evident, it is often argued that trials involving genocide or crimes against humanity are less about judging a person than about establishing the truth of the events. While the prosecution of Eichmann in Jerusalem in 1961, for example, was almost universally held to be necessary, few thought that the necessity lay in the need of punishing Eichmann, the person. He was, after all, only a cog in the Nazi killing machine. Instead, the trial was held to be necessary in order to bring to publicity the full extent of the horrors of the "Nazi war against the Jews,"[4] especially as that aspect of the German criminality had, in the view of many, received only insufficient attention in the Nuremberg process. For the State of Israel, the trial was to bring to light a central aspect of the nation's history, and

to take a step towards explaining how it all could have happened.[5] What was to be Eichmann's fate after the trial would be of secondary consequence. Indeed, Elie Wiesel suggested that Eichmann should be simply set free, while Arendt advocated handing him over to the United Nations.[6] His death would in no way redress the enormity of the crime in which he had been implicated. It might even diminish the extent to which the special nature of that crime lay in its collective nature as part of the official policy of the German nation.

The view of criminal justice – also the Milosevic trial – as an instrument of truth and memory has been stated precisely in response to criticisms about criminal law's apparently obsessive concentration on the accused. This aspect of it was highlighted during the early years of the Yugoslavia Tribunal as it proved impossible to bring those accused of war crimes to trial in The Hague. The Tribunal resorted to the procedure that allows the reading of the indictment in open court and the issuing of an international arrest warrant in the absence of the accused.[7] The reasoning behind a "tribunal de verbe" as the procedure was opened on 27 June 1996 against Karadzic and Mladic has been summarised as follows:

> Incapable jusqu'ici de rendre la justice, contraint de laisser sans châtiment des crimes contre l'humanité et un génocide, le travail du TPI prenait subitement une réelle consistance: la vérité pouvait au moins être dite devant les juges et les victimes reconnues comme telles, face au monde.[8]

Recording "the truth" and declaring it to the world through the criminal process has been held important for reasons that have little to do with the punishment of the individual. Instead, it has been thought necessary so as to enable the commencement of the healing process in the victim: only when the injustice to which a person has been subjected has been publicly recognised, the conditions for recovering from trauma are present and the dignity of the victim may be restored. Facing the truth of its past is a necessary condition to enable a wounded community – a community of perpetrators and victims – to recreate the conditions of viable social life.[9] Nuremberg, Eichmann and the three French trials (as well as more recent processes focusing on torture in Algeria) have each been defended as necessary for didactic purposes, for establishing an impartial account of the past and for teaching younger generations of the dangers involved in particular policies.[10]

It is hard to assess the psychological credibility of such justifications. In Germany, the didactic effects of Nuremberg have been obscure. At the time of the process itself 78 per cent of the German population regarded the trial as "just" while a similar poll four years later showed only 38 per cent to have this opinion. Many reasons must have contributed to such change of perception: allied policy in occupied Germany, attitudes towards de-Nazification and the sense of Nuremberg as victor's justice.[11] German legal literature of the immediate postwar period usually treated the International Military Tribunal as an occupation court (*Besatzungsgericht*) rather than as an international tribunal.[12] The trials held in the American occupation zone during 1946–9, too, were intended "to reform and re-educate the German people."[13] However, they were compromised from the outset. Influential members of the US judiciary – including judges from the tribunals themselves – had serious doubts about the constitutionality and procedural fairness of the trials and congressional support for them was thin. Under such conditions, little sympathy could be expected for the trials from the German population.[14] In 1952, only 10 per cent of Germans approved of them.[15] "To be tried by a Nuremberg Military Tribunal signified at least in the Federal Republic of Germany no dishonour."[16]

Over the years, the German government, communities and individuals have taken far-reaching steps to keep alive and come to terms with the memory of the crimes of the Hitler regime.[17] But criminal justice has not been at the forefront of *Vergangenheitsbewältigung*. The Auschwitz process that terminated in Frankfurt in 1965 had only slight popular response, despite widespread press and TV coverage. In that same year, the Ministries of Justice of the Länder commenced a systematic effort to prosecute Nazi criminals: though the annual number of new dossiers rose in peak years to over 2,000, the highest number of annual convictions was 39,

and declined by 1976 to fewer than ten a year.[18] Empirical confirmation about the positive effects of truth-telling is not much more available from other sources, either. The most significant effort in this regard, the South African Truth and Reconciliation Commission (TRC), was hugely controversial when it was set up, and much of that controversy persists. In a recent poll in South Africa, only 17 per cent of the interviewed persons felt that process had had a positive effect while altogether two-thirds expressed the opinion that race relations after the TRC had deteriorated.[19]

Undoubtedly, many kinds of truth may be sought through criminal trials. The "denial of the Holocaust," for instance, has been criminalized in a number of countries in part to honour the memory of the victims, in part to uphold the conventions of truthfulness and good faith that found the discursive basis of the state. The 1985 law in the Federal Republic of Germany that prohibits "lying about Auschwitz" not only seeks to preserve the memory of the Holocaust but also and perhaps above all the legitimacy of the new Germany by keeping open the gap between it and its Nazi predecessor.[20] The more distant the events, the more fragile their truth becomes and thus, it may seem, the more necessary to protect it by the law. And yet, as Lawrence Douglas points out, the agnostic formalism of the law that accepts all historical accounts as *prima facie* of equal value may, in an adversarial process, end up inadvertently legitimating "negationism" as a position on which reasonable men may disagree.[21]

In a similar way, the strategy chosen by Milosevic in The Hague reveals the danger of thinking about international criminal trials in historical or didactic terms. This was the gist of Arendt's controversial critique of the Eichmann trial. For her, the trial's problems arose from the introduction of historical, political, and educational objectives into it.

> The purpose of the trial is to render justice, and nothing else; even the noblest ulterior purposes – "the making of a record of the Hitler regime . . ." can only detract from the law's main business: to weigh the charges brought against the accused, to render judgment and to mete out due punishment.[22]

By contrast, Arendt wrote, the Eichmann trial had become a "show trial,"[23] staged by the Prime Minister, David Ben-Gurion to support political motives which had nothing to do with criminal trials as Arendt understood them, as being about the guilt or innocence of individuals.

But should Arendt have the final word? Many of the problems of applying criminal law in response to massive injustice have become evident in the reactions to her critiques. Surely, as many of those involved in the process that led to the signature of the Statute for the International Criminal Court in 1998 seem to have assumed, the value of the new court lies in its deterrent message, the way in which it serves to prevent future atrocities.[24] The force of this argument is, however, doubtful. In the first place, if crimes against humanity really emerge from what Kant labelled "radical evil," an evil that exceeds the bounds of instrumental rationality, that seeks no objective beyond itself, then by definition, calculations about the likelihood of future punishment do not enter the picture. Indeed, there is no calculation in the first place. But even if one remained suspicious about the metaphysics of "radical evil" (as Arendt herself later became) the deterrence argument would still fail to convince inasmuch as the atrocities of the 20th century have not emerged from criminal intent but as offshoots from a desire to do good.[25] This is most evident in regard to the crimes of communism, the Gulag, the Ukraine famine, liquidation of the "Kulaks." But even the worst Nazi nightmares were connected to a project to create a better world. Commenting upon the speeches of Heinrich Himmler to the SS in 1942, Alain Besançon concluded that even the death camps were operated "au nom d'un bien, sous le couvert d'une morale."[26] But if the acts do not evidence criminal intent, and instead come about as aspects of ideological programmes that strive for the good life, however far in the future, or to save the world from a present danger, then the deterrence argument seems beside the point.[27] In such cases, criminal law itself will come to seem a part of the world which must be set aside, an aspect of the "evil" that the ideology seeks to eradicate.

As criminal lawyers know well, fitting crimes against humanity or other massive human rights violations into the deterrence frame requires some rather implausible psychological generalisations. Either the crimes are aspects of political normality – Arendt's "banality of evil" – in which case there is no *mens rea*, or they take place in exceptional situations of massive destruction and personal danger when there is little liberty of action.[28] This is not to say that in such cases, people act as automatons, losing capacity for independent judgement. Many studies have elucidated the way individuals react to pressure created by either normality or exceptionality, and are sometimes able to resist. But it is implausible to believe that criminal law is able to teach people to become heroes, not least because what "heroism" might mean in particular situations is often at the heart of the confrontation between the political values underlying the criminal justice system (perhaps seen as victor's justice) and the system that is on trial.

And then there is of course the very politics behind the establishment and functioning of a tribunal in the aftermath of a great crisis that may not always support the grandiloquent rhetoric that accompanies, on the victors' side, the work of justice, so conveniently underwriting their views and post-conflict preferences. By the end of the 1940s, Allied preferences had shifted dramatically. There was no political support for the trials of German industrialists and proceedings against high-ranking professional soldiers were followed with some embarrassment. Fear of communism, Germanophilia, sometimes anti-semitism, as well as administrative problems connected with further punishments, made the principal Allied powers wary of further purges in Germany and keen to establish normal relations with it.[29] At least some of this supported the widespread German opposition to the Allied war crimes trial programme of 1946–9: "Germans saw themselves as victims and not as perpetrators."[30]

In the Yugoslavian situation, too, it may not be exclusively the result of manipulation by the local leaders that the populations often seem to have little faith in the truth propounded by the Tribunal. The fluctuation of Western support, the visible impunity enjoyed by a large number of important Balkan war criminals, and the failure to prosecute the NATO bombings of Serbia of 1999 have provided space for cynicism and denial. Four years after the horrors of Srebrenica, Serbs residing in the area persist in claiming that "[n]othing happened here. . . . It is all propaganda."[31]

For such reasons, studies on the transformations of authoritarian regimes into more or less liberal democracies in central and eastern Europe, South America and South Africa have suggested a much more complex understanding of the role of criminal trials as not merely about punishment or retribution, nor indeed about deterrence, but as an aspect of a larger "transitional justice" that, in the words of one commentator, sometimes "perform . . . a successful 'final judgement' in the religious sense, a performance that would ultimately enable the state itself to function as a moral agent."[32] Under this view, it is the symbolism of the criminal trial – and the eventual judgement – that enables the community ritually to affirm its guiding principles and thus to become a workable "moral community."

But no uniform jurisprudence has emerged on the use of criminal trials of former political leaders in transition situations. Perhaps the main generalisation that can be made is that such trials have been few, they have been targeted very selectively, the convictions have been moderate and amnesties have been widely used.[33] The legal principles have been vigorously contested, the main controversy focusing on to what extent such trials are only political instruments to target former adversaries on the basis of laws that were not in force at the time they were acting.

But whether the trials use superpositive law (such as the "Radbruch formula" in Germany) or retrospective interpretation of pre-transition law,[34] it seems clear that in order to attain the symbolic, community-creating effect it is supposed to have, criminal law need not be applied to everyone. It is sufficient that a few well-published trials are held at which the "truth" of the past is demonstrated, the victims' voices are heard and the moral principles of the (new) community are affirmed.[35]

This may sometimes become a logistic necessity, too. In 1946, for instance, over 100,000 suspected war criminals resided in the British and American occupation zones in Germany. And in 2001 the Rwandan prisons housed approximately 120,000 detainees. A full trial of each individual was in both cases an impossibility. In the Rwandan situation, an attempt is being made to use "Gacaca courts," popular tribunals akin to truth commissions to expedite the work of justice and the prospect of reconciliation.[36] Clearly, at least sometimes victims do not so much expect punishment (though of course that is not insignificant) but rather a recognition of the fact that what they were made to suffer was "wrong," and that their moral grandeur is symbolically affirmed.[37] For such purposes, "show trials" are quite sufficient, especially if they are supplemented with other measures such as compensations, disqualifications, administrative measures, truth commissions, opening of archives, etc. However, such supplementary measures are not available at the international level. And here is the problem with the analogy between international courts and transitional justice. The reasons that make "show trials" – that is to say, trials of only few political leaders – acceptable, even beneficial, at the national level, while others are granted amnesty, are not present when criminal justice is conducted at the international plane. When trials are conducted by a foreign prosecutor, and before foreign judges, no moral community is being affirmed beyond the elusive and self-congratulatory "international community." Every failure to prosecute is a scandal, every judgement too little to restore the dignity of the victims, and no symbolism persuasive enough to justify the drawing of the thick line between the past and the future.[38]

In other words, if the argument of deterrence is unpersuasive as a justification of international criminal justice, and if the symbolic, community-creative rationales can be invoked only with the greatest difficulty, the temptation is great to see the point of the Milosevic trial in its truth-telling function, against the critiques by Arendt and others. Perhaps, the argument might go, the trial is important neither because it may end up punishing Milosevic, because it makes potential dictators or their henchmen think twice, nor because it enables the recreation of Balkan societies as moral communities. Perhaps, we might think, the significance of this "trial of the century" lies in the way it will bring to general knowledge the truth of what really happened – however and by whom that "truth" is then used by anyone at the national or the international level.

II. Of Truth and Context

As criminal lawyers have always known, legal and historical truth are far from identical. The wider the context in which individual guilt has to be understood, and the more such understanding defers to the contingencies of historical interpretation, the more evident the limits of criminal procedure for reaching the "truth."[39] One of the few uncontroversial merits of truth commissions vis-à-vis criminal justice has been stated to lie in the way the former are able to canvass much more widely and deeply the criminality under scrutiny and thus to offer more "opportunities for closure, healing and reconciliation."[40] This is not to say that there would be no intrinsic relationship between the two types of truth, historical and criminal. In the domestic society, and in the context of a domestic criminal trial, that relationship rarely becomes questioned. Even if a crime is exceptionally shocking – "serial killing" for example – there is normally little doubt about how to understand the relevant acts in their historical context. The only problem is "did the accused do it?" No further question about how to understand what he did, how to place his behaviour in relation to the overall behaviour of those around him, emerges. The truth of the broader context is one, or at least relatively uncontested. In transitional periods, however, the debate about past normality takes on a contested, political aspect. How to deal with the routine spying by citizens of one another, shooting at those wishing to escape, or systematic liquidation of political opponents? How to judge the actions of individuals living and working in a "criminal" normality (Unrechtsstaat): how much "heroism" is needed? What about (mere) passivity? And last but not least – can those judge who have not lived under such conditions?[41]

Much of this applies in the international sphere, too, where problems of interpretation are even more difficult. For any major event of international politics – and situations where the criminal responsibility of political leaders is invoked are inevitably such – there are many truths and many stakeholders for them. In the Milosevic trial, for instance, the narrative of "Greater Serbia" collides head-on with the self-determination stories of the seceding populations, while political assessments of "socialism" and "nationalism" compete with long-term historical and even religious frames of explanation. Much of the Western view depends on a (liberal) understanding of the sombre effects of the allegedly atavistic irrationalism underlying the different Balkan identifications – a view that dramatically plays down the political aspects of the conflict and the role of interest-groups (including the liberal one) in fomenting ethnic hostility. How to understand the actions of the leaders of the Yugoslav communities – whether they were "criminal" or not – depends on which framework of interpretation one accepts.[42]

Political Realists such as Hans Morgenthau always highlighted the weaknesses of the legal process in coming to grips with large events of international politics. Already in 1929, Morgenthau concluded that the role of formal dispute settlement had to remain limited in the international context because it inevitably focused only on some in itself minor aspect of an overall situation. A legal "dispute" for him was always just a part – and sometimes a very marginal part – of what he called a political "tension."[43] The narrower the focus, the less the process would convey any in-depth understanding of the situation and the less reason to think that it will bring about a credible political result. Because the legal process inevitably distorted the political context, it was not only useless but counterproductive for the purpose of providing a basis for peace and reconciliation.

The effort to end the "culture of impunity" emerges from an interpretation of the past – the Cold War in particular – as an unacceptably political approach to international crises. Focusing on the individual abstracts the political context, that is to say, describes it in terms of the actions and intentions of particular, well-situated individuals. Indeed, this is precisely what the Prosecutor in the Milosevic trial, Carla del Ponte, said she was doing in The Hague in February 2002. The (Serb) nation was not on trial, only an individual was. But the truth is not necessarily served by an individual focus.[44] On the contrary, the meaning of historical events often exceeds the intentions or actions of particular individuals and can be grasped only by attention to structural causes, such as economic or functional necessities, or a broad institutional logic through which the actions by individuals create social effects. Typically, among historians, the "intentionist" explanations of the destruction of European Jewry are opposed by "functional" explanations that point to the material and structural causes that finally at the Wannsee conference of 1942 – but not until then – turned Nazi policy towards full-scale extermination. When Arendt and others were criticising the Eichmann trial, they pointed to the inability of an individual focus to provide an understanding of the way the Shoah did not come about as a series of actions by deviant individuals with a criminal mind but through *Schreibtisch* acts by obedient servants of a criminal state.

This is why individualisation is not neutral in its effects. Use of terms such as "Hitlerism" or "Stalinism" leaves intact the political, moral and organisational structures that are the necessary condition of the crime.[45] To focus on individual leaders may even serve as an alibi for the population at large to relieve itself from responsibility. Something of this took place in the trials of Nazi criminals in Germany after World War II. The failure of the Allied powers to agree on a "trial of industrialists" may have reflected emerging concern in the West about the appearance of a new enemy – the Soviet Union – and the need to enlist a democratic Germany on their side. But it dramatically downplayed the degree of participation by German economy and society in the Nazi crimes.[46] As the prosecutions moved to German courts, Allied legislation, particularly Control Council Law No. 10, was set aside as contrary to the principle of non-retroactivity. Recourse was made to the German Penal Law whose relevant provisions had to do with murder and manslaughter. These described the relevant criminality in purely individual terms. Murder, under the interpretation of the *Bundesgerichtshof*, had to take place with a "murderous intent" (*Mordlust*) or "in a malicious and brutal manner" in a way that completely failed to grasp the kind of writing desk action of which most Nazi criminality consisted and in which individuals could (rightly) believe themselves as fully replaceable if they did not carry out their tasks in accordance with the rules that themselves were criminal.[47] By the time of the Auschwitz trials in Frankfurt in 1963–5, the crime of manslaughter had already been subject to the statute of limitations so that the defendants could only be tried for murder, and because of a definition of murder that referred to individual intent failed to apply to any but the most brutal operators of the extermination system, most of the Nazis not only escaped judgement but were integrated as loyal citizens of the Bonn republic.[48]

The point here is not to try to settle the epistemological controversy about whether the individual or the contextual (functional, structural) focus provides the better truth but, rather, that neither can *a priori* override the other and that in some situations it is proper to focus on individuals while in other cases – such as Nazi criminality, and perhaps in taking stock of *Stasi* collaboration in the GDR – the context provides the better frame of interpretation. But if that is so, then there is no guarantee that a criminal process *a priori* oriented towards individual guilt such as the Milosevic trial necessarily enacts a lesson of historical truth. On the contrary, it may rather obstruct this process by exonerating from responsibility those larger (political, economic, even legal) structures within which the conditions for individual criminality have been created – within which the social normality of a criminal society emerges.

As the German historian Martin Broszat has pointed out, the "one-sided personalisation" and rigid conceptualisation of criminal categories may lead not only to a different kind of truth but also a different way of distributing accountability from that produced by a contextually oriented historical study in a situation such as Germany under the Hitler regime.[49] If one is participating in a collective venture with a sense of historical mission and a moral purpose ("happiness of mankind") such as "communism," for instance, then little is gained by a retrospective interpretation of the effects of that effort – between 85 to 100 million innocent killed – in terms of the evil acts of some number of individuals. The logic of "tentation du bien, mémoire de mal" at work in communism can only be reached through trying to grasp the collective process that combines utopianism and scientism with a revolutionary spirit.[50]

Notes

1 The description of the campaign for ending the culture of impunity as an aspect of the legalist–domestic analogy is usefully discussed in G. Bass, *Stay the Hand of Vengeance. The Politics of War Crimes Tribunals* (2000), 8–36.

2 Quoted in N. Frei, "Le retour du droit en Allemagne. La justice et l'histoire contemporaine après l'Holocauste – un bilan provisoire," in F. Brayard (ed.), *Le génocide des Juifs entre procès et histoire 1943–2000* (2000), 57.

3 L. Kohler and H. Kohler (eds), *Hannah Arendt – Karl Jaspers. Correspondence 1926–1969* (1996), 410. Quoted also in L. Douglas, *The Memory of Judgment. Making Law and History in the Trials of the Holocaust* (2001), 174–5. Here Jaspers was undoubtedly drawing upon his *Die Schuldfrage* (1946).

4 In her *The Nazi War Against the Jews: 1933–1945* (1975), Lucy Davidowicz stresses the extent to which the Holocaust was not an accidental offshoot but a deliberate choice of the Hitler regime.

5 This was certainly the perspective taken by the Prosecutor, Gideon Hausner, whom Arendt saw as simply "obeying his master," David Ben-Gurion, the Prime Minister; H. Arendt, *Eichmann in Jerusalem. A Report on the Banality of Evil*, rev. and enlarged edition (1963), 5. For an excellent recent discussion of this aspect of the trial, cf. Douglas, see note 3, 97 et seq., 150–82.

6 Arendt, see above, 270–1.

7 Rule 61 of the Rules of the Tribunal: "Procedure in case of failure to execute a warrant."

8 P. Hazan, *La justice face à la guerre. De Nuremberg à la Haye* (2000), 134.

9 Cf. e.g. J. Verhoeven, "Vers un ordre répressif universel?" *AFDI* 45 (1999), writing about criminal justice in terms of "une fonction qui l'on dirait 'consolatrice', d'ordre thérapeutique et pédagogiqce . . . la quiétude et la sérénité," 55 et seq., (60). In regard to the Rwandan genocide of 1994, D. D. Ntanda Nserko, "Genocidal Conflict in Rwanda and the ICTR," *NILR* 48 (2001), 62 et seq.

10 For a summary of such justifications, cf. A. Cassese, "On the Current Trend towards Criminal Prosecution and Punishment for Breaches of International Humanitarian Law," *EJIL* 9 (1998), 2 et seq. (9–10).

11 Frei, see note 2, 62–7.

12 S. Jung, *Die Rechtsprobleme der Nürnberger Prozesse* (1992), 89–92, 109–11.

13 F. M. Buscher, *The US War Crimes Trials Programme in Germany, 1946–1955* (1989), 69.

14 During 1946–9, twelve US military tribunals sitting in Nuremberg heard cases of 185 to 199 defendants (numbers vary according to source) while a US Army European Command set up its own process, conducted at Dachau that tried 1672 individuals. The trials were vehemently criticised by various United States and German organisations. Though the processes ended in a large number of convictions, most of the sentences were later reduced and a large number of the convicted amnestied in 1951. The summary of the history of those trials is negative: ". . . the war crimes programme did little to change German attitudes. Cries of foul play and 'victor's justice' accompanied the proceedings. . . . The constant attacks against the Allies, especially the United States as the main instigator of those proceedings in the late 1940's by Germany's church leaders, politicians, veterans' and refugee organizations demonstrated that the war crimes programme had not reeducated and democratized the Germans," Buscher, see note 13, 22. For the domestic US critiques, cf. ibid., 29–47. For the uses of administrative reviews and amnesties, cf. ibid., 49–89.

15 Buscher, see note 13, 91.

16 Jung, see note 12, 5.

17 For a detailed review, cf. e.g. A. Grosser, *Le crime et la mémoire* (1989), 87–132.

18 Cf. A. Rückerl, *NS-Verbrechen vor Gericht. Versuch einer Vergangenheitsbewältigung* (1984), 330; Grosser, see note 17, 112–13, 121.

19 E. Kiss, "Moral Ambition Within and Beyond Political Constraints. Reflections on Restorative Justice," in R. J. Rotberg and D. Thompson, *Truth v. Justice. The Morality of Truth Commissions* (2000), 88, and Rotberg, "Truth Commissions and the Provision of Truth, Justice, and Reconciliation," ibid., 19.

20 L. Douglas, "Régenter le passé: Le négationnisme et la loi," in Brayard, see note 2, 218–23.

21 Douglas, see note 20, 227–38.

22 Arendt, see note 5, 251.

23 Arendt, see note 5, 4–5.

24 Thus one advocate: ". . . punishment of war criminals should be motivated primarily by its deterrent effect, by the impetus it gives to improved standards of international conduct," C. M. Bassiouni, *Crimes against Humanity in International Law* (1992), 14. A particularly thoughtful argument is in P. Akhavan, "Beyond Impunity. Can International Criminal Justice Prevent Future Atrocities?" *AJIL* 95 (2001), 7 et seq.

25 Cf. especially T. Todorov, *Tentation du bien, mémoire du mal* (2000).

26 A. Besançon, *Le malheur du siècle. Sur le commun-isme, le nazisme et l'unicité de la Shoah* (1998), 45.

27 Cf. J. Klabbers, "Just Revenge? The Deterrence Argument in International Criminal Law," in *Finnish YBIL* 11 (2000).

28 For a recent analysis, cf. I. Tallgren, "The Sensibility and Sense of International Criminal Law," in *EJIL* 13 (2002).

29 Cf. D. Bloxham, *Genocide on Trial, War Crimes Trials and the Formation of Holocaust History and Memory* (2001), 38–56.

30 Buscher, see note 13, 110.

31 Hazan, see note 8, 245–7.

32 J. Borneman, *Settling Accounts. Violence, Justice and Accountability in Postsocialist Europe* (1997), 23.

33 Cf. R. G. Teitel, *Transitional Justice* (2000), especially 51–9.

34 For this controversy after German unification, especially in relation to the GDR border guard trials and the trials of Honecker and the former Politbüro members, cf. J. McAdams, *Judging the Past in Unified Germany* (2001), 23–54.

35 Teitel, see note 33, 46–9, 66.

36 Cf. K. C. Moghadli, "No Peace without Justice. The Role of International Criminal and Humanitarian Law in Conflict Settlement and Reconciliation," paper given at a conference "From Impunity to a Culture of Accountability," Utrecht 26–28 November 2001.

37 Cf. e.g. P. Bouretz, "Prescription: table ronde du 22 janvier 1999," *Droits* 31 (2000), 53.

38 For this criticism in regard to the ICTY, cf. Hazan, see note 8, 239–63.

39 Cf. M. Wildt, "Des vérités qui diffèrent. Historiens et procureurs face aux crimes de Nazis," in Brayard, see note 2, 251–7. Cf. also D. Lochak, "Prescription, remarques dans une table ronde du 22 janvier 1999," *Droits* 31 (2000), 49–54.

40 Kiss, see note 19, 69.

41 For discussion of this difficulty in the German situation, cf. Borneman, see note 32, 80–96, 99–100; McAdams, see note 34, 47–54.

42 For the role of such interpretations in the Milosevic trial, cf. K. Čavoški, "Juger l'histoire," in P. Marie Gallois and J. Vergès, *L'apartheid judiciaire au TPI, arme de guerre* (2002), 77–89.

43 H. Morgenthau, *Die internationale Rechtspflege, ihr Wesen und ihre Grenzen* (1929), 62–72 and *passim*. For the general context and a discussion, cf. M. Koskenniemi, *The Gentle Civilizer of Nations. The Rise and Fall of International Law 1870–1960* (2002), 440–5.

44 Wildt, see note 39, 251.

45 As pointed out in Grosser, see note 17, 76–7.

46 Cf. Bloxham, see note 29, 28–32.

47 For an account of the procedural difficulties in prosecuting former Nazis in Germany under the common criminal law, cf. Rückerl, see note 18, 261–88.

48 Cf. D. O. Pendas, " 'Auschwitz, je ne savais pas ce que c'était'. Le procès d'Auschwitz à Francfort et l'opinion public allemande," in Brayard, see note 2, 85–93. Cf. also Douglas, see note 3, 188–90.

49 H. Graml and K. D. Henke, *Nach Hitler. Der schwierige Umgang mit unserer Geschichte. Beiträge von Martin Broszat* (1987), 47–9.

50 Todorov, see note 25, 36–41; Besançon, see note 26, 59–64.

42

Atrocity, Punishment, and International Law

Mark Drumbl

Deterrence

Deterrence theory justifies punishment not because it is deserved, but rather because punishment consequentially builds a safer world.[1] Insofar as deterrence assumes that individuals will be dissuaded from offending (or reoffending) because they fear getting punished, it posits that law is capable of fulfilling a social engineering function. Deterrence can be specific to individual offenders or general to the community of potential offenders. There is some scattered reference to the merits of specific deterrence in the jurisprudence of institutions that punish extraordinary international criminals.[2] However, the focus overwhelmingly is on general deterrence, namely the notion that if one person is punished, this will reduce the likelihood that another person in that same place or somewhere else will offend in the future.[3] As an ICTR Trial Chamber intoned, punishment "dissuade[s] for ever[] others who may be tempted in the future to perpetrate such atrocities [. . .]."[4] The UN Secretary-General has explicitly endorsed the value of the international criminal tribunals in "deter[ring] further horrors."[5]

Can criminal law deter atrocity? Although there are scattered anecdotal reports that suggest that potential extraordinary international criminals are deterred by the punishment of others following criminal trials,[6] no systematized or conclusive evidence has been proffered.[7] In any event, any anecdotal research must absorb the reality that at times atrocity has continued to occur in places following the creation of criminal tribunals to punish perpetrators. The ICTY stands out as an example. It was created in 1993. However, some of the gravest atrocities in the former Yugoslavia, including the Srebrenica massacre (1995) and Kosovo ethnic cleansing (1998), occurred while the ICTY was in full operation. Assuredly, it is somewhat facile to conclude that deterrence may not be actualized just because atrocity continues after the establishment of a punishing institution. After all, we can never know how much worse atrocity might have been if no institution ever had been created. That said, all things considered, just because we may have some cause to think that some deterrence has been achieved does not mean that the extant paradigm effectively deters. Other approaches to sanctioning universally repugnant crimes might be more adept in attaining deterrent aspirations.

One reality that deterrence theory must contend with is the very low chance that offenders ever are accused or, if accused, that they ever are

Mark Drumbl, chapter 6 from *Atrocity, Punishment and International Law* (Cambridge University Press, 2007), pp. 169–80. © 2007 by Mark A. Drumbl. Reprinted with permission from the author and Cambridge University Press.

taken into the custody of criminal justice institutions. Selectivity is especially corrosive to the
deterrent value of prosecution and punishment.
Criminologists long have posited that it is the
chance of getting caught and the promptness
of punishment, and not the severity of punishment, that affects behavior.[8] International
tribunals are particularly vexed by the difficulties
they experience in capturing indictees. Insofar
as international tribunals lack their own police
force or agents of enforcement, they can become
dependent on the cooperation of the same
national authorities whose jurisdiction they may
have ousted. In its early years, the ICTY was
stymied by the difficulty it experienced in capturing
indictees. ICTY officials tenaciously persevered,
however, and, as of December 2005, only 6 out
of a total of 161 indictees remain at large
(although, for the moment, this group includes
high-profile suspects such as Mladić and
Karadzić).[9] Eighteen of the ICTR indictees
remain at large (the ICTR has arrested seventy-
two individuals). Before closing up shop, the
East Timor Special Panels were able to prosecute
only 87 of 370 indicted individuals. Many indictees
roam around free in Indonesia.

Moreover, being brought into custody to face
trial is one thing; actually being convicted is
another. International criminal law's focus on
individual culpability provable beyond a reasonable doubt – a hallmark of liberal legalism –
sharply reduces the number of people who can
plausibly be brought into the dock because there
always is a risk that insufficiently compelling
evidence will lead to an acquittal. This risk is
cited as one of the reasons in favor of introducing vicarious liability theories into international
criminal law, such as JCE, to which the field
exhibits considerable skittishness. Although JCE
may promote deterrence by increasing the number of potential convicts, any such increase is a
minor one at the margins. There are only a small
number of defendants for whom JCE has played
a material difference in terms of the prospect
of conviction.

In some cases, national institutions are more
successful in obtaining custody over accused
offenders. In Rwanda, well over one hundred
thousand accused have been taken into custody.
However, in other contexts few (and sometimes
no) suspects are indicted or taken into custody

by national authorities. National institutions often
are crimped in the exercise of criminal punishment by amnesties that, in certain cases, may
be implemented for eminently laudable goals
of political transition or peace. In other cases,
national authorities simply elect to forget the past.

In sum, the chances of getting caught for
committing egregious violations of human
rights – certainly for heads of state and superior
officers – are higher today than they were prior
to the establishment of institutions at the international level. That said, notwithstanding the
fact that the prospect of getting caught is greater
than it once was, it still remains tiny.

At this juncture, an interlocutor committed to
deterrence theory might respond: if the problem
is limited to a lack of institutions, constabulary,
and finances, that problem is easy to rectify.
Just create more institutions! Provide more
money! And, thereby, increase the likelihood of
getting caught. Accordingly, so goes the argument,
shortcomings with deterrence are not intrinsic
to the theory. Instead, they derive from the functionally inadequate way in which the theory
currently is implemented: the deterrence objective is attainable, but remains underachieved by
virtue of administrative limitations.

At first blush, it seems plausible that creating
new institutions might go some way to augment
deterrence. However, I remain unconvinced that,
fundamentally, the existence of more liberal
legalist punishing institutions would *effectively*
deter committed extraordinary international
criminals. This is because deterrence's assumption
of a certain degree of perpetrator rationality,
which is grounded in liberalism's treatment of the
ordinary common criminal, seems particularly
ill fitting for those who perpetrate atrocity. This
assumption already is hotly debated within the
context of isolated common crime. However,
its viability is even more problematic in the context of the chaos of massive violence, incendiary
propaganda, and upended social order that
contours atrocity. Do genocidal fanatics, industrialized into well-oiled machineries of death,
make cost–benefit analyses prior to beginning
work? In the specific case of terrorism, will a
suicide bomber be deterred by fear of punishment in the event of capture? Although certain
people may be deterred from killing or raping
in pursuit of eliminationist goals by a fear of

imminent retaliation (i.e., an enemy army coming around the corner), there is little to suggest that the threat of punishment by a distant international court would deter. I am not alone in my skepticism.[10] Mégret opines that "[i]t beggars belief to suggest that the average crazed nationalist purifier or abused child soldier . . . will be deterred by the prospect of facing trial."[11] He adds that this assumption is "a typical case of liberalism's hegemonious tendency of constructing the other in its own self-image, preferably along the lines of some reductionist form of economic rational choice theory."[12]

Let us examine two painful realities that jeopardize the assumption of perpetrator rationality amid cataclysmic events. These are: first, gratification; and, second, survival.

First, many perpetrators *want* to belong to violent groups.[13] They find comfort and solidarity in these groups. For many participants, violence has meaning and is compelling. Although certain group organizers may be coldly motivated by bureaucratic ambitions (such as Adolf Eichmann's goal of advancing his career) that might be deterred by the threat of eventual punishment or demotion, many individuals organized as foot soldiers of evil share an affective motivation for discriminatory killing. They are captured by angry social norms or, at least, are captivated by them. As Jaime Malamud-Goti observes, many participants believe that they are acting for the benefit of the collective, not their own personal gain.[14] It is simply not evident that the risk of punishment will deter people from engaging in violent behavior that they, at the time, believe is morally justifiable and perhaps even necessary – if not downright gratifying.[15]

Even assuming *arguendo* that rational choice were possible in the cataclysm of mass violence, for some people the value of killing or dying for a cause exceeds the value of living peacefully without the prospect of punishment. Participants often are motivated by immediate approval from their peers. Cravings for such approval easily can outweigh the dissuasive effect of distant, and often hypothetical, punishment by an alien international criminal tribunal. Why incur immediate ostracism in situations where, as perpetrators themselves note, one person's insubordination would have made no difference anyway? Alette Smeulers reports:

Many perpetrators [. . .] convince themselves that they do not really have any control and that it would not have made a difference if they had stood up and refused to carry out the order. Stangl, commander of Treblinka, said: If I had sacrificed myself, if I had made public what I felt and had died . . . it would have made no difference. Not an iota. It would all have gone on just the same, as if it and I had never happened.[16]

Second, amid the social disintegration and group-based reconstitution that usually precedes mass violence, individuals often end up joining a marauding group because to do so is the only viable survival strategy. Anthropologists have documented such motivations in a variety of contexts, including among child soldiers in Sierra Leone.[17] After all, if one is not part of the group, one is alone. Being alone makes it all the easier to become victimized or perceived as belonging with or sympathetic to the "other." Fears of aloneness are particularly pronounced among many militia recruits – orphaned children, adolescents, and young men without families: in many cases poor and without occupational skills. Even those individuals for whom violence is not gratifying may willingly join, insofar as participating in massacre can guarantee survival to the next morning. There is something luxurious, if not utopian, in the notion that individuals in such desperate circumstances are amenable to being deterred by the prospect of some distant international or domestic institution that might punish them several years after their side might lose the conflict they currently are embroiled in. This requires a heavy burden of proof on the part of deterrence theorists. This burden has not been satisfactorily discharged. Although individuals who join a marauding group for petty material gain might be deterred by the criminal law, the same cannot be said for those who join to survive. And those who join for survival purposes become much more committed and rigorous in their killing than those who join merely to acquire incidental material trinkets.

Accordingly, criminal trials face significant obstacles in achieving their goal of deterring killers. Criminal trials face even greater difficulty in reaching benefiting bystanders [. . .]. Essentially, liberal criminal law leaves the masses unaccountable: its narrow focus persists *despite* the fact that support and acquiescence of the masses is the singular prerequisite for atrocity truly to become epidemic. Violence becomes normalized when neighbors avert their gaze, draw the blinds, and excitedly move into a suddenly available apartment. This broad public participation, despite its catalytic role, is overlooked by criminal law, thereby perpetuating a myth and a deception. The myth is that a handful of people are responsible for endemic levels of violence. The deception, which inures to the benefit of powerful states and organizations, involves hiding the myriad political, economic, historical, and colonial factors that create conditions precedent for violence.[18]

Because the silence of the majority, the acquiescence of the bystander, the enrichment of neighbors, and the nonfeasance of international organizations never is implicated by a system based on criminalization, any such system does little to deter these essential prerequisites to mass violence. Although the trial represents closure, this closure may be chimeric; and, more ominously, prematurely might divert attention from more expansive reconstruction efforts or dull our sensibilities regarding the inadequacies of criminal trials in unearthing many of the root causes of systemic violence. On the other hand, a broader-based approach that contemplates diverse, including collectively based, sanctions might reduce the appeal of passively acquiescing and, thereby, turn some erstwhile bystanders into gatekeepers who shutter out and shut down conflict entrepreneurs before it becomes too late. I contend that the passive support of the public that benefits from eliminationism but is not intoxicated by it might, to some degree at least, be dissipated by regulatory structures that sanction passive support. [. . .] Although it is not evident that collective sanctions actually will dissuade public acquiescence (perhaps the passive public also lies beyond deterrence?), what is evident is that a regulatory system based on select criminalization, which never even reaches the key constituency of the passive public, forecloses this possibility and with it a valuable line of research and inquiry.

International criminal law is deeply paradoxical: it courageously operates in opposition to state interests while stubbornly protecting state interests.[19] To the extent that international criminal law pins blame for atrocity on a small number of horrible individuals, who generally control a state apparatus, it achieves some justice and curbs atrocity as a tool of a state's foreign or domestic policy. However, if in the process of attributing guilt it pulls our gaze away from the many other actors involved in the tapestry of atrocity – including malfeasant, complicit, or distracted states and their officials, along with decisionmakers in international organizations – then it will do little to root out atrocity's multicausal origins. A fuller picture of responsibility for wrongdoing will emerge only to the extent that we resist simple, and comforting, criminal explanations and reach deeper to a more embarassing place. The institutionalization of some accountability through criminal trials – and the conversations these trials produce – must not lull us into thinking we have attained justice, but should prod us to go much further.

Expressivism

Expressivists contend that trial, conviction, and punishment appreciate public respect for law. The expressivist punishes to strengthen faith in rule of law among the general public, as opposed to punishing simply because the perpetrator deserves it or because potential perpetrators will be deterred by it. Expressivism also transcends retribution and deterrence in claiming as a central goal the crafting of historical narratives, their authentication as truths, and their pedagogical dissemination to the public. Overall, expressive objectives receive less attention than retribution or deterrence in the jurisprudence of institutions that pursue extraordinary international criminals, although they are reliably invoked as justifications for imposing sanction.[20]

Much of expressive theory relates to trial and conviction. For example, Judge Patricia Wald observes that taking indictees into custody and prosecuting them "put[s] the flesh of situational application on the bareboned definitions of war crimes, crimes against humanity, and genocide [. . .]."[21] It is tempting for the expressivist who extols the norm-generating and dramaturgical function of law to focus on trial and conviction. However, punishment, too, has significant messaging value – both as an end in and of itself and, also, as contributing to the force of prosecution and conviction. David Garland posits that punishment "communicates meaning . . . about power, authority, legitimacy, normality, morality, personhood, social relations, and a host of other tangential matters."[22] The fact that consequences follow a guilty verdict makes law all the more real to the community.[23] This sends a message that the law is to be taken seriously. Emile Durkheim observed that by expressing condemnation, punishment in fact could strengthen social solidarity.[24] Punishment internalizes – and even reinforces – social norms among the public and, thereby, from the expressivist perspective proactively promotes law-abiding behavior. Moreover, punishment can serve a prophylactic purpose – carrying with it significant therapeutic value for victims.

If punishment signals the absolute immutability of core values – for example, the universal repugnance of discriminatory group-based killings – then initial plans by conflict entrepreneurs to inveigle and habituate killers may stall. Punishment can thereby impede the early indoctrination phases in which average citizens become assimilated into the machinery of mass violence. This objective of punishment differs from deterring individuals from killing after they have become habituated into killing by desire or desperation. Whereas it seems problematic to deter – through fear of distant and deferred punishment – violence once it is imminent or has already begun, it seems somewhat more plausible to inhibit the mainstreaming of hatemongering as politics owing to the consolidation, through law and punishment, of a social consensus regarding the *moral unacceptability* of such politics. Law and punishment may be able to decelerate indoctrination because potential indoctrinees to the inchoate stages where hate is normalized have come to see discrimination-based massacre as manifestly illegal. Assuredly, it is difficult to combat the dizzying effects of propaganda. But if punishment can create principled citizens who value a normative structure that repudiates group-based eliminationism, then the size and attentiveness of the propagandists' audience would drop. In this vein, punishment operates as moral educator.[25]

Legal process can narrate history and thereby express shared understandings of the provenance, particulars, and effects of mass violence; punishing the offender contributes yet another layer of authenticity to this narration. Truth-telling (or, more colloquially, "discovering the truth") has been acknowledged by international criminal tribunals and is itself tied to a number of other goals, including the consequentialist goal of national reconciliation.[26] Discovering the truth also is frequently evoked by atrocity victims as an important objective of retrospective legal interventions. Trials create archives of information: either through documents, as at Nuremberg, or through testimony, as at Eichmann's trial in Jerusalem. The ICTY's dogged prosecution of the Srebrenica massacre led to "an archive of eyewitness accounts and often gruesome photographs and videos."[27] These materials can turn tragedy into a teaching moment. Trials can educate the public through the spectacle of theater – there is, after all, pedagogical value to performance and communicative value to dramaturgy.[28] This performance is made all the more weighty by the reality that, coincident with the closing act, comes the infliction of shame, sanction, and stigma upon the antagonists. Prosecution and punishment in response to extraordinary crimes can thereby serve a broader didactic purpose that meets the interests of history and memory.[29]

The ICTR's judicial characterization of the massacre that took place in Rwanda in 1994 as genocide serves the purpose of indelibly memorializing the violence; the ICTY Appeals Chamber also very consciously used its judgment in *Krstić* as a vehicle to pursue declaratory objectives so as to officialize the Srebrenica tragedy as genocide.[30] Prosecution and punishment can manufacture an authoritative version of the truth and, thereby, narrate a story that later becomes history. The IMT at Nuremberg put a repertoire of Nazi barbarities on display and condemned – before the international community – those of its architects who had survived so as, in the words of Robert Jackson, to "establish incredible events by credible evidence."[31] Now, sixty years later, the Nuremberg judgment remains a fixed anchor of our children's education.

There is good reason to believe that the punishment inflicted by an international tribunal operating prominently on the global agenda at the

cusp of history has enhanced expressive value in
asserting the importance of law, the stigmatiza-
tion of the offender who transgresses that law, and
the authenticity of the historical narrative that
ensues. International trials have a better chance
of becoming the kinds of "popular trials" that
define a debate, remind us of the content and value
of law, or serve as intergenerational "signposts"
in history.[32] This is in part because international
trials reach a global audience.[33] Their liberal
legalist modalities are intelligible to communities
in the epicenters of global power. Their reliance
on due process may help justice to be seen to
be done. On the other hand, too much due
process may give rise to technical proceedings
seen to be overly tilted in favor of iniquitous
defendants, who become able to grandstand and
humiliate witnesses.

The didactic value of international proceedings
is not preordained. The Tokyo Tribunal has
not become a pedagogical anchor in a manner
comparable to the Nuremberg Tribunal. Contemporary international institutions must be careful
not to overlook the audience that matters more
than any other – namely, directly afflicted populations. Perceptions among such populations
that contemporary institutions lack clean hands
will not be dissipated by fastidious adherence
to due process alone. In determining a process
to be just, audiences will assess much more than
simply whether it accords with liberal legalism.

Other than *Eichmann*, national trials or Nazi
atrocity – whether conducted by civilian or
military instrumentalities – have not reached
Nuremberg's expressivist level.[34] That said,
national proceedings regarding Nazi atrocity did
produce salient expressive content, even when
it came to the implication of non-Germans. The
Barbie, *Touvier*, and *Papon* trials were, at least for
the French nation, didactically valuable popular
events. Other proceedings, despite resulting in
lenient sentences completely disproportionate
to the gravity of the underlying offenses, narrated
the horrors of the Nazi concentration camps to
a bewildered public. These proceedings – many
of which were undertaken by West German courts
– filled a critical gap in the historical tapestry insofar as the Nuremberg prosecutions were directed
toward Nazi aggressive war, not crimes against
humanity or the Holocaust.[35] Furthermore, one
of the strengths of certain national institutions

is the diversity of mechanisms they rely upon
to didactically weave narratives. In Rwanda, for
example, the *partie civile* lawsuits adduce and
personalize stories of suffering and loss in a
victim-centered manner. *Mato oput* in Uganda
relies on ritual to reintegrate offenders while
respecting their own suffering, which seems
particularly apt in the case of child soldiers.

Assuredly, whether liberal criminal trials narrate
historical truths that, in turn, have expressive
legitimacy remains a contested question.[36] I
believe they are capable of such a function,
although I certainly recognize that alternate
forms of accountability may have equivalent or
even enhanced truth-telling capacity. I also
recognize that criminal prosecution, followed
by incarceration, is limited in its truth-telling
function. In particular, four specific aspects
of criminal process and sanction challenge the
quality of the narrative output. These aspects
are: (1) selective truths; (2) interrupted perform-
ances; (3) management strategies; and (4) plea
bargains. I consider each of these in turn.

Selective truths

Criminal trials are deliberately selective in terms
of the truths they produce. The application of
modern rules of evidence and procedure frames
this selectivity. These rules favor the production of logical and microscopic truths over the
dialogic and experiential truths that emerge
phenomenologically from restorative justice
initiatives.[37] For Miriam Aukerman, the formalism and rigidity of trials make them at times
"excruciatingly boring."[38]

The rules may create more than just tedium.
Although bolstering the authenticity of the narrative, these rules paradoxically also may crimp
it. For example, Martti Koskenniemi writes that
evidentiary rules and due process may undermine memory by allowing the accused to belittle
accusers in cross-examination and reduce their
accusations to "panicky 'I don't know' statements."[39] Rules may truncate victim storytelling,
thereby sowing disappointment;[40] but, on the
other hand, may control the extent to which
victim storytelling serves ulterior political purposes unrelated to the guilt or innocence of the
accused. Rules also exclude as nonprobative certain facts that local audiences might find deeply

relevant and, in this regard, distort the historical narrative. The situation of Belgian courts adjudging Rwandan *génocidaires* constitutes an example. Although the Belgian prosecutions should be lauded for bringing systematic human rights abusers to justice, they also rewrite the historical record by presenting Belgium as a font of justice, instead of weaving into the judicial narrative the much more complicated role Belgian colonial interventions played in exacerbating ethnic divisions in Rwanda that laid the groundwork for eventual genocide.

Expressive value is further threatened by the reality that this value often is externalized from afflicted local communities owing to the distance and mistrust evident between such communities and international criminal tribunals. Procedural differences between liberal criminal trials and expectations among local populations, in particular non-Western populations, also diminish the prophylactic value of verdict and punishment.

Interrupted performances

The death of Slobodan Milošević in the midst of his trial (which, at the time of his death, had gone on for four years) illustrates the frailties of criminal process. To be sure, a trial that stops short of verdict and punishment is not denuded of all expressive value. Prosecuting Milošević allowed a worldwide public to learn in dribs and drabs of the charges against him and the details of the atrocities he allegedly coordinated. Instrumentally speaking, some of the testimonial and documentary evidence introduced during the Milošević proceedings will be used against other defendants. But Milošević's death denied the possibility of a final sentence: infallible and authoritative. The curtain fell before the closing act. When the antagonist dies before the protagonist's pursuit is complete, the script becomes frustrated. The performance reaches an end, but it is an anticlimax. A formal adversarial trial cannot continue posthumously, at least not under current understandings of internationalized due process.

Milošević's premature death is an obstacle to the ICTY's narration of an overarching story of death and destruction in the Balkans. The ICTY has mitigated the impact of this obstacle by indicting 161 individuals in total; and, quickly following Milošević's death, by moving ahead with other high-profile trials, including regarding atrocity at Srebrenica and in Kosovo. That said, the ICTY had plea-bargained with other defendants, giving up reduced sentences in exchange for the promise of prized testimony against Milošević. These bargains crimped the expressive value of punishing those defendants in the hopes of a blockbuster impact in ringingly convicting Milošević.

The expressive vulnerabilities of criminal trials, and the impact of an interrupted performance, can be minimized to the extent that the net of accountability is broadened. In particular, if accountability ranges beyond high-profile criminal trials, the resultant greater methodological diversification diminishes the risk that an interrupted performance scuttles the overall truth-telling process.

The prosecution of leaders rendered frail through the passage of time necessarily involves a race against time. The sooner justice is delivered the better. Wily defendants can dither, piddle, and delay. Popular trials create a platform that places the defendant onto the world's center stage. If the defendant can make the trial all about himself, and selfishly control the stage though grandstanding, histrionics, and manipulation, then the proceedings drift away from the victims and their terrible losses.

Management strategies

The Milošević trial's performativity was susceptible to interruption in part because the trial had dragged on for so long. The Iraqi High Tribunal (IHT) applied some lessons learned from the languidness of the Milošević proceedings to its prosecution of Ba'ath Party leaders, including Saddam Hussein.

First, IHT judges exhibited greater vigilance than their ICTY counterparts in controlling the courtroom and the content of the discussions. On the one hand, tight control secures managerial and bureaucratic goals, streamlines process, dissipates inflammatory controversy, and preserves judicial authority. On the other hand, though, as levels of control become too tight, they may strangle the judicial record and thereby inflict credibility costs. Flattening the narratives to protect power drains some of their transformative content.

Second, IHT prosecutors elected to proceed through a series of minitrials instead of, as had been the case with Milošević, one overwhelming omnibus sixty-six count proceeding. The first minitrial, which led to convictions for crimes against humanity and war crimes against seven defendants (and a variety of sentences, including a death sentence for Saddam Hussein), involved the killings – at the hands of the Iraqi state – of 148 residents of the Shiite village of Dujail.[41] In 1982, Dujail had been the site of a failed assassination attempt against Hussein. In response, Iraqi security forces detained suspects. The Iraqi Revolutionary Court subsequently sentenced these villagers to death. Executions were carried out. Hussein's signature was on the orders.

Subsequent IHT minitrials do involve a higher-stakes context: for example, proceedings related to the Anfal (Arabic for "spoils of war") campaign, which had resulted in the allegedly genocidal massacre of at least (a conservative estimate) 50,000 Kurdish civilians in 1988, and the crushing of the 1991 Shiite uprising in the south. By proceeding sequentially, IHT prosecutors ensure cyclical episodes of gratification and closure, thereby reducing the risks that long-term proceedings lead to a deferred all or nothing outcome. They allow different victim groups, for example Kurds and Shias, to express outrage at the travesties inflicted upon them through context-specific proceedings. This is a prudential move. However, it is not without its own drawbacks. It results in a dramaturgical methodology in which the narrative is told through iterated vignettes. IHT officials need to be diligent that the digestible parts add up to a compelling, overarching whole. If discontinuous lower-stakes convictions remain narratively fragmented, then the IHT may, in the name of prudence, have forsaken the opportunity to leave a hardier historical footprint. Moreover, hanging Hussein for the Dujail conviction before the remaining minitrials took place induced an interrupted performance detrimental to the expressive value of these other proceedings.

Pleading out

Can plea bargains attain truth-telling objectives? Indeed, offenders who plead guilty may admit wrongdoing, apologize, express remorse, dignify victims, and provide details regarding the crimes. Self-convicting offenders may even implicate others, although this is not always the case (nor is there any guarantee of the veracity of the evidence subsequently proffered).[42] With regard to high-level accused, where the exacting nature of the criminal law requires the leader to be traced to the bodies interred in the mass grave, plea bargains can offer a partial print of the truth whose value exceeds that of the acquittal that might result should the prosecution be unable to meet the high threshold of proof demanded in the pursuit of microscopic and logical truths.

Although the ad hoc tribunals affirm that plea bargains contribute to truth-telling objectives,[43] certain institutionalized aspects of plea bargaining at the ad hoc tribunals whittle down the narrative value of plea-bargained convictions and sentences. Although some agreements contain a detailed factual basis, in other cases the offender pleads guilty to fairly bare allegations. In the latter case, the offender avoids contending with the gruesome, detailed evidence that would be admitted at trial. Deronjić's plea agreement, which was judicially affirmed, cursorily established the truth only regarding the tragedy that encompassed one village on one particular day, thereby burying several other potential truths – namely, accusations involving other spaces and places in Bosnia.[44]

Charge bargaining, in particular, jeopardizes expressive storytelling. Plavšić, in an agreement affirmed by the ICTY, pled guilty to one umbrella count of persecution as a crime against humanity and the Prosecutor dropped the remaining seven charges, including two counts of genocide and complicity in genocide.[45] In Milan Simić's case, the ICTY Prosecutor "agreed to withdraw several counts, including the most serious – persecution as a crime against humanity relating to Simić's mayor-like role [. . .]."[46] Simić, a paraplegic, was sentenced to five years' imprisonment. Combs notes that "such a sentence would have been unthinkable had the factual basis for Simić's conviction encompassed all the conduct for which he was initially charged."[47] As discussed earlier in the context of retribution, charge bargains push certain allegations off the agenda, thereby precluding the truth of those allegations from being officially unearthed. It is true that pleading guilty to an umbrella charge of persecution, a result that obtains in certain plea bargains, permits a broad array of facts, which may well support the substance of all of the original charges, to be included in the judicial record. However, the practice of the ad hoc tribunals has been spotty in this regard.

Conclusion

The preference for incarceration following what liberal international lawyers deem to be an acceptable criminal trial on the whole falls short of its penological objectives, in particular retribution and deterrence. This may be because those objectives are too ambitious. It may also be because the criminal law, standing alone, simply is not enough nor can ever be enough.

Notes

1 Cesare Beccaria, *On Crimes and Punishment* (1764) (Young trans., 1986).

2 *Prosecutor v. Kordić and Čerkez*, IT-95-14/2-A, ¶ 1076 (ICTY Appeals Chamber, Dec. 17, 2004) (noting that "both individual [n.b. specific] and general deterrence serve as important goals of sentencing"; also discussing reintegrative deterrence).

3 Miriam J. Aukerman, "Extraordinary Evil, Ordinary Crime," 15 *Harv. Ham. Rts J.* 39, 65 n.148 (2002) ("in the transitional justice context 'deterrence' almost always refers to 'general deterrence'").

4 *Prosecutor v. Rutaganda*, Case No. ICTR-96-3-T, ¶ 456 (ICTR Trial Chamber, December 6, 1999), aff'd on appeal, *Prosecutor v. Rutaganda*, Case No. ICTR-96-3-A (ICTR Appeals Chamber, May 26, 2003).

5 Report of the Secretary-General, *In Larger Freedom – Towards Development, Human Rights, and Security for All*, UN Doc. A/59/2005, ¶ 138 (March 21, 2005).

6 See, e.g., William W. Burke-White, "Complementarity in Practice: The International Criminal Court as Part of a System of Multi-level Global Governance in the Democratic Republic of Congo," 18 *Leiden J. Int'l L.* 557, 587 (2005) (noting also the methodological limitations to his research and the impossibility of turning to these data to provide statistically meaningful evidence that the ICC has had direct deterrent effect).

7 Jerry Fowler, "A New Chapter of Irony: The Legal Implications of the Darfur Genocide Determination," 1:1 *Genocide Studies and Prevention* 29, 36 (2006). There also is vivid debate regarding the suitability of deterrence as a justification for punishment under ordinary common criminal law. See, e.g., James Gilligan, *Violence*, 94–6 (1996) (arguing that rational self-interest models that underlie deterrence theory are based on ignorance of what violent people really are like); H. L. A. Hart, "Prolegomenon to the Principles of Punishment," in H. L. A. Hart, *Punishment and Responsibility: Essays in the Philosophy of Law*," 1–27 (1968) (doubting the validity of deterrence in domestic contexts to ordinary common criminals).

8 John Braithwaite, *Crime, Shame and Reintegration*, 69 (1989); David Chuter, *War Crimes*, 271 (2003); Michael Tonry, "The Functions of Sentencing and Sentencing Reform," 58 *Stan. L. Rev.* 37, 52 (2005).

9 ICTY Press Release, ICTY President Pocar Addresses the Security Council (December 15, 2005).

10 Martha Minow, *Between Vengeance and Forgiveness*, 50 (1998) ("Individuals who commit atrocities on the scale of genocide are unlikely to behave as 'rational actors,' deterred by the risk of punishment"); Judith Shklar, *Legalism: Law, Morals, and Political Trials*, 187 (rev. ed., 1986) (wondering "whether international criminal law can fulfill in any degree the great function of criminal law – the deterrence of potential criminals"). See also Stuart Beresford, "Unshackling the Paper Tiger, 1 *J. Int'l Crim. Law Rev.* 43 (2001); Christopher Rudolph, "Constructing an Atrocities Regime: The Politics of War Crimes Tribunals," 55 *Int'l Org.* 655, 683–4 (2001); Immi Tallgren, "The Sensibility and Sense of International Criminal Law," 13 *Eur. J. Int'l L.* 561 (2002); David Wippmann, "Atrocities, Deterrence, and the Limits of International Justice," 23 *Fordham Int'l L.J.* 473, 474 (1999).

11 F. Mégret, "Three Dangers for The International Criminal Court," XII *Finnish Y.B. Int'l L.* 203 (2001).

12 Id.

13 Robert D. Kaplan, *The Coming Anarchy*, 44–5 (2000).

14 Jaime Malamud-Goti, "Transitional Governments in the Breach: Why Punish State Criminals?" 12 *Hum. Rts. O.* 1 (1990).

15 Michael Ignatieff, *The Lesser Evil*, 121 (2004).

16 Alette Smeulers, "What Transforms Ordinary People into Gross Human Rights Violators?," in *Understanding Human Rights Violations – New*

Systematic Studies, 239, 247 (Carey & Poe eds., 2004) (citations omitted).

17 See, e.g., Krijn Peters & Paul Richards, "Fighting with Open Eyes: Youth Combatants Talking About War in Sierra Leone," in *Rethinking the Trauma of War*, 76, 109 (Bracken & Petty eds., 1998) (noting that child soldiers "seek to stay alive using their strength and ingenuity as best they can"); Kimberly Lanegran, "Developments in International Law Regarding Recruitment of Child Combatants from the Special Court for Sierra Leone," 4 (2006) (unpublished manuscript on file with the author, cited with permission).

18 Mark J. Osiel, *Mass Atrocity, Ordinary Evil, and Hannah Arendt*, 157 (2001); see also Amy Chua, *World on Fire*, 9, 124 (2004) (arguing that the simultaneous global spread of democracy and markets is a major aggravating cause of ethnic violence, in particular in countries with a market-dominant ethnic minority and a poor majority of a different ethnic group).

19 Klabbers notes a similar phenomenon at the national level: "[i]n Barbie, the French Cour de Cassation ended up exempting France (and, by extension, democratic states generally), from any possible complicity in crimes against humanity by linking such crimes to states practicing 'a hegemonic political ideology.'" Jan Klabbers, "Book Review," 15 *Eur. J. Int'l L.* 1055, 1056 (2004).

20 In Rajić, an ICTY Trial Chamber held that "punishment aims at reinforcing the validity and the effectiveness of the breached rules of international humanitarian law vis-à-vis the perpetrator, the victims and the public." *Prosecutor v. Rajić*, Case No. IT-95-12-S, ¶ 69 (ICTY Trial Chamber, May 8, 2006). In the Rauter case, expressivism was explicitly cited by the Netherlands Special Court of Cassation as an important purpose of punishment. Trial of Hans Albin Rauter (Netherlands Special Court in The Hague, May 4, 1948, and Netherlands Special Court of Cassation, January 12, 1949), reprinted at 14 *Law Reports of Trials of War Criminals* 89, 109 (1949).

21 Patricia Wald, "Book Review," 99 *Am. J. Int'l L.* 720, 725 (2005).

22 David Garland, *Punishment and Modern Society: A Study in Social Theory*, 252 (1990).

23 As the Nuremberg judges insisted, "only by punishing individuals who commit [crimes against international law] can the provisions of international law be enforced." International Military Tribunal (Nuremberg), Judgment and Sentences (Oct. 1, 1946), reprinted in 41 *Am. J. Int'l L.* 172, 221 (1947).

24 Emile Durkheim, *The Division of Labor in Society* (1933).

25 For further writing on punishment as moral education, see H. L. A. Hart, *Punishment and Responsibility*, 255 (1968); Andrew von Hirsch, *Censure and Sanctions*, 10 (1993).

26 Antonio Cassese, "Reflections on International Criminal Justice," 61 *Mod. L. Rev.* 1, 1 (1998).

27 Molly Moore, "Trial of Milošević Holds Lessons for Iraqi Prosecutors," *Washington Post* (October 18, 2005), at A19.

28 See generally David Luban, "Beyond Moral Minimalism," 20 *Ethics & International Affairs* 353 (2006).

29 Lawrence Douglas, *The Memory of Judgment* (2001) (writing within the context of the Holocaust).

30 *Prosecutor v. Krstić*, Case No. IT-98-33-A, ¶ 34 (ICTY Appeals Chamber, April 19, 2004).

31 Telford Taylor, *The Anatomy of the Nuremberg Trials*, 54 (1992).

32 Robert Hariman, *Popular Trials: Rhetoric, Mass Media, and the Law*, 2, 18 (ed. 1990).

33 Proceedings conducted locally also can be broadcast to a global audience. The process of diffusion, however, can be more complex.

34 There are important differences between the proceedings held in Nuremberg and Adolf Eichmann's trial in Jerusalem. Whereas Nuremberg principally involved documentary evidence, Eichmann turned on victim testimony; whereas Nuremberg focused on Nazi aggression, Eichmann focused on crimes against the Jewish people.

35 Nuremberg required a nexus between the existence of an aggressive war and crimes against humanity. This was so, according to William Schabas, owing to unease on the part of the Allies that the independent criminalization of crimes against humanity might restrict Allied governments with regard to their own national minorities or in the colonies. William A. Schabas, *An Introduction to the International Criminal Court*, 42 (2d ed., 2004). The requirement of a nexus between aggressive war (or any armed conflict at all) and crimes against humanity has since departed international criminal law.

36 See, e.g., Tristram Hunt, "Whose Truth? Objective Truth and a Challenge for History," 15 *Crim. L.F.* 193, 197 (2004) (discussing the work of historian Richard Evans, who argues that phenomena such as the "judicialization of history" that arise from retrospective criminal law bring a crass categorization among perpetrators, bystanders, and victims that actually presents obstacles to understanding the past, appreciating the diffuseness of historical synthesis, and educating for the

future); Eric Stover, "Witnesses and the Promise of Justice in The Hague," in *My Neighbor, My Enemy: Justice and Community in the Aftermath of Mass Atrocity*, 104, 116 (Stover & Weinstein eds., 2004) (noting that, although the ICTY has convened four trials based on attacks by Bosnian Croats on the ethnically mixed village of Ahmici, a study reveals that there is "absolutely no indication that these trials have in any way transformed the way in which Croats in the village interpret what happened"). David Mendeloff questions the instrumental usefulness of obtaining "truth." He notes that "we actually know very little about the impact of truth-telling or truth-seeking on peace." "Truth-seeking, Truth-telling, and Postconflict Peacebuilding," 6 *Int'l St. Rev.*, 356 (2003). See also id. at 365: "[T]he truth-telling literature relies heavily on anecdotal evidence." Mendeloff observes situations where "collective forgetting" might have proven "conducive to harmony and cooperation," such as post-Franco Spain and Mozambique. Id. at 367.

37 According to South African Justice Albie Sachs, microscopic and logical truths are exacted on a "beyond a reasonable doubt" standard derived from a sequential proof of facts. Albie Sachs, Lecture at Columbia University School of Law (Apr. 13, 1999), cited and discussed in Mark A. Drumbl, "Punishment, Postgenocide: From Guilt to Shame to Civis in Rwanda," 75 *N.Y.U. L. Rev.* 1221, 1283 (2000) (notes on file with author). For Sachs, experiential and dialogic truths are different. They emerge phenomenologically when people come forward and tell their stories. Restorative mechanisms – whether in the form of truth commissions or traditional dispute resolution – may constitute comfortable sites for such storytelling. Through a process of accretion over time, these expressions of experience create an overarching historical narrative that can displace preexisting narratives that normalized or legitimized violence. For Sachs, courts do not encourage experiential or dialogic truths.

38 Aukerman, op. cit., at 73.

39 Martti Koskenniemi, "Between Impunity and Show Trials," 6 *Max Planck Yearbook of U.N. Law* 1, 33 (2002) (discussing Milošević proceedings).

40 Elizabeth Neuffer, *The Key to My Neighbor's House*, 298 (2002).

41 The IHT's Dujail judgment was announced in November 2006. Written reasons were issued in December 2006. The trial attracted considerable concern regarding its apparent departure from internationalized due process standards and the fact that three defense lawyers and a witness had been assassinated. Sentences for convicted defendants ranged from death to term imprisonment (15 years). An appeals court affirmed most of the IHT sentences, including Saddam Hussein's, in December 2006. Hussein was executed. In the IHT judgment, only 4 (of 283) pages dealt with sentence (in addition, there was a brief discussion in Part 2 of the judgment regarding the legality of punishment). The IHT offered no explanation as to the purposes of sentencing. In addition to being brief, the sentencing discussion was rote and repetitive. The IHT listed the convicts and their convictions, ordered as to type of conviction, and then stipulated a penalty. The IHT did not explain, for the public, exactly why some of the defendants received lesser sentences than others. To be sure, a discerning reader could total the numbers of convictions, and the crimes for which convictions were issued, and come to some conclusion that the gravity of certain convictions exceeded that of others or that an accumulation of convictions mechanically led to a harsher sentence. However, such inferences never were explicated. The IHT did not mention aggravating or mitigating factors. It remains unclear whether what the IHT took as aggravating factors in sentencing were identical to factors it considered in finding liability (the Nuremberg judges did this, but the ICTY, which sentences less severely than the IHT, has repudiated such double-dipping).

42 For example, Plavšić refused to involve anyone else in the violence or testify in any other cases. She took responsibility for her own actions, but stated that this responsibility was hers "alone" and was not to be "extend[ed] to other leaders who have a right to defend themselves." N. Combs, "International Decisions," 97 *Am. J. Int'l L.* 934 (2003) (citing reports). The bargained-for testimony of another defendant who pled guilty was subsequently found to be evasive and even false. See, e.g., *Prosecutor v. Momir Nikolić*, Case No. IT-02-60/1-A, ¶ 106 (ICTY Appeals Chamber, March 8, 2006) ("[T]he mere fact that the Deronjić Trial Chamber gave significant weight to the accused's co-operation notwithstanding certain false statements does not illustrate that the Trial Chamber in this case abused its discretion in reaching a different result."); see also *Prosecutor v. Krstić*, Case No. IT-98-33-A, ¶ 94 (ICTY Appeals Chamber, April 19, 2004) (hesitating to rely independently on Deronjić's plea-bargained testimony in the proceedings against Krstić owing to discrepancies in Deronjić's testimony and the ambiguity surrounding some of the statements he had made).

43 See, e.g., *Prosecutor v. Sikirica*, Case No. IT-95-8-S, ¶ 149 (ICTY Trial Chamber, Nov. 13, 2001) ("... a guilty plea contributes directly to one of the fundamental objectives of the international tribunal: namely, its truth-finding function"); *Prosecutor v. Todorović*, Case No. IT-95-9/1-S, ¶ 81 (ICTY Trial Chamber, July 31, 2001) (stating that "a guilty plea is always important for the purpose of establishing the truth in relation to a crime").

44 *Prosecutor v. Deronjić*, Case No. IT-02-61-S, ¶ 4 (ICTY Trial Chamber, March 30, 2004) (Schomburg, J., dissenting).

45 Combs, "International Decisions," op. cit., at 931. Other cases where charges were dropped include

Prosecutor v. Bisengimana, Case No. ICTR-00-60-T, ¶¶ 136–7 (ICTR Trial Chamber, April 13, 2006); *Prosecutor v. Mrdja*, Case No. IT-02-59-S, ¶¶ 4–5 (ICTY Trial Chamber, March 31, 2004) (dropping charge of crime against humanity as part of the plea bargain). Babić also pled guilty to one count of persecution as a crime against humanity in exchange for agreement by the ICTY Prosecutor to drop four other charges. Babic Admits Persecuting Croats, BBC News (Jan. 27, 2004), available at http://news.bbc.co.uk/2/hi/europe/3433721.stm.

46 Combs, "Procuring Guilty Pleas," op. cit., at 91.

47 Id. at 91–2.

43

Defending International Criminal Trials

Larry May

International criminal law is under assault from both realists and communitarians.[1] International law generally is often portrayed as a pipe dream at best and a dangerous distraction at worst. Such criticisms will have an effect on whether there are to be international trials for the crime of aggression. To defend international criminal trials diverse authors have proposed various normative rationales: some proposing deterrence, some proposing retribution, and others proposing truth and reconciliation. Yet, each of these theories has been shown to fall short of defending the entirety of international criminal law. In this paper, I will provide a limited defense of international criminal trials conducted in a neutral locale such as The Hague, not by reference to a single normative principle, such as deterrence or retribution or truth and reconciliation, but by reference to a combination of principles applicable differently for different contexts. I do not claim that the sum of these defenses is larger than its parts, but only that it may be possible to construct a partial defense on the basis of each that overlaps sufficiently to justify most of international criminal law.

The task of defending international criminal trials for the crime of aggression is made more difficult by the fact that there has been only one significant set of trials for this crime, namely the trials at Nuremberg. And today, there are no trials even planned since the members of the international community cannot seem to agree about what constitutes State aggression or about what entity should make the decision about whether a State has indeed engaged in aggression in a particular case. I believe that such trials should be held much less frequently than those for crimes against humanity and for war crimes. Nonetheless, international criminal trials for aggression and crimes against peace can be defended in a limited way. In this paper I will support the view that some international criminal trials for aggression can be justified.

The paper is divided into four parts. In the first section, I will summarize the arguments advanced by Martti Koskenniemi concerning the seeming inability to find a normative ground for international criminal trials. In the second section, I will attempt to respond to Koskenniemi, agreeing with him about the difficulty of providing such a normative grounding, but disagreeing that the task cannot succeed. In the third section, I will consider the nuanced arguments of Mark Drumbl on these themes and try to respond to him as well.

Larry May, "Defending International Criminal Trials," from *Aggression and Crimes Against Peace* (Cambridge University Press, 2008). © 2008 by Larry May. Reprinted with permission from Cambridge University Press.

I am sympathetic to both Koskenniemi's and Drumbl's critiques. In the fourth section, I consider the challenge of trying to make international criminal trials less prone to the charge that they are politicized. Throughout, I will mount a limited defense of international trials for aggression, while recognizing that these trials pose the most difficult problems of all.

I. Koskenniemi's Critique of International Criminal Law

The distinguished Finnish legal scholar, Martti Koskenniemi, has mounted a significant critique of the project of international criminal law in his essay, "Between Impunity and Show Trials."[2] There are two parts to his challenging and rigorous exposition. First, he argues that the standard normative groundings offered in defense of international criminal law: deterrence, retribution, and truth are each seriously flawed as bases of international criminal law. Second, he argues that political leaders brought before international tribunals, as was true of Slobodon Milosevic brought before the ICTY, will try to politicize the trials even more than they already are. The only alternative seems to be to silence these leaders by not allowing them to defend themselves. And yet this alternative will also merely point up the political nature of these trials, and make them look even more like show trials. In this section I will summarize Koskenniemi's important objections to the project of international criminal law.

Let me take up the issue of retribution first. Koskenniemi claims to agree with Hannah Arendt that "punishing an individual does not come close to measuring up" to the tragedies, such as crimes against humanity, for which the individuals are charged.[3] Koskenniemi also cites Karl Jaspers who held that "something other than law [was] at stake here – and to address it in legal terms was a mistake."[4] Koskenniemi agrees, calling Jaspers' insight "plainly evident" and then arguing that this is also true today:

[I]t seems clear that whether or not Milosevic goes to prison is in no way an "adequate" response to the fact that over 200,000 people lost their lives – while millions more were affected – by the succession of wars in the former

Yugoslavia. If the trial has significance, then that significance must lie elsewhere than in the punishment handed down.[5]

For Koskenniemi, the crimes are too enormous, or at least the tragedies that the crimes are based on are too enormous, to be adequately dealt with in retributive terms by the punishment of just one person, or even a group of people.

Koskenniemi says little else about retribution in his essay, leading me to think that this is not the main basis of his critique of international criminal law. One can imagine a more concerted effort to buttress the claims advanced by Koskenniemi. It could be claimed that putting one, or even several people, in prison pales by comparison with the number of those killed in mass atrocity. Even if the trials could employ capital punishment, how many times would the person in the dock have to be killed to make up for the deaths and suffering of so many victims? Standard international prison terms of ten years seem not to do justice to crimes involving mass atrocity. Such an argument, which seeks to establish that standard punishments cannot adequately reflect what perpetrators of mass atrocity deserve, might buttress Koskenniemi's case against seeing international criminal trials grounded in the moral principle of retribution.

Another matter that is treated briefly is that of deterrence. Koskenniemi argues that deterrence is unlikely if the crimes in question "emerge from what Kant labeled 'radical evil,' an evil that exceeds the bounds of instrumental rationality."[6] And even if this "metaphysical" idea of radical evil is not accepted, says Koskenniemi, "the deterrence argument would still fail to convince inasmuch as the atrocities of the 20th century have not emerged from criminal intent but as offshoots from a desire to do good."[7] Koskenniemi makes the point crystal clear when he says:

As criminal lawyers know well, fitting crimes against humanity or other massive human rights violations into the deterrence frame requires some rather implausible psychological generalizations. Either the crimes are aspects of political normality – Arendt's "banality of evil" – in which case there is no *mens rea*, or they take place in exceptional situations of massive destruction and personal anger when there is little liberty of action. . . . [I]t is implausible to believe that criminal law is able to teach people to become heroes, not least because what "heroism" might mean in particular situations is often at the heart of the confrontation between political values underlying the criminal justice system (perhaps seen as victor's justice) and the system that is on trial.[8]

If the locals see the trials held so far from home as "mere propaganda," those trials and the ensuing punishments will be highly unlikely to deter anyone.

Koskenniemi's argument against grounding international criminal trials in the normative principle of deterrence is more subtle than his argument against grounding such trials in retribution. But to defend such a view persuasively one would have to devote much attention to the actual "facts on the ground" in order to show that such trials have not and are unlikely to have deterrent effects. Others have attempted to provide reasons to doubt the deterrent effects of international criminal trials,[9] but the main problem is that there have not been enough of these trials for a statistically significant sample in any study that did more than speculate about deterrent effects. For all we know, the ICC may very well have a strong deterrent effect. In any event, Koskenniemi seems to be more interested in another rationale, to which we now turn.

In my view, Koskenniemi's most important critique concerns the inability of supporters of international criminal trials to defend these trials by reference to the search for truth and reconciliation. And here we need to distinguish several distinct strains in his argument: there is the question of whether international criminal trials do or are likely to get at the truth, and then there is the symbolic argument that in any event people may feel better, perhaps reconciling somewhat with their attackers, for having made the effort to get at the truth even if the truth was elusive or impossible to ascertain by means of criminal trials. Both arguments dovetail nicely but since in the next section I will insist on separating them, I will also keep them separate in this expository discussion.

Once again appealing to the common knowledge of lawyers, Koskenniemi offers the following set of claims:

As criminal lawyers have always known, legal and historical truth are far from identical. The wider the context in which individual guilt has to be understood, and the more such understanding defers to the contingencies of historical interpretation, the more evident the limits of criminal procedure for reaching the "truth."[10]

The argument behind these claims is that in domestic law all we need to do is to answer the question: "did the accused do it?" Beyond that question, no "further question about how to understand what he did, how to place his behavior in relation to the overall behavior of those around him, emerges."[11] Thus, according to Koskenniemi, the truth of domestic trials is "relatively uncontested."[12]

But, Koskenniemi argues, in trials for mass atrocity crimes, "there are many truths and many stakeholders for them. In the Milosevic trial, for instance, the narrative of 'Greater Serbia' collides head-on with the self-determination stories of the seceding populations, while political assessments of 'socialism' and 'nationalism' compete with long-term historical and even religious frames of explanation."[13] Criminal trials privilege the individual over the contextual, and yet at the international level neither can "a priori override the other" and the individual frame may not "enact a lesson of historical truth."[14] Trials would need to pay as much attention to contexts as to individuals if they were to stand any likelihood of getting at the truth.

In addition, the victims will not necessarily feel better because trials are ongoing, since the symbolism of international trials is so hard to divorce from "victor's justice" or even from political "show trials." Indeed, in order to turn the tide of "symbolism" well-schooled defendants will attack the legal system itself, or will attempt to fix the blame on other institutions, especially Western institutions like the United Nations that are responsible for forcing the trial to be waged concerning such politically charged matters. It is not at all clear which symbolic message, the message that the defendants committed horrible acts that have now received their comeuppance or that the defendants were mere scapegoats in a show trial, will be received by the often highly nationalistic audience back home. The symbolic value of trials may be just the reverse of what is hoped for when such trials are planned.

This final point relates to Koskenniemi's worries about having especially heads of State defend themselves. Either these leaders will be allowed to play to the audience back home or they will have to be silenced, pointing out that these really were "show trials" after all. There is a very serious problem of establishing that international criminal trials are fair if the defendant is not allowed to speak in his or her own defense. It is rather like the Chicago Seven trial where Bobby Seale was strapped to a chair and gagged, a perfect symbol of a trial that had no more positive symbolic value than if Seale had been subjected to summary justice. The higher-ranking is the official in the dock, the greater is the likelihood that he or she will be a skilled rhetorician, able to transform the trial into an indictment of Western institutions that are conspiring against nationalist movements at home. The only option other than to set oneself up for a show trial is to allow impunity. In neither case, argues Koskenniemi, does it look good for the normative grounding of international criminal law.

II.   The Diversity of Norms Defense

One way to respond to Koskenniemi is to agree that no one norm is able to justify the project of international criminal law, but that different aspects of that project may be justified by different norms, allowing an overarching justification that utilizes a diversity of norms. In this section I will sketch this response. The idea is that a partial defense of international criminal law can be constructed from a combination of the norms of retribution, deterrence, and reconciliation, but not by any one of these norms alone. As will become evident, I agree with many of the points that Koskenniemi has made, but I disagree that he has provided a devastating critique of the project of international criminal law. I leave to a later section of this paper a discussion of the symbolic argument and the problem of having political leaders in the dock defending themselves.

Koskenniemi makes a good case for thinking that the enormity of the harms and wrongs that mass atrocity involves do not translate well into individual criminal sentences. Retribution

directed at individuals cannot fully make amends for such atrocities as are involved in ethnic cleansing or waging aggressive war. I do not dispute this point. But what criminal trials can sometimes do is to punish individuals for their roles in such atrocities. And here I would also agree with Koskenniemi that the roles that are played are not as important as are the contexts, or circumstances, within which those who played the roles acted. As I have argued, mass atrocities occur due to the coordinated efforts of many individual human persons. It is patently unfair to hold one of these individuals responsible for the entire atrocity. Indeed, it is normatively unjustified to do so.

What an individual can be held responsible for is that person's participation in a mass atrocity. I am skeptical of the importance of retribution in criminal law generally. But I do agree that there is a sense in which individuals who participate in wrongdoing should have their comeuppance. And in this respect, I think that international criminal trials can be partially justified in that sometimes these trials can accomplish this objective. It is important that individuals pay for the harms and wrongs they have participated in. By this I mean that a retributive model can justify some international trials insofar as the part played by individuals in the dock can match the punishment they are sentenced to. Since individuals did not, and generally cannot, cause mass atrocities on their own, international courts should look only to the part each individual played – and standard punishments can sometimes be adequate retribution for those parts. But this is only a partial grounding for international trials since, as Jan Klabbers has pointed out,[15] sometimes international atrocities do not divide up neatly. It is often difficult to say which part each person played in the atrocity and in any event it is normally not practicable to prosecute all of the individuals who so participated. Hence there is a gap between the horror of the crime and the extent of punishment. I return to this point in the next section.

Deterrence is similarly problematical in international trials since normally not all of even the major participants can be prosecuted. But this is a problem in all of criminal law. Inevitably, many people who participate in crimes will not be prosecuted or punished. Surely this fact will diminish the deterrence effects of criminal law. But deterrence is, in my view, primarily about increasing the risks that a perpetrator has of suffering a serious consequence for committing a harm or wrong. And in this sense, there can be some deterrence that results from international criminal trials. Even if the population that one wishes to deter does not recognize the legitimacy of the tribunal, the punishments handed down can still deter. We are all motivated, at least to a certain extent, by fear of adverse consequences. There are also conflicting motivations that may offset the adverse consequences threatened by punishment and hence block the deterrent effect. But this is true of all criminal law. In the end, whether international criminal law deters less than domestic law is an empirical question that can only be answered after there is enough evidence. At the moment, there have been so few international trials and so few sentences that it is mere speculation whether or not there is a robust deterrent effect here.

So, we need to look to the similarities and differences between domestic and international criminal law in order to see if there are likely to be impediments to deterrence in the international setting. The major difference, Jan Klabbers argues, is that many international crimes are not committed from evil but from good motives, whereas domestic criminals act from evil motives.[16] But I would argue that there are important similarities as well. Human rights violators may still have *mens rea* insofar as they realize that what they are doing is wrong and they nonetheless aim at violating the law. Criminality is established by looking at intentions not motives. And deterrence can still sometimes operate to stop people from intentionally violating the law, either domestic or international, regardless of whether their motives were good or evil. Even those who act from what they believe to be good motives can be deterred from so acting by threat of punishment.

Deterrence is only a partial grounding for international criminal law since motives do affect how deterrence operates. If one's motives and intentions are bad then deterrence has the most efficacy. The deterrence effects will likely be diminished when people are motivated by patriotism or nationalism, even as they recognize that their actions violate a law. But I don't see any

reason to think that people cannot sometimes be deterred nonetheless from breaking the law if they recognize that they may still be subject to punishment. Liability to punishment changes the weights of the reasons that people have to act in various ways. Those who are otherwise strongly motivated to break the law may still pause to do so if the risk of punishment is great enough. Deterrence, like retribution, can give us a partial defense of international criminal law in that in many cases the threat of punishment will have an effect on behavior, at least lessening the likelihood of harmful behavior if not completely eliminating such behavior. Deterrence is less likely in certain situations than others to have a dramatic effect on the incidence of international crime, but there are situations nonetheless where it is likely to have such an effect, giving us a partial justification for international criminal trials. Just as retribution will succeed in some cases, so deterrence is likely to succeed in some cases as well.

I next turn to the truth and reconciliation norm. Koskenniemi is surely right there as well, at least partially, since trials are sometimes not the best or even a particularly good way to get at the truth. This looks to be even more of a problem when trials are highly politicized, as sometimes happens in international criminal trials. It will not be possible to give a complete normative grounding for these trials by reference to such norms. But if we are only looking for partial grounding things look different. For some trials, at both the domestic and international level, surely do allow for the truth to be told, that is, for some victims to feel reconciled with perpetrators, and for some perpetrators to prove their innocence. It is true that the "truth" of the matter may indeed be skewed by ideological differences among the principal parties in any given war. But this need not block all truth and reconciliation.

Some of the standard procedures in criminal trials may need to be adjusted or changed to make it more likely that truth will be achieved in some international criminal trials. Let us think about this matter from the standpoint of the defendant. In highly politicized trials, the procedures should give defendants ample opportunity to prove that they have been set-up or scapegoated. Prosecutorial overreaching should be curtailed, as should attempts to block, by procedural maneuvering, the introduction of exculpatory evidence. I have argued for similar procedural changes in US domestic law, especially in highly publicized criminal cases where it will be otherwise hard for the defendant to tell his or her story in a way that brings out the defendant's innocence.[17] Of course, procedural safeguards will not always prevent the manipulation rather than the accurate telling of the truth just as procedural safeguards cannot always prevent miscarriages of justice.

The truth that I have in mind here is not what victims' families often most desire. International trials are limited affairs – they can try to tell us whether a given defendant did in fact participate in an atrocity and to what extent. Criminal trials serve the limited task of allowing victims and their families to confront particular people who are believed to be the ones who perpetrated horrible acts. But of course, there is often a larger story to be told about what brought about an atrocity and some victims want that story to be told. Trials have only limited value in disclosing these larger truths, but sometimes the combination of smaller truths will add up to something significant for the victims and their families nonetheless. And in at least one sense, concerning the defendants, the small-scale truth of innocence is highly important.

One must ask what are the alternatives that are likely to do a better job of uncovering some of the truth and providing for some reconciliation between the parties. I have elsewhere admitted that trials sometimes are not the best for obtaining truth and securing reconciliation.[18] Sometimes amnesty for truth programs are better at securing truth and even better at achieving reconciliation. But these proceedings must be initiated internally, and hence are not always an alternative to international criminal trials. And in any event, amnesty for truth programs are not always better than criminal trials at ferreting out the truth. Indeed, there are circumstances where trials are clearly better, such as where a society has been so oppressed that people will only speak out about the truth if their identities are hidden in the way that witnesses have been protected in trials for several centuries. Whether considerations of truth and reconciliation will normatively ground international trials depends on the alternatives that are available and on whether these alternatives are likely to be any better at uncovering the truth

and achieving reconciliation than are the trials in question, especially to get this evidence made public in a timely manner.

Sometimes historians are better at getting at the larger truth of atrocities, while historians are often not as good as lawyers at getting at particular truths. In many cases, historians cannot get access to the relevant specific facts about who did what. In a trial, both parties have the ability to demand evidence be produced that may have been intentionally hidden. Historians are unlikely to get access to that information for many years if not generations. The system that allows both sides, through their lawyers, to confront witnesses and subject evidence to careful scrutiny, in real time as it were, is not available to historians. So, there is a kind of truth that historians are not necessarily better at, and there is no good reason to think that the goal of ferreting out the truth is generally best served by historians than by trials.

International trials are sometimes the only way, or at least the only practicable way, for victims to be able to tell their stories and for alleged perpetrators also to tell their stories. Indeed, it seems to me that the best normative grounding for international criminal trials comes in these last resort cases, where for various reasons no other reasonable alternatives are open to allow for the truth, or at least some of it, to be disclosed, and for reconciliation between the parties, or at least some of the parties, to be achieved. And here we have one more partial normative grounding for international criminal trials.

While I agree with Koskenniemi that there is no single grounding norm for international criminal law, I think that a combination of diverse norms, including retribution, deterrence, and reconciliation can provide such a grounding in enough cases to constitute enough of a normative grounding nonetheless. And I'm not sure why anyone would think that it is likely that there would be such a single grounding norm for any criminal trial. For there have been centuries if not millennia of criticism of retribution and deterrence models for justifying punishment. We should not expect things to be any better in the international domain. My proposal is that if we consider the partial normative grounding offered by each of these norms, something approaching an overlapping good-enough rationale for such trials can be constructed. Of course, it will always be possible to criticize specific international trials on each of these counts, but the consideration of each of these norms makes the ground under international criminal law considerably firmer than Koskenniemi has led us to believe. I next examine a very recent attempt to provide a nuanced critique of the normative underpinnings of international criminal law by Mark Drumbl.

III. Drumbl's Arguments about Retribution and Deterrence

Mark Drumbl has written an excellent book-length treatment of these topics where he develops some of the arguments we have been considering in very interesting directions.[19] Specifically, I find his arguments about selectivity of prosecution and the rational capacity of those to be deterred to warrant special consideration in my ultimate attempt to provide a limited defense of international criminal trials for aggression and other international crimes. Drumbl also develops an expressivist argument in favor of those trials that I partially endorse, as will become clear in the next section of this paper.

Drumbl argues that selectivity and leniency of punishment undermine the retributive goals of international criminal law by creating what he calls "a retributive shortfall." The selectivity argument is that not all of the worst of international criminal acts are punished, and this underscores "the difficulty of ascribing retributive purposes to international criminal law as a whole when a 'confluence of political concerns,' and not the inherent gravity of the crimes, prods the punishment of offenders."[20] Since "too few people or entities receive just deserts" there is "a retributive shortfall" that results.[21] The "tiny subset of alleged perpetrators" calls attention to the fact that retributive goals are not well served by international criminal law. At least in part this is because prosecutors make decisions about who to prosecute not on grounds of deservingness but on such factors as the cooperation of States, utility of convicting low-level perpetrators for strategic purposes, and availability of material resources.[22]

Drumbl also argues that lenient sentences undermine the retributive goals of international criminal law. On the assumption that international crimes are supposed to be the worst of crimes, because they involve multiple or mass criminal acts, one would expect the sentences to match the gravity of the crimes. Yet, it turns out that international sentences fall far short of what one would expect for the worst of crimes. As Drumbl argues, "the data reveal that at both the national and international levels, sentences for multiple international crimes are generally not lengthier than what national jurisdictions award for a single serious ordinary crime."[23] Drumbl also argues that even if one does not see quantity of sentence as definitive of sanctions, and looks also to conditions of imprisonment and stigma associated with sentence, international criminal sanctions do not exceed those of national tribunals.[24]

I would grant that there is a retributive shortfall in international criminal law today, and that it is unlikely to get much better in the near future. But it is not clear to me that because international criminal law cannot now convict and punish all wrongdoers that this means that one important function, and rationale, for international criminal law is not retribution. To say that there is a retributive shortfall is to commit one only to say that more needs to be done in this area of law than is currently being done. Prosecutors always face limited material resources, and can hence not bring to trial all of those who deserve to be punished for their crimes. And while this is worrisome, it need not undercut the retributive rationale of the prosecutions that do take place. If two people deserve to be punished and only one of them is caught, this does not affect the fact that the one that is caught deserves to be prosecuted, and if convicted, punished. The retributive rationale of the trial of the second person is not undermined by the failure to catch the first person.

A more serious worry is that political decisions are made that allow those to be put in the dock who are not the worst offenders. If there are harsher sentences administered for lesser than for graver crimes, retribution is seriously undermined as well. This raises fairness issues and can cut into the retributive rationale of international criminal law. But as far as I can tell, there is nothing endemic to international criminal law that would not allow for such political interference, or unfairness, to be diminished if not eliminated in the future. Similarly, the wide variation in sentences and the seeming lightness of sentences given in international, as opposed to national, tribunals, is also not endemic to international criminal law. Until the passage of the federal sentencing guidelines in the United States, a similar disparity of punishments as well as a comparative lightness of sentence in certain jurisdictions existed. But the uniform guidelines solved many of these problems. There is no structural impediment to stiffer sentences or to uniformity of sentencing in international law just as there is no structural impediment to it in national legal systems. There is, and will remain, limited resources guaranteeing that not all who are guilty can be prosecuted – but that is true in all of criminal law, not merely in international criminal law.

Drumbl also offers a very powerful argument against the deterrence rationale of international criminal law. He forces us to consider a more subtle argument here than considered in the previous sections of this paper. Drumbl argues that those who perpetrate atrocities are not as likely to be deterred as common criminals because there are factors that undermine their rationality; specifically, their calculations about gratification and survival are undermined by the context of atrocity. Since the perpetrators of atrocities are not fully rational, they will not be as easily deterred as common criminals are. In the remainder of this section I will set out and respond to Drumbl's powerful arguments here.

Drumbl first points out that many perpetrators of atrocities find solidarity in being members of violent groups. As Drumbl says: "They are captured by angry social norms or, at least, are captivated by them."[25] And based on this motivation, these perpetrators of atrocities come to believe that they are acting for a collective cause. Drumbl then makes two points. First, it is unlikely that rational choice can occur during the violence that surrounds them. Second, "the value of living or dying for a cause" exceeds the worries about being punished. And in addition, the circumstances of mass violence make individuals feel that they could not have made a difference in any event. These considerations make it much less likely that these perpetrators can be deterred in the way in which common criminals are.[26]

The other consideration that Drumbl focuses on is survival. Many people join violent groups because they feel they don't have any choice in the matter. Drumbl says that "Even those individuals for whom violence is not gratifying may willingly join, insofar as participating in massacre can guarantee survival to the next morning."[27] When one's own survival is in jeopardy, it seems unlikely that a person would be deterred by "the prospect of some distant international" institution "that might punish them" several years from now.[28] In Drumbl's view, deterrence theory "leaves the masses unaccountable."[29] It isn't just leaders, but "broad public participation" that perpetuates mass violence, and the public is unlikely to be deterred by international criminal sanctions.

Again, while I share Drumbl's concerns, I do not find them to show that international criminal law cannot be partially justified by reference to deterrence. First, I would note that Drumbl has not addressed the political or military leaders that will be the overwhelming majority of people brought before the ICC. Those people are not typically rendered less rational by considerations of gratification or survival. And despite what Drumbl says, it is the leaders that are most in need of being deterred if atrocities are to be diminished, especially those related to the crime of aggression, since it is the leaders that plan, initiate, and motivate most atrocities. It is hard to say whether such leaders have been deterred in the past, but there is no evidence that I am aware of that shows that threat of international punishment has not had a deterrent effect, and good reasons to think that it will have such an effect. For, leaders like Pinochet, Milosevic, and Saddam seem quite resistant to serving prison sentences, going to great lengths to avoid being captured and tried. This seems to indicate that they are rational and care about potential loss of freedom.

The minor players also play a crucial role in atrocities, and I am not unsympathetic to some of the worries Drumbl voices about the chances of deterring them. It is certainly true that many small fry are influenced by gratification or fear, although I don't see why Drumbl thinks that these factors, which after all affect nearly all humans, affect these small fry to such an extent that they lose their rational capacities. I agree that the small fry are harder to deter, but for my argument to go through, international criminal law does not have to have strongly deterrent effects on everyone, since deterrence is only a partial justification. In any event, as we will next see, there are also good reasons to support international criminal law in terms of what Drumbl calls expressivism. Even if there were no deterrent effects of international criminal sanctions, the sanctions may be justifiable for the condemnation expressed to the world.

IV. A Limited Defense

I now turn to symbolic issues, and especially to the way those issues are affected when we have political leaders who choose to defend themselves before international tribunals, or at least where such leaders are allowed to speak in their own behalf. The positive symbolic value of international criminal trials is indeed often offset by the countervailing message that a political leader in the dock is able to deliver to his or her fellow citizens back home. I wish to discuss the problem of having a political leader defend himself or herself, and like Milosevic, turn the trial into a mechanism for challenging the legitimacy of international tribunals. I will also address an alternative to having to muzzle a leader who tries to disrupt the trial making it difficult to get the evidence presented and weighed objectively, or as objectively as commonly happens in criminal trials.

David Luban has argued that the normative point of international criminal trials is norm projection, namely, "International public trials declare, in the most public way possible, that the condemned deeds are serious transgressions . . . through the dramaturgy of the trial process, not through treatises or speeches."[30] I have been assuming so far that the point of international criminal trials was pretty much the same as that of any other form of criminal law, namely, deterrence, retribution, and truth. But I actually agree with Luban that norm projection can also be a goal of International Criminal Law, although I disagree that this is primarily accomplished through the dramaturgy of the trial process. Rather, there are book-length treatises being written as the judgments from these courts – indeed the first few judgments of the ICTY were

considerably longer than the book of which this current paper is a part.

Similar to Luban, Drumbl has argued that the best strategy of justifying international criminal law concerns its expressive dimension, although he also notes various problems with such a rationale. Drumbl worries that the kind of narrative that trials can provide is often adversely affected by the nature of trials themselves, namely, that trials can only selectively expose the facts that are relevant to the case against a particular defendant. This is certainly true, but even the selective telling of the story of a narrative has some expressive value and can contribute to the overall diversity of norms defense of international criminal law. Plea-bargaining and the death of a defendant can disrupt the telling of a narrative, as well, argues Drumbl.[31] Perhaps plea-bargaining should be disallowed in high-profile international criminal trials – there certainly is nothing structural to prevent such a prohibition.[32] The death of a defendant cannot be so easily addressed, although the telling of the narrative is often able to proceed with some other defendant in the dock, just as was true when Hitler killed himself before he could be put on trial. Drumbl also worries that trials can get highjacked, as they were by Milosevic, a topic I will return to later.

The problem is that individuals are being put in prison as a result of these international trials. I agree with Koskenniemi that these trials are not and should not be thought of as "show trials" where the international community merely makes a scapegoat of certain people. So, if there is a dramaturgy of international criminal law, it will have to be one that does not merely use defendants as part of the drama, thereby disregarding their rights. Nonetheless, I agree with Luban and Drumbl that some international criminal trials can be justified morally as norm projection, although perhaps with less dramaturgy than they allow.

The Milosevic and Saddam Hussein trials are good illustrations of what the International Criminal Court is likely to face in the future when strong political leaders are put in the dock and charged with mass atrocities. Koskenniemi is right to think that such leaders will be highly motivated to change the nature of the trial, and to try to indict the tribunal, or the Western powers that back the tribunal, rather than to address the evidence within the confines of the rules established for international criminal trials. Milosevic managed to drag the trial out for so long that he eventually died before the trial concluded. And in any event, his standing with the people back home rose rather than fell as the trial progressed. He was seen as a martyr, who stood up for his people, rather than as the butcher that the prosecutors hoped to portray him. Of course, the truth probably was somewhere in the middle, and it is a shame that prosecutors feel compelled to overstate the case against defendants, thereby making it more likely that defendants will then overstate the case against the tribunal back home.

Yet, over time such a problem may dissipate as more and more States ratify the Rome Statute of the ICC, and as clearer rules against prosecutorial overreaching are put in place. As more States and defendants see the Court as a fair forum to help solve various problems with their neighbors, it will be harder to indict the Court as if it is one more instance of Western colonialism or hegemony. In my view, the International Criminal Court needs to gain widespread acceptance, especially in non-Western countries in order best to thwart the specter of political leaders in the dock continuously indicting the ICC itself instead of being forced to respond to the evidence of their putative misdeeds. Political leaders know better than most others when it makes sense to play certain emotionally charged cards and when to hold them back. One of the best long-term strategies to confront the truly daunting problem of what to do about the grandstanding of such leaders is for the ICC to garner the broadest of public support. Since over one hundred States have ratified the Rome Treaty of the ICC, this process seems to be well along already.

Some, like Koskenniemi, will claim that highly politicized trials will never appear fair to both sides. If hegemony and colonialism remain strong in the world, then it is indeed likely that the ICC will merely reflect the dominant powers in the world. But neither the strong critics of the ICC, like Koskenniemi, nor the much weaker critics, like me, can predict the future with any certainty. Courts always reflect, to a certain extent, the reigning political powers of the time. Yet, if there are conflicting powers, Courts have a

fighting chance to escape the influence of just one power and to attain a modicum of fairness, or at least be perceived so by both parties to a dispute. In the long run, my hope is that the ICC will emerge from under the influence of strong powers and be perceived by victims and defendants alike, although not necessarily all of them, as a fair tribunal of the sort that it would be pointless to vilify instead of mounting substantive arguments in favor or opposed to the accusations of guilt of those in the dock.

In the short run, the problems addressed at the beginning of this section remain of pressing importance. One strategy, again only a partial strategy, is to appoint back-up counsel for those political leaders who demand to represent themselves. Such a strategy is likely to be partially effective at restraining the more bellicose of leaders, since back-up counsel will be in a position to point out the countervailing effects of bad behavior on the part of these leaders. But the behavior that is truly problematic, namely that which is not clearly bad behavior, but behavior aimed at making a geopolitical point, will still be hard to deal with. We must recognize that sometimes the geopolitics of the trial may be relevant to proving that the trial is indeed a show trial. We must distinguish the mere cynical playing to the home audience's virulent nationalism, from the serious attempt to show the people back home that the trial is indeed a set-up. For this reason, muzzling defendants should never be countenanced. Nonetheless, it may be necessary in some cases to try temporarily to keep the political speech-making of the defendant to a minimum, and allow the back-up counsel to act in his or her stead, until the defendant, or the prosecutor for that matter, is then willing to address the relevant evidence being brought before the Court.[33]

My proposal will no doubt be seen as unsatisfactory to those who are generally opposed to international criminal law in particular and international law in general. For they will find such trials to be political through-and-through, and will regard even my attempt to restrict one or both sides from politicizing the trials as merely a heavy-handed bias in favor of another type of politicizing that routinely goes on in international law. I am indeed bothered by such criticisms. I would be equally worried about such criticisms voiced against domestic as against international trials. But to give voice to criticisms is not to establish the legitimacy of those criticisms. We must examine whether it is true that international trials are merely, or primarily, the reflection of political bias. And in any event we must look closely at each trial to see whether there is evidence of political bias. In some cases this task will be easier than in others, although in no cases at the moment do trials seem to be completely free from the charge of some political bias. The key consideration, in my opinion is to resist the temptation to make the proceedings into "show trials" for publicizing what seems to be political extremism of one State or one party.

To try to portray the trials as having at least the appearance of fairness, these trials must minimize the politicizing of the trials by either the defendants or the prosecutors. Specifically, I advocate not allowing the joining of defendants together, especially that type of joining that was done at the main Nuremberg trial where all of the major defendants were tried together making it seem as if what any one defendant did was not the main point at issue. In addition, I advocate not allowing the joining of charges together, as was done in the Milosevic trial where it then took years to present the prosecution's case, potentially frustrating the defendant who had to wait so long to present his side of the story.

In many cases, politics can be kept to a minimum if the number of defendants and the number of charges are kept to a minimum, allowing the focus of the trial to be on very specific acts of just one party, and not giving the appearance that the trial is really about what the whole society has done over a very long period of time. It is true, though, that accepting my proposals will make the pursuit of the truth of the causes of the larger atrocity harder to ascertain by means of trials. There will be truths nonetheless that will emerge, and the kind of truth that is less prone to be challenged as blatantly political, namely that truth concerning whether a given defendant did participate in an atrocity and to what extent. But those victims looking for trials to provide a broader truth about these atrocities will sometimes have to give ground in order to maintain a respect for the defendants' rights and the rule of law.

There is a sense in which many of the criticisms I have been considering of international trials are even more apt in cases of the crime of aggression. The idea that one State has acted aggressively and another State has acted only defensively, especially in situations where two States have been feuding for decades, is extremely hard to ascertain without at least the appearance of bias toward one of the parties. It is for this reason, among others, that I have advocated caution in proceeding against State leaders for the crime of aggression. And the caution should be greater than that exercised for crimes against humanity or war crimes trials. Yet, I continue to believe that some criminal trials for the crime of aggression should be conducted, so that whatever the retributive, deterrent, or expressivist effects had by such a trial can manifest themselves. But here even more restrictions on scope must be implemented to make sure that we do not fall prey to the charge of conducting "show trials" that will, for instance, often further widen the divide between Western and non-Western societies.

In this paper, I argued that prosecutions for leaders who initiate such wars should occur, although prosecutions for lower-ranking military and political leaders should proceed more cautiously. I defended such trials, and international criminal trials generally, not by reference to a single normative principle, such as deterrence or retribution or reconciliation, but by reference to a combination of principles applicable differently for different contexts. I also recognized that trials are not likely to satisfy all of the parties, for they are compromises of a sort, where both parties have to settle for a more limited truth, namely, whether a given defendant did participate in an atrocity and to what extent. For some international criminal trials, it may be best that the defendant goes free even though there remains some evidence that he or she did participate in some atrocities, especially the waging of aggressive war, where it is so hard to figure out who did what. In order for such trials to be defended against the critics from various diverse political persuasions, such trials must be greatly restricted in scope.

We stand at a crossroads in the movement for international law and justice. I see myself as squarely in the middle of the debate about which direction to take. On one side are those who argue for cosmopolitan justice; and on the other side are those realists who urge that we retreat from any kind of morally grounded international interference in the affairs of sovereign States. I defend a limited scope for international trials. One of the most important limitations is that we respect the international rule of law and not merely prosecute on the basis of our heartfelt moral outrage in the face of mass atrocities. Human rights are indeed important and need to be protected, especially when it is a State that seeks to abridge these rights. But it is not as clear as it might seem that individuals should be held legally accountable in international proceedings for each and every human rights abuse committed by a State. If we limit our scope, we will have a better chance of defending international trials for the most egregious of human rights abuses.

Notes

1   I do not subscribe to either communitarianism or realism. I suppose my own view comes closest to what Simon Caney has called "the 'society of states' approach." See his book, *Justice Beyond Borders*, Oxford: Oxford University Press, 2005, pp. 10–13.

2   Martti Koskenniemi, "Between Impunity and Show Trials," *Max Planck Yearbook of United Nations Law*, vol. 6, 2002, pp. 1–35.

3   Ibid., p. 2.

4   Lotte Kohler and Hans Kohler, editors, *Hannah Arendt – Karl Jaspers. Correspondence 1926–1969*, 1996, p. 410, quoted in ibid., p. 2, note 3.

5   "Beyond Impunity and Show Trials," p. 3.

6   Ibid., p. 8.

7   Ibid.

8   Ibid., pp. 8–9.

9   See Mark Drumbl, *Atrocity, Punishment, and International Law*. New York: Cambridge Univer-

sity Press, 2007. I address Drumbl's arguments in section III of this paper.

10   Koskenniemi, "Beyond Impunity and Show Trials," p. 12.

11   Ibid.

12   Ibid.

13   Ibid.

14   Ibid., p. 15.

15   Private correspondence.

16   See Jan Klabbers, "Just Revenge? The Deterrence Argument in International Criminal Law," *Finnish Yearbook of International Law*, vol. XII, 2001, pp. 249–67, especially p. 253.

17   Larry May and Nancy Viner, "Actual Innocence and Manifest Injustice," *St Louis University Law Journal*, vol. 49, no. 2, 2004, pp. 481–97.

18   See Larry May, *Crimes Against Humanity: A Normative Account*, New York: Cambridge University Press, 2005, chapter 13.

19   Mark Drumbl, *Atrocity, Punishment, and International Law*.

20   Ibid., p. 151.

21   Ibid., p. 153.

22   Ibid., p. 152.

23   Ibid., p. 155.

24   See ibid., p. 157.

25   Ibid., p. 171.

26   Ibid., pp. 171–2.

27   Ibid., p. 172.

28   Ibid.

29   Ibid.

30   David Luban, "Beyond Moral Minimalism," *Ethics & International Affairs*, vol. 20, no. 3, 2006, pp. 354–5.

31   Drumbl, *Atrocity, Punishment, and International Law*, pp. 187–94.

32   See Nancy Combs' excellent book on this topic, *Guilty Pleas in International Criminal Law*, Stanford, CA: Stanford University Press, 2007.

33   The ICTY's Judge Richard May was a master of controlling the microphones, temporarily cutting off both defendants and prosecutors who strayed too far from the consideration of the evidence in their speech-making. I am uncomfortable with this form of censorship, but it may be a temporary solution that is worth considering.

44

Opening Statement before the International Military Tribunal (1945)

Justice Robert H. Jackson

On November 21, 1945, in the Palace of Justice at Nuremberg, Germany, Justice Robert H. Jackson, Chief of Counsel for the United States, made his opening statement to the International Military Tribunal in Case No. 1, The United States of America, the French Republic, the United Kingdom of Great Britain and Northern Ireland, and the Union of Soviet Socialist Republics v. Hermann Wilhelm Göring, et al.

May it please Your Honors:

The privilege of opening the first trial in history for crimes against the peace of the world imposes a grave responsibility. The wrongs which we seek to condemn and punish have been so calculated, so malignant, and so devastating, that civilization cannot tolerate their being ignored, because it cannot survive their being repeated. That four great nations, flushed with victory and stung with injury stay the hand of vengeance and voluntarily submit their captive enemies to the judgment of the law is one of the most significant tributes that Power has ever paid to Reason.

This Tribunal, while it is novel and experimental, is not the product of abstract speculations nor is it created to vindicate legalistic theories. This inquest represents the practical effort of four of the most mighty of nations, with the support of 17 more, to utilize international law to meet the greatest menace of our times – aggressive war. The common sense of mankind demands that law shall not stop with the punishment of petty crimes by little people. It must also reach men who possess themselves of great power and make deliberate and concerted use of it to set in motion evils which leave no home in the world untouched. It is a cause of that magnitude that the United Nations will lay before Your Honors.

In the prisoners' dock sit twenty-odd broken men. Reproached by the humiliation of those they have led almost as bitterly as by the desolation of those they have attacked, their personal capacity for evil is forever past. It is hard now to perceive in these men as captives the power by which as Nazi leaders they once dominated much of the world and terrified most of it. Merely as individuals their fate is of little consequence to the world.

What makes this inquest significant is that these prisoners represent sinister influences that will lurk in the world long after their bodies have returned to dust. We will show them to be living symbols of racial hatreds, of terrorism and violence, and of the arrogance and cruelty

Justice Robert H. Jackson, "Opening Statement before the International Military Tribunal," International Military Tribunal, Nuremberg, November 21, 1945. *Source*: www.roberthjackson.org/Man/theman2-7-8-1/.

of power. They are symbols of fierce nationalisms and of militarism, of intrigue and war-making which have embroiled Europe generation after generation, crushing its manhood, destroying its homes, and impoverishing its life. They have so identified themselves with the philosophies they conceived and with the forces they directed that any tenderness to them is a victory and an encouragement to all the evils which are attached to their names. Civilization can afford no compromise with the social forces which would gain renewed strength if we deal ambiguously or indecisively with the men in whom those forces now precariously survive.

What these men stand for we will patiently and temperately disclose. We will give you undeniable proofs of incredible events. The catalog of crimes will omit nothing that could be conceived by a pathological pride, cruelty, and lust for power. These men created in Germany, under the "Führerprinzip", a National Socialist despotism equalled only by the dynasties of the ancient East. They took from the German people all those dignities and freedoms that we hold natural and inalienable rights in every human being. The people were compensated by inflaming and gratifying hatreds towards those who were marked as "scapegoats". Against their opponents, including Jews, Catholics, and free labor, the Nazis directed such a campaign of arrogance, brutality, and annihilation as the world has not witnessed since the pre-Christian ages. They excited the German ambition to be a "master race", which of course implies serfdom for others. They led their people on a mad gamble for domination. They diverted social energies and resources to the creation of what they thought to be an invincible war machine. They overran their neighbors. To sustain the "master race" in its war-making, they enslaved millions of human beings and brought them into Germany, where these hapless creatures now wander as "displaced persons". At length bestiality and bad faith reached such excess that they aroused the sleeping strength of imperiled Civilization. Its united efforts have ground the German war machine to fragments. But the struggle has left Europe a liberated yet prostrate land where a demoralized society struggles to survive. These are the fruits of the sinister forces that sit with these defendants in the prisoners' dock.

In justice to the nations and the men associated in this prosecution, I must remind you of certain difficulties which may leave their mark on this case. Never before in legal history has an effort been made to bring within the scope of a single litigation the developments of a decade, covering a whole continent, and involving a score of nations, countless individuals, and innumerable events. Despite the magnitude of the task, the world has demanded immediate action. This demand has had to be met, though perhaps at the cost of finished craftsmanship. To my country, established courts, following familiar procedures, applying well-thumbed precedents, and dealing with the legal consequences of local and limited events seldom commence a trial within a year of the event in litigation. Yet less than 8 months ago today the courtroom in which you sit was an enemy fortress in the hands of German SS troops. Less than 8 months ago nearly all our witnesses and documents were in enemy hands. The law had not been codified, no procedures had been established, no tribunal was in existence, no usable courthouse stood here, none of the hundreds of tons of official German documents had been examined, no prosecuting staff had been assembled, nearly all of the present defendants were at large, and the four prosecuting powers had not yet joined in common cause to try them. I should be the last to deny that the case may well suffer from incomplete researches and quite likely will not be the example of professional work which any of the prosecuting nations would normally wish to sponsor. It is, however, a completely adequate case to the judgment we shall ask you to render, and its full development we shall be obliged to leave to historians.

Before I discuss particulars of evidence, some general considerations which may affect the credit of this trial in the eyes of the world should be candidly faced. There is a dramatic disparity between the circumstances of the accusers and of the accused that might discredit our work if we should falter, in even minor matters, in being fair and temperate.

Unfortunately, the nature of these crimes is such that both prosecution and judgment must be by victor nations over vanquished foes. The worldwide scope of the aggressions carried out by these men has left but few real neutrals.

Either the victors must judge the vanquished or we must leave the defeated to judge themselves. After the first World War, we learned the futility of the latter course. The former high station of these defendants, the notoriety of their acts, and the adaptability of their conduct to provoke retaliation make it hard to distinguish between the demand for a just and measured retribution, and the unthinking cry for vengeance which arises from the anguish of war. It is our task, so far as humanly possible, to, draw the line between the two. We must never forget that the record on which we judge these defendants today is the record on which history will judge us tomorrow. To pass these defendants a poisoned chalice is to put it to our own lips as well. We must summon such detachment and intellectual integrity to our task that this trial will commend itself to posterity as fulfilling humanity's aspirations to do justice.

At the very outset, let us dispose of the contention that to put these men to trial is to do them an injustice entitling them to some special consideration. These defendants may be hard pressed but they are not ill used. Let us see what alternative they would have to being tried.

More than a majority of these prisoners surrendered to or were tracked down by the forces of the United States. Could they expect us to make American custody a shelter for our enemies against the just wrath of our Allies? Did we spend American lives to capture them only to save them from punishment? Under the principles of the Moscow Declaration, those suspected war criminals who are not to be tried internationally must be turned over to individual governments for trial at the scene of their outrages. Many less responsible and less culpable American-held prisoners have been and will continue to be turned over to other United Nations for local trial. If these defendants should succeed, for any reason, in escaping the condemnation of this Tribunal, or if they obstruct or abort this trial, those who are American-held prisoners will be delivered up to our continental Allies. For these defendants, however, we have set up an International Tribunal and have undertaken the burden of participating in a complicated effort to give them fair and dispassionate hearings. That is the best-known protection to any man with a defense worthy of being heard.

If these men are the first war leaders of a defeated nation to be prosecuted in the name of the law, they are also the first to be given a chance to plead for their lives in the name of the law. Realistically, the Charter of this Tribunal, which gives them a hearing, is also the source of their only hope. It may be that these men of troubled conscience, whose only wish is that the world forget them, do not regard a trial as a favor. But they do have a fair opportunity to defend themselves – a favor which these men, when in power, rarely extended to their fellow countrymen. Despite the fact that public opinion already condemns their acts, we agree that here they must be given a presumption of innocence, and we accept the burden of proving criminal acts and the responsibility of these defendants for their commission.

When I say that we do not ask for convictions unless we prove crime, I do not mean mere technical or incidental transgression of international conventions. We charge guilt on planned and intended conduct that involves moral as well as legal wrong. And we do not mean conduct that is a natural and human, even if illegal, cutting of corners, such as many of us might well have committed had we been in the defendants' positions. It is not because they yielded to the normal frailties of human beings that we accuse them. It is their abnormal and inhuman conduct which brings them to this bar.

We will not ask you to convict these men on the testimony of their foes. There is no count in the Indictment that cannot be proved by books and records. The Germans were always meticulous record keepers, and these defendants had their share of the Teutonic passion for thoroughness in putting things on paper. Nor were they without vanity. They arranged frequently to be photographed in action. We will show you their own films. You will see their own conduct and hear their own voices as these defendants re-enact for you, from the screen, some of the events in the course of the conspiracy.

We would also make clear that we have no purpose to incriminate the whole German people. We know that the Nazi Party was not put in power by a majority of the German vote. We know it came to power by an evil alliance between the most extreme of the Nazi revolutionists, the most unrestrained of the German reactionaries, and the most aggressive of the German militarists. If the German populace had willingly accepted the Nazi program, no Storm-troopers would have been needed in the early days of the Party and there would have been no need for concentration camps or the Gestapo, both of which institutions were inaugurated as soon as the Nazis gained control of the German State. Only after these lawless innovations proved successful at home were they taken abroad.

The German people should know by now that the people of the United States hold them in no fear, and in no hate. It is true that the Germans have taught us the horrors of modern warfare, but the ruin that lies from the Rhine to the Danube shows that we, like our Allies, have not been dull pupils. If we are not awed by German fortitude and proficiency in war, and if we are not persuaded of their political maturity, we do respect their skill in the arts of peace, their technical competence, and the sober, industrious, and self-disciplined character of the masses of the German people. In 1933 we saw the German people recovering prestige in the commercial, industrial, and artistic world after the set-back of the last war. We beheld their progress neither with envy nor malice. The Nazi regime interrupted this advance. The recoil of the Nazi aggression has left Germany in ruins. The Nazi readiness to pledge the German word without hesitation and to break it without shame has fastened upon German diplomacy a reputation for duplicity that will handicap it for years. Nazi arrogance has made the boast of the "master race" a taunt that will be thrown at Germans the world over for generations. The Nazi nightmare has given the German name a new and sinister significance throughout the world which will retard Germany a century. The German, no less than the non-German world, has accounts to settle with these defendants.

The fact of the war and the course of the war, which is the central theme of our case, is history. From September 1st, 1939, when the German armies crossed the Polish frontier, until September 1942, when they met epic resistance at Stalingrad, German arms seemed invincible. Denmark and Norway, the Netherlands and France, Belgium and Luxembourg, the Balkans and Africa, Poland and the Baltic States, and parts of Russia, all had been overrun and conquered by

swift, powerful, well-aimed blows. That attack on the peace of the world is the crime against international society which brings into international cognizance crimes in its aid and preparation which otherwise might be only internal concerns. It was aggressive war, which the nations of the world had renounced. It was war in violation of treaties, by which the peace of the world was sought to be safe-guarded.

This war did not just happen – it was planned and prepared for over a long period of time and with no small skill and cunning. The world has perhaps never seen such a concentration and stimulation of the energies of any people as that which enabled Germany 20 years after it was defeated, disarmed, and dismembered to come so near carrying out its plan to dominate Europe. Whatever else we may say of those who were the authors of this war, they did achieve a stupendous work in organization, and our first task is to examine the means by which these defendants and their fellow conspirators prepared and incited Germany to go to war.

In general, our case will disclose these defendants all uniting at some time with the Nazi Party in a plan which they well knew could be accomplished only by an outbreak of war in Europe. Their seizure of the German State, their subjugation of the German people, their terrorism and extermination of dissident elements, their planning and waging of war, their calculated and planned ruthlessness in the conduct of warfare, their deliberate and planned criminality toward conquered peoples, – all these are ends for which they acted in concert; and all these are phases of the conspiracy, a conspiracy which reached one goal only to set out for another and more ambitious one. We shall also trace for you the intricate web of organizations which these men formed and utilized to accomplish these ends. We will show how the entire structure of offices and officials was dedicated to the criminal purposes and committed to the use of the criminal methods planned by these defendants and their co-conspirators, many of whom war and suicide have put beyond reach.

It is my purpose to open the case, particularly under Count One of the Indictment, and to deal with the Common Plan or Conspiracy to achieve ends possible only by resort to Crimes against Peace, War Crimes, and Crimes against

Humanity. My emphasis will not be on individual barbarities and perversions which may have occurred independently of any central plan. One of the dangers ever present is that this trial may be protracted by details of particular wrongs and that we will become lost in a "wilderness of single instances". Nor will I now dwell on the activity of individual defendants except as it may contribute to exposition of the common plan.

The case as presented by the United States will be concerned with the brains and authority back of all the crimes. These defendants were men of a station and rank which does not soil its own hands with blood. They were men who knew how to use lesser folk as tools. We want to reach the planners and designers, the inciters and leaders without whose evil architecture the world would not have been for so long scourged with the violence and lawlessness, and wracked with the agonies and convulsions, of this terrible war.

[. . .]

To apply the sanctions of the law to those whose conduct is found criminal by the standards I have outlined, is the responsibility committed to this Tribunal. It is the first court ever to undertake the difficult task of overcoming the confusion of many tongues and the conflicting concepts of just procedure among divers systems of law, so as to reach a common judgment. The tasks of all of us are such as to make heavy demands on patience and good will. Although the need for prompt action has admittedly resulted in imperfect work on the part of the Prosecution, four great nations bring you their hurriedly assembled contributions of evidence. What remains undiscovered we can only guess. We could, with witnesses' testimony, prolong the recitals of crime for years – but to what avail. We shall rest the case when we have offered what seems convincing and adequate proof of the crimes charged without unnecessary cumulation of evidence. We doubt very much whether it will be seriously denied that the crimes I have outlined took place. The effort will undoubtedly be to mitigate or escape personal responsibility.

Among the nations which unite in accusing these defendants the United States is perhaps in a position to be the most dispassionate, for, having sustained the least injury, it is perhaps the least animated by vengeance. Our American cities have not been bombed by day and by night, by humans, and by robots. It is not our temples that had been laid in ruins. Our countrymen have not had their homes destroyed over their heads. The menace of Nazi aggression, except to those in actual service, has seemed less personal and immediate to us than to European peoples. But while the United States is not first in rancor, it is not second in determination that the forces of law and order be made equal to the task of dealing with such international lawlessness as I have recited here.

Twice in my lifetime, the United States has sent its young manhood across the Atlantic, drained its resources, and burdened itself with debt to help defeat Germany. But the real hope and faith that has sustained the American people in these great efforts was that victory for ourselves and our Allies would lay the basis for an ordered international relationship in Europe and would end the centuries of strife on this embattled continent.

Twice we have held back in the early stages of European conflict in the belief that it might be confined to a purely European affair. In the United States, we have tried to build an economy without armament, a system of government without militarism, and a society where men are not regimented for war. This purpose, we know now, can never be realized if the world periodically is to be embroiled in war. The United States cannot, generation after generation, throw its youth or its resources on to the battlefields of Europe to redress the lack of balance between Germany's strength and that of her enemies, and to keep the battles from our shores.

The American dream of a peace-and-plenty economy, as well as the hopes of other nations, can never be fulfilled if those nations are involved in a war every generation so vast and devastating as to crush the generation that fights and burden the generation that follows. But experience has shown that wars are no longer local. All modern wars become world wars eventually. And none of the big nations at least can stay out. If we cannot stay out of wars, our only hope is to prevent wars.

I am too well aware of the weaknesses of juridical action alone to contend that in itself your decision under this Charter can prevent future wars. Judicial action always comes after the event. Wars are started only on the theory and in the confidence that they can be won. Personal punishment, to be suffered only in the event the war is lost, will probably not be a sufficient deterrent to prevent a war where the warmakers feel the chances of defeat to be negligible.

But the ultimate step in avoiding periodic wars, which are inevitable in a system of international lawlessness, is to make statesmen responsible to law. And let me make clear that while this law is first applied against German aggressors, the law includes, and if it is to serve a useful purpose it must condemn aggression by any other nations, including those which sit here now in judgment. We are able to do away with domestic tyranny and violence and aggression by those in power against the rights of their own people only when we make all men answerable to the law. This trial represents mankind's desperate effort to apply the discipline of the law to statesmen who have used their powers of state to attack the foundations of the world's peace and to commit aggressions against the rights of their neighbors.

The usefulness of this effort to do justice is not to be measured by considering the law or your judgment in isolation. This trial is part of the great effort to make the peace more secure. One step in this direction is the United Nations organization, which may take joint political action to prevent war if possible, and joint military action to insure that any nation which starts a war will lose it. This Charter and this trial, implementing the Kellogg–Briand Pact, constitute another step in the same direction and juridical action of a kind to insure that those who start a war will pay for it personally.

While the defendants and the prosecutors stand before you as individuals, it is not the triumph of either group alone that is committed to your judgment. Above all personalities there are anonymous and impersonal forces whose conflict makes up much of human history. It is yours to throw the strength of the law back of either the one or the other of these forces for at least another generation. What are the real forces that are contending before you?

No charity can disguise the fact that the forces which these defendants represent, the forces that would advantage and delight in their acquittal, are the darkest and most sinister forces in society – dictatorship and oppression, malevolence and passion, militarism and lawlessness. By their fruits we best know them. Their acts have bathed the world in blood and set civilization back a century. They have subjected their European neighbors to every outrage and torture, every spoliation and deprivation that insolence, cruelty, and greed could inflict. They have brought the German people to the lowest pitch of wretchedness, from which they can entertain no hope of early deliverance. They have stirred hatreds and incited domestic violence on every continent. These are the things that stand in the dock shoulder to shoulder with these prisoners.

The real complaining party at your bar is Civilization. In all our countries it is still a struggling and imperfect thing. It does not plead that the United States, or any other country, has been blameless of the conditions which made the German people easy victims to the blandishments and intimidations of the Nazi conspirators.

But it points to the dreadful sequence of aggressions and crimes I have recited, it points to the weariness of flesh, the exhaustion of resources, and the destruction of all that was beautiful or useful in so much of the world, and to greater potentialities for destruction in the days to come. It is not necessary among the ruins of this ancient and beautiful city with untold members of its civilian inhabitants still buried in its rubble, to argue the proposition that to start or wage an aggressive war has the moral qualities of the worst of crimes. The refuge of the defendants can be only their hope that international law will lag so far behind the moral sense of mankind that conduct which is crime in the moral sense must be regarded as innocent in law.

Civilization asks whether law is so laggard as to be utterly helpless to deal with crimes of this magnitude by criminals of this order of importance. It does not expect that you can make war impossible. It does expect that your juridical action will put the forces of international law, its precepts, its prohibitions and, most of all, its sanctions, on the side of peace, so that men and women of good will, in all countries, may have "leave to live by no man's leave, underneath the law."

Questions

1   Considering Mill's example of public drunkenness, explain the difference between offense and injury, and how it relates to his "harm principle." Why do you think this distinction is important for Mill's normative theory of criminal law?

2   Explain why disgust is important for Devlin's argument for public morality, and how it justifies criminal liability.

3   In your own view, is there such a thing as public morality and what role should it play in debates about individual freedoms and criminal liability?

4   In expressivist terms, how significant is the fact that trials take place rather than summary executions of those who lose wars?

5   Is international criminal punishment more problematic than domestic criminal punishment in terms of deterrence?

Part VII

Contracts

Introduction

According to this concept, law should protect agreements that are freely entered into. Here, more than in any other field of law, we see how the "bindingness" of law is based on the self-binding acts of individuals. A dispute nonetheless continues about why people are bound to perform their contracts and about why the law is justified in intervening in what appear to be the private actions of individuals trying to regulate their own lives. It is often said that contract law is the cornerstone of free society, and yet, contract law is also criticized as being the basis of economic exploitation by the powerful against the poor.

We begin this section with a selection from Thomas Hobbes's seventeenth-century classic, *Leviathan*. Hobbes defines a contract as a "mutual transferring of right." One can transfer a right either by delivering a good to another person or by transferring the right with the promise that the good will follow. However, Hobbes argues that a mere promise is not a transfer of right: A promise indicates what one will do in the future, but a contract occurs in the present. For a contract to occur, something must be transferred in the present. Hobbes says that it is the right that must transfer, and there must be some clear sign that this has occurred. In legal systems, societies have established rules for the transfer of rights that allow someone to distinguish mere promises from a contract. In the Anglo-American tradition, "consideration" is the sufficient sign that a binding contract has been made.

Hobbes provides one of the most widely cited justifications for the institution of contracts. In the state of nature, prior to the formation of societies, people had no constraints on their avaricious behavior. As a result, each person felt that she had a right to do anything to the other. But this created extreme uncertainty and fear, because no one could trust anyone else. Yet, people saw the need for trust and peace in order to prosper. Because of the lack of trust, agreements were impossible; nonetheless, people were naturally driven to seek them to better their lives. People wanted to trust one another, but the first person to do so would be taking too great a risk. Societies, especially coercive governments, were created to enforce contracts and make it reasonable for people to enter into and perform their contracts. Without such arrangements, people would still be in the state of nature, hoping for peace and prosperity but unable to achieve these goals. Without contracts, people's lives would be "solitary, poor, nasty, brutish and short."[1]

In "The Practice of Promising," P. S. Atiyah expands on Hobbes's analysis, linking the obligation to perform contracts and keep promises to the performer's expected benefit. Atiyah points out that in law a person justifiably fails to perform a contract either if there has already been a breach by the other party or if the expected benefit of performing has greatly diminished. Indeed, the reason to keep contracts and promises has more to do, he suggests, with the idea that someone else has relied on the expected performance to his or her detriment. In those cases where there has been no loss from relying on the promise of another, judges are unlikely to demand that the breaching party suffer any sanction. Atiyah argues that one cannot ascertain the moral justification of performing contracts or promises unless one determines why the promise was made. Promises are made and kept not out of general concern for morality but because of what the promisor expects to get by performing.

Charles Fried, in "Contract as Promise," provides a sustained argument against views like those of Atiyah, contending that contract law hinges on the moral doctrine that a person's explicit, intentional act of promising is morally binding and therefore also legally enforceable. Here, commitment is the most important idea, much more important than expected benefit or reliance. Reliance cannot fully account for why the law enforces contracts, for, most frequently, expectation, not reliance, serves as the basis of compensation for breached contracts. Expectation is simply the position one would have been in had the contract been performed rather than breached. To account for this scheme of legal compensation, we are required to look beyond the interests of the parties to what they have actually committed to.

Fried sees contracts as exemplifying a distinctly liberal principle – namely, that people should be free to live their lives as they see fit. When a person chooses to make a promise or contract, he transforms an act from something that was previously morally neutral into something that is now morally required. Our free choices make a difference in the world, and we should be held responsible for both the good and the bad that occur as the result of our free choices. If we commit ourselves to perform a certain act, then we should be held liable if we do not so perform. Fried is thus led to conclude that contracts derive their moral justification from their intimate relationship to promises.

In "Legally Enforceable Commitments," Michael D. Bayles proposes a set of reasonable limits for determining which contract should be legally enforced. Specifically, Bayles proposes three principles that should govern the legal enforcement of contracts. First, he argues that

involuntary transfers should be disallowed; only voluntary transfers of goods should be legally enforced. Second, zero-sum transactions should be enforced only if doing so is necessary to prevent loss to one of the parties. Contracts should normally be limited to mutually beneficial transactions, and contracts that involve a loss to both parties should not be allowed. Third, the legal enforcement of contracts should be limited to those that are for the "collective good."

A good example of a dispute about the place of law in contractual situations concerns whether a contract can be so lopsided and coercive as to be morally "unconscionable" and considered void on that basis alone. The standard account of unconscionability is that it involves unequal bargaining power, where one of the parties will almost surely not benefit from the transaction. In "Unconscionability and Contracts," Alan Wertheimer argues that many contracts involve unequal bargaining power; indeed, the authors of the Uniform Commercial Code say that the purpose of the unconscionability doctrine is not to eliminate the risk of loss of bargaining that people may voluntarily choose to incur but, rather, "to prevent oppression and unfair surprise."

Concern about unconscionability typically arises when one party uses a standard form contract that allows no room for bargaining. This is increasingly prevalent in the practice of rental agreements and sales contracts, and often takes place when the landlord or merchant is economically powerful and the tenant or buyer not terribly knowledgeable. Often, these types of contract look as if there is a bargaining inequality. But what exactly is the problem with standard form contracts? Wertheimer says that many such contracts are perfectly fair. Indeed, he points out that the take-it-or-leave-it character of standard form transactions often does not substantially differ from most other commercial transactions. Wertheimer suggests that the only way to save the idea of unconscionable contract is to argue that such agreements are ideally bad for society even if no person is specifically harmed.

In many parts of the world, unconscionability of contract is not recognized as a legal doctrine. In "South African Contract Law: The Need for a Concept of Unconscionability," Lynn Berat argues that South Africa should embrace the doctrine of unconscionability. South Africa has especially high numbers of both wealthy businesses and people in abject poverty. Law should protect the vulnerable when their interests conflict with those of the powerful. Berat's essay provides a useful summary of the main differences between systems of law that follow a Roman model and those that follow an Anglo-Saxon model. The Roman model focuses only on whether there has in fact been an agreement. South Africa has a hybrid system; it is part Roman and part Anglo-Saxon. The Roman influence predominates in contract law. As a result, contracts are not invalidated unless they are clearly fraudulent or signed under duress. Berat argues that considerations of fraud and duress will help protect some buyers, but many others will not have their economic rights fully protected until South Africa adopts the unconscionability doctrine.

The final piece of this section is the US court case *Williams v. Walker-Thomas Furniture Co.* This case concerns an installment contract for the purchase of furniture that stipulated that if a payment was missed, the furniture could be repossessed, along with any other furniture purchased from the same company that still had an outstanding balance. There was nothing fraudulent about the agreement. After the buyer defaulted on one payment, the furniture company attempted to repossess all the furniture that the buyer had purchased over the previous four years. In holding for the buyer, the court stressed the unequal bargaining position of the parties, saying that in such situations there "is little real choice" on the part of the buyer. For this reason, the court found the terms of the contract to be unconscionable. In the dissenting opinion, Circuit Judge Danaher argues that more caution is needed given that the buyer "seems to have known precisely where she stood."[2]

Notes

1 Thomas Hobbes, *Leviathan*, ch. 13.
2 Williams v. Walker-Thomas Furniture Co., United States Court of Appeals, District of Columbia Circuit, 1960, 350 F.2d 450.

45

Of the First and Second Natural Laws, and of Contracts

Thomas Hobbes

Right of nature what. THE RIGHT OF NATURE, which writers commonly call *jus naturale*, is the liberty each man hath, to use his own power, as he will himself, for the preservation of his own nature; that is to say, of his own life; and consequently of doing any thing, which in his own judgment, and reason, he shall conceive to be the aptest means thereunto.

Liberty what. By LIBERTY, is understood, according to the proper signification of the word, the absence of external impediments: which impediments, may oft take away part of a man's power to do what he would; but cannot hinder him from using the power left him, according as his judgment, and reason shall dictate to him.

A law of nature what. Difference of right and law. A LAW OF NATURE, *lex naturalis*, is a precept or general rule, found out by reason, by which a man is forbidden to do that, which is destructive of his life, or taketh away the means of preserving the same; and to omit that, by which he thinketh it may be best preserved. For though they that speak of this subject, use to confound *jus*, and *lex*, *right* and *law*: yet they ought to be distinguished; because RIGHT, consisteth in liberty to do, or to forbear: whereas LAW, determineth, and bindeth to one of them: so that law, and right, differ as much, as obligation, and liberty; which in one and the same matter are inconsistent.

Naturally every man has right to every thing. The fundamental law of nature. And because the condition of man, as hath been declared in the precedent chapter, is a condition of war of every one against every one; in which case every one is governed by his own reason; and there is nothing he can make use of, that may not be a help unto him, in preserving his life against his enemies; it followeth, that in such a condition, every man has a right to every thing; even to one another's body. And therefore, as long as this natural right of every man to every thing endureth, there can be no security to any man, how strong or wise soever he be, of living out the time, which nature ordinarily alloweth men to live. And consequently it is a precept, or general rule of reason, *that every man, ought to endeavour peace, as far as he has hope of obtaining it; and when he cannot obtain it, that he may seek, and use, all helps, and advantages of war.* The first branch of which rule, containeth the first, and fundamental law of nature; which is, *to seek peace, and follow it.* The second, the sum of the right of nature; which is, *by all means we can, to defend ourselves.*

The second law of nature. From this fundamental law of nature, by which men are commanded to endeavour peace, is derived this second law; *that a man be willing, when others*

Thomas Hobbes, "Of the First and Second Natural Laws, and of Contracts," from *Leviathan*, chapter 14.

are so too, as far-forth, as for peace, and defence of himself he shall think it necessary, to lay down this right to all things; and be contented with so much liberty against other men, as he would allow other men against himself. For as long as every man holdeth this right, of doing anything he liketh; so long are all men in the condition of war. But if other men will not lay down their right, as well as he; then there is no reason for any one to divest himself of his: for that were to expose himself to prey, which no man is bound to, rather than to dispose himself to peace. This is that law of the Gospel; *whatsoever you require that others should do to you, that do ye to them.* And that law of all men, *quod tibi fieri non vis, alteri ne feceris.*

What it is to lay down a right. To *lay down* a man's *right* to any thing, is to *divest* himself of the *liberty*, of hindering another of the benefit of his own right to the same. For he that renounceth, or passeth away his right, giveth not to any other man a right which he had not before; because there is nothing to which every man had not right by nature: but only standeth out of his way, that he may enjoy his own original right, without hindrance from him; not without hindrance from another. So that the effect which reboundeth to one man, by another man's defect of right, is but so much diminution of impediments to the use of his own right original.

Renouncing a right, what it is. Transferring right what. Obligation. Duty. Injustice. Right is laid aside, either by simply renouncing it; or by transferring it to another. By *simply* RENOUNCING; when he cares not to whom the benefit thereof reboundeth. By TRANSFERRING; when he intendeth the benefit thereof to some certain person, or persons. And when a man hath in either manner abandoned, or granted away his right; then is he said to be OBLIGED, or BOUND, not to hinder those, to whom such right is granted, or abandoned, from the benefit of it: and that he *ought*, and it is his DUTY, not to make void that voluntary act of his own: and that such hindrance is INJUSTICE, and INJURY, as being *sine jure*; the right being before renounced, or transferred. So that *injury*, or *injustice*, in the controversies of the world, is somewhat like to that, which in the disputations of scholars is called *absurdity*. For as it is there called an absurdity, to contradict what one maintained in the beginning: so

in the world, it is called injustice, and injury, voluntarily to undo that, which from the beginning he had voluntarily done. The way by which a man either simply renounceth, or transferreth his right, is a declaration, or signification, by some voluntary and sufficient sign, or signs, that he doth so renounce, or transfer; or hath so renounced, or transferred the same, to him that accepteth it. And these signs are either words only, or actions only; or, as it happeneth most often, both words, and actions. And the same are the BONDS by which men are bound, and obliged: bonds, that have their strength, not from their own nature, for nothing is more easily broken than a man's word, but from fear of some evil consequence upon the rupture.

Not all rights are alienable. Whensoever a man transferreth his right, or renounceth it; it is either in consideration of some right reciprocally transferred to himself; or for some other good he hopeth for thereby. For it is a voluntary act: and of the voluntary acts of every man, the object is some *good to himself.* And therefore there be some rights, which no man can be understood by any words, or other signs, to have abandoned, or transferred. As first a man cannot lay down the right of resisting them, that assault him by force, to take away his life; because he cannot be understood to aim thereby, at any good to himself. The same may be said of wounds, and chains, and imprisonment; both because there is no benefit consequent to such patience; as there is to the patience of suffering another to be wounded, or imprisoned; as also because a man cannot tell, when he seeth men proceed against him by violence, whether they intend his death or not. And lastly the motive, and end for which this renouncing, and transferring of right is introduced, is nothing else but the security of a man's person, in his life, and in the means of so preserving life, as not to be weary of it. And therefore if a man by words, or other signs, seem to despoil himself of the end, for which those signs were intended; he is not to be understood as if he meant it, or that it was his will; but that he was ignorant of how such words and actions were to be interpreted.

Contract what. The mutual transferring of right, is that which men call CONTRACT.

There is difference between transferring of right to the thing; and transferring, or tradition, that is delivery of the thing itself. For the thing may be delivered together with the translation of the right; as in buying and selling with ready-money; or exchange of goods, or lands: and it may be delivered some time after.

Covenant what. Again, one of the contractors, may deliver the thing contracted for on his part, and leave the other to perform his part at some determinate time after, and in the mean time be trusted; and then the contract on his part, is called PACT, or COVENANT: or both parts may contract now, to perform hereafter: in which cases, he that is to perform in time to come, being trusted, his performance is called *keeping of promise*, or faith; and the failing of performance, if it be voluntary, *violation of faith.*

Free gift. When the transferring of right, is not mutual, but one of the parties transferreth, in hope to gain thereby friendship, or service from another, or from his friends; or in hope to gain the reputation of charity, or magnanimity; or to deliver his mind from the pain of compassion; or in hope of reward in heaven; this is not contract, but GIFT, FREE-GIFT, GRACE: which words signify one and the same thing.

Signs of contract express. Promise. Signs of contract, are either *express* or *by inference.* Express, are words spoken with understanding of what they signify: and such words are either of the time *present*, or *past*; as, *I give, I grant, I have given, I have granted, I will that this be yours*: or of the future; as, *I will give, I will grant*: which words of the future are called PROMISE.

Signs of contract by inference. Signs by inference, are sometimes the consequence of words; sometimes the consequence of silence; sometimes the consequence of actions; sometimes the consequence of forbearing an action: and generally a sign by inference, of any contract, is whatsoever sufficiently argues the will of the contractor.

Free gift passeth by words of the present or past. Words alone, if they be of the time to come, and contain a bare promise, are an insufficient sign of a free-gift, and therefore not obligatory. For if they be of the time to come, as *tomorrow I will give*, they are a sign I have not given yet, and consequently that my right is not transferred, but remaineth till I transfer it by some other act. But if the words be of the time present, or past, as, *I have given*, or *do give to be delivered to-morrow*, then is my to-morrow's right given

away to-day; and that by the virtue of the words, though there were no other argument of my will. And there is a great difference in the signification of these words, *volo hoc tuum esse cras*, and *cras dabo*; that is, between *I will that this be thine tomorrow*, and, *I will give it thee tomorrow*: for the word *I will*, in the former manner of speech, signifies an act of the will present; but in the latter, it signifies a promise of an act of the will to come: and therefore the former words, being of the present, transfer a future right; the latter, that be of the future, transfer nothing. But if there be other signs of the will to transfer a right, besides words; then though the gift be free, yet may the right be understood to pass by words of the future: as if a man propound a prize to him that comes first to the end of a race, the gift is free: and though the words be of the future, yet the right passeth: for if he would not have his words so be understood, he should not have let them run.

Signs of contract are words both of the past, present, and future. In contracts, the right passeth, not only where the words are of the time present, or past, but also where they are of the future: because all contract is mutual translation, or change of right; and therefore he that promiseth only, because he hath already received the benefit for which he promiseth, is to be understood as if he intended the right should pass: for unless he had been content to have his words so understood, the other would not have performed his part first. And for that cause, in buying, and selling, and other acts of contract, a promise is equivalent to a covenant; and therefore obligatory.

Merit what. He that performeth first in the case of a contract, is said to MERIT that which he is to receive by the performance of the other; and he hath it as *due*. Also when a prize is propounded to many, which is to be given to him only that winneth; or money is thrown amongst many, to be enjoyed by them that catch it; though this be a free gift; yet so to win, or so to catch, is to *merit*, and to have it as DUE. For the right is transferred in the propounding of the prize, and in throwing down the money; though it be not determined to whom, but by the event of the contention. But there is between these two sorts of merit, this difference, that in contract, I merit by virtue of my own power, and the contractor's need; but in this case of free gift, I am enabled to merit only by the benignity of the giver: in contract I merit at the contractor's hand that he should depart with his right; in this case of gift, I merit not that the giver should part with his right; but that when he has parted with it, it should be mine, rather than another's. And this I think to be the meaning of that distinction of the Schools, between *meritum congrui*, and *meritum condigni*. For God Almighty, having promised Paradise to those men, hoodwinked with carnal desires, that can walk through this world according to the precepts, and limits prescribed by him; they say, he that shall so walk, shall merit Paradise *ex congruo*. But because no man can demand a right to it, by his own righteousness, or any other power in himself, but by the free grace of God only; they say no man can merit Paradise *ex condigno*. This I say, I think is the meaning of that distinction; but because disputers do not agree upon the significance of their own terms of art, longer than it serves their turn; I will not affirm any thing of their meaning: only this I say; when a gift is given indefinitely, as a prize to be contended for, he that winneth meriteth, and may claim the prize as due.

Covenants of mutual trust, when invalid. If a covenant be made, wherein neither of the parties perform presently, but trust one another; in the condition of mere nature, which is a condition of war of every man against every man, upon any reasonable suspicion, it is void: but if there be a common power set over them both, with right and force sufficient to compel performance, it is not void. For he that performeth first, has no assurance the other will perform after; because the bonds of words are too weak to bridle men's ambition, avarice, anger, and other passions, without the fear of some coercive power; which in the condition of mere nature, where all men are equal, and judges of the justness of their own fears, cannot possibly be supposed. And therefore he which performeth first, does but betray himself to his enemy; contrary to the right, he can never abandon, of defending his life, and means of living.

But in a civil estate, where there is a power set up to constrain those who would otherwise violate their faith, that fear is no more reasonable; and for that cause, he which by the covenant is to perform first, is obliged so to do.

The cause of fear, which maketh such a covenant invalid, must be always something arising after the covenant made; as some new fact, or other sign of the will not to perform: else it cannot make the covenant void. For that which could not hinder a man from promising, ought not to be admitted as a hindrance of performing.

Right to the end, containeth right to the means. He that transferreth any right, transferreth the means of enjoying it, as far as lieth in his power. As he that selleth land, is understood to transfer the herbage, and whatsoever grows upon it: nor can he that sells a mill turn away the stream that drives it. And they that give to a man the right of government in sovereignty, are understood to give him the right of levying money to maintain soldiers, and of appointing magistrates for the administration of justice.

No covenant with beasts. To make covenants with brute beasts, is impossible; because not understanding our speech, they understand not, nor accept of, any translation of right; nor can translate any right to another; and without mutual acceptation, there is no covenant.

Nor with God without special revelation. To make covenant with God, is impossible, but by mediation of such as God speaketh to, either by revelation supernatural, or by his lieutenants that govern under him, and in his name: for otherwise we know not whether our covenants be accepted, or not. And therefore they that vow any thing contrary to any law of nature, vow in vain; as being a thing unjust to pay such a vow. And if it be a thing commanded by the law of nature, it is not the vow, but the law that binds them.

No covenant, but of possible and future. The matter, or subject of a covenant, is always something that falleth under deliberation; for to covenant, is an act of the will; that is to say, an act, and the last act of deliberation; and is therefore always understood to be something to come; and which is judged possible for him that covenanteth, to perform.

And therefore, to promise that which is known to be impossible, is no covenant. But if that prove impossible afterwards, which before was thought possible, the covenant is valid, and bindeth, though not to the thing itself, yet to the value; or, if that also be impossible, to the unfeigned endeavour of performing as much as is possible: for to more no man can be obliged.

Covenants how made void. Men are freed of their covenants two ways; by performing, or by being forgiven. For performance, is the natural end of obligation; and forgiveness, the restitution of liberty; as being a retransferring of that right, in which the obligation consisted.

Covenants extorted by fear are valid. Covenants entered into by fear, in the condition of mere nature, are obligatory. For example, if I covenant to pay a ransom, or service for my life, to an enemy; I am bound by it: for it is a contract, wherein one receiveth the benefit of life; the other is to receive money, or service for it; and consequently, where no other law, as in the condition of mere nature, forbiddeth the performance, the covenant is valid. Therefore prisoners of war, if trusted with the payment of their ransom, are obliged to pay it: and if a weaker prince, make a disadvantageous peace with a stronger, for fear; he is bound to keep it; unless, as hath been said before, there ariseth some new, and just cause of fear, to renew the war. And even in commonwealths, if I be forced to redeem myself from a thief by promising him money, I am bound to pay it, till the civil law discharge me. For whatsoever I may lawfully do without obligation, the same I may lawfully covenant to do through fear: and what I lawfully covenant, I cannot lawfully break.

The former covenant to one, makes void the later to another. A former covenant, makes void a later. For a man that hath passed away his right to one man to-day, hath it not to pass to-morrow to another: and therefore the later promise passeth no right, but is null.

A man's covenant not to defend himself is void. A covenant not to defend myself from force, by force, is always void. For as I have showed before, no man can transfer, or lay down his right to save himself from death, wounds, and imprisonment, the avoiding whereof is the only end of laying down any right; and therefore the promise of not resisting force, in no covenant transferreth any right; nor is obliging. For though a man may covenant thus, *unless I do so, or so, kill me*; he cannot covenant thus, *unless I do so, or so, I will not resist you, when you come to kill me.* For man by nature chooseth the lesser evil, which is danger of death in resisting; rather than the greater, which is certain and present death in not resisting. And this is granted to be true by all men, in that they lead criminals to execution, and prison, with armed men, notwithstanding that such criminals have consented to the law, by which they are condemned.

No man obliged to accuse himself. A covenant to accuse oneself, without assurance of pardon, is likewise invalid. For in the condition of nature, where every man is judge, there is no place for accusation: and in the civil state, the accusation is followed with punishment; which being force, a man is not obliged not to resist. The same is also true, of the accusation of those, by whose condemnation a man falls into misery; as, of a father, wife, or benefactor. For the testimony of such an accuser, if it be not willingly given, is presumed to be corrupted by nature; and therefore not to be received: and where a man's testimony is not to be credited, he is not bound to give it. Also accusations upon torture, are not to be reputed as testimonies. For torture is to be used but as means of conjecture, and light, in the further examination, and search of truth: and what is in that case confessed; tendeth to the ease of him that is tortured; not to the informing of the torturers: and therefore ought not to have the credit of a sufficient testimony: for whether he deliver himself by true, or false accusation, he does it by the right of preserving his own life.

To an end of an oath. The form of an oath. The force of words, being, as I have formerly noted, too weak to hold men to the performance of their covenants; there are in man's nature, but two imaginable helps to strengthen it. And those are either a fear of the consequence of breaking their word; or a glory, or pride in appearing not to need to break it. This latter is a generosity too rarely found to be presumed on, especially in the pursuers of wealth, command, or sensual pleasure; which are the greatest part of mankind. The passion to be reckoned upon, is fear; whereof there be two very general objects: one, the power of spirits invisible; the other, the power of those men they shall therein offend. Of these two, though the former be the greater power, yet the fear of the latter is commonly the greater fear. The fear of the former is in every man his own religion, which hath place in the nature of man before civil society. The latter hath not so; at least not place enough, to keep men to their promises; because in the condition of mere nature, the inequality of power is not discerned, but by the event of battle. So that before the time of civil society, or in the interruption thereof by war, there is nothing can strengthen a covenant of peace agreed on, against the temptations of avarice, ambition, lust, or other strong desire, but the fear of that invisible power, which they every one worship as God; and fear as a revenger of their perfidy. All therefore that can be done between two men not subject to civil power, is to put one another to swear by the God he feareth: which *swearing*, or OATH, is a *form of speech, added to a promise; by which he that promiseth, signifieth, that unless he perform, he renounceth the mercy of his God, or calleth to him for vengeance on himself.* Such was the heathen form, *Let* Jupiter *kill me else, as I kill this beast.* So is our form, *I shall do thus, and thus, so help me God.* And this, with the rites and ceremonies, which every one useth in his own religion, that the fear of breaking faith might be the greater.

No oath but by God. By this it appears, that an oath taken according to any other form, or rite, than his, that sweareth, is in vain; and no oath: and that there is no swearing by any thing which the swearer thinks not God. For though men have sometimes used to swear by their kings, for fear, or flattery; yet they would have it thereby understood, they attributed to them divine honour. And that swearing unnecessarily by God, is but profaning of his name: and swearing by other things, as men do in common discourse, is not swearing, but an impious custom, gotten by too much vehemence of talking.

An oath adds nothing to the obligation. It appears also, that the oath adds nothing to the obligation. For a covenant, if lawful, binds in the sight of God, without the oath, as much as with it: if unlawful, bindeth not at all; though it be confirmed with an oath.

46

The Practice of Promising

P. S. Atiyah

From time to time I have commented critically on the methodology of various writers who have sought answers to questions about the nature and sources of promissory obligation without any sociological inquiry into the institution of promising as it currently exists in a modern Western society. I have commented that this approach seems particularly odd when it comes from philosophers who argue that promises derive their binding force from the "practice of promising," but make no attempt to inquire into the rules of this practice. In this chapter I propose to make some preliminary inquiry into the "practice of promising" as it exists in modern England. This in no way professes to be a serious sociological study of promising; in particular, my data come mainly (though not exclusively) from the Law Reports and are no doubt unrepresentative for that reason. This is conceded without reservations; but it remains true that much may be learnt about the morality of promising from some acquaintance with the law, and the legal treatment of promises. It is right to stress that, when people's interests are seriously affected by what they regard as a breach of a promise, they can and do have recourse to the Courts for justice; and although judges are not free to do justice precisely as they please, there

is no doubt that in most cases of this nature, the justice which the Courts administer is very largely congruent with the moral sense of the community. Although it may differ from the sort of verdict often to be found in philosophical writings, this is, I believe, because lawyers and judges are more aware of the complexity and subtlety of the problems which are involved. The law is thus more sophisticated in its morality than many non-lawyers might think; it is difficult to substantiate this assertion without a substantial treatment of the law of contract and this is obviously not the place for that. But it is a place for a beginning to be made.

The Strength of the Promise-keeping Principle

I want to begin by suggesting that the strength of the principle that promises must be kept is not nearly so great as seems to be assumed by many writers. Neither in the community at large, nor in the law, I suggest, is the principle accorded that sanctity which many philosophers still think is due to it.[1] Historically, it is of course true that in the middle of the last century the sanctity of contract was widely regarded, by lawyers and

P. S. Atiyah, "The Practice of Promising," from *Promises, Morals, and the Law* (Oxford University Press, 1981), pp. 138–76.

others, as the keystone of the social and legal edifice. But the law has moved a long way since then, and this movement certainly appears to have been a response to changing social attitudes; philosophers who still write about the duty to keep promises with the high moral tone that one often finds (for example in Ross, Hare, Hart, Warnock, or Rawls[2]) appear to be reflecting the moral attitudes of the last century rather than those of the present day. It is perhaps significant that a philosopher who has recently made a serious attempt to study the law of contract discovered somewhat to his surprise that in the law, "the opprobrium attached to [promise breaking] is not often great."[3]

So far as the rules of law are concerned, it must be stressed that the sanctions for breach of promise, or (contract) are usually very mild by comparison with many of the sanctions at the law's disposal. It is very rare that the law provides for the *punishment* of the contract-breaker. Neither imprisonment nor fines are available as remedies for breach of contract, nor is it customary (except in certain limited categories) for Courts actually to order contracting parties to perform their contracts.[4] In the great majority of contractual actions the law merely provides for the payment of sums which are due, or for damages in default. And damages are almost invariably assessed on purely compensatory principles, that is to say, they are limited by the extent of the promisee's loss. They cannot include an element of "exemplary" or "punitive" damages such as are sometimes allowed in other kinds of actions. It is true (as we have seen) that the promisee's "loss" is understood sufficiently widely to encompass his lost expectations, but that is normally the limit of the promisor's liability.

But this is not all, because (as I have also pointed out) where the promisee has not relied upon the promise, and no payment has been made to the promisor, so that the promisee's claim is purely for the loss of his expectations, it will often happen that no damages are recoverable at all. If the promisee can obtain substitute performance elsewhere at no additional cost, he is expected, as a reasonable man, to do so, and not to insist upon performance by the promisor. This explains why, in cases like *Lazenby Garages v. Wright*, [. . .] a car dealer who is able to resell a car which the buyer has refused to take and pay

for, may be unable to claim any damages at all. So in cases like this the sanction for breach of contract is, in fact, nil.

Moreover, empirical studies of business attitudes to contracts and contract-breaking, both in England and in the United States, suggest that business men in fact expect and tolerate a considerable amount of contract-breaking, at all events on matters which they do not regard as of fundamental importance. A leading American contracts scholar has recently been moved to say that "it is perfectly clear that a great deal of promise breaking is tolerated and expected. Indeed, it is so widely tolerated that a realist would have to say that beneath the covers we are firmly committed to the desirability of promises being broken, not just occasionally but quite regularly."[5]

This kind of evidence may not tell us much about social attitudes to the morality of promising. But there is also evidence from other legal cases that public bodies, at least, appear to have less compunction about promise-breaking today than perhaps they would have done a hundred years ago. Promises are frequently made by corporate bodies or other associations of people (such as Governments) as well as by individuals. And when there is a change in those who represent such bodies, personal moral scruples about promise keeping may be non-existent. Thus (for example) where a local council contracted (that is, promised) to sell council houses to certain tenants, and then, following an election, a new council took office pledged to a new policy, the new council declined to fulfil these contracts. They were sued by one tenant and put up a manifestly untenable defence; they appealed to the Court of Appeal where again, they strenuously defended on the flimsiest of grounds; and when they lost again, they sought leave to appeal to the House of Lords – unsuccessfully.[6] And it is, perhaps, not irrelevant to remember also that in 1975 the Labour Government invited the people of Britain to decide, in the Common Market referendum, whether they wished to affirm or repudiate the treaty obligations solemnly entered into by their elected representatives only a few years earlier. One factor which played virtually no part in the public debates[7] was that the country's representatives had actually signed the Treaty of Accession, and thus pledged the nation's word. The public debates treated the whole issue as though the question was one which arose *de novo*, and as though the merits of joining the Community were up for discussion.

When we turn to the actual rules of law for the "enforcement" of promises, we also find (as I have previously mentioned) that there are different degrees of bindingness. As was stressed in a seminal article on the theory of contractual liability, "the 'binding' effect of a promise is a matter of degree, proceeding in an ascending scale which embraces, in order, the restitution, reliance and expectation interests."[8] If this sounds a little cryptic for those unacquainted with this legal terminology, all that it means is that the legal right of a promisee to obtain recompense for value actually rendered to the promisor ranks highest, that his right to be compensated for loss incurred through reliance on a promise, ranks second, and that his right to compensation for his disappointed expectations ranks lowest in the scale. Some philosophers have recognized that the binding force of promises may vary in a similar sort of way,[9] but the implications of this have not (I think) been properly grasped. At the lowest, recognition of these differing degrees of bindingness must involve acceptance that pure expectations are not generally thought deserving of a high degree of protection, and in some cases are not thought worthy of protection at all. On this view, the breach of a promise which has not been paid for or relied upon is a relatively venial wrong, and in some instances (for example where alternative arrangements can readily be made by the promisee), not of sufficient importance to warrant legal protection. But the point may involve deeper implications, as can be seen if we turn to examine some of the generally accepted justifications for breaking promises.

Justifications for Promise-breaking

Few philosophers have attempted to analyse the circumstances in which a breach of promise may be found morally justifiable. When they discuss this question at all, it is usually in terms of trivial cases such as a social promise to meet or dine with a friend, which is broken because the promisor's son is taken ill. Now in law, by far the most important justification for breaking

a promise is that a return promise has itself been broken in whole or in part. It is the breach by one party of his contractual duties which is the principal justification for breach by the second party of *his* duties. This was originally justified by lawyers at the end of the eighteenth century in the same way that they (and the Natural Lawyers) explained why promises induced by fraud or supervening events might be discharged; that is to say, they argued that it was "impliedly" intended that the promises were conditional upon mutual performance. Thus if one party refused to perform, the other party's promise did not have to be performed, because he had not promised to perform in that event. It later came to be felt that this argument from "implication" was too fanciful to explain the many difficult situations which had to be differentiated by law, and that other considerations explained the legal approach. In particular, judges were, and are, much influenced by the belief that it is *unjust* for a party to be compelled to perform a promise if he has not received (or may not receive) substantially the benefits that he has bargained for.[10]

It thus seems that not only is the receipt of a benefit itself one of the principal grounds for holding a promise to be binding, not only that the duty to recompense for benefits is a strong source of legal obligation even in the absence of a promise; but also that the failure to receive an anticipated benefit is a strong ground for treating the duty to perform a promise as no longer binding. So here too there seems confirmation for the idea that perhaps it is not the promise itself which creates the obligation, so much as the accompanying incidents, such as the rendering of benefits (or in other circumstances, acts of detrimental reliance).

Why are Promises Made and Kept, or Broken?

The above discussion serves as a convenient link to some other questions which are little discussed in the philosophical writings about promises. Why do people make promises? Why do they keep them? Why do they break them? It is evident from the previous discussion that one common reason why people break promises is that a return promise has been, or is very likely to be, broken by the promisee. And this itself is some indication of the fact that people who make promises very often – perhaps usually – do so because they want to get something from the promisee which they can only get by doing so. It seems too often to be assumed by philosophers that the paradigm of a promise is the charitable or wholly benevolent promise, the promise which involves no return at all.[11] This is surely wrong. It is of course difficult to be sure, in the absence of empirical research, what are the most common types of promises, and why these are given, but it seems highly probable that they are promises given as the price of something the promisor wants. Promises of this kind do not confer an uncovenanted benefit on the promisee. On the contrary, it is the promisor who often benefits from such a promise, for it is a means of deferring a liability, rather than of creating an obligation. To take a simple illustration, a person wishes to buy goods but has not the cash to pay the price; he asks the seller to give him credit, that is to say, to accept a promise of payment in lieu of actual payment. In a case of this nature, the buyer's obligation to pay the price surely derives from his purchase of the goods, rather than from his promise; and, as I have previously argued, the implication of a promise to pay the price may be the result, rather than the cause of holding the transaction to be a purchase. Of course, it must be clear that the transaction is not a gift (and that no doubt depends on the intentions and relationship of the parties), but once this possibility is ruled out, the voluntary acceptance or receipt of the goods by the buyer is the necessary and sufficient condition for his liability. An explicit promise alone is neither of these things. If the promise was given and the seller failed to deliver the goods, the buyer (as explained above) would not be bound to perform his promise; and if the buyer requested the seller to supply the goods and voluntarily accepted them when supplied, he would be liable to pay the price even in the absence of an explicit promise. No doubt it would be said that he had "impliedly" promised, but it is not clear why the implication needs to be made, and the buyer's obligation to pay the price would exist even if he promised without any intention of keeping his promise.

Cases of this nature – that is the giving of promises in lieu of immediate performance of a duty – are very common indeed. But there are other similar cases where the promisor's duty is not deferred, and yet he makes the promise to obtain some benefit which he desires. Two parties enter into a contract on 1 January for the purchase and sale of a house on 1 February. Each promises something to the other because he wants what the other is willing to give. The case differs from that discussed in the previous paragraph because the performance of the two promises is intended to be simultaneous; neither party will perform before the other, and no credit is to be given. But this does not alter the fact that each promise is given because of what it brings; and this also is borne out by the rule that prima facie a failure by one party to perform will discharge the other. Thus many promises are given because the promisor expects to derive some benefit from the promise. But it may be possible to put the matter more generally: promises are given to induce people to act upon them. In the cases so far discussed, the action which the promisor *wants* is something beneficial to him. In these cases, the promisor *wants* the promisee to act in reliance on the promise. But there may be cases in which the action will be of little or no benefit to him except in the trivial sense that if he wants it, it must be assumed that it will be *some* benefit to him. Because this case is conceptually wider than the previous one, it is the one which lawyers and philosophers have tended to concentrate upon. Action in reliance is more generally recognized as a "consideration" in the law than conduct beneficial to the promisor; and a parallel is to be found in much philosophical writing. But it is important to appreciate that in a large proportion of cases, perhaps most cases, the action in reliance which the promisor seeks to induce the promisee to undertake, is something beneficial to the promisor, directly or indirectly.

Now it is apparent that where the promisor has not yet actually obtained what he wants at the time when performance of his promise is due, he will (unless he has changed his mind in the interim) normally be motivated to perform his promise for precisely the same reason that he originally gave it – namely, that he wants to induce the promisee to act in some way likely to be beneficial to him. Thus, in the example of the contract for the purchase and sale of the house, both parties will normally be motivated to perform their promises on the day set for performance for the same reason that they originally gave their promises, that is the seller wants money in preference to the house, and the buyer wants the house in preference to the money.

It should, I hope, be apparent now why it seems to me idle to discuss the source of the moral obligation to perform a promise without having some regard to the question *why* promises are given, and *why* they are (normally) performed. If we assume that promises are binding because of some inherent moral power, or even if we assume that they are binding because of the expectations they rouse, or that they are binding because of the existence of a practice of promising, we are in danger of overlooking that *most* promises are performed because it is in the interests of the promisor to perform. The legal and moral sanction thus turns out to be needed for some cases only; and (I would venture to guess) for a small minority of cases. It is needed for those cases where the promisor has obtained credit, or full performance of what he sought to obtain by his promise; and it is needed for those cases where the promisor changes his mind after giving his promise, and before he performs it. Of course, even in these cases, it may be in the long-term interests of the promisor to perform. As many writers have observed, the loss of credit and trustworthiness which results from promise-breaking may make it in the long-term interests of the promisor to perform, even in the two situations I have mentioned.

The importance of this, I suggest, is that it should influence our view of the paradigm case. In much philosophical writing, it seems to be assumed that the paradigmatic case is of a promise which is wholly gratuitous and is given for charitable or benevolent purposes. It seems to me far more likely that the source of both legal and moral obligations concerning the binding force of promises is derived from the more common case where the promisor obtains, or expects to obtain, some advantage from his promise, and that cases of charitable and benevolent promises are the result of extrapolating from the common case. [. . .]

The Intentions of the Promisor

I want now to draw attention to certain difficulties which arise concerning the intention of the promisor. There is, of course, the obvious and initial difficulty arising from promises which the promisor has no intention of performing. Are these to be called genuine promises? Those who believe that the essence of a promise is the intentional commitment, the intentional acceptance of an obligation, plainly have difficulty with the case of the fraudulent or dishonest promise. I have previously pointed out that there would in fact be no insuperable difficulty in arguing that the promisor in such a case is under a duty, not because he has promised, but because he has deceived. However, this is certainly not the legal approach. A lawyer would unhesitatingly say that a dishonest promise was a promise, and that the promisor is liable because he has promised, and not because he has deceived. Hence he is legally liable for disappointing the promisee's expectations, and not just for loss incurred in reliance. If the dishonest party had not made an apparent promise, but a dishonest statement of a different character, this would not be so. I think it probable that current English "positive" morality would broadly agree with the law in regarding a dishonest promisor as bound because he had promised, and not because he had deceived, though obviously that point cannot be settled by general argument.

Nevertheless, the nature of the intention which a promisor must have – even leaving aside this particular problem – is a much more difficult question than seems to be generally assumed. One of the few writers to discuss this issue is Searle,[12] who argues that a promisor must intend that his words "will place him under an obligation" to do what he promises. Thus, he says, Mr Pickwick did not promise to marry Mrs Bardell because "we know that he did not have the appropriate intention."[13] A lawyer's reaction to this would be that although *we* may know that he did not intend to marry Mrs Bardell (because the author has told us), Mrs Bardell did not know this fact. And since, in everyday life, there is no benevolent author to tell us what other people's intentions are, we are in fact entitled to assume that their intentions are what they appear to be.

The jury's verdict in *Bardell v. Pickwick* – if we can assume that they honestly thought that Mrs Bardell had reasonably construed Mr Pickwick's words as an offer of marriage – was thus sound in law.[14] This may be thought to show that a promisor must at least intend to act in such a way as to make it reasonable to construe him as intending to promise, rather than that he should merely intentionally act. But the significance of this distinction depends on what "reasonable construction" involves. It may involve merely implying a promise because the kind of conduct in question usually is accompanied by an intention voluntarily to assume an obligation. But it may, *per contra*, involve "implying" a promise because the neutral, impartial judge thinks that in all the circumstances, an obligation ought to be imposed on the promisor.

No doubt Mr Pickwick's was an extreme case. But there is also no doubt that it is very common for the law to hold a person bound by a promise when he never intended to give one. Sometimes, as in Mr Pickwick's case, this may well be because the promisee has reasonably understood the words and conduct of the putative promisor as indicating that the promisor does mean to make a promise. Even here, of course, if no such intention is actually present, it is not self-evident what is the source of the obligation. Some moralists, while agreeing that in such circumstances, a duty or obligation may rest on the promisor, would derive the duty from some other source than a promise.[15] And it is perhaps significant also that some legal writers think that the law goes too far in protecting pure expectations when they are the result of a mistake or misunderstanding of this kind. If, for instance, the mistake is discovered before the promisee has acted on the promise, and before any payment has been rendered for it, it is not obviously just that the promise should still be held binding. In legal theory, the promise probably is still binding, but I think it fair to say that a Court would probably find that theory unpalatable, and would strive to avoid it if it could do so. But, in light of what has already been said in this book, this does not show a legal hankering after a subjective theory of liability. What it shows is that – here as elsewhere – the protection of those who have paid for, or relied upon promises, is generally accorded a much higher priority, than the protection of bare disappointed expectations.

It must now be noted that in the law there are many circumstances in which a promise is implied, not only where there is probably no intention to give one, but where it cannot even be said that the words and behaviour of the promisor, reasonably construed, would give rise to the inference that he intended to give one. A simple example arises in the law of sale, where a seller is often treated as "impliedly" promising to supply goods of merchantable quality, goods fit for their purpose, and so on. Obligations of this kind appear to be imposed on sellers as an expression of the sense of justice arising from social policy; they appear to have little to do with the real intentions of most sellers.

Promises with variable content

I now want to say a little about a variety of other difficulties which experience with the law shows to be involved in the notion of intention in this particular sphere. Too many writers appear (at least in dealing with promises[16]) to assume that the state of mind of a person who promises to do something is a relatively simple matter; whether he is honest or not, it seems to be widely assumed that sharp lines can be drawn between the person who intends to do something and the person who does not. Unfortunately this is not the case. There are many acutely difficult questions here. For example, a person may sign a written document which contains many printed clauses, and which purports to be a contract. Each clause may even begin by saying "I hereby promise" or words to that effect. The promisor may, or may not read all or part of the document; he probably has some understanding of the general nature of the document, but it is unlikely that he knows in any detail what the clauses contain or what they mean or what is their legal result. I find it very difficult to say what this person's intentions are in relation to such matters. Lawyers have in the past tended to assume (with little articulated justification) that to sign a document is, in a sense, to indicate one's acceptance of all that it contains. The signer, by placing his signature at the foot of the document, *intends* to bind himself to all that it contains.[17] He may thus be said to promise to do whatever the document requires him to do. But this conclusion creates great difficulties. Suppose the document contains some wholly unexpected and grossly unfair clause, such as has never been included in contracts of this nature, would it still be said that the signature amounts to a promise to do whatever the document requires? Or suppose that the document contains clauses which are today declared to be void by Act of Parliament, for the very purpose of protecting unwary customers who sign such documents without reading them? To the lawyer it matters little whether or not one says that the signer has promised to perform the void clause, because in either event, it is not binding. But to the moralist, it may matter whether we say, "there is no promise here at all," or, "there is a promise but the promisor is legally relieved from performance." And surely the moralist needs to be aware of these problems. Can he really assert that clauses made void by Parliament under consumer protection legislation, are still morally binding and ought to be kept? But if such promises are not morally binding, while other promises (of whose content the promisor is equally ignorant) are binding, how can the explanation be sought in the intention of the promisor?

There are other difficulties. Contracts sometimes contain clauses under which one party may vary the duty of the other party. An example only too well known to many householders today, is the power of a building society to alter the terms of a mortgage by increasing the interest rate payable, after due notice given. Suppose a person has entered into a mortgage of this character, at an initial rate of 7 per cent, but ten years later finds himself paying 12 per cent. Would it be said that he has promised to pay 12 per cent? Or that he intended to pay 12 per cent? Certainly, he is legally bound to pay 12 per cent; he is treated as having contracted to pay for it, but it is not clear to me whether one would say that he had *promised* to pay it, still less that he *intended* to pay it. The reality would seem to be that he intentionally entered into a certain transaction and that one of the consequences of that transaction, to which he is committed, is that he is now bound to pay the higher interest rate.

Stronger cases can be found in the law. For example, a person joins a club or society, or takes shares in a company. The association (whatever its form) will have rules which bind the members, and the person joining will be bound by them, even though he does not read them or know anything about them. Thus far the case is no different from the one discussed earlier. But the rules of an association will almost always contain procedures for their own alteration, and frequently these procedures will envisage alteration by some majority vote of the members. Suppose that a person joins a tennis club with an annual subscription of £5; we may readily agree that he has promised to pay £5 a year, and that he fully intends to do so. But suppose now that the club, by majority vote, with our friend dissenting, increases the subscription to £10. Are we to say that, so long as he remains a member, he has promised to pay £10 annually; are we to say that when he joined he intended to pay whatever subscription was due, from time to time, as duly required by the club rules? Of course, a member may resign from a tennis club, and if he does not resign, we may say he must be "assumed" to have acquiesced in the new subscription and so has impliedly promised to pay it. For most practical purposes this is no doubt legitimate enough; but what is not legitimate is to *equate* this person's state of mind with that of the man who says, "I promise to pay £10." Still more difficult cases can be found where the opportunity to escape the consequences of the new rule by resignation does not exist. For example, a member of a company who holds shares of class A is outvoted on a resolution which has the result of reducing the value of class A shares and increasing the value of class B shares. To "resign" or sell his shares is no solution to this person's problems. The reduction in the value of his shares is already an accomplished fact. Is he bound by the result? Are we to say that, when he joined the company, he must be deemed to have accepted the consequences of any change duly passed by appropriate legal procedures?

Now all these cases raise questions as to the precise relationship which subsists between the intentions of the promisor and the content of the promise. These illustrations show that, in law at least, a person who enters into a transaction may be held bound by many consequences of the transaction even though he does not intend those consequences. Obligations of this kind surely cannot be justified by saying that the promisor "intended" to assume them. The reality is that he intends to enter into a transaction, the consequences of which are imposed upon him by the law. It seems difficult to argue that, in principle, the moral solution to these cases differs from the legal solution. No doubt there may be moral dissent from some extreme legal cases; but it surely cannot be doubted that (for example) a mortgagor is morally, no less than legally, bound to pay the interest rate properly required of him, even though it is far higher than the one he originally promised to pay.

One further problem needs mention. In law, breach of a contract often has the result of making the promisor liable to pay damages. The way in which the damages are assessed often depends on a number of legal rules which may, in some situations, involve much complexity. If, in the cases discussed in the previous paragraphs, we are willing to say that all the consequences of the original contract, or promise, must be "deemed" to have been covered by the promise, or by the promisor's intentions, are we now to say the same for the legal consequences? It would seem remarkably odd to say that a person who is guilty of a breach of contract must be deemed to have promised (and intended?) to pay damages for breach, as assessed by the Courts. Yet the total consequences of the promise are an elaborate mesh of the actual words used (particularly written words) and of the law. Some promises are read in by the law which are not explicitly stated; some promises which are explicitly stated are struck out by the law as void; other promises are subject to legal interpretation which may alter their literal or prima-facie import; and the calculation of the damages, as I have said, may involve some complex legal rules.

Who Makes Promises, to Whom, and Who is Bound by Them?

There are further sociological matters about the practice of promising on which the law provides some guidance; and here again, I believe, it will be found that some of the assumptions made in much philosophical writing are too simplistic, for lack of attention paid to these data. Let me begin with the question, Who makes promises? Philosophers nearly always assume that promises are only made by individual human beings. But this is not true. Promises are made by people acting collectively in all manner of institutional groups. Promises are made by companies, associations, schools, hospitals, universities, Governments, and many other institutions. This fact is relevant to the moral issues arising from promising for a number of obvious, and perhaps less obvious reasons. First, it makes it necessary to recognize that one person (the agent) can make a promise which binds another person (the principal), something which many philosophers seem reluctant to recognize. Second, it is much more difficult to attribute a "real" intention to a collective group than to a single individual promisor. For one thing, the intentions of (say) the members of a Board or a Committee, acting on behalf of an institution, may not all be the same. For another thing, institutions often act through agents (in the legal sense) such as executives, directors, secretaries, and so forth. Agents sometimes commit their principals by promises which the principal (or superior agents) did not wish, or intend, to make. Legally, there are rules for determining when a principal can be bound by an agent who thus acts in excess of his authority, but there is no doubt that this is a common legal phenomenon. All this naturally strengthens the legal tendency to ignore "real" intentions, and focus on apparent intentions – on what is said and done, rather than what was "actually" intended.

A second reason why the nature of institutional promisors is often relevant to the moral issues is this. Institutions often have specified formal procedures for making decisions. Boards of directors, College Governing Bodies, Committees of various kinds, normally have formal meetings, and keep records of their decisions. When a body of this kind announces its intentions, or makes a decision which it then communicates to the persons concerned, the line between a mere statement of intent and a promise becomes somewhat blurred. A public announcement in the form "The Committee [Board, Government, etc.] has decided . . ." is much closer to being a promise than a comparable statement by a private individual. Decisions of this character are usually more trustworthy than declarations of intent by a single individual, because the former are so much more difficult to change than the latter. An extreme example of this may, perhaps, be found in legislative procedures. There is a sense in which an Act of Parliament is a declaration of Parliament's will and intention that the persons concerned should behave in the manner laid down in the Act. In the British constitutional system, such a declaration of intent does not preclude Parliament from changing its mind tomorrow and repealing the first Act. But parliamentary procedure is a formal process, governed by many technical rules of procedure, and, in the majority of cases, taking several months to transform a Bill into an Act. It is, in the result, reasonable to assume that laws will remain unchanged, save at longish intervals (except of course after an election!), and the public are generally entitled to adjust their conduct on the assumption that they can rely upon the existing law. Indeed, we can go further, because it is reasonable to say that legislation tells the citizen how he must and also how he may behave. Those who adjust their behaviour in reliance on the legality of a course of conduct are entitled to feel aggrieved if they are not given adequate time to adjust to changes in the law. It would indeed not be wholly fanciful to suggest that the legislature, by laying down the lines of proscribed behaviour, is impliedly promising that those who do *not* cross the lines will not be subject to penalties.[18] The implication of a promise in such a case arises from the nature of decision-making procedures, and the way in which Parliament declares its intent. It may, of course, be said that any such implied promise would be fictitious, but that depends upon the nature and purpose of implied promises. No doubt it would be fictitious to impute to Parliament any actual intent to assume a legal obligation not to change the law without adequate notice. But it would not be a fiction to argue that Parliament passes laws in order to tell citizens how to behave in various respects; and that if the citizen complies with these instructions, and assumes that if he observes the law he will not be subject to penalties, it would be morally wrong for Parliament to punish him. If we think that that would be morally wrong, it is because we think that people are justified in relying on the law as from time to time enacted, and that such reliance should be protected. So Parliament may well come under a moral obligation to respect such

reliance. It seems to be largely a matter of taste whether we say that such an obligation derives from an "implied promise."

One final point may be made here about the parties to a promise. It is not uncommon in law for a promise to become binding on some third party, other than the promisor. For example, contractual problems may bind the executors of the promisor after his death; in effect the promisor's successors take his property burdened with his liabilities, and these liabilities include promissory, or at least contractual liabilities. Or, again, it is sometimes possible for an owner of a piece of land to burden the land with a promise (for example, not to build on it, or not to build certain types of property), and this promise will bind subsequent owners of the land provided that certain simple formalities as to registration have been complied with. Cases of this nature may be of some importance to the basis of the promissory liability for the moralist as well as the lawyer. For one thing, they illustrate what is often thought to be an impossibility, namely that a promisor can promise that someone else will do something; but they also illustrate cases where it is plain that the liability of a person on a promise must be based on something other than his consent. The third party who succeeds to, or buys, property thus burdened with another's promises, will often know of the burden when he takes the property, and may in some sense be assumed to acquiesce in it; but this is not necessarily the case. The purchaser of land burdened with a registered covenant is bound by it even if he knew nothing of it at all: the onus is on him to discover it by searching the register. Of course, it can be said that the reasons for holding such a third party bound by a promise may be quite different from those affecting the promisor himself. But in practice it will usually be found that, in the absence of consent, there will be present one or both of the other two bases of contractual liability, viz. that the third party has derived some benefit, for which the promise is, in a broad sort of way, the *quid pro quo*; or alternatively that the promisee has acted upon the promise in such a way that it would seem unreasonable and unjust if the third party was not bound by it. So once again, it seems that the duty to recompense benefits and to compensate for losses incurred by actions in

reliance may actually embrace liabilities thought
to be promissory, and which certainly are promissory in origin. [. . .]

Notes

1 A few writers have themselves criticized the
   general philosophical tradition on this point, e.g.
   Narveson, *Morality and Utility* (Johns Hopkins
   University Press, 1967), p. 193; John Finnis, *Natural
   Law and Natural Rights* (Oxford University Press,
   1980), p. 308.

2 Even J. L. Mackie, *Ethics* (Penguin, 1991), p. 123,
   surprisingly argues that "Hobbes' third law of
   nature, that men perform their covenants made, is
   an eternal and immutable fragment of morality."

3 R. Bronaugh, "Contracting: An Essay in Legal
   Philosophy" (unpublished Oxford B. Litt. thesis,
   1976), p. 29.

4 In practice, contracts for the purchase and sale
   of houses, or land, are normally "specifically
   enforceable" by order of the Court: failure to
   comply is punishable by imprisonment.

5 I. Macneil, "The Many Futures of Contract," 47
   Southern Calif. Law Rev. 691, 729 (1974). Indeed,
   Holmes, J. used to argue that a contracting
   party was *entitled* to break his contract and pay
   damages in lieu, if he chose. This view did not
   win many adherents among lawyers, but in
   particular circumstances it reflects the reality of
   legal rules.

6 *Storer v. Manchester City Council* (1974) 1 WLR
   1403.

7 So far as I am aware, the only prominent figure
   to raise this issue (in a televised debate at the
   Oxford Union) was Mr Heath, who had personally signed the Treaty.

8 Fuller and Perdue, "The Reliance Interest in
   Contract Damages," 46 *Yale Law J.* 52 and 373, 396
   (1936); cf. John Finnis, op. cit., pp. 308 ff., for a
   very different view.

9 For example, Ross, *The Right and the Good*
   (Hackett, 1988), p. 100. Warnock (*The Object of
   Morality* (Methuen, 1971), p. 94) attempts to distinguish *obligations* (which one is *bound* to perform)
   and other "duties" (which one *ought*, but is not
   bound, to do). This distinction seems untenable:
   the bindingness of *all* oughts is surely a matter
   of degree.

10 Patterson, "Constructive Conditions in Contracts,"
   42 *Columbia Law Rev.* 903 (1942). In modern
   English law, it is well established that a breach of
   contract by one party discharges the other, *either*
   (1) if that is the effect of the agreement, expressly
   or by implication, *or* (2) if the breach substantially
   deprives the other of the benefit he expected to
   receive under the contract.

11 Rawls, *A Theory of Justice* (Belknap Press, 1971),
   at pp. 344–50, rightly stresses that promises
   are "often" made to secure something which
   the promisor wants. I believe this is a major
   understatement.

12 "What is a Speech Act?," in *The Philosophy of
   Language* (Oxford University Press, 1971),
   pp. 50–1.

13 Searle also says that even an insincere promisor
   must intend that his words "will make him
   responsible for intending to do" what he has said
   he will do. I must confess my inability to understand the state of mind of a promisor who has
   this intention. [. . .]

14 I said as much in my *Introduction to the Law of
   Contract* (2nd edn., Oxford University Press,
   1971), p. 4.

15 For example, Sidgwick, *Methods* (Dover Publications, 1966), p. 304.

16 Of course, in dealing with the criminal law, a
   considerable literature (both legal and philosophical) has grown up around the question of
   intention.

17 See, for example, Lord Pearson in *Saunders v.
   Anglia Building Society* (1971) AC 1004 at 1036.

18 L. Fuller, *The Morality of Law* (Yale University Press,
   1964), pp. 61–2.

47

Contract as Promise

Charles Fried

It is a first principle of liberal political morality that we be secure in what is ours – so that our persons and property not be open to exploitation by others, and that from a sure foundation we may express our will and expend our powers in the world. By these powers we may create good things or low, useful articles or luxuries, things extraordinary or banal, and we will be judged accordingly – as saintly or mean, skillful or ordinary, industrious and fortunate or debased, friendly and kind or cold and inhuman. But whatever we accomplish and however that accomplishment is judged, morality requires that we respect the person and property of others, leaving them free to make their lives as we are left free to make ours. This is the liberal ideal. This is the ideal that distinguishes between the good, which is the domain of aspiration, and the right, which sets the terms and limits according to which we strive. This ideal makes what we achieve our own and our failures our responsibility too – however much or little we may choose to share our good fortune and however we may hope for help when we fail.[1]

Everything must be available to us, for who can deny the human will the title to expand even into the remotest corner of the universe? And when we forbear to bend some external object to our use because of its natural preciousness we use it still, for it is to our judgment of its value that we respond, our own conception of the good that we pursue. Only other persons are not available to us in this way – they alone share our self-consciousness, our power of self-determination; thus to use them as if they were merely part of external nature is to poison the source of the moral power we enjoy. But others *are* part of the external world, and by denying ourselves access to their persons and powers, we drastically shrink the scope of our efficacy. So it was a crucial moral discovery that free men may yet freely serve each others' purposes: the discovery that beyond the fear of reprisal or the hope of reciprocal favor, morality itself might be enlisted to assure not only that you respect me and mine but that you actively serve my purposes.[2] When my confidence in your assistance derives from my conviction that you will do what is right (not just what is prudent), then I trust you, and trust becomes a powerful tool for our working our mutual wills in the world. So remarkable a tool is trust that in the end we pursue it for its own sake; we prefer doing things cooperatively when we might have relied on fear or interest or worked alone.[3]

Charles Fried, "Contract as Promise," from *Contract as Promise* (Harvard University Press, 1981), pp. 7–27. © 1981 by the President and Fellows of Harvard College. Reprinted with permission of Harvard University Press.

The device that gives trust its sharpest, most palpable form is promise. By promising we put in another man's hands a new power to accomplish his will, though only a moral power: What he sought to do alone he may now expect to do with our promised help, and to give him this new facility was our very purpose in promising. By promising we transform a choice that was morally neutral into one that is morally compelled. Morality, which must be permanent and beyond our particular will if the grounds for our willing are to be secure, is itself invoked, molded to allow us better to work that particular will. Morality then serves modest, humdrum ends: We make appointments, buy and sell, harnessing this loftiest of all forces.

What is a promise, that by my words I should make wrong what before was morally indifferent? A promise is a communication – usually verbal; it says something. But how can my saying something put a moral charge on a choice that before was morally neutral? Well, by my misleading you, or by lying.[4] Is lying not the very paradigm of doing wrong by speaking? But this won't do, for a promise puts the moral charge on a *potential* act – the wrong is done later, when the promise is not kept – while a lie is a wrong committed at the time of its utterance. Both wrongs abuse trust, but in different ways. When I speak I commit myself to the truth of my utterance, but when I promise I commit myself to *act*, later. Though these two wrongs are thus quite distinct there has been a persistent tendency to run them together by treating a promise as a lie after all, but a particular kind of lie: a lie about one's intentions. Consider this case:

I.   I sell you a house, retaining an adjacent vacant lot. At the time of our negotiations, I state that I intend to build a home for myself on that lot. What if several years later I sell the lot to a person who builds a gas station on it? What if I sell it only one month later? What if I am already negotiating for its sale as a gas station at the time I sell the house to you?[5]

If I was already negotiating to sell the lot for a gas station at the time of my statement to you, I have wronged you. I have lied to you about the state of my intentions, and this is as much a lie as a lie about the state of the plumbing.[6] If,

however, I sell the lot many years later, I do you no wrong. There are no grounds for saying I lied about my intentions; I have just changed my mind. Now if I had *promised* to use the lot only as a residence, the situation would be different. Promising is more than just truthfully reporting my present intentions, for I may be free to change my mind, as I am not free to break my promise.

Let us take it as given here that lying is wrong and so that it is wrong to obtain benefits or cause harm by lying (including lying about one's intentions). It does not at all follow that to obtain a benefit or cause harm by breaking a promise is also wrong. That my act procures me a benefit or causes harm all by itself proves nothing. If I open a restaurant near your hotel and prosper as I draw your guests away from the standard hotel fare you offer, this benefit I draw from you places me under no obligation to you. I should make restitution only if I benefit *unjustly*, which I do if I deceive you – as when I lie to you about my intentions in example I.[7] But where is the injustice if I honestly intend to keep my promise at the time of making it, and later change my mind? If we feel I owe you recompense in that case too, it cannot be because of the benefit I have obtained through my promise: We have seen that benefit even at another's expense is not alone sufficient to require compensation. If I owe you a duty to return that benefit it must be because of the promise. It is the promise that makes my enrichment at your expense unjust, and not the enrichment that makes the promise binding. And thus neither the statement of intention nor the benefit explains why, if at all, a promise does any moral work.

A more common attempt to reduce the force of a promise to some other moral category invokes the harm you suffer in relying on my promise. My statement is like a pit I have dug in the road, into which you fall. I have harmed you and should make you whole. Thus the tort principle might be urged to bridge the gap in the argument between a statement of intention and a promise: I have a duty just because I could have foreseen (indeed it was my intention) that you would rely on my promise and that you would suffer harm when I broke it. And this wrong then not only sets the stage for compensation of the harm caused by the misplaced reliance, but also supplies the moral predicate for restitution of any benefits I may have extracted from you on the strength of my promise.[8] But we still beg the question. If the promise is no more than a truthful statement of my intention, why am *I* responsible for harm that befalls you as a result of my change of heart? To be sure, it is not like a change in the weather – I might have kept to my original intention – but how does this distinguish the broken promise from any other statement of intention (or habit or prediction of future conduct) of mine of which you know and on which you choose to rely? Should your expectations of me limit my freedom of choice? If you rent the apartment next to mine because I play chamber music there, do I owe you more than an expression of regret when my friends and I decide to meet instead at the cellist's home? And in general, why should my liberty be constrained by the harm you would suffer from the disappointment of the expectations you choose to entertain about my choices?

Does it make a difference that when I promise you do not just happen to rely on me, that I communicate my intention to you and therefore can be taken to know that changing my mind may put you at risk? But then I might be aware that you would count on my keeping to my intentions even if I myself had not communicated those intentions to you. (*You* might have told me you were relying on me, or you might have overheard me telling some third person of my intentions.) It might be said that I become the agent of your reliance by telling you, and that this makes my responsibility clearer: After all, I can scarcely control all the ways in which you might learn of my intentions, but I *can* control whether or not I tell you of them. But we are still begging the question. If promising is no more than my telling you of my intentions, why do we both not know that I may yet change my mind? Perhaps, then, promising is like telling you of my intention and telling you that I don't intend to change my mind. But why can't I change my mind about the latter intention?

Perhaps the statement of intention in promising is binding because we not only foresee reliance, we invite it: We intend the promisee to rely on the promise. Yet even this will not do. If I invite reliance on my stated intention, then

that is all I invite. Certainly I may hope and intend, in example I, that you buy my house on the basis of what I have told you, but why does that hope bind me to do more than state my intention honestly? And that intention and invitation are quite compatible with my later changing my mind. In every case, of course, I should weigh the harm I will do if I do change my mind. If I am a doctor and I know you will rely on me to be part of an outing on which someone may fall ill, I should certainly weigh the harm that may come about if that reliance is disappointed. Indeed I should weigh that harm even if you do not rely on me, but are foolish enough not to have made a provision for a doctor. Yet in none of these instances am I bound as I would be had I promised.[9]

A promise invokes trust in my future actions, not merely in my present sincerity. We need to isolate an additional element, over and above benefit, reliance, and the communication of intention. That additional element must *commit* me, and commit me to more than the truth of some statement. That additional element has so far eluded our analysis.

It has eluded us, I believe, because there is a real puzzle about how we can commit ourselves to a course of conduct that absent our commitment is morally neutral. The invocation of benefit and reliance are attempts to explain the force of a promise in terms of two of its most usual effects, but the attempts fail because these effects depend on the prior assumption of the force of the commitment. The way out of the puzzle is to recognize the bootstrap quality of the argument: To have force in *a particular case* promises must be assumed to have force generally. Once that general assumption is made, the effects we intentionally produce by a particular promise may be morally attributed to us. This recognition is not as paradoxical as its abstract statement here may make it seem. It lies, after all, behind every conventional structure: games,[10] institutions and practices, and most important, language.

Let us put to one side the question of how a convention comes into being, or of when and why we are morally bound to comply with its terms, while we look briefly at what a convention is and how it does its work. Take the classical example of a game. What the players do is defined by a system of rules – sometimes quite vague and informal, sometimes elaborate and codified. These rules apply only to the players – that is, to persons who invoke them. These rules are a human invention, and their consequences (castling, striking out, winning, losing) can be understood only in terms of the rules. The players may have a variety of motives for playing (profit, fun, maybe even duty to fellow players who need participants). A variety of judgments are applicable to the players – they may be deemed skillful, imaginative, bold, honest, or dishonest – but these judgments and motives too can be understood only in the context of the game. For instance, you can cheat only by breaking rules to which you pretend to conform.

This almost canonical invocation of the game example has often been misunderstood as somehow applying only to unserious matters, to play, so that it is said to trivialize the solemn objects (like law or promises) that it is used to explain. But this is a mistake, confusing the interests involved, the reasons for creating and invoking a particular convention, with the logical structure of conventions in general. Games are (often) played for fun, but other conventions – for instance religious rituals or legal procedures – may have most earnest ends, while still other conventions are quite general. To the last category belongs language. The conventional nature of language is too obvious to belabor. It is worth pointing out, however, that the various things we do with language – informing, reporting, promising, insulting, cheating, lying – all depend on the conventional structure's being firmly in place. You could not lie if there were not both understanding of the language you lied in and a general convention of using that language truthfully. This point holds irrespective of whether the institution of language has advanced the situation of mankind and of whether lying is sometimes, always, or never wrong.

Promising too is a very general convention – though less general than language, of course, since promising is itself a use of language.[11] The convention of promising (like that of language) has a very general purpose under which we may bring an infinite set of particular purposes. In order that I be as free as possible, that my will have the greatest possible range consistent with the similar will of others, it is necessary that there be a way in which I may commit myself. It

is necessary that I be able to make nonoptional a course of conduct that would otherwise be optional for me. By doing this I can facilitate the projects of others, because I can make it possible for those others to count on my future conduct, and thus those others can pursue more intricate, more far-reaching projects. If it is my purpose, my will that others be able to count on me in the pursuit of their endeavor, it is essential that I be able to deliver myself into their hands more firmly than where they simply predict my future course. Thus the possibility of commitment permits an act of generosity on my part, permits me to pursue a project whose content is that *you* be permitted to pursue *your* project. But of course this purely altruistic motive is not the only motive worth facilitating. More central to our concern is the situation where we facilitate each other's projects, where the gain is reciprocal. Schematically the situation looks like this:

> You want to accomplish purpose A and I want to accomplish purpose B. Neither of us can succeed without the cooperation of the other. Thus I want to be able to commit myself to help you achieve A so that you will commit yourself to help me achieve B.

Now if A and B are objects or actions that can be transferred simultaneously there is no need for commitment. As I hand over A you hand over B, and we are both satisfied. But very few things are like that. We need a device to permit a trade over time: to allow me to do A for you when you need it, in the confident belief that you will do B for me when I need it. Your commitment puts your future performance into my hands in the present just as my commitment puts my future performance into your hands. A future exchange is transformed into a present exchange. And in order to accomplish this all we need is a conventional device which we both invoke, which you know I am invoking when I invoke it, which I know that you know I am invoking, and so on.

The only mystery about this is the mystery that surrounds increasing autonomy by providing means for restricting it. But really this is a pseudomystery. The restrictions involved in promising are restrictions undertaken just in order to increase one's options in the long run, and thus are perfectly consistent with the principle of autonomy – consistent with a respect for one's own autonomy and the autonomy of others. To be sure, in getting something for myself now by promising to do something for you in the future, I am mortgaging the interest of my future self in favor of my present self. How can I be sure my future self will approve?* This is a deep and difficult problem about which I say more later in this chapter. Suffice it to say here that unless one assumes the continuity of the self and the possibility of maintaining complex projects over time, not only the morality of promising but also any coherent picture of the person becomes impossible.

The Moral Obligation of Promise

Once I have invoked the institution of promising, why exactly is it wrong for me then to break my promise?

My argument so far does not answer that question. The institution of promising is a way for me to bind myself to another so that the other may expect a future performance, and binding myself in this way is something that I may want to be able to do. But this by itself does not show that I am morally obligated to perform my promise at a later time if to do so proves inconvenient or costly. That there should be a system of currency also increases my options and is useful to me, but this does not show why I should not use counterfeit money if I can get away with it. In just the same way the usefulness of promising in general does not show why I should not take advantage of it in a particular case and yet fail to keep my promise. That the convention would cease to function in the long run, would cease to provide benefits if everyone felt free to violate it, is hardly an answer to the question of why I should keep a particular promise on a particular occasion.

David Lewis has shown[12] that a convention that it would be in each person's interest to observe if everyone else observed it will be established and maintained without any special mechanisms of commitment or enforcement. Starting with simple conventions (for example that if a telephone conversation is disconnected, the person who initiated the call is the one who calls back) Lewis extends his argument to the case of language. Now promising is different, since (unlike language, where it is overwhelmingly in the interest of all that everyone comply with linguistic conventions, even when language is used to deceive) it will often be in the interest of the promisor *not* to conform to the convention when it comes time to render his performance. Therefore individual self-interest is not enough to sustain the convention, and some additional ground is needed to keep it from unraveling. There are two principal candidates: external sanctions and moral obligation.

David Hume sought to combine these two by proposing that the external sanction of public opprobrium, of loss of reputation for honesty, which society attaches to promise-breaking, is internalized, becomes instinctual, and accounts for the sense of the moral obligation of promise.[13] Though Hume offers a possible anthropological or psychological account of how people feel about promises, his is not a satisfactory *moral* argument. Assume that I can get away with breaking my promise (the promisee is dead), and I am now asking why I should keep it anyway in the face of some personal inconvenience. Hume's account of obligation is more like an argument *against* my keeping the promise, for it tells me how any feelings of obligation that I may harbor have come to lodge in my psyche and thus is the first step toward ridding me of such inconvenient prejudices.

Considerations of self-interest cannot supply the moral basis of my obligation to keep a promise. By an analogous argument neither can considerations of utility. For however sincerely and impartially I may apply the utilitarian injunction to consider at each step how I might increase the sum of happiness or utility in the world, it will allow me to break my promise whenever the balance of advantage (including, of course, my own advantage) tips in that direction.

---

*Note that this problem does not arise where I make a present sacrifice for a future benefit, since by hypothesis I am presently willing to make that sacrifice and in the future I only stand to gain.

The possible damage to the institution of promising is only one factor in the calculation. Other factors are the alternative good I might do by breaking my promise, whether and by how many people the breach might be discovered, what the actual effect on confidence of such a breach would be. There is no a priori reason for believing that an individual's calculations will come out in favor of keeping the promise always, sometimes, or most of the time.

Rule-utilitarianism seeks to offer a way out of this conundrum. The individual's moral obligation is determined not by what the best action at a particular moment would be, but by the rule it would be best for him to follow. It has, I believe, been demonstrated that this position is incoherent: Either rule-utilitarianism requires that rules be followed in a particular case even where the result would not be best all things considered, and so the utilitarian aspect of rule-utilitarianism is abandoned; or the obligation to follow the rule is so qualified as to collapse into act-utilitarianism after all.[14] There is, however, a version of rule-utilitarianism that makes a great deal of sense. In this version the utilitarian does not instruct us what our individual moral obligations are but rather instructs legislators what the best rules are.[15] If legislation is our focus, then the contradictions of rule-utilitarianism do not arise, since we are instructing those whose decisions can *only* take the form of issuing rules. From that perspective there is obvious utility to rules establishing and enforcing promissory obligations. Since I am concerned now with the question of individual obligation, that is, moral obligation, this legislative perspective on the argument is not available to me.

The obligation to keep a promise is grounded not in arguments of utility but in respect for individual autonomy and in trust. Autonomy and trust are grounds for the institution of promising as well, but the argument for *individual* obligation is not the same. Individual obligation is only a step away, but that step must be taken.[16] An individual is morally bound to keep his promises because he has intentionally invoked a convention whose function it is to give grounds – moral grounds – for another to expect the promised performance.[17] To renege is to abuse a confidence he was free to invite or not,

and which he intentionally did invite. To abuse that confidence now is like (but only *like*) lying: the abuse of a shared social institution that is intended to invoke the bonds of trust. A liar and a promise-breaker each *use* another person. In both speech and promising there is an invitation to the other to trust, to make himself vulnerable; the liar and the promise-breaker then abuse that trust. The obligation to keep a promise is thus similar to but more constraining than the obligation to tell the truth. To avoid lying you need only believe in the truth of what you say when you say it, but a promise binds into the future, well past the moment when the promise is made. There will, of course, be great social utility to a general regime of trust and confidence in promises and truthfulness. But this just shows that a regime of mutual respect allows men and women to accomplish what in a jungle of unrestrained self-interest could not be accomplished. If this advantage is to be firmly established, there must exist a ground for mutual confidence deeper than and independent of the social utility it permits.

The utilitarian counting the advantages affirms the general importance of enforcing *contracts*. The moralist of duty, however, sees *promising* as a device that free, moral individuals have fashioned on the premise of mutual trust, and which gathers its moral force from that premise. The moralist of duty thus posits a general obligation to keep promises, of which the obligation of contract will be only a special case – that special case in which certain promises have attained legal as well as moral force. But since a contract is first of all a promise, the contract must be kept because a promise must be kept.

To summarize: There exists a convention that defines the practice of promising and its entailments. This convention provides a way that a person may create expectations in others. By virtue of the basic Kantian principles of trust and respect, it is wrong to invoke that convention in order to make a promise, and then to break it.

What a Promise is Worth

If I make a promise to you, I should do as I promise; and if I fail to keep my promise, it is fair that I should be made to hand over the equivalent of the promised performance. In contract doctrine this proposition appears as the expectation measure of damages for breach. The expectation standard gives the victim of a breach no more or less than he would have had had there been no breach – in other words, he gets the benefit of his bargain.[18] Two alternative measures of damage, reliance and restitution, express the different notions that if a person has relied on a promise and been hurt, that hurt must be made good; and that if a contract-breaker has obtained goods or services, he must be made to pay a fair (just?) price for them.[19] Consider three cases:

II-A. I enter your antique shop on a quiet afternoon and agree in writing to buy an expensive chest I see there, the price being about three times what you paid for it a short time ago. When I get home I repent of my decision, and within half an hour of my visit – before any other customer has come to your store – I telephone to say I no longer want the chest.
II-B. Same as above, except in the meantime you have waxed and polished the chest and had your delivery van bring it to my door.
II-C. Same as above, except I have the use of the chest for six months, while your shop is closed for renovations.

To require me to pay for the chest in case II-A (or, if you resell it, to pay any profit you lost, including lost business volume) is to give you your expectation, the benefit of your bargain. In II-B if all I must compensate is your effort I am reimbursing your reliance, and in II-C to force me to pay a fair price for the use I have had of the chest is to focus on making me pay for, restore, an actual benefit I have received.

The assault on the classical conception of contract, the concept I call contract as promise, has centered on the connection – taken as canonical for some hundred years – between contract law and expectation damages. To focus the attack on this connection is indeed strategic. As the critics recognize and as I have just stated, to the extent that contract is grounded in promise, it seems natural to measure relief by the expectation, that is, by the promise itself. If that link can be threatened, then contract itself may be grounded elsewhere than in promise, elsewhere

than in the will of the parties. In his recent comprehensive treatise, *The Rise and Fall of Freedom of Contract*, Patrick Atiyah makes the connection between the recourse to expectation damages and the emerging enforceability of executory contracts – that is, contracts enforced, though no detriment has been suffered in reliance and no benefit has been conferred. (Case II-A is an example of an executory contract.) Before the nineteenth century, he argues, a contractual relation referred generally to one of a number of particular, community-sanctioned relations between persons who in the course of their dealings (as carriers, innkeepers, surgeons, merchants) relied on each other to their detriment or conferred benefits on each other. It was these detriments and benefits that had to be reimbursed, and an explicit promise – if there happened to be one – was important primarily to establish the reliance or to show that the benefit had been conferred in expectation of payment, not officiously or as a gift. All this, Atiyah writes, turned inside out when the promise itself came to be seen as the basis of obligation, so that neither benefit nor reliance any longer seemed necessary and the proper measure of the obligation was the promise itself, that is, the expectation. The promise principle was embraced as an expression of the principle of liberty – the will binding itself, to use Kantian language, rather than being bound by the norms of the collectivity – and the award of expectation damages followed as a natural concomitant of the promise principle.

The insistence on reliance or benefit is related to disputes about the nature of promising. As I have argued, reliance on a promise cannot alone explain its force: There is reliance because a promise is binding, and not the other way around. But if a person is bound by his promise and not by the harm the promisee may have suffered in reliance on it, then what he is bound to is just its performance. Put simply, I am bound to do what I promised you I would do – or I am bound to put you in as good a position as if I had done so. To bind me to do no more than to reimburse your reliance is to excuse me to that extent from the obligation I undertook. If your reliance is less than your expectation (in case II-A there is no reliance), then to that extent a reliance standard excuses me from the very obligation I undertook and so weakens the force of an obligation I chose to assume. Since by hypothesis I chose to assume the obligation in its stronger form (that is, to render the performance promised), the reliance rule indeed precludes me from incurring the very obligation I chose to undertake at the time of promising. The most compelling of the arguments for resisting this conclusion and for urging that we settle for reliance is the sense that it is sometimes harsh and ungenerous to insist on the full measure of expectancy. (This is part of Atiyah's thrust when he designates the expectation standard as an aspect of the rigid Victorian promissory morality.) The harshness comes about because in the event the promisor finds the obligation he assumed too burdensome.

This distress may be analyzed into three forms: (1) The promisor regrets having to pay for what he has bought (which may only have been the satisfaction of promising a gift or the thrill of buying a lottery ticket or stock option), though he would readily do the same thing again. I take it that this kind of regret merits no sympathy at all. Indeed if we gave in to it we would frustrate the promisor's ability to engage in his own continuing projects and so the promisor's plea is, strictly speaking, self-contradictory. (2) The promisor regrets his promise because he was mistaken about the nature of the burdens he was assuming – the purchaser in case II-A thought he would find the money for the antique but in fact his savings are depleted, or perhaps the chest is not as old nor as valuable as he had imagined, or his house has burned down and he no longer needs it. All of these regrets are based on mistaken assumptions about the facts as they are or as they turn out to be. [...] [T]he doctrines of mistake, frustration, and impossibility provide grounds for mitigating the effect of the promise principle without at all undermining it.

Finally there is the most troublesome ground of regret: (3) The promisor made no mistake about the facts or probabilities at all, but now that it has come time to perform he no longer values the promise as highly as when he made it. He regrets the promise because he regrets the value judgment that led him to make it. He concludes that the purchase of an expensive antique is an extravagance. Compassion may lead a promisee

to release an obligation in such a case, but he releases as an act of generosity, not as a duty, and certainly not because the promisor's repentance destroys the force of the original obligation. The intuitive reason for holding fast is that such repentance should be the promisor's own responsibility, not one he can shift onto others. It seems too easy a way of getting out of one's obligations. Yet our intuition does not depend on suspicions of insincerity alone. Rather we feel that holding people to their obligations is a way of taking them seriously and thus of giving the concept of sincerity itself serious content. Taking this intuition to a more abstract level, I would say that respect for others as free and rational requires taking seriously their capacity to determine their own values. I invoke again the distinction between the right and the good. The right defines the concept of the self as choosing its own conception of the good. Others must respect our capacity as free and rational persons to choose our own good, and that respect means allowing persons to take responsibility for the good they choose. And, of course, that choosing self is not an instantaneous self but one extended in time, so that to respect those determinations of the self is to respect their persistence over time. If we decline to take seriously the assumption of an obligation because we do not take seriously the promisor's prior conception of the good that led him to assume it, to that extent we do not take him seriously as a person. We infantilize him, as we do quite properly when we release the very young from the consequences of their choices.[20]

Since contracts invoke and are invoked by promises, it is not surprising that the law came to impose on the promises it recognized the same incidents as morality demands. The connection between contract and the expectation principle is so palpable that there is reason to doubt that its legal recognition is a relatively recent invention. It is true that over the last two centuries citizens in the liberal democracies have become increasingly free to dispose of their talents, labor, and property as seems best to them. The freedom to bind oneself contractually to a future disposition is an important and striking example of this freedom (the freedom to make testamentary dispositions or to make whatever present use of one's effort or goods one desires are other examples), because in a promise one is taking responsibility not only for one's present self but for one's future self. But this does not argue that the promise principle itself is a novelty – surely Cicero's, Pufendorf's and Grotius's discussions of it[21] show that it is not – but only that its use has expanded greatly over the years.

Remedies in and around the Promise

Those who have an interest in assimilating contract to the more communitarian standards of tort law have been able to obscure the link between contract and promise because in certain cases the natural thing to do *is* to give damages for the harm that has been suffered, rather than to give the money value of the promised expectation. But it does not follow from these cases that expectation is not a normal and natural measure for contract damages. First, these are situations in which the harm suffered is the measure of damages because it is hard to find the monetary value of the expectation. A leading case, *Security Stove & Mfg. Co. v. American Railway Express Co.*,[22] illustrates the type. The plaintiff stove manufacturer had arranged to have a new kind of stove shipped by the defendant express company to a trade convention, at which the plaintiff hoped to interest prospective buyers in his improved product. The president and his workmen went to the convention, but the defendant failed to deliver a crucial part of the exhibit in time, and they had nothing to show. Plaintiff brought suit to recover the cost of renting the booth, the freight charges, and the time and expenses lost as a result of the fruitless trip to the convention. The recovery of these items of damages, which (with

the possible exception of the prepaid booth rental) seem typical examples of reliance losses, is generally agreed to have been appropriate. There was no way of knowing what results the plaintiff would have obtained had he succeeded in exhibiting his product at the convention. There was no way of knowing what his expectancy was, and so the court gave him his loss through reliance. But this illustrates only that where expectancy cannot be calculated, reliance may be a reasonable surrogate. It is reasonable to suppose that the plaintiff's expectation in *Security Stove* was at least as great as the monies he put out to exhibit his goods – after all, he was a businessman and is assumed to have been exhibiting his goods to make an eventual profit. If it could somehow be shown that the exhibit would have been a failure and the plaintiff would have suffered a net loss, the case for recovery would be undermined, and most authorities would then deny recovery.*[23]

Second are the cases in which the amount needed to undo the harm caused by reliance is itself the fairest measure of expectation.

> III-A. Buyer approaches manufacturer with the specifications of a small, inexpensive part – say a bolt – for a machine buyer is building. Manufacturer selects the part and sells it to buyer. The bolt is badly made, shears, and damages the machine.

The value of the thing promised, a well-made bolt, is negligible, but to give buyer his money back and no more would be a grave injustice. Here it does seem more natural to say that the manufacturer induced buyer's reasonable reliance and should compensate the resulting harm. But it is equally the case that it is a fair implication of the simple-seeming original transaction that manufacturer not only delivered and

*A case like this may be seen as involving no more than the allocation of the burden of proof as to the expectation. The plaintiff shows his reliance costs and says that prima facie his expectation was at least that great. The burden then shifts to the defendant to show that indeed this was a losing proposition and the expectation was less than the reliance. It seems only fair that since the defendant's breach prevented the exhibition from taking place and thus prevented the drama on which the expectation depended from being played out, the defendant should at least bear the risk of showing that the venture would have been a failure.

promised to transfer good title to the bolt, but promised at the same time that the bolt would do the job it was meant to do.*[24]

It is for the (perhaps wholly innocent) breach of this implied promise that we hold manufacturers liable. The soundness of this analysis is brought home if we vary the facts slightly:

> III-B.   Same as above, except buyer purchases the bolt over the counter in a local hardware store, saying nothing about its use.

To make the owner of the hardware store or the manufacturer of the bolt responsible for large damages in this case seems unfair. One can say that this is because they could not *foresee* harm of this magnitude arising out of their conduct. (A tort locution: The man who negligently jostles a package containing a bomb could not *foresee* and is not responsible for harm of the ensuing magnitude when the package explodes.) But one can as well cast the matter again in contractual terms, saying that they did not undertake this measure of responsibility. After all, if in the first version of this example the buyer and manufacturer had agreed that manufacturer would be responsible only up to a certain amount, say ten times the cost of the bolt, such a limitation would generally be respected. So in certain cases tort and contract ideas converge on the same result.[25] In III-A we may say that buyer justifiably relied on manufacturer. He relied in part because of the (implied) promise or warranty, and of course it *is* a primary function of promises to induce reliance.

Consider finally this variation:

> III-C.   Manufacturer makes not bolts but tinned goods. Buyer buys a can of peas at a grocer's and serves them to a guest who chips a tooth on a stone negligently included in the can.

Manufacturer promised the guest nothing. (In legal terminology there is between them no privity of contract.) Yet manufacturer should be responsible for the guest's injuries, just as the driver of a car should be responsible for the injuries of a pedestrian whom he negligently hits, though there too privity of contract is lacking.[26] One may say that the guest reasonably relied on the purity of the peas he ate, just as a pedestrian must rely on the due care of motorists. But I never argued that promise is the *only* basis of reliance or that contract is the only basis of responsibility for harms to others.

Third, there are cases in which wrongs are committed and loss is suffered in and around the attempt to make an agreement. In these cases too reliance is the best measure of compensation. A striking example is *Hoffman v. Red Owl Stores:*[27] A prospective Red Owl supermarket franchisee sold his previously owned business and made other expenditures on the assumption that his negotiations to obtain a Red Owl franchise would shortly be concluded. The award of reliance damages was not a case of enforcement of a promise at all, since the parties had not reached the stage where clearly determined promises had been made. Reliance damages were awarded because Red Owl had not dealt fairly with Hoffman. It had allowed him to incur expenses based on hopes that Red Owl knew or should have known were imprudent and that Red Owl was not prepared to permit him to realize. Red Owl was held liable not in order to force it to perform a promise, which it had never made, but rather to compensate Hoffman for losses he had suffered through Red Owl's inconsiderate and temporizing assurances.[28] There is nothing at all in my conception of contract as promise that precludes persons who behave badly and cause unnecessary harm from being forced to make fair compensation. Promissory obligation is not the only basis for liability; principles of tort are sufficient to provide that people who give vague assurances that cause foreseeable harm to others should make compensation. Cases like *Hoffman* are seen to undermine the conception of contract as promise: If contract is

*In law the latter promise is called a warranty – a promise not merely that the promisor will do something in the future, but a taking of responsibility over and above the responsibility of well-meaning honesty that something is the case. For instance, a dealer may warrant that a violin is a Stradivarius. This means more than that he in good faith believes it to be one: he is promising that if it is not, he will be responsible. Uniform Commercial Code (hereafter cited UCC) §2–714. Cf. Smith v. Zimbalist, 2 Cal. App.2d 324, 38 P.2d 170 (1934), hearing denied 17 Jan. 1935.

really discrete and if it is really based in promise, then whenever there has been a promise in the picture (even only a potential promise) contractual principles must govern the whole relation. To state the argument is to reveal it as a non sequitur. It is a logical fallacy of which the classical exponents of contract as promise were themselves supremely guilty in their reluctance to grant relief for fraud or for mistakes that prevented a real agreement from coming into being. Modern critics of contractual freedom have taken the classics at their word. Justice often requires relief and adjustment in cases of accidents in and around the contracting process, and the critics have seen in this a refutation of the classics' major premise. In chapter 5, which deals with mistake, impossiblility and frustration, I will show in detail how the excessive rigidity of the classics played both them and the concept of contract as promise false. Here it is sufficient to introduce the notion that contract as promise has a distinct but neither exclusive nor necessarily dominant place among legal and moral principles. A major concern of this book is the articulation of the boundaries and connection between the promissory and other principles of justice.*

The tendency to merge promise into its adjacent concepts applies also to the relation between it and the principle of restitution, which holds that a person who has received a benefit at another's expense should compensate his benefactor, unless a gift was intended. This principle does indeed appeal to a primitive intuition of fairness. Even where a gift was intended, the appropriateness at least of gratitude if not of a vague duty to reciprocate is recognized in many cultures. Aristotle refers the principle to the imperative that some balance be retained among members of a society, but this seems to restate the proposition rather than to explain it.[29] Since restitution, like reliance, is a principle of fairness that operates independently of the will of the parties, the attempt to refer promissory obligation to this principle is another attempt to explain away the self-imposed character of promissory obligation. I have already argued that this cannot be done without begging the question. Certainly the restitution principle cannot explain the force of a promise for which no benefit has yet been or ever will be given in return. (The legal recognition of such gift promises is tangled in the confusions of the doctrine of consideration.) The reduction of promise to restitution (or to restitution plus reliance) must fail. There are nevertheless breaches of promise for which restitution is the correct principle of relief.[30]

IV.   In a case like *Security Stove*, where the freight charges have been prepaid but the goods never picked up or delivered as agreed, let us suppose the express company could show that the contemplated exhibit would have been a disaster and that the stove company was much better off never having shown at the fair. Perhaps in such a case there should be no award of reliance damages, but should the express company be allowed to keep the prepayment? Should it be able to argue that the stove company is lucky there was a breach?

In terms of both expectation and harm the stove company should get nothing. Its expectation is shown to be negative, and it suffered no harm. And yet it is entirely clear that Railway Express should make restitution. They did nothing for the money and should not keep it. But is this enforcing the promise? Not at all.

---

*There is a category of cases that has become famous in the law under the rubric of promissory estoppel or detrimental reliance. In these cases there has indeed generally been a promise, but the basis for *legal* redress is said to be the plaintiff's detrimental reliance on the promise. Courts now tend to limit the amount of the redress in such cases to the detriment suffered through reliance. But these cases also do not show that reliance and harm are the general basis for contractual recovery. Rather these cases should be seen for what they are: a belated attempt to plug a gap in the general regime of enforcement of promises, a gap left by the artificial and unfortunate doctrine of consideration. See Fuller and Eisenberg, supra note 25, at 159–61.

V. I owe my plumber ten dollars, so I place a ten-dollar bill in an envelope, which I mistakenly address and send to you.

On what theory can I get my ten dollars back from you? You made no promise to me. You have *done* me no wrong, and so that is not the ground of my demand that you return the money – though you wrong me now if you do not accede to my demand. The principle is a general one: It is wrong to retain an advantage obtained without justification at another's expense. And what justification can you offer for keeping the ten dollars?*[31] What justification can Railway Express offer for keeping the freight charges in case IV? That it has done the stove company a favor by spoiling the exhibit? But this is no favor the stove company asked for and not one that Railway Express had a right to thrust on it. And surely Railway Express cannot say it received the money properly under a contract, since it has utterly repudiated that contract. The contract drops out leaving Railway Express without a justification. In this state of affairs the stove company wins.

Promise and restitution are distinct principles. Neither derives from the other, and so the attempt to dig beneath promise in order to ground contract in restitution (or reliance, for that matter) is misconceived. Contract is based on promise, but when something goes wrong in the contract process – when people fail to reach agreement, or break their promises – there will usually be gains and losses to sort out. The *Red Owl* case is one illustration. Here is another:

I. Britton signs on to work for Turner for a period of one year at an agreed wage of $120 to be paid at the end of his service. After nine months of faithful service he quits without justification, and Turner without difficulty finds a replacement for him.

On one hand Britton has not kept his promise; on the other Turner has had a substantial benefit at his expense.[32] The promise and restitution principles appear to point in opposite directions in this situation. In chapter 8 I consider at length the way these two principles work together, when and why one or the other of them has priority. For the present it is sufficient to note that it is the very distinctness of the principles that causes such questions to arise. Certainly nothing about the promise principle, the conception of contract as promise, entails that all disputes between people who have tried but failed to make a contract or who have broken a contract must be decided solely according to that principle.

Notes

1 On the right and the good the critical discussion is John Rawls, *A Theory of Justice*, §§68, 83–5 (Cambridge, 1971), which harks back to Immanuel Kant, *Groundwork of the Metaphysics of Morals* (Paton trans. Harper Torchbooks ed. New York, 1964) where the contrast is made between the right and happiness. See also W. D. Ross, *The Right and the Good* (Oxford, 1930); Ronald Dworkin, "Liberalism," in *Public and Private Morality* (S. Hampshire ed. Cambridge, England, 1978). On the relation between liberalism and responsibility, see Friedrich Hayek, *The Constitution of Liberty*, ch. 5 (Chicago, 1960); Charles Fried, *Right and Wrong*, 124–6 (Cambridge, 1978); Rawls, supra at 519. For a different view see C. B. Macpherson, *The Political Theory of Possessive Individualism – Hobbes to Locke* (Oxford, 1962).

2 Immanuel Kant, *The Metaphysical Elements of Justice*, 54–5 (Ladd trans. Indianapolis, 1965).

3 See Charles Fried, *An Anatomy of Values*, 81–6 (Cambridge, 1970); Henry Sidgwick, *Elements of Politics*, quoted in Friedrich Kessler and Grant Gilmore, *Contracts*, 4 (2d ed. Boston, 1970).

4 Sissela Bok, *Lying: Moral Choice in Public Life* (New York, 1978); Fried, supra note 1, ch. 3.

5 This example is based on Adams v. Gillig, 199 N.Y. 314, 92 N.E. 670 (1930).

6 See generally Page Keeton, "Fraud: Statements of Intention," 15 *Texas L. Rev.* 185 (1937).

7 See generally Robert Goff and Gareth Jones, *The Law of Restitution*, ch. 1 (2d. ed. London, 1978).

8 For a strong statement of the tort and benefit principles as foundations of contract law, see

---

*That you thought it was a present, spent it, and would now have to dip into the grocery budget to pay me back? Well, that might be a justification if it were true.

Patrick Atiyah, *The Rise and Fall of Freedom of Contract*, 1–7 (Oxford, 1979). A remarkable article stating the several moral principles implicit in contract law is George Gardner, "An Inquiry into the Principles of the Law of Contracts," 46 *Harv. L. Rev.* 1 (1932).

9 For a review of Anglo-American writing on promise from Hobbes to modern times, see Atiyah, supra note 8, at 41–60, 649–59. There has been a lively debate on the bases for the moral obligation of promises in recent philosophical literature. Some philosophers have taken a line similar to that of Atiyah and Gilmore, deriving the obligation of promise from the element of reliance. The strongest statement is Neil MacCormick, "Voluntary Obligations and Normative Powers," *Proceedings of the Aristotelian Society*, supp. vol. 46, at 59 (1972). See also Pall Ardal, "And That's a Promise," 18 *Phil. Q.* 225 (1968); F. S. McNeilly, "Promises Demoralized," 81 *Phil. Rev.* 63 (1972). G. J. Warnock, *The Object of Morality*, ch. 7 (London, 1971), offers an effective refutation along the lines in the text, but his affirmative case proposes that the obligation of a promise rests on the duty of veracity, the duty to make the facts correspond to the promise. For an excellent discussion of this last suggestion and a proposal that accords with my own, see Don Locke, "The Object of Morality and the Obligation to Keep a Promise," 2 *Canadian J. of Philosophy* 135 (1972). Locke's emphasis on trust seems a clearer and sounder version of H. A. Prichard's proposal that the obligation of a Promise rests on a more general "agreement to keep agreements." *Moral Obligation*, ch. 7 (Oxford, 1957).

10 A number of the philosophers who disagree with the Atiyah–MacCormick argument emphasize the conventional aspect of the invocation of the promissory form, as well as the self-imposed nature of the obligation. E.g. Joseph Raz, "Voluntary Obligations," *Proceedings of the Aristotelian Society*, supp. vol. 46, at 79 (1972); Raz, "Promises and Obligations," in *Law, Morality and Society* (Hacker, Raz eds. Oxford, 1977); John Searle, *Speech Acts*, 33–42, 175–88 (Cambridge, 1969); Searle, "What Is a Speech Act?" in *The Philosophy of Language* (John Searle ed. Oxford, 1971). The locus classicus of this view of promising is John Rawls, "Two Concepts of Rules," 64 *Phil. Rev.* 3 (1955). The general idea goes back, of course, to Ludwig Wittgenstein, *Philosophical Investigations*, §23. For Hume's account of the conventional nature of promissory obligation, see *A Treatise of Human Nature*, 516–25 (Selby-Bigge ed. Oxford, 1888).

11 Stanley Cavell's contention in *The Claim of Reason*, 293–303 (Oxford, 1979) that promising is not a practice or an institution, because unlike the case of a game one cannot imagine setting it up or reforming it and because promising is not an office, seems to me beside the point. Kant's discussion, supra note 2, shows that morality can mandate that there be a convention with certain general features, as does Hume's discussion supra note 10, though Hume's morality is a more utilitarian one.

12 David Lewis, *Convention* (Cambridge, 1969).

13 Supra note 10.

14 Here I side with David Lyons, *The Forms and Limits of Utilitarianism* (Oxford, 1965) in a continuing debate. For the most recent statement of the contrary position, see Richard Brandt, *A Theory of the Good and Right* (Oxford, 1979). For an excellent introduction, see J. J. C. Smart and Bernard Williams, *Utilitarianism: For and Against* (Cambridge, England, 1973). I argue that it is a mistake to treat Rawls's discussion of promising in "Two Concepts of Rules," supra note 10, as an instance of rule-utilitarianism in my review of Atiyah, 93 *Harv. L. Rev.* 1863n18 (1980). See also Charles Landesman, "Promises and Practices," 75 *Mind* (n.s.) 239 (1966).

15 This was in fact Bentham's general perspective. See also Brandt, supra note 14.

16 Compare Rawls, supra note 1, ch. 6, where it is argued that (*a*) the deduction of the principles of justice for institutions, and (*b*) a showing that a particular institution is just are not sufficient to generate an obligation to comply with that institution. Further principles of natural duty and obligation must be established.

17 See Locke, supra note 9; Prichard, supra note 9; Raz, supra note 10.

18 American Law Institute, *Restatement (1st) of the Law of Contracts* [hereafter cited as *Restatement* (1st) or (2d)], §329, Comment a: "In awarding compensatory damages, the effort is made to put the injured party in as good a position as that in which he would have been put by full performance of the contract . . ."; E. Allan Farnsworth, "Legal Remedies for Breach of Contract," 70 *Colum. L. Rev.* 1145 (1970); Gardner, supra note 8; Charles Goetz and Robert Scott, "Enforcing Promises: An Examination of the Basis of Contract," 80 *Yale L. J.* 1261 (1980).

19 See Fuller and Perdue, "The Reliance Interest in Contract Damages," 46 *Yale L. J.* 52, 373 (1936, 1937); Gardner, supra note 8.

20 For discussions of these issues see Fried, supra note 3, at 169–77; Rawls, supra note 1, §85; and

478 CHARLES FRIED

the essays in *The Identities of Persons* (Amelie Rorty ed. Berkeley, 1976) and *Personal Identity* (John Perry ed. Berkeley, 1975).

21 See Atiyah, supra note 8, at 140–1 for a discussion of these early sources. See my review of Atiyah, 93 *Harv. L. Rev.* 1858, 1864–5 (1980) for a further discussion of these and other early sources.

22 227 Mo. App. 175, 51 S.W.2d 572 (1932).

23 *Restatement* (1st) §333(d).

24 Gardner, supra note 8, at 15, 22–3.

25 This is the problem that is standardly dealt with in contract texts under the rubric of consequential damages, or the principle in *Hadley v. Baxendale* 9 Exch. 341 (1854). See Gardner, supra note 8, at 28–30. Holmes, in Globe Refining Co. v. Landa Cotton Oil Co., 190 U.S. 540 (1903) explained the limitation of liability for consequential damages in terms of the agreement itself: The defendant is liable only for those risks he explicitly or tacitly agreed to assume. This conception has been generally rejected in favor of a vaguer standard by which defendant is liable for any risks of which he had "reason to know" at the time of the agreement. UCC §2–715 comment 2. Holmes's test seems more consonant with the thesis of this work. See Pothier, *The Law of Obligations*, quoted in Lon

Fuller and Melvin Eisenberg, *Basic Contract Law* 27 (3rd ed. St. Paul, 1972). The difference between the two positions is not great: first, because it is always within the power of the parties to limit or expand liability for consequential damages by the agreement itself, UCC §2–719(3); second, because the "reason to know" standard means that the defendant at least has a fair opportunity to make such an explicit provision.

26 UCC §2–318; William Prosser, *Torts*, ch. 17 (4th ed. St. Paul, 1971).

27 133 N.W.2d 267, 26 Wis.2d 683 (1965).

28 See Stanley Henderson, "Promissory Estoppel and Traditional Contract Doctrine," 78 *Yale L.J.* 343, 357–60 (1969); see generally Friedrich Kessler and Edith Fine, "*Culpa in Contrahendo*, Bargaining in Good Faith, and Freedom of Contract: A Comparative Study," 77 *Harv. L. Rev.* 401 (1964).

29 *Nicomachean Ethics*, bk. V, iv–v.

30 See John Dawson, "Restitution or Damages?," 20 *Ohio St. L.J.* 175 (1959); Gardner, supra note 8, at 18–27.

31 Goff and Jones, supra note 7, at 69; the problem raised in the footnote is treated at 88–9.

32 Britton v. Turner, 6 N.H. 281 (1834).

48

Legally Enforceable Commitments

Michael D. Bayles

Introduction

A continuing issue of contract law is what purported promises, agreements, or contracts should be legally enforced. Classic common-law theory usually addresses this issue through the doctrine of consideration: only those promises for which consideration is given are legally enforceable. The intent to enter contractual relations has also often been mentioned as another factor but its importance is questionable. In the absence of consideration, an intent to enter contractual relations would not suffice; and if a court finds consideration, it will also find an implied intent to contract unless there is a very explicit statement to the contrary.

My aim here is to consider what commitments should be legally enforceable. Although the terms "promisor" and "promisee" will be used, the term "commitment" is used to avoid possible limitations imposed by the concepts of promise and agreement. If one person sells a boat to another representing it as fourteen feet long, it seems odd to say that the seller promises that it is fourteen feet long; however, the seller certainly makes a commitment to its being that long. In other situations the "promisor" might not say anything but the "promisee" reasonably relies on a commitment. Without any linguistic communication, however, one might hesitate to say a promise was made.

Normative Analysis

The purpose herein is to consider what commitments *should* be legally enforced, not to determine which ones have been or will be enforced.[1] Because there is little agreement on methods for establishing such normative claims, it is important to state the method used even though space does not permit a defense of the method.

The central normative question is: What principles would rational persons accept courts using to decide cases in a society in which they expected to live?[2] As acceptable principles could and should vary with the type of society, the society is assumed to be an industrialized Western one with a common-law system. The crucial concepts to clarify are those of principles and rational persons.

Principles and rules can be distinguished from each other.[3] On the one hand, rules apply in an all-or-nothing way; if they apply to a situation, they determine its evaluation. For example, a law requiring two witnesses to a will not in the handwriting of the testator is a rule. If a will has only

Michael D. Bayles, "Legally Enforceable Commitments," *Law and Philosophy*, vol. 4, no. 3 (December 1985), pp. 311–42 (excerpts). © 1985. Reprinted with permission from Springer Science and Business Media.

one witness, it is invalid. In contrast, when principles apply, they do not necessarily determine an evaluation. For example, it might be a principle that people should be free to dispose of their property by devise as they wish. It does not necessarily follow that a freely made will should be upheld because a contrary principle, for example, that a person should make adequate provision for children, might also apply. On the other hand, because principles do not apply in an all-or-nothing way and can conflict, principles have "weight." Conflicting principles must be weighed or balanced against one another, and some have more weight than others. Because rules apply in an all-or-nothing fashion, they do not have to be weighed or balanced against one another.

Some scholars reject this distinction between principles and rules, contending that principles differ from rules only by being more general.[4] In this view, both rules and principles have weight and can be balanced against one another. This contention does not affect the following arguments because the essential features are the possibility of weighing or balancing and different levels of generality. The following discussion presents some principles for different types of commitments.

A rational person uses logical reasoning and all relevant available information in acquiring desires and values, deciding what to do, and accepting legal principles.[5] Logical reasoning is not restricted to deductive logic but also includes inductive logic or scientific method. A rational person considers arguments for and against principles, accepting the sound arguments and rejecting the unsound ones. All relevant available information is all pertinent information that a person in the situation can obtain. It is information, not knowledge, that a rational person has. People are rational if they use the best information available, even if it later turns out to be incorrect; indeed, it would be irrational to use information that, on the basis of presently available evidence, appeared incorrect even if it were later found to be correct. Information is relevant to the acceptability of a legal principle if it indicates that the principle's use by courts has or lacks some normative characteristic, such as fairness, or that the probable consequences of such use, including effects on third parties, would be good or bad.

Some normative basis must be used in determining what legal principles are justifiable or acceptable, but it need not be a moral or legal one. Much legal analysis and justification is in terms of people's interests. There is little reason to believe that these interests or desires (the difference is not important here) are irrational. Herein certain basic desires are assumed to be rational, namely, those for wealth, security, bodily and mental integrity (including life), prestige or reputation, and freedom. Most of these have been justified elsewhere.[6]

Finally, it is assumed that rational persons could be either party to a case. This assumption is implicit in the very question being asked, for it concerns the acceptability of legal principles for a society in which one expects to live. In contract cases, many principles can be used by plaintiff or defendant. In arguing for a legal principle, one must then consider its acceptability from both parties' points of view.[7] This type of argument is common in courts. An example is the following argument by Judge Turnage for the rule that rejection of a purchased option does not terminate the right to accept later unless the other party has materially changed position.

> This rule fully protects the rights of both parties. It extends to the optionor the protection he requires in the event a rejection of the option is communicated to him and he thereafter changes his position in reliance thereon to his detriment. At the same time it protects the right of the option holder to have the opportunity to exercise his option for the full period for which he paid, absent the material change in position.[8]

This argument shows that it is a reasonable rule whichever party one might be. One has no reason to think that people are more likely to have written than purchased an option.

Contract Law

Contracts are often defined as promises or agreements enforceable at law.[9] Contract law might then be taken to be the law pertaining to the enforcement of promises or agreements. However, this narrow conception of contract law is inadequate for material normally included in contract law, let alone for evaluating the law. Many court cases normally included in contract law do not, for one reason or another, involve enforceable agreements or promises. Indeed, often it is found that no contract has been made. In short, contract law concerns more than enforceable contracts and agreements; it also concerns failed attempts to make them. This narrow conception of contract has made possible talk of the death of contract,[10] because nontraditional principles have come to play such an important role in failed attempts to contract.

An extremely broad conception of contract law is the law pertaining to private transfer of property or services. So conceived, contract law includes many subjects not usually thought to belong to it, such as wills and inheritance, gifts, restitution, fraud, and conversion of property. This extremely broad conception of contract law can be subdivided by the use of two distinctions. The first is simply whether an intended transfer is a present or future one. The second distinction is among "plus sum," "zero sum," and "minus sum" interactions. In plus sum interactions, more value exists after the interaction than before; that is, value is increased. The general concept of a plus sum interaction has three subcases. One party might lose but the other gain more than the first loses; one party might remain the same and the other gain; and both parties might gain. If Arnold purchases a watch from a store, then presumably both he and the store benefit and the interaction is a plus sum one of the last type. In zero sum interactions, the same amount of value exists after the interaction as before. If two people each mistakenly take the other's similar umbrella from a stand, the interaction is a zero sum one. An interaction would also be a zero sum one if one party gained precisely what the other lost. In minus sum interactions, less value exists after the interaction than before. If two people have an automobile accident, value is decreased. Either one party is the same and the other worse off or both are worse off.

How one classifies some interactions depends on how value is conceived. For example, gifts are usually treated as zero sum interactions, probably because there is only a one way transfer. But the parties to a gift transfer might think of it as a plus sum interaction. The recipient of a book might value it more than a donor who

has already read it. The donor might value the recipient having the book and indicate this by paying to mail the book to the donee. Voluntary gifts can then increase economic value and be plus sum interactions. Gift interactions can also be minus sum ones, for example, when a recipient places less value on a gift than the donor or the market. One often receives gifts that one did not want and puts away in a drawer or closet. Perhaps on average gifts are zero or modest plus sum interactions, the plus sum ones barely offsetting the minus sum ones.

With these two distinctions, transfers of property or services can be classified as follows.

	ZERO SUM	PLUS SUM
PRESENT	gift inter vivos gift causa mortis	barter cash sales
FUTURE	conditional deeds succession	executory contracts

All of the transfers in the zero sum column are considered in property law. Gifts causa mortis and deeds with conditional delivery are placed near the border of present and future, because gifts causa mortis are present transfers with a right to revoke, whereas conditional deeds involve future transfers when the condition is met.

Logically, one might expect contract law to concern all the transfers in the plus sum column. However, there are two main problems with that. First, the concept of a plus sum interaction needed is a special one. Contract law is not limited to interactions which are in fact plus sum ones; it includes cases when something goes wrong and the interaction is not a plus sum one. One must view the interaction from a prospective or *ex ante* perspective; it is expected to be a plus sum interaction. As noted above, one party can lose and the interaction still be a plus sum one if the other party gains more than the first loses. Nonetheless, if the interaction is voluntary, rational parties expect it to be beneficial to them, although they need not expect or even consider whether it will be beneficial to the others. The concept then is of mutually expected beneficial plus sum interactions. Each party hopes to get something that is of more value to it than what is given. Because each party expects to benefit, based on the parties' expectations, *ex ante* the interaction is a plus sum one of the third type – in which both parties gain. Court cases arise when something goes wrong and the transfer does not occur or is for some other reason not mutually beneficial as expected.

Second, many commentators claim that contracts necessarily involve a promise.[11] If promises always relate to the future, then contract law excludes all present transfers such as barter.[12] This creates a problem for cash sales of goods as in purchasing groceries. Of course many sales of goods are partially "executory," for example, one party is to perform at a future date. Moreover, even most present sales involve commitments to the future, for example, warranties. Nonetheless, a cash payment for goods "as is" (no warranties) is included in the Uniform Commercial Code[13] and thus part of what is usually considered contract law. We have placed cash sales of goods in the present category, but near the border because of the future effect of warranties. If one party in a sale is to perform in the future, then sales of goods belong to executory contracts as that term is meant in the table, namely, as all those in which at least one party makes a commitment to something in the future.

Finally, "interaction" rather than the more usual "transaction" has been used because of its durational openness. "Transaction" suggests a discrete event, whereas "interaction" can apply to a long-term relationship. Much traditional contract law focuses on brief interactions between strangers. Yet, in the contemporary world, many contracts, such as employment, franchise, and installment contracts, pertain to a course of dealing between parties.[14] Although many of these long-term or relational contracts are treated in special fields, such as labor law, it is desirable to develop contract principles that can cover both them and discrete transactions.

Thus, the main function of contract law is to regulate mutually expected beneficial interactions transferring property or services between private persons[15] and to provide civil remedies when they go wrong. Failed mutually expected plus sum interactions usually become zero sum or minus sum ones. Most minus sum interactions are treated in tort law, but because many failed mutually expected plus sum interactions become

minus sum ones, there is an overlap of tort and contract principles, especially for remedies. This does not mean that tort and contract law are the same; they take different perspectives. Tort law takes an *ex post* view of interactions as minus sum ones. Criminal law also regulates plus sum and minus sum interactions, but it can be distinguished by its remedy – punishment.

Aims

Most theories of contract law adopt a single aim: the enforcement of agreements or promises, maximizing economic value, or fulfilling reasonable expectations. An advantage of this approach is that it provides a unity to the field. However, human beings, and courts composed of them, are not such single-minded machines. People can have more than one purpose for their activities or institutions and reconcile or balance them when they conflict. Consequently, none of these theories alone provides an adequate basis for evaluating the law. Nevertheless, it is useful to briefly examine their claims, and then to bring together the insights they provide.

Agreement and Promise

The classical view is that contract law is to enforce the agreement or promises of the parties. On the agreement version, the purpose of contract law is to carry out the wills of parties who intended to be legally bound by an agreement.[16] On the promise version, the purpose of contract law is to enforce the moral obligation to keep promises when the institution of promising is intentionally invoked.[17] Three claims are central to both versions. (1) The parties intend to bind themselves. (2) The parties freely choose to bind themselves. (3) Legal enforcement increases freedom or autonomy by enabling people to make definite arrangements for the future.[18]

There are problems with this view as the sole purpose of contract law. First, much of contract law concerns situations when, for one reason or another, agreements or valid promises were not made. The purpose of enforcing agreements or promises thus does not reach them. The heroic approach is to call such situations contractual accidents or gaps falling outside of contract law proper.[19] But this is like saying principles of building construction pertain only when they are followed and have no relevance to situations when they are not.

Second, the first two claims are sometimes denied in the law. Parties can be legally bound although they did not intend to bind themselves legally. Indeed, it is not at all unusual for parties to find they have legally binding contracts or promises when they did not so intend. Contrarily, some contracts are not legally enforced even if the parties want and intend them to be, for example, gambling contracts. Whether one is legally bound depends on the rules of law, although often one can avoid legal obligations by explicitly stating that one is not making legal commitments. It follows that parties do not always freely choose to bind themselves. One should distinguish two aspects of freely binding oneself – entering a contract and choosing the terms of a contract. Terms of a contract are often set by law (for example, a marital contract), but one is free to enter it or not. In a few cases, a contract is not even entered freely. Different conceptions of freedom can pertain here, but on almost any of them some contracts are not entered freely, for example, an agreement with a judge not to do some act.[20]

One's overall freedom is increased by being able to make legally binding agreements. One has options to bind oneself in the future. But it is the ability to bind others to one, not the ability to bind oneself, that is the most valuable aspect of contract, although being able to bind oneself and doing so might be necessary to get others to bind themselves. One is freed from worry and actions to ensure the promised performance. Thus, enforcement of agreements or promises cannot be the sole aim of contract law, because it simply fails to cover a multitude of situations arising in it. Nonetheless it, and especially the freedom it provides, can still be purposes of contract law.

Maximizing Economic Value

Economic analysts view law, at least private law, as designed to maximize economic value or wealth.[21] The point or test of legal enforcement (imposition of liability) is to create incentives for value maximizing conduct in the future.[22] A more contract specific and sophisticated aim is to "maximize the net beneficial reliance derived from promise-making activity."[23] "Beneficial reliance" is reliance on commitments that are kept so that one benefits. "Detrimental reliance" is reliance when a commitment is not kept and one loses. A balance must be struck between the benefits from fulfilled commitments and the losses from unfulfilled ones. In reciprocal or bargained for contracts, these two considerations can be balanced by the parties in their negotiations. For example, if Bradford is negotiating a contract to loan Caswell a sum of money, the interest to be charged will reflect Bradford's estimate of the likelihood of Caswell repaying. The greater the risk of nonrepayment (loss), the higher the interest (benefit) will be. In non-reciprocal contracts, the law must be more active, because these considerations are not balanced by the parties adjusting the terms.

On this economic view, freedom is subordinated to increasing wealth. Freedom of parties is not important for its own sake but because value is determined by the free preferences of persons. Free choice in entering contracts and fixing their terms is essential, because it ensures that both parties expect to benefit from them and value is thus increased. If a person did not (freely) intend to make a commitment, then its enforcement is not justified, because there is not reason to believe the person thought it would be beneficial.[24] The economic view supports a freedom the promise theory does not, namely, the freedom to breach contracts. If a party finds that another deal can provide more benefit even if damages are paid, then that party is free to break the contract. Indeed, to maximize value, the party should do so. Similarly, if the original judgment about expected benefit from the contract were incorrect and one would lose from completing the deal, one is free to and should breach if the damages would be less than the costs of performance.

The economic view focuses on the fact that contracts are mutually expected to be beneficial, that is, value increasing interactions. One has good reasons to accept the economic purpose. Laws facilitating mutually expected beneficial plus sum interactions are desirable, since one can expect to benefit whichever party one is. Moreover, one has no reason to object to rules that enable others to break contracts provided one receives benefits equivalent to what one would have received had the contract been performed. However, economic theorists tend to discount the costs of breach by the other party, in particular, the costs of suing for compensation. Possible legal expenses and judicial error are costs of another's breach that must be subtracted from the benefits of the contract. Consequently, one would not accept allowing others to breach whenever, after subtracting one's expected benefits, they gain.

Maximizing beneficial reliance comes close to maximizing the trust which promise theorists see as central. On a promise view, the principles of mutual trust and respect are the basis for enforcing promises.[25] Beneficial reliance amounts to action in trust that promises will be fulfilled. Thus, both views fasten on essentially the same element but describe it in different terminology – mutual trust and beneficial reliance. They have different views as to the ultimate purpose or benefit of enforcement. Promise theorists view the benefit as freedom, while economic theorists view it as material gain. The difference is subtle, because an important point of contractual freedom is to be able to improve one's situation materially by arranging the future. However, freedom to contract includes the freedom to make expected detrimental commitments as well as beneficial ones, although a rational self-interested person would not do so.

Reasonable Expectations

Another view contends that "the fundamental purpose of contract law is the protection and promotion of expectations reasonably created."[26] In a contractual setting, only those reasonable expectations of which the other party was or should have been aware are to be protected.[27] This view emphasizes one being responsible for another reasonably relying on, or having expectations due to, one's words or actions.[28] If one is or should have been aware that one's actions would create expectations in another, then one is responsible for fulfilling (not frustrating) those expectations.

The central problem for this view is to specify when expectations and reliance are reasonable.[29] One might determine reasonableness of contractual

expectations and reliance by social practices. Courts often use commercial customs and practices as a basis for interpreting contracts.[30] However, for many contracts no such commercial basis exists. Instead, one has to turn to what the average person would have expected or to a normative theory about reasonable expectations. Using the expectations of the average person will not provide a sound normative basis for contract law. Even if one thinks it valuable to satisfy people's expectations, this will not help. The average person's expectations are often determined, directly or indirectly, by what the law is. Thus, the argument might be circular: the law should be such and such because that complies with what people expect, but they expect that because the law is such and such. A normative basis should thus enable one to evaluate the expectations of people. The concept of a rational person as used here can fulfill that role. But then the view simply amounts to claiming that contracts should be enforced when rational persons have good reasons for doing so. This does not provide an aim for contract law.

The aim of protecting reasonable expectations and reliance is closely related to the aims of the promise and economic views. Reasonable expectations arise from promises, and their protection and promotion largely involves enforcing the promises. Promoting and protecting reasonable reliance is similar to the economic view's concern to maximize beneficial reliance. The economic theory, however, provides a criterion for determining when and how reliance should be protected, thereby specifying what reliance is reasonable. The reasonable expectations view does not provide guidance here.

Specific Aims

With different language and emphasis, each of the views is concerned to promote and protect mutually expected beneficial plus sum interactions involving the transfer of property or services and the interests arising therein. It is possible to pick out specific aims common to these views and to add one that they ignore. Both the promise and economic views emphasize freedom to enter contracts and fix their terms. Although the reasonable expectations view does not emphasize freedom, it does emphasize responsibility for the exercise of freedom, for expectations and reliance voluntarily created. Consequently, the freedom to transfer property and services in mutually expected beneficial interactions is common to each. This aspect is contained in the following principle. *(1) The principle of freedom of transfer: (a) property and services should be voluntarily transferable from one person to another; and (b) involuntary transfers should be not be allowed.* This principle is a very general one, covering gifts and testamentary dispositions as well as contracts.[31]

The expected benefit of entering interactions involving commitments rests on the assurance that they will be fulfilled. The views' emphasis on trust, beneficial reliance, and fulfillment of reasonable expectations all support legal assurance. Promises are more trustworthy if supported by law; beneficial reliance is more likely when the law enforces most commitments; and expectations and reliance are reasonable if the law will protect them. Not all commitments need be or should be legally enforced. Much depends on whether the interaction is expected to be a plus sum, zero sum, or minus sum one. One has good reasons for the promotions and enforcement of commitments in mutually expected beneficial plus sum interactions, because one can expect to benefit from them. This rationale does not apply to zero sum and minus sum interactions. In an expected minus sum interaction, at least one party and often both will lose, so one has no reason to support commitments to them. In zero sum interactions, either both parties will be left as they were or one will gain what the other loses. With an equal chance of being either party, one would be indifferent to them. Again, however, whether an interaction is zero sum depends on what counts as value. If one counts the psychological satisfaction of a donor or the greater value to the donee, then the giving of gifts can be a plus sum interaction. One might thus rationally desire to bind oneself legally to giving a gift in the future. Moreover, as a potential donee in a zero sum interaction, one does not want it turned into a minus sum interaction with oneself the loser.

(2) The principle of enforceable commitments: commitments in transfers of property or services should be supported and enforced (a) in mutually expected beneficial plus sum interactions, and (b) in zero sum interactions if (i) it is necessary to prevent *loss due to reasonable reliance by intended beneficiaries or (ii) donors indicate they are enforceable.* This principle encapsulates the reasoning of the previous paragraph. It extends to wills and gratuitous conditional deeds, for by making such instruments a donor indicates that they are enforceable. It also protects reasonable reliance on gratuitous promises. This principle assumes that, in accordance with the principle of freedom of transfer, the commitments are voluntary.

Of course, as with all principles, there can be sufficient reasons against complying with it. In law, a crucial concern is not bothering with de minimis or trivial matters. This consideration is largely met by the costs imposed on parties in lawsuits for enforcement of commitments. Although none of the views considered makes note of the point, one also has another good reason to limit enforcement of commitments. *(3) The principle of collective good: enforcement of commitments should be limited by social policies for the collective good.* Courts have always so limited commitments, refusing to enforce contracts contrary to public policy. One stands to benefit from justifiable policies of this sort. Although one might want to enter into an arrangement involving a commitment contrary to such a policy, for most people the chances of this being so are small. Even if one would want to make or receive such a commitment in a particular case, it does not follow that a legal principle of enforcing such commitments would benefit one. One would have to consider the detrimental effects on one as a member of society from their enforcement. Consequently, for almost everyone, the expectable benefits from the principle outweigh the expectable benefits of not having it. However, few policies are likely to restrict enforcement, because mutually beneficial interactions do not usually impose harm on others. The primary instances of this occur when collective restraint from conduct is necessary for some good, for example, refraining from anticompetitive business practices. [. . .]

Notes

1   See Michael D. Bayles, "Introduction: The Purposes of Contract Law," *Valparaiso University Law Review* 17 (1983): 613–15.

2 See also Richard B. Brandt, "A Motivational
   Theory of Excuses in the Criminal Law," in
   J. Roland Pennock and John W. Chapman (eds.),
   Criminal Justice: Nomos XXVII (New York:
   New York University Press, 1985), p. 169.

3 Ronald Dworkin, *Taking Rights Seriously* (Cam-
   bridge: Harvard University Press, 1977), pp. 22–8;
   Michael D. Bayles, *Principles of Legislation* (Detroit:
   Wayne State University Press, 1978), pp. 42–4.

4 Joseph Raz, "Legal Principles and the Limits of
   Law," *Yale Law Journal* 81 (1972): 823–54.

5 Richard B. Brandt, *A Theory of the Good and the
   Right* (Oxford: Clarendon Press, 1979), pp. 10–
   16; Bayles, *Principles of Legislation*, pp. 51–4.

6 Bayles, *Principles of Legislation*.

7 See also David A. J. Richards, "Human Rights
   and the Moral Foundations of the Substantive
   Criminal Law," *Georgia Law Review* 13 (1979):
   1414–15, 1436.

8 Ryder v. Wescoat, 535 S.W. 2d 269 (Mo. Ct. App.
   1976).

9 Arthur Linton Corbin, *Corbin on Contracts*, 1 vol.
   edn. (St Paul, Minn.: West Publishing Co., 1952),
   p. 5; G. H. Trietel, *The Law of Contract*, 5th edn.
   (London: Stevens & Sons, 1979), p. 1.

10 Grant Gilmore, *The Death of Contract* (Columbus,
   Ohio: Ohio State University Press, 1974).

11 John D. Calamari and Joseph M. Perillo, *The
   Law of Contracts*, 2d edn. (St Paul, Minn.: West
   Publishing Co., 1977), p. 1; Corbin, *Corbin on
   Contracts*, p. 7.

12 Corbin, *Corbin on Contracts*, p. 6.

13 U.C.C. sec. 2–316 (3) (d) (1978).

14 See generally Ian R. Macneil, *The New Social Contract* (New Haven and London: Yale University
   Press, 1980).

15 See Anthony T. Kronman, "Contract Law and Distributive Justice," *Yale Law Journal* 89 (1980): 472.

16 G. H. Fridman, "On the Nature of Contract,"
   Valparaiso University Law Review 17 (1938): 631.

17 Charles Fried, *Contract as Promise* (Cambridge:
   Harvard University Press, 1981), p. 16; see also
   P. S. Atiyah, *An Introduction to the Law of Contract*,
   3rd edn. (Oxford: Clarendon Press, 1981), p. 3.

18 Fridman, "Nature of Contract," p. 636; Fried,
   Contract as Promise, pp. 20–1.

19 Fried, *Contract as Promise*, p. 69.

20 Atiyah, *Law of Contract*, p. 23.

21 Richard A. Posner, *The Economics of Justice*
   (Cambridge: Harvard University Press, 1983),
   pp. 88–115.

22 Richard A. Posner, *Economic Analysis of Law*, 2d
   edn. (Boston: Little, Brown and Co., 1977), p. 68.

23 Charles J. Goetz and Robert E. Scott, "Enforcing
   Promises: An Examination of the Basis of Contract," *Yale Law Journal* 89 (1980): 1321.

24 Anthony T. Kronman and Richard A. Posner,
   "Introduction: Economic Theory and Contract
   Law," in Anthony T. Kronman and Richard A.
   Posner (eds.), *The Economics of Contract Law*,
   (Boston: Little, Brown and Co., 1979), p. 5.

25 Fried, *Contract as Promise*, p. 17.

26 Barry Reiter and John Swan, "Contracts and the
   Protection of Reasonable Expectations," in Barry
   J. Reiter and John Swan (eds.), *Studies in Contract
   Law* (Toronto: Butterworths, 1980), p. 6.

27 Reiter and Swan, "Contracts," p. 7.

28 Barry Reiter, "Contracts, Torts, Relations and
   Reliance," in Barry J. Reiter and John Swan (eds.),
   Studies in Contract Law (Toronto: Butterworths,
   1980), p. 242.

29 P. S. Atiyah, *Promises, Morals, and Law* (Oxford:
   Clarendon Press, 1981), p. 68.

30 *Restatement (Second) of Contracts*, secs. 219–22
   (1979).

31 See also Fried, *Contract as Promise*, p. 39.

49

Unconscionability and Contracts

Alan Wertheimer

Introduction

McNamara, a television and stereo dealer, advertised a color television on a "rent to own" plan – a plan that required "no deposit," "no credit," and "no long term obligation."[1] After seeing the advertisement, Carolyn Murphy, a welfare recipient, leased a 25-inch Philco color television from McNamara, agreeing to pay a $20 delivery charge and 78 weekly payments of $16, after which she would own the set, having paid $1,268 for a set which retailed for $499. After paying $436 over a six month period, Ms. Murphy saw a newspaper article criticizing the plan and stopped making payments. McNamara sought to repossess the set and threatened to file criminal charges if Ms. Murphy failed to return it. Ms. Murphy filed for an injunction against repossession, claiming that the agreement was unconscionable and therefore unenforceable. The court granted the injunction: ". . . an agreement for the sale of consumer goods entered into with a consumer having unequal bargaining power, which agreement calls for an unconscionable purchase price, constitutes an unfair trade practice. . . ."[2]

In nullifying Murphy's contract with McNamara, the court seems to say that it will not allow one party to exploit another party even if the parties appear to agree to the transaction and even if the relation is (arguably) mutually advantageous. It is unfairness, not harm, that seems to do the work. But what made this contract unconscionable? And if a contract can be both unconscionable and mutually advantageous should such contracts be unenforceable? Those are the sorts of questions which I would like to explore in this paper. I hope to use the doctrine of unconscionability in contracts as a lens through which to get a clearer understanding of exploitation – its essential characteristics and its moral force.

At the most general level, contract law can be justified in two principal ways.[3] First, it may be said that contract law facilitates individual autonomy or freedom.[4] To be autonomous is to be able to plan and control one's life, and that includes the ability to form binding relationships with others, an ability which is facilitated by contract law. Second, contract law can also be justified in consequentialist or utilitarian terms. From this perspective, contract law promotes social utility by allowing individuals to put their resources to more valued uses.[5]

The contrast between these background justifications for contract law is (roughly) replicated in the way in which we might evaluate the

Alan Wertheimer, "Unconscionability and Contracts," *Business Ethics Quarterly*, vol. 2, no. 4, October 1922, pp. 479–96.

morality of contracts. We can, it seems, evaluate an agreement or contract in terms of its *process*, that is, the way in which it was formed, and its *substance*, that is, its result or content. On the one hand, we might say that the process is morally legitimate if the parties come to their agreement freely and with (relatively) full information. On the other hand, we might say that the result is morally legitimate if it is mutually advantageous or, as economists would say, Pareto superior.

Yet we can and do ask another question about substance. We can ask whether a contract represents a fair exchange of value. If we assume, for the sake of argument, that it is possible to evaluate contracts in terms of fairness, it is still *another* question as to why enforceable contracts must be fair, assuming they are freely entered into and mutually advantageous. The autonomy view of contract need *not* assume that contracts are an instance of pure procedural justice, and the utilitarian view need not deny that there can be an independent criterion of fairness. These views need only maintain that a contract should be regarded as *binding* if it is voluntary or Pareto superior, not that it is therefore just.

Now on the standard contemporary view of freedom of contract, a valid contract requires (1) parties with capacity, (2) manifested assent, and (3) consideration.[6] The principal common law defenses to a contract – duress, fraud, misrepresentation, incapacity, mistake – focus on capacity and assent, on the "process" or "voluntariness" of the contract, rather than its substance, defenses which are obviously required by the autonomy view. Interestingly, the utilitarian view of contract law emphasizes the same procedural dimensions. Gifts and deliberate self-sacrifice aside, people will not freely enter into an agreement unless they expect it to be advantageous to them. On the consequentialist account of contract law, the principal exceptions to the enforcement of contracts will be those that defeat the assumption that the agreement is (at least *ex ante*) reasonably regarded as Pareto superior. On this view, a contract procured through coercion or fraud should be nullified not because it is involuntary, but because fraud negates the presumption that the contract is beneficial to the defrauded party.

Now it might be thought that whereas capacity and assent refer to "process" criteria, "consideration" has to do with the substance or fairness of the agreement. But that would be a mistake. Consideration must flow between the parties to establish that an agreement or exchange has occurred (rather than a one-sided promise), but the *adequacy* or *amount* of the consideration is irrelevant. The terms of a contract may be harsh, but "the Chancery mends no man's bargain."[7]

This is not the whole truth. For it is also said that when we examine what judges *do* as well as what they *say*, we will find that "relief from contractual obligations is frequently given on the ground of unfairness. . . ."[8] For example, in a famous maritime case, *The Port Caledonia and the Anna*, a vessel in difficulty asked for assistance from a nearby tug. The tugmaster's terms were £1,000 or no rope. The master of the vessel agreed to pay the £1,000. In refusing to uphold the agreement (the court awarded the tugmaster £200 for his efforts) the court said this: "I have to ask myself whether the bargain that was made was so inequitable, so unjust, and so unreasonable that the court cannot allow it to stand."[9] But this sort of case, indeed, the sorts of cases which characterized unconscionability in equity courts, are not much help in contemporary cases of unconscionability, for the traditional equity case involved a claim that one party took advantage of some *special weakness* of the other party in a unique transaction rather than a more impersonal imbalance of economic power, the sort of situation which framed *Murphy v. McNamara*.[10]

Contemporary Unconscionability

The contemporary doctrine of unconscionability has received its most explicit development in Section 2–302 of the Uniform Commercial Code – "Unconscionable Contract or Clause." It reads as follows:

> (1) If the court as a matter of law finds the contract or any clause of the contract to have been unconscionable at the time it was made the court may refuse to enforce the contract, or it may enforce the remainder of the contract without the unconscionable clause, or it may so limit the application of any unconscionable clause as to avoid any unconscionable result.[11]

By adopting the UCC, state legislatures gave courts a statutory mandate to invalidate unconscionable contracts. But it is less clear what that meant.[12] The text of 2–302 strongly suggests that unconscionability is a matter of result rather than process. Yet the language of the provision notwithstanding, the official *commentary* on 2–302 says that the doctrine of unconscionability is "designed to prevent oppression and unfair surprise . . . and not the disturbance of risks because of superior bargaining power." Here, it seems, process is more important than result. But rather than pursue doctrinal statements, let us instead consider the way in which unconscionability has been understood in some contemporary cases.

Henningsen v. Bloomfield Motors (1960).[13] Mr. Henningsen purchased a Plymouth, manufactured by Chrysler Corporation, from Bloomfield Motors. Ten days later, Mrs. Henningsen was injured while driving the car. According to an insurance adjuster, something went "wrong from the steering wheel down to the front wheels." The Henningsens sued for damages on grounds of negligence and upon breach of express and implied warranties. The trial court dismissed the negligence counts, but an award was granted on the grounds of implied warranty of merchantability. Bloomfield Motors and Chrysler appealed, claiming that the purchase order which Mr. Henningsen signed contained, albeit in fine print, the uniform warranty of the Automobile Manufacturers Association, which disclaimed any responsibility for injuries.

In finding for Henningsen, the Court paid homage to the principle of freedom of contract, but also emphasized that the disclaimer was contained in a "standard form." According to the Court, "freedom of contract" is most at home when a contract is the result of "free bargaining of parties . . . who meet each other on a footing of approximate economic equality" rather than the "standardized mass contract . . . used primarily by enterprises with strong bargaining power and position" and which is presented to the consumer on a take-it-or-leave-it basis.

Williams v. Walker-Thomas Furniture Co. (1965).[14] Williams, who was on welfare, purchased a number of items from Walker-Thomas under an installment agreement, which provided that "all payments now and hereafter made by [purchaser] shall be credited pro rata on all outstanding leases, bills and accounts due the Company by [purchaser] at the time each such payment is made."[15] In effect, the "add-on" provision gave Walker-Thomas the right to repossess old items until the new item was paid off. In 1962, Williams bought a stereo set of stated value of $514.95. She owed $164 on prior purchases. When she defaulted, Walker-Thomas sought to repossess all the items purchased since 1957. On appeal, the US Court of Appeals held that "where the element of unconscionability is present at the time a contract is made, the contract should not be enforced."[16] And an unconscionable contract, said the court, includes "an absence of meaningful choice on the part of one of the parties together with contract terms which are unreasonably favorable to the other party."[17]

Gianni v. Gantos (1986).[18] In June 1980, Gantos, a clothing retailer, submitted to Gianni, a clothing manufacturer, an order for women's holiday clothing to be delivered on October 10, 1980. The back of the purchase order contained this clause: "Buyer reserves the right to terminate by notice to Seller all or any part of this Purchase Order with respect to Goods that have not actually been shipped by Seller. . . ." In late September, 1980, and before any clothing had been shipped, Gantos canceled the order. Faced with the prospect of holding inventory that it could not sell, Gianni subsequently agreed to a 50% price reduction if Gantos would accept the goods. A lower court held the agreement invalid on the grounds that the cancellation clause was unconscionable.

According to the court, the parties did not have equal bargaining power because the "holiday order" comprised about 20% of Gianni's annual business and Ganto's sales were 20 times those of Gianni. A buyer for Gantos testified that such clauses were, in fact, standard in the business because "the buyer in our industry is in the driver's seat."[19]

Lloyds Bank Ltd. v. Bundy (1974).[20] Herbert Bundy, an elderly farmer, and his only son, Michael had been customers of a branch of Lloyds Bank for many years. Michael formed a company which banked at the same branch. Michael's company was not doing well and, on several occasions, Herbert Bundy gave the bank additional security for the son's overdrafts. In

December, 1969, Michael visited Herbert along with Mr. Head, a new assistant manager of the bank. Mr. Head told Herbert that the bank would continue to support his son only if he secured the son's overdrafts with all of his remaining assets – his farm – but it did not offer any additional line of credit. Herbert said that he was 100% behind his son. Without seeking further advice, he signed the papers. When the son's business failed, the bank sought possession of the farm.

The Court of Appeals ruled that the contract was unenforceable, primarily because it resulted from a serious inequality of bargaining power. In addition, it was said that the terms were unfair because neither the father nor the son received adequate consideration, that Herbert's judgment had been impaired by his love for his son, that Herbert did not and was not urged to consult an independent advisor, and that there was a conflict of interest between the bank and the father which the bank failed to acknowledge.

Macaulay v. Schroeder Music Publishing Co. Ltd. (1974).[21] Macaulay, an unknown young songwriter, entered into a standard form agreement with Schroeder, whereby Schroeder acquired the right to publish all songs written by Macaulay for a five year period and, if Macaulay earned royalties exceeding £5,000 during the five year period, the agreement would be automatically extended for another five years. By contrast, Schroeder could terminate the contract at any time. Acting as a court of appeals, the House of Lords ruled that the contract was void because the terms of the contract were unreasonably asymmetrical and because the terms were contained in a standard form, rather than having been reached through a process of negotiation or bargaining.[22]

Process and/or Result? With this as background we are now in a (somewhat) better position to consider this question: What *kind* of defect is unconscionability? Is it a defect in process and/or result? There are both textual and conceptual reasons for regarding a defect in *result* as a necessary if not sufficient condition of unconscionability. The textual support can be found in the statute and cases we have considered. I say that there are conceptual reasons for regarding a

defect in result as necessary to unconscionability because we can well imagine a relevant defect in voluntariness that would *not* entail unconscionability, as when, for paternalistic reasons, A coerces B to agree to terms that are manifestly in B's interests and (otherwise) eminently fair.

Process

Even if a defect in result is *necessary* for unconscionability, is it *sufficient*? Or is a defect in process also necessary? One thing, I think, is clear. If unconscionability involves a defect in process, it is *not* a straightforward defect of voluntariness. There are three reasons to adopt this view. First, the standard defenses to a contract, such as duress and fraud, not only compromise voluntariness, they constitute reasons to doubt that a contract is advantageous to B as compared with the precontractual baseline. By contrast, the typical modern unconscionability case claims that the contract is *unjust*, and not that it is not advantageous at all. Second, if unconscionable contracts were involuntary, there would be no need to develop a principle of unconscionability. The standard defenses could do all the work. Third, there is no reason to think that freedom of contract was, in fact, violated in the typical case of unconscionability.

Now some disagree with the previous claim. Joel Feinberg, for example, argues that *Henningsen* can be understood as a case of duress because "the weaker party has no reasonable alternative to the terms offered by the stronger party and is thus forced to choose what to him appears the lesser evil. . . ."[23] I disagree. There may be *a* sense in which the offeree is "forced" to contract in some unconscionability cases, but it is quite distinct from the way in which coercion and duress are understood in the law. A contract signed at the point of a gun is made under duress not merely because A has "no reasonable choice" but to sign, but, and this is crucial, because A proposes to do something which is independently wrong – to shoot B – if B refuses to sign.[24] That B agrees to A's terms because B has no better alternative or even a decent alternative has *never* been definitive of coercion or duress. We do not say, for example, that a wage contract is involuntary just because B has to work and has no better alternative or that a patient's consent to surgery is invalid just because B wants to live and the only alternative is death.

Consider some of the other cases we have examined. Even if Murphy could not have purchased a television on more favorable terms, say because she was a poor credit risk and could not make a down-payment, we can hardly say that McNamara coerced her into signing the contract. Indeed, she had a reasonable alternative to this agreement – not to buy a television at all. And much the same could be said about the "add-on" clause in *Williams*. What of *Gianni and Macaulay*? Gantos was not proposing to harm Gianni if Gianni did not accept the contract on Gantos' terms. And the same was true for Schroeder. To say "these are my terms – take it or leave it" may be objectionable in certain circumstances, but it hardly seems coercive.

Contrast these cases with the *Port Caledonia*. In this case, we might say that the vessel agreed to pay £1,000 for a rope under duress, not because it had no reasonable alternative, but because the tugmaster had an *obligation* to rescue the vessel on better terms, that it was not morally or legally free to sail away. But in seeing why this case might constitute coercion, we see why the other cases do not. For it seems preposterous to say that McNamara, Walker-Thomas, Gantos and Schroeder had an independent obligation to deal with their respective parties on better terms or that they were not free to walk away from the deal.

If I am right in arguing that unconscionability does not require a defect in voluntariness, it does not follow that unconscionability turns on result alone.[25] Unconscionability might require a different sort of procedural defect, but then we would have to explain just what this procedural defect involves and why – when combined with a defect in result – it deserves a special status.

Result

Let us assume that a contract is minimally advantageous to B as compared with the pre-contractual baseline. There are two ways in which we might regard the *terms* of a contract as unconscionable: (1) *harshness* – the terms may be particularly harsh for B; (2) *disproportionality*

– A's benefit from the agreement is exorbitant or disproportionate to B's gain. It is a further question as to whether, as Joel Feinberg suggests, an unconscionable contract must be both harsh *and* disproportionate.

When courts find that a contract is unconscionably harsh, they tend to focus on the non-monetary terms of the contract as contrasted with the monetary price. In principle, of course, there can be no rigid distinction between monetary and non-monetary terms. A contract represents a package of price, quality, financial provisions, and risks. Harsh *terms* may be compensated by a relatively generous *price*. Suppose, for example, that a couple prefers to hire a live-in nanny who will agree not to entertain boy-friends at home.[26] If the couple is prepared to pay a wage premium in order to hire on its preferred terms, then there is hardly anything unconscionable with the arrangement, even if it would otherwise be viewed as excessively demanding.[27] The nanny cannot legitimately complain that the terms are unfair, particularly if she could have secured her preferred terms for a lower wage.

Why do unconscionability cases tend to focus on terms rather than (monetary) price?[28] First, because price is a continuous variable whereas non-monetary terms have a binary quality, it may be easier to make judgments about the unconscionability of contractual terms. Second, although a price may be *exorbitant*, it does not typically establish an *oppressive relation* that endures over time. By contrast, some contractual terms establish just such relations. Third, there may be more explicit bargaining over price than over terms. Henningsen probably did bargain over price with Bloomfield Motors, and, if not, he could easily have taken his business elsewhere if he could get a better deal. On the other hand, he had no opportunity to bargain over the warranty with Bloomfield or anyone else. And so we have the appearance of a harsh result which one party cannot alter.

I say we have the "appearance" of a harsh result because, as we say, appearances can be deceiving. When harsh terms are clearly compensated monetarily, as with the nanny, we are less apt to regard them as unacceptable. But no such comparison is possible when the *same* terms are used among competitors. Nonetheless, it is possible that automobile buyers have, in effect, been compensated (without their asking to be compensated in *this* way) in advance – that, in principle, Chrysler would have been willing to allow Henningsen to purchase a far more inclusive warranty, one which included insurance for injuries, for an added premium. If so, we would need to ask why consumers do not get to choose high price/easy terms over low price/harsh terms, but the fact remains that Henningsen received a price discount for accepting harsh terms.

To put the point slightly differently, what appear to be extremely harsh terms – *ex post* – may not be harsh when considered *ex ante*. Consider *Macaulay*. Macaulay signed on with Schroeder – putting himself at risk for a ten year commitment – when he was an unknown songwriter. It is entirely possible that a music publisher will make a profit on only 10% of their unknown songwriters. Schroeder is willing to lose money on 90% of such clients only because it makes a significant profit on the other 10%.[29] The successful songwriter may feel exploited, but only because his vision is limited. The reasonableness of contractual terms must be evaluated against the background of the risks involved.

And this gives rise to the second point, namely, that what *appear* to be harsh terms may better reflect the buyer's risk than the seller's greed. (Re)consider the "add-on" provision of Williams's agreement with Walker-Thomas.[30] Given the high probability that Williams would default, given that her purchases were likely to depreciate quickly and that repossession of the sole item in case of default would entail a loss for Walker-Thomas, it is possible that the only way for her to have received more favorable *terms* was for her to pay a higher down-payment on the goods involved.[31]

One final point about harshness. It would be a mistake to claim that a contract is unconscionably harsh only when B's utility is not significantly enhanced as contrasted with the pre-contractual position. For some, nay most, allegedly unconscionable contracts are ones in which B's utility is *greatly* enhanced, as when the vessel gained its rescue for £1,000. If this is so, either harshness is not a straightforward function of utility gain or many contracts which

have been thought to be unconscionably harsh are, in fact, not unconscionably harsh.

Let us now consider disproportionality. It is commonly thought that an agreement is exploitative or unconscionable when A gets much more value from the exchange than B, that a fair transaction is "one in which the surplus is divided (approximately) equally."[32]

But how should we conceptualize equal gain? A famous example asks how a rich man and a poor man should agree to share $200.

> The rich man could argue for a $150–$50 split in his favor because it would grieve the poor man more to lose $50 than the rich man to lose $150 ... an arbitrator, keeping in mind the needs of the rich man and the poor man, might suggest the reverse split.[33]

If we measure a party's gain in terms of utility, then the rich man's argument is extremely persuasive. Similarly, in the *Port Caledonia*, there is every reason to think that the vessel gained more utility from being rescued than the tugmaster received from £1,000. So if unconscionability has to do with A's and B's relative gains, we must rely on independent or "objective" criteria for measuring their gains, or claim that A's gain is exorbitant even if A gains *less* than B (because, say, in a normal transaction, B *should* gain much more than A), or conclude that many allegedly unconscionable contracts are not in fact unconscionable.

Suppose we say that A's gain is disproportionate if its profits are – by some general standard – supracompetitive. This standard would not yield unconscionability in cases such as *Henningsen*, *Gianni*, and *Macaulay*, for despite concerns about the terms of the contracts, there is simply no evidence that these businesses generated supracompetitive profits. But what of businesses which prey on the poor as in *Murphy* and *Williams*? Here, too, there is no reason to think that these contracts generate exorbitant profit margins. Indeed, if these businesses were especially profitable, we would have to explain why potential competitors allow sellers to garner monopoly profits rather than enter the business themselves and, *ex hypothesi*, drive the price down. There are, then, two possibilities: (1) if unconscionability requires supracompetitive profits, then many contracts which are thought to be unconscionable are not; (2) if these contracts are unconscionable, then unconscionability does *not* require exorbitant or disproportionate profits.

Standard Forms

We have seen that allegations of unconscionability often refer to allegedly onerous provisions which are contained in standard form contracts. What *precisely* was the problem in *Macaulay* or *Henningsen* or *Williams*? True, in some cases, the offeror may have known more about the content and effects of the contract than the offeree. And an asymmetry of information may well create an exploitable inequality between the parties. But, and by contrast with claims that are frequently made about the use of standard forms, it is simply *not* true that the "take-it-or-leave-it" character of standard forms typically arises in non-competitive industries. Critics of standard forms have failed to note that virtually *all* transactions occur on a "take-it-or-leave-it" basis in a truly competitive market. In a truly competitive market, *no one gets to negotiate anything.*[34] Everyone is a "price taker." The seller must offer the equilibrium price and the buyer must either pay the price or do without.

On this view, the use of standard forms occurs in a competitive market because they reduce transaction costs. To require or even encourage bargaining in individual transactions would be expensive, and the offeree would end up paying some if not all of those costs or would be driven out of the market entirely. In principle, then, the use of standard forms in a competitive market should be beneficial to the *class* of offerees, although not always to particular offerees.

If this is so, how can we also explain the apparently onerous terms to which the courts have objected in *Henningsen*, *Macaulay*, *Williams*, and the like? If Mr. Henningsen would have preferred a better warranty, albeit perhaps at a higher price, why was it not offered by Bloomfield Motors or another dealer? If the "add-on" provision in Williams's contract with Walker-Thomas Furniture was, in fact, a bad deal, why wasn't some competitor offering a better deal –

not out of kindness, but in order to make a buck?[35]

One possibility is that these markets are not competitive, but there is no evidence that this is so. A second possibility is that market imperfections remain even in a reasonably competitive market, and that a more perfect market would have produced a better package of price and terms. But there is, of course, a third possibility, namely, that when all is said and done the allegedly onerous terms provide the maximum benefit to the offeree – given the risks inherent in contracting with the offeree.[36] If we employ the doctrine of unconscionability to benefit the exploited party, then we need to engage in careful economic analysis to determine whether the allegedly harsh terms actually optimize the weaker party's benefits – given his or her background positions.

Inequality of Bargaining Power

Let us take another tack, by considering the notion of "inequality of bargaining power" the concept that appears to be the *gravamen* of virtually all unconscionability cases, despite the fact that it has received precious little analysis as to its defining characteristics or its normative force. At the broadest level, there are two questions to which we want answers: (1) What constitutes an inequality of bargaining power? (2) What are the normative upshots of such inequalities?

What gives A greater bargaining power than B?[37] We can begin by distinguishing between *bargaining ability*, which is a function of one's personal characteristics (e.g., information, toughness, patience, perceptiveness, etc.) and *bargaining potential*, which is primarily a function of one's external resources or circumstances. Put colloquially, bargaining ability concerns how well one plays one's cards, whereas bargaining potential is a function of the cards themselves.[38]

Now some unconscionability cases appear to involve problems of bargaining ability. Herbert Bundy's agreement was set aside because he made an agreement for which he incurred risks but for which he received virtually nothing in return. To the extent that "inequality of bargaining power" refers to defects in capacity, it is relatively unproblematic. For it represents a defect in voluntariness and efficiency.[39] But what of those "one-sided" contracts which result from an inequality of bargaining *potential*? How can we explain *Henningsen, Gianni*, and *Macaulay* – all of which allegedly involved an inequality of bargaining power? There is no reason to doubt anyone's competence or rationality in these cases. Nonetheless, the courts appear to be claiming that there were gross asymmetries between the parties with respect to bargaining *potential* and that these asymmetries led to an unjust result.

What constitutes inequality in bargaining potential? Two potential candidates – size and necessity – can be set aside. Consider size. Although the image of the lonely individual facing the large corporation seems to have figured in several decisions, this model is quite misleading. I do not think that the contemporary (1991) automobile buyer is at a disadvantage in bargaining (through the dealer) with General Motors.[40] For size is irrelevant when the "larger" party needs the "smaller" party more than the other way around. Necessity is similarly irrelevant. The fact that B needs a good – even in order to live – does not give A any special power over B if there is a competitive market among sellers of the good.[41]

It might be thought that the more resources one brings to a bargaining situation, the greater one's bargaining power. But this, too, is incorrect.

> *The Investment Case.* B needs $500 for a venture that will yield $1,000. B is prepared to contribute $400, which is all that he has, but he needs $100 from A, who is quite wealthy.

Although B is contributing more resources, A has more bargaining potential. Suppose that A proposes that the $1,000 be divided thus: A gets $400, B gets $600. This gives A a 300% return on his investment, while B gets a 50% return on his investment. This may look unfair. It may *be* unfair. But A's threat to walk if B does not accept his proposal is credible precisely because a proportional split (where A receives $200 and B receives $800) does *not*, in fact, do much for A – given his current position.

The general point is, then, that bargaining potential is not a function of size or necessity or resource contribution. It is a function of a party's "threat advantage" – his willingness not to contract if his proposal is not accepted. And that is largely a function of a party's utilitarian gain from the precontractual baseline. A has a threat advantage because A stands to lose less if agreement is not reached. Put slightly differently, it is precisely because the stronger party gets *less* utility from a proposed bargain that he is able to get a greater share of objective resources.

Assume that A has greater bargaining potential than B. What follows – normatively speaking? I want briefly to make five points. First, we need a moral principle of fair division. For unless we can say something about how the surplus *ought* to be divided, we cannot say that an agreement is *morally* one sided – however unequal the distribution appears.

Second, although rational choice theory has made important contributions to a special normative problem – what ideally rational bargainers would do in a bargaining situation – there is no reason to think that a rational choice solution to the bargaining problem provides us with the best principle of fair division.

Third, there are no unproblematic solutions to the normative problem. Although this is not the place to probe this question in detail, let me mention but two principles which we might consider. At first glance, equal utility gain is an attractive moral principle. It is frequently said that a contract is just when it benefits both parties to the same extent. Unfortunately, and as we have already seen, equal utility may well prescribe exactly the sorts of distributions that motivated the concern with inequality of bargaining potential.

And so we might look to the proportionality principle – "one that distributes the cooperative surplus in proportion to the contributions of individuals...."[42] Even if this principle were morally attractive, it raises thorny questions as to how to measure a party's contribution. Should a party's contribution be evaluated in "objective" terms or in terms of utility, in which case each $100 from B is worth *more* than $100 from A? And should a party's contribution be understood as its *pre-cooperative* value or its value to the cooperative activity? Is A's contribution of $100 a contribution of $100 (as compared with B's contribution of $400) or is it a contribution which made it possible to realize a $500 gain? In *The Port Caledonia*, for example, should we say that the tug is contributing a rope (which, *ex hypothesi*, is not worth that much) or is he contributing that which *saves a vessel* (which, *ex hypothesi*, is worth a lot)? And what is the vessel contributing? Its needs for rescue?

I do not want to deny that there may be solution(s) to the problem of fair division. I do want to claim that absent some principle of fair division, it is not clear that the alleged injustices that arise from inequalities of bargaining power are, in fact, unjust.

And that gives rise to the fourth point, the problem of background endowments. Even if the parties abide by reasonable principles of fair division, the resulting bargain may be unjust if the background conditions are unjust. Indeed, even scrupulous adherence to principles of fair bargaining may simply pass through unjust background endowments.

The fifth point about inequalities of bargaining power is this. That a bargain results in an unjust distribution does not entail that we should prevent such injustices from occurring. If it is desirable to allow B to improve his situation, and if we assume that the background injustices notwithstanding, A is under no moral requirement to provide that improvement, then it is at least arguable that contract law should uphold bargains that result from inequalities of bargaining potential. It is one thing to disallow contracts in which the strong "push the weak to the wall," as in *Bundy*, and quite another to disallow contracts in which the strong find the weak "*at* the wall," and where the contract will give the weak a little distance.

Conclusions

So let us take stock.

The first point is this. Some allegedly unconscionable contracts are not only not obviously unconscionable, they may be eminently fair. I see no reason to think that Schroeder took unfair advantage of Macaulay or to doubt that the *ex ante* value of the contract reflected the genuine risks of dealing with unknown songwriters. Similarly, and without knowing more, it is entirely possible that Gantos's contract with Gianni is best understood as an assignment of risk for which

Gianni was compensated in the price it receives from retailers to whom it sells. More generally, it is a gross mistake to think that we can assess the fairness of an agreement by simple inspection of its terms. Unlike pornography, we cannot always tell unconscionability when we see it.

But other cases are more troublesome and we may remain concerned about the contract even after engaging in careful analysis. Let us classify putatively unconscionable contracts on two criteria: (1) whether the contract is beneficial to B as contrasted with the precontractual baseline; (2) whether the contract is extremely profitable to A. In principle, then, we can identify four types of unconscionable contracts: (a) harmful/high profit; (b) harmful/low profit; (c) beneficial/high profit; (d) beneficial/low profit.

As we have seen, contracts of type (a) and (b) will occur when B does not understand or lacks the capacity to understand the terms of the contract or the value of the goods that have been purchased or when B is placed under such stress that he cannot resist entering into a non-advantageous transaction (hence rules providing for a "cooling off" period for contracts made with door-to-door salespersons). In these cases, unconscionability is a relatively unproblematic form of paternalism, where we seek to protect B from harming himself because we have reason to doubt the full voluntariness of his decision.

There is, however, no reason to assume that contracts which are harmful to B typically generate high profits for A. There is, for example, no reason to assume that Lloyds bank was making a high profit in its dealings with Bundy. Rather, its behavior may have been unconscionable precisely because it sought to avoid a loss when it should have swallowed it. Consider *Murphy* as a type (b) contract, say because the cost of the rental plan exceeded the value of the television to Murphy and because "rent to own" plans are not extraordinarily profitable, because many televisions are returned after a short period having depreciated greatly in value. In that case, the contracts were unconscionable not because A's profits are exorbitant, but because we would prefer that *no one* deal with consumers on terms that are likely to prove harmful to them. If one cannot profitably deal with a class of consumers on better terms, it is better that one not deal with them at all.

Let us now consider type (c) cases, where A makes a high profit yet the agreement is beneficial to B. This will typically occur when there is some sort of market imperfection. Consider *The Port Caledonia*. Given the choice between contracting with the tug on "extortionate" terms and not contracting at all, the vessel will prefer the "freedom to choose." But the vessel might prefer to be *prevented* from entering into an "extortionate" agreement with the tug if the tug would then rescue the vessel on better terms. Here the argument for unconscionability is not paternalistic but *strategic*. It is in the vessel's interest (or the class of vessels) to have its bargaining range limited, not because the vessel doesn't *know* what is in its interest, but because limiting its options puts it in a stronger bargaining position.[43] Here the doctrine of unconscionability effectively seeks to replicate the results of a more perfect market. It supplies the price that the tug would have charged had there been a competitive market for rescues.

But the most interesting and difficult cases are the beneficial/low profit contracts. *Henningsen* and *Williams* may both exemplify this situation, but there are important differences between them. In one type of case, perhaps illustrated by *Henningsen*, there is an information and collective action problem which can be solved on Pareto superior terms. In the second type, perhaps illustrated by *Williams*, no Pareto superior moves are available.

Suppose that most car buyers would be better off with a less limited warranty, even if it required them to pay a higher price. For some reason, automobile manufacturers have settled on low price/harsh terms contracts, but they are quite prepared to offer high price/soft terms contracts so long as this does not put them at a competitive disadvantage. If we declare that the low price/harsh terms contracts are void for unconscionability, then most buyers will be better off and the manufacturers will not be worse off. Declaring the contracts unconscionable serves to create a larger social surplus – where the buyer gets virtually all of the increase. This may be an eminently sensible reason to interfere with the market, but it has little to do with inequalities of bargaining power or wrongful exploitation.

There is another type (d) case which deserves to be mentioned. Suppose that some automobile buyers have much greater bargaining ability than others. Because all dealers encounter a comparable mix of good and bad bargainers, they must "take advantage" of the bad bargainers if they are to stay in business. If we prevent dealers from exploiting the bad bargainers, say by reducing price dispersion, then the bad bargainers would gain, but the good bargainers would lose. For the bad bargainers were not actually being exploited by the dealers, they were being exploited by the good bargainers. It may well turn out that many cases of unconscionability are like this: prohibiting people from entering unconscionable contracts shifts the benefits *among* the offerees, but not between the class of offerees and the offerors.

But the most difficult cases arise when contractual terms are minimally beneficial to B, generate only competitive profits to A, and no Pareto superior contracts are available. Suppose (what is probably not quite true) that Williams's contract with Walker-Thomas accurately and fairly reflected the risks of dealing with very poor customers and that Williams did not underestimate the costs involved or overestimate the value of the appliance. This was a problem of poverty, not ignorance. Let us also assume, for the sake of argument, that the background endowments are *unjust*, that Williams would not be (so) poor in a just society.

Should we refuse to enforce such contracts on grounds of unconscionability? Assuming that we could reliably distinguish these contracts from the others, then if the only justification of unconscionability is to protect the exploited party, then the answer seems to be no. There are, however, several additional types of arguments for refusing to enforce unconscionable contracts in such cases which might be mentioned.

The first and welfarist line of argument maintains that unconscionable contracts have negative externalities, they generate psychic disutility for other members of the society. I am inclined to think that these considerations have some *causal* importance in explaining the appeal of unconscionability law, but it is hard to see why they have any moral significance. For it may well be said that if we are not prepared to rectify the unjust background conditions themselves, it would be self indulgent to prevent people from improving on their admittedly unjust situation just because such contracts make us uncomfortable.

A second line of argument takes justice a bit more seriously. This view notes that principles of justice affect social behavior and helps to explain the sorts of transactions that do and do not occur. There is a growth industry in economics dedicated to the proposition that rational actor models do not explain everything, that sellers will often accept less than they would receive if they acted as rational maximizers and that buyers will often refuse to pay an "exorbitant" price even though a rational actor model would predict that they would. On this view, principles of fair division are important social and cultural goods. And from that perspective, the doctrine of unconscionability can be understood as one way that society signals its commitment to principles of fair division. Once again, it is important to note that this line of argument justifies a doctrine of unconscionability by appeal to its effects on third parties.

Thirdly, I wish to mention a class of perfectionist arguments although I shall not defend them here. These arguments maintain that it would be wrong to allow parties to enter into certain forms of relation even though they prefer to do so and even though it would improve their welfare. These arguments could take at least two different forms. First, we could argue that a person is *morally* harmed – degraded – when he enters into an unjust relation that there is a sense in which entering into an unconscionable contract is, in *some* sense, bad for B. The problem here is that absent some argument, there is no reason to believe that this is so.

A second view takes a different tack. On that view, unconscionable agreements may be bad even if they are bad for no one. On this view, unconscionability is "a free-floating evil."[44] It might be said that it is wrong to allow unjust relations to occur, even when (as contrasted with the world in which they do not occur) they are not bad for anyone – just as some versions of retributivism claim that it is good that wrong-doers are punished even when it's not good for anyone. I do not know if one or both of these perfectionist lines of argument can be sustained.

But something like them may have to be sustained if we are going to justify prohibiting at least some unconscionable contracts.

Notes

1 Murphy v. McNamara, 38 Conn. Super. 183, 416 A. 2d 170 (1979). The injunction was granted, but McNamara was permitted to file suit for the difference between the amount Murphy had already paid and the value of the set.

2 *Id.* at 416 A. 2d at 177.

3 Some may argue that there is, in the final analysis, no distinction between these justifications. For the purpose of the present argument, I do not need to take a position on that argument.

4 See Charles Fried, *Contract As Promise* (Cambridge, MA: Harvard University Press, 1981).

5 The classic defense of this view is Richard Posner, *Economic Analysis of Law* (Boston: Little, Brown, 1977).

6 Arthur Leff, "Unconscionability and the Code – The Emperor's New Clause," 115 *U. Pa. L. Rev.* 485, 486 (1967). These are necessary but not sufficient requirements of a valid contract. An agreement which meets these criteria may be unenforceable on paternalistic grounds, as when a tenant is not permitted to waive a warranty of habitability, because it threatens to harm third parties, or because society has decided that certain goods should not be "commodified" – for example, votes, drugs, or sex. More generally, an agreement which is against "public policy" is not enforceable, even though it may meet the tests of capacity, assent, and consideration.

7 Lord Nottingham in *Maynard v. Moseley* 3 Swans, 651, at 655, 36 Eng. Rep. 1009 (1676), cited in S. M. Waddams, *The Law of Contracts*, 326 (2d ed. 1984).

8 S. M. Waddams, *The Law of Contracts*, 326.

9 *The Port Caledonia and the Anna* (1903), pp. 184, 190. Quoted in S. M. Waddams, "Unconscionability in Contracts," 39 *Mod. L. Rev.* 369, 385 (1976). Also see Lord Goff of Chieveley and Gareth Jones, *The Law of Restitution* 267 (3d ed. 1986).

10 In addition, equity cases typically involved a claim of *specific performance*. Unlike many modern cases of unconscionability, equity cases did not generally involve a dispute about the price of a transaction or an effort to have the transaction go through on more favorable terms. Rather, the promise demanded transfer of the land and the

11 Thomas M. Quinn, et al., *Uniform Commercial Code Commentary and Law Digest* 2–94 (1978).

promisor sought to overturn the transaction in its entirety. See Leff, *supra* note 6.

12 It seems that unconscionability is defined as "a matter of *law*" rather than a matter of *fact* in order to make it easier to appeal a lower court's decision.

13 32 N.J. 385, 161A2d 69 (1960).

14 350 F.2d 445 (D.C. Cir. 1965).

15 *Id.*, at 447.

16 *Id.*, at 449.

17 *Id.*, at 450, quoting 1 Corbin, *Contracts* §128 (1963). Although the Court did not claim that the contract was unconscionable in light of these criteria, it concluded that the District Court had a legal basis for considering the question. Judge Danaher, dissenting, maintained that Williams knew just where she stood, that the pricing and credit policies may have been reasonably consistent with the risk of default. *Id.*, at 450.

18 151 Mich. App. 598, 391 N.W. 2d 760 (1986).

19 *Id.*, at 762.

20 3 W.L.R. 501 (1974).

21 1 W.L.R. 1308 (1974).

22 Actually, the Court noted that the agreement had been signed "with a few alterations" – implying that at least some negotiation had, in fact, occurred. *Id.*, at 1309.

23 *Id.*, pp. 251–2.

24 See my *Coercion* (Princeton: Princeton University Press, 1987), chapter 2.

25 ". . . despite indications of increasing freedom for courts to manipulate contract terms, the concept of unconscionability still directs judicial inquiry to the bargaining behavior of the parties." Lewis Kornhauser, "Unconscionability in Standard Forms," 64 *Cal. L. Rev.* 1151, 1162 (1976).

26 I borrow this example from Brian Barry, "Lady Chatterley's Lover and Doctor Fischer's Bomb Party: Liberalism, Pareto Optimality and the Problem of Objectionable Preferences," in his collection, *Democracy, Power and Justice* (Oxford: Clarendon Press, 1989), p. 374.

27 *Id.*

28 I shall use the term "price" to refer to *monetary* price in what follows although it is obvious that the terms are part of the overall price of a contract.

29 For an interesting analysis of this case, see M. J. Trebilcock, "The Doctrine of Inequality of Bargaining Power in the House of Lords," 26 *U. Toronto L.J.* 359 (1976).

30 See Richard Epstein, "Unconscionability: A Critical Appraisal," 18 *J. L. & Econ.* 293 (1975).

31 See *Id.*, at 307.

32 Robert Frank, *Passions within Reason* (New York: W. W. Norton, 1988), p. 164.

33 Duncan Kennedy, "Distributive and Paternalist Motives in Contract and Tort Law With Special Reference to Compulsory Terms and Unequal Bargaining Power," 41 *Md. L. Rev.* 563, 616 (1982).

34 [*sic* – missing]

35 As Duncan Kennedy puts it, "If there is competition among sellers, and good information about buyer preferences, sellers will offer whatever terms they think buyers will pay for." "Distributive and Paternalist Motives in Contract and Tort Law," *id.*

36 Richard Posner, *Economic Analysis of Law*, p. 85.

37 As Thomas Schelling reminds us, we must be very cautious. " 'Bargaining power,' 'bargaining strength,' 'bargaining skill' suggest that the advantage goes to the powerful, the strong, or the skillful. It does, of course, if those qualities are defined to mean only that negotiations are won by those who win. But if the terms imply that it is an advantage to be more intelligent . . . or to have more financial resources, more physical strength . . . or more ability to withstand losses, then the term does a disservice. These qualities are by no means universal advantages in bargaining situations; they often have a contrary value." *The Strategy of Conflict* (New York: Oxford University Press, 1963), p. 22.

38 The distinction between bargaining ability and bargaining potential cannot be pressed too far. It appears, for example, that blacks and women pay more for new cars than white males, not because of animus, but because profit-maximizing dealers believe that blacks and women are less likely to shop around. If so, a black or a woman may have less bargaining power not because of some characteristic *qua* individual, but because of other people's perceptions. In this sense, we might count the *perception* of one's bargaining ability as an *external* resource. If this belief were false, and if only some dealers had this belief, then blacks and women would not pay more. They would go to other dealers. Yet if many dealers have this false belief, then the market will still settle on a higher price for blacks and women. Ian Ayres, "Fair Driving: Gender and Race Discrimination in Retail Car Negotiations," 104 *Harv. L. Rev.* 817, 845 (1991).

39 I say *relatively* unproblematic, because it is not clear whether a contract should be nullified if A neither caused nor knowingly took advantage of B's incapacity.

40 Nor is Bethlehem Steel at a disadvantage in dealing with the (much larger) United States

government when the government needs its ship-building capacity during a war.

41 As Duncan Kennedy remarks, "If there are many sellers of a necessity, none of them will be able to charge more than the going package of price and terms without losing all his buyers." *Supra*, note 35 at 618–19.

42 Jody S. Kraus and Jules L. Coleman, "Morality and the Theory of Rational Choice," in Peter Vallentyne (ed.), *Contractarianism and Rational Choice* (New York: Cambridge University Press, 1991), p. 267.

43 "What we have here is a situation in which someone may be better off doing a certain deal than not doing it if he is permitted to do it, but would be better off still if he were not permitted to do it." Brian Barry, "Lady Chatterley's Lover and Doctor Fischer's Bomb Party: Liberalism, Pareto Optimality, and the Problem of Objectionable Preferences," in Jon Elster and Aanund Hylland (eds.) *Foundations of Social Choice Theory* (Cambridge: Cambridge University Press, 1986), p. 21.

44 Joel Feinberg, *Harmless Wrongdoing* (New York: Oxford University Press, 1988).

50

South African Contract Law: The Need for a Concept of Unconscionability

Lynn Berat

I. Introduction

Despite a decade of economic difficulties, caused in part by the imposition of sanctions, South Africa remains the economic powerhouse of southern Africa.[1] Now, as the ruling National Party and major opposition groups such as the African National Congress[2] ("ANC") seek to arrive at a new dispensation of the country's wealth, the future shape of the economy is a vexing issue.[3] South Africa's escape from its downward economic spiral requires economic growth. Such growth is especially important if Africans, who for decades have occupied an inferior position in South African society, are to participate fully in South Africa's economic life. To achieve this goal, contract law will have to be altered. In particular, the courts should develop a doctrine of unconscionability to safeguard the interests of the millions of Africans entering into contracts and other business transactions for the first time. As many Africans are disadvantaged by little or no education,[4] and are daunted by the prospect of dealing with an unfamiliar legal system,[5] it is imperative that such a doctrine exist to protect their rights. Currently, South African contract law contains no specific concept

of unconscionability. The concept's position is the same as that in the United States in 1952, when jurist Arthur Corbin wrote:

> There is sufficient flexibility in the concepts of fraud, duress, misrepresentation, and undue influence, not to mention differences in economic bargaining power, to enable the courts to avoid enforcement of a bargain that is shown to be unconscionable by reason of gross inadequacy of consideration accompanied by other relevant factors.[6]

Indeed, these doctrines, which reflect South Africa's hybrid legal heritage, form the South African analogue to unconscionability. It now seems imperative that a more explicit concept of unconscionability similar to that found in the United States' Uniform Commercial Code[7] ("UCC") be developed in transformed South Africa. This Article examines South Africa's hybrid legal heritage. It provides an overview of contract formation in South Africa and discusses the concepts of fraud, duress, and undue influence. Finally, this Article suggests that South Africa adopt a commercial code, giving special attention to formulating a concept of unconscionability.

Lynn Berat, "South African Contract Law: The Need for a Concept of Unconscionability," *Loyola of Los Angeles International and Comparative Law Journal*, vol. 14, 1992, pp. 507–27. © 1992. Reprinted with permission from ILR-Loyola Law School.

A. The South African legal heritage

Scholars have characterized South African law as a hybrid or mixed legal system,[8] consisting mainly of Roman, Roman-Dutch, and English law.[9] Roman law evolved over twelve centuries, from around 753 BC, the traditional date of Rome's founding, to AD 565, the date of Emperor Justinian's death.[10] Continuing through medieval times, Roman law had a major influence upon European institutions.[11] The late thirteenth century through the end of the sixteenth century marked the period of reception of Roman law into the law of the Netherlands. The resulting Roman-Dutch law "is a conglomerate of Roman law, Germanic customary law, feudal law, canon law," and natural law concepts. It enjoyed its classical period from the sixteenth century to the late eighteenth century.

The Dutch East India Company brought this classical Roman-Dutch law to the Cape of Good Hope in 1652, when it took possession of the Cape and founded a station there for its ships traveling the Netherlands to the Dutch East Indies route. Roman-Dutch law continued as the Cape's common law during the period of Dutch East India Company rule from 1652 to 1795. In 1795, Great Britain occupied the Cape, fearing that the French Republic would seize it. The Dutch East India Company formally capitulated to the British on September 16, 1795. The Articles of Capitulation empowered the Raad van Justitie, renamed the Court of Justice, to administer Roman-Dutch law in civil and criminal matters. In 1802, Britain entered into a truce with Napoleon, and, in March of that year, signed the Treaty of Amiens, restoring all of its recent colonial conquests except Ceylon and Trinidad. Thus, Great Britain ceded its authority to the Netherlands, which had become the Batavian Republic by that time. The British, however, remained cautious of Napoleon's colonial designs, and by 1806 again controlled the Cape.

British rule did not signal the end of Roman-Dutch law at the Cape. The Cape Articles of Capitulation of January 10 and 18, 1806, provided that "the Burghers and Inhabitants shall preserve all their Rights and Privileges which they have enjoyed hitherto."[12] Some scholars claim this provision ensured the perpetuation of Roman-Dutch law.[13] The well-established principle of English law that "the laws of a conquered country continue in force, until they are altered by the conqueror" also protected Roman-Dutch law.[14] However, the legal system at the Cape did not escape English influences. Indeed, the British government envisioned English law gradually assimilating Roman-Dutch law. In 1823, the British government appointed a commission to review colony affairs. Reporting in 1826 on judicial matters at the Cape, the commission suggested that the existing procedure should assimilate English procedure, future legislation should follow principles of English jurisprudence, and the courts should gradually adopt English common law.

In the years after 1826, this policy engendered numerous legislative changes that greatly affected procedure, evidence, and succession. For example, Ordinance No. 40 of 1928 restyled Cape criminal procedure in the manner of English criminal procedure. Ordinance No. 72 of 1830 adopted the English law of evidence with minor modifications. Civil procedure also experienced a remodeling along English lines, although some Roman-Dutch procedures remained. In 1833, Ordinance No. 104 replaced the Roman-Dutch law of universal succession of heirs with the English system of executorship. In 1845, Ordinance No. 15 established the English underhand form of will. Additionally, the Law of Inheritance Amendment Act and the Succession Act removed various restrictions on testamentary transfers.

The English legal system greatly influenced mercantile law, company law, and insolvency law. Cape statutes adopted English statutes verbatim by reference or by repromulgation. These included the Merchant Shipping Act of 1855; the General Law Amendment Act of 1879, governing maritime and shipping law, fire, life, and marine insurance, stoppage in transit, and bills of lading; the Joint Stock Companies Limited Liability Act of 1861; and the Companies Act of 1892.

English law also had a non-legislative impact. The English language dominated the courts, English judges occupied the bench, and English legal training was required for advocates. The use of the English system of government also meant the introduction of English principles of constitutional law. Although Roman-Dutch law remained the basic common law of the Cape, by the end of the nineteenth century, it had been thoroughly infused with English law.

Meanwhile, in the nineteenth century, Roman-Dutch law spread from the Cape to the Afrikaner republics of the Transvaal and the Orange Free State and to the British colony of Natal.[15] All three adopted the Roman-Dutch system, but English law, operating through the law of the Cape Colony, soon modified it.[16] After the 1899–1902 South African War,[17] in 1910, the two former Afrikaner republics and the two British colonies formed the Union of South Africa,[18] which remained until the Union transformed itself into the Republic of South Africa in 1961.[19] The pronouncement about the common law notwithstanding, the South African legal system had clearly become a "three-layer cake" of Roman, Roman-Dutch, and English law.[20] These influences continue to manifest themselves in modern South African contract law.

II.   Contracts and Their Legal Effects

In Roman law, only four types of agreements constituted enforceable contracts. These were (1) *contracts re*, in which a party delivered a thing (*res*) to the other and could, therefore, claim redelivery or counterperformance from the other; (2) *contracts literis*, in which a creditor made an entry in his or her domestic account books relating to a debt owed to the creditor and that entry made the debt enforceable; (3) *contracts verbis*, in which the agreement was made orally in the form of question and answer; such a contract was called a *stipulatio* and was enforceable because of its form; and (4) *contracts consensu*, in which agreement was enough to make a contract of sale, partnership, hire, or mandate binding.

Roman law required agreement and *causa*, or cause, to constitute a valid contract. *Causa* could be found in *contracts re* by delivery of the thing; in *contracts literis* by the entry in the books; in *contracts verbis* by the form of words used; and in *contracts consensu* by the agreement itself. An agreement that did not fall into one of these four classes was not enforceable and was called a *nudum pactum*. The rule appeared in the maxim, *Ex nudo pacto non oritur actio*, meaning no action arises from a bare agreement. Not

enforceable by action, a *nudum pactum* gave rise to a natural obligation and could be used as a defense.

The *causa* requirement grew increasingly meaningless because of a European-developed rule that made all serious agreements actionable. By the seventeenth century, this had become the rule in Holland. Nevertheless, some writers still followed the older terminology and insisted that *causa* was necessary for contracts to be valid. In England, the courts did not require *causa* for a valid contract. However, except with regard to sealed covenants, the courts demanded that there be consideration, a counterperformance, or quid pro quo. By the nineteenth century, English ideas had so influenced legal thought at the Cape that many believed Roman-Dutch references to *causa* meant the same thing as consideration did to the English.[21] The courts in the Transvaal dismissed this view.[22] The issue remained controversial until 1919, when the Appellate Division of the South African Supreme Court ("Appellate Division") accepted the Transvaal view.[23]

Under modern South African law, a contract is an agreement between or among persons that gives rise to personal rights and corresponding obligations.[24] Although a contract is an agreement legally binding on the parties,[25] not all agreements bind the parties. Rather, an agreement is a contract only if it has a number of essential elements: (1) the agreement is for future performance or non-performance by one or more of the parties; (2) the parties have the legal capacity to contract; (3) the parties seriously intend to bind themselves; (4) with few exceptions, the agreement is executed with some formality and in writing; and (5) the agreement is not contrary to statutory law, public policy, or good morals in its formation, performance, or purpose.

If these five elements are present, the agreement becomes a legally binding contract. However, "legally binding" does not mean that the law inevitably compels the parties to perform their promises or undertakings, because the law cannot or will not compel certain types of performance. Each party to a contract acquires a right against the other party for the agreed upon performance, as well as for a corresponding obligation. Each party has a duty to perform this obligation, which gives the other party a cause of action for specific performance when the party fails to perform. Should the other party not comply with court-ordered specific performance, then the plaintiff has a cause of action for damages. However, a court will not order specific performance for certain types of contracts, such as unenforceable contracts, contracts void *ab initio*, and voidable contracts.

An unenforceable contract is one on which no action can be brought. No legal obligations may be imposed, but a natural obligation remains. Since 1969, when the South African government passed the Prescription Act,[26] only wagering contracts or bets have constituted unenforceable contracts.

A contract is void *ab initio* if it lacks one or more of the elements necessary to the formation of a contract. Such an agreement has no legal effect from its inception. An agreed upon performance prohibited by law is an example of this kind of contract. Others include contracts lacking a definite agreement on the terms of performance, or contracts involving an insane party. These agreements give no legal rights to either party. One or both of the parties cannot later ratify these agreements. In addition, registration will not validate an agreement that is void *ab initio*. A court order is not necessary to set it aside because the agreement is deemed to be worthless. Although a void contract gives neither side a cause of action, if one party has performed the terms of the agreement, the court may sometimes grant the party redress by restoring the property or by granting monetary compensation.

Unlike contracts void *ab initio*, voidable contracts contain all of the essential elements of an agreement. However, some flaw exists at the time the agreement was made, which entitles the parties to repudiate the contract and ask that both parties be restored, if possible, to their original positions. Such reinstatement is termed *restitutio in integrum*. A flawed contract is voidable at the option of the prejudiced party. Yet, unless and until the prejudiced party justifiably repudiates it, the contract is prima facie valid and binding on the parties. A court order declaring the contract rescinded is not necessary, as it only determines that party's right to end the contract. The flaws that make a contract voidable are of three types: fraudulent or non-fraudulent misrepresentations, duress, and undue influence.

These three flaws form the South African equivalent of the doctrine of unconscionability as applied in the United States and elsewhere. The interplay between duress and undue influence evidences the continuing tensions between Roman-Dutch and English law present in South Africa's mixed legal heritage.

III. Unconscionability South African-Style: Misrepresentation, Duress, and Undue Influence

A. Misrepresentation

In the formation of contracts, a party's mistaken motive is irrelevant and does not prevent the parties to the contract from reaching an agreement.[27] However, an action may lie if the mistake was caused by misrepresentation.[28] A party who has been persuaded by misrepresentation to enter into a contract or to accept terms to which he or she otherwise would not have agreed is entitled to relief if the representation was intentional, negligent, or innocent.

1. Fraudulent misrepresentation

Fraudulent misrepresentation is a precontractual false statement of fact intentionally made by one party to a contract, that induces the other party to enter into the contract or to agree to terms to which he or she would not have agreed had the truth been known.[29] Fraudulent misrepresentation requires five elements. First, there must be a precontractual false statement of fact. This statement can include the expression of an opinion that is not honestly held.[30] The statement need not be explicit, and conduct can suffice,[31] as can silence, if the silence fails to rectify an incorrect impression.[32] Second, the misrepresentation must be wrongful, meaning unlawful. A fraudulent misrepresentation is a tort, called a *delict*, in South Africa.[33] For tort liability, the act complained of must have been wrongful. Thus, if the misrepresentation was unlawful under the circumstances, liability arises. However, the courts pay particular attention only to cases where the misrepresentation was based on a wrongful omission.[34] Wrongfulness is assumed where misrepresentation by words or other positive conduct induced the contract or led a party to accept terms to which he or she otherwise would not have agreed.[35] Third, the misrepresentation must be made fraudulently. Misrepresentations are made fraudulently when the maker does not honestly believe the truth of his or her statement and intends the other party to act on it.[36] Fourth, the misrepresentation must induce the other party to conclude the contract or to agree to its terms. A court will not find liability for fraudulent misrepresentation unless there is proof of a causal link between the misrepresentation and the act of the misled party in concluding the contract or agreeing to certain terms. Fifth, the misrepresentation must be made by the other party to the contract or by a third party acting in collusion with, or as an agent of, one of the parties to the contract. A fraudulent inducement from an independent third party does not affect the contract.

The parties to a contract cannot agree between themselves to exclude remedies for fraudulent misrepresentation. Furthermore, the misrepresenting party cannot claim that the aggrieved party, as a reasonable person, should not have been misled. A contracting party who has been the victim of a fraudulent misrepresentation has a choice of two remedies: The party may accept the contract or rescind it and receive *restitutio in integrum*. The right to choose a remedy is clear where the party would not have entered into the contract without the misrepresentation. This is *dolus dans causam contractum*, or causal fraud. Incidental fraud, or *dolus incidens in contractum*, is found in situations where no causal fraud occurred. Instead, the party agreed to terms which he or she otherwise would not have agreed. The South African law regarding incidental fraud is unclear.

A party may choose rescission as a defense against the other party's action on the contract or upon filing an action. Whether he or she accepts or rescinds the contract, the aggrieved party has an action in tort for any loss suffered. A party must elect to rescind within a reasonable time after the party learns of the misrepresentation, or lose the right. Once a party elects a remedy, he or she must abide by it. If a party chooses rescission, he or she must restore to the other party that which he or she received under the contract. However, the court may decline to follow this rule if justice requires.

The measure of the injured party's damages is the difference between the party's current financial situation and the financial situation he or she would have been in had the misrepresentation not been made. If the party chooses rescission and restitution, damages are usually calculated on the basis of wasted costs. However, if the contract is upheld, calculation becomes more difficult, with the method depending upon the circumstances. The court always endeavors to determine the detriment suffered by the aggrieved party because of the misrepresentation. Nevertheless, two generalizations may be made. First, in a causal fraud case, the court typically determines damages by subtracting the value of the performance made by the misrepresenting party from the value of the performance made by the aggrieved party. The court then adds any consequential loss suffered by the aggrieved party. Second, in an incidental fraud case, the court often calculates damages by subtracting the price that would have been paid if there had been no misrepresentation from the price actually paid. The court then adds any consequential loss.

2. Non-fraudulent misrepresentation

Non-fraudulent misrepresentation is the negligent or innocent misrepresentation by one party to a contract that induces the other party to enter into a contract or to agree to terms to which the party would not have agreed had he or she known the truth. Thus, non-fraudulent misrepresentation has the same elements as fraudulent misrepresentation, except that the misrepresentation is made negligently or innocently[37] rather than intentionally.

Under Roman law, a party could plead the *exceptio doli* to a claim on a contract concluded on the basis of an innocent misrepresentation. Although Roman-Dutch law accepted this rule, neither Roman nor Roman-Dutch law provided a cause of action for innocent misrepresentation. In 1907, South African law departed from this position and allowed the innocent party to sue for rescission and restitution, but did not permit the recovery of damages. Twenty years later, the Appellate Division determined that the parties can, by prior agreement, exclude remedies for non-fraudulent misrepresentation.

In 1959, the Orange Free State Provincial Division held that there was no reason for denying a claim for restitutional damages to a buyer who had entered into a contract of sale as a result of the seller's material, innocent misrepresentation. The courts in the Transvaal and Natal also adopted this position.

Finally, in 1973, the Appellate Division addressed remedies for non-fraudulent misrepresentation in *Phame (Pty) Ltd. v. Poizes*. The court established two rules concerning remedies regarding sales contracts. First, a buyer can claim either rescission or restitution with the *actio redhibitoria*. The buyer can claim restitutional damages, abatement of the purchase price, with the *actio quanti minoris* if he or she has been misled by a seller's misrepresentation that constituted a *dictum et promissum*.[38] The party to whom the misrepresentation is made may raise the *exceptio redhibitoria* or the *exceptio quanti minoris* as a defense to an action by the seller. Second, if the seller's misrepresentation is not a *dictum et promissum*, or if the representation is made to a party to a contract other than a sales contract, the party to whom the misrepresentation is made may claim rescission and restitution or may raise the *exceptio doli* as a defense to an action by the other party. In such cases, no action for restitution arises.

B. Duress

Duress, which derived from Roman-Dutch law, occurs when a person acts through fear of actual or threatened danger. Three elements must exist to establish a claim of duress. First, there must be a threat of imminent or inevitable harm to the life, person, honor, or property of a person or family member.[39] Threats of criminal prosecution will suffice.[40] Likewise, threats to destroy or forfeit property, known as duress of goods, permit the property owner to repudiate any contract extorted by the threats.[41]

The second element of duress is an unlawful threat.[42] A threat is unlawful if the threatened conduct is unlawful in itself or the purpose of the threat is unlawful, such as attempting to obtain something to which one is not entitled.[43] A creditor's threat to institute civil proceedings to enforce his or her rights is not unlawful as long as the creditor does not try to obtain something to which he or she is not entitled. A party entering into a contract under these circumstances cannot set it aside on the grounds of duress.

It is unlawful to threaten a person with criminal prosecution in order to enforce a private debt if the other party did not commit the crime or if the creditor is using the threat to obtain something to which the creditor is not entitled. A split of authority exists as to whether the same result occurs if the debtor committed the crime and the creditor seeks only that to which he or she is entitled. For example, South African jurist Wessels wrote that "[t]he threat to prosecute a person for a crime involving imprisonment unless he enters into a contract is sufficient mortal violence to justify the setting aside of the contract." In contrast, the Transvaal Provincial Division of the Supreme Court and the Durban and Coast Local Division of the Supreme Court believe that if the debtor committed the crime and the creditor seeks no more than that to which he or she is entitled, the threat of criminal proceedings is lawful. The Cape Provincial Division has not yet decided the issue, but, should the case arise, the court is likely to determine that the threat of criminal procedure is *contra bonos mores* or against public policy, even if the debtor has committed the crime and the creditor seeks no more than that which the creditor is due. All South African courts should adopt this view. It seems inappropriate that the criminal process, aimed at protecting society at large, can be used to enforce private rights. Moreover, irrespective of duress, every threat of criminal prosecution implies that there will not be future prosecution if the desired contract is concluded. All such contracts implicitly are agreements to stop prosecutions or to compound crimes and will be void as against public policy.

The third element of duress is that the threat must have induced the threatened party to enter into the contract or to agree to terms to which he or she otherwise would not have agreed. Hence, the threat and the contract must have a causal link. Many jurisdictions also require the victim's reasonable fear, although the victim's fear does not make the contract voidable. On the other hand, obtaining the victim's consent by improper means does make the contract voidable.[44] Indeed, it is difficult to imagine how the unreasonableness of the victim's fear has inferential value in deciding whether the threats actually induced the formation of the contract. If reasonable fear were required, any distinction made by courts between threats to an individual and duress of goods where the victim can claim duress only if he or she acted under protest, would also relate to proving a causal link between the threat and the victim's subsequent conduct.

With regard to remedies under Roman Law, a duress victim could use the *exceptio quod metus causa* as a defense against an action on the contract into which he or she had entered.[45] A victim could also claim *restitutio in integrum* in cases where he or she had already performed the contractual terms.[46] In addition, a victim could obtain damages with delictual *actio quod metus causa*.[47] Roman-Dutch law followed these precedents,[48] and, following its Roman-Dutch heritage, South African law allows the threatened party to accept the contract or have it set aside.[49] In electing to avoid the contract, the threatened party may either raise duress as a defense or claim *restitutio in integrum*. Regardless of whether the threatened party accepts or rejects the contract, the threatened party may receive delictual damages in compensation for his or her negative interest.

C. Undue influence

Like English common law, South African law holds that a contract made under duress is voidable.[50] However, the English common law is much narrower than its South African counterpart. The English concept comprises only cases of actual or threatened physical violence to, or unlawful constraint of, the contracting party's person. The narrowness of the English common law concept of duress resulted in intervention by courts of equity, which, through application of the doctrine of constructive fraud, had broader jurisdiction over contracts made without free consent than did the common law courts. The equity courts developed a doctrine of undue influence, which provided relief in cases where a contract was procured through improper pressure that did not rise to the level of duress. It also provided relief in cases where a special relationship existed between the contracting parties. The two types of cases are indistinguishable. Where no special relationship exists between the parties, the party alleging undue influence must prove that

the other party imposed improper pressure on him or her. Where a special relationship does exist, a presumption of undue influences arises, which the alleged undue influencer must rebut. Many relationships give rise to the presumption, including those of parent–child, guardian–ward, religious adviser–disciple, physician–patient, attorney–client, and trustee–*cestui que* trust.

After the South African War, the courts in the Cape and Natal, and the Appellate Division first referred to undue influence as a ground for setting aside a contract. Some of the courts accepted unquestioningly the proposition that the doctrine of undue influence formed part of South African law. In 1948, the Cape Provincial Division of the Supreme Court determined that undue influence had a basis in South African law. In reaching its decision, the Court drew on previous decisions of South African courts, the writings of several scholars, the views of various writers on the grounds for *restitutio in integrum*, and on the fact that undue influence prevented true consent. Six years later, in *Preller v. Jordaan*, the Appellate Division accepted the view that undue influence provided a ground for *restitutio in integrum*. That decision marked the unambiguous acceptance in South African law of the rule that a party can avoid a contract if the other party used undue influence to induce him or her to enter into it. The acceptance of this rule diverges from Roman-Dutch practice, which is demonstrated by the minority judgment of Van den Heever in *Preller*, and by the writings of South African jurist De Wet in an examination of the sources the court relied upon in *Preller*.

Despite acceptance of the general rule, the specific elements of undue influence remain unclear. The English courts vaguely define undue influence as "some unfair and improper conduct, some coercion from outside, some overreaching, some form of cheating, and generally, though not always, some personal advantage obtained by" the guilty party. The South African courts have not been more precise. In *Preller*, the court found that the grounds for *restitutio in integrum* were broad enough to include the case

where one person obtains an influence over another which weakens the latter's powers of resistance and renders his will compliant, and where such person then uses his influence in an unconscionable manner to persuade the other to agree to a prejudicial transaction which he would not have concluded with normal free will.

Then, in *Patel v. Grobbelaar*, the Appellate Division affirmed the Transvaal Provincial Division's decision requiring a plaintiff asserting undue influence to prove three elements: (1) the defendant exerted influence over him or her; (2) the influence weakened his or her resistance and made him or her compliant; and (3) the defendant used his or her influence unscrupulously to induce the plaintiff to agree to a transaction which was prejudicial to him or her and which he or she would not otherwise have entered.

In terms of remedies for undue influence, the injured party may elect to accept the contract or to rescind it and claim *restitutio in integrum*. The courts have not decided whether the party also has an action for damages. However, if undue influence is to be accepted as duress, a plaintiff would have an action for damages.

IV. The Need for a Commercial Code with Emphasis on Unconscionability

As South Africa struggles to cast off apartheid's sordid legacy, there is much discussion of a new constitution that will guarantee human rights and equality before the law.[51] There is also great debate over whether such a document should guarantee economic rights. This debate, however, centers on land and wealth redistribution, and does not involve contract formation or the sanctity of contracts.

Nevertheless, there are pressing reasons for those crafting a new legal order for the country to pay particular attention to contract law. To create a just society, the South African economy will have to expand dramatically. Expanding the economy will require infusions of foreign capital, but such investment alone will not be enough to undo the underlying problems of high unemployment, poverty, and despair. Domestic economic growth will also have to be fueled by greater African participation, primarily through small business creation and heightened presence in the consumer economy. In such an environment, contracts, whether between businesses, between businesses and individuals, or between individuals, will assume a new importance as the foundations facilitating economic change. Inevitably, contract disputes will arise, particularly because middle class South African blacks starting new businesses will not have established advice networks to rely on for assistance in making deals. Consequently, it seems likely that many contract disputes will find their way to court.

Historically, in South Africa, white judges enforced laws created by whites in courts catering to white interests; hence, it will be important for courts to be responsive to those wronged in contract disputes. This is essential not only for economic stability but also for the creation of much needed respect for the rule of law in general. The courts' responsiveness is even more urgent because whites will continue to dominate the economy, the judiciary, and the bar in the foreseeable future. Therefore, both South African courts and those creating a new legal order for the country should make an effort to define a coherent doctrine of unconscionability that favors the rights of victims.

In terms of case law, courts should adopt a concept of unconscionability that seeks to merge, where possible, the existing doctrines of misrepresentation, duress, and undue influence. The success of this merger will partly depend upon the continuing position of Roman-Dutch law in the South African legal order, an issue not yet decided.[52] Even so, the hybrid legal heritage does not pose too formidable an obstacle to the development of a judicial doctrine of unconscionability.

Looking beyond the case law, any new government should adopt a commercial code, perhaps modeled on the United States' Uniform Commercial Code,[53] that would have explicit provisions on unconscionability. Such provisions, developed in consultation with judges, commercial lawyers, and consumer advocates, would help guide judges in devising their standards. To better serve South Africa's undereducated African population, the code should avoid legal jargon as much as possible. Once adopted, the government should publicize the code by distributing summaries for laypersons published in the official language, which is likely to be English,[54] as well as in Afrikaans and various African languages. The government should mobilize trade unions, consumer groups, and those conducting secondary school street law programs to familiarize people with the code. Both entrepreneurs and consumers alike will then become comfortable with commercial law and enter into transactions that will benefit the economy and, therefore, all South Africans.

V. Conclusion

South Africa has a hybrid legal system that combines elements of Roman, Roman-Dutch, and English law. That mixed heritage is readily apparent in South African contract law, which has never developed the concept of unconscionability as found in the law of the United States and other countries, but instead relies upon the doctrines of misrepresentation, duress, and undue influence. As debates rage in South Africa about the post-apartheid legal order, many of the ills besetting the country demand eradication. The post-apartheid order must involve the increased participation of Africans both as business owners and consumers. To encourage that participation, there should be a doctrine of unconscionability that favors the victims of unconscionable contracts. This should be developed in two ways. First, the courts should harmonize existing doctrines and develop a concept of unconscionability. Second, those responsible for commercial law in any new government should adopt a commercial code that employs a concept of unconscionability; such a code must avoid legal jargon and be explained to laypersons through various education programs. Only by encouraging Africans to feel that the economy belongs to them will the growth so necessary to South Africa's stability and survival be able to occur.

Notes

1   See Lynn Berat, "Undoing and Redoing Business in South Africa: The Lifting of the Comprehensive Anti-Apartheid Act of 1986 and the Continuing Validity of State and Local Anti-Apartheid Legislation," 6 *Conn. J. Int'l. L.* 7 (1991).

2   The African National Congress is described in Tom Lodge, *Black Politics in South Africa since 1945* (1983).

3   See Berat, supra note 1, at 9–11; Lynn Berat, "The Courts and the Economy in a New South Africa: A Call for an Indexation Model," 15 *B.C. Int'l & Comp. L. Rev.* 1 (1992).

4   See generally Francis Wilson & Maphela Ramphele, *Uprooting Poverty: The South African Challenge* (1988).

5   The future of customary law, as opposed to the western-based South African national system, remains unresolved. For a discussion of this problem, see Lynn Berat, "Customary Law in the New South Africa: A Proposal," 15 *Fordham Int'l. L.J.* 92 (1991).

6   Arthur Corbin, *Corbin on Contracts*, 188 (1952).

7   Section 2-302 provides:

>   (1) If the court as a matter of law finds the contract or any clause of the contract to have been unconscionable at the time it was made the court may refuse to enforce the contract, or it may enforce the remainder of the contract without the unconscionable clause as to avoid any unconscionable result.
>
>   (2) When it is claimed or appears to the court that the contract or any clause thereof may be unconscionable the parties shall be afforded a reasonable opportunity to present evidence as to its commercial setting, purpose and effect to aid the court in making its determination.

UCC §2-302 (1990).

8   Imre Zajtay & W. J. Hosten, "The Permanence of Roman Law Concepts in the Continental Legal System and South African Law," 2 *Comp. & Int'l L.J. S. Afr.* 181, 197 (1969).

9   See John Dugard, *Human Rights and the South African Legal Order*, 8 (1978).

10 See W. J. Hosten et al., *Introduction to South African Law and Legal Theory*, 132 (1983) (discussing South Africa's mixed system of law).

11 Wolfgang Kunkel, *An Introduction to Roman Legal and Constitutional History*, 168–78 (1966). For more on Roman law, see Fritz Schultz, *History of Roman Legal Science* (1946).

12 Cape Colony, Articles of Capitulation, Nos. 11, 12 (1806).

13 See, e.g., H. D. J. Bodenstein, "English Influences on the Common Law of South Africa," 32 *S. Afr. L.J.* 337, 339 (1915); N. J. De Wet, "Die Romeins-Hollandse Reg in Suid-Afrika no 1806," 21 *Tydskrif Vir Hedenaagse Romeins-Hollandse Reg* 239, 239 n.2 (1958).

14 Campbell v. Hall (1774) 1 Cowp. 204, 209 (Eng. K.B.); see Dugard, supra note 9, at 8.

15 For a constitutional history of the Afrikaner Republics, see Leonard Thompson, "Constitutionalism in the South African Republics," *Butterworth's S. Afr. L. Rev.* 49 (1954).

16 Hosten et al., supra note 10, at 201–3.

17 See Lynn Berat, "Constitutionalism and Mineral Law in the Struggle for a New South Africa: The South African War Revisited," 15 *Suffolk Transnat'l L.J.* 61 (1992).

18 See Leonard Thompson, *The Unification of South Africa 1902–1910*, at 459 (1960).

19 Thompson, *A History of South Africa* (1990), at 188.

20 Zajtay & Hosten, supra note 8, at 197. One judge wrote:

> Our country has reached a stage in its national development when its existing law can better be described as South African than Roman-Dutch. . . . No doubt its roots are Roman-Dutch, and splendid roots they are. But continuous development has come through adaptation to modern conditions, through case law, through statutes, and through the adoption of certain principles and features of English law. . . . The original sources of the Roman-Dutch law are important, but exclusive preoccupation with them is like trying to return the oak tree to its acorn.

Ex parte de Winnaar (1959) 1 S.A. 837, 839 (S. Afr. N.P.D.).

21 See Conradie v. Roussouw (1919) A.D. 279 (S. Afr.).

22 See e.g., Rood v. Wallach (1904) T.S. 187, 209 (S. Afr.).

23 Conradie (1919) A.D. at 317.

24 J. C. De Wet & A. H. Van Wyk, *Die Suid-Afrikaanse Kontraktereg en Handelsreg*, 4 (1978).

25 However, parties can sometimes be bound by a contract even though they are not really in agreement. George v. Fairmead (Pty) Ltd. (1958) 2 S.A. 465 (S. Afr. App. Div.).

26 Republic of South Africa, Prescription Act No. 68 (1969).

27 For example, X buys a 1966 Ford Mustang from Y. Both believe the car has a V8 engine, but later determine that it has a V6 engine.

28 See H. R. Hahlo & Ellison Kahn, *The Union of South Africa: Development of its Laws and Constitution*, 463 (1960).

29 Id.

30 A. J. C. Copeling, "Copyright in Ideas?," 28 *Tydskrif Vir Hedendaagse Romeins-Hollandse Reg* 3 (1965).

31 Displaying a used car among new ones is an example of conduct constituting fraudulent misrepresentation.

32 M. A. Miller, "Fraudulent Non-Disclosure," 74 *S. Afr. L.J.* 177, 179–80 (1957).

33 Trotman v. Edwick (1951) 1 S.A. 443 (S. Afr. App. Div.); De Jager v. Grunder (1964) 1 S.A. 446 (S. Afr. App. Div.); Ranger v. Wykerd (1977) 2 S.A. 976 (S. Afr. App. Div.).

34 Failing to speak is wrongful if there was a duty to speak. On the duty to speak, see Bodemer v. American Ins. Co. (1961) 2 S.A. 662, 669 (S. Afr. App. Div.) (a contract *uberrimae fidei* imposes duty to speak); Glaston House (Pty) Ltd. v. Inag (Pty) Ltd. (1977) 2 S.A. 846, 867–9 (S. Afr. App. Div.) (duty to speak if seller knows of latent defects in item sold).

35 The misrepresentation must be related to the material facts. Karroo v. Farr (1921) A.D. 413, 415 (S. Afr.). Puffing alone is not actionable. Dig 4.3.37 (Ulpian, Sabinus, bk. 44); Voet Commentarius 21.1.3.

36 Rex v. Myers (1948) 1 S.A. 375, 382 (S. Afr. App. Div.).

37 According to the South African law of *delict*, negligent misrepresentation gives rise to the *delictual actio legis Aquiliae*, legal action, for damages in the same manner as a fraudulent misrepresentation. Herschel (1954) 3 S.A. at 464.

38 One example is a material statement by the seller to the buyer during the negotiations that bears on the quality of the thing sold and goes beyond mere praise and commendation.

39 Grotius, *Inleiding*, 3.48.6; Van Leeuwen, *Cens For*, 1.4.41.2–3; Broodryk v. Smuts (1942) Natal L.R. 47 (S. Afr.); Jans Rautenbach Produksies (Edms) Bpk v. Wijma (1970) 4 S.A. 31 (S. Afr. T.P.D.); Shepstone v. Shepstone (1974) 1 S.A. 411 (S. Afr. D. & C.L.D.).

40 See, e.g., Broodryk (1942) Natal L.R. at 47; Jans Rautenbach Produksies (Edms) Bpk (1970) 4 S.A. 31; Arend v. Astra Furnishers (Pty) Ltd. (1974) 1 S.A. 765 (S. Afr. C.P.D.).

41 Hendricks v. Barnett (1975) 1 S.A. 765 (S. Afr. N.P.D.). For example, if a person in a position of authority unlawfully compels the owner of certain goods to pay or agree to pay him or her money by threatening that failure to pay will result in a forfeiture of the goods, the goods' owner is not bound if he or she protests at the time.

42 Voet 4.2.10; Broodryk (1942) Natal L.R. at 47; Jans Rautenbach Produksies (Edms) Bpk (1970) 4 S.A. at 31; Arend (1974) 1 S.A. at 765.

43 See P. J. J. Olivier, "Onregmatige Vreesaanjaging," 28 *Tydskrif Vir Hedendaagse Romeins-Hollandse Reg* 187, 203 (1965).

44 Grotius, *De Iure B Ac P*, 2.11.7; De Wet & Van Wyk, *Die Suid-Afrikanse Kontraktereg en Handelsreg*, 4 (1978), at 44.

45 See Mauerberger v. Mauerberger (1948) 4 S.A. 902, 903–5 (S. Afr. C.P.D.).

46 Grotius, *Inleiding*, 3.48.6; Grotius, *De Iure B Ac P*, 2.11.7; Van Leeuwen, *Cens For*, 1.1.13.5–7; Voet, *Commentarius*, 4.2.1.

47 Grotius, *Inleiding*, 3.48.6; Grotius, *De Iure B Ac P*, 2.11.7; Van Leeuwen, *Cens For*, 1.1.13.5–7; Voet, *Commentarius*, 4.2.1.

48 Grotius, *Inleiding*, 3.48.6; Grotius, *De Iure B Ac P*, 2.11.7; Van Leeuwen, *Cens For*, 1.1.13.5–7; Voet, *Commentarius*, 4.2.1.

49 Broodryk, 1942 Natal L.R. at 47; Jans Rautenbach Produksies (Edms) Bpk (1970) 4 S.A. at 31; Shepstone (1974) 1 S.A. at 411; Ilanga Wholesalers (1974) 2 S.A. at 292; Arend (1974) 1 S.A. at 765.

50 G. C. Cheshire & C. H. S. Fifoot, *The Law of Contract*, 285–90 (1981).

51 On the constitutional debate, see Lynn Berat, "A New South Africa?: Prospects for an African-ist Bill of Rights and a Transformed Judiciary," 13 *Loy. L.A. Int'l & Comp. L.J.* 467, 467–84 (1991).

52 On the future of Roman-Dutch law, see, e.g., Albie Sachs, *The Future of Roman-Dutch Law in a Non-Racial Democratic South Africa: Some Preliminary Observations* (1989).

53 UCC (1990).

54 On the language question, see Neville Alexander, "Language Planning in South Africa with Special Reference to the Harmonization of the Varieties of Nguni and Sotho," Paper Presented at the South African Research Program Seminar, Yale University (Feb. 20, 1991); Neville Alexander, "The Sociology of Language Planning for a Democratic South Africa," Paper Presented at the South African Research Program Seminar, Yale University (Oct. 17, 1990).

51

Williams v. Walker-Thomas Furniture Co. (1965)

J. Skelly Wright, Circuit Judge: Appellee, Walker-Thomas Furniture Company, operates a retail furniture store in the District of Columbia. During the period from 1957 to 1962 each appellant in these cases purchased a number of household items from Walker-Thomas, for which payment was to be made in installments. The terms of each purchase were contained in a printed form contract which set forth the value of the purchased item and purported to lease the item to appellant for a stipulated monthly rent payment. The contract then provided, in substance, that title would remain in Walker-Thomas until the total of all the monthly payments made equaled the stated value of the item, at which time appellants could take title. In the event of a default in the payment of any monthly installment, Walker-Thomas could repossess the item.

The contract further provided that "the amount of each periodical installment payment to be made by [purchaser] to the Company under this present lease shall be inclusive of and not in addition to the amount of each installment payment to be made by [purchaser] under such prior leases, bills or accounts; *and all payments now and hereafter made by [purchaser] shall be credited pro rata on all outstanding leases, bills and accounts* due, the Company by [purchaser] at the time each such payment is made." (Emphasis added.) The effect of this rather obscure provision was to keep a balance due on every item purchased until the balance due on all items, whenever purchased, was liquidated. As a result, the debt incurred at the time of purchase of each item was secured by the right to repossess all the items previously purchased by the same purchaser, and each new item purchased automatically became subject to a security interest arising out of the previous dealings.

On May 12, 1962, appellant Thorne purchased an item described as a Daveno, three tables, and two lamps, having total stated value of $391.10. Shortly thereafter, he defaulted on his monthly payments and appellee sought to replevy all the items purchased since the first transaction in 1958. Similarly, on April 17, 1962, appellant Williams bought a stereo set of stated value of $514.95.[1] She too defaulted shortly thereafter, and appellee sought to replevy all the items purchased since December, 1957. The Court of General Sessions granted judgment for appellee. The District of Columbia Court of Appeals affirmed, and we granted appellants' motion for leave to appeal to this court.

Appellants' principal contention, rejected by both the trial and the appellate courts below, is

Williams v. Walker-Thomas Furniture Co., 350 F.2d 445 (1965).

that these contracts, or at least some of them, are unconscionable and, hence, not enforceable. In its opinion in Williams v. Walker-Thomas Furniture Company, 198 A.2d 914, 916 (1964), the District of Columbia Court of Appeals explained its rejection of this contention as follows:

Appellant's second argument presents a more serious question. The record reveals that prior to the last purchase appellant had reduced the balance in her account to $164. The last purchase, a stereo set, raised the balance due to $678. Significantly, at the time of this and the preceding purchases, appellee was aware of appellant's financial position. The reverse side of the stereo contract listed the name of appellant's social worker and her $218 monthly stipend from the government. Nevertheless, with full knowledge that appellant had to feed, clothe and support herself and seven children on this amount, appellee sold her a $514 stereo set.

We cannot condemn too strongly appellee's conduct. It raises serious questions of sharp practice and irresponsible business dealings. A review of the legislation in the District of Columbia affecting retail sales and the pertinent decisions of the highest court in this jurisdiction disclose, however, no ground upon which this court can declare the contract in question contrary to public policy. We note that were the Maryland Retail Installment Sales Act, Art. 83, §§128–53, or its equivalent, in force in the District of Columbia, we could grant appellant appropriate relief. We think Congress should consider corrective legislation to protect the public from such exploitive contracts as were utilized in the case at bar.

We do not agree that the court lacked the power to refuse enforcement to contracts found to be unconscionable. In other jurisdictions, it has been held as a matter of common law that unconscionable contracts are not enforceable.[2] While no decision of this court so holding has been found, the notion that an unconscionable bargain should not be given full enforcement is by no means novel. In Scott v. United States, 79 U.S. (12 Wall.) 443, 445 20 L.Ed. 438 (1870), the Supreme Court stated:

...If a contract be unreasonable and unconscionable, but not void for fraud, a court of law

will give to the party who sues for its breach damages, not according to its letter, but only such as he is equitably entitled to. . . .[3]

Since we have never adopted or rejected such a rule,[4] the question here presented is actually one of first impression.

Congress has recently enacted the Uniform Commercial Code, which specifically provides that the court may refuse to enforce a contract which it finds to be unconscionable at the time it was made. 28 D. C. Code §2–302 (Supp. IV 1965). The enactment of this section, which occurred subsequent to the contracts here in suit, does not mean that the common law of the District of Columbia was otherwise at the time of enactment, nor does it preclude the court from adopting a similar rule in the exercise of its powers to develop the common law for the District of Columbia. In fact, in view of the absence of prior authority on the point, we consider the congressional adoption of §2–302 persuasive authority for following the rationale of the cases from which the section is explicitly derived.[5] Accordingly, we hold that where the element of unconscionability is present at the time a contract is made, the contract should not be enforced.

Unconscionability has generally been recognized to include an absence of meaningful choice on the part of one of the parties together with contract terms which are unreasonably favorable to the other party.[6] Whether a meaningful choice is present in a particular case can only be determined by consideration of all the circumstances surrounding the transaction. In many cases the meaningfulness of the choice is negated by a gross inequality of bargaining power.[7] The manner in which the contract was entered is also relevant to this consideration. Did each party to the contract, considering his obvious education or lack of it, have a reasonable opportunity to understand the terms of the contract, or were the important terms hidden in a maze of fine print and minimized by deceptive sales practices? Ordinarily, one who signs an agreement without full knowledge of its terms might be held to assume the risk that he has entered a one-sided bargain.[8] But when a party of little bargaining power, and hence little real choice, signs a commercially unreasonable contract with little or no knowledge of its terms, it is hardly likely that his consent, or even an objective manifestation of his consent, was ever given to all the terms. In such a case the usual rule that the terms of the agreement are not to be questioned[9] should be abandoned and the court should consider whether the terms of the contract are so unfair that enforcement should be withheld.[10]

In determining reasonableness or fairness, the primary concern must be with the terms of the contract considered in light of the circumstances existing when the contract was made. The test is not simple, nor can it be mechanically applied. The terms are to be considered "in the light of the general commercial background and the commercial needs of the particular trade or case."[11] Corbin suggests the test as being whether the terms are "so extreme as to appear unconscionable according to the mores and business practices of the time and place" (1 Corbin, op. cit. supra Note 2).[12] We think this formulation correctly states the test to be applied in those cases where no meaningful choice was exercised upon entering the contract.

Because the trial court and the appellate court did not feel that enforcement could be refused, no findings were made on the possible unconscionability of the contracts in these cases. Since the record is not sufficient for our deciding the issue as a matter of law, the cases must be remanded to the trial court for further proceedings.

So ordered.

Danaher, Circuit Judge (dissenting):

The District of Columbia Court of Appeals obviously was as unhappy about the situation here presented as any of us can possibly be. Its opinion in the *Williams* case, quoted in the majority text, concludes: "We think Congress should consider corrective legislation to protect the public from such exploitive contracts as were utilized in the case at bar."

My view is thus summed up by an able court which made no finding that there had actually been sharp practice. Rather the appellant seems to have known precisely where she stood.

There are many aspects of public policy here involved. What is a luxury to some may seem an outright necessity to others. Is public oversight to be required of the expenditures of relief funds? A washing machine, e.g., in the hands of a relief client might become a fruitful source of income. Many relief clients may well need credit, and certain business establishments will take long chances on the sale of items, expecting their pricing policies will afford a degree of protection commensurate with the risk. Perhaps a remedy when necessary will be found within the provisions of the "Loan Shark" law, D.C.Code §§26–601 *et seq.* (1961).

I mention such matters only to emphasize the desirability of a cautious approach to any such problem, particularly since the law for so long has allowed parties such great latitude in making their own contracts. I dare say there must annually be thousands upon thousands of installment credit transactions in this jurisdiction, and one can only speculate as to the effect the decision in these cases will have.

I join the District of Columbia Court of Appeals in its disposition of the issues.

Notes

1   At the time of this purchase her account showed a balance of $164 still owing from her prior purchases. The total of all the purchases made over the years in question came to $1,800. The total payments amounted to $14,000.

2   Campbell Soup Co. v. Wentz, 3 Cir., 172 F.2d 80 (1948); Indianapolis Morris Plan Corporation v. Sparks, 132 Ind.App. 145, 172 N.E.2d 899 (1961); Henningsen v. Bloomfield Motors, Inc., 32 N.J. 358, 161 A.2d 69, 84–96, 75 A.L.R.2d 1 (1960). *Cf.* 1 Corbin, *Contracts* §128 (1963).

3   See Luing v. Peterson, 143 Minn. 6, 172 N.W. 692 (1919); Greer v. Tweed, N.Y. C.P., 13 Abb.Pr., N.S., 427 (1872); Schnell v. Nell, 17 Ind. 29 (1861); and see generally the discussion of the English authorities in Hume v. United States, 132 U.S. 406, 10 S.Ct. 134, 33 L.Ed. 393 (1889).

4   While some of the statements in the court's opinion in District of Columbia v. Harlan & Hollingsworth Co., 30 App.D.C. 270 (1908), may appear to reject the rule, in reaching its decision upholding the liquidated damages clause in that case the court considered the circumstances existing at the time the contract was made, see 30 App.D.C. at 279, and applied the usual rule on liquidated damages. See 5 Corbin, *Contracts* §§1054–75 (1964); *Note,* 72 *Yale L.J.* 723, 746–755 (1963). Compare Jaeger v. O'Donoghue, 57 App.D.C. 191, 18 F.2d 1013 (1927).

5 See Comment §2–302, Uniform Commercial Code (1962). Compare *Note*, 45 *Va.L.Rev.* 583, 590 (1959), where it is predicted that the rule of §2–302 will be followed by analogy in cases which involve contracts not specifically covered by the section. *Cf.* 1 *State of New York Law Revision Commission, Report and Record of Hearings on the Uniform Commercial Code*, 108–10 (1954) (remarks of Professor Llewellyn).

6 See Henningsen v. Bloomfield Motors, Inc., *supra* Note 2; Campbell Soup Co. v. Wentz, *supra* Note 2.

7 See Henningsen v. Bloomfield Motors, Inc., supra Note 2, 161 A. 2d at 86, and authorities there cited. Inquiry into the relative bargaining power of the two parties is not an inquiry wholly divorced from the general question of unconscionability, since a one-sided bargain is itself evidence of the inequality of the bargaining parties. This fact was vaguely recognized in the common law doctrine of intrinsic fraud, that is, fraud which can be presumed from the grossly unfair nature of the terms of the contract. See the oft-quoted statement of Lord Hardwicke in Earl of Chesterfield v. Janssen, 28 Eng.Rep. 82, 100 (1751):

> . . . [Fraud] may be apparent from the intrinsic nature and subject of the bargain itself; such as no man in his senses and not under delusion would make. . . .

And *cf.* Hume v. United States, *supra* Note 3, 132 U.S. at 413, 10 S.Ct. at 137, where the Court characterized the English cases as "cases in which one party took advantage of the other's ignorance of arithmetic to impose upon him, and the fraud was apparent from the face of the contracts." See also Greer v. Tweed, *supra* Note 3.

8 See *Restatement, Contracts* §70 (1932); *Note*, 63 *Harv. L.Rev.* 494 (1950). See also Daley v. People's Building, Loan & Savings Ass'n, 178 Mass. 13, 59 HE. 452, 453 (1901), in which Mr. Justice Holmes, while sitting on the Supreme Judicial Court of Massachusetts, made this observation:

> . . . Courts are less and less disposed to interfere with parties making such contracts as they choose, so long as they interfere with no one's welfare but their own. . . . It will be understood that we are speaking of parties standing in an equal position where neither has any oppressive advantage or power. . . .

9 This rule has never been without exception. In cases involving merely the transfer of unequal amounts of the same commodity, the courts have held the bargain unenforceable for the reason that "in such a case, it is clear, that the law cannot indulge in the presumption of equivalence between the consideration and the promise." 1 *Williston, Contracts* §115 (3d ed. 1957).

10 See the general discussion of "Boiler-Plate Agreements" in Llewellyn, *The Common Law Tradition*, 362–71 (1960).

11 Comment, Uniform Commercial Code §2–307.

12 See Henningsen v. Bloomfield Motors, Inc., *supra* Note 2; Mandel v. Liebman, 303 N.Y. 88, 100 N.E.2d 149 (1951). The traditional test as stated in Greer v. Tweed, *supra* Note 3, 13 Abb.Pr., N.S., at 429, is "such as no man in his senses and not under delusion would make on the one hand, and as no honest or fair man would accept, on the other."

Questions

1 Should contracts be overturned on grounds of unconscionability? Explain what is unconscionability. In the *Port Caledonia* what facts are salient in thinking that the contract was unconscionable?

2 Should the contract in *Williams v. Walker-Thomas Furniture* be declared unconscionable on the same basis as the *Port Caledonia* contract?

3 Why does Atiyah think that reliance and restitution damages are more important than expectation?

4 What type of damage does Fried think is the most important? How would he respond to Atiyah?

5 Why does Bayles argue that zero-sum transactions should be enforced only if doing so is necessary to prevent loss to one of the parties?

Part VIII

Constitutional Law

Introduction

Contemporary disputes in constitutional law center on well-known philosophical topics, such as rights, equality, privacy, fairness, and the interpretation of texts. A constitution is supposed to provide grounding for a legal system and groundings are often drawn in broadly philosophical terms. Constitutions provide the abstract principles that guide judges and legislators. The analysis of abstract principles is, of course, the proper domain of philosophy. Consider the question of what is the proper relationship between a given government and its citizens. Clearly, this question has both philosophical and constitutional implications, both of which will be explored in this section.

We begin with Ronald Dworkin's "Constitutional Cases." Dworkin focuses our attention on two issues concerning how to interpret a constitution properly. First, how faithful must interpreters be to the intentions of those who wrote and adopted the given constitution? Second, how narrowly should one view "the moral rights that individuals have against society"? Though both issues are often lumped under the heading of "strict" construction, as opposed to "liberal" construction, of a constitution, Dworkin argues that we should not confuse these issues. In trying to be faithful to the framers' intent, one can be a strict constructionist but not view moral rights narrowly in the legal context, if it turns out that the framers intended to give a broad construal of moral rights in law.

The distinction between two ways of being strict in interpreting a constitution comes to a head when a constitution includes intentionally vague clauses concerning moral rights, such as the clause in the US Constitution guaranteeing "equal protection of the laws." It would not be faithful to the framers' intentions to conceive this provision of equal rights narrowly if the framers intended a broad moral base for the system of laws that the Constitution grounded. Dworkin argues further that this was the framers' intent in forming the US Constitution. He then argues for an "activist" court that puts moral concerns high on its agenda. Only in this way will courts be faithful to the founding moral principles of US democracy.

One type of "strict" interpretation of a constitution takes an historical approach, by which one makes the intent of the authors or framers of a constitution definitive when one is deciding how to interpret and apply a constitution to present-day cases. In "Does the Constitution mean What It Always Meant?" Stephen R. Munzer and James W. Nickel advance several arguments against the historical approach. They argue that changes in government over time, as well as changes in circumstances, make it difficult to adhere strictly to the framers' intent. On the other hand, the authors argue against a complete rejection of any attention to the framers' intent. Such a view presents clearly counterintuitive results – matters clearly mandated by the

Constitution can be rejected. They thus argue for a middle ground on how strictly to interpret the Constitution.

Munzer and Nickel also argue against Dworkin's view of constitutional interpretation. They contend that even the vague clauses of a constitution, such as equal protection of the laws, "have more content than Dworkin allows." These are not mere concepts that the framers intended to have no fixed meaning. As such, we need to pay attention to what the framers intended these concepts to capture. The authors propose a view more faithful to the framers' intent than is Dworkin's view, but which also recognizes US government changes over time because of democratic debate. How we interpret the Constitution should reflect this democratic deliberation.

The Chinese Constitution recognizes an even broader array of people's rights against the government than does the US Constitution. Even so, the United States often criticizes the Chinese government for not respecting the rights of its citizens. According to R. P. Peerenboom, one reason for this is that the Chinese do not conceive of rights as "trumps" against all other concerns. This view proceeds from China's historical reliance on the philosophy of Confucianism, which does not recognize universal moral norms. Further, Confucian philosophy is community oriented and contextual. As such, the Chinese interpret rights in their own constitution according to these values.

Does the lack of universal scope of Chinese constitutional rights make them inferior to Western rights that are said to be "inalienable" and to extend to all citizens? In "What's Wrong with Chinese Rights?" Peerenboom argues that the Chinese conception of rights is not necessarily inferior to the Western conception. Despite the rhetoric of Western rights theorists, rights are not extended to everyone in every situation in Western countries either. For example, a person has a right to free speech, but no right to yell "fire" in a crowded theater. In addition, Peerenboom argues that when rights are tailored to the particular circumstances of different communities, they will better serve the purpose for which they were designed – namely, to serve the common good.

In India, judges regularly rule that the eradication of poverty is their main mandate, a striking

position given that this view is so clearly unsupported by the Indian Constitution. Jeremy Cooper, in "Poverty and Constitutional Justice: The Indian Experience," argues that the Indian Supreme Court is justified in so acting, because such action is necessary for there to be social justice in the country. Further, Cooper argues, if the courts are to have any claim for respect, they must actively support the most downtrodden members of society. That is, courts cannot both falter in their pursuit of social justice for the poor and also claim justice as their main moral underpinning. Here we have an argument for very strong "activism" in judicial decision-making.

The next essay deals with whether judges ought to apply principles of morality to decide questions of private sexual practice. In "Natural Law: Alive and Kicking?," Rory O'Connell documents how this conception of morality has played itself out in Irish court decisions concerning homosexuality. He argues that this debate still focuses on what principles of morality one should apply to law. O'Connell comments that judicial activism concerning sexual rights will have very different results depending on which conception of morality judges actively apply. While US courts have "emphasized the 'dignity and freedom of individuals,'" Irish courts are concerned with the "supremacy of God['s] law." In Ireland, God's natural law is held to be superior to even the Irish Constitution. In matters of sexual privacy, appeals to dignity and freedom allow courts to extend privacy rights, whereas appeals to natural laws will have the opposite result in these cases. Judicial activism fueled by concerns for morality can look very different depending on the country and culture.

The final two essays in this section look at constitutional law in the international context. In these, we examine what is referred to as the constitutional norms of the international system of law. The norms that we focus on are called *jus cogens*. These norms are mandatory and peremptory in the sense that they cannot be overridden by any other norm not of the same type. *Jus cogens* norms are binding not because of the consent of states, but because of their intrinsic superiority. In this category are included norms against aggression, the denial of self-determination, genocide, crimes against humanity, slavery, racial discrimination, and apartheid. The question of the source of such norms is problematic, since the entire legal system seems to be one based in consent of the states not on anything intrinsically binding. In "Peremptory Norms as International Public Order," Alexander Orakhelashvili argues that the source of *jus cogens* norms must be in morality. He then surveys the main categories of *jus cogens* norms in an attempt to show that they are instrumental in supporting the moral norm of public order in the international arena.

In "The Gender of *Jus Cogens*," Hilary Charlesworth and Christine Chinkin examine the status and justification of *jus cogens* norms, pointing out that such norms are supposed to be universally binding and applicable to everyone. They contend, though, that such norms do not provide the same protection for woman as for men. In particular, they focus on the fact that most lists of *jus cogens* norms include racial discrimination but not sexual discrimination. Charlesworth and Chinkin also focus on the fact that most *jus cogens* norms concern the public as opposed to the private sphere, and yet women's

rights are most often concerned with the latter. In the end they also focus on such rights as reproductive freedom and sexual equality that they believe should be enshrined as *jus cogens* norms in order for the system of *jus cogens* norms to avoid the charge of bias.

We conclude this section with the US case, *Plessy v. Ferguson*. In this, the Supreme Court considered the case of a man who was seven-eighths Caucasian but who was treated by Louisiana as a non-white. He was accused of sitting in the whites-only section of a train. Plessy challenged the law under which he was arrested as unconstitutional. He stated that it violated his Fourteenth Amendment right to equal protection of the law. The Court decided that equal protection was not envisioned by the framers to "abolish distinctions based on color," but only to make the races equal. Upholding the doctrine of "separate but equal," the majority ruled against Plessy, because he had an opportunity to ride in just as good a train car set aside for non-whites. In the dissenting opinion, Justice Harlan states that the law should be color-blind, a position which was used to attack the separate but equal doctrine.

52

Constitutional Cases

Ronald Dworkin

1.

When Richard Nixon was running for President he promised that he would appoint to the Supreme Court men who represented his own legal philosophy, that is, who were what he called "strict constructionists". The nominations he subsequently made and talked about, however, did not all illuminate that legal philosophy; jurisprudence played little part in the nation's evaluation of Haynesworth and Carswell, let alone those almost nominated, Hershell Friday and Mildred Lilly. But the President presented his successful choices, Lewis Powell and William Rehnquist, as examples of his theory of law, and took the occasion to expand on that theory for a national television audience. These men, he said, would enforce the law as it is, and not "twist or bend" it to suit their own personal convictions, as Nixon accused the Warren Court of doing.

Nixon claimed that his opposition to the Warren Court's desegregation decisions, and to other decisions it took, were not based simply on a personal or political distaste for the results. He argued that the decisions violated the standards of adjudication that the Court should follow. The Court was usurping, in his views, powers that rightly belong to other institutions, including the legislatures of the various states whose school systems the Court sought to reform. He was, of course, not alone in this view. It has for some time been part of general conservative attitudes that the Supreme Court has exceeded its rightful authority. Nixon, Ford and many Congressmen and representatives have canvassed ways to limit the Court's authority by legislation. Nixon, for example, asked for a Congressional statute that would have purported to reverse important decisions, including the decision in *Swann v. Charlotte-Mecklenburg Board of Education* which gave federal courts wide powers to use busing orders as a remedy for certain forms of *de facto* segregation, and Senator Jackson and others have for some time campaigned for a constitutional amendment to the same point.

I shall not be concerned with the correctness of any of the Court's controversial decisions, nor with the wisdom of these various attempts, so far unsuccessful, to check its powers by some form of legislation or amendment. I am concerned rather with the philosophy of constitutional

Ronald Dworkin, "Constitutional Cases," from *Taking Rights Seriously* (Cambridge, Mass: The Belknap Press of Harvard University Press, 1977), pp. 131–49. © 1977, 1978 by Ronald Dworkin. Reprinted with permission from Harvard University Press.

adjudication that the politicians who oppose the Court suppose that they hold. I shall argue that there is in fact no coherent philosophy to which such politicians may consistently appeal. [. . .]

Nixon is no longer president, and his crimes were so grave that no one is likely to worry very much any more about the details of his own legal philosophy. Nevertheless in what follows I shall use the name 'Nixon' to refer, not to Nixon, but to any politician holding the set of attitudes about the Supreme Court that he made explicit in his political campaigns. There was, fortunately, only one real Nixon, but there are, in the special sense in which I use the name, many Nixons.

What can be the basis of this composite Nixon's opposition to the controversial decisions of the Warren Court? He cannot object to these decisions simply because they went beyond prior law, or say that the Supreme Court must never change its mind. Indeed the Burger Court itself seems intent on limiting the liberal decisions of the Warren Court, like *Miranda*. The Constitution's guarantee of "equal protection of the laws", it is true, does not in plain words determine that "separate but equal" school facilities are unconstitutional, or that segregation was so unjust that heroic measures are required to undo its effects. But neither does it provide that as a matter of constitutional law the Court would be wrong to reach these conclusions. It leaves these issues to the Court's judgment, and the Court would have made law just as much if it had, for example, refused to hold the North Carolina statute unconstitutional. It would have made law by establishing, as a matter of precedent, that the equal protection clause does not reach that far.

So we must search further to find a theoretical basis for Nixon's position. It may be silly, of course, to suppose that Nixon has a jurisprudence. He might simply have strung together catch phrases of conservative rhetoric, or he might be recording a distaste for any judicial decision that seems to extend the rights of individuals against constituted authority. But Nixon is, after all, a lawyer, and in any event his conservative views are supported by a great many lawyers and some very distinguished legal scholars. It is therefore important to see how far this conservative position can be defended as a matter of principle and not simply of prejudice.

2.

The constitutional theory on which our government rests is not a simple majoritarian theory. The Constitution, and particularly the Bill of Rights, is designed to protect individual citizens and groups against certain decisions that a majority of citizens might want to make, even when that majority acts in what it takes to be the general or common interest. Some of these constitutional restraints take the form of fairly precise rules, like the rule that requires a jury trial in federal criminal proceedings or, perhaps, the rule that forbids the national Congress to abridge freedom of speech. But other constraints take the form of what are often called "vague" standards, for example, the provision that the government shall not deny men due process of law, or equal protection of the laws.

This interference with democratic practice requires a justification. The draftsmen of the Constitution assumed that these restraints could be justified by appeal to moral rights which individuals possess against the majority, and which the constitutional provisions, both "vague" and precise, might be said to recognize and protect.

The "vague" standards were chosen deliberately, by the men who drafted and adopted them, in place of the more specific and limited rules that they might have enacted. But their decision to use the language they did has caused a great deal of legal and political controversy, because even reasonable men of good will differ when they try to elaborate, for example, the moral rights that the due process clause or the equal protection clause brings into the law. They also differ when they try to apply these rights, however defined, to complex matters of political administration, like the educational practices that were the subject of the segregation cases.

The practice has developed of referring to a "strict" and a "liberal" side to these controversies, so that the Supreme Court might be said to have taken the "liberal" side in the segregation cases and its critics the "strict" side. Nixon has this distinction in mind when he calls himself a "strict constructionist". But the distinction is in fact confusing, because it runs together two different issues that must be separated. Any case that arises under the "vague" constitutional guarantees can be seen as posing two questions: (1) Which decision is required by strict, that is to say faithful, adherence to the text of the Constitution or to the intention of those who adopted that text? (2) Which decision is required by a political philosophy that takes a strict, that is to say narrow, view of the moral rights that individuals have against society? Once these questions are distinguished, it is plain that they may have different answers. The text of the First Amendment, for example, says that Congress shall make *no* law abridging the freedom of speech, but a narrow view of individual rights would permit many such laws, ranging from libel and obscenity laws to the Smith Act.

In the case of the "vague" provisions, however, like the due process and equal protection clauses, lawyers have run the two questions together because they have relied, largely without recognizing it, on a theory of meaning that might be put this way: If the framers of the Constitution used vague language, as they did when they condemned violation of "due process of law", then what they "said" or "meant" is limited to the instances of official action that they had in mind as violations, or, at least, to those instances that they would have thought were violations if they had had them in mind. If those who were responsible for adding the due process clause to the Constitution believed that it was fundamentally unjust to provide separate education for different races, or had detailed views about justice that entailed that conclusion, then the segregation decisions might be defended as an application of the principle they had laid down. Otherwise they could not be defended in this way, but instead would show that the judges had substituted their own ideas of justice for those the constitutional drafters meant to lay down.

This theory makes a strict interpretation of the text yield a narrow view of constitutional rights, because it limits such rights to those recognized by a limited group of people at a fixed date of history. It forces those who favor a more liberal set of rights to concede that they are departing from strict legal authority, a departure they must then seek to justify by appealing only to the desirability of the results they reach.

But the theory of meaning on which this argument depends is far too crude; it ignores a distinction that philosophers have made but lawyers have not yet appreciated. Suppose I tell my children simply that I expect them not to treat others unfairly. I no doubt have in mind examples of the conduct I mean to discourage, but I would not accept that my "meaning" was limited to these examples, for two reasons. First I would expect my children to apply my instructions to situations I had not and could not have thought about. Second, I stand ready to admit that some particular act I had thought was fair when I spoke was in fact unfair, or vice versa, if one of my children is able to convince me of that later; in that case I should want to say that my instructions covered the case he cited, not that I had changed my instructions. I might say that I meant the family to be guided by the *concept* of fairness, not by any specific *conception* of fairness I might have had in mind.

This is a crucial distinction which it is worth pausing to explore. Suppose a group believes in common that acts may suffer from a special moral defect which they call unfairness, and which consists in a wrongful division of benefits and burdens, or a wrongful attribution of praise or blame. Suppose also that they agree on a great number of standard cases of unfairness and use these as benchmarks against which to test other, more controversial cases. In that case, the group has a concept of unfairness, and its members may appeal to that concept in moral instruction or argument. But members of that group may nevertheless differ over a large number of these controversial cases, in a way that suggests that each either has or acts on a different theory of *why* the standard cases are acts of unfairness. They may differ, that is, on which more fundamental principles must be relied upon to show that a particular division or attribution is unfair, in that case, the members have different conceptions of fairness.

If so, then members of this community who give instructions or set standards in the name of fairness may be doing two different things. First they may be appealing to the concept of fairness, simply by instructing others to act fairly; in this case they charge those whom they instruct with the responsibility of developing and applying their own conception of fairness as controversial cases arise. That is not the same thing, of course, as granting them a discretion to act as they like; it sets a standard which they must try – and may fail – to meet, because it assumes that one conception is superior to another. The man who appeals to the concept in this way may have his own conception, as I did when I told my children to act fairly; but he holds this conception only as his own theory of how the standard he set must be met, so that when he changes his theory he has not changed that standard.

On the other hand, the members may be laying down a particular conception of fairness; I would have done this, for example, if I had listed my wishes with respect to controversial examples or if, even less likely, I had specified some controversial and explicit theory of fairness, as if I had said to decide hard cases by applying the utilitarian ethics of Jeremy Bentham. The difference is a difference not just in the *detail* of the instructions given but in the *kind* of instructions given. When I appeal to the concept of fairness I appeal to what fairness means, and I give my views on that issue no special standing. When I lay down a conception of fairness, I lay down what I mean by fairness, and my view is therefore the heart of the matter. When I appeal to fairness I pose a moral issue; when I lay down my conception of fairness I try to answer it.

Once this distinction is made it seems obvious that we must take what I have been calling "vague" constitutional clauses as representing appeals to the concepts they employ, like legality, equality, and cruelty. The Supreme Court may soon decide, for example, whether capital punishment is "cruel" within the meaning of the constitutional clause that prohibits "cruel and unusual punishment". It would be a mistake for the Court to be much influenced by the fact that when the clause was adopted capital punishment was standard and unquestioned. That would be decisive if the framers of the clause had meant to lay down a particular conception of cruelty, because it would show that the conception did not extend so far. But it is not decisive of the different question the Court now faces, which is this: Can the Court, responding to the framers' appeal to the concept of cruelty, now defend a conception that does not make death cruel?

Those who ignore the distinction between concepts and conceptions, but who believe that the Court ought to make a fresh determination of whether the death penalty is cruel, are forced to argue in a vulnerable way. They say that ideas of cruelty change over time, and that the Court

must be free to reject out-of-date conceptions; this suggests that the Court must change what the Constitution enacted. But in fact the Court can enforce what the Constitution says only by making up its own mind about what is cruel, just as my children, in my example, can do what I said only by making up their own minds about what is fair. If those who enacted the broad clauses had meant to lay down particular conceptions, they would have found the sort of language conventionally used to do this, that is, they would have offered particular theories of the concepts in question.

Indeed the very practice of calling these clauses "vague", in which I have joined, can now be seen to involve a mistake. The clauses are vague only if we take them to be botched or incomplete or schematic attempts to lay down particular conceptions. If we take them as appeals to moral concepts they could not be made more precise by being more detailed.[1]

The confusion I mentioned between the two senses of "strict construction" is therefore very misleading indeed. If courts try to be faithful to the text of the Constitution, they will for that very reason be forced to decide between competing conceptions of political morality. So it is wrong to attack the Warren Court, for example, on the ground that it failed to treat the Constitution as a binding text. On the contrary, if we wish to treat fidelity to that text as an overriding requirement of constitutional interpretation, then it is the conservative critics of the Warren Court who are at fault, because their philosophy ignores the direction to face issues of moral principle that the logic of the text demands.

I put the matter in a guarded way because we may *not* want to accept fidelity to the spirit of the text as an overriding principle of constitutional adjudication. It may be more important for courts to decide constitutional cases in a manner that respects the judgments of other institutions of government, for example. Or it may be more important for courts to protect established legal doctrines, so that citizens and the government can have confidence that the courts will hold to what they have said before. But it is crucial to recognize that these other policies compete with the principle that the Constitution is the fundamental and imperative source of constitutional law. They are not, as the "strict constructionists" suppose, simply consequences of that principle.

3.

Once the matter is put in this light, moreover, we are able to assess these competing claims of policy, free from the confusion imposed by the popular notion of "strict construction". For this purpose I want now to compare and contrast two very general philosophies of how the courts should decide difficult or controversial constitutional issues. I shall call these two philosophies by the names they are given in the legal literature – the programs of "judicial activism" and "judicial restraint" – though it will be plain that these names are in certain ways misleading.

The program of judicial activism holds that courts should accept the directions of the so-called vague constitutional provisions in the spirit I described, in spite of competing reasons of the sort I mentioned. They should work out principles of legality, equality, and the rest, revise these principles from time to time in the light of what seems to the Court fresh moral insight, and judge the acts of Congress, the states, and the President accordingly. (This puts the program in its strongest form; in fact its supporters generally qualify it in ways I shall ignore for the present.)

The program of judicial restraint, on the contrary, argues that courts should allow the decisions of other branches of government to stand, even when they offend the judges' own sense of the principles required by the broad constitutional doctrines, except when these decisions are so offensive to political morality that they would violate the provisions on any plausible interpretation, or, perhaps, when a contrary decision is required by clear precedent. (Again, this put the program in a stark form; those who profess the policy qualify it in different ways.)

The Supreme Court followed the policy of activism rather than restraint in cases like the segregation cases because the words of the equal protection clause left it open whether the various educational practices of the states concerned should be taken to violate the Constitution, no clear precedent held that they did, and reasonable men might differ on the moral issues involved. If the Court had followed the program of judicial restraint, it would therefore have held in favor of the North Carolina statute in *Swann*, not against it. But the program of restraint would not always act to provide decisions that would please political conservatives. In the early days of the New Deal, as critics of the Warren Court are quick to point out, it was the liberals who objected to Court decisions that struck down acts of Congress in the name of the due process clause.

It may seem, therefore, that if Nixon has a legal theory it depends crucially on some theory of judicial restraint. We must now, however, notice a distinction between two forms of judicial restraint, for there are two different, and indeed incompatible, grounds on which that policy might be based.

The first is a theory of political *skepticism* that might be described in this way. The policy of judicial activism presupposes a certain objectivity of moral principle; in particular it presupposes that citizens do have certain moral rights against the state, like a moral right to equality of public education or to fair treatment by the police. Only if such moral rights exist in some sense can activism be justified as a program based on something beyond the judge's personal preferences. The skeptical theory attacks activism at its roots; it argues that in fact individuals have no such moral rights against the state. They have only such *legal* rights as the Constitution grants them, and these are limited to the plain and uncontroversial violations of public morality that the framers must have had actually in mind, or that have since been established in a line of precedent.

The alternative ground of a program of restraint is a theory of judicial *deference*. Contrary to the skeptical theory, this assumes that citizens do have moral rights against the state beyond what the law expressly grants them, but it points out that the character and strength of these rights are debatable and argues that political institutions other than courts are responsible for deciding which rights are to be recognized.

This is an important distinction, even though the literature of constitutional law does not draw it with any clarity. The skeptical theory and the theory of deference differ dramatically in the kind of justification they assume, and in their implications for the more general moral theories of the men who profess to hold them. These theories are so different that most American politicians can consistently accept the second, but not the first.

A skeptic takes a view, as I have said, that men have no moral rights against the state and only such legal rights as the law expressly provides. But what does this mean, and what sort of argument might the skeptic make for his view? There is, of course, a very lively dispute in moral philosophy about the nature and standing of moral rights, and considerable disagreement about what they are, if they are anything at all. I shall rely, in trying to answer these questions, on a low-keyed theory of moral rights against the state [...]. Under that theory, a man has a moral right against the state if for some reason the state would do wrong to treat him in a certain way, even though it would be in the general interest to do so. So a black child has a moral right to an equal education, for example, if it is wrong for the state not to provide that education, even if the community as a whole suffers thereby.

I want to say a word about the virtues of this way of looking at moral rights against the state. A great many lawyers are wary of talking about moral rights, even though they find it easy to talk about what is right or wrong for government to do, because they suppose that rights, if they exist at all, are spooky sorts of things that men and women have in much the same way as they have non-spooky things like tonsils. But the sense of rights I propose to use does not make ontological assumptions of that sort: it simply shows a claim of right to be a special, in the sense of a restricted, sort of judgment about what is right or wrong for governments to do.

Moreover, this way of looking at rights avoids some of the notorious puzzles associated with the concept. It allows us to say, with no sense of strangeness, that rights may vary in strength and character from case to case, and from point to point in history. If we think of rights as things, these metamorphoses seem strange, but we are used to the idea that moral judgments about what it is right or wrong to do are complex and are affected by considerations that are relative and that change.

The skeptic who wants to argue against the very possibility of rights against the state of this sort has a difficult brief. He must rely, I think, on one of three general positions: (a) He might display a more pervasive moral skepticism, which holds

that even to speak of an act being morally right or wrong makes no sense. If no act is morally wrong, then the government of North Carolina cannot be wrong to refuse to bus school children. (b) He might hold a stark form of utilitarianism, which assumes that the only reason we ever have for regarding an act as right or wrong is its impact on the general interest. Under that theory, to say that busing may be morally required even though it does not benefit the community generally would be inconsistent. (c) He might accept some form of totalitarian theory, which merges the interests of the individual in the good of the general community, and so denies that the two can conflict.

Very few American politicians would be able to accept any of these three grounds. Nixon, for example, could not, because he presents himself as a moral fundamentalist who knows in his heart that pornography is wicked and that some of the people of South Vietnam have rights of self-determination in the name of which they and we may properly kill many others.

I do not want to suggest, however, that no one would in fact argue for judicial restraint on grounds of skepticism; on the contrary, some of the best known advocates of restraint have pitched their arguments entirely on skeptical grounds. In 1957, for example, the great judge Learned Hand delivered the Oliver Wendell Holmes Lectures at Harvard. Hand was a student of Santayana and a disciple of Holmes, and skepticism in morals was his only religion. He argued for judicial restraint, and said that the Supreme Court had done wrong to declare school segregation illegal in the *Brown* case. It is wrong to suppose, he said, that claims about moral rights express anything more than the speakers' preferences. If the Supreme Court justifies its decisions by making such claims, rather than by relying on positive law, it is usurping the place of the legislature, for the job of the legislature, representing the majority, is to decide whose preferences shall govern.

This simple appeal to democracy is successful if one accepts the skeptical premise. Of course, if men have no rights against the majority, if political decision is simply a matter of whose preferences shall prevail, then democracy does provide a good reason for leaving that decision to more democratic institutions than courts, even when these institutions make choices that the judges themselves hate. But a very different, and much more vulnerable, argument from democracy is needed to support judicial restraint if it is based not on skepticism but on deference, as I shall try to show.

4.

If Nixon holds a coherent constitutional theory, it is a theory of restraint based not on skepticism but on deference. He believes that courts ought not to decide controversial issues of political morality because they ought to leave such decisions to other departments of government. If we ascribe this policy to Nixon, we can make sense of his charge that the Warren Court "twisted and bent" the law. He would mean that they twisted and bent the principle of judicial deference, which is an understatement, because he would be more accurate if he said that they ignored it. But are there any good reasons for holding this policy of deference? If the policy is in fact unsound, then Nixon's jurisprudence is undermined, and he ought to be dissuaded from urging further Supreme Court appointments, or encouraging Congress to oppose the Court, in its name.

There is one very popular argument in favor of the policy of deference, which might be called the argument from democracy. It is at least debatable, according to this argument, whether a sound conception of equality forbids segregated education or requires measures like busing to break it down. Who ought to decide these debatable issues of moral and political theory? Should it be a majority of a court in Washington, whose members are appointed for life and are not politically responsible to the public whose lives will be affected by the decision? Or should it be the elected and responsible state or national legislators? A democrat, so this argument supposes, can accept only the second answer.

But the argument from democracy is weaker than it might first appear. The argument assumes, for one thing, that state legislatures are in fact responsible to the people in the way that democratic theory assumes. But in all the states, though in different degrees and for different reasons, that is not the case. In some states it

is very far from the case. I want to pass that point, however, because it does not so much undermine the argument from democracy as call for more democracy, and that is a different matter. I want to fix attention on the issue of whether the appeal to democracy in this respect is even right in principle.

The argument assumes that in a democracy all unsettled issues, including issues of moral and political principle, must be resolved only by institutions that are politically responsible in the way that courts are not. Why should we accept that view of democracy? To say that that is what democracy means does no good, because it is wrong to suppose that the word, as a word, has anything like so precise a meaning. Even if it did, we should then have to rephrase our question to ask why we should have democracy, if we assume that is what it means. Nor is it better to say that that view of democracy is established in the American Constitution, or so entrenched in our political tradition that we are committed to it. We cannot argue that the Constitution, which provides no rule limiting judicial review to clear cases, establishes a theory of democracy that excludes wider review, nor can we say that our courts have in fact consistently accepted such a restriction. The burden of Nixon's argument is that they have.

So the argument from democracy is not an argument to which we are committed either by our words or our past. We must accept it, if at all, on the strength of its own logic. In order to examine the arguments more closely, however, we must make a further distinction. The argument as I have set it out might be continued in two different ways: one might argue that judicial deference is required because democratic institutions, like legislatures, are in fact likely to make sounder decisions than courts about the underlying issues that constitutional cases raise, that is, about the nature of an individual's moral rights against the state.

Or one might argue that it is for some reason fairer that a democratic institution rather than a court should decide such issues, even though there is no reason to believe that the institution will reach a sounder decision. The distinction between these two arguments would make no sense to a skeptic, who would not admit that someone could do a better or worse job at identifying moral rights against the state, any more than someone could do a better or worse job of identifying ghosts. But a lawyer who believes in judicial deference rather than skepticism must acknowledge the distinction, though he can argue both sides if he wishes.

I shall start with the second argument, that legislatures and other democratic institutions have some special title to make constitutional decisions, apart from their ability to make better decisions. One might say that the nature of this title is obvious, because it is always fairer to allow a majority to decide any issue than a minority. But that, as has often been pointed out, ignores the fact that decisions about rights against the majority are not issues that in fairness ought to be left to the majority. Constitutionalism – the theory that the majority must be restrained to protect individual rights – may be a good or bad political theory, but the United States has adopted that theory, and to make the majority judge in its own cause seems inconsistent and unjust. So principles of fairness seem to speak against, not for, the argument from democracy.

Chief Justice Marshall recognized this in his decision in *Marbury v. Madison*, the famous case in which the Supreme Court first claimed the power to review legislative decisions against constitutional standards. He argued that since the Constitution provides that the Constitution shall be the supreme law of the land, the courts in general, and the Supreme Court in the end, must have power to declare statutes void that offend that Constitution. Many legal scholars regard his argument as a *non sequitur*, because, they say, although constitutional constraints are part of the law, the courts, rather than the legislature itself, have not necessarily been given authority to decide whether in particular cases that law has been violated.[2] But the argument is not a *non sequitur* if we take the principle that no man should be judge in his own cause to be so fundamental a part of the idea of legality that Marshall would have been entitled to disregard it only if the Constitution had expressly denied judicial review.

Some might object that it is simple-minded to say that a policy of deference leaves the majority to judge its own cause. Political decisions are made, in the United States, not by one stable majority but by many different political institutions each representing a different constituency which itself changes its composition over time. The decision of one branch of government may well be reviewed by another branch that is also politically responsible, but to a larger or different constituency. The acts of the Arizona police which the Court held unconstitutional in *Miranda*, for example, were in fact subject to review by various executive boards and municipal and state legislatures of Arizona, as well as by the national Congress. It would be naïve to suppose that all of these political institutions are dedicated to the same policies and interests, so it is wrong to suppose that if the Court had not intervened the Arizona police would have been free to judge themselves.

But this objection is itself too glib, because it ignores the special character of disputes about individual moral rights as distinct from other kinds of political disputes. Different institutions do have different constituencies when, for example, labor or trade or welfare issues are involved, and the nation often divides sectionally on such issues. But this is not generally the case when individual constitutional rights, like the rights of accused criminals, are at issue. It has been typical of these disputes that the interests of those in political control of the various institutions of the government have been both homogeneous and hostile. Indeed that is why political theorists have conceived of constitutional rights as rights against the "state" or the "majority" as such, rather than against any particular body or branch of government.

The early segregation cases are perhaps exceptions to that generality, for one might argue that the only people who wanted *de jure* segregation were white Southerners. But the fact remains that the national Congress had not in fact checked segregation, either because it believed it did not have the legal power to do so or because it did not want to; in either case the example hardly argues that the political process provides an effective check on even local violations of the rights of politically ineffective minorities. In the dispute over busing, moreover, the white majority mindful of its own interests has proved to be both national and powerful. And of course decisions of the national government, like executive decisions to wage war or congressional attempts to define proper police policy, as in the

Crime Control Act of 1968, are subject to no review if not court review.

It does seem fair to say, therefore, that the argument from democracy asks that those in political power be invited to be the sole judge of their own decisions, to see whether they have the right to do what they have decided they want to do. That is not a final proof that a policy of judicial activism is superior to a program of deference. Judicial activism involves risks of tyranny; certainly in the stark and simple form I set out. It might even be shown that these risks override the unfairness of asking the majority to be judge in its own cause. But the point does undermine the argument that the majority, in fairness, must be allowed to decide the limits of its own power.

We must therefore turn to the other continuation of the argument from democracy, which holds that democratic institutions, like legislatures, are likely to reach *sounder* results about the moral rights of individuals than would courts. In 1969 the late Professor Alexander Bickel of the Yale Law School delivered his Holmes Lectures at Harvard and argued for the program of judicial restraint in a novel and ingenious way. He allowed himself to suppose, for purposes of argument, that the Warren Court's program of activism could be justified if in fact it produced desirable results.[3] He appeared, therefore, to be testing the policy of activism on its own grounds, because he took activism to be precisely the claim that the courts have the moral right to improve the future, whatever legal theory may say. Learned Hand and other opponents of activism had challenged that claim. Bickel accepted it, at least provisionally, but he argued that activism fails its own test.

The future that the Warren Court sought has already begun not to work, Bickel said. The philosophy of racial integration it adopted was too crude, for example, and has already been rejected by the more imaginative leaders of the black community. Its thesis of simple and radical equality has proved unworkable in many other ways as well; its simple formula of one-man-one-vote for passing on the fairness of election districting, for instance, has produced neither sense nor fairness.

Why should a radical Court that aims at improving society fail even on its own terms? Bickel has this answer: Courts, including the Supreme Court, must decide blocks of cases on principle, rather than responding in a piecemeal way to a shifting set of political pressures. They must do so not simply because their institutional morality requires it, but because their institutional structure provides no means by which they might gauge political forces even if they wanted to. But government by principle is an inefficient and in the long run fatal form of government, no matter how able and honest the statesmen who try to administer it. For there is a limit to the complexity that any principle can contain and remain a recognizable principle, and this limit falls short of the complexity of social organization.

The Supreme Court's reapportionment decisions, in Bickel's view, were not mistaken just because the Court chose the wrong principle. One-man-one-vote is too simple, but the Court could not have found a better, more sophisticated principle that would have served as a successful test for election districting across the country, or across the years, because successful districting depends upon accommodation with thousands of facts of political life, and can be reached, if at all, only by the chaotic and unprincipled development of history. Judicial activism cannot work as well as government by the more-or-less democratic institutions, not because democracy is required by principle, but, on the contrary, because democracy works without principle, forming institutions and compromises as a river forms a bed on its way to the sea.

What are we to make of Bickel's argument? His account of recent history can be, and has been, challenged. It is by no means plain, certainly not yet, that racial integration will fail as a long-term strategy; and he is wrong if he thinks that black Americans, of whom more still belong to the NAACP than to more militant organizations, have rejected it. No doubt the nation's sense of how to deal with the curse of racism swings back and forth as the complexity and size of the problem become more apparent, but Bickel may have written at a high point of one arc of the pendulum.

He is also wrong to judge the Supreme Court's effect on history as if the Court were the only institution at work, or to suppose that if the Court's goal has not been achieved the country is worse off than if it had not tried. Since 1954, when the Court laid down the principle that equality before the law requires integrated education, we have not had, except for a few years of the Johnson Administration, a national executive willing to accept that principle as an imperative. For the past several years we have had a national executive that seems determined to undermine it. Nor do we have much basis for supposing that the racial situation in America would now be more satisfactory, on balance, if the Court had not intervened, in 1954 and later, in the way that it did.

But there is a very different, and for my purpose much more important, objection to take to Bickel's theory. His theory is novel because it appears to concede an issue of principle to judicial activism, namely, that the Court is entitled to intervene if its intervention produces socially desirable results. But the concession is an illusion, because his sense of what is socially desirable is inconsistent with the presupposition of activism that individuals have moral rights against the state. In fact, Bickel's argument cannot succeed, even if we grant his facts and his view of history, except on a basis of a skepticism about rights as profound as Learned Hand's.

I presented Bickel's theory as an example of one form of the argument from democracy, the argument that since men disagree about rights, it is safer to leave the final decision about rights to the political process, safer in the sense that the results are likely to be sounder. Bickel suggests a reason why the political process is safer. He argues that the endurance of a political settlement about rights is some evidence of the political morality of that settlement. He argues that this evidence is better than the sorts of argument from principle that judges might deploy if the decision were left to them.

There is a weak version of this claim, which cannot be part of Bickel's argument. This version argues that no political principle establishing rights can be sound, whatever abstract arguments might be made in its favor, unless it meets the test of social acceptance in the long run; so that, for example, the Supreme Court cannot be right in its views about the rights of black children, or criminal suspects, or atheists, if the community in the end will not be persuaded to recognize these rights.

This weak version may seem plausible for different reasons. It will appeal, for instance, to those who believe both in the fact and in the strength of the ordinary man's moral sense, and in his willingness to entertain appeals to that sense. But it does not argue for judicial restraint except in the very long run. On the contrary, it supposes what lawyers are fond of calling a dialogue between the judges and the nation, in which the Supreme Court is to present and defend its reflective view of what the citizen's rights are, much as the Warren Court tried to do, in the hope that the people will in the end agree.

We must turn, therefore, to the strong version of the claim. This argues that the organic political process will secure the genuine rights of men more certainly if it is not hindered by the artificial and rationalistic intrusion of the courts. On this view, the rights of blacks, suspects, and atheists will emerge through the process of political institutions responding to political pressures in the normal way. If a claim of right cannot succeed in this way, then for that reason it is, or in any event it is likely to be, an improper claim of right. But this bizarre proposition is only a disguised form of the skeptical point that there are in fact no rights against the state.

Perhaps, as Burke and his modern followers argue, a society will produce the institutions that best suit it only by evolution and never by radical reform. But rights against the state are claims that, if accepted, require society to settle for institutions that may not suit it so comfortably. The nerve of a claim of right, even on the demythologized analysis of rights I am using, is that an individual is entitled to protection against the majority even at the cost of the general interest. Of course the comfort of the majority will require some accommodation for minorities but only to the extent necessary to preserve order; and that is usually an accommodation that falls short of recognizing their rights.

Indeed the suggestion that rights can be demonstrated by a process of history rather than by an appeal to principle shows either a confusion or no real concern about what rights are. A claim of right presupposes a moral argument and can be established in no other way. Bickel paints the judicial activists (and even some of the heroes of judicial restraint, like Brandeis and Frankfurter, who had their lapses) as eighteenth-century philosophers who appeal to principle because they hold the optimistic view that a blueprint may be cut for progress. But this picture confuses two grounds for the appeal to principle and reform, and two senses of progress.

It is one thing to appeal to moral principle in the silly faith that ethics as well as economics moves by an invisible hand, so that individual rights and the general good will coalesce, and law based on principle will move the nation to a frictionless utopia where everyone is better off than he was before. Bickel attacks that vision by his appeal to history, and by his other arguments against government by principle. But it is quite another matter to appeal to principle *as* principle, to show, for example, that it is unjust to force black children to take their public education in black schools, even if a great many people *will* be worse off if the state adopt the measures needed to prevent this.

This is a different version of progress. It is moral progress, and though history may show how difficult it is to decide where moral progress lies, and how difficult to persuade others once one has decided, it cannot follow from this that those who govern us have no responsibility to face that decision or to attempt that persuasion.

5.

This has been a complex argument, and I want to summarize it. Our constitutional system rests on a particular moral theory, namely, that men have moral rights against the state. The difficult clauses of the Bill of Rights, like the due process and equal protection clauses, must be understood as appealing to moral concepts rather than laying down particular conceptions; therefore a court that undertakes the burden of applying these clauses fully as law must be an activist court, in the sense that it must be prepared to frame and answer questions of political morality.

It may be necessary to compromise that activist posture to some extent, either for practical reasons or for competing reasons of principle. But Nixon's public statements about the Supreme Court suggest that the activist policy must be abandoned altogether, and not merely compromised, for powerful reasons of principle. If we

try to state these reasons of principle, we find that they are inconsistent with the assumption of a constitutional system, either because they leave the majority to judge its own cause, or because they rest on a skepticism about moral rights that neither Nixon nor most American politicians can consistently embrace.

So Nixon's jurisprudence is a pretense and no genuine theory at all. It cannot be supported by arguments he can accept, let alone by arguments he has advanced. Nixon abused his legal credentials by endorsing an incoherent philosophy of law and by calling into question the good faith of other lawyers because they do not accept what he cannot defend.

The academic debate about the Supreme Court's power of judicial review must, however, have contributed to Nixon's confusion. The failure to draw the distinctions I have described, between appealing to a concept and laying down a conception, and between skepticism and deference, has posed a false choice between judicial activism as the program of moral crusade and judicial restraint as the program of legality. Why has a sophisticated and learned profession posed a complex issue in this simple and misleading way?

The issue at the heart of the academic debate might be put this way. If we give the decisions of principle that the Constitution requires to the judges, instead of to the people, we act in the spirit of legality, so far as our institutions permit. But we run a risk that the judges may make the wrong decisions. Every lawyer thinks that the Supreme Court has gone wrong, even violently wrong, at some point in its career. If he does not hate the conservative decisions of the early 1930s, which threatened to block the New Deal, he is likely to hate the liberal decisions of the last decade.

We must not exaggerate the danger. Truly unpopular decisions will be eroded because public compliances will be grudging, as it has been in the case of public school prayers, and because old judges will die or retire and be replaced by new judges appointed because they agree with a President who has been elected by the people. The decisions against the New Deal did not stand, and the more daring decisions of recent years are now at the mercy of the Nixon Court. Nor does the danger of wrong decisions lie entirely on the side of excess; the failure of the Court to act in the McCarthy period, epitomized by its shameful decision upholding the legality of the Smith Act in the *Dennis* case, may be thought to have done more harm to the nation than did the Court's conservative bias in the early Roosevelt period.

Still, we ought to design our institutions to reduce the risk of error, so far as this is possible. But the academic debate has so far failed to produce an adequate account of where error lies. For the activists, the segregation decisions were right because they advanced a social goal they think desirable, or they were wrong because they advanced a social goal they dislike. For the advocates of restraint they were wrong, whether they approve or disapprove that social goal, because they violated the principle that the Court is not entitled to impose its own view of the social good on the nation.

Neither of these tests forces lawyers to face the special sort of moral issue I described earlier, the issue of what moral rights an individual has against the state. The activists rest their case, when they argue it at all, on the assumption either that their social goals are self-evidently good or that they will in the long run work for the benefit of everybody; this optimism exposes them to Bickel's argument that this is not necessarily so. Those who want restraint argue that some principle of legality protects constitutional lawyers from facing any moral issues at all.

Constitutional law can make no genuine advance until it isolates the problem of rights against the state and makes that problem part of its own agenda. That argues for a fusion of constitutional law and moral theory, a connection that, incredibly, has yet to take place. It is perfectly understandable that lawyers dread contamination with moral philosophy, and particularly with those philosophers who talk about rights, because the spooky overtones of that concept threaten the graveyard of reason. But better philosophy is now available than the lawyers may remember. Professor Rawls of Harvard, for example, has published an abstract and complex book about justice which no constitutional lawyer will be able to ignore.[4] There is no need for lawyers to play a passive role in the development of a theory of moral rights against the state, however, any more than they have been passive in the development of legal sociology and legal economics. They must recognize that law is no more independent from philosophy than it is from these other disciplines.

Notes

1   It is less misleading to say that the broad clauses of the Constitution "delegate" power to the Court to enforce its own conceptions of political morality. But even this is inaccurate if it suggests that the Court need not justify its conception by arguments showing the connections between its conception and standard cases, as described in the text. If the Court finds that the death penalty is cruel, it must do so on the basis of some principles or groups of principles that unite the death penalty with the thumbscrew and the rack.

2   I distinguish this objection to Marshall's argument from the different objection, not here relevant, that the Constitution should be interpreted to impose a legal *duty* on Congress not, for example, to pass laws abridging freedom of speech, but it should not be interpreted to detract from the legal *power* of Congress to make such a law valid if it breaks its duty. In this view, Congress is in the legal position of a thief who has a legal duty not to sell stolen goods, but retains legal power to make a valid transfer if he does. This interpretation has little to recommend it since Congress, unlike the thief, cannot be disciplined except by denying validity to its wrongful acts, at least in a way that will offer protection to the individuals the Constitution is designed to protect.

3   Professor Bickel also argued, with his usual very great skill, that many of the Warren Court's major decisions could not even be justified on conventional grounds, that is, by the arguments the Court advanced in its opinions. His criticism of these opinions is often persuasive, but the Court's failures of craftsmanship do not affect the argument I consider in the text. (His Holmes lectures were amplified in his book *The Supreme Court and the Idea of Progress*, 1970.)

4   *A Theory of Justice*, 1971 – see Chapter 6.

53

Does the Constitution Mean
What It Always Meant?

Stephen R. Munzer and James W. Nickel

Introduction

One does not have to dig very deeply into the
literature of American constitutional law to
suspect that many constitutional provisions do
not mean today what their framers thought they
meant.[1] This mutability of constitutional norms
is not surprising; the document is nearly two
centuries old, has few formal amendments, and
was framed in a different social and political
age. The Constitution has remained vital largely
because its provisions have proved adaptable
to the changing needs of a developing society.
It does not mean what it always meant.[2] But this
phenomenon of constitutional change raises a
number of perplexing questions. How can the
Constitution change when the text and the intentions of its framers remain static? What are the
methods of constitutional change short of formal
amendment? When and how should such change
occur?

This Article attempts to develop an account
of constitutional change that addresses these
questions. It presents our Constitution as a text-
based institutional practice. It thus is opposed
to theories, like the "historical approach,"[3]
which see the Constitution simply as an original

text together with an accretion of historically
correct interpretations, and to theories like Karl
Llewellyn's,[4] which see it as just a complicated
institution. No progress can be made in understanding what the Constitution is unless we
recognize that our constitutional system is a
unique, intricate product of text and institutional
practice and that the notions of "meaning," "interpretation," and "fidelity" to the Constitution must
reflect that duality.

In Part I, we examine three established theories of constitutional interpretation and change
and identify the deficiencies of each. In Part II,
we propose a more adequate theory. Analytically,
our account tries to explain informally what it
is, in terms of the philosophy of language, for the
"meaning" of the Constitution to change, and how
various models must be used to understand that
change. Recognizing such change, the account
analyzes patterns of judicial innovation, the nature
of constitutional "interpretations" and "fidelity"
to the Constitution, and the criteria for being part
of our constitutional law. The normative part of
our account is an attempt, not to develop a set
of principles for generating results in concrete
cases, but to show how the functions of the
Constitution help establish when constitutional

Stephen R. Munzer and James W. Nickel, "Does the Constitution Mean What It Always Meant?" *Columbia Law Review*,
vol. 77, no. 7, November 1977, pp. 1029–62. © 1977 by Columbia Law Review Association, Inc. Reproduced with permission of Columbia Law Review Association, Inc. in the format Textbook via Copyright Clearance Center.

change is proper and who should make it. It thus seeks to locate the boundaries of constitutional argument within that part of political theory referred to as constitutionalism.

I. Three Theories of the Constitution and its Development

A. The historical approach

The historical approach to constitutional interpretation regards the words and intent of the authors of the Constitution as the sole source of constitutional law.[5] Under this approach, the Constitution is to be interpreted in the same manner as any other historical text. One looks to the intent of the authors and to the textual language as understood at the time the document was drafted. One may also rely on prior interpretations provided they comport with the words and intent of the framers. Most versions of the historical approach would permit one, in hard cases, to appeal to a broad conception of intent and to conjecture about what the framers would have decided had they faced a certain issue, even though they did not or could not have actually done so. The important point, however, is that the original meaning of a constitutional provision must always be controlling.

The historical approach has several seemingly powerful points in its favor. It explains the preoccupation of lawyers with the language of the document and the prominence of the search for original understandings – two features of our constitutional practice that, for brevity, we shall call the "textual focus." Furthermore, it may seem that since the authors of the Constitution proposed, and the people accepted, a certain document as the supreme law of the land, what was meant at that time should still be legally controlling. Lastly, the idea that a written document can, apart from amendments, change in its meaning or content may seem incoherent.

There are, however, decisive grounds for rejecting the historical approach. Analytically, it cannot account for the actual extent of change in our constitutional law. While it is true that the meaning of a term ("connotation") can remain constant even though the objects to which it applies ("denotation") may change,[6] this simple distinction is not helpful when new items included under a term are significantly dissimilar from those previously recognized.[7] It is also true that conjectures invoking the broad intent of the framers are permitted by the historical approach. But the reliability and fecundity of such conjectures should not be overestimated. Even if we can establish that the goal of the authors of, say, the first amendment, was to ensure that public issues could be fully and freely discussed, this provides us with little guidance in balancing this goal against competing goals such as ensuring public security,[8] or in dealing with nonpolitical literature.[9] Moreover, many important doctrinal developments cannot plausibly be accommodated by this method of analysis. It is, for example, most doubtful that the use of the equal protection clause to bar many forms of nonracial discrimination[10] can be justified by an appeal to the intentions of the authors of that clause.

If one seeks to avoid this conclusion by appealing to the *very* broad intent of the framers – for example, by imputing to them a desire to create a just society – serious problems arise. One is that claims about such broad goals are apt to be at best weakly supported by the historical evidence. Hence it will be difficult to know whether the justices are carrying out the will of the framers or deciding on other grounds. In addition, such appeals to very broad intent can easily serve as masks for judicial decision-making based solely on judges' perceptions of desirable social goals. It is therefore doubtful that any "historical approach" can produce large amounts of new constitutional doctrine that is any different in practice from a straightforward policy-oriented approach.

The normative deficiencies of the historical approach are even more striking. First, a constitutional system that makes formal amendments very difficult and does not allow for gradual change through interpretation is likely to become rigid and out-of-date. If one accepts that change in governmental structures is inevitable and often desirable, provision must be made for such change.

Second, strict reliance on the historical approach would require us to abandon – or at least to regard as mistaken while continuing to follow – large parts of current constitutional doctrine. As has been argued in detail by Professor Thomas

C. Grey,[11] numerous developments in our constitutional law cannot plausibly be justified in terms of original understandings. To many it would be unacceptable, for example, to retrench the protections of privacy and equality afforded by expansive interpretations of the Bill of Rights. And even those not enamoured of the work of the recent Court may perhaps concede that a great deal of doctrinal and social disruption would result if one were to turn back the clock.

Third, the nature of historical materials and the uses judges can make of them create serious problems for the historical approach. Foremost among these is the likelihood that the historical materials will be incomplete, inaccurate, or conflicting.[12] In addition, the intentions of individuals are notoriously difficult to ascertain, and it is especially difficult to identify the intentions of a large *group* such as the authors of the Constitution.[13] Even when there might be sufficient evidence for an expert historian to arrive at a clear result, a judge may not be equipped to do so or to evaluate another's claim to have done so. Moreover, given the difficulty of securing amendments, practitioners of the historical approach may, consciously or subconsciously, be moved to use slanted or fabricated history to justify results they favor on other grounds.[14] This procedure may lead to acceptable results in particular cases, but its misuse of historical materials might hinder critical examination of the real reasons for the decision and lead to doctrinal distortions to be contended with in the future. Of course, any procedure involving the assessment of evidence is vulnerable to error and mishandling; the point is that the risks are exacerbated with historical evidence because judges are not trained historians and operate under pressures that may deflect them from historically generated results. Furthermore, it should be noted that there is a special danger in allowing a controversial case to turn on an historical claim if the claim is not beyond dispute. Since good historical research is not within the competence of most judges, the antecedent probability of mistakes is high. This increases the chances that professional historians will challenge and refute the Court's reading of history, thus undermining the basis, or ostensible basis, for the decision.[15]

A fourth normative difficulty with the historical approach is that the original intent, even when it can be determined by judges, will sometimes be unpersuasive. Because conditions have changed greatly since the Constitution was written, we should expect that some of the results and rationales for decisions generated by a historical interpretation will be unappealing. It is not clear why the will of the people of two hundred years ago should, aside from the wisdom that will contains, completely control our constitutional practices today. The current authoritativeness of original understandings depends in part on the strength of the framers' reasons for their choices and the applicability of those reasons today.

B. Institutional theories

When one recognizes the deficiencies of the historical approach, a natural reaction is to view the Constitution as part of the practice of ongoing government. A theory reflecting this view is presented in an important but neglected essay by Karl Llewellyn.[16] It is part of a legal realist program which emphasizes patterns of official behavior and discounts the significance of legal rules or verbal formulations of the law.[17] Llewellyn opposes his theory to what is in effect a version of the historical approach.[18] He argues that although some current practices can trace their roots to the text, many changes in constitutional doctrine since 1789 are so sweeping that it is impossible to represent them as textual interpretations.[19] For him, "[w]hat is left, and living, is not a code, but an *institution*."[20]

Llewellyn's theory is elaborated as follows: An "institution" is a set of patterns of behavior, partly similar and partly complementary and competing, among a group of people. That institution which we call the Constitution involves the activities of interested groups and the general public as well as those directly concerned with governing.[21] The Constitution is not, however, the entirety of this behavior but only its *fundamental* part. More precisely, it consists of those regular practices which resist easy change and which have some important function in governmental operations.[22] Nevertheless, no hard and fast line can be drawn between the Constitution and "mere working government"; there will be penumbral patterns of behavior which cannot be firmly placed on either side. Still, it is possible to say that practices such as political patronage and conference committees in Congress are definitely part of the Constitution, while affairs such as the Inaugural Ball are not.[23] Thus "it is not essential that [a] practice . . . be in any way related to the Document"[24] to be part of the Constitution.

Much in Llewellyn's account is genuinely illuminating. In particular it was an achievement to show how institutional practices could affect our constitutional law. Yet Llewellyn's insights are contaminated by mistaken assumptions in two respects. First, he assumes that if rules or constitutional provisions do not give utterly plain and easily applicable guidance, they give no guidance worth the name.[25] Since few provisions give clear-cut answers to particular problems, he writes off much judicial interpretation as legerdemain.[26] Llewellyn's critique, however, holds only against a very formalistic conception of legal rules, and overlooks the fact that constitutional rules, though rarely completely clear, are as a general matter sufficiently informative to shape behavior.[27] A judge might try to apply the cruel and unusual punishment clause by turning in part to linguistic and conceptual analyses of cruelty as well as by looking at prior decisions. Once constitutional rules and language are seen in this light, it becomes less plausible to assert, as Llewellyn implies, that our constitutional law often has only a fleeting connection with the text and its interpretations.

Llewellyn's second mistaken assumption is that *fundamentality* of institutional practice is the touchstone of what is constitutional, but in fact this criterion spawns several counterintuitive results. One is that some clear mandates of the constitutional text, such as the prohibition of titles of nobility,[28] would not be considered part of the Constitution because they are not basic to the workings of the government. Another is that some matters fundamental to government would be regarded as having constitutional status even though they do not. Examples include political patronage and conference committees as well as major regulatory statutes such as the federal antitrust laws.[29] It is plainly a mistake to elevate these items to the same class as the power to declare war or the guarantee of freedom of speech. A final counterintuitive result is that all fundamental institutional practices are in Llewellyn's account seen as vulnerable to or insulated from change in the same way, namely,

through alteration in or maintenance of the behavior patterns of those involved in government. However, matters that we regard as having constitutional status generally exhibit a different sort of entrenchment from other practices. If a matter is constitutional, then its abrogation typically is an appropriate subject for formal amendment and not for statutory change. Thus abolition of Congress's power to declare war could be made by formal amendment, though one might allow that this could be changed in other ways as well. In contrast, the elimination of political patronage or conference committees would not be appropriate for the formal amendment process; for these matters a statute would be ample.[30]

It may be replied that these criticisms of Llewellyn turn merely on different senses of the word "constitution." In Llewellyn's sense, the results detailed above are not counterintuitive but just obvious consequences of his theory. This reply may have some surface plausibility, yet we do not think that the issues posed by constitutional change can be adequately confronted if they are seen as merely involving the proprieties of, or irresolvable differences between, linguistic usage. For what is ultimately at stake is the best way of accounting for and formulating prescriptions in regard to an important range of legal phenomena. If so, it is a disadvantage of Llewellyn's theory that it does little to elucidate the textual focus of our constitutional law and that it seems committed to the normative proposition that there is no particular reason why the text and its meaning should figure importantly in constitutional decision-making.

If the defects of Llewellyn's theory stem in large measure from his rejection of the textual focus, it is in order to consider what might be viewed as an attempt by Professor Charles A. Miller to overcome them by combining the historical and institutional approaches.[31] Miller distinguishes between a *Constitution*, which is "a formal written document describing a pattern of legal rules and institutions that function for political purposes," and a *constitution*, which is "a pattern of political relationships which may be, but need not be, defined in legal instruments."[32] Miller suggests that the United States has both a Constitution and a constitution.[33] The textual focus of our constitutional practice relates to the former,[34] and Miller appears to think that the meaning of the Constitution is static.[35] Nevertheless, growth and development can occur because the United States "Constitution" is narrower than its "constitution," and the political relationships which constitute the latter can change. Thus, "should it be insisted that a written document must stay the same, it is the constitution rather than the Constitution of the United States that changes."[36]

Miller's position is in one respect an improvement on Llewellyn's, since he recognizes the importance of the text in our constitutional practice. But his theory is flawed in that it fails to challenge Llewellyn's unsupported assumption that the meaning of the constitutional document cannot change without formal amendment. Moreover, Miller fails to show how the immutable Constitution embodied in the document is related to the protean "constitution" comprising our political institutions. Thus it is impossible to be certain which notion would prevail, in Miller's view, when they yielded contradictory results in particular instances. One must suspect, however, that Miller's homage to the textual focus is ultimately mere lip-service, since the rules of our living political institutions would apparently prevail in his eyes over the precepts of an ancient document.

C. Dworkin on concepts and conceptions

An attempt to avoid the pitfalls of both the historical and institutional views is found in Professor Ronald Dworkin's theory of legal concepts. The theory rests on a distinction between *concepts* and *conceptions*[37] and is, though highly suggestive, sketchy and imprecise at many points. The statement presented here seems to us the most plausible reading of Dworkin's view, though perhaps he might prefer to develop it differently. The object of the distinction is to justify the claim that the core meaning of the Constitution remains unchanged even when judges diverge from the specific content that the framers would have found there. To appeal to a conception is to appeal to a specific understanding or account of what the words one is using mean. To appeal to a concept is to invite rational discussion and argument about what words used to convey some general idea mean. Concepts are not tied

to the author's situation and intentions in the way that conceptions are.[38] Broad phases such as "cruel and unusual punishment," "freedom of speech," "due process," and "equal protection" tend to be vague and abstract. While Dworkin is apparently not committed to thinking of the concepts denoted by these phrases as utterly lacking in content, their content is not usually specific enough to decide troubling cases involving issues such as capital punishment. They are "contested" concepts; their proper content is always disputable.[39] Even though people may agree on some paradigm cases of what is and is not cruel and unusual punishment, the boundaries of this concept are always open to dispute.

Two points should be noted concerning the abstract character of concepts. One is that Dworkin does not suggest that it is impossible to argue rationally about their proper content. He develops elaborate categories to show how an ideal judge would choose among competing conceptions of legal concepts. Briefly stated, Dworkin's idea is that a judge should choose the conception implied by the most coherent account of the principles underlying the legal system and all the non-mistaken legislation and decisions within it.[40] The second point is that concepts alone, because they are abstract, do not generally yield specific results in difficult cases. A conception of the true meaning of the concept must be added. A conception explains why the paradigm cases are instances of the concept and ties their character to some feature of the case at bar, thus generating a particular result.[41]

The authors of our Constitution undoubtedly had conceptions of their own, but in Dworkin's view these are not binding on later interpreters and need not be used in deciding cases now. Dworkin holds that the framers did not intend[42] to give their own conceptions any special weight: "If those who enacted the broad clauses had meant to lay down particular conceptions, they would have found the sort of language conventionally used to do this, that is, they would have offered particular theories of the concepts in question."[43] For example, Dworkin's view is that the authors of the Constitution were not giving, or even trying to give, instructions not to use some particular set of punishments when they prohibited cruel and unusual punishment in the eighth amendment. They were rather telling officials always to consider whether a proposed punishment is compatible with the best current views about what is cruel. It is as if they were saying, "You have to figure out for yourselves what cruelty amounts to in your time and circumstances, but punishments are to be used only if they are not cruel in terms of the conceptions you arrive at." Since the framers were merely offering for guidance the general concepts, and not their own conceptions of them, it is sometimes justifiable to use conceptions different from those the framers used, and so reach results different from those they would have reached. Hence one can arrive at innovative results without being open to the charge of infidelity to the Constitution.[44]

Thus, Dworkin's distinction between concepts and conceptions is used to make the claim that the framers gave their own paradigms and theories of the broad terms they were using "no special standing."[45] This is not merely the innocuous thesis that the framers knew that the exact content of some of their language would be determined as the new government got started and judges began deciding cases. It is the considerably stronger claim that the broad clauses do not have, and were not intended to have, a sufficiently definite content for it to be possible to use them, without the addition of a current conception, in deciding difficult cases now.

Dworkin's theory has the advantage of explaining how change can occur consistent with the textual focus of our constitutional practice. Nevertheless, it seems mistaken in several connected ways.[46] First, even the broad clauses of the Constitution have more content than Dworkin allows, and he gives no adequate reason why that content should not be considered more fully relevant in constitutional argument and decision-making. Ordinarily in interpreting someone's instructions one attends not only to the concepts used but also to the instructor's intentions and situation. In so doing one often finds that an apparently vague word or phrase has a relatively clear meaning in the context. For example, a person may be using a vague phrase in a context where it has a more precise meaning because of a customary or explicit definition. Thus, a vague phrase like "fair hearing" may have a relatively definite meaning within a school system in which there are established customary standards as to

what constitutes a fair hearing in dismissal proceedings. Many constitutional commentators have assumed that the phrases of the Constitution can and should be interpreted in the way this example suggests and therefore that, when terms the framers used had a previous legal usage – for example, "bill of attainder,"[47] "cruel and unusual,"[48] or "due process of law"[49] – that usage is relevant. Dworkin has done nothing to criticize this kind of constitutional commentary, or to support his claim that the framers were merely offering concepts and not their own conceptions for guidance, save to note the vagueness of the language they used and the inconvenience of this approach if one wants to reach the conclusion that capital punishment is unconstitutionally cruel. Although such evidence is not decisive[50] – and admittedly becomes less valuable over time – Dworkin does not adequately allow for the *relevance* of historical language, intent, and context. It is true that these are pertinent, in his scheme, to the identification of the concepts the framers were using. But in our view that does not exhaust their relevance. Historical language, intent, and context also bear on the *conceptions* the framers had of those concepts, and hence on the instructions they were giving. If such considerations are to be ignored, this should not in any case be on the weak grounds that Dworkin suggests.

Second, Dworkin claims that whether a person intends to give his own views special standing makes a difference in the "kind of instructions given,"[51] but this is really a matter of degree. It is not easy to classify the clauses of the Constitution into just the two kinds that Dworkin's theory allows. The amount of particular guidance that the framers intended to give seems to vary from provision to provision.[52] There are *many* things that a person using a general concept to give instructions might be doing. He might be offering the general concept and nothing more, while giving no hints as to intended interpretation or scope; he might be using the concept and giving a few indications as to how he wants it generally to be applied (for example, whether he wants it applied broadly or narrowly); or he might be offering a concept and including with it a substantial number of instructions as to how it is to be applied in certain controversial cases.

Third, Dworkin's account of fidelity to the Constitution is insufficiently candid. Dworkin's strategy for making fidelity compatible with substantial constitutional change involves extruding some content from the original document and its amendments.[53] As a result, the very constitutional materials to which new decisions are likely to be unfaithful are conveniently absent. Remaining is a framework broad enough to allow for decisions quite different from those generated by original understandings. Dworkin tries to justify this approach by suggesting that it is only what the framers intended, but this suggestion is doubly questionable. First, Dworkin's claim is undefended and implausible. Here two questions about the framers should be carefully distinguished: whether the framers intended that a court should occupy itself with searches for their conceptions, and whether the framers intended that a court should knowingly adopt its own conceptions rather than theirs. We have argued in effect that Dworkin's negative answer to the former question is dubious in many instances.[54] But even if one allowed his answer, it would not follow that Dworkin is right in giving an affirmative response to the latter question. The framers might have anticipated that later their own conceptions would sometimes be unrecoverable but might not have licensed a court to substitute its own conceptions when their conceptions are readily ascertainable. Second, Dworkin's claim puts the focus of argument in the wrong place. The grounds for continued adherence to the basic structure of the Constitution as well as to the framers' conceptions when recoverable should be articulated in terms of current political considerations rather than giving controlling power to the intentions of people who are long dead. The important thing is not what was originally intended, but what has subsequently been done with the document and the role it now plays.

II. Toward a More Adequate Theory of Constitutional Change

Having criticized three theories of constitutional change and development we are now able to identify the central problem that must be confronted in developing a more adequate theory.

That problem is the tension between change in constitutional norms and the textual focus. If a new theory is to improve on past efforts, it must account for a changing Constitution while explaining the central role of the text without depleting that text of its original content The theory offered here attempts to accomplish this task. Analytically, it holds that authoritative interpretations can modify the meaning of the Constitution and that the present content of the document results from the interaction over time of framers judges, legislators, and executive officials. Change occurs in the meaning of the Constitution itself, not merely in its interpretations or in the meaning of certain words belonging to the English language. Normatively, the theory that constitutional change through interpretation is necessary and desirable and some guidance as to when such change is in order, can be found in the functions of the Constitution.

A. The Problem of a written constitution

The root of the problem of meaning-change stems from the idea that we have a written constitution. That idea is in some sense obviously right. But is it completely right? To grapple with this question it is instructive to consider a syllogism advanced by Justice Brewer: "The Constitution is a written instrument. As such its meaning does not alter. That which it meant when adopted it means now."[55] The conclusion of this argument follows logically from the premises. Thus to deny the conclusion one must deny at least one of the premises. The first premise says that ours is a written constitution; the second says that a written constitution cannot change in its meaning. These premises will be considered in turn.

1. *A Partially Written Constitution.* If our Constitution were simply a body of unwritten customary rules, little difficulty would be encountered in understanding how its meaning could change.[56] Rules without complete canonical formulations can plainly be modified by the informal formulations they receive from time to time. Some may doubt whether this is true of written constitutions, especially since the point of writing down rules may be to limit such change. Reflection reveals, however, that the clauses of the US Constitution are, in at least two ways, only

partial formulations of constitutional law. First, these clauses do not give the full or exact scope of all constitutional rules specified in the text; to determine that one must, among other things, read the relevant cases. Second, they do not even mention some constitutional rules, namely those which, like the right to travel and the right of privacy,[57] are not found in any particular provision of the text.

2. *The Need for Change in the Written Constitution.* The conclusion that the Constitution is composed of both a written text and formulations of additional rules does not allow us fully to rebut Justice Brewer's argument. It might still be asserted that the written Constitution has retained precisely the meaning it had when ratified, and that only those constitutional rules which lack a canonical formulation in the original document have undergone a change in meaning or content. This will not do, however, if a phrase from the written Constitution is now to describe a rule that is radically different from the rule that the phrase originally formulated. If a provision P of the Constitution originally gave an accurate description of rule R of constitutional law, and that rule has changed substantially so that it is now a different rule R', it is hard to imagine how P can without change in meaning now be a full and accurate description of R'. For P to be an accurate description of R' it must have a different meaning from that which it had when it was an accurate description of R. For example, the freedom of speech and press guaranteed by the first amendment was originally concerned essentially with political speech and perhaps allied forms of communication expressing ideas in science, art, morality, religion, etc. So understood, that amendment did not give any protection to commercial speech such as advertising.[58] Under recent decisions, however, certain forms of advertising receive some shelter under the first amendment.[59] Thus, to state the matter generally, we must either abandon words used in the text as the accurate descriptions of much-modified rules, or admit that the words do not now mean what they meant.

3. *Authoritative Interpretation As the Instrument of Change.* The issue in analyzing Justice Brewer's second premise is not whether something that an authoritative interpreter does can change what a constitutional provision meant; its original meaning is a historical fact not subject to change. It is rather a question of whether the action of an authoritative interpreter can change what the provision will thereafter mean.[60] Now to some an affirmative answer will seem beset by an insuperable difficulty, namely, the fact that philosophers often think of the meaning of an utterance as being fixed for the present and for the future by the author's language and intent. It is not, of course, problematic to say that change occurs in the meanings of words in a language; the meaning of "wonderful," for example, is now somewhat different from what it was prior to the eighteenth century. But it is problematic to say that an utterance which a particular person made at a particular time can have one meaning at that time and another meaning later.[61]

Yet even if utterance meaning in the standard case is unalterable, for two reasons that is no bar to change in the meaning of the constitutional text. The first is that the original document cannot be counted an "utterance" in the usual sense. The standard or paradigm case of an utterance is when one person speaks or writes a sentence on a particular occasion; its meaning is typically a function of the utterer's intentions together with the context and the senses assigned to those words in grammatical combinations in a given language. In contrast, the sentences of the Constitution were products of more than one person (draftsmen, framers, ratifiers) and more than one time (successive drafting, debating, adoption, and ratification stages). No doubt in the process statements were made which are susceptible of being analyzed as standard utterances. But the eventual product is not thus susceptible: if the text of the Constitution is an utterance or set of utterances at all, it is not so in the standard sense. Its original meaning may, it is true, still be a function of the various intentions, contexts, and words that led to it. Yet if so, given the number of persons involved at different times and in different situations, that meaning will be an extraordinarily complex function of those elements.

The second reason is that the original text serves through authoritative interpreters to give ongoing guidance in changing circumstances. Perhaps the idea that the meaning of a text composed of standard utterances cannot change is satisfactory where no one is empowered to make official determinations of its meaning, or where the language is not intended to provide a reason for action, or where directives supplied by the text apply only in a finite number of static situations. But if we turn our attention to law, it does not seem so strange that the current meaning of a constitutional provision should be the result of the activities of both the authors and the officials who applied it. Authoritative interpreters, in their institutional capacity of determining what a provision means in unanticipated situations, supplement or modify the meaning or content of the provision. The institutional practice involved in the use and interpretation of constitutional language is one in which the responsibility for creating the current meaning of a constitutional provision is spread among different people at different times; the power of creating meaning is broken into shares. The original authors of the Constitution determined the meaning it would have unless and until it was changed or developed through amendment or decision, and thereby set out the general direction of its future development. The meaning of the Constitution changes as it is interpreted. Authoritative interpretations of the text often create a new meaning for it, and the original meaning, or whatever had previously replaced it, ceases to be the current meaning. Hence we say that the current meaning of a constitutional provision is the result of interaction over time between the framers and its authoritative interpreters. This interaction is a dynamic process; it may often take the form of cooperation, but there may at times be tug-of-war or outright conflict between different interpreters.

It is now clear that both premises of Justice Brewer's argument must be rejected. Our Constitution is first of all not merely a written instrument. Viewed more accurately it is a text-based institutional practice in which authoritative interpreters can create new constitutional norms. Secondly, the meaning of a written document like the text of the Constitution can intelligibly be said to change. The "meaning" possessed by the text differs from utterance meaning as standardly conceived, and was originally the product of many persons. That initial meaning has subsequently been altered in an interactive institutional process. . . .

Notes

1　For discussion of specific areas of constitutional growth, see Grey, "Do We Have an Unwritten Constitution?," 27 *Stan. L. Rev.* 703, 710–14 (1975).

2　As used in this Article the word "meaning" does not, save in a few places where the context so indicates, refer to the sense that a word, phrase or sentence bears in a given language ("language meaning"). Nor is it identical with the intention with which a word, phrase or a sentence is uttered by a particular speaker on a particular occasion ("utterance meaning"). The meaning of the Constitution and its clauses is indeed related to utterance meaning, but differs from it in at least two ways. First, their meaning is initially the product, not of a single speaker at a single time, but of a complex of intentions on the part of framers, ratifiers, and perhaps others at different times. Second, while it is often maintained that utterance meaning cannot change, the meaning of the Constitution and its clauses, in our view, is susceptible of being amplified and altered by later authoritative interpretations. The best vehicle for analyzing constitutional meaning as just explained may be one of the speech, act or intentional theories of meaning current among analytic philosophers of language. See, e.g., J. L. Austin, *How to Do Things with Words* (1962); S. Schiffer, *Meaning* (1972); J. Searle, *Speech Acts* (1969). But we know of no such theory which has been developed to accommodate constitutional meaning, nor are we simply borrowing notions that every philosopher of language would accept. Part II of this Article offers an extended, though still informal and imprecise, account of constitutional meaning and how it can change. A formal and rigorous theory cannot be attempted here.

3　See text accompanying notes 5–15 infra.

4　Llewellyn, "The Constitution as an Institution," 34 *Colum. L. Rev.* 1 (1934). See text accompanying notes 16–30 infra.

5　Advocates of this approach include William Crosskey and, most recently, Raoul Berger. See, e.g., 1 & 2 W. Crosskey, *Politics and the Constitution* (1953); Berger, "The Imperial Court," *NY Times*, Oct. 9, 1977, §6 (Magazine), at 38 (article drawn from forthcoming book). Judicial statements abound. See, e.g., Harper v. Virginia Bd. of Elections, 383 U.S. 663, 677–8 (1966) (Black, J., dissenting); West Coast Hotel Co. v. Parrish, 300 U.S. 379, 402–3 (1937) (Sutherland, J., dissenting); South Carolina v. United States, 199 U.S. 437, 448–9 (1905); Dred Scott v. Sandford, 60 U.S. (19 How.) 393, 426 (1857) (Taney, C. J.). There are extensive statements of historical and non-historical approaches by Justice Sutherland and Chief Justice Hughes, respectively, in Home Bldg. & Loan Ass'n v. Blaisdell, 290 U.S. 398 (1934).

6   For example, the meaning of "house" does not change when houses are built or destroyed. See generally J. S. Miu, *A System of Logic*, 19–25 (8th ed. 1872). Justice Sutherland used this distinction as a way of allowing for new applications of constitutional provisions: "The provisions of the Federal Constitution, undoubtedly, are pliable in the sense that in appropriate cases they have the capacity of bringing within their grasp every new condition which falls within their meaning. But, their meaning is changeless; it is only their *application* which is extensible." Home Bldg. & Loan Ass'n. v. Blaisdell, 290 U.S. 398, 451 (1934) (dissenting opinion) (emphasis on original; footnote omitted). See also Village of Euclid v. Ambler Realty Co., 272 U.S. 365, 687 (1926) (Sutherland, J.).

7   For example, the power to "regulate Commerce . . . among the several States," *US Const* art. I, §8, cl. 3, was early held sufficient to authorize Congress to charter corporations for the construction of a railroad, Roberts v. Northern Pac. R.R., 158 U.S. 1, 21 (1895), or a bridge, Luxton v. North River Bridge Co., 153 U.S. 525 (1894). Later concern with national economic problems and "undesirable" local activities gradually led the Supreme Court to accept the commerce clause as support for legislation of widely different sorts. See, e.g., United States v. Darby, 312 U.S. 100 (1941) (wage and hour legislation); NLRB v. Jones & Laughlin Steel Corp., 301 U.S. 1 (1937) (labor practices). Sometimes the economic effect was tangential, as in Wickard v. Filburn, 317 U.S. 111 (1942) (penalty on wheat produced and consumed at home upheld). In addition, legislation was allowed to prohibit "immoral" practices having a fleeting connection, if any, with interstate commercial activity. See, e.g., United States v. Five Gambling Devices, 346 U.S. 441 (1953) (registration of gambling machines); Hoke v. United States, 227 U.S. 308 (1913) (prostitution); The Lottery Case, 188 U.S. 321 (1903) (lottery tickets). The commerce clause was also used to justify civil rights legislation. See Heart of Atlanta Motel, Inc. v. United States, 379 U.S. 241 (1964); Katzenbach v. McClung, 379 U.S. 294 (1964).

8   See, e.g., Dennis v. United States, 341 U.S. 494 (1951); Gitlow v. New York, 268 U.S. 652 (1925).

9   See, e.g., Virginia State Bd. of Pharmacy v. Virginia Citizens Consumer Council, Inc., 425 U.S. 748 (1979) (first amendment protection of commercial speech).

10 See, e.g., Sugarman v. Dougall, 413 U.S. 634 (1973); *In re* Griffiths, 413 U.S. 717 (1973); Graham v. Richardson, 403 U.S. 365 (1971) (equal protection clause protects aliens).

11 Grey, supra note 1, at 710–14.

12 See Wofford, "The Blinding Light: The Uses of History in Constitutional Interpretation," 31 *U. Chi. L. Rev.* 502, 503–6 (1964).

13 Wofford offers a useful discussion of the problems of the various intents of the framers, ratifiers, and so on. Id. at 507–9. For difficulties concerning intents of groups, see MacCallum, "Legislative Intent," 75 *Yale L.J.* 754 (1966). In regard to whether the particular intentions of framers should be considered, Dworkin has suggested – in the related area of statutory construction – that we should not be concerned with the mental state of particular legislators, but instead consider what interpretation of a statute best fits within the legislature's general responsibilities. R. Dworkin, "Hard Cases," in *Taking Rights Seriously*, 81, 108 (1977) (hereinafter cited as Dworkin, "Hard Cases").

14 These matters are ably documented in Kelly, "Clio and the Court: An Illicit Love Affair," 1965 *Sup. Ct. Rev.* 119.

15 See Wofford, supra note 12, at 528.

16 Llewellyn, supra note 4. Llewellyn indicates, id. at 1–2 & nn. 1–2, that his view is also shared by A. Bentley, *The Process of Government* (1908), and H. McBain, *The Living Constitution* (1927).

17 See, e.g., K. Llewellyn, *The Bramble Bush* (2d ed. 1951); Llewellyn, "A Realistic Jurisprudence – The Next Step," 30 *Colum. L. Rev.* 431 (1930).

18 He refers to the theory he opposes as "the orthodox theory." Llewellyn, supra note 4, at 3–4.

19 Llewellyn notes that the money and borrowing powers of article I, §8, cls. 2 & 5, have been held, over time, to allow first a national bank, later the Federal Reserve System, and eventually securities affiliates. The connection of the last with the document, he observes wryly, "escapes my untrained eye; the giddy trapeze-work of constitutional theory is not for mere commercial lawyers." Id. at 14 n. 28.

20 Id. at 6 n. 13 (emphasis added).

21 Id. at 17–26.

22 Id. at 26–31.

23 Id. at 26–33.

24 Id. at 30.

25 Thus he writes: "If rules decided cases, one judge would be as good as another, provided only the cases had been adduced before him." Id. at 7.

26 "Only because the Supreme Court has been so good at three-card monte, has made so much seem to be where it was not, have the Document and [the

orthodox] Theory been able to survive so long."
Id. at 17 (emphasis in original; footnote omitted).

27 As H. L. A. Hart has argued, while legal rules and language do not bind rigidly, and while they exhibit open texture and may have exceptions not exhaustively specifiable in advance, they still provide guidance. H. L. A. Hart, *The Concept of Law*, 135–6 (1961).

28 *US Const.* art. I, §9, cl. 8.

29 The first two examples may be found in Llewellyn, supra note 4, at 29–30. Indeed, since Llewellyn wrote, certain patronage dismissals have been held unconstitutional. See Elrod v. Burns, 427 U.S. 347 (1976). The Sherman Act is seen as having constitutional stature in Miller, "Change and the Constitution," 1970 *L. & Soc. Ord.* 231, 247–8. Miller's approach to constitutional law – presented also in Miller, "Notes on the Concept of the 'Living' Constitution," 31 *Geo. Wash. L. Rev.* 881 (1963) – has many features in common with Llewellyn's.

30 These issues are taken up later in our own account of constitution-identity....

31 C. Miuer, *The Supreme Court and the Uses of History*, 149–69 (1969).

32 Id. at 150 (footnote omitted).

33 Id. at 150–1.

34 Id. at 153.

35 Id. at 150–1. But see note 36 infra.

36 C. Miller, supra note 31, at 151 (footnote). Miller seems to suppose that written documents cannot change in meaning. Id. at 150–1. However, he subsequently appears to question such an assumption, Id. at 151 n. 3, and later says that "since the Constitution was adopted ... the meaning of the text has changed." Id. at 155. Hence it is at least possible that he has no uniform position on this issue. Miller may have fallen into this confusion by failing to distinguish between the meaning of words in a language. One might try to make his position consistent by suggesting that at some points he regards the document to be static in terms of utterance meaning and that at others he is speaking of the language meaning of words used in the text. For further consideration of the distinction between utterance meaning and language meaning in the context of our own theory, see note 2 supra; text accompanying note 61 infra.

37 See R. Dworkin, "Constitutional Cases," in *Taking Rights Seriously*, supra note 13, at 131 (hereinafter cited as Dworkin, "Constitutional Cases.")

38 Dworkin introduces the distinction as follows:

> Suppose I tell my children simply that I expect them not to treat others unfairly. I no doubt have in mind examples of the conduct I mean to discourage, but I would not accept that my "meaning" was limited to these examples, for two reasons. First, I would expect my children to apply my instructions to situations I had not and could not have thought about. Second, I stand ready to admit that some particular act I thought of when I spoke was in fact unfair, or vice versa, if one of my children is able to convince me of that later; in that case I should want to say that my instructions covered the case he cited, not that I had changed my instructions. I might say that I meant the family to be guided by the *concept* of fairness, not by any specific *conception* of fairness that I might have had in mind.

Id. at 134 (emphasis in original).

39 See Dworkin, "Hard Cases," supra note 13, at 103–7, 126–7, and passim. Dworkin, id. at 103 n. 1, adopts this notion from Gallie, "Essentially Contested Concepts," 56 *Proc. Aristotelian Soc'y* 167 (1955–6).

40 This idea is linked to Dworkin's position that, in virtually all instances, lawsuits have uniquely correct results and judicial decisions declare pre-existing rights. See Dworkin, "Hard Cases," supra note 13, at 81, 87, 105; Dworkin, "No Right Answer?," in *Law, Society, and Morality: Essays on Honour of H. L. A. Hart*, 58 (P. Hacker & J. Raz eds. 1977). This position cannot be discussed here, but it is the subject of Munzer, "Right Answers, Preexisting Rights, and Fairness," 11 *Ga. L. Rev.* 1055 (1977), and the response in Dworkin, "Seven Critics," id. at 1201, 1241–50. This last essay may modify Dworkin's coherence theory of justifying decisions, as it now appears to be allowed that the best justification may give greater weight to "sound political morality" than to "fit" with institutional history. Id. at 1252–5.

41 The following passage illustrates Dworkin's view of what is involved in having a moral concept and suggests the nature of a conception:

> Suppose a group believes in common that acts may suffer from a special moral defect which they call unfairness, and which consists in a wrongful division of benefits and burdens, or a wrongful attribution of praise or blame. Suppose also that they agree on a great number of standard cases of unfairness and use these as benchmarks against which to test other, more controversial cases. In that case, the group has a concept of unfairness, and its members may appeal to that concept in moral instruction or agreement. But members of that group may nevertheless differ over a large number of these controversial cases, in a way that

suggests that each either has or acts on a different theory of *why* the standard cases are acts of unfairness. They may differ, that is, on which more fundamental principles must be relied upon to show that a particular division or attribution is unfair. In that case, the members have different conceptions of fairness.

Dworkin, "Constitutional Cases," supra note 37 at 134–5 (emphasis in original).

42   In general, Dworkin views the "intent of the legislators" as a contested concept. Claims about what was intended are not to be settled exclusively on historical grounds but in terms of which postulated intent would best meet the legislature's constitutional responsibilities. Dworkin, "Hard Cases," supra note 13, at 108. The authors of the Constitution had no such responsibilities. Hence an account of the background rights they were relying on has to be in terms of what they did and, perhaps, of how the Constitution was subsequently developed. It is unclear whether the claim that they did not intend to give their own conceptions any special standing is to be settled solely on historical grounds, though plainly Dworkin thinks that the kind of language they used is relevant evidence.

43   Dworkin, "Constitutional Cases," supra note 37, at 136.

44   Those who ignore the distinction between concepts and conceptions, but who believe that the Court ought to make a fresh determination of whether the death penalty is cruel, are forced to argue in a vulnerable way. They say that ideas of cruelty change over time, and that the Court must be free to reject out-of-date conceptions; this suggests that the Court must change what the Constitution enacted. But in fact the Court can enforce what the Constitution says only by making up its own mind about what is cruel.

Id. Fidelity to the Constitution is therefore compatible with introducing constitutional doctrine that is substantially different from what preceded it and from what the framers would have accepted.

For the application of Dworkin's account to current constitutional issues, see D. Richards, *The Moral Criticism of Law* (1977). Richards accepts Dworkin's approach to constitutional adjudication and the concepts/conceptions distinction, id. at 41–4, 52–3, but gives them a historical twist, and argues that the contract theory of morality in J. Rawls, *A Theory of Justice* (1971), provides the best conceptions of moral concepts embedded in the Constitution. On the relations between their

legal theories, compare Richards, "Rules, Policies, and Neutral Principles: The Search for Legitimacy in Common Law, Constitutional Adjudication," 11 *Ga. L. Rev.* 1069 (1977): with Dworkin, "Seven Critics," id. at 1201, 1250–8. Richards' position is critically examined in Munzer, "Book Review," *Rutgers L. Rev.* (1978).

45   See Dworkin, "Constitutional Cases," supra note 37, at 135.

46   We cannot take up here the question, belonging to logical theory and the philosophy of language, of whether it is possible in principle to distinguish concepts from conceptions, and if so how that is to be done.

47   *US Const.* art. I, §9, cl. 3; art. I, §10, cl. 1.

48   *US Const.* amend. VIII.

49   *US Const.* amends. V; XIV, §1.

50   See text accompanying notes 11–15 supra.

51   Dworkin, "Constitutional Cases," supra note 37, at 135.

52   For a discussion of theories of the Constitution which emphasize the differences between general and specific clauses, see C. Miller, supra note 31, at 162–5. See also United States v. Lovett, 328 U.S. 303, 321 (1946) (Frankfurter, J., concurring); Home Bldg. & Loan Ass'n v. Blaisdell, 290 U.S. 398, 426 (1934). A special difficulty for theories that divide all clauses into general (or vague) and specific is that judges sometimes do not agree how a given clause should be classified. See Wofford, supra note 12, at 515–18.

53   Dworkin seems to try to have it both ways. He wants particular legal concepts to be empty enough to allow for innovation and development, but the whole of the legal materials to be rich enough to rule out strong discretion. One might wonder whether such poverty of the parts is compatible with such richness of the whole. We would emphasize that we are not questioning Professor Dworkin's candor; only whether his theory allows for as much candor about innovative decisions as do our constitutional practice and any acceptable account of it.

54   See text accompanying notes 42–50 supra.

55   South Carolina v. United States, 199 U.S. 437, 448 (1905). These premises are the foundation of the historical approach. See notes 5–15 and accompanying text supra. There we analyzed the operation of a theory based on this foundation. In this section we examine the validity of its underlying premises.

56   Such an approach to constitutional development is suggested by Charles A. Miller's distinction between the *Constitution* as formal written document and the *constitution* as a pattern of political

relationships. See C. Miller, supra note 31, at 149–69. Miller's analysis is a reaction to the sort of argument Justice Brewer makes, and is critically discussed at text accompanying notes 31–6 supra.

57 See, e.g., Shapiro v. Thompson, 394 U.S. 618 (1969) (constitutional right to travel established); Griswold v. Connecticut, 381 U.S. 479 (1965) (constitutional right of privacy established).

58 See, e.g., Valentine v. Chrestensen, 316 U.S. 52 (1942).

59 See Bates v. State Bar of Ariz., 97 S.Ct. 2691 (1977) (advertising by lawyers); Virginia State Bd. of Pharmacy v. Virginia Citizens Consumer Council, Inc., 425 U.S. 748 (1976) (advertising by pharmacists). Without merit is the objection that change in meaning need not be invoked if either the earlier or the later decisions are mistaken. For while an authoritative interpretation can sometimes properly be criticized as a mistake, such criticism does not deprive the interpretation of constitutional status unless it quickly leads to the overturning of the interpretation or makes such overturning likely. . . .

60 We do not take up here how retroactively applied interpretations are to be analyzed. Perhaps some such interpretations can be seen as declarations of the "correct" meaning of a constitutional clause. But often this declaratory analysis of retroactivity will be most implausible, and some different account will be needed of how the legal significance of past events can now be changed. A theory of the appropriate sort, which may be conjoined with our view of constitutional change, is developed in Munzer, "Retroactive Law," 6 *J. Legal Stud.* 373 (1977).

61 As one contemporary philosopher of language has written:

> A speech has a date and duration, not so its meaning. When a speech is over nothing can change what is meant. What has been said cannot be unsaid, though later remarks can contradict it. Even the ambiguities in this evening's speech must remain such forever, though tomorrow's press conference may clarify the speaker's intentions. Though the speech may be differently translated in different countries or different periods, no one could judge the correctness of each new translation unless he assumed the meaning of the original speech to remain the same. Though expositions of what has been said can change they can also be criticized, and the question whether a given exposition is loose or close, fair or biased, accurate or inaccurate, would not arise unless the meaning itself were invariant under exposition.

L. J. Cohen, *The Diversity of Meaning*, 3 (2d ed. 1966).

54

What's Wrong with Chinese Rights? Toward a Theory of Rights with Chinese Characteristics

R. P. Peerenboom

The question "What's wrong with Chinese rights?" implies that there are Chinese rights. A quick glance at the constitution of the People's Republic of China suggests that a Chinese citizen shares the full complement of rights that members of modern, western liberal democracies have come to hold so dear: freedom of speech, press, association, religious belief and practice; inviolability of the person; protection from unlawful arrest and search of person, and so on.[1] Indeed, some claim that Chinese citizens enjoy rights unknown to their American counterparts: job placement and security, free access to medical care, and other "economic rights" are most often cited.[2]

Yet despite this seemingly rosy picture, the cry for human rights in China has grown steadily louder since the Tiananmen tragedy and the collapse of socialism in Eastern Europe and the former USSR. To be sure, qualifications are in order. The cry rises largely from foreigners and a coterie of Chinese dissidents and intellectuals, many now living abroad in exile.[3] As an on-site observer of the 1989 demonstrations, I was particularly struck by the low priority given to human rights by many of the protesters, reports of western journalists notwithstanding. While a few students and intellectuals called for human rights (and even fewer could state what that meant), the vast majority of the demonstrators seemed motivated primarily by economic concerns, with inflation and corruption heading the list.[4] Those rights that the demonstrators did seek – freedom of the press, greater voice in electing officials – were grounded in pragmatic concerns: a free, investigative press would keep tabs on and expose corrupt officials; elections would allow for the expulsion of those exposed.[5]

Further, the call for "human rights" in China tends to elide several issues. The rhetoric of human rights is often that of universal, inalienable, absolute rights – and indeed often that of so-called "natural" rights. But is that actually what Chinese need or want? As rhetoric, rights talk is glorious: all people are created equal, each individual possesses an inviolable right to life, liberty, and the pursuit of happiness.[6] But this is rhetoric – powerful, effective, socially significant rhetoric, but rhetoric nonetheless. As such, it has been criticized, at least in unqualified form, as nonsense on stilts.[7] More importantly, such a conception of human rights is at odds with reality in which intuitions about human dignity and individual rights are at odds with equally

R. P. Peerenboom, "What's Wrong with Chinese rights? Toward a Theory of Rights with Chinese Characteristics," *Harvard Human Rights Journal*, vol. 6, 1993, pp. 29–57. © 1993. Reprinted with permission from Harvard Human Rights Journal.

strong intuitions about utilitarian consequences, the overall social good, and duties to others.[8] The result is a compromise: one has a right to free speech, yet one cannot cry "fire" in a theater, to cite a familiar example.

Notwithstanding the stirring words of the Declaration of Independence and distinguished philosophers, all states impose limits on individual rights in the name of public interest. Indeed, the Universal Declaration of Human Rights explicitly provides:

> In the exercise of his rights and freedoms, everyone shall be subject only to such limitations as are determined by law solely for the purpose of securing due recognition and respect for the rights and freedoms of others and of meeting the *just requirements of morality, public order and the general welfare* in a democratic society.[9]

Rhetoric aside, we constantly perform a complex calculus by which the rights or protected interests of individuals are weighed against the good of the collective (and other rights). Reasonable people differ as to the proper balance to effect; that diverse cultures would reach different conclusions is only natural.[10]

Examining the criticisms of China's human rights record raises three related questions. Are critics calling for a new kind of Chinese right – absolute, inalienable, ahistorical, human cum natural rights – or simply a different calculus where the rights of individuals are not so readily traded off to promote the "collective good"?

Similarly, does the problem lie in the outcome of the calculus or in the manner in which the calculus is made? While the Tiananmen massacre shocks the conscience, the more basic problem may be how the tragic decisions that culminated in tanks rolling through the streets of Beijing were reached: that is, via an authoritarian one-party system rather than a democratic process.

Finally, it is not so much the *how* of the calculus but the *who*. Though some intellectuals call for democracy, one still encounters with alarming frequency the traditional paternalistic attitude that the "masses" are not sufficiently educated to shoulder the responsibilities of democracy.[11] This suggests that in the eyes of many, what is needed is not an institutional change from

dictatorship to democracy, but simply a change in dictators: just replace old guard conservatives with free-market reformers and all will be well.[12]

Whatever one's response to these questions, there can be little doubt that individuals in the PRC need some protection against the all-powerful state. There must be real constraints imposed on the government. If we were to impose these constraints through the vehicle of rights, then the PRC needs i) a stronger system of enforceable rights – rights in practice, not just name, and ii) a coherent theory of Chinese rights – a theory of rights justified on Chinese terms.

In Part I, I examine institutional obstacles to a workable system of rights in China. In Part II, I explore some of the philosophical assumptions that underwrite western rights theories. In Part III, I contrast these assumptions with the underlying premises of Confucianism. I do so because I believe Confucianism continues even today to be the basis of the Chinese world view, despite the attempts of the socialist government to eradicate such "feudal" thinking. Hence any workable theory of rights justifiable on Chinese terms will in all likelihood emerge out of and be consistent with the basic premises of Confucianism. Of course Confucianism is not the only intellectual influence. Thus I discuss socialism in Part IV. In Part V, I critique China's socialist regime not on the alien terms of western rights theories but from a Chinese perspective on rights. In Part VI, I sketch the contours of a Chinese rights theory and speculate as to the possibilities of its realization.[13]

I. Institutional Obstacles

A central obstacle to the protection of rights in China is the primacy of the Party over the rule of law. Party control eviscerates the rule of law, prevents the development of a genuinely independent judiciary, and renders meaningless the concept of constitutional review. According to the constitution, the Party is to follow the law,[14] yet in practice, the Party remains the law.[15] This is to be expected, given the basic premises of socialism. Mao once described law and courts as "instruments with which one class oppresses another. As far as the hostile classes are concerned these are instruments of oppression. They are violent and certainly not 'benevolent things.' "[16] As a tool of socialism, the law must serve the Party rather than individuals. That such ideas retain their currency despite repeated calls for a rule of law independent of Party control is scarcely surprising. What is perhaps somewhat surprising is the articulation of such views by the most senior members of the judiciary. For example, a major newspaper recently quoted Justice Minister Cai Cheng as declaring: "Chinese law must be at the service of class struggle... [T]here can be no question of 'the law being supreme'.... China must jettison the concept of 'the supremacy of the law' because the judicial code and system must be at the service of the proletariat class."[17]

There will be no way to protect the rights and interests of individuals if political might makes right – as the history of many other countries demonstrates. If rights are to become meaningful in China, limitations on Party power are essential.

To justify state abuse of individual rights, the Party can turn to article 51 of the constitution, itself a major impediment to practicable rights: "The exercise of citizens of the PRC of their freedoms and rights may not infringe upon the interests of the state, of society, and of the collective, or upon the lawful freedoms and rights of other citizens."[18] This manifestly asserts the hierarchy of state over individual, undermining the *raison d'être* of rights as a guarantee that "each person possesses an inviolability founded on justice that even the welfare of society as a whole cannot override."[19]

Another institutional impediment, related to but distinct from the issue of an independent judiciary and rule of law, is the lack of constitutional review. In the United States, the judiciary has emerged as the body that reviews governmental actions for conformity with the Constitution, but other arrangements are possible.[20] What matters is not so much the particular method, but that some agency other than the one that created the law be given the power of review. The 1982 PRC constitution gives the power to interpret and enforce the constitution not to the judiciary or an independent constitutional review body but to the standing committee of the supreme legislature, the National People's Congress. Because it is the National People's Congress that drafts and adopts laws in the first place,

"[i]t seems unlikely that the standing committee would interpret any statute or amendment as inconsistent with the constitution or the basic principles of the statutes (such as Criminal Law)."[21]

Constitutional review is one element of what some scholars have termed "constitutionalism." Although constitutionalism has not been definitively defined, the lack of it is generally considered fatal to human rights. Noting that variations are possible and no authoritative definition exists, Louis Henkin, a prominent champion of this new *ism*, offers several core elements: government according to the constitution; separation of powers; popular sovereignty and democratic government; constitutional review; independent judiciary; civilian control of the military; individual rights; and limitations on suspension, derogation, or amendment of the constitution by political organs.[22] Obviously China fails several, if not all, of these threshold tests. For example, the government has not only suspended the constitution but regularly promulgated new ones.[23] More importantly, by all accounts the government has disregarded all of its constitutions at one time or another.[24] In addition, separation of powers is nonexistent. As noted, the Party dominates all aspects of government, including the military.

Taken collectively, wholesale violation of these elements is perhaps a good indicator of the absence of a strong commitment to individual rights.[25] More debatable is whether possessing any single element or combination of elements is either necessary or sufficient to ensure human rights. England, for instance, does not even have a written constitution, and many states allow suspension of the constitution during times of crisis.[26] Conversely, the PRC at least nominally provides for separation of powers and functions.[27] How can England, a country without a written constitution, succeed in providing human rights while the PRC, constitution in hand, fails? "In the end," concludes Henkin, "constitutionalism depends on political, social and economic stability and a political culture that is committed to constitutionalism."[28] Perhaps most importantly, for human rights to be respected, there must be rights consciousness, a culture of rights, an attitude among the people that the government cannot do to them as it wishes.[29] The people must learn to stand up to the government and insist on their rights. They must demand that the judiciary and the body responsible for constitutional review perform their designated functions in the face of opposition from political powers. This attitude is sorely lacking in China.[30]

Many in the United States turn to the judiciary when they feel their rights have been violated. However for historical reasons, many Chinese continue to shy away from and fear the courts.[31] Chinese tradition frowned on judicial resolution of conflicts.[32]

Conflicts were to be resolved through informal, extrajudicial means such as mediation spearheaded by a local elder.[33] To end up in court was shameful and risky. The pitfalls of even successful litigation are enshrined in the Chinese proverb: "Win your lawsuit but lose your money."[34] Traditional distrust of and reluctance to rely on the formal legal system remain an impediment to the development of a rights attitude and culture in China.[35]

Even assuming that these obstacles could be overcome – the influence of the Party diminished, article 51 rewritten (or limited by interpretation), constitutional review established, and the deep-rooted fear of the courts overcome – it is unlikely that a strong theory of individual rights would emerge in China. To understand this, one must examine the philosophical assumptions that lie at heart of the Chinese world view. Perhaps the best way to do this is to begin with a brief overview of the underpinnings of western rights theories.

II. Underpinnings of Human Rights Theories

Western theories of human or natural rights have as a whole been foundational and universal in character.[36] They tend to be written as if equally applicable to contemporary Asia as to seventeenth-century Europe or twentieth-century United States. For instance, one popular form of expression is that human rights are "self-evident."[37] As Henry Rosemont has noted, "it is a bedrock presupposition of our moral, social, and political thinking that human beings have rights, solely by virtue of being human . . . [T]he concept of human beings as right-bearers is not itself in serious question in contemporary Western moral, social and political philosophy."[38] This, like so many other self-evident axioms of western social and political philosophy, is far from obvious in a Chinese context. The oft-noted late arrival of the concept "right" to China, along with classical Confucianism's emphasis on rites[39] rather than rights, suggests that within a Chinese cultural and philosophical milieu, it is far from self-evident that everyone enjoys rights that even the good of society as a whole cannot override.

A second source of human rights is God. So-called natural rights are often said to be God-given. Many today dismiss such a suggestion as preposterous, truly nonsense on stilts. Rights, they argue, do not rain down from heaven: they are political creations. In any case, the Chinese can hardly be expected to ground a rights theory upon Judeo-Christian religious conceptions.

A third scenario is the Hobbesian/Lockean fable of the ascent of humans from a brutal and savage state of nature to the civilized wonder of a social life where each person's autonomy and dignity is safeguarded by a strong theory of rights. The story begins with atomistic, rational individuals free from any duty to others, who realize the gains in safety and self-protection from cooperation and consent to limit individual freedom. By signing a mythical social compact, one limits one's liberty in exchange for certain rights. Just what these rights are varies from thinker to thinker. The same basic story-line underwrites the minimalist libertarian state of Locke and Nozick;[40] the autocratic, sovereign-dominated Leviathan of Hobbes;[41] the majoritarianism of Rousseau;[42] and, in a slightly altered version, the contemporary liberal democracy of Rawls.[43]

If one allows that society is an arena in which self-interested individuals compete for scarce resources and goods, some set of principles, rules, or laws may be needed to protect the rightful claims of individuals to goods or liberties from invasion by others. By contrast, Confucianism rejects both the atomistic individual and inevitable competition assumptions. But before turning to Confucianism, one further point merits comment. Contemporary rights thinking revolves around the distinction between Kantian deontic principles and utilitarian consequences or social policy.[44] Those who take rights seriously side with Dworkin in privileging principle over policy.[45] Those more concerned with the distributive effects of legal and political decisions give primacy to policy. A third, more pragmatic faction refuses to privilege either side, insisting instead on a situational analysis where one effects justice by balancing the rights of individuals to pursue their own ideals against the social consequences of individual choice.[46]

Confucianism, however, rejects both the atomistic individual and inevitable competition assumptions. Part of my project shall be to argue that the situational character of Confucian ethics and the pragmatism of Chinese leaders make unlikely the pressing concern with deontic principles necessary to underwrite a strong theory of individual rights. Indeed, the context-specificity of Confucian ethics militates against any attempt to pass off historically and culturally contingent political policies and theories as universal, ahistorical absolutes.[47]

III.   Confucianism

In asking how individuals become obligated to the state (and each other), Hobbes achieved the equivalent of a Copernican revolution in social and political thought. Previously the assumption was that the individual was born a member of a state. A human being, in the words of Aristotle, was a political animal, part and parcel of a polis.[48] Few doubted that the interests of the state naturally preceded those of the individual. The question in Plato's Republic was "How can one best serve the state," not "What can the state do for me."[49]

Chinese thinking to this day is dominated by this pre-Hobbesian world view. State interests override the interests and rights of any given individual. The apparent one-sidedness of this relationship is diminished to some extent, however, by a second basic assumption in Chinese thought: that the interests of the state and individual are in, or at least can be brought into, harmony.

One of the primary concerns of Tocqueville and Mill was that individuals and minorities would be overwhelmed by the more powerful majority and state.[50] In contrast, early rights advocates in China saw no contradiction between individual rights and the goals of the state.[51] On the contrary, the belief was that unleashing

individual initiative would further the interests of the state. Convinced of the fundamental harmony of state and individual, Chinese leaders and intellectuals never developed a strong theory of rights to protect the individual against the dominant interests of the majority and state.

In fact, Chinese leaders tended to view rights as derivative from the state. As R. Randle Edwards explains, "China's leaders today, like the imperial and bureaucratic rulers of the past, hold that rights flow from the state in the form of a gratuitous grant that can be subjected to conditions or abrogation by the unilateral decision of the state."[52] In contrast, most western theorists maintain that the state is designed to protect rights which derive from one's status as a human being. To override these rights, the state must meet stringent political and legal standards and demonstrate compelling state interests.[53]

By drawing a distinction between human beings *qua* members of a biological species and humans *qua* social beings, classical Confucianism rejects the assumption that individuals are entitled to certain inalienable rights from birth. The well-publicized and much debated distinction between masses (*min*) and persons (*ren*) as well as that between the small person (*xiao ren*) and the exemplary person (*jun zi*)[54] suggests that one must earn rights by achieving some minimal level of personhood, of humanity.[55] That is, entitlement to the privileges and benefits offered by society requires demonstration of credentials as a participating member of society. As David Hall and Roger Ames remark:

A person is not entitled to political participation because he is born into an exclusive *jen* [human being] class. Rather, he becomes *jen* as a consequence of that personal cultivation and socialization that renders him particular. Being a person is something one does, not something one is; it is an achievement rather than a given.[56]

The achievement, it should be emphasized, is a social one. For Confucius, one *becomes* a human being, a humane person, by virtue of participation in society. Personhood and humanity are functions of socialization. At birth, before the process of enculturation, of becoming humane, we are not different than the other beasts.[57] It is this joining with others, overcoming one's natural conditionality (*ming*) in creating a different and better society, which is distinctive about humans. If one cannot overcome the passions, instincts and desires that human beings share with beasts, then one fails to achieve humanity, to become the kind of person society has an interest in protecting and granting even minimal rights.[58]

The Confucian (and socialist) challenge then is to inspire in members of society the desire to achieve a humane society and to encourage them to direct their energies toward the attainment of a harmonious social order where the interests of individuals and of the state are reconciled. This requires a willingness to participate in collective living, to search for a cooperative solution, to become humane (*ren*). It is in this sense that humanity is not something that can be conferred by law or by right of birth.

Confucianism would consider it a failure for society to aim at securing a minimum level of basic rights for alienated individuals unable or unwilling to participate cooperatively in collective living. If one accepts that there is no way to overcome the self-interested passions and desires of the animal world, then there is no hope for a humane society. Confucius realized that laws cannot force people to be humane.[59] For society to achieve collective humanity, the people that *constitute* it must be willing to put aside narrow self-interest and see their interests as inextricably tied to societal interests.

The ethical focus, therefore, cannot be on determining and implementing a universal system of laws that establishes a minimum standard of basic rights for individuals alienated from each other and society. Rather, the ethical orientation must be directed to the achievement of the highest quality of life made possible by the joint efforts of humans cooperating in collective living.[60] The call is for realization of excellence in inter-personal relations (*ren*).[61]

Rights may serve well to provide a minimum level of protection for the individual. But rights, particularly as conceived and enforced in the United States, are no panacea: such rights are negative, not positive rights.[62] They are rights against the state, providing freedom *from* state intervention, but they generally do not entitle

one *to* substantive benefits.[63] For instance, one has no legal claim to the economic rights enumerated in the Universal Declaration of Human Rights.[64]

Furthermore, rights are but half of the picture – the other half is duties. One indication of the different orientation of Confucian China and the United States is the contrasting conceptions of the relation between, and relative importance of, rights and duties. In the United States, much is made of rights, but duties, if discussed at all, are considered merely as corollaries to rights: in Hohfeldian terms, if one has a claim right, then others, including the state, have a duty not to interfere with that right.[65] There is generally no legal duty to the state or to fellow citizens. There is, for instance, no constitutional obligation to render aid to another;[66] indeed, in all but two states, one need not throw a life-jacket to a drowning person even though the inconvenience would be trivial.[67]

Emphasizing duties rather than rights, Chinese tradition turns Hohfeld on his head: rights are corollaries to duties.[68] For instance, a child has a duty of piety to his parents; as a result, parents have a "claim right" to support. Not surprisingly, the current constitution requires children to support their parents.[69] Individuals have legal duties not only to their parents but also to each other and the state.[70]

More broadly, the Confucian concept of *ren* is a duty to act appropriately in relation to others. At first blush, Confucianism appears to promote not natural rights but natural duties. Human beings, born into a family, a society, a state, owe duties to other members by virtue of birth. Some Confucians have even attempted to ground the hierarchical five primary social relations in a hierarchical natural order: just as heaven is above earth and yang superior to yin, so is the ruler above the official, the husband superior to wife,[71] and so on.[72]

Yet at the heart of a duty lies not simply the natural relation but also deference. One becomes an authority, a person to whom others will defer, in part by age and natural relation but, more importantly, by earning the respect of others. To do so, one must show cultural and moral achievement and demonstrate to others that they are better off following one's advice than had they set out on their own.[73] In times of conflict, people turn to the authoritative person (*jun zi*) as the one best able to envision a solution and thereby restore harmony.

In the Confucian world, there are no ahistorical or abstract rational beings. Confucianism concurs in this regard with Edmund Pincoffs, who maintains that "individualism makes sense only against a background of social organization. There is no human situation that consists of an aggregate of unrelated individuals. . . . We come into a world that is already organized; . . . we understand ourselves through our reflection in the perceptions of others. . . ."[74]

The historicized, relational character of the Chinese self/person makes it difficult to isolate the basic ethical unit, the individual, to whom ahistorical, universal rights would attach. Identity constantly changes, varying with the context; duties and, correspondingly, rights/rites are also constantly being redefined as other actors change. A son owes deference and filial piety to his father; the father owes deference and piety to his son. Confucianism requires sensitivity to the particular person and the web of relations that define the person. Whereas Kantian rights are based on the fundamental dignity and equality of every human being, Confucian rites give full play to the relational differences that distinguish each person. Thus, ethical duties radiate out in concentric circles – at the center, oneself, then one's parents, the rest of the nuclear family, relatives, friends, neighbors, state, nation, world – the larger the circle, the lesser the duty. The notion that generic rights or duties attach to individuals *simpliciter* is alien to the more graded and finely tuned rites-oriented mind.

Of central importance to the historically rich Confucian world view and its non-rights based method of conflict resolution are the *li*. The *li* – conventionally translated as rites – may be understood more broadly to include the full range of social customs, ethical norms, and political principles embodied in the complex relations, organizations, and institutions of society. They are culture-specific norms, the contingent, ever-changing values of a particular society. But the *li* are important not merely as the amassed wisdom of the ages, but also because they are the communally-owned repository of shared meaning and value on which people can draw in times of conflict. However different people may be, there

are still deep chords of affinity which bind them together as a result of a shared past. By tapping the areas of commonality, one may be able to find the ground upon which to build consensus, to forge new harmony.

Placing the burden of achieving or failing to achieve a humane society on the members of society fosters an environment in which compromise and innovative solutions can occur. The absence of any fixed, external, or privileged standards deprives one of a foundation on which to ground a dogmatic position.

There is then little room for the privileging of deontological principles that underwrite contemporary liberal rights theory. To the pragmatic Chinese mind, to ignore social consequences is sheer folly. Indeed, it is not at all clear that deontic principles make much sense in a Chinese context; to paraphrase Cardozo, rights (or duties) in the air are no rights (or duties) at all:[75] rights and duties can only arise out of a particular context. Consequently, one must approach afresh each new conflict between principle and policy, between rights and consequences.[76]

To insist on one's rights in a Chinese context is a cultural *faux pas* – one must be willing to negotiate, to compromise. Even when the legal system is invoked, the emphasis most often remains on compromise. Most contractual disputes are resolved through mediation or arbitration, in which "the court's judgment is not phrased in terms of a holding or a directive. Rather, after mediation by the court, the record indicates that the parties agreed to the particular resolution."[77] To be sure, court mediation in China may often be considerably less than voluntary.[78] Significantly, however, it seems the court wants to at least maintain the appearance that the parties themselves have come to a harmonious resolution on mutually agreeable terms (just as our courts strive to keep alive the myth of impartial, apolitical justice).[79]

The emphasis placed on compromise, mutual agreement, and harmony even in the legal context suggests that substantive justice tends to take precedence over formal justice. When a mutually acceptable solution cannot be reached, or the interests of the individual and the state cannot be reconciled, then the lack of procedural rights is particularly worrisome, as in the trials of the 1989 student demonstrators.[80]

Indeed, one may object to this picture of a harmonious Confucian society on several fronts. First, extralegal methods of resolving conflict such as informal mediation may not fully respect legal rights and interests. In the absence of formal oversight, abuse and corruption are possible. One side may be able to take advantage of personal connections (*guan xi*) to influence the mediator. Even if the process is not corrupt, the social pressure from neighbors and colleagues to accept a solution that compromises legal rights and interests may be overwhelming.

Second, a key assumption of mediation and the Confucian approach to conflict resolution more generally is that harmony is possible and interests reconcilable. But perhaps Mill was right in posing private and public, individual interest and state interest as fundamental antinomies.[81] Third, even if harmony is theoretically possible, in practice, people must be willing to seek a solution amenable to all. This attitude seems sorely lacking in the present-day China. Today, the number of encounters between strangers is ever increasing; perhaps an inevitable consequence is a breakdown in the kind of cooperative behavior and attitudes required by Confucianism. Fourth, even assuming sufficient altruism and a willingness to compromise, there must be sufficient common ground on which to build a solution acceptable to all. Such common ground may not exist in many instances in China.

A fifth problem is that Confucius' ethical gaze was so trained on the lofty heights attainable by humankind that he neglected to provide for even a minimal level of institutional protection for the individual against the state and others. The emphasis on duty, rather than on rights, leaves the individual vulnerable to the whims of the state. A related objection is that the Confucian system encourages authoritarianism. In the absence of external ethical or internal political constraints, the authoritative Confucian leader all too readily becomes an authoritarian despot. The Confucian system confers great discretionary power on the ruler, relying on the moral character of the ruler and internal monitoring by officials to ensure that the state serves the people. Far from being politically benign, the rhetoric of harmony is easily manipulable in the service of dictators.

IV. Socialism

Socialism may take many forms, some of which are more rights-friendly than others, but Marxism, at least Marx's Marxism, is not an ideology hospitable to rights. Marx viewed rights as an illusion, crumbs thrown to the alienated worker to dupe her or him into accepting the legitimacy of the state and the current economic order. Rights play no role in the ideal communist society, for the state withers away and with it the need for rights as protections from the state. Nor would rights be needed to protect against others, because self-interested individuals coveting the property of others would no longer exist. Once one does away with private property, which leads to class conflict and "the struggle of the isolated individual against the relationship of dominance,"[82] a new socialist human being is created, more other-regarding than the self-interested capitalist ancestor. Similarly, because everyone would be provided for, positive rights would be unnecessary. The result for Marx – as for Confucius – is that harmony would prevail. Each person would achieve full potential in a self-regulating society. Order would emerge from the bottom up, out of the particular historical conditions, rather than being imposed from above in accordance with allegedly universal or natural principles that in fact only represent the interests of the ruling class.[83]

For the present, rights and law may be useful tools to serve socialism's ends. Beyond doubt, law has served as an important tool in the factional power struggles of socialist China.[84] Official attitudes toward the judiciary and law have swung radically. Even so, rights have never been taken seriously in any period. Emphasis on "formal" law has resulted in harsher penalties in practice, with the Party exerting control over the legal process in order to realize its political objectives.[85] On the other hand, the less formal approaches have often been equally detrimental to individual rights.

At one end of the informal spectrum lay mediation, with disputes resolved outside the courts, either with a village elder's assistance or under the guidance of local Party officials, neighborhood committees, or the police.[86] Other informal sanctions during the Maoist years varied from private criticism and education to public criticism, censure, and struggle.[87] There were in fact different forms of struggle. The lesser exposed one to "intense vituperation from those in attendance, amid shaking fists, shouts, and accusing fingers";[88] the more severe forms often resulted in physical violence.

Political status determined treatment, for Mao distinguished contradictions between the people and the enemy from contradictions among the people.[89] Conflicts among the people were to be handled through "democratic" means – education and persuasion – with formal legal punishment meted out only to those resistant to persuasion and rehabilitation. But severe sanctions and dictatorial methods were to be employed in dealing with enemies such as "reactionaries, exploiters, counterrevolutionaries, landlords, bureaucrat-capitalists, robbers . . . and other scoundrels who disrupt social order."[90] Thus the more serious forms of informal sanction, such as struggle, were reserved for those with bad political backgrounds or guilty of political crimes. The scope of "political" crime, however, could be extraordinarily broad.

In any event, none of these various "informal" means of social control focused particularly on individual rights. To the contrary, insisting upon one's rights would only have subjected a person to greater abuse for maintaining incorrect political views.

On a more theoretical level, throughout the socialist period, rights have been seen as political expedients, granted by the state as needed and revoked when necessary. Furthermore, duties coexist with rights: for example, the duty as well as the right to work and receive education.[91] More ominously, one has the duty to safeguard the security, honor, and interests of the motherland.[92] Indeed, duties are owed primarily to the state rather than to other individuals.[93] Commentators have criticized the tendency in the PRC to emphasize duties at the expense of rights.[94] But the existence of duties *per se* does not account so much for the detriment to the individual as the fact that duties are owed to the *state* and the demands upon the individual in the name of socialism are essentially unlimited, defined primarily by the transitory dictates of the Party.

One positive aspect of socialism, however, is the importance invested in economic and social rights. The PRC constitution provides not only the right to a job, education, and vocational training, but to rest, medical care, and material support for the elderly, ill, or disabled.[95] Indeed, one of Beijing's major complaints has been that international rights organizations have focused myopically on political rights, ignoring China's commitment to economic rights and actual improvements in the basic material living conditions of many citizens. There is some truth to that assertion, but it is far from the whole story.

V.   A Critique, on Chinese Terms

Discussion of China's record on human rights all too often ends up with both sides talking past rather than to each other.[96] Westerners, particularly the United States and its representatives, denounce China for abuse of political freedoms and rights. Chinese retort that the foremost human right is the right to subsistence.[97] By all accounts, China has made remarkable economic progress, given its huge population and history of imperialist exploitation and decades of war with rights-conscious western nations. Indeed, the Chinese may well wonder at the authenticity of western protestations given the severe mistreatment of Chinese citizens by the imperial powers.[98] Even today, states far wealthier than China fail to provide the economic rights mandated by the Universal Declaration and arguably achieved to some extent in the PRC.

Despite the rhetoric of universal human rights, the reality is that different states have different conceptions and practices with respect to rights, reflecting their own cultural, philosophical, political, ethical, and economic traditions. Thus a more productive approach than simply attempting to impose one's own particular rights ideology on another sovereign state is to engage the other on its own terms. To do so is not to endorse an anything-goes cultural relativism or to deny the legitimacy of judging another culture. At minimum, a country must stand up to scrutiny on its own terms: it must be able to withstand criticism of both its theory (or underlying philosophies) and empirical practice. More importantly, many terms are shared terms. One need not be an ethical absolutist to decry the massacre of unarmed students and citizens in and around Tiananmen Square.[99]

To begin with the positive, China may be praised for the progress it has made in its efforts to secure economic rights for citizens. There is, of course, room for improvement. Citizens have a right to a job, but it may not be a job to which they are inclined or suited. In practice, the duty to work means that people are assigned jobs, at times in cities far from their spouse's place of work. In addition, medical care could be improved and a more comprehensive welfare system implemented. But these are to a large measure social policy choices; how one society directs resources will differ from another.[100]

China's most noticeable failure is in the area of political rights. Beijing's assertions that "the people are the real masters of the country with the right to run the country's economic and social affairs"[101] is of course absurd. Nor can one take seriously the government's attempt to portray the current system as one of free elections with politically independent multiple parties, or its claim that "the Party conducts its activities within the framework of the Constitution and the law."[102] The assertion that there is no censorship in China and that the government upholds the principle of "letting a hundred flowers blossom and a hundred schools of thought contend" is patently false.[103] To declare that there are no political prisoners in China (only "counter-revolutionaries") is insulting not only to the courageous demonstrators of 1989 but to those around the world who witnessed the events on television.[104]

Although the constitution and other laws nominally provide various rights, many are not legally enforceable in practice. For instance, while the recently promulgated Administrative Law allows citizens to sue the government,[105] the government has never lost a politically sensitive case.[106] Thus, another reason why citizens often do not pursue their legal rights is their belief that to do so is futile.

Beijing's issuance of a lengthy statement on human rights denying this familiar catalogue of complaints demonstrates that it is aware of a problem. In many instances, the PRC baldly lied rather than attempt to justify human rights abuses, which indicates a failure according not to alien western principles but to China's own standards. The Chinese Constitution provides for these rights – they are the self-selected goals and commitments of the government itself. Failure to realize them is a failure of the current regime to make good on its own promises.

With rights violations so widespread, Beijing cannot simply attempt to explain away particular instances. One government justification argues that China is a poor country, and economic stability must therefore take priority over all else, including political rights.[107] Though there may be a kernel of truth to this argument, it cannot justify the many specific instances of censorship, suppression of political speech, imprisonment of political activists, and so on. Not every attempt to exercise a political right threatens economic progress, but such attempts threaten the continued rulership of the current regime, and socialism itself.

The problem, therefore, is systemic. As noted, socialism is hostile to genuine political rights. Thus one can scarcely be surprised at the host of institutional impediments to rights discussed previously: Party domination of both the legislature and judiciary (despite constitutional provisions of independence); elevation of the interests of the state over the rights of the individual as sanctioned in article 51; use of the language of duty to override rights, and so on. Enjoyment of genuine rights apparently is incompatible with the continued existence of statist socialism in China. Beijing's only possible remaining justification is that the future benefits of socialism outweigh the present costs of exploiting, lying to, and abusing the people. But the collapse of socialism around the world and the bankruptcy of Communism as a practicable ideal cut against any such justification.

In any event, even if the current regime, or a postsocialist China, decides to take rights seriously, these rights will be rights with Chinese characteristics. That a Chinese rights culture will share western philosophical conceptions is highly doubtful. Many of the basic elements of traditional Chinese thought and practice militate against a strong theory of rights: the historical conception of person where one is born into a family, community, and state rather than the Hobbesian view of rights-bearing individuals preceding the state; the notion that rights are grants from the state rather than manna from heaven; the rejection of deontological and universal principles in favor of contingent, culture-sensitive ethics; the lack of foundational external restraints on authoritarian political rulers; the preference for informal mediation rather than appeal to the courts for enforcement of rights.

What then will rights with a Chinese face look like? Will such a theory provide rights that genuinely protect the individual in practice? Although one cannot be sure, certain guesses may be ventured.

VI.   A Chinese Theory of Rights

Given the pragmatic, anti-foundational character of much of Chinese philosophy, and of Confucianism in particular, any rights theory justifiable on Chinese terms will almost assuredly be a contingent one. There will be no attempt to pass off Chinese rights as universal rights – rights in China will be viewed as a product of Chinese culture, traditions, and historical and economic conditions.[108] As such, they may or may not be appropriate for other countries.[109] Further, rights will differ not only between China and other states but within China from one period to the next. This of course is the reality everywhere in the world. What will differ is that in China jurisprudential rhetoric may match reality.[110]

Second, Chinese rights will be more communitarian in theory and in practice. The traditional emphasis on social harmony and duties will be manifested in a theory that imposes duties as well as confers rights. Rights will provide a minimum level of protection for the individual against others and the state; duties will point to social solidarity and possibilities for human achievement. One will owe duties to fellow citizens as well as to the state, although not as in statist socialism to the *socialist* state as such. In contrast to PRC practice today, duties will not be used to limit rights in the name of the socialist cause but rather to supplement rights as ethical standards and guideposts.

Third, rights will continue to be looked upon as inspirational ethical themes to be realized in light of the particular situation by individuals seeking a harmonious solution to problems rather than simply as minimalist protections against the state and others.[111] Thus, rights will be one

resource, a starting point, for resolving conflicts. The goal will still be to move beyond strident insistence on rights to the detriment of others to creative solutions acceptable to all. Of course, in some cases, such solutions may not be possible. This may be because those involved are unwilling to put aside narrow self-interest – in which case there may yet be hope for persuasion – or it may be because there simply are not sufficient resources to satisfy everyone, or because some issues do not lend themselves to compromise. In such instances, where the ideal of harmony cannot be attained and the best solution is a more modest one, rights will play an important role in ensuring that certain individual interests are afforded at least special consideration and perhaps some minimum level of protection.

Fourth, given the historicized conception of the self in which a person is born into a complex social matrix, one would expect a relational theory of rights. One's rights (and duties) will vary depending on the relation of the parties. Not all rights and duties will be created equal; there will be greater duties to (and claim greater rights from) one's family than fellow citizens. Indeed, there will be greater duties to some citizens than others: for instance, the duty to neighbors or colleagues may be more stringent than those to strangers.

One constraint on the full realization of a highly articulated relational model of rights is the limited capacity of the formal legal system to take into account the particulars of the parties. Thus, a fifth aspect of Chinese rights culture will be the continued reliance on informal means for conflict resolution. Although far from perfect, traditional methods such as mediation offer many advantages. Both parties save face, fully participate in the proceeding, and shape the ultimate solution. The process, usually faster and cheaper than more formal methods, allows for a more particularized justice and for the restoration of social harmony, with both sides feeling they have received their due.

A sixth characteristic of Chinese rights and one positive result of socialism will be the continued prominence given to economic rights. Citizens have come to expect certain economic and material benefits from the state. Any regime that assumes power would be hard pressed to justify the elimination of medical care, for instance. The provision of a minimum level of material support is also consistent with the ideals, if not the historical reality, of Chinese traditions. Now that the people have actually observed that it is possible for the state to provide a minimum standard of living for all, they will not accept the old excuse that China is simply too poor.

A seventh characteristic is that rights will continue to be instrumental, construed as political and ethical tools for achieving the ultimate goal of harmony. The extreme deontological position that an individual possesses an inviolability that even the good of society as a whole cannot override is out of step with Chinese ethical traditions.

An eighth characteristic and a corollary of the rejection of the extreme deontological rights position is that the balance between the rights of the individual and the interests of the collective will probably be more inclined toward the latter than in the United States, though to what extent is difficult to predict.

As for whether Chinese rights will continue to be considered grants from the state, that too is uncertain. The idea that humans are born into this world with a full complement of rights as well as duties might take hold in the popular mind – as may the idea that the state is to serve the people rather than the rulers. Surely, greater contact with the world outside China will tend to reinforce such notions. If assimilated, such beliefs will make more likely the development of a viable rights culture in China.[112]

The seeds of a rights culture have already been planted in China, at least to the extent that the litany of rights provided in the constitution is not simply empty rhetoric. International pressure and a desire to enjoy the benefits of membership in the community of civilized nations may push China marginally further in the direction of a more rights-oriented public policy. Arguably, international pressure has already produced results. One can point not only to the government White Paper on rights but also to the release of prisoners tied to visits of foreign diplomats or to congressional votes on key issues such as most-favored nation status.[113]

However, the government will do what is necessary to maintain power – most importantly, maintaining economic progress and a higher standard of living. For this it needs foreign assistance.[114] Thus, in dealing with foreigners, Beijing must play high stakes poker. Whenever possible, the government goes on the attack, citing past imperialist abuses and contemporary rights failures within foreigners' own countries, or it stonewalls, simply denying that there are political prisoners or human rights abuses in China. Only when the potential economic gains are high and the international pressure unrelenting does Beijing make concessions to the international community, releasing a few prisoners here, making a conciliatory statement there. Ultimately, little changes within the Great Wall, as indicated by the recent statements of Justice Minister Cai Cheng rejecting the rule of law for the supremacy of the Party.[115]

Even if post-socialist China implements a contingent, communitarian rights program like the one outlined, the question remains whether it will be of much use. When push comes to shove, will the rights promulgated in the future constitution be worth the paper they are written on? When the interests of the individual conflict with those of the state, will the latter inevitably prevail, as they have throughout much of Chinese history?

The danger of an avowedly contingent theory of rights is that once one allows rights to be compromised to secure other normative considerations, the Pandora's box is open. Powerful political parties may abuse this window of discretionary opportunity to inappropriately override legitimate individual rights. Since absolute power in the hands of the foolhardy – or self-interested – is a real and ominous possibility, there should be many and stringent institutional safeguards. Decisions as to when state interests are sufficiently compelling to override constitutional rights granted to individuals should not be in the hands of a single branch of government, much less a single person. Constitutional review and a truly independent judiciary seem imperative. Whether these institutional adjustments alone or in combination with other changes are sufficient is difficult to predict. At a minimum, a rights culture with a heightened rights consciousness on the part of the people also seems essential. If the people do not stand up for their rights, the courts surely will not.

Conclusion

Not all rights theories are theories of natural rights. Nor does taking human rights seriously necessarily entail that rights be considered absolute and inalienable, a trump against any and all interests of the state, or as invariably of greater moral weight than matters of policy or social consequences. Indeed, no system takes human rights that seriously in practice.

There can be little doubt that the calculus as to the proper balance of individual autonomy versus social good will differ between the United States and China, as it does between the United States and every other country in the world. Although the ultimate ability of a contingent, communitarian rights theory to protect Chinese citizens against their government is uncertain, one thing is clear: the rhetoric of absolute, ahistorical, universal rights is at odds with China's philosophical and cultural traditions. The hope that China will adopt wholesale American rights ideology is misplaced. China may adopt a more rights-oriented public policy, but even then, rights in China will remain rights with Chinese characteristics.

Notes

1 Zhongguo Renmin Gongheguo Xianfa [Constitution of the People's Republic of China] arts. 33–40 (1982) [hereinafter PRC Const.]. For a discussion of Chinese rights, see Louis Henkin, "The Human Rights Idea in Contemporary China: A Comparative Perspective," in *Human Rights in Contemporary China*, 25–6 (R. Randle Edwards et al., eds., 1986); Andrew J. Nathan, "Political Rights in the Chinese Constitutions," in id. at 79–80.

2 See PRC Const., supra note 1, arts. 42–6.

3 In the years since Tiananmen, the topic of human rights has been increasingly debated in China. For a useful overview of current issues and theories, see Dangdai Renquan, *Contemporary Human Rights* (The Legal Research Institute of the Chinese Academy of Social Sciences, ed., 1992).

4 Two of the more popular slogans were dadao guandao (smash profiteering) and fandui fubai (oppose corruption). A poll conducted in early May of 865 Beijing residents found that 71%

believed corruption to be the main cause of instability in China. See Seth Faison, "Poll Shows Support for Demonstration," *S. China Morning Post*, May 12, 1989, at 1. See also Nicholas Kristof, "China Erupts: The Reasons Why," *NY Times Magazine*, June 4, 1989, at 26, 28 (noting that dissatisfaction stemmed not only from a desire for democracy, but also from economic frustration).

5 For a similar view, see Jane Macartney, "The Students: Heroes, Pawns, or Power-Brokers?," in *The Broken Mirror: China After Tiananmen*, 3, 5, 12, 13 (George Hicks, ed., 1990). Andrew Nathan has noted that intellectuals attempted to limit the movement's agenda to issues of freedom of speech and dialogue with the government. Freedom of speech is, of course, particularly important to academics. See Andrew Nathan, "Tiananmen and the Cosmos," *New Republic*, July 19, 1991, at 31, 32. See also Marsha L. Wagner, "The Strategies of the Student Democracy Movement in Beijing," in *Tiananmen: China's Struggle for Democracy*, 43, 59, 74–6 (Marsha L. Wagner & Winston L. Y. Yang, eds., 1990) (students wanted a more honest government but continued to believe the Party and government officials could be reformed through moral suasion).

6 *The Declaration of Independence* (US 1776). In Dworkinian terms, the rights of the individual trump the overall good of society; in Nozickian, "individuals have rights and there are things no person or group may do to them"; in Rawlsian, "each person possesses an inviolability founded on justice that even the welfare of society as a whole cannot override." See Ronald Dworkin, *Taking Rights Seriously* (1977); Robert Nozick, *Anarchy, State and Utopia*, ix (1974); John Rawls, *A Theory of Justice*, 3 (1971).

7 Jeremy Bentham, "Anarchical Fallacies," in 2 *Collected Papers* (1843), reprinted in *Human Rights* 32 (A. I. Meldin, ed., 1970).

8 In response to Kant's injunction against treating humans as things, Oliver Wendell Holmes candidly remarked, "If a man lives in society, he is liable to find himself so treated." Oliver W. Holmes, *The Common Law*, 38 (Mark DeWolfe Howe, ed., Belknap Press of Harvard University 1963) (1881). Indeed, "No society has ever admitted that it could not sacrifice individual welfare to its own existence." Id. at 37.

9 Universal Declaration of Human Rights, art. 29(2) UN GAOR, UN Doc. A/811 (1948) (emphasis added). The US also limits rights in the name of the public good. Our system first distinguishes

between rights. Some are classified as "fundamental" or "preferred" – for example, freedom of religion and speech. But even these fundamental rights are not absolute or inalienable; they may be overridden if on strict scrutiny the court finds a compelling state interest. Other rights, for example economic rights, may be infringed on finding nothing more than a minimally rational basis for the trumping legislation. Griswold v. Connecticut, 381 U.S. 479, 486 (1965) (Goldberg, J., concurring); Poe v. Ullman, 367 U.S. 497, 522 (1961) (Harlan, J., dissenting).

10 The point is not that China may justify or be excused for Tiananmen simply by waving a banner of cultural relativism. Some things – such as the torture of student activists – are clearly not acceptable, *by anyone's standards*, western or Chinese (be they Confucian or socialist). See "Activist Details Human Jail Abuse," *S. China Morning Post*, June 1, 1992, at 10.

11 Cf. Andrew Nathan, "Tiananmen and the Cosmos," supra note 5, at 32, 35 (noting that intellectuals wanted democracy without the demos). Indeed, in a June 3, 1989 interview, the student leader Wuer Kaixi stated that "the Chinese people lack consciousness of democracy, and do not understand democracy." *Ming Pao*, June 17, 1989; *Foreign Broadcast Information Service*, June 20, 1989, at 24–7 (hereinafter FBIS).

12 Witness the support for so-called new or neo-authoritarianism in the PRC modeled on the economically free-market and politically authoritarian approach of Taiwan, Singapore, and South Korea. See Xin Quanweizhuyi, *New Authoritarianism* (Liu Jun & Li Lin, eds., 1989); see also Michel Oksenberg et al., eds., *Beijing Spring, 1989: Confrontation & Conflict*, 123–49 (1990).

13 The claim is not that Chinese intellectual traditions alone will determine the nature and course of human rights in China. No doubt Chinese rights are and will continue to be influenced by a host of other factors, including domestic and foreign political and economic realities. But see infra notes 113–15 and accompanying text. Nor do I claim that Chinese intellectual traditions "lock in" a particular form of rights – or that, for instance, the Chinese cannot escape from the walls of Confucian political philosophy. The thesis is simply that these intellectual traditions, particularly Confucianism, will most likely exert considerable influence on Chinese human rights.

14 PRC Const., supra note 1, art. 5; see also "Human Rights in China," 34 *Beijing Rev.*, Nov.

4–10, 1991 at 8, 14 (hereinafter *White Paper*). (This is Beijing's official statement on human rights.)

15 See Nathan, supra note 1, at 101–2, 108–12; see also Andrew Nathan, "Sources of Chinese Rights Thinking," in *Human Rights in Contemporary China*, supra note 1, at 125, 132–7; Shao-Chuan Leng & Hungdah Chiu, *Criminal Justice in Post-Mao China*, 98–104 (1985); Li Maoguan, "Why Laws Go Unenforced," 32 *Beijing Rev.* 17–18 (1980). While in theory the 1982 Constitution limits Party authority, the ultimate authority of the Party is explicit in the 1975 and 1978 constitutions. Further, during all periods since 1949, the Party has in practice dominated the People's Congresses, courts and other organs of state. For continuing problems in the establishment of a truly independent judiciary, see *Report of the Australian Human Rights Delegation to China*, 14–26, 27–9 (1991).

16 Mao Zedong, *On People's Democratic Dictatorship*, 16–17 (1951).

17 Willy Wo-lap Lam, "Justice Minister Rejects 'Supremacy of the Law,'" *S. China Morning Post*, Nov. 12, 1991, at 12.

18 PRC Const., supra note 1, art. 51.

19 Rawls, supra note 6. Whether state interest may trump individual interest, and if so, under what conditions, are discussed infra. As noted in supra notes 6–7 and accompanying text, all states impose limits on individual rights in the name of the public good.

20 See Louis Favoreu, "Constitutional Review in Europe," in *Constitutionalism and Rights* 38, 47–54 (Louis Henkin & Albert Rosenthal, eds., 1990).

21 Leng & Chiu, supra note 15, at 43. PRC Const., supra note 1, at 43. See also Nathan, supra note 1, at 120.

22 Louis Henkin, "Constitutions and the Elements of Constitutionalism," paper prepared for the American Council of Learned Societies Conference on Constitutionalism and the Transition to Democracy in Eastern Europe, Pecs, Hungary (June 18–20, 1990) (on file at Chinese Legal Studies Center, Columbia University), passim.

23 China has had four constitutions since 1949. The first was promulgated in 1954, followed by new ones in 1975, 1978, and 1982. For a comparison, see Nathan, supra note 1, at 80–1.

24 For abuses of the constitution and the criminal process arising out of the Tiananmen "incident" see Jerome Cohen, "Tiananmen and the Rule of Law," in *The Broken Mirror*, supra note 5, at 325–6. Ironically, one important motivation behind the return to a rule of law called for by

Deng and other leaders in the late 1970s was personal experience of widespread legal abuse during the Cultural Revolution. See Leng & Chiu, supra note 15, at 35–7 (noting also the importance of rule of law to the "four modernizations" and economic reform).

25 Simply as an analytical matter, wholesale rejection of constitutionalism necessarily entails rejection of rights because one element of constitutionalism is individual rights. Indeed, to the extent that a commitment to rights is a necessary condition of constitutionalism, the argument is circular: constitutionalism is necessary for rights, and rights are necessary for constitutionalism. If individual rights are not a necessary element, one can avoid the apparent circularity by defining constitutionalism without reference to rights for the purpose of the discussion.

26 Even the International Covenant on Civil and Political Rights, UN GAOR, 21st Sess., Annex, 1496th plen. mtg. at art. 4 (1966), provides that "[i]n time of public emergency which threatens the life of the nation," States may "take measures derogating from their obligations under the present Covenant to the extent strictly required by the exigencies of the situation."

27 See e.g., PRC Const., supra note 1, art. 126 (providing for an independent judiciary).

28 Henkin, supra note 1, at 19.

29 As Peter Lin notes, even a consciousness of rights is not sufficient. In addition,

there must be a widespread, entrenched, and "self-sacrificial" commitment by the elites to act consistently with the values and standard of rationality generally accepted by the people. Such a commitment involves "self-sacrifice" because the governing elites have to forgo the advantage they could otherwise gain by abusing their power, in exchange for a system from which all will benefit.

Peter Lin, "Between Theory and Practice: The Possibility of a Right to Free Speech in the People's Republic of China," 4 *J. Chinese L.* 257, 268 (1990).

30 To be sure, some have stood up and continue to stand up to the government. One need only recall the unforgettable image of the sole demonstrator standing resolutely in front of a row of tanks. Similarly, the existence of underground newspapers and dissidents both in China and living abroad in exile demonstrates that some Chinese are prepared to oppose the government. Even more direct evidence is the recent phenom-

enon of politically motivated lawsuits against the government. See Sheryl WuDunn, "Chinese Bite Back at Beijing with Lawsuits," *NY Times*, Sept. 13, 1992, at 9 (noting that the government is unlikely to lose a politically sensitive lawsuit).

Nevertheless, such pockets of resistance remain the exception and not the rule. The few people willing to challenge the political authority of the government directly fall far short of the kind of broad-based social support that Henkin sees as necessary to constitutionalism.

31 *See* Li Maoguan, supra note 15, at 18–19.

32 "In hearing litigation," remarked Confucius, "I am no different from any other man. But if you insist on a difference, it is, perhaps, that I try to get the parties not to resort to litigation in the first place." Confucius, *Lun Yü [Analects]*, 12:13 (hereinafter *Analects*). For an English translation, see D. C. Lau, *Confucius: The Analects* (1979). Citations to the *Analects* follow the numbering of Lau.

33 For informal or "extralegal" methods of conflict resolution in contemporary China, see Victor H. Li, *Law Without Lawyers*, 14–16, 44–65 (1978); Jerome A. Cohen, *The Criminal Process in the People's Republic of China 1949–1963*, 97–199 (1968).

34 Sybille Van Der Sprenkel, *Legal Institutions in Manchu China*, 135 (1966). For an excellent "insider's view" of the Chinese legal system of the Qing, see Huang Liu-hong, *A Complete Book Concerning Happiness and Benevolence* (Djang Chu, trans. & ed., 1984). Huang describes frankly the corruption plaguing every level of the judicial system.

35 There is some evidence that the historical stereotypes are losing their validity. In 1989, Chinese brought 1.85 million civil cases. This represented a 24% increase over 1988 and a sevenfold jump over 1978. Edward Epstein, "China's Legal Reforms," in *China Review* 9.33 (Kuan Hsin-Chi & Maurice Brosseau, eds., 1991) (citing *Renmin Erbao* [People's Daily], Apr. 10, 1990, at 2). Nevertheless, traditional attitudes continue to exert an influence, as noted by Li Maoguan, supra note 15.

36 More accurately, civil and political rights are understood as universal, abstract, and natural whereas social, economic, and collective rights are understood as contingent, nonuniversal, and decidedly secondary. See Ann Kent, "Waiting for Rights: China's Human Rights and China's Constitutions, 1949–1989," 13 *Hum. Rts. Q.* 170, 174 (1991). I do not mean to imply that all rights theories, even political rights theories, are

universal natural rights theories. Nevertheless, I consider such theories in this section for several reasons. First, the rhetoric of rights theories is often that of universal, natural rights. The claim that China needs human rights is often the claim that China needs universal human rights. Second, such theories have been and remain extremely influential in the western tradition. Third, understanding how assumptions underlying such theories are at odds with Chinese political tradition helps explain why China is more likely to adopt the kind of contingent, communitarian rights theory described in part VI. Of course, westerners may also favor similar theories. Indeed, communitarian theories are currently in vogue. I do not claim that such theories must be unique to China or that no western thinkers have advanced similar views.

37 The poverty of this "justification" is itself evident from Alasdair MacIntyre's observation that:

> there is no expression in any ancient or medieval language correctly translated by our expression "a right" until near the close of the middle ages: the concept lacks any means of expression in Hebrew, Greek, Latin or Arabic, classical or medieval, before 1400, let alone in Old English, or in Japanese even as late as the mid-nineteenth century.

Alasdair MacIntyre, *After Virtue*, 69 (1984).

38 Henry Rosemont, "Why Take Rights Seriously? A Confucian Critique," in *Human Rights and the World's Religions*, 167 (Leroy Rounder, ed., 1988). Some western thinkers have begun to challenge the notion that humans possess rights simply by virtue of birth.

39 *Li*, conventionally translated as rites, refers to the full range of social customs, ethical norms, and political principles that inform interpersonal relations, social institutions, and normative discourse in China.

40 John Locke, *Two Treatises of Government*, bk. II, chs. VIII–XV, 361–99 (Peter Laslett, ed., 1960) (3d ed. 1698); Nozick, supra note 6, at 10–25.

41 Thomas Hobbes, *Leviathan*, P. I, chs. 13–15, 17–19, P. II, ch. 26, 183–217, 223–39, 313 (Crawford B. Macpherson, ed., 1951) (1651).

42 Jean-Jacques Rousseau, *On Social Contract*, bk. IV, ch. 2, in *The Essential Rousseau*, 88 (Lowell Bair, tr., 1974) (1762).

43 Rawls, supra note 6, at 11–17. The Rawlsian variant adds a twist or two: rational agents in the "original position" now make life-choices from behind a veil of ignorance. Id. at 17–22, 136–41.

However, the key assumptions remain the same. One is still in a world of atomistic individuals in competition for scarce goods, a world where individual rights and liberties precede obligations to the state and to each other.

44 See Philip Soper, "Dworkin's Domain," 100 *Harv. L. Rev.* 1166, 1180–1 (1987).

45 Dworkin, supra note 6, at 219–24.

46 See R. Kent Greenwalt, "Law's Empire," 84 *J. Phil.* 284, 290 (1987) (book review); see also R. P. Peerenboom, "A Coup D'Etat in Law's Empire: Dworkin's Hercules Meets Atlas," 9 *Law & Phil.* 95, 108–11 (1990).

47 Of course, not all western ethical theories are foundational and universalist in character. For instance, situational ethics and the normative views of American pragmatists such as Dewey share much in common with Confucianism. See Randall P. Peerenboom, *Law and Morality in Ancient China: The Silk Manuscripts of Huang-Lao*, ch. IV (1993). Similarly, many writers now accept that normative theories and systems are contingent. Indeed, even Rawls has conceded that his arguments for justice as fairness are framed to apply to the "'basic structure' of a modern constitutional democracy." John Rawls, "Justice As Fairness: Political not Metaphysical," 14 *Phil. & Pub. Affs.* 223, 224 (1985). See also John Rawls, "Kantian Constructivism in Moral Theory," 77 *J. Phil.* 515, 518 (1980); John Rawls, "The Idea of an Overlapping Consensus," 7 *Oxford J. Legal Studies* 1 (1987) ("[T]he aims of political philosophy depend on the society it addresses"). He then proceeds to list seven features of modern constitutional democracies, including "the fact that the political culture of a society with a democratic tradition implicitly contains certain fundamental intuitive ideas from which it is possible to work up a political conception of justice suitable for a constitutional regime." Id. at 4–5.

48 Aristotle, *Politics*, in *The Complete Works of Aristotle*, bk. I, ch. 2, at 1987 (Jonathan Barnes, ed., 1984) ("[M]an is by nature a political animal"). He adds, "([H]e who is unable to live in society, or who has no need because he is sufficient for himself, must be either a beast or a god." Id. at 1988. For a similar view, see Confucius, *Analects*, supra note 32, at 18:7 ("One cannot associate with birds and beasts. Am I not a member of this human race? Who, then, is there for me to associate with?") For the Confucian view of the self as a nexus of relations – social, political, cultural, religious, and so forth – see infra notes 57–61, 74 and accompanying text.

49   Plato, *The Republic*, in *Plato: The Collected Dialogues*, 575–844 (Edith Hamilton & Huntington Cairns, eds., 1961).

50   Their worries were in part a response to the autocratic, all-powerful sovereign of Hobbes and the majoritarian universal will of Rousseau. See Alexis de Tocqueville, "Democracy in America," ch. 15, in *Alexis de Tocqueville: Democracy, Revolution, and Society*, 99–101 (John Stone & Stephen Mennell, eds., 1980) (1835) (warning against the "tyranny of the majority"). See also John Stuart Mill, *On Liberty*, ch. 4, 141–62 (Gertrude Himmelfarb, ed., 1982) (1859).

51   Andrew Nathan, *Chinese Democracy*, 50–1 (1985).

52   R. Randle Edwards, "Civil and Social Rights: Theory and Practice in Chinese Law Today," in *Human Rights in Contemporary China*, supra note 1, at 44–5.

53   The compelling interest standard applies to "fundamental" or "preferred" rights. Non-fundamental rights are measured by a mere minimum rationality test: the legislature must have had some intelligible reason for enacting the rights limiting legislation. See supra note 9 and accompanying text. Of course, this points to one of the major conceptual equivocations underlying rights talk. Not all rights are created equal. One must distinguish between explicit constitutional rights, implicit constitutional rights, legislative rights, legal rights, and nonlegal rights (social rights or rights in theory – philosophical rights – and so forth).

54   Linguistic distinctions continue to be important. Ann Kent notes that despite the restrictive nature of the 1982 constitution, Chinese citizens experienced in practice an expansion of civil and political rights during the early to mid-1980s. Consonant with greater liberties was a shift from collective to individual consciousness, as symbolized by the increasing use of *gongmin* (citizen) as opposed to the previously dominant *qunzhong* (masses). Kent, supra note 36, at 188.
      During the 1989 protests, some of the working class demonstrators referred to themselves as *shimin* (urbanites or civilians). Significantly, intellectuals continued to refer to these demonstrators as *qunzhong* (masses) or *laobaixing* (common people), reinforcing the appearance, if not the reality, of anti-democratic elitism. Nathan, supra note 5, at 32.

55   Mary Anne Warren was one of the first in the contemporary western literature to draw a similar distinction between "genetic humans" and "persons." See Mary Anne Warren, "On the Moral and Legal Status of Abortion," 57 *Monist* 43–61 (1973).

56   Davld L. Hall & Roger T. Ames, *Thinking Through Confucius*, 139 (1987).

57   See *Analects*, supra note 32, at 18:6, 10:17. Humans, of course, have the potential to differentiate themselves from animals. This may provide a justification for extending some degree of moral consideration to children, though it does little for the severely impaired. The relatively high degree of infanticide, the almost non-existence of opposition to abortion, and the fact that in traditional Chinese law children were provided little protection against their parents, suggest that children were not full-fledged members of society and that one's right to consideration was indeed linked to social achievement. In the Qin, for example, the father was permitted to kill or mutilate his son as long as he first petitioned for approval. A. F. P. Hulsewe, *Remnants of Han Law*, 8 (1985). If the child was born deformed, infanticide was permitted. Id. at 139. Harsh treatment of one's offspring was also permitted in other dynasties. See Gu Tang Lu Shuyi, *The Tang Code and Commentaries*, arts. 253, 256; for an English translation, see Wallace Johnson, *The Tang Code*, 21, 31–2 (1979).

58   The view that some members of society have no claim right on society even to life is not completely alien to the American mind: presumably some such notion underlies the popular appeal of capital punishment in the United States. The difference is that in China one must first earn one's rights whereas in the United States one starts with rights but can forfeit them through socially inappropriate behavior.

59   "Lead the people by edicts, keep them in line with penal law, and they will avoid punishments but have no sense of shame. Lead them with virtue, keep them in line with the rites, and they will not only have a sense of shame but will order themselves harmoniously." *Analects*, supra note 32, at 2:3.

60   In a Confucian world, ethical standards – of which rights are one species – serve not so much as aspirational norms as inspirational themes. See A. S. Cua, *Dimensions in Moral Creativity*, 124 (1978). That is, one is not simply to conform to a particular rule or standard. Rather one is to embody and give expression to the underlying ideal in one's own way, in light of one's own circumstances. To act appropriately in a given circumstance, one must "appropriate" the ethical value – one must make that value one's own. As a consequence, one has a great deal

of discretion in how one translates an ethical rule or norm into practice.

The inspirational character of Confucian ethics explains in part an observation of Andrew Nathan, namely, that rights in Chinese constitutions are programmatic – "that is, they are presented as goals to be realized." See Nathan, supra note 1, at 121. What are minimal ethical and political restraints imposed on the government in the west become in Confucian China ethical ideals through which social beings can realize a humane society. These ideals must be translated into practice and given expression in light of the particular circumstances. Thus, in seeking harmony, one begins but does not end with rights.

61 Thus, one is transformed from a human being qua animal to a social person entitled to deference and respect. As A. S. Cua observes, "concept of ren is the concept of an ideal of moral excellence. ... The focus is on man himself and what he can morally accomplish in relation to others." Cua, supra note 60, at 68.

62 See David Currie, "Positive and Negative Constitutional Rights," 53 U. Chi. L. Rev. 864 (1986).

63 See, e.g., DeShaney v. Winnebago County Dep't of Social Servs., 489 U.S. 189, 196 (1989).

[The Due Process Clause's] purpose was to protect the people from the State, not to ensure that the State protected them from each other.... Consistent with these principles, our cases have recognized that the Due Process Clauses generally confer no affirmative right to governmental aid, even where such aid may be necessary to secure life, liberty, or property....

64 Universal Declaration of Human Rights, supra note 9, arts. 22–25 (right to work, social security, and an adequate standard of living, including food, clothing, housing, and medical care).

65 See Westley Newcomb Hohfeld, "Fundamental Legal Conceptions as Applied in Judicial Reasoning," 23 Yale L.J. 16, 31–2 (1913).

66 US tort law does impose specific duties on some individuals in certain circumstances based on a "special relationship" between the parties. For instance, innkeepers have certain duties toward their guests, as do jailors to their prisoners, and hosts to guests invited onto the premises. See Restatement (Second) of Torts, §314A (1965). Similarly, one who attempts to aid another but leaves that person worse off or who intentionally prevents a third party from coming to the aid of someone injured may be held liable. Id. at

§§322, 323, 324A, 326, 327. Further, a small number of states have enacted good samaritan laws. See infra note 67. Nevertheless, in the vast majority of states, the general rule is that in the absence of a special relation, "the fact that the actor realized or should realize that action on his part is necessary for another's aid or protection does not of itself impose upon him a duty to take such action." Restatement, at §314.

67 See Vt. Stat. Ann. tit. 12, sec. 519 (1973); Minn. Stat. sec. 604.05 (1984). More than a dozen European states have good samaritan laws that impose criminal sanctions for failing to provide aid to one in peril. For good samaritan laws in Europe, see Rudzinski, "The Duty to Rescue: A Comparative Analysis," in The Good Samaritan and the Law, 91 (J. Ratcliffe, ed., 1966).

68 Of course, this is largely a matter of rhetorical emphasis. On the Hohfeldian view, claim rights and duties are but two sides of the same coin. Nevertheless, the rhetorical difference is illuminating. See Wang Jiafu et al., "Lun Fazhi Gaige [On Reform of the Legal System]," 2 Faxue Yanjiu 1, 8 (1989) (arguing that while rights entail duties and duties entail rights, rights should nonetheless occupy the leading position).

69 PRC Const., supra note 1, art. 49 (also providing that parents have a duty to rear and educate their minor children).

70 Id. arts. 42, 46, 49, 54–6.

71 The issue of Confucianism's role in the historical subordination of women in China is a difficult one. No doubt the traditional hierarchical status relationships of Confucianism contributed to discrimination against women in practice. Nevertheless, Confucian theory does not mandate such a result. As a contextual ethical system, it is able to pay greater heed to women's interests, in keeping with their changed circumstances and status in contemporary society. That said, women's issues will most likely remain a concern.

72 The five primary relations are ruler/official, husband/wife, parent/child, older brother/ younger brother, friend/friend. Only the last is not hierarchical. One of the first to ground the five relations in the natural order was Dong Zhongshu. See Wingtsit Chan, A Sourcebook in Chinese Philosophy, 277–8 (1963).

73 Thus one condition for deference is that the authority, the person in the superior position, respect the interests of the deferring party. Obviously the leaders in Beijing did not meet this condition in dealing with the students and workers in 1989. Indeed, the failure of creativity

resulting in the excessive and unnecessary use of force by the *authoritarian* regime reveals their bankruptcy as *authoritative* Confucian rulers.

74 Edmund Pincoffs, *Quandaries and Virtues*, 8 (1986).

75 Palsgraf v. Long Island Railroad Co., 162 N.E. 99 (N.Y. 1928) (citing Frederick Pollock, *Torts*, 455 (1891)) ("Proof of negligence in the air, so to speak, will not do").

76 Lest anyone believe that socialist China has succeeded in eradicating Confucian values, consider the government's official statement on human rights:

> China is in favor of strengthening international cooperation in the realm of human rights on the basis of mutual understanding and seeking a common ground while reserving differences. However, no country in its effort to realize and protect human rights can take a route that is divorced from its history and its economic, political and cultural realities. . . . It is also noted in the resolution of the 46th conference on human rights that no single mode of development is applicable to all cultures and peoples. It is neither proper nor feasible for any country to judge other countries by the yardstick of its own mode or to impose its own mode on others. . . . Consideration should be given to the differing views on human rights held by countries with different political, economic and social systems, as well as different historical, religious and cultural backgrounds. International human rights activities should be carried on in the spirit of seeking common ground while reserving differences, mutual respect, and the promotion of understanding and cooperation.

White Paper, supra note 14, at 8. Present are many of the key features of Confucianism: rejection of abstract, universal dogmas and ethical principles; attention to the particular historical context of the parties; attempt to find and build on common ground in order to realize a solution amenable to all parties; belief in multiple possible resolutions to social and political conflicts; focus on persuasion and rejection of force. Indeed, if one had to summarize Confucian teaching in a single sentence, one would be hard pressed to do better than Beijing's twice repeated slogan: seek common ground while reserving differences, maintain mutual respect, and promote understanding and cooperation. Again, by their own self-selected standards, the leaders in Beijing failed utterly in violently oppressing the 1989 demonstrators.

77 Roderick Macneil, "Contract in China: Law, Practice, and Dispute Resolution," 38 *Stan. L. Rev.* 303, 333 (1986).

78 See Donald Clarke, "Dispute Resolution in China," 5 *J. Chinese L.* 245, 245–6 (1991).

79 Macneil, supra note 77, at 342. See also Economic Contract Law of the People's Republic of China, art. 32 (adopted Dec. 13, 1981) (if both parties have "committed mistakes," they should "share responsibility" according to "actual circumstances").

80 See infra note 102.

81 See Mill, supra note 50.

82 Karl Marx, *The German Ideology*, quoted in Cohen, supra note 33, at 75.

83 Unlike Marx, Mao rejected the utopian "theory of no clashes." Instead, he called for permanent revolution to ensure that the bureaucracy remained faithful to the needs of the masses and to prevent the emergence of class conflicts. See Mao Tsetung, "The Vision of the Great Leap," in *The People's Republic of China: A Documentary History of Revolutionary Change*, 381, 385–7 (Mark Selden, ed., 1979).

84 For an overview of law in Maoist China, see Alice E.-S. Tay, "The Struggle for Law in China," 21 *U. Brit. Colum. L. Rev.* 561 (1987).

85 See Note, "Concepts of Law in the Chinese Anti-Crime Campaign," 98 *Harv. L. Rev.* 1890 (1985).

86 As noted earlier, legal rights are often compromised in the mediation process. See supra note 78 and accompanying text.

87 See Cohen, supra note 33, at 20.

88 Id.

89 Mao Tsetung, "On the Correct Handling of Contradictions among the People," in *Selected Works of Mao Tsetung*, 391 (1977).

90 Id. at 393.

91 PRC Const., supra note 1, arts. 42, 46.

92 Id. art. 54; see also art. 33 ("Every citizen enjoys the rights and at the same time must perform the duties prescribed by the Constitution and the law").

93 See id. arts. 42, 46, 52, 54–6. But see art. 49 (duty of parents to rear and educate children and duty of children to support parents).

94 See, e.g., Wang et al., supra note 68, at 8.

95 PRC Const., supra note 1, arts. 43–5.

96 If indeed they talk to each other at all. Recently, Britain's Home Office refused to see a human rights delegation from China, fearing that the Chinese group was planning to criticize Britain's human rights record, particularly with respect to Northern Ireland. Under pressure from the Foreign Office, the Home Office relented. Refusal

to see the delegation might have jeopardized Prime Minister Major's request to send Britain's own human rights delegation to China. Geoffrey Crothall, "UK Averts Incident by Agreeing to See China Team," *S. China Morning Post*, Feb. 14, 1992, at 1.

97 *White Paper*, supra note 14, at 9.

98 For an account of these atrocities and human rights abuses inflicted on Chinese citizens, see id. at 10.

99 The theoretically interesting metaethical issue is whether one may legitimately judge another individual or culture according to values not shared by that individual or culture. Because I rely on shared and indigenous Chinese values, I need not address the issue. For a defense of "evaluative universalism," where one judges another culture according to the values one believes in, see Andrew Nathan, "The Place of Values in Cross-Cultural Studies: The Example of Democracy in China," in *Ideas Across Cultures*, 293–317 (Paul A. Cohen & Merle Goldman, eds., 1990). Little is to be gained from judging another culture according to exogenous values if the other side refuses to engage in dialogue on those terms or believes its own values to be superior. That such coercive methods would succeed with Beijing is unlikely. See infra notes 113–15 and accompanying text.

100 Ann Kent argues that notwithstanding previous achievements, China in the 1980s experienced several setbacks in the actual realization of economic rights. For instance, the right to work was increasingly out of step with the realities of the fledgling commodity or market economy spawned by reform policies. Further negative developments included: "(1) the commodification of social welfare; (2) the increase of the rural–urban gap in the provision of social services; (3) the devolution of responsibility for social welfare and social security; and (4) the lack of a comprehensive unemployment insurance system." See Kent, supra note 36, at 193–9.

101 *White Paper*, supra note 14, at 13.

102 Id. at 14–15. For an account of Beijing's abuse of PRC criminal procedure laws in the treatment of 1989 demonstrators, see Asia Watch, "Rough Justice in Beijing: Punishing the 'Black Hands' of Tiananmen Square," in *News from Asia Watch*, Jan. 27, 1991, at 4–7.

103 *White Paper*, supra note 14, at 15–16, 19. Witness the treatment of Zhang Yimou's films. See Lynn Pan, "A Chinese Master," *NY Times Magazine*, Mar. 1, 1992, at 30. Foreign reporters are also subject to restrictions. For a discussion of post-Tiananmen suppression of freedom of expression, see Asia Watch, "Punishment Season: Human Rights in China After Martial Law," in *The Broken Mirror*, supra note 5, at 383–6; for limits on the press, see International League for Human Rights & the Ad Hoc Study Group on Human Rights in China, "Winter in Beijing: Continuing Repression Since the Beijing Massacre," Feb. 18, 1990, at 20–2.

104 *White Paper*, supra note 14, at 24. One report based on Chinese documents estimated that, as of 1991, as many as 100,000 people were imprisoned for opposing the government. See Charles Lane, "The Last Gulag," *Newsweek*, Sept. 23, 1991, at 26.

105 See Zhonghua Renmin Gongheguo Xingzheng Susong Fa (Administrative Litigation Law of the PRC) (promulgated, April 4, 1989), *Renmin Ribao*, Apr. 10, 1989, at 2, trans. in *China Law and Practice*, June 5, 1989, at 37–57.

106 See supra note 30.

107 Cf. *White Paper*, supra note 14, at 11–12.

108 In this respect, Marxism's emphasis on historical materialism coincides with Confucianism's sensitivity to the particular conditions of society, reinforcing the view of rights as contingent. Even some scholars who argue for an expansive theory of human rights based on the commonality (*gongtongxing*) of all people reflect the influence of Marxism in maintaining that rights are a product of the particular historical, economic, and material conditions of a society. See, e.g., Li Buyun, "Lun renquan de sanzhong cunzai xingtai [On Three Forms of Existence of Human Rights]," 65 *Faxue Yanjiu* [*Studies in Law*] 11, 13 (1992).

109 It is true that all state[s] may share some similar rights. Such rights, however, would be contingent on political, cultural, and economic factors.

110 As Nathan points out, a prominent feature of Chinese rights is that they have varied from one constitution to the next. He attributes this to the belief of authors of the Chinese Constitutions that rights are grants from the state, and hence may be added or subtracted at the will of the state. Nathan, supra note 1, at 121. The conception of social order as historically contingent and evolving may also explain this phenomenon: as the society changes, so must rights.

111 See supra note 60 and accompanying text.

112 There is no inherent contradiction between an instrumental, harmony-based theory of rights and the view that such rights attach to human beings qua human beings. One could believe that one is born with certain rights that protect one

against certain intrusions by the state and others and yet do not trump all social consequences.

113 However, the extent to which the international community can exercise influence over China is limited. Having suffered through 100 years of imperialist oppression, China is highly sensitive to foreign criticism and intrusions in sovereign affairs. One need only reflect on Tiananmen to appreciate Beijing's disdain for world opinion. More importantly, the leaders of the PRC are fully aware that foreign commitment to human rights is not deep. When economic goals conflict with concern for human rights abuse, economics wins out all too often. In light of such short-term self-interest and transitory commitment, the PRC need but stay the course.

114 It bears noting that even in the immediate days following Tiananmen, Beijing insisted that its open-door policies would continue unabated. See, e.g., Deng Xiaoping's remarks on June 9, 1989, *Beijing Rev.*, June 12–25, 1989, at 4.

115 See supra note 17 and accompanying text.

55

Poverty and Constitutional Justice: The Indian Experience

Jeremy Cooper

I. Introduction

In 1933, the British House of Lords affirmed its view that "poverty is a misfortune for which the law cannot take any responsibility at all."[1] In 1986, Justice Bhagwati, Chief Justice of the Indian Supreme Court, described the function of a Supreme Court, in relation to poverty and oppression, in a somewhat different vein:

> The judges in India have asked themselves the question: Can judges really escape addressing themselves to substantial questions of social justice? Can they simply say to litigants who came to them for justice and the general public that accords them power, status and respect, that they simply follow the legal text when they are aware that their actions will perpetuate inequality and injustice? Can they restrict their enquiry into law and life within the narrow confines of a narrowly defined rule of law? Does the requirement of constitutionalism not make greater demands on the judicial function?[2]

The history of litigation in the Indian Supreme Court throughout the past decade has demonstrated that the answer to all of the above rhetorical questions has been a clear and unambiguous no, the Judges cannot. Throughout the 1980s, whenever a citizen of India has come to the Indian Supreme Court, seeking relief under the constitution, the court seems consistently to have asked itself the same fundamental question: Will the granting of the relief asked by the plaintiff advance the goal of social justice? If the answer is affirmative, the litigant is granted the relief requested. If the answer is negative, the relief is refused.[3] This article seeks to describe and explain the background of this phenomenon, and to explore the promises and limitations found in this strategy for poverty lawyers in other jurisdictions.

India has a total area of 3,287,782 square kilometers and a population in excess of 700 million, of whom only 100 million live in cities or towns. Although there are considerable gaps between rich and poor, the vast majority of the Indian population is poor. An enormous variety of races and peoples live within the political boundaries of the state, and despite a large Hindu majority, there are large minorities of other religions, including Moslems, Christians, Sikhs, Buddhists, and Jains. India's legal system is among the oldest in the world.[4] The Constitution of India,

Jeremy Cooper, "Poverty and Constitutional Justice: The Indian Experience," *Mercer Law Review*, vol. 44, 1993, pp. 611–35. © 1993. Reprinted with permission from Mercer Law Review.

created in 1950, gave its Supreme Court the powers to nullify actions of the Executive and the Legislature, when the action breaches fundamental human rights.[5] These powers are as wide ranging as those afforded in 1787 by the United States Constitution's Founding Fathers to the United States Supreme Court, a Court described by one international law expert as "the world's first human rights tribunal."[6] The traditions of the Indian Supreme Court between 1950 and 1980 were proud, with many strong judgements meted from its chambers.[7] However, the primary focus of their judgements was not poverty or social justice.[8] Indeed, the contrary was more often the case, as was observed by Dwivedi in 1973, when characterizing the Indian Supreme Court of that period as "an arena of legal quibbling for men with long purses."[9] The legal system had itself been "transplanted from a foreign colonial power based on foreign ideals and values and imposed on a country with vastly different indigenous value systems, traditions and customs."[10] The court tried to follow the arcane methods of the British House of Lords. It is not surprising therefore that during the period from 1950–80, the Indian Supreme Court was frequently accused of obstructing social reform.[11] In the 1980s, however, due largely to the collective philosophy of a group of radical judges who formed the majority view of the court at that time, a primary function of the Indian Supreme Court became "the liberation of the poor and oppressed through judicial initiatives" with the overt assistance of "the social activists and public interest litigators."[12] In a decade, the Indian Supreme Court became the last resort for the oppressed and bewildered.[13]

As part of this process, numerous public interest groups mobilized to take advantage of a likely favourable judicial response to protect a whole range of vulnerable, or victimised groups, including prisoners held without trial, bonded labourers, pavement dwellers, litigants without legal aid, women bought and sold as chattels, children forced into jails for homosexual activities, slave labourers paid wages in the form of toxic drugs causing an incurable disease, tortured young prisoners in state jails, and abused inmates of children's homes.[14] The blend of social and judicial activism allowed the Indian Supreme Court finally to break free from its conservative traditions, and what Dhavan has

described as "the conflicts between Nehru's political mandate approach and subsequent affirmations of juridical constitutionalism" were at least temporarily resolved in favour of judge led human rights litigation.[15] In the words of Chief Justice Bhagwati:

> With a legal architecture designed for a colonial administration and a jurisprudence structured around a free-market economy, the Indian judiciary could not accomplish much in fulfilling the constitutional aspirations of the vast masses of underprivileged people during the first three decades of freedom. During the last five or six years however, social activism has opened up a new dimension of the judicial process, and this new dimension is a direct emanation from the basic objectives and values underlying the Indian Constitution.[16]

The next part of this article traces the background to the above stated period of judicial activism and assesses its achievements.

II. Background

The background to the development in India of a Supreme Court committed to pro-active litigation designed to achieve social justice on behalf of the poor is to be found in an influential report on the lack of national judicare published by a high level committee in India in 1977.[17] A crucial section of this report reads as follows:

> In our expensive court system, it is impossible for the lower income groups and the poor to enforce rights. The poor people of a village may be prevented from walking along a public pathway by a feudal chief, immigrant workers may be denied fair wages, women workers as a class may be refused equal wages. Collective wrongs call for class action. The rule of *locus standi* requires to be broad-based and any organisation or individual must be able to start such legal action.[18]

This committee, which included two distinguished Indian Supreme Court Judges, Justice Bhagwati and Justice Krishna Iyer, was committed from the outset to a path of reform that was to be based on high-profile litigation, at a time when governments throughout the world were engaged in similar debates on the broadening of access to justice, but few were seeking the path of group litigation as their chosen priority.[19] However, this particular path was not entirely new to Indian jurisprudence. It had already been seen as an appropriate priority in the Indian context by the Bhagwati Committee of Gujerat on Legal Aid in 1971, by the Krishna Iyer Committee on Processual Justice to the People in 1973, and the Rajasthan Law Reform Committee in 1975.[20] Indeed, the latter committee had gone so far as to proclaim that "public interest litigation can prove to be the glory of our legal and judicial system," and the Krishna Iyer Committee had been happy to expand the concept of public interest litigation to embrace socio-legal research on problems affecting the poor, the initiation of law and judicial reforms, and the auditing of the work of state financed social welfare organisations.[21]

The recommendations contained in the 1977 report were largely accepted by the Bhagwati Committee for Legal Aid Implementation, set up in 1980 to give practical effect to the report. By 1982, a leading Indian jurist could already write that

> today, over a hundred matters being litigated mostly in the Supreme Court and the High Courts relate to problems affecting directly the rights of perhaps a hundred thousand or more people who, in the ordinary course of nature, would never have come before the courts for redressal of their just grievances.[22]

Few, if any other jurisdictions in the world could claim such a radical transformation in such a short period of time. What was it that occurred in India at this time that brought about this change?

Perhaps the most remarkable aspect of this process was the shift that occurred in this period in the Indian Supreme Court's perception of its own function with regard to human rights protection. Far from being a merely defensive fortress for the protection of the traditionally accepted "fundamental" human rights, such as equality before the law and personal liberty, the Indian Supreme Court adopted a highly visible role as the initiator of affirmative action to force national and state governments to accept the existence of a whole range of positive rights, hitherto more or less unrecognised outside the canons of international statements of human rights principles.[23] In the space of a mere five years, the Indian Supreme Court, in a string of dazzling judgements, asserted inter alia, the fundamental right of Indian citizens to speedy trial, against bondage, to livelihood, against environmental pollution, to human dignity, and to legal aid.[24] In their judgements in this period of judicial activism, the Indian Supreme Court Justices deliberately adopted a style of interpretation that they argued "shared the passion of the Constitution for social justice."[25] Their credo was the conviction that "in a developing society judicial activism is essential for participative justice. . . . Justices are the constitutional invigilators and reformers (who) bring the rule of law closer to the rule of life."[26]

III.   The Strategies

At the heart of the reforms that made possible the outgrowth of judicial activism in the 1980s was a two-pronged assault on traditional conceptions of constitutional court practice. The first strategy has involved rethinking judicial interpretation in the context of constitutional rights and social justice and the second a dynamic approach to civil procedure. Let us examine each of these in turn.

A.   Judicial interpretation, constitutional rights, and social justice

Throughout the 1980s, the Indian Supreme Court has argued that it has the social responsibility of imaginatively interpreting constitutional rights to reflect social justice, and to operate neither narrowly nor statically. Rights are dynamic and should be treated as such. Justice Bhagwati developed this philosophy at the Bangalore Judicial Colloquium where reviewing the development of human rights he said:

> Civil and political rights . . . do not exist for the large masses of people in the developing countries who are suffering from poverty, want and

destitution. . . . It is only if social and economic rights are ensured to these large masses of people that they will be able to enjoy civil and political rights and become equal participants in the democratic process.[27]

In sharp contrast, the American Professor, Geoffrey Hazard, described the contribution of civil justice to social justice as "diffuse, microcosmic, and dull."[28] He argues that this more or less meets the expectations of the poor that the legal system is supposed to serve, leaving the true resolution of the question of social justice where it belongs: "on the conscience of the community."[29] However, Stephen Sedley, a highly experienced public interest advocate practising in England (now a High Court judge), demonstrates that this "dull function" of the justice system is more complex than it may first appear when he writes, "Left-wing critiques of judicial decision making often fail to grasp the complexity of judicial aims and the divergences that may exist between those aims and the myopic ends of the politicians for whom the judges probably vote."[30] Crucially, Sedley's experience when appearing before the highest judges in the land, in a series of politically and socially embattled cases, lead him to caution that "[t]he judiciary may be reactionary, but it is not the Tory Party in horsehair, and it is eminently capable of biting the hand that feeds it."[31] In another article on the same theme, he states that "there is no defensible simple equation of conservative judges, with conservative lawmaking. . . . The radicalism of modern political conservatism in Britain has in many respects overtaken that of the judiciary."[32] This view is energetically supported by another leading commentator on the function of British judges, Professor Simon Lee, author of a seminal text, *Judging Judges*.[33] However, a contemporary Australian judge of high status, Justice Michael Kirby, argues from another perspective, one drawn more from a sense of the function of a judge, than the politics he or she may embody, when he states, "The sense of frustration about the overly activist court . . . may in the ultimate cause, and even justify, unrest and the very civic disorder which it has traditionally been a function of the judiciary to avoid and replace."[34] In the 1980s the justices of the Indian Supreme Court have not shared the scepticism of Hazard,

the cautioning balance of Sedley and Lee, nor the pragmatic restraint of Kirby.[35] Furthermore, they have totally rejected in the Indian context the stronger statements of the academic left contained in the conclusions of such writers as Ewing and Gearty, who having investigated the arguments in favour of creating a legally enforceable Bill of Rights in the United Kingdom, conclude "[w]e consider that the arguments against a judicially enforceable Bill of Rights are overwhelming."[36] The Indian judges argue that it is the luxury of the academic to argue such points, and the duty of the courts to prove them wrong.[37]

It is clear that the primary function of the Indian Supreme Court in constitutional rights litigation has been to stimulate government and other public bodies to adopt proper practices, under the closet scrutiny of social activist organisations. The results for the parties are ultimately of secondary importance. But a further function of the Indian Supreme Court's work for the poor and oppressed could perhaps be described as the opening of a dialogue on oppression, as an attempt to influence and redefine public opinion.[38] Bickel has observed that in the United States:

> virtually all important decisions in the Supreme Court are the beginnings of a conversation between the Court and the people and their representatives. They are never, at the start, conversations between equals. The Court has an edge, because it initiates things with some immediate action, even if limited. But conversations they are, and to say that the Supreme Court lays down the law of the land is to state the ultimate result, following upon a complex series of events, in some cases and in others it is a form of speech only. The effectiveness of the judgement universalised depends on consent and administration.[39]

Interpreting the Constitution
How then has the Indian Supreme Court set about this dual purpose of regulating public bodies through social activism and opening of further dialogue on the nature of constitutional rights in its judgements?

At the heart of the Indian Supreme Court's judicial activism in the 1980s has been a perception that constitutional interpretation fundamentally differs, almost mystically, from statutory interpretation. Justice Bhagwati expressed this distinction at the Commonwealth Law Conference in Jamaica in 1986, in the following terms:

> It must be remembered that a constitution is a totally different kind of enactment than an ordinary statute. It is an organic instrument defining and regulating the power structure and power relationship: it embodies the hopes and aspirations of the people; it projects certain basic values and it sets out certain objectives and goals. It cannot therefore be interpreted like any ordinary statute. It must be interpreted creatively and imaginatively with a view to advancing the constitutional values and spelling out and strengthening the basic human rights of the large masses of people in the country, keeping in mind all the time that it is the constitution, the basic law of the land, that we are expounding and that ultimately, as one great American judge felicitously said, "the Constitution is what we say it is."[40]

Let us look at this approach in practice by reference to some of the key decisions of the Indian Supreme Court in this period.[41] Perhaps the most celebrated decision of the early 1980s was the case of *People's Union for Democratic Rights v. Union of India.*[42] This case centered on the exposure of illegal employment practices that were being carried out on a grand scale, as the country prepared to host the highly prestigious Asian Games. The practices were first unearthed by social activists, and presented to the Indian Supreme Court by way of an epistolary petition.[43] In order to comply with the exacting international standards necessary to host this prestigious event, the Indian Government had to embark upon a large range of construction projects including the building of flyovers, stadia, swimming pools, hotels, and the Asian Games Village Complex.[44] The Government duly contracted the work out to a number of agencies, some of whom flaunted the labour laws on such matters as minimum wages and equal wages for men and women, and the prohibition on the employment of children under fourteen. In addition, many of the workers were denied proper living conditions and medical and other facilities to which they were entitled by law. The significant point about the case for our purposes, was that it was brought not against the contractors, who were clearly and flagrantly breaching labour laws, but was brought against the Indian Government for failing to uphold various fundamental human rights of its citizens. This was despite the fact that the contractors were already being prosecuted under various criminal acts, for their wrongdoing. Constitutionally, the Indian Supreme Court could only accept a direct petition of this kind if it could demonstrate a breach of a fundamental right under the Constitution.[45] At this point, the new creativity emerged.

Article 23 of the Indian Constitution enacts the fundamental right prohibiting "traffic in human beings and forced labour."[46] A narrow "statutory interpretation" of this section would not conclude that the facts as presented in this particular case revealed such a breach. The Indian Supreme Court thought otherwise. It argued that:

> in a country like India, where there is so much poverty and unemployment and there is no equality of bargaining power, a contract of service may appear on the face of it voluntary, but it may in reality be involuntary. . . . Where a person is suffering from hunger or starvation, when he has no resources at all to fight disease or to feed his wife and children, or even to hide their nakedness, where utter and grinding poverty has broken his back and reduced him to a state of helplessness and despair and where no other employment is available to alleviate the rigor of his poverty, he would have no choice but to accept any work, that comes his way, even if the remuneration offered to him is less than the minimum wage . . . the labour (thus) provided to him would be "forced labour."[47]

The Indian Supreme Court further justified this decision by reference to what it considered the "broader purposes of the Constitution," which were defined as "ushering in a new socio-economic order."[48] In these circumstances, the Court argued that the word "force" must be construed to include not only physical or legal force, but also force arising from the compulsion of economic circumstances which leaves no choice of alternatives to a person in want.[49]

The Indian Supreme Court's interpretation of Article 21 of the Indian Constitution provides further insight into this new activity in judicial interpretation. Article 21 of the Indian Constitution enacts a further fundamental right that "no person shall be deprived of his life or personal liberty except by procedure established by law."[50] The Indian Supreme Court formed the view, in the course of its deliberations in the early 1980s, that the state was dragging its heels in providing access to justice. In the words of Justice Bhagwati, "large masses of the people were leading a life of destitution . . . on account of a lack of awareness, assertiveness and availability of machinery, and were priced out of the legal system and thus denied access to justice."[51] In a leading case, *M. M. Hoskot v. State of Maharasta 1978*,[52] the Indian Supreme Court held it to be in breach of Article 21 to try a criminal case, imperilling the life or personal liberty of an individual, without giving him proper and adequate legal representation.[53] Furthermore, if a magistrate did not inform the accused of this right, the conviction could be set aside.[54] In another case involving Article 21, the Indian Supreme Court decided that "life" does not mean merely physical existence, but also includes "the use of every limb or faculty through which life is enjoyed."[55] Implicit in this right was the right to "live with basic human dignity and all that goes along with it, including the right to the basic necessities of life and also the right to carry on such functions and activities as constitute the base minimum expression of the human self."[56] Thus, the Court elevated this right to the status of fundamental right. In another Article 21 case, the Court concluded that the "right to life" also included the "right to a livelihood."[57] In another case, Article 21 was said to include the right to be "free from exploitation," and

> at the least, therefore, it must include protection of the health and strength of workers, men and women, and of the tender age of children against abuse, opportunities and facilities for children to develop in a healthy manner and in conditions of freedom and dignity, educational facilities, just and humane conditions of work and maternity relief. These are the minimum requirements which must exist in order to enable a person to live with human dignity.[58]

B. A dynamic approach to civil procedure

The relationship between civil procedure and substantive law has always given rise to controversy of interpretation.[59] In 19th and turn of the century jurisprudence, the function of procedure was by and large perceived as neutral, and mechanical, giving rise to such anodyne definitions as that of Jeremy Bentham – "procedure is the course taken for the execution of the laws,"[60] and Collins M.R. "the relation of the rules of practice to the work of justice is intended to be that of handmaid rather than mistress."[61] Later proceduralists have been more willing to assert the dynamic function of civil procedure in promoting or thwarting access to justice. Cappelletti, for example, has described civil procedure as "like a mirror, in which the great issues of liberty and justice, the great themes of the relationship between individuals, groups, and states, are faithfully reflected."[62] The justices of the Indian Supreme Court grasped the dynamic potential of civil procedure to transform the workings and even the basic function of a constitutional court with fortitude, and in several outstanding judgements in the early 1980s made a series of overarching decisions regarding procedure that laid the groundwork for future poverty litigation.

In a major statement of the Indian Supreme Court's philosophy with regard to its encouragement of public interest litigation on behalf of the poor and oppressed, Bhagwati, in a 1982 judgement, summarised the necessary reforms as threefold: (1) *locus standi* should be made available to anybody who can show a bona fide observation of a legal injury or wrong done to any person or group, if that person or group cannot themselves approach a court by reason of poverty, disability, or a socially or economically disadvantaged position; (2) the defendant in a private action can be the state, for failing to protect the constitutional rights of the injured citizen, even though the immediate technical defendant is a private individual or body, such as a private employer; and (3) whatever the status of the parties to the action, the remedy must be appropriate to the social problem involved, and if no enforceable remedy exists, a new one must be invented.

Let us examine each of these three components of the Indian Supreme Court philosophy, as articulated by Bhagwati, in turn, beginning with the momentous changes in *locus standi*, and the collation of evidence thereafter.[63]

Locus standi

At the heart of the procedural reforms enacted by the Indian Supreme Court in this period was a revolutionary approach to *locus standi*. The approach was in essence more of a revolution in interpretation than in substance, for the traditional common law rider that *locus standi* can only be granted to those with "sufficient interest" in the outcome of the proceedings was retained. The interpretation of what amounts to "sufficient interest" was revolutionary. In a landmark case in 1981, Bhagwati delivered the following judgement for the court:

> Today a vast revolution is taking place in the judicial process; the theatre of law is fast changing and the problems of the poor are coming to the forefront. The Court has to innovate new methods and devise new strategies for the purpose of providing access to justice to the large masses of people who are denied their basic human rights. . . . The only way in which this can be done is by entertaining writ petitions and even letters from public spirited individuals seeking judicial redress for the benefit of persons who have suffered [injuries]. . . . We hope and trust that the High Courts of the country will also adopt this proactive, goal-oriented approach.[64]

The provision: epistolary jurisdiction The implications contained in this judgement for the future jurisprudence of civil procedure go far beyond the confines of India. Proceduralists throughout the world, should undergo a uniform catching of breath, if they grasp the full implications of this radical approach to the limits of *locus standi*. Speaking to the Administrative Law Bar Association in London in 1990, Sir Konrad Schiemann, Justice of the English High Court remarked that "neither (England) nor any other (country) has . . . a legal system under which anyone could obtain a ruling from a court on any subject upon which he or she desired a ruling."[65] But by 1981, India had already opened

the doors to such a possibility. What this remarkable judgement meant in practice was as follows:

> Where a legal wrong or a legal injury is caused [or threatened] to a person or to a determinate class of persons . . . and such person[s] . . . [are] by reason of poverty, helplessness or disability or socially or economically disadvantaged position, unable to approach the Court for relief, any member of the public can maintain an application for an appropriate direction, order or writ in the High Court under Article 226 and in case of breach of any fundamental right of such person or determinate class of persons, in [the Supreme Court] under Article 32 seeking judicial redress for the legal wrong or injury caused to such person or determinate class.[66]

What clearly emerges from this statement is the breaking down of the procedural barrier of *locus standi* coupled with the reservation of a fast stream, direct access to the Indian Supreme Court provision for cases involving "fundamental rights" as defined in Part III of the Indian Constitution.[67]

This provision is particularly radical because of the further ruling that a person acting *pro bono publico* can initiate proceedings in the public interest simply by writing a letter (described as the epistolary jurisdiction). A judge may issue public interest proceedings by his own motion, *suo moto*.[68] The court justified this procedure as "a major breakthrough . . . in bringing justice closer to the large masses of people."[69] It was noted that the Court

> for a long time had remained the preserve of the rich and the well-to-do, and had been used only for the purpose of protecting the rights of the privileged classes. As a result of this innovative use of judicial power . . . the portals of the court [were] thrown open to the poor, the ignorant and the illiterate.[70]

The epistolary jurisdiction is more important for its symbolic reaching out to the common man, and to its confirmation that access to justice is upheld as a fundamental right by the Indian Supreme Court itself, than for its extensive practical use. In the first four years of its availability, little more than seventy cases are recorded as having availed of its potential.[71] The epistolary jurisdiction has been particularly welcomed and used by investigative journalists who have written articles about social injustices they have uncovered, which when issues of fundamental rights have been involved have subsequently been translated by social action groups into direct writs to the Indian Supreme Court.[72] One of the first uses of this jurisdiction was by a Supreme Court advocate, who filed a writ in 1980, based on a series of journalistic articles in a national daily, *The Indian Express*, exposing certain nefarious practices in Bihar, involving pre-trial prisoners.[73] In the same year, two professors of law wrote a letter to the same newspaper, exposing barbaric conditions in a protective home for women, which the Indian Supreme Court translated into a writ petition under Article 21 of the Indian Constitution.[74] Following this, a law student and a social worker adopted a similar strategy to expose barbarism in a women's home in Delhi, and three journalists exposed and filed a writ concerning a market in which women were bought and sold as chattels. Other social activist groups, lawyers, social workers, and academics have used the same jurisdiction to similar effect.[75]

Whilst the epistolary jurisdiction allows individuals not directly involved in an injustice to petition the court without incurring the expense of pursuing the litigation, it alone would be of little value without some subsidiary provision regarding the collection of evidence and financing of the case thereafter. The Indian Supreme Court developed a strategy to cover this difficulty. The Court's strategy has been the appointment of socio-legal commissions of enquiry to visit the sites of alleged injustice and to collect all necessary evidence, at the court's own expense.[76] Such commissions of enquiry may employ social activists, teachers, researchers, journalists, or government and judicial officers.[77] Any evidence thus collected is regarded as prima facie evidence, and is submitted to all interested parties inviting affidavit response.[78] The case will then be adjudicated on the basis of all the "evidence" thus accumulated.[79]

Abuse of process Dangers of possible abuse of the liberal *locus standi* provisions are also dealt with in the judgement when the court stated

that applicants must be acting bona fide.[80] If it appears that applicants are acting "for personal gain or private profit or out of political motivation or other oblique consideration,"[81] the court can reject the application. Herein lies the abuse of process provision that in practice is rarely used in India.[82] A wider range of possible abuses of the open system of access to the jurisdiction of courts, afforded by ultra liberal standing rules, has been canvassed by Schiemann.[83] Schiemann focuses on the negative impact that open access might have upon a cautious administrator who, fearful of litigation from an unknown quarter, might "concentrate less on the quality of his decision, and more on making it 'judge proof.' "[84] Schiemann notes also the problems of paying for the expanded litigation that open access will encourage, and the risk that flamboyant publicists and pressure groups might convert the courts into some form of debating platform, despite the certain knowledge that they will lose their case.[85] Despite raising the disadvantages, however, Schiemann largely answers these criticisms when he muses that

> the undesirability of putting certain actions beyond legal challenge by anyone is self evident. The politically, financially or socially strong can oppress the weak, safe in the knowledge that the courts cannot interfere. This is undesirable not only because oppression is undesirable, but also because if the law is openly flouted without redress in the courts the law is brought into contempt as being a dream without substance.[86]

If this is the conclusion of a judge operating in the relative affluence of English "social injustice," it seems safe to say that in a country operating on a scale of poverty and related economic problems such as India, the abuse of process provisions that are necessary in more affluent jurisdictions seem to be of little relevance or application.

Sufficient interest

> If no specific legal injury is caused to a person or to a determinate class or group of persons by the act or omission of the State or any public authority and the injury is caused only to *public interest* . . . any member of the public acting bona fide and having *sufficient interest*

can maintain an action for redressal of such public wrong. . . . What is *sufficient interest* to give standing to a member of the public would have to be determined by the Court in each individual case. It is not possible for the Court to lay down any hard and fast rule.[87]

It is perhaps in the interpretation of this section of the judgement that the most far-reaching and radical practices have occurred. No universal agreement exists as to the definition of the term "public interest" despite a tremendous amount of scholarship devoted to the subject.[88] What emerges from the Indian case-law is that if the Indian Supreme Court considers that litigation in any particular matter is "in the public interest," the court will grant de facto *locus standi* to the applicant on the basis of a perceived "sufficient interest." The terms "sufficient interest" and "in the public interest" are effectively merged into one and the same. This is going further than any equivalent court has dared to do elsewhere. Prior to this advance, the concept of sufficient interest had already been given a more liberal hue in a common law setting by Lord Denning, in a 1976 Court of Appeal case in England, *R. v. Greater London Council, ex parte Blackburn*.[89] The Indian Supreme Court have always seen this brilliant, but maverick, English judge as an inspiration, and a man in their own mould. In this case, Mr. Blackburn, a ratepayer, had successfully applied to the court for an order to enforce the council's statutory duty to prohibit the exhibition of pornographic films in the London area, a duty which the council had previously refused to exercise.[90] In granting *locus standi* to Mr. Blackburn, and thereafter the right to enforce the statutory duty, Lord Denning wrote the following:

I regard it as a matter of high constitutional principle that, if there is good ground for supposing that a government department or a public authority is transgressing the law or is about to transgress it, in a way which offends or injures thousands of Her Majesty's subjects [sic], then any one of those offended or injured can draw it to the attention of the courts of law and seek to have the law enforced, [then] the courts in their *discretion* can grant whatever remedy is appropriate.[91]

This liberal approach to the concept of standing was broadly adopted by the British House of Lords in a landmark case in 1981, *I.R.C. v. The National Federation of Self-Employed & Small Businesses Ltd*.[92] By a curious coincidence, this case was being heard at almost the same time as the Indian Supreme Court was laying down its judgement on the issue of standing and sufficient interest. In the case before the House of Lords, the court had to decide whether a group representing self-employed people had sufficient interest in a decision by the Inland Revenue to grant an "amnesty" to another group of notorious tax defaulters, to be granted *locus standi* to challenge the decision of the Inland Revenue.[93] The House of Lords decided that the group did have sufficient interest. Lord Diplock concluded that

it would . . . be a grave lacuna in our system of public law if a pressure group, like the federation or even a single public-spirited taxpayer, were prevented by outdated technical rules of locus standi from bringing the matter to the attention of the court to vindicate the rule of law and get the unlawful conduct stopped.[94]

A leading administrative law academic and appeal court judge, Lord Justice Woolf, reflected upon the significance of this judgment in the following terms:

Since the decision of the House of Lords . . . I know of no case where the court has come to a conclusion that there is a breach of the law being committed by a public body which requires rectifying but because the person making the application has insufficient standing, leave should not be granted.[95]

Subsequent case law in England has, however, cast doubt upon the wisdom of Lord Justice Woolf's unfettered optimism.[96]

Locus standi *and justiciability*

[T]he Court [has] to bear in mind that there is a vital distinction between locus standi and justiciability and it is not every default on the part of the State or a public authority that is justiciable. The Court must take care to see that it does not overstep the limits of its judicial function and trespass into areas which are reserved to the Executive and the Legislature by the Constitution.[97]

The state as defendant

Trubek has argued that constitutional rights, rooted in a liberal understanding of society, do less to improve the welfare of the disadvantaged than to entrench the existing maldistribution of wealth and power.[98] This view is sustained and developed by Katz in his study of 100 years of the history of poverty law programmes in Chicago.[90] Katz reaches the disturbing conclusion that the most aggressive and creative of the poverty lawyers have proved to be less successful at eliminating poverty than reorganizing the poor into a formal category.[100] These observations illustrate the danger contained in the second of Bhagwati's philosophical/procedural axioms. Nevertheless, it remains pivotal to the entire system.

In Singh's analysis of the effectiveness of judicial activism as a means of employing rule of law rhetoric as a weapon against both poverty and lawlessness, he has observed that the primary function of such activity, in India, is "to raise the standards of governmental accountability towards . . . human values and not necessarily the widening of the adjudication process to the mass of the people."[101] Herein lies the justification for rights based strategies, that may be the subject of more sceptical scrutiny in the highly developed, and more mechanically administered welfare states operating in more affluent countries than India. Cassels has observed, in this context, that "litigative strategies can never substantially redistribute wealth or power, nor penetrate and affect the economic·and cultural conditions which define the reality of Indian life."[102] The fact that these strategies do nevertheless frequently expose the lawlessness of public bodies does serve a useful political function, particularly when that public body is the government.

Galanter has described disputes requiring access to a forum such as the Indian Supreme Court, namely one that is "external to the original social setting of the dispute, at a location at which some specialised learning or expertise will be brought to bear,"[103] as a manifestation of a legal centralist model of justice dispensation, and not, in Galanter's view, a model that is in any way essential to the achievement of justice in a given society.[104] What is important in the Indian context is the fact that the legal centralist model function symbolically and politically, as the embodiment of human rights aspiration, through the mouths of a genuine political elite, the justices of the Indian Supreme Court, and as such can perform the function of the watchdog of governmental accountability referred to above. The history of the Indian Supreme Court has demonstrated unequivocally that it is a political institution.[105]

The separation, both cultural and physical, of this powerful political institution from the mass of those whom it seeks to serve, is significant in that "[t]o the foreign observer, one of the most striking aspects of the Indian legal system is the extent to which formal legal arrangements exist in almost metaphysical isolation from social reality."[106] In practical terms, the political and the symbolic function of the court's decisions have exercised a far greater influence on Indian society than the formal decision between the parties. The willingness of the court to concentrate its energies in the field of social justice has opened the door to facilitate what the Trubeks have described as a people's "aspiration for . . . civil justice."[107] They argue that

> when the state seeks to protect interests without groups, it confronts problems very different from those encountered when it seeks to protect the more traditional interests of organised sectors of society. Effective protection of any interest means much more than giving formal guarantees of rights. These rights must be translated into tangible benefits, and this can only occur in the day-to-day operation of government and private entities regulated by government.[108]

This perspective clearly raises serious questions as to what precisely is to be understood by the concept of facilitation. Do the judges create the concept of civic justice in people's minds, or do they merely give a formal expression to pre-existent notions? The debate goes far beyond the confines of this Article, and indeed can be said to be the central debate underpinning much political and legal/constitutional discussion that is currently taking place in central and eastern Europe. For our purposes, the function of the epistolary jurisdiction is primarily to permit the people to define for themselves what they perceive as civil injustice, and for the court to exercise its discretion, tempered by practical constraints, in the prioritisation of its treatment of such decisions, as manifest in the petitions that come before it. Set out below are some examples of the operation of this axiom in practice in the Indian context.

In a country in which direct action is constantly on the agenda as the most likely alternative to legal process, and as a means to achieve a solution to a social or political problem, the symbolic function of the Supreme Court in replacing, and thereby diverting the threat of direct action cannot be over-emphasised. One writer suggested in the 1980s in this context that the legalisation of politics threatens to divert, manage, and contain the demands of social activists for a more humane social order.[109] Thus, the Indian Supreme Court allows for a process of "continued and effective participation in the ongoing stream of governmental decisions"[110] in a way that no other organ of the state can achieve. For Indian social activists, it is the best thing available.

Appropriate remedies

Whatever the strength and originality of the new procedures developed by the Indian Supreme Court in the 1980s to allow greater access for the poor to its chamber, there would have been little point in allowing such access without also evolving new remedies for giving relief. As Bhagwati himself pointed out. "The suffering of the disadvantaged could not be relieved by mere issuance of prerogative writs of certiorari, prohibition or mandamus, or by making orders granting damages or injunctive relief, where such suffering was the result of continuous repression and denial of rights."[111]

The process of developing appropriate remedies involves two aspects. The first aspect is the principle of flexibility, whereby a specific remedy is developed to meet the facts of the injustice uncovered by the court. One case dealt with the discovery of a large scale, illegal debt bondage network, akin to the most primitive form of slavery.[112] The remedy of the courts was to make an order giving various directions for identifying, releasing, and rehabilitating labourers held in debt bondage, and for ensuring thereafter that all labour laws would be observed, that they would all receive a minimum wage, wholesome drinking water, medical assistance, and appropriate schooling facilities for their children, along with legal awareness training.[113]

In another series of cases involving the scandal of people being held pre-trial for longer periods than the maximum possible sentence for their alleged offence, the Supreme Court directed the Bihar state government to prepare an annual census of the prisoners on trial in their state, and to submit it annually to the High Court, which would declare for the early disposal of all cases in which prisoners were being held for an unreasonably long period.[114] In a third case, again in the state of Bihar, in which prisoners under trial had been blinded by the police, the Court ordered that these prisoners should be given vocational training in an institute for the blind, and paid compensation for the rest of their lives.[115] In a fourth case, involving the abuse by male police officers of women in custody, the court directed that there should be a separate lock-up for women, supervised by women police officers, and that a written notice should be placed in each lock-up informing the arrested person of their rights.[116]

The second aspect in the development of effective remedies relates to enforcement. The remedy may be tailor-made to match the problem, but unenforceable and therefore worthless. In the words of Bhagwati:

> The orders made by the Court are obviously not self-executing. They have to be enforced through State agencies; if the State agencies are not enthusiastic in enforcing the Court orders and do not actively cooperate in that task, the object and purpose of the public interest litigation would remain unfulfilled.[117]

The main device adopted by the Court to try to ensure enforcement of their orders has been the creation of special monitoring agencies, who report back to the court on the effectiveness of the ordered enforcement procedure. Thus in the case concerning the protection of women in police custody, the Court instructed a woman judicial officer to make regular visits to the police stations in question and to report to the High Court on whether the directives were being obeyed.[118] In the case involving bonded labourers, the Supreme Court appointed the Joint-Secretary in the Ministry of Labour to visit the quarries where the bonded labour network had existed, after three months, with a similar purpose.[119] In a case involving environmental pollution caused by a gas leak from a chemical plant, an even more stringent monitoring system was set up by the Court.[120]

> On the basis of recommendations of four separate court-appointed technical teams the court ordered specific technical, safety and training improvements. It required the allocation of trained staff to defined safety functions. To monitor the plant the court set up an independent committee to visit the plant every two weeks, and also ordered the government inspector to make surprise visits once a week. . . . [It] "suggested" that the government establish an Ecological Sciences Resource Group to assist the court. . . . [It] required the company and its managers to deposit security to guarantee compensation to any who might be injured as a result of the enterprise's activity.[121]

The remedies are thus an imaginative and bold step down the road of constitutional court activism and enforcement of rights. Their effectiveness is challenged by some, and is in any event piecemeal, and under-researched.[122] The Indian Supreme Court has accepted that unless and until the attitudes of public administrators change significantly, the vigilance and dedication of social activists on the ground will remain of greater importance than any Supreme Court eloquence in protecting the poor.[123] They have not yet proved Hazard wrong.[124]

IV.   Conclusion

> I often wonder whether we do not rest our hopes too much upon constitutions, upon laws and upon courts. These are false hopes; believe me, they are false hopes. Liberty lies in the hearts of men and women; where it dies there is no constitution, no law, no court can save it; no constitution, no law, no court can even do much to help it. While it lies there it needs no constitution, no law, no court to save it.[125]

The words of Judge Learned Hand ring as true today as they did when he first uttered them in 1953. And they are just as true in India, as they are anywhere else. In particular, it would be misleading to assume that the "Indian Experiment" in public interest litigation has been an unmitigated success. Some quarters are especially critical: "The Indian legal system, in its current condition, is far from meeting its constitutional obligation of promoting justice. In fact, it actually operates to deny justice to a majority of the Indian population, the rural and the urban poor."[126] "Public Interest Litigation is failing in India in more ways than one."[127] Specifically, the number of cases using the epistolary jurisdiction has been relatively small,[128] and has served to clog up the court dockets. The time taken to bring public interest cases to the Supreme Court is inordinate, and has been heavily criticised.[129] The leading exponents of public interest judicial activism, Justices Bhagwati and Krishna Iyer, are no longer in the court, and their replacements are more cautious and conservative; epistolary litigants are normally allocated a legal aid lawyer, not the lawyer of their choice; and litigants are not able to select the judge that might be more sympathetic to their cause.[130] Nevertheless, these cautionary statements remain cautionary, not debilitating. These statements certainly do not undermine the tremendous achievements of the Indian Supreme Court over the past decade in demonstrating the potential possessed by any constitutional court to bring about significant improvements in the general level of social justice at any one time, nor do they undermine the continuing symbolic function of the Supreme Court, to lead the way as champions of simple concepts of justice.

Extrapolation of policy for one country from the experiences of another is never a wise philosophy, particularly when the social, political, and economic differences are as great as they are between India and the Western countries in which constitutional courts make at least a pretence of asserting fundamental human rights through the process of judicial decision making. Nevertheless, some of the clear conclusions that emerge from the recent Indian experience are of such universality that they bear discussion and debate "in fora" far wider than the Indian sub-continent.[131] First, it is clear that the same words in constitutions can be interpreted in widely differing ways, according to the desire of the judges to make them work in a particular way. Second, procedural restraints on access to the courts are by and large, judge-made, and the potential to open up access rests in large part with the same judges. Wherever debates on *locus standi* take place, at least in the common law world, the terms of reference are remarkably similar. The judges take it upon themselves to decide whether a particular party should, or should not, be heard. Third, if judges have the personal, social, or political will to do so, they have enormous scope to expand the type of remedies they wish to see operating in their courts, and the types of evidence that they wish brought before them. Fourth, as history comes full circle, and critics, echoing contemporary debates in the United States, intimate that public interest litigation in India is not today what it was three years ago, the words of John Curran in 1790, are as true today as they were when uttered in those fomenting years of revolutionary politics some 200 years ago: "The condition upon which God hath given liberty to man is eternal vigilance; which condition if he break, servitude is at once the consequence of his crime, and the punishment of his guilt."[132]

It has been shown in the course of this Article that to use its public interest function effectively, a court must not only be fearless in stating its objectives, but set out a reform agenda designed to achieve those objectives. This agenda will involve a willingness to see and use the creative potential of civil procedure as a tool for reform rather than technical barrier to justice. It will require bold and imaginative initiatives to create enforcement mechanisms and procedures appropriate to the problem in hand. It will require the appointment of the right judges, bearing in mind that in developing countries "judges will frequently be among the very few highly educated citizens available for leadership."[133] Above all, it will involve a conscious and overt acceptance by constitutional court justices, wherever they may sit, that theirs is the power to make law,[134] and this is a power that they should not squander negatively. In the words of one of the British House of Lords judges, Lord Reid: "There was

a time when it was thought almost indecent to suggest that Judges make law – they only declare it. . . . But we do not believe in fairy tales any more."[135]

Notes

1   Wolfgang Friedman, *Law in a Changing Society*, 122 (1972).
2   P. Bhagwati, "Chief Justice on What Justices Should Do," *The Times of India*, Sept. 21, 1986, at 9.
3   B. Agarwala, "The Legal Philosophy of P.N. Bhagwati," 14 *Ind. L. Rev.* 136, 140 (1987).
4   Judges and the Judicial Power, vi (Rajeev Dhavan et al., eds., 1985).
5   Upendra Baxi, *The Indian Supreme Court and Politics*, 10 (1980); S. P. Sathe, *Constitutional Amendments 1950–1988: Law and Politics* (1989).
6   P. Sieghart, *The Lawful Rights of Mankind*, 29 (1985).
7   H. Seervai, *Constitutional Law of India* (1987); Sathe, supra note 5.
8   Rajeev Dhavan, *The Supreme Court and Parliamentary Sovereignty: A Critique of its Approach in Recent Constitutional Cases* (1976); Rajeev Dhavan, "Managing Legal Activism: Reflections on India's Legal Aid Programme," 15 *Anglo. Am. L. Rev.* 281, 297 (1986).
9   Keshavananda Bharati v. State of Kerala, 1973 All India Reporter (A.I.R.) 1461, 1485 (S.C.).
10 M. Williams, "Increasing Access to Justice: A Search for Alternatives," *The Lawyers*, Jan. 1990, at 4.
11 M. Menon, "Public Interest Litigation: A Major Breakthrough in the Delivery of Social Justice," 9 *J. Bar Council of India* 150, 155 (1982).
12 P. Singh, "Access to Justice: Public Interest Litigation and the Indian Supreme Court," 10–11 *Delhi L. Rev.* 56 (1981–2).
13 Upendra Baxi, "Taking Suffering Seriously: Social Action Litigation in the Supreme Court of India," 29 *Review of the International Commission of Jurists* 37 (1982).
14 Id. at 42–3.
15 Letter from Rajeev Dhavan, to Jeremy Cooper (Apr. 4, 1992).
16 P. N. Bhagwati, "Judicial Activism and Public Interest Litigation," 23 *Colum. J. Transnat'l L.* 561, 568 (1985).
17 *Report on National Juridicare* (Ministry of Law, Justice and Company Affairs, Govt. of India, 1977); Dhavan, supra note 8, at 293.

18 Dhavan, supra note 8, at 293.

19 See *Access to Justice* (Mauro Cappelletti & B. Garth, eds. 1979–81).

20 Dhavan, supra note 8, at 293–4.

21 Menon, supra note 11.

22 Id. at 151.

23 The principal international human rights instrument of relevance is The International Bill of Human Rights consisting of The Universal Declaration of Human Rights 1948 (adopted and proclaimed by General Assembly Resolution 217 A (iii)), The International Covenant on Civil and Political Rights 1976, and The International Covenant on Economic, Social and Cultural Rights 1976 (adopted by General Assembly of the United Nations by Resolution 2200).

24 Hoskot v. State of Maharasta, 1978 A.I.R. 1548, 1553 (S.C.); People's Union for Democratic Rights v. India, 1982 A.I.R. 1473, 1487 (S.C.); Olga Tellis v. Bombay Mun. Corp. 1986 A.I.R. 180, 193 (S.C.); Rural Litigation & Entitlement Kendra, Dehradun v. State of U.P., 1985 A.I.R. 652, 656 (S.C.); Mullin v. Administrator, Union Territory of Delhi, 1981 A.I.R. 746, 753 (S.C.); Barse v. State of Moharoshta, 1983 A.I.R. 378, 382 (S.C.); Suk Das v. Union Territory of Arunchal Pradesh, 2 S.C.C. 401, 408 (1986).

25 V. Krishna Iyer, "Democracy of Judicial Remedies: A Rejoinder to Hidayatullah," 4 S.C.C. 1 (1984); A. Bhattacharjee, "Judicial Activism and the World Judges Conference," 3 S.C.C. 1 (1984); P. Bhagwati, "Unorganised Rural Labour," 3 S.C.C. 44 (1984); P. Singh, "Judicial Socialism and Promises of Liberation," 28 *J. of Indian Law Institute* 338 (1988).

26 Singh, supra note 25, at 339.

27 P. Bhagwati, "Inaugural Address by the Convenor," in *Commonwealth Secretariat*, xx–xix (1988).

28 Geoffrey C. Hazard, "Social Justice through Civil Justice," 36 *U. Chi. L. Rev.* 699, 712 (1969).

29 Id.

30 Stephen Sedley, "Free Speech for Rupert Murdoch," *London Review of Books*, Dec. 19, 1991 at 3, 3.

31 Id.

32 Stephen Sedley, "Hidden Agendas: The Growth of Public Law in Britain and Canada," in *Socialist Lawyer*, 12 (1990).

33 See generally Simon Lee, *Judging Judges* (1988).

34 M. Kirby, "The Role of the Judge in Advancing Human Rights by Reference to Human Rights Norms," in *Commonwealth Secretariat*, 67 (1988).

35 But see P. Singh, "Thinking about the Limits of Judicial Vindication of Public Interest," 3 S.C.C. 1 (1985).

36 This brief quotation does not do justice to the serious and trenchant critique put forward by Ewing and Gearty in their analysis of the dangers of a judge enforced Bill of Rights in the United Kingdom. It is submitted, however, that the arguments contained in their excellent paper, are highly specific to the United Kingdom. K. Ewing & C. Gearty, *Democracy or a Bill of Rights* (1990).

37 Id.

38 Dhavan, supra note 8, at 299.

39 A. Bickel, *The Supreme Court and the Idea of Progress* (1970).

40 P. N. Bhagwati, "Fundamental Rights in their Economic, Social, and Cultural Context," in *Commonwealth Secretariat*, 57 (1988).

41 M. P. Jain, "Justice Bhagwati and Indian Administrative Law," 16 *The Banaras Law Journal* 1 (1980).

42 1982 A.I.R. 1473 (S.C.).

43 Id. at 1476.

44 Id. at 1479.

45 Id. at 1476, 1479.

46 India Const. art. 23.

47 P. N. Bhagwati, *Observe Labour Laws: An Historic Judgment of Supreme court of India*, 28–9 (1982).

48 Id. at 5–6.

49 Id. at 29.

50 India Const. art. 21.

51 Bhagwati, supra note 40, at 65.

52 1978 A.I.R. 1548 (S.C.).

53 Id. at 1554.

54 Id. at 1556.

55 Bhagwati, supra note 40, at 65.

56 Olga Tellis v. Bombay Mun. Corp., 1985 A.I.R. 180, 193 (S.C.).

57 Hoskot v. State of Maharasta, 1978 A.I.R. 1548, 1553 (S.C.).

58 Morcha v. India, 1983 A.I.R. 802, 811–12 (S.C.); Jamie Cassels, "Judicial Activism and Public Interest Litigation in India: Attempting the Impossible," 37 *Am. J. Comp. L.* 495, 503–4 (1989).

59 See Hein Kötz, "Civil Litigation and the Public Interest," 1 *Civil Justice Quarterly* 237 (1982); J. A. Jolowicz, "On the Nature and Purposes of Civil Procedural Law," in *International Perspectives on Civil Justice* 27 (I. R. Scott, ed. 1990).

60 Jeremy Bentham, *Principles of Judicial Procedure, Works*, Vol. 2.

61 Per Collins M.R. in Re Coles and Ravenshear 1907 1 K.B. at 4.

62 Mauro Cappelletti, "Some Reflexions on the Role of Procedural Scholarship Today," in *The Eighth World Conference on Procedural Law Justice and Efficiency, General Reports and Discussions*, 441, 442 (W. Wedekind, ed. 1989).

63 Judges Appointment and Transfer Case, 1982 A.I.R. 149 (S.C.).

64 Gupta v. President of India, 1982 A.I.R. 149, 189 (S.C.).

65 Sir Konrad Schiemann, "Locus Standi," *Public Law*, 342, 342 (1990).

66 See supra note 63.

67 S. P. Sathe, *Fundamental Rights and Amendment of the Indian Constitution*, 53 (1968); S. P. Sathe, supra note 5, at 16–22; P. Tripathi, "Perspectives on the American Constitutional Influence on the Constitution of India," in *Constitutionalism in Asia: Asian Views of the American Influence*, 56 (Beer, ed. 1979); Mauro Cappelletti, "The Law Making Power of the Judge, and Its Limits: A Comparative Analysis," 8 *Monash Univ. L. Rev.* 15 (1981–2); Dhavan, supra note 8.

68 P. Jaswal, *Public Interest Litigation: Some New Developments in India*, Address at the Human Rights Seminar, SOAS, London University, February 17, 1992.

69 Bhagwati, supra note 16, at 572.

70 Id. at 571–2.

71 Jaswal, supra note 68.

72 Bhagwati, supra note 16, at 572; Baxi, supra note 13, at 39.

73 Baxi, supra note 13, at 39.

74 Cassels, supra note 58, at 495; Baxi, supra note 13, at 39.

75 Baxi, supra note 13, at 39–40.

76 Bhagwati, supra note 16, at 574.

77 Id.

78 Id.

79 Id. at 575.

80 Tripathi, supra note 67.

81 Id.

82 Id.

83 Schiemann, supra note 65, at 342.

84 Id. at 348.

85 Id.

86 Id. at 343.

87 S. P. Gupta v. President of India, 1982 A.I.R. 149, 190, 192 (S.C.) (emphasis added).

88 J. Cooper, *Keyguide to Information Sources in Public Interest Law* (1991).

89 3 All E.R. 184 (1976).

90 Id. at 186.

91 Id. at 192.

92 2 All E.R. 93 (1981)

93 Id. at 96.

94 Id. at 107.

95 H. Woolf, "Locus Standi in Practice," in *International Perspectives on Civil Justice*, 262 (I. Scott, ed. 1990).

96 I am grateful to my colleague Bill Bowring for bringing to my attention a spate of recent cases in the English Court of Appeal, which have drawn back from further developing the open access of locus standi, intimated by Lord Justice Woolf in the quotation, in particular the cases of R. v. Secretary of State for the Environment, ex parte The Rose Theatre Trust Co., 1990 1 All E.R. at 754.

97 S. P. Gupta v. President of India, 1982 A.I.R. 149, 195 (S.C.); see Carol Harlow, "Public Interest Litigation in England: The State of the Art," *Public Interest Law* 90 (J. Cooper & R. Dhavan, eds. 1986).

98 D. Trubek, "Public Policy Advocacy: Administrative Government and Representation of Diffuse Interests," in *Access to Justice*, 443–94 (M. Cappelletti, B. Garth, eds. 1979–81).

99 Jack Katz, *Poor People's Lawyers in Transition* (1982).

100 Id.

101 Singh, supra note 25, at 340–1.

102 Cassels, supra note 58, at 515.

103 Marc Galanter, "Justice in Many Rooms: Courts, Private Ordering, and Indigenous Law," 19–20 *Journal of Legal Pluralism* 1, 1 (1981–2).

104 Id.

105 Dhavan, supra note 8, at 296; Baxi, supra note 5, at 147; George Gadbois, "The Supreme Court of India As a Political Institution," in *Judges and the Judicial Power*, 250, 250–1 (Rajeev Dhavan et al., eds. 1985).

106 Cassels, supra note 58, at 515.

107 L. Trubek & D. Trubek, "Civic Justice through Civil Justice: A New Approach to Public Interest Advocacy in the United States," in *Access to Justice in the Welfare State*, 119, 119 (Mauro Cappelletti, ed. 1981).

108 Id. at 120 (footnote omitted).

109 See inter alia Michael Mandel, "The Rule of Law and Legalisation of Politics in Canada," 13 *Int. Journal of the Sociology of Law* 273 (1985).

110 Trubek & Trubek, supra note 107, at 121.

111 Bhagwati, supra note 16, at 575.

112 Bandhua Mukti Morcha v. Union of India, 1984 A.I.R. 802 (S.C.).

113 Id. at 828.

114 Upendra Baxi, "The Supreme Court under Trial: Undertrials and the Supreme Court," S.C.C. 35 (1980).

115 Khatri v. State of Bihar, 1981 A.I.R. 928, 934 (S.C.).

116 Sheela Barse v. State of Maharashtra, 1983 A.I.R. 378, 382 (S.C.).

117 Bhagwati, supra note 16, at 576–7.

118 Sheela Barse, 1983 A.I.R. at 382.

119 Bandhua Mukti Morcha v. Union of India, 1984 A.I.R. 802, 831 (S.C.).

120 Mehta v. India, 2 S.C.C. 176, 196–200 (1986).

121 Cassels, supra note 58, at 506.

122 Id. at 517.

123 Sheela Barse v. State of Maharashtra, 1983 A.I.R. 378, 379–80 (S.C).

124 Hazard, supra note 28, at 699.

125 *Learned Hand, Spirit of Liberty: Papers and Addresses of Learned Hand*, cited in J. McCluskey, *Law, Justice and Democracy*, Reith Lectures 1987, at 60.

126 Williams, supra note 10, at 4.

127 Dhavan, supra note 15.

128 Jaswal, supra note 68.

129 B. Pande, "The Food Petitions: Is There the Right to Basic Human Needs?," *The Lawyers*, September 1989, at 4.

130 Jaswal, supra note 68.

131 It is significant however that in the past twelve months, activists in Bangladesh and in Pakistan are starting to group together with a view to encouraging their own Supreme Courts to adopt a similar stance to that of India.

132 John Philpot Curran, from his speech "The Right of Election of Lord Mayor of Dublin," made on 10th July, 1790, in the City of Dublin, Ireland.

133 Kirby, supra note 34, at 71.

134 Cappelletti, supra note 67; K. Rohl, *The Judge As Mediator* (University of Wisconsin-Madison Disputes Processing Research Program Working Paper, 1988–9).

135 Lord Reid, "The Judge As Law Maker," 12 *Journal of the Society of Public Teachers of Law* 22, 22 (1972–3).

56

Natural Law: Alive and Kicking? A Look at the Constitutional Morality of Sexual Privacy in Ireland

Rory O'Connell

1. Introduction

Whilst for two centuries, the paradigm of legal discussion had been the separation of law and morality, there are those who wish to return to pre-Kantian, pre-Benthamite days of a unity, or at least a connection, of law and morality. Roland Dworkin, Carlos Nino and Robert Alexy are but three of the theorists who dispute the paradigm of separation. They dismiss the title "natural law" for their theories, but in so far as the term designates the belief that law includes a strong moral element, the term applies. How does a system of law which recognizes a strong connection between the two, actually work? Here I examine the issue of sexual morality in Irish constitutional law, where judges operate with a very moralized conception of law.

The reader should look for three elements in this article. First, the actual role played by moral reasoning in the decisions of the courts. Second, the nature of the decisions as a debate between different judges and different philosophies. Third, the judicial contribution of two sorts to the ongoing public debate on the same issues. Judges both demonstrate the concrete effects of the existing rules and principles of law, and offer visions of different underlying justifications

which may serve to either re-interpret or revise those rules and principles.

Please note two elements of Irish law. The Irish system is a common law one, with all the trappings: a Supreme Court cum Constitutional Court, a unified court system, a moderate doctrine of precedent, and multiple Supreme Court opinions. Second, the courts have, since 1965, asserted the power to deem certain human rights to be fully fledged constitutional rights, even though nowhere mentioned in the text (*Ryan v. Ireland* (1965) I.R. 294). This they have done invoking Art. 40, section 3, sub-section 1 (Art. 40.3.1) of the Constitution, which implies that the Constitution protects all personal rights, not merely those specifically mentioned.

2. The Birth of Constitutional Privacy: *M'Gee*

One finds no mention of the right of privacy in the Irish Constitution. Nevertheless, it is a constitutional right, born of a confrontation between personal circumstances and the blunt prohibition of the positive law, and finding its solution in a piece of moral–legal reasoning at the highest level.

Rory O'Connell, "Natural Law: Alive and Kicking? A Look at the Constitutional Morality of Sexual Privacy in Ireland," *Ratio Juris*, vol. 9, no. 3, Summer 1996, pp. 258–82. © 1996 by Ratio Juris. Reprinted with permission from Blackwell Publishing.

Mrs Mary M'Gee was a young married woman with four children. At least one of those births had been a complicated one, and her doctor advised her that any more pregnancies would seriously harm her. She decided, with her husband, that they should use some form of contraception. Customs officers seized the spermicidal jelly she sought to import relying on section 17 of the 1935 Criminal Law (Amendment) Act, which banned the sale or importation (but not the use or manufacture) of contraceptives. This section was enacted, by an overwhelming majority, two years before the adoption of the 1937 Constitution. Since no one manufactured contraceptives in the Ireland of 1973, there was no legal means to acquire them. Mrs M'Gee argued in the High Court that section 17 violated her enumerated constitutional right to marital privacy. The judge disagreed. According to him, to determine whether a right was protected, one had to determine what was the will of the people in 1937, when they adopted the Constitution. The constitutional principles of 1973 must not differ too much from the morality of traditional 1937 society. The section must not have violated the beliefs of the people of 1937, because only two years before, Parliament had adopted the law almost unanimously. So the section did not conflict with the Constitution. Now Mrs M'Gee had but one recourse – to appeal to the Supreme Court (*M'Gee v. Ireland* (1974) I.R. 284).

Four (of five) judges agreed that the provision violated the hitherto unknown right of marital privacy (though they disagreed on the reasoning). Perhaps none of them realized the implications their decision would have on the lives of many people, from gay men to 14-year-old rape victims, and more generally on Irish public life. (I consider here only two main judgements.)

Henchy J., like two other judges, based his opinion on Art. 40.3.1. Henchy J. stresses that the purpose of s. 17 was to protect the communal notion of sexual morality (ibid., 324). The "totality of the prohibition aims at nothing less" than to prohibit *in effect* the use of contraceptives, given the absence of any manufacturer of contraceptives in Ireland. Henchy J. then sets out the unenumerated rights doctrine. A particular right has constitutional status if it "inheres" in the citizen "by virtue of his human personality" (ibid., 325). This must be shown considering the

Constitution as a whole, and in light of the constitutional social order, and the concrete conditions of the person involved. It is not possible to list fully these rights.

The section subjects the couple to the criminal law because of their decision. It condemns them "to a way of life ... fraught with worry, tension, and uncertainty" (ibid., 326). Henchy J. continues:

And this in the context of a Constitution which in its preamble proclaims as one of its aims the dignity and freedom of the individual; which in sub. s. 2 of s. 3 of Article 40 casts on the State a duty to protect as best it may from unjust attack and in the case of injustice done to vindicate the life and person of every citizen; which in Article 41 ... guarantees to protect it [the family] in its constitution and authority as the necessary basis of social order and as indispensable to the welfare of the nation and the State; and which also in Article 41, pledges the State to guard with special care the institution of marriage, ... (*M'Gee v Ireland* (1974) I.R. 284, 326)

The objection to s. 17 is that "the law, by prosecuting her, will reach into the privacy of her marital life in seeking to prove her guilt" (ibid., 326). The section violates both Art. 40.3.1's guarantee of privacy in marriage, and Art. 41's protection of the family (ibid., 328).

For Walsh J. the central issue is whether the legislature can make contraceptives absolutely unavailable (ibid., 308). He explains that the Constitution places justice over law. Rights are not created by law; the Constitution merely "confirms their existence and gives them protection" (ibid., 310). When it comes to fundamental rights, the courts may review Parliament's determination of the common good.

Walsh J. bases his decision on Art. 41 which requires the State to protect the family. It is of the essence that the couple be allowed to determine for themselves the number of children to have, if any (ibid., 311). The religion of other parties, and the moral beliefs of the citizens do not amount to an exigency justifying intervention:

The private morality of its citizens does not justify intervention by the State into the activities of those citizens unless and until the common good requires it. (*M'Gee v. Ireland* (1974) I.R. 284, 312)

There can be no imposition of a code of morality on a married couple (ibid., 313). Interference would only be justified as the only possible means to prevent such an effect on public morality that amounts to the subversion of the common good (ibid., 314). The ban on importation is invalid.

Walsh J. comments on the nature of the Constitution and the judiciary. The Constitution envisages that "we are a religious people" (Preamble, Art. 6). So human rights are part of the natural law "of God promulgated by reason" which is "the ultimate governor of all the laws of men." Art. 44 insists that we live in a pluralist state, where all religions are entitled to Constitutional protection (ibid., 317). In a pluralist society, judges cannot turn to religious experts or churches for an explanation of the natural law. This is a task for the judiciary, guided by the structure of the Constitution, and the "Aristotelian" and "Christian" virtues of justice, prudence and charity (ibid., 318–19). Any judicial interpretation may be reviewed in the light of developing values (ibid., 319).

Walsh amplifies his view in several articles. The Constitution represents the fundamental values of the sovereign people, which they have reserved from the political process and entrusted to the judiciary (Walsh 1987a, 87, 108). It is written in the present tense and judges must so interpret it – it is not "concerned with what has been, but with what may be" (Walsh 1987b, 195). Of course it is a law which includes "social and political objectives ... [and] certain moral concepts" and thus embroils judges in contemporary "social, economic, philosophical and political debates" (ibid., 192). The judge must explore questions of justice, so he must rely on "instinct or intuition, ... his own moral sense and his own intelligence." Both judges and law makers must act according to "prevailing ideas of justice" with which they are imbued "by training and experience" (Walsh 1987a, 106. Cf. Dworkin 1986, 249–50, 257–8, 398).

He regards the 1937 Constitution as endorsing a natural law approach first seen in *State (Ryan) v. Lennon*, ((1935) I.R. 370), where Kennedy C. J., dissenting, argued that Art. 2a of the 1922

Constitution was invalid because the creation of a special military court violated the natural law (ibid., 89–91). Walsh J. notes the disasters of positivism in Nazi Germany and South Africa and the importance of natural law values in international human rights law. So far this leaves open the question as to whether he is talking of secular (e.g., Lockean) or religious (e.g., Thomistic) natural law. He then states that the Constitutional version of natural law is theological, but not Catholic (ibid., 94). According to Walsh J. all democracies reject the idea that "the state of God or that state power is right" – they are committed to defending rights (ibid., 95). Given the role of judges as defenders of the Constitution, they may deploy any remedy they deem necessary to defend a fundamental right (Walsh 1987b, 193; *State (Quinn) v. Ryan* (1965) I.R. 70).

What are we to make of the role of moral or political argument in this case? First the Supreme Court rejects the High Court claim that the Constitution is limited by the morals of 1937, either those embraced by the people who drafted or who adopted it. The Constitution must be given a present tense interpretation, in the light of today's values. From whence are those values to be derived? Clearly Parliament's conception of justice is not decisive. Yet it would appear that even the conceptions of justice of the people of today, and of the judges are not to be chosen simply because of who believes in them. Rather:

> The judges must, therefore ... interpret these rights in accordance with their ideas of prudence, justice and charity ... no interpretation of the Constitution is intended to be final for all time. It is given in the light of prevailing ideas and concepts. (*M'Gee v. Ireland* (1974) I.R. 294, 319)

Judges must interpret the Constitution's conception of justice – during which they must rely on their own and others' ideas on the question (cf. Dworkin 1986, 254–8).

A second point is whether the right to marital privacy is founded on Art. 40.3.1 or Art. 41. Article 40.3.1 is inspired by secular rationalist thought, and Art. 41 by Aquinian thought (Costello 1956, 1962). Art. 41 states that the family exists as an institution prior to positive law and has "inalienable and imprescriptible" rights, which the State must protect. Divorce is forbidden. Furthermore the State recognizes the value of woman's work in the home, and guarantees that mothers shall not be forced to work outside the home. Article 40.3.1 requires the State to respect, and in so far as is practicable, defend and vindicate personal rights in general.

Walsh J. chooses Art. 41, and emphasises the value of marriage, whilst the other three members of the majority invoke Art. 40.3.1 which protects all personal rights (Henchy J. agrees that Art. 41 is also violated). Walsh J. specifies that the statute violates Art. 41's guarantee of marital privacy, Art. 40.1's guarantee of equality, and Art. 40.3.1's guarantee of a right to protection of health, but not any personal right of privacy in Art. 40.3.1.

In basing the decision on Art. 41, Walsh J. makes it impossible for anyone to use that part of his reasoning to found a right to privacy outside of marriage. The majority, by basing the decision on Art. 40.3.1, makes it clear that it is a personal right which inheres in every citizen, and leaves open for consideration whether it extends beyond a right to privacy in marital relations. As M'Carthy J. (who was State counsel in *M'Gee*) later noted, the majority upheld the *right of (personal) privacy in a case involving marriage (Norris)*. That is, the right to privacy should not be limited to marriage. The three judge majority chose a basis for the right to privacy which left no doubt that it was personal, not marital right. Possibly this difference reflects differing philosophical visions: one an approach centering on individual autonomy, one centering on perfectionist or communitarian beliefs of the importance of family.

When considering the doctrine of unenumerated rights, the judges dramatically reject several less radical conceptions of rights. They reject the pre-1965 judicial belief that it is for Parliament to protect rights. They assert that the state does not merely protect positive rights, whether explicitly mentioned or necessarily implied. Rather it protects rights which derive from a synthesis between the Constitution and justice. There is no clear-cut technical reason to opt for one or other of these approaches to rights. The soundest argument in favour of each relies on a vision of political morality. Those who believe

that the value of the law rests in clear terms being applied by non-political judges worry about the unenumerated rights doctrine, those who believe that some rights are more important than legal certainty endorse the doctrine (Kelly 1967, Introduction; Chubb 1991, ch. 6). The majority makes it clear that the Constitution has outgrown the mindset of its drafters, and embraces the notion that law and state must first pay homage to justice. Walsh J. explicitly states that the Constitution places justice above the law (*M'Gee v. Ireland* (1974) I.R. 284, 310). Henchy J. stresses that the Constitution protects those rights which inhere "in the citizen in question by virtue of his human personality" (ibid., 325), not simply because of a term of the Constitution. The judges pursue a synthesis of justice and the Constitution, which is required by the Constitution itself, as interpreted (ibid., 318, 325).

Which view of justice should be relied on in determining personal rights: theological, liberal, perfectionist, communitarian? Do the judges accept Kenny J.'s assertion in *Ryan* ((1965) I.R. 294), that rights are rooted in the "Christian and democratic nature of the State" and if so what do they mean by it?

Henchy J. believes that personal rights are rooted in the human personality, which gives rights in certain social situations. In this case a wife and mother made a conscientious decision, about an important area of her life. The State was not entitled to frustrate that decision, even indirectly. Behind this argument is a conception of justice which centers on individual autonomy. The individual may effectuate decisions about intimate matters, even if society disapproves.

Walsh J.'s opinion poses a dilemma for Irish jurists. He asserts that justice is superior to the law, and that "the individual has natural and human rights over which the State has no authority" (*M'Gee v. Ireland* (1974) I.R. 284, 310). On this basis, Art. 41 recognizes the right of a married couple to decide whether to have children and how many (ibid., 311). The State cannot interfere with this decision simply because the private morality of some or most people disapproves (ibid., 312–13). This argument would seem more appropriate in the context of an Art. 40 personal right. Why should a right not to have a moral rule imposed on one, be particularly connected with a familial right? In other parts, the emphasis on the family may suggest a communitarian or other perfectionist approach: The marital couple (not the individual) is the most important entity, and so valued is it, that it is exempt from the restrictions which apply outside marriage. However this seems contrary to the strongly anti-perfectionist streak just referred to.

After disposing of the case, Walsh J. made several comments on religion which might be misinterpreted. He refers to his own statement in *Quinn's Supermarket* ((1972) I.R. 1, a religious freedom case), that the Constitution recognizes that the people are religious, but also that they live in a pluralist State (*M'Gee v. Ireland* (1974) I.R. 294, 317). However the super constitutional status of rights is founded on their being part of the natural law, whose superiority to positive law is implicit in the Preambular reference to Christianity and the constitutionally recognized authority of God (ibid., 318). Nevertheless pluralism requires that judges determine the contents of these rights in accordance with the virtues of prudence, justice and charity (ibid., 318–19).

There are two possible interpretations of this argument. The first is that constitutional rights must be interpreted according to Christian or Judaeo-Christian concepts of justice. The second is that the argument recognizes that our notions of justice and natural rights have their genesis in religious concepts, but that these concepts have now been bequeathed to the Constitution (and liberal tradition). The concepts of justice and rights are therefore the property of the Constitution, and must be interpreted by judges with respect for the contemporary views of these concepts, with respect for the Constitutional text, and the pluralist nature of the State.

Which interpretation later judges would accept, of course depends on their own normative outlook. This debate would have far reaching reverberations in Irish public life, which would only climax in 1992. But now I turn to the second stage of this debate.

3. And the Death of Privacy?

Mr (now Senator) David Norris, was a man with a serious problem. A congenital homosexual, he was seriously oppressed by laws penalizing homosexual acts. Sections 61 and 62 of the 1861 Offence Against the Person Act punished sodomy (anal intercourse) and attempts to commit it (whether between a man and a man or between a man and a woman), and section 11 of the 1885 Criminal Law (Amendment) Act punished "gross indecency" between men. The penalty for the latter was a jail sentence of up to two years. Someone convicted of the first could be jailed for any period up to life.

Mr Norris had not been prosecuted under either section when he sought a declaration in the High Court of their unconstitutionality. However as a congenital homosexual, and gay rights activist, he had suffered psychological trauma, and discrimination. It was impossible for him to develop a homosexual relationship. At one stage his psychiatrist advised him to leave the country. Instead he publicly campaigned for an end to the Victorian era in Ireland.

Norris argued that the laws violated his unenumerated right to individual privacy (*Norris* (1984) I.R. 36). He called 10 witnesses to show that the effects of such laws on homosexual people were severely negative. The State did not adduce any evidence to show that homosexuality was a threat to society's morals, health or any other significant interest. Nevertheless the State won.

According to M'William J., the role of the court is to determine whether there exist reasonable grounds for the legislature to believe that principles of morality, order and social policy require a particular legislative provision. If such grounds exist, then the legislation is valid (ibid., 46, 48). M'William J. interprets Walsh J., in *M'Gee*, as saying that constitutional morality is associated with the morality of the Irish Christian churches (ibid., 48). M'William J. says, referring to Christian dogma, that since the function of the sexual organs is reproduction, it is reasonable to believe "that sexuality outside marriage should be condemned, and that sexuality between people of the same sex is wrong" (ibid., 45).

Norris appealed to a Supreme Court composed of O'Higgins C.J., Finlay P., Henchy, Griffin, M'Carthy JJ. The judges gave two different answers to the question left unresolved by Walsh J.'s comments in *M'Gee*. The Chief Justice delivered the majority judgement, with which

Finlay P. and Griffin JJ. agreed. The other two saved the pride of Irish jurists.

For O'Higgins C.J., the court's role is not to reform the law, but merely to interpret it "with objectivity and impartiality" (ibid., 53). He notes that the laws concern conduct of a kind usually regarded . . . as abnormal and unnatural" (ibid., 51) and considers the development of the law in the UK. He describes as "understandable" the reluctance of the UK legislature to change the law on a matter involving "deep religious and moral beliefs" (ibid., 61). The Chief Justice emphasizes that organized religions have despised homosexuality as "a perversion of the biological function of the sexual organs and an affront both to society and to God." St Paul and all Christian churches have condemned it (ibid., 61). O'Higgins C.J. thus endorses the sectarian interpretation of Walsh J. in M'Gee.

The Chief Justice, citing a book by a Prof. West, describes a homosexual lifestyle as being "sad, lonely, and harrowing," promiscuous, frustrating, unstable, depressing and leading to a high incidence of suicide attempts (ibid., 62). O'Higgins C.J. did not mention that Prof. West was called as a witness by Mr. Norris, and had said that the statutes had these "prejudicial effects" for homosexuals, without achieving any significant social interest (ibid., 74, per Henchy J.). O'Higgins C.J. also said that the book mentions that the effect of decriminalisation was an increase in homosexual behavior and an increase in sexually transmitted diseases (ibid., 62). He did not mention Prof. West's comment on oath, that decriminalisation in England had not led to either result (ibid., 74).

O'Higgins C.J. then considers the effect of decriminalization of homosexual behaviour on marriage. He notes that the 1957 English Wolfenden Committee, which recommended decriminalisation in England and Wales, thought that there might be adverse effects for marriage, as homosexual behavior by the husband might lead to marital breakdown. The report also thought that decriminalisation might discourage moderately inclined homosexual people from marrying. In other words, "homosexual behavior and this encouragement may not be consistent with respect and regard for marriage" and it is reasonable to assume that permitting such behaviour harms marriage (ibid., 63).

O'Higgins C.J. rejects the notion that the right to privacy means that the law has no business interfering with private morality.

> The preamble to the Constitution proudly asserts the existence of God in the Most Holy Trinity and recites that the people of Ireland humbly acknowledge their obligation to "our Divine Lord, Jesus Christ." It cannot be doubted that the people, . . . were proclaiming a deep religious conviction and faith and an intention to adopt a Constitution consistent with . . . Christian beliefs. (Norris (1984) I.R. 36, 64)

O'Higgins rejects as unreasonable the idea, that the people in 1937 thought they were sweeping away anti-homosexual laws which had enforced Christian morality for centuries. In 1937 such conduct was prohibited in all parts of the United Kingdom and Ireland. So the right to privacy does not set up an area of exclusion. The State has an:

> . . . Interest in the general moral well-being of the community and [is] . . . entitled, where it is practicable to do so, to discourage conduct which is morally wrong and harmful to a way of life and to values which the State wishes to protect. (Norris (1984) I.R. 36, 64)

Thus among the immoral acts which the State can forbid, even when done in private, are abortion, incest, suicide pacts, suicide attempts, mercy killing. These can be prohibited even when no harm is done to anyone else. And in fact, homosexual practices may cause harm, at least to oneself, for they may lead one into a homosexual existence, the horrors of which O'Higgins C.J. believes he has described. And such conduct may lead to an increase in venereal disease, which is a threat to the public health. Also homosexual practices are harmful to marriage, or at least potentially so and marriage is an institution the state is sworn to uphold (Art. 41) (ibid., 65). For these reasons, the State may punish homosexual practices.

Henchy J. dissented. After noting the "Christian" nature of the state, the reference to "prudence, justice and charity," "dignity and freedom of the individual," and "democratic State" in the Preamble and Art. 5, he explains that the "vital human component" in the Constitutional order must be accorded:

> ... Such a range of personal freedoms or immunities are necessary to ensure his dignity and freedom as an individual in the type of society envisaged. (*Norris* (1984) I.R. 36, 71)

These rights inhere in the human personality and include a complex of rights which create a zone of privacy:

> A secluded area of activity or non-activity which may be claimed as necessary for the expression of an individual personality, for purposes not always necessarily moral or commendable, but meriting recognition in circumstances which do not engender considerations such as State security, public order or morality, or other essential components of the common good. (*Norris* (1984) I.R. 36, 72)

As in *M'Gee* the condemnation of the activity by religious groups is constitutionally irrelevant.

The court must decide whether there are reasons of public order and morality which require the intrusion into the zone of privacy with such disastrous effects for the plaintiff. Given that the statute was passed by a Parliament unaware of the Constitution, and that it indiscriminatingly criminalises all homosexual acts between males, there is a heavy onus on the State to justify that intervention into the private zone.

Henchy J. spends five pages examining the testimony of eminent Irish, British and US psychiatrists, sociologists, theologians (ibid., 72–6). The State called no witnesses; it introduced no evidence at all. All of the testimony was to the effect that: Criminalisation severely hurt homosexuals; there was no harm to society by its decriminalisation; decriminalisation would have beneficial effects for homosexuals and society generally. He observes that the case turns on one issue: Are the harmful effects to society of decriminalising homosexual behaviour less significant than the harmful effects to homosexuals of maintaining the Victorian statutes? If the latter harms are demonstrated by evidence to be significant, and the former harms are shown to be negligible, then the decision must be for the plaintiff (ibid., 77). Since "the unrebutted

consensus of the evidence was against" any justification of the laws, the judge was bound to give judgement for Norris. He should not substitute his own beliefs on homosexuality to justify such an extreme law (ibid., 77). The trial judge went astray in not relying on the evidence, but on the attitude of the Irish Christian Churches in determining the constitutionality of the law. Acts condemned by religious bodies might undermine the common good, and so merit punishment. However even then the State could not seek to eliminate them by the criminal law.

> To do so would upset the necessary balance which the Constitution posits between the common good and the dignity and freedom of the individual. What is deemed necessary to his dignity and freedom by one man may be abhorred by another as an exercise in immorality. The pluralism necessary for the preservation of constitutional requirements in the Christian democratic State envisaged by the Constitution means that sanctions of the criminal law may be attached to immoral acts only when the common good requires their proscription as a crime. (*Norris* (1984) I.R. 36, 78)

He notes that decriminalisation is not synonymous with approval of certain acts, but rather indicates that the common good does not require such a severe encroachment into the private sphere. At the very least, the law would have to make an exception for homosexual people.

M'Carthy J. also forcefully dissented. He argues that the courts must use a "present tense" and not a historical approach when interpreting the Constitution:

> ... The Constitution is a living document, its life depends not merely upon itself but upon the people from whom it came and to whom it gives varying rights and duties. (*Norris* (1984) I.R. 36, 96)

M'Carthy J. then examines several cases relating to unenumerated rights.[1] He insists that rights are not based on Christianity, though they are related to Christ's "great doctrine of charity" which the Irish Constitution has inherited (ibid., 99). They are rooted in the human personality,

and the State must treat them "with due observance of prudence, justice and charity, so that
the dignity and freedom of the individual may
be assured" (Preamble) (ibid., 100).

The right to privacy was identified by the
majority in *M'Gee*. There are many examples
of privacy in the Constitution (e.g., secret ballot,
property, inviolability of dwelling). These are but
aspects of the general right to personal privacy,
rooted in Art. 40.3.1 (ibid., 100). In *M'Gee*, the
majority upheld the *personal* right of privacy
in marriage, not simply the right of a married
couple to privacy: Their decision was based on
Art. 40.3.1 not Art. 41 (Family).

Here that right is infringed by law which
says that one man may masturbate in private, a
man and a woman may masturbate in private,
a woman may masturbate in private, an entire
society of women may do so – but two men
may not (ibid., 101). Unlike issues of protecting
others, or of maintaining military discipline,
there is no compelling state interest involved in
preventing two consenting men from mastur-
bating in private. The State has not justified
"state interference of a most grievous kind (the
policeman in the bedroom)" (ibid., 102).

Again in this decision, we find the strong
impact of moral reasoning. I start with the Chief
Justice. The exact basis of his opinion is unclear.
There are several rationales which might justify
his decision, but only two of these merit serious
attention.

The first argument is a communitarian/
historicist one. This would suggest that the Constitution is founded on the community's vision
of the good life, which the 1937 generation
bequeathed to its successors. To maintain the
continuity of that tradition, one must not change
the constitutional requirements too much from
the values of 1937. If the 1937 community
regarded certain activities as so abhorrent that
it punished them with life imprisonment, and
if, in its communal charter it included references to philosophies which condemned those
practices, then judges may not extend the protection of the Constitution to them.

There is a significant flaw with this approach.
The majority do not state that *M'Gee* is overruled.
M'Gee is one of many cases where judges gave
the Constitution a "present tense interpretation." It must not be shackled to the consciences

of an earlier generation. The 1937 generation
accepted laws banning the importation or sale
of contraceptives. They accepted that accused
persons could be subject to preventive detention,[2]
that a special criminal status could be created for
homeless persons,[3] and that women could be
exempt from jury service.[4] All these provisions had
been declared unconstitutional. Such an approach
in *Norris* would have required the judges to
explain why they were departing from the present
tense approach of so many cases.

The more likely argument is a perfectionist
one asserting the natural inferiority of homosexuality to heterosexuality. O'Higgins C.J. starts
his discussion by referring to homosexual acts
as "abnormal and unnatural." He notes that
organized Christian religion has condemned
homosexual acts consistently through history.
He then examines the alleged harms caused by
homosexual behaviour. There is no evidence of
these harms, and the majority's willingness to
accept their reality underscores their attitude
to the worth of homosexuals.

O'Higgins C.J. then explains that homosexual
acts are not covered by the right to privacy. Why
not? First, because the Constitution acknowledges the supremacy of Christian values. Second,
the State may protect the "general moral well-being
of the community" and punish what is "morally
wrong." Thus homosexual acts are the same
as other victimless acts such as abortion, incest,
suicide, and mercy killing, which the State may
punish because they are wrong. Other than
the reference to traditional condemnation as a
"perversion of the biological functions" and an
insult to God and society, O'Higgins C.J. does
not give concrete substantiated examples of the
harms caused by homosexuality.

The majority says that homosexual acts are to
be condemned even if they take place in private,
and harm no one. They may be condemned
even though that has seriously harmful effects
on gay men, without achieving any benefit for
society, simply because they are morally wrong.
The tenor of O'Higgins' argument is similar
to Finnis' natural law approach. Homosexuality,
like masturbation, is a form of sexuality which
cannot substantiate two basic goods (friendship
and procreation). This choice to use oneself
for purposes not related to these goods is "dis-
integrative manipulation" of oneself, and has

been condemned by all reasonable societies (Finnis 1985, 1993). The choice is always wrong regardless of its concrete effects on health or marriage. And the choice to do something immoral can be punished regardless of the absence of a concrete harm to the common good. The majority accepts the sectarian interpretation of Walsh J.'s *M'Gee* decision, and repudiates his comments on pluralism.

The dissenters are loyal to the vision of constitutional morality in *M'Gee*. They insist that the Constitution must be interpreted in the present tense; that respect for individual autonomy precludes invading the bedroom because of a conventional social morality; that the beliefs of no church forms any part of constitutional law. They refer to Christianity only as the historical tradition which bequeathed to modern liberalism certain core values (*Norris* (1984) I.R. 36, 99).

There are three elements to the dissenting opinions. First, there is the close attention to the concrete facts, which is tied into the second element, the emphasis that the individual counts. The minority say that *the State, through means direct and indirect, has seriously hurt the plaintiff; it must now justify its actions to him.* The focus on the reality of a situation is a key element of post 1970s liberal thought (Dworkin 1993; Dworkin 1985, 353–9).

The dissenters believe that the individual, as a "vital human" in a democratic society, must be accorded a zone of non-interference where she can develop. As Rawls puts it: "Each person possesses an *inviolability* founded on justice that even the welfare of society as a whole cannot override" (Rawls 1971, 3. Italics added). The State must not interfere in this zone, even though what takes place within is immoral. To interfere on this ground would violate the pluralism envisaged by the Constitution, endorsed by the Supreme Court in *M'Gee* and *Quinn's Supermarket* ((1972) I.R. 1). The State may only interfere if it can prove that there is a sufficiently weighty requirement of State security, public order or public morality which requires such intervention, and that such weighty requirement counterbalances the serious harm caused to gay men.

The third element is an anti-perfectionist approach (neutrality), rooted in human equality. Each person is an equal; to respect this the State may not regard some conceptions of the good as superior or inferior to others (Dworkin 1985, 181–213). This is what the dissenters insist, when they deny the people of the State to interfere simply because it objects strongly to the individual's practices within the confines of her constitutionally protected domain. It is also found in earlier decisions of the Supreme Court, most notably in *Quinn's Supermarket* ((1972) I.R. 1), and *M'Gee* ((1974) I.R. 294). Such is the requirement of pluralism which runs as a "golden thread" through the decisions of Walsh, Henchy and M'Carthy JJ. in the triad of decisions.

The Irish State did eventually end its persecution of homosexuality, but only after the European Court of Human Rights reminded it of its duty (*Norris* (1991) 13 E.H.R.R. 186; 1993 Criminal Law (Sexual Offences) Act). The 1993 debate on the amendment of the laws included contributions from some conservative groups who explicitly relied on the perfectionist vision proposed by the *Norris* majority in their opposition to the reform. The then Prime Minister argued for reform, insisting, as had Henchy and M'Carthy JJ., that the principle of equality demands respect for the orientation of the gay minority. So the competing visions of the Court found their way into the political dialogue, with the dissenting view (eventually) winning out.

The visionary conflict continued in other areas. *Norris* did not establish a particular vision even in the courts of the 1980s. Three years after *Norris*, the High Court decision of Hamilton P. (now Chief Justice) in *Kennedy v. Ireland* ((1987) I.R. 587, a telephone tapping case), seemed to resurrect the liberal opinions of the dissenters. Hamilton P. held that the right to privacy was a constitutional right, founded on the duty to assure the dignity and freedom of the individual in a democratic state. Certainly his opinion suggests that the anti-perfectionist liberal vision of *M'Gee* and the *Norris* dissenters is not buried. However he himself gives us ground to think otherwise.

4. Life versus Privacy

We turn now to the most explosive issue in any discussion of the right of privacy – abortion. The *M'Gee* vision provoked public debate on the right to privacy. Some activists were concerned that some judge, relying on US precedent (*Roe v. Wade* (1973) 410 US 113), might discover a right to an abortion lying within the right to privacy and invalidate sections 58, 59 of the 1861 Offences Against the Person Act, which prohibit abortion. This fear led to a decisive political debate on the amendment of the Constitution.

At one stage, someone tried to argue that the proposed amendment was invalid. The courts refused to get involved in the debate on the amendment: *Finn* ((1983) I.R. 154). The people may enact any wording as part of the Constitution. The judicial role is limited to elaborating on the effects of past decisions, or proposing new underlying visions to existing rules and principles. Judges do not debate on the formation of the sovereign will itself. (But see O'Hanlon 1992, 1993.)

Following this debate, the people approved the Eighth Amendment of the Constitution in 1983. This inserted Art. 40.3.3 immediately after Art. 40.3.2 (Personal Rights):

> The State acknowledges the right to life of the unborn and, with due regard to the equal right to life of the mother, guarantees in its law to respect, and as far as practicable, by its laws to defend and vindicate the right. (Art. 40.3.3)

In the 12 years which followed Parliament ignored its constitutional duty to legislate on this topic and instead the judges strove to elaborate the meaning of the sub-section in practice.

In 1986, a private organization, the Society for the Protection of the Unborn Child (SPUC), sought to prevent two agencies assisting women who wished to go to England for an abortion (*Att. Gen. (SPUC) v. Open Door* (1987) I.R. 477). (The English 1967 Abortion Act is more liberal than the Irish Law.)

SPUC sought three remedies: First, a declaration that the activities of the defendants were unlawful in view of Art. 40.3.3; second, a declaration that the defendants were engaged in a conspiracy to corrupt public morals; third, an injunction prohibiting the defendants from assisting pregnant women to obtain an abortion.[5]

The case went before Hamilton P. He notes that the right to life of the unborn is one of the rights of the natural law. The Constitution does not create the right; it recognizes it and guarantees to protect it (ibid., 481). The courts must protect it, whether the threat comes from the state or private individuals (ibid., 483). Courts can protect such rights even if the legislature had not given them a statutory form (ibid., 488–9; *State (Quinn) v. Ryan* (1965) I.R. 70). Should no procedure exist to protect adequately a right, then the courts will create one (*Open Door* (1987) I.R. 477, 489). Although the courts may go to great lengths to protect rights, Hamilton P. decided not to create what might amount to a new crime, that of assisting someone to commit an abortion abroad.

Hamilton P. considered a "crime" allegedly existing at common law, the unwritten law laid down by Superior Courts as binding: conspiracy to corrupt public morals (a conspiracy is a simple agreement by two or more people to do something; one may be guilty of conspiracy even if one has done nothing). In fact this "crime" was invented by the English House of Lords in the 1960s in *Shaw v. DPP* ((1962) Appeal Cases 220). Further, the House of Lords held that people may be convicted of conspiracy to corrupt public morals, *even where the conduct they were promoting was not itself a crime* (*Knuller* (1973) A.C. 446).

Hamilton P. accepted that conspiracy to corrupt public morals was a crime in Irish law (*Open Door* (1987) I.R. 477, 494). Furthermore, it was not necessary that the conduct promoted itself be criminal (ibid., 495). However, he refused to grant a declaration saying that the defendants were guilty of the crime. That would usurp the function of a criminal court sitting with a jury (ibid., 497).

Hamilton P. then considered whether the plaintiff was entitled to a declaration that the activities were unlawful, as a violation of the right to life. He observes that the defendant agencies are assisting women in obtaining an abortion in England (ibid., 499). Abortion is a violation of a right, and it is not rendered constitutional by committing it abroad (ibid., 493). Every citizen must obey the law and not interfere with constitutional rights (ibid., 496). The right to life must be protected, and no other lesser right (to privacy, to expression or to information) may interfere with it (ibid., 500). He granted an injunction, prohibiting the defendants from assisting women to obtain an abortion. There was an unsuccessful appeal to the Supreme Court (*Open Door* (1988) I.L.R.M. 18, 27).

There are two issues in the decision of Hamilton P.: the recognition of the crime of conspiracy to corrupt public morals, and the use of an injunction to restrain the provision of information relating to abortion. I treat here only of the first.

When discussing *Norris*, I argued that the dissenters were moved by a belief that the individual is important, and that there is a heavy onus on the State to justify its interventions into her zone of autonomy. In *Kennedy*, Hamilton P. apparently accepted this. Yet when importing a crime of conspiracy he attaches no weight to the rights of privacy or expression. Consider this novel crime. In this case, Hamilton P. suggests that it strikes into a private conversation between a pregnant woman and her counsellor concerning a most intimate matter. The justification for this intrusion is that they may be discussing the promotion of immorality. The crime is not limited to conspiracy to attack fundamental rights. It is not limited to conspiracy to do something unlawful. It is not limited to conspiracy to do something immoral. It applies to conspiracies to *promote* immorality. This is a blunt rejection of the proposition in *M'Gee* ((1974) I.R. 284) and the dissent in *Norris* ((1984) I.R. 36), that something may not be condemned as illegal simply because it is perceived as immoral. It might be legitimate for Parliament to punish conspiracy to attack fundamental rights, or to do something unlawful. But if Hamilton P. is saying that one can punish conspiracy to do or promote something immoral, he is saying that *M'Gee* should be overruled. For in *M'Gee*, the court said that Parliament could not criminalise the intention of Mrs M'Gee and her husband to do something perhaps immoral. Indeed *M'Gee* goes further: Parliament could not, even by indirect means, punish the effectuation of the intention. This new crime is far more extensive in scope than the law in *M'Gee*: It covers the joint intention to advocate something, not only the doing of something.

Furthermore the invasion of the private sphere is done in a very vague manner. It is unconstitutional for any crime to be so vague that someone does not know whether she is within

its terms or not (*King* (1981) I.R. 223). This applies with even greater force when the activity punished may well be the exercise of a right (*King*). The phrase "conspiracy to corrupt public morals" gives no indication as to what sort of conduct or expression is covered. It thus violates the proscription of vague criminal laws. Suppose that two people admit in public that they are homosexual lovers. Is this conspiracy to corrupt public morals? Suppose that two men hold hands in public. Is this conspiracy to corrupt public morals? There is no precision as to whether this offence, never considered by an Irish legislature or executive, or judge prior to this case, may strike in the zone of privacy upheld in *M'Gee* and *Kennedy* ((1987) I.R. 587). It is an arbitrary criminalisation of potentially large areas of expression and private conduct. The recognition of this crime is support for the perfectionist element of *Norris* ((1984) I.R. 36).

In other cases in the 1980s, the courts confirmed these rules: No one is allowed to give information which will assist a woman to obtain an abortion abroad. This applies at least to counselling groups, and student unions (*Coogan* (1989) I.R. 734: *Grogan* (1989) I.R. 753). The right to life cannot be defeated by any lesser right, such as privacy, or expression. However debate on the merits of abortion was permitted. And, apparently, travel abroad was also permitted.

So by 1990 it appears that the judges had put a particular interpretation on the Constitution – one which subordinated the rights to privacy and expression to one particular right. Furthermore the solution was socially acceptable in that it simultaneously expressed public disapproval of abortion, while allowing women (those who could afford it) to have abortions in England.

5. Life versus Life

This is not the conclusion of the story. In a case combining a tragic personal situation, and abstract Constitutional principles, a different evaluation emerges. In *Attorney General v. X*, ((1992) 1 I.R. 1) the Government's legal adviser sought an injunction restraining a 14-year-old rape victim from leaving the State to have an abortion. The girl was inclined towards suicide due to the pressures of the pregnancy.

Costello J. in the High Court, granted the injunction. He reiterated that constitutional rights are judicially enforceable even if not regulated by statute (ibid., 10). He held that the threat to the life of the foetus was more serious than the threat to the life of the girl, which was declared by Art. 40.3.3 to be equal to the life of the foetus. There was evidence that the girl would commit suicide if the abortion did not take place. Costello J. considered that this threat was different from the threat to the life of the foetus: If an abortion took place, the foetus would certainly die, whereas if it did not, it was not certain the young girl would kill herself (ibid., 12).

Costello J. rejected an argument rooted in the Constitutional right against preventive detention (*People v. O'Callaghan* (1966) I.R. 510). He also rejected a challenge based on the EC right to travel abroad to receive services (*Luisi and Carbone* (1984) 1 E.C.R. 377, case 286/82), arguing that the injunction was justified by a public policy exception to that right, which he derived from an analogy with the case of free movement of workers (*R. v. Bouchereau* (1977) 2 E.C.R. 1999, case 30/77). The judge also considers that such an injunction would be a proportional limit on rights under the European Convention on Human Rights.

The High Court prohibited the girl or her family from arranging an abortion, and prohibited the girl from leaving the state for nine months. Costello J. provided a reasoned explanation of what the constitutional principles required in the case. In affirming those principles, he also laid down a challenge to those who stood by them.

Seven days later, the Supreme Court heard an appeal. After two days, amidst the largest amount of publicity ever to attach to any case, the Court granted the appeal. A week later the judges explained why.

Finlay C.J. spoke first. He reviews the facts, and refers to the judicial duty to protect fundamental rights even in the absence of legislation (*Att. Gen. v. X* (1992) 1 I.R. 1, 50–1). He refers to the statements of Walsh J. in *M'Gee*, about the superiority of justice, to the remarks of O'Higgins C.J. in *State (Healy) v. O'Donoghue*, ((1976) I.R. 325) on the duty to judge according to developing notions of prudence, justice, and charity (*Att. Gen. v. X* (1992) 1 I.R. 1, 52–3). He

emphasises that judges must construe the constitution harmoniously. He says that the appropriate test to apply in this case was:

> . . . If it is established as a matter of probability that there is a real and substantial risk to the life, as distinct from the health, of the mother, which can only be avoided by the termination of her pregnancy, such termination is permissible . . . (*Att. Gen v. X*, (1992), 1 I.R. 1, 54)

In this case, the young girl was suicidal. Since suicide is something which it is not possible to guard against, this constitutes such a real and substantial risk, and the girl was entitled to an abortion, and to leave the State to obtain one. Egan and O'Flaherty JJ. concur with most of the Chief Justice's reasoning on the right to life.

Finlay C.J. then considers the unenumerated right to travel abroad. He observes that, if the protection of fundamental rights cannot be reconciled one with the other, then the courts must protect the most important right (ibid., 57). The right to life clearly prevails over the right to travel abroad, and the courts may suspend the right to travel abroad, to protect the right to life. Egan J. agrees (ambiguously) with Finlay C.J. on this issue (ibid., 92).

M'Carthy J. also granted the appeal. He dislikes the notion of a hierarchy of rights (ibid., 78). Even the right to life is not absolute: The Constitution apparently allows the death penalty. He rejects a hierarchical approach: The real question is how to defend and vindicate the two rights as far as practicable (Art. 40.3.3 only imposes the duty to defend and vindicate rights as far as practicable). In his opinion, where there is a real and substantial risk to the life of the mother, then defending the right of the unborn may not be practicable (ibid., 80).

M'Carthy J. then considers the right to travel. He rejects the balancing exercise. One does not balance rights but ascertains whether citizens have them or not. If they do, then they may exercise them, regardless of their purpose (ibid., 38). The mere fact that someone intended to do something when abroad (even murder) cannot be invoked to curtail the right to travel. So only M'Carthy J. defends the position of Henchy J. in *Norris*, that persons may exercise rights even though for an immoral purpose.

Hederman J. delivered a thoughtful, indeed forceful dissent. He emphasises that the State has a far-ranging duty to protect life "which is the essential value of every legal order and essential to the enjoyment of all other rights." This duty includes positive duties: For instance, the right to life may be invoked to require the State to deal with life-threatening pollution. Indeed, Hederman J. says that not only may all persons invoke the right to life, but further, people may invoke it on others' behalf (ibid., 71).

Art. 40.3.3 of the Constitution makes it clear that the foetus is entitled to live. Hederman J. allows one exception – an operation, "the sole purpose of which is to save the life of the mother" cannot be considered "a direct killing of the foetus" even if the inevitable consequence of the operation is the death of the foetus (ibid., 72). However the mother may not invoke her right to privacy in abortion cases, for "the unborn life is an autonomous human being protected by the Constitution" (ibid., 72). The right to self-determination does not include the right to end life.

In this case, the State's duties extend to restricting the right to travel of the young girl. Such a restriction, though offensive to the Con-stitution, is not so offensive as the "irrevocable step of the destruction of life" (ibid., 73). Before an abortion may be permitted to save the life of a pregnant woman, it must be shown, by weighty, cogent evidence, that it is the only way to save her life. In this case the threat to the girl's life is the threat of suicide. The appropriate response is to put the girl under supervision. It is not acceptable to destroy one human life to dissuade someone else from taking a life, even her own (ibid., 76).

This case carries forward themes from earlier cases. I draw your attention to the dissent of Hederman J., with its emphasis on the value of life as overriding other concerns, and the overall role of perfectionist–sectarian reasoning in the opinions.

Hederman J.'s dissenting opinion is interesting for its reliance on what appears to be some form of secularized Catholic beliefs, rather similar to the approach promoted by Finnis (1980). He describes life as first and foremost a value to which the Constitution is dedicated. This recalls Finnis' theory which is a value not a rights based

theory. For Finnis (and apparently Hederman J.) rights and duties flow from the supreme values. Secondly, Hederman J. is clearly of the opinion that one has a duty never to act against a basic value. Third, Hederman J., like Finnis, relies on the Catholic doctrine of "double effect" to describe some actions which result in the death of the foetus as not being an abortion even though the death is the natural and probable consequence. And, of course, like Finnis, he believes that the foetus is entitled to the protection of the right to life. In drawing these comparisons, I do not suggest that Hederman J.'s library includes the collected works of the Oxford scholar. Rather I note that he relies on certain contested moral theories, which happen to have been expressed by Finnis. In considering the accept-ability of Hederman's opinion, we are surely allowed to consider the debate surrounding the most sophisticated defender of that view.

The second point is the more important. In *Norris*, there were strong suggestions of a per-fectionist, even sectarian, underpinning to the reasoning of the judges. *Open Door* seemed to confirm that vision (even though *Kennedy* disputed it). The most striking feature of the X case, is that the reasoning of the judges is secular; even Hederman J. does not rely on religious argu-ments to bolster his dissent. Furthermore, the majority judges do not seem to rely on any perfectionist theory (or at least not any per-fectionist theory with a strong concept of the good). They rely on a discussion of the rights involved. No one suggests that abortion may be prohibited because it is immoral or unpopular, or violates God's law. Rather it is prohibited because it violates the right to life of the unborn. Indeed the majority upheld a *right* to an abortion, that is a right to do something perceived as immoral. Again, the argument of some of the judges that the right to life could be limited to protect the right to life, is not one which relies on any perfectionist theory. Clearly the type of reasoning found in *Norris* is no longer acceptable (for the moment).[6]

The Supreme Court provided a controversial concretisation of the moral legal principles of Irish abortion law. They did not simply say (as many would have said) that the girl was free to go, even though abortion is a violation of a human right. Nor did they say, as Finnis and the Catholic church, that the termination of a pregnancy to save the life of the girl, is not an abortion. Either view would have played mere lip service to the constitutional doctrine of a hierarchy of rights, the constitutional right of the foetus, and the constitutional supremacy of life.

The decision posed many questions which Parliament tried to avoid answering by proposing referenda to the people. Although some people demanded the abolition of any right to abortion, the Government proposed three amendments to the people. These amendments provided that Art. 40.3.3 did not limit either the right to travel or the right to receive information about services lawfully available abroad, and provided that an abortion was not justified to prevent a suicide. If all these had been accepted, it would mean that a judge in an X type case would have to say to a suicidal woman – "you have no right to an abortion – but you may go to have one anyway." This solution the people rejected; rather they voted in favour of the first two proposals, and against the third. The right to abortion in limited cases remains, but now judges and legislators must reconsider the abortion rules developed in *Open Door*.[7] So the dialogue originating in *M'Gee* continues.

6. Conclusion

I have now presented some key cases of Irish constitutional law, where law interacts with morality. What is the moral of the story?

The first thing to note is that the cases form, not merely a narrative but a debate. In *M'Gee* ((1974) I.R. 284) the majority judges of the Supreme Court upheld the claim to an unenumerated right to privacy, on the basis of a moral approach which stressed the autonomy of the individual. The majority rejected the notion that the conventional morality of society (of 1937 or 1973) could define the limits of individual freedom, at least in certain important areas of human life.

However, we then came to *Norris* ((1984) I.R. 36) where the opposite occurs. A three judge majority rely on a perfectionist theory of morality, to limit the right to sexual freedom of gay men and others wishing to have anal intercourse. This despite the serious damage

inflicted on those who were affected, despite the failure of the State to adduce any evidence that such stern prohibitions were necessary.

One should not conclude that this perfectionist approach swept all before it. In *Kennedy* ((1987) I.R. 587) Hamilton P. relied on the moral vision presented by the dissenters in *Norris*, to condemn a violation by the State of individual privacy. But then in *Open Door* ((1987) I.R. 477), he goes to the opposite extreme. Without any discussion of its roots in Irish law, he imports the "crime" of conspiracy to corrupt public morals. This "crime" is entirely contrary to the spirit of a legal system which respects the right to privacy. Like the *Norris* majority, it surrenders individual autonomy to the whim of conventional morality.

The decision in the X case ((1992) 1 I.R. 1) suggests a different solution to the debate. The majority judgements of the Supreme Court make it clear that it is the nature of rights, and their relationship with the constitutional text, and not conventional (or religious) morality, which is determinative. The Supreme Court recognized a limited right to an abortion, not conceded by conventional morality. The perfectionist reasoning of *Norris* is nowhere to be found.

However the debate is not just a legal one between judges. It is also a public one, to which the judiciary contribute. The right to privacy protected the decision to use contraceptives. At the time there was a serious public debate, with many people demanding the decriminalisation of the sale and importation of contraception. Parliament declined to deal with the issue. It was left to the Court to decide, and establish the State's commitment to pluralism and autonomy.

However that decision, and its reasoning, led some people to launch a public campaign to give constitutional protection to the foetus. This issue was publicly debated, and the sovereign people made known its decision in 1983. (As noted above the courts declined to review the legality of a procedurally correct amendment proposal: *Finn* (1983) I.R. 154; *Abortion Information* (1995) 2 I.L.R.M. 81) Normally one would expect the public debate to continue, with Parliament fleshing out the guidelines left vague by the new amendment. However Parliament did nothing.

Instead the issue was thrown back to the courts, to resolve weighty public problems in the context of specific cases. The courts produced some answers, which Parliament left undisturbed. The general acceptance of society was ruptured when Costello J. produced a thoroughly reasoned decision, which demonstrated how the principles perceived to be underpinning the abortion laws led to a result no one wanted – the confinement of a 14-year-old rape victim in the State. The general acceptance was shattered this time – with public demands that the girl be let free. The Supreme Court perceived the principles to be applied differently from Costello J. Unlike many members of the public, the judges did not advocate a thoroughly hypocritical solution. Constrained by notions of legal consistency, the judges ended the injunction, and explained that the wording of the people's amendment created a right (albeit in limited circumstances) to an abortion. They thus provided a consistent elaboration of the public rules.

The debate did not thereby terminate. As explained above, the elaboration provided by the Court led to a major debate on the amendment of the Constitution, during which the people rejected one change to the solution in X, but accepted two changes to the Constitution, which overruled Open Door. In 1995 Parliament enacted the Regulation of Information Act to implement the amendments. In a key decision the Supreme Court upheld its validity, giving it a reading favourable to the free flow of information (*Abortion Information* (1995) 2 I.L.R.M. 81).

The contributions of the judiciary seem to be of two types: the visionary and the elaboratory. In some decisions, judges consider the specific rules available to them, and the principles which underpin them, and try to elaborate the requirements and impact of these in a concrete case. Thus they provide an example of what the political decisions of the people lead to. For instance, in *Open Door*, the courts say in effect: "If you believe in the right to life of the foetus, you are committed to restricting the rights of women." Costello's judgement in X ((1992) 1 I.R. 1), is a particularly good instance. If you accept that there is a hierarchy of rights topped by life (*Shaw*, (1982) I.R. 1), that the foetus has the right to live equal to the rights of others (Art. 40.3.3), and that courts may do anything to

protect the hierarchically superior right (ibid.), then you must accept Costello's application in the concrete case.

Yet other decisions involve visionary debates: What view of political morality should inspire our interpretations of the Constitution? In *M'Gee* a strongly liberal theory was defended, which also found expression in the dissenting opinions in *Norris*. Yet *Norris* and *Open Door* offer a more perfectionist vision. Although X does not revert to the liberal vision of an earlier age, it also does not embrace the perfectionism of *Norris*. Regarding the issue in *Norris*, the dissenters' vision won out in the political debate.

So our judges both implement and suggest. They solve present problems with reasoning rooted in the past, but with an eye to the future (Dworkin 1986, 225, ch. 11).

However we must sometimes reconstruct the reasoning of the judges, where they do not make it transparent or fully coherent. When we do reconstruct that reasoning, we better understand the vision and its implications for concrete cases. And such reconstruction forces us to pose other questions not adequately treated of in the judges' reasoning. For instance, most people agree that it makes an important difference whether the right to life is considered to be rooted in a value, or a right properly so-called (Dworkin 1993, 11–13). Yet the judges in the abortion cases do not seem to be entirely aware of the need to answer this question.

The notion of moralized constitutionalism as a legal debate and a contribution to a public debate on political morality, is the central point of this article. However there are other questions to note. Clearly the majority judges in *Norris* and *M'Gee* relied on very different notions of political morality in reaching their decisions. The judges in *M'Gee* paid great respect to the principles of autonomy and pluralism; those in the later case, to more perfectionist notions.

This poses a question to those who argue for a moralized conception of law. Exactly what criteria are to be used to decide which vision of political morality is to guide interpretation? Should judges decide in a practical discourse what is the most appropriate morality, and then present it to the rest of us? Or should they opt for the theory closest to the wording and tenor of the text? Or should they defer to the perceived conventional morality of the society? How would such philosophers have advised the judges in *Norris* who had to decide between those provisions of the Constitution which emphasize the "dignity and freedom of the individual" and those sections which emphasize the supremacy of God?

A final point to note is that the Irish example demonstrates that judicial activism and judicial moralization of the law cut both ways. One may not simply applaud moralization when liberals carry the day (*M'Gee*) and complain when conservatives do (*Norris*). A more nuanced theory which specifies the criteria for judging the acceptability of either vision is needed. On the issue of activism, do defenders of activism wish to stand over *Open Door*; do defenders of deference to legislative judgement wish to praise *Norris*? Where does this issue even fit in when Parliament simply ignores a problem (*Open Door, X*)?

With this article I have tried to give a vivid picture of how law develops in a system accepting a moralized conception of law. The reader may be amused, horrified, or impressed. But the question of law and morality is, for Irish lawyers at least, no academic distraction, but a practical reality. The final word I leave to Hamilton C.J. in the recent *Abortion Information* case, of which regrettably considerations of space and time preclude a full consideration. Although denying that there was a "natural law" superior to the Constitution, the Chief Justice continued:

> . . . The courts . . . in determining . . . the rights which are *superior to positive law or which are imprescriptible or inalienable* . . . must interpret them in accordance with *their ideas of prudence, justice and charity* (*Abortion Information* (1995) 2 I.L.R.M. 81, 107, italics added)

Notes

1   In *Ryan* ((1965) I.R. 294, right to health), Kenny J. describes unenumerated rights as being justified by the "Christian and democratic nature of the State." In *G. v. An Bord Uchtála* ((1980) I.R. 32, rights of unmarried mothers, and children born out-

side of marriage), Walsh J. cites approvingly the opinion of Henchy J. in *M'Gee* that unenumerated rights vest in people as a consequence of their human personality. In *State (C.) v. Frawley* ((1976) I.R. 365, the right not to be subject to torture or inhuman and degrading treatment) and *State (M.) v. Attorney General* ((1979) I.R. 73, the right to leave the State), Finlay P. refers to the phrase of Kenny J. in *Ryan* about the Christian ethos of the State.

2   Declared unconstitutional in *People v. O'Callaghan* ((1966) I.R. 501).

3   Declared unconstitutional in *King v. Attorney General* ((1981) I.R. 223).

4   Declared unconstitutional in *DeBúrca v. Attorney General* ((1976) I.R. 38).

5   An injunction is a court order backed up with the threat of summary punishment in the event of non-compliance.

6   This is confirmed by *F. v. F.* ((1994) 2 I.L.R.M. 401), where the High Court refused to hear evidence from moral theologians, insisting that it is for judges, not religious experts to determine the meaning of the Constitution, in the light of evolving values. The judge thus dismisses the degree of importance attached to beliefs claiming a religious provenance, in *Norris* ((1984) I.R. 36). Indeed he describes Walsh J.'s opinion in *M'Gee* ((1974) I.R. 284), as decisively rejecting any influence by theology or religion or constitutional development.

7   The Supreme Court rejected the opportunity to do so in *Att. Gen. (SPUC) v. Open Door* ((1994) I.L.R.M. 256), for procedural reasons. In 1995 Parliament finally enacted the Regulation of Information Act, which the Supreme Court upheld as valid: *Abortion Information* ((1995) 2 I.L.R.M. 81) in a decision much criticized by conservative interest groups.

References

Chubb, Basil. 1991. *The Politics of the Irish Constitution*. Dublin: Institute of Public Administration.

Costello, Declan. 1956. The Natural Law and the Constitution. *Studies* 45:403.

Costello, Declan. 1962. Book Review. *Studies* 51:201.

Dworkin, Ronald. 1985. *A Matter of Principle*. Cambridge: Harvard University Press.

Dworkin, Ronald. 1986. *Law's Empire*. London: Fontana.

Dworkin, Ronald. 1993. *Life's Dominion*. London: Harper Collins.

Finnis, John. 1980. *Natural Law and Natural Rights*. Oxford: Oxford University Press.

Finnis, John. 1985. Personal Integrity, Sexual Morality and Responsible Parenthood. *Anthropos* 1:43.

Finnis, John. 1993. Is Homosexual Conduct Wrong? Disintegrity. *The New Republic*, 15th November.

Kelly, John. 1967. *Fundamental Rights in the Irish Law and Constitution*. Dublin: Figgis.

Kelly, John, Gerald Hogan and Gerry Whyte. 1994. *The Irish Constitution*. Dublin: Jurist.

O'Hanlon, Roderick. 1992. Natural Rights and the Irish Constitution. *Irish Law Times* 8.

O'Hanlon, Roderick. 1993. The Judiciary and the Moral Law. *I.L.T.* 129.

Rawls, John. 1971. *A Theory of Justice*. Oxford: Oxford University Press.

Walsh, Brian. 1987a. The Constitution and Constitutional Rights. In *The Constitution of Ireland*. Ed. Litton. Dublin: Institute of Public Administration.

Walsh, Brian. 1987b. The Constitution: A View from the Bench. In *DeValera's Constitution and Ours*. Ed. Farrell. Dublin: Gill and MacMillan.

57

Peremptory Norms as International Public Order

Alexander Orakhelashvili

Peremptory Norms as an Aspect of the Hierarchy of Norms

The hierarchy of norms in international law raises a variety of questions.[1] One norm could prevail over another because it emerged later in time; or because it applies as between certain States in contrast to general international law; or because the States which established that norm have so intended, for example by stipulating that the parties to a given treaty shall not consent to any treaty obligation contradicting that treaty,[2] and if they nevertheless do so, the original treaty will prevail, as specified, for instance, in Article 103 of the UN Charter which gives the Charter obligations primacy over inconsistent agreements. The precise scope of Article 103 is a subject of debates in doctrine and practice, but it is indisputable that it establishes the case of normative hierarchy by giving precedence to certain norms over others.

A specific kind of normative hierarchy is observable in international institutional law between constitutive instruments of international organizations and acts enacted within those organizations.[3]

These instances of hierarchy are based on the conception of international law as a consent-based system of norms derived from the will of States. Assumptions that a later norm prevails over an earlier one or that it does not so prevail because the States concerned have so wished, or that a norm applicable between a limited number of States can trump general international law all imply that the will of States determines the priority of norms. This means that there is no categorical hierarchy of international instruments, for no instrument is inherently superior to another. The issues of hierarchy arise only in the specific cases when the clauses of different instruments come into conflict with each other and the rule which prevails does so because this was so wished by the relevant States for this specific case.

The only visible exception can be found in Article 53 of the 1969 Vienna Convention on the Law of Treaties,[4] stating that treaties in conflict with peremptory norms[5] are void and defining a peremptory norm as "a norm accepted and recognised by the international community of States as a whole as a norm from which no derogation is permitted and which can be modified only by a subsequent norm of general international law having the same character". Peremptory norms prevail not because the States involved have so decided but because they are

Alexander Orakhelashvili, *Peremptory Norms in International Law* (Oxford University Press, 2006), pp. 7–11, 48–53. © 2006 by A. Orakhelashvili. Reprinted with permission from Oxford University Press.

intrinsically superior and cannot be dispensed with through standard inter-State transactions. The specific character of such hierarchy is also manifested by the nullity that is attached to the transactions conflicting with peremptory norms.

The rationale behind the distinction between peremptory and ordinary rules is described by the Special Rapporteur of the UN International Law Commission Fitzmaurice:

> The rules of international law in this context fall broadly into two classes – those which are mandatory and imperative in all circumstances (*Jus cogens*) and those (*jus dispositivum*) which merely furnish a rule for application in the absence of any other agreed regime, or, more correctly, those the variation or modification of which under an agreed regime is permissible, provided the position and rights of third States are not affected.[6]

In other words, the rules of *jus cogens* have to apply whatever the will and attitude of States, while the applicability of the rules of *jus dispositivum* can be excluded or modified in accordance with the duly expressed will of States.

Such regulation causes peremptory norms to prevail over treaties, thereby creating an exception to the *lex specialis* rule. This is a hierarchy related to international public order as a phenomenon of general international law and hence different from any institutional *lex superior*.[7] As Rozakis affirms, one of the effects of the introduction of peremptory law in the international legal system is that it partly transforms international law – a horizontal and consensual legal order – into a vertical system of law. Such a system includes rules with different hierarchical standing, that is superior and inferior rules. The superior rules determine the frame within which the inferior rules can be valid, while the inferior rules must comply with the content of superior rules.[8] In domestic law, peremptory norms are not necessarily hierarchically superior to other norms:[9] positive law, whatever its rank, can prevail over contracts. But in international law there can be no *jus cogens* unless it is superior to ordinary norms because the latter constitute positive law, not just transactions between legal persons.

In international law where legal norms are produced by the agreement of States no cases

should arguably be admitted where one norm by itself, and not because of the relevant States' will and determination, prevails over another norm. This means that the factors must be sought for which make the relevant norm so special as to enable it to effectuate an exception from the otherwise valid and dominant consensual pattern.

Peremptory norms as defined in the Vienna Convention on the Law of Treaties can have multiple functions, bearing in mind the nature of the international community.[10] They operate as peremptory norms proper, constraining the contractual capacity of legal persons. Conceivably, they also operate as constitutional norms.[11] In national law, *jus cogens* and constitutional norms can be distinguished, even if they overlap in substance, because constitutional norms establish the overall framework for legislative and administrative regulation while peremptory norms relate to private contracts. In the decentralized international legal system, agreements expressly or tacitly concluded by individual States are the primary source of positive law. Peremptory norms, prevailing over such agreements, necessarily implicate a constitutional element.[12] Given that individual States appear in international law as law-makers, the concept of *jus cogens* resembles conceptually not merely peremptory norms limiting the contractual freedom legal persons but also the constitutional limitations in terms of on what the law-makers can freely enact. Such constitutional character of a norm is a matter of the substance of that norm, whether enshrined in written or unwritten sources of law.

All said on this subject is only to indicate that peremptory norms can have the potential to build the constitutional element in international law, not that they necessarily have this potential. The constitution of the international community would conceivably encompass, apart from *jus cogens*, the UN Charter, the international bill of human rights, and the Vienna Convention on the Law of Treaties, that is the instruments which regulate in international relations the subject-matters which are regulated in national law by national constitutions. But there is no clear evidence that the international community as a whole views these instruments as its constitution.

The identification of international *jus cogens* with legislative norms is also a tempting option, as it reflects the subjection of contractual agreement to the legislative will.[13] However, this analogy would assume the logically anterior factors that simply do not occur in international law. Legislation is a process of the enactment of juridical instruments by an organ that has been specifically authorized to perform its function as a legislator. The absence of such in the international legal system makes it impossible to see *jus cogens* as an element of international legislation. Moreover, many peremptory norms are based on unwritten law.

Finally, peremptory norms operate as a public order protecting the legal system from incompatible laws, acts and transactions. As with every legal system, international law can be vulnerable to infiltration of the effect of certain norms and transactions which are fundamentally repugnant to it. It seems that the general concept of public order most suitably reflects the basic characteristics of international *jus cogens*. This concept not only reflects the domestic law analogy, but it is the most suitable, if not the only, analogy that can be adapted, without the disruption of the inherent character of the concept itself, to the decentralized character of the international legal system.

[. . .]

The Basis for the Peremptory Character of Norms

It is crucial to determine which factor causes a legal interest to become the community concern and be protected by a peremptory norm. It is widely accepted that the concept of public order is based on morality and its function is to outlaw the acts and transactions offending against the morality accepted in the given legal system.[14] Sentiments of the just and unjust impose themselves as absolute values.[15] National legislative clauses directly refer to moral criteria,[16] and even in legal systems without such clauses, public order outlaws immoral acts and transactions. For instance, in *Kuwait Air Corp.* the general conceptions of morality and humanity were identified as aspects of public policy.[17] Public order may refer both to the rules of positive law and generally recognized principles of morality which are not necessarily part of positive law.[18]

Although the starting-point distinction can be made between the mere concept of morality and peremptory norms mentioned in Article 53 of the Vienna Convention as legal norms,[19] the crucial question is the relevance of the morality factor in conferring the peremptory character to legal norms.

In international law, it is arguable that when a right of a particular actor or entity is very important in terms of morality, it can be assumed to embody the community interest and hence limit the will and discretion of individual States. The Inter-American Commission affirmed that peremptory norms are accepted "as necessary to protect the public interest of the society of nations or to maintain the levels of public morality recognised by them".[20]

Morality can arguably itself explain a norm's peremptory character. According to Special Rapporteur Lauterpacht, in order to operate as norms of public policy, these norms "need not necessarily have crystallised in a clearly accepted rule of law"; they may alternatively "be expressive of rules of international morality so cogent" that an international tribunal would consider them as part of the general principles of law in terms of Article 38 of the International Court's Statute.[21] Special Rapporteur Fitzmaurice attributed similar effects to *jus cogens* and humanity and good morals with regard to treaty invalidity, further emphasizing that

> it is not possible . . . to state exhaustively what are the rules of international law that have the character of *jus cogens*, but a feature common to them, or to a great many of them, evidently is that they involve not only legal rules but considerations of morals and international good order.[22]

Public policy is not determinable by mere reference to norms of positive law, but refers also to the prevailing social and moral attitudes of the community.[23] McNair refers in terms of *jus cogens* to "some rules of law or some principles of morality which individuals are not permitted by law to ignore or to modify by their agreements".[24] This is a reference to positive law and morality as two separate but mutually complementary concepts. Verdross explains *jus cogens* by reference to the ethics of the international community.[25] As Cassese submits, even if the content of *jus cogens* may be unclear on occasions, it may have effect due to its moral and psychological weight, and invalidate conflicting acts and transactions merely on the ground of their immorality.[26] According to Judge Schücking in *Oscar Chinn*, tribunals would never apply a legal instrument the terms of which are contrary to public morality.[27]

Lauterpacht also links public order to morality, emphasizing that States cannot change by treaties the rules of customary law by laying down immoral obligations.[28] At the same time, mere immorality is not sufficient, "it must be such as to render its enforcement contrary to public policy and to socially imperative dictates of justice".[29]

Specific Norms of International Public Order

In order to qualify as peremptory, a norm, while protecting a given actor, legal person or value, must safeguard interests transcending those of individual States, have a moral or humanitarian connotation, because its breach would involve a result so morally deplorable as to be considered absolutely unacceptable by the international community as a whole, and consequently not permitting division of these interests into bilateral legal relations. It remains to identify the norms and principles meeting these criteria.

The prohibition of the use of force

The fundamental importance of State interests to survive, exist independently and effectively protect its population can justify the elevation of such interests to the interests of the international community as a whole and their protection through peremptory norms.[30] The law related to the use of force in international relations which is based on the UN Charter and relevant customary law is the principal implication of those considerations.

The prohibition of the use of force by States undoubtedly forms part of *jus cogens*.[31] Judge Nagendra Singh emphasized that the principle of the non-use of force, being "the very cornerstone of the human effort to promote peace", is part of

jus cogens.[32] Judge Sette-Camara also pointed out that this principle is part of "peremptory rules of customary international law which impose obligations on all States".[33] In *Oil Platforms*, Judge Simma affirmed that the norms of general international law on the unilateral use of force are undeniably of a peremptory nature.[34] Judge Elaraby emphasized in his Separate Opinion in the *Palestinian Wall* case that the prohibition of the use of force, as the most important principle that emerged in the twentieth century, is undoubtedly part of *jus cogens*.[35]

The inherent right of States to self-defence is also part of *jus cogens*. The International Court considered in *Nuclear Weapons* that the right of a State to resort to self-defence follows from the fundamental right of every State to survival and hesitated to qualify this right even by reference to non-use of nuclear weapons.[36] Self-defence implies the right to defend itself and organize State machinery in a way necessary and sufficient for protecting life, property and well-being of citizens.[37]

It seems that jus *ad bellum* as a whole is peremptory. *Jus ad bellum* concerns the right of States to use force and defines the circumstances of such use. It thereby comes in touch with the outer limits of the very prohibition of the use of force and any judgment as to whether the use of force is legal has to do with the question whether that use of force is justified under Article 2(4) of the UN Charter and its customary counterpart. Therefore, if the very prohibition of the use of force is peremptory, then every principle specifying the limits on the entitlement of States to use force is also peremptory. To illustrate, in *Oil Platforms* the International Court in fact affirmed the peremptory character of the entire *jus ad bellum* as it examined and affirmed the limits these norms impose on the interpretation of bilateral treaties.

The principle of self-determination and its incidences

The right of peoples to self-determination is undoubtedly part of *jus cogens* because of its fundamental importance,[38] even if its peremptory character is sometimes disputed.[39] The UN General Assembly made a number of statements based on the peremptory status of the right of peoples to self-determination. In the preamble of

Resolution 1803(XVII), the General Assembly pointed out that "economic and financial agreements between the developed and developing countries must be based on the principles of equality and of the right of peoples and nations to self-determination". In Resolution 35/118, the General Assembly "categorically reject[ed] any agreement, arrangement or unilateral action by colonial or racist Powers which ignores, violates, denies or conflicts with the inalienable rights of peoples under colonial domination to self-determination and independence". This attitude clearly views the principle of self-determination as the limitation on the permissible content of treaties and hence the public order principle of peremptory status.[40] The ILC and the UN Human Rights Commission have likewise affirmed the peremptory character of the principle of self-determination.[41]

It seems that certain incidences of the principle of self-determination, such as permanent sovereignty over natural resources, are part of *jus cogens*.[42] As Brownlie suggests, the provisions of the UN General Assembly Resolution 1803 regarding the Permanent Sovereignty over Natural Resources constitute the part of the catalogue of peremptory norms.[43] Authors such as Sztucki and Schrijver contend that a State, in exercise of its permanent sovereignty, can conclude contracts which would derogate from the principle, and hence the principle is not peremptory.[44] The Arbitral Tribunal in *Aminoil* expressed a similar view, but only to assert that permanent sovereignty over natural resources does not prohibit the State's subscribing to the stabilisation clauses that are often included in State contracts.[45] The Arbitral Tribunal in *Texaco* does not deny the *jus cogens* character of permanent sovereignty and adopts a subtler solution that in entering into a concession contract a State does not necessarily contradict that sovereignty. *Jus cogens* would extend to the agreements concluded between States and foreign private companies if these agreements "in fact alienate the sovereignty of the State over [its natural] resources". Some State contracts are not alienations, but just the exercise of sovereignty over natural resources.[46]

But this reasoning is defective for several reasons. First, the principle of permanent sovereignty is an integral element of the principle of self-determination, and is so regarded by the UN General Assembly.[47] Second, it is the very essence of the principle that a State should be free to dispose of its natural resources in the exercise of its sovereignty. This normative core is the basis of the peremptory nature of the principle. Contracts concluded in the exercise of permanent sovereignty are not derogations from the principle; rather, there would be derogation if a State entered into an agreement through which it waived the right to take decisions on all or part of its natural resources.[48] Third, several peremptory norms, such as the prohibition of the use of force or the principle of self-determination itself, enable the actor protected by a given norm to exercise the choice in performance of rights under that norm: a State could invite another State to intervene; it could even decide to become part of another State, and none of these would contradict the relevant peremptory norms. The peremptory character of the above-mentioned norms has not been doubted because they give the protected actors the right to choose, and the validity of such argument with regard to sovereignty over natural resources should be assessed accordingly.

Fundamental human rights

Most of the cases of *jus cogens* are "cases where the position of the individual is involved".[49] Human rights norms protect not the individual interests of a State but the interests of mankind as such and the interests they protect are not at the disposal of States, nor can these interests be damaged by reprisals or reciprocal non-compliance.[50] This reflects the fact that, unlike individual rights pure and simple, human rights protect the individual as such, regardless of the link to the rights and interests of any State, and hence protect the community interest. Human rights are not just individual rights; they are right not disposable by States, individually or in concert.

[. . .]

Notes

1   On hierarchy of norms in general, see Akehurst, The Hierarchy of Norms in International Law,

BYIL (1974–5), 273–86; Pauwelyn, *Conflict of Norms in Public International Law* (2003), 13, 96–8; Shelton, International Law and "Relative Normativity", Evans (ed.), *International Law* (2003), 145–72; Thirlway, The Sources of International Law, Evans (ed.), *International Law* (2003), 136–7.

2 For examples see Sztucki, *Jus Cogens and the Vienna Convention on the Law of Treaties* (1974), 29–40.

3 E.g. UN Charter, Articles 24–5; see further Jenks, The Conflict of Law-Making Treaties, 30 *BYIL* (1951), 440; Guggenheim, La Validité et la nullité des acles juridiques internationanx, *RDC* (1949), 198, 201.

4 Kadelbach, *Zwingendes Völkerrecht* (1992), 26–30; Akehurst (1974–5), 281–2; Dupuy, L'unité de l'ordre juridique international, 297 *RdC* (2002), 281, speaking of the new type of hierarchy; Pauwelyn (2003), 22, 98, speaking of "the only instance of *a priori* hierarchy"; Thirlway, The Law and Procedure of the International Court of Justice, *BYIL* (1990), 143.

5 Also denoted as imperative, absolute, mandatory, categorical, cogent, overriding, inalienable, compelling, conclusive, fundamental, self-determined norms, *Black's Law Dictionary* (1990), 1136; Hannikainen, *Peremptory Norms in International Law: Historical development, criteria, present status* (1988), 21; Eek, Peremptory Norms and Private International Law, 139 *RdC* (1973), 10–11; Parker and Neylon, *Jus Cogens*: Compelling the Law of Human Rights, 12 *Hastings International and Comparative Law Review* (1989), 415; Bassiouni, *Crimes Against Humanity in International Criminal Law* (1999), 210. All these terms point to the rigidity of these norms and their ability to produce legal effects irrespective of, and even against, the will of the relevant legal persons. As for the term *jus cogens*, which originates from the Roman law where it denoted the norms which cannot be derogated from by private contracts, it is used interchangeably with the term "peremptory norms". It has been so used in the work of the UN International Law Commission on the law of treaties. For an overview see Sztucki (1974), 103–6.

6 Fitzmaurice, Third Report on the Law of Treaties, II YbILC 1958, 40. See also Fitzmaurice, The Law and Procedure of the International Court of Justice, *BYIL* (1959), 224. As Judge Verdross pointed out in the *Ringeisen* case before the European Court of Human Rights, Article 26 of the European Convention on Human Rights, dealing with the exhaustion of local remedies with regard to the cases submitted to the European Convention organs, can be considered to prevail over the rules and practices related to the exhaustion of local remedies as accepted under general international law. This is so, because the rule requiring the exhaustion of local remedies is not part of *jus cogens*. Separate Opinion of Judge Verdross, *Ringeisen*, para. 1, further stressing that it was "superfluous to undertake an analysis of international practice on the matter". In other words, Article 26 applied as *lex specialis*.

7 Meron, *Human Rights Law-Making in the United Nations* (1986), 177, suggests that the reach of hierarchically superior instruments adopted within an institution is limited to the legal system of the parent organization and should not be confused with *jus cogens*. See also Pauwelyn (2003), 99.

8 Rozakis, *The Concept of* Jus Cogens *in the Law of Treaties* (1976), 19–20; see also Joint Dissenting Opinion, *Al-Adsani*, para. 1; Christenson, *Jus Cogens*: Guarding Interests Fundamental to the International Society, 28 *Virginia Journal of International Law* (1988), 600–1. In another context involving *jus cogens*, the Joint Separate Opinion in *Arrest Warrant (Congo v Belgium)* emphasized that, in prosecuting crimes affecting the community interest, States act as community agents and this vertical notion of authority is significantly different from otherwise the horizontal pattern of international law, para. 51.

9 Hannikainen (1988), 11.

10 The notion of such functions can be borrowed from national law, Virally, Reflexions sur le 'jus cogens', 12 *Annuaire Français de Droit International* (1966), 7.

11 *Per contra* Hannikainen (1988), 11.

12 "With public international law developing into much more than a law of bilateral and multilateral treaty relationships the threshold to a constitutional structure has long been crossed." Frowein, Reactions by Not Directly Affected States to Breaches of Public International Law, 248 *RdC* (1994), 365; Münch, Bemerkungen zum ius cogens, *Voelkerrecht als Rechtsordnung – Internationale Gerichtsbarkeit – Menschenrechte: Festschrift Mosler* (1983), 617, affirms that even an unorganized society can have a constitution. It is also generally true that, as Jenks writes, "The hierarchic principle represents the transposition to international life of the principle which determines the validity of legislation governed by a written constitution." Jenks, The Conflict of Law-Making Treaties, 30 *BYIL* (1951), 436. As Janis suggests, the compelling law, *jus cogens*, "is not a

form of customary international law, but a form of international constitutional law, a norm which sets the very foundations of the international legal systems". Janis, The Nature of Jus Cogens, 3 Connecticut JIL (1988), 363.

13 Domb, Jus Cogens and Human Rights, 6 Israel Yearbook of Human Rights (1976), 108.

14 Rolin, Vers un ordre public réellement international, in Hommage d'une generation des Juristes au President Basdevant (1961), 444; Nussbaum Deutsches Internationales Privatrecht (1974), 60–1, 64, 67; Pillet and Niboyet, Manuel de Droit International Privé (1924), 417; Wolff (1954), 62; Kegel Internationales Privatrecht (1987), 325, emphasizing that the same considerations of morality apply to the nullity of contracts and application of foreign laws; Kropholler, Internationales Privatrecht (1997), 224; Niederer, Einführung in die Allgemeine Lehren des Internationalen Privatrechts (1956), 285–7; Bleckmann, Sittenwidrigkeit wegen Verstoßes gegen den ordre public international, 34 ZaöRV (1974), 112–13, 118, 128; Raape Internationales Privatrecht (1961), 95; Zitelmann Internationales Privatrecht (1897), 334; Blom, Public Policy in Private International Law and Its Evolution in Time, 50 Netherlands International Law Review (2003), 374.

15 Meyer, Droit internationale privé (1994), 140.

16 Article 138 of the German Civil Code and Article 30 of the Einführungsgesetz, Article 6 of the French Civil Code (placing good morals and public order on the same footing), Article 12 of the Preliminary Provisions to the Italian Civil Code. Levi (1994), 58; Zweigert and Kötz, An Introduction to Comparative Law (1998), 380–2; Bernier, Droit Public and Ordre Public, 15 Transactions of the Grotius Society (1930), 90.

17 Kuwait Air Corp., 116 ILR 571.

18 Kegel (1987), 326; Levi, The International Ordre Public, 62 Revue de Droit International (1994), 57, 66–7.

19 Domb (1976), 107–8.

20 Victims of the Tugboat "13 de Marzo", para. 79; Roach, Resolution No. 3/87, Case No. 9647, para. 55, 8 HRLJ (1987), 352; Mangas, para. 144; Gormley (1985), 123–4; Reuter, Introduction to the Law of Treaties (1972), 111.

21 YbILC (1953-II), 155.

22 YbILC (1958-II), 41, treaties conflicting with one of these categories are similarly void even inter partes.

23 Levi (1994), 56; Virally Réflexions sur le "jus cogens", 12 Annuaire Français de Droit International (1966), 11, stresses that the morality factor reinforces the link between international

jus cogens and public order as recognized in national law.

24 McNair (1961), 213. See also Hall, A Treatise on International Law (1924), 383.

25 Verdross, Forbidden Treaties in International Law, AJIL (1937), 572.

26 Cassese, Self-Determination of Peoples (1994), 174; cf. Jaenicke, Zur Frage des Internationalen Ordre Public, 7 Berichte der Deutschen Gesellschaft fur Volkerrecht (1967), 92, and the Swiss attitude at the Vienna Conference, UNCLT First Session (1969), 324.

27 PCIJ Series A/B, No. 63,150.

28 Lauterpacht, Collective Papers (1970), 234.

29 Lauterpacht (1970), 358.

30 As the ILC emphasized, the prohibition of the use of force protects the interests of the international community as a whole even though it overlaps with protecting the survival and security of individual States, commentary to Article 48, para. 10, ILC Report 2001, 322; Jaenicke (1967), 86.

31 As confirmed by ICJ, Nicaragua, ICJ Reports, 1986, 100–1 and ILC, YbILC (1966-II), 248; ILC Report 2001, commentary to Article 40, 283, para. 4. The German Bundesverwaltungsgericht has also confirmed that the prohibition of the use of force is part of jus cogens, BverwG 2 WD 12.04, para. 4.1.2.6. See also Dinstein, War, Aggression and Self-Defence (2001), 94.

32 ICJ Reports, 1986, 153.

33 ICJ Reports, 1986, 199.

34 Separate Opinion, para. 9: see also Separate Opinion of Judge Koojmans, para. 44; Dissenting Opinion of Judge Elaraby, para. 1.1.

35 Judge Elaraby, Separate Opinion, Wall, para. 3.1.

36 ICJ Reports, 1996, 263.

37 Verdross, Forbidden Treaties in International Law; 31 AJIL (1937), 574–5, refers to a memorandum of the Austrian Government of 2 March 1936 on the re-establishment of compulsory military service despite the limitations imposed by the peace treaties after the First World War. Verdross also suggests that "It would be immoral to oblige a State to remain defenceless", id. Mosler, Jus Cogens in Volkerrecht, 25 Schweizcrischers Jarhbuch fur Internationales Recht (1968), 10; Schwelb, Some Aspects of Interntional Jus Cogens, 51 AJIL (1967), 966–7.

38 Judge Ammoun, Barcelona Traction, ICJ Reports, 1970, 72, emphasized that the right to self-determination is based on the "norm of the nature of jus cogens, derogation from which is not permissible under any circumstances". See also Shaw, Title to Territory in Africa (1986), 91; Gros-Espiel, Self-Determination and Jus Cogens,

Cassese (ed.), *UN Law/Fundamental Rights* (1979), 167–71; Dugard, *Recognition and the United Nations* (1987), 158ff; Cassese, *Self-Determination of Peoples* (1994), 171–2; Parker and Neylon (1989), 440–1.

39 Crawford, *Creation of States in International Law* (1979), 81; Weisbrud, The Emptiness of *Jus Cogens*, as Illustrated by the War in Bosnia-Herzegovina, 17 *Michigan Journal of International Law* (1995), 23–4; Scheuner, Conflict of a Treaty Provision with a Peremptory Norm of International Law and Its Consequences, 27 *Zeitschrift für ausländisches öffentliches Recht und Völkerrecht* (1967), 525; Scheuner, Conflicts of Treaty Provisions with a Peremptory Norm of General International Law, 29 *Zeitscheift fur Auslandisches Offentliches Recht und Volkerrdecht* (1969), 34.

40 See also the attitude of the General Assembly with regard to the agreements violating the right of the Palestinian people to self-determination, and see further Hannikainen (1988), 382.

41 YbILC (1963-II), 22; UN Human Rights Commission Resolutions 1997/4, 1998/4, 2003/3. Craven, The European Community Arbitration Commission on Yugoslavia, *BYIL* (1995), 380–1, suggests that while the principle of self-determination is peremptory in the colonial context, it is unclear whether the same could be said of its non-colonial context. Craven refers to the statement of Judge Dillard in *Namibia* (*ICJ Reports* 1971) that self-determination as a norm applies to decolonization. But the scope of applicability is not the same thing as the normative quality. Today it is absolutely clear that the principle of self-determination benefits peoples also outside the colonial context, as was affirmed in *East Timor*, *ICJ Reports* 1995, 105–6, and *Palestinian Wall*, General List No. 131, paras 88, 122 (respectively on East Timor and Palestine). At the same time, the UN Human Rights Commission affirmed the peremptory status of this principle with regard to Palestine, that is in a non-colonial context.

42 Jaenicke (1967), 94. Another peremptory incidence can be the special combatant status of armed defenders of self-determination, Brownlie, *Principles of Public International Law* (2003), 78.

43 Brownlie, *Principles* (2003), 489.

44 Scrijver, *Sovereignty Over Natural Resources* (1997), 375; Sztucki, *Jus Cogens and the Vienna Contention on the Law of Treaties* (1974), 44; see also Paavistra, Internationalization and Stabilization of Contracts versus State Sovereignty, *BYIL* (1989), 340.

45 *Aminoil*, 66 ILR 587–8.

46 *Texaco*, para. 78, 53 ILR 482.

47 In Resolution 1803 (1962), the General Assembly stressed that permanent sovereignty over natural resources is "a basic constituent of the right to self-determination". Parker and Neylon (1989), 440, emphasize that in order to realize self-determination, political independence must be coupled with permanent sovereignty over natural resources. Sornarajah, *The International Law on Foreign Investment* (2004), 327 also emphasizes the intrinsic link between the right to self-determination on the one hand and the permanent sovereignty over natural resources, or economic sovereignty, on the other.

48 In addition, the contracts disposing the natural resources concluded by unrepresentative rulers are also invalid, Sornarajah (2004), 42.

49 Fitzmaurice, 2 YbILC 1958, 40; see also Barberis, La liberté de traiter des Etats et le *jus cogens*, 30 *Zeitschrift für ausländisches öffentliches Recht und Völkerrecht* (1970), 44.

50 Barile, The Protection of Human Rights in Article 60, paragraph 5 of the Vienna Convention on the Law of Treaties, *International Law at the Time of its Codification, Essays in Honour of Roberto Ago*, vol. II (1987), 3–4.

58

The Gender of *Jus Cogens*

Hilary Charlesworth and Christine Chinkin

I.   Introduction: The Doctrine of *Jus Cogens*

The modern international law doctrine of *jus cogens* asserts the existence of fundamental legal norms from which no derogation is permitted.[1] It imports notions of universally applicable norms into the international legal process. The status of norms of *jus cogens* as general international law, Onuf and Birney argue, "is not a logical necessity so much as a compelling psychological association of normative superiority with universality."[2] A formal, procedural definition of the international law concept of the *jus cogens* is found in the Vienna Convention on the Law of Treaties.[3] Article 53 states that:

> [A] peremptory norm of general international law is a norm accepted and recognized by the international community of States as a whole as a norm from which no derogation is permitted and which can be modified only by a subsequent norm of general international law having the same character.[4]

Such a category of principles has had an uneasy existence in international law as "peremptory" norms do not fit well with the traditional view of international law as a consensual order. If the basis of international law, whether customary or conventional, is the agreement of states, how can states be bound by a category of principles to which they may have not freely consented? On what basis can peremptory norms be distinguished from other rules of international law? Thus Prosper Weil has criticized the theory of *jus cogens* both for forcing states "to accept the supernormativity of rules they were perhaps not even prepared to recognize as ordinary norms"[5] and for generally weakening the unity of the international legal system by introducing notions of relative normativity.[6] As Martii Koskenniemi points out, however, the actual terms of Article 53 contain two distinct strains, non-consensualist ("descending") and consensualist ("ascending"): "*jus cogens* doctrine shows itself as a compromise. . . . [P]eremptory norms bind irrespective of consent . . . but what those norms are is determined by consent."[7]

Article 53, together with Article 64 which provides that treaties conflicting with new peremptory norms of international law become void, was one of the most contentious provisions at the Vienna Conference. Much of the support

Hilary Charlesworth and Christine Chinkin, "The Gender of *Jus Cogens,*" *Human Rights Quarterly,* vol. 15 (1993), pp. 63–76. © 1993 by The Johns Hopkins University Press. Reprinted with permission from The Johns Hopkins University Press.

for the inclusion of the concept of *jus cogens* in the Vienna Convention came from socialist and third world states which saw it as some protection from the unmitigated operation of the principle of *pacta sunt servanda*.[8] Some Western nations were particularly critical of the inclusion of this provision on grounds of its challenge to the principle of state sovereignty, its vagueness, the problem of definition of *jus cogens* norms, and the lack of state practice to support it.[9]

Defenders of the notion of *jus cogens* often explain its basis as the collective international, rather than the individual national, good.[10] On this analysis, principles of *jus cogens* play a similar role in the international legal system to that played by constitutional guarantees of rights in domestic legal systems. Thus states, as national political majorities, accept the limitation of their freedom of choice "in order to reap the rewards of acting in ways that would elude them under pressures of the moment."[11] Among those jurists who accept the category of *jus cogens*, however, continuing controversy remains over what norms qualify as principles of *jus cogens*.

Our concern in this article is neither with the debates over the validity of the doctrine of *jus cogens* in international law nor with particular candidates for *jus cogens* status. Rather, we are interested in the structure of the concept detailed by international law scholars. We argue that the concept of the *jus cogens* is not a properly universal one as its development has privileged the experiences of men over those of women, and it has provided a protection to men that is not accorded to women.

II.   The Function of *Jus Cogens* in International Law

The clearest operation of the doctrine of *jus cogens* in international law is set out in the Vienna Convention on the Law of Treaties: "A treaty is void if, at the time of its conclusion, it conflicts with a peremptory norm of general international law."[12] The freedom of states to enter into treaties is thus limited by fundamental values of the international community. Despite fears that the inclusion of this provision would subvert the principle of *pacta sunt servanda* and act to destabilize the certainty provided

by treaty commitments, *jus cogens* doctrine has been only rarely invoked in this context.[13] It thus has had little practical impact upon the operation of treaties, although it may possibly exert some restraining influence on the conclusion of treaties.

Inconsistent principles of customary international law cannot stand alongside *jus cogens*.[14] Some jurists have argued that all states have a legal interest, and consequently standing, to complain in international fora about violations of the *jus cogens* by another state.[15] Allusions to *jus cogens*-type norms and their procedural and substantive implications in the jurisprudence of the International Court of Justice, however, have been occasional and ambiguous.[16]

Much of the importance of the *jus cogens* doctrine lies not in its practical application but in its symbolic significance in the international legal process. It assumes that decisions with respect to normative priorities can be made and that certain norms can be deemed to be of fundamental significance. It thus incorporates notions of universality and superiority into international law.[17] These attributes are emphasized in the language used in describing the doctrine: *jus cogens* is presented as "guarding the most fundamental and highly-valued interests of international society";[18] as an "expression of a conviction, accepted in all parts of the world community, which touches the deeper conscience of all nations";[19] as fulfilling "the higher interest of the whole international community."[20] Indeed, Suy describes *jus cogens* as the foundation of international society without which the entire edifice would crumble.[21]

In the international legal literature on *jus cogens*, the use of symbolic language to express fundamental concepts is accompanied by abstraction. Writers are generally reluctant to go beyond the abstract assertion of principle to determine the operation and impact of any such norms. A tension thus exists between the weighty linguistic symbolism employed to explain the indispensable nature of *jus cogens* norms and the very abstract and inconclusive nature of their formulation. Some writers have argued that the doctrinal discussion of *jus cogens* has no echo at all in state practice.[22]

The search for universal, abstract, hierarchical standards is often associated with masculine modes of thinking. Carol Gilligan, for example, has contended that different ways of reasoning are inculcated in girls and boys from an early age. Girls tend to reason in a contextual and concrete manner; boys in a more formal and abstract way.[23] Most systems of knowledge prize the "masculine" forms of reasoning. The very abstract and formal development of the *jus cogens* doctrine indicates its gendered origins. What is more important, however, is that the privileged status of its norms is reserved for a very limited, male centered, category. *Jus cogens* norms reflect a male perspective of what is fundamental to international society that may not be shared by women or supported by women's experience of life. Thus the fundamental aspirations attributed to communities are male and the assumptions of the scheme of world order assumed by the notion of *jus cogens* are essentially male. Women are relegated to the periphery of communal values.

Our aim here is not to challenge the powerful symbolic significance of *jus cogens* but to argue that the symbolism is itself totally skewed and gendered. In doing so we propose a much richer content for the concept of *jus cogens*; if women's lives contributed to the designation of international fundamental values, the category would be transformed in a radical way. Our focus will be the category of human rights often designated as norms of *jus cogens*.[24]

III.   Human Rights as Norms of *Jus Cogens*

The "most essential"[25] human rights are considered part of the *jus cogens*. For example, the American Law Institute's Revised Restatement of Foreign Relations Law lists as violations of *jus cogens* the practice or condoning of genocide, slave trade, murder/disappearances, torture, prolonged arbitrary detention or systematic racial discrimination.[26] This list has been described as "a particularly striking instance of assuming American values are synonymous with those reflected in international law."[27] At a deeper level, Simma and Alston argue that "it must be asked whether any theory of human rights law which singles out race but not gender discrimination, which condemns arbitrary imprisonment

but not death by starvation, and which finds no place for a right of access to primary health care is not flawed in terms both of the theory of human rights and of United Nations doctrine."[28]

The development of human rights law has challenged the primacy of the state in international law and given individuals a significant legal status. It has, however, developed in an unbalanced and partial manner and promises much more to men than to women. This phenomenon is partly due to male domination of all international human rights fora,[29] which itself fashions the substance of human rights law in accordance with male values. At a deeper level, it replicates the development of international law generally.

A.   The gender bias of human rights law

International law assumes, and reinforces, a number of dichotomies between public and private spheres of action.[30] One is the distinction drawn between international ("public") concerns and those within the domestic ("private") jurisdiction of states. Within the category of international concerns there is a further public/private distinction drawn. International law is almost exclusively addressed to the public, or official, activities of states, which are not held responsible for the "private" activities of their nationals or those within their jurisdiction. The concept of imputability used in the law of state responsibility is a device to deem apparently "private" acts "public" ones. This more basic dichotomy has significant implications for women. Women's lives are generally conducted within the sphere deemed outside the scope of international law, indeed also often outside the ambit of "private" (national) law.[31]

Although human rights law is often regarded as a radical development in international law because of its challenge to that discipline's traditional public/private dichotomy between states and individuals, it has retained the deeper, gendered, public/private distinction. In the major human rights treaties, rights are defined according to what men fear will happen to them, those harms against which they seek guarantees. The primacy traditionally given to civil and political rights by Western international lawyers and philosophers is directed towards protection for men within their public life – their relationship with government. The same importance has not been generally accorded to economic and social rights which affect life in the private sphere, the world of women, although these rights are addressed to states. This is not to assert that when women are victims of violations of the civil and political rights they are not accorded the same protection,[32] but that these are not the harms from which women most need protection.

All the violations of human rights typically included in catalogues of *jus cogens* norms are of undoubted seriousness; genocide, slavery, murder, disappearances, torture, prolonged arbitrary detention, and systematic racial discrimination. The silences of the list, however, indicate that women's experiences have not directly contributed to it. For example, although race discrimination consistently appears in *jus cogens* inventories, discrimination on the basis of sex does not.[33] And yet sex discrimination is an even more widespread injustice, affecting the lives of more than half the world's population. While a prohibition on sex discrimination, as racial discrimination, is included in every general human rights convention and is the subject of a specialized binding instrument, sexual equality has not been allocated the status of a fundamental and basic tenet of a communal world order.

Of course women as well as men suffer from the violation of the traditional canon of *jus cogens* norms. However the manner in which the norms have been constructed obscures the most pervasive harms done to women. One example of this is the "most important of all human rights",[34] the right to life set out in Article 6 of the Civil and Political Covenant[35] which forms part of customary international law.[36] The right is concerned with the arbitrary deprivation of life through public action.[37] Important as it is, the protection from arbitrary deprivation of life or liberty through public actions does not address the ways in which being a woman is in itself life-threatening and the special ways in which women need legal protection to be able to enjoy their right to life. Professor Brownlie has pointed to the need for empirical, rather than purely abstract, studies on which to base assertions of rights.[38] Such an approach highlights the inadequacy of the formulation of the international legal right to life.

A number of recent studies show that being a woman may be hazardous even from before birth due to the practice in some areas of aborting female fetuses because of the strong social and economic pressure to have sons.[39] Immediately after birth womanhood is also dangerous in some societies because of the higher incidence of female infanticide. During childhood in many communities girls are breast-fed for shorter periods and later fed less so that girls suffer the physical and mental effects of malnutrition at higher rates than boys.[40] Indeed in most of Asia and North Africa, women suffer great discrimination in basic nutrition and health care leading to a disproportionate number of female deaths.[41] The well-documented phenomenon of the "feminization" of poverty in both the developing and developed world causes women to have a much lower quality of life than men.[42]

Violence against women is endemic in all states; indeed international lawyers could observe that this is one of those rare areas where there is genuinely consistent and uniform state practice. An International Tribunal on Crimes Against Women, held in Brussels in 1976, heard evidence from women across the world on the continued oppression of women and the commission of acts of violence against them.[43] Battery is the major cause of injury to adult women in the United States, where a rape occurs every six minutes.[44] In Peru, 70 percent of all crimes reported to police involve women as victims.[45] In India, 80 percent of wives are victims of violence, domestic abuse, dowry abuse or murder.[46] In 1985, in Austria, domestic violence against the wife was given as a factor in the breakdown of marriage in 59 percent of 1,500 divorce cases.[47] In Australia, a recent survey indicated that one in five men believed it acceptable for men to beat their wives;[48] while surveys by the Papua New Guinea Law Reform Commission found that up to 67 percent of wives had suffered marital violence.[49]

The United Nations system has not ignored the issue of violence against women. For example, the United Nations Commission on the Status of Women has noted its great concern on this matter and the Economic and Social Council has adopted resolutions condemning it.[50] The General Assembly itself has supported concerted, multidisciplinary action within and outside the United Nations to combat violence against women and has advocated special measures to ensure that national systems of justice respond to such actions.[51] A United Nations report on violence against women observes that "[v]iolence against women in the family has . . . been recognized as a priority area of international and national action. . . . All the research evidence that is available suggests that violence against women in the home is a universal problem, occurring across all cultures and in all countries."[52] But although the empirical evidence of violence against women is strong, it has not been reflected in the development of international law. The doctrine of *jus cogens*, with its claim to reflect central, fundamental aspirations of the international community, has not responded at all to massive evidence of injustice and aggression against women.

The great level of documented violence against women around the world is unaddressed by the international legal notion of the right to life because that legal system is focussed on "public" actions by the state. A similar myopia can be detected also in the international prohibition on torture.[53] A central feature of the international legal definition of torture is that it takes place in the public realm: it must be "inflicted by or at the instigation of or with the consent or acquiescence of a public official or other person acting in an official capacity."[54] Although many women are victims of torture in this "public" sense,[55] by far the greatest violence against women occurs in the "private" nongovernmental sphere.

Violence against women is not only internationally widespread, but most of it occurs within the private sphere of home, hearth and family.[56] In the face of such evidence, many scholars now have moved from an analysis of domestic violence based on the external causes of such violence to a structural explanation of the universal subordination of women: "wife beating is not just a personal abnormality, but rather has its roots in the very structuring of society and the family; that in the cultural norms and in the sexist organization of society."[57]

Violence against, and oppression of, women is therefore never a purely "private" issue. As Charlotte Bunch noted, it is caused by "the structural relationships of power, domination and privilege between men and women in society. Violence against women is central to maintain-

ing those political relations at home, at work and in all public spheres."[58] These structures are supported by the patriarchal hierarchy of the nation state. To hold states accountable for "private" acts of violence or oppression against women, however, challenges the traditional rules of state responsibility.[59] The concept of imputability proposed by the International Law Commission in its draft articles on state responsibility does not encompass the maintenance of a legal and social system in which violence or discrimination against women is endemic and where such actions are trivialized or discounted.[60] It could be argued that, given the extent of the evidence of violence against women, failure to improve legal protection for women and to impose sanctions against perpetrators of violence against women should engage state responsibility.[61]

The problematic structure of traditionally asserted *jus cogens* norms is also shown in the more controversial "collective" right to self-determination.[62] The right allows "all peoples" to "freely determine their political status and freely pursue their economic, social and cultural development."[63] Yet the oppression of women within groups claiming the right of self-determination has never been considered relevant to the validity of their claim or to the form self-determination should take.[64] An example of this is the firm United States support for the Afghani resistance movement after the 1979 Soviet invasion without any apparent concern for the very low status of women within traditional Afghani society.[65] Another is the immediate and powerful United Nations response after Iraq's 1990 invasion of Kuwait. None of the plans for the liberation or reconstruction of Kuwait were concerned with that state's denial of political rights to women. Although some international pressure was brought to bear on the Kuwaiti government during and after the invasion to institute a more democratic system, the concern did not focus on the political repression of women and was quickly dropped.

The operation of the public/private distinction in international human rights law operates to the detriment of women. In a sense, the doctrine of *jus cogens* adds a further public/private dimension to international law as *jus cogens* norms are those which are central to the functioning of the entire international community and are thus "public" in contrast to the "private" or less fundamental human rights canon. In this way, women's lives are treated as being within a doubly private sphere, far from the concerns of the international legal order.

B. *A feminist rethinking of* jus cogens

In the context of human rights, what can a feminist contribution to the jurisprudence of *jus cogens* be? For example, should we seek to define a "fourth generation" of women's human rights? Such a development could lead to segregation and marginalization of exclusively women's rights and would be unlikely to be accepted as *jus cogens*. It has been argued that the central task of feminist theory in international relations is to understand the world from the perspective of the socially subjugated.[66] One method of doing this in international law is to challenge the gendered dichotomy between public and private worlds and to reshape doctrines based on it. For example, existing human rights law can be redefined to transcend the distinction between public and private spheres and truly take into account women's lives as well as men's.[67] Considerations of gender should be fundamental to an analysis of international human rights law.[68]

Feminist rethinking of *jus cogens* would also give prominence to a range of other human rights; the right to sexual equality, to food, to reproductive freedom, to be free from fear of violence and oppression, and to peace. It is significant that these proposals include examples from what has been described as the third generation of human rights, which includes claimants to rights that have been attacked as not sufficiently rigorously proved, and as confusing policy goals with law-making under existing international law.[69] This categorization of rights to which women would attach special value might be criticized as reducing the quality and coherence of international law as a whole.[70] Such criticism underlines the dissonance between women's experiences and international legal principles generally. In the particular context of the concept of *jus cogens*, which has an explicitly promotional and aspirational character, it should be possible for even traditional international legal theory to accommodate rights that are fundamental to the existence and dignity of half the world's popula-

tion. Professor Riphagen's nonhierarchical analysis of *jus cogens*[71] accommodates the inclusion of these rights even more readily.

IV. Conclusion

Fundamental norms designed to protect individuals should be truly universal in application as well as rhetoric, and operate to protect both men and women from those harms they are in fact most likely to suffer. They should be genuine human rights, not male rights. The very human rights principles that are most frequently designated as *jus cogens* do not in fact operate equally upon men and women. They are gendered and not therefore of universal validity. Further, the choices that are typically made of the relevant norms and the interpretation of what harms they are designed to prevent reflect male choices which frequently bear no relevance to women's lives. On the other hand, the violations that women do most need guarantees against do not receive this same protection or symbolic labelling. The priorities asserted are male-oriented and are given a masculine interpretation. Taking women's experiences into account in the development of *jus cogens* norms will require a fundamental rethinking of every aspect of the doctrine.

It has been argued that the "New World Order" promised as a positive and progressive development from the realignment of the superpowers and the apparent renaissance of the United Nations in fact continues the same priorities as the old world order.[72] The gendered nature of the international legal order is not yet on the agenda in the discussions of any truly new world order. Without full analysis of the values incorporated in *jus cogens* norms or the impact of their application, further work to make them effective in a new international legal order will in fact only continue the male orientation of international law.

Notes

1 *Jus cogens* norms have also been recognized in many domestic legal systems. See Eric Suy, *The Concept of Jus Cogens in Public International Law*, in 2 *The Concept of Jus Cogens in International Law*

17, 18–22 (Carnegie Endowment for International Peace, 1967); J. Sztucki, *Jus Cogens and the Vienna Convention on the Law of Treaties*, 6–11 (1972). On the existence of the doctrine of *jus cogens* in international law before the 1969 Vienna Convention, see Alfred von Verdross, *Forbidden Treaties in International Law*, 31 Am. J. Int'l L. 571 (1937); Egon Schwelb, *Some Aspects of International Jus Cogens as Formulated by the International Law Commission*, 61 Am. J. Int'l L. 946, 948–60 (1967); *International Law Commission Report 1982*, at 132, UN Doc. A/37/10 (1982); Lauri Hannikainen, *Peremptory Norms (Jus Cogens) in International Law*, chs. 1, 2 (1988).

2 N. G. Onuf & Richard K. Birney, *Peremptory Norms of International Law: Their Source, Function and Future*, 4 Denver J. Int'l L. & Pol'y 187, 190 (1974).

3 Vienna Convention on the Law of Treaties, 1155 U.N.T.S. 331, 63 Am. J. Int'l L. 875, 891 (1969).

4 Article 53 purports to define the notion of *jus cogens* only for the law of treaties within the Vienna Convention itself, but is generally regarded as having wider significance. See also *Vienna Convention on the Law of Treaties between States and International Organizations or between International Organizations 1986*, art. 53, 25 I.L.M. 572 (1986). Apart from these provisions, explicit references to *jus cogens* in other treaties are rare. See also International Law Commission, *Draft Articles on State Responsibility*, arts. 18(2), 29(1), 33(2), 2 Y.B. Int'l L. Comm'n 30 (1980).

5 Prosper Weil, *Towards Relative Normativity in International Law*, 77 Am. J. Int'l L. 413, 427 (1983). See also Georg Schwarzenberger, *International Jus Cogens*, 43 Texas L. Rev. 455 (1965).

6 Weil, *supra* note 5, at 423–30. Compare W. Riphagen, *From Soft Law to Jus Cogens and Back*, 17 Victoria U. Wellington. L. Rev. 81, 92 (1987) (arguing that relationship between "soft" international law, "hard" international law, and principles of *jus cogens* is not hierarchical, and that "soft" law and principles of *jus cogens* are more accurately seen as closely connected "entry points" to the legal system).

7 Martii Koskenniemi, *From Apology to Utopia* 283 (1989). An example of the operation of the "compromise" *jus cogens* doctrine is the prohibition on apartheid. Although the chief practitioner of apartheid, South Africa, never "consented" to its prohibition, the principle is widely accepted as universally binding as *jus cogens*. See Ted L. Stein, *The Approach of the Different Drummer: The Principle of the Persistent Objector in International Law*, 26 Harv. Int'l L.J. 457, 482 (1985).

8 John H. Spencer, *Review of the Tenth and Eleventh Sessions of the Asian-African Legal Consultative Committee, held in 1969 and 1970*, 67 Am. J. Int'l L. 180, 181 (1973); Richard D. Kearney, *The Future Law of Treaties*, 4 Int'l Lawyer 823, 830 (1970); Robert Rosenstock, *Peremptory Norms – Maybe Even Less Metaphysical and Worrisome*, 5 Denver J. Int'l L. & Pol'y 167, 169 (1975).

9 Hannikainen, *supra* note 1, at 172–3; Richard D. Kearney & Robert E. Dalton, *The Treaty on Treaties*, 64 Am. J. Int'l L. 495, 535–8 (1970); I. M. Sinclair, *Vienna Conference on the Law of Treaties*, 19 Int'l & Comp. L.Q. 47, 66–9 (1970).

10 *E.g.*, Hannikainen, *supra* note 1, at 1–2. Hannikainen writes that "'the international community of States as a whole' . . . is entitled to assume in extremely urgent cases, to protect the overriding interests and values of the community itself and to ensure the functioning of the international legal order, the authority to require one or a few dissenting States to observe a customary norm of general international law as a peremptory customary norm." *Id.* at 241.

11 Laurence H. Tribe, *American Constitutional Law* 10 (1978). See Jonathan I. Charney, *The Persistent Objector Rule and the Development of Customary International Law*, 56 Brit Y.B. Int'l L. 1, 19–20 (19).

12 Vienna Convention on the Law of Treaties, *supra* note 3, art. 53. See also *id.* art. 64 (providing that if a new peremptory norm of general international law emerges, any existing treaty which is in conflict with it becomes void and terminates); art. 66 (allowing submission of disputes concerning the application or interpretation of arts. 53 or 64 to the International Court of Justice); art. 71 (setting out the consequences of nullity on the grounds of *jus cogens*).

13 It has been argued that the Treaty of Guarantee of August 16, 1960, between Cyprus, on the one hand, and Greece, Turkey and the United Kingdom on the other, violated the *jus cogens* norm prohibiting the threat or use of force by reserving the right for the Guarantee powers to take action to reestablish the state of affairs created by the Treaty, and that United Nations resolutions on the issue implicitly acknowledge this. Schwelb, *supra* note 1, at 952–3. On assertions of invalidity of the 1979 Camp David agreements on the basis of conflict with norms of *jus cogens*, see Giorgio Gaja, *Jus Cogens Beyond the Vienna Convention*, 172 Recueil Des Cours 271, 282 (1981). For other examples see Gordon Christenson, *Jus Cogens: Guarding Interests Fundamental to International Society*, 28 Va. J. Int'l L. 585, 607 (1988). The Portuguese application against Australia in the

International Court of Justice (Application Instituting Proceedings, filed in the Registry of the Court February 22 1991) obliquely raises *jus cogens* issues in the context of the bilateral Timor Gap Treaty between Indonesia and Australia. 29 I.L.M. 469 (1990).

14 Ian Brownlie, *Principles of Public International Law* 514–15 (4th ed. 1990). See also Jordan Paust, *The Reality of Jus Cogens*, 7 Conn. J. Int'l L. 81, 84 (1991).

15 *E.g.*, Hannikainen, *supra* note 1, at 725–6; Oscar Schachter, *General Course in International Law*, 178 Recueil Des Cours 182–4 (1982).

16 See, e.g., *Barcelona Traction*, 1970 I.C.J. 321, 325 (sep. op. Judge Ammoun); *Namibia* (Advisory Opinion), 1971 I.C.J. 72–5 (sep. op. Judge Ammoun); *US Diplomatic and Consular Staff in Tehran* 1980 I.C.J. 30–1, 40–1, 44–5; *Military and Paramilitary Activities in and Against Nicaragua*, 1986 I.C.J. 14, 100–1. (All discussed in Hannikainen, *supra* note 1, at 192–4.)

17 See generally Onuf & Birney, *supra* note 2.

18 Christenson, *supra* note 13, at 587.

19 Ulrich Scheuner, *Conflict of Treaty Provisions with a Peremptory Norm of General International Law and its Consequences*, 27 Zeitschrift Fur Auslandisches Offentliches Recht und Volkerrecht 520, 524 (1967).

20 Alfred Verdross, *Jus Dispositivum and Jus Cogens in International Law*, 60 Am. J. Int'l L. 55, 58 (1966).

21 Suy, *supra* note 1, at 18. Similarly, the West German Federal Constitutional Court referred to *jus cogens* as "indispensable to the existence of the law of nations as an international legal order." Cited in Christenson, *supra* note 13, at 592.

22 See, e.g., Sztucki, *supra* note 1, at 93–4 ("[I]n the light of international practice, the question whether the concept of *jus cogens* has been 'codified' or 'progressively developed' in the [Vienna] Convention, may be answered only in the sense that there has been nothing to codify"); David Kennedy, *The Sources of International Law*, 2 Am. U.J. Int'l L. & Pol'y 1, 18 (1987).

23 Carol Gilligan, *In a Different Voice: Psychological Theory and Women's Development* 25–51 (1982). For a discussion of this characteristic in the context of traditional international relations theory, see J. Ann Tickner, *Hans Morgenthau's Principles of Political Realism: A Feminist Reformulation*, 17 Millenium: J. Int'l Stud. 429, 433 (1988).

24 Although many asserted norms of *jus cogens* are drawn from the international law of human rights, *jus cogens* is usually defined as more extensive. For example, the International Law

Commission's Special Rapporteur, Sir Humphrey Waldock, proposed three categories of *jus cogens* norms: those prohibiting the threat or use of force in contravention of the principles of the United Nations Charter; international crimes so characterized by international law; and acts or omissions whose suppression is required by international law. Sir Humphrey Waldock, *Second Report on the Law of Treaties*, 2 Y.B. Int'l L. Comm'n 56–9, U.N. Doc. A/CN.4/156 and Add. 1–3 (1963). See also Roberto Ago, Recueil Des Cours 320, 324 (1971); Scheuner, *supra* note 19, at 526–67.

25 Scheuner, *supra* note 19, at 526.

26 *Restatement (Third) of the Foreign Relations Law of the United States*, §702 (1987). Compare Marjorie M. Whiteman, *Jus Cogens in International Law, With a Projected List*, 7 Ca. J. Int'l & Comp. L. 609, 625–6 (1977).

27 Bruno Simma & Philip Alston, *The Sources of Human Rights Law: Custom, Jus Cogens & General Principles*, 12 Aust. Y.B. Int'l L. 82, 94 (1992).

28 *Id.* at 95.

29 For example, within the United Nations, apart from the Committee on the Elimination of all Forms of Discrimination Against Women (whose 18 members are all women), there are a total of 13 women out of 90 "independent experts" on specialist human rights committees. See Hilary Charlesworth, Christine Chinkin & Shelley Wright, *Feminist Approaches to International Law*, 85 Am. J. Int'l L. 613, 624 n.67 (1991).

30 For a fuller discussion, see *id.* at 625–8.

31 As Professor O'Donovan has pointed out, however, the "private" sphere associated with women is in fact often tightly controlled by legal regulation of taxation, health, education and welfare. Katherine O'Donovan, *Sexual Divisions in Law* 7–8 (1985).

32 Indeed Article 3 of the International Covenant on Civil and Political Rights states they will be accorded equal treatment with men. International Covenant on Civil and Political Rights, *adopted* 16 Dec. 1966, *entered into force* 23 Mar. 1976, C.A. Res. 2200 (XXI), 21 UN GAOR Supp. (No. 16), at 52, UN Doc. A/6316, 999 U.N.T.S. 171 (1966).

33 Compare Brownlie, *supra* note 14, at 513 n.29 (stating that principle of non-discrimination as to sex "must have the same [*jus cogens*] status" as principle of racial non-discrimination). See also Hannikainen, *supra* note 1, at 482.

34 Yoram Dinstein, *The Right to Life, Physical Integrity and Liberty*, in *The International Bill of Rights: The Covenant on Civil and Political Rights* 114 (L. Henkin ed., 1981).

35   See also Universal Declaration on Human Rights, *signed* 10 Dec. 1948, C.A. Res. 217A (III), art. 3, UN Doc. A/810, at 71 (1948); European Convention for the Protection of Human Rights and Fundamental Freedoms, 213 U.N.T.S. 221, art. 2 (1950).

36   Dinstein, *supra* note 34, at 115.

37   There is debate among various commentators as to how narrowly the right should be construed. Fawcett has suggested that the right to life entails protection only from the acts of government agents. J. E. S. Fawcett, *The Application of the European Convention on Human Rights* 30–1 (1969). Dinstein notes that it may be argued under Article 6 that "the state must at least exercise due diligence to prevent the intentional deprivation of the life of one individual by another." He seems however to confine the obligation to take active precautions against loss of life only in cases of riots, mob action, or incitement against minority groups. Dinstein, *supra* note 34, at 119. Ramcharan argues for a still wider interpretation of the right to life, "plac[ing] a duty on the part of each government to pursue policies which are designed to ensure access to the means of survival for every individual within its country." B. G. Ramcharan, *The Concept and Dimensions of the Rights to Life*, in *The Rights to Life in International Law* 1, 6 (B. C. Ramcharan ed., 1985). The examples of major modern threats to the right to life offered by Ramcharan, however, do not encompass violence outside the "public" sphere. *Id.* at 7–8.

38   Ian Brownlie, *The Rights of Peoples in Modern International Law*, in *The Rights of Peoples* 1, 16 (J. Crawford ed., 1988).

39   United Nations, *The World's Women, 1970–1990: Trends and Statistics* 1 n.2 (1991); Charlotte Bunch, *Women's Rights as Human Rights: Towards a Re-Vision of Human Rights*, 12 Hum. Rts. Q. 486, 488–9 n.3 (1990).

40   Bunch, *supra* note 39, at 489; United Nations, *supra* note 39, at 59.

41   Amartya Sen, *More Than 100 Million Women Are Missing*, NY Rev. Books, 30 Dec. 30 1990, at 61.

42   See, e.g., *Women are Poorer*, 27 (3) UN Chronicle 47 (1990).

43   *Crimes Against Women: The Proceedings of the International Tribunal* (D. Russell ed., 1984). Richard Falk has pointed out the importance of such grass roots initiatives in contributing to the normative order on the international level (without referring to this Tribunal). Richard Falk, *The Rights of Peoples (In Particular Indigenous Peoples)*, in *The Rights of Peoples* 17, 27–9 (J. Crawford ed., 1988). Compare Crawford, *The Rights of Peoples: Some Conclusions*, in *id.* at 159, 174–5.

44   Bunch, *supra* note 39, at 490.

45   *Id.*

46   *Id.*

47   United Nations, *supra* note 39, at 19.

48   Australian Government, Office of the Status of Women, *Community Attitudes Towards Domestic Violence in Australia* 2 (1988).

49   United Nations, *Violence Against Women in the Family* 20 (1989).

50   UN E.S.C. Res. 1982/22, 1984/14.

51   C.A. Res. 40/36 (1985), cited in United Nations, *supra* note 49, at 4.

52   United Nations, *supra* note 49, at 4.

53   A more detailed analysis of the international law prohibition on torture from a feminist perspective is contained in Charlesworth, Chinkin & Wright, *supra* note 29, at 628–9.

54   United Nations Convention against Torture and Other Cruel, Inhuman or Degrading Treatment or Punishment, G.A. Res. 39/46 (Dec. 10, 1984), art. 1(1), draft reprinted in 23 I.L.M. 1027 (1984), substantive changes noted in 24 I.L.M. 535 (1985), also reprinted in *Human Rights: A Compilation of International Instruments*, at 212, UN Doc. ST/HR/1/Rev.3 (1988).

55   See, e.g., Amnesty International, *Women in the Front Line: Human Rights Violations Against Women* (1991).

56   United Nations, *supra* note 49, at 18–20.

57   Quoted in *id.* at 30.

58   Bunch, *supra* note 39, at 491.

59   See Gordon Christenson, *Attributing Acts of Omission to the State*, 12 Mich. J. Int'l L. 312 (1991).

60   The International Law Commission's controversial definition of an international crime in Draft Article 19 (3)(c), *supra* note 4, is also significantly limited in its coverage: it refers to a "serious breach on a widespread scale of an international obligation of essential importance for safeguarding the human being, such as those prohibiting slavery, genocide, apartheid."

61   See Americas Watch, *Criminal Injustice: Violence Against Women in Brazil* (1991).

62   This norm is not accepted by all commentators as within the *jus cogens*, but has considerable support for this status. See Brownlie, *supra* note 14, at 513.

63   International Covenant on Civil and Political Rights, *supra* note 32, at 1.

64   See Christine Chinkin, *A Gendered Perspective to the Use of Force in International Law*, 12 Aust.

Y.B. Int'l L. 279 (1992); Charlesworth, Chinkin & Wright, *supra* note 29, at 642–3.

65 See Charlesworth, Chinkin & Wright, *supra* note 29, at 642–3.

66 Sarah Brown, *Feminism, International Theory, and International Relations of Gender Inequality*, 17 Millenium: J. Int'l Stud. 461, 472 (1988).

67 For example, in the context of the right to life, the wide terms of the Human Rights Committee's General Comment on Article 6 of the International Covenant on Civil and Political Rights could be exploited to argue for the prevention of domestic violence as an aspect of this right. See UN Doc. CCPR/C/21/Rev.1 (1989), at 4–6 (1989). See also General Recommendation No. 19 of the Committee on the Elimination of Discrimination Against Women, UN Doc. CEDAW/C/1992/L.I/

Add.15 (1992), which describes gender based violence as a form of discrimination against women.

68 Interesting work already exists in this area. For example, on the prohibition on apartheid, see Cheryl L. Poinsette, *Black Women under Apartheid: An Introduction*, 8 Harv. Women's L.J. 93 (1985); Penny Andrews, *The Legal Underpinnings of Gender Oppression in Apartheid South Africa*, 3 Aust. J.L. & Soc'y 92 (1986).

69 See, e.g., Brownlie, *supra* note 38, at 16.

70 *Id.* at 15.

71 See *supra* note 6.

72 See, e.g., Philip Alston, *Human Rights in the New World Order: Discouraging Conclusions from the Gulf Crisis*, in *Whose New World Order: What Role for the United Nations?* 85 (M. Bustelo & P. Alston eds., 1991).

59

Plessy v. Ferguson (1896)

JUSTICE BROWN *delivered the opinion of the Court.*

This case turns upon the constitutionality of an act of the general assembly of the State of Louisiana, passed in 1890, providing for separate railway carriages for the white and colored races. [. . .]

The first section of the statute enacts "that all railway companies carrying passengers in their coaches in this state shall provide equal but separate accommodations for the white and colored races, by providing two or more passenger coaches for each passenger train, or by dividing the passenger coaches by a partition so as to secure separate accommodations: *Provided,* That this section shall be construed to apply to street railroads. No person or persons shall be permitted to occupy any coaches other than the ones assigned to them, on account of the race they belong to."

By the second section it was enacted "that the officers of such passenger trains shall have power and are hereby required to assign each passenger to the coach or compartment used for the race to which such passenger belongs: any passenger insisting on going into a coach or compartment to which by race he does not belong, shall be liable to a fine of $25 or in lieu thereof to imprisonment for a period of not more than twenty days in the parish prison." [. . .]

The information filed in the criminal district court charged in substance that Plessy, being a passenger between two stations within the State of Louisiana, was assigned by officers of the company to the coach used by the race to which he belonged, but he insisted upon going into a coach used by the race to which he did not belong. Neither in the information nor plea was his particular race or color averred.

The petition for the writ of prohibition averred that petitioner was seven-eighths Caucasian and one-eighth African blood; that the mixture of colored blood was not discernible in him, and that he was entitled to every right, privilege, and immunity secured to citizens of the United States of the white race; and that, upon such theory, he took possession of a vacant seat in a coach where passengers of the white race were accommodated, and was ordered by the conductor to vacate said coach and take a seat in another assigned to persons of the colored race, and having refused to comply with such demand he was forcibly ejected with the aid of a police officer, and imprisoned in the parish jail to answer a charge of having violated the above act.

The constitutionality of this act is attacked upon the ground that it conflicts both with the Thirteenth Amendment of the Constitution,

Plessy v. Ferguson, 163 U.S. 537; 41 L. Ed. 256; 16 S. Ct. 1138 (1896).

abolishing slavery, and the Fourteenth Amendment, which prohibits certain restrictive legislation on the part of the States.

1 That it does not conflict with the Thirteenth Amendment, which abolished slavery and involuntary servitude, except as a punishment for crime, is too clear for argument. [. . .]

A statute which implies merely a legal distinction between the white and colored races – a distinction which is founded in the color of the two races, and which must always exist so long as white men are distinguished from the other race by color – has no tendency to destroy the legal equality of the two races, or reestablish a state of involuntary servitude. Indeed, we do not understand that the Thirteenth Amendment is strenuously relied upon by the plaintiff in error in this connection.

2 By the Fourteenth Amendment, all persons born or naturalized in the United States, and subject to the jurisdiction thereof, are made citizens of the United States and of the State wherein they reside; and the States are forbidden from making or enforcing any law which shall abridge the privileges or immunities of citizens of the United States, or shall deprive any person of life, liberty, or property without due process of law, or deny to any person within their jurisdiction the equal protection of the laws. [. . .]

The object of the Amendment was undoubtedly to enforce the absolute equality of the two races before the law, but in the nature of things it could not have been intended to abolish distinctions based upon color, or to enforce social, as distinguished from political, equality, or a commingling of the two races upon terms unsatisfactory to either. Laws permitting and even requiring their separation in places where they are liable to be brought into contact do not necessarily imply the inferiority of either race to the other, and have been generally, if not universally, recognized as within the competency of the state legislatures in the exercise of their police power. The most common instance of this is connected with the establishment of separate schools for white and colored children, which have been held to be a valid exercise of the legislative

power even by courts of States where the political rights of the colored race have been longest and most earnestly enforced.

One of the earliest of these cases is that of *Roberts v. Boston*, 5 Cush. 198, in which the supreme judicial court of Massachusetts held that the general school committee of Boston had power to make provision for the instruction of colored children in separate schools established exclusively for them, and to prohibit their attendance upon the other schools. [. . .] It was held that the powers of the committee extended to the "establishment of separate schools for children of different ages, sexes, and colors." [. . .] Similar laws have been enacted by Congress under its general power of legislation over the District of Columbia [. . .] as well as by the legislatures of many of the States, and have been generally, if not uniformly, sustained by the courts. [. . .]

Laws forbidding the intermarriage of the two races may be said in a technical sense to interfere with the freedom of contract, and yet have been universally recognized as within the police power of the State, *State v. Gibson*, 36 Ind. 389 (10 Am. Rep. 42).

The distinction between interfering with the political equality of the negro and those requiring the separation of the two races in schools, theaters, and railway carriages, has been frequently drawn by this court. Thus in *Strauder v. West Virginia*, 100 U.S. 303, it was held that a law of West Virginia limiting to white male persons, twenty-one years of age and citizens of the State, the right to sit upon juries, was a discrimination which implied a legal inferiority in civil society, which lessened the security of the right of the colored race, and was a step towards reducing them to a condition of servility. . . .

Much nearer, and, indeed almost directly in point, is the case of the *Louisville, N.O. & T.R. Co. v. Mississippi*, 133 U.S. 587, wherein the railway company was indicted for a violation of a statute of Mississippi, enacting that all railroads carrying passengers should provide equal, but separate, accommodations for the white and colored races, by providing two or more passenger cars for each passenger train, or by dividing the passenger cars by a partition, so as to secure separate accommodations. The case was presented in a different aspect from the one under consideration, inasmuch as it was an indictment against the railway company for failing to provide the separate accommodations, but the question considered was the constitutionality of the law. In that case, the supreme court of Mississippi, 66 Miss. 662, had held that the statute applied solely to commerce within the State, and, that being the construction of the state statute by its highest court, was accepted as conclusive. "If it be a matter," said the court, "respecting commerce wholly within a state, and not interfering with commerce between the states, then, obviously, there is no violation of the commerce clause of the Federal Constitution. [. . .] No question arises under this section as to the power of the state to separate in different compartments interstate passengers, or to affect in any manner, the privileges and rights of such passengers. All that we can consider is, whether the state has the power to require that railroad trains within her limits shall have separate accommodations for the two races; that affecting only commerce within the states is no invasion of the powers given to Congress by the commerce clause." [. . .]

[I]t is [. . .] suggested by the learned counsel for the plaintiff in error that the same argument that will justify the state legislature in requiring railways to provide separate accommodations for the two races will also authorize them to require separate cars to be provided for people whose hair is of a certain color, or who are aliens, or who belong to certain nationalities, or to enact laws requiring colored people to walk upon one side of the street, and white people upon the other, or requiring white men's houses to be painted white, and colored men's black, or their vehicles or business signs to be of different colors, upon the theory that one side of the street is as good as the other, or that a house or vehicle of one color is as good as one of another color. The reply to all this is that every exercise of the police power must be reasonable, and extend only to such laws as are enacted in good faith for the promotion of the public good, and not for the annoyance or oppression of a particular class. [. . .]

So far, then, as a conflict with the Fourteenth Amendment is concerned, the case reduces itself to the question whether the statute of Louisiana is a reasonable regulation, and with respect to this there must necessarily be a large discretion on the part of the legislature. In determining the

question of reasonableness it is at liberty to act with reference to the established usages, customs, and traditions of the people, and with a view to the promotion of their comfort, and the preservation of the public peace and good order. Gauged by this standard, we cannot say that a law which authorizes or even requires the separation of the two races in public conveyances is unreasonable or more obnoxious to the Fourteenth Amendment than the acts of Congress requiring separate schools for colored children in the District of Columbia, the constitutionality of which does not seem to have been questioned, or the corresponding acts of state legislatures.

We consider the underlying fallacy of the plaintiff's argument to consist in the assumption that the enforced separation of the two races stamps the colored race with a badge of inferiority. If this be so, it is not by reason of anything found in the act, but solely because the colored race chooses to put that construction upon it. The argument necessarily assumes that if, as has been more than once the case, and is not unlikely to be so again, the colored race would become the dominant power in the state legislature, and should enact a law in precisely similar terms, it would thereby relegate the white race to an inferior position. We imagine that the white race, at least, would not acquiesce in this assumption. The argument also assumes that social prejudices may be overcome by legislation, and that equal rights cannot be secured to the negro except by an enforced commingling of the two races. We cannot accept this proposition. If the two races are to meet on terms of social equality, it must be the result of natural affinities, a mutual appreciation of each other's merits and a voluntary consent of individuals. [. . .] Legislation is powerless to eradicate racial instincts or to abolish distinctions based upon physical differences, and the attempt to do so can only result in accentuating the difficulties of the present situation. If the civil and political rights of both races be equal, one cannot be inferior to the other civilly or politically. If one race be inferior to the other socially, the Constitution of the United States cannot put them upon the same plane.

It is true that the question of the proportion of colored blood necessary to constitute a colored person, as distinguished from a white person, is one upon which there is a difference of opinion in the different States, some holding that any visible admixture of black stamps the person as belonging to the colored race (*State v. Chavers*, 5 Jones, L. II); others that it depends upon the predominance of blood (*Gray v. State*, 4 Ohio 354; *Monroe v. Collins*, 17 Ohio St. 665); and still others that the predominance of white blood must only be in the proportion of three fourths (*People v. Dean* 14 Mich. 406; *Jones v. Com.* 80 Va. 544). But these are questions to be determined under the laws of each State and are not properly put in issue in this case. Under the allegation of his petition it may undoubtedly become a question of importance whether, under the laws of Louisiana, the petitioner belongs to the white or colored race.

The judgment of the court below is therefore affirmed.

[JUSTICE BREWER did not hear the argument or participate in the decision of this case.]

JUSTICE HARLAN, *dissenting*. [. . .]

[W]e have before us a state enactment that compels, under penalties, the separation of the two races in railroad passenger coaches, and makes it a crime for a citizen of either race to enter a coach that has been assigned to citizens of the other race.

Thus the State regulates the use of a public highway by citizens of the United States solely upon the basis of race.

However apparent the injustice of such legislation may be, we have only to consider whether it is consistent with the Constitution of the United States. [. . .]

In respect of civil rights, common to all citizens, the Constitution of the United States does not, I think, permit any public authority to know the race of those entitled to be protected in the enjoyment of such rights. Every true man has pride of race, and under appropriate circumstances, when the rights of others, his equals before the law, are not to be affected, it is his privilege to express such pride and to take such action based upon it as to him seems proper. But I deny that any legislative body or judicial tribunal may have regard to the race of citizens when the civil rights of those citizens are involved. Indeed such legislation as that here in question is inconsistent, not only with that

equality of rights which pertains to citizenship, national and state, but with the personal liberty enjoyed by everyone within the United States. [The Thirteenth, Fourteenth and Fifteenth Amendments] removed the race line from our governmental systems. They had, as this Court has said, a common purpose, namely, to secure "to a race recently emancipated, a race that through many generations have [*sic*] been held in slavery, all the civil rights that the superior race enjoys." They declared, in legal effect, this court has further said, "that the law in the states shall be the same for the black as for the white: that all persons, whether colored or white, shall stand equal before the laws of the states, and, in regard to the colored race, for whose protection that amendment was primarily designed, that no discrimination shall be made against them by law because of their color." We also said; "The words of the Amendment, it is true, are prohibitory, but they contain a necessary implication of a positive immunity, or right, most valuable to the colored race – the right to exemption from unfriendly legislation against them distinctively as colored – exemption from legal discriminations, implying inferiority in civil society, lessening the security of their enjoyment of the rights which others enjoy, and discrimination which are steps towards reducing them to the condition of a subject race." [. . .]

It was said in argument that the statute of Louisiana does not discriminate against either race, but prescribes a rule applicable alike to white and colored citizens. But this argument does not meet the difficulty. Everyone knows that the statute in question had its origin in the purpose, not so much to exclude white persons from railroad cars occupied by blacks, as to exclude colored people from coaches occupied or assigned to white persons. Railroad corporations of Louisiana did not make discrimination among whites in the matter of accommodation for travelers. The thing to accomplish was, under the guise of giving equal accommodation for whites and blacks, to compel the latter to keep to themselves while traveling in railroad passenger coaches. No one would be so wanting in candor to assert the contrary. The fundamental objection, therefore, to the statute is that it interferes with the personal freedom of citizens. "Personal liberty," it has been well said, "consists in the power of locomotion, of changing situation, or removing one's person to whatsoever place one's own inclination may direct, without imprisonment or restraint, unless by due course of law," 1 Bl. Com. 134. If a white man and a black man choose to occupy the same public conveyance on a public highway, it is their right to do so, and no government, proceeding alone on grounds of race, can prevent it without infringing the personal liberty of each.

It is one thing for railroad carriers to furnish, or to be required by law to furnish, equal accommodations for all whom they are under a legal duty to carry. It is quite another thing for government to forbid citizens of the white and black races from traveling in the same public conveyance, and to punish officers of railroad companies for permitting persons of the two races to occupy the same passenger coach. If a State can prescribe as a rule of civil conduct, that whites and blacks shall not travel as passengers in the same railroad coach, why may it not so regulate the use of the streets of its cities and towns as to compel white citizens to keep on one side of the street and black citizens to keep on the other? Why may it not, upon like grounds, punish whites and blacks who ride together in street cars or in open vehicles on a public road or street? Why may it not require sheriffs to assign whites to one side of the courtroom and blacks to the other? And why may it not also prohibit the commingling of the two races in the galleries of legislative halls or in public assemblages convened for the political questions of the day? Further, if this statute of Louisiana is consistent with the personal liberty of citizens, why may not the State require the separation in railroad coaches of native and naturalized citizens of the United States, or of Protestants and Roman Catholics?

The answer given at the argument to these questions was that regulations of the kind they suggest would be unreasonable, and could not, therefore, stand before the law. Is it meant that the determination of questions of legislative power depends upon the inquiry whether the statute whose validity is questioned is, in the judgment of the courts, a reasonable one, taking all the circumstances into consideration? A statute may be unreasonable merely because a sound public policy forbade its enactment. But I do not understand that the courts have anything

to do with the policy or expediency of legislation. A statute may be valid, and yet upon grounds of public policy may well be characterized as unreasonable. Mr Sedgwick correctly states the rule when he says that the legislative intention being clearly ascertained, "the courts have no other duty to perform than to execute the legislative will, without any regard to their views as to the wisdom or justice of the particular enactment." Sedgw. Stat. & Const. L. 324. [. . .]

The white race deems itself to be the dominant race in this country. And so it is, in prestige, in achievements, in education, in health, and in power. So, I doubt not that it will continue to be for all time, if it remains true to its great heritage and holds fast to the principles of constitutional liberty. But in view of the Constitution, in the eye of the law, there is in this country no superior, dominant, ruling class of citizens. There is no caste here. Our Constitution is color-blind, and neither knows nor tolerates classes among citizens. In respect of civil rights, all citizens are equal before the law. The humblest is the peer of the most powerful. The law regards man as man, and takes no account of his surroundings or of his color when his civil rights as guaranteed by the supreme law of the land are involved. It is therefore to be regretted that this high tribunal, the final expositor of the fundamental law of the land, has reached the conclusion that it is competent for a state to regulate the enjoyment by citizens of their civil rights solely upon the basis of race.

In my opinion, the judgment this day rendered will, in time, prove to be quite as pernicious as the decision made by this tribunal in the *Dred Scott Case*. [. . .] The recent amendments of the Constitution, it was supposed, had eradicated the principles (announced in that decision) from our institutions. But it seems that we have yet, in some of the states, a dominant race, a superior class of citizens, which assumes to regulate the enjoyment of civil rights, common to all citizens, upon the basis of race. The present decision, it may well be apprehended, will not stimulate aggressions, more or less brutal and irritating, upon the admitted rights of colored citizens, but will encourage the belief that it is possible, by means of state enactments, to defeat the beneficent purposes which the people of the United States had in view when they adopted the recent amendments of the Constitution. [. . .] Sixty millions of whites are in no danger from the presence here of eight millions of blacks. The destinies of the two races in this country are indissolubly linked together, and the interests of both require that the common government of all shall not permit the seeds of race hate to be planted under the sanction of law. What can more certainly arouse race hate, what more certainly create and perpetuate a feeling of distrust between these races, than state enactments which in fact proceed on the ground that colored citizens are so inferior and degraded that they cannot be allowed to sit in public coaches occupied by white citizens? That, as all will admit, is the real meaning of such legislation as was enacted in Louisiana.

The sure guaranty of the peace and security of each race is the clear, distinct, unconditional recognition by our governments, national and state, of every right that inheres in civil freedom, and of the equality before the law of all citizens of the United States without regard to race. State enactments, regulating the enjoyment of civil rights, upon the basis of race, are cunningly devised to defeat legitimate results of the war, under the pretense of recognizing equality of rights, and can have no other result than to render permanent peace impossible and to keep alive a conflict of races, the continuance of which must do harm to all concerned. [...]

The arbitrary separation of citizens, on the basis of race, while they are on a public highway, is a badge of servitude wholly inconsistent with the civil freedom and the equality before the law established by the Constitution. It cannot be justified upon any legal grounds.

If evils will result from the commingling of the two races upon public highways established for the benefit of all, they will be infinitely less than those that will surely come from state legislation regulating the enjoyment of civil rights upon the basis of race. We boast of the freedom enjoyed by our people above all other peoples. But it is difficult to reconcile that boast with a state of the law which, practically, puts the brand of servitude and degradation upon a large class of our fellow citizens, our equals before the law. The thin disguise of "equal" accommodations for passengers in railroad coaches will not mislead anyone, or atone for the wrong this day done. [...]

I am of opinion that the statute of Louisiana is inconsistent with the personal liberty of citizens, white and black, in that State, and hostile to both the spirit and letter of the Constitution of the United States. If laws of like character should be enacted in the several States of the Union, the effect would be in the highest degree mischievous. Slavery as an institution tolerated by law would, it is true, have disappeared from our country, but there would remain a power in the States, by sinister legislation, to interfere with the full enjoyment of the blessings of freedom: to regulate civil rights, common to all citizens, upon the basis of race; and to place in a condition of legal inferiority a large body of American citizens, now constituting a part of the political community, called the people of the United States, for whom and by whom, through representatives, our government is administered. Such a system is inconsistent with the guarantee given by the Constitution to each state of a republican form of government, and may be stricken down by Congressional action, or by the courts in the discharge of their solemn duty to maintain the supreme law of the land anything in the Constitution or laws of any State to the contrary notwithstanding.

For the reasons stated, I am constrained to withhold my assent from the opinion and judgment of the majority.

Questions

1 Why might one think that the prohibition on racial discrimination should be a *jus cogens* norm, but that the prohibition of sexual discrimination should not be so considered?

2 According to Dworkin's theory of constitutional adjudication, there is a difference between a concept and a conception. Why is this distinction important for trying to determine how to interpret "vague" clauses concerning moral rights, such as the US Constitution's equal protection clause?

3 What is judicial activism? Why are Munzer and Nickel critical of judicial activism?

4 How do you think Justice Bhagwati, Chief Justice of the Indian Supreme Court, would interpret the equal protection clause of the US Constitution?

5 Considering O'Connell's arguments, what do you think should be the criteria used to decide the sources of public morality used by a judge to interpret the law? What reasons are there to think that the use of public morality is problematic in constitutional interpretation?